Street by Street

C000064834

DERBYSHIRE

PLUS ALTON TOWERS, ASHBY-DE-LA-ZOUCH, BURTON UPON TRENT, CASTLE DONINGTON, MANSFIELD, SUTTON IN ASHFIELD, UTTOXETER

Enlarged Areas Chesterfield, Derby

Ist edition May 2001

© Automobile Association Developments Limited 2001

This product includes map data licensed from Ordnance Survey® with the permission of the Controller of Her Majesty's Stationery Office. © Crown copyright 2000. All rights reserved. Licence No: 399221.

Published by AA Publishing (a trading name of Automobile Association Developments Limited, whose registered office is Norfolk House, Priestley Road, Basingstoke, Hampshire, RG24 9NY. Registered number 1878835).

Mapping produced by the Cartographic Department of The Automobile Association.

A CIP Catalogue record for this book is available from the British Library.

Printed by G. Canale & C. s.p.a., Torino, Italy

The contents of this atlas are believed to be correct at the time of the latest revision. However, the publishers cannot be held responsible for loss occasioned to any person acting or refraining from action as a result of any material in this atlas, nor for any errors, omissions or changes in such material. The publishers would welcome information to correct any errors or omissions and to keep this atlas up to date. Please write to Publishing, The Automobile Association, Fanum House, Basing View, Basingstoke, Hampshire, RG21 4EA.

Ref: MX088

Key to map pages — ii-iii

Key to map symbols — iv-1

Enlarged scale pages — 2-5

Street by Street — 6-295

Index – towns & villages — 296-297

Index – streets — 298-333

Index – featured places — 333-338

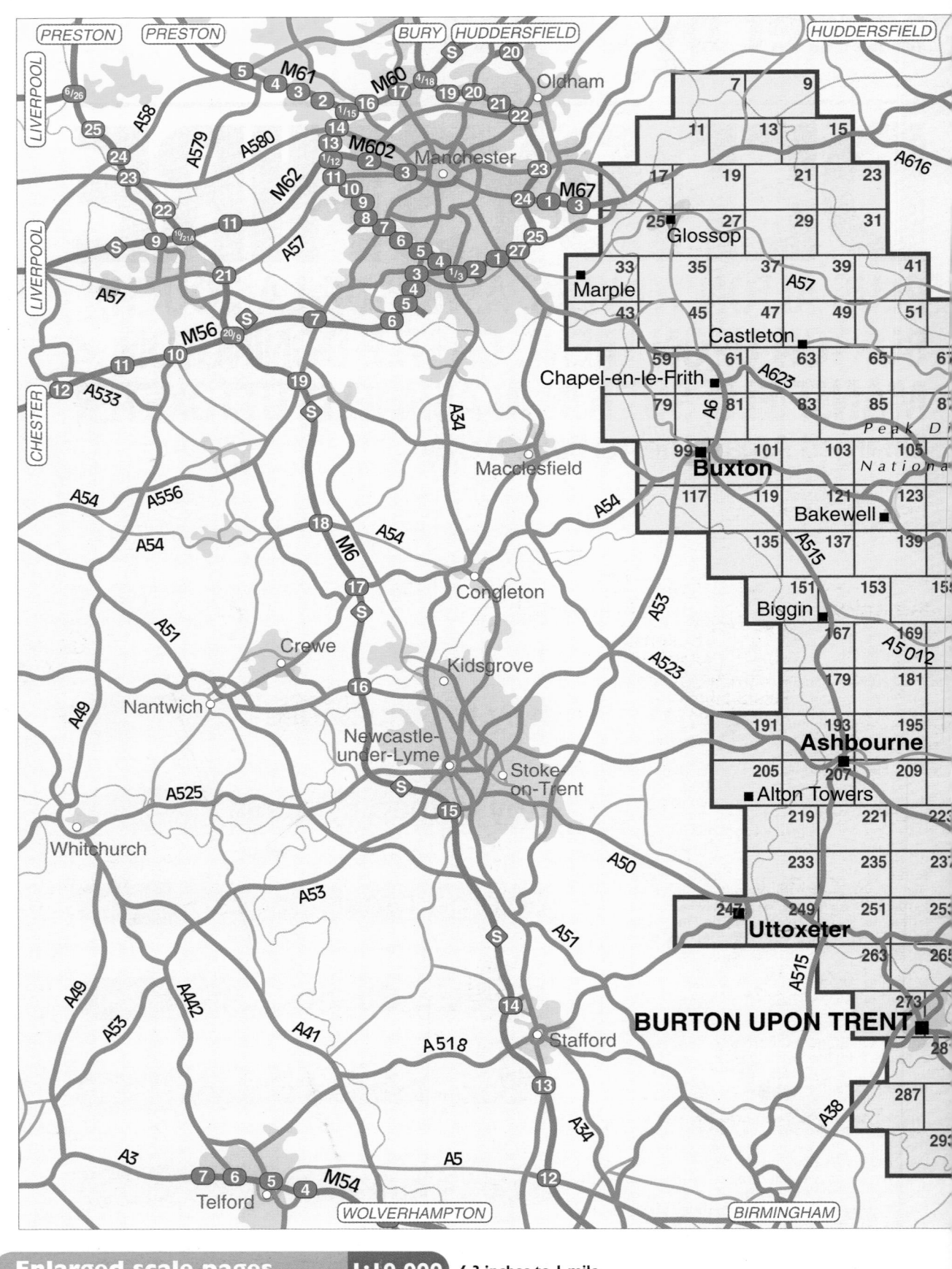

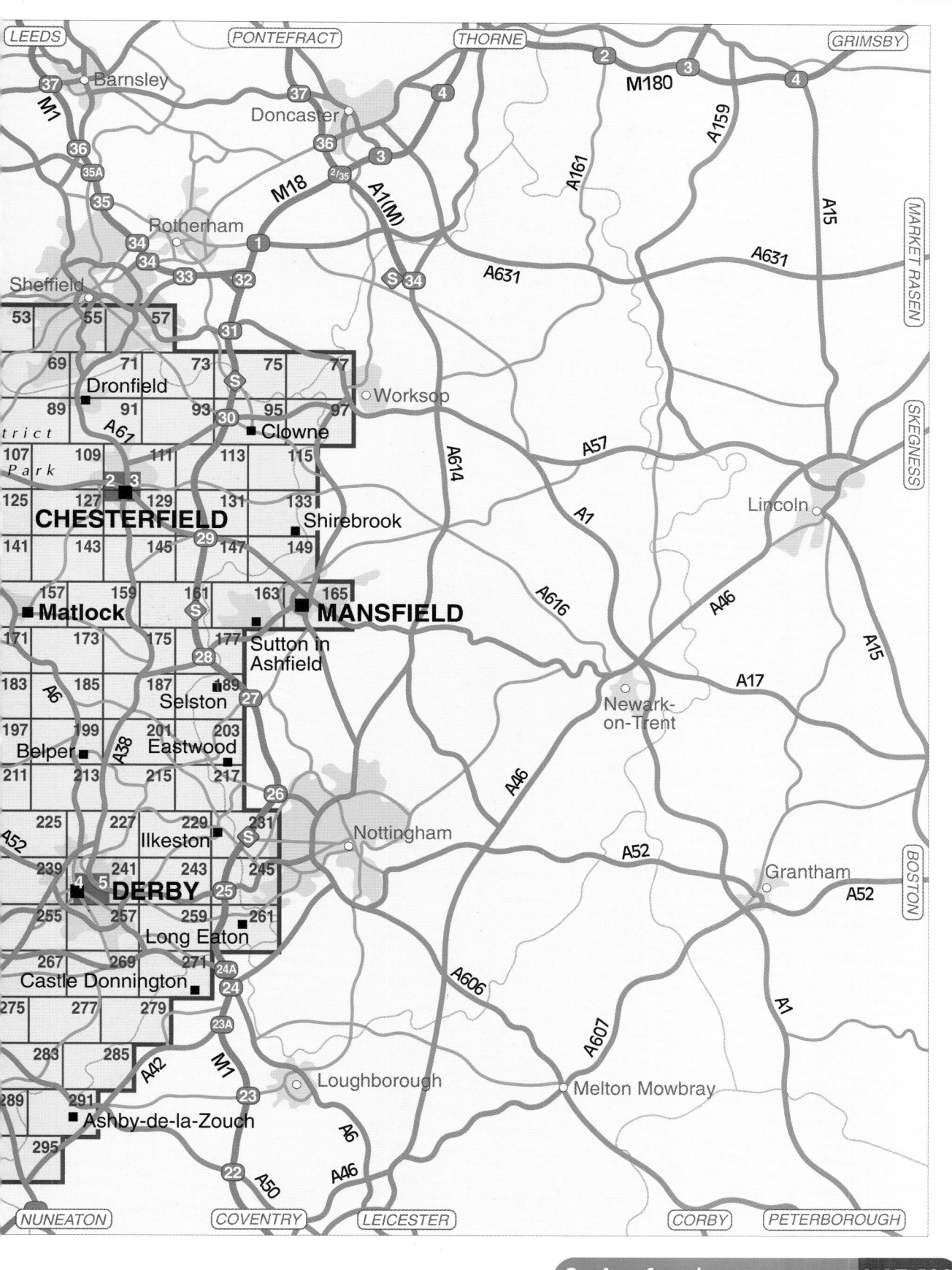

LEEDS · PONTEFRACT · THORNE · GRIMSBY

Barnsley

M1
37
36
35A
35
34
34
33
32

Sheffield

Rotherham

37
Doncaster
36
2/35
3
1
S 34
M18
A1(M)

M180
2
3
4

A161
A159
A631
A15

MARKET RASEN

53 | 55 | 57
31

69 | 71 | 73 | 75 | 77
Dronfield
S
89 | 91 | 93 | 95 | 97
A61
30
Clowne
t r i c t
107 | 109 | 111 | 113 | 115
P a r k
2 3
125 | 127 | 129 | 131 | 133
CHESTERFIELD
Shirebrook
141 | 143 | 145 | 147 | 149
29

157 | 159 | 161 | 163 | 165
Matlock
S
171 | 173 | 175 | 177
Sutton in
28
Ashfield
183 | 185 | 187 | 189
A6
Selston
27
197 | 199 | 201 | 203
Belper
A38
Eastwood
211 | 213 | 215 | 217

225 | 227 | 229 | 231
A52
Ilkeston
S
239 | 241 | 243 | 245
4 5
255 | 257 | 259 | 261
DERBY
25
Long Eaton
267 | 269 | 271
Castle Donnington
24A
24
275 | 277 | 279
23A
283 | 285
A42
M1
289 | 291
23
295
Ashby-de-la-Zouch
22
A50
A46
A6

Worksop

A614
A57
A616
A46
A1

Lincoln

SKEGNESS

Newark-
on-Trent
A17
A15
A46

Nottingham
A52
Grantham
A52

BOSTON

A606
A607
A1

Loughborough
Melton Mowbray

NUNEATON · COVENTRY · LEICESTER · CORBY · PETERBOROUGH

3.6 inches to 1 mile   **Scale of main map pages 1:17,500**

0 ——— 1/2 ——— miles ——— 1
0 ——— 1/2 ——— 1 ——— kilometres ——— 1 1/2 ——— 2

iv

Junction 9	Motorway & junction
Services	Motorway service area
	Primary road single/dual carriageway
Services	Primary road service area
	A road single/dual carriageway
	B road single/dual carriageway
	Other road single/dual carriageway
	Restricted road
	Private road
← ←	One way street
	Pedestrian street
	Track/ footpath
	Road under construction
⊏ - - - - ⊐	Road tunnel
P	Parking

P+🚌	Park & Ride
🚌	Bus/coach station
	Railway & main railway station
	Railway & minor railway station
⊖	Underground station
⊖	Light railway & station
+++++++++++	Preserved private railway
LC	Level crossing
•—•—•—•—•	Tramway
- - - - - - - -	Ferry route
....	Airport runway
— · — · — · —	Boundaries- borough/ district
⋎⋎⋎⋎⋎⋎⋎⋎⋎	Mounds
93	Page continuation 1:17,500
7	Page continuation to enlarged scale 1:10,000

	River/canal lake, pier			Toilet with disabled facilities
	Aqueduct lock, weir			Petrol station
465 Winter Hill	Peak (with height in metres)		PH	Public house
	Beach		PO	Post Office
	Coniferous woodland			Public library
	Broadleaved woodland		i	Tourist Information Centre
	Mixed woodland			Castle
	Park			Historic house/ building
	Cemetery		Wakehurst Place NT	National Trust property
	Built-up area		M	Museum/ art gallery
	Featured building		†	Church/chapel
	City wall			Country park
A&E	Accident & Emergency hospital			Theatre/ performing arts
	Toilet			Cinema

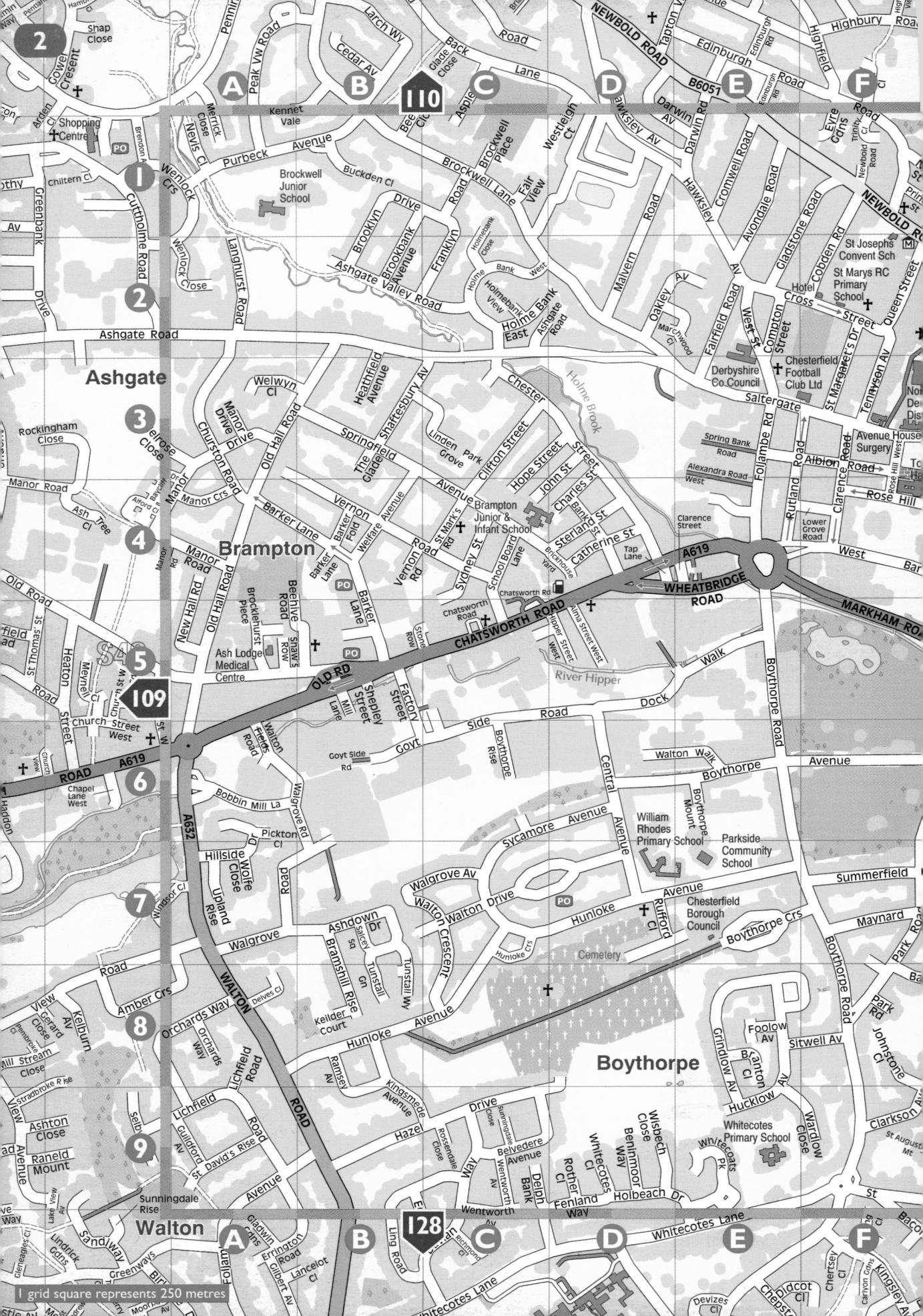

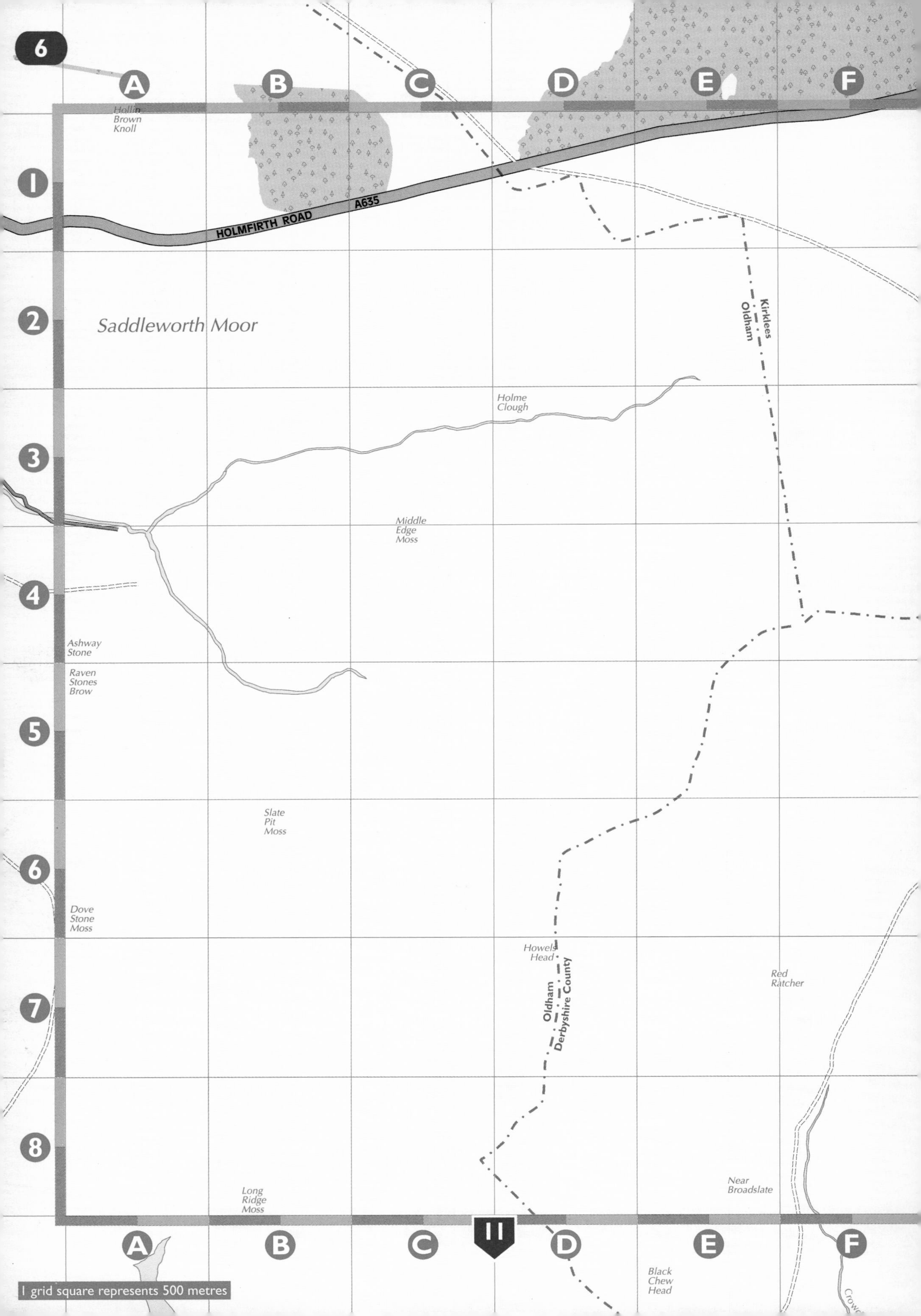
A
B
C
D
E
F
1
2
3
4
5
6
7
8
Hollin Brown Knoll
HOLMFIRTH ROAD
A635
Saddleworth Moor
Kirklees
Oldham
Holme Clough
Middle Edge Moss
Ashway Stone
Raven Stones Brow
Slate Pit Moss
Dove Stone Moss
Howels Head
Oldham
Derbyshire County
Red Ratcher
Near Broadslate
Long Ridge Moss
Black Chew Head
11
1 grid square represents 500 metres

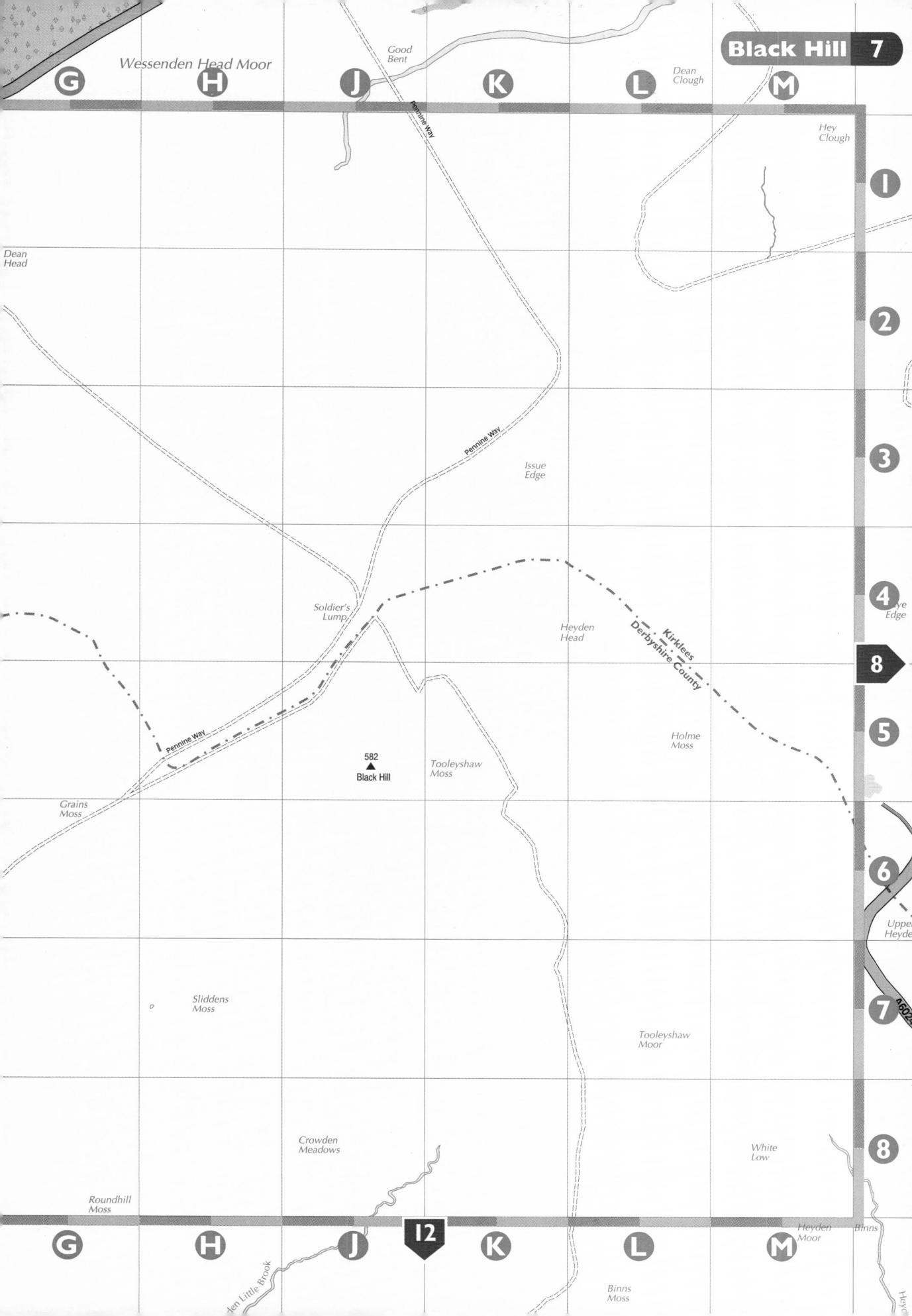

Wessenden Head Moor

Good Bent

Dean Clough

Hey Clough

Dean Head

Pennine Way

Pennine Way

Issue Edge

Soldier's Lump

Heyden Head

Kirklees

Derbyshire County

ye Edge

Holme Moss

Pennine Way

582 ▲ Black Hill

Tooleyshaw Moss

Grains Moss

Uppe Heyde

Sliddens Moss

Tooleyshaw Moor

White Low

Crowden Meadows

Roundhill Moss

Heyden Moor

Binns

Binns Moss

G H J K L M

I 2 3 4 8 5 6 7 8

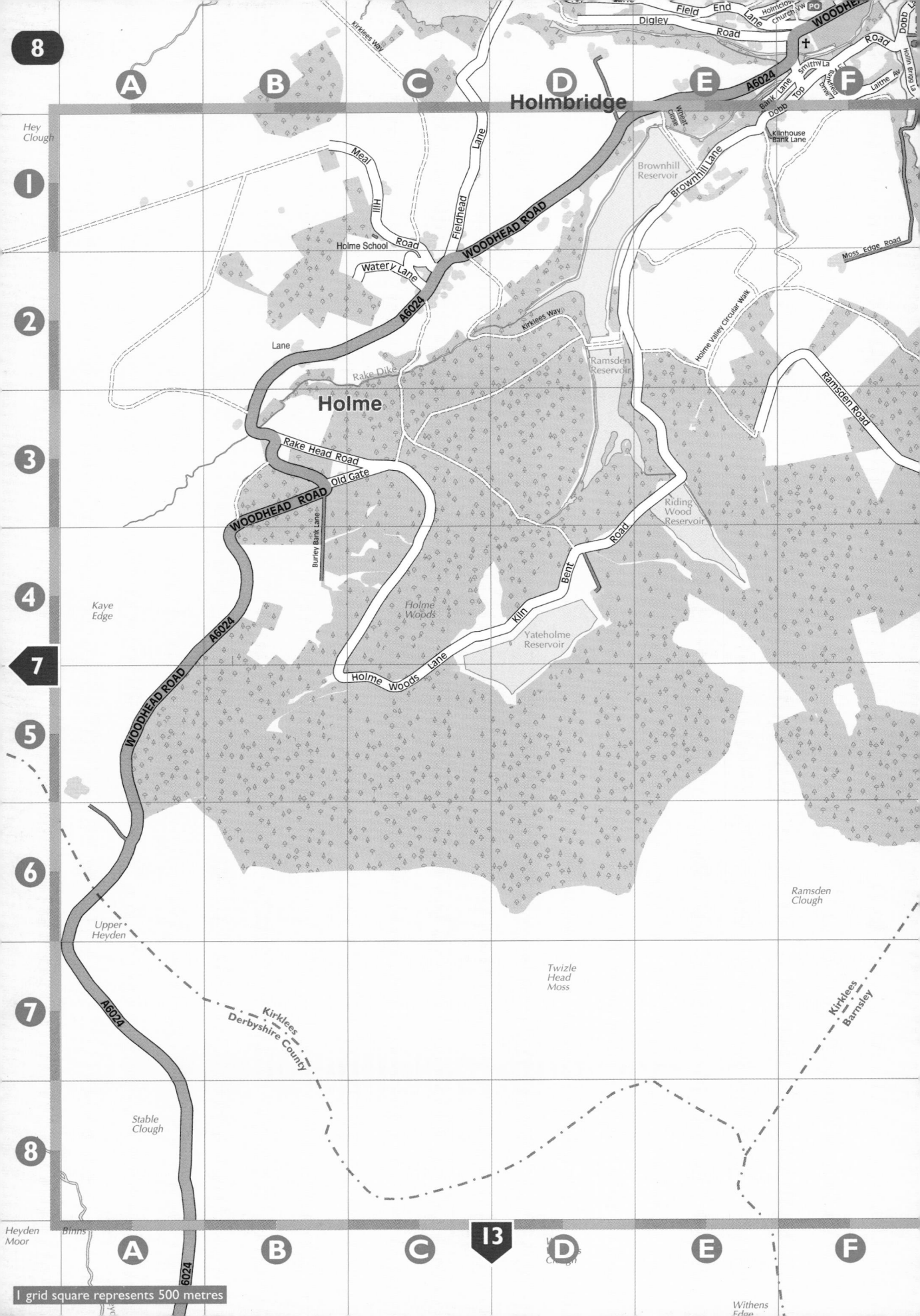

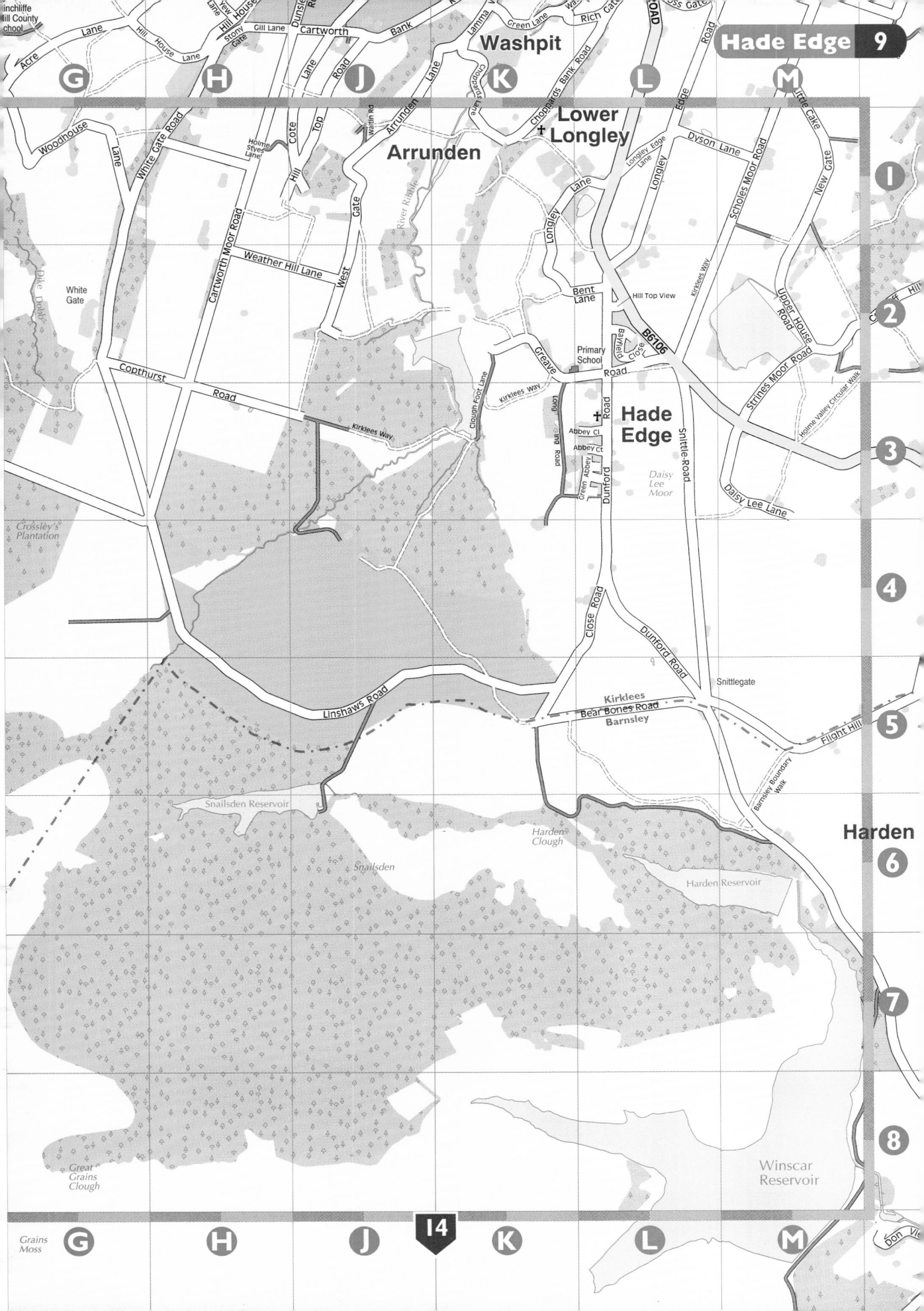

Washpit

Lower Longley

Arrunden

Hade Edge

Harden

White Gate

Crossley's Plantation

Dike Delph

Snailsden Reservoir

Snailsden

Harden Clough

Harden Reservoir

Winscar Reservoir

Great Grains Clough

Grains Moss

Daisy Lee Moor

Primary School

Snittlegate

Kirklees Barnsley

Hill Top View

inchliffe Hill County chool

Woodhouse Lane

White Gate Road

Cartworth Moor Road

Weather Hill Lane

West Gate

Copthurst Road

Kirklees Way

Clough Foot Lane

Greave Road

Long Ing Road

Dunford Road

Close Road

Linshaw's Road

Bear Bones Road

Daisy Lee Lane

Snittle Road

Dunford Road

Close Road

Longley Edge Road

Longley Edge Lane

Longley Lane

Scholes Moor Road

Upper House Road

New Gate

Dyson Lane

Strines Moor Road

Kirktees Way

Bent Lane

Bayfield Close

Green Abbey

Abbey Cl

Abbey Ct

Holme Styes Lane

Hill Top

Cote Gate

Wattin Rd

Arrunden Lane

Choppards Bank Road

Choppards Lane

Rich Gate

Green Lane

Cross Gate

Lamma Lane

Acre Lane

Hill House Lane

Yew Lane

Stony Gate

Gill Lane

Cartworth Road

Bank

River Ribble

Holme valley Circular Walk

Barnsley Boundary Walk

Flight Hill

B6106

Don Vil

G H J K L M

G H J K L M

I

1

2

3

4

5

6

7

8

14

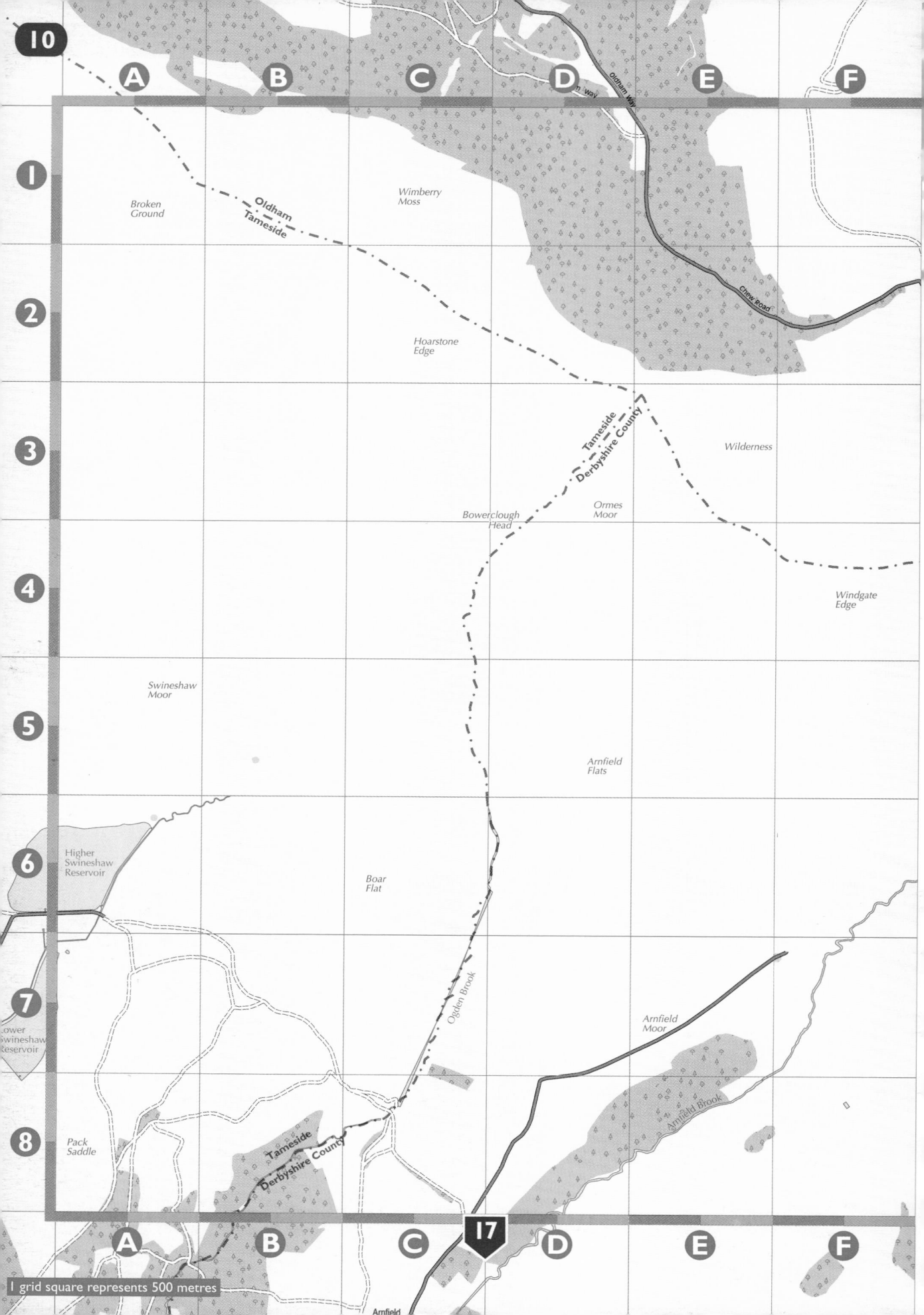

10

A   B   C   D   E   F

1   Broken Ground   Oldham Tameside   Wimberry Moss

2   Hoarstone Edge   Chew Road

3   Bowerclough Head   Tameside Derbyshire County   Ormes Moor   Wilderness

4   Windgate Edge

5   Swineshaw Moor   Arnfield Flats

6   Higher Swineshaw Reservoir   Boar Flat

7   Lower Swineshaw Reservoir   Ogden Brook   Arnfield Moor   Arnfield Brook

8   Pack Saddle   Tameside Derbyshire County

A   B   C   17   D   E   F

Arnfield

1 grid square represents 500 metres

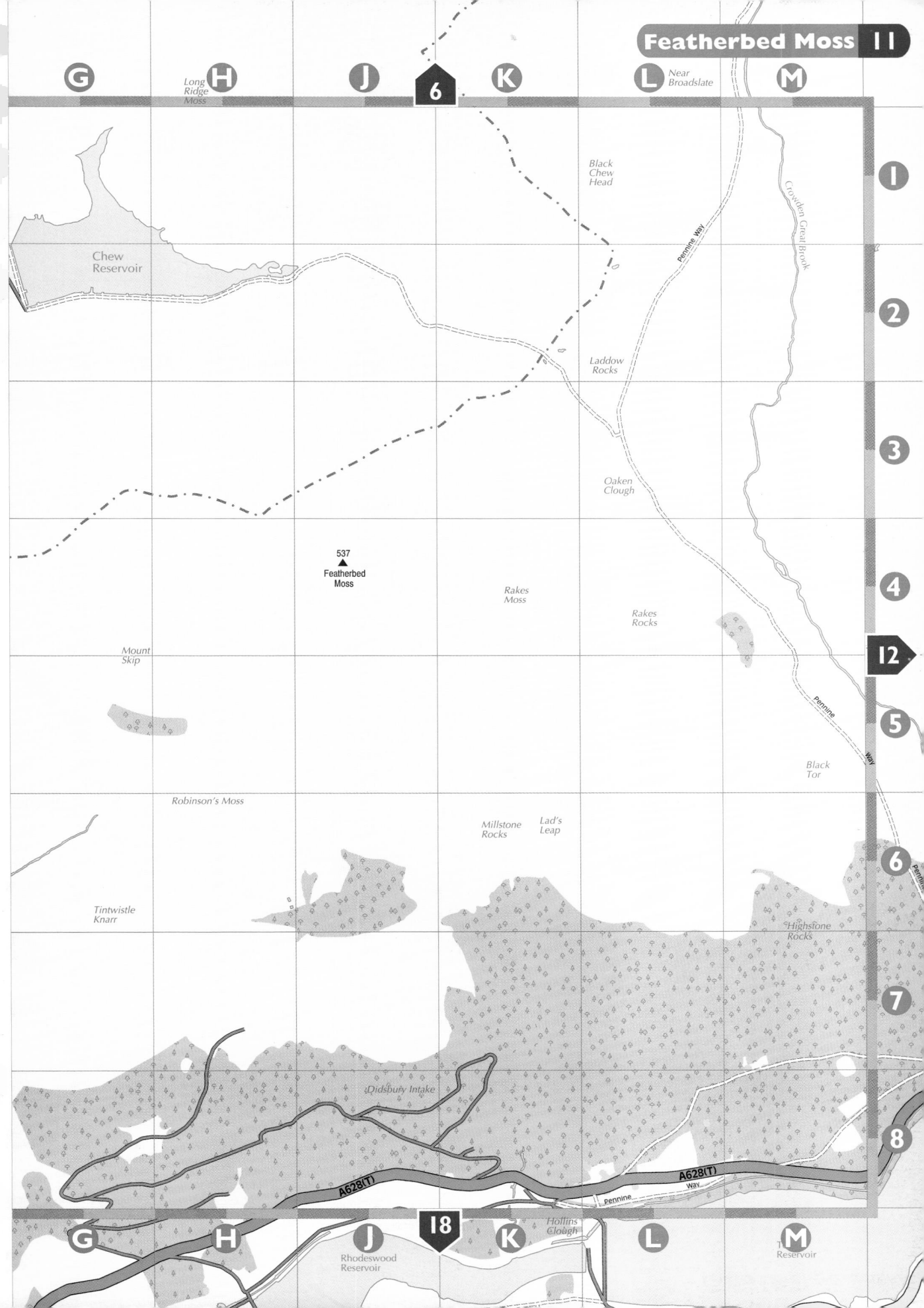

G   H   J   **6**   K   L   M

Long Ridge Moss

Near Broadslate

Black Chew Head

I

Chew Reservoir

Crowden Great Brook

Pennine Way

2

Laddow Rocks

3

Oaken Clough

537 ▲
Featherbed Moss

Rakes Moss

4

Rakes Rocks

Mount Skip

I2

Pennine

5

Black Tor

Way

Robinson's Moss

Millstone Rocks

Lad's Leap

6

Pennine

Tintwistle Knarr

Highstone Rocks

7

Didsbury Intake

8

A628(T)

A628(T)

Pennine   Way

G   H   J   **18**   K   L   M

Hollins Clough

Rhodeswood Reservoir

Reservoir

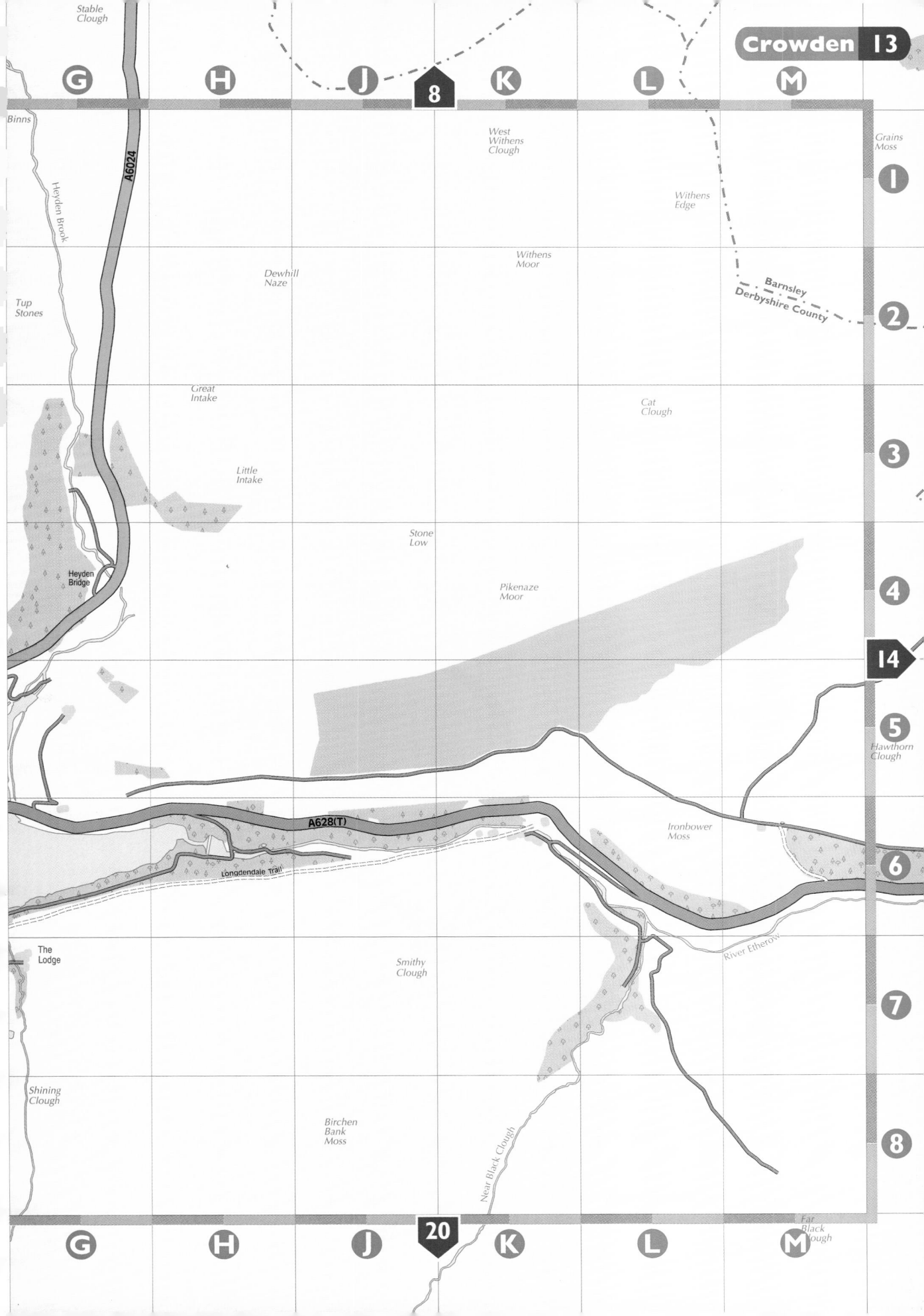

14

A   B   C   9   D   E   F

1   Grains
     Moss

2   Upper
     Dead
     Edge

     Wike Head

3   Upper
                                                     Windleden
                                                     Reservoirs

     Longside
4   Moss

13
                                        Windle Edge

5   Hawthorn   A628(T)   Gallows
     Clough   Moss
                                      Longdendale Trail

6   Long
     Side   A628(T)

7   Rose   Far
     Clough   Small
                 Clough

                 Barnsley
                 Derbyshire County

8   Featherbed
                                                     Moss

ack
ough

     A   B   C   21   D   E   F

                          Swains
                          Head

Winscar
Reservoir

Longdend...

1 grid square represents 500 metres

Dunford Road

River Don

Windle Edge

Don View

Dunford Bridge

s Trail

G H J K L M

I

Lower
Windleden
Reservoirs

Thurlstone
Moors

Wogden
Clough

2

3

A628(T)

4

Barmings

Fiddlers
Green

Long
Moor
Clough

Hordron Road

5

6

Langsett
Moors

Little Don River or The Porter

7

Near
Cat
Clough

8

Harden
Moor

Howden
Edge

Barnsley
Sheffield

B8
1 Dunne La

A7
1 Fernhill Cl

A   B   C   **11**   D   E   F

A62   A628(T) Way

Pennine

Hollins Clough

Torside Reservoir

1

Rhodeswood Reservoir

B6105

Pennine Way

Reaps

Old House

Valehouse Reservoir

2

Deepclough

Bramah Edge

Peaknaze Moor

3

B6105

Devil's Elbow

Ogden Clough

Longdendale

4

Reservoir

Peak Naze

Reservoir

17

Blackshaw Clough

Glossop Low

5

Blake Moor

Blackshaw Farm

Small Clough

Cemetery

6

Swineshaw Reservoir

Road

WOODHEAD

Road

7

Shire Hill Hospital

Bute Street

Moorside

ROAD

Heath Road

Bowden Road

Kingsmoor Flgs

Hanwards Cl

Ramsden

Shire Wy

Castle Hl

Thorpe St

Hawkshead Road

Hope

Charles Lane

Upper Street

Wesley St

All Saints School

Blackshaw Rd

Well Gate

Hope St

B6105

Church Street

Church St

Church St South

Shepley

Street

8

Derbyshire Co Council

Glossopdale Community College

Road

Hall Meadow Rd

Kingsmoor Road

Park Close

Old Hall Close

PO

Old Glossop

Mossy Lea Farm

Fauvel Road

NORFOLK STREET

King Edward St

Duke

Norfolk C of E School

Manor Park Road

York Street

EAST

26

Lord St

Fitzalan St

Charles St

Henry St

HIGH STREET

Woodcock Grove

Queen's Drive

Pingrove

Cowbrook Avenue

SHEFFIELD ROAD

WOODCOCK ROAD A57

Woodcock

Smithy Fd

Manor House Surg

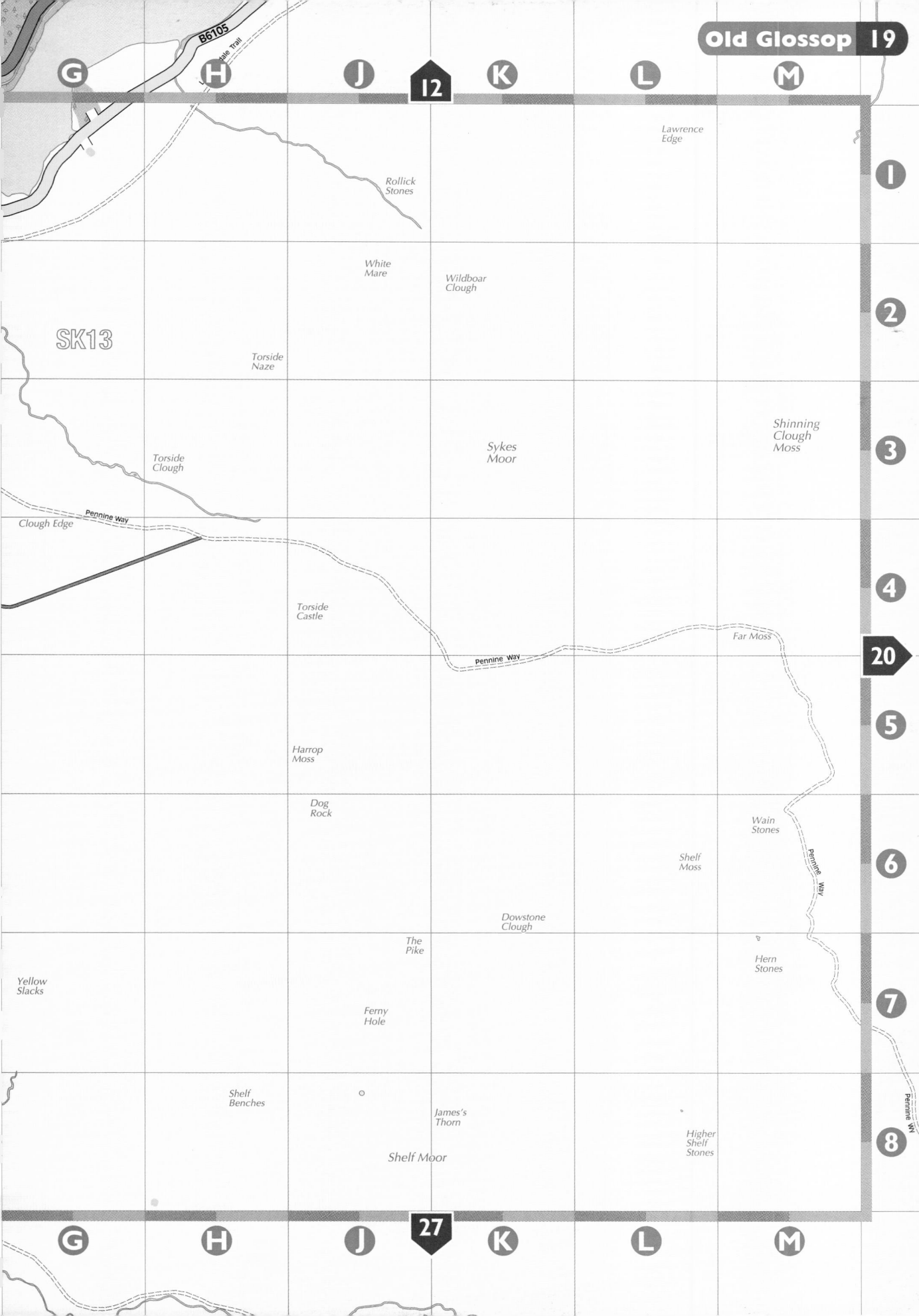

G H J K L M

12

I
2
3
4
20
5
6
7
8

Lawrence
Edge

Rollick
Stones

White
Mare

Wildboar
Clough

SK13

Torside
Naze

Shinning
Clough
Moss

Sykes
Moor

Torside
Clough

Pennine Way

Clough Edge

Torside
Castle

Pennine Way

Far Moss

Harrop
Moss

Dog
Rock

Wain
Stones

Shelf
Moss

Pennine Way

Dowstone
Clough

The
Pike

Hern
Stones

Yellow
Slacks

Ferny
Hole

Shelf
Benches

James's
Thorn

Pennine W

Higher
Shelf
Stones

Shelf Moor

27

G H J K L M

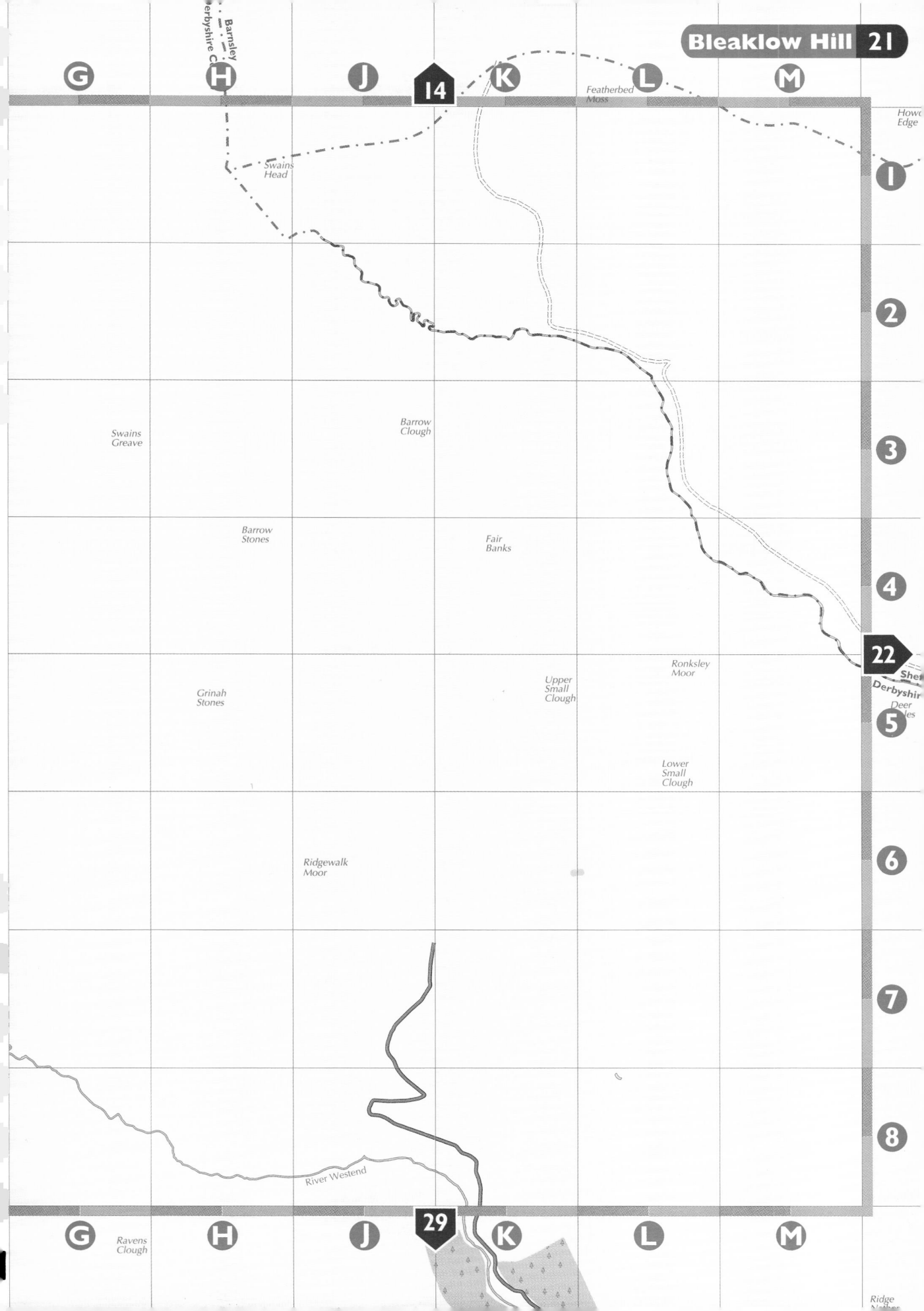

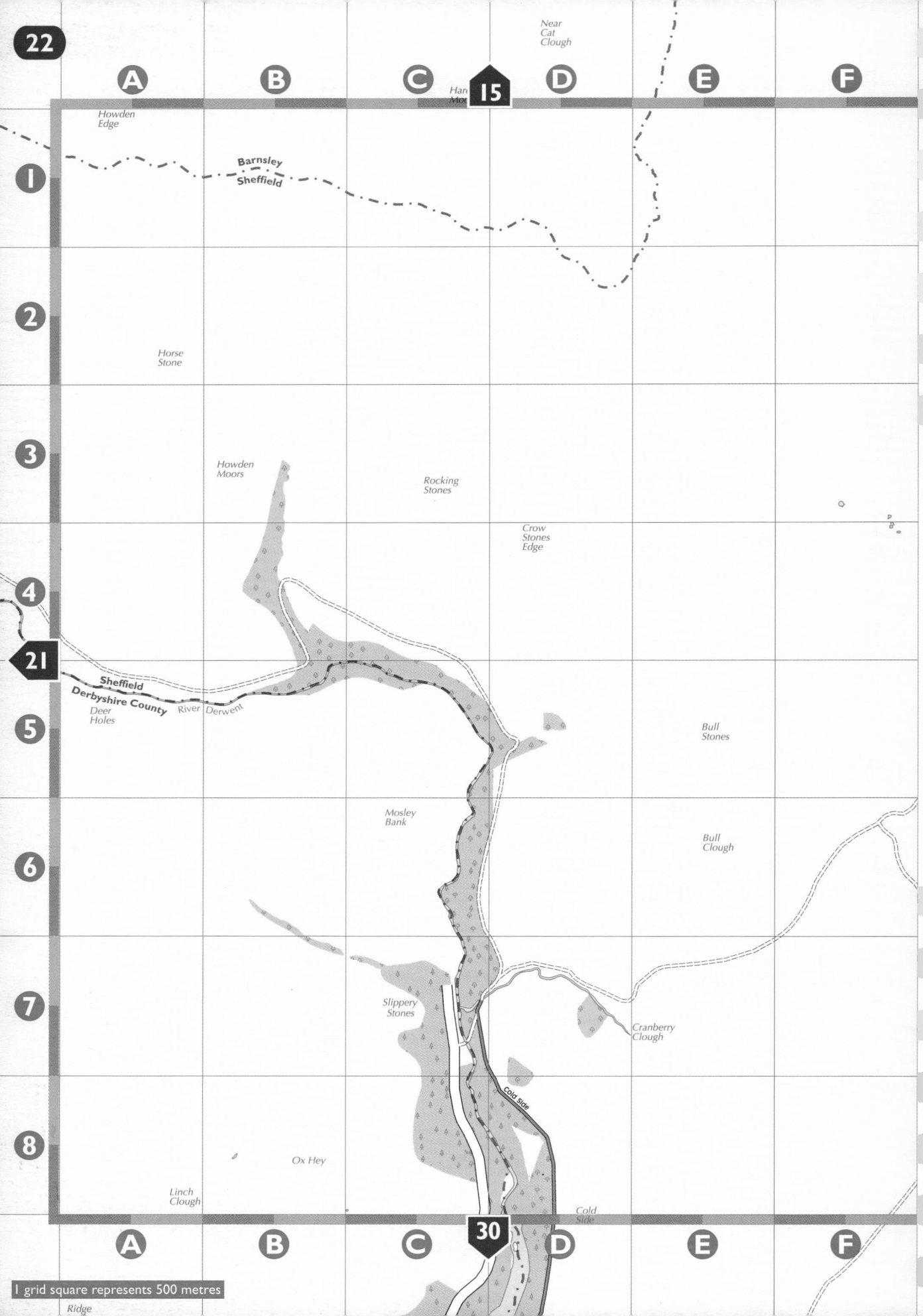

G H J K L M

Mickleden Edge

1

Fenny
Common

2

Pike Lowe
Stones

Bull
Clough

Pike
Lowe

3

Cut Gate

4

o

Upper
Commons

5

Ewden Bec

6

546
▲
Margery
Hill

Stainery
Clough

7

8

Middle
Moss

Penistone
Stile

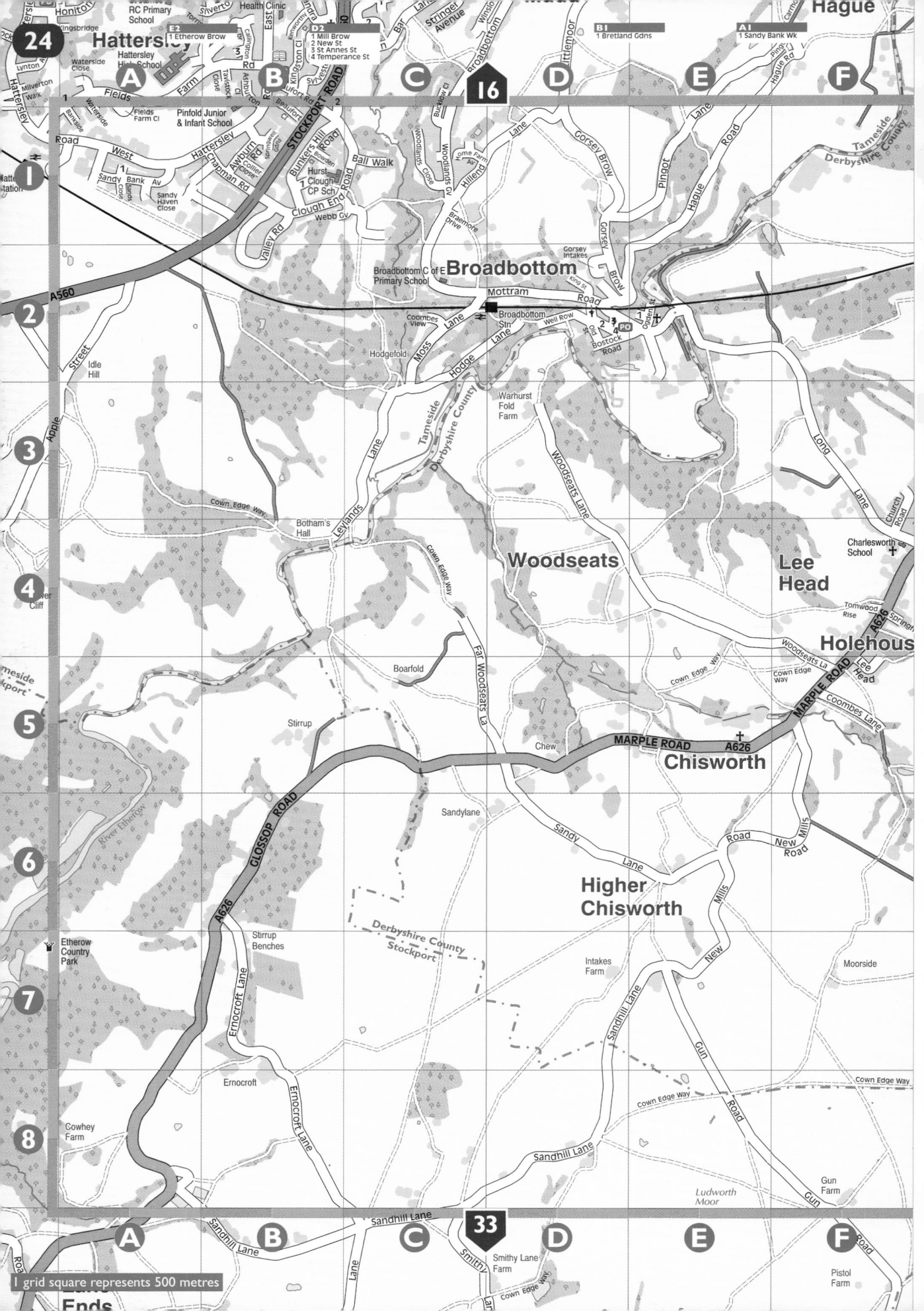

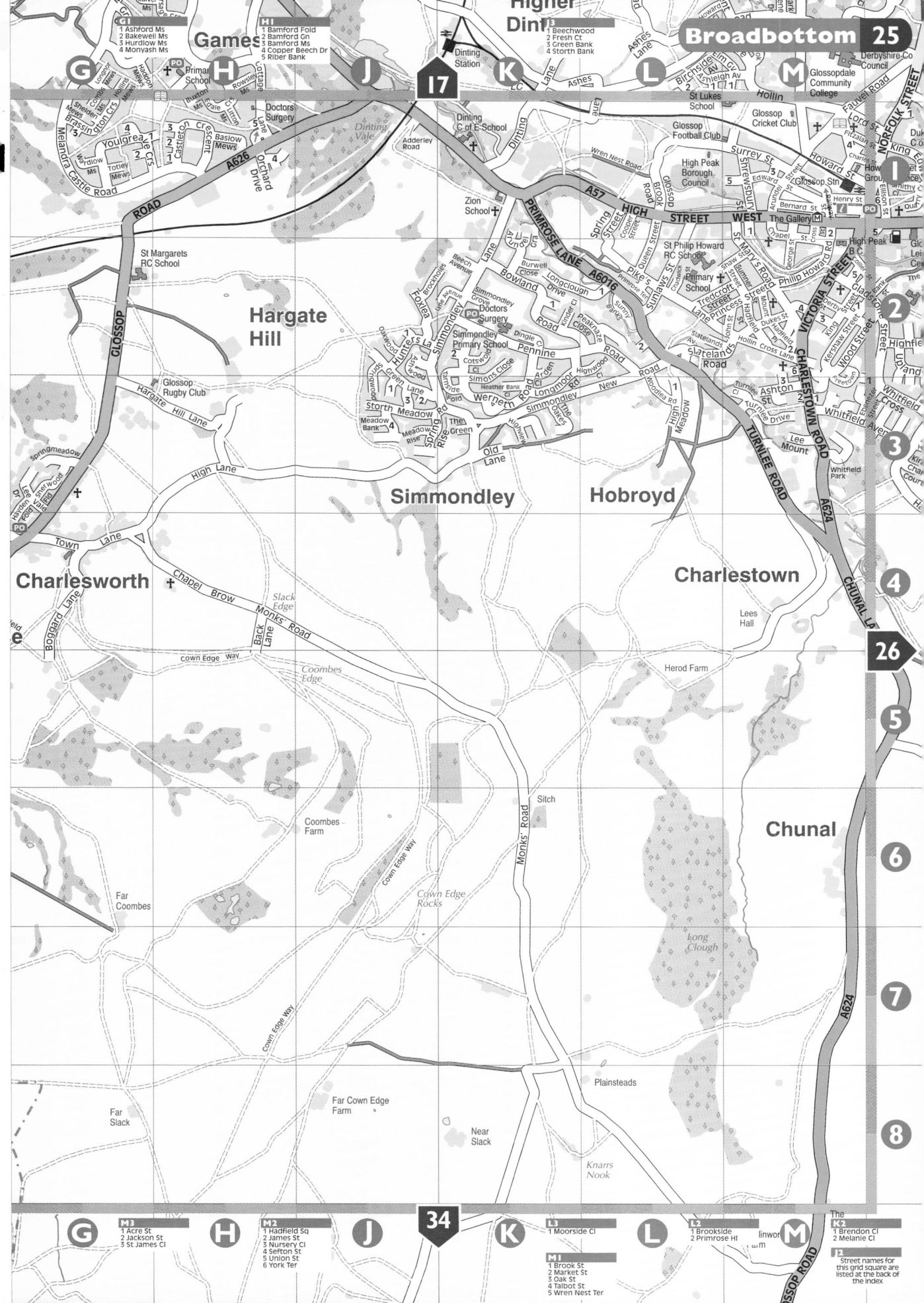

Glossopdale
Community
College

Derbyshire Co
Council

A   B   C   18   D   E   F

Old
Glossop

NORFOLK STREET

Hall Meadow CI
Kingsmoor Park Close

Duke of Norfolk
C ofE School

Fauvel Road

Ford St
Fitzalan St
Charles St

King Edward AV

Riverside

Manor

Smithy
Qua

House Surg

Corn St
Jordan St

York Street

Manor Park Road

Church St South

Wesley St

Woodcock
Grove

Queen's
Drive

Pyegrove

Pyegrove

Woodcock
Farm

WOODCOCK ROAD A57

SNAKE PASS

Howard Street
Group Practice

Henry St

PO

I

SHEFFIELD ROAD

HIGH STREET EAST

A57

Thomas Street

Sills St

Brook Meadow

Cowbrook
Avenue

Hurstbrook
CI

Birch
Grn

Hurst Road

Derbyshire

Hotel

Glossop &
District
Golf Club

Hurst
Reservoir

GLOSSOP

Glossop
Leisure
Centre

Lower
Bank

The Bank

St Marys
RC School

Shrewbrook
Drive

Croft Manor

Cross
Cliffe

Cross Cliffe

Slant

Croft Manor

Millerscale Court

Hillwood Dr

Shireton

Millerscale

Winnats
CI

Hatherage Drive

2   3   1

10

9

11   8

Shirebrook

Wiltshire Dr

Hampshire

Yorkshire
Way

Warwick
Close

Level

GLORIA STREET

Kershaw Street

Wood Street

Highfield Road

Morley
Street

Carr Farm

12

6

Rose
Way

Leicester Drive

Shropshire Way

Riverbank

2

Highbank Rd

Southview
Road

Bracken
Way

Hurstnook
Farm

Level

2

Uplands

Cliffe Road

Whitfield
Cross

Whitfield
Avenue

Padfield Ga

Derbyshire

3

Whitfield
Park

King
Charles
Court

Hob'n
Mdw

Jumble

Moorfield

A624

CHUNAL LANE

25

Hague Street

Kidd Road

Gnat Hole

Wood's
Cabin

5

6

Span
Clough

Hurst Brook

Bray
Clough

Black
Moor

7

A6

Whitethorn
Clough

Shaw
Moor

8

The
Grouse

Chunal
Moor

Harry
Hut

Pennine Way

A   B   C   35   D   E   F

I grid square represents 500 metres

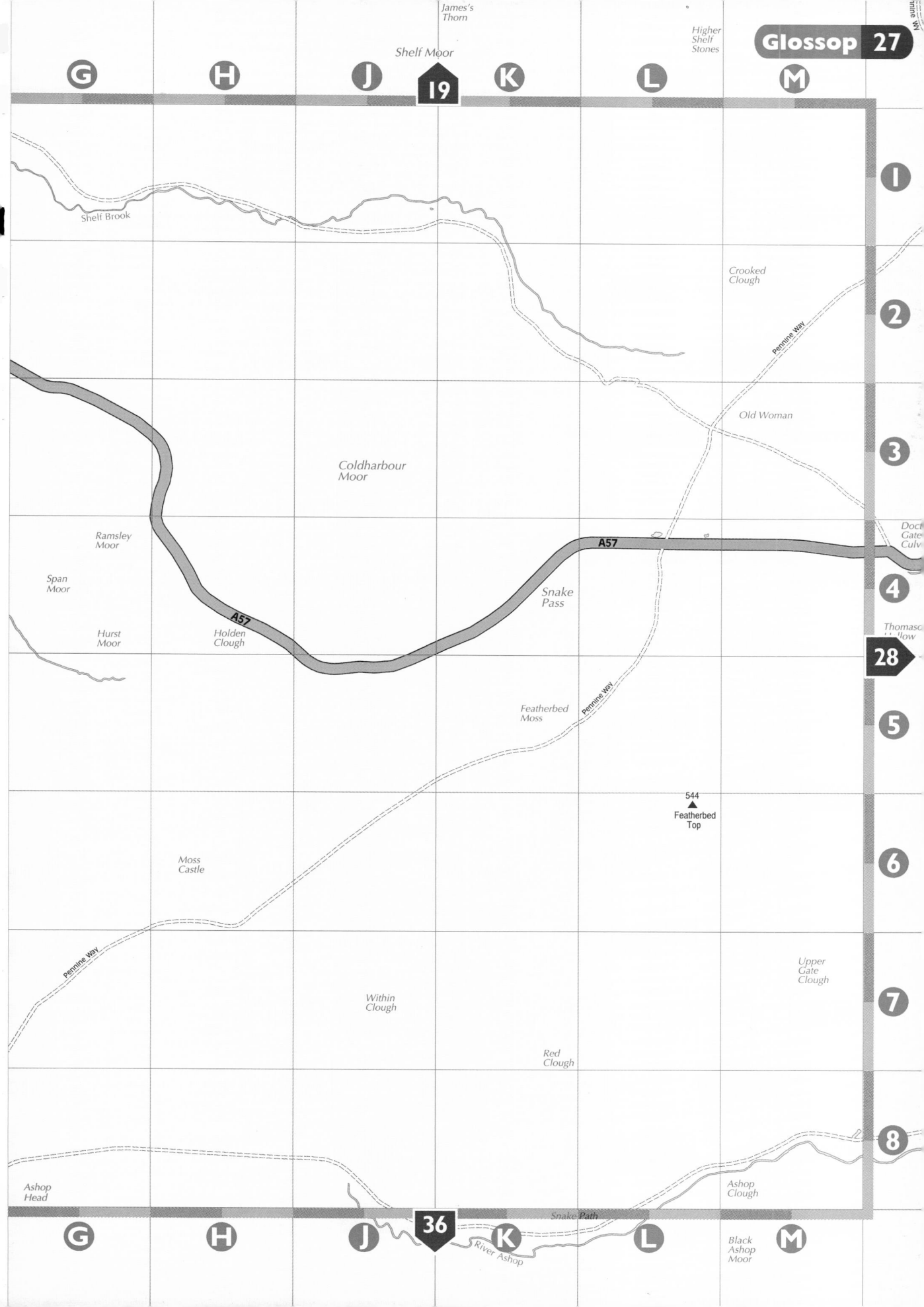

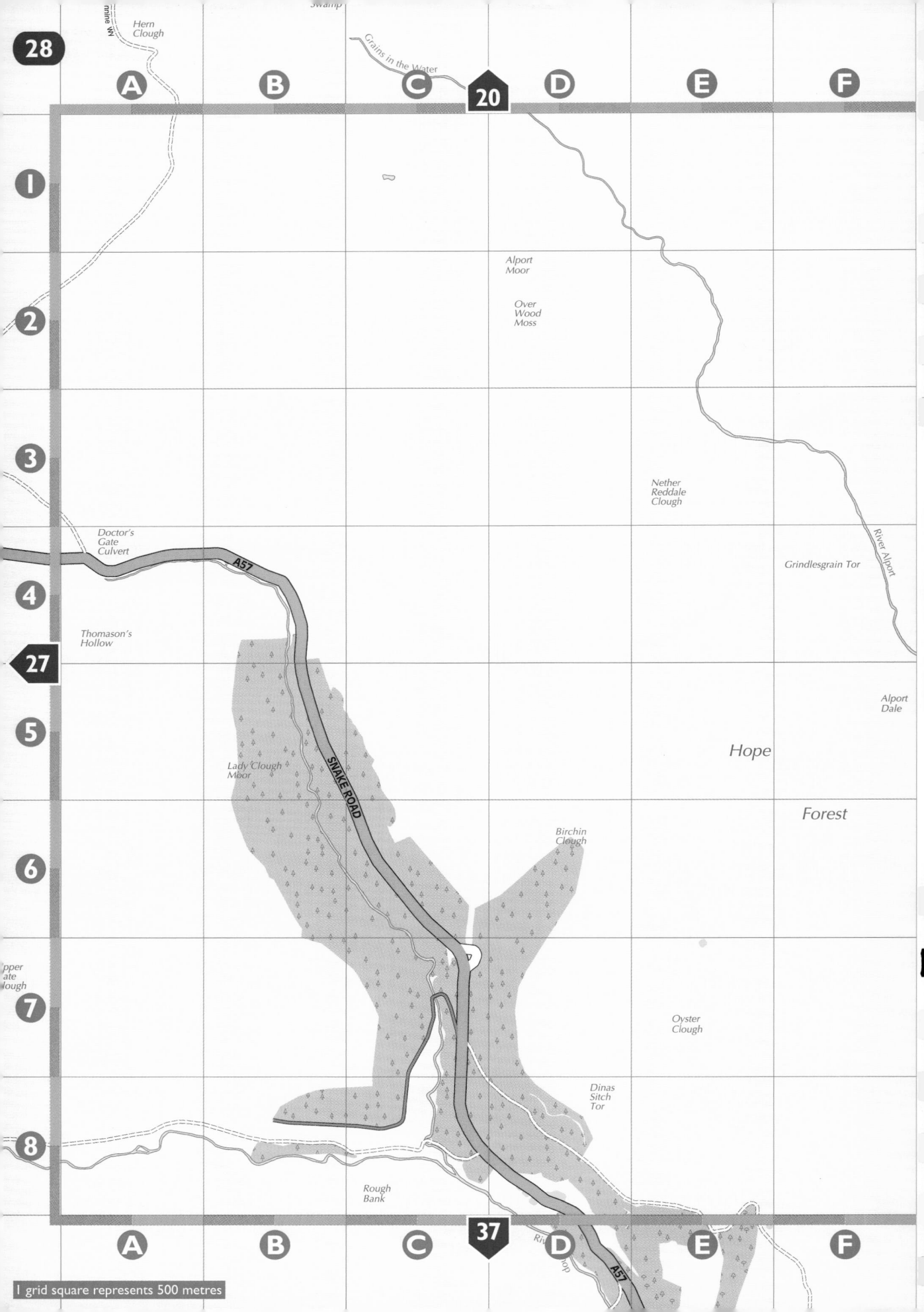

28

A   B   C   **20**   D   E   F

Hern Clough

Swamp

Grains in the Water

1

Alport Moor

2

Over Wood Moss

3

Nether Reddale Clough

River Alport

Doctor's Gate Culvert

A57

Grindlesgrain Tor

4

Thomason's Hollow

27

Alport Dale

5

Lady Clough Moor

SNAKE ROAD

Hope

Forest

Birchin Clough

6

pper ate ough

7

Oyster Clough

Dinas Sitch Tor

8

Rough Bank

37

Ri

A   B   C   D   E   F

A57

1 grid square represents 500 metres

G H River West J `21` K L M

`1`
Ridge
Nether
Moor

Ravens
Clough

`2`
Banktop
Hey

Black
Clough

Westend
Moor

`3`

`4`

Fagney
Clough

`30`

`5`

Green
Clough

Ferny
Side

Birchin
Hat

`6`
Birchinlee
Pasture

Alport
Castles

The
Tower

`7`

Alport
Castles Farm

Cowms
Rocks

River Alport

Hucklow
Lees Barn

`8`

Rowlee
Pasture

Swint
Clough

Hey
Edge

G H J `38` K L M

Knots

Cowms

30

A B C **22** D E F

Linch
Clough

Ox Hey

I

Ridge
Nether
Moor

Cow
Hey

Cold
Side

2

Howden Clough

Sheffield
Derbyshire County

3

Howden
Reservoir

Fox's
Piece

4

29

Beaver's
Croft

Howden
Dam

Green
Clough

5

Upper Derwent Valley

Little
Howden
Moor

Birchinlee
Pasture

Birchinlee

6

Abbey
Bank

7

Derwent
Reservoir

Ouzelden
Clough

8

Gores Farm

Derwent
Dale

Gores
Heights

A B C **39** D E F

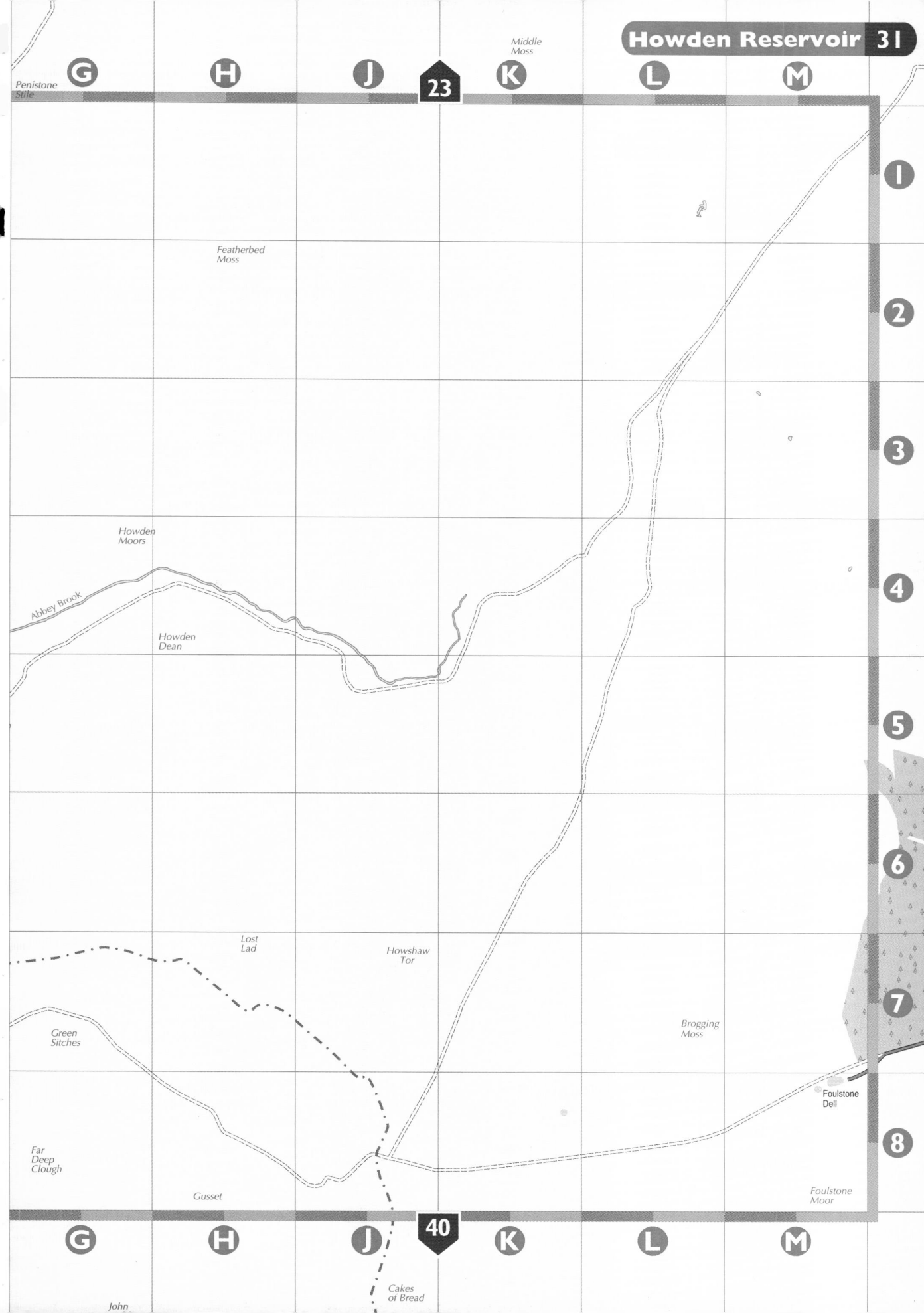

Penistone
Stile

Middle
Moss

Featherbed
Moss

Howden
Moors

Abbey Brook

Howden
Dean

Lost
Lad

Howshaw
Tor

Green
Sitches

Brogging
Moss

Foulstone
Dell

Far
Deep
Clough

Gusset

Foulstone
Moor

John

Cakes
of Bread

ROMIL

A **B** **C** **D** **E** **F**

Gainsborough
Gals

Cherry
Tree

Stockport
Metropolitan
Borough

1 **2** **3** **4** **5** **6** **7** **8**

SK6

Ley Hey Park

Marple Bridge

MARPLE

Hawk Green

Marpleridge

Windlehurst

1 grid square represents 500 metres

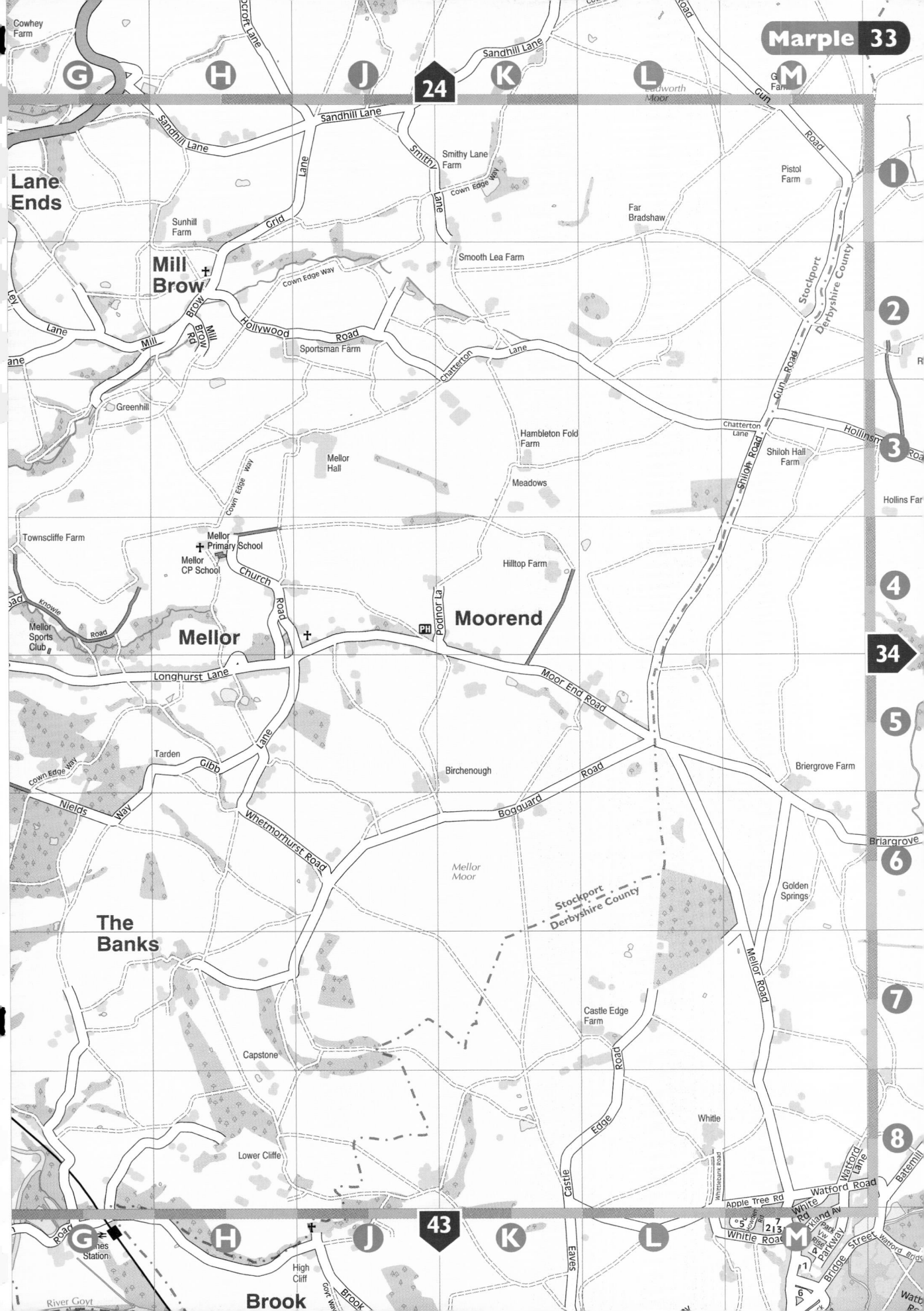

G H J K L M

24

Cowhey Farm

Sandhill Lane

Ledworth Moor

G Farm

I

Lane Ends

Sandhill Lane

Sandhill Lane

Smithy Lane

Smithy Lane Farm

Cown Edge Way

Far Bradshaw

Pistol Farm

Stockport Derbyshire County

Gun Road

2

Sunhill Farm

Grid Lane

Mill Brow

Smooth Lea Farm

Cown Edge Way

Hollywood Road

Sportsman Farm

Chatterton Lane

Chatterton Lane

Gun Road

Shiloh Hall Farm

Hollinsm

3

Hollins Far

Greenhill

Hambleton Fold Farm

Mellor Hall

Meadows

Shiloh Road

4

Townscliffe Farm

Cown Edge Way

Mellor Primary School

Mellor CP School

Hilltop Farm

Church Road

Podnor La

PH

Moorend

34

Mellor Sports Club

Knowle Road

Mellor

Longhurst Lane

Moor End Road

5

Tarden

Gibb Lane

Birchenough

Road

Briargrove Farm

Cown Edge Way

Nields Way

Whetmorhurst Road

Bogguard Road

Golden Springs

Briargrove

6

The Banks

Mellor Moor

Stockport Derbyshire County

Mellor Road

7

Capstone

Castle Edge Farm

Castle Edge Road

Whitle

Whitebank Road

8

Lower Cliffe

...nes Station

G

43

H

J

K

Eaves

L

M

Apple Tree Rd

Whitle Road

Watford Lane

Batemill

Watford Road

5

213

...land AV

...Parkway

Bridge Street

Watford Brds

River Goyt

Goyt Way

Brook

High Cliff

Brook

Brook

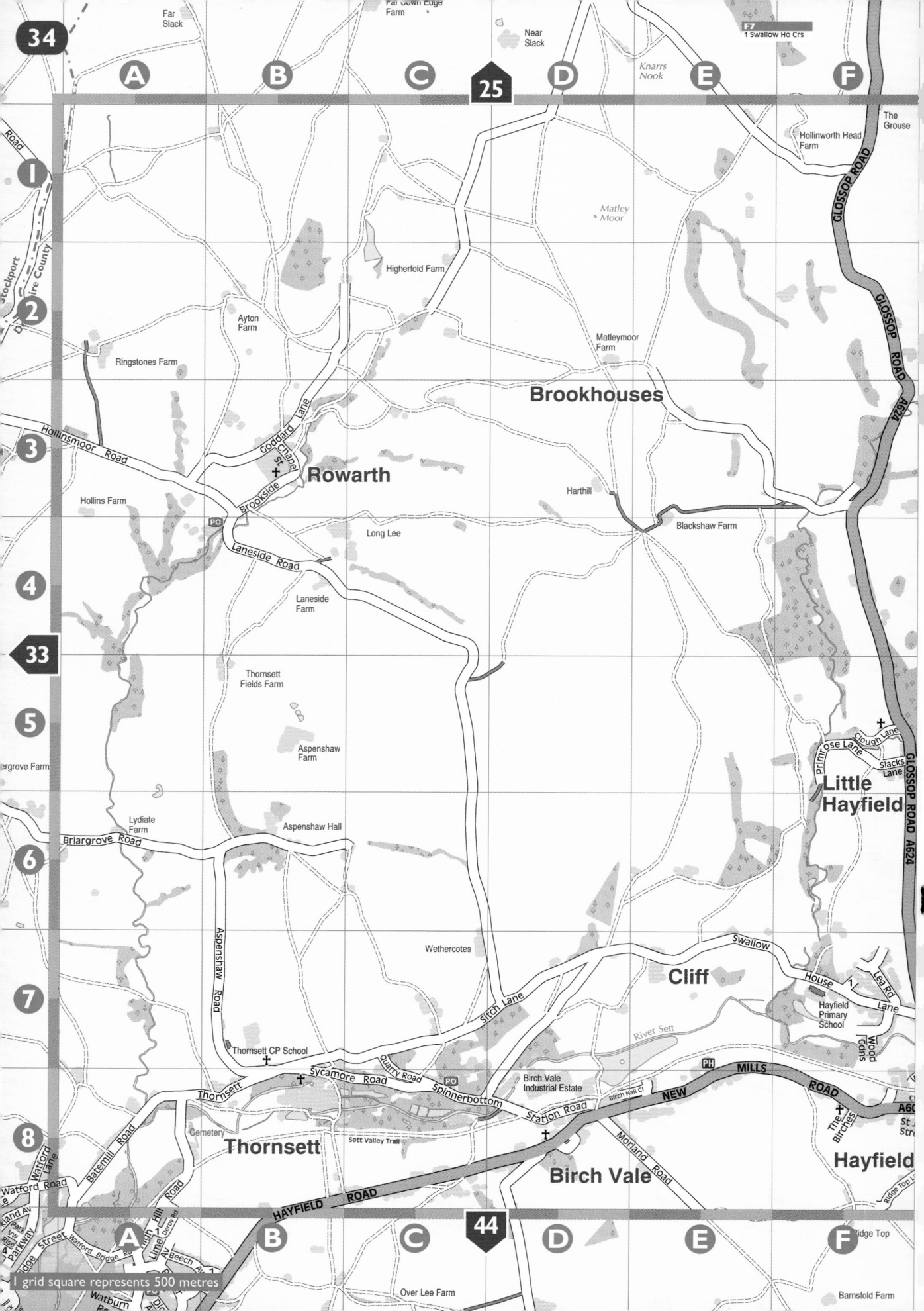

G7
1 Wainhouse Brow
2 Walk Mill Rd

G8
1 Fishers Br
2 The Ridgeways

G H J **26** K L M

Ashop Head

1

2

3

4

36

5

6

7

8

The Intakes

Hollingworth Clough

The Knott

William Clough

Spray House Farm

Leygatehead Moor

Nab Brow

White Brow

Park Hall

Middle Moor

Kinder Reservoir

Park Lane

Farlands Booth

Oldpits Plantation

River Kinder

Kinder Road

The Cote

Fairy Bank Crs

SK22

Kinder Bank

Market Street

Fairy Bank Rd

Highfield Rd

North Rd

Cote Lane

Hill Houses

Hayfield Parish Council

Bank

Vicarage Lane

Doctors Surgery

The Old Bank Surgery

Church St

Chapel St

Spring Vale

Kinder Road

Edale Road

PH

Oaks Av

Valley Road

Tunstead House

Highgate Road

A624 CHAPEL

G H J **45** K L M

Highgate Head

The Ashes

Ⓐ　　　　Ⓑ　　　　Ⓒ　⬣　Ⓓ　　　　Ⓔ　　　　Ⓕ
　　　　　　　　　　　　　　27

Ashop
Head

Snake Path

Ashop
Clough

River Ashop

Black
Ashop
Moor

Ⓘ

The Edge

②

Pennine Way

③

Sandy Heys

Mermaid's
Pool

Kinder
Downfall

④

Kinder　　　　Scout

㉟

River Kinder

Pennine Way

631
▲
The
Peak

⑤

⑥

Cluther Rocks

Pennine Way

⑦

Broad Clough

Kinder Low

Edale Head

Pym Chair

Crowden Tower

Noe Stool

⑧

The Cloughs

Kinderlow End

Ⓐ　　　　Ⓑ　　　　Ⓒ　⬣　Ⓓ　　　　Ⓔ　　　　Ⓕ
　　　　　　　　　　　　　　46

Pennine Way

G   H   J   28   K   L   M

Rough
Bank

Q

River Ashop

A57

Upper
House Farm

SNAKE ROAD A57

1
Cowms
Moor

2

Fairbrook Naze

Fair Brook

3
Wood
Moor

Middle
Seal
Clough

Seal
Flats

Seal
Edge

4

Seal
Stones

Blackden
Moor

38

Crowden Head

5

6
Nether
Tor

Upper
Tor

Edale
Moor

Ring
Roge

7
Golden
Clough

Fox
Holes

Grindslow
Knoll

Grinds Brook

8
The
Nab

G   H   J   47   K   L   M

Grindslow Home

Grindsbrook

A   B   C   D   E   F

29

Swint Clough

Hey Ridge

Knots

Hucklow Lees Barn

Rowlee Pasture

I

Cowms Moor

2

Wood Cott

A57

River Ashop

A57

†

3

The Wicken

Gillot Hey Farm

Rowlee Farm

Upper Ashop

4

Ashop Moor

Blackley Hey

37

Blackden Edge

Crookstone Knoll

5

Madwoman's Stones

6

Nether Moor

Ringing Roger

Jaggers Clough

7

8

The Nab

Lady Booth Brook

Rowland Cote

Carr Home

Clough Farm

48

Nether Booth

River Noe

A   B   C   D   E   F

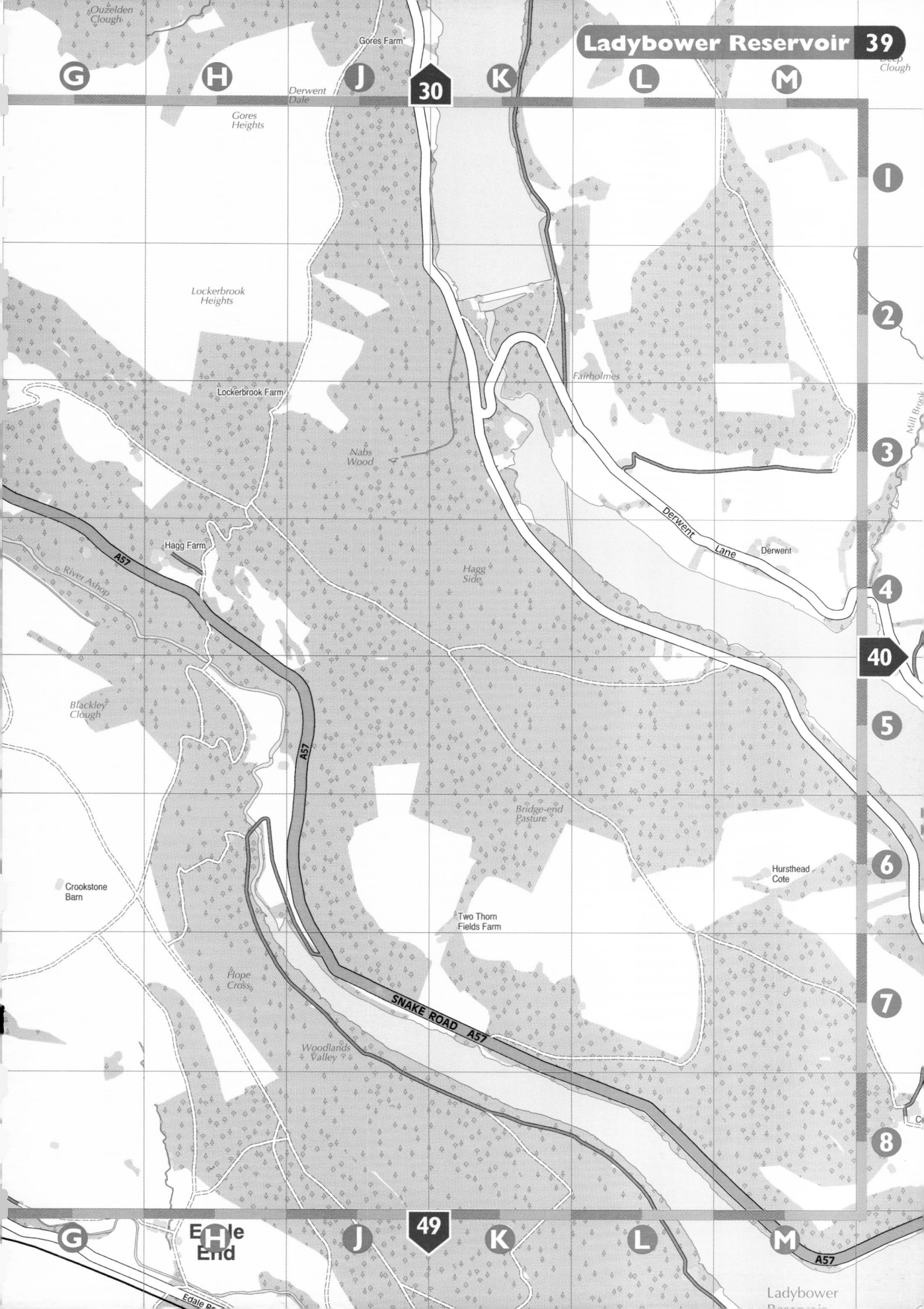

G   H   J   30   K   L   M

Ouzelden Clough

Gores Farm

Derwent Dale

Gores Heights

I

Lockerbrook Heights

Deep Clough

2

Mill Brook

Fairholmes

3

Derwent Lane

Derwent

Lockerbrook Farm

Nabs Wood

A57

River Ashop

Hagg Farm

Hagg Side

4

40

Blackley Clough

A57

5

Bridge-end Pasture

Hursthead Cote

6

Crookstone Barn

Two Thorn Fields Farm

7

Hope Cross

SNAKE ROAD   A57

Woodlands Valley

8

G   Edale End   J   49   K   L   M   A57

Ladybower

Far
Deep
Clough

A

Gusset

B

C

31

D

E

F

Foulstone
Moor

1

John
Field
Howden

Cakes
of Bread

2

Dovestone
Clough

Derwent
Edge

Sheffield
Derbyshire County

Strines
Moor

Dovestone
Tor

Mill Brook

3

Salt
Cellar

White
Tor

4

Wheel
Stones

39

Ashes
Farm

5

Derwent
Moors

Ladybower
Reservoir

6

head

Hurkling
Stones

Highshaw
Clough

7

Cutthroat
Bridge

Hordron
Edge

8

Crookhill Farm

Ladybower
Tor

Ashopton

Ladybower
House

Priddock
Wood

A

B

C

50

D

A57

A6013

E

F

ybower
servoir

I grid square represents 500 metres

G H J K L M

G **H** PH Strines **J** **K** **L** **M**

I
2
3
4
5
6
7
8

Strines
Resevoir

Sugworth Road

Bradfield
Moors

Sugworth
Hall

Bents
House

Moor
Lodge

Strines
Edge

Sheffield
Derbyshire County

Sugworth Road

Ughill Moors

Stake Hill Road

Rising
Clough

Moscar
Cross

Moscar Cross Road

Moscar
House

Heathy Lane

Moscar
Lodge

**Hollow
Meadows**

A57

A57

Moscar
Fields

Stanage
End

G **H** **J** 5I **K** **L** **M**

Jarvis
Clough

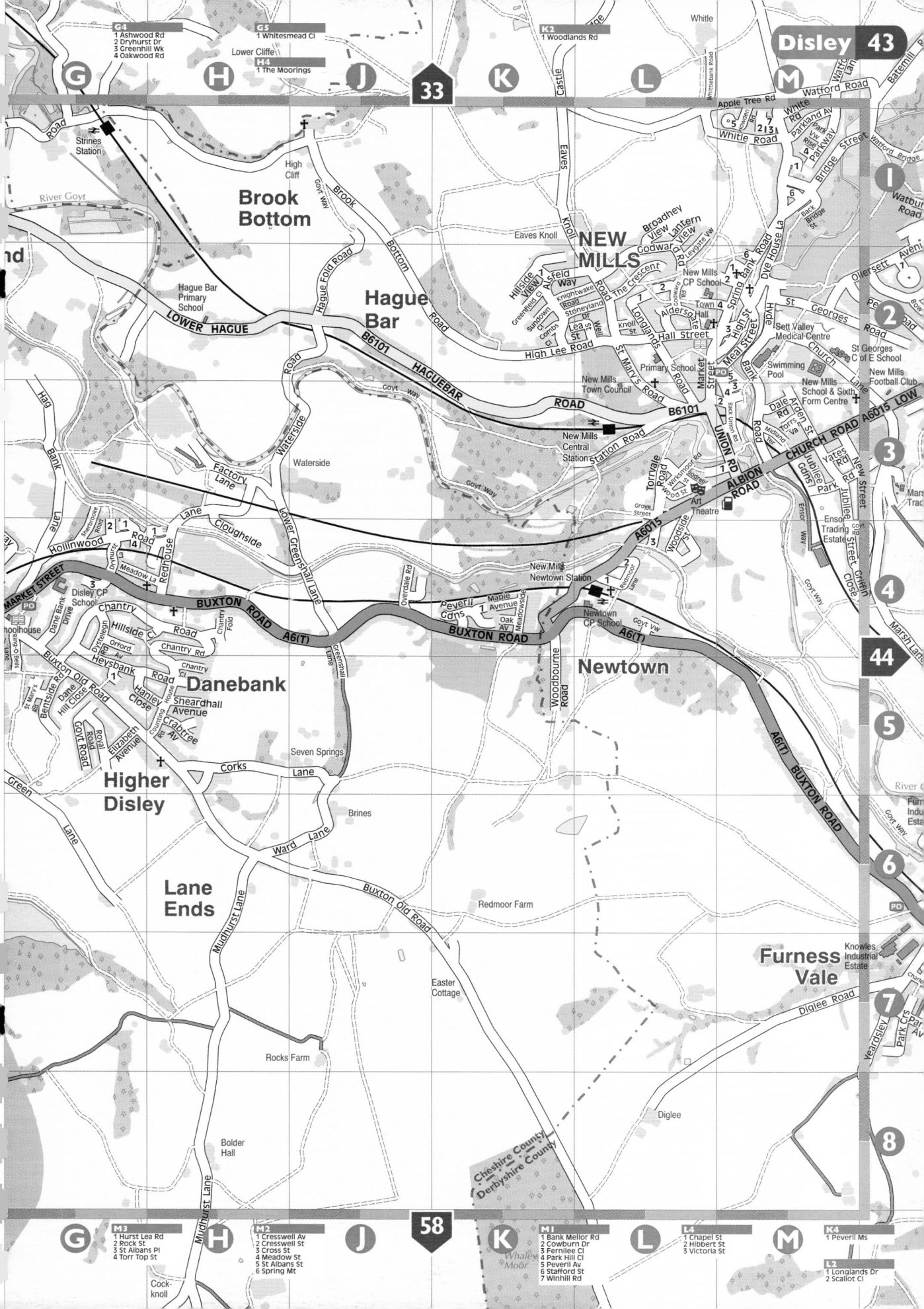

G4
1 Ashwood Rd
2 Dryhurst Dr
3 Greenhill Wk
4 Oakwood Rd

G5
1 Whitesmead Cl

Lower Cliffe

H4
1 The Moorings

K2
1 Woodlands Rd

33

River Goyt

Strines Station

Brook Bottom

High Cliff

NEW MILLS

Hague Bar Primary School

LOWER HAGUE

Hague Bar

B6101

HAGUEBAR ROAD

Goyt Way

High Lee Road

New Mills Town Council

Waterside

Factory Lane

New Mills Central Station

Station Road

B6101

Goyt Way

Broadhey View
Lantern View
Godwar
Hillside VIEW
Alsfeld Way
Greenfield Cl
Sundown Cl
Combs
Knightwake Road
Stoneyland Dr
Lea St
Knoll St
Longlands
The Crescent
New Mills CP School
Town Hall
Aldersage
Primary School
St Mary's Road
Well

Watford Road

Apple Tree Rd

Parkland Av
White Rd
Whitle Road
Bridge Street
Park Parkway
Watford Bridge

I

Watbur Road

Ollersett Avenu
Pe
Bow

2

St Georges Road

St Georges C of E School
Sett Valley Medical Centre
Swimming Pool
Church
New Mills Football Club
New Mills School & Sixth Form Centre

Market Street
Meal Street
Bank
Back Union Rd
UNION RD
ALBION ROAD
CHURCH ROAD A6015 LOW
Dale Rd
Arden Rd
Torrs
Midland
Jubilee Gdns
Yates Rd
Jubilee Park
New Street
Ensor Trading Estate
Ensor St
Griffin Close
Goyt

3

Mars
Trad

4

Hollinwood

MARKET STREET

PO
Schoolhouse

Disley CP School

Chantry
Hillside
Dysteleigh
Orford Av
Chantry Road
Chantry Fold
Chantry Ci
Chantry Cl

Danebank

Sheardhall Avenue

Crabtree Av

Corks Lane

Higher Disley

Lane Ends

Mudhurst Lane

Torvale Road
Wirksmoor Rd
Wood St
Grove Street
A6015
Woodside
Art Theatre

New Mills Newtown Station

Peveril Gdns
Maple Avenue
Oak Av
Meadowside

BUXTON ROAD A6(T)

Lower Greenshall Lane

Greenshall Lane

Overdale Rd

Redhouse

Meadow La

Dane Bank Drive
Heysbank Road
Hanley Close
Dane Hill Close Road
St Mary's
Bentside Rd
Buxton Old Road
Royal Oak
Goyt Road
Elizabeth Avenue
Green Lane

Seven Springs

Brines

Ward Lane

Buxton Old Road

Redmoor Farm

Easter Cottage

Rocks Farm

Bolder Hall

Cock-knoll

Newtown CP School
Redmoor Lane
Woodbourne Road

Newtown

A6(T) BUXTON ROAD

44

5

River G

Furn Indu Esta

6

PO

Furness Vale

Knowles Industrial Estate

Goyt Way

Diglee Road

Yeardsley
Park Crs
Par Av

7

Diglee

Cheshire County
Derbyshire County

8

G

M3
1 Hurst Lea Rd
2 Rock St
3 St Albans Pl
4 Torr Top St

H

M2
1 Cresswell Av
2 Cresswell St
3 Cross St
4 Meadow St
5 St Albans St
6 Spring Mt

J

58

K

M1
1 Bank Mellor Rd
2 Cowburn Dr
3 Fernilee Cl
4 Park Hill Cl
5 Peveril Av
6 Stafford St
7 Winhill Rd

L

L4
1 Chapel St
2 Hibbert St
3 Victoria St

M

K4
1 Peveril Ms

L2
1 Longlands Dr
2 Scallot Cl

Whaley Moor

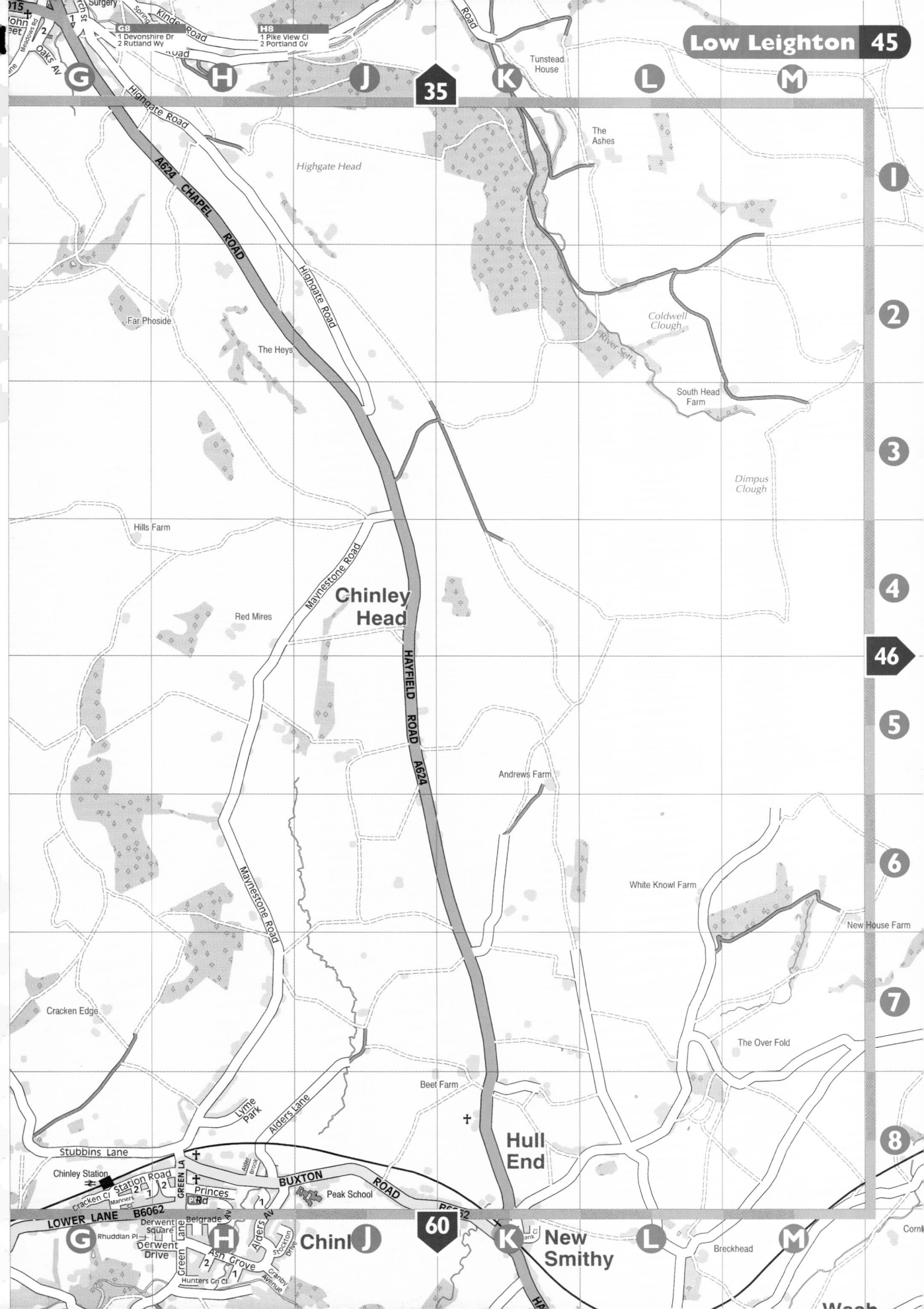

G H J 35 K L M

I

2

3

4

46

5

6

7

8

G H Chinl J 60 K New Smithy L M

Tunstead House

The Ashes

Highgate Head

Coldwell Clough

River Sett

South Head Farm

Dimpus Clough

Far Phoside

The Heys

Hills Farm

HIGHGATE ROAD

A624 CHAPEL ROAD

Highgate Road

Maynestone Road

Red Mires

Chinley Head

HAYFIELD ROAD

A624

Andrews Farm

White Knowl Farm

New House Farm

Maynestone Road

Cracken Edge

The Over Fold

Beet Farm

Hull End

Lyme Park

Alders Lane

Stubbins Lane

Chinley Station

Cracken Cl

Station Road

GREEN LA

Princes Rd

Manners Cl

Derwent Square

Belgrade

Alder Brook

BUXTON ROAD

Peak School

B6062

Breckhead

Cornl

LOWER LANE B6062

Rhuddlan Pl

Derwent Drive

Ash Grove

Alders Av

Stockton Drive

Granby Avenue

Hunters Gn Cl

Meadows Br

Oaks Av

Surgery

Kinder Road

Road

G8 1 Devonshire Dr 2 Rutland Wy

H8 1 Pike View Cl 2 Portland Gv

Weak

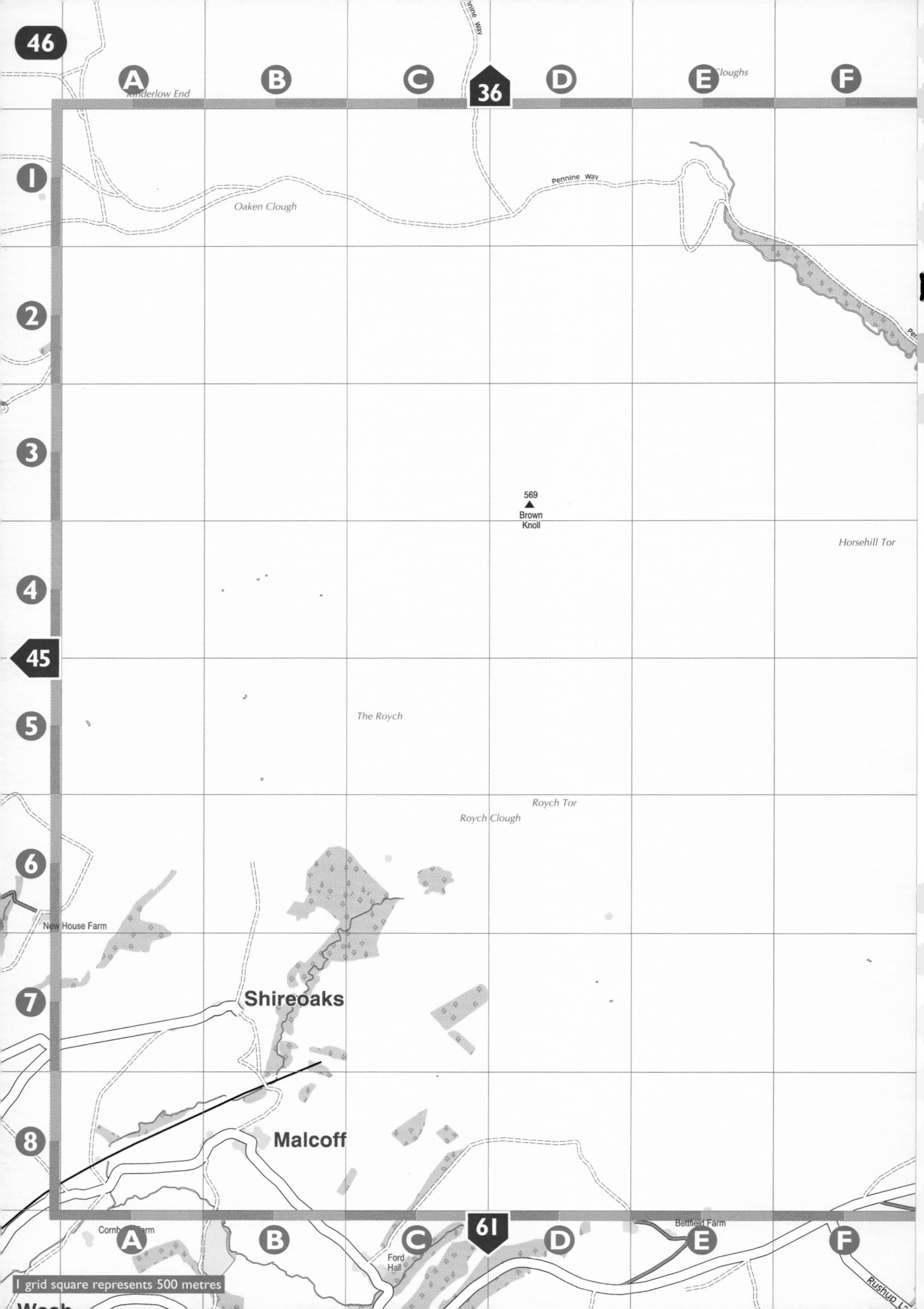

A Kinderlow End
B
C
36
D
E Cloughs
F

I

Pennine Way

Oaken Clough

2

3

569
▲
Brown
Knoll

Horsehill Tor

4

45

5

The Roych

Roych Tor
Roych Clough

6

New House Farm

7

Shireoaks

8

Malcoff

A Cornb... Farm
B
C Ford
Hall
61
D
E Bettfield Farm
F

Rushup L...

1 grid square represents 500 metres

Week

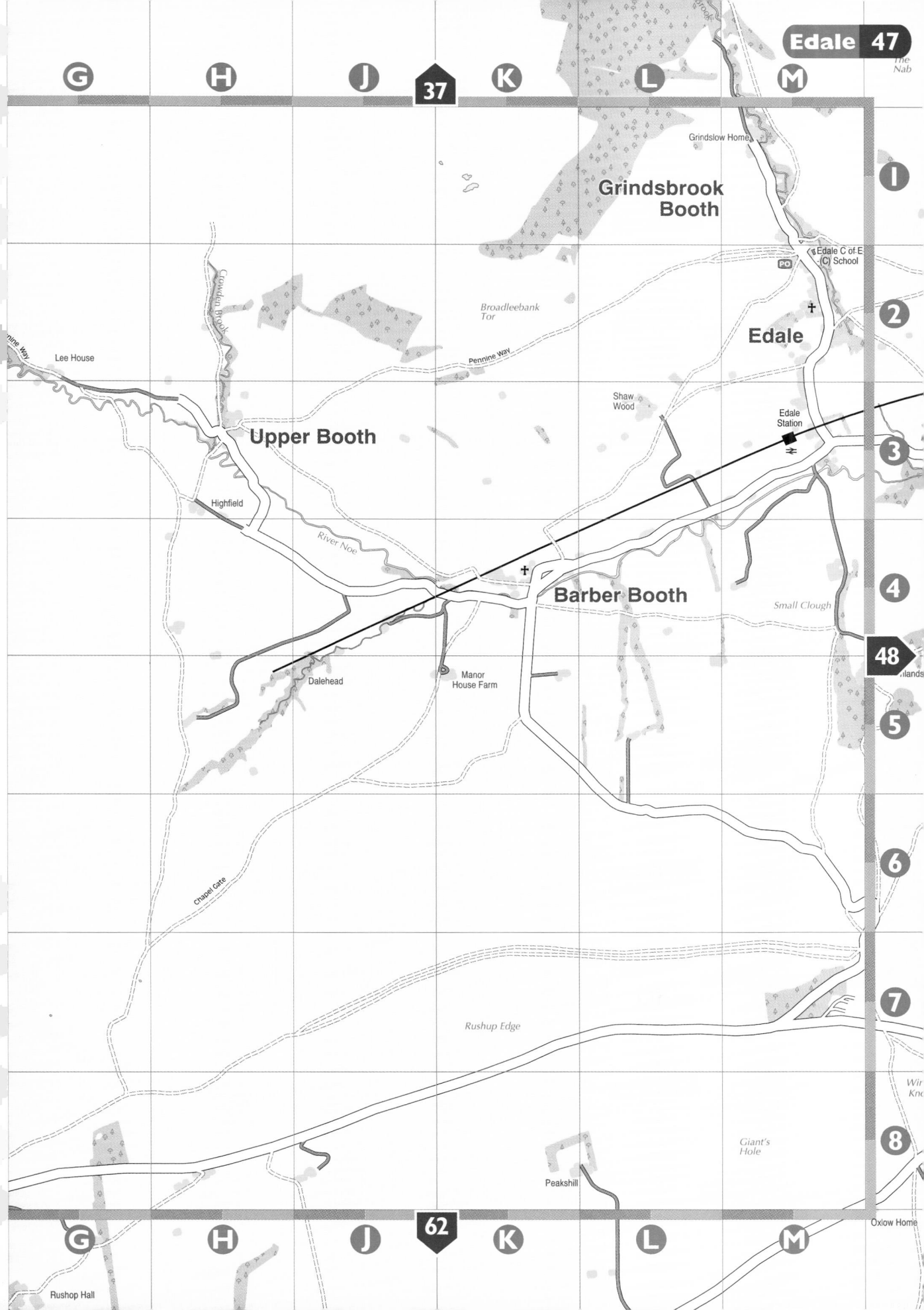

G H J K L M

39

Edale End

Ladybower Reservoir

I

Fiddle Clough

A57

Normans Farm

Harrop Farm

2

S33

Oaker Farm

Hope Brink

Ward's Piece

Thornhill Brink

3

Fullwood Holmes

Fullwood Stile Lane

464 ▲ Win Hill

Losehill Farm

Fullwood Stile Farm

4

Townhead

Twitchill Farm

50

5

Birchfield

Spring Home Farm

Aston

PH

Cemetery

6

Hope County Primary School

Eccles Close

River Noe

Hope

Castleton Road

PO

The Crescent

CASTLETON ROAD

Hope Valley College

STATION ROAD

Hope Station

Aston Lane

7

Peakshole Water

Station Road

Warehouse Lane

Pindale Road

on

8

Road

Brough

G H J K L M

64

Pin Dale

Works

RETFIELD ROAD

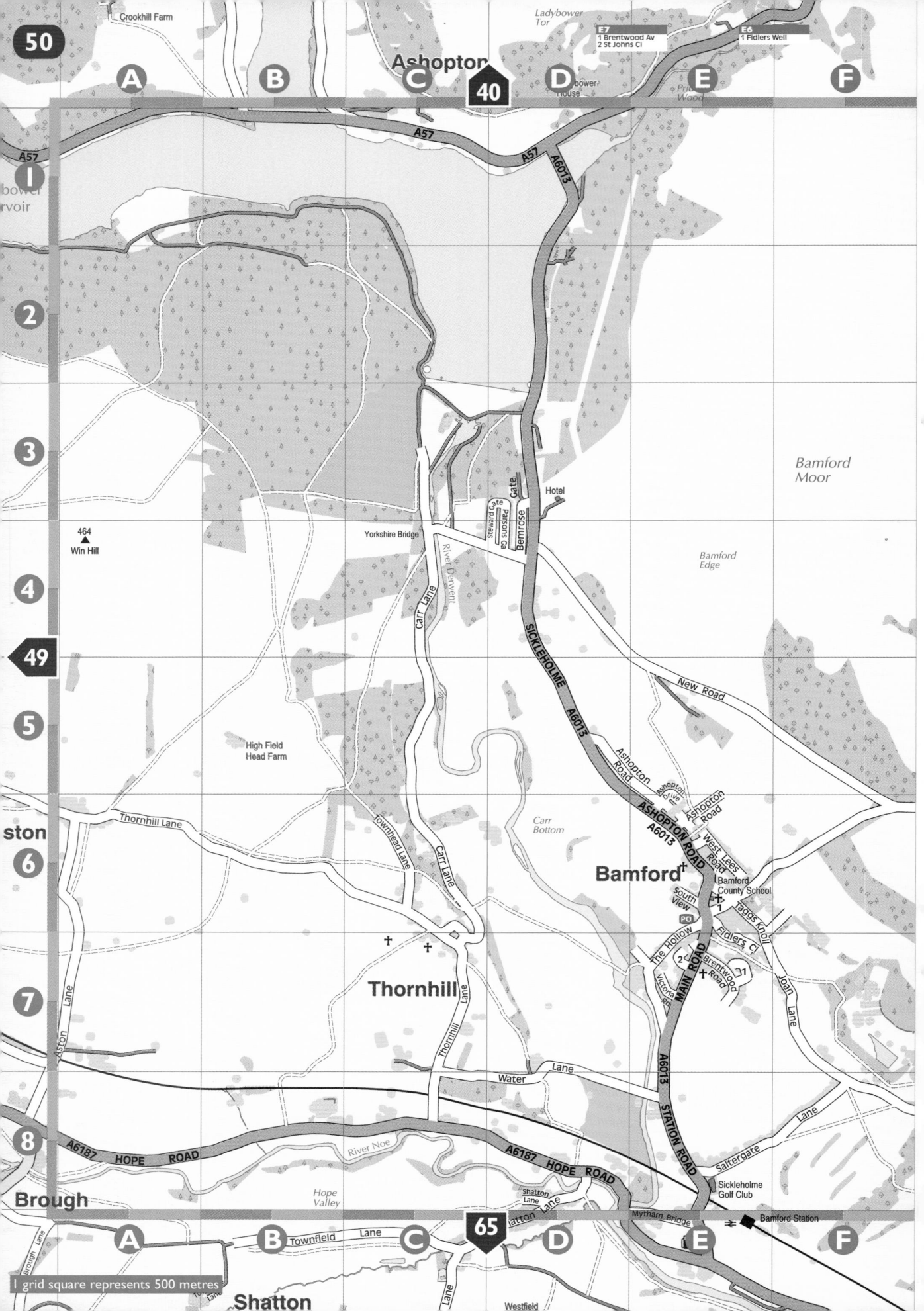

G   H   J   41   K   L   M

Jarvis
Clough

Moscar
Moor

High Lad
Ridge

Crow
Chin

457
High Neb

Stanage Edge

Stanedge
Lodge

Sheffield
Derbyshire County

Buck Stone

Long Causeway

52

The Cough

Sheepwash
Bank

Dennis
Knoll

Greens House

Robin
Hood's Cave

Gatehouse

Upper
Hurst Farm

North
Lees

Hook's
Car

Hurstclough Lane

Nether
Hurst

Birley Lane

Brookfield
Manor

G   H   66   J   K   L   M

Cunliffe House

Thornseat

Birley Farm

Kimber
Car Head

Stanage

A B C D E F

Ash
Cabin
Flat

I Brown
Edge

Redmires Road

2 Hallam
Moors

Wyming
Brook Farm

Redmires
Reservoirs

3 Fairthorn
Lodge

dge

4

51

Stanedge
Pole

5

White
Path
Moss

6 Robin
Hood's Cave

Friar's Ridge

Sheffield
Derbyshire County

Hook's
Car

7 Cowper
Stone

Overstones
Farm

8

Toothill
Farm

A B C D E F

Gallow

Burbage
Moor

I grid square represents 500 metres

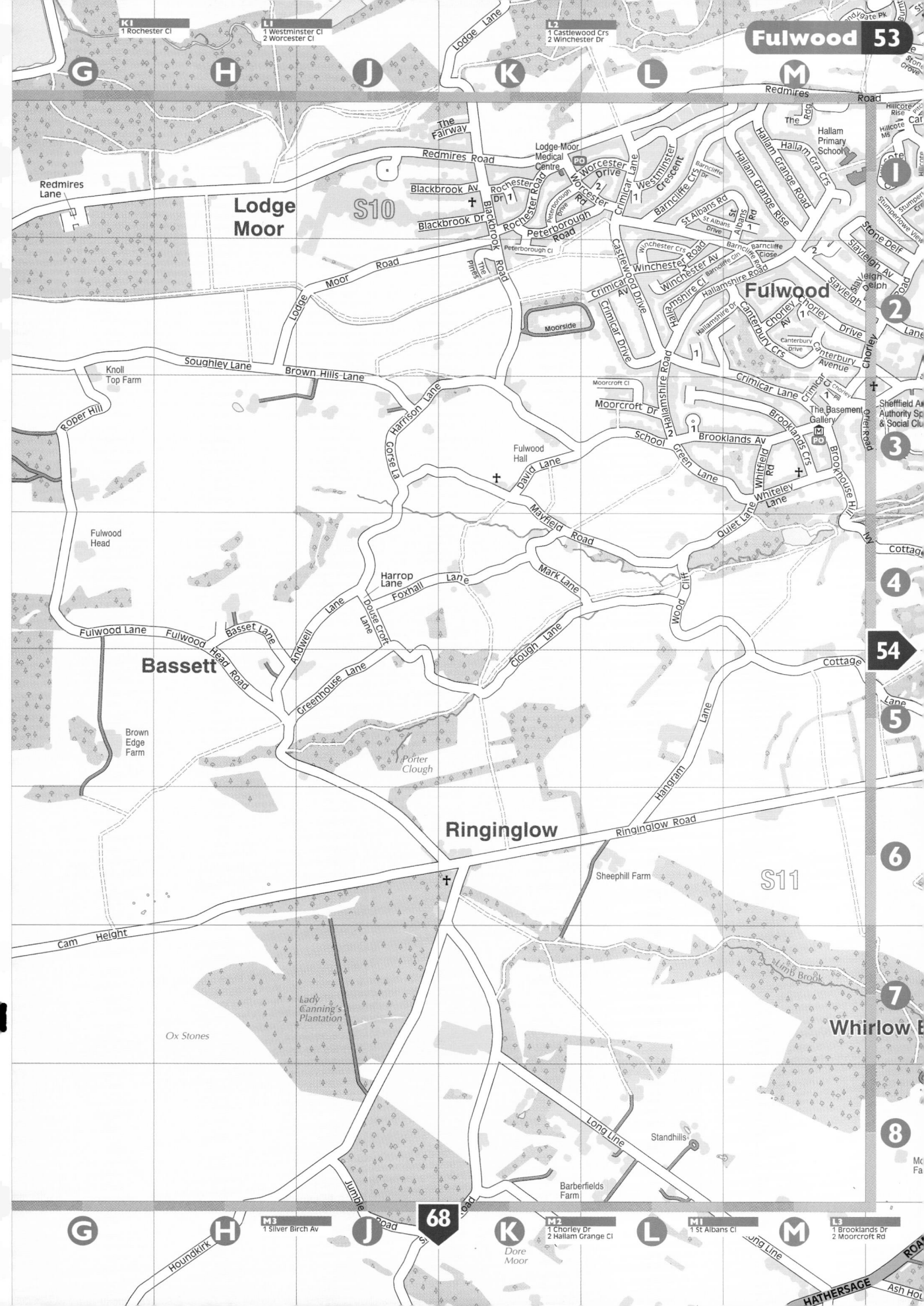

G H J K L M

1 Rochester Cl

Redmires Road

Hillcote Rise
Hillcote Ms

The Rdg

Stone Delf

Stumperlowe View
Stumperlowe

Slayleigh Av

Slayleigh Delph

I

1
1 Westminster Cl
2 Worcester Cl

1
1 Castlewood Crs
2 Winchester Dr

The Fairway

Redmires Road

Lodge-Moor Medical Centre

PO

Worcester Drive

Blackbrook Av

Rochester Road

Castlewood Av

Crimicar Lane

Westminster Crescent

Hallam Gra Crs

Hallam Grange Rise

Hallam Grange Road

Hallam Primary School

Hallam Cl

Fulwood

2

Redmires Lane

Lodge Moor

S10

Blackbrook Dr

Blackbrook Road

Peterborough Drive

Peterborough Road

Winchester Cres

Winchester Av

Winchester Road

St Albans Rd

St Albans Drive

St Albans

Barncliffe Crs

Barncliffe Dr

Barncliffe Rd

Barncliffe Close

Barncliffe Road

Chorley Av

Chorley Rd

Chorley Drive

Chorley

Slayleigh Av

The Pines

Peterborough Cl

Lodge Moor Road

Moorside

Crimicar Drive

Castlewood Drive

Hallamshire Av

Hallamshire Dr

Hallamshire Road

Canterbury Crs

Canterbury Avenue

Canterbury Drive

Crimicar Lane

Chorley

Orrel Road

Sheffield Au Authority Sp & Social Clu

3

Soughley Lane

Brown Hills Lane

Knoll Top Farm

Harrison Lane

Gorse La

Moorcroft Cl

Moorcroft Dr

Hallamshire Road

School Green Lane

The Basement Gallery

Brooklands Av

Brooklands Crs

Whitfield Rd

M PO

Brookhouse Hill

Fulwood Hall

David Lane

Whiteley Lane

Quiet Lane

Ivy Cottage

Cottage

4

Roper Hill

Fulwood Head

Mayfield Road

Mark Lane

Wood Cliff Lane

54

Harrop Lane

Foxhall Lane

Andwell Lane

Douse Croft Lane

Clough Lane

Cottage

5

Fulwood Lane

Fulwood Head Road

Basset Lane

Bassett

Greenhouse Lane

Porter Clough

Hangram Lane

6

Brown Edge Farm

Ringinglow

Ringinglow Road

S11

Sheephill Farm

Cam Height

Limb Brook

7

Lady Canning's Plantation

Ox Stones

Whirlow E

Long Line

Standhills

8

Barberfields Farm

Jumble Road

68

Houndkirk Road

Dore Moor

Long Line

HATHERSAGE ROA Ash Hou

G H J K L M

M3
1 Silver Birch Av

M2
1 Chorley Dr
2 Hallam Grange Ci

M1
1 St Albans Cl

L3
1 Brooklands Dr
2 Moorcroft Rd

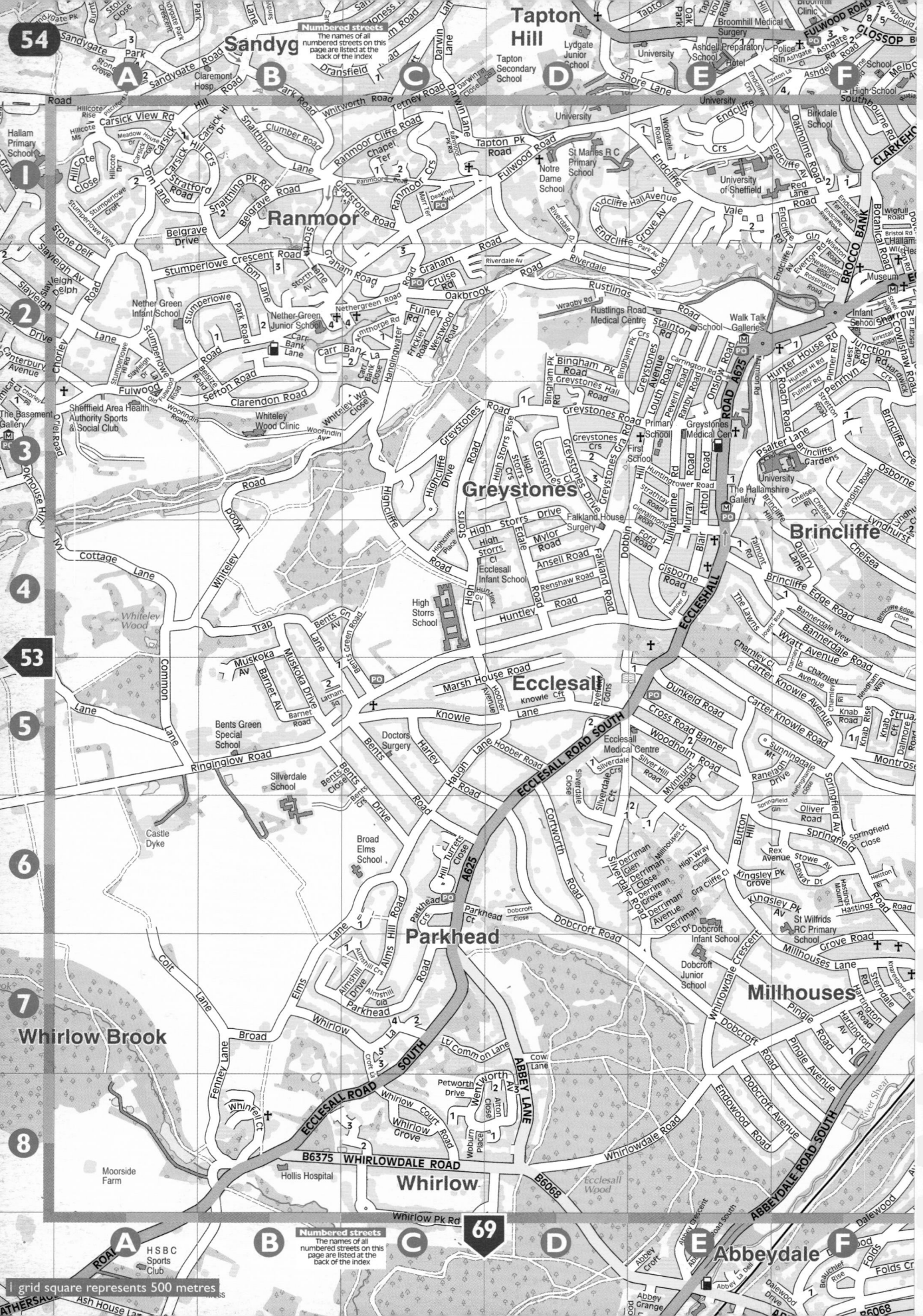

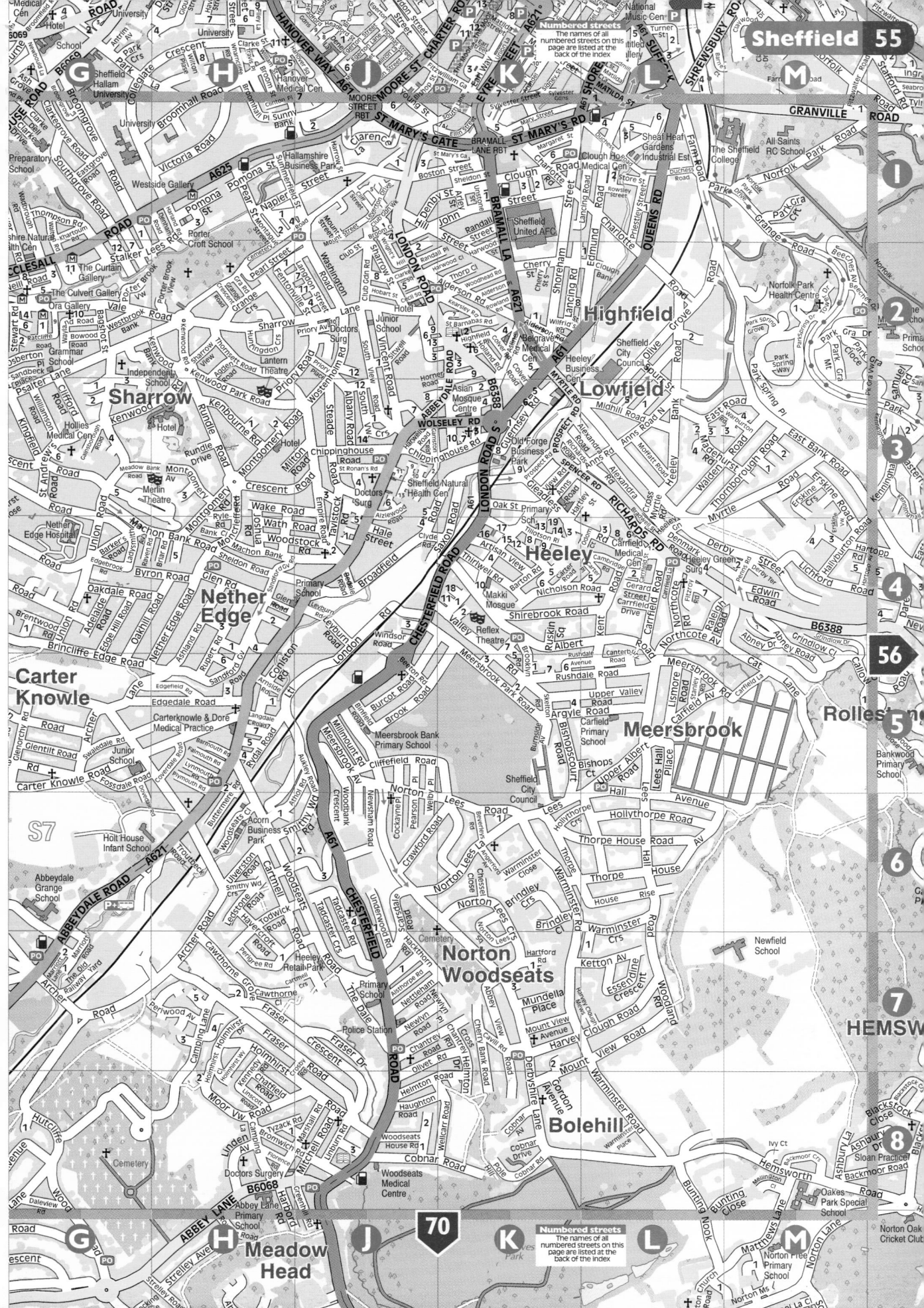

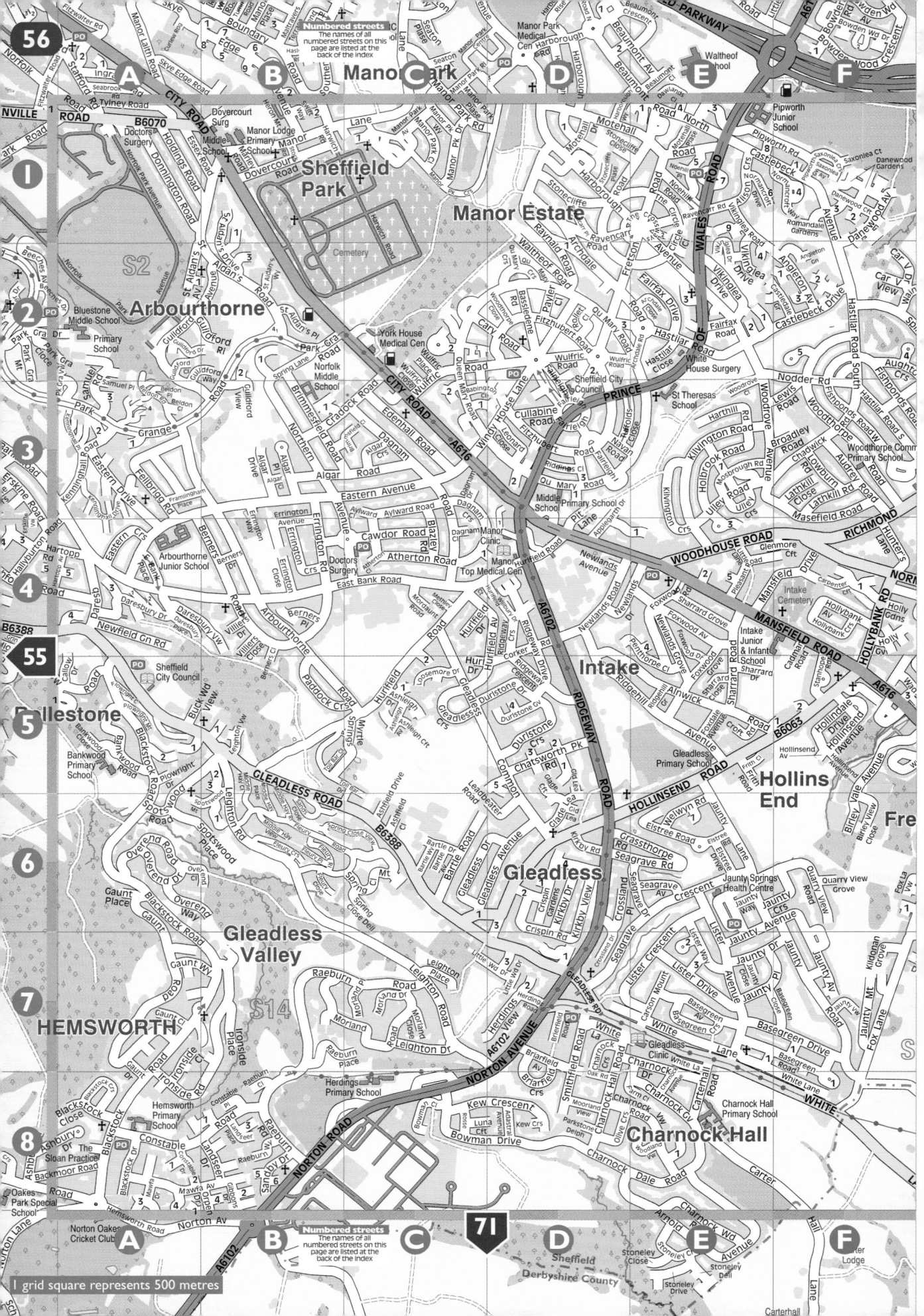

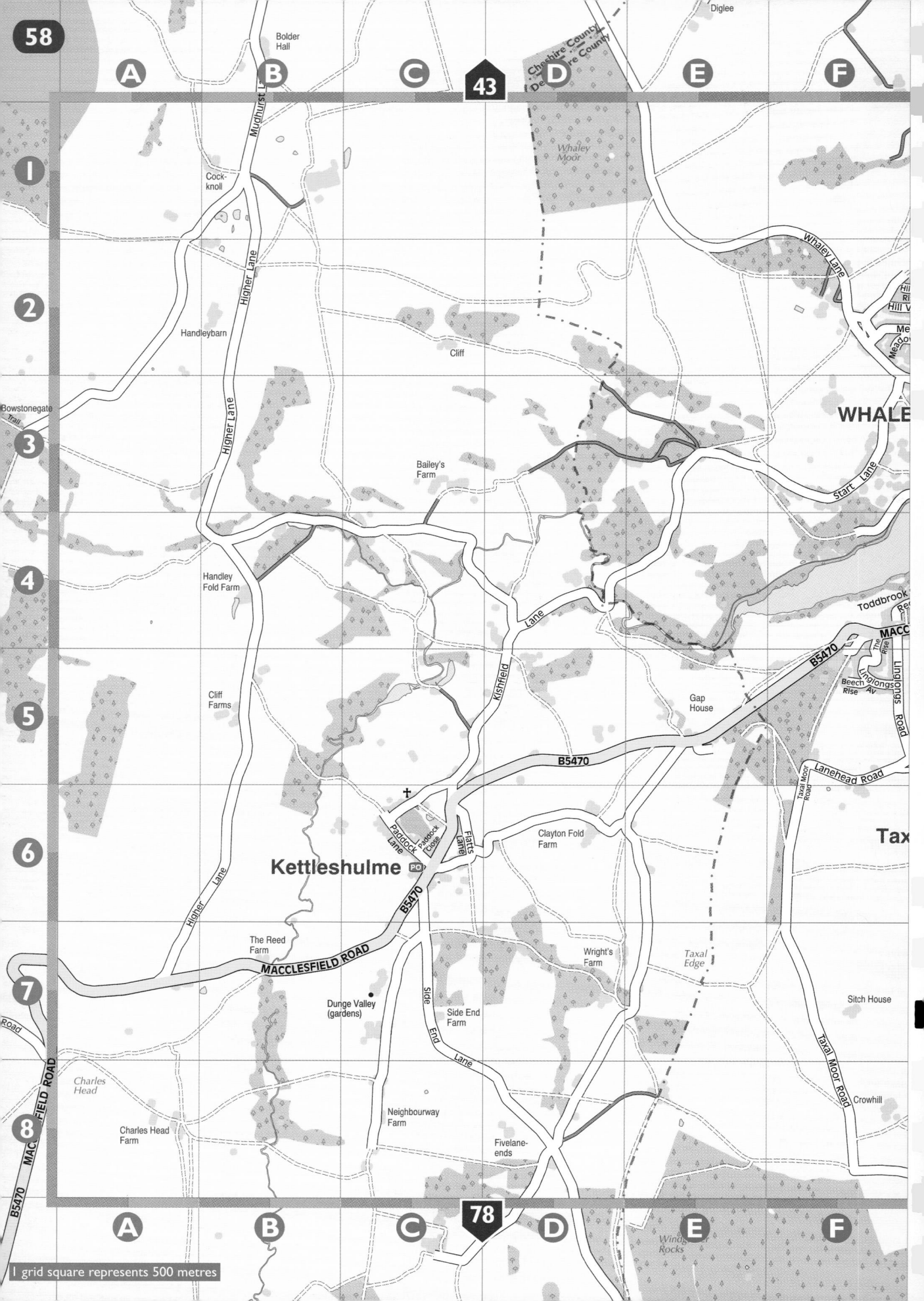

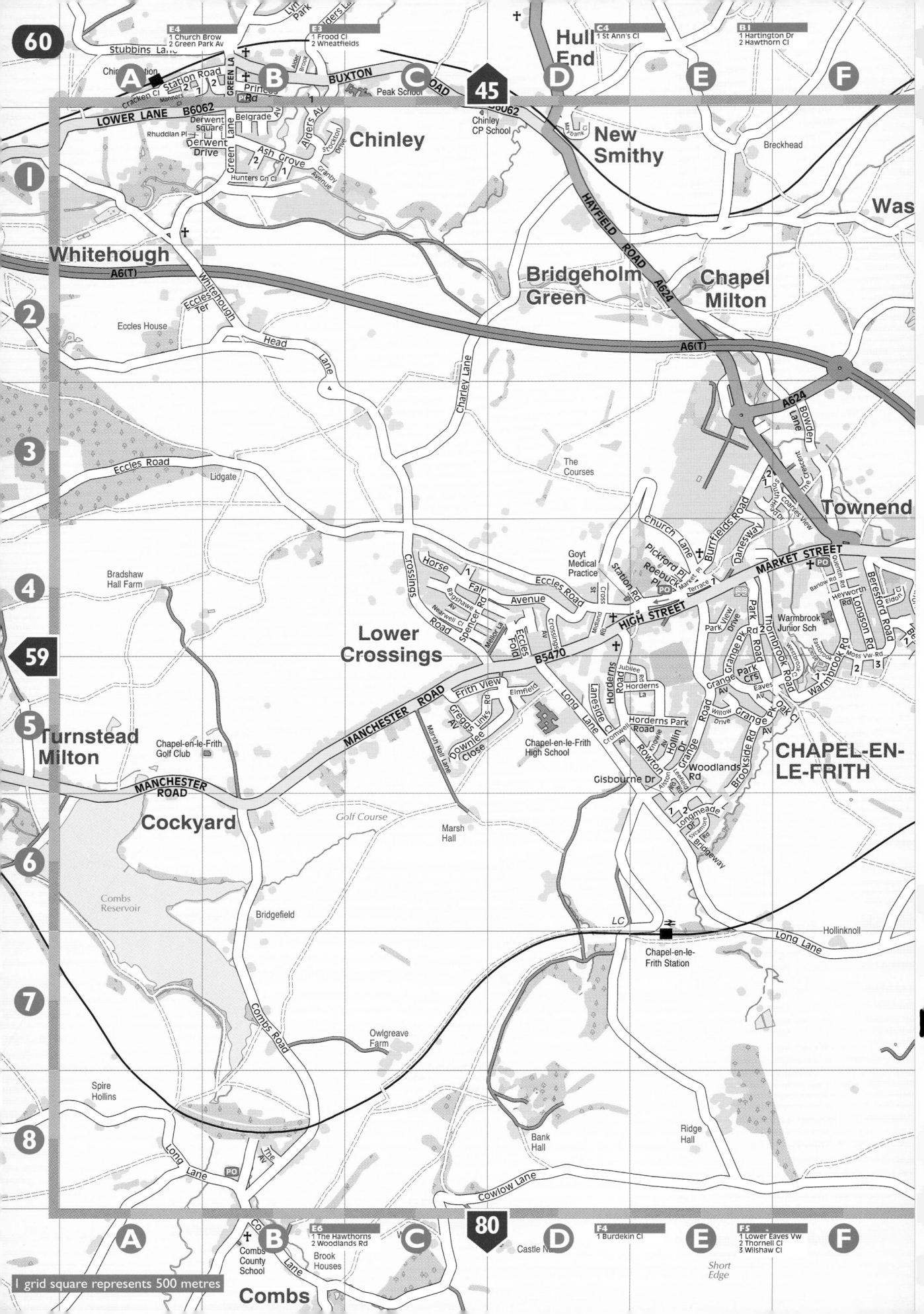

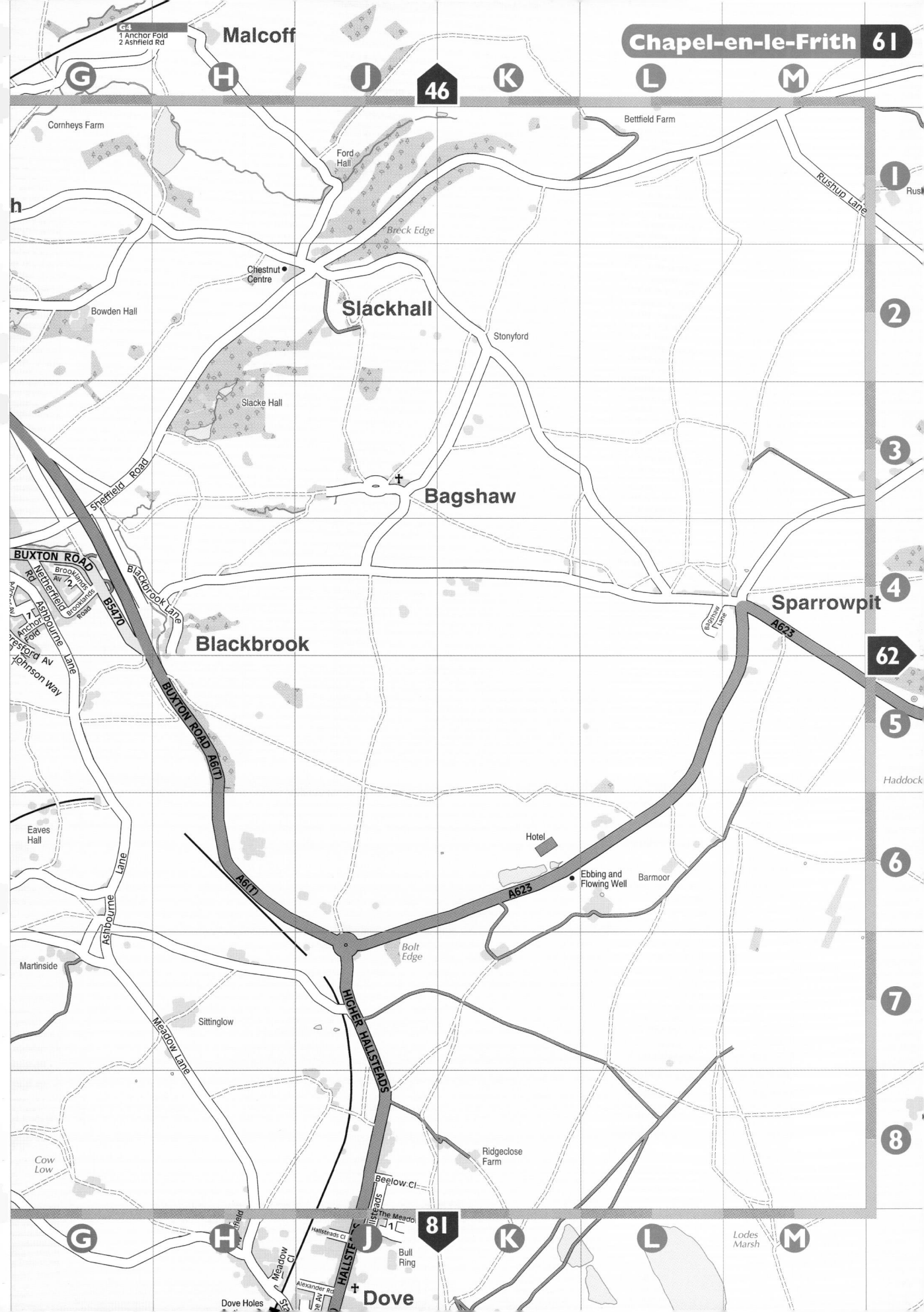

G4
1 Anchor Fold
2 Ashfield Rd

Malcoff

G   H   J   46   K   L   M

Cornheys Farm

Bettfield Farm

Rushup Lane

I

Ford Hall

Breck Edge

Chestnut Centre

Bowden Hall

Slackhall

Stonyford

2

Slacke Hall

3

† **Bagshaw**

Sheffield Road

Blackbrook Lane

Sparrowpit

Bagshaw Lane

A623

4

BUXTON ROAD

B5470

Netherfield Rd

Brooklands Av

Brookanos Road

Ashbourne Rd

Anchor Fold

Cresford Av

Johnson Way

Blackbrook

62

Haddock

5

BUXTON ROAD A6(T)

Eaves Hall

Hotel

A623

Ebbing and Flowing Well

Barmoor

6

A6(T)

Ashbourne Lane

Bolt Edge

Martinside

Meadow Lane

Sittinglow

HIGHER HALLSTEADS

7

Cow Low

Ridgeclose Farm

8

Beelow Cl

The Meado

HALLSTEADS

Lodes Marsh

G   H   Hallsteads Cl   J   81   K   L   M

Meadow Cl

Bull Ring

Alexander Rd

† **Dove**

Dove Holes

A B C **47** D E F

D7
1 Church Cl
1t's
Hole

Peakshill

Rushop Hall

Rushup Lane

Rushup Lane

Whitelee

Bull
Pit

Perryfoot

Perry
Dale

Eldon
Hole

Conies
Dale

arrowpit

61

Harratt
Grange

Ox Low

Haddock Low

A623

Conies Farm

Eldon Lane

Eldon Lane

Oxlow
Rake

Pedicote
Farm

A623

**Old
Dam**

Old Dam Lane

Beytonsdale

Church Lane

Dam Hall

Old Dam Lane

Chamber Farm

† Church Lane

Peak Forest
C of E
School

**Peak
Forest**

⌂
1 †

HERNSTONE

Ivy House

Lodesbarn

Backlane Farm

Damside
Farm

LANE

A623

Laneside
Farm

A B **82** C D E F

Batham Gate

Dam Cliff

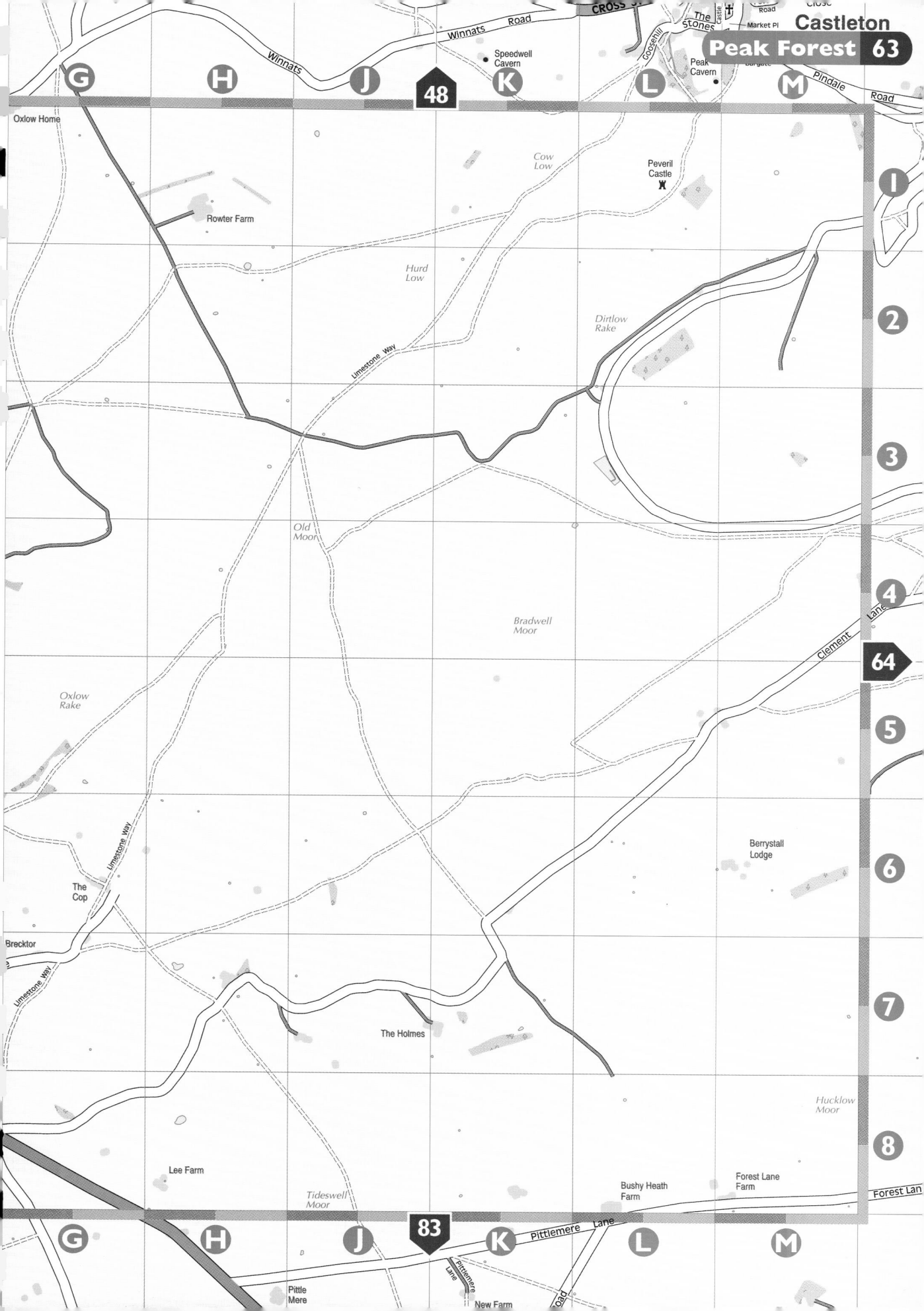

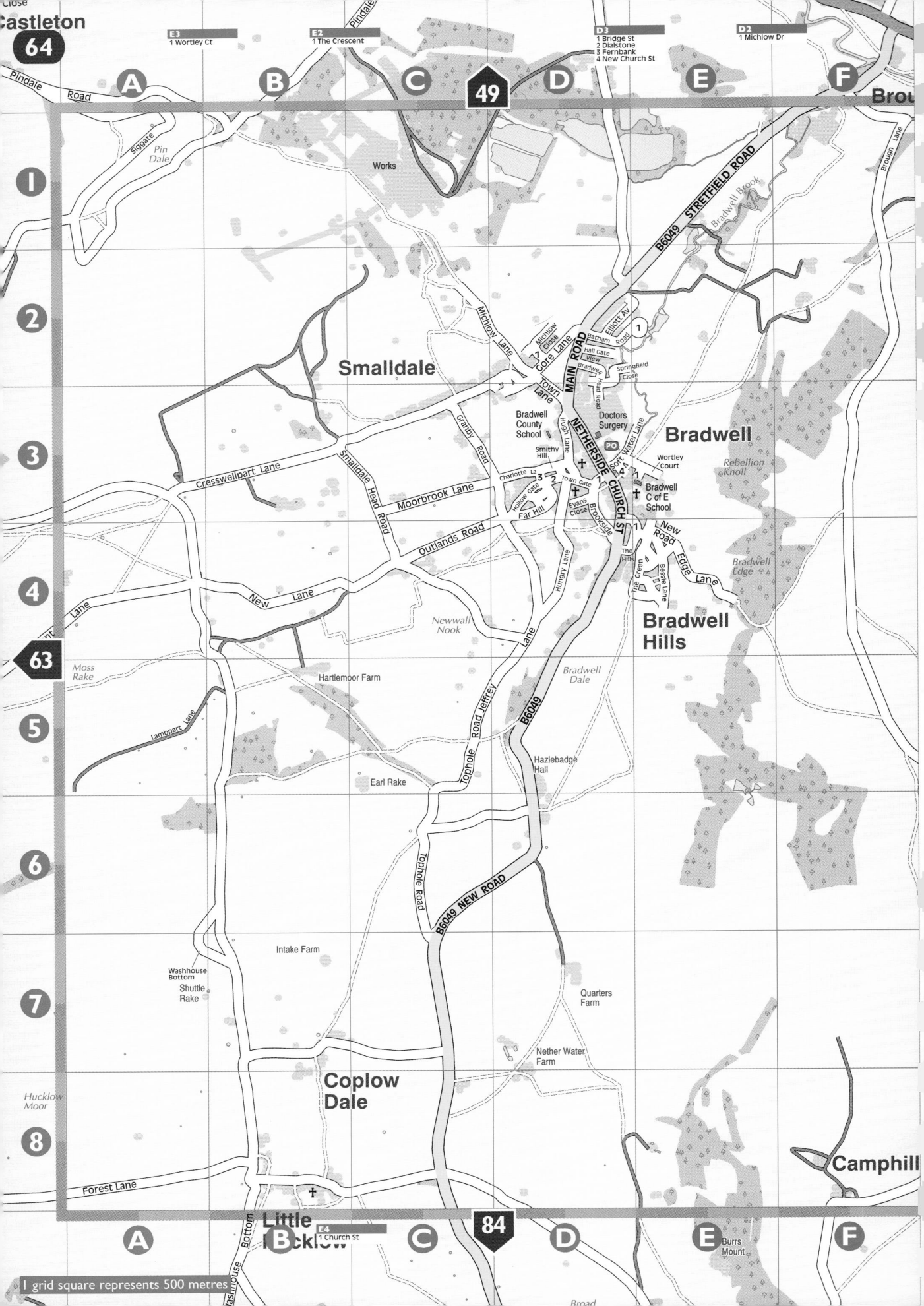

E3
1 Wortley Ct

E2
1 The Crescent

D3
1 Bridge St
2 Dialstone
3 Fernbank
4 New Church St

D2
1 Michlow Dr

A **B** **C** **49** **D** **E** **F**

Pindale Road

Brou

1

Sigoate

Pin Dale

Works

Michlow Lane

STRETFIELD ROAD

B6049

Bradwell Brook

Brough Lane

2

Smalldale

Michlow Close

Gore Lane

Town Lane

MAIN ROAD

Elliott Av

Batham Gate

Hall View

Bradwell Head Road

Springfield Close

1

3

Cresswellpart Lane

Granby Road

Smalldale Head Road

Moorbrook Lane

Bradwell County School

Smithy Hill

Charlotte La

Hollow Gate

Far Hill

3

2

Town Gate

Hugh Lane

NETHERSIDE CHURCH ST

PO

Soft Water Lane

4

1

Evans Close

Brookside

Doctors Surgery

Wortley Court

Bradwell

Bradwell C of E School

Rebellion Knoll

4

New Lane

Outlands Road

Hungry Lane

Tophole Road Jeffrey

Newwall Nook

The Hills

The Green

Bessie Lane

New Road Edge Lane

Bradwell Hills

Bradwell Edge

Lane

Moss Rake

Hartlemoor Farm

Lambpart Lane

5

Earl Rake

B6049

Bradwell Dale

Hazlebadge Hall

6

Tophole Road

B6049 NEW ROAD

7

Washhouse Bottom

Shuttle Rake

Intake Farm

Quarters Farm

Nether Water Farm

8

Hucklow Moor

Coplow Dale

Camphill

Forest Lane

Fashhouse Bottom

A **B** **84** **C** **D** **E** **F**

Little **Hucklow**

E4
1 Church St

Burrs Mount

Broad

A6187 HOPE ROAD

River Noe

STATION ROAD

Lane

Saltergate

Sickleholme
Golf Club

Mytham Bridge

Bamford Station

Cunli

G H J 50 K L M

Townfield Lane

Shatton Lane

Shatton Lane

Shatton

Westfield

Garner
House

Elmore
Hill Farm

Townfield
Lane

River Derwent

I

2

Hope
Valley

Shatton
Moor

Shatton
Lane

Shatton
Edge

Offerton
Hall

3

Over
Dale

Shatton Lane

Abney
Moor

Offerton
Moor

4

66

5

Duper
Lane

Duper Lane

Oaks Farm

6

Abney

Abney
Clough

Highlow

Abney
Moor

Cockey
Farm

Stoke Ford

7

Bolton Brook

Abneylow

Abney
Grange

Bretton
Clough

8

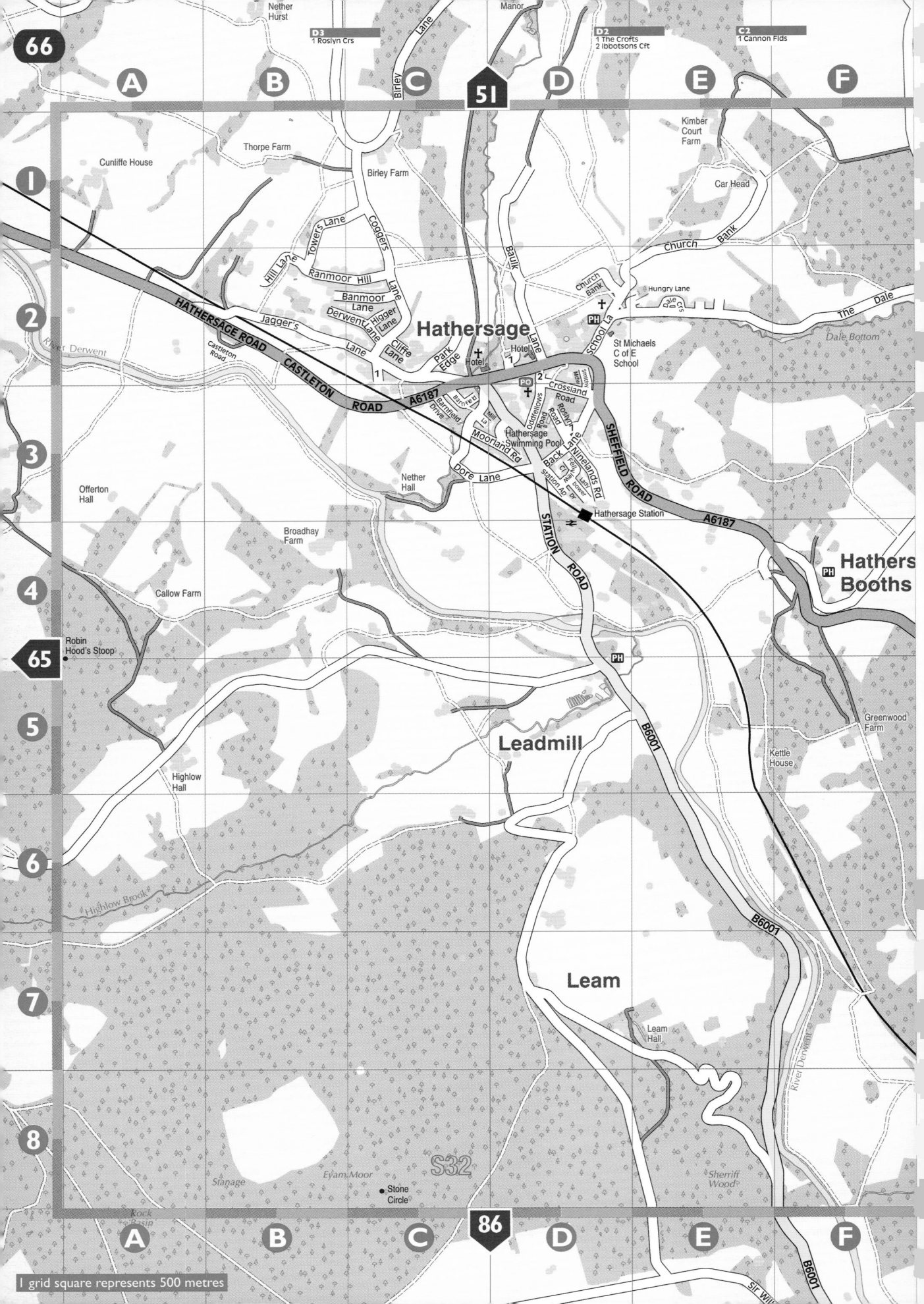

A B C 53 D E F

I

2

3

4

67

5

6

7

8

A B C 88 D E F

Houndkirk Road

Jumble Road

Sheephill Road

Dore Moor

F4 1 Overdale Rl

F2 1 Causeway Gdns

Standhills

Barberfields Farm

Long Line

HATHERSAGE

A625

Cross Lane

Fern Glen Farm

Brickhouse Lane

Causeway

Kerwin Road

Kerwin Lane

Newfield Lane

Kerwin Drive

Kerwin Close

Heather Lea

Newfield Croft

Heather Lea Avenue

Newfield Crs

B Ho

Houndkirk Moor

Whitelow

Whitelow Lane

High Greave

Roundseats Farm

Knowle Gn

Whitelow Lane

Townhead

Knowle Gn

Middlefield

Middlefield Cl

Overall

Ro

Blacka Moor View

Blacka Moor

Blacka Moor Crs

HATHERSAGE ROAD

A625

Shorts Lane

Old Hay Gardens

Hallfield Farm

Totley Bents

Old H Lane

Hillfoot

Strawberry Lee Lane

Penny

Moss Road

Totley All Saints C of Primary School

Lane Head Road

BASLOW ROAD

Sheffield

Derbyshire County

Totley Moor

S17

Brown Edge

Totley

BASLOW ROAD

A621

stoc

Over Ris

Ove

Moor Edge Farm

Moorwood's Hall Farm

Moorwood Lane

A621

Moor

B6054

Salter Sitch

Flask Edge

ley

ss

or

rbag

I grid square represents 500 metres

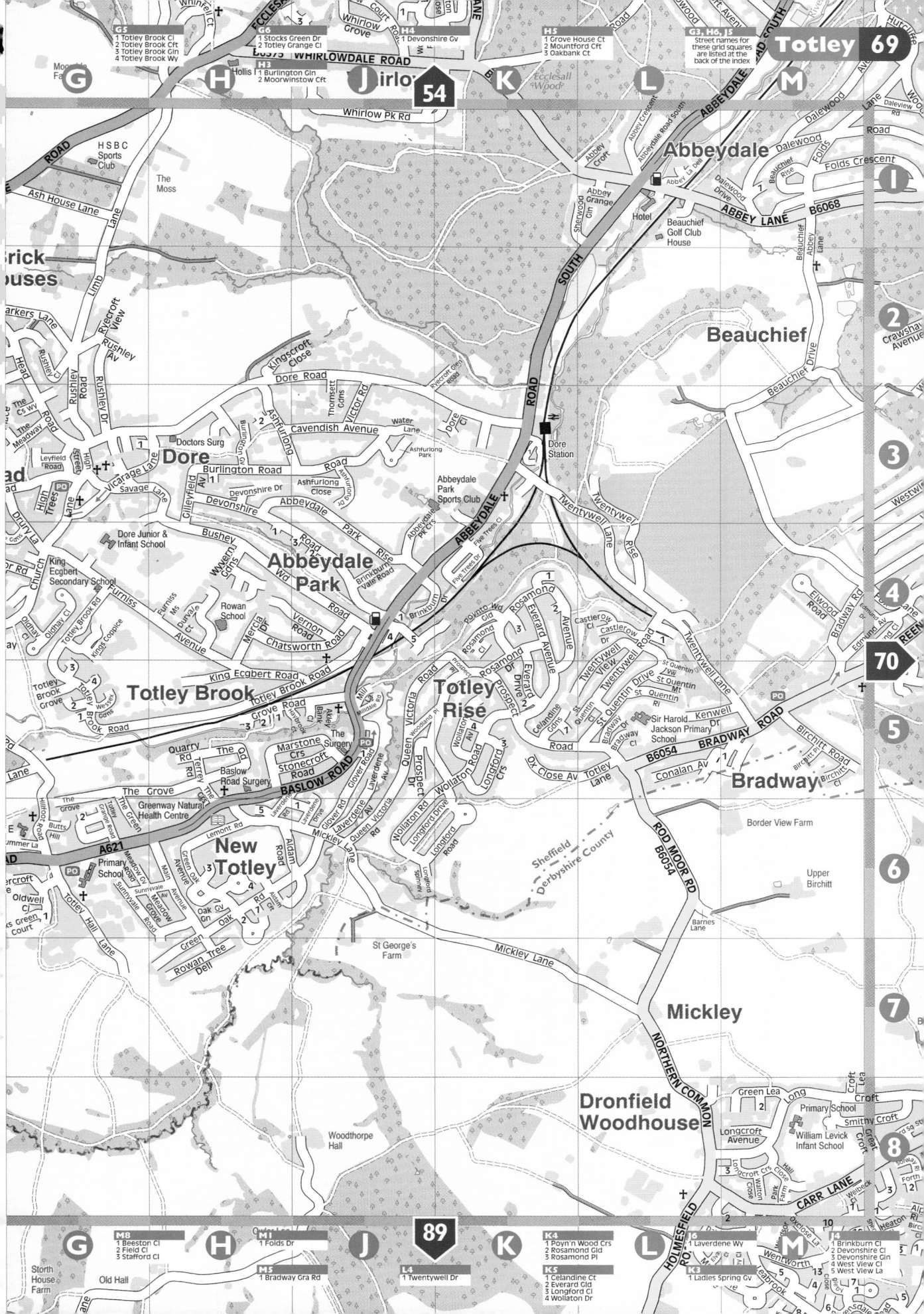

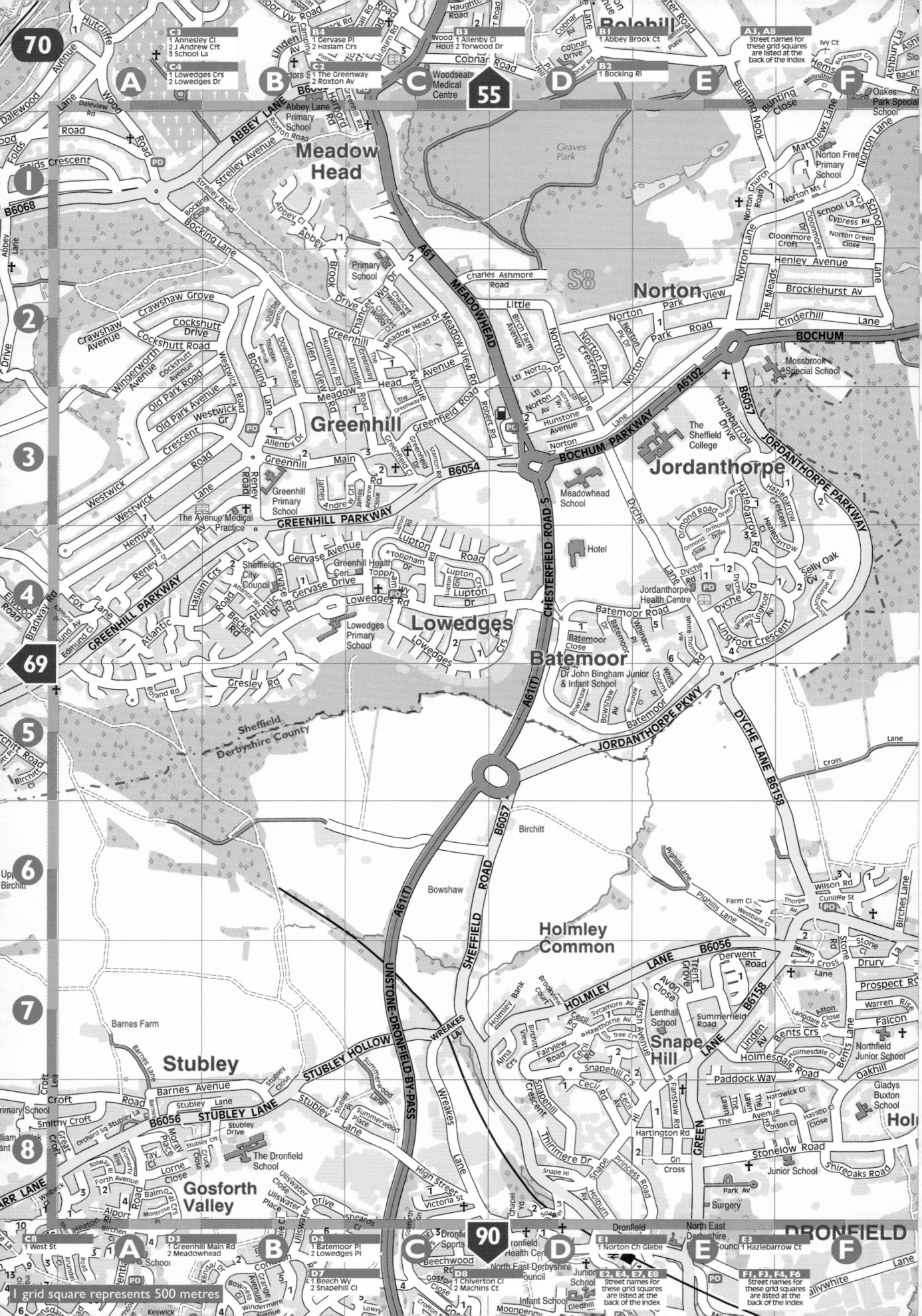

A B C 57 D E F

Owlthorpe

School
Health Centre
Birley Moor Drive
Newstead Drive
Birley

E8
1 Randall St

E3
1 Meadow Crs

E7
1 Sandown Cl

D2
1 Bishopdale Dr
2 Parkgate Cl
3 Parkgate Cft

E2
1 Owlthorpe Cl

D1
1 Bishopdale Ct

Birley Moor Drive
Birley
Dent Lane

Moorthorpe
Royston

Moorhole

Sheffield
Derbyshire County

Moor Valley
Close

Birdfield

B6054
B6054

Phoenix Court
Phoenix Road
Lowfield Avenue
Weifield
HIGH LANE

Highlane

Ridgeway Primary School

Kent House Close

Main Road

PO

Wren Park Close

Ridgeway

QUARRY HILL

A616
MOSBOROUGH MOOR A616 HIGH STREET

Rose Hill Drive
Rose Hill Avenue

Mosborough Medical Centre

Plumbley

Bridle Stile

Plumbley Lane

Sloade

Litfield Farm

Ford

Ridgeway Moor

Ridgeway Moor

71

Birleyhay

Geer Lane

Ford Lane

The Moss

Lady Ida's

Bramleyhill Farm

Lady Ida's Drive

Birchwood Road

Ford Road

Bramley

Back Lane

Greenhall Road
Green Chase

Eckington School

Fernbank Drive

Staniforth Avenue

ECKINGTON

School Lane

Marsh Lane Primary School

Bramley Moor

ROAD

B6056

Marsh Lane

Main Road

PO

DRONFIELD ROAD

WEST STREET

Birkhill Primary School

Quarry Hill

Warren Crescent
Woodnook Grove
Lightwood Road

Bolehill Lane

Bolehill

Bramleymoor Lane

Bramley Road

CHESTERFIELD ROAD

A B 92 C D E F

F2
1 Moor Farm Garth

F3
1 Bridle Stile Cl
2 Plumbley Hall Rd

F7
1 Greenfields

F8
1 Fanshaw Dr
2 Hazel Rd
3 Valley View Cl

1 grid square represents 500 metres

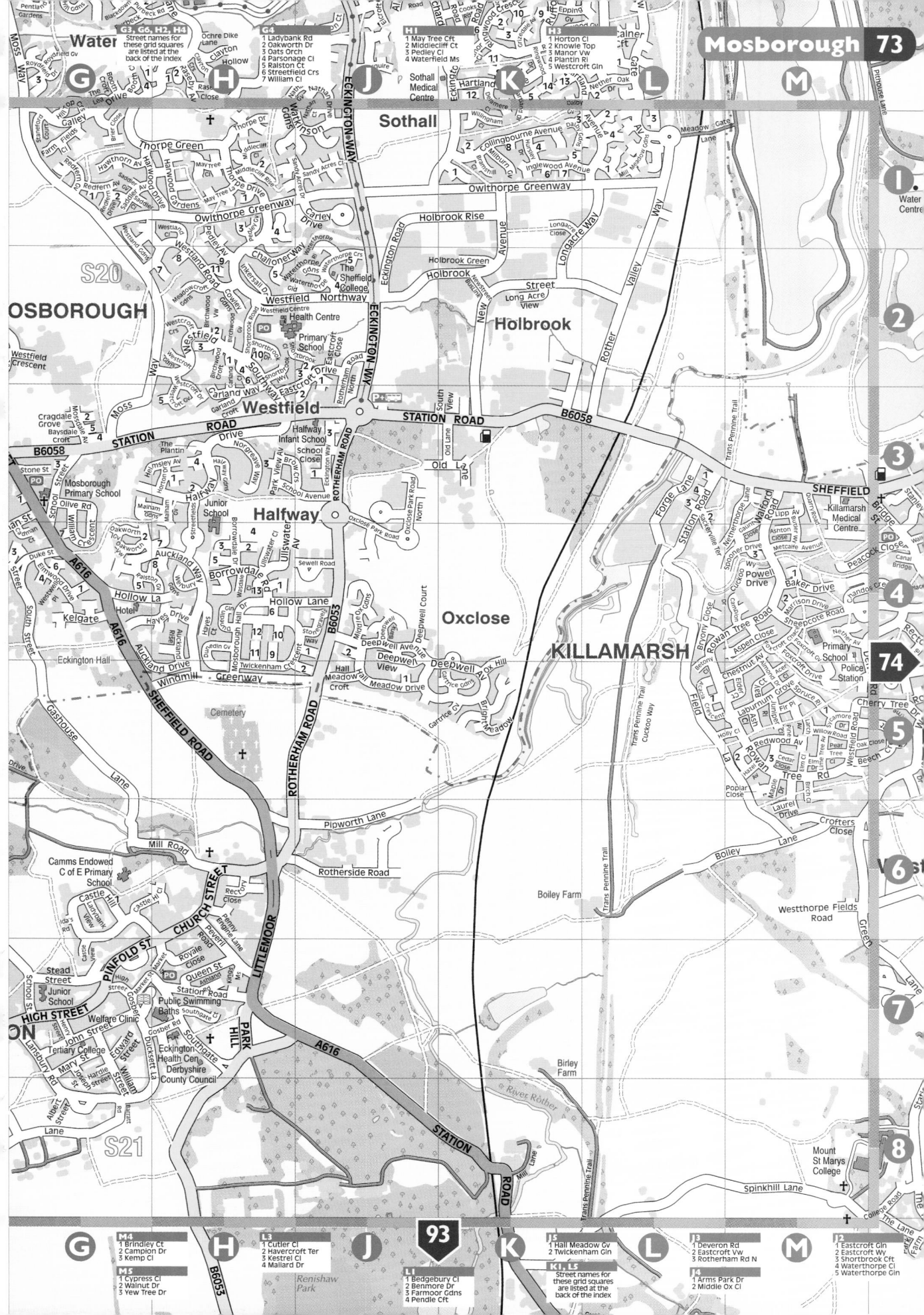

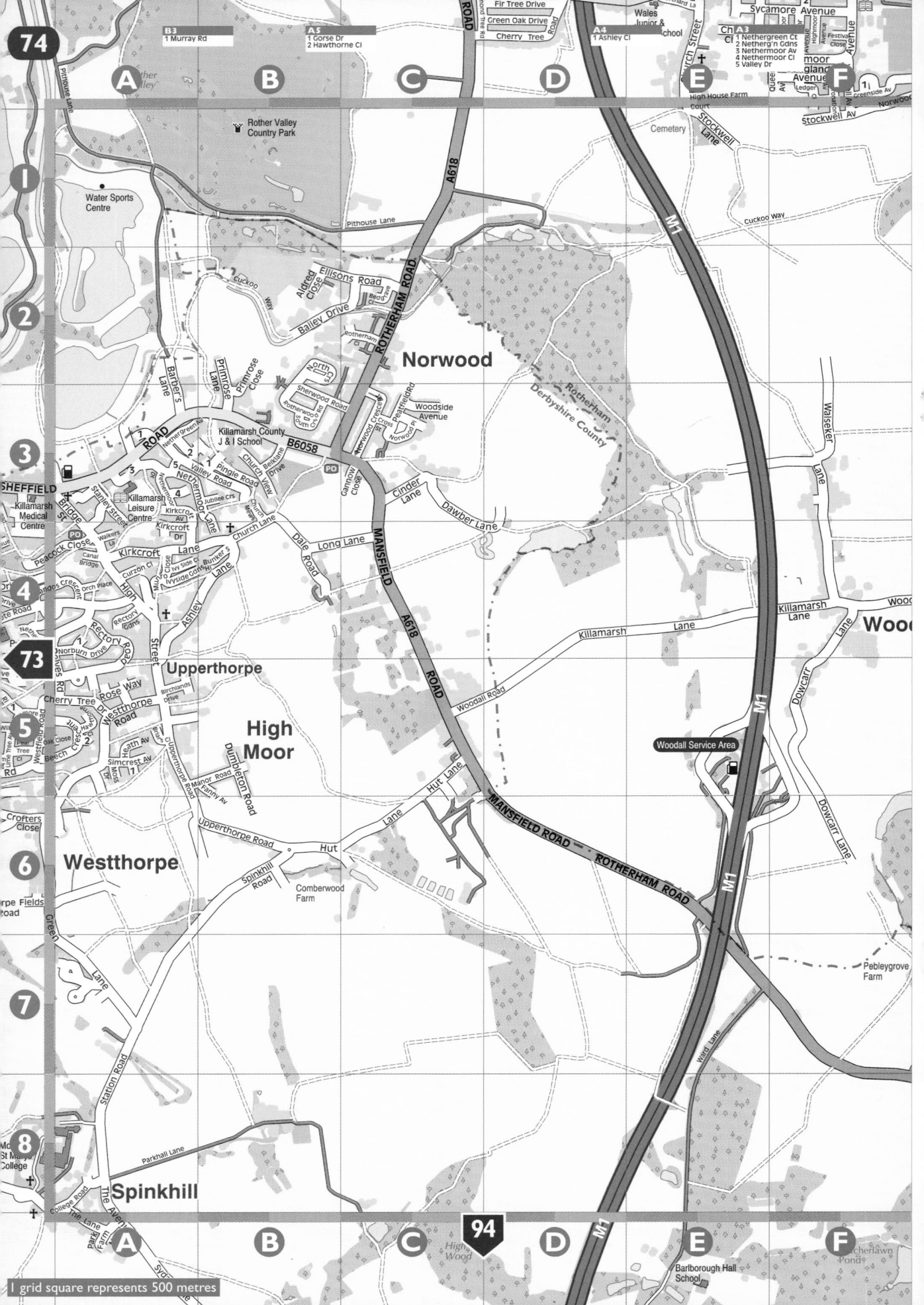

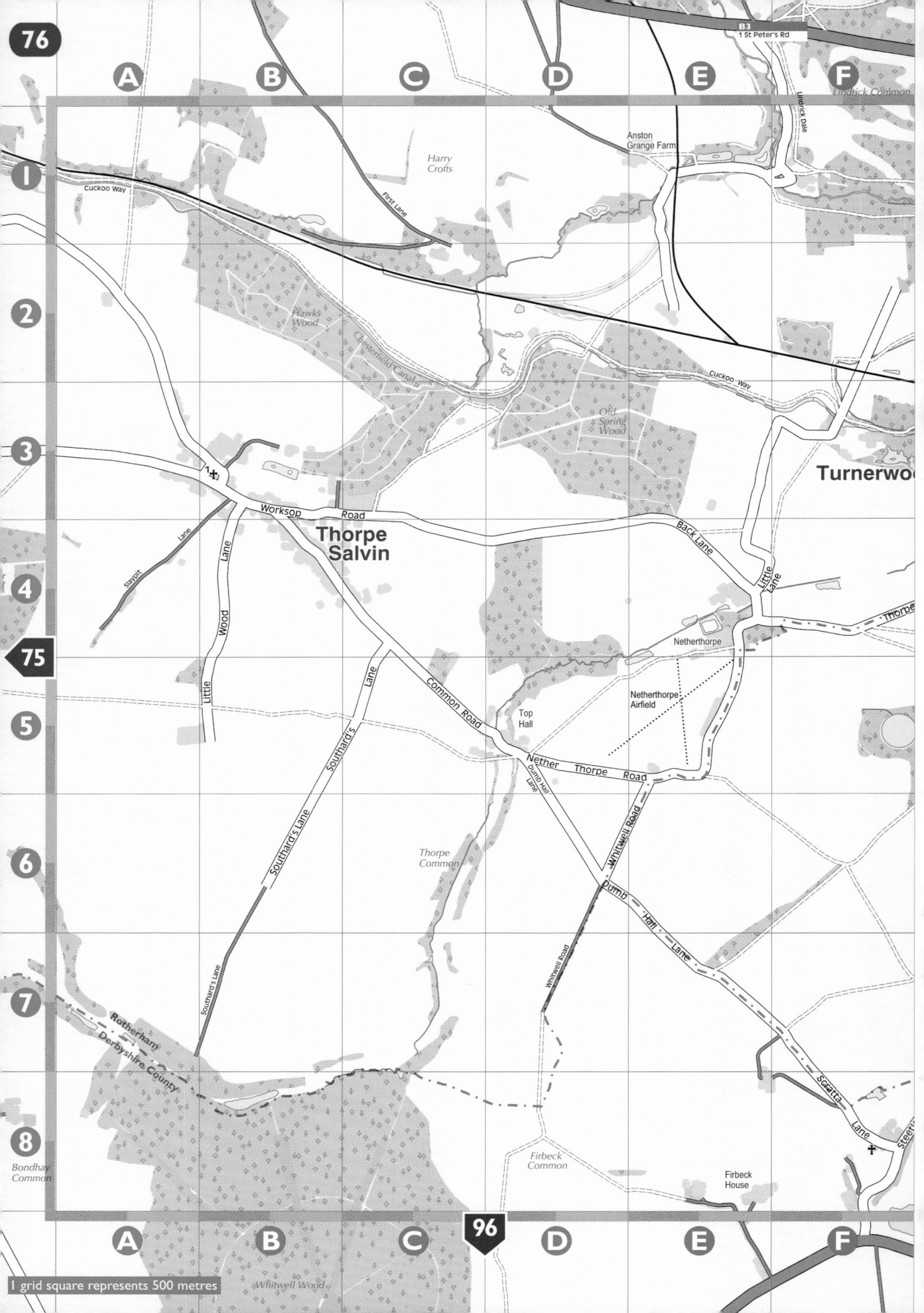

A B C D E F

Lindrick Common

Lindrick Dale

Anston
Grange Farm

1

Cuckoo Way

Harry
Crofts

First Lane

2

Hawks
Wood

Chesterfield Canal

Cuckoo Way

Old
Spring
Wood

3

Turnerwood

Worksop   Road

Back Lane

Thorpe
Salvin

Little   Lane

Thorpe

Lane

Little

Wood

Lane

stayolt   Lane

Netherthorpe

4

75

Netherthorpe
Airfield

5

Common Road

Southard's

Lane

Top
Hall

Nether   Thorpe   Road

Dumb Hall
Lane

Whitwell Road

6

Southard's Lane

Thorpe
Common

Dumb   Hall   Lane

Whitwell Road

7

Rotherham

Derbyshire County

8

Bondhay
Common

Firbeck
Common

Firbeck
House

Scratta
Lane

Steetit

A B C D E F

96

1 grid square represents 500 metres

J3
1 Cherry Tree Av
2 Pembroke Rd
3 Pilgrim Ct
4 Potters Nook
5 York Pl

K5
1 Tylden Wy

L5
1 Tylden Rd

G H J K L M

I

2

3

4

5

6

7

8

Owday Wood

Worksop Road

Woodsetts Lane

GATEFORD ROAD

Owday Lane

Rogers Piece

Linanick Golf Club

Brancliffe Grange

Moses View

Brancliffe Lane

St Lukes C of E School

Shireoaks Common

Shireoaks Common

GATEFORD ROAD

B6041

Applewood

Manston Close

Wellesle

Kellett Rd

Shireoaks

Cartwright Street

Glenthorn Close

PO

Monks Way

Common

Leeds Road

Cornwall Road

Woodside Road

Elmtree Close

Walnut Avenue

Shireoaks Common

Gateford Common

Swan Ct

Hewson St

Quarry Grove

Machin St

Newton Close

Kirkpatrick Drive

Mosgrove Close

Sandmartins

Fieldfare

The Bramblings

Goldcrest Rise

Plover Dene

Kingfisher Walk

Starlin Court

Apley

Fulmar Way

Gateford

Dawber

Shireoaks Station

Shireoaks

Cuckoo Way

Shireoaks Business Centre

Claylands Avenue

Redwing

Starling Gv

Dunlin Ct

Kingfisher Wk

Avocet Grove

Starlings

Way

Dukeries Close

Gateford Ga

The Hall

Shireoaks Miners Welfare & Sports Club

Shireoaks Road

A57(T)

Tranker Lane

Dukeries Close

Dukeries Industrial Estate

Spring Lane

Royds Crs

Boughton Road

PO

Tylden

Rhodesia

Shireoaks Road

Shireoaks Road

SANDY LA

Chesterfield Canal

Steetley Lane

Primary School

Cecil Close

Winifred St

Marjorie

Maple St

Mary Street

Elizabeth Crs

5

High Grounds Way

High Grounds Rd

6

Holme Carr

Spring Lane

Lady Lee Farm

River Royton

Stubbing

Steetley Lane

Teague Piece

Underwood Gdns

Ackford

Beaumont

7

Cusworth Ri

Halliday Cl

Newca

Featherbed

Lodge Farm

St Annes Way

St Annes

Wallingbrook

Hillwood Cl

Oakwood Mews

Westwood Rd

Glebe

Saint

Manor

Briar

Leam

Drive

Anne

Meadow

Lea

Mayfield

Pasture Cl

Mill Cl

Ladylea Close

The Dene

Meadow Drive

Meadow Road

Birchfield Dr

Alpine

8

ley Lane

Harness

West Wood

Menagerie Wood

MAN

ROAD

A60

A619

Harfoulds

G H J K L M

M4
1 Lark Spinney

M3
1 Chaffinch Ms
2 Cuckoo Holt
3 Greenfinch Dl
4 Heron Gld
5 Magpie Cl
6 The Mallards

58

A   B   C   D   E   F

Crowhill

Charles Head
Farm

Neighbourway
Farm

Fivelane-
ends

Windgather
Rocks

1

Summer Close

2

Dunge
Farm

Hollowcowhey
Farm

Goyt
Forest

Todd Brook

3

Green
Booth

Green
Stack

Bank Lane

4

Lane

Jenkin
Chapel

The
Street

Ewrin Lane

Saltersford
Hall

Embridge Causeway

5

Ewrin Lane

Hooleyhey Lane

Redmoor

6

Hooleyhey Lane

aload
ervoir

7

Derbyshire County
Cheshire County

8

Hooleyhey Lane

Shooters
Clough

A   B   C   D   E   F

1 grid square represents 500 metres

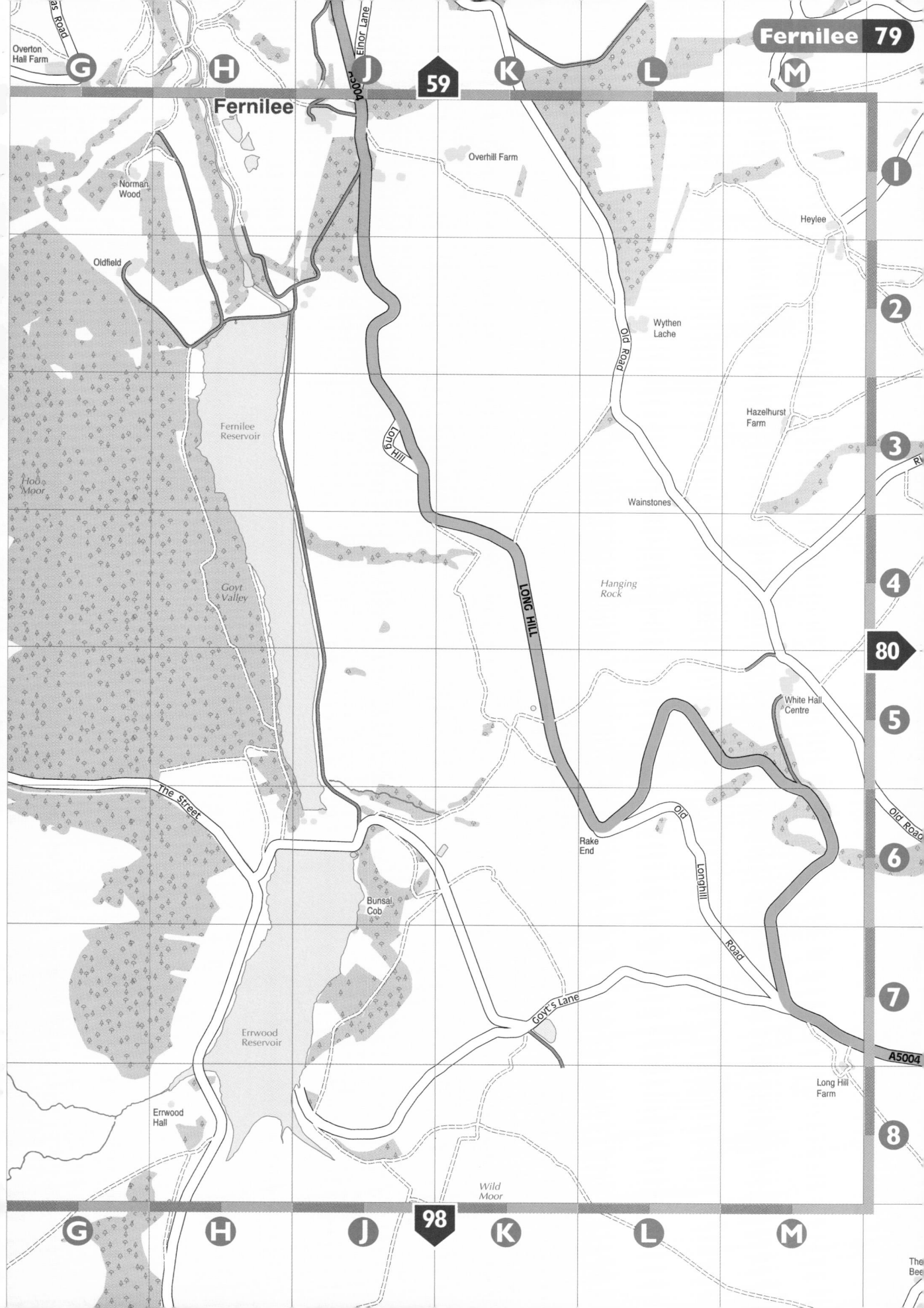

G H J **59** K L M

I

2

3

4

80

5

6

7

A5004

8

Fernilee

Overton
Hall Farm

Elnor Lane

Overhill Farm

Norman
Wood

Heylee

Oldfield

Wythen
Lache

Old Road

Hazelhurst
Farm

Fernilee
Reservoir

Long Hill

Wainstones

Hoo
Moor

Goyt
Valley

Hanging
Rock

LONG HILL

White Hall
Centre

The Street

Rake
End

Old

Longhill

Road

Old Road

Bunsal
Cob

Goyt's Lane

Errwood
Reservoir

Long Hill
Farm

Errwood
Hall

Wild
Moor

80

A   Long Lane   B   C   60   D   E   F

PO   The Av   Combs Lane   Brook Houses   Whitehills   Castle Naze   Short Edge

I   Combs County School   Combs   Hob Tor

2   Pyegreave

Greave House   Allstone Lee

3   Bag House Farm   Ridge Lane

4   Broadlee Farm   501 ▲ Hob Tor

79

Hall   Combs Moss

5

Old Road

6

7   A5004   LONG HILL   Lightwood Reservoirs   Cuckoo Tors   Edge Road

Long Hill Farm   Moss House Farm   Brown

8   Cold Springs Farm   Lightwood Road   Ladycroft

A   B   A5004   99   C   MANCHEST   D   E   F

The   John Duncan School   Williamson Avenue

I grid square represents 500 metres

Cow Low

G H J **61** K L M

1 Beaumont Dr
2 Hallsteads

Ridgeclose Farm

Lodes Marsh

I

Highfield Av

Meeow Cl

The Meadows

2

Hallsteads Cl

HALLSTEADS

Bull Ring

Meadow Cl

Alexander Rd

Dove Holes Station

Station Rd

Horseshoe Av

A6(T)

Dove Holes

Lodes Lane

Sr

3

Beech Lane

PO

Dale Road

Smalldale Road

BUXTON ROAD

Doveholes Dale

4

A6(T)

Longridge Lane

Gate Road

82

Batham

Church AV

School Rd

Peak Dale

Blackedge Farm

Peak Dale Primary School

Meadow Av

PO

5

Upper End

Ferndale Road

New St.

Gate

Ferndale Avenue

Upper End Road

6

Batham

Longridge Lane

Tomthorn

Turner Lodge Farm

Waterswallows Lane

Hardybarn

Waterswallows Road

7

Hardybarn Lane

Water Swallows

Green Lane

Green Lane

8

Waterswallows Road

Daisymere Lane

Fairfield Common

A6(T)

Redg

Townend Farm

Da Far

Peter's Rd

North Rd

or Rd

Barms

Town End

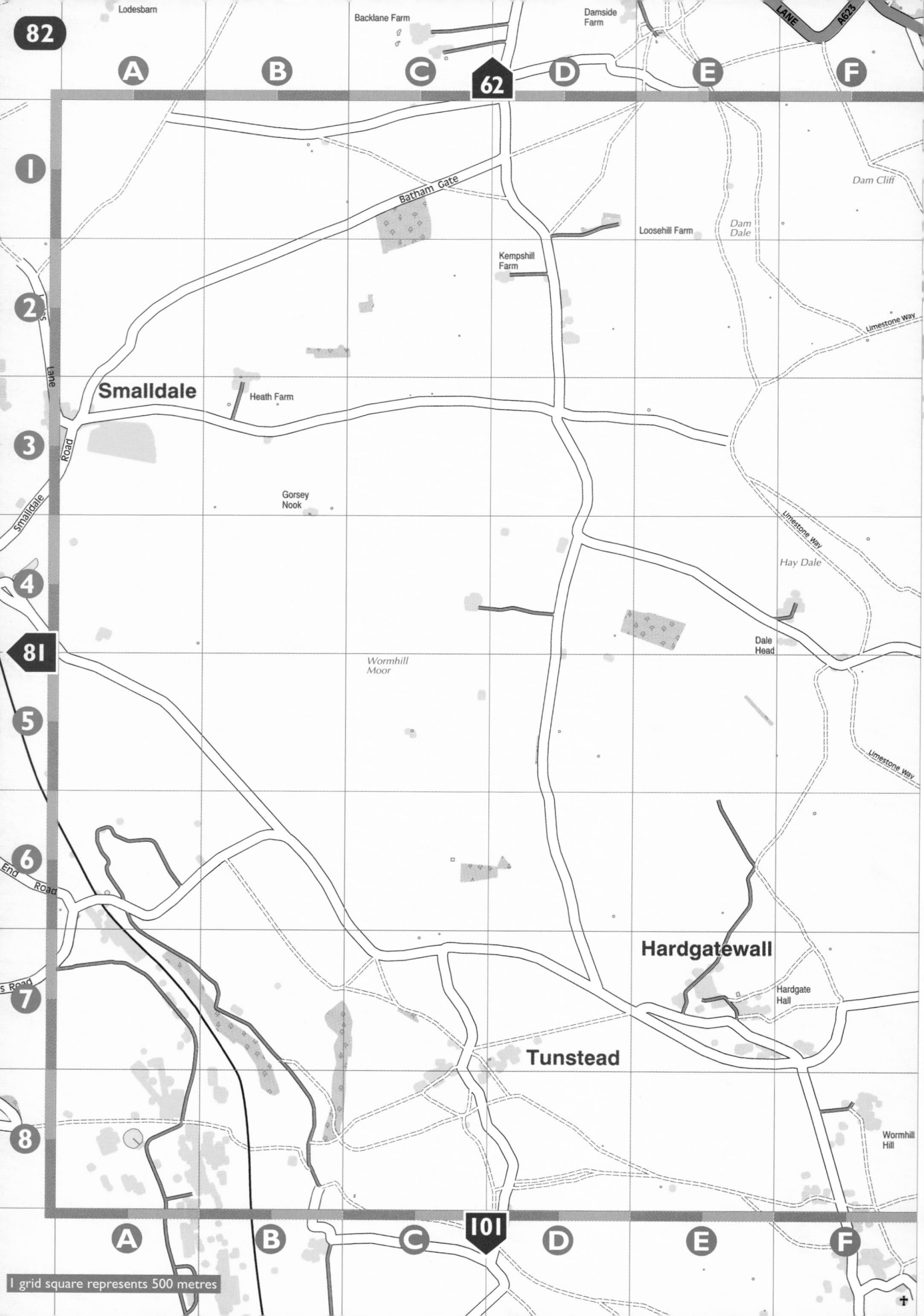

A   B   C   62   D   E   F

1

Lodesbarn

Backlane Farm

Damside
Farm

LANE   A623

Dam Cliff

Batham Gate

Dam
Dale

Loosehill Farm

Kempshill
Farm

Limestone Way

2

Smalldale

Heath Farm

3

Smalldale Road   Lane

Gorsey
Nook

Limestone Way

Hay Dale

4

81

Wormhill
Moor

Dale
Head

Limestone Way

5

6

End   Road

Hardgatewall

's Road

7

Hardgate
Hall

Tunstead

8

Wormhill
Hill

A   B   C   **101**   D   E   F

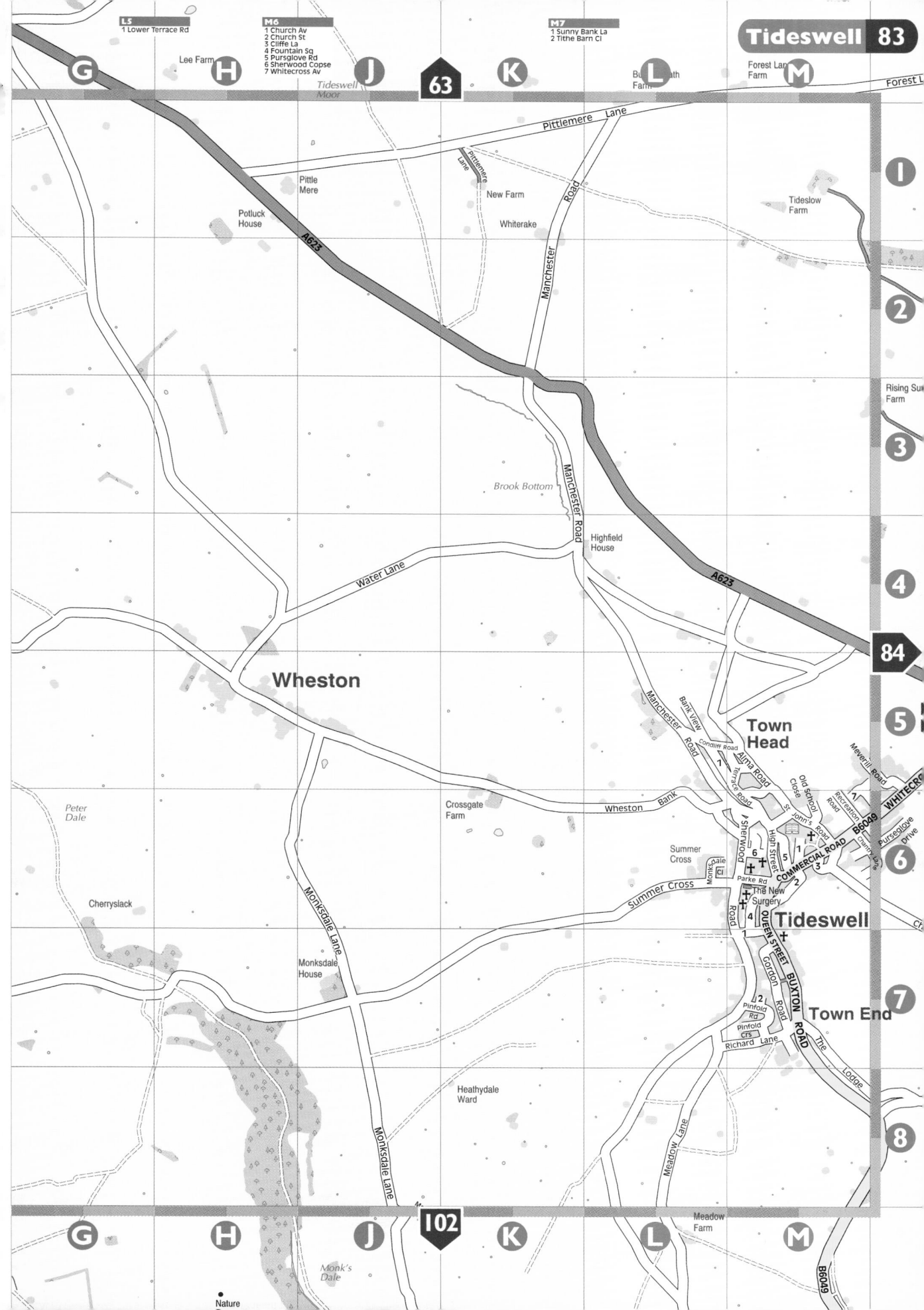

L5
1 Lower Terrace Rd

M6
1 Church Av
2 Church St
3 Cliffe La
4 Fountain Sq
5 Pursglove Rd
6 Sherwood Copse
7 Whitecross Av

M7
1 Sunny Bank La
2 Tithe Barn Cl

G   H   J   63   K   L   M

I
2
3
4
84
5
6
7
8

Lee Farm
Forest Lane Farm
Forest L

Tideswell Moor
Pittlemere Lane
Pittle Mere
New Farm
Pittlemere Lane
Whiterake
Tideslow Farm
Bushy Heath Farm

Potluck House
A623
Manchester Road

Rising Sun Farm

Brook Bottom
Manchester Road
Highfield House
A623

Water Lane

Wheston

Peter Dale

Crossgate Farm

Manchester Road
Bank View
Condliff Road
Town Head
Alma Road
Terrace Road
St John's Road
Old School Road
Recreation Road
Meverill Road
WHITECROSS
B6049
Pursglove Drive

Summer Cross
Wheston Bank
Sherwood Road
High Street
Commercial Road
Chapel Lane

Cherryslack
Monksdale Lane
Monksdale Cl
Parke Rd
Summer Cross
The New Surgery
Tideswell

Monksdale House
Queen Street
Gordon Road
Buxton Road
Town End
Pinfold Rd
Pinfold Crs
Richard Lane
The Lodge

Heathydale Ward

Monksdale Lane

Meadow Lane
Meadow Farm
B6049

Monk's Dale
Nature

G   H   J   102   K   L   M

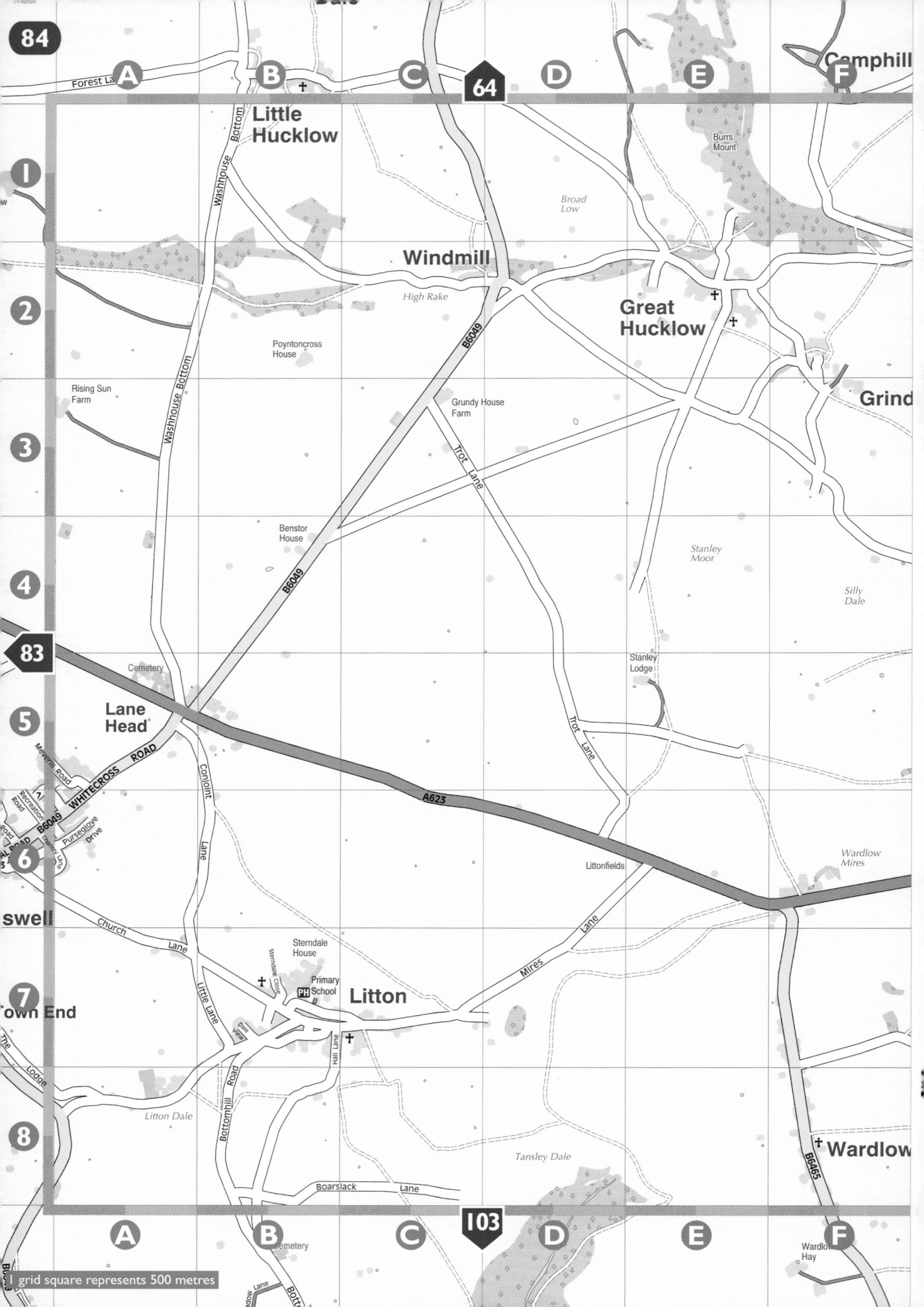

A B C 64 D E F Camphill

Forest La

Little
Hucklow

Washhouse Bottom

1

Burrs
Mount

Broad
Low

Windmill

High Rake

2

B6049

Great
Hucklow

Grind

Poyntoncross
House

Rising Sun
Farm

Washhouse Bottom

3

Grundy House
Farm

Trot Lane

Benstor
House

B6049

Stanley
Moor

4

Silly
Dale

83

Cemetery

Stanley
Lodge

5

Lane
Head

Trot Lane

Meverhill Road

WHITECROSS ROAD

Conjoint Lane

Recreation Road

B6049

Purseglove Drive

A623

6

swell

Littonfields

Wardlow
Mires

Church Lane

Mires Lane

Sterndale
House

Primary
School

PH

Litton

7

own End

Little Lane

Sterndale Close

Dale View

Hall Lane

The Lodge

Litton Dale

Bottomhill Road

8

Tansley Dale

Wardlow

B6465

A B 103 C D E F Wardlow
Hay

Boarslack Lane

Cemetery

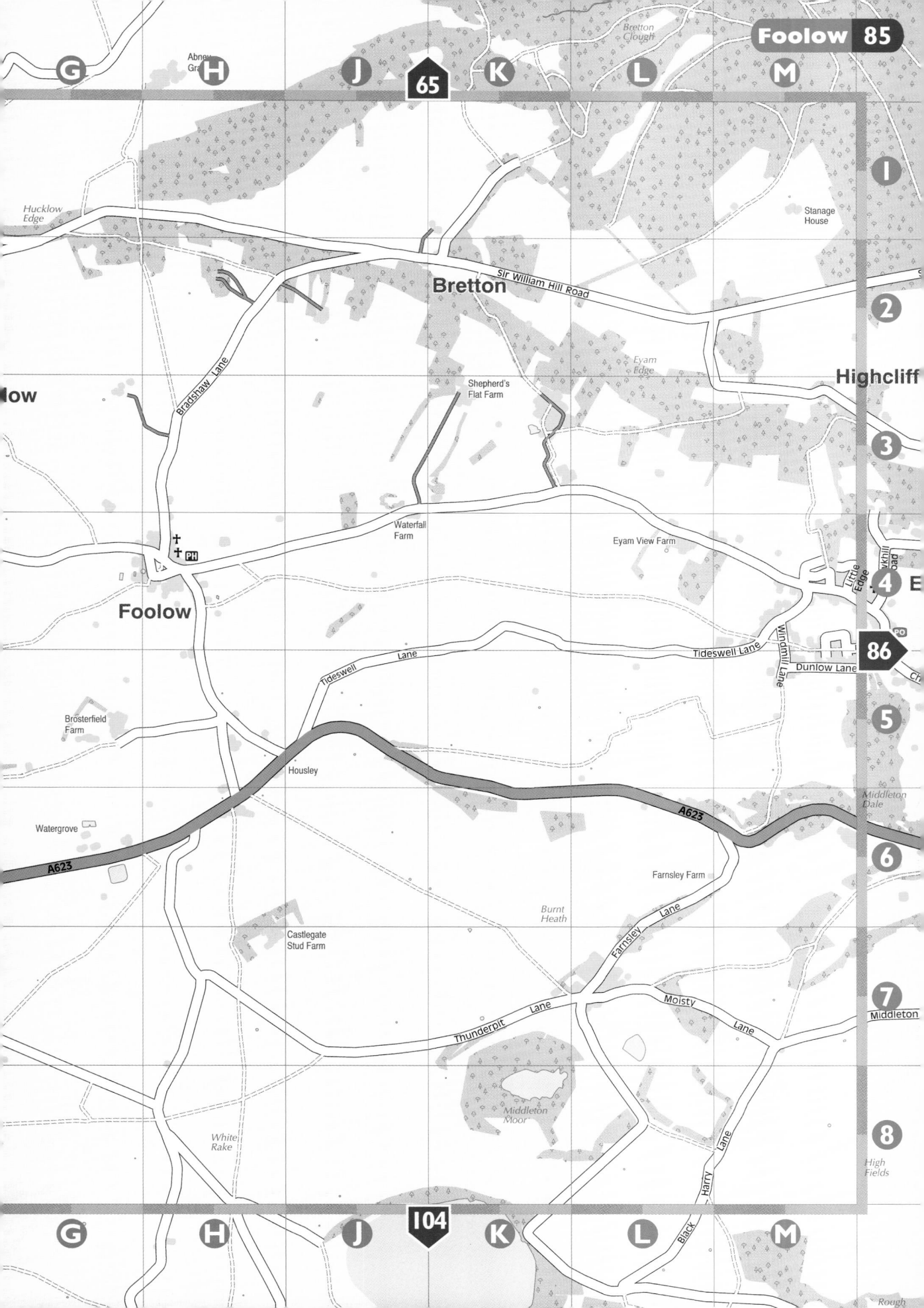

G H J 65 K L M

I

2

Highcliff

3

Bretton

Sir William Hill Road

Hucklow Edge

Stanage House

Eyam Edge

Bradshaw Lane

Shepherd's Flat Farm

low

Waterfall Farm

Eyam View Farm

Little Edge

†
† PH
△

Foolow

Tideswell Lane

Windmill Lane

Dunlow Lane

PO

4 E

86

5

Brosterfield Farm

Tideswell   Lane

Middleton Dale

Housley

A623

Watergrove

A623

Farnsley Farm

6

Burnt Heath

Farnsley   Lane

Castlegate Stud Farm

Moisty   Lane

7 Middleton

Thunderpit   Lane

Middleton Moor

White Rake

Harry   Lane

8

High Fields

G H J 104 K L *Black* M

Rough

G H J **67** K L M

G2
1 St Helen's Cft

H8
1 Chapel Wk

B6054

Nether Padley

PH
Hotel

Padley Hl

Maynard Road

Tedness Road

B6521

St Helen's Close

Padley Road

7

White Edge Moor

The Haywood

went lery

A625

1

2

3

4

88

5

Stoke Flat

White Edge

Big Moor

Froggatt Edge

Green Side Lane

A625

Froggatt

Curbar Edge

6

Riddings Lane

Ridding House Farm

7

Swine Sty

The Croft

Warren Lodge

Clodhall Lane

8

Curbar

The Bent

Dukes Drive

Pinfold Hl

The Green

The Hillock

Bar Road

Curbar Hill

River

1

Riverside

G + H J **106** K L M

Curbar County School

Lane

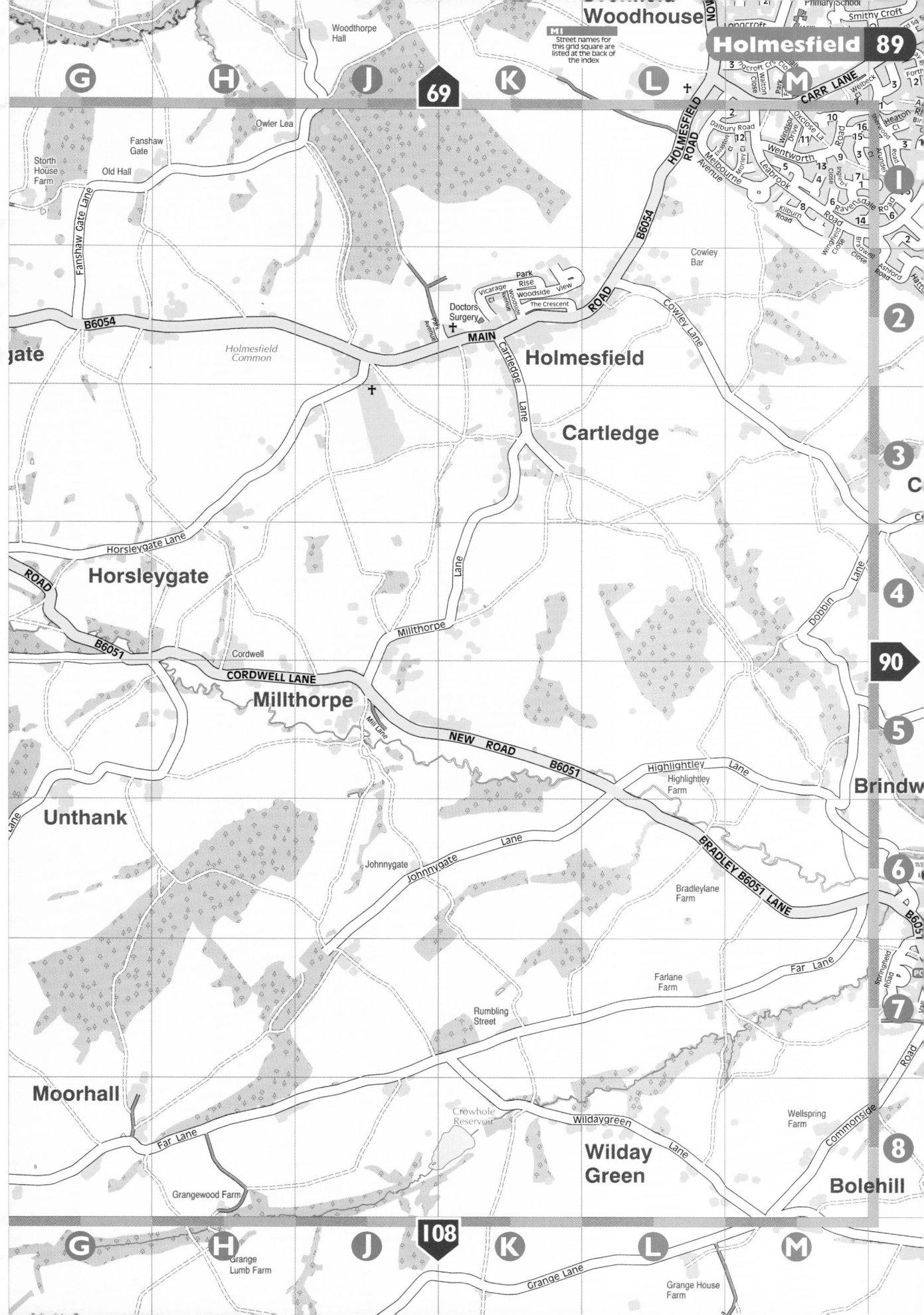

G H J **69** K L M

Woodhouse

Woodthorpe Hall

Street names for this grid square are listed at the back of the index

M1

CARR LANE

Primary School

Smithy Croft

Longcroft

Heaton

Longcroft Crs

Clio

HOLMESFIELD ROAD

Dalbury Road

Oxclose La

Windsor Drive

Wentworth

Park Close

Melbourne Avenue

Leabrook

Kilburn Road

Inglev

Wingfield Close

Bradwell Close

Ravensdale

Arundel Road

Ashford Road

Harr

B6054 ROAD

Owler Lea

Fanshaw Gate

Storth House Farm

Old Hall

Fanshaw Gate Lane

Cowley Bar

Cowley Lane

1

2

Park Rise

Vicarage CI

Woodside Avenue

Woodside View

The Crescent

Doctors Surgery

MAIN

Pk Avenue

B6054

B6054 ROAD

gate

B6054

Holmesfield Common

✝

Holmesfield

Cartledge Lane

Cartledge

3

C

Lane

Dobbin Lane

4

ROAD

Horsleygate Lane

Horsleygate

Millthorpe

Lane

B6051

Cordwell

90

5

Millthorpe

CORDWELL LANE

Mill Lane

NEW ROAD B6051

Highlightley Lane

Highlightley Farm

Brindw

B6051

Unthank

Lane

Johnnygate

Johnnygate

BRADLEY B6051 LANE

Bradleylane Farm

6

Springfield Road

PC

7

Far Lane

Far Lane

Rumbling Street

Farlane Farm

Wellspring Farm

Commonside Road

Moorhall

Far Lane

Crowhole Reservoir

Wildaygreen

Lane

Wilday Green

8

Bolehill

Grangewood Farm

G H J **108** K L M

Grange Lumb Farm

Grange Lane

Grange House Farm

mesdale

H4 1 Ramshaw Rd
Summerley Farm

H6 1 Mary Ann St

K1 1 Moorland Vw
2 Quarry Rd

G H J 71 K L M

I

Moortop Farm

Apperknowle

Back Lane
Gipsy Lane
Hawley Street
Chapel Lane
High Street
PO
New Road
Moortop Road
Long Lane
Morton Lane

Primary School
Town End
Staton Lane
Ash Lane

2
West Handle

Crow Lane
Unstone Grange

St John's Road
St Marys School
Church St
Hundall Lane

Unstone
PO
Crow Lane

3

Unstone Junior School

Hundall

Pool's Lane

Half Acre Lane
Chesterfield Rd
UNSTONE HILL
B6057
MAIN ROAD

4
Handley Lane

Unstone Green

North Close
Brierley Road
Central Cl
Old Whittington Lane
Green Cl
South Close
Loundes Road
Windmill Lane

92

Sylvia Road
Hardhurst Road
Birch Holt Grove
Alice Way
Robert Close
Cheetham Avenue
Whittington Lane

Ramshaw Farm

Hundall Lane

5

Glasshouse Lane

River Drone
SHEFFIELD ROAD
B6057
Unstone Road

Glasshouse Lane
Glasshouse Farm

Infant Sch

6

Hotel

The Brushes

New Whittington

STREET
B6052
Junior Sch

BY-PASS A61(T)

Chesterfield Caravan & Leisure Centre
Carlisle Close

SHEFFIELD ROAD

Rodge Croft
Church Street
Church Lane
North
Compass Crescent
Burnbridge Road
Brearley Street
May Av

7

Broombank Road
Broombank Park
Holly House School
Revolution House
Mary Swanick Primary School
Whittington Medical Centre
Meadows Community School
HIGH Street
Oak Bank Av
Ashcroft Dr
Potters Cl
Caxton Close
Meadow Close

Sheepbridge Business Centre
Dunston Trading Estate
Foxwood Road

Sheepbridge

William St
Broomhill
Prospect
George St
Victoria St
Holland Road
Fowler Road
Laurence Cl
Howard Drive
Ivy Cl
PO
B6052
WHITTINGTON HILL North
The Glebe Way
Hilltop Rd
Danby Av
Gipsy Lane
RoeCar Close
Station Lane
Ashcroft Drive
Station Lane Industrial Estate
Station Lane

8

G H **110** J K L **Whittington** M

DUNSTON ROAD
B6057
A61(T)

M7 1 Sims Cft

Whittington Way
Newbridge Avenue
Layton Av
Discovery Way
Whitting Vale Rd

L8 1 Glossop's Cft
2 Pynot Rd
3 Webster Cft

Old Whittington

K8 1 Cavendish St N
2 Doveridge Cl
3 High St
4 Old Bakery Cl
5 Rutland St
6 Swanwick St

Colton Cl
Millennium Way

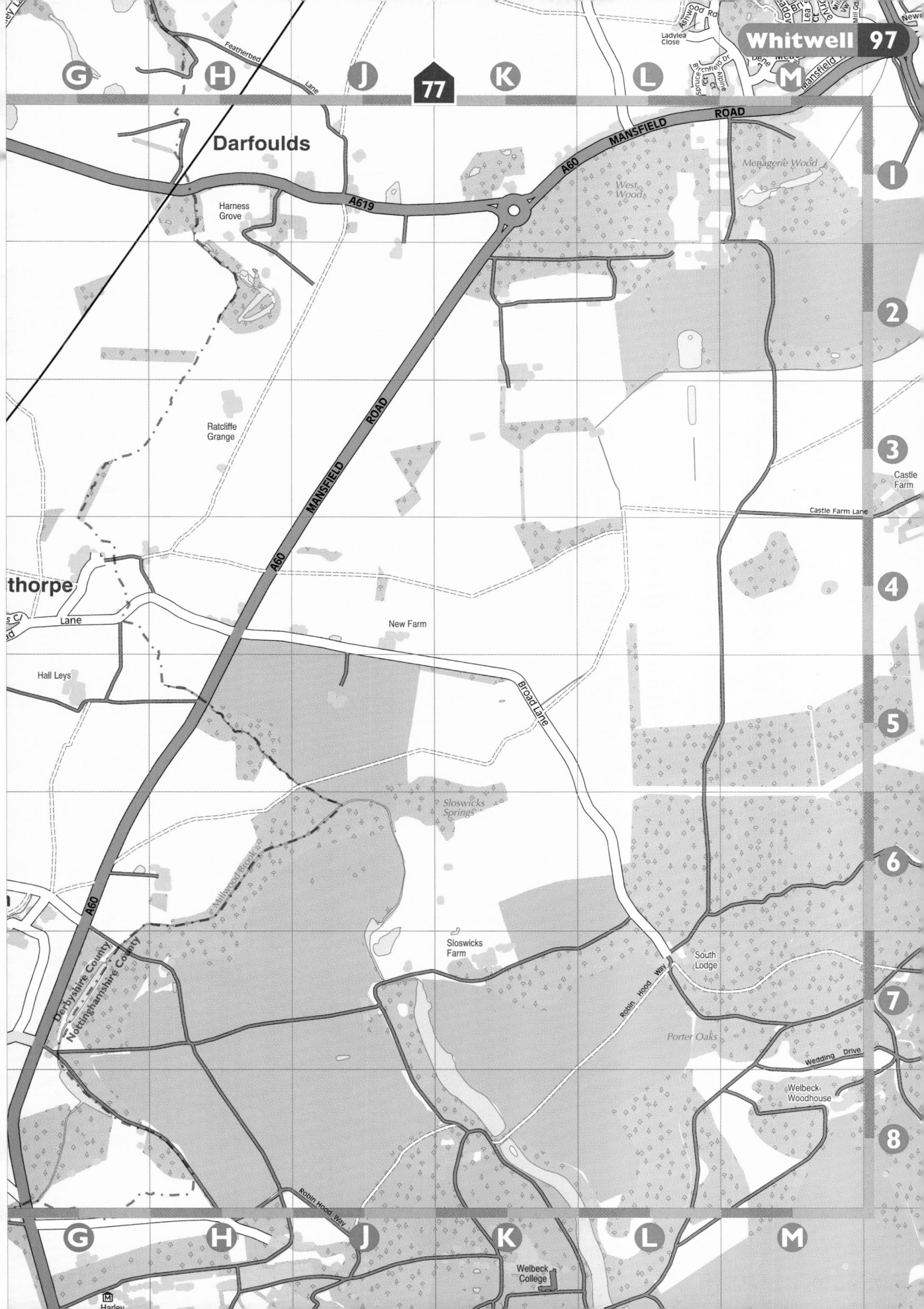

98

A   B   C   D   E   F

I

2

3

4

5

6

7

8

A   B   C   D   E   F

Errwood
Hall

Wild
Moor

Stake
Side

Stake
Clough

Goyt's
Moss

Deep
Clough

Berry Clough

A54

A537

Derbyshire County
Cheshire County

Moss
Chain

MACCLESFIELD   MAIN   ROAD   A54

Axe Edge
Moor

551
▲
Axe Edge

Whetstone
Ridge

Danebower
Hollow

116

1 grid square represents 500 metres

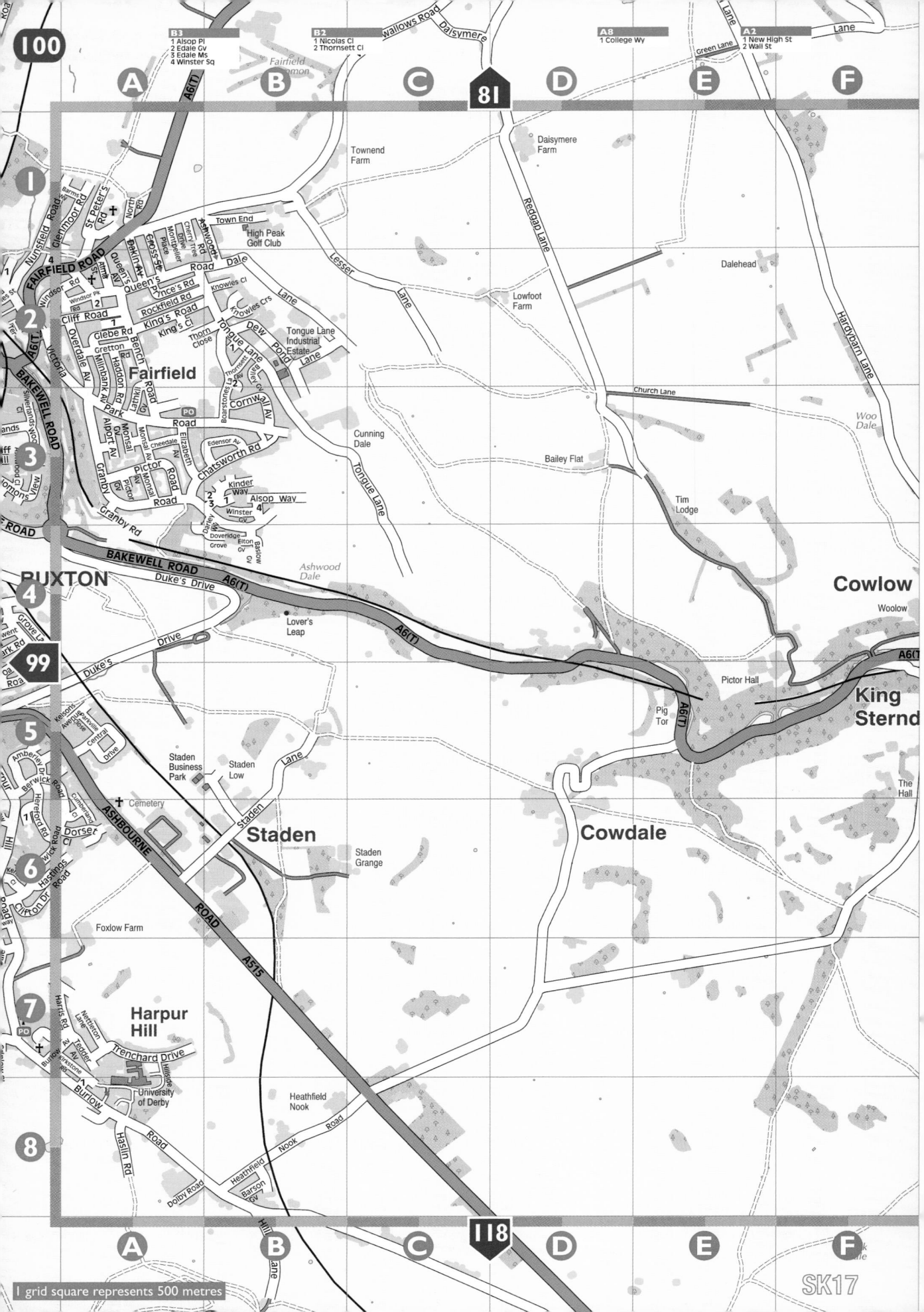

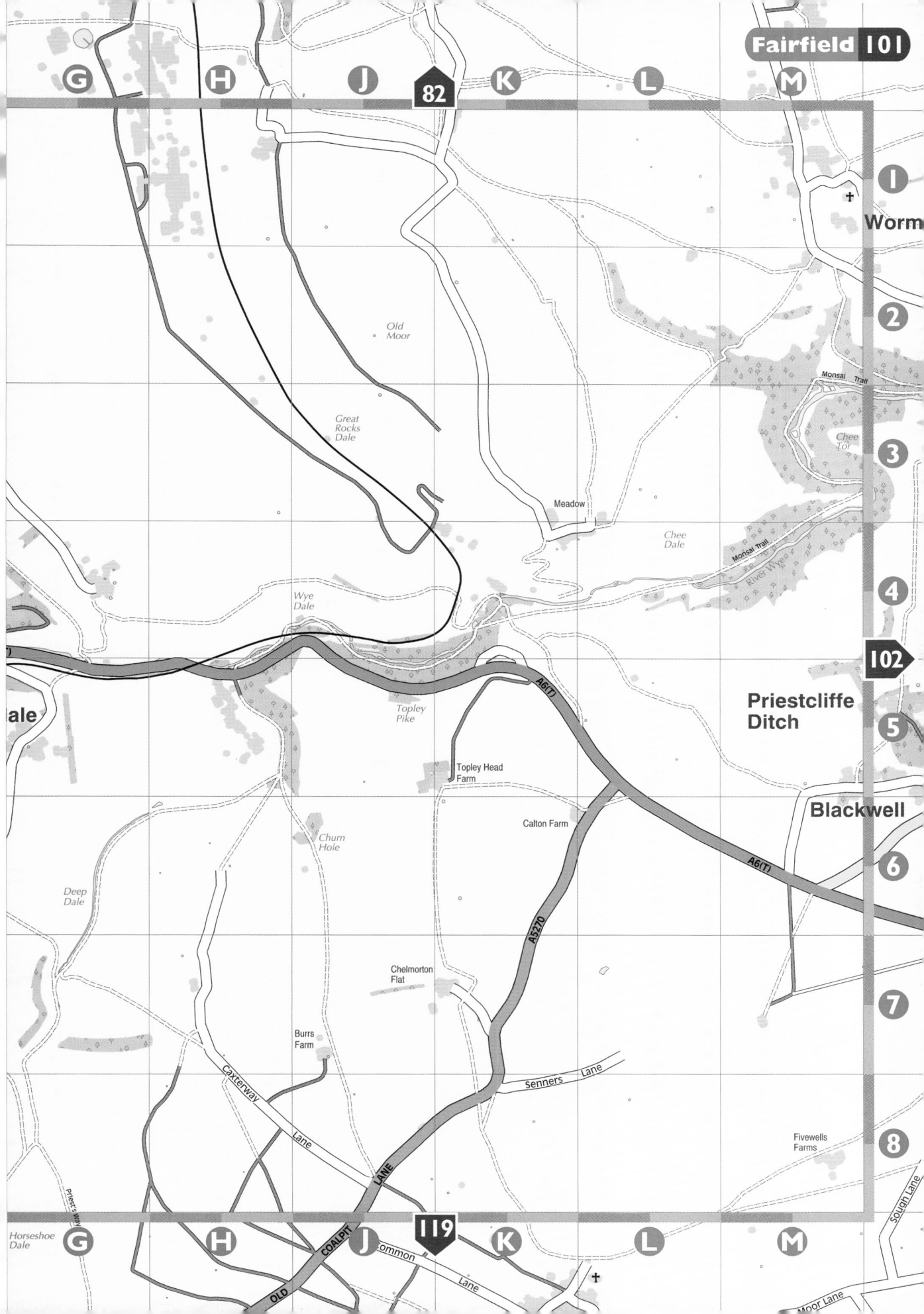

G H J K L M

82

I

Worm

2

Monsal Trail

3

Chee Tor

Old Moor

Great Rocks Dale

Meadow

Chee Dale

Monsal Trail

River Wye

4

Wye Dale

102

ale

A6(T)

Topley Pike

Priestcliffe Ditch

5

Topley Head Farm

Calton Farm

Blackwell

Churn Hole

A6(T)

6

Deep Dale

A5270

Chelmorton Flat

7

Burrs Farm

Fivewells Farms

8

Caxterway Lane

Senners Lane

Priest's Way

Horseshoe Dale

OLD COALPIT LANE

Common Lane

South Lane

Moor Lane

G H J K L M

119

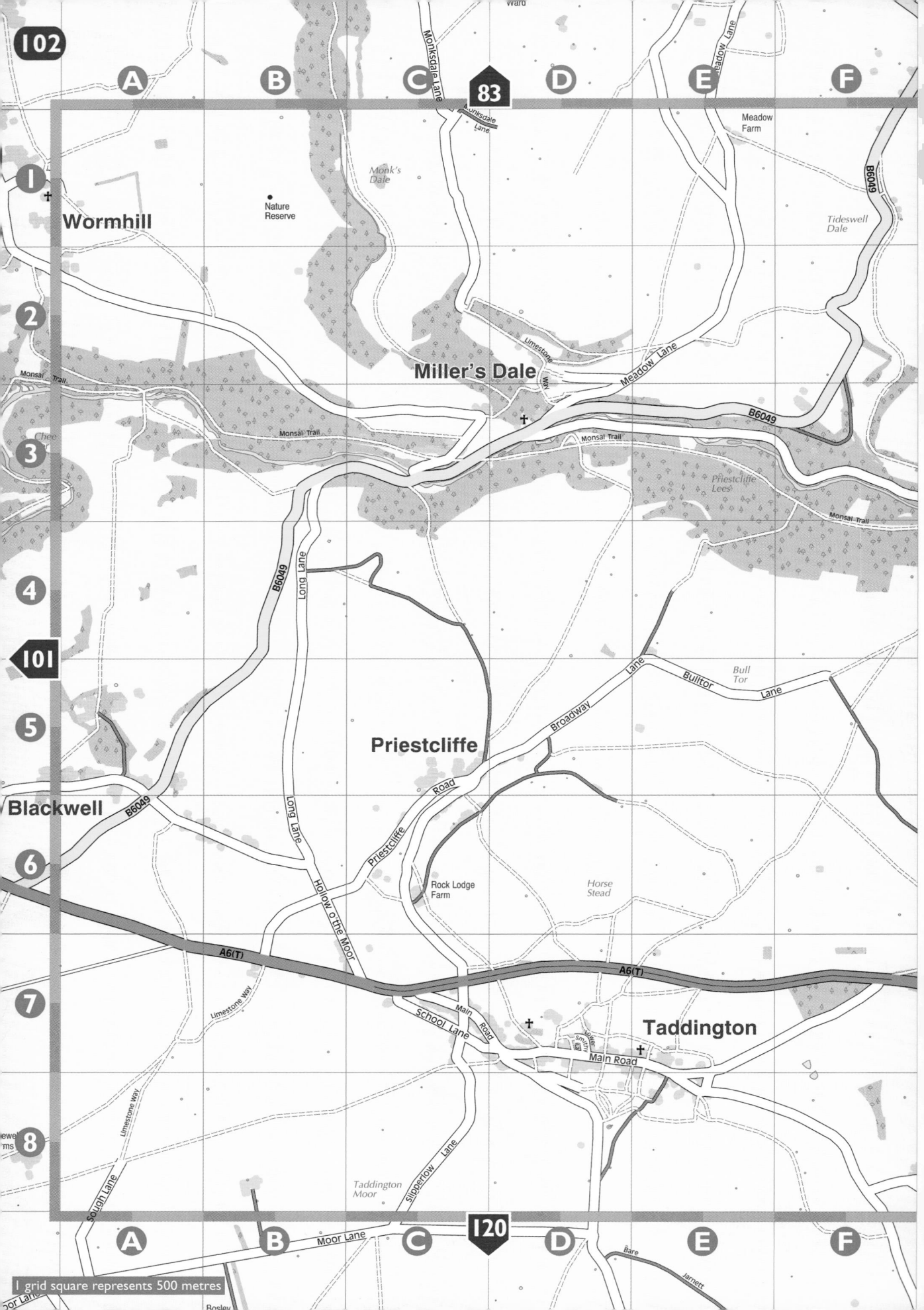

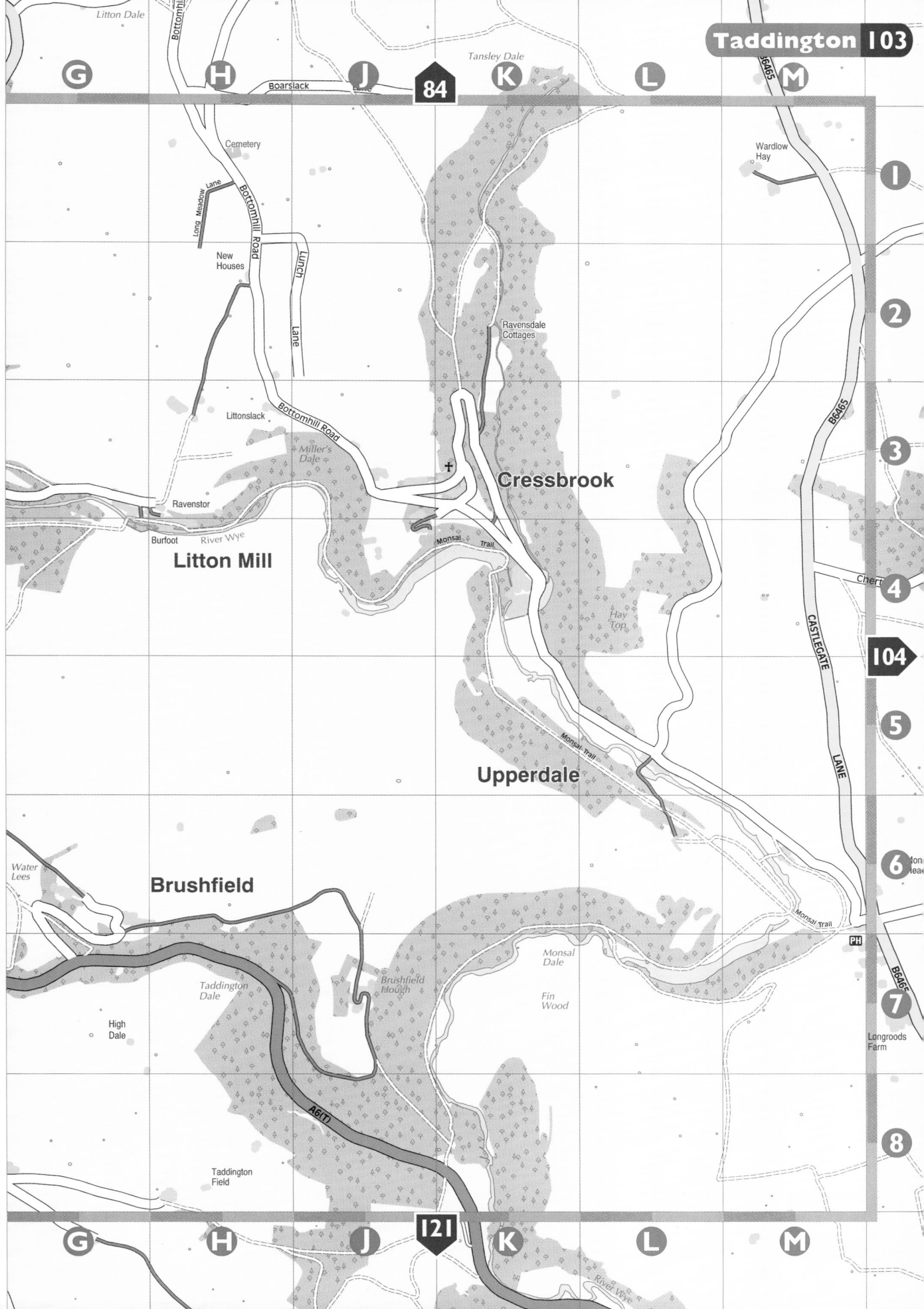

Litton Dale

Bottomhill

Boarslack

Tansley Dale

G H J 84 K L M

Wardlow Hay

B6465

1

Cemetery

Long Meadow Lane

Bottomhill Road

New Houses

Lunch Lane

2

Ravensdale Cottages

3

Littonslack

Bottomhill Road

Miller's Dale

Cressbrook

Chert

4

Ravenstor

Burfoot   River Wye

Monsal   Trail

Litton Mill

Hay Top

CASTLEGATE LANE

104

Monsal Trail

5

Upperdale

Water Lees

6

Mon lea

Brushfield

Monsal Trail

PH

B6465

Monsal Dale

7

Taddington Dale

Brushfield Hough

Fin Wood

High Dale

Longroods Farm

A6(T)

Taddington Field

8

G H J 121 K L M

River Wye

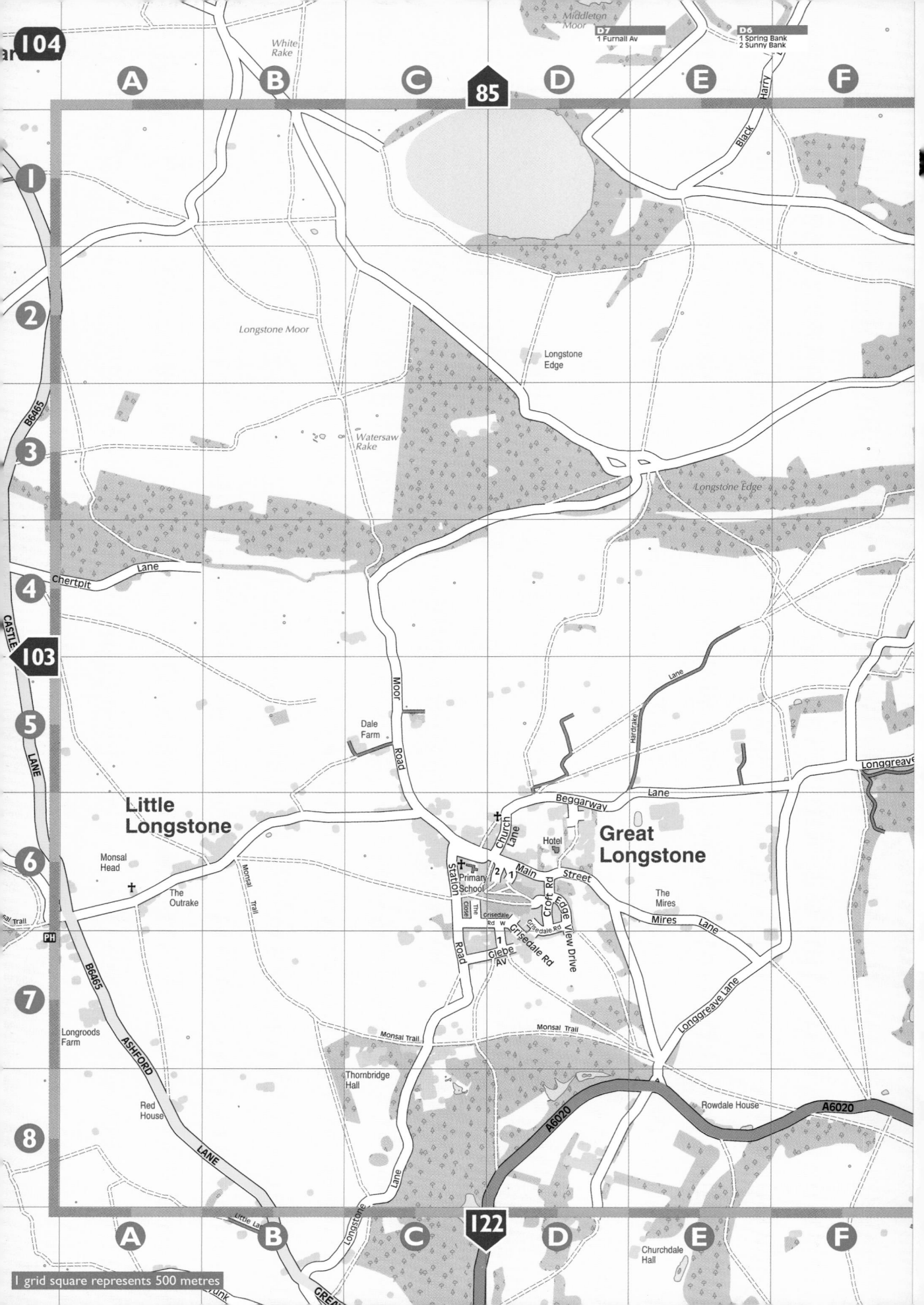

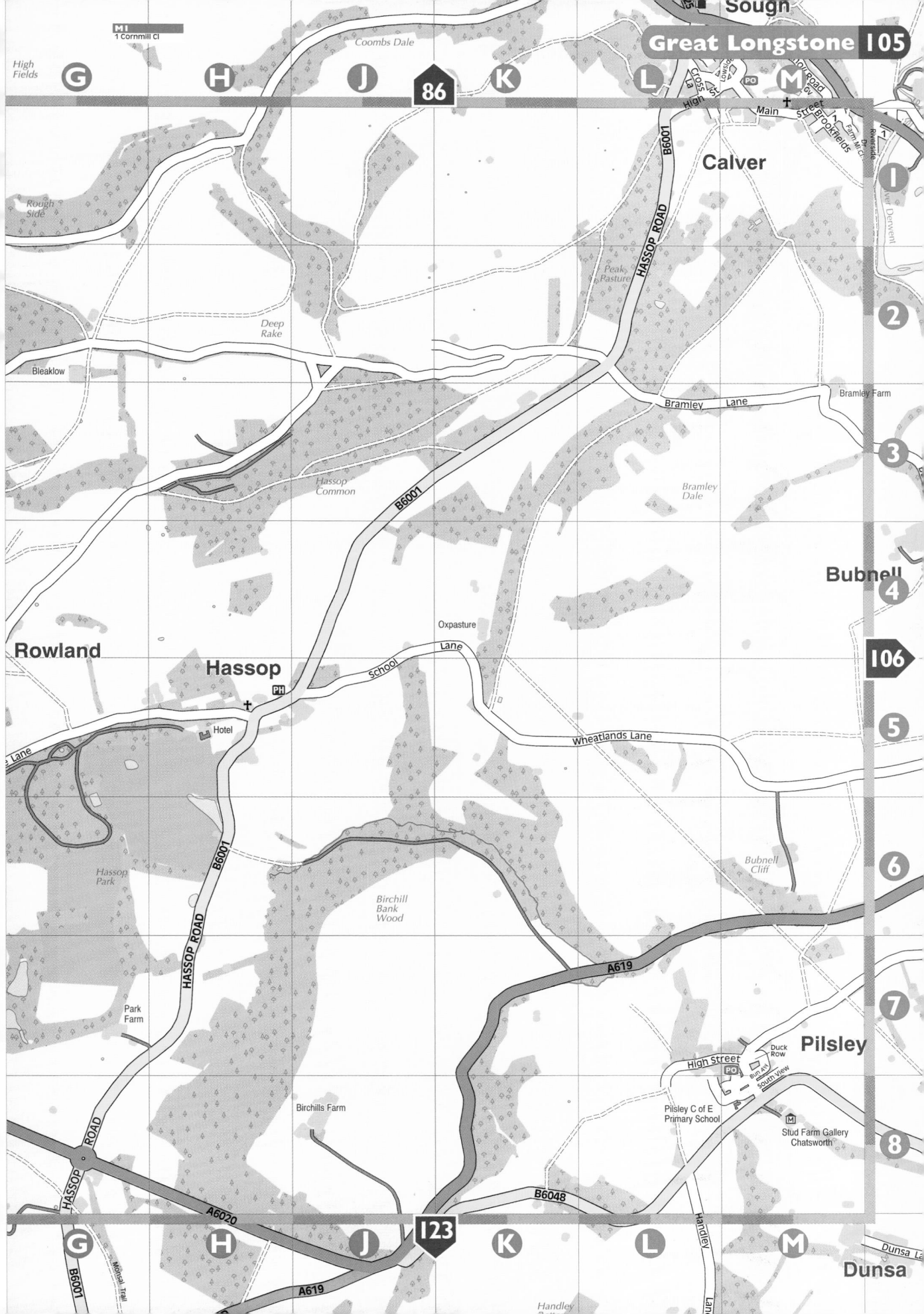

G   H   J   `86`   K   L   M

MI
1 Cornmill CI

Coombs Dale

High
Fields

Rough
Side

Deep
Rake

Bleaklow

Hassop
Common

B6001

HASSOP ROAD

Peak
Pasture

Bramley Lane

Calver

Main Street

Brookfields

PO

Cross St

High

B6001

Bramley Farm

Bramley
Dale

Bubnell

Rowland

Hassop

PH

†

Hotel

Oxpasture

School   Lane

Wheatlands Lane

`106`

Bubnell
Cliff

B6001

HASSOP ROAD

Hassop
Park

Birchill
Bank
Wood

A619

Park
Farm

Birchills Farm

Pilsley C of E
Primary School

High Street

PO

Duck
Row

South View

Pilsley

Stud Farm Gallery
Chatsworth

HASSOP ROAD

B6001

A6020

G   H   `123`   J   K   L   M

A619

B6048

Handley Lane

Dunsa La

Dunsa

Handley

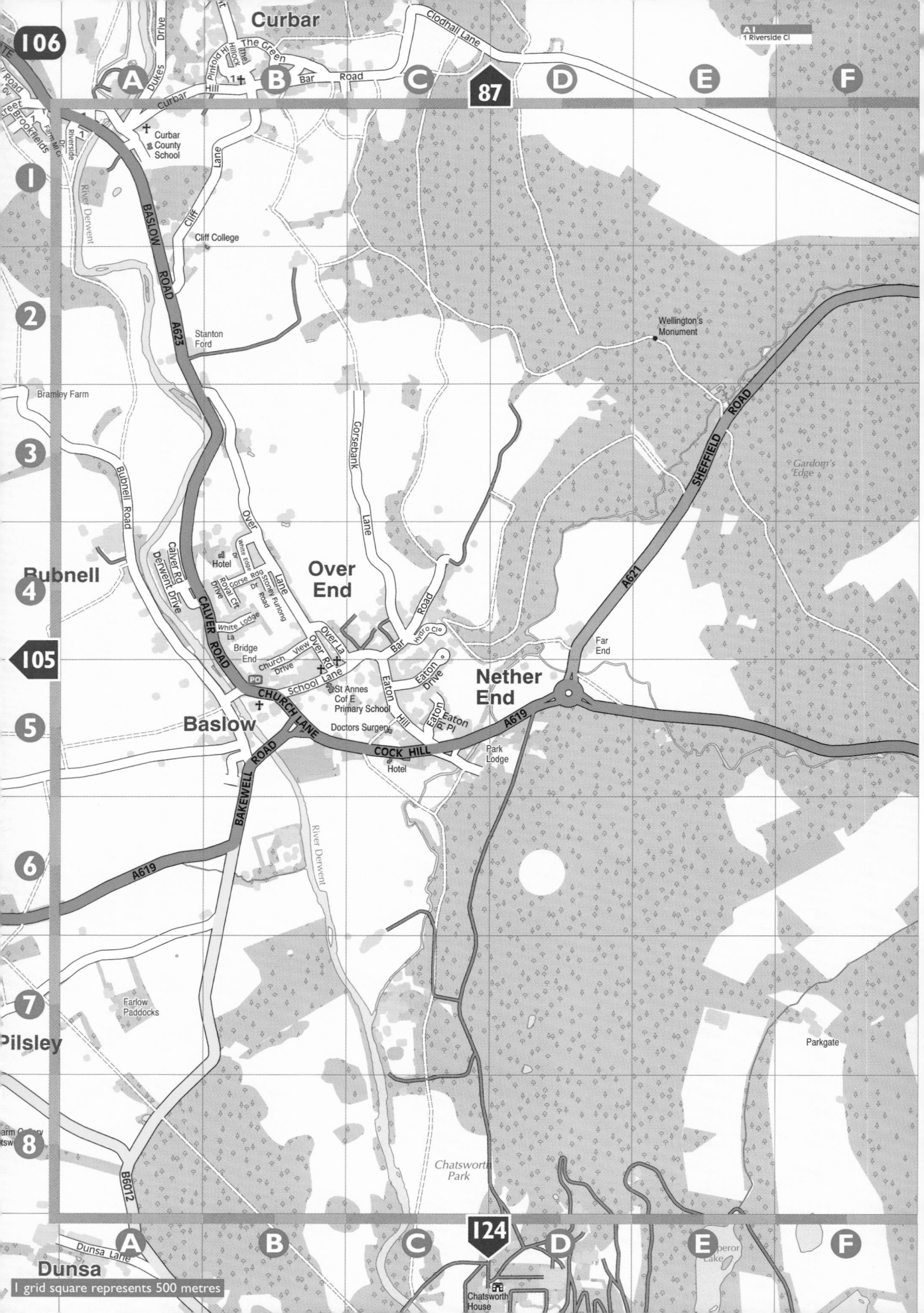

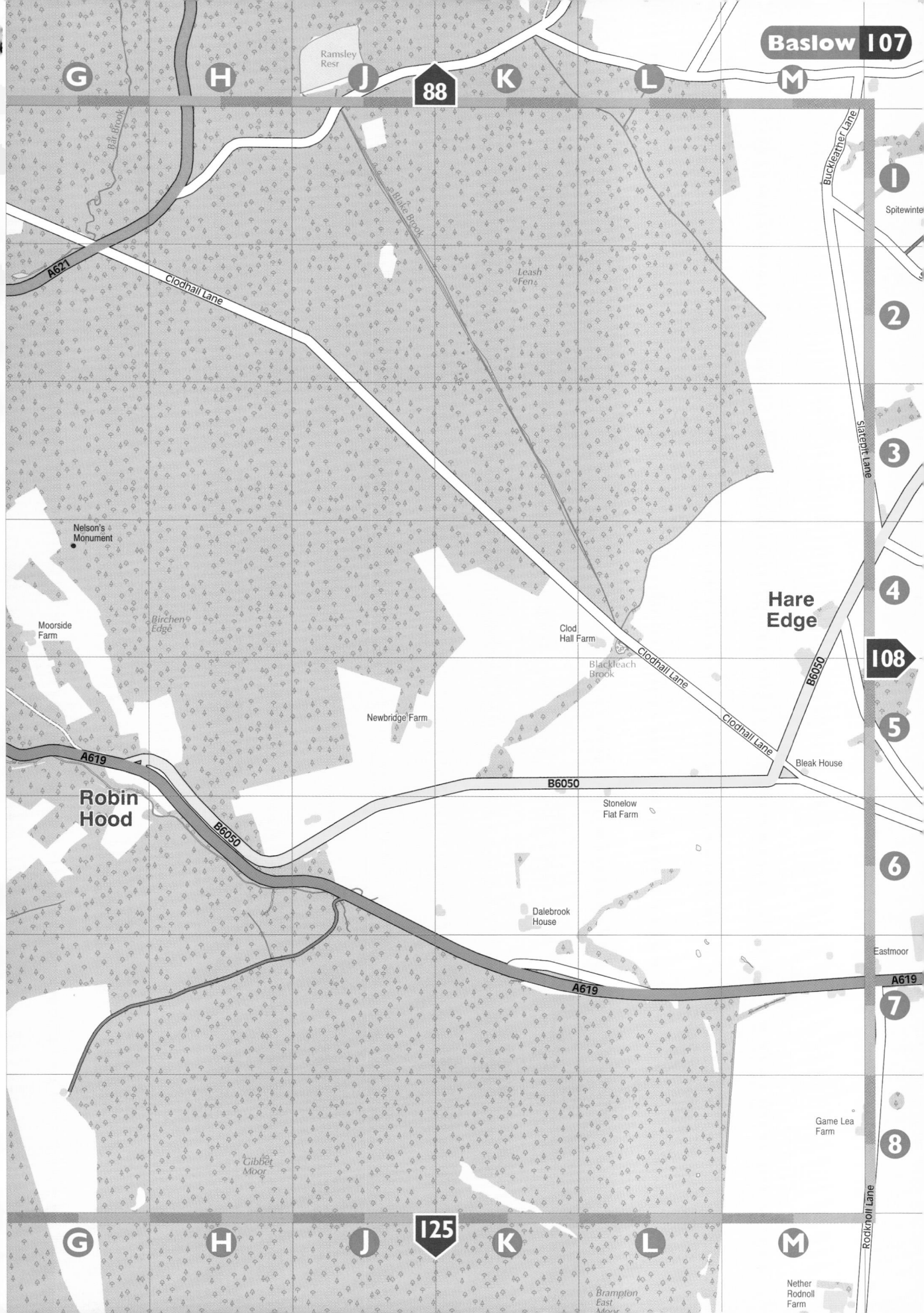

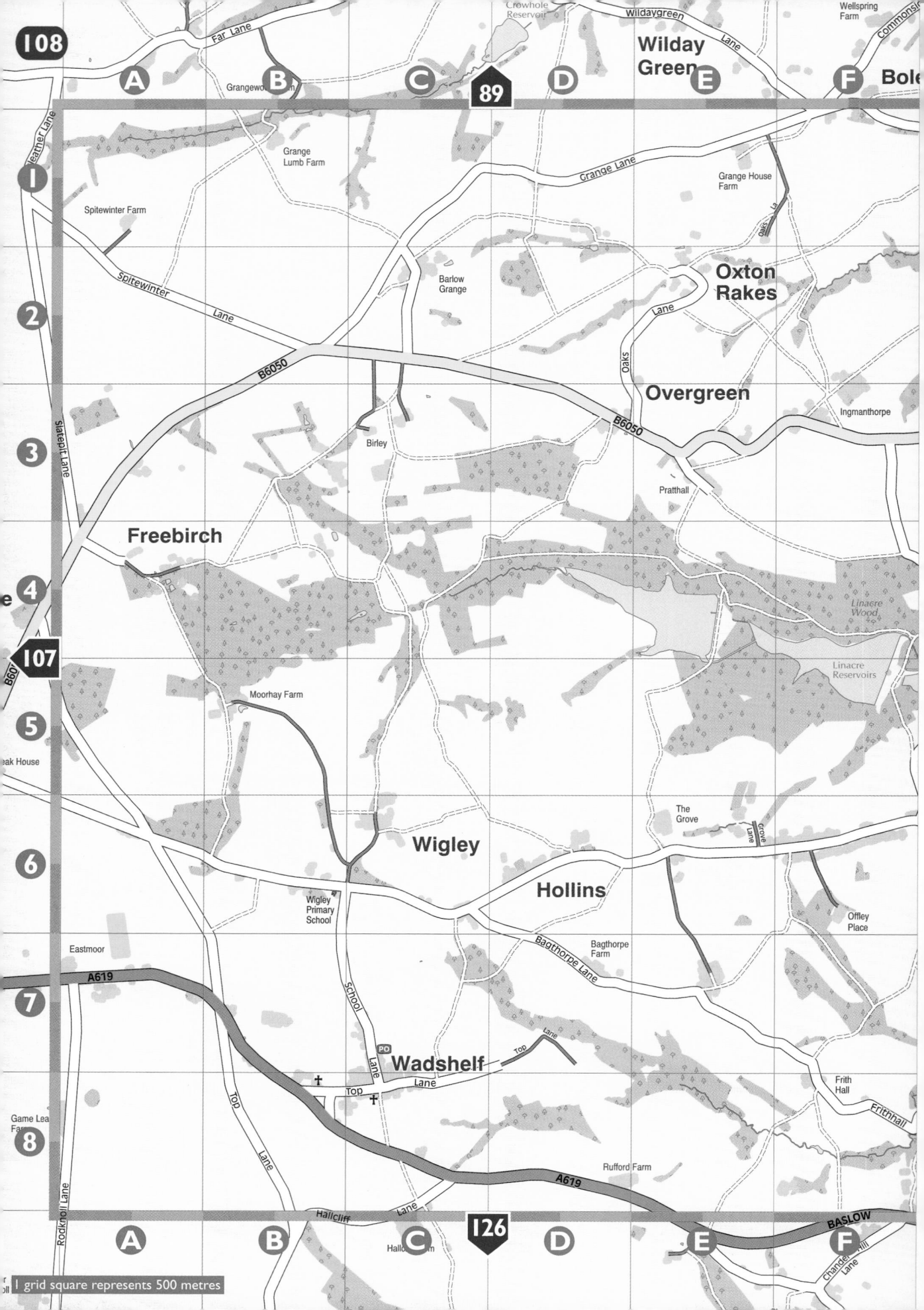

G2
1 Belle Vue Cl
2 Capel Ri
3 Fairfield Cl
4 Langdale Sq
5 Selmer Ct
6 Wayside Ct

H2
1 Lydden Cl

H3
1 Well Spring Cl

G3
Street names for
this grid square are
listed at the back of
the index

J2
1 Cambridge Rd
2 Cornwall Av

92

Chesterfield Canal

Hollingwood

Railway Staff
Social & Sports Club

New
Brimington

I

Gregory Lane

King Street

Queen Street

Cowpingle Lane

Hollingwood Junior
& Infant School

2

CHESTERFIELD ROAD

Infant School

BRIMINGTON

RINGWOOD ROAD

3

CHESTERFIELD RD CHURCH ST
HALL RD

A619

Inkersall
Primary
School

Ink
Gr

4

Furnace Lane

West
Wood

II2

Tapton
Grove

Limetree Close

Brimington
Common

5

Grove
Road

Infant
School

Brooke Drive

Eliot
Cl

6

Works Farm

Westmoor Road

Calow

Calow C of E
Junior School

7
Arkwright
Primary
School

Hady

Hady
School

HighView Close

A632

TOP ROAD

Rose
Avenue
Surgery

CHESTERFIELD ROAD

Arkwright
Town

8
A632

DE
CK
LANE

129

G H J K L M

M4
1 Beeley Cl
2 Thoresby Pl

M2
1 Grangemill Pl
2 Paisley Cl

M3
1 Amber Cft
2 Holbrook Pl
3 Monyash Cl

K7
1 Laburnum Ct

J6
1 Chesterton Cl

J8
1 Old School La

M1
1 Northmoor Cl

Bolehill

Netherthorpe

Woodthorpe

A **B** **C** **D** **E** **F**

Staveley
Council Office
High Street
Medical Centre

Netherthorpe
Comprehensive
School

D2
1 Poolsbrook Sq

Church St
Rectory
Porter St
Devonshire St

MARKET ST
DUKE STREET
Telford
Watermoury
Grove
Huntsman
Road

Belmont Dr
Ireland St
Whitehead St
Bird St
Netherthorpe
Arrow St
Tudor St

Ralph Road

PO

93

Bridle Road

Seymour Lane

I

Darley Barlow
Road
Lime Avenue
Staveley
Health Clinic

Infants
School
Staveley Junior
School

Staveley Urban
District Council

Brierley Close

Ireland
Close

Fan

STAVELEY

Stephenson Road

Hayford Way

Cemetery Lane

St Johns Road
St Johns Road
Circular Road
West Vw
College Avenue
Freicheville Street
St Musard
Place

Cemetery

Inkersall Road

Erin Road

Poolsbrook Av
Poolsbrook Vw
Staveley
Poolsbrook Crescent

Erin Road

PO
The Grove

2

Division
Westwood
Bond Street
Cavendish Street
Middlecroft
Avenue
Fern
Longshaw
Mantold
Lane
Foxstone
Ladybower
Chatsworth
Court
Haddon Place
Elton
Close
Calver Crescent
Burbage

Middlecroft

Griffin Cl
Adelphi Way
Meadows
Meadows Dr

St Josephs
RC Primary
School

1

Cottage Close

3

Lumsdale Road
Wensley Way
Logan
Winster Road
Middlecroft Road

Middlecroft
Leisure
Centre

Springwell
Community
School

Poolsbrook
Country Park

Poolsbrook

4

Bradwell
Place
Winnat
Place
Avondale Road
Pindale Avenue
Peak
Place
Hucklow
Avenue
Clumber Pl

**Inkersall
Green**

Pools Brook

The Oaks

Erin Road

5

III

Bamford
Tinsley
Way
Milton
Close
Ribel
Close

Inkersall Road

North Grove
Poolsbrook Road
West Crs
North Crescent
East Crescent
Whittington

Duckmanton
Primary
School

Markham Road

6

Tom Lane

Staveley Road

Blue Lodge Farm

Duckmanton

Duckmanton Road
PO
South Crs
Old Peverel Road

Rectory Road

Markham Lane

**Long
Duckmanton**

Robertson's Avenue

7

Works Farm

Cherry Tree Drive
Beech Grove
St Peters Close
Rectory Close

A632

A632

B6418 BUTTERM

Arkwright
Primary
School

Oak Tree
Beech
Lime Tree
Penrose Crescent
Hardwick Dr
School Lane

Longcourse Lane

8

**Arkwright
Town**

A632
Laurel Avenue
Rosling Way
PO

A632

DEEPSICK LANE

Sutton Lane

Duckmanton

Longcourse Fm

130

M1

A **B** **C** **D** **E** **F**

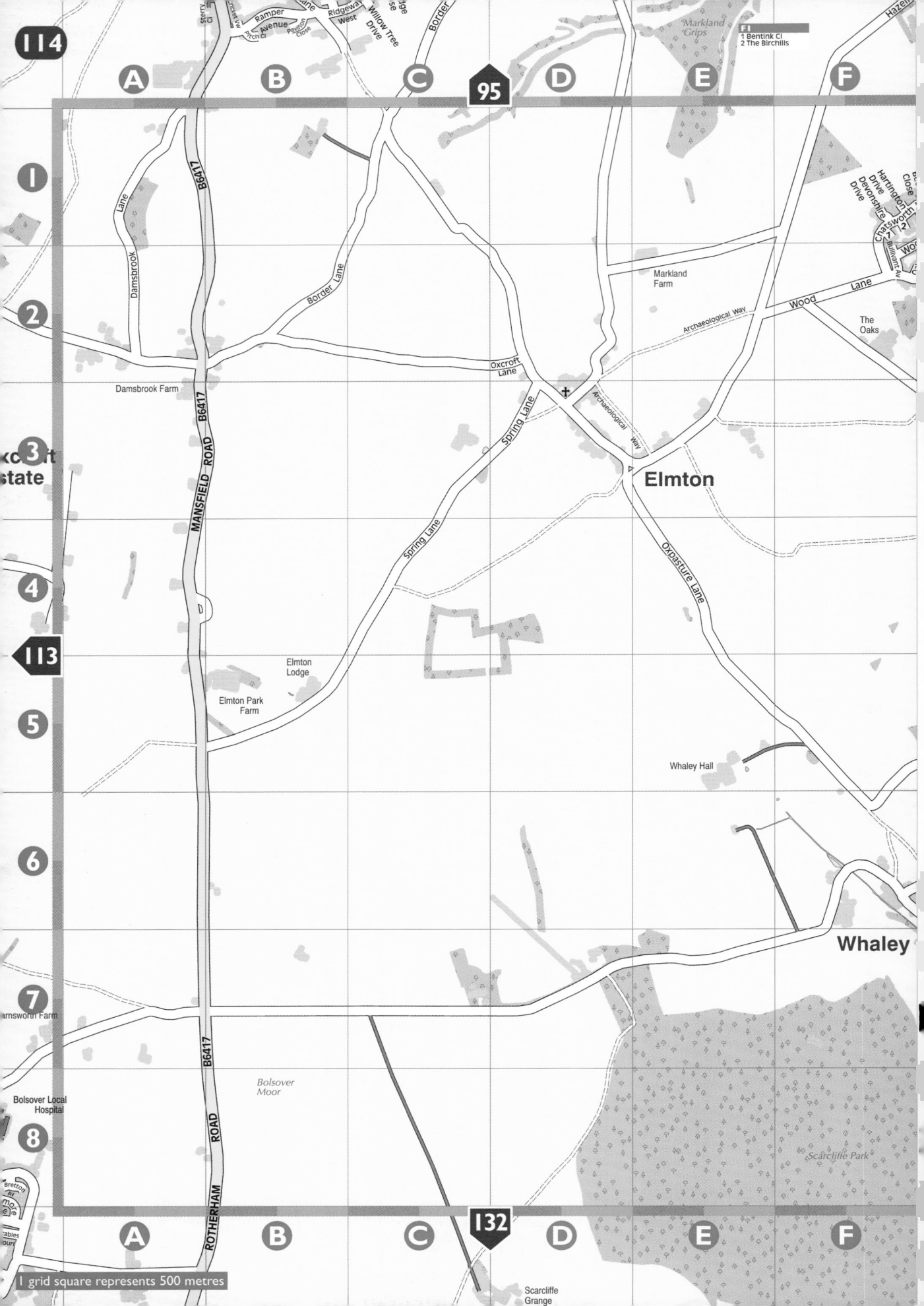

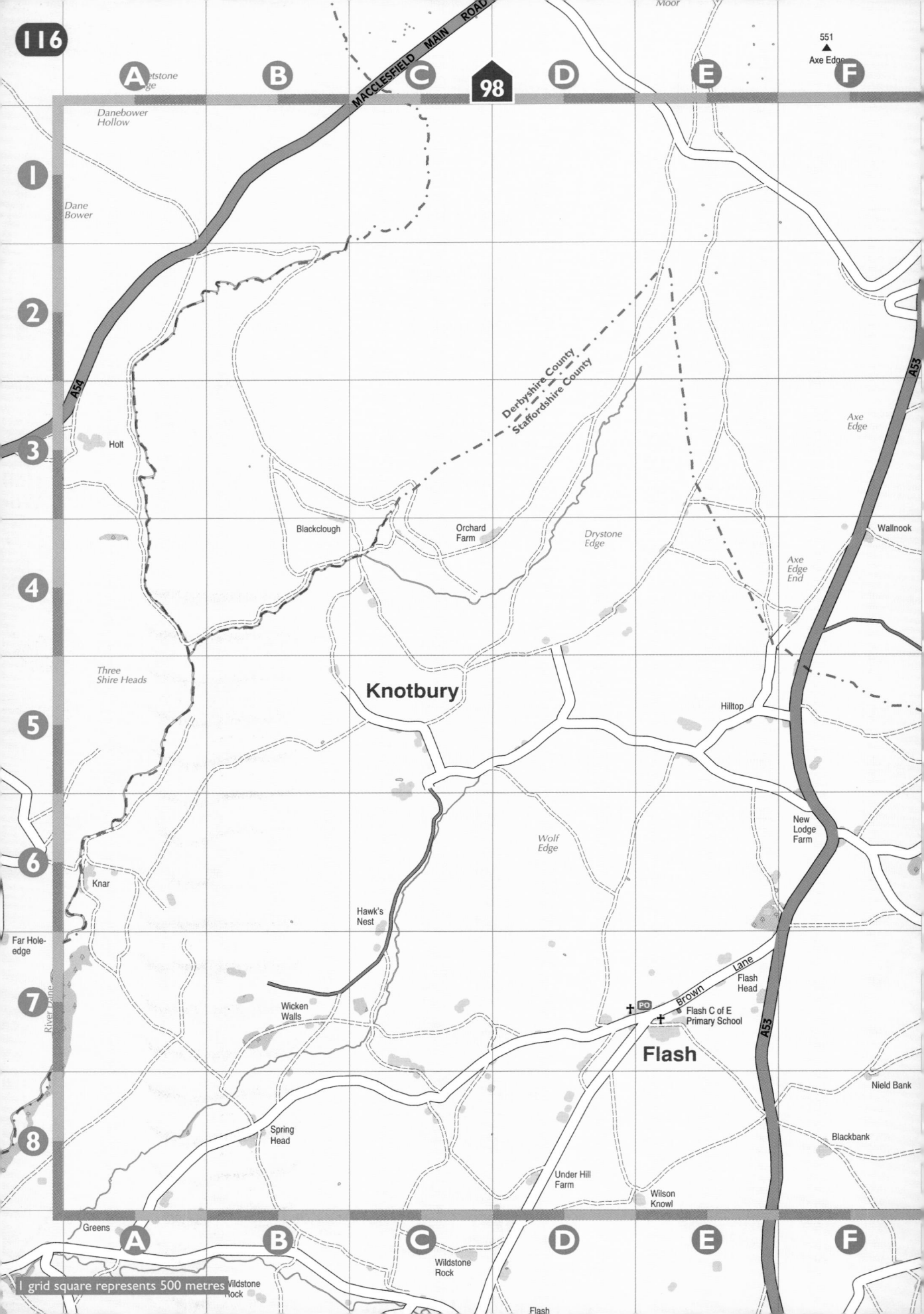

116

A B C D E F

MACCLESFIELD MAIN ROAD

98

551
▲
Axe Edge

Danebower
Hollow

1

Dane
Bower

2

A54

3

Holt

Derbyshire County
Staffordshire County

Axe
Edge

Blackclough

Orchard
Farm

Drystone
Edge

Wallnook

A53

4

Axe
Edge
End

Three
Shire Heads

Knotbury

Hilltop

5

New
Lodge
Farm

6

Knar

Wolf
Edge

Far Hole-
edge

Hawk's
Nest

Brown   Lane

Flash
Head

7

River Dane

Wicken
Walls

† PO
† Flash C of E
Primary School

Flash

A53

Nield Bank

8

Spring
Head

Blackbank

Under Hill
Farm

Wilson
Knowl

Greens

A B C D E F

Wildstone
Rock

Wildstone
Rock

Flash

1 grid square represents 500 metres

G H J 99 K University of Sheffield L M

1

2

3

118

4

5

6

7

8

I

Turncliff

Leap Edge

The Frith

Fairthorn

Brand Side

Thirkelow

Brand Top

Dove Head

Howe Green

River Dove

Brand End

Booth Farm

Stoop Farm

Tor Rock

Colshaw

Gamballs Green

Leycote

Fough

Summerhill

Hollins Farm

Tenterhill

Hollinsclough Rake

Moor Side

River Dove

Dun Cow's Grove

Moseley

Hollinsclough Rake

Hollinsclou School

Hollinsclough

G H J K L M

Thick Withins

Edgetop

Hollinsclough

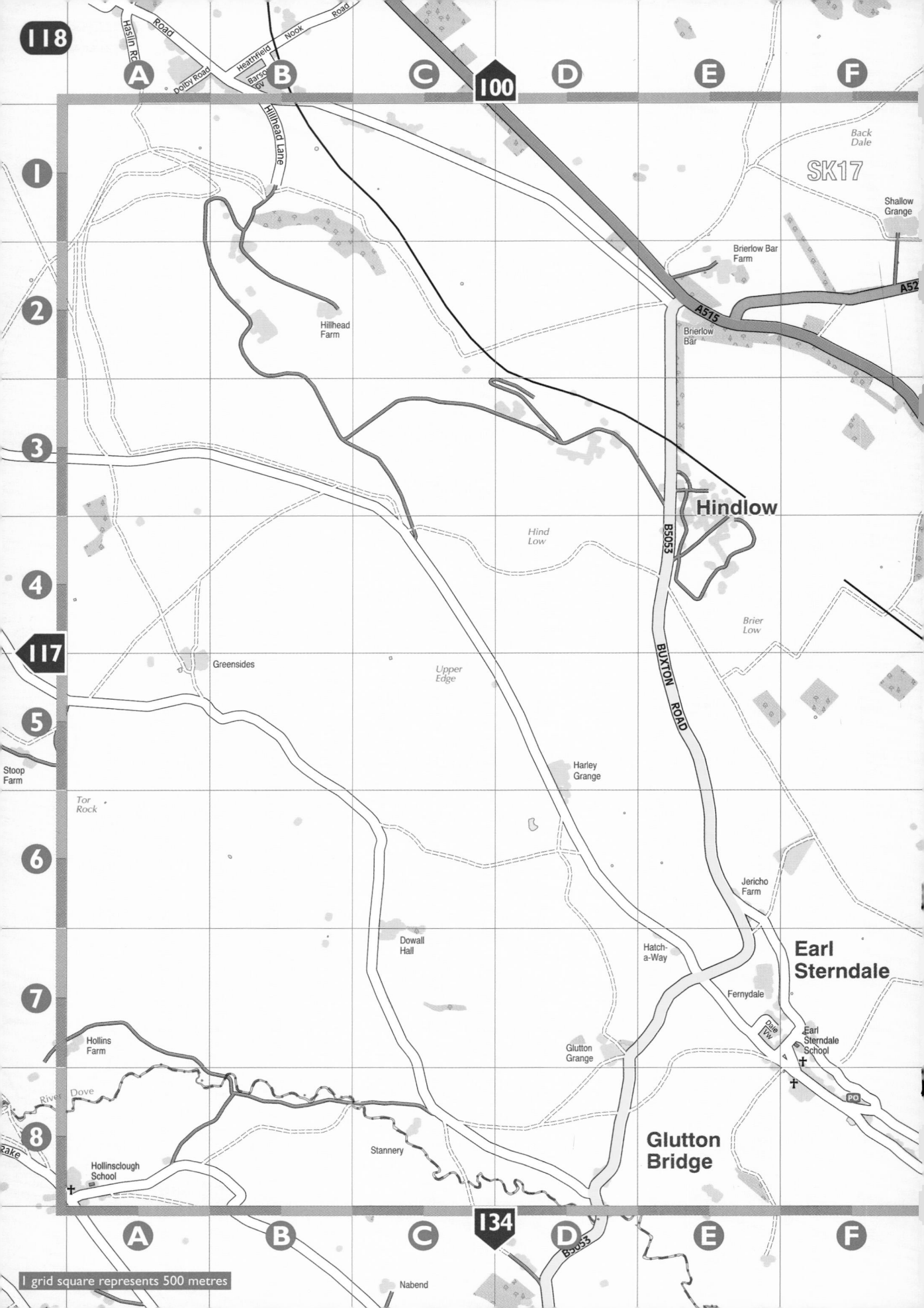

118

A   B   C   **100**   D   E   F

1

Haslin Rd   Dolby Road   Heathfield   Barson   Nook Road   Hillhead Lane

SK17

Back Dale

Shallow Grange

I

2

Brierlow Bar Farm

A52

A515

Brierlow Bar

Hillhead Farm

3

Hindlow

Hind Low

B5053

4

Brier Low

117

Greensides   Upper Edge

BUXTON ROAD

5

Stoop Farm

Tor Rock

Harley Grange

6

Jericho Farm

Earl Sterndale

7

Dowall Hall

Hatch-a-Way

Fernydale

Dale Vw

Earl Sterndale School

Hollins Farm

8

River Dove

Glutton Grange

Glutton Bridge

PO

ake

Hollinsclough School

Stannery

A   B   C   **134**   D   B5053   E   F

Nabend

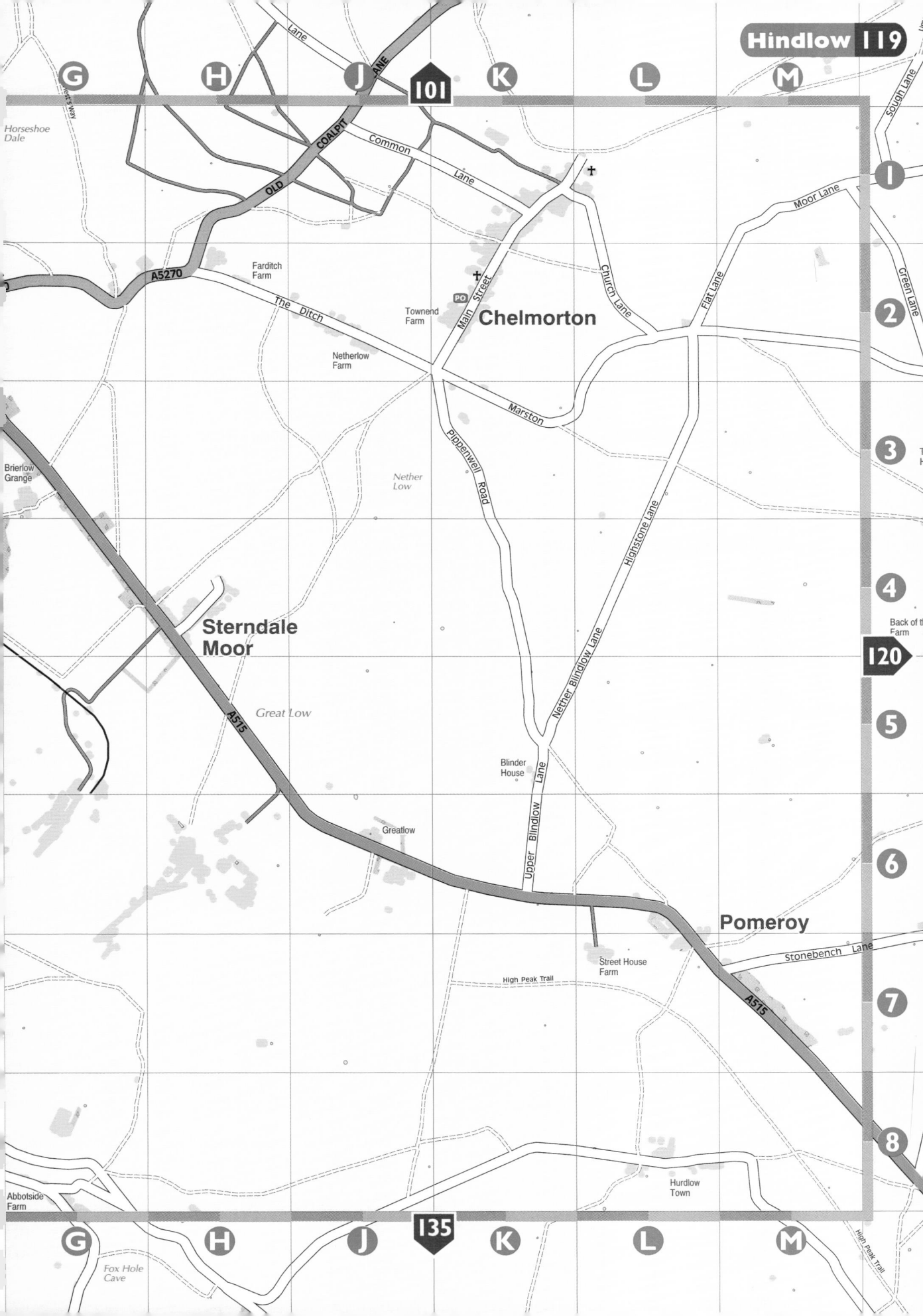

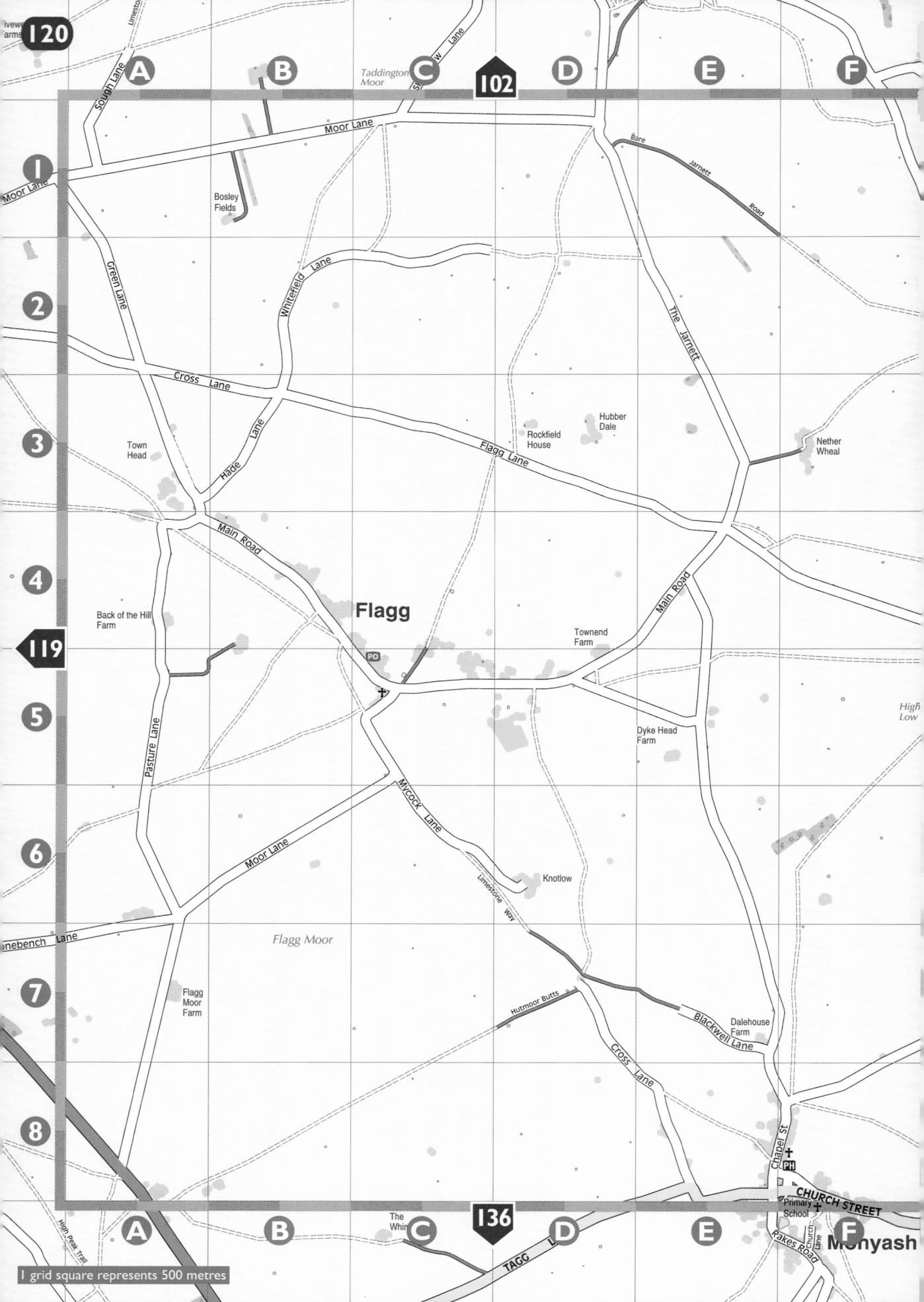

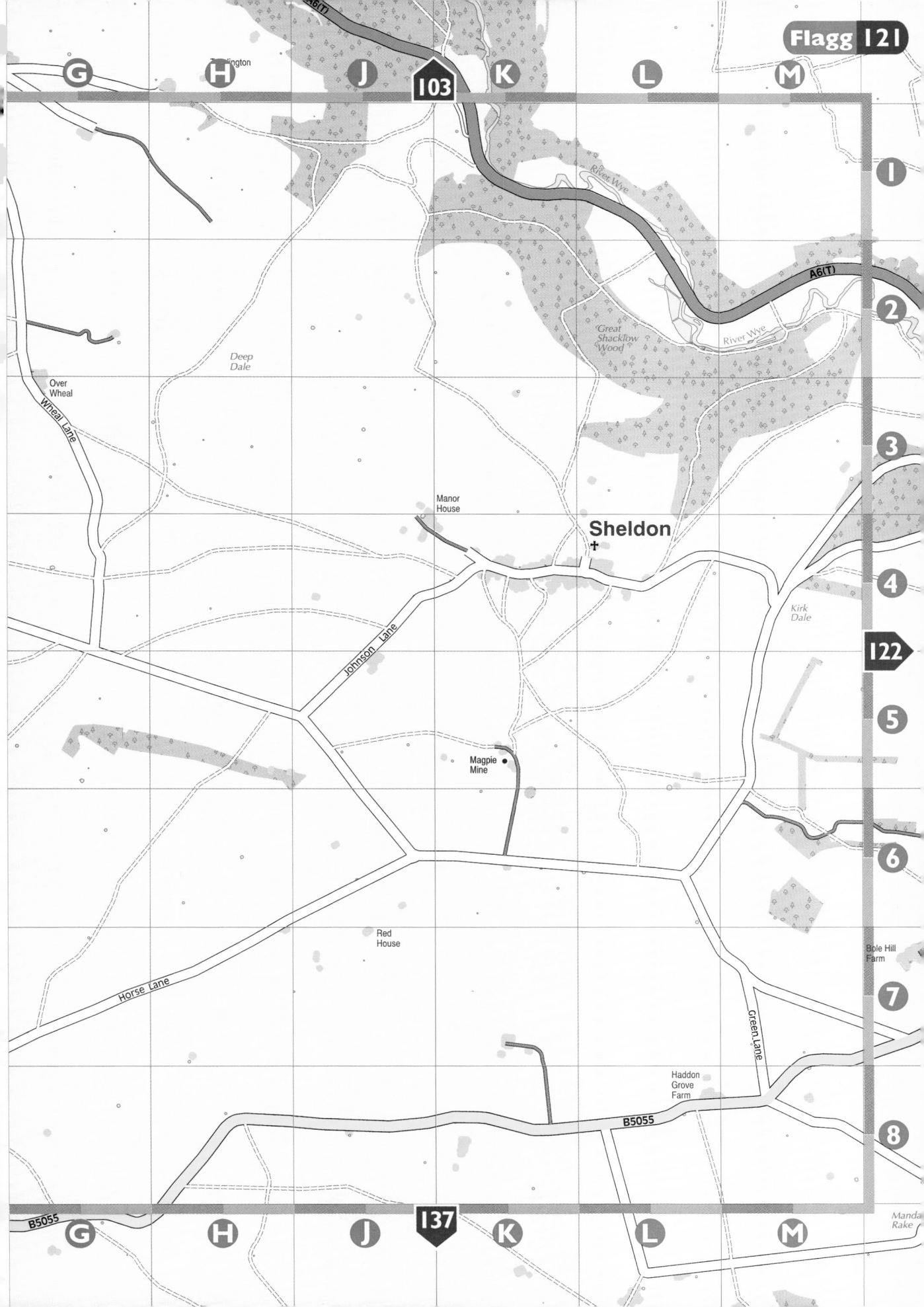

G H J K L M

Tallington

103

River Wye

A6(T)

River Wye

I

2

'Great
Shacklow
Wood'

3

Over
Wheal

Deep
Dale

Wheal Lane

Manor
House

Sheldon

Kirk
Dale

4

122

Johnson Lane

5

Magpie
Mine

6

Bole Hill
Farm

7

Red
House

Horse Lane

Haddon
Grove
Farm

Green Lane

B5055

8

Manda
Rake

B5055

G H J 137 K L M

G4
1 Castle Mount Crs
2 Mill St

G5
1 Church Alley
2 Woodside Dr

H4
1 Castle Mount Wy

Pilsley C of E
Primary School

G H J 105 K L6048 L M

A6020

Dunsa La

Dunsa

I

A619

BASLOW RD

Monsal Trail

Handley
Bottom

Handley Lane

2

Eweclose

B6001

Monsal Trail

Brookfield Lane

A619

BASLOW

Ballcross
Farm

Handley Lane

3

Aldern Way

Castle Drive

Newholme
Hospital

Bakewell
Golf
Club

New Piece Wood

Holme Lane

ROAD

Castle Mount Crs

Station Road

STATION ROAD

Burre Close

Lady
Manners
School

4

124

Calton
Pastures

NORTHCHURCH ST

Milford
Brook
Side

Castle St

BRIDGE ST

The
Brooklands

Brooklands
Bank

Monsal Trail

Bath St

Infant
Sch

North
Church St

Water

Granby
Gallery

The
Agricultural
Business Centre

Agricultural
Showground

Manners Wood

5

Houses

CHURCH ST

KING ST

PH

Doctors
Surg

MATLOCK STREET

Chapel
Lane

Granby Cr

A6(T)

Agricultural Way

Coombs Road

Butts Road

The Av

Woodside
Drive

Woodside
Close

Wye Bank

Wye Bank

Wye Grove

6

Cemetery

Park Road

Burton
Edge

Wyedale View Drive

Wyedale
Close

Wyedale Crs

Stoney
Close

Bakewell
Methodist
Junior School

Burton
Closes

Haddon
Drive

Burton Cl Dr

Coombs
Road

Coombs Farm

Intake Lane

Haddon
House

HADDON

ROAD

Haddon
Park Farm

7

Park Road

Bowling
Green Farm

8

Noton Barn
Farm

G H J 139 K Haddon
Hall (NT) L M H6
1 Burton Close Dr

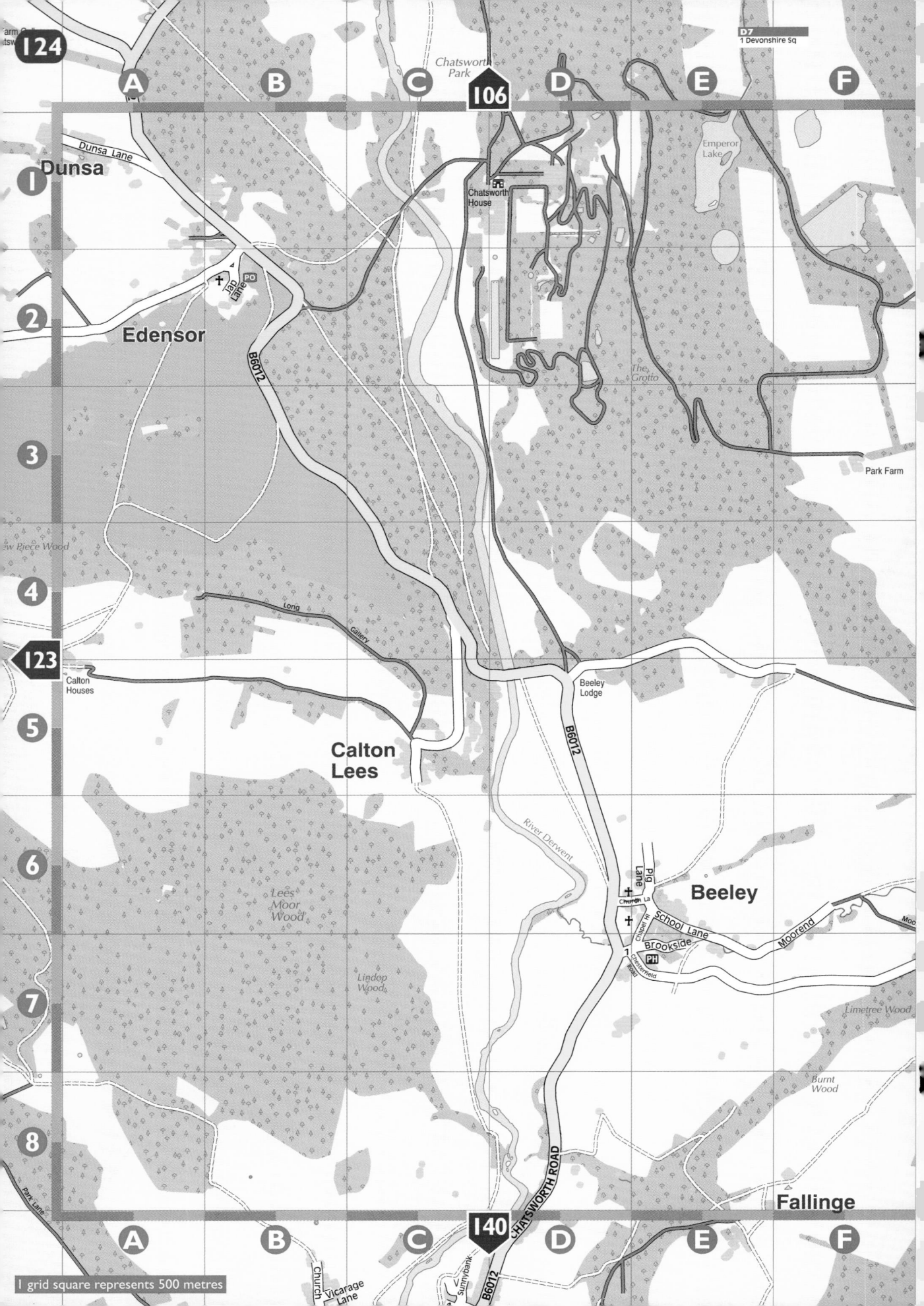

A B C D E F

Chatsworth
Park

Emperor
Lake

1

Dunsa

Dunsa Lane

Chatsworth
House

2

Edensor

PO

B6012

The
Grotto

3

Park Farm

w Piece Wood

4

Long

Gallery

Calton
Houses

Beeley Lodge

B6012

5

Calton
Lees

River Derwent

6

Lees
Moor
Wood

Beeley

Pig
Lane

Church La

School Lane

Brookside

Moorend

Moo

PH

Chesterfield

1

Chapel Hill

Lindop
Wood

Limetree Wood

7

Burnt
Wood

8

CHATSWORTH ROAD

Fallinge

Park Lane

A B C D E F

B6012

Church

Sunnybank

Vicarage Lane

1 grid square represents 500 metres

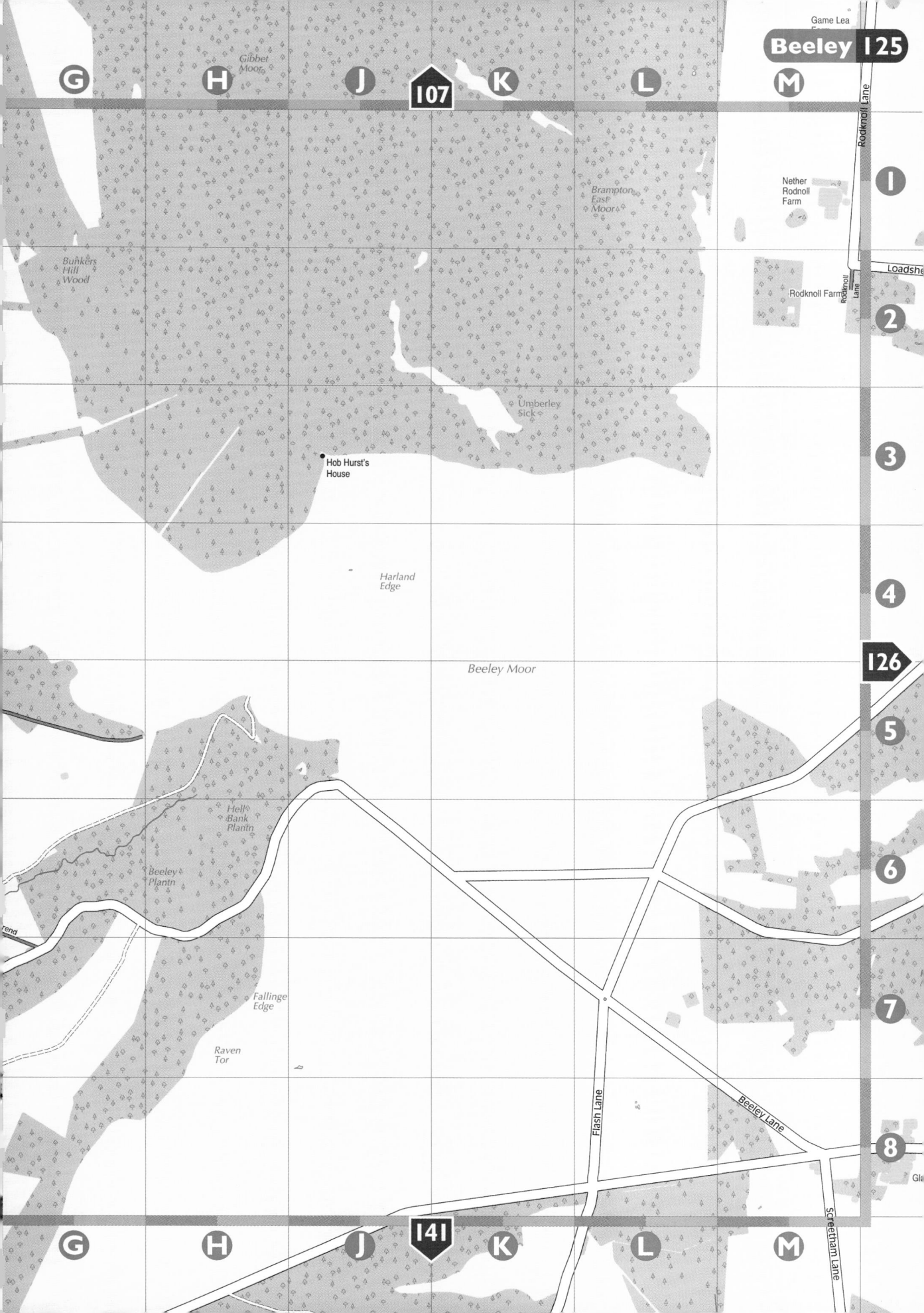

G   H   J   K   L   M

107

Game Lea Farm

I

Nether Rodknoll Farm

Rodknoll Farm

Rodknoll Lane

Loadshe

2

Bunkers Hill Wood

Brampton East Moor

3

Umberley Sick

Hob Hurst's House

Harland Edge

4

Beeley Moor

126

5

Hell Bank Plantn

6

Beeley Plantn

rend

Fallinge Edge

7

Raven Tor

Flash Lane

Beeley Lane

8

Screetham Lane

G   H   J   K   L   M

141

Gla

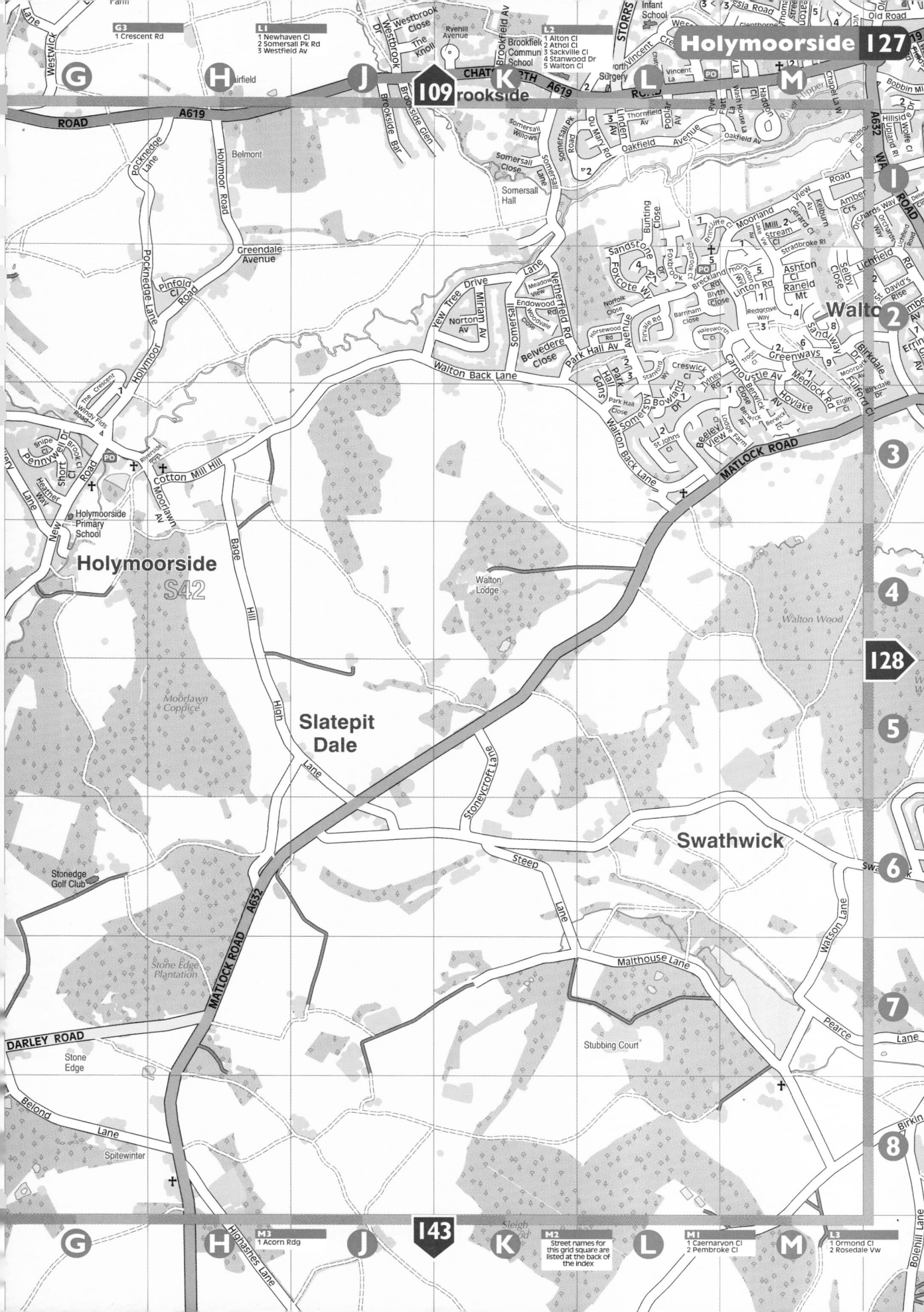

G3
1 Crescent Rd

L1
1 Newhaven Cl
2 Somersall Pk Rd
3 Westfield Av

L2
1 Alton Cl
2 Athol Cl
3 Sackville Cl
4 Stanwood Dr
5 Walton Cl

G **H** **J** **109** **K** **L** **M**

Westbrook Close
Westbrook Dr
The Knoll
Ryehill Avenue
Brookfield Av
Brookfield Communn School
CHAT
A619
STORRS
Infant School
Westsla Road
Glenthorpe
Old Road

Westwick
Lane
Hairfield
Brookside Glen
Brookside Bar
rookside
ROTH
A619
ROAD
North Vincent
Surgery
Vincent
PO
Chapel La W
Bobbin Ml
Upper

I

ROAD
A632
WA
Hillside
Wolfe Rd
Orchards Way

G ROAD A619

Pocknedge Lane
Holymoor Road
Belmont
Somersall Willows
Somersall Pk
Somersall Lane
Du Mary Rd
Moorland
View
Kelburn
Amber Crs
Gerard Cl
Orchards Way
St. David's Rise
Lichfield Rd

1

Greendale Avenue
Somersall Close
Oakfield Avenue
Moorland Av
Mill Stream Cl
Stradbroke Ri

Pinfold Cl
Pocknedge Road
Somersall Hall
Sandstone Cl
Bunting Close
Timcliffe
Foxbrook Rd
PO
Thornfield Av
Poplar
Haddon
Wash House La
Windsor Dr

Yew Tree Drive
Lane
Meadow View
Netherfield Rd
Foxcote Wy
Breckland Rd
Linton Rd
Ashton Cl
Selby Cl
Raneld Mt
Amber Crs
Walto

2

Holymoor Road
Pinfold Cl
Norton Av
Miriam Av
Woodvale Cl
Endowood Rd
Norfolk Close
Firvale Rd
Blyth Close
Redgrove Way
Sandiway
Birkdale
Elfin Cl
Fulford Cl

The Crescent
Windy Flds Road
Snipe
Pennywell Dr
Short Brook Cl
Road
PO
Riverside
Cotton Mill Hill
Moorlawn Av
Belvedere Close
Park Hall Av
Park Hall
Gdns
Creswic W
Stanton Cl
Camoustie Av
Troon
Medlock Rd
Hoylake
Elgin
Birkdale

Heather Way
New Lane
Holymoorside Primary School
Walton Back Lane
Horsewood Rd
Haleswth
Barnham Close
Somersby
Bowland Dr
Tiney Rd
Beeley
Berwick
Bar Wick
Birkdale Dr

Holymoorside
S42
Bage Hill
Walton Back Lane
St Johns Cl
Park Hall Close
St. John's
Beeley View
Loop Farm
MATLOCK ROAD

3

Walton Lodge
Walton Wood

4

128

Moorlawn Coppice
High Lane
Slatepit Dale

5

Stonedge Golf Club
Stoneycroft Lane
Swathwick

6
Swa

Stone Edge Plantation
MATLOCK ROAD
A632
Steep Lane
Malthouse Lane
Watson Lane

7

DARLEY ROAD
Stone Edge
Stubbing Court
Pearce Lane
Birkin

8

Belong
Lane
Spitewinter
Bolehill La

G **H** **M3** **J** **143** **K** **M2** **L** **M1** **M** **L3**

M3
1 Acorn Rdg

M2
Street names for this grid square are listed at the back of the index

M1
1 Caernarvon Cl
2 Pembroke Cl

L3
1 Ormond Cl
2 Rosedale Vw

Highstairs Lane
Sleigh od

G2
1 Eastleigh Ct
2 Granville Cl

G3
1 Nicholas St

G4
1 Hazelhurst

G H J **III** K L M

I

Hady School
HighView Close
Lee Road
Kenyon Road
Barnes Road
Dingle Lane
The Clough
Dalewood
Calow Lane

Bolehill

Cock Alley

Smith Crs
Taylor Crs
Spital Lane
Heathcote Drive
Ashfield Road
Calow Brook
Holythorpe Cl
Hoole St
Meakin St
Handby St
Chapel La E
Park Vw
Blackthorn Close
Talbot Crs
Talbot Street
Gorse Valley Way
Gorse Valley Rd
Heather Dale Rd
Valley View Close
Valley View

Hallfhash Lane
Back Lane

Calow Green

2

MANSFIELD ROAD

Community School
Burgess Rd
Norwood Av
Hillcrest
Mansfield Road

Hasland

Manor Farm

Woodnook Farm

3

Hall
Arbour
Foxwood Cl
Coppice Cl
Pauls Av
Linden Drive
Broomfield Av
Norwood Av
Southfield AV
Broomfield Avenue

Winsick

B6039

Sutton Spring Wood

4

Churchside Lane
Cemetery

CHURCHSIDE B6038

HASSOCKY LANE

B6425

MOOR LANE B6425

DEEPSICK LANE

Muster Brook

I30

5

Corbriggs

A617

NORTH

River Rother

Five Pits Trail

Grassmoor Country Park

MANSFIELD

6

WINGFIELD

Keats Way
Scott Close
Westhill La
Shakespeare Street
Tennyson Way
Burns Dr
Cotswold Drive
Danbury Drive
Cross Street
MacDonald Cl
New Street
Wenlock Dr
Chiltern Close
Dymond Grove

Temple Normanton

Springwood St
Elm St
Postmans Lane
Temple Normanton Primary School

ROAD
B6039

7

Mill Lane
Whitmore Avenue
Furnace Close
Broom Drive
Grange Walk
Henry St
Chapel Rd
Chapman Lane
Cornwall Dr
Norfolk AV
Durham Avenue
Oak Road
Birch Cl

Birkin Lane

Philadelphia

Cemetery
Church Street

Birkin Lane

8

Grassmoor
Grassmoor Primary School
Gill's Lane
Old Church School
Birkin Lane
Vernon Rl
Smithy Place
Southend

Five Pits Trail

Lings Farm

I45

J7
1 Devon Cl

H7
1 Frederick St
2 Wingerworth St

H4
1 Norwood Cl

H3
1 Heather Gdns
2 Heather Vale Cl

B6038

CHESTERFIELD B6039

Five Pits
Park Rd
Enterprise Drive

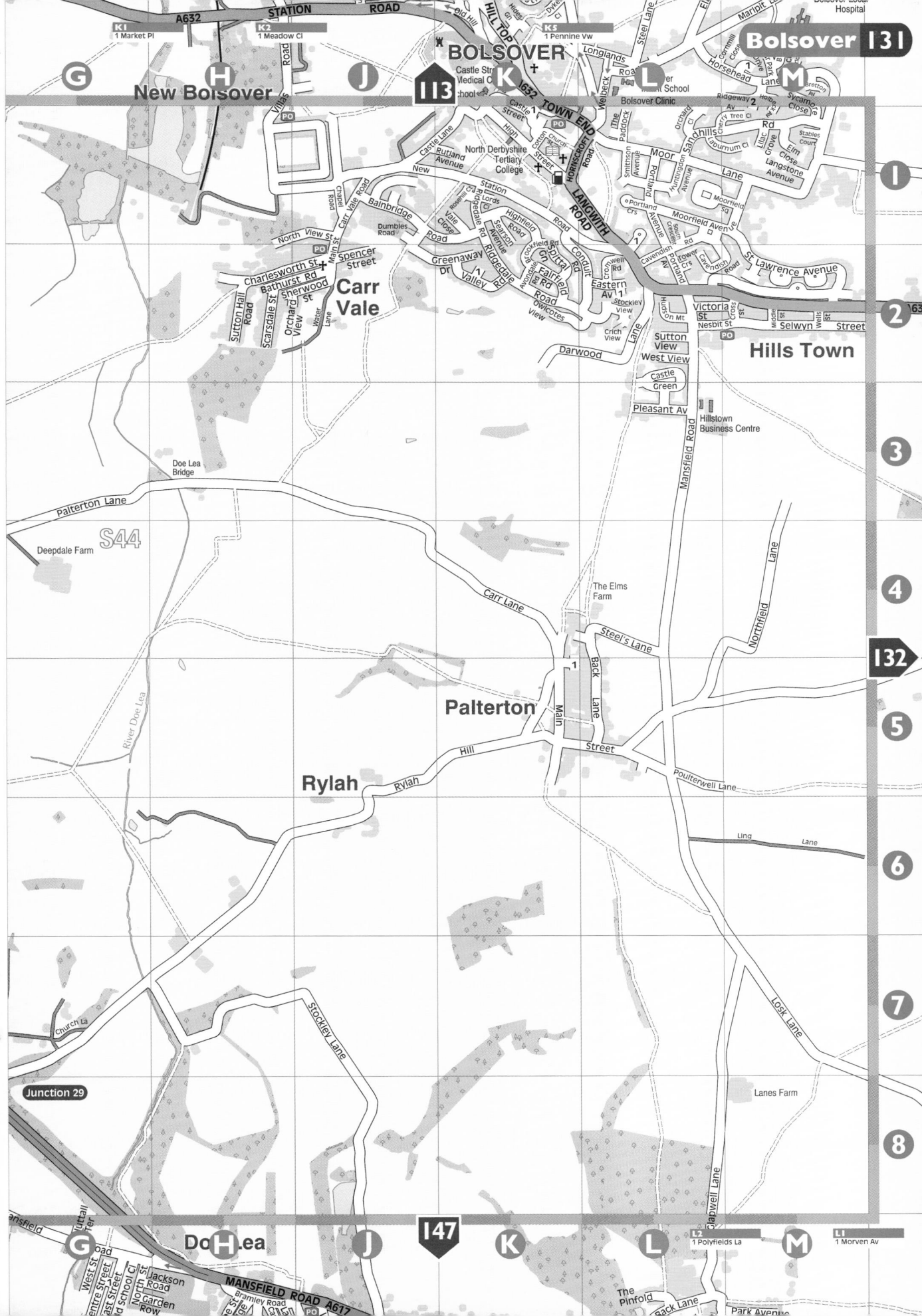

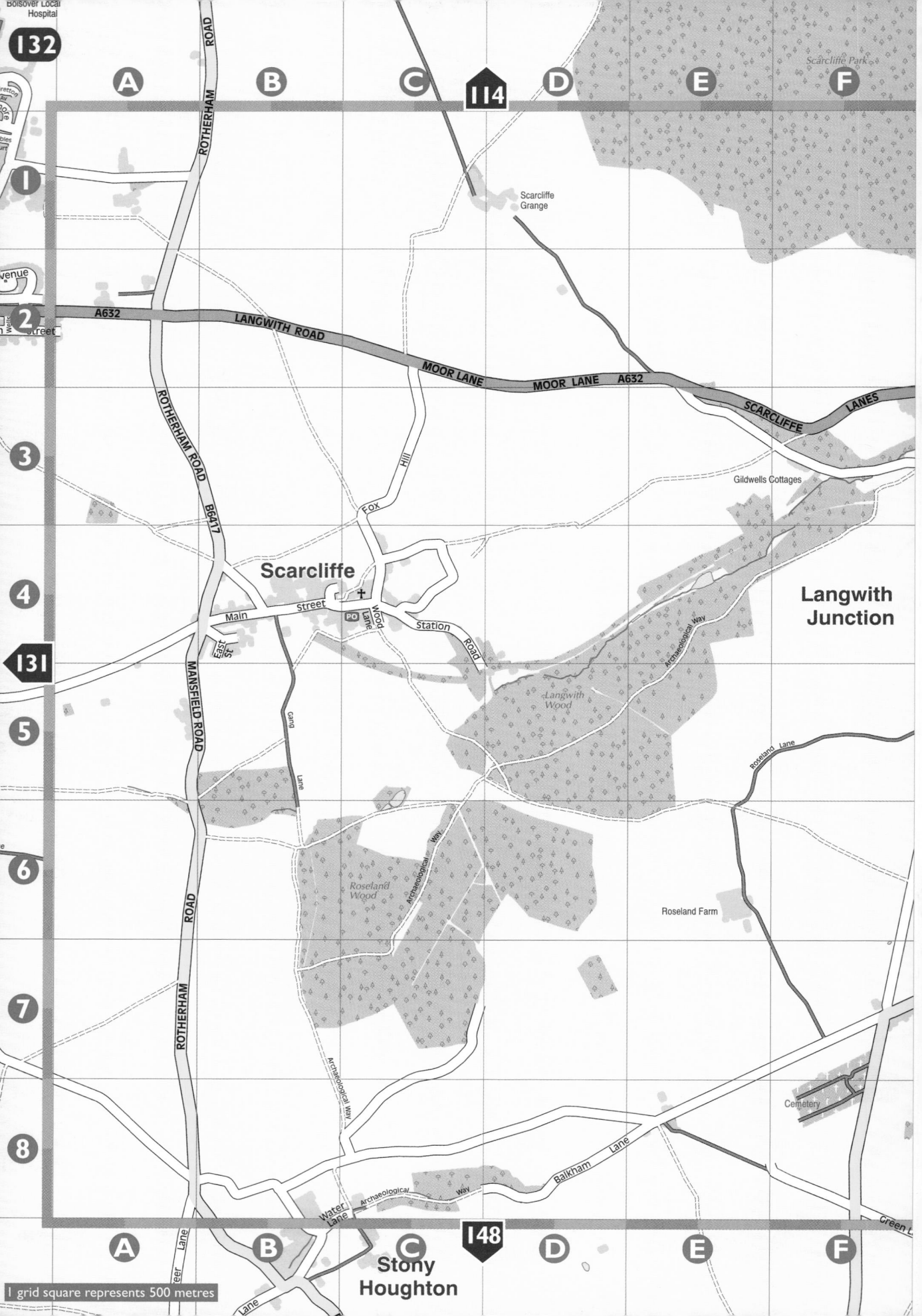

G8 1 Newbarn Cl
H4 1 The Bassett 2 Orange Cl
H5 1 Almond Av

Whaley Thorns Station
Main Street
Pasture Hill Farm
Langwith Lodge

I

Main Road

Nether Langwith

A632

River Poulter
Dale Cl
Langwith Maltings
Hartington Street
Devonshire Drive
Hardwick St
Compton St
Cavendish St

Langwith

Boom Hills Wood

2

3

Upper Langwith

Lord Stubbins Wood

Highfield Avenue
Haddon Cl
Vaughan Pl
Albine Road
Station Road
Chatsworth Av
The Crs
Burlington Av

William Wood Lane

4

East View Industrial Estate

Warsop Cottage Farm

William Wood Farm
Spring Lane

Recreation Vw
Brookfield County Junior School
Stubbins Wd La
Eland Road

Shirebrook Community School
Rowan Dr
Valley Rd
Brookfield Crs
The Close
Langwith Road

5

Wars

Park Junior School
Arcadia Avenue
Springfield Av
Thickley Close
St Josephs Catholic School

North St

6

Carter

Chestnut Drive
Kissing Gate Leisure Centre
College
Health Centre
Station Rd
STATION RD B6407
Shirebrook Station
Vernon Ct
Merchant St

B6407

Carter Lane
West
KG EDWARD ST
PORTLAND ROAD
Sookholme Rd
Herewood Close

MAIN STREET B6407
York Rd
Long Lane
Sookholme Road

LONGSTER LANE

7

SHIREBROOK

Sherwood Dr
Swanwick Av
South Av
Vale Drive
Acreage Lane

Shirebrook Business Park

Bath Lane

8

Sookhol

Sookholme Bath

K6 1 New Linden St
Hodhill Farm
J7 1 Nicholson's Rw
Wood La.
J6 1 Bank Cl 2 Sookholme Cl
H7 1 Church Ct 2 Vicarage Cl
H6 1 Hardwick Av 2 Mayflower Ct

Glutton
Bridge

E4
1 Carder Gn
2 Chapel St
3 Market Pl
4 Queen St

Hollinsclough
School

Stannery

Nabend

Moss
Carr

Underhill

Derbyshire County
Staffordshire County

Tunstead

Under
the Hill

BUXTON ROAD

B5053

Fawside
Edge

Lane Head

St Bartholomews
C of E Primary
School

Church Street

Gauledge
Lane

Fawside

PO

High Street

Longnor

Windyridge

dings
th

Heath
House

Leek Road

The
Cottage

Hillend

The Lane

Fawfieldhead

Waterhouse
Farm

River Manifold

School
Clough

Brownspit

Hallhill

The Ferns

Bank
House

The Low

The
Bent

Ridge
Farm

Bridge
End

Ludburn

Boosley
Grange

The
Holmes

1 grid square represents 500 metres

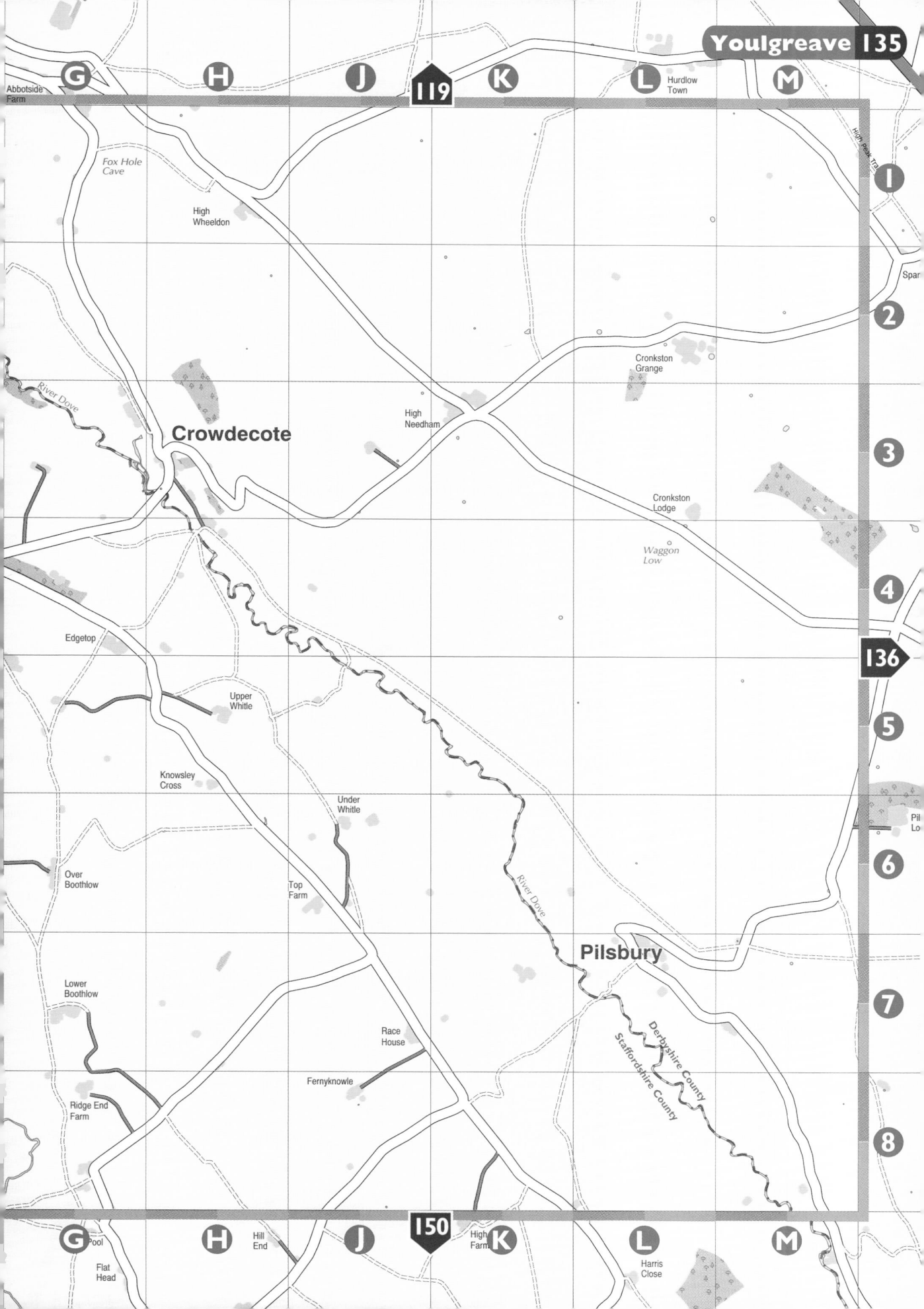

G
H
J
119
K
L
Hurdlow Town
M

Abbotside Farm

High Peak Trail

I

Fox Hole Cave

Spar

High Wheeldon

2

River Dove

Cronkston Grange

Crowdecote

High Needham

3

Cronkston Lodge

Waggon Low

4

Edgetop

136

Upper Whitle

5

Knowsley Cross

Under Whitle

Pil Lo

6

Over Boothlow

Top Farm

River Dove

Pilsbury

Lower Boothlow

7

Race House

Derbyshire County

Staffordshire County

Ridge End Farm

Fernyknowle

8

G
Pool
H
Hill End
J
150
K
High Farm
L
M

Flat Head

Harris Close

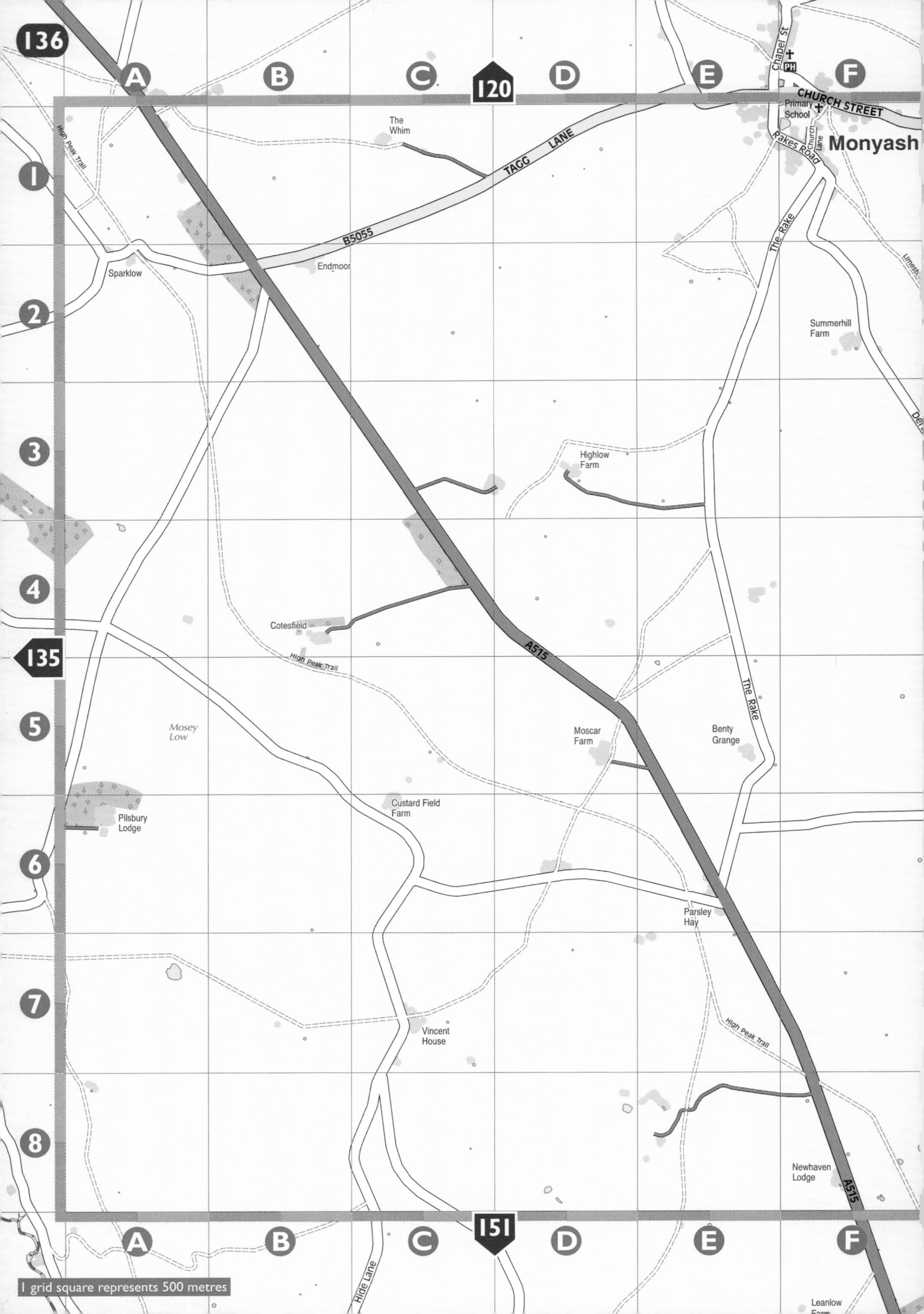

136

A B C **120** D E F

1

High Peak Trail

The Whim

TAGG LANE

Chapel St
PH

CHURCH STREET

Primary
School

Rakes Road

Monyash

B5055

Endmoor

Sparklow

The Rake

2

Summerhill
Farm

Limeston

Del

3

Highlow
Farm

4

Cotesfield

135

High Peak Trail

A515

5

Mosey
Low

Moscar
Farm

The Rake

Benty
Grange

6

Custard Field
Farm

Pilsbury
Lodge

Parsley
Hay

7

Vincent
House

High Peak Trail

8

Newhaven
Lodge

A515

A B Hide Lane C **151** D E F

Leanlow
Farm

1 grid square represents 500 metres

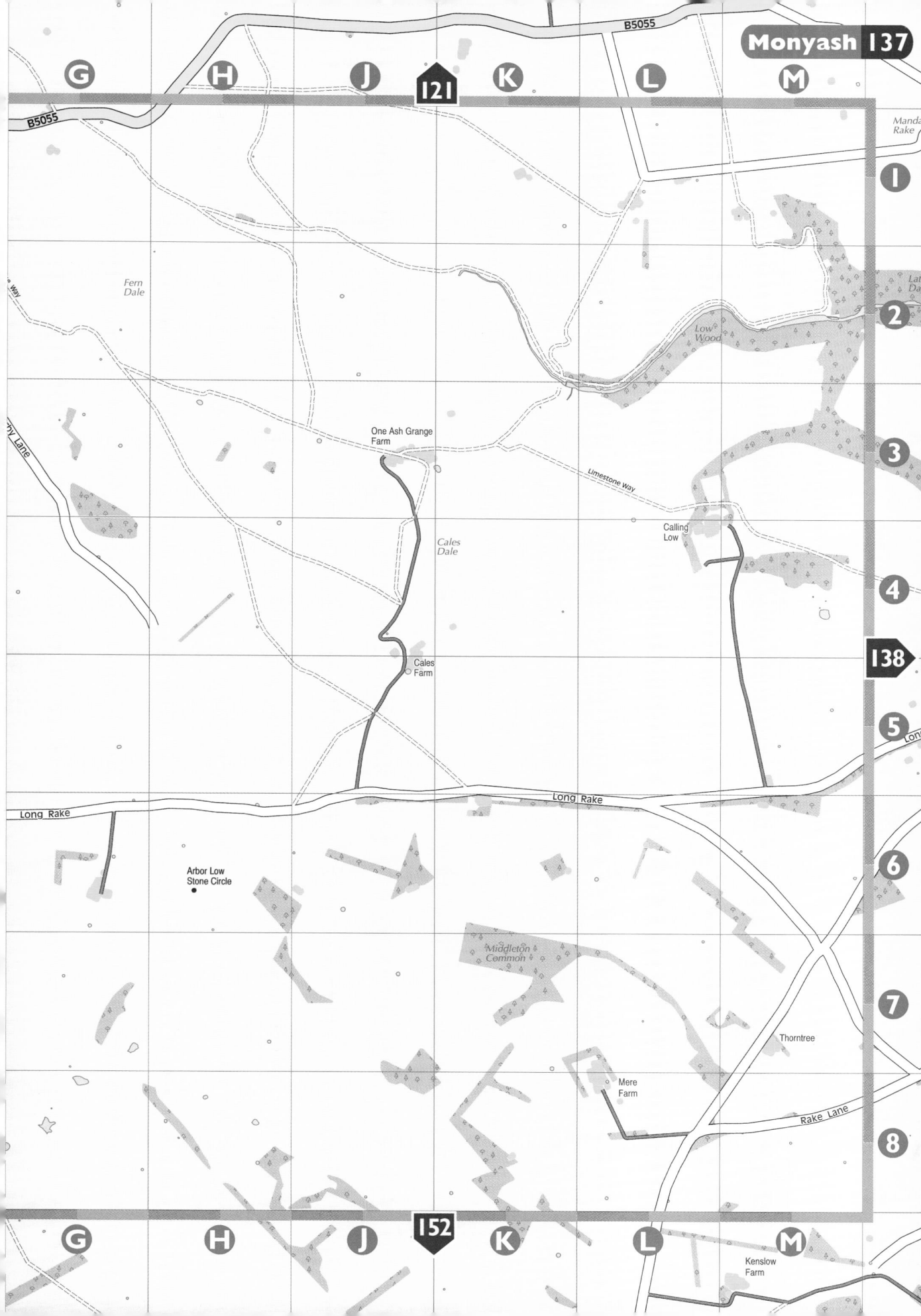

G   H   J   **121**   K   L   M

B5055

B5055

I

Manda
Rake

Fern
Dale

Lath
Da

2

Low
Wood

...Way

3

One Ash Grange
Farm

Limestone Way

Cales
Dale

Calling
Low

4

Cales
Farm

138

5   Lon

Long Rake

Long Rake

6

Arbor Low
Stone Circle

Middleton
Common

7

Thorntree

Mere
Farm

Rake Lane

8

G   H   J   **152**   K   L   M

Kenslow
Farm

A   B   C   D   E   F

Over
Haddon

Monyash   Road

New
Close Farm

F5
1 Brookleton

Wellgate La

Mandale
Rake

1

Lathkill
Dale

River Lathkill

Meadow
Place Grange

2

Conksbury

3

Raper Lodge

Back   Lane

River Lathkill

4

Back   Lane

Conksbury   Lane

Coalpit   Lane

Doctors
Surg

Alport La

Conksbury Av

Moor   Lane

Moor   Lane

Youlgreave All Saints
C of E Primary School

Bi

Moor   Lane

The
Orchard

New   Road

5

Long Rake

Limestone   Way

Grove
Place

West Croft
Close

PO

Chapel
Close

Church   La

Holywell La

Barnes
La

Bankside

Brassington
Close

Youlgreave

Lomberdale
Hall

River Bradford

Limestone   Way

Mawstone
Lane

6

Limestone   Way

Hopping   Lane

Mawstone Farm

Village Hall
School

7

Middleton

Mawstone Lane

Hopping Farm

Mawstone Lane

Rake Lane

The
Pinfold

stree

Whitfield   Lane

Weadow   Lane

8

Rake Lane

A   B   C   D   E   F

Lowfield Farm

1 grid square represents 500 metres

M5
1 The Lane

G   H   J   123   K   L   M

I

2

River Wye

Haddon
Hall (NT)

Bowling
Green Farm

Haddon
Fields

B5056

Stantonhall Lane

Cong

3

Dark Lane

Alport Lane

Bowers
Hall

Pilhough Lane

4

Alport

140

Bradford

Stanton in Peak
C of E Primary School

Cemetery

Millfield
Farm

B5056

School La

Middle
Street

Stanton
in Peak

The Green

Lees Road

5

Greenfields
Farms

Hollow Farm

6

Birchover Road

Cow Close
Farm

7

Eagle
Tor

Birchover Road

8

Harthill
Moor Farm

The

Mires

B5056

Barn Farm

G   H   J   154   K   L   M

Robin
Hood's

B5056

PH

Main   Street

Barton Hill

E7
1 Arkwright Cl
2 Bowler Rd
3 Old Hall Cl

E7
1 Crowstones Rd
2 Laburnum Cl
3 Rowan Cl
4 Stanton Cl

C2
1 Old Station Cl

C1
1 Riverbank
2 Schofield Ct

A   B   C   D   E   F

Fallinge

I

Park Lane

Church

Vicarage
Lane

St Katherines
Close

Lane

Rowsley

Sunnybank

Hinckley
Ct

CHATSWORTH ROAD

B6012

Chesterfield
Road

Rowsley
Wood

Derek Topp
Gallery

Hotel

A6(T)

2

River Wye

Wye Farm

Primary
School

School Lane

Old station
close

Woodhouse Rd

Lane

Peaktor

Woodhouse Road

River Derwent

Copywood

3

Congreave

Lane

Cote

Tinkersley

Hilloc

4

139

Pilhough

Lane

Pilhough Road

Woodhouse
Road

DALE ROAD NORTH

A6(T)

Harrison
Way

Carlton
Av

Thorncliffe Av

Northwood
Lane

The
Av

Lumb Lane

Northwood

5

Green
s Road

Lees Road

Dungreave
Avenue

Peak Railway

Whitworth
Road

Stancliffe
Hall
School

6

Birchover

Hillcarr
Wood

Sir Joseph's
La

Bent Lane

Long Hill

Gill La

Moor La

Hallmoor Road

Strathallan
Av

Derwent
Av

northwood
Cl

Darley
Av

Peveril
School

7

Stanton
Moor
Plantation

Nine
Ladies

Stanton
Lees

Lees Road

Molyneaux
Business Park

Green La

PO

Hawksley Av

St Helen sOker

Oker Av

South Pk Av

St Joseph's

Butts Rd

Willow Wy

Yew Tr Cl

Broad Av

Whitworth Av

Stancliffe Av

Newell
Wy

John Turner
Road

Darley
Broad
Av

Nether
Wy

Tree Park

Glasgow Park

DALE ROAD NORTH

8

Lees Road

Hill
Wood

Churchtown

Darley Churchtown
C of E Primary School

River Derwent

Church Road

Darley Dale

Peak Railway

LC

STATION RD

MAIN ROAD

Old

am Farm

A   B   C   D   E   F

1 grid square represents 500 metres

G H J **125** K L M

I

2

B5057

3

The
Woodlands

Bent Lane

Bumper
Castle

Back Lane

Flash Lane

4

Nursery Farm

I42

Jagger's Lane

Flash
Dam

Burley
Fields Farm

Woodside Farm

SYDNOPE HILL B5057

5

Sydnope
Hall

Farley Lane

Hall
Dale

Butcher's La

6

Lane

Sydnope
Stand

Darley Hillside

Halldale Lane

7

Hallmoor Road

**Two
Dales**

B5057

Denacre Lane

Knab Rd

Tax Farm

Wheatley
Rd

Porteous

The Park

Painter's
Wy

Lady Grove
Road

Columber
Wy

Warney Rd

CHESTERFIELD RD

Medical Cen

Doctors Surg

PO

A6(T)

Oddford Lane

Darley Dale
Primary School

8

Matlock M

Greenaway Lane

Holt Road

G DALE ROAD **H** **156** **J** **K** **L** **M**

Road

Red House Stables
Working Carriage
Museum

Hotel

St Elphins
School

Blind Lane

Farley

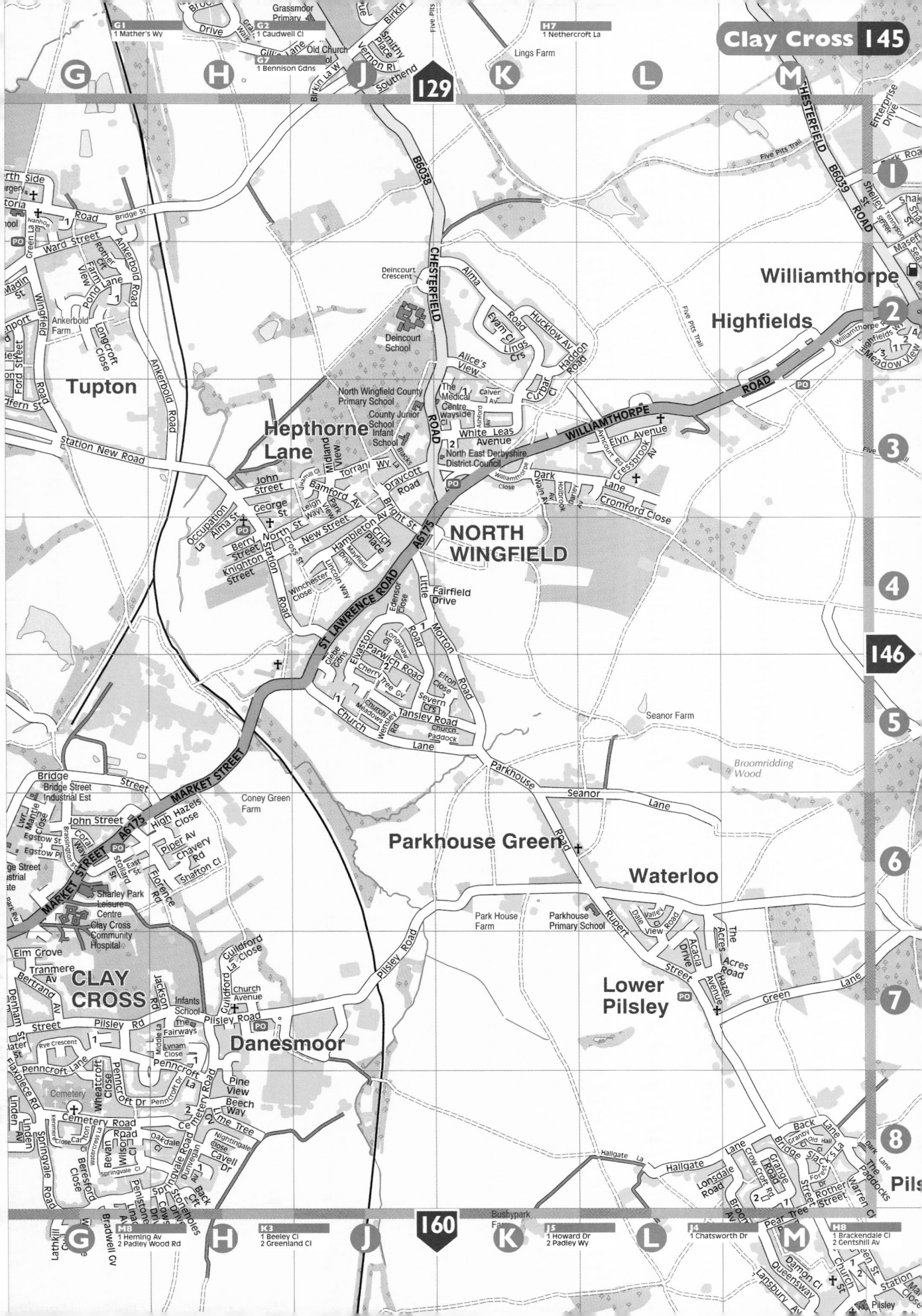

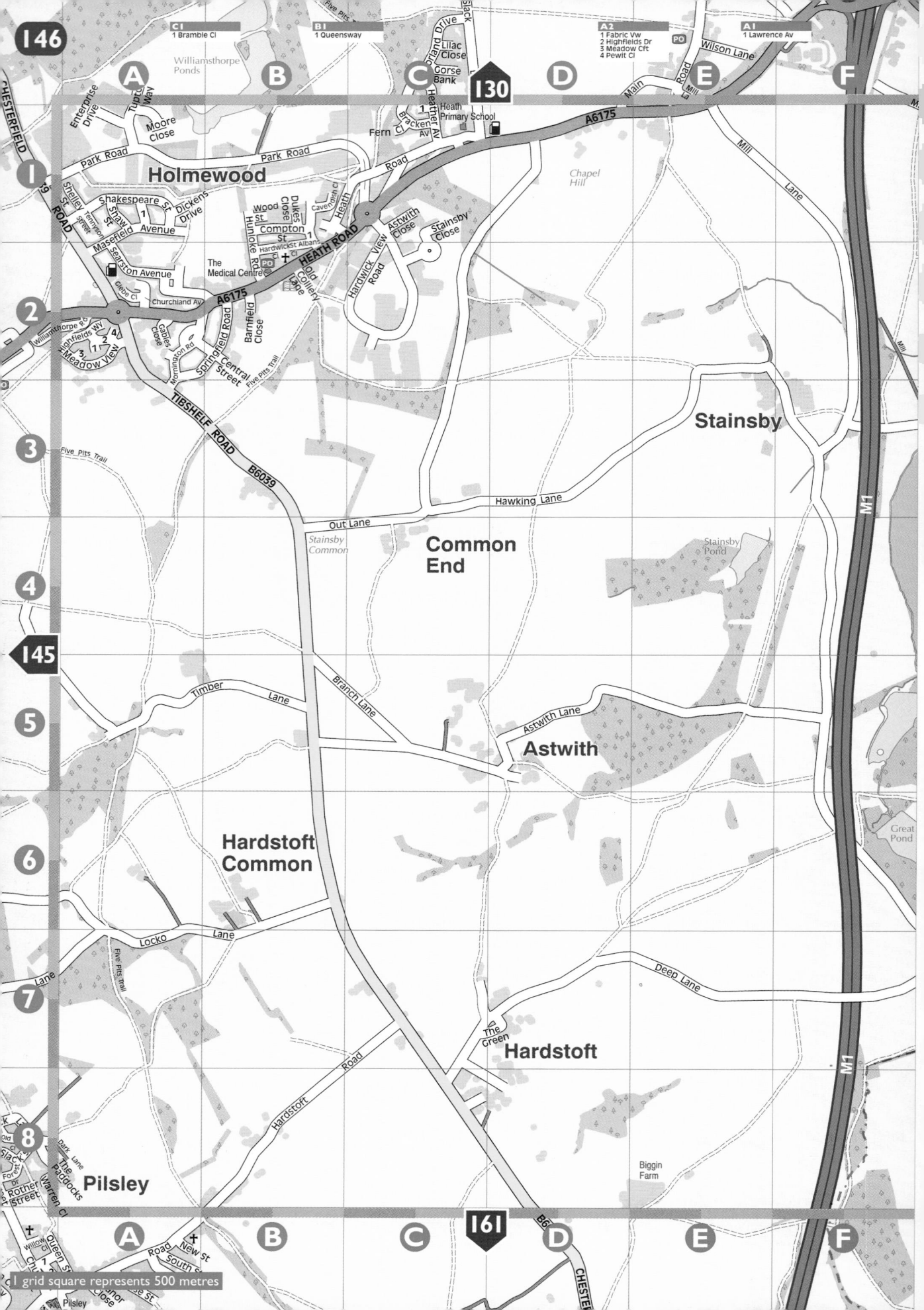

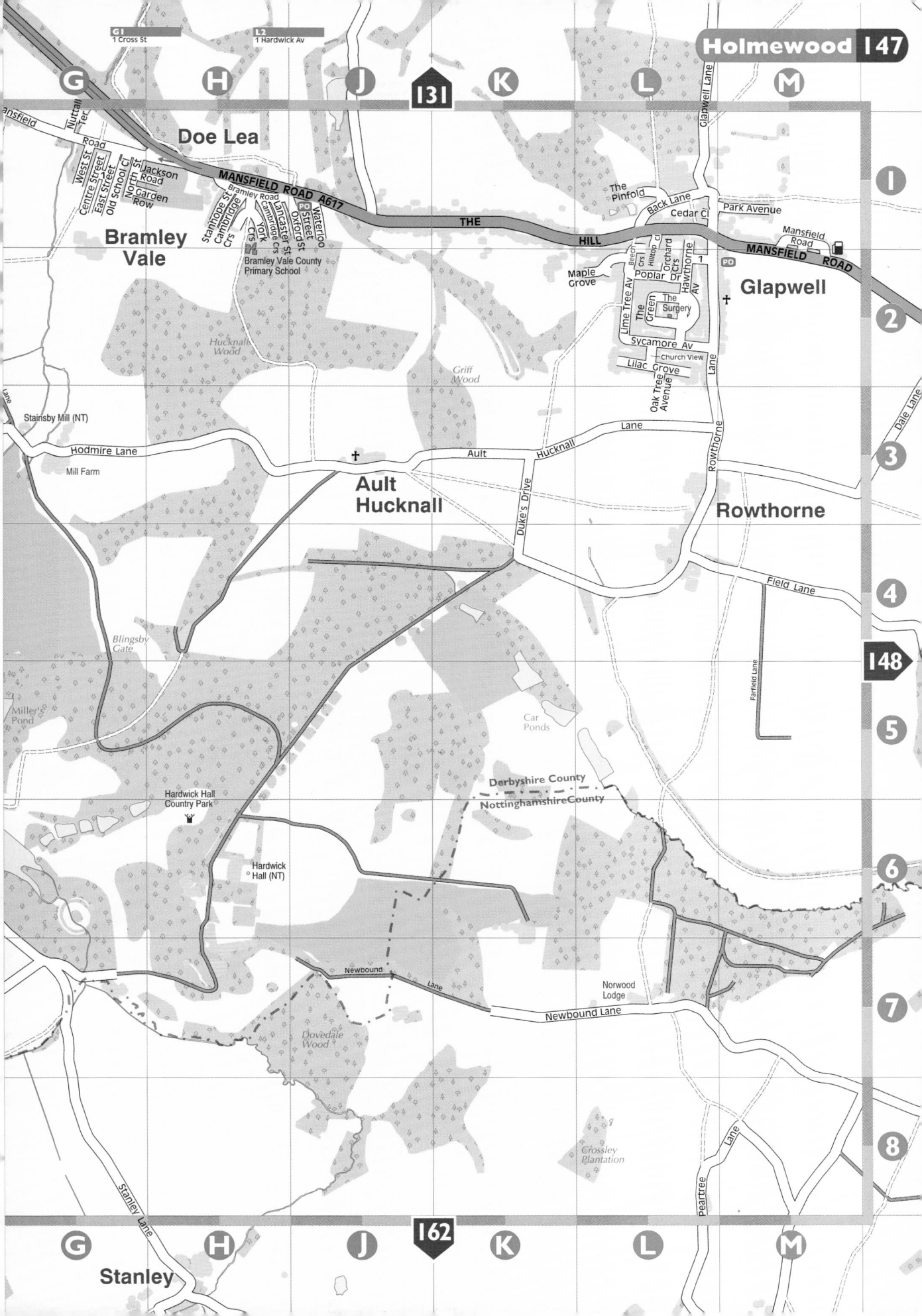

G1
1 Cross St

L2
1 Hardwick Av

G   H   J   `131`   K   L   M

Mansfield

Nuttall Ter

Doe Lea

Road

West St
Centre Street
East Street
Old School Cl
North St
Garden Row

Jackson Road

MANSFIELD ROAD A617

Stanhope St
Cambridge Crs
York Crs
Lancaster St
Cambridge Crs
Oxford St
Waterloo Street
Bramley Road

**Bramley
Vale**

Bramley Vale County
Primary School

The Pinfold

Back Lane

Cedar Cl

Park Avenue

THE   HILL

Beech Crs
Hilltop Cl
Orchard Crs
Hawthorne Av
1

MANSFIELD ROAD

Mansfield
Road

PO

Maple
Grove

Lime Tree Av
Poplar Dr
The Green
The Surgery

Glapwell

Sycamore Av

Church View

Lilac Grove

Oak Tree Avenue

Rowthorne Lane

I

2

Stainsby Mill (NT)

Hodmire Lane

Mill Farm

Griff
Wood

Hucknall
Wood

Lane

Ault

Hucknall

Duke's Drive

**Ault
Hucknall**

Rowthorne

Dale Lane

Field Lane

Farfield Lane

3

4

`148`

Blingsby
Gate

Miller's
Pond

Car
Ponds

5

Hardwick Hall
Country Park

Hardwick
Hall (NT)

Derbyshire County
NottinghamshireCounty

6

Newbound

Lane

Newbound Lane

Norwood
Lodge

Peartree Lane

7

Dovedale
Wood

Crossley
Plantation

8

Stanley Lane

Stanley

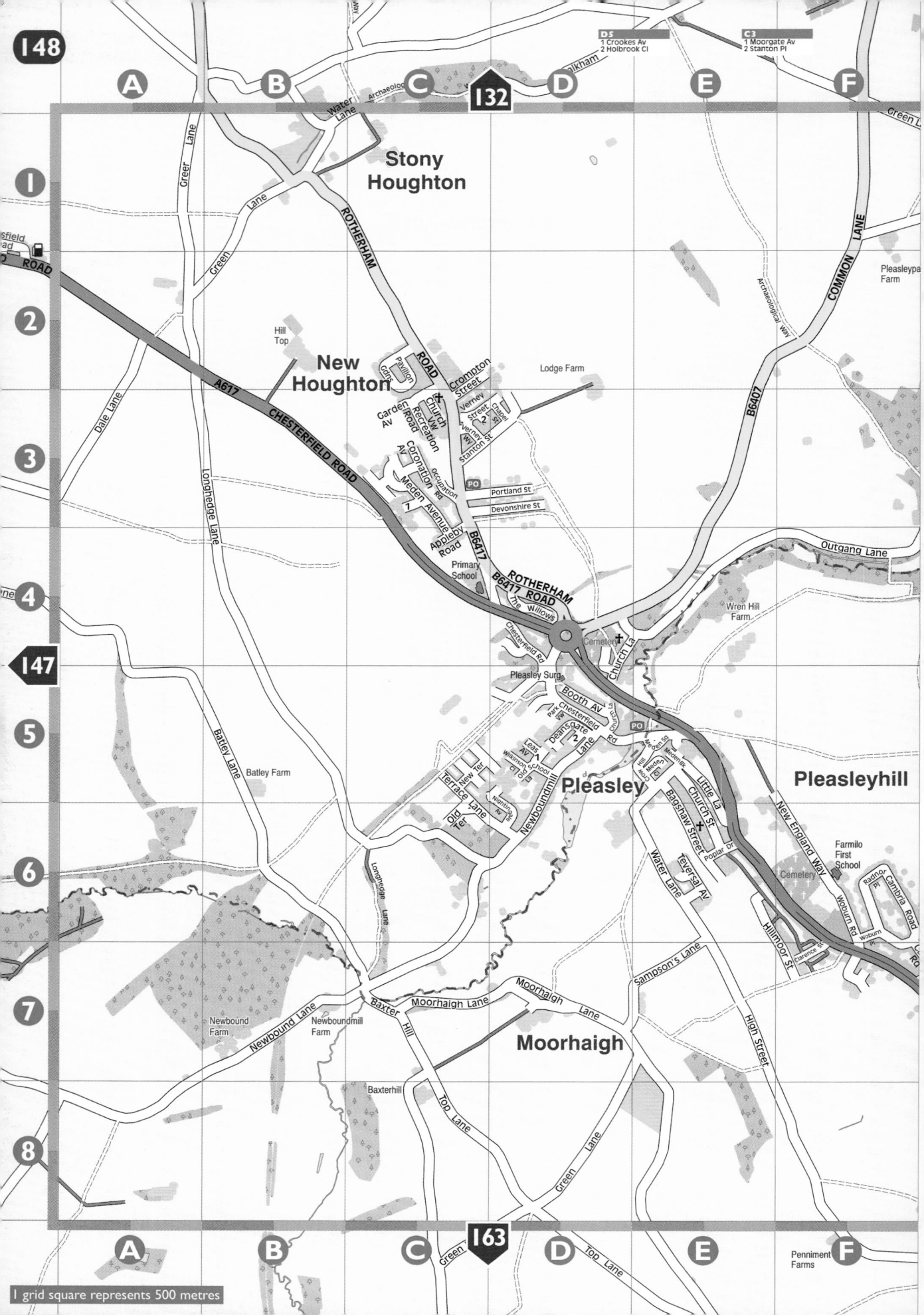

133

164

Radmanthwaite

Mansfield Woodhouse

NG19

G8
1 Boothbright Crs
2 Wilberforce Rd

H8
1 Ballater Cl
2 Banchory Cl
3 Clumber Ct

K6
1 Laburnum Gv

L4
1 Sandringham Ct

L5
1 Alexandra Av

M8
1 Gladstone St
2 Woodhouse Ct

M6
1 Portland Ct Ms

M4
1 Cranbrook Ct
2 Exford Ct
3 Purbeck Cl

M5
1 Park Hall Gdns
2 Pine Cl

L7
1 Orchard Vw
2 Spring Hl
3 West Hill Pk

L6
1 Mallatratt Pl
2 Oak Tree Crs

G H J K L M

135

Ludburn

Ridge End
Farm

Pool

Flat
Head

Hill
End

High Sheen
Farm

Harris
Close

Sprink

Marsh
H...

Slate House
Farm

Moorhouse

Sheen

PO

Brund

Hulme
House

gginstall

Fold
Farm

Pown Street

Bridge-end

Townend

River Dove

Lowend

Banktop

Hayesgate

The
Raikes

MILL LANE

Hole
End

B5054

B5054

Hulme
End

B5054

Lower Hurst
Farm

Cowlow Lane

Manifold Way

West
Side

Upper
Hurst

Harecops

Beresford Lane

Dale

Ecton

Ecton
Hill

Archford
Moor

Newhaven Lodge

G H J **136** K L M

I

Hide Lane

Leanlow Farm

2

Long Dale

Hartington-moor Farm

Tissington Trail

B5054

3

Bank Top Farm

Hand Dale

Moat Hall

Hide Lane

Tissington Trail

4

Bank Side

Hartington

Dig Street

152

Harrots Lane

Church St

Stonewell Lane

Hardings Lane

Hartington C of E School

B5054

5

PO

Heathcote

Parsons Cl

Hall Bank

High Cross

Reynards Lane

MILL LANE

Highfield Lane

Crossland Sides

6

Highfield Lane

Dale End

Cotterill Farm

Liffs Road

Percival Close

Biggin

Brighton

7

gin of E Schoo

Derbyshire County

Staffordshire County

Drury Lane

Greenhead Crescent

Biggin Grange

Beresford Dale

Woollaton Lane

8

Dalehead

Wo Gre head

G H J **166** K L M

ffs Road

Back Lar

Wolfscote

Biggin

A   B   C   137   D   E   F

1

2

A054

3

4

151

5

6

7

8

A   B   C   167   D   E   F

Rake Lane

Kenslow Farm

The Oldhams

High Peak Trail

Brundcliffe

Newhaven Cottage

Friden

High Peak Trail

Smerrill Moor

Old House

A5012

Newhaven Farm

A515

Newhaven

Stanedge Grange

A515

Tissington Trail

Ivy House

High Peak Trail

Upperhouse Farm

Percival Close

Biggin C of E School

Drury Lane

Greenhead Crescent

ton Lane

Greenhead

Woollaton Lane

Tissington Trail

Cardlemere Lane

Bank House

Back Lane

1 grid square represents 500 metres

G   H   J   **138**   K   L   M

Whitfield

addow Lane

Lowfield Farm

Smerrill Grange

Rock Farm

Mount Pleasant Farm

Dale End

Gratton Lane

Oddo House Farm

Long Dale

Gratton Dale

Gratton Moor

Gratton Moor Farm

154

Elton Common

Mouldridge La

Mouldridge Grange

Pikehall

A5012

A5012

Parwich Lane

Mouldridge Lane

Astonhill

New Barn

G   H   J   **168**   K   L   M

Gotham

High Peak Trail

1 2 3 4 5 6 7 8

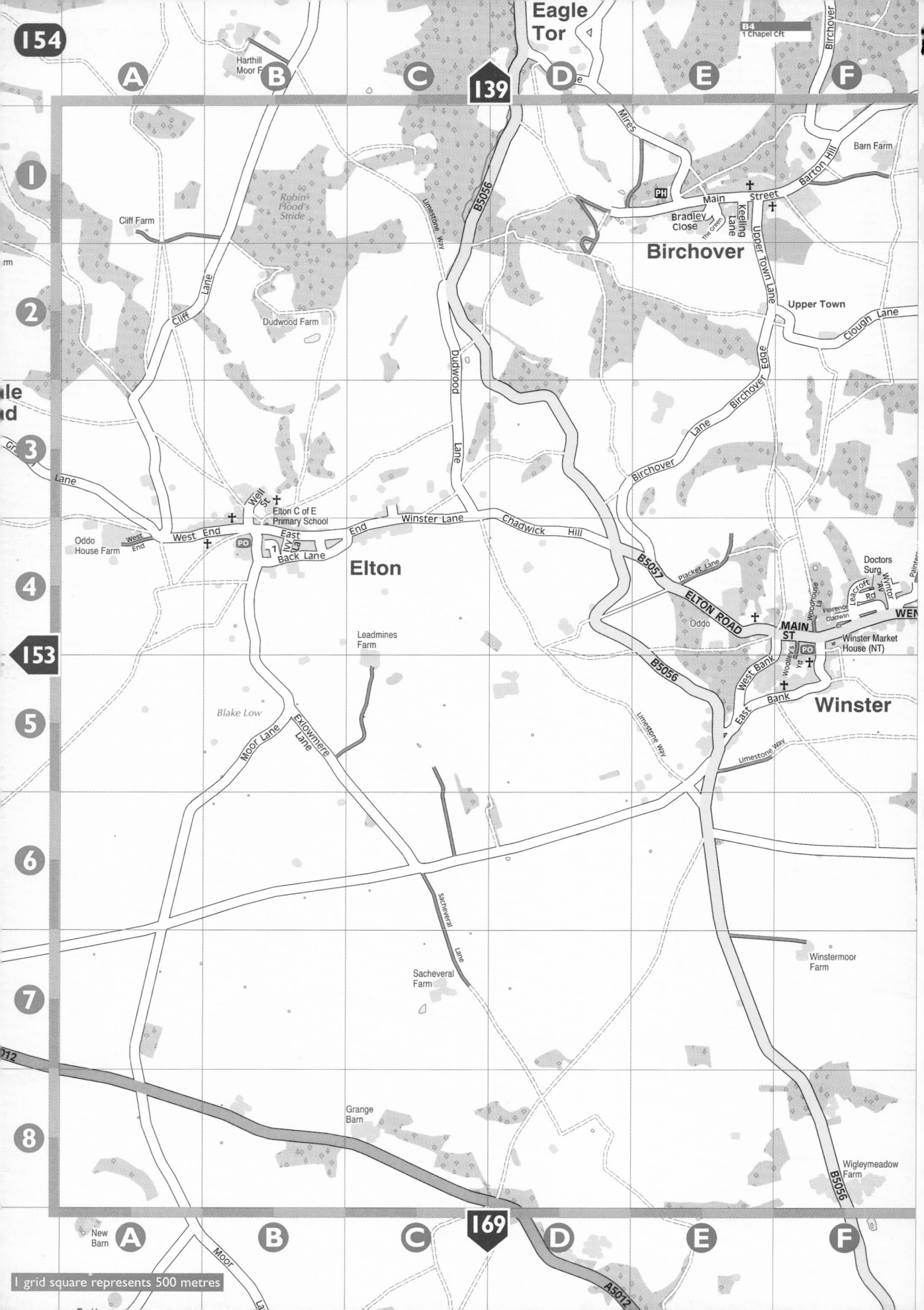

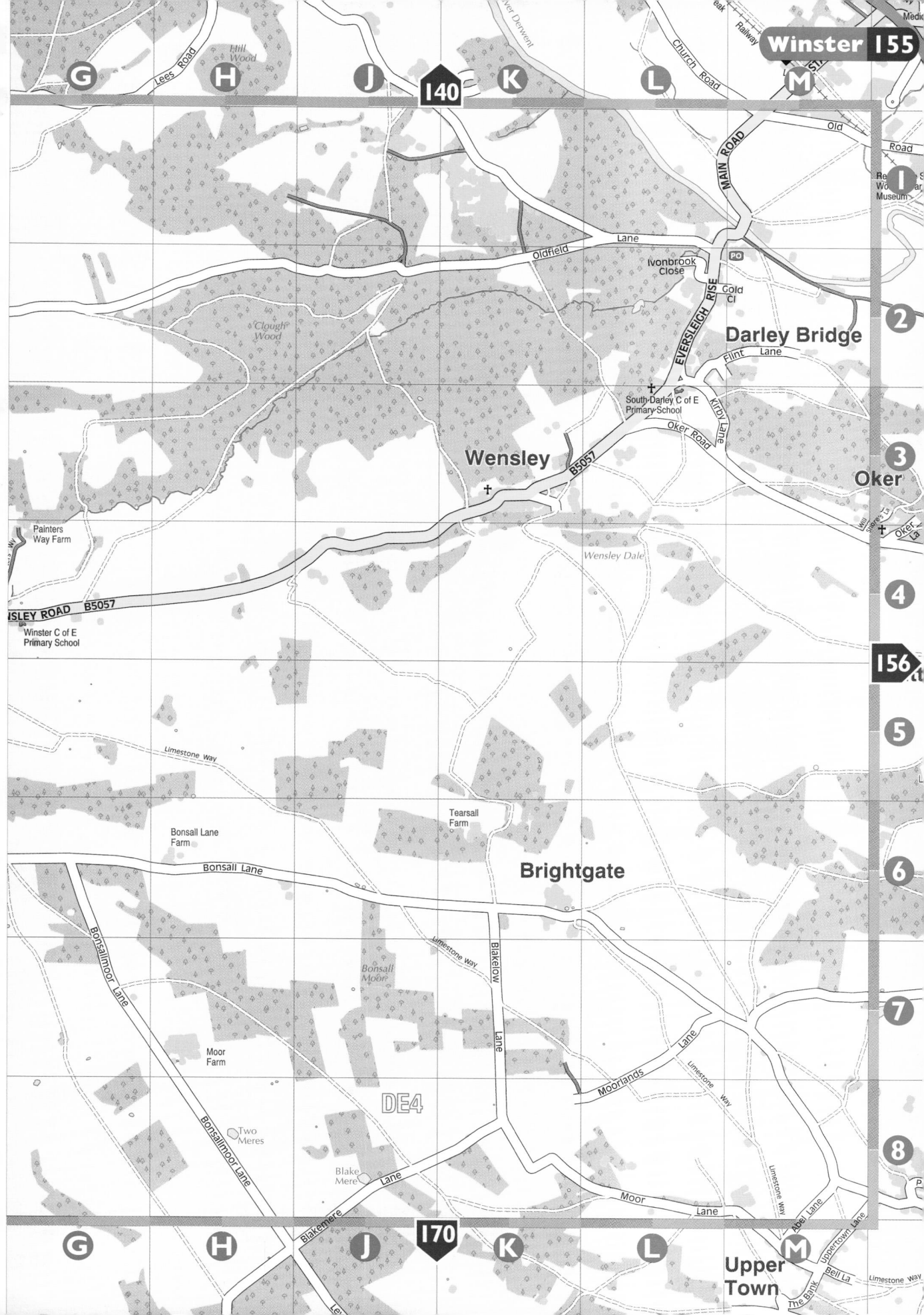

140

G H J K L M

Lees Road

Hill Wood

River Derwent

Church Road

MAIN ROAD

Old Road

Medi...

R... W... Museum

1

Lane

Oldfield

Ivonbrook Close

PO

EVERSLEIGH RISE

Gold Cl

2

Darley Bridge

Flint Lane

Clough Wood

South Darley C of E Primary School

Kirby Lane

Oker Road

3

Oker

Wensley

B5057

Wensley Dale

Wm Shore's La

Oker...

Painters Way Farm

...NSLEY ROAD B5057

4

Winster C of E Primary School

156

...t

5

Limestone Way

Tearsall Farm

Bonsall Lane Farm

Brightgate

6

Bonsall Lane

Bonsallmoor Lane

Limestone Way

Blakelow Lane

Bonsall Moor

7

Moor Farm

Moorlands

Limestone Way

DE4

Two Meres

8

Blake Mere

Lane

Moor Lane

Limestone Way

Abel Lane

Bell La

The Bank

Uppertown Lane

Blakemere Lane

Le...

170

G H J K L M

Upper Town

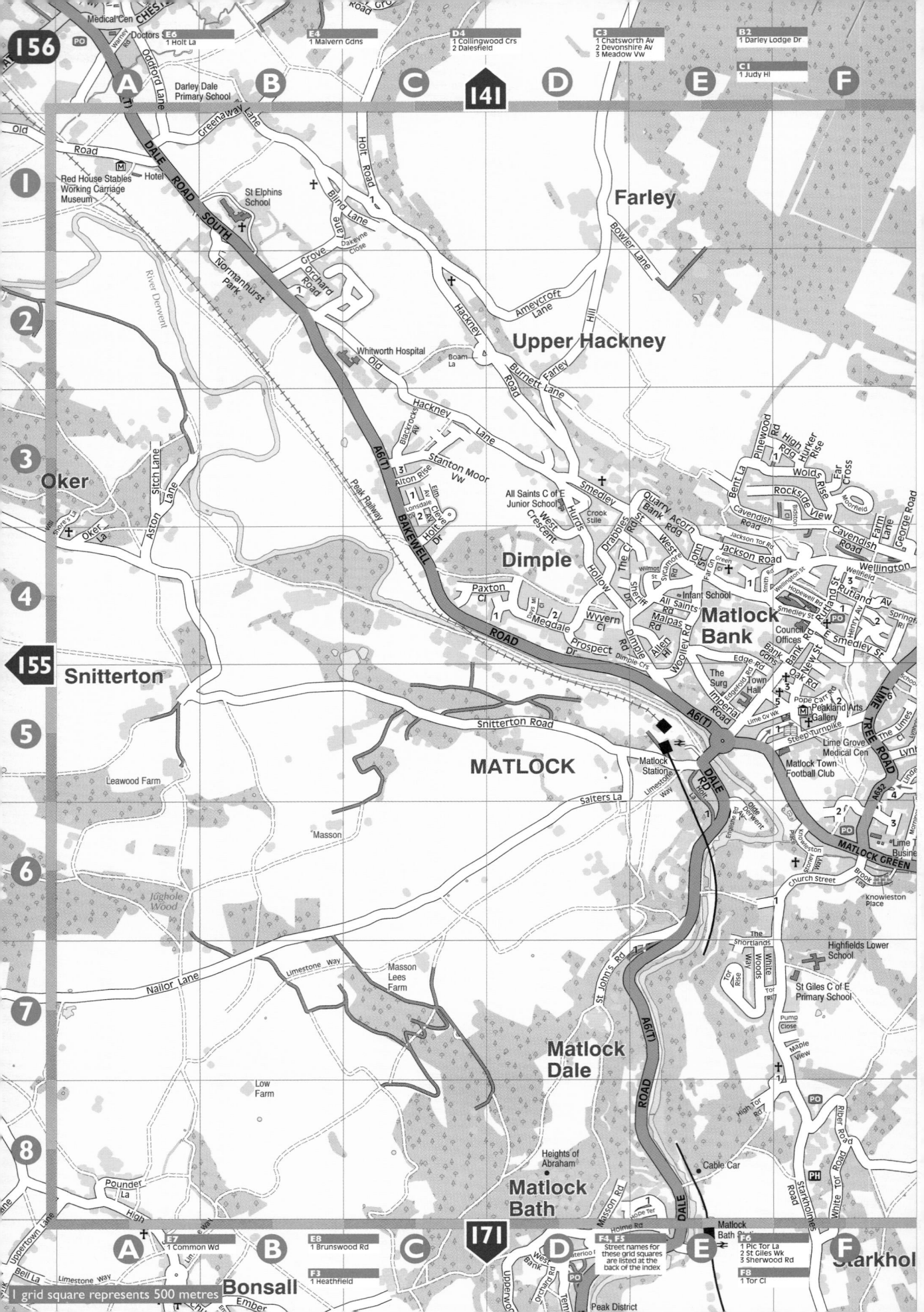

G H J 142 K L M

I
2
3
4
158
5
6
7
8

Holestone Gate Road
Holeston

Cuckoostone
House

Cuckoo
Stone

Cuckoostone Lane

CHESTERFIELD ROAD

A632

Matlock
Golf Club

Quarry Lane

Bentley Bridge

Sandy Lane

Bentley Close

Gritstone Rd

Highfields
School

Lumsdale

CHESTERFIELD ROAD

A632

Street

Luns Hi
Rise

Highfield Dr

Mooredge
Dr

Asker
Lane

Bull
Lane

Hawleys Cl

St Joseph
Roman Catholic
Primary School

Matlock
County Infant
School

Hilltops
View

Matlock
Junior School

Hazel
Gv

Lumsdale
Crescent

Hurst
Rise

Mettesford

Overdale

Fairholmes
Rise

holmes Road

Hurst

Lumsdale

Lumsdale

Lumsdale

Smuse Lane

Lumsdale

Portland
Grange
Farm

Foxholes

Knabhall Lane

Lane

Lant Lane

Lant
Lodge Farm

Lant Lane

South Carolina
Farm

Tansley
Moor

Allen Lane

Knabhall Lane

Oaksedge
Lane

Tansley
Knoll

Whitelea Lane

The
Knoll

The
Rocks

PO

River Vw

Cl

Church St

Green Lane

Mais
Close

Mooredge

Brookfield Industrial
Estate

Brookfield Way

Old
Coach
Road

Tawney Croft

Tansley County
Primary School

Goldhill

Tansley

Park Close

ALFRETON

ROAD

A615

Matlock Cliff

Oak Tree Gdns

Holly
La

Ashley Cl

Alders Lane

Thatcher's Lane

Startin

Thatcher's
La

NOTTINGHAM

ROAD

B6014

RED
HILL

Red Hill Lane

Cunnery

Cunnery Lane

Riber

Riber Castle
Wildlife Park

Hotel

Carr Lane

Hearthstone

Hearthstone

Green Lane

mes

G H J 172 K L M

Littlemoor

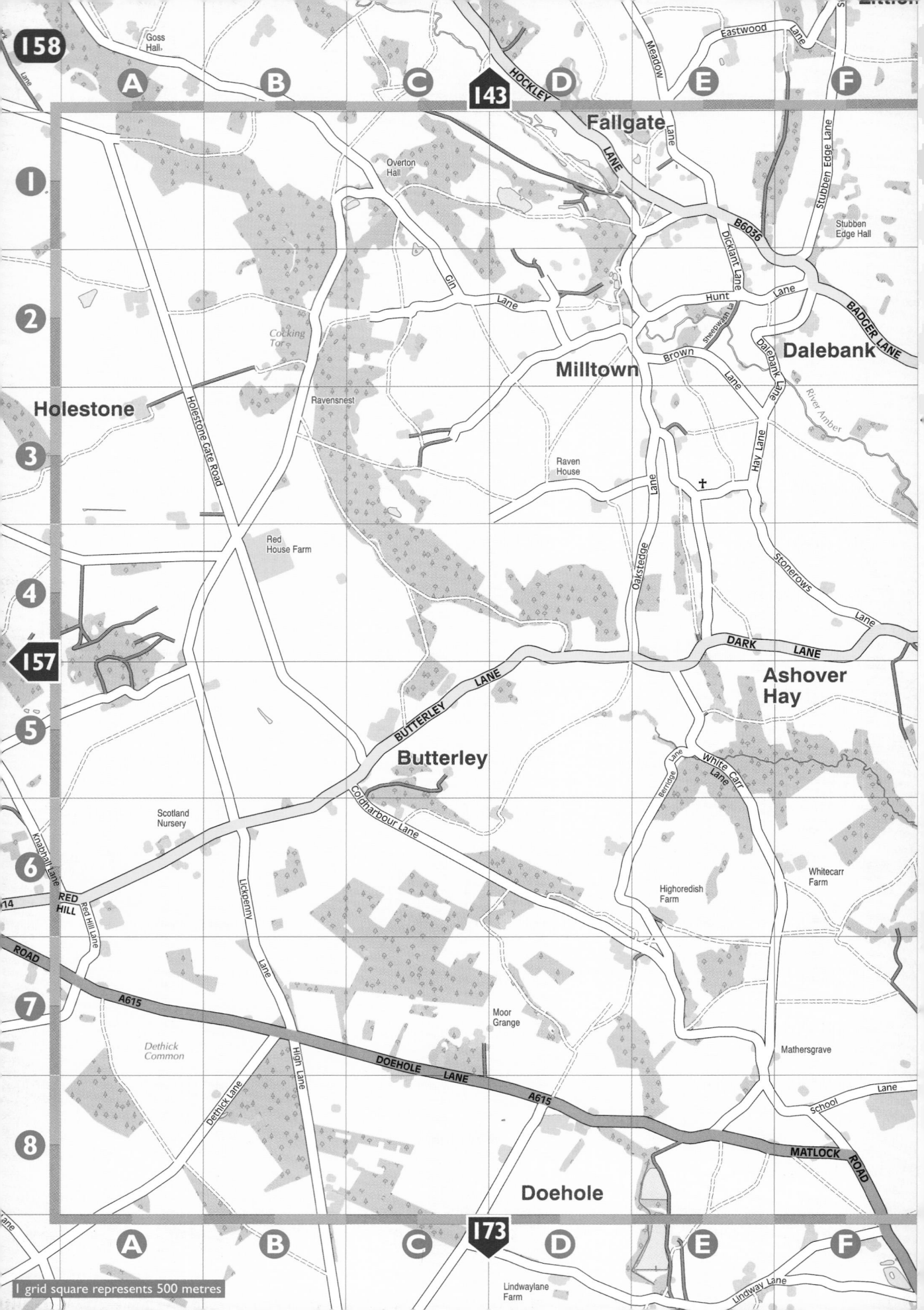

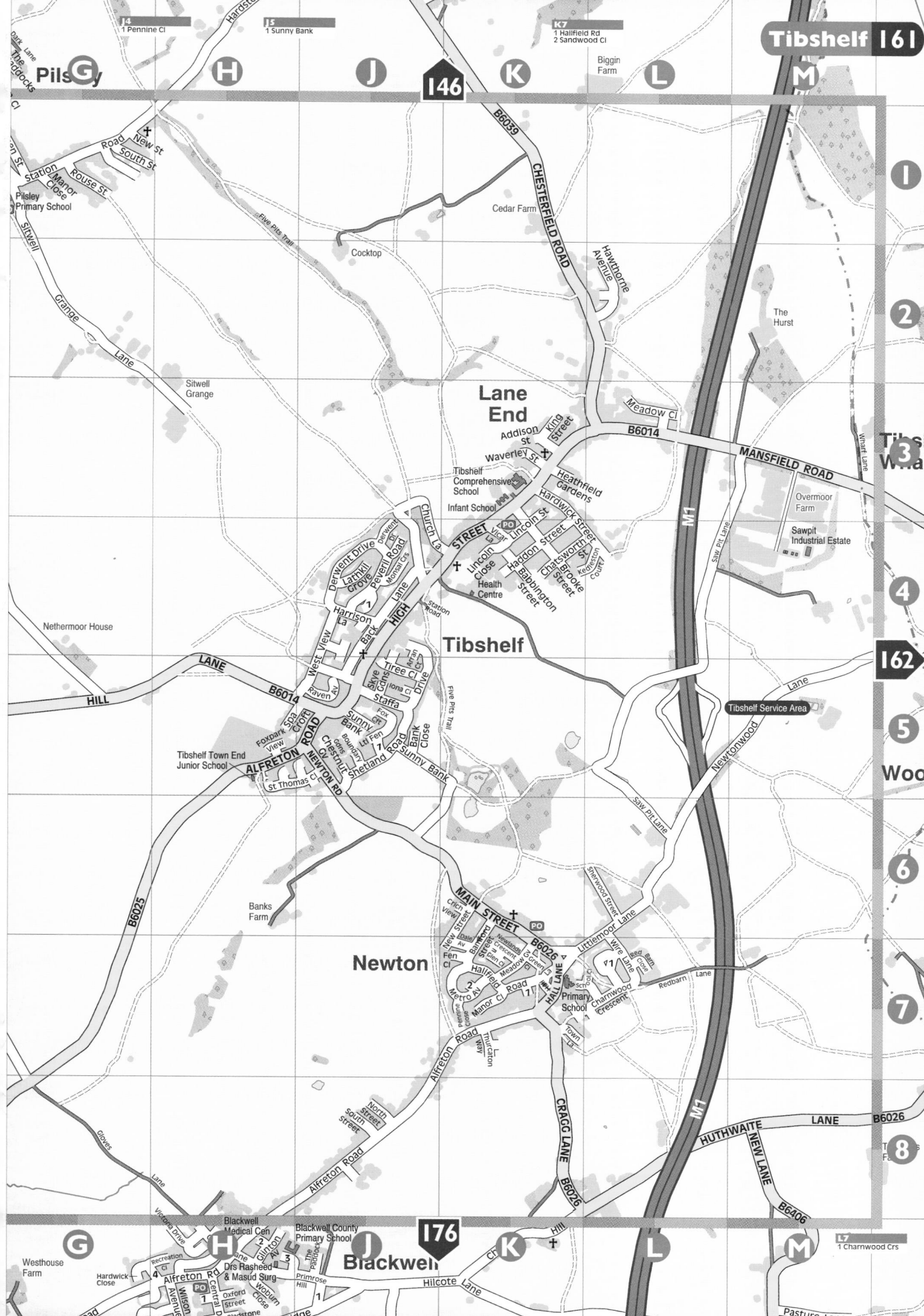

G G7
1 Carrfield Cl
2 Westbourne Cl

G8
1 Doreen Dr
2 Percy St

H6
1 Hathersage Wy

H7
1 Davies Av

H8
1 Church Ms
2 Duke St
3 Firemen's Rw
4 High St
5 Lammas Cl
6 Victoria St

Bull Farm
First School

148

164

NG17

G H J K L M

G7
1 Fairfield Rd
2 The Hillocks
3 Sheepwash La

H J
K6
1 Clipstone Av

1 Welford Cl

K4
1 Moorland Cl

K5
1 Dale Cl
2 Whilton St

L
1 Low St
2 Parliament St

J6
1 Alexandra Av
2 New Cross St

Street names for
this grid square are
listed at the back of
the index

Forest Town

The Brunts School

Heatherley Primary School

Forest Town Primary Sch

Primary Sch

KINGSWAY

Ravensdale School

RAVENSDALE ROAD

Sherwood Hall Upper School

SHERWOOD HALL ROAD B6030

The Surgery

CLIPSTONE RD

Crown Farm Way

Long Stoop Way

Eakring Road

Windmill Ridge Middle School

Carter Lane First School

First School

ROCK HILL A617

SOUTHWELL ROAD WEST

CARTER LANE

Eakring Road

The Links

First School

Oak Tree Lane Leisure Centre

Oak Tree Lane Health Centre

WINDSOR ROAD

SOUTHWELL ROAD WEST A617

Wynndale Drive JMI School

Berry Hill First School

Woodland Drive

Berry Hill Middle School

Athletics Club

North Park

The Avenue

Anglia Way Industrial Estate

St Peters C of E First School

Thorpe Road

Wilford Road

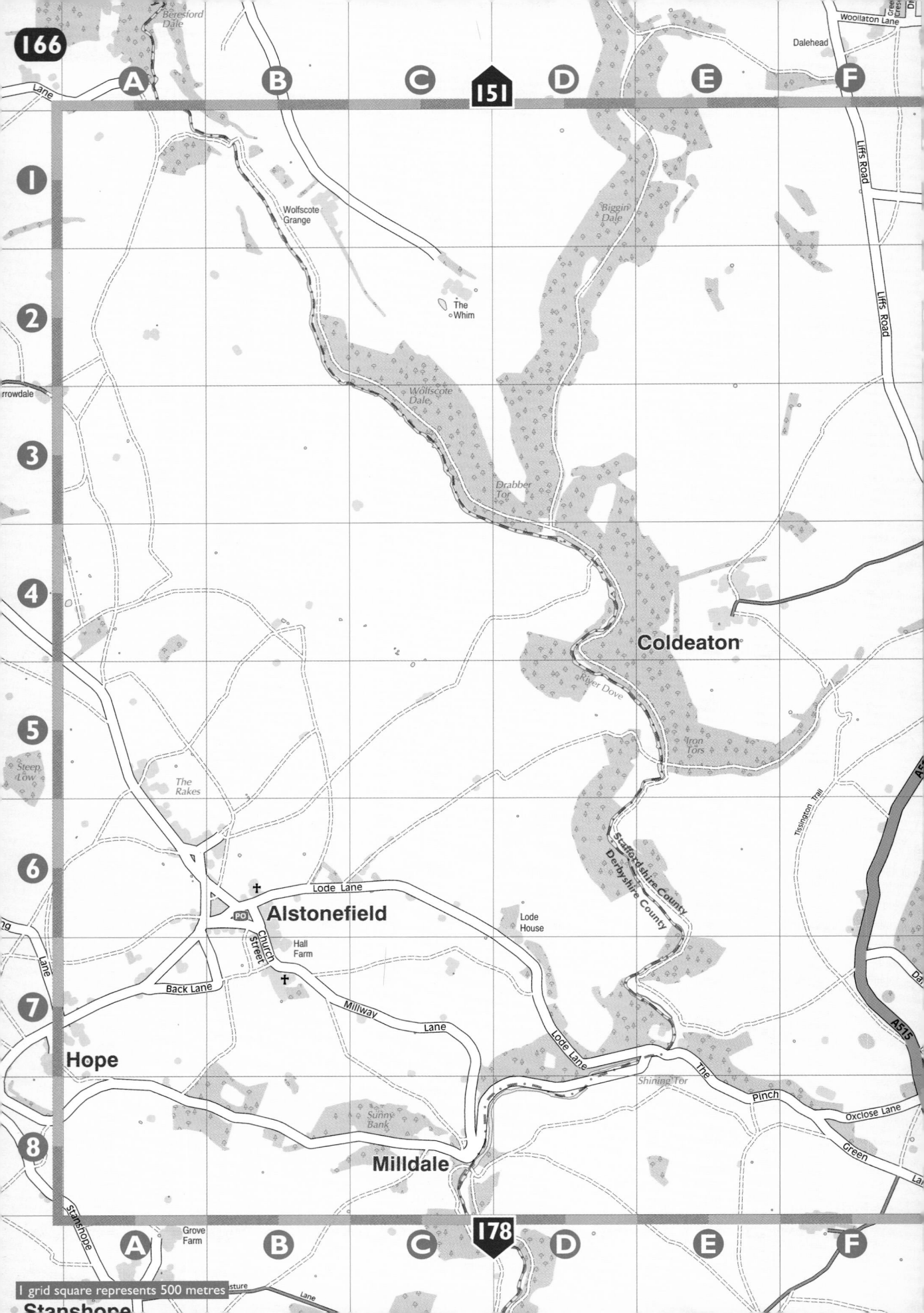

A B C **151** D E F

1

2

3

4

5

6

7

8

Beresford Dale

Woollaton Lane

Dalehead

Lane

Liffs Road

Liffs Road

Wolfscote Grange

'Biggin' Dale

The Whim

Wolfscote Dale

rrowdale

Drabber Tor

Coldeaton

River Dove

Steep Low

The Rakes

Iron Tors

Tissington Trail

A515

Lode Lane

Alstonefield

PO

Lode House

Staffordshire County

Derbyshire County

Church Street

Hall Farm

Back Lane

Millway Lane

Lode Lane

Hope

Shining Tor

The Pinch

Oxclose Lane

ng Lane

Green La

Sunny Bank

Milldale

Stanshope

Grove Farm

A B C **178** D E F

Stanshope

sture Lane

Greenhead

Woollaton Lane

Tissington Trail

Bank House

rdlemere Lane

152

G   **H**   **J**   **K**   **L**   **M**

1

Back Lane

Back Lane

Bigginmoor Farm

A515

Uppermoor Farm

2

Tissington Trail

White Cliffe Farm

3

Liffs Road

Tissington Trail

Middlemoor Farm

4

168

Crosslow Lane

Alsop Moor Cottages

Hawkslow Farm

5

Oxdales Farm

Crosslow Lane

A515

6

Eaton Dale

Crosslowbank

Dale End Farm

Lane

7

Alsop en le Dale

†

Peakway

Foufinside

Dam Lane

8

Tissington Trail

Dam Lane

Parwich Lees

Parwich Primary School

G   **H**   **J**   **K**   **L**   **M**

Gag Lane

A515

179

Dam Lane

Parwich

eymeadow

A   B   C   D   E   F

Two
Meres

Bonsallmoor Lane

Blake
Mere

155

Blakemere

Moor   Lane

Upper
Town

Abel La

Uppertown Lane

Bell La

The Bank

Limestone Way

Horsedale
Farm

Slaley Lane

Th

I

Leys Lane

Tophill
Farm

Tophill   Lane

Grange Dale

2

Green   Lane

Leys

Grange

Lane

Leys Lane

Leys Lane

Slaley

3

Whitelow

Cross Lane

+   Ible

Whitecliffe
Farm

GELLIA

Middleton
Wood

Wood

Lane

VIA

4

A5012

Lane

Via Gellia

Wood

Griffe
Grange
Valley

A5012

B5023   NEW

ROAD

Cemetery

Burfo

5

Griffe
Grange
Farm

Hopton
Wood

Water L

The Mo

Doghole Lane

Rain's Lane

6

Pearsons
Farm

Griffe
Walk
Farm

Griffe
Grange

7

New
Harboro'
Farm

High Peak T

8

High Peak Trail

High Peak Trail

182

Broxendale
Farm

A   B   C   D   E   F

ton
Pasture

1 grid square represents 500 metres

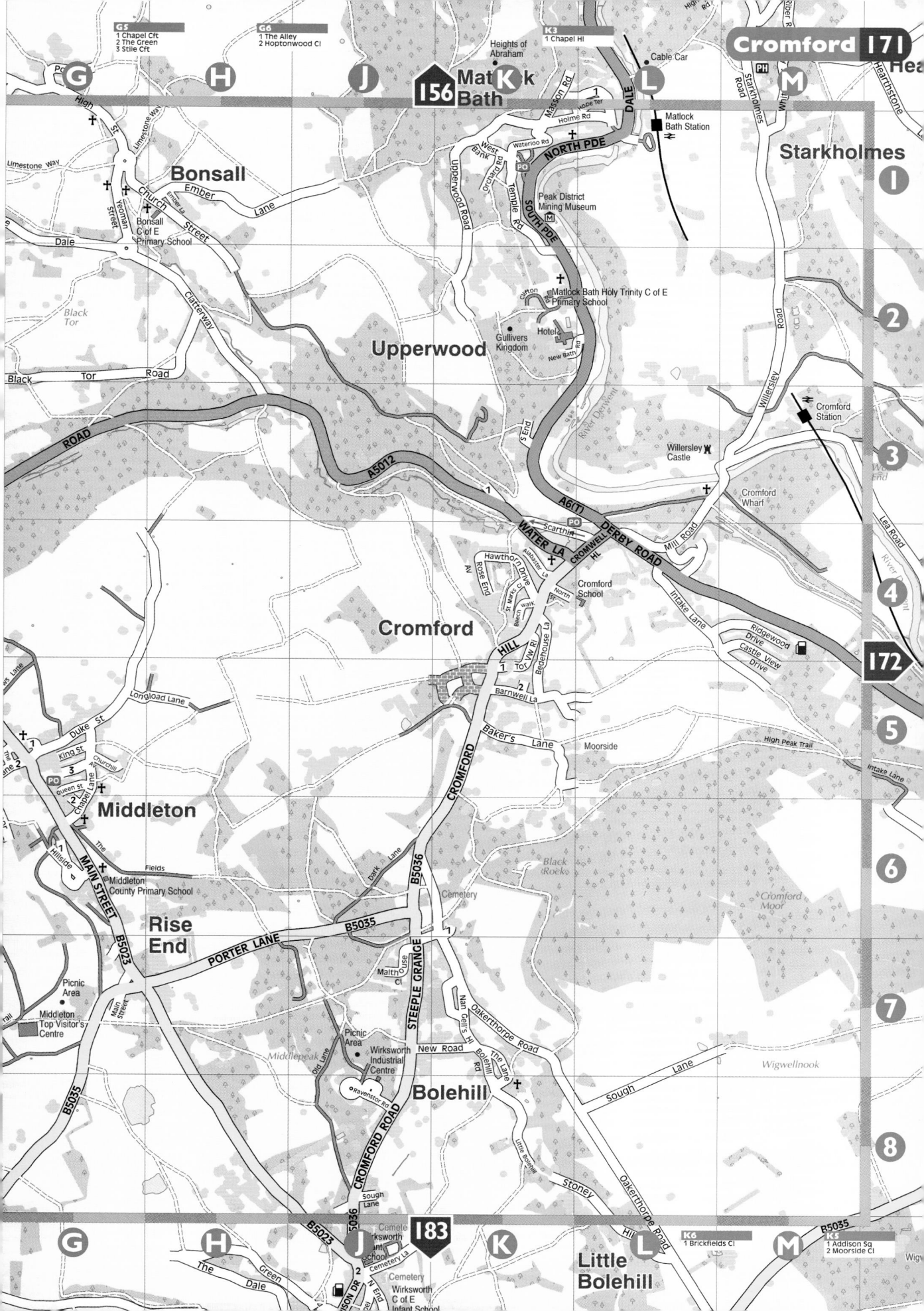

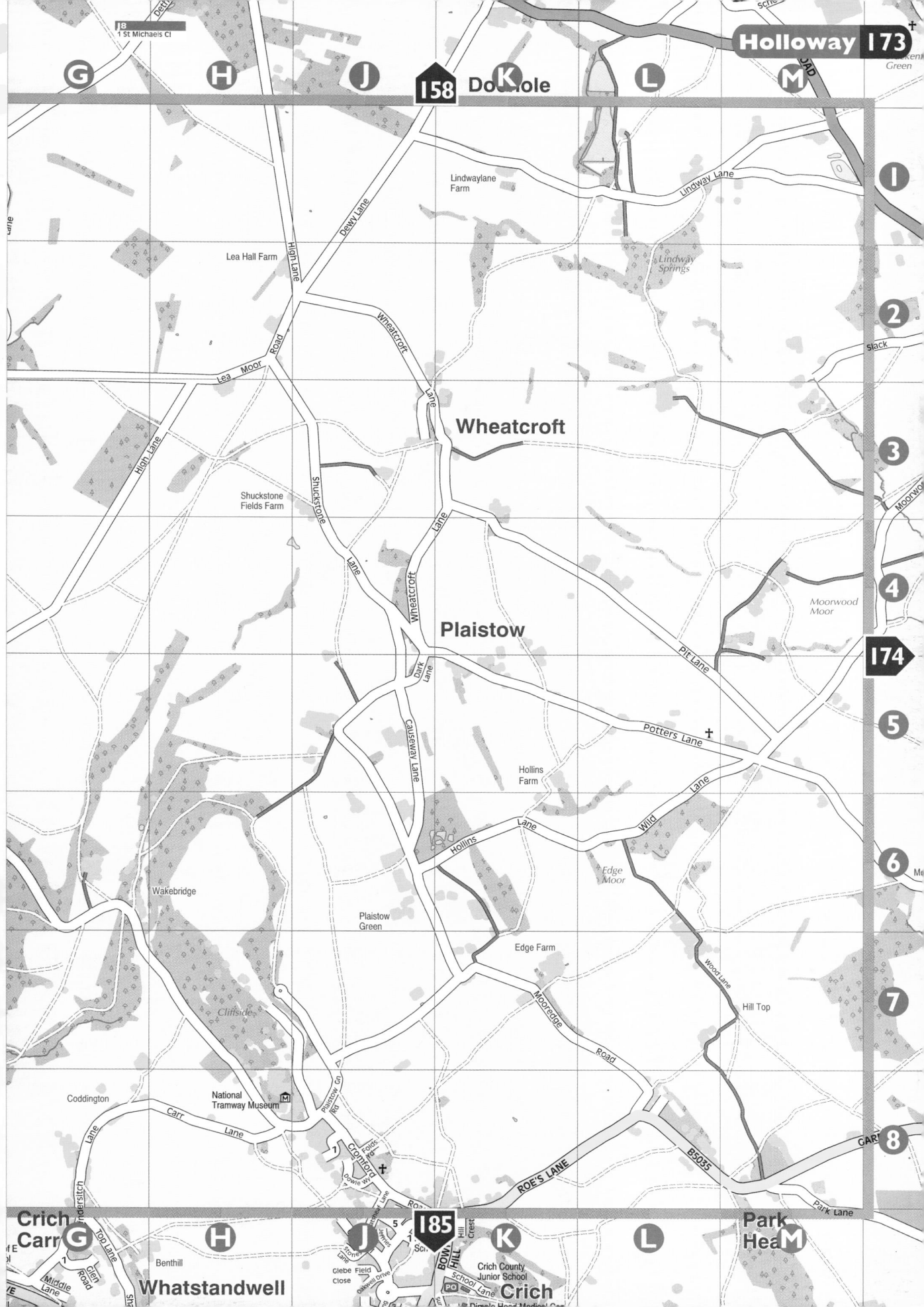

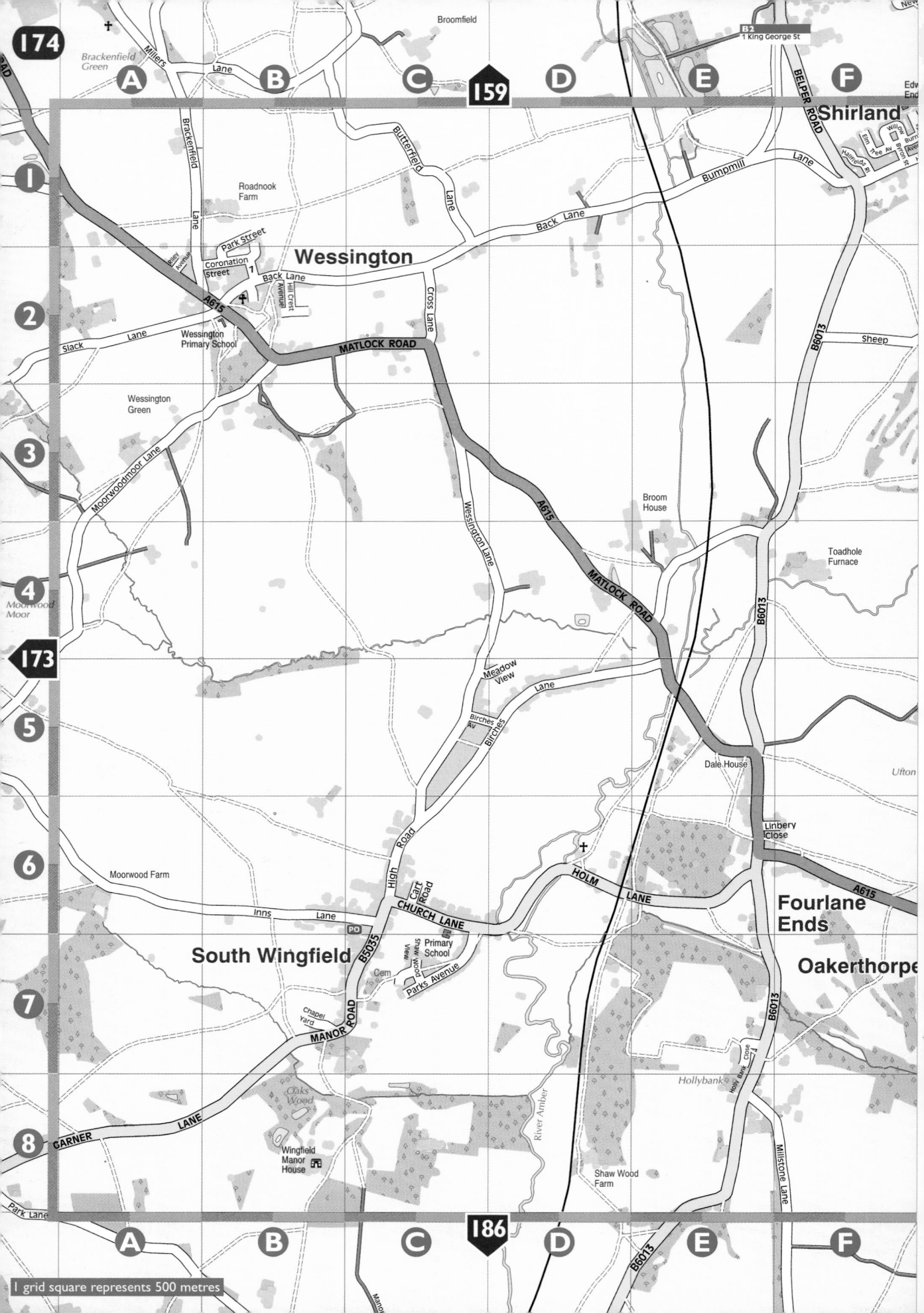

A B C 159 D E F

Shirland

Broomfield

B2
1 King George St

BELPER ROAD

Brackenfield
Green

Millers
Lane

Roadnook
Farm

Brackenfield Lane

Butterfield Lane

Back Lane

Bumpmill Lane

Halfields Rd

1

Park Street

Wessington

Coronation
Street 1

Back Lane

Hill Crest Avenue

Cross Lane

B6013

Sheep

2

A615

Slack Lane

Wessington
Primary School

MATLOCK ROAD

Wessington
Green

Moorwoodmoor Lane

Wessington Lane

A615

Broom
House

3

Moorwood
Moor

MATLOCK ROAD

Toadhole
Furnace

B6013

4

Meadow
View

Lane

Birches AV

Birches

Dale House

Ufton

5

Moorwood Farm

High Road

Cart Road

HOLM LANE

Linbery
Close

A615

Fourlane
Ends

6

Inns Lane

CHURCH LANE

PO

Primary
School

Shaw Wood View

Parks Avenue

B5035

Cem

MANOR ROAD

South Wingfield

Chapel
Yard

River Amber

Oakerthorpe

7

GARNER LANE

Oaks
Wood

Wingfield
Manor
House

Hollybank

Holly Bank Close

Millstone Lane

B6013

8

Park Lane

Shaw Wood
Farm

A B C 186 D E F

B6013

Manor

1 grid square represents 500 metres

G **H** **J 160** **K** **L** **M**

MAIN ROAD
ard Revill
owed School

Wellington Pl
Church St

Rowan
Lilac Way Aspen

Drive
allfieldgate Lane

Park Lane
Bevan Street
St Leonards Pl
Park

**Hallfield
Gate**

DE55

Cross Lane

Westhouses
Primary School

Astover
View

Sidings Way
Church
Close

Lane
Dam

Meadow
Farm

Pit Lane
Lane

Golf Club

Delves

Pit Lane

Westhouses

B6025
TIBSHELF ROAD

PARK LANE
ALFRETON ROAD

Silver Birch
Crescent
Park Mill Drive

PO

Park Lane

I

2

3

4

Shirland
Lodge

B6025
Alfreton Brook

I76

Ufton Fields
Farm

Fields

Pond
Wood

Meadow Lane
Industrial Estate

Dunsford
Road

Tavistock
Square

Elite
Business Park

Lydford Road

Christ the King
RC School

Acre Ridge
Industrial Estate

Salcombe
Wood St North

Alfreton Station

Westhouse

5

CARNFIE

Carnfiel
Hall

6

Beech Avenue
Cedar Av
Birch

Bishop Street

Hardy Street
Arthur Street

Frederick

Rodger's Lane
Firs Avenue

Willow
Cl

Willows Avenue
Oak

Beech

Meadow

Parkin Street
Priory Road

Catherine Street

MANSFIELD ROAD

ALFRETON

Infant
School

Charles Street
Bonsall La

Cem
Rowland St

Limes
Medical Cen
Doctors Surg

Elms
Firs Gdns

John St
Wilson St

B6019
Ellesmere Av

Oakland Dr

PO

Leys County
Junior School

Ley Gardens

Church Street

Chesterfield Close

Alfreton Leisure Centre

The Horse Fair
Gallery

Alfreton
Indoor
Mkt Hall

PO

HIGH STREET B6019
Chapel St

Central Rd

Cross St
George
Street

Wycliffe Road

Alma Street
Orange Street

Prospect Street

Preston Avenue

Addison
Drive

Byron Av

Shakespeare

Milton Av

Parkwood
School

KING STREET
A61(T)

Haddon
Close

Lincoln
Street

Independent

Hill

Street
Marshall St
South/ce St
Church

Infant
School

Police
Station

Alfreton
Clinic

Orange
Street

Secondary
School

Victoria Street

North St

Connaught
Ct

Alfreton Town
Football Club

Mercer
Crs

Cowham
Close

Rugby

Normanton
Road

Henry
Crs

Alfreton
Golf Club

WINGFIELD ROAD

COOKER LANE
DERBY ROAD

EACH WELL LANE

Watchorn Lane

Park Street
Nuttall St

Providence
Place

Long
Ewart
Lane

Meadow Road

Derwent Grove

Alfred Street

A38(T)

Woodbridge
Junior School

West End
Close

West
End

Brook
Av

Brook
Close

Pease Hill
Peak

The Green

Outseats Drive

Flowery

Leys Lane

Abbott Road

Birchwood Road

Dale
Cl

Rugdale

Elmwood

7

Cotes
Park

8

Hotel

Venture Crescent

Whites
Close

Wimsey

Hill St

Keys Road

Hockley Way

Wimsey Way

Monk
Road

NOTTINGHAM ROAD

Cotes
Park

West

Carnham Clo

Ashfield

Old Swanwick

G **H** **J I87** **K** **L** **M**

A38(T)
Y ROAD

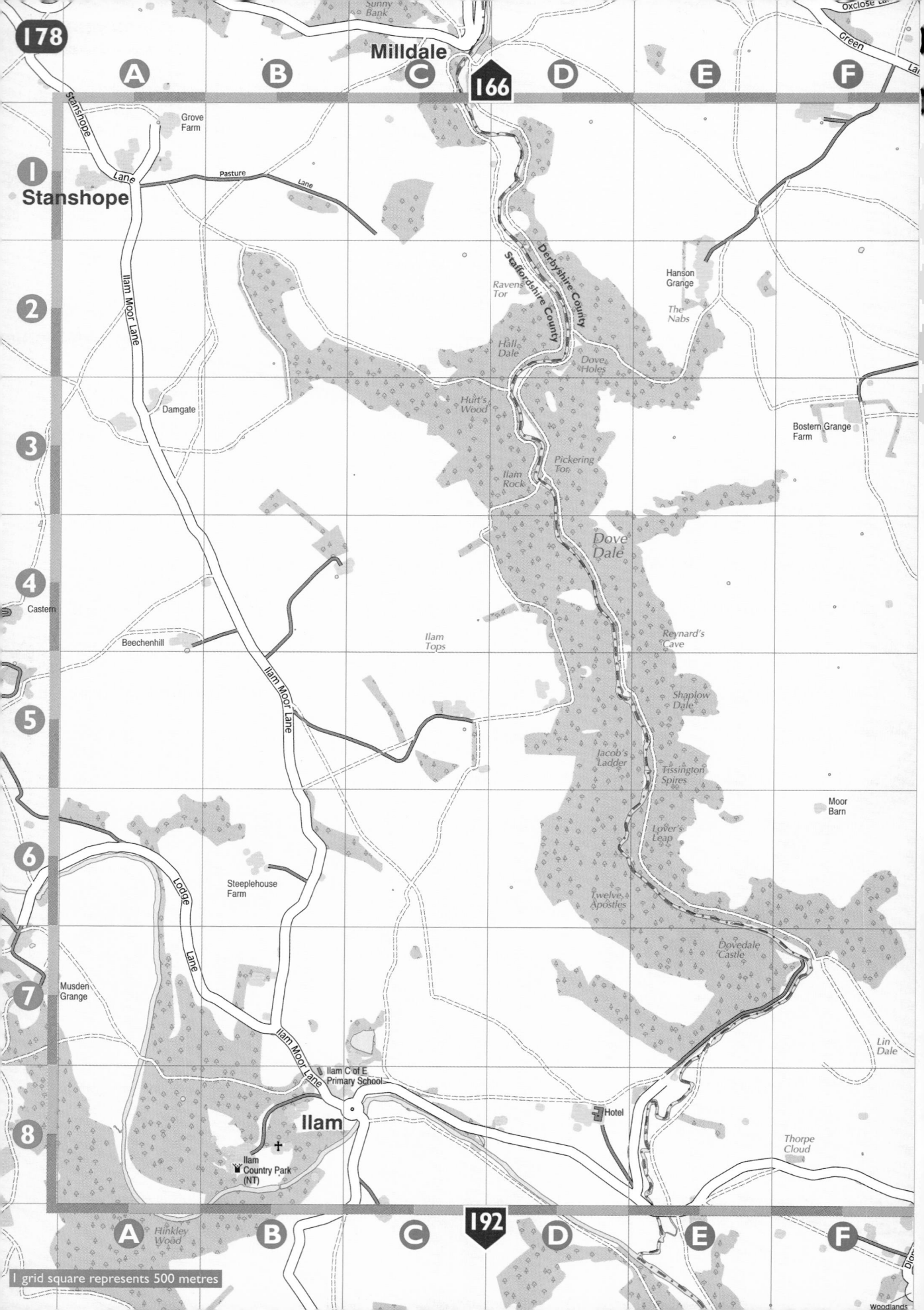

178

I **Stanshope**

Milldale

166

A B C D E F

1

2

3

4

5

6

7

8

A B C D E F

192

Stanshope Lane

Grove Farm

Pasture Lane

Ilam Moor Lane

Damgate

Castern

Beechenhill

Ilam Moor Lane

Lodge Lane

Musden Grange

Steeplehouse Farm

Ilam Moor Lane

Ilam C of E Primary School

Ilam

Ilam Country Park (NT)

Hinkley Wood

Ravens Tor

Staffordshire County

Derbyshire County

Hall Dale

Dove Holes

Hurt's Wood

Ilam Rock

Pickering Tor

Ilam Tops

Dove Dale

Reynard's Cave

Shaplow Dale

Jacob's Ladder

Tissington Spires

Lover's Leap

Twelve Apostles

Dovedale Castle

Hotel

Hanson Grange

The Nabs

Bostern Grange Farm

Moor Barn

Lin Dale

Thorpe Cloud

Sunny Bank

Oxclose La

Green La

Woodlands

Dr

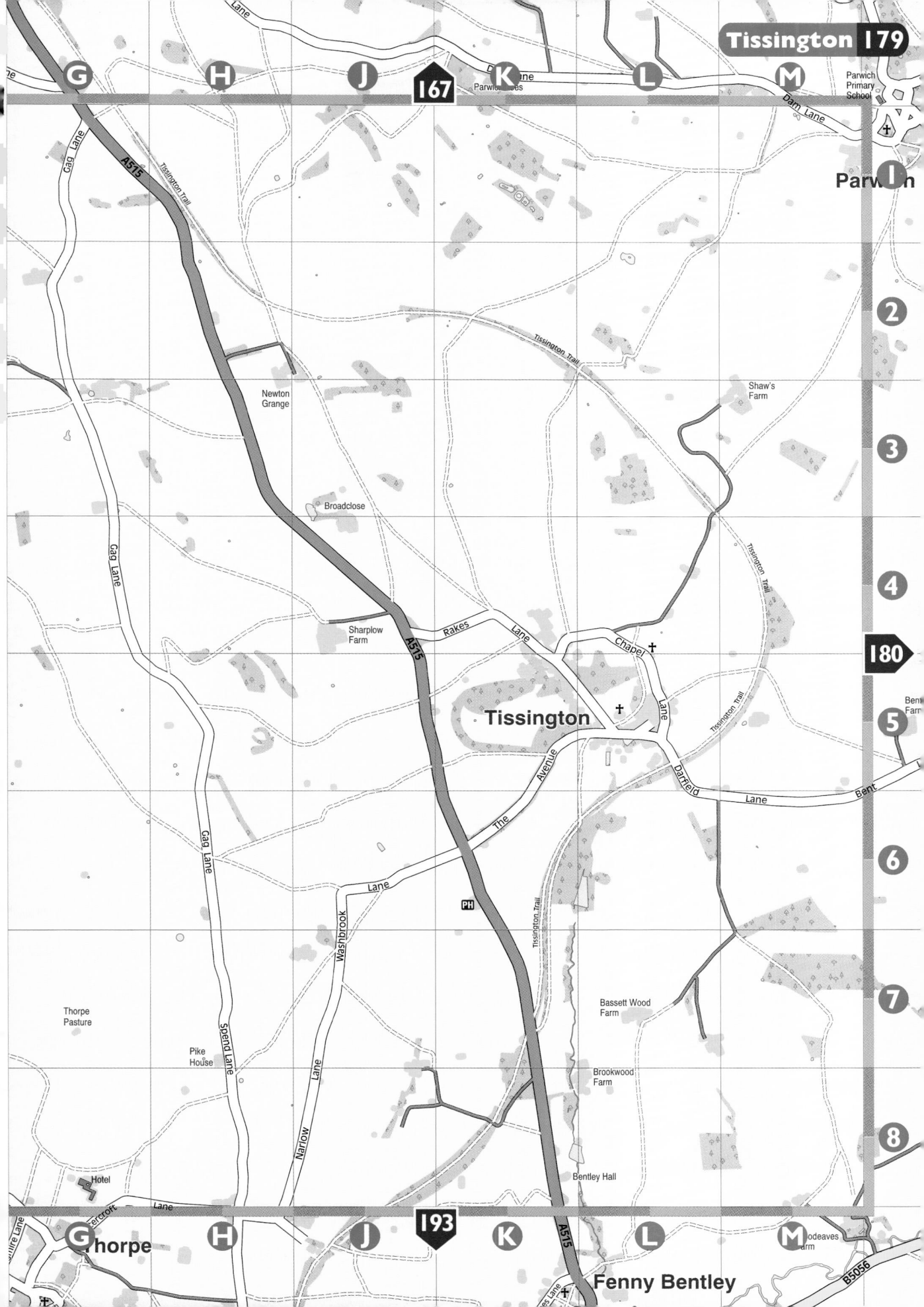

G
H
J
167
K
L
M

Parwich Primary School

Parwich

1

2

Shaw's Farm

3

Cag Lane

A515

Tissington Trail

Newton Grange

Broadclose

4

180

Beni Farm

5

Sharplow Farm

Rakes Lane

Chapel

Tissington

Lane

Darfield Lane

Bent Lane

6

The Avenue

Cag Lane

Washbrook Lane

Narlow Lane

Spend Lane

PH

Tissington Trail

Bassett Wood Farm

7

Thorpe Pasture

Pike House

Brookwood Farm

8

Hotel

Bentley Hall

odeaves Farm

G Thorpe
H
J
193
K
A515
L
M

Fenny Bentley

B5056

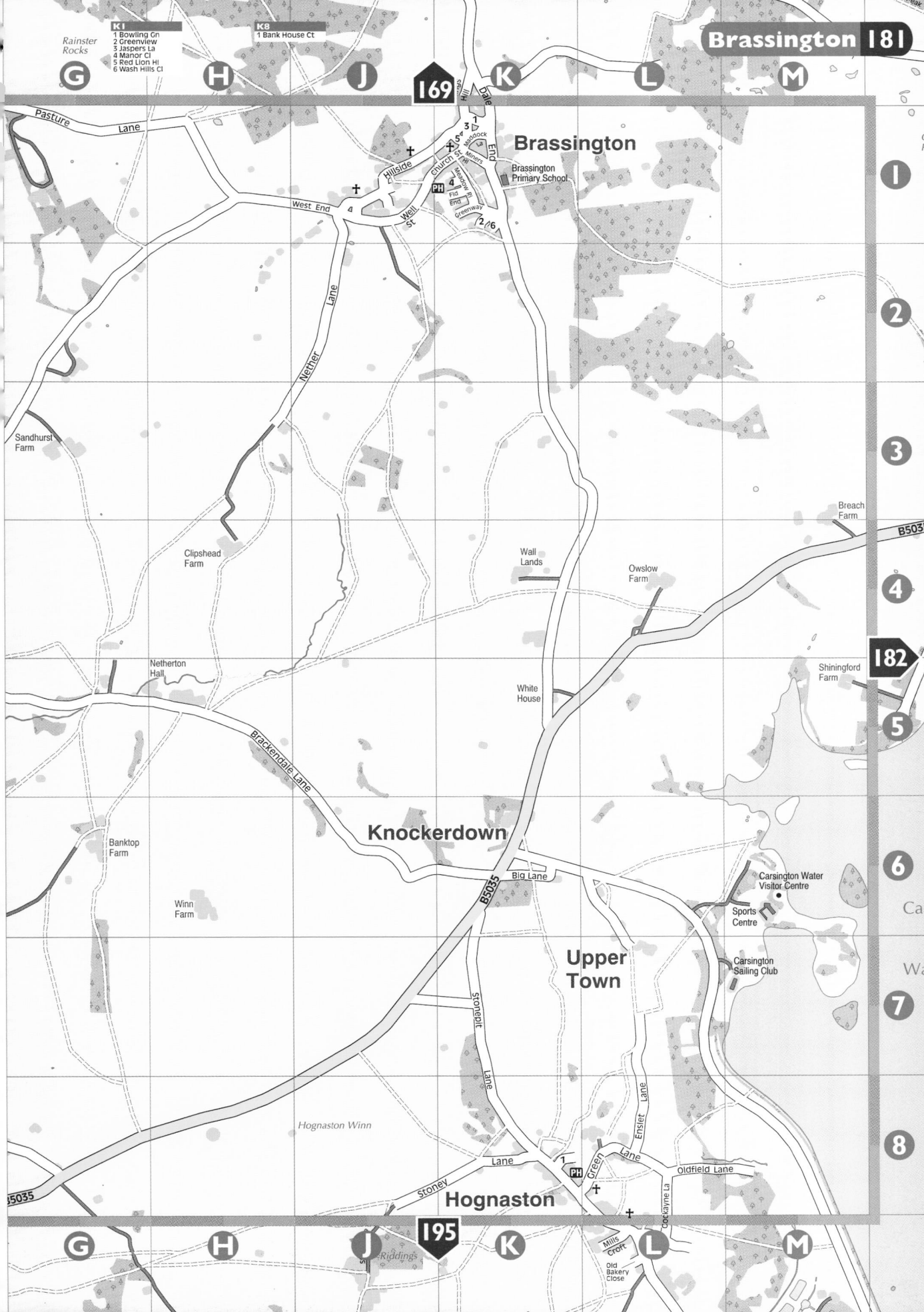

K1
1 Bowling Gn
2 Greenview
3 Jaspers La
4 Manor Cl
5 Red Lion Hl
6 Wash Hills Cl

K8
1 Bank House Ct

Rainster Rocks

G H J K L M

Pasture Lane

169

Brassington

Hillside

Dale End

Miners

West End

Church St

Well St

PH

Meadow

Fld End

Greenway

Brassington Primary School

Nether Lane

Sandhurst Farm

Clipshead Farm

Breach Farm

B5035

Wall Lands

Owslow Farm

182

Shiningford Farm

Netherton Hall

White House

Brackendale Lane

Banktop Farm

Knockerdown

Winn Farm

B5035

Big Lane

Carsington Water Visitor Centre

Sports Centre

Ca

Upper Town

Carsington Sailing Club

Wa

Stonepit Lane

Hognaston Winn

Green Lane

Enslet Lane

Oldfield Lane

Cockayne La

Stoney Lane

PH

Hognaston

195

Riddings

Mills Croft

Old Bakery Close

G H J K L M

I
2
3
4
5
6
7
8

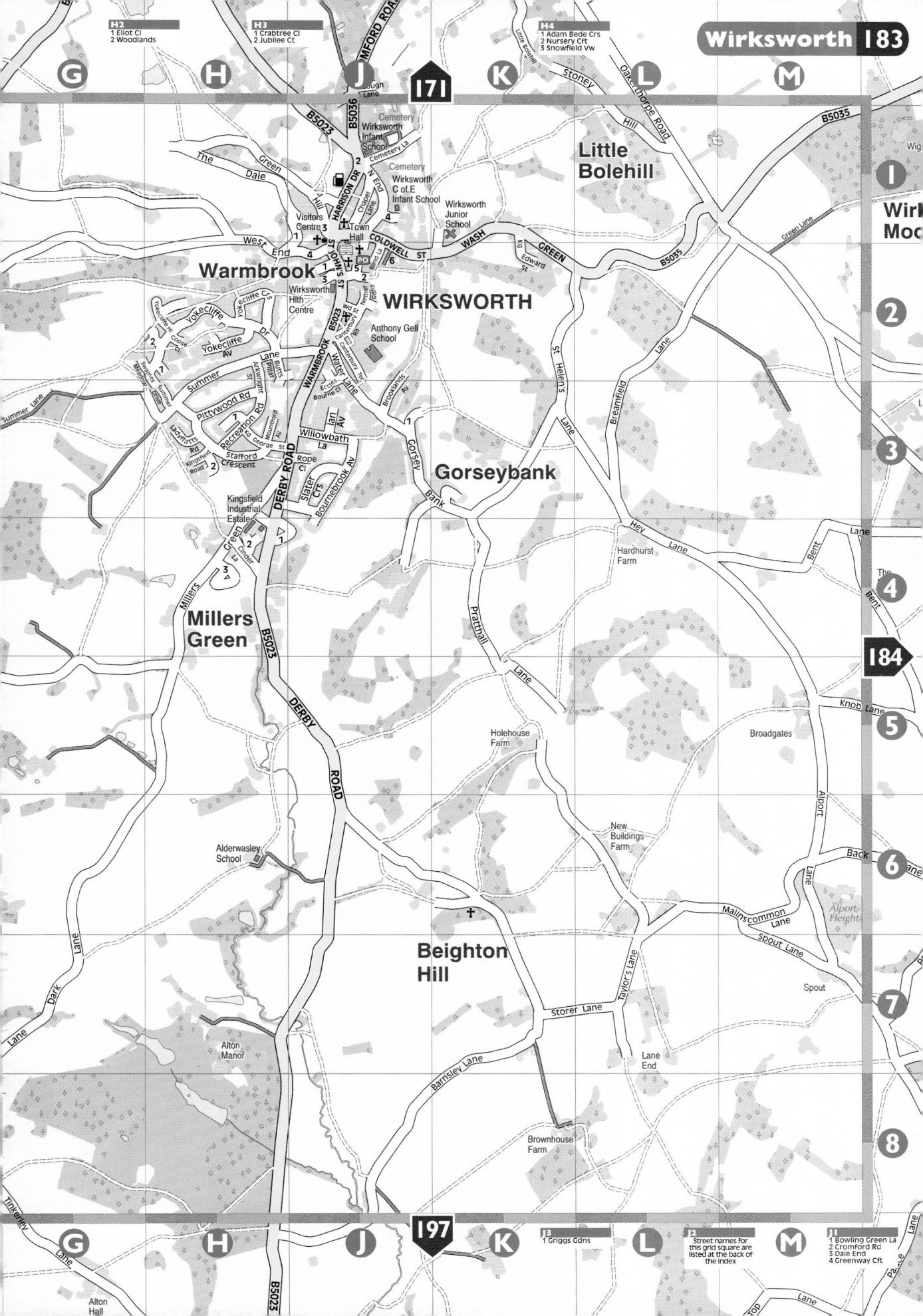

H2
1 Eliot Cl
2 Woodlands

H3
1 Crabtree Cl
2 Jubilee Ct

H4
1 Adam Bede Crs
2 Nursery Cft
3 Snowfield Vw

I

Wir
Moc

2

3

184

5

6

7

8

Cemetery
Wirksworth
Infant
School

Cemetery La

Cemetery

Wirksworth
C of E
Infant School

Wirksworth
Junior
School

Little
Bolehill

Green Lane

B5035

B5035

Oakerthorpe Road

Stoney Hill

Little Bolehill

The Dale

The Green

Dale Hill

B5023

B5036

N End

Harrison Dr

Chapel La

Visitors
Centre

Town
Hall

West End

St Johns St

Coldwell St

Wash

Green

Edward St

St Helen's Lane

Warmbrook

Wirksworth
Hlth Centre

Yokecliffe Crs

Yokecliffe Av

Yokecliffe Dr

Cooper Ct

Summer Lane

Summer

Pittywood Rd

Lanriatts Rd

Kingsfield Road

Stafford Crescent

Recreation Rd

Mountford

George St

Arkwright St

Butts

Eccles Bourne

Wd St

WIRKSWORTH

Anthony Gell
School

Warmbrook

Water Lane

Canterbury Ter

Willowbath La

Ian Av

Bournebrook Av

Slater Cfs

Rope Cl

Brooklands Av

Gorsey Bank

1

Gorseybank

Breamfield Lane

Lane

Hey Lane

Hardhurst
Farm

Bent Lane

Lane

The Bent

Knob Lane

Broadgates

Alport Lane

Kingsfield
Industrial
Estate

Green La

Cinder La

Derby Road

B5023

**Millers
Green**

Millers

Pratthall Lane

Holehouse
Farm

New
Buildings
Farm

Malinscommon Lane

Spout Lane

Alport
Heights

Back Lane

Spout

Alderwasley
School

Derby Road

B5023

**Beighton
Hill**

Storer Lane

Taylor's Lane

Barnsley Lane

Lane
End

Dark Lane

Alton
Manor

Brownhouse
Farm

J3
1 Griggs Gdns

J2
Street names for
this grid square are
listed at the back of
the index

J1
1 Bowling Green La
2 Cromford Rd
3 Dale End
4 Greenway Cft

Tinkerley Lane

Alton
Hall

B5023

Pa

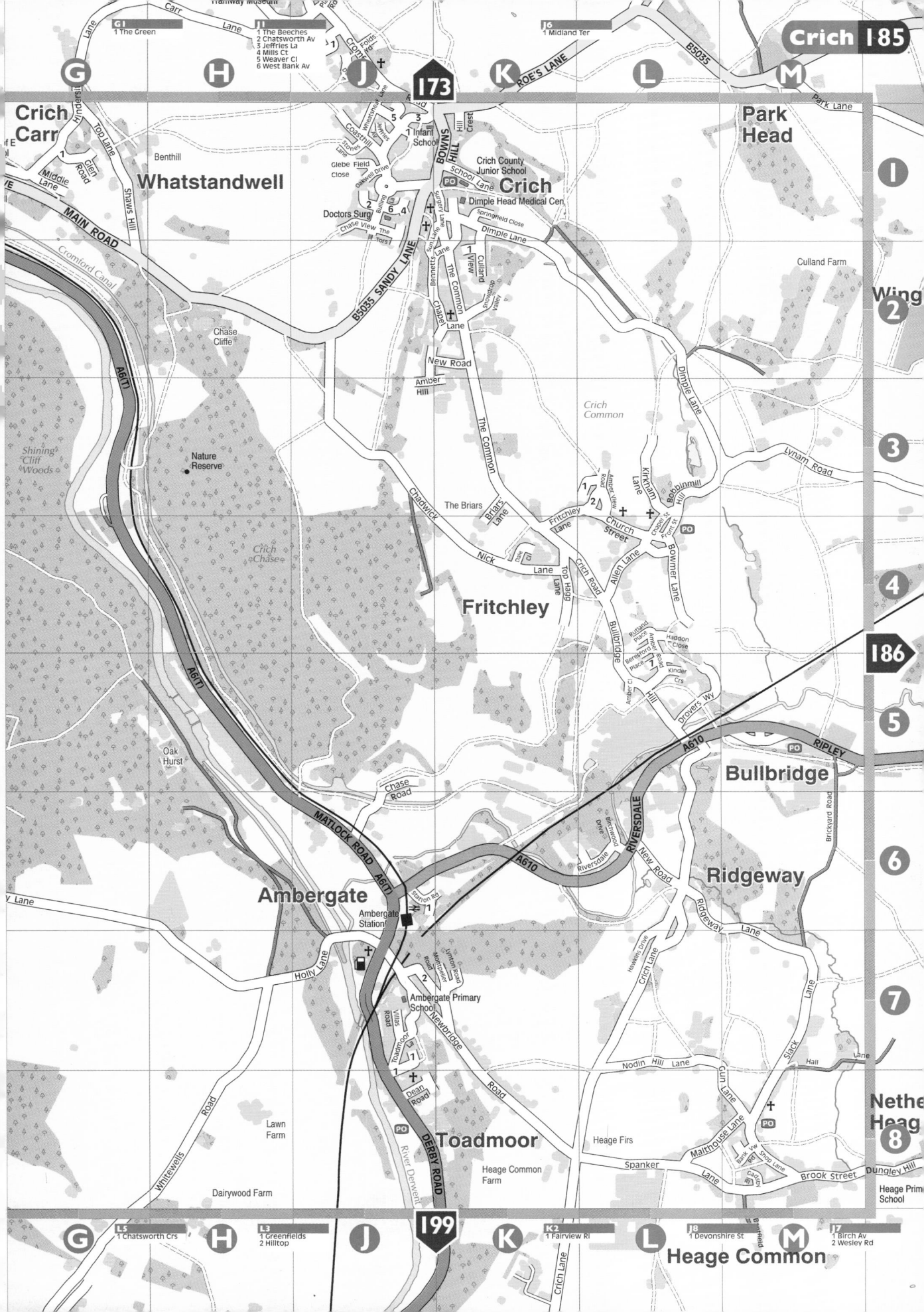

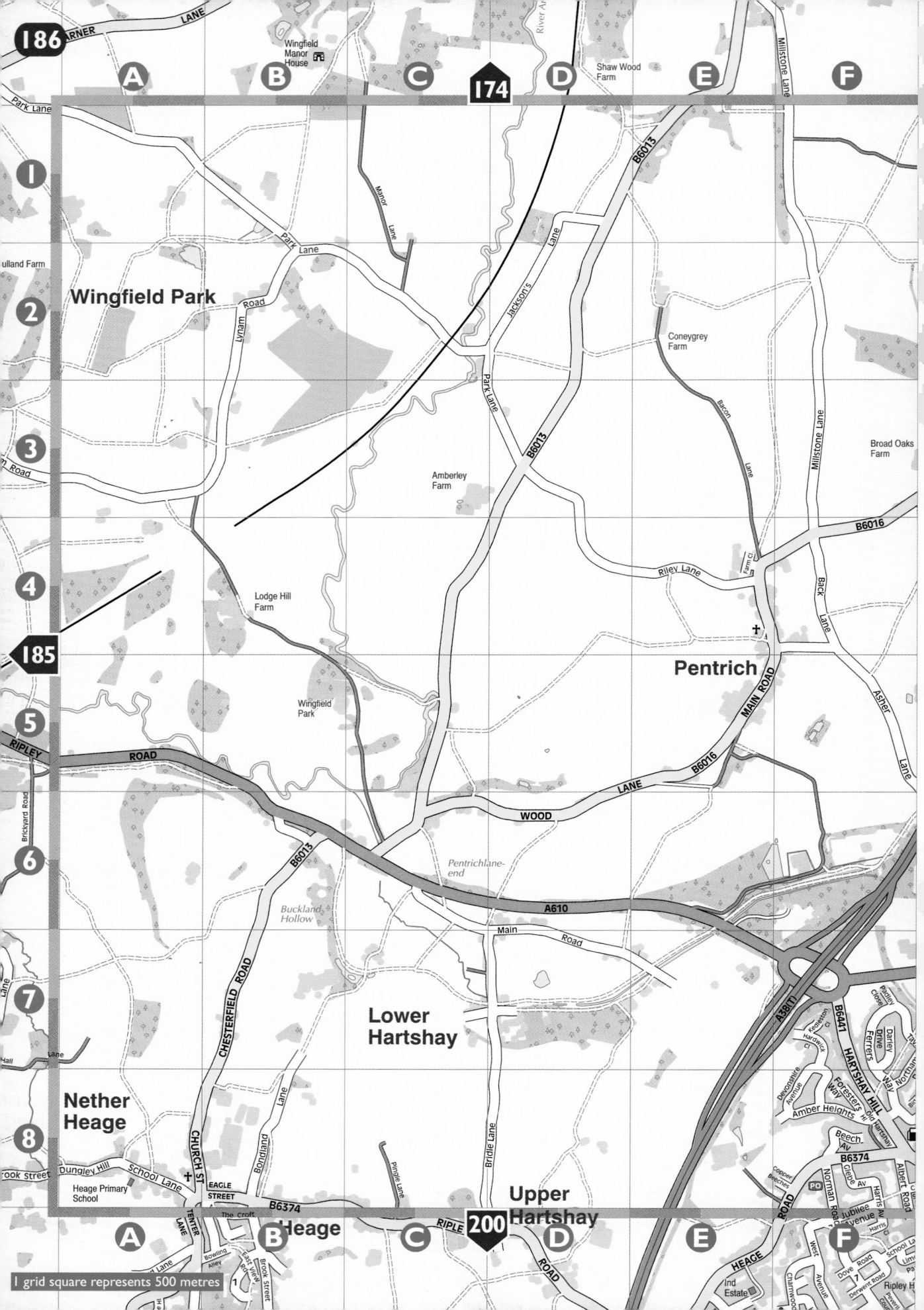

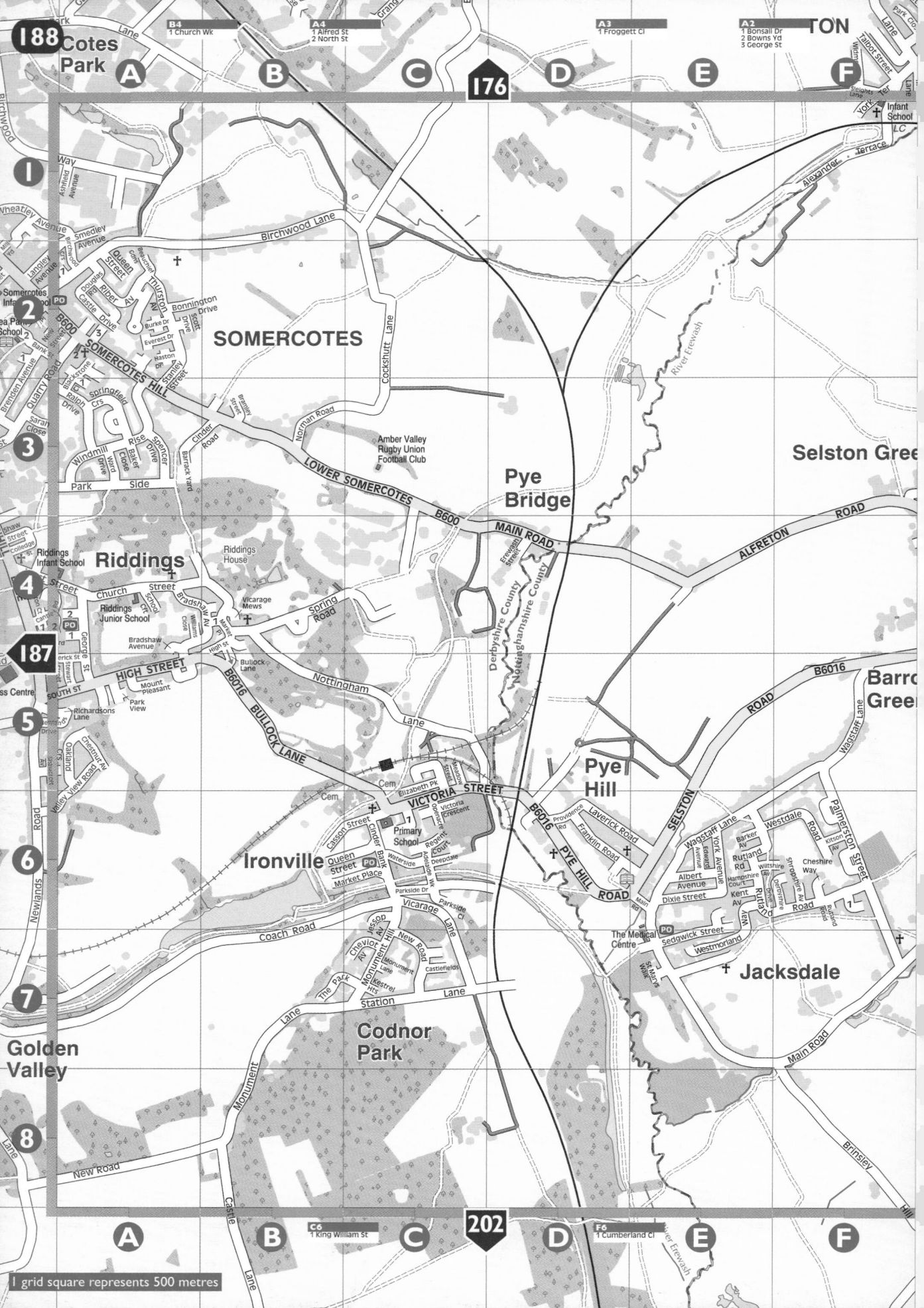

Cotes Park

176

TON

1 Church Wk

1 Alfred St
2 North St

1 Froggett Cl

1 Bonsall Dr
2 Bowns Yd
3 George St

Infant School

SOMERCOTES

Birchwood Lane

Wheatley Avenue

Ashfield Avenue

Smedley Avenue

Langley Avenue

Somercotes Infant School

ea Park School

Brenden Avenue

Somercotes Hill

Bank Street

Springfield Drive

Windmill Drive

Rise Drive

Baker Close

Spencer

Park Side

Barrack Yard

Cinder Road

Bonnington Drive

Norman Road

Cockshutt Lane

River Erewash

Selston Green

Amber Valley Rugby Union Football Club

LOWER SOMERCOTES

B600

Pye Bridge

MAIN ROAD

ALFRETON ROAD

Riddings Infant School

Riddings

Riddings House

Riddings Junior School

Church Street

School Croft

Bradshaw Av

Vicarage Mews

Spring Road

Derbyshire County

Nottinghamshire County

187

HIGH STREET

Bradshaw Avenue

Mount Pleasant

Bullock Lane

Nottingham Lane

B6016

Pye Hill

B6016

Barrow Green

B6016 ROAD

SOUTH ST

Richardsons Lane

Oakland

Chestnut Av

Valley View Road

Newlands Road

BULLOCK LANE

Cem

Cem

Elizabeth Pk

VICTORIA STREET

Primary School

Ironville

Casson Street

Queen Street

Market Place

Waterside

Victoria Crescent

Regent Court

Deepdale

Selston

Laverick Road

Franklin Road

Providence Rd

Pye Hill Road

Wagstaff Lane

York Avenue

Barker Av

Albert Avenue

Dixie Street

Kent Av

Westdale Road

Rutland Rd

Wiltshire Av

Hampshire Court

Derbyshire Av

Shropshire Av

Cheshire Way

Palmerston Street

Kitson Av

Rutland Road

The Medical Centre

Sedgwick Street

Westmorland

Jacksdale

St Mary's Walk

Parkside Dr

Vicarage Lane

Parkside Cl

Coach Road

Jessop Av

Cheviot Av

Monument Hill

New Road

Castlefields

Golden Valley

The Park

Monument Lane

Kestrel Hts

Station Lane

Codnor Park

Monument

Castle Lane

New Road

Brinsley

Main Road

River Erewash

202

1 King William St

1 Cumberland Cl

I grid square represents 500 metres

A B C D E F

I

roomyshaw

2

3

4

5

6

7

8

Duke's Lane

Waterhouses C of E Primary School

Crowtrees Industrial Es

Bishops Valley Rd

Portland PI

Waterhouses Medical Practice

Field House Farm

Greensides

Crowtrees

Hotel

Waterhouses

PH

Whitefield Lane

Manifold Way

A523(T)

Middlehills Farm

Earlsway

Butt's Lane

Cemetery

Cow Lane

Church Lane

Church Bank

PH

Cauldon

Moorend

Duke's Lane

Stoney Lane

Windy Harbour

Cauldon Low

A52

PO

Road

Hoften's Cross

Ellastone Road

Westfields

Moorfields

Main

B5417

Moorside

Wardlow

Tenement Farm

Wredon

† A B C 204 D E F

Threelows

The Walk

G H J K L M

Upper Musden

Doglane Farm

Calton
PO ✝
Back Lane
Back Lane

Stony Lane

Lane

Dogmoor La

A523(T)

Common Lane

Calton Green

Dog Lane

Green Lane

Hazelton Clump

The Waterings Farm

Huddale Lane
Huddale

Dale Lane

Miles Knoll

A523(T)

Latham Hall

Caltonmoor House

A52(T)

The Dale

Common Lane

192

Forest Farm

Bullgap Lane

Stanton Dale Farm

A52

Dale Lane

Dale Abbey Farm

A52

A52

Walk Farm

Thorswood House

Bullgap Lane

Brown Edge

Bullgap Lane

Nibs End Farm

Lane

Stubbs Lane

Lane

Thorswood

Blake Low

G H J K L M

205

Blakelov Lane

The Stitchings

Slade Hollow

Sladehollow Lane

Bankside

✝

Star

I 1
2
3
4
192
5
6
7
8

192

A   **Ilam**   B   C   **178**   D   E   F

Thorpe Cloud

Ilam Cou... Park (NT)

Hinkley Wood

1

Woodlands Close

Hazelton Clump

2

Limestone Way

Coldwall Bridge

terings

Blore

Coldwall

3

Yerley Hill

Limestone Way

Woodhouses

4

Lees House Farm

A52(T)

191

Hillend Farm

5

Swinscoe

Bullpap Lane

PO

Townend Lane

PH

Hotel

Marten Hill

Bulloa...

6

A52(T) SWINSCOE HILL

Limestone Way

7

The Orchards

Brown Edge

Cornpark

8

Lane

Lordspiece

Scrubs

206

Stanton Lane

Harlow Farm

A52(T)

SWINSCOE HILL

A   B   C   D   E   F

I grid square represents 500 metres

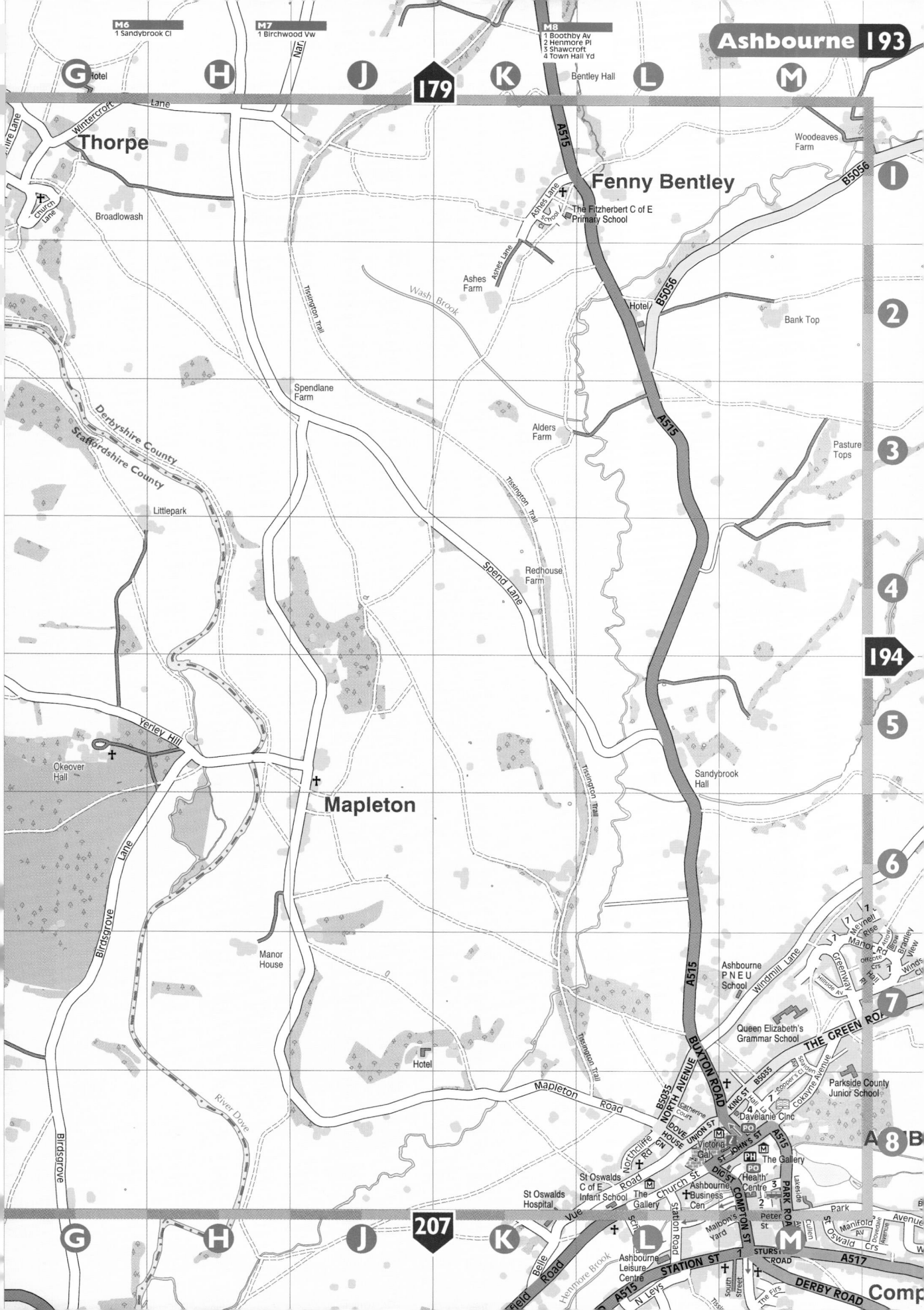

M6
1 Sandybrook Cl

M7
1 Birchwood Vw

M8
1 Boothby Av
2 Henmore Pl
3 Shawcroft
4 Town Hall Yd

G   H   Nan.   J   179   K   Bentley Hall   L   M   I

Hotel

Wintercroft Lane   Lane

Thorpe

Broadlowash

Church Lane

Ashes Lane
C of E School

Fenny Bentley

The Fitzherbert C of E
Primary School

Woodeaves Farm

B5056

2

Wash Brook

Ashes Lane

Ashes Farm

Hotel

B5056

Bank Top

Tissington Trail

Spendlane Farm

Alders Farm

A515

Pasture Tops

3

Derbyshire County

Staffordshire County

Littlepark

Tissington Trail

Spend Lane

Redhouse Farm

194

4

Yeley Hill

Okeover Hall

Mapleton

Sandybrook Hall

5

Birdsgrove Lane

Manor House

Tissington Trail

Ashbourne P N E U School

Meynell Rise
Manor Rd
Bradley
Greenway
Winds
THE GREEN ROAD

6

7

Queen Elizabeth's Grammar School

Hotel

Mapleton   Road

River Dove

Birdsgrove

BUXTON ROAD

North Avenue

B5035

A515

Parkside County Junior School

King St
Cokayne Avenue

A8 B

Catherine Court

Davelanie Clnc

Dove House Gn

Northcliffe Rd

Union St

Victoria Gdn

PO

M   The Gallery

PH   'Health' Centre

Compton St

Park Road

Lakeside

St Oswalds C of E Infant School

The Gallery

Ashbourne Business Cen

Church Road

Peter St
Sturston Rd
St Oswald Av

St Oswalds Hospital

Station Road

Vue

Belle Road

Hennmore Brook

Ashbourne Leisure Centre

STATION ST

A515

N Levs

Malbons Yard

The Firs

DERBY ROAD

Manifold Av
Dovedale Avenue

A517

A **B** **C** **D** **E** **F**

Woodeaves Farm

5056

Ravenscliffe

Riddings Park

Woodside

Knivetonwood

Wood Lane

A7 1 Copley Cft

Longr

Closes Farm

The Hallsteads

A6 1 Woodlands Brow

Standlow Lane

Lane

Kniveton C of E Primary School

Kniveton

Old Hall

1

Top

Rowfields Hall Farm

B5035

Foxholes Lane

Brookhouse Farm

2

ture s

Breck Farm

Pethills

3

Herdmans Close Farm

Herdsmans Close

Foxhole Farm

Kniveton Brook

4

Underwood Farm

5

Offcote House

Offcote Grange

Kniveton Lane

B5035

Ashbourne Green

The Grove

6

The Green Hall

Meynell Rise

Manor Rd

Arrow

Brook

Bradley View

Offcote Crs

Windsor Close

Greenway

Hall

Ox Close

7

THE GREEN ROAD

yre Avenue

Parkside County Junior School

8

ASHBOURNE

Sturston Hall

Park

Beresford Av

Cullen

St Oswald

Manifold Av

Avenue

W Crs

Brookside

Okeover Av

Mill Lane

Nether Sturston

A **B** **C** **D** **E** **F**

A517

BELPER ROAD

ompton

A517

Bradley Wood

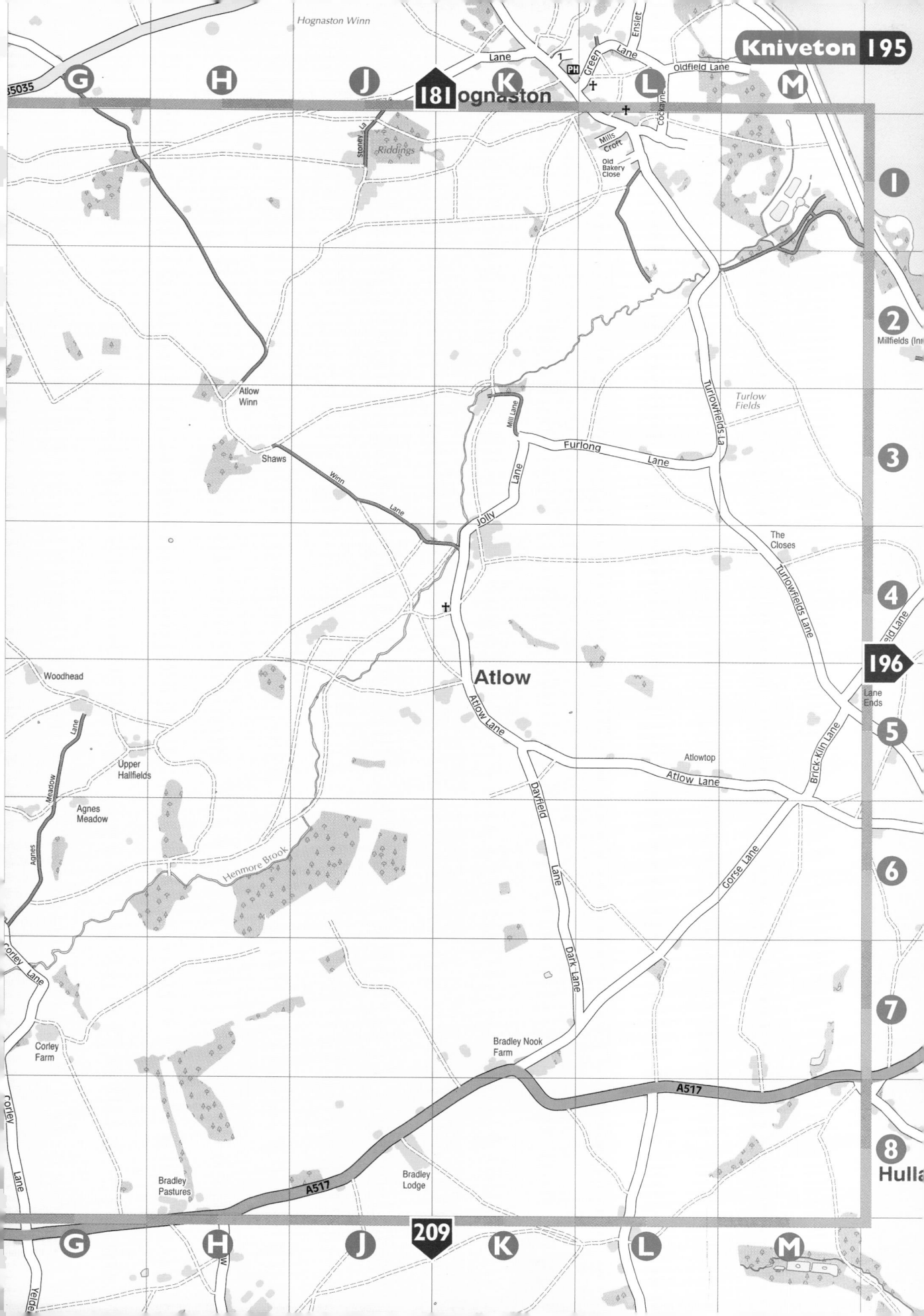

G   H   J   **181** K   L   M

Hognaston Winn

Lane

181 ognaston

PH

Green Lane

Enslet Lane

Oldfield Lane

Cockayne

Mills Croft

Old Bakery Close

Stoney La

Riddings

I

Millfields (Inn

2

Turlowfields La

Turlow Fields

3

Atlow Winn

Mill Lane

Furlong Lane

Shaws

Winn Lane

Jolly Lane

The Closes

Turlowfields Lane

4

196

Lane Ends

Woodhead

Atlow

Atlow Lane

Atlowtop

Atlow Lane

Brick Kiln Lane

5

Meadow Lane

Upper Hallfields

Agnes Meadow

Agnes

Henmore Brook

Dayfield Lane

Dark Lane

Gorse Lane

6

Corley Lane

7

Corley Farm

Bradley Nook Farm

A517

8

Bradley Pastures

A517

Bradley Lodge

Hulla

Yelde

W

G   H   J   **209**   K   L   M

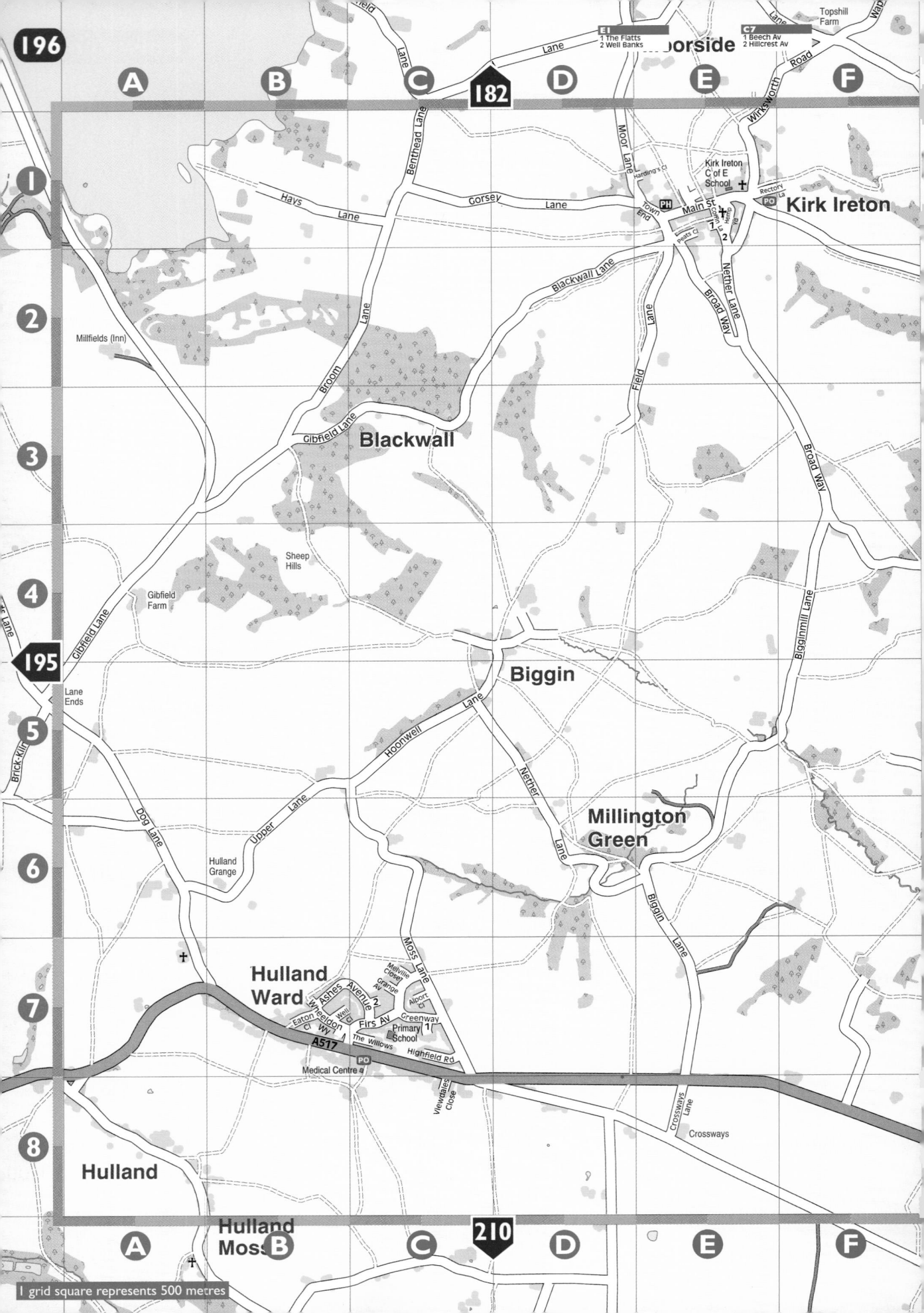

A   B   C   182   D   E   F

1

2

3

195

4

5

6

7

8

E1
1 The Flatts
2 Well Banks

C7
1 Beech Av
2 Hillcrest Av

Topshill
Farm

orside

Wirksworth   Road

Lane

Moor Lane

Harding's Cl

Kirk Ireton
C of E
School

Town
End

PH

Main St

PO

Rectory La

Kirk Ireton

Nether Lane

Broad Way

Peats Cl

7

2

Hays   Lane

Gorsey   Lane

Benthead Lane

Blackwall Lane

Field   Lane

Broom   Lane

Millfields (Inn)

Gibfield Lane

Blackwall

Sheep
Hills

Gibfield
Farm

Gibfield Lane

Lane Ends

Brick Kiln

Broad Way

Bigginmill Lane

Biggin

Hoonwell   Lane

Nether   Lane

Millington
Green

Biggin   Lane

Dog Lane

Upper   Lane

Hulland
Grange

Hulland
Ward

Ashes   Avenue

Wheeldon

Eaton
Cl

Firs Av

Well

Wy

Moss   Lane

Melville
Close

Grange
Av

2

Alport   Close

Greenway

1

Primary
School

The Willows

A517

Highfield Rd

Medical Centre   PO

Viewdales   Close

Crossways   Lane

Crossways

Hulland

Hulland
Moss

A   B   210   C   D   E   F

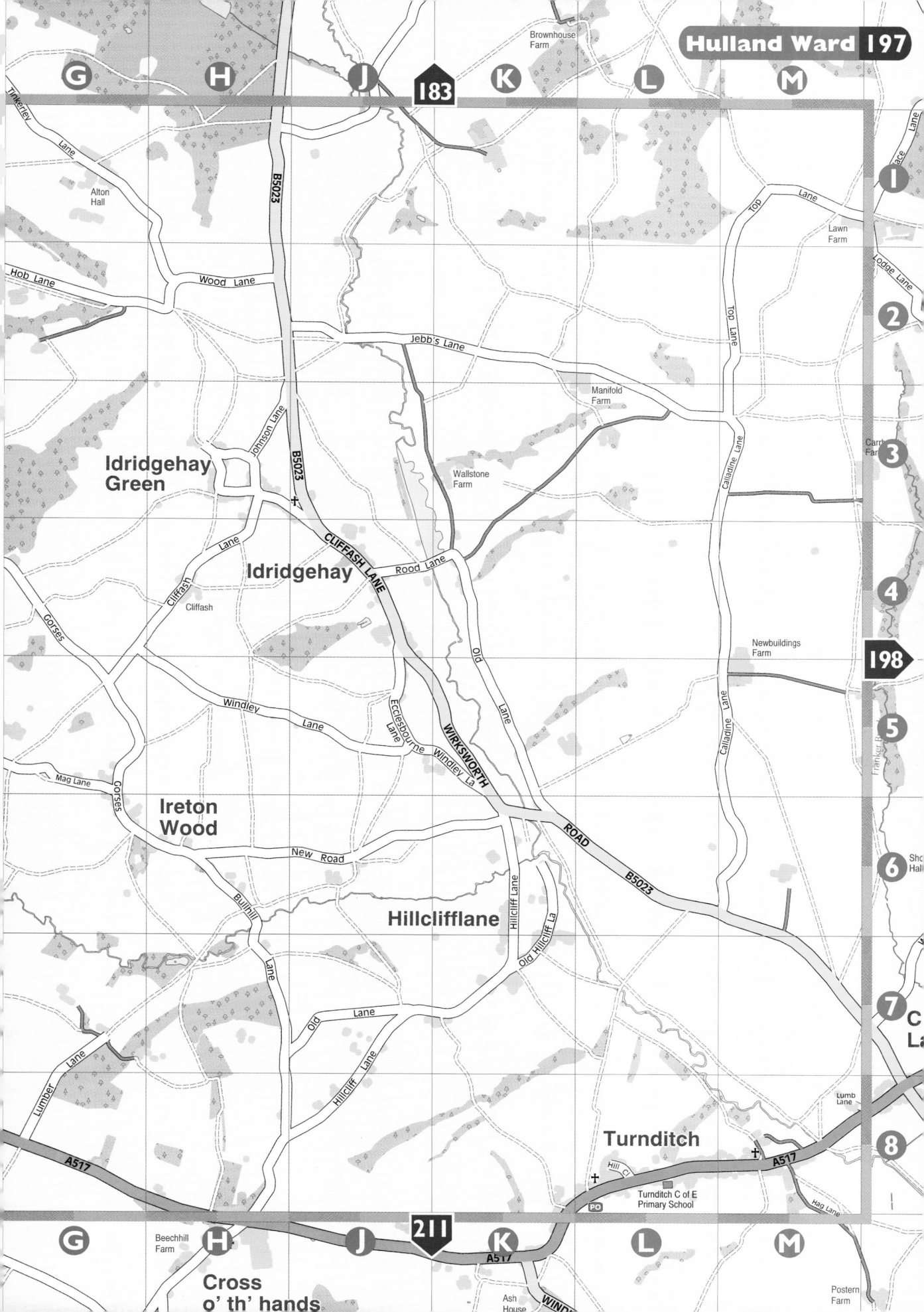

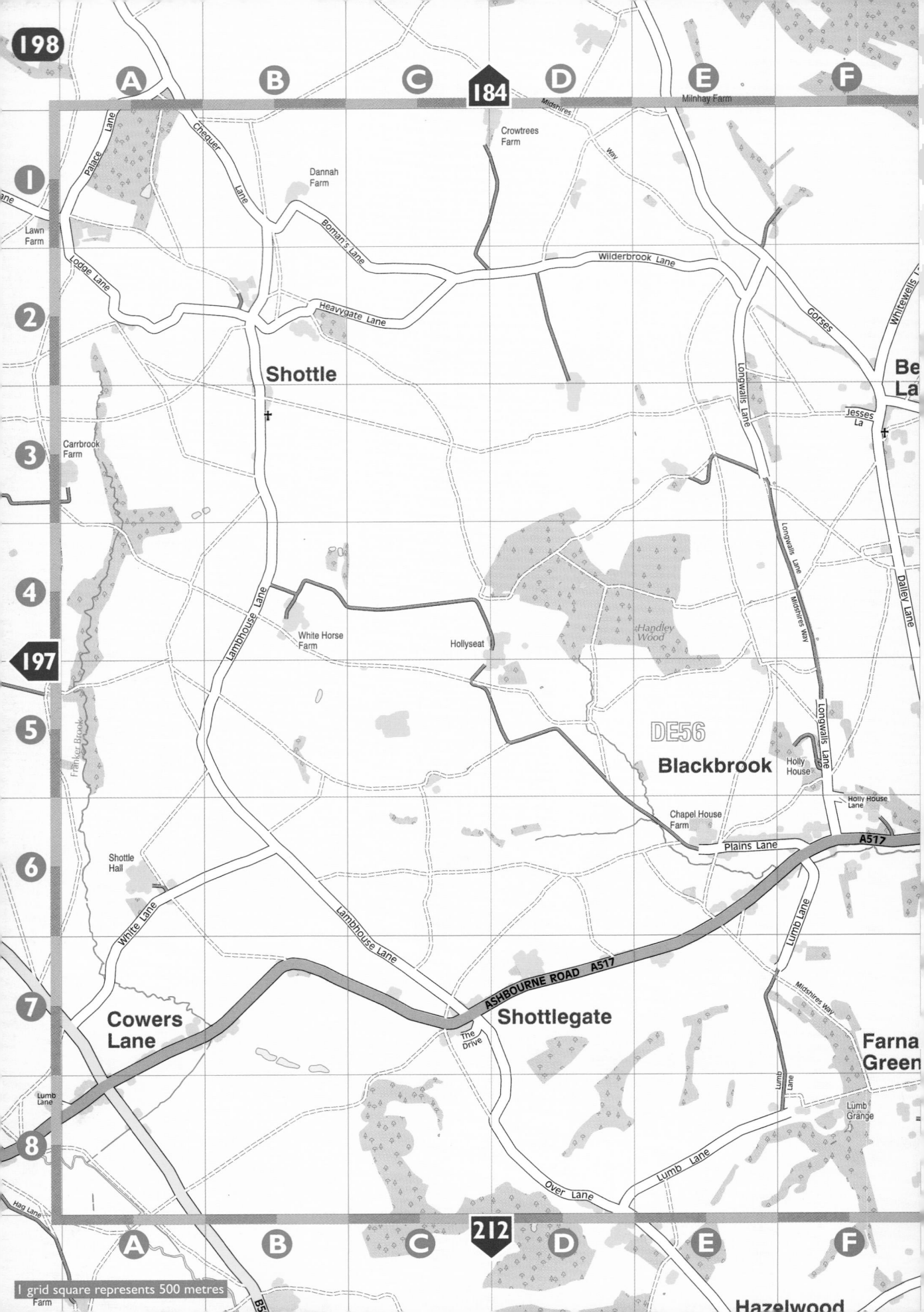

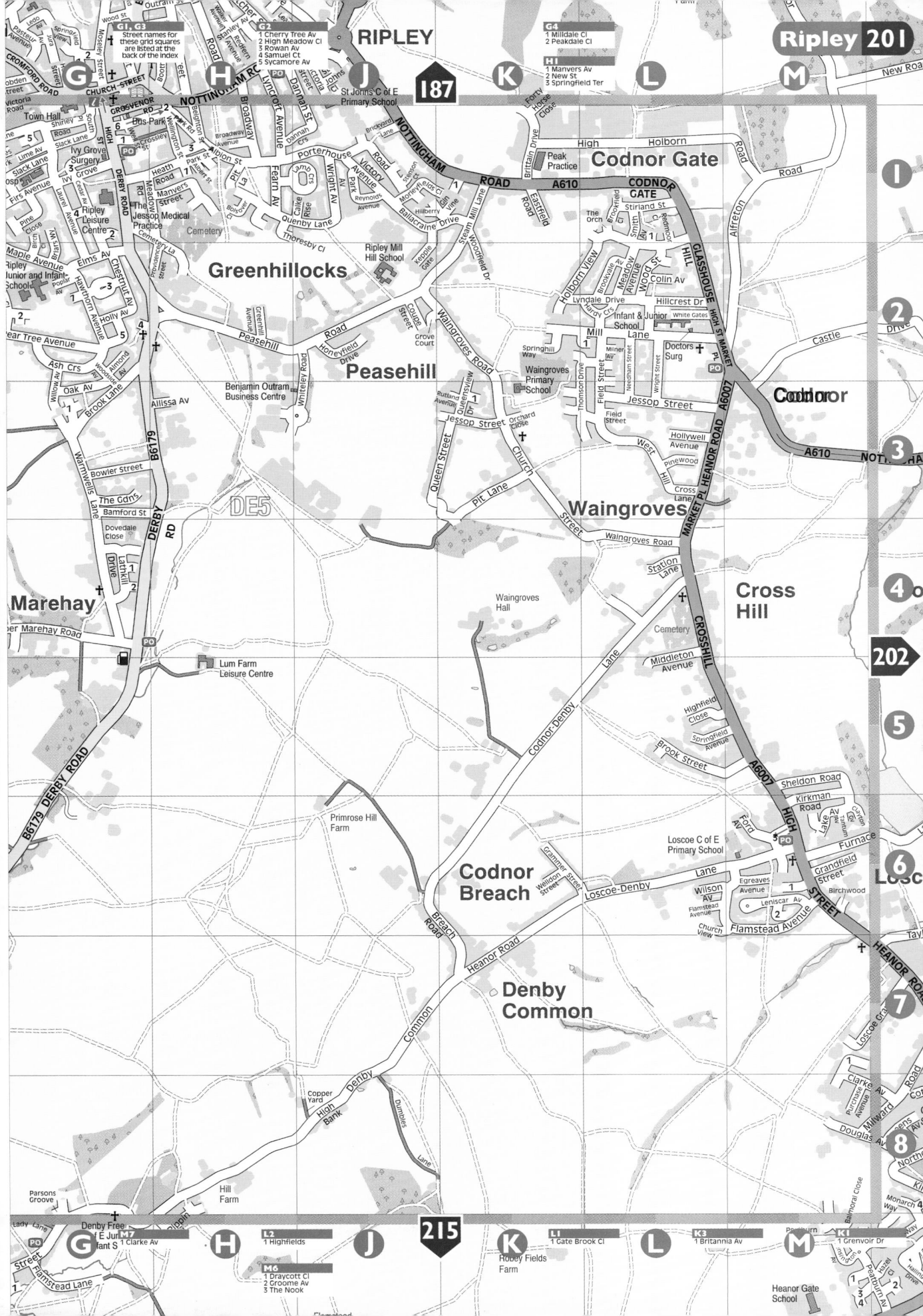

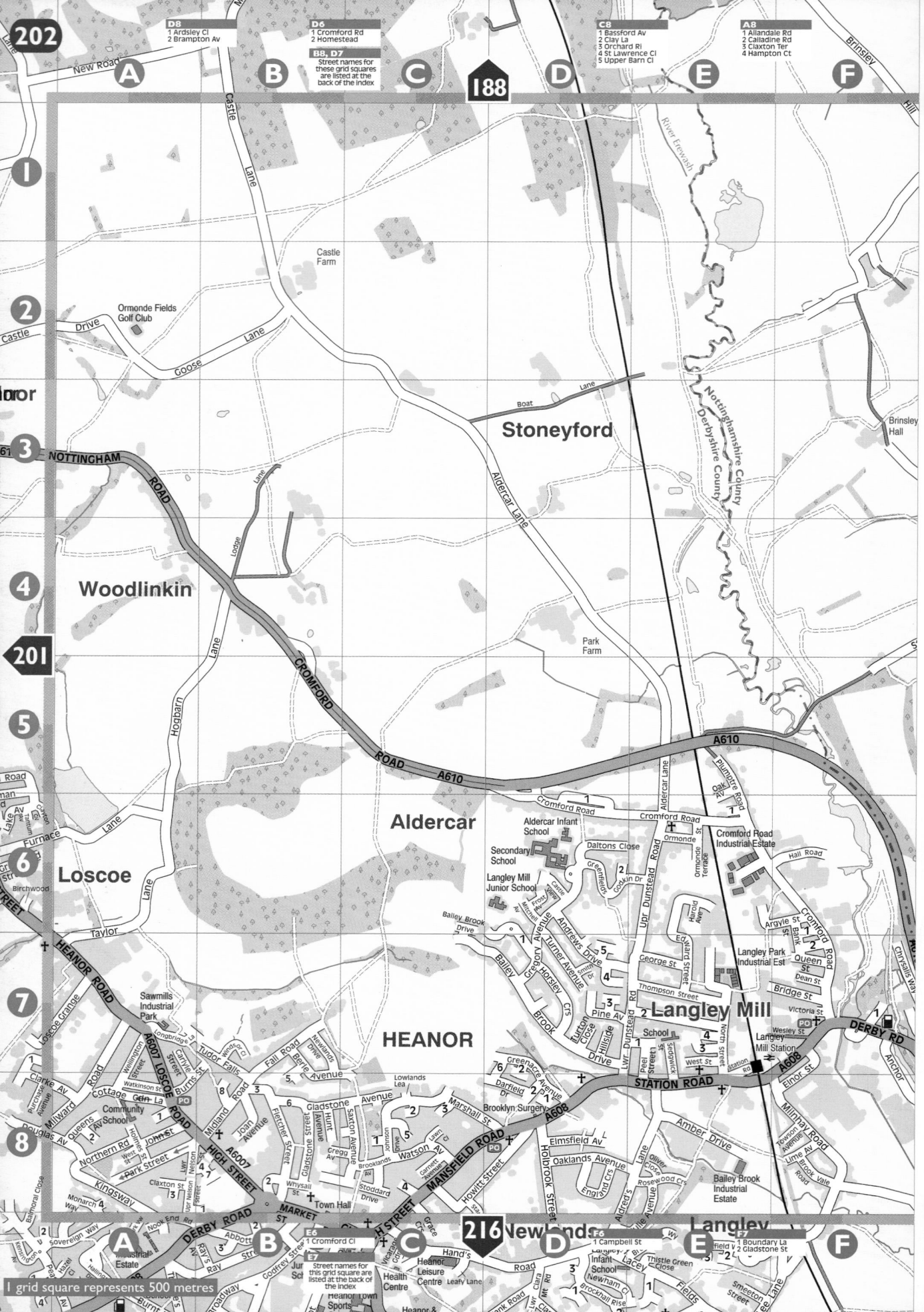

1 grid square represents 500 metres

G **P** **H** Spot **J** **189** **K** **L** **M**

I

New Brinsley

Frances Street

Main Street

Clumber Av

St John's Cl

Broad Oak Dr

James St

Hobs Cl

Lawrence Dr

The Moor

Cherry Tree Lane

Moor Road

Red Lane

Winter Closes

Underwood C. of E. Primary School

Main Crescent

Wilcox Drive

Mainside

WILLEY LANE

Felly Mill Lane (South)

Haggs Farm

Willey Spring

2

Queens Dr

Kings Dr

Brinsley Primary School

Brinsmoor Rd

Brinsley

CORDY LANE

CHURCH LANE

A608

B600

High Park Wood

3

NG16

WILLEY

Willey Wood Farm

LANE

Oaks Farm

Moorgreen Reservoir

4

Hall Lane

Coney

Clinton Avenue

Church Walk

Mill Farm

Lamb Close

Nature Reserve

Lamb Close Drive

5

MANSFIELD ROAD

Coneygrey Farm

MOORGREEN

6

Cockerhouse Road

Eastwood Hall

Eastwood Town Cricket Club

Moorgreen Ind Park

Engine Lane

B600

M

EASTWOOD

A608

Park Crs

Thorpe Road

Coach Drive

Robey Drive

Greenhills Road

Green Friar

Three Tun Gdns

Robey Close

Garden Road

Lower Beauvale

Dorothy Av

Kirby Rd

Brunel Avenue

Bosworth Drive

Hackworth Cl

Lindley St

Telford Drive

Metcalf Road

7

Beauvale

MOORGREEN

B6010

Meadowbank Way

Dawlish Court

Eastwood Comprehensive School

Coppice Drive

Princes Street

Grange View

Moorfields Avenue

Estwic Av

Atherfield Gardens

Wood Street

Lynncroft Primary School

Lower School

Walker Street

Kirby Street

Mill Street

Beauvale Road

Greasley Beauvale D H Lawrence Infant School

Greasley Sports Centre

Greasley Beauvale Junior School

DOVECOTE ROAD

8

NEW DERBY ROAD

A608 DERBY ROAD

Bailey

Scalby Cl

South Street

GV Road

Blackthorne Ct

Larch Crs

Woodland Way

Ivy Lane

Church Street

Ratcliffe Street

Swift Street

Medical Cen

Parkham Gallery

Eastwood Junior School

The Surgery

The Lawrence Mus

Community College

Midland Road

Pickering

William Av

Queens Road N

Plumptre Way

Nottingham Road

Broxtowe Borough Council

Lawrence Av

Parkview Surg

Three Tunes Road

Percy Street

Lynncroft

Norman Crs

The Crs

Edward Rd

Barber St

Abbey Road

Vale Close

Fairdale

Oakdale

Richmond

Heather

Dunster Road

Hazelwood

Peters

Bartons Close

Greenacres Close

Eastwood Health Cen

Hill Top

B6010

Brookhill Junior

Brookhill Leys Infant School

Newthorpe

G **H** **L7** **J** **217** **K** **K7** **L** **J7** **M**

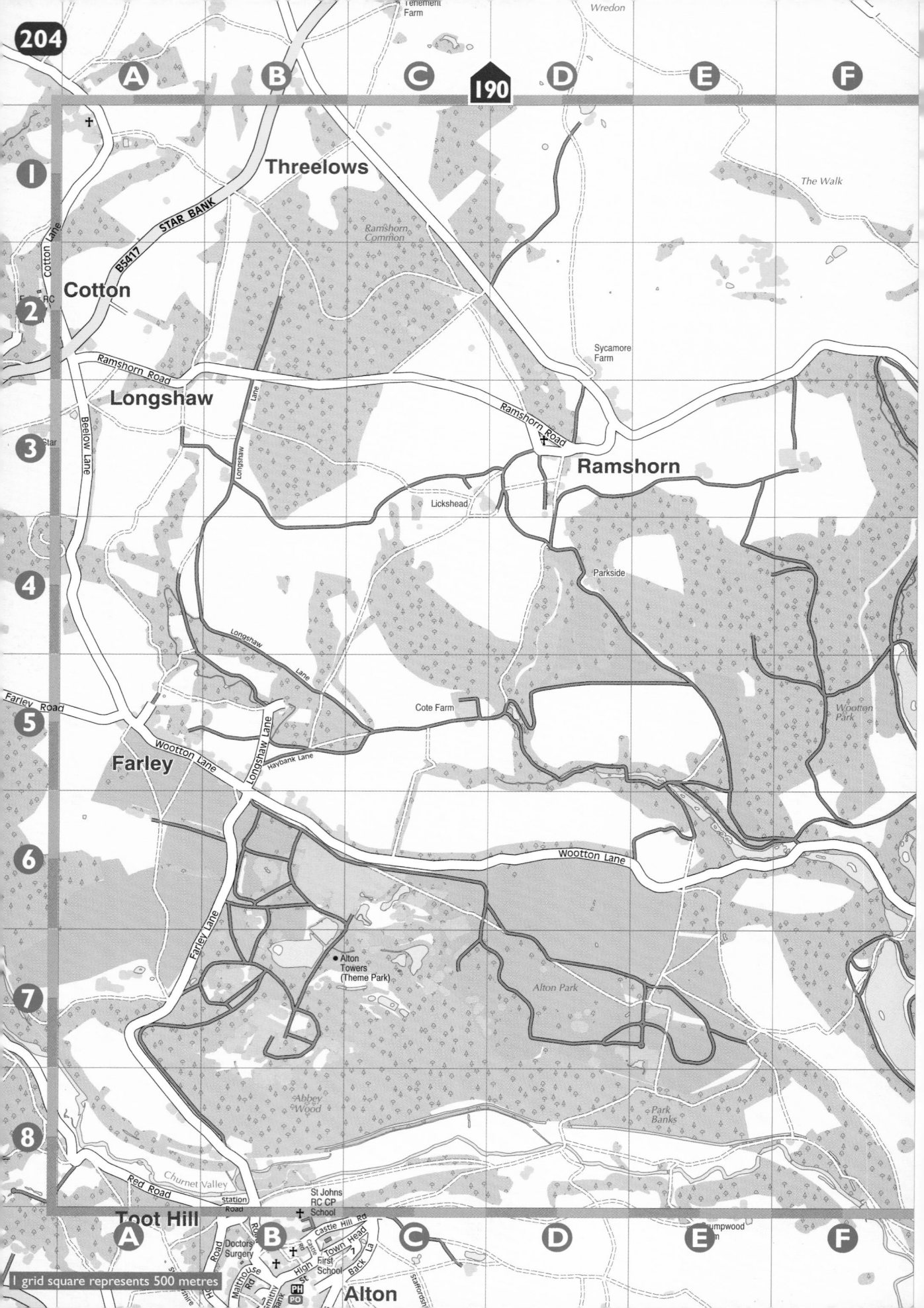

190

A B C D E F

I

Threelows

2 Cotton

RC

B5417 STAR BANK Cotton Lane

Wredon

The Walk

Ramshorn Common

Ramshorn Road Sycamore Farm

Ramshorn Road Longshaw

3 Longshaw Beelow Lane Star

Lane

Lickshead

Ramshorn

4 Parkside

Longshaw Lane

5 Farley Road Wootton Lane Cote Farm Wootton Park

Farley Longshaw Lane Haybank Lane

6 Wootton Lane

Farley Lane

7 Alton Towers (Theme Park) Alton Park

8 Abbey Wood Park Banks

Churnet Valley Red Road Station Road

Toot Hill St Johns RC CP School Castle Hill Rd Trumpwood

Maltshouse Rd High St Town Head Back La Staffordsh

Smithy Bank PH PO First School

Alton

A B C D E F

1 grid square represents 500 metres

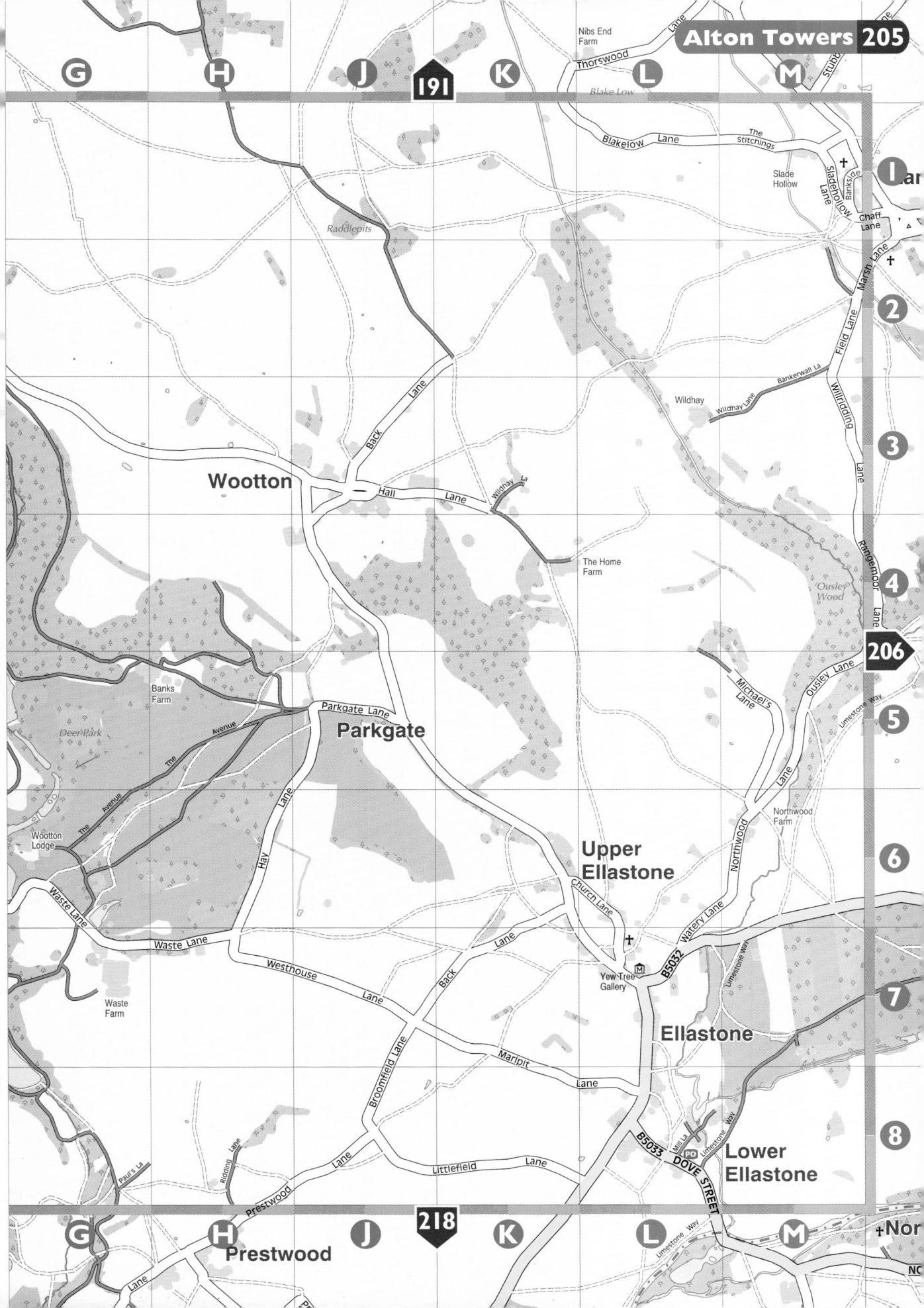

G H J **191** K L M

Nibs End Farm
Thorswood
Blake Low

Blakelow Lane
The stitchings

Slade Hollow
Sladehollow Lane
Banks de
Chaff Lane

I lar

Marsh Lane

Field Lane

2

Raddlepits

Wildhay
Wildhay Lane
Bankerwall La
Willridding Lane

3

Back Lane

Wootton
Hall Lane
Wildhay La
The Home Farm

Rangemoor Lane
'Ousley Wood

4

206

Michael's Lane
Ousley Lane
Limestone Way

5

Banks Farm
Deer Park
Avenue

Parkgate Lane

Parkgate

Northwood Farm

6

Wootton Lodge
The Avenue

Upper Ellastone
Church Lane

Northwood Lane
Watery Lane

Hay Lane
Waste Lane

Waste Lane
Westhouse Lane

Back Lane

+

Yew Tree Gallery
B5032

Ellastone

Limestone Way

7

Waste Farm

Broomfield Lane
Ridding Lane

Marlpit Lane

B5033
Mill La
PO
DOVE STREET
Limestone Way

Lower Ellastone

8

Paul's La

Prestwood Lane

Littlefield Lane

G H J **218** K L M +Nor

Prestwood

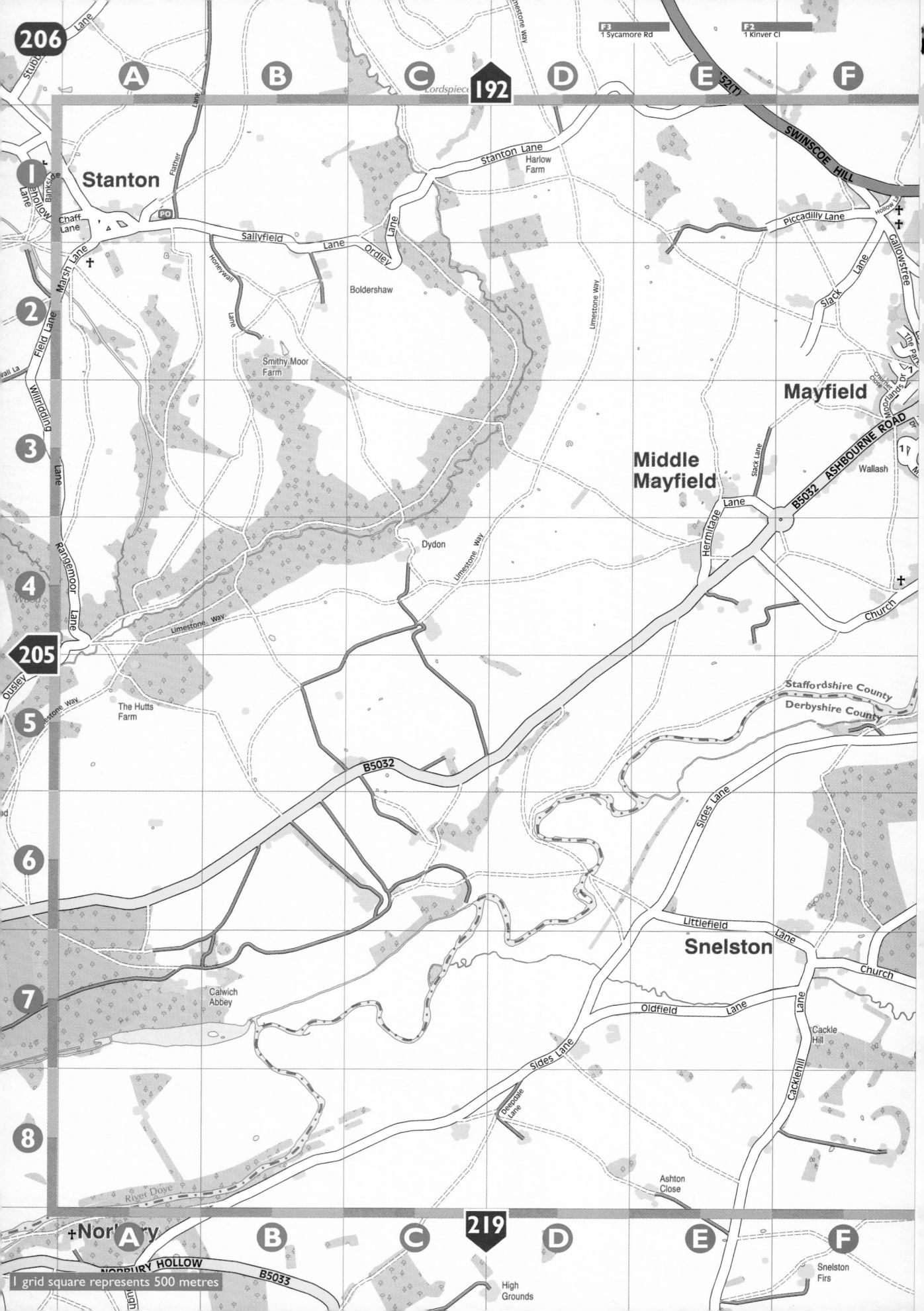

A B C **192** D E F

192

1 Sycamore Rd   F3
1 Kinver Cl   F2

SWINSCOE HILL
52(T)

1

Stanton
Banks Lane
Hollow La
Piccadilly Lane
Gallowstree La

2
Marsh Lane
Chaff Lane
Sallyfield   Lane   Lane
Ordley
Honeywall
Lane
Boldershaw
Stanton Lane
Harlow Farm
Limestone Way
Slack Lane
The Park

Mayfield

3
Willridding Lane
Smithy Moor Farm
Rangemoor Lane
Middle Mayfield
Slack Lane
B5032 ASHBOURNE ROAD
Wallash

4
Wood
Limestone   Way
Dydon
Limestone   Way
Hermitage   Lane
Church

205
Ousley
Limestone   Way
The Hutts Farm
Staffordshire County
Derbyshire County

5

B5032

6
Sides   Lane
Littlefield   Lane

7
Calwich Abbey
Snelston
Oldfield   Lane
Lane
Church
Lane
Cackle Hill
Cacklehill

8
Sides   Lane
Deepdale Lane
Ashton Close
Snelston Firs

Nor Ay   A   B   **219**   C   D   E   F

NORBURY HOLLOW
B5033
High Grounds

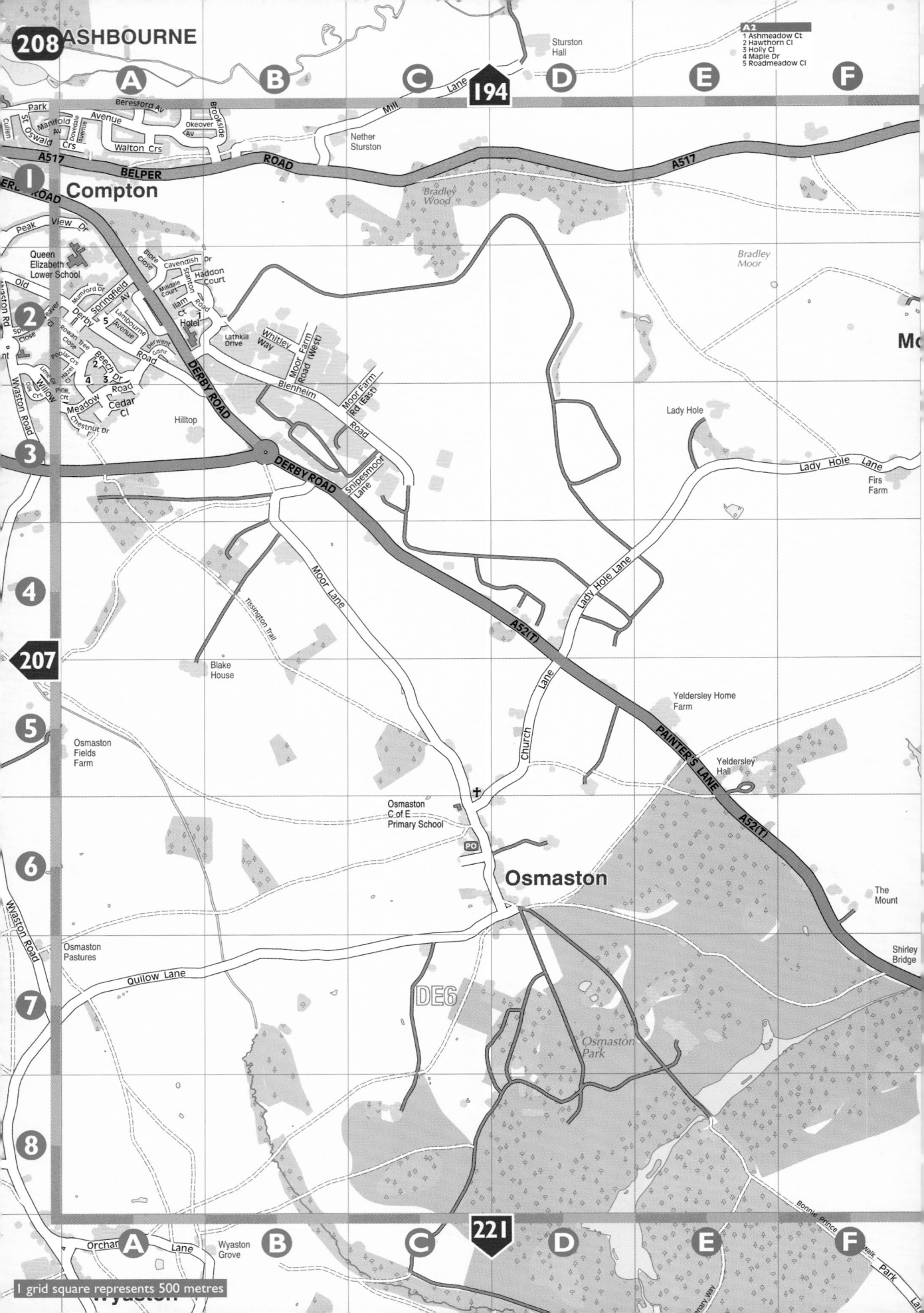

Hulla

G   H   J   K   L   M

A517

195

I

Bradley
Pastures

Yew

Crowtrees

Tree

Bradley

The
Knob

2

Lane

Houghpark

Hole in
the Wall

Bradley C of E
Primary School

Pinfold   Lane

Brunswood

orend

Hadley

Lane

Lane

3

Milldam Lane

Dogkennel Lane

Old Hall
Farm

Yeldersley Lane

4

nneyford Brook

210

Rough Lane

Yeldersley Lane

Bradley
Oldpark

5

**Yeldersley
Hollies**

6

Coppice
Farm

Rough

Lane

Knowles
Fine Art
Gallery M

Knowles
Farm

7

Alder
Carr

PAINTER'S LANE

Shirley
Common

St Mary's
Home

8

Hall Lane

A52(T)

222

PAINTE   LANE

G   H   J   K   L   M

Brick Kiln

Yeldersley

Ednaston
Manor

Birch
House

Bratsl

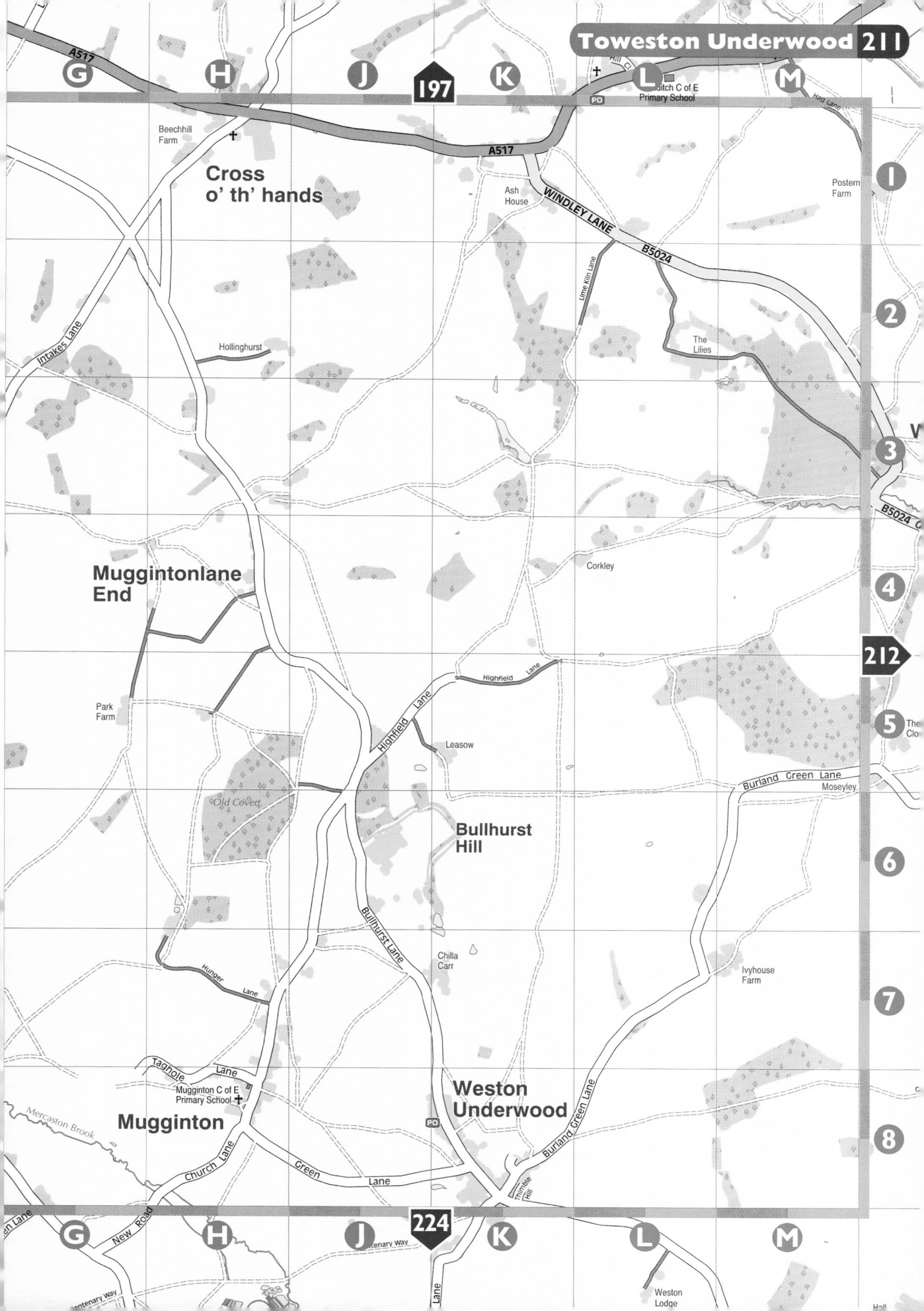

G H J **197** K L M

A517

Beechhill
Farm

Cross
o' th' hands

Ash
House

WINDLEY LANE

B5024

Lime Kiln Lane

Postern
Farm

Dutch C of E
Primary School

PO

Hag Lane

Hollinghurst

The
Lilies

Intakes Lane

Muggintonlane
End

Corkley

B5024

212

Highfield Lane

Park
Farm

Leasow

Highfield Lane

The
Clo

Burland Green Lane

Moseyley

Old Covert

**Bullhurst
Hill**

Chilla
Carr

Ivyhouse
Farm

Bullhurst Lane

Hunger
Lane

Taghole Lane

Mugginton C of E
Primary School

Mugginton

**Weston
Underwood**

PO

Burland Green Lane

Mercaston Brook

Church Lane

Green Lane

Thimble Hill

G New Road H J **224** K L M

Centenary Way

Weston
Lodge

I 2 3 4 5 6 7 8

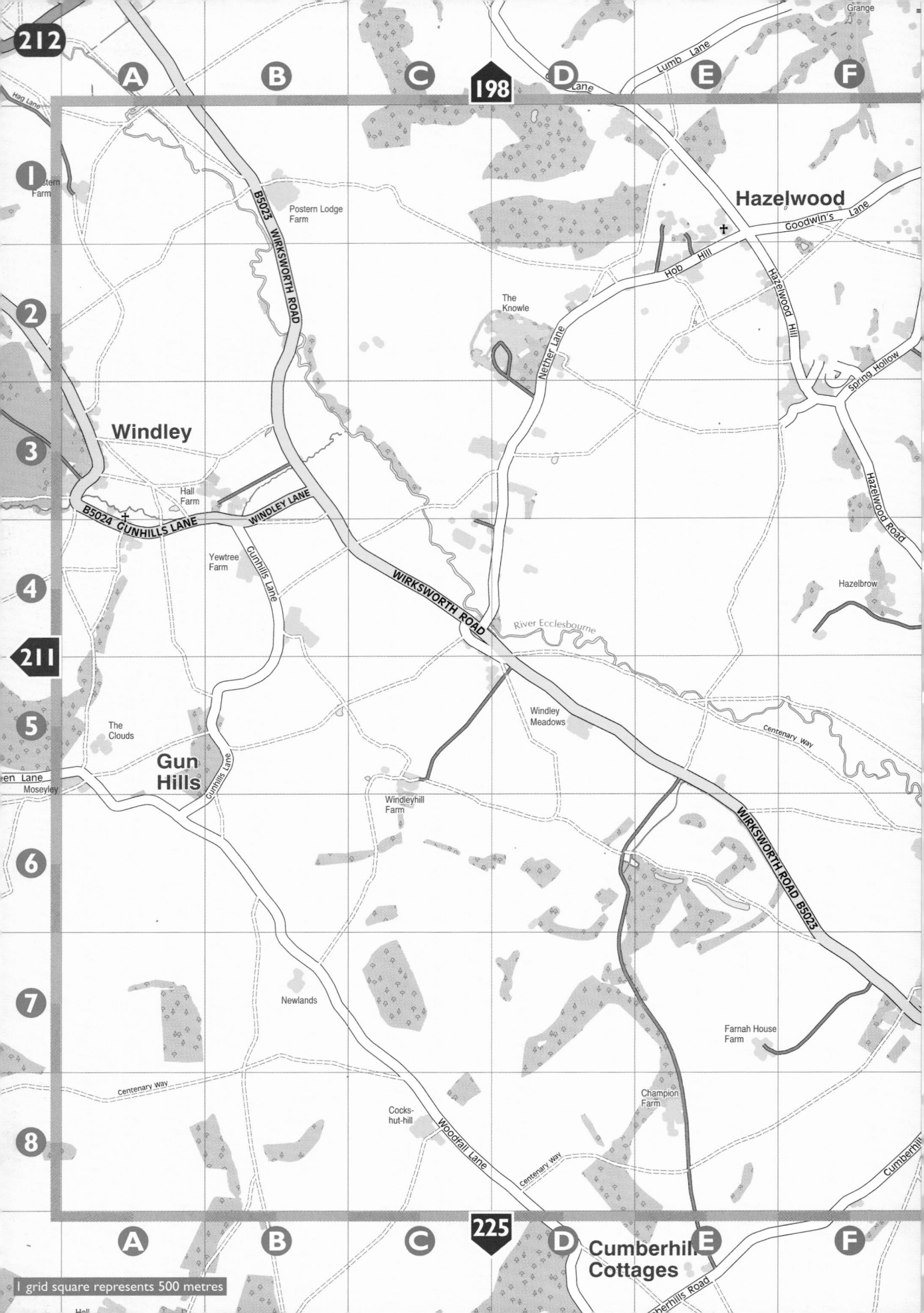

212

A **B** **C** **D** **E** **F**

198

1

Hag Lane

Postern
Farm

Hazelwood

2

B5023 WIRKSWORTH ROAD

Postern Lodge
Farm

The Knowle

Hob Hill

Goodwin's Lane

Hazelwood Hill

Lumb Lane

Grange

3

Windley

Hall
Farm

B5024 GUNHILLS LANE

WINDLEY LANE

Nether Lane

Spring Hollow

Hazelwood Road

4

Yewtree
Farm

Gunhills Lane

WIRKSWORTH ROAD

River Ecclesbourne

Hazelbrow

211

5

The
Clouds

Gun
Hills

Gunhills Lane

Windley
Meadows

Centenary Way

Green Lane
Moseyley

6

Windleyhill
Farm

WIRKSWORTH ROAD B5023

Farnah House
Farm

7

Newlands

Champion
Farm

8

Centenary Way

Cocks-
hut-hill

Woodfall Lane

Centenary Way

Cumberhill

A **B** **C** **D** **E** **F**

225

Cumberhill
Cottages

Cumberhills Road

1 grid square represents 500 metres

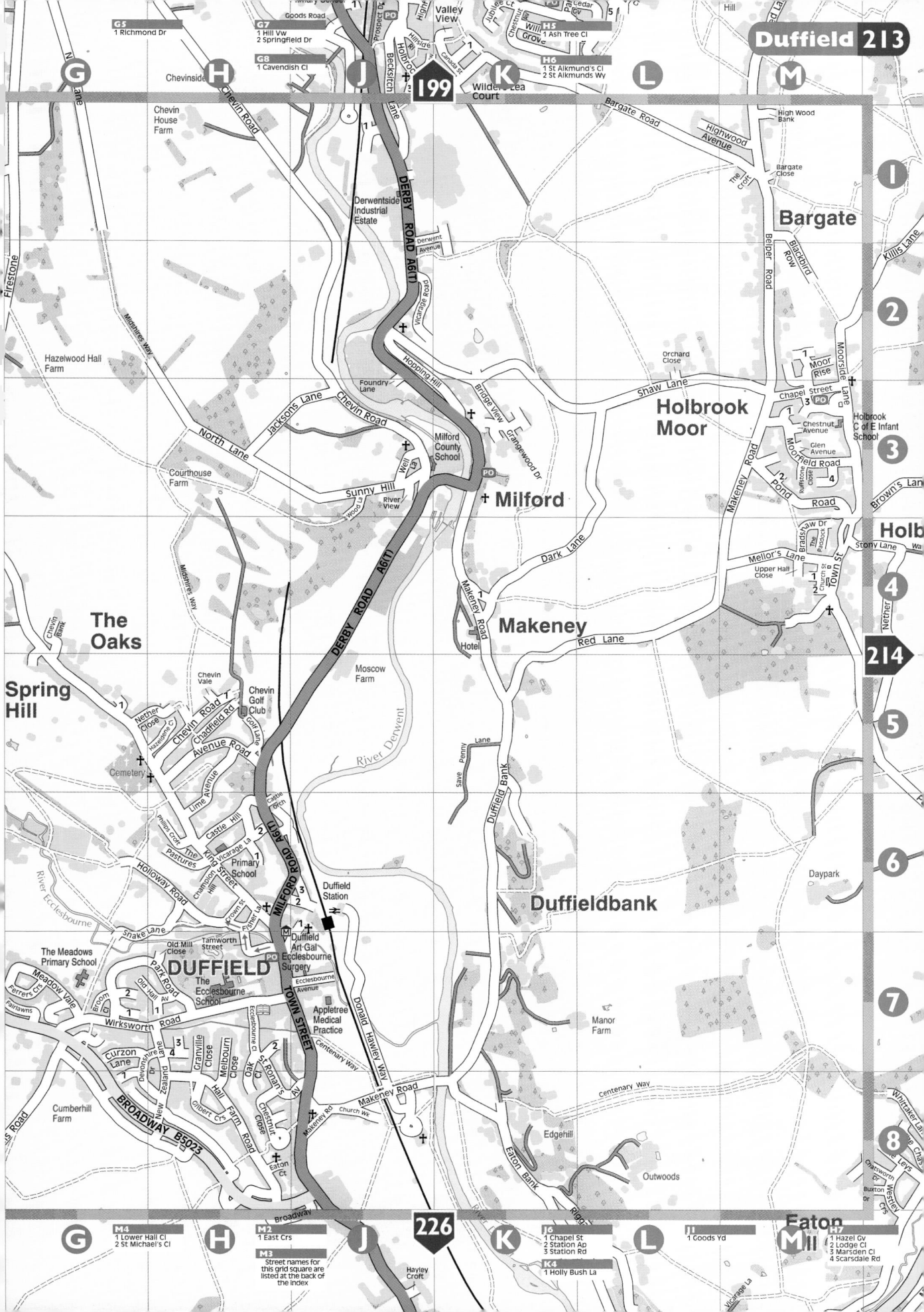

G H J 201 K L M

G1
1 Oaklands Cl

G4
1 The Orchard

J4
1 Richardson Dr

Parsons
Groove

Lady
Lane

PO

Street

Flamstead Lane

Denby Free
C of E Junior
& Infant School

Pippin
Hill

Flamstead
House

Robey Fields
Farm

Heanor Gate
School

Peatburn
Avenue

Heanor Gate

Adale Rd

Marina
Road

The Grange

The Beeches

Twyford
Close

Sinclair
Close

HEANOR ROAD

Holly Mount
Farm

A608

Old Pit Lane

Redmoor
Farm

Hirst
Farm

Meadow
Close

Cem

CHURCH LANE

Horsley
Woodhouse
Primary Sch

A609

Calladine
Lane

Stainsby
Avenue

DOBHOLES LANE

MAIN ROAD

PO

Kerry Drive

Dix Av

Radford
Road

Stafford
Cl

Richardson Endowed
Primary School

Smalley

Prospect
Farm

216

Vicarage
Cl

Glebe Av

Wilmot Drive

Laurel
Crs

St Johns
Road

Pine
Close

Stainsby
House

Bell Lane

Wood Lane

Whitehouse
Farm

Bell Lane

Woodside

Smalley
Hall

MAIN ROAD

A608

Smalley
Green

Woodside

Hill

Smalley
Common

Simonfield

ILKESTON ROAD A609

Spencer
Street

Glendon
Drive

Simon Fields
Close

Tansley Avenue

BELPER ROAD

G H J 228 K L M

M1
1 Banksburn Cl
2 Kings Cl
3 Platts Av
4 Poynter Cl

K8
1 Blunt St
2 Oakfield Ct

Primary
School

PO

Barker Close

G H J **206** K L M

I

+Norbury

NORBURY HOLLOW   B5033

Snelston
Firs

2

River Dove

Roughlow Lane

Bowlingalley Lane

Mill Lane

Lid Lane

Lid Lane

Bag Lane

Greenlane
Farm

High
Grounds

GREEN

LANE   B5033

Shapes Lane

Virginsalley Lane

**Snelston
Common**

COCKSHEAD

3

Norbury C of E
Primary School

Roston

The Hollow

PO

**Roston
Common**

Birchwood
Park

4

220

Birchwoodmoor

5

Hollies Lane

Hollies Lane

6

Woodhay
Farm

Sand
Farm

Long
Chimneys

7

Marston
Park

Daisybank
Farm

8

G **H** Thurvaston **J** **233** K L M

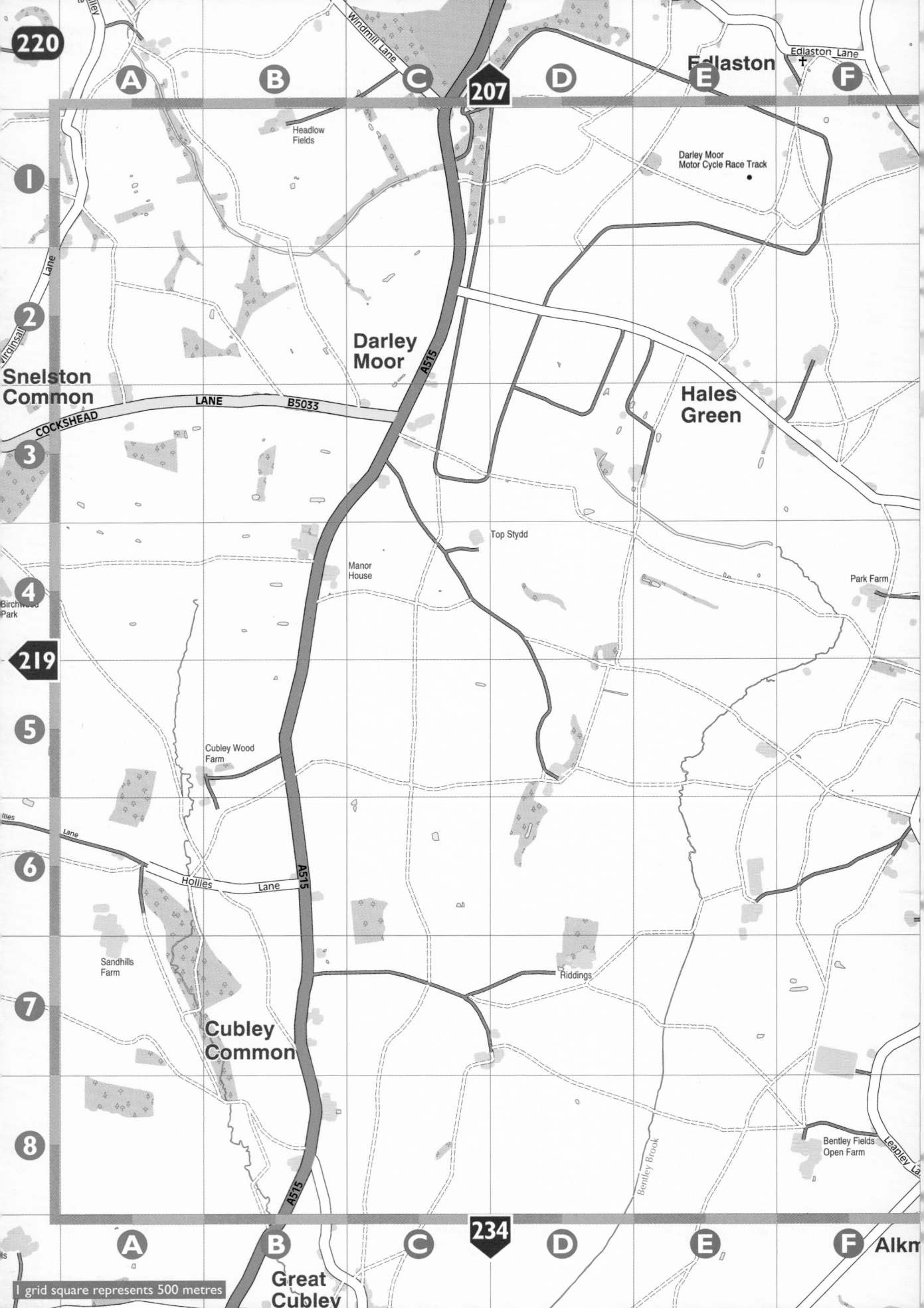

220

A   B   C   207   D   E   F

Edlaston

Edlaston Lane

1

Darley Moor
Motor Cycle Race Track

2

Snelston
Common

COCKSHEAD   LANE   B5033

Darley
Moor

Hales
Green

3

Top Stydd

Manor
House

Park Farm

4

Birchwood
Park

219

5

Cubley Wood
Farm

A515

6

Hollies   Lane   A515

Sandhills
Farm

Riddings

7

Cubley
Common

8

Bentley Fields
Open Farm

Bentley Brook

Leapley La

A   B   C   234   D   E   F   Alkm

Great
Cubley

1 grid square represents 500 metres

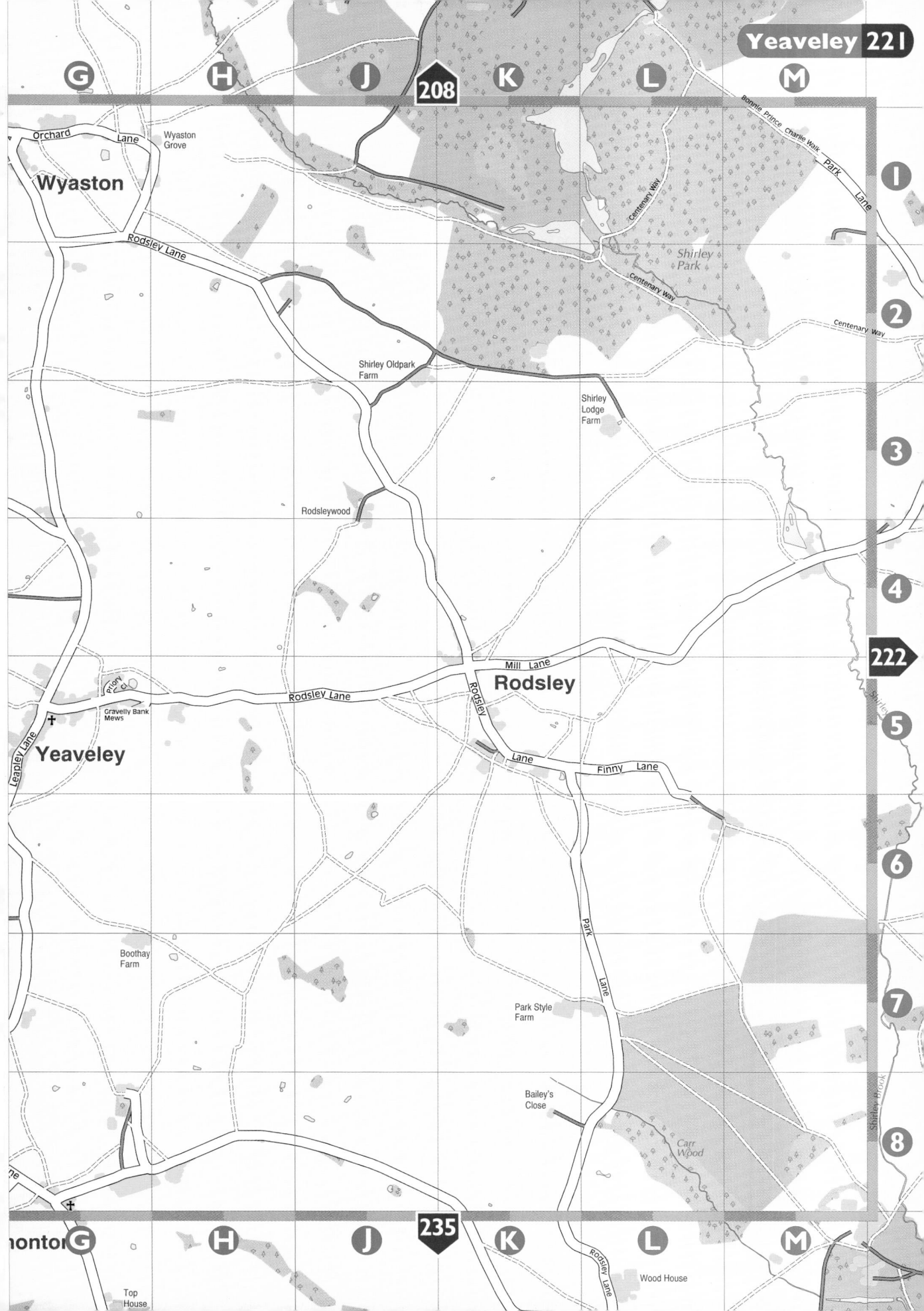

G H J K L M

208

I
2
3
4
222
5
6
7
8

Orchard Lane
Wyaston Grove
Wyaston
Rodsley Lane

Bonnie Prince Charlie Walk
Park Lane
Centenary Way
Shirley Park
Centenary Way
Centenary Way

Shirley Oldpark Farm
Shirley Lodge Farm

Rodsleywood

Mill Lane
Rodsley
Rodsley Lane
Rodsley Lane

Prion Cl
Gravelly Bank Mews
Yeaveley
Leapley Lane

Rodsley Lane
Finny Lane

Shirley

Boothay Farm

Park Lane

Park Style Farm

Bailey's Close

Shirley Brook

Carr Wood

monton G H J K L M

235

Wood House

Top House

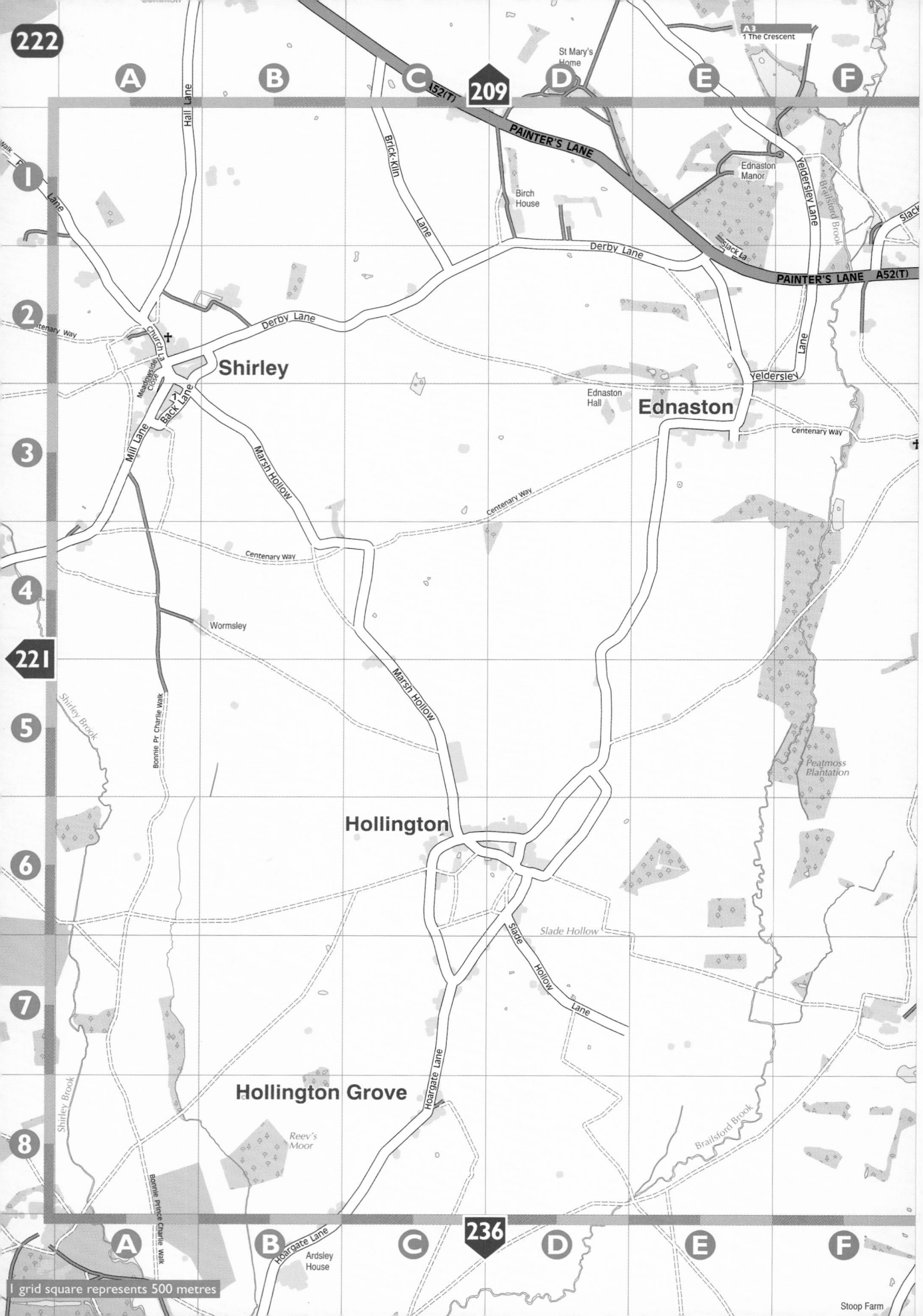

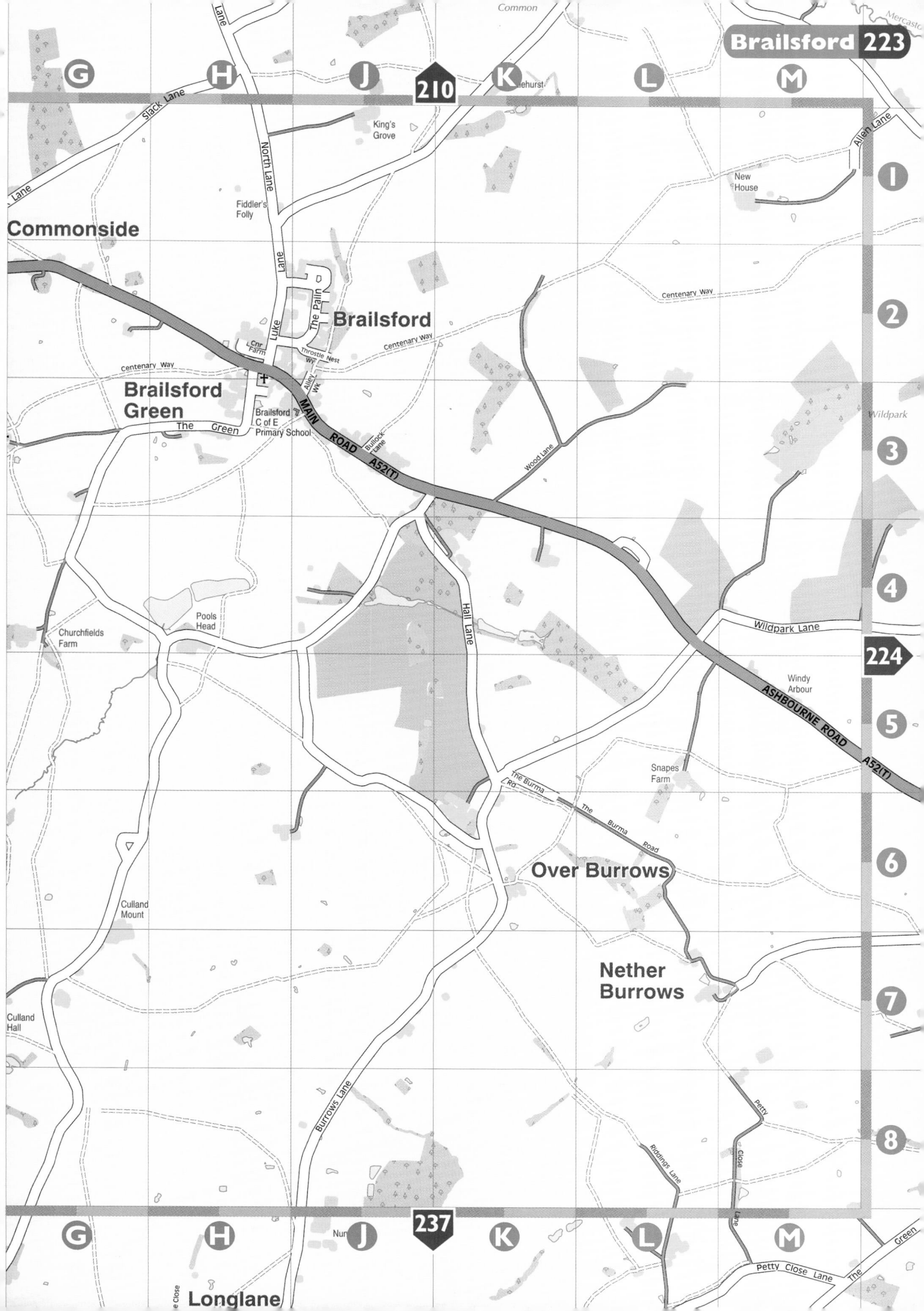

G   H   J   **210**   K   L   M

Common

Slack Lane

Lane

North Lane

King's Grove

Allen Lane

Mercasto

New House

1

Fiddler's Folly

Luke Lane

The Palm

Commonside

Brailsford

Centenary Way

2

Cnr Farm

Throstle Nest

Centenary Way

Centenary Way

Brailsford Green

Brailsford C of E Primary School

Alley Wk

Bullock Lane

Wood Lane

Wildpark

3

The Green

MAIN ROAD A52(T)

Hall Lane

4

Wildpark Lane

Pools Head

Churchfields Farm

Windy Arbour

224

ASHBOURNE ROAD A52(T)

5

The Burma Rd

Snapes Farm

Culland Mount

The Burma Road

Over Burrows

6

Culland Hall

Nether Burrows

7

Petty

Burrows Lane

Riddings Lane

Close Lane

8

G   H   **237**   J   K   L   M

Nun

Petty Close Lane

The Green

Close

Longlane

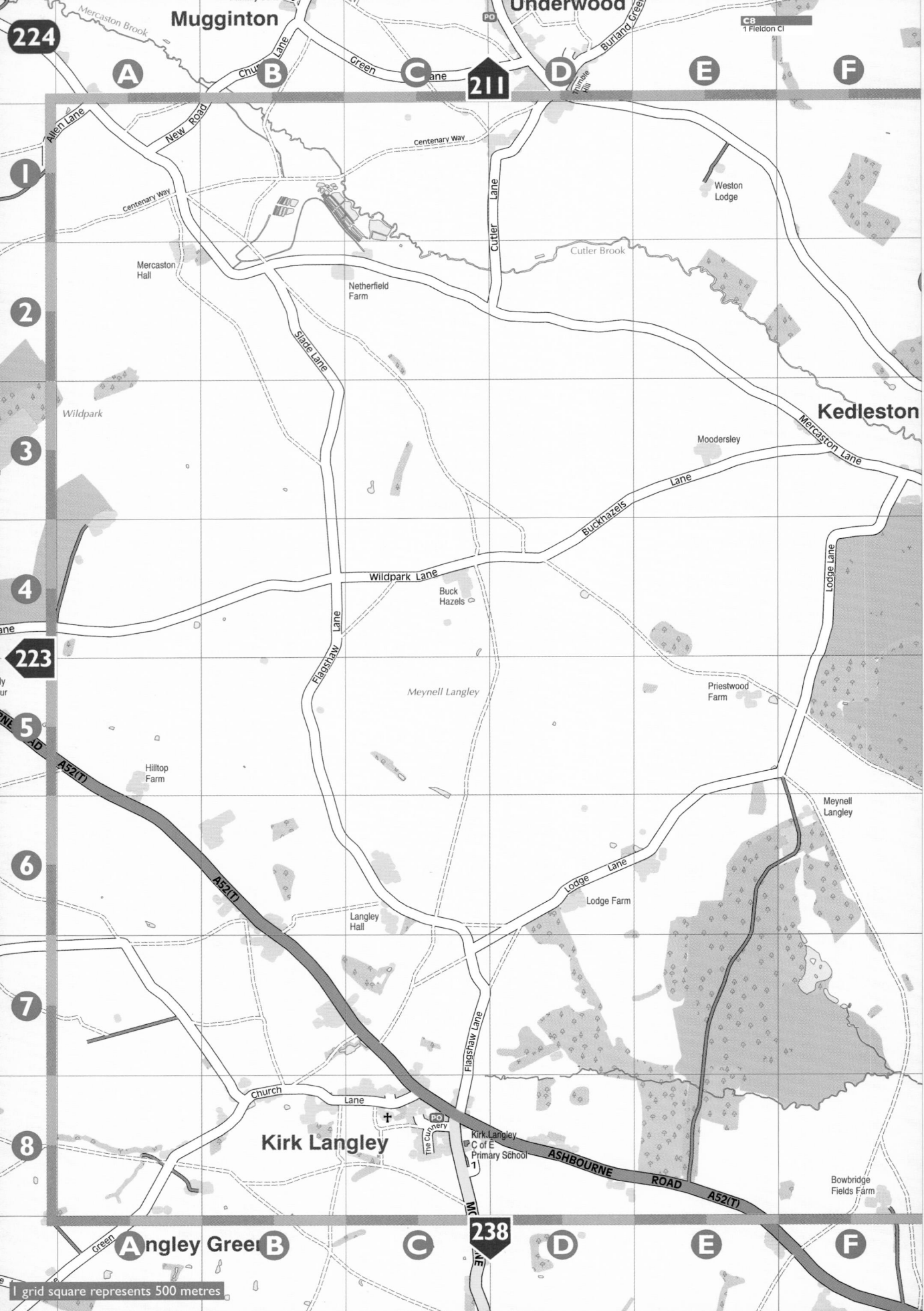

M5
1 Old Vicarage La

M7
1 Netherwood Ct
2 Rosemount Ct

M8
1 Bellingham Ct
2 Quarndon Heights
3 Quarndon Vw
4 Ribblesdale Cl
5 Stoodley Pike Gdns
6 Widdybank Cl

Cocks-hut-hill

Woodfall Lane

Centenary Way

Cumberhills Cottages

Cumberhills Road

Hall Close

Beech Avenue

Park Nook

Ireton Farm

Kedleston Road

Quarndon Hill

The Common

Quarndon

Coach Drive

Hay Wood

Kedleston Road

Kedleston Park Golf Club

Golf Course

Primary School

Barn Cl

Church Road

226

Kedleston Park

Inn Lane

Old Church Cl

Brook Cl

Kedleston Hall (NT)

Kedleston Road

Crabtree Cl

Curzon

Bancroft Dr

Cobthorn

Ravensdale Rd

Ashbrook

Blenheim

Hardwick AV

Kingsley

Drive

Askerfield Avenue

Quarn Drive

Upper Vicarwood

Welbeck Grove

Scarsdale AV

Haddon

DE22

Somme Rd

Memorial Road

Lower Vicarwood

Menin Road

Kedleston Road

Lens Rd

Markeaton Brook

Ypres Road

Erewash Dr

Lambley Dr

Otterburn

Amber Road

City of Derby

Derbyshire County

Markeaton Stones

Kedleston Road

Carsington

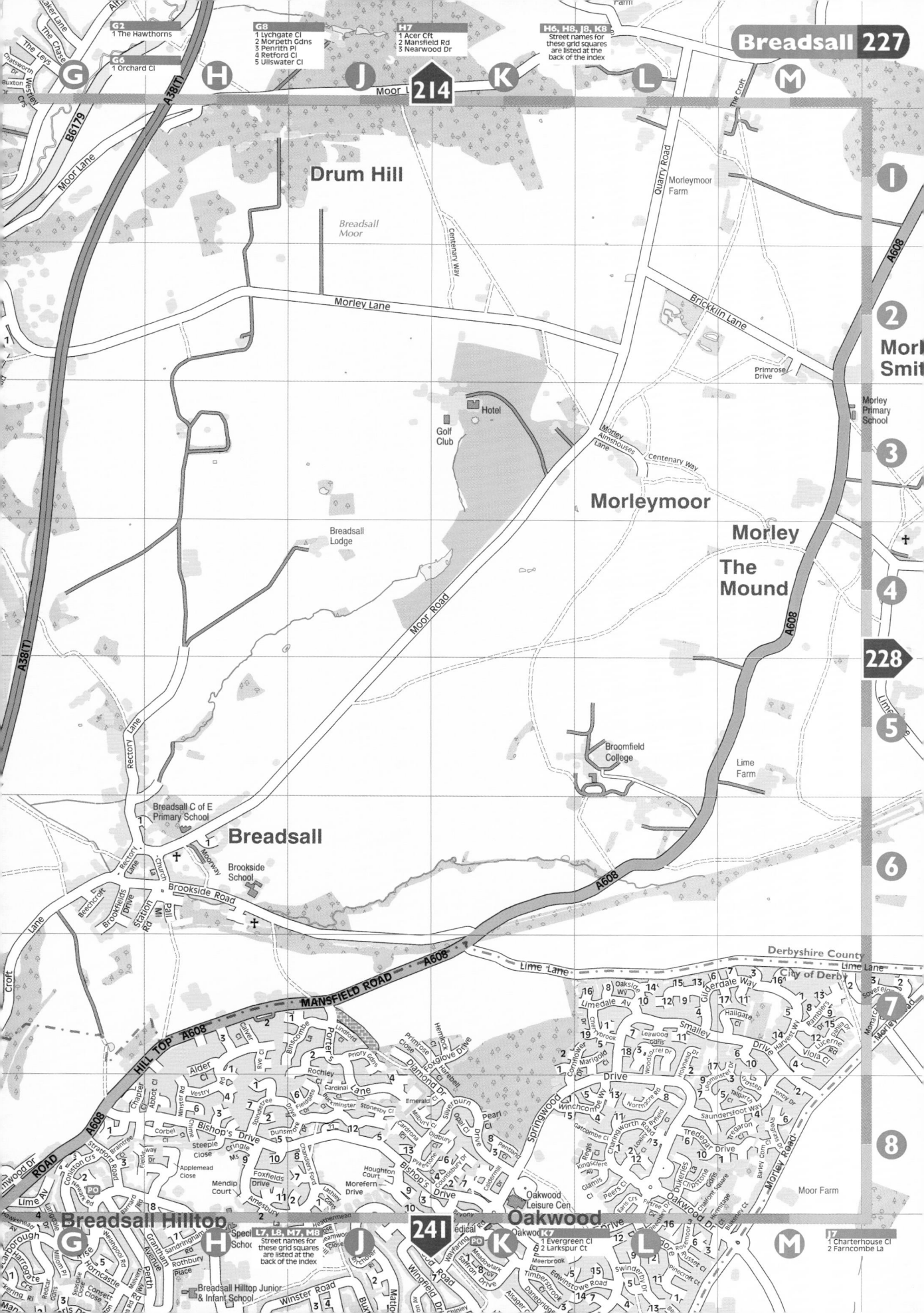

G **H** **J** 214 **K** **L** **M**

Moor Lane

1
A608

2
Mor
Smit

3

4

228

5

6

7

8

Drum Hill

Breadsall
Moor

Morley Lane

B6179

A38(T)

Moor Lane

Quarry Road

Morleymoor
Farm

Brickkiln Lane

Primrose
Drive

Morley
Primary
School

Morley
Primary
School

Golf
Club

Hotel

Morley
Almshouses
Lane

Centenary Way

Centenary Way

Morleymoor

Morley

**The
Mound**

Breadsall
Lodge

Moor Road

A608

Broomfield
College

Lime
Farm

Rectory Lane

Breadsall C of E
Primary School

Breadsall

Brookside
School

Brookside Road

Moorway

Church La

Station Rd

Mill

Pall

Beechcroft

Brookfields Drive

Lane

Croft

A608

Mansfield Road

A608

Lime Lane

Lime Lane

Derbyshire County
City of Derby

The Croft

The Leys

Chatsworth
Westley
Buxton

Crs

Gt Dr

A38(T)

The Chase

Barker Lane

A608

A608

Breadsall Hilltop

G **H** 241 **J** **K** **L** **M**

Oakwood
Leisure Cen

Oakwood

Oakwood Dr

Morley Road

Moor Farm

Breadsall Hilltop Junior
& Infant School

Winster Road

Hill Top A608

A608 Road

Lime Av

PO

G2
1 Burnham Cl
2 Chertsey Ct
3 Richmond Cl
4 Sunninghill Cl
5 Twyford Cl
6 Weybridge Cl
7 Windsor Ct

H2
Street names for this grid square are listed at the back of the index

H3
1 Burncroft Pl
2 School Sq

Turnberry Close

216

243

230

Birkdale Close

Barli

Westfield
Holme Cl

Avenue

Knivetor Park

Nutbrook Trail

Nutbrook Trail

Centenary Way

D

Dallin
Prima
Scho

Sowb
Farm

Chatsworth Pl

A609 HIGH LANE CENTRAL

Lawcore Lane

HIGH LANE WEST

Kiln Cl

Lechlade Close

Surtwon Way

Whilton

Chiltern

Derbyshire Avenue

Basseton Cl

Eliver

2

2

Derwent Av

4

West Hallam

Etton Court

Newbridge Way

Walton

Marlowe Crs

Elizabeth

Henley

7

1

Hurley Court

3

5

Crescent

Hardwick

Peveril

Fernlea Close

6

Lathkill Close

Caversham Way

Hampton

Harlow Ct

Ashton

Kingstock

Scargill Road

Holme Cft

Scargill C of E Primary School

Nursery West

Centenary Way

Beech Lane

The Dales Medical Cen

Hallam Medical Cen

PO

Orchard Close

Cat And Fiddle Lane

The Village Hall Ct

Stanley Grange

Cat And Fiddle Lane

Cat & Fiddle Farm

A609

Hagg Lane

Hagg Farms

Arbour Hill

The Flourish

The Village

Croft Cl

Moor Lane

Gateway Christian School

Tattle Hl

Dale Abbey

Midshires Way

Midshires Way

Whitefurrows

Centenary Way

HIGH LANE EAST

A609

Nutbrook Cricket Club

Foxhole Farm

A6096 LADYWOOD ROAD

Ladywood Farm

Bassett Farm

Dale Moor

Woodpecker Hill

Dale Road

Grove Farm

Thacker Barn

Abbot Road

St John Houghton RC School

Sharp Close

Bunting Close

Friars Court

Windale Drive

Dumbles Close

Lock Close

Godfrey

Bankfield Drive

Sunningdale Dr

Bradfield

Oliver

Limetree Rise

Kirk Hallam

Highfield Drive

Ridgeway Drive

Coole Way

PO

Hillary Place

1

3

Avondale Rd

Ascot Cl

Tilton Cl

Ravondale Rd

Queen Elizabeth Tudor Place

Kenilworth

Windermere

Depedale Cl

Glendon Rd

Nuthall Circle

Wirksworth

Buckminster Rd

Thorpe Crs

Woolston Rd

Dallin Road

M5
1 Crosshill Dr
2 Festival Rd
3 Hardwick Pl
4 Meerbrook Pl
5 Ribblesdale

M4
1 Priory Cl
2 Westfield Cl

L5
1 Chatsworth Pl

A B C **218** D E Abbotsholme School ✝ F

Woodseat

1

B5030

Staffordshire County
Derbyshire County

River Dove

2

Sedsall

Havenhouse Farm

3

Brookend

Eaton Dovedale

Waldley

River Dove

Eaton Wood

4

B5030

Derbyshire County
Staffordshire County

5

Eaton Hall Farm

Upwoods Farm

6

Staffordshire Way

7

Holmlea Farm

Staffordshire County
Derbyshire County

8

A50(T)

A50

Upwoods Road

Derby

Field Farm

A B **248** C D E Marston Lane Babbs Lane F

Oak Dr
West Dr
Park Dr
Lake Dr
Crs East Dr
Cook Lane
Hawthorn Cl
Sand Lane
Marston Lane
Bak
Cross Coven

A50

River D

1 grid square represents 500 metres

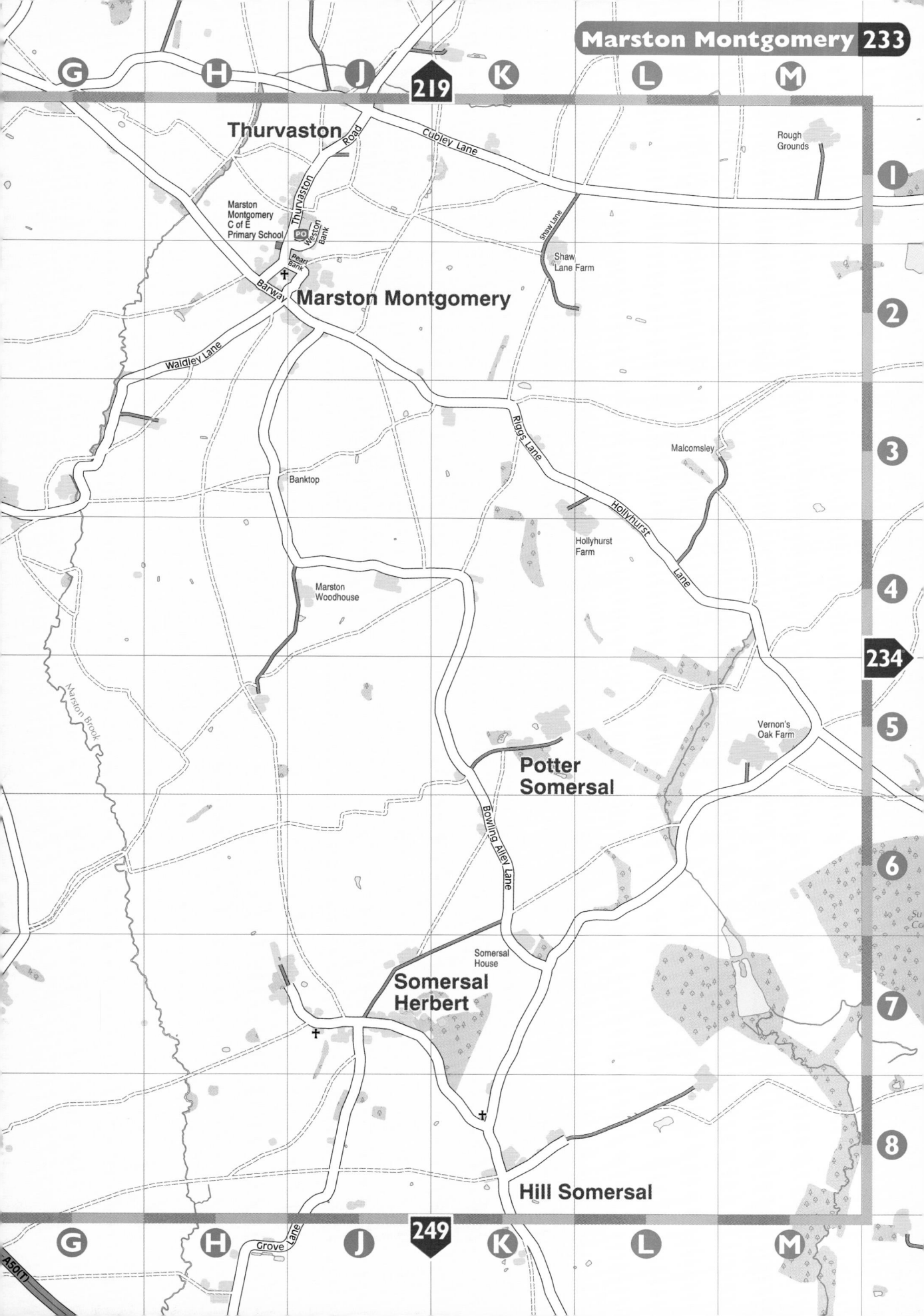

G H J 219 K L M

I

Thurvaston

Cubley Lane

Rough
Grounds

Marston
Montgomery
C of E
Primary School

PO

Weston
Bank

Shaw Lane

Shaw
Lane Farm

2

Pearl
Bank

Barway

Marston Montgomery

Waldley Lane

Riggs Lane

Malcomsley

3

Banktop

Hollyhurst
Farm

Hollyhurst Lane

234

Marston
Woodhouse

4

Marston Brook

Vernon's
Oak Farm

5

Potter
Somersal

Bowling Alley Lane

6

Somersal
House

Somersal
Herbert

7

Hill Somersal

8

G H Grove Lane J 249 K L M

A50(T)

G H J **221** K L M

Carr Wood

Rodsley Lane

Wood House

nonton

Top House Farm

Silverhill Farm

I

Longfo Paroch Primar

2

Longfo

3

Middleton Park

Alkmonton Old Hall

Ashbourne Road

Heathy Close

Mammerton

4

Dairy House Farm

236

Grove Farm

5

Boylestonfield

6

Barton

ylestone

7

Bartonpark

Gorsty Fields

8

Sapperton

Barton Hall

G H J **251** K L M

Lodg Farm

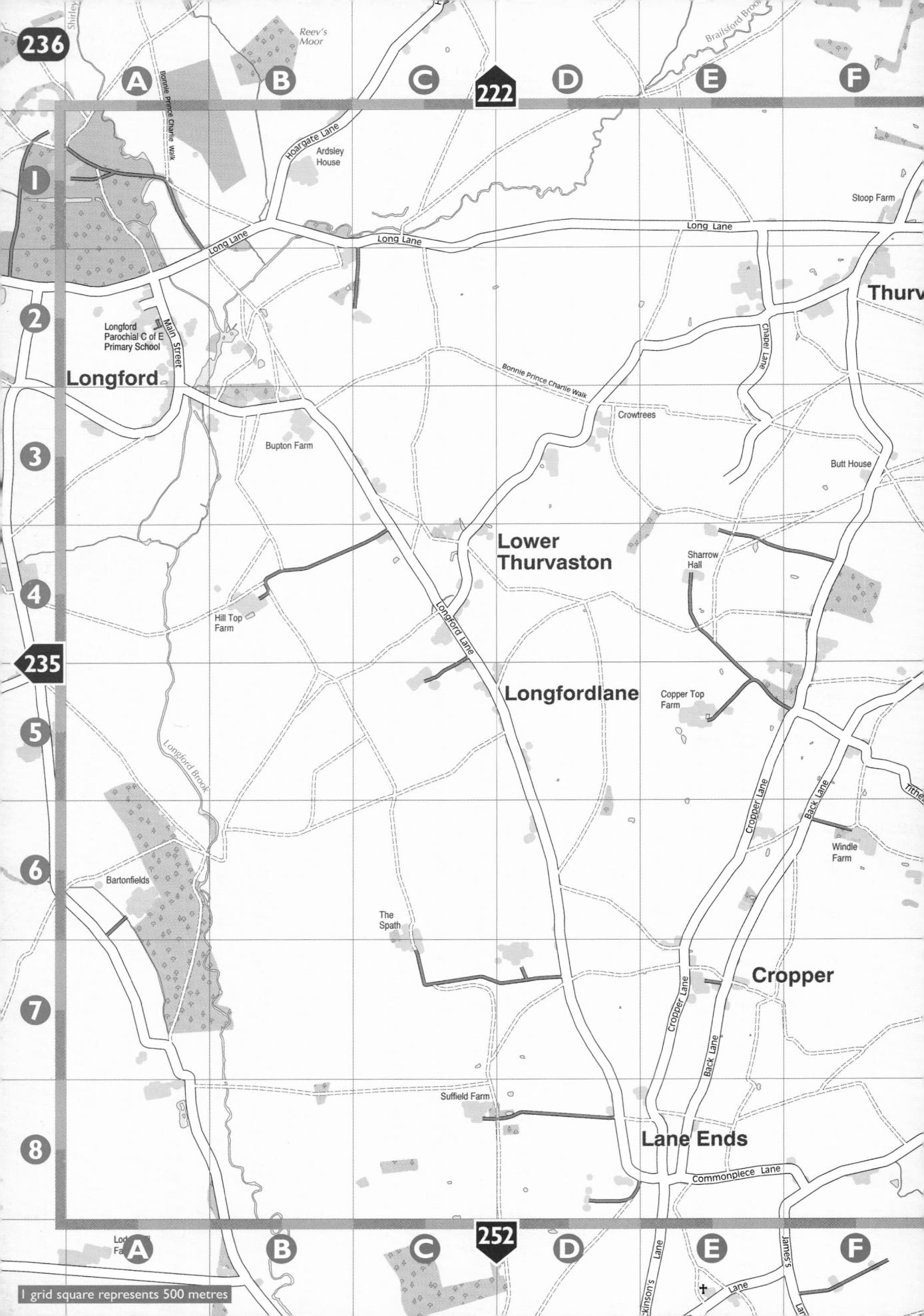

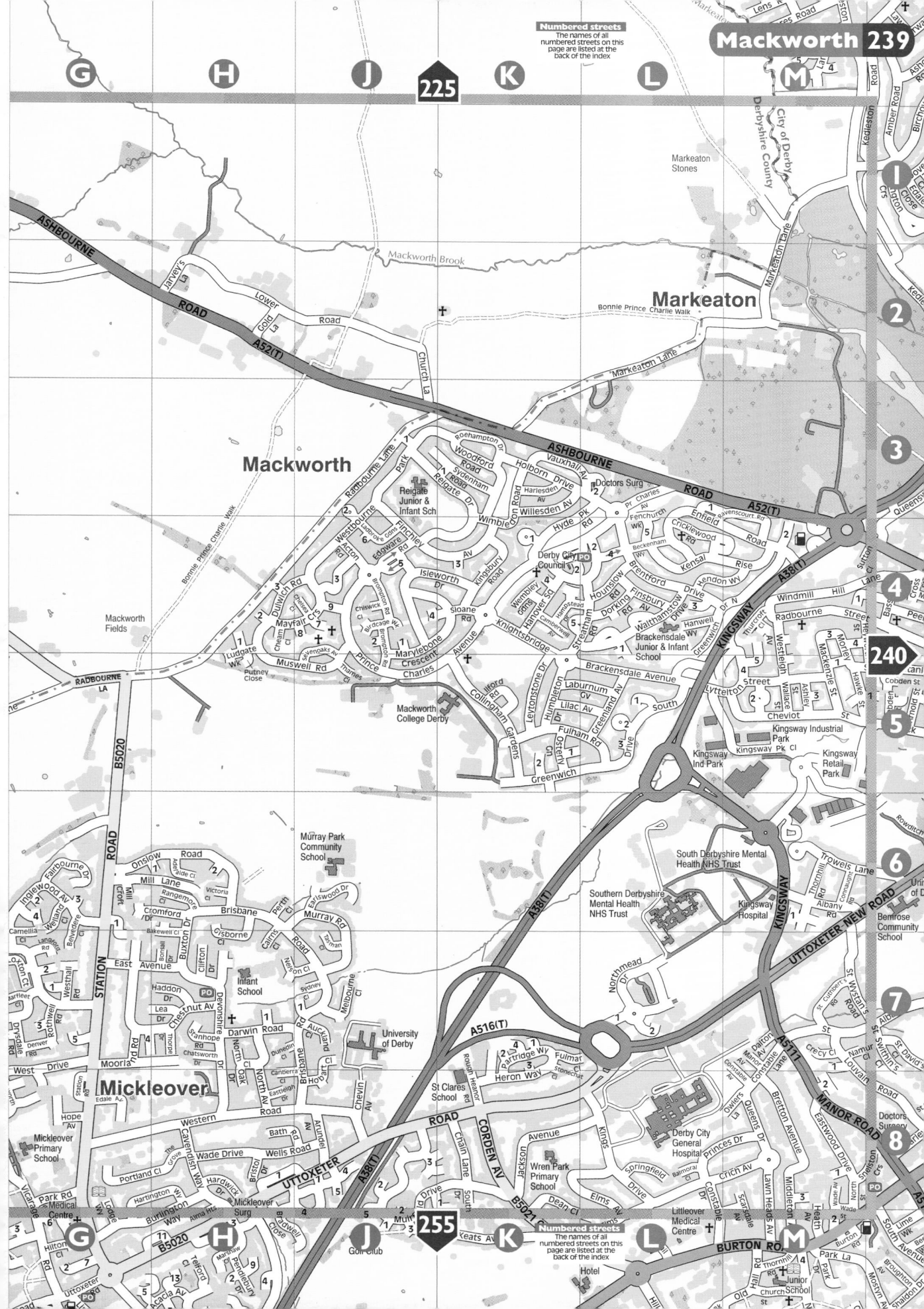

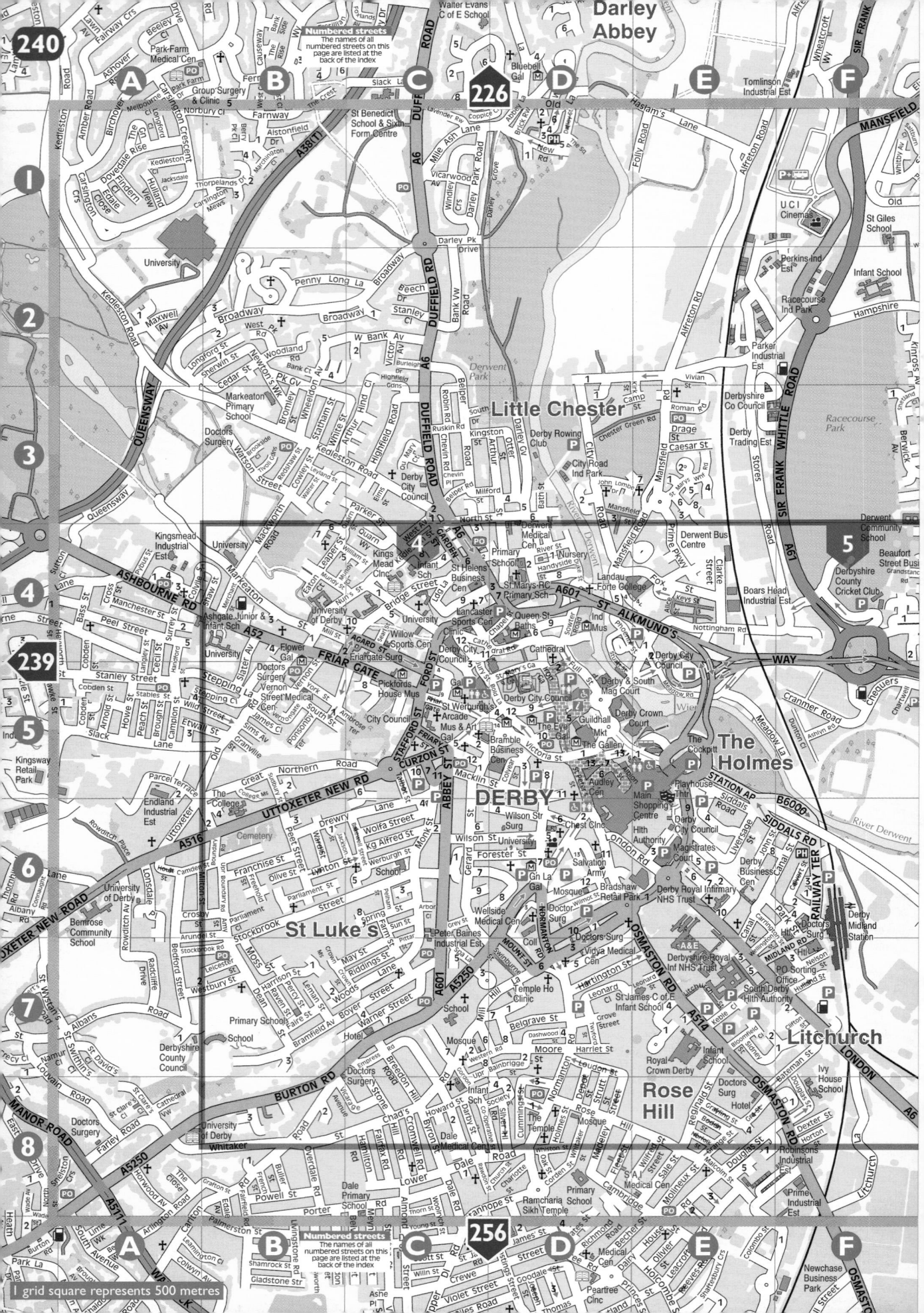

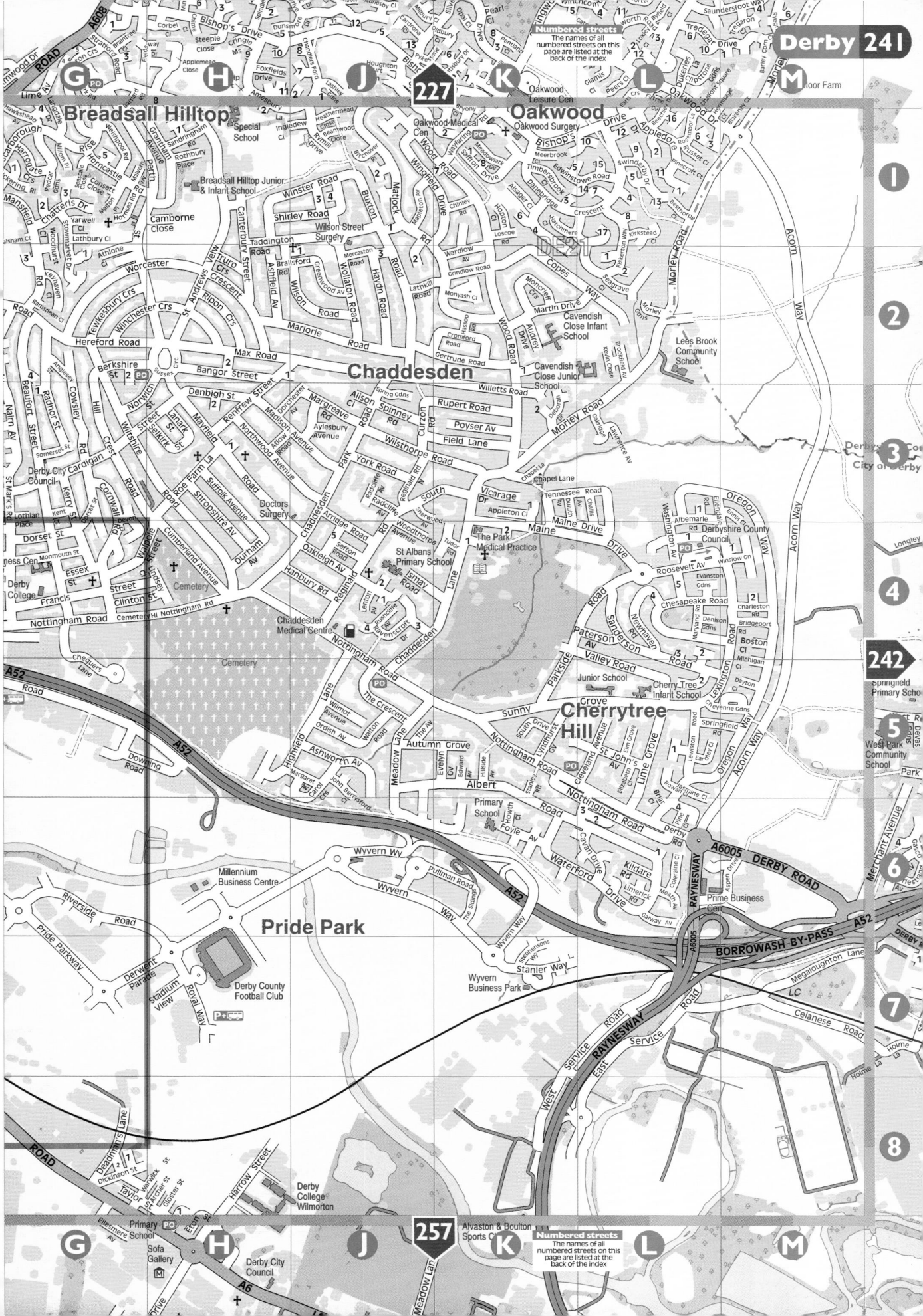

A B C 228 D E F

Moor Farm

Dunnshill

1

Deer Park

The Lake

Bartlewood Farm

2

A6096

Brunswood Farm

3

Derbyshire County
City of Derby

Spondon Wood

Spondon Wood Farm

Moor Lane

Longley Lane

Chaffinch Close

Deer Pk Vw
Goldcrest Dr
Redstart

Fallow Rd

Huntley Avenue

ROAD

DALE ROAD

4

Longley La   Lousie Greaves

Sancroft Avenue
Stone Chesterton Road
Nicholas

Hamilton

Sancroft

Dolphin Elancourt Deincourt

Hazel Drive Birch

Avondale Rd
Royal Hill Rd
Marina Dr
Charles St

Coniston
Ullswater
Brecon

Grasmere
Frazer Cl
Rudyard
Stewart
Orchard Ct

Moor Croft Close

MOOR STREET

Windsor Dr

Dale Rd
Dale Rd
DALE

A6096

Holyrood Close

Spondon

City of Derby

Homefarm
Green Lane
Oak
Columbell

5

Springfield
Primary School

West Road
Devas Gdns
Sunningdale

Beeches

Chapel Lane
Brunswood

Strathaven Cl
Brockley
Oxford St
Coxon St

Reader
St

Farningham
Cl

Lawnside
Caernarvon
Beaumaris

Hampton

Bakehouse

Ockbrook
School

Pares
Top

Bare Lane

West Park
Community
School

Park Road

St Werburghs
C of E School

Chapel St
Beech
Act

Poplar

PO

Doctors Surg

Cemetery

Borrow Wood
Junior & Infant School

Lane
The Settlement shop
Stones
Paddock

PO

6

Merchant Avenue

Fowler
Av
Gascoigne
Dr
Gilbert

Church Street
Potter St
Hallowes
Sitwell
Av
Lodge La

Stoney Lane
South Av
The Meadow

Arundel Dr
Clover

Hill Cl
The
Covert

Borrowash Rd
Sandringham Drive
Lochinvar
Argyll
Burnside Dr
Sundew
The Pingle

Derbyshire County
City of Derby

Moravian
Settlement

Victoria Avenue
Church Street
Hill Cl
Elloe
Cole
Orchard
Collier Lane

PO

PASS
A52

DERBY RD

Leeway
Drury Av
Vancouver
Lodge La
WILLOWCROFT RD

Kirk Leys Av North
Kirk
Moult Av
Leys Avenue South
Park Leys Ct
Ladybower
Gravel Pit Lane
Hillside Rd
Hillside Crs
Stoney Lane
Trent Rd
Derwent
Ormskirk Rd
Lane
Haddon
Drive

BORROWASH BY-PASS A52(T)

BORROWASH BY-PASS

7

Aloughton Lane

Anglers La
Station Road
Stoney Cross
Langley Rd
Vincent
Cambridge street
Arnhem
Craddock Av
Dovedale Rd
Edmund Road
Terrace
Savernoll Rd
Borrowfield
Road
Monsal
Kirk Dl Av
Millside Rd
Eagle Dr
Deepdale
Litton Dr
Borrowash Road

Asterdale
School

Asterdale
Leisure
Centre

Field Cl
Greenway
Cl

BORROWASH BY-PASS

Beech
Av
Chestnut
Gv
Derwent
Av

Spondon
Station

PO

A6005 NOTTINGHAM ROAD

Nottingham Rd

A6005

Hawthorne Avenue

Victoria
Avenue
Deans
Dr
Kimberley Road
Ladysmith
Rd

Ashbrook
Junior &
Infant School

Chervil
Ashbrook
Rutland Av

Hermitage

Woodland
Avenue
Devonshire Av
Harrington
Charnwood Av
Priory
Way

Tanese
Road
Holme La
Holme

8

River Derwent

The Park
Medical
Practice

DERBY ROAD

BORROWASH

Princess Dr
Mano
Dovecote

Elm Street
Nursery Cl
PO

STATION ROAD
Royal
St Stephens
Central Avenue
Ashmeadow
Weyacres

Briar Cl
Cem
Windsor
Cl
The Spinney

A B 258 C D E F

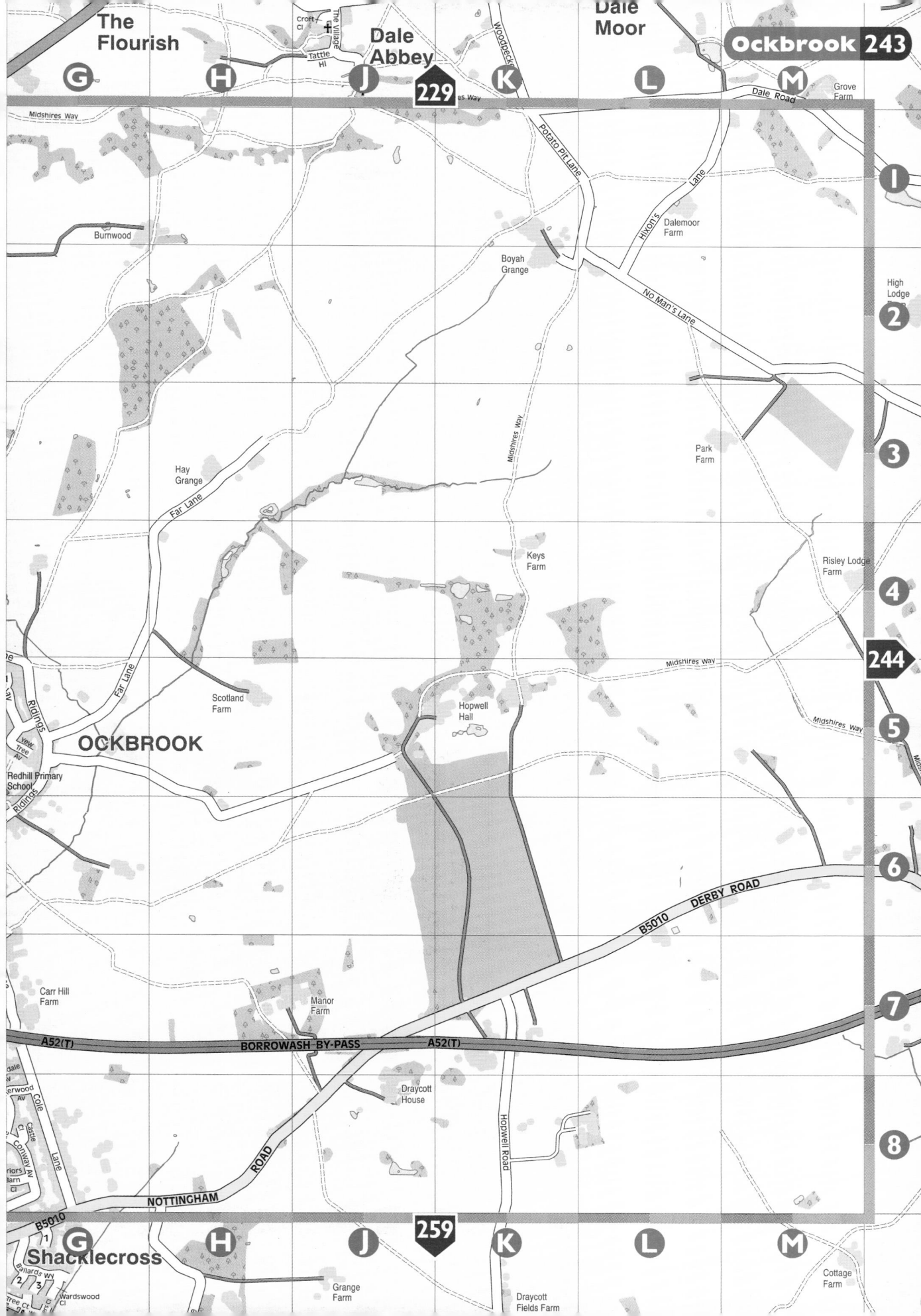

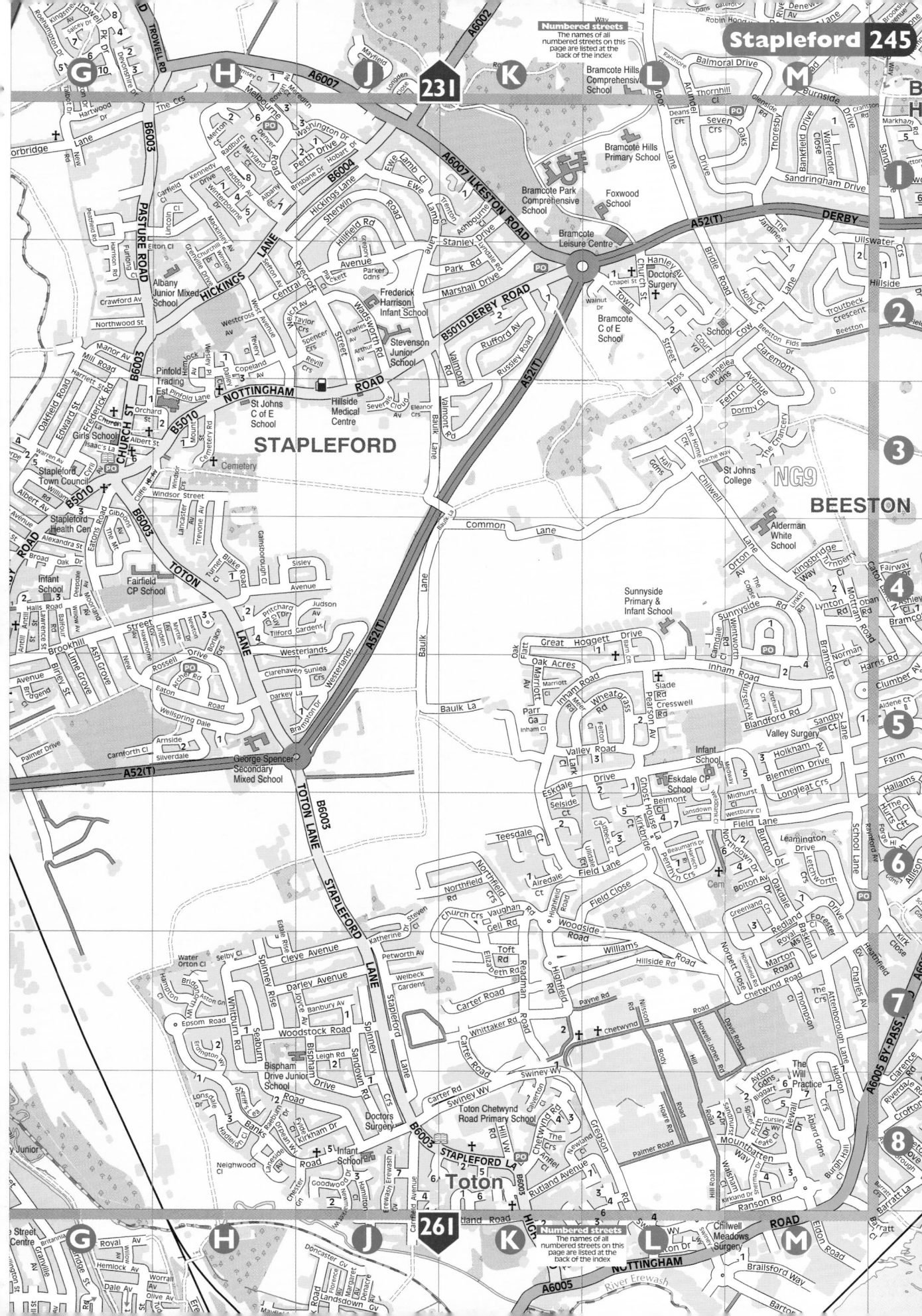

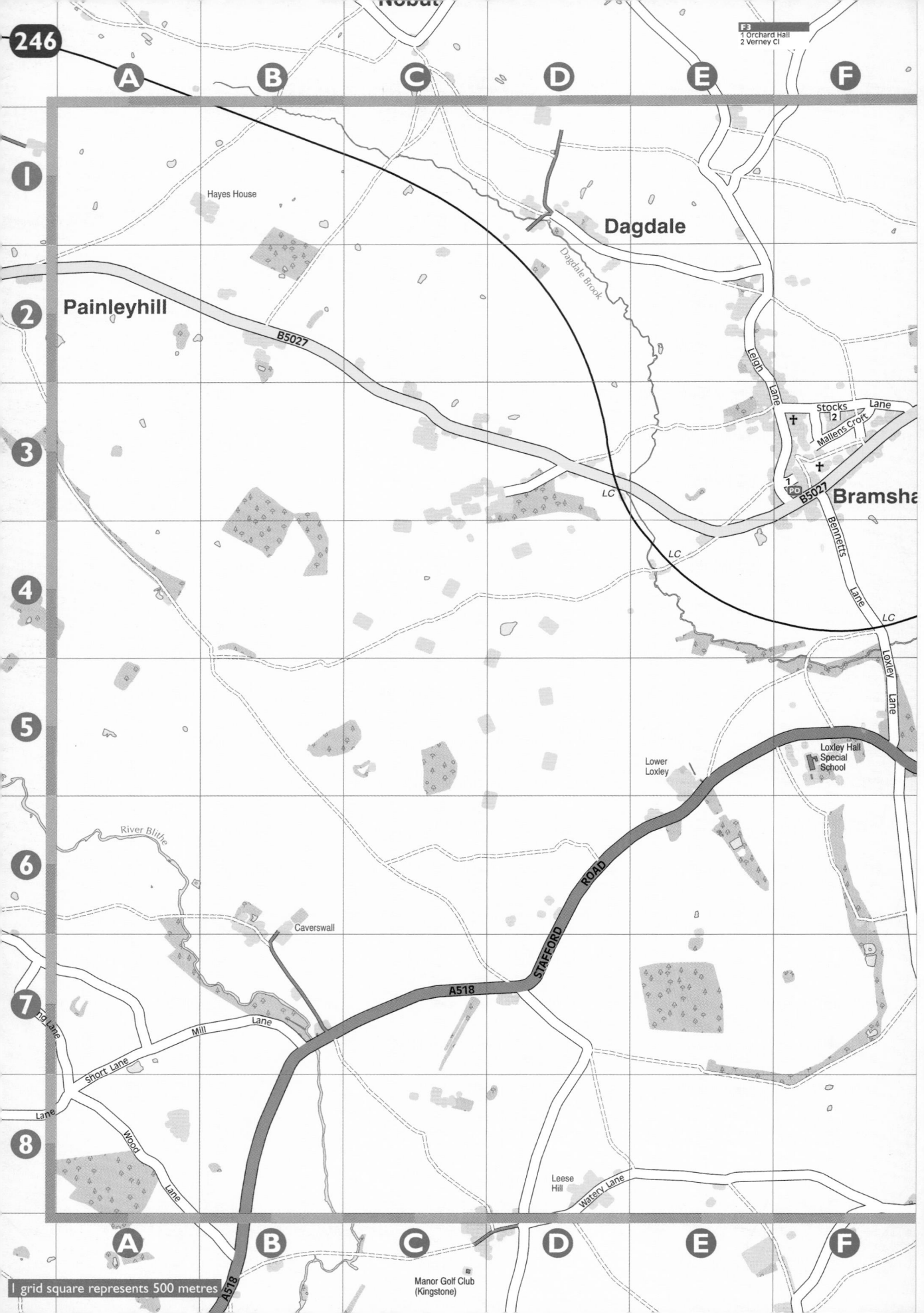

A   B   C   D   E   F

Nobut

1 Orchard Hall
2 Verney Cl

Hayes House

Dagdale

Dagdale Brook

Painleyhill

B5027

Leigh Lane

Stocks Lane
2
Mallens Croft

LC

PO
B5027

Bramsha

Bennetts Lane

LC

LC

Loxley Lane

Loxley Hall
Special
School

Lower
Loxley

River Blithe

STAFFORD ROAD

Caverswall

Mill Lane

Short Lane

A518

ng Lane

Lane

Wood Lane

Leese
Hill

Watery Lane

A B C D E F

I grid square represents 500 metres

A518

Manor Golf Club
(Kingstone)

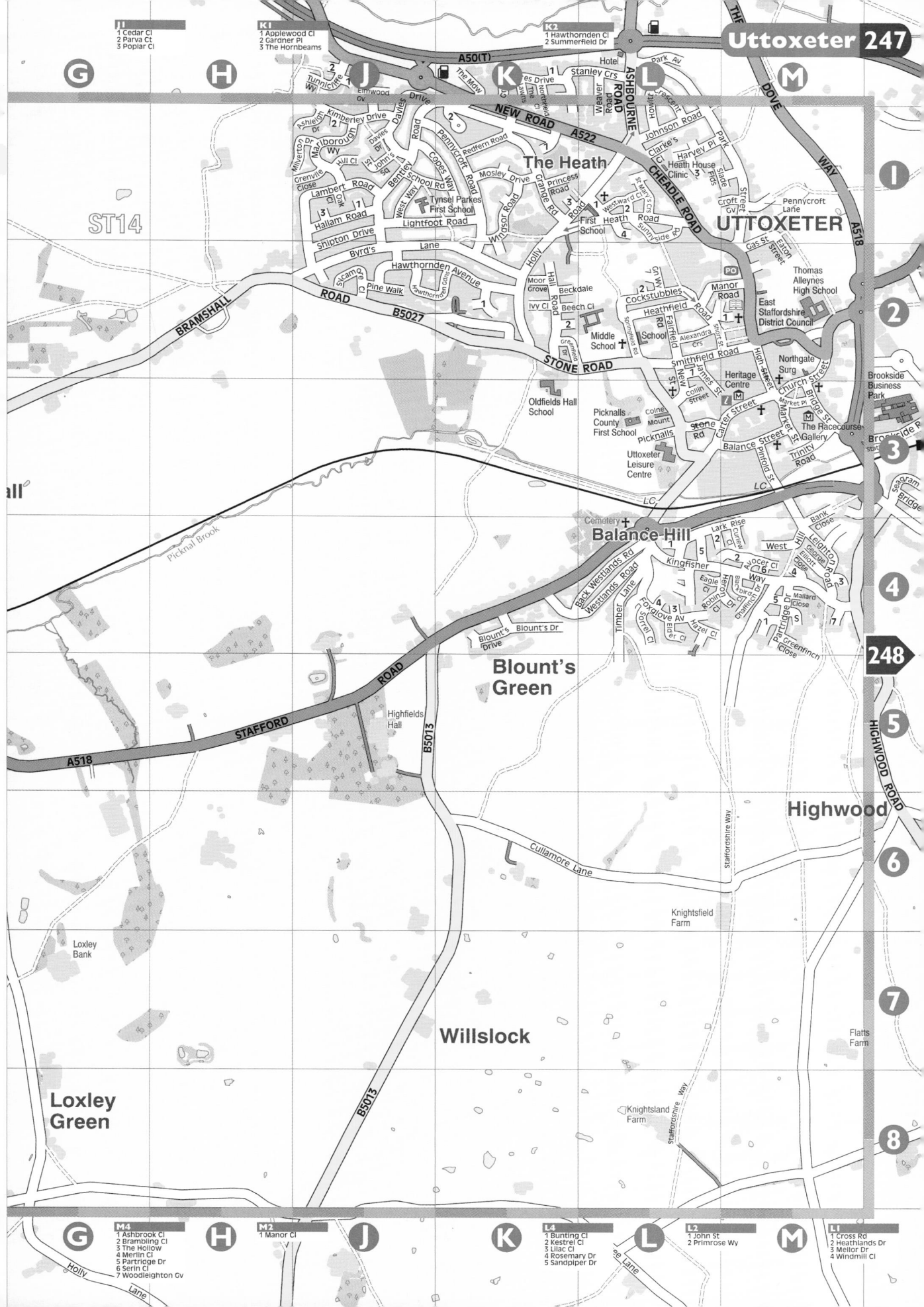

Map labels

J1
1 Cedar Cl
2 Parva Ct
3 Poplar Cl

K1
1 Applewood Cl
2 Gardner Pl
3 The Hornbeams

K2
1 Hawthornden Cl
2 Summerfield Dr

G   H   J   K   L   M

A50(T)

NEW ROAD   A522

Hotel

The Heath

UTTOXETER

ST14

Marlborough Wy

Kimberley Drive

Ashleigh Dr

Milverton Dr

Grenville Close

Davies Drive

Pennycroft Road

Copes Way

Mosley Drive

Redfern Road

Grange Rd

Princess Road

Lambert Road

Bentley Road

School Rd

West Way

John's Sq

Hill Cl

Oak

Hallam Road

Shipton Drive

Byrd's

Tynsel Parkes First School

Lightfoot Road

Windsor Road

Holly

Lane

Sycamore Cl

Pine Walk

Hawthornden Avenue

Hawthornden Gdns

Hawthornden Close

BRAMSHALL ROAD   B5027

STONE ROAD

Moor Grove

Beckdale

Ivy Cl

Beech Cl

Greening Rd

Cockstubbles

Heathfield Rd

Fairfield School

Middle School

Smithfield Road

Alexandra Crs

Stonefield Rd

Manor Road

Cheadle Road

First Heath School

Summerside Rd

Heath House Clinic

Croft Gv

Pennycroft Lane

Gas St

Eaton Street

Thomas Alleynes High School

East Staffordshire District Council

PO

Northgate Surg

Heritage Centre

James St

Collin Street

Church Street

Market St

The Racecourse Gallery

Market St

Bridge St

High Street

New St

Oldfields Hall School

Picknalls County First School

Picknalls

Colne Mount

Stone Rd

Carter Street

Balance Street

Pinfold St

Trinity Road

Uttoxeter Leisure Centre

LC

LC

Brookside Business Park

Brookside R

Seagram Bridge

Cemetery

Balance Hill

Lark Rise

Curlew

Back Westlands Rd

Westlands Road

Kingfisher

Avocet Cl

West Way

Bank Close

West Hill

Leighton Road

George Close

Elliott

Eagle

Robin

Blackbird Cl

Chaffinch

Mallard Close

Partridge

Greenfinch

Foxglove Av

Sorrel Cl

Hazel Cl

Elder Cl

Timber Lane

Blount's Drive

Blount's Dr

Blount's Green

Highfields Hall

STAFFORD ROAD   B5013

A518

Cuilamore Lane

Staffordshire Way

Knightsfield Farm

Highwood

HIGHWOOD ROAD

Picknal Brook

Loxley Bank

Willslock

Knightsland Farm

Loxley Green

Holly Lane

M4
1 Ashbrook Cl
2 Brambling Cl
3 The Hollow
4 Merlin Cl
5 Partridge Dr
6 Serin Cl
7 Woodleighton Gv

M2
1 Manor Cl

L4
1 Bunting Cl
2 Kestrel Cl
3 Lilac Cl
4 Rosemary Dr
5 Sandpiper Dr

L2
1 John St
2 Primrose Wy

L1
1 Cross Rd
2 Heathlands Dr
3 Mellor Dr
4 Windmill Cl

G   H   J   K   L   M

A   B   234   C   D   E   F

1

2

Oaks
Green

3

A515

Sudbury Park

4

Oak Cott

5

A50(T)

Sudbury Hall (NT)

Dove River Practice
PO

Club La

School Lane

Sudbury Primary School

Sudbury

6

Main   Road

Dovebank

7

Aston Bridge

A515

8

Hotel

LC

Cave Cott

Mackley House

Muse Lane

Twisses

Lees Hall Farm

Marjory Lane

Dalebrook

Aston Heath

Aston   Lane

Breach   Lane

Broomhill Farm

Aston

Main Road

A50(T)

A50(T)

Uttoxeter   Road

Woodland Drive

Leathersley Lane

Leathersley Farm

Broom's Lane

A   B   262   C   D   E   F

Moat Farm

Sapperton

G H J **235** K L M

I

2

3

4

252

5

6

7

8

K2
1 Auden Cl
2 Fearn Cl

L2
1 Chapel La
2 Meadow Ri

Crowfoot Lane

Sapperton Lane

Ashbourne Road

Church Road

Church Broughton C of E Primary School

Bent Brook

Bent House

Tipper's Lane

Main St

Badway Lane

Littlefield Road

Church Broughton

Old Hall Lane

PO

Bent Lane

The Bent

Foston Mill Farm

Cotefield

Bottom Lane

Cote Lane

Boggy Lane

Heathtop

Woodhouse Lane

Mill Lane

Woodyard Lane

Hay Lane

Coplow Lane

Foston Brook

Boggy Lane

Heath House

Miry Lane

Church Road

Woodyard Lane

Foston

Park Av

Packenham Boulevard

Uttoxeter Road

A511

A50(T)

A50(T)

A511

Heath House

A511

Breach

Broughton Road

Watery Lane

Uttoxeter Road

A511

Guinea Farm

UTTOXETER ROAD A511

Brook Lane

Church Lane

Malthouse

Sawpit Lane

DERBY ROAD

Green Acres Lane

The Shieling

The Hays

Brook Cl

Coopers

Woodmans Crt

STATION ROAD A511

Tree Road

G H J **263** K L M

Scropton

PO

LC

Scropton Road

Barton Hall

G8
1 Cherry Tree Cl

H8
1 Churchill Dr
2 Falaise Wy
3 Lancaster Dr
4 Montgomery Cl
5 Shaef Cl
6 Utah Cl

L6
1 Ash View Cl
2 Mansfields Cft

G **H** **J** **237** **K** **L** **M**

Bearwardcote Hall

I

Dalbury

2

Trusley
Brook Farm

bury Hollow

Baldfields Farm

Highfields
Farm

3

Heage Lane

Hepnalls

Ash   Lane

Willowpit
Lane

Etwall Brook

Ashe
Hall

4

Hilton
Fields

Park Farm

A516(T)

Sutton   Lane

254

5

Church Hill

Lawn Avenue

Slade Close

Ashe
Lane

John Port
School

PO

Sandypits

Lane

6

Willowpit Lane

Etwall
Leisure
Centre

Hilton Road

Etwall

Mill Meadow
Way

Etwall
Primary
School

Derby   Road

The Bancroft

Chestnut Grove

Ett's Way

Pine Cl

Windmill Road

Oaklands Road

Belfield

Elms
Grove

7

A516(T)

Hilton Lodge

DERBY ROAD

Springfield Road

Eggington   Road

A50(T)

Hilton
Industrial
Estate

DERBY ROAD

A5132

Pegasus Way

Lucas Lane

Eggington Road

Grove Park

Jacksons   Lane

8

EGGINGTON ROAD

Normandy Road

New Road

Rodney
Cl

Halifax
Cl

Blakeley Lane

Blakeley Lodge

Hilton

Mulberry Way

Peacroft Ct

Primary
School

Bancroft Close

Hawthorn Cl

The Mease

EGGINGTON ROAD

265

M7
1 Courtland Rd

M6
1 Beech Dr
2 Gerard Gv
3 John Port Cl
4 Sycamore Cl

L7
1 Blakelow Dr
2 Melville Ct

G **H** **J** **265** **K** **L** **M**

Wyston
Brook

Avon Way

DE65

Hargate

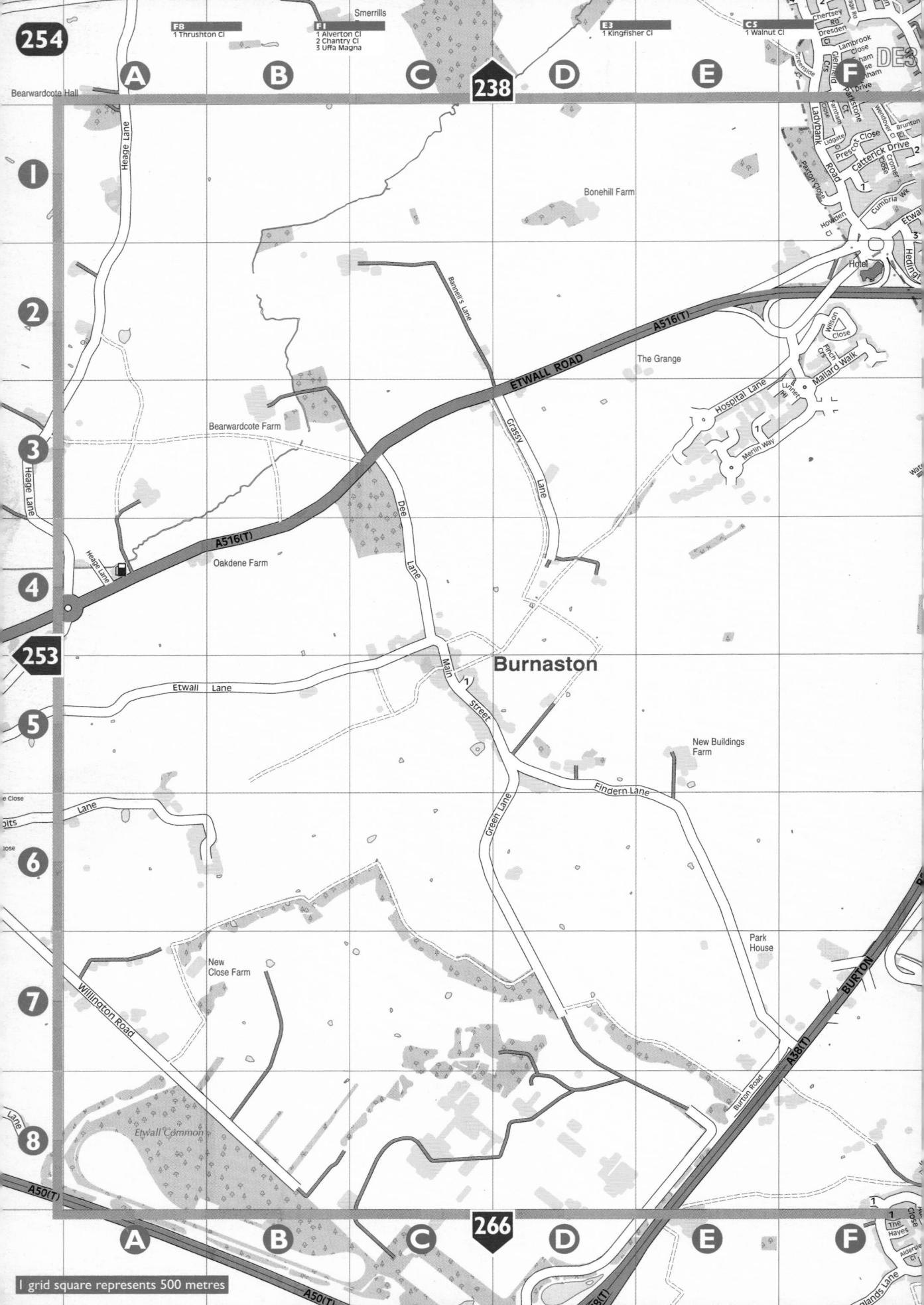

A   B   C   238   D   E   F

DE3

F8
1 Thrushton Cl

F1
1 Alverton Cl
2 Chantry Cl
3 Uffa Magna

Smerrills

E3
1 Kingfisher Cl

C5
1 Walnut Cl

Chertsey
Dresden

Lambrook
Close

Prescot Close

Catterick Drive

Ladybank

Bearwardcote Hall

1

Bonehill Farm

2

Heage Lane

Bannell's Lane

ETWALL ROAD

A516(T)

The Grange

Hospital Lane

Merlin Way

Mallard Walk

3

Heage Lane

Bearwardcote Farm

Grassy Lane

Dee Lane

A516(T)

Oakdene Farm

Heage Lane

4

253

Etwall   Lane

Main Street

Burnaston

New Buildings Farm

5

Lane

Green Lane

Findern Lane

Park House

BURTON

6

Willington Road

New Close Farm

Burton Road

A38(T)

7

Lane

Etwall Common

A50(T)

8

A   B   266   C   D   E   F

The Hayes

A50(T)

A38(T)

I grid square represents 500 metres

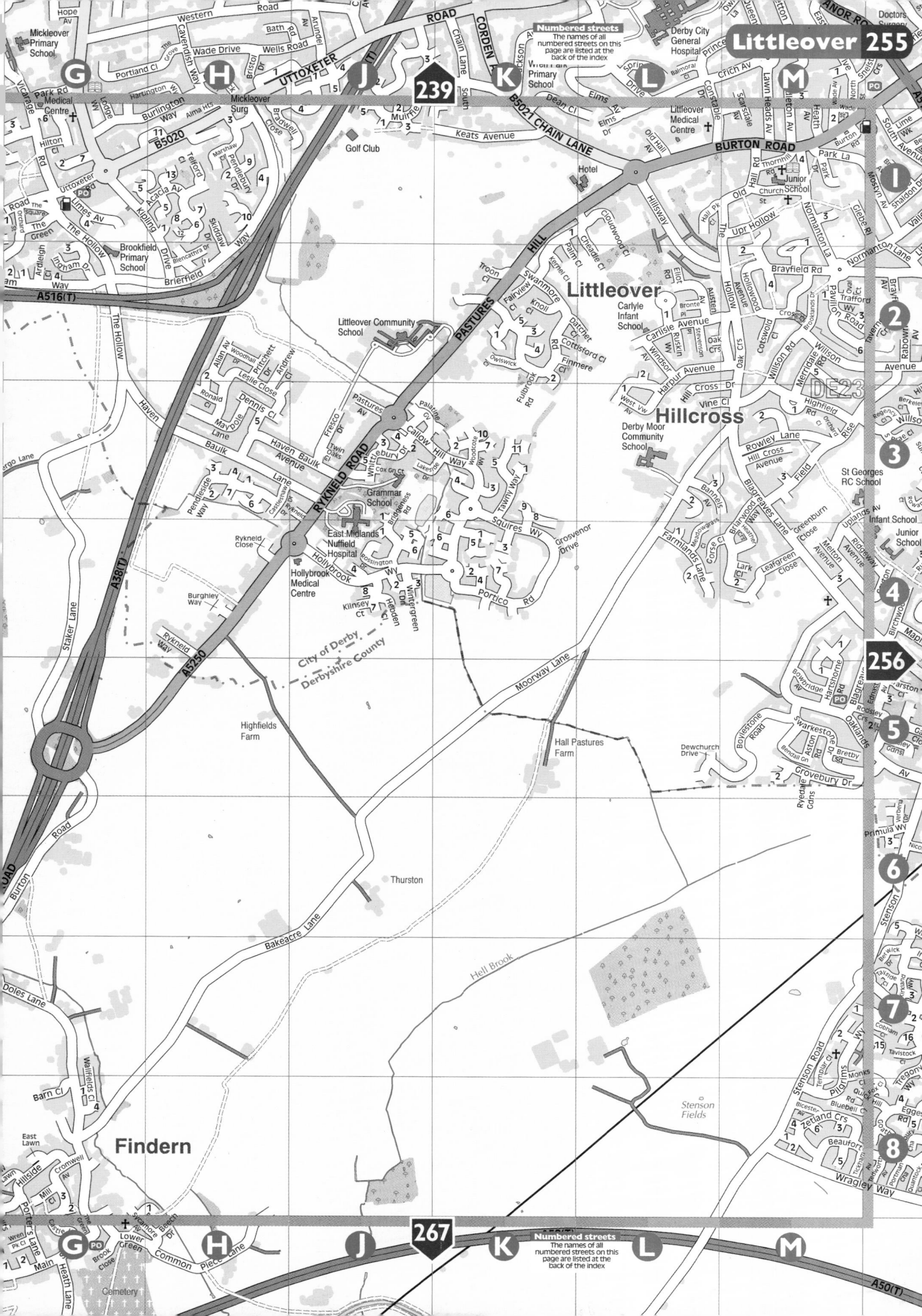

G2
1 Alexandra Rd
2 The Pingle

G4
1 Wyvern Av

G5

H1
1 Howard Cl

H2
1 Midland St

Toton Chetwynd
Road Primary School

H6, H3
Street names for
these grid squares
are listed at the
back of the index

STAPLEFORD

245

Doctors
Surgery

Infant
School

NG10

I
2
3
4
5
6
7
8

Trentlock

Thrumpton

M1
1 Paisley Gv

K4
1 Junction Rd

L1
Street names for
this grid square
are listed at the
back of the
Index

K3
1 Armitage Dr
2 Barton Rd
3 Litchfield Cl

K1
1 Evesham Ct
2 Kensington Cl

K2
1 The Hollows

J1
1 Wallace Gdns

L3
1 Rugeley Av
2 Warwick Rd

M2
1 Acton Gv
2 St Laurence Ct

H5
1 Belvoir Cl
2 Farm Cl
3 Gainsborough Cl
4 Stone Mdw

G H J K L M

251

272

264

L4
1 Bourne Cl

M1
1 Bradshaw Mdw
2 Bramley Ct
3 Ley Cft
4 Russet Cl

M2
1 Castleview
2 Oakwood Cl

Guinea Farm

DERBY ROAD

The Shieling

Coopers Cft

Woodmans Cft

Appletree Road

Holme Cl

Heath Fields
Primary School

Foston Cl

Field Av

Heath Way

Yew Tree Road

STATION RD

STATION ROAD

Church

Av

Hoon Rd

Merc

1

2

Scropton

LC

PO

Scropton   Road

Mill La

Brookside
Farm

Derbyshire County
Staffordshire County

Green Ends Lane

Scropton   Road

2

1

Station Road
Industrial Estate

Castle
View Industrial Estate

Scropton Old
Road

LC

Tutbury & H

Marston
Old Lane

Dove
Side

BRIDGE ST A511

3

Tutbury Cricket
Club

Bridge Street

Castle

Cemetery

Castle Street

Church St

Monk St

High Street

Corn Mill Lane

The Cl

Hillside

Tutbury Health
Centre

Duke St

Fishpond
Lane

PO

PH

Hotel

Burton Street

Dove

4

Richard
Wakefield C of E
Primary School

Cornmill
Bank

Fauld
Industrial Estate

Fauld   Lane

Park   Lane

Wakefield Avenue

Norman
Road

1

3

2

7

Ludgate Street

Ironwalls Lane

264

Woodhouse
Farm

Holt's

Millview
Avenue

Chatsworth
Drive

5

A511

Bus

TUTBURY

Redhill Lane

Ferrers
Close

The Park Pale

Belmot Road

Babbington
Cl

Portway Drive

Green

Lane

1

Owen's Bank

Ferrers
Av

Lancaster
Drive

Pinfold Close

6

Hayes   Lane

Castle

Belmot   Road

Chapel House
Farm

7

Rolleston
Park

Castle Hayes
Park Farm

Bushton Lane

8

Hare
Holes Farm

Bushton

Lower Castle
Hayes Far

Belmot   Road

Bushton
Lane

272

M5
1 Cromwell Cl

M4
1 Norman Keep
2 Queens Rl
3 Rushton Cl
4 Silk Mill La

G H J K L M

A5132 DERBY

EGGINTON ROAD

G Hilton

1 Twentylands

H1
1 Bentley Rd
2 Blithe Cl
3 Dale Brook
4 Huntspill Rd
5 Marston Brook
6 Mill Fleam
7 Sandford Brook

H2
1 Stour Cl

Jacksons Lane

A50(T)

I

Blakeley Lodge

J 253 K L M A50(T)

EGGINGTON ROAD

Field Cl

Peacroft Lane

Mulberry Way

The Mease

DE65

1 2

Hawthorn Cl

Wyston Brook

Calder Close

Welland Road

Avon Way

Tinsell Brook

Nene Way

Washford Rd

The Mease

A5132

Oldfield Lane

Hargate Manor

Eggington Road

2

LC

LC

Egginton Comm 3

HILTON ROAD

A5132 CARRIERS

Derby Airfield

Hilton Brook

Blacksmith's Lane

Etwall Road

Ash Grove Lane

4

River Dove

Blacksmith's Lane

Elmhurst

Fishpond Lane

Duck Street

Main Street

William Newton Close

266

PO

Egginton 5

Grange Court

Smedley Court

Egginton Primary School

Station Road

Watford Road

South Hill

Fairfield Avenue

Dovecliff Road

Church Road

Rectory Mews

6

A38(T)

Dovecliff Road

Derbyshire County
Staffordshire County

7

Craythorne Farm

Craythorne Road

Clay Mills

Forge Lane

Rose Av

Claymills Road

Shrewsbury Road

DERBY ROAD

A38(T)

8

Tintagel Close

Tristram Grove

Lancelot Drive

Guinevere Avenue

Hall Green Avenue

Gunmore Dr

Priory Lands

St Mary's Drive

Primary School

Church Road

Jordan Avenue

Bladon View

A38(T)

Wentworth Drive

Crown Special

Bitham Lane

Bridgeside

Crest

Almond

Gretton

Hillfield

Main Street

Fairham Rd

Hu

DERBY ROAD

K5
1 Dove Gv

J8
1 Dovecliff Crs
2 Lovatt Cl

H8
1 Arthurs Ct
2 Camelot Cl
3 Galahad Dr
4 Gawain Gv
5 Knights Ct
6 Lohengrin Ct

A50(T)

A   B   254   C   D   E   F

Etwall

The Hayes

1

Longlands Lane

Boundary Road

2

B5008

A50(T)

A50(T)

A38(T)

Hill Farm

Willingham Lane

3

BURTON   ROAD

ETWALL   ROAD

Findern Lane

LC   LC

Willington

Cemetery

CARRIERS Lane

4

ROAD

A5132

A38(T)

Derwent

Willow Gv

CANAL   BRIDGE

Orchard Close

The Potlocks

Fern Clos

265

THE   CASTLE   WAY   A5132

DERBY   ROAD

A38(T)

Green Close

PO

Willington Stn

Willington Surgery

Ivy Close

Saxon Gv

Tawny Drive

The Green

Oaks Road

Mercia Drive

Beech   Avenue

Hall

St. Michael's

Church

Primary School

Vere   Old Hall

TWYFORD ROAD

Twyford Cl

Trent Avenue

Sealey Close

Ford La

Lane

Coach Way

Ferry Green

Riverbank

B5008   REPTON   ROAD

Bargate Lane

5

6

WILLINGTON   ROAD

Repton Sports Club

7

Tanner's Lane

Repton School

Repton School

PO

Brook School

8

Reptor

Repton School

The Pastures

Chestnut Way

The Fell

Parson's Hills

BURTON   ROAD

A   B   275   C   D   E   F

B5008

Cokhay

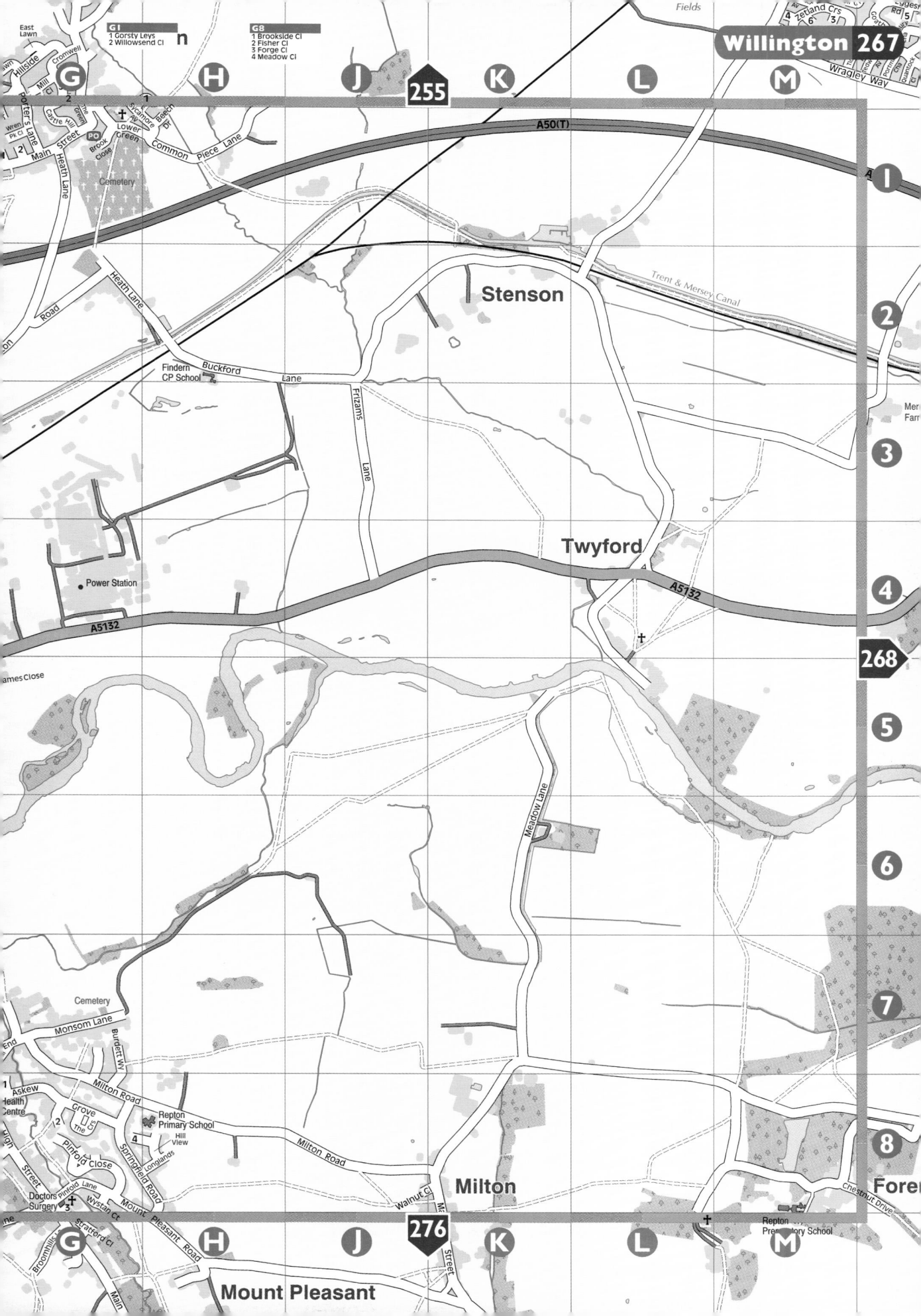

G1
1 Gorsty Leys
2 Willowsend Cl

G8
1 Brookside Cl
2 Fisher Cl
3 Forge Cl
4 Meadow Cl

G   H   J   255   K   L   M   I

A50(T)

Trent & Mersey Canal

Stenson

2

3

East Lawn

Hillside   Mill Cl   Cromwell   n

Porter's Lane   Castle Hill Street   The Green   Sycamore   Beech Dr   Lower Green

Main Street   Heath Lane   PO   BROOK CLOSE   Common Piece Lane

Wren   Pk Cl

Cemetery

Road   Heath Lane

Findern CP School   Buckford   Lane   Fritzams Lane

Mer Farm

Twyford   4

A5132

268

James Close   Power Station   A5132

5

Meadow Lane   6

7

Cemetery   Monsom Lane   Burdett Wy

Askew Health Centre   Grove   The   Repton Primary School   Hill View   Milton Road

Milton Road   Longlands

Milton Road

8

Fore

Doctors Surgery   Pinfold Close   Pinfold Lane   Wysan Ct   Mount Pleasant Road   Springfield Road   Walnut Cl   Milton   Chestnut Drive   Repton Preparatory School

Broomhills   Street   Stratford Cl   Main

Mount Pleasant

Wragley Way

Arleston

A50(T)

Arleston Farm

Ashlea Farm

City of Derby
Derbyshire County

D5
1 Beaumont Cl

Lea Farm

D4
1 Walnut Cl

Moor Lane

A50(T)

The Lowes Farm

Merry Bower Farm

Barrow-hill

Moor Lane

Trent & Mersey Canal

Sinfin Lane

SWARKESTONE ROAD

BARROW LANE

A5132

A5132

Twyford Road

Brookfield

The Nook

Chapel Lane

Doctors Surgery

Club La

Lane

Cemetery

Sale & Davys
C of E
School

Hall Park

Church

Lane

Barrow upon Trent

Green Lane

River Trent

Ingleby

Foremark

Chestnut Drive

ry School

Ingleby Toft

A   B   C   D   E   F

1 grid square represents 500 metres

G H J K L M

`257`

Chellaston

1 Groves Nook
2 Rye Butts

1 Chellaston Pk Ct
2 Lee Farm Cl
3 Penhaligan's Cl
4 Small Meer Cl

1 Chapel La
2 Church Cl
3 High St
4 Pit Close La
5 Tudor Field Cl
6 Woodgate Dr

Marsh Flatts

`1`

`2`

Weston Fields Farm

Spring Farm

`3`

Glebe Farm

`4`

Swarkestone

The Hall

`270`

`5`

Hill Farm

Trent & Mersey Canal

`6`

Stanton by Bridge

Swarkestone Boat Club

River Trent

`7`

The Hills

`8`

G H J K L M

`278`

Kings Newton

DE73

K2
1 Parklands Dr
2 Weston Rl

Glebe
Farm

A   B   C   258   D   A50(T)   E   F

I

Marsh
Flatts

Lane

Chellaston

Aston Hill

Aston Hill
Farm

2

Knob
Farm

Weston Fields Farm

Lane

Holden
Avenue

Compton Avenue

Long Croft Cl

Leas Cl

Aston-on-Trent
Primary School

Derby

Road

Walnut Cl

Moor Lane

Hanger
Bank
Cem

Aldersdale
Cl

Bird's Nest
Farm

Fox Covert
Farm

Aston-
on-Trent

Aston

3

Ellison
Avenue

Valerie
Road

Bell
Avenue

PO

Posy
Lane

Rectory Cotts

Manor
Farm

Ash

Clarkes
Lane

Road

Willow
Close

Park View

Shardlow Road

Willow
Way

Park

Aston Hall Drive

Trent & Mersey Canal

4

Weston Road

Aston Hall
Hospital

Weston
Grange

269

5

Wilmot
Av

Street

The
Av

Weston-on-Trent

River Trent

Main

Trent

Lane

Park
Lane

Weston-on-Trent
Parochial
Primary School

6

Rectory
Farm

Trent & Mersey Canal

King's

Mill

Lane

King's Mills

Hotel

Home
Farm

7

River Trent

Donington
Hall

8

A   B   279   C   D   E   F

Hall Leys Lane

E3
1 The Green
2 Shirley Pk

Newton's
Corner

Shire County
Shire County

Wilne

K1
1 Cavendish Ct
2 The Maltings

K6
1 Loudoun Pl
2 Rawdon Cl
3 Selina Cl
4 The Spinney

K7
1 Carrs Cl
2 Delven La
3 Lothian Pl
4 Peartree Cl

G H Shardlow J 259 K L M

Manor Farm

PO LONDON
Clover

Shardlow Business Park

The Grove Hospital

Shardlow County Primary School

Glenn Wy
Arts Nook
W End Drive

Cowlishaw Cl

Wavelyn

LONDON ROAD

The Wharf

Wilne

Millfield

Midshires Way

1

Marina

River Trent

Cavendish Bridge

2 NORTH

Aston Lane

Roydon Hall Farm

A50(T)

Trent & Mersey Canal

Canal Bank

PH

LONDON ROAD

Donington Lane

A50(T)

Rycrof

3

Acre Lane

River Trent

Derbyshire County
Leicestershire County

Back Lane

LC

Station Road

Donington Lane

4

Trent Lane Industrial Estate

Station Road

5

Sycamore Road

Willow Road

Gasny Av

Newbold Drive

Hawthorn Road

Trent Lane

Station Road

Victoria Street

Hemingt Primary

PO

Short Lane

Walton Hl
Campion Hill
Spittal Hill

Tanyard Close

The Horse Shoes

Main Street

Hill

6

Bentley Road
Hazelrigg

Shirley Cl
Darsway

2
7

Huntingdon Dr

3

Haulton

Harcourt Place

Tanyard Close

Bondgate

Castle Hill

1 3

Hemington

Fox Road
Foxbrook Dr

Saffrel Cl
Staunton

School Lane

3

Orchard CP School

4

Drive

The Hollow

Borough St

The Barroon

Charnwood Avenue

Cem

Roby Lea
Minton Rd

Queens Wy

The Green

Grange

3

Road

Tipnall

4

Doctors Surg

PO

Clapgun Street

Garden Crs

Moira Dale

Studbrook Close

Kirkland Close

Cordwell

Ferrers Close

Orchard Avenue

Aidan

Gate

+

Eastway

7

Park Lane

Bosworth

Starkle Avenue

Park Av

Paddock Cl

Shields Crescent

Towles Pastures

Park Lane

Delven Lane

2

Hotel

+

St Edwards Junior School

Castle Donington Community College

CASTLE DONINGTON

Cheribough Road

Cooks Av

Barn Close

Hall Farm Close

Orly Av

Bakewell Drive

Hastings St

Eaton Road

Harvey

2

Meadow Crs

1

High Street

Crabtree Close

Hallam Fields

St Edward's Rd

Stonehill

Cedar Road

DE74

8

G H J PH Hill Top K L M K8
1 Cavendish Cl

L8
1 Routh Av
2 Windmill Cl

Hill Top m

Hill Top

Disery

L7
1 The Biggin
2 Mount Pleasant
3 St Anne's La

L6
1 The Moat
2 Monteith Pl
3 Montford Ms

263

A B C D E F

1
2
3
4
5
6
7
8

A B C D E F

Belmot Road

Lower Castle
Hayes Farm

Anslow Road

Belmot Farm

Stockley
Park

Bushton

Bushton Lane

Whitestone

Main Street

Mosley County
Primary School

Anslow

Outwoods
Lane

Anslow
Gate

Nankirk Lane

Hopley Road

Chapel Lane

Rough
Hay

East Lodge

Bellhouse Lane

B5017

Callingwood

Callingwood Lane

HENHURST

PO

HILL

Henhurst Ridge

Aviation Lane

Postern Road

Knightley
Park

Tatenhill Common

Lane

Pool Green
Farm

Cuckoo Cage Lane

Tatenhill
Common

Main Street

Tatenhill

I grid square represents 500 metres

G   H   J   264 TUTBURY   K   L   M

J6
1 Anglesey St

L1
1 Beowulf Covert
2 The Fletches

L3
1 Glenfield Ri
2 Hornton Rd
3 Morley's Hi

K3
1 Highfield Cl

L2
1 Hornbrook Cl

Cross Lane

Lount Farm

Newgatefield

Lount Lane

Longhedge Lane

Beam Hill

Beam Close

Harehedge Lane

A511

William Hutson Junior School

Castle Park Infants School

Crown Special School I

The Belfry

Nene
Severn
Way
Athelstan
Goodwood

Rolleston Road

Bitham Lane

Bitham Special School

De Ferrers High School

Kenilworth

St Mary's Dr

St Luke's Road

St Patricks Rd

St David's Dr

St John's Rd

Ferrers Avenue

2

3

Outwoods Lane

Beamhill Road

Upper Outwoods Farm

Kitling

Greaves Lane

PO

Castle Rd

Hornbrook Road

St Andrew's Dr

Green La

St George's Field

Field Rise

Beaconsfield Road

Clinic

HORNINGLOW ROAD NORTH

Horninglow

Horninglow Co Infants Speech & Language Unit

A38(T)

3

Field Lane

Field Lane

Field Lane

Glen Ri

Denton Rise

Enderby Rise

Charnwood Road

Lewis Drive

Bosworth drive

Dover Road

Northfield Rd

Carlton Street

Westfield Road

Rowton

Longmead

Craven St

Balfour St

4

Welford Rise

Oadby Rise

Harbury Street

Ashford Road

Foston Avenue

Norton Road

Swannington Street

Calais

Ibstock

Addie Rd

Warwick Street

Horninglow Surg.

Horninglow Surg.

Denton Road

Faversham Road

Hardaxton Street

Belvedere Road

Outwoods

Patch Cl

Carver Road

Breach

4

Outwoods Road

St Margarets

A&E

Queens Hospital

Belvoir Cl

Belvoir Road

St Modwens RC Primary School

Mona Road

Beadmore Rd

Breach Cl

The Carousels

Steel Fabs Industrial Estate

William Street

Arthur St

Victoria Crs

274

5

Anslow Lees

B5017

FOREST ROAD

Reservoir Road

A38(T)

Belvedere County Junior School

Outwoods Street

Dallow Close

Dallow Crescent

PO

Primary School

Dallow Street

Victoria Street

Edward Street

A511

5

Highcroft Dr

PO

Lordswell Road

Primary School

Price Court

Waterloo Street

Waterloo

Princess

Albert St

Burton Muslim Mosque

Derby Street

Derby Street East

DERBY STREET

6

Anglesey street

SHOBNALL

ROAD

Robirch Sports Centre

Lyme Ct

Waverley Lane

Jennings

Shobnall Cl

Infants School

Hill Con Way

Curtis Way

Grange

Gordon

Richmond

Casey

Byrkley Street

St Paul's St W

S B K Sports Club

Rangemore Street

Grange

Kg Edward Pl

East Staffordshire District Council

A5121

Curzon street

Millers Lane

WELLINGTON ST

6

Shobnall

Sinai Park

Lord's Well

The Rough

SHOBNALL

ROAD

The grange

SHOBNALL ROAD

Insley Industrial Estate

John Carr Industrial Est

Greenline Business Park

A5121

BOROUGH RD

Burton upon Trent Station

Fire Brigade Sports Club

Stanley St

Mosley Street

Duke Street

B5416 STATION STREET

Infant Welfare Clinic

Moor Street

7

Anglesey street

Crown Industrial Estate

B5017

A5189

Anglesey County

Canal St

Dale Street

Alfred St

Christchurch Infants School

Park street

Alma St

James St

Sheffi

Orchard St

Burton Club

8

M6
1 Hallams Rw

M2
1 St Aidan's Cl
2 St Chad's Cl
3 St Jude's Wy
4 St Mark's Rd
5 St Martin's Cl

L4, M1, M3
Street names for these grid squares are listed at the back of the index

L1
1 Butler Ct
2 Curzon St West
3 St Paul's Sq

L6
1 Needwood St
2 Ravens Wy

Lawns Farm

Trent Meadows Medical Cen

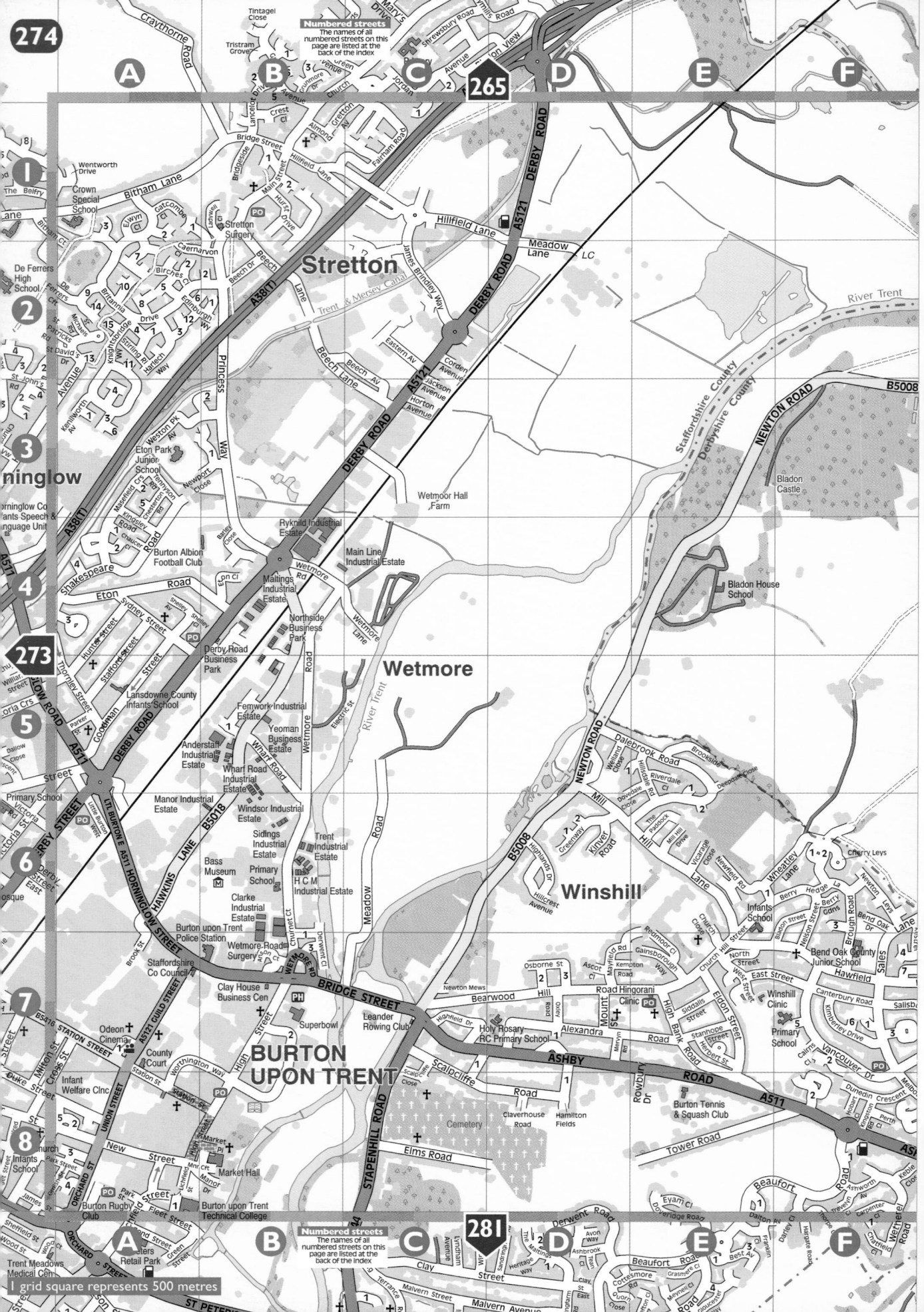

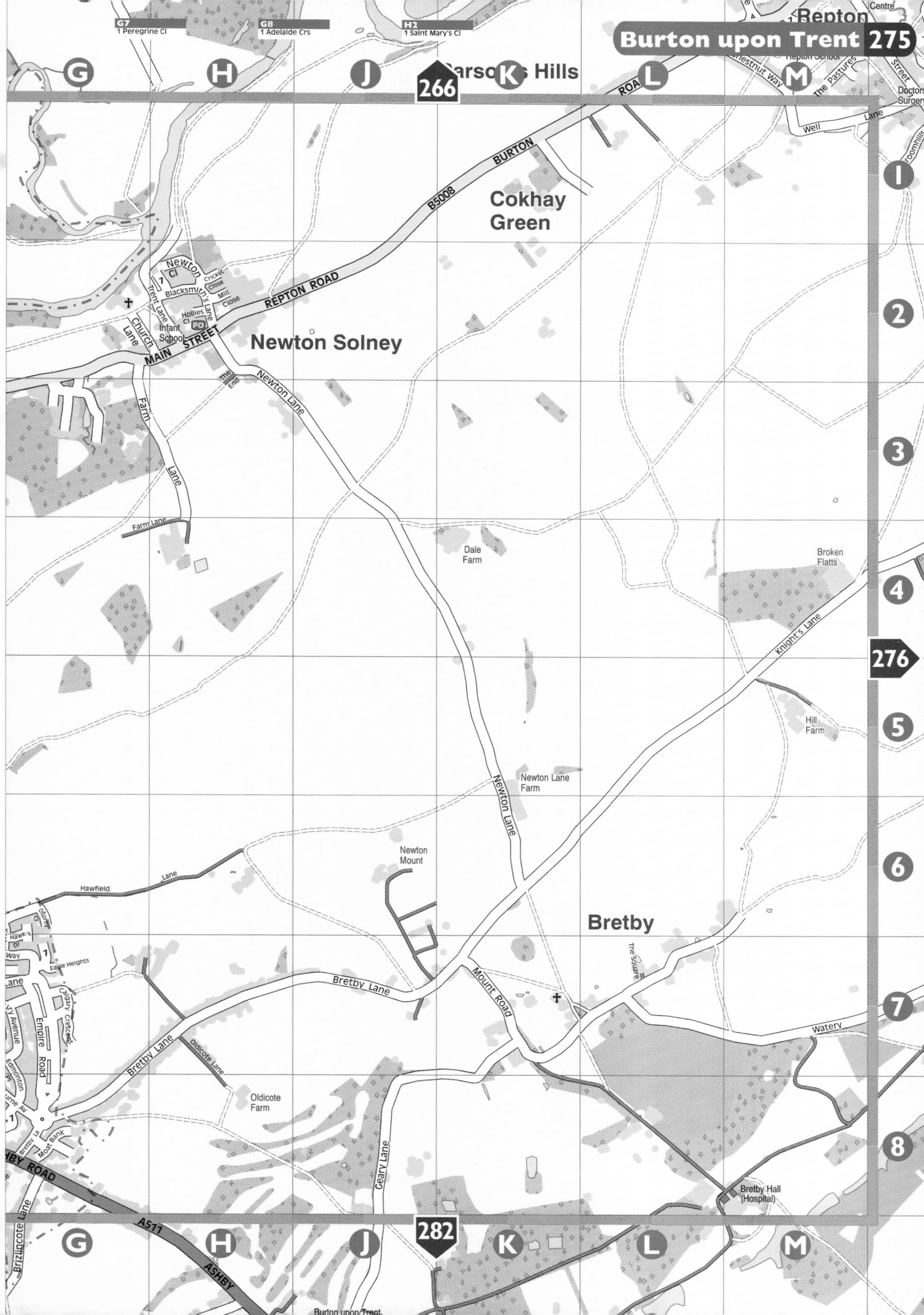

G7
1 Peregrine Cl

G8
1 Adelaide Crs

H2
1 Saint Mary's Cl

G

H

J

266

Barsons Hills

K

ROA

L

Repton

Chestnut Way

Repton School

M

The Pastures

Toormilk Street

Doctors Surger

Well Lane

I

BURTON

B5008

Cokhay Green

Newton Cl

Cricket Close

Blacksmith's Lane

Mill Close

REPTON ROAD

Trent Lane

Hollies Cl

PO

Church Lane

Infant School

MAIN STREET

The End

Newton Lane

Newton Solney

Farm Lane

Farm Lane

Dale Farm

Broken Flatts

Knight's Lane

276

Hill Farm

Newton Lane Farm

Newton Lane

Lane

Hawfield

Newton Mount

Oslyn Cl

Hawk's Dr

Eagle Heights

Calvary Crescent

Empire Road

Oldicote Lane

Bretby Lane

Bretby Lane

Bretby

The Square

Mount Road

Watery

Oldicote Farm

Geary Lane

Bretby Hall (Hospital)

Brizlincote Lane

McAt Bank

HBY ROAD

A511 ASHBY

G

H

J

282

K

L

M

Burton upon Trent

ForeG ark

H   J   K   L   M

268

Ingleby Toft

I

Warsick Lane

Seven
Spouts
Farm

Robin
Wood

2

Knowle Hill
Farm

3

A514

Woodside

4

278

STANTON HILL

5

Dame Catherine
Harpurs School

Chapel Street

Melbourne Lane

Broadstone

Rose

MAIN   STREET

Grange

Church La

Rose
La

BURTON   ROAD

A514

PO   Banton's
Lane

Harpur
Avenue

Ticknall

White
Leys

6

Narrow Lane

B5006 HIGH STREET

LANE

SCADDOWS

Foremarke Park
Farm

7

ASHBY ROAD

The
Scaddows

8

284

Staunton
Lane

Poker's
Leys

G   H   J   K   L   M

Smith's
Gorse

E3
1 Bishops Ct
2 Market Pl
3 Palmerston Ct
4 Salisbury La

E2
1 Blakemore Av

D3
1 Hatton Ct
2 Moira St
3 Orchard Cl
4 Quick Cl
5 Thomas Cook Cl

D2
1 Benbow Av
2 Blackthorn Cl
3 The Croft
4 Hardacre Cl
5 Lampad Cf
6 Redway Cft

269

King's
Newton

Trent Lane
Sleepy

Main Street

Breach Lane

DE73

Jawbone La

Station Road

Derby Road

No Cherrold
Ct

PH

Cem

Woodlands
Ct

Smith Av

Melton Av

Windsor Av

Woodlands
Ct

The Woodlands

Pack Horse Road

Oaklands Wy

Huntingdon Ct

Melbourne
Junior & Infant
School

Acacia Drive

Doctors
Surg

Woodlands

Coronation
Cl
Grange
Cl

Derby

Queensway

Beech Av

Cockshut Lane
Business
Centre

Selina
Hill

Victoria Street

Alma St

Chapel Street

Jubilee Cl

Castle Lane

Commerce Street

North St

South Street

Dunnicliffe La

Union St

George Street

Castle Street

Castle
Mews

Highfield
House

Hope St

PO

Potter Street

Blackwell

St Brides

Cockshut Lane

MELBOURNE

Selina St

High Street

Church Street

Melbourne Hall

Riding Bank

Washington
Close

Peniston
Rise

Penn Lane

Ashby Road

Shaw
House

ROBINSON'S HILL B587

B587

A514

Bleak
House

Shepherd's Lane

Bog Lane

Derby Hills House
Farm

Broadstone Lane

White
Leys

Woodhouses

Staunton
Harold
Reservoir

Melbourne

Sir Henry's Lane

The Coppice

Burney Lane

Green Lane

Calke
Abbey (NT)

Spring
Wood

285

B587

Scotlands
Farm

E4
1 Church Sq

Calke

1 grid square represents 500 metres

H4
1 Wilson Rl

H7
1 Hollow Rd

H8
1 The Crescent
2 The Green
3 Rectory Cl
4 Studfarm Cl

G H J K L M

270

1

Newton's Corner

Derbyshire County
Leicestershire County

Donington Park
Motor Racing Circuit

The Do
acing

2

Donington Park
Farm

3

WALTON

Is

†

Wilson Hall
Farm

Slade Lane

4

Forty Foot Lane

Short Hill

Dog Lane

Street

Main

Wilson

A453

5

Green Lane

Breedon Priory
Golf Club

Road

Pool Road

Parks

Derbyshire County
Leicestershire County

MOOR LANE

6

Moor Lane

The Bulwarks

†

Squirrel Lane

Lane

Dovecote

Tonge Lane

Tonge

7

Tonge Lane

Berry Avenue

Peters Close

Field Lane

A453

Melbourne Lane

1
3
4 1
2
PO
2
The Dell
Street
Main
The Dovecote
3
St Hardulphs
School

8

Ashby Road

1

Hastings Close

A453

A42(T)

**Breedon
on the Hill**

Worthington Lane

Doctor's

G H J K L M

J8
1 Cross St
2 Hillside Ct
3 Saxon Cl

Breedon Lodge

River Trent

Stapenhill

ST PETER'S BRIDGE A5189

St Peters Retail Park

Burton Rugby Club

Burton upon Trent Technical College

New Street

ORCHARD ST

UNION

Lichfield Street

Fleet Street

Bond Street

Green Street

Watson Street

Bailey Street

Orchard St

G1 1 Rose Cot Gdns

G3 1 Bedford Rd

H2 1 Ferry St

H3 1 Willow Pl

H4 1 Dorset Cl
2 Hazelwood Rd

J1 1 The Cloisters
2 St Peters Ct

Cemetery

Claverhouse Road

Hamilton Fields

Tower Road

Burton Tennis & Squash Club

Elms Road

Brizlincote Lane

Beaufort Road

Derwent Road

Doveridge Road

Evam Cl

Dunstall Brook

Windsor Dr

Clay Street

Lyndham

Malvern Street

Malvern Avenue

Lane

Clay St East

Ashbrook

Cottesmore Rd

Grafton Rd

Grasmere Cl

Meynell Cl

Gloucester Way

Spring Terrance

Asti St

Holme Farm

Brizlincote Street

Woods Lane

Merrydale Rd

Mayfield Drive

Marlborough Crescent

Outfield Rd

Holly Green

Holly Street

Five Lands Road

Convent Close

Greenvale Cl

Marston Rise

Violet Lane County Infants School

Little Theatre Co

Hill Street School

Heath Road

Ford Street

Greenwood Street

Frederick Street

Ferry Street

The Dingle

Main Street

Ivy Lodge Close

Saxon St

Paulet County High School

Staffordshire County / Derbyshire County

DE15

Waterside

Northumberland Road

Norfolk Road

Suffolk Road

Huntingdon Road

Lincoln Road

Waterside County Junior School

Bradley Street

Baker Street

Short Street Infants School

Rosliston Road

Wheatlands Road

Newtree Crs

Edge Hill Junior School

Bluestone Lane

Robert Sutton RC High School

Bretlands Way

Mead Walk

Mead Crs

Manor Crs

Manor Road

Cumberland Road

Somerset Road

Essex Road

Rutland

Kent

Devon Close

Sussex Rd

Worcester Road

Cornwall Rd

Rosliston Road

Hawthorn Crescent

Ridgeway

Fyrfield Rd

Pinewood

Laburnum

Lilac Gv

Cherrytree Rd

Weir Bank

Birchfield

Blackthorn

Lime Cl

Sandalwood Rd

Rosewood Road

Brackenwood Road

Sycamore

Laurel Grove

Maple Grove

Stapenhill Football Club

Piddocks Road

Bridle Lane

WOODLAND ROAD

A444

Stanton County Primary School

B5353

Stanton

Walton Road

Rosliston Road South

Stanton House

Royle Farm

Breach Farm

G | Street names for these grid squares are listed at the back of the index

L1, M1

H K2 1 Clematis Crs

K3 1 Honeysuckle Vw

K1 1 Barleycorn Cl
2 Hopmeadow La
3 Woods La

J3 1 Chestnut Rd

J2 1 Cricketers Cl

Morris Croft

G H J 276 K L M

I

2

3

284

5

6

7

8

H6
1 Wood Farm La

I7
1 Heron Dr
2 Kingfisher Av
3 Nightingale Dr
4 Partridge Dr
5 St Stephens Ct
6 Stanley Cl
7 Swift Cl

J8
1 Princess Cl
2 Smallthorn Pl

Greysich Farm

The Buildings Farm

A514

Coal La

Coppice House Farm

Nether Hall

Springhill

Brook St

Ticknall La

Repton Road

Dunnsmoor   Lane

PO

Kendricks Cl

Hartshorne

Hartshorne C of E Primary School

Church St

Lower Midway

Seawood Road

Longlands Rd

The Sandcliffe

Sandlands

York Cl

Coventry Cl

Malmesbury

Hereford Gdns

Winchester Drive

Exeter Cl

Dunnsmoor Way

Warwick Dr

Guildford

Lichfield Av

Durham Cl

Truro Cl

Sarisbury Drive

Lincoln Wy

Broomy Furlong

Tower Road

Dinmore Grange

A514

Slack Lane

MAIN STREET

MANCHESTER LANE

Eureka Primary School

PO

James Street

Dundee Rd

Eureka Road

Sandcroft Cl

A511

ROAD

WOODVILLE ROAD

Goseley Dale

Short Hazels

Manchester Lane

DE11

Granville Community School

Sharpswood Manor

Sorrel Drive

Campion Road

Celandine Place

Sage Drive

Goseley Avenue

Goseley Crs

Hartshill Road

Eastdale Road

Mount Road

Bretby View

Short Hazels

Bernard Street

Court St

Frederick St

Cranville Street

Burton Rd Surgery

Rose Hill

HARTSHORNE ROAD

A514

The Cinema

Wren

Dove Cl

Brookdale

Limestone Close

Bemrose

Bantock

Falcon Cl

Edward St

Blacksmith's Lane

Woodhouse Business Centre

WOODVILLE ST

SWADLINCOTE ROAD   A514

Woodville

Kiln Way

Swallow Rd

Belvedere Rd

Merlin Way

Plover Av

Finch Cl

Viking Business Centre

Kestrel Rd

Station Road

Millfield St

Beech Drive

A511

Field Lane

Boundary

Vicarage Road

Woodville County Infant School

Woodville C of E Junior School

New Road

Foster Rd

HIGH STREET

Sun Street

Holly

Canner Cl

Albion Street

Thorn Street

Chapel Street

Buckley

South

Blackfordby House

Heath

Pool Street

Occupation Lane

shire County

shire County

G H ROAD J 290 K J Rift Lane L M

K8
1 The Shrubbery

K3
1 Pear Tree Cl

Blackfordby C of E School

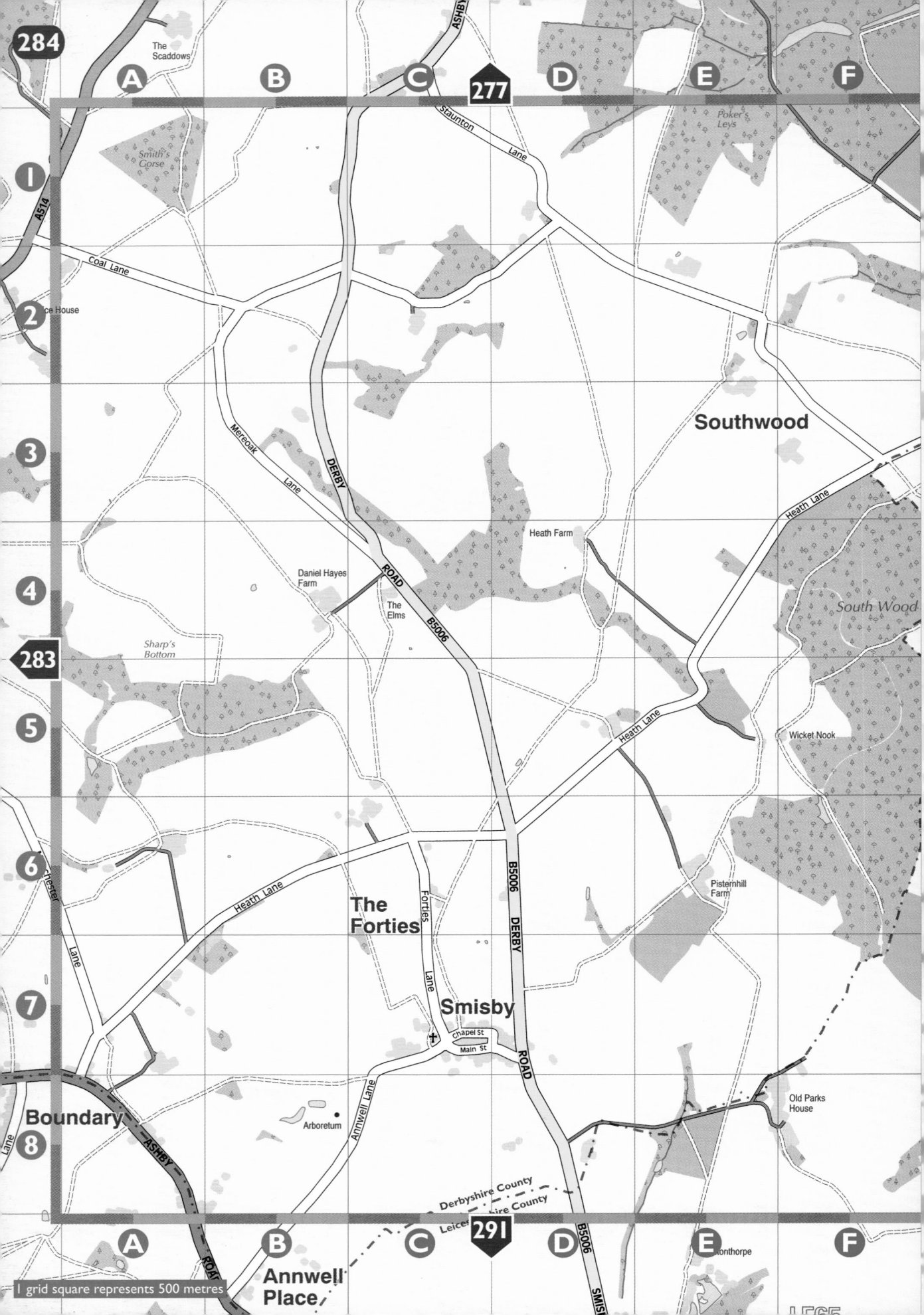

A
B
C
277
D
E
F

The Scaddows

I
A514
Smith's Gorse

Poker's Leys

Staunton Lane

Coal Lane

2
ce House

Southwood

3
Mereoak Lane
DERBY
Heath Lane

4
Daniel Hayes Farm
ROAD
The Elms
B5006
Heath Farm
South Wood

Sharp's Bottom

5
Heath Lane
Wicket Nook

6
Chester Lane
Heath Lane
B5006
DERBY
Pisternhill Farm

The Forties
Forties Lane

7
Smisby
Chapel St
Main St
ROAD
B5006
Old Parks House

Boundary
8
Lane
ASHBY
Arboretum
Annwell Lane
onthorpe

Derbyshire County
Leicestershire County

A
B
C
291
D
SMIS
B5006
E
F

Annwell Place

G2
1 Leedhams Cft

M4
1 Vicarage Wk

Grove Farm

G **H** **J** 280 **K** **L** **M**

Warren Fm

I

Walton-on-Trent

Main Street

Barr Hall

Ladle End Lane

Bells End Road

Orchard Close

Harbin Road

Lane

PO

1

Walton-on-Trent C of E Primary School

Standing Butts Close

Fairfield

Rosliston Road

2

Walton Hill Farm

3

Burton Road

Coton Road

Holdon Croft

The Glebe

Rosliston

PO

4

Oaklands Farm

Primary School

1

Yew Tree R

Main St

W St

288

Borough Fields

5

Field House

Catron Lane

Coton La

Lads Grave

6

Overfields Farm

Church Croft

PO

Elms Road

Glebe

Burton Road

Summerfields

Church Street

New Road

Elmsleigh

Main Street

Mill Street

Pri St

Co in t

7

Donkhill Farm

2

Mansditch Farm

8

Little Liverpool

G **H** **J** 292 **K** **L** **M**

The Crosses

Grafton House

G H J **282** K L M

K1 Appleby Industrial
1 Darley Cl
2 Derwent Cl
3 The Holdings

L1
1 Leyburn Cl

Beresford Dale

Wye Dale

Darley Worscote Dale

Hillside Gardens

Woodlands

Pennine Way
Junior
L6
1 Edward St

Charles St

Market St

York

Common Rd

Robin Hood
Place

John

Derbyshire County
Leicestershire County

I
Albert

**Castle
Gresley**

Burton Road

Swadlincote Lane

Home Farm Ct

Knob
Fields

Mount Road

A444

Burton
Rd

Bridge
St

Chapel
Street

PO

Arnold
Close

Linton Road

Bass's Crescent

Pine
Walk

Cedar
Road

Oak Cl

The Scots

Arthur St

**Mount
Pleasant**

Castle Road

Princess Street

Station Street

Bank St

Spring
Close

Guild St

Colliery Road

Industrial
Estate

Meynell St

Ashbourne
Drive

Regent Street

Oxford Street

Talbot
Street

Queen St

Chapel
St

Church

Railway
Side

Gresley Rovers
Football Club

Primary
School

Mickleton
Close

Rockcliffe
Close

The
Downs

Penbridge Rd

Udale Gv

Arnside Rd

Silkstone Cl

Covert
Place

Main Street

B586

MUSHROOM LANE

The
Close

Edward
Street

Albert Village
County School

**Church
Gresley**

2

Mount Pleasant Road

Infant School

Burton Road

A444

Fields
Lane

Greenfields

Park Road

Occupation Road

3

Manor
House

Close

**Linton
Heath**

Linton Heath

4

Main Street

Winchester
Drive

Sycamore
Cl

Windsor
Rd

Helston
Close

Emery
Close

Weatherhill
Field

PO

Patrick
St

Primary
School

290

Spring
Co

5

Colliery Lane

Seal Wood Lane

Sealwood Lane

Green Lane

Burton Road

A444

Spring Cottage

S

Co

6

Alexandra
Road

1

Coronation
Street

Woodlands Crs

Scamham
Rd

WOODVILLE ROAD

B5004

Overseal
CP School

Slackey Lane

**Gorsey
Leys**

Hall Croft Avenue

Surgery

Manor
School

MOIRA ROAD

B5003

7

Overseal

Bramble Wk

MAIN STREET

Valley Road

Clifton
Close

Lullington Road

Squirrel
Walk

PO

ACRESFORD ROAD

Shortheath

**She
Hea**

8

Grange
Wood

Grangewood
Hall

Gunby Hill

L7
1 Ashley Cl

Derby

Leice

292

287

A B C D E F

1

Mansditch
Farm

Little
Liverpool

The
Crosses

Grafton
House

Pessall
Farm

2

Homestall
Wood

Pessall Brook

Raddle Farm

Pessall Lane

3

Lady
Leys

Radfields
m

4

Raddle Lane

Edingale Fields
Farm

Green Lane

Westbrook
Farm

Close
Croft
PO

5

Edingale

Lullington Road

Main Road

Church Lane

Hatch
Lane

Church
Hollow

Schofield
Lane

Staffordshire County
Derbyshire County

West Brook

6

Mill Lane

Poplars
Farm

7

Main Road

Church
Side

Syerscote
Lane

Mease Lane

8

Manor Lane
PO

Haunton

A B C D E F

Twizles Lane

Syerscote Lane

I grid square represents 500 metres

G
H High Flatts Farm
J
288
K
L
M

1
2
3
4
294
5
6
7
8

Grange Wood

Woodfields Farm

Grangewood Lodge

West View Farm

Home Farm

Hollows Farm

The Grange

Dag Lane

PO

Lullington

Seal Brook

Bald Hill's Farm

River Mease

Mill Farm

Lullington Road

Stones Bridge

Seal Fields Farm

Clifton Hall

Derbyshire County
Staffordshire County

Main Street

Tudor Rd
St Rd
Church St
St Andrews Cl
David's St
Nethersea Road

St Andrews C of E CP School

Smithy Lane

Chestnut Lane

Clifton Campville

Coppice Lane

Clifton Lodge

G
H
J
K
L
M

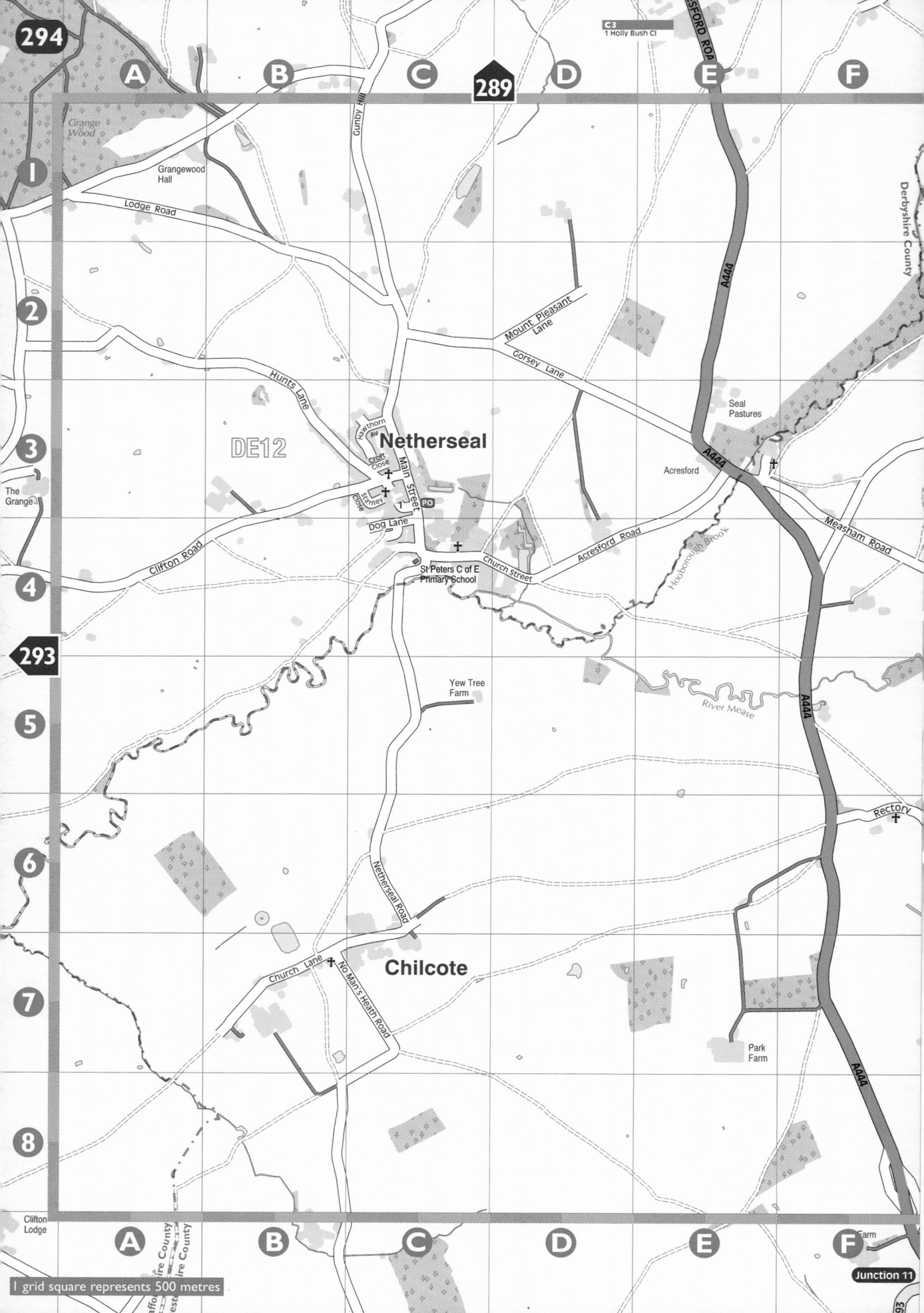

Abbeydale 69 L1
Abbeydale Park 69 H4
Abney 65 J6
Albert Village 290 A1
Aldercar 202 C6
Alder Moor 264 C7
Alderwasley 184 C2
Aldwark 169 J3
Alfreton 175 H6
Alkmonton 234 F1
Allenton 256 F6
Allestree 226 C7
Alma 189 K5
Alport 139 G4
Alsop en le Dale 167 H7
Alstonefield 166 B6
Alton 143 M5
Alvaston 257 L3
Ambaston 258 F4
Annwell Place 291 H1
Anslow 272 F3
Anslow Gate 272 B3
Anslow Lees 273 G5
Apperknowle 91 L1
Arbourthorne 56 A2
Arkwright Town 111 M8
Arrunden 9 J1
Ashbourne 194 A8
Ashby-de-la-Zouch ... 291 L3
Ashford in the Water 122 B3
Ashgate 109 M7
Ashopton 40 C8
Ashover 143 H6
Ashover Hay 158 E5
Aston 49 M6
Aston 250 C6
Aston-on-Trent 270 E2
Astwith 146 D5
Atlow 195 K5
Ault Hucknall 147 J3
Awsworth 217 M6
Bagshaw 61 J3
Bagthorpe 189 J7
Bakestone Moor 96 A5
Bakewell 122 F4
Balance Hill 247 L4
Ballidon 168 D8
Bamford 50 D6
The Banks 33 G6
Barber Booth 47 K4
Bargate 213 M1
Barlborough 94 E2
Barlow 90 C8
Barrow Hill 92 D6
Barrowhill 218 C4
Barrows Green 188 F5
Barrow upon Trent ... 268 C3
Barton Turn 286 E1
Baslow 106 A5
Bassett 53 G5
Batemoor 70 D5
Beam Hill 273 K1
Beauchief 69 L2
Beauvale 203 M7
Beeley 124 E6
Beeston 245 M3
Beighton Hill 183 J7
Belper 199 L5
Belper Lane End 198 F2
Belph 96 F6
Biggin 151 M7
Biggin 196 D5
Birchover 154 E2
Birch Vale 34 M4
Birdholme 128 C3
Birleyhay 72 K3
Blackbrook 61 H4
Blackbrook 198 E5
Blackfordby 290 F1
Blackwall 196 C3
Blackwell 101 M6
Blackwell 176 C1
Blore 192 C3
Blount's Green 247 K5
Bolehill 55 K8
Bolehill 89 M8
Bolehill 129 L1
Bolehill 171 J8
Bolsover 113 K8
Bonsall 171 H1
Boothgate 200 B3
Borrowash 242 E8
Boulton 257 K4
Boulton Moor 257 K7
Boundary 283 M8
Boylestone 234 F6
Boylestonfield 235 H5
Boythorpe 2 D8
Brackenfield 159 G7
Bradbourne 180 F5
Bradford 138 F5
Bradley 209 J2
Bradway 69 M5
Bradwell 64 E3
Bradwell Hills 64 E4
Brailsford 223 J2
Brailsford Green 223 G3
Bramley 72 C7
Bramley Vale 147 G1
Brampton 2 A4
Bramshall 246 F3
Branston 280 B3
Brassington 181 K1
Breadsall 227 H6
Breadsall Hilltop 241 G1
Breaston 259 M2
Breedon on the Hill . 279 H8
Bretby 275 L6
Bretton 85 K2
Brick Houses 68 F2
Bridgeholm Green 60 D2
Bridgemont 44 B8
Brightgate 155 K6
Brimington 111 J3
Brimington Common . 111 K5
Brincliffe 54 F4
Brindwoodgate 89 M5
Brinsley 203 H3

Broadbottom 24 C2
Broadholm 199 K3
Brockhurst 142 F4
Brook Bottom 43 H1
Brookfield 17 G7
Brookhouses 34 D3
Brookside 109 K8
Brough 49 M8
Brund 150 B3
The Brushes 91 J6
Brushfield 103 H6
Bubnell 105 M4
Bullbridge 185 M5
Bullhurst Hill 211 K6
Burbage 99 H3
Burnaston 254 C5
Burntheath 252 E6
Burton upon Trent ... 274 B7
Butterley 158 C5
Butterley 187 H7
Buxton 99 M4
Buxworth 59 K1
Caldwell 288 C3
Calke 285 H1
Callingwood 272 A6
Callow 182 E6
Callow 111 J7
Calow 129 K2
Calow Green 129 K2
Calton 191 H1
Calton Lees 124 B5
Calver 105 L1
Calver Sough 86 F8
Camphill 64 F8
Canholes 99 H5
Carr Vale 131 J2
Carsington 182 B3
Carter Knowle 55 G5
Cartledge 89 K3
Castle Donington 271 M8
Castle Gresley 289 H1
Castleton 48 F8
Cauldon 190 D3
Cavendish Bridge 271 M2
Chaddesden 241 J2
Chapel-en-le-Frith ... 60 F5
Chapel Milton 60 E2
Charlestown 25 L4
Charlesworth 25 G4
Charnock Hall 56 D8
Chellaston 269 K1
Chelmorton 119 K2
Cherrytree Hill 241 K5
Chesterfield 3 G6
Chilcote 294 C7
Chinley 60 C1
Chinley Head 45 J4
Chisworth 24 E5
Chunal 25 M6
Church Broughton 251 K3
Church Gresley 289 L1
Church Mayfield 207 G4
Churchtown 140 D7
Church Wilne 259 L6
Cinderhill 200 A8
Clay Cross 145 G7
Clay Mills 265 K7
Cliff ... 34 .... E7
Clifton 207 H4
Clifton Campville 293 J8
Clowne 95 G6
Coal Aston 71 G6
Cock Alley 129 K1
Cockyard 60 A5
Codnor 201 M3
Codnor Breach 201 K6
Codnor Gate 201 L1
Codnor Park 188 C7
Coisley Hill 57 K4
Cokhay Green 275 K1
Coldeaton 166 E4
Colshaw 117 H6
Combs 80 B1
Common End 146 C4
Common Side 90 A7
Commonside 162 B8
Common Side 216 B2
Commonside 222 F1
Compton 208 A1
Coplow Dale 64 B8
Corbriggs 129 J5
Cossall 230 F1
Cossall Marsh 217 M8
Cotes Park 176 A8
Cotmanhay 217 H6
Coton in the Clay 262 C3
Coton in the Elms ... 288 A7
Coton Park 288 F2
Cotton 204 A2
Cowdale 100 D6
Cowers Lane 198 A7
Cowhill 199 K8
Cowley 90 A3
Cowlow 100 F4
Craythorne 265 G8
Cressbrook 103 K3
Creswell 96 C8
Crewton 257 J2
Crich 185 K1
Crich Carr 185 G1
Crist 59 L2
Cromford 171 J4
Cropper 236 E7
Cross Hill 201 M4
Cross o'th hands 211 H1
Crowdecote 135 H3
Crowden 12 B7
Crowhole 90 A6
Cubley Common 220 B7
Cumberhills Cottages 225 K1
Curbar 87 H8
Cutthorpe 109 H3
Dagdale 246 D1
Dalbury 253 L1
Dale Abbey 229 J8
Dalebank 158 F2
Dale End 153 M3
Dale Moor 229 L8
Dalestorth 163 K4

Danebank 43 H5
Danesmoor 145 H7
Darfoulds 97 H1
Darley Abbey 226 D8
Darley Bridge 155 L2
Darley Hillside 141 G6
Darley Moor 220 C2
Deepclough 18 A2
Denby 214 F1
Denby Bottles 214 D1
Denby Common 201 K7
Derby 4 E5
Dimple 156 D4
Disley 42 E4
Doehole 158 D8
Doe Lea 147 H1
Donisthorpe 295 H1
Dore 69 H3
Dove Green 189 H4
Dove Holes 81 J1
Doveridge 248 D2
Draycott 259 J3
Draycott in the Clay 262 A5
Dronfield 90 F1
Dronfield Woodhouse 69 L8
Drum Hill 227 J1
Duckmanton 112 C5
Duffield 213 H7
Duffieldbank 213 K6
Dunford Bridge 15 G1
Dunsa 123 M1
Dunsill 162 C2
Dunston 109 M2
Eagle Tor 139 K8
Earl Sterndale 118 F7
Eastwood 203 H7
Eaton Hill 226 F1
Ecclesall 54 D5
Eckington 72 F7
Edale 47 M2
Edale End 49 H1
Edensor 124 A2
Edingale 292 A5
Edlaston 207 L8
Ednaston 222 E3
Efflinch 286 A3
Eggington 265 M5
Eggington Common ... 265 M3
Ellastone 205 L7
Elmton 114 E3
Elton 154 C4
Elvaston 258 D5
Emmett Carr 93 M2
Etwall 253 L6
Eyam 86 A4
Fackley 162 D3
Fairfield 100 A2
Fallgate 158 D1
Fallinge 124 F8
Farhill 143 L6
Farlands Booth 35 K6
Far Laund 199 M4
Farley 156 D1
Farley 204 A5
Farnah Green 198 F7
Fauld 262 F5
Fawfieldhead 134 B6
Fenny Bentley 193 L1
Fernilee 79 H1
Findern 255 G8
Flagg 120 C4
Flash 116 E7
Flaxholme 226 C1
The Flourish 229 G8
Foolow 85 G4
Ford 72 A4
Foremark 268 A4
Forest Town 165 L1
The Forties 284 C6
Foston 251 G5
Fourlane Ends 174 F6
Frecheville 56 F6
Freebirch 108 A4
Friden 152 C4
Friezeland 189 L8
Fritchley 185 K4
Froggatt 87 G5
Fulwood 53 M2
Fulwood 177 M2
Furness Vale 43 M7
Gallows Inn 230 E4
Gamesley 17 H8
Gateford Common 77 L3
Giltbrook 217 M2
Glapwell 147 M2
Gleadless 56 D6
Gleadless Valley 56 B7
Glossop 26 B2
Glutton Bridge 118 E8
Golden Valley 187 M7
Gorseybank 183 K3
Gorsey Leys 289 M6
Goseley Dale 283 K5
Gosforth Valley 70 A8
Gowhole 44 B6
Grangemill 169 L2
Grassmoor 129 H8
Great Cubley 234 B1
Great Hucklow 84 D2
Great Longstone 104 D6
Great Wilne 259 L8
Greenhill 70 B3
Greenhillocks 201 H2
Greenside 71 L7
Greystones 54 C3
Grindleford 86 E2
Grindlow 84 F3
Grindsbrook Booth ... 47 L1
Gun Hills 212 A5
The Gutter 199 M6
Hackenthorpe 57 H6
Hade Edge 9 L3
Hadfield 17 J6
Hady 111 G8
Hague Bar 43 J2
The Hague 16 F8
Hales Green 220 E3
Halfway 73 H3

Hallam Fields 230 D6
Hallfield Gate 175 G1
Hallowes 90 F2
Hammersmith 187 G6
Hanbury 262 D6
Hanbury Woodend ... 262 B8
Handley 159 H2
Harden 9 M6
Hardgatewall 82 E7
Hardstoft 146 D7
Hardstoft Common ... 146 B6
Hare Edge 107 M4
Harehill 234 D7
Hargate Hill 25 H2
Harlesthorpe 95 H5
Harpur Hill 100 A7
Harthill 75 J4
Hartington 151 C4
Hartshorne 283 K3
Hasland 129 C3
Hassop 105 H5
Hatton 264 A1
Haunton 292 E8
Hawk Green 32 B7
Hayfield 34 F8
Hazelwood 212 E1
Heage 200 B3
Heage Common 199 L1
Heanor 202 C7
Heanor Gate 215 M2
Hearthstone 157 G8
Heath 130 D8
Heathcote 151 L5
Heath End 285 C3
The Heath 247 K1
Heathtop 251 K4
Heeley 55 K4
Hemsworth 55 M7
Hepthorne Lane 145 H3
Higham 159 M7
Highcliffe 85 M3
Higher Chisworth 24 C6
Higher Dinting 17 K8
Higher Disley 43 G5
Highfield 55 L2
Highfields 145 L2
High Lane 42 B3
Highlane 72 B2
High Moor 74 B5
Highwood 247 M6
Hilcote 176 F1
Hillclifflane 197 J6
Hillcross 255 L3
Hill Somersal 233 K8
Hills Town 131 M2
Hill Top 90 D3
Hilltop 143 H5
Hill Top 203 L8
Hilton 253 G8
Hindlow 118 E3
Hobroyd 25 L3
Hockley 128 D3
Hodthorpe 96 F4
Hoften's Cross 190 B6
Hognaston 181 K8
Holbeck 73 K2
Holbrook 214 A4
Holbrook 213 L3
Holbrook Moor 213 L3
Holehouse 24 F4
Holestone 157 M3
Hollington 222 C6
Hollington Grove 222 B8
Hollingwood 111 L1
Hollingworth 16 F5
Hollins 108 D6
Hollinsclough 117 L8
Hollins End 56 E5
Holloway 172 E5
Hollow Meadows 41 M6
Holme 8 B3
Holmesdale 70 F8
Holmesfield 89 K2
The Holmes 5 H4
Holmewood 146 A1
Holmley Common 70 D6
Holymoorside 127 G4
Hope 49 J6
Hope 166 A7
Hopton 182 C3
Horninglow 273 M3
Horsleygate 89 G4
Horsley Woodhouse . 214 F4
Horwich End 59 H5
Hulland 196 A8
Hulland Moss 210 B1
Hulland Ward 196 B7
Hull End 45 K8
Hulme End 150 C7
Hundall 91 L3
Huthwaite 162 B7
Ible 170 B3
Idridgehay 197 H4
Idridgehay Green 197 G3
Ilam 178 B8
Ilkeston 217 G8
Ingleby 268 D7
Inkersall Green 112 A4
Intake 56 D5
Ireton Wood 197 H6
Ironville 188 B6
Jacksdale 188 E7
Jordanthorpe 70 E3
Kedleston 224 F3
Kelstedge 143 G6
Kettleshulme 58 B6
Kilburn 214 D2
Killamarsh 73 K4
King's Mills 270 E6
King's Newton 278 F1
King Sterndale 100 F5
Kirk Hallam 229 M5
Kirk Ireton 196 F1
Kirk Langley 224 B8

Kniveton 194 D1
Knockerdown 181 J6
Knotbury 116 C5
Ladmanlow 99 H6
Ladybrook 164 B3
Landslow Green 16 E3
Lane End 161 K3
Lane Ends 33 G1
Lane Ends 43 H6
Lane Ends 236 E8
Lane Head 84 A5
Langley 216 E1
Langley Common 238 E2
Langley Green 238 A1
Langley Mill 202 E7
Langwith 133 J2
Langwith Junction ... 132 F4
Larklands 230 D3
Lea 172 E3
Leabrooks 187 L3
Leadmill 66 D5
Leam 66 D7
Lee Head 24 F4
Lees 237 L3
Ley Hey Park 32 B3
Lidgate 88 F2
Lightwood 71 J2
Limekiln Field 113 L7
Linton 288 F4
Linton Heath 289 H4
Litchurch 5 J8
Little Bolehill 183 L1
Little Chester 240 D3
Little Cubley 234 B2
Little Eaton 226 F2
Little Hallam 230 B4
Little Hayfield 34 F5
Little Hucklow 84 B1
Little Longstone 104 A6
Littlemoor 143 M8
Littleover 255 K2
Litton 84 C7
Litton Mill 103 H4
Lodge Moor 53 H1
Longcliffe 169 J6
Long Duckmanton ... 112 C6
Long Eaton 260 F3
Longford 236 A2
Longfordlane 236 D5
Longlane 237 H1
Longnor 134 C2
Longshaw 204 A3
Longway Bank 172 C7
Loscoe 202 A6
Loundsley Green 109 L4
Lount 285 K7
Lowedges 70 C4
Lower Crossings 60 C4
Lower Ellastone 205 M8
Lower Hartshay 186 C7
Lower Kilburn 214 C3
Lower Longley 9 K1
Lower Midway 283 H4
Lower Pilsley 145 L7
Lower Thurvaston ... 236 D4
Lowfield 55 K3
Low Leighton 44 F4
Loxley Green 247 C8
Lullington 293 H3
Lumsdale 157 H4
Mackworth 239 H5
Makeney 213 K4
Malcoff 46 B8
Manor Estate 56 C1
Mansfield 164 C3
Mansfield Woodhouse 149 K7
Mapleton 193 J6
Mapperley 216 C2
Marchington 249 H8
Marehay 201 C4
Markeaton 239 L2
Maripool 216 C2
Marple 32 B4
Marple Bridge 32 C3
Marpleridge 32 C8
Marsh Lane 72 C7
Marston Montgomery 233 J2
Marston on Dove 264 E2
Martin Hill 192 D5
Mastin Moor 93 M7
Matley 16 C4
Matlock Bank 156 E4
Matlock Bath 156 D8
Matlock Cliff 157 G6
Matlock Dale 156 D7
Mayfield 206 F3
Meadow Head 70 B1
Measham 295 L5
Meersbrook 55 L5
Melbourne 278 C3
Mellor 33 H4
Mercaton 210 F7
Mickleover 239 G8
Mickley 69 L7
Middlecroft 112 A2
Middle Handley 92 C2
Middle Mayfield 206 E3
Middleton 138 B7
Middleton 171 G6
Milford 213 K3
Mill Brow 33 H2
Milldale 166 C8
Miller's Dale 102 C2
Millers Green 183 H4
Millhouses 54 E7
Millington Green 196 D6
Millthorpe 89 G5
Milltown 158 D2
Milton 267 G8
Moira 290 C6
Money Hill 291 L2
Monyash 136 F1
Moorend 33 K4
Moorend 208 F2
Moorfield 26 C4
Moorhaigh 148 D7
Moorhall 89 C8
Moorhole 72 D1

Moorside	182	E8
Moravian Settlement	242	E6
Morley	227	M4
Morleymoor	227	L3
Morley Park	200	D4
Morley Smithy	228	A2
Morton	160	C5
Mosborough	72	F2
Mottram in Longdendale	16	E6
Mottram Rise	16	B3
Mount Pleasant	199	G4
Mount Pleasant	276	B1
Mount Pleasant	289	C3
Mudd	16	D8
Mugginton	211	G8
Muggintonlane End	211	G4
Nether Booth	48	D1
Nether Burrows	223	L7
Nether Edge	55	H4
Nether End	106	C5
Nether Handley	92	C4
Nether Heage	186	A8
Netherland Green	248	B8
Nether Langwith	133	K1
Nether Loads	126	E2
Nether Moor	144	D1
Nether Padley	87	G1
Netherseal	294	C3
Netherthorpe	93	K8
Newbold	110	B3
New Bolsover	113	G8
New Brimington	111	H1
New Brinsley	203	H1
New Eastwood	217	J2
Newhall	282	B4
Newhaven	152	B5
New Horwich	59	H4
New Houghton	148	B2
Newlands	216	D1
New Mills	43	L2
New Sawley	260	E5
New Smithy	60	D1
New Stanton	230	B7
Newthorpe	217	M1
Newthorpe Common	217	M3
Newton	161	J7
Newton Solney	275	H2
New Totley	69	H6
Newtown	43	L5
New Whittington	91	M6
Norbury	219	G1
Normanton	256	A3
Normanton Spring	57	H4
Norris Hill	290	F4
Northedge	143	L3
North Wingfield	145	K4
Northwood	140	E5
Norton	70	E2
Norton Woodseats	55	K7
Norwood	74	C2
Oakerthorpe	174	F7
Oaks Green	249	M3
The Oaks	213	G4
Oakthorpe	295	K4
Oakwood	241	K1
Ockbrook	243	C5
Oker	155	M3
Old Brampton	109	G6
Old Dam	62	E6
Old Glossop	18	B8
Old Tupton	144	E3
Old Whittington	110	E1
Ollerbrook Booth	48	B2
Openwoodgate	200	A7
Orgreave	57	M1
Osleston	237	G4
Osmaston	208	D6
Osmaston	257	G3
Outwoods	273	L4
Over Burrows	223	K6
Over End	106	B4
Overend	142	D4
Overgreen	108	E3
Over Haddon	122	D8
Overseal	289	K7
Owen's Bank	263	K5
Owler Bar	88	D2
Owlthorpe	57	L8
Oxclose	73	K4
Oxcroft Estate	113	M3
Oxton Rakes	108	E2
Packington	291	K8
Padfield	17	M5
Painleyhill	246	A2
Palmer Moor	249	H3
Palterton	131	K5
Parkgate	205	J5
Parkhead	54	C7
Park Head	185	M1
Park Nook	225	K2
Parkhouse Green	145	J6
Parson's Hills	266	D8
Parwich	179	M1
Peak Dale	81	L5
Peak Forest	62	C7
Pear Tree	256	D2
Peasehill	201	J2
Penny Green	96	F6
Pentrich	186	E5
Perryfoot	62	B3
Pikehall	153	G7
Pilhough	140	A4
Pilsbury	135	L7
Pilsley	105	M7
Pilsley	146	A8
Pilsley Green	160	F2
Pinxton	176	E8
Plain Spot	189	H8
Plaistow	173	K4
Pleasley	148	D5
Pleasleyhill	148	F5
Plumbley	72	E3
Pomeroy	119	M6
Poolsbrook	112	C3
Potter Somersal	233	K5
Press	144	A3
Prestwood	218	B1
Pride Park	241	H6
Priestcliffe	102	C5
Priestcliffe Ditch	101	M5
Pye Bridge	188	D3
Pye Hill	188	D5
Quarndon	225	M3
Quarndon Common	226	A2
Quixhill	218	B3
Radbourne	238	A5
Radmanthwaite	149	G7
Ramshorn	204	D3
Ranmoor	54	B1
Rawson Green	200	C8
Renishaw	93	K3
Repton	266	F8
Rhodesia	77	J5
Riber	157	H7
Richmond	57	H2
Riddings	188	A4
Ridgeway	72	B2
Ridgeway	185	L6
Ridgeway Moor	72	B4
Ringinglow	53	K6
Ripley	187	J8
Rise End	171	H6
Risley	244	B6
Robin Hood	107	G6
Rocester	218	C7
Rodsley	221	K5
Roe Cross	16	C5
Rolleston	55	M5
Rolleston on Dove	264	F6
Rose Hill	5	G9
Rosliston	287	M4
Roston	219	G3
Roston Common	219	L4
Rough Hay	272	D5
Rowarth	34	B3
Rowland	105	G4
Rowsley	140	C2
Rowthorne	147	L3
Rylah	131	J5
St Luke's	4	B6
Sandiacre	244	D4
Sapperton	250	F1
Sawley	260	C6
Scarcliffe	132	B4
Scotches	199	H4
Scropton	263	H1
Selston	189	H3
Selston Common	189	K4
Selston Green	188	F3
Shacklecross	259	G1
Shardlow	259	H8
Sharrow	55	G3
Shatton	65	H1
Sheen	150	D3
Sheepbridge	91	G8
Sheffield Park	56	B1
Sheldon	121	L4
Shellbrook	291	G4
Shelton Lock	257	H7
Shipley	216	D3
Shipley Common	217	G2
Shirebrook	133	J7
Shireoaks	46	B7
Shireoaks	77	H3
Shirland	174	F1
Shirley	222	B2
Shobnall	273	J7
Short Heath	290	A8
Shottle	198	B2
Shottlegate	198	D7
Shuttlewood	113	K4
Simmondley	25	J3
Sinfin	256	B7
Skegby	163	J3
Slackhall	61	J2
Slaley	170	F3
Slatepit Dale	127	J5
Sleet Moor	187	K2
Smalldale	64	B2
Smalldale	82	A3
Smalley	215	J5
Smalley Common	215	K8
Smalley Green	215	J7
Smisby	284	C7
Smithy Houses	200	E7
Snape Hill	70	E7
Snelston	206	E7
Snelston Common	219	M2
Snelston Hall	207	G7
Snitterton	156	A5
Somercotes	188	B2
Somersal Herbert	233	J7
Sookholme	133	M8
Sothall	73	J1
South Normanton	176	C4
South Wingfield	174	A7
Southwood	284	E3
Sparrowpit	61	M4
Spinkhill	74	A8
Spital	3	M7
Spitalhill	207	M3
Spondon	242	D5
Spring Cottage	290	A5
Spring Hill	213	G5
Staden	100	B6
Stainsby	146	E3
Stanfree	113	L2
Stanhope Brentby	282	C1
Stanley	162	A1
Stanley	228	F4
Stanley Common	228	D2
Stanton	206	A1
Stanton by Bridge	269	G7
Stanton-by-Dale	244	B2
Stanton Gate	244	F2
Stanton Hill	162	E4
Stanton in Peak	139	L5
Stanton Lees	140	C7
Stapenhill	281	J2
Stapleford	245	H3
Starkholmes	171	M1
Staveley	112	C1
Stenson	267	K2
Sterndale Moor	119	H4
Stonebroom	160	D7
Stonegravels	110	D5
Stoneyford	202	D3
Stoney Middleton	86	C7
Stony Houghton	148	C1
Street Lane	200	E5
Strelley	231	M2
Stretton	159	M3
Stretton	274	B2
Stretton en le Field	295	C6
Strines	42	F1
Stubbley	70	A7
Sudbury	250	B6
Sunny Hill	256	A5
Sutton Forest Side	163	L7
Sutton in Ashfield	162	E2
Sutton on the Hill	252	E2
Sutton Scarsdale	130	C4
Swadlincote	282	C6
Swanwick	187	H4
Swarkestone	269	H4
Swathwick	127	L6
Swinscoe	192	C5
Taddington	102	E7
Tansley	157	L6
Tansley Knoll	157	K5
Tapton	110	F4
Taxal	58	F6
Temple Normanton	129	K6
Teversal	162	F1
Thornhill	50	C7
Thornsett	34	B8
Thorpe	193	G1
Thorpe Salvin	76	B4
Threelows	204	B1
Thrumpton	261	M7
Thulston	258	D6
Thurvaston	233	H1
Thurvaston	236	F2
Tibshelf	161	K4
Tibshelf Wharf	162	A3
Ticknall	277	K6
Tideswell	83	M6
Tintwistle	17	L3
Tissington	179	K5
Toadmoor	185	J8
Tomthorn	81	J6
Totley	68	F6
Totley Brook	69	G5
Totley Rise	69	J5
Toton	245	K8
Townend	60	F3
Town End	83	M7
Townhead	68	F3
Town Head	83	M5
Trentlock	261	H7
Troway	71	K6
Trowell	230	F7
Trusley	237	J7
Tunstead	82	D7
Tupton	145	G3
Turnditch	197	L8
Turnerwood	76	F3
Turnstead Milton	59	M5
Tutbury	263	K4
Two Dales	141	H7
Twyford	267	K4
Underwood	189	J8
Unstone	91	H3
Unstone Green	91	G4
Unthank	89	G6
Upper Birchwood	176	D7
Upper Booth	47	H3
Upperdale	103	K5
Upper Ellastone	205	L6
Upper End	81	L5
Upper Hackney	156	D2
Upper Hartshay	186	D8
Upper Langwith	133	G3
Upper Loads	126	B3
Upper Midway	282	F3
Upper Newbold	109	K2
Upper Padley	67	G7
Upperthorpe	74	A5
Uppertown	142	D3
Upper Town	170	F1
Upper Town	181	K7
Upperwood	171	J2
Uttoxeter	247	L1
Wadshelf	108	C7
Waingroves	201	K3
Waldley	232	F3
Walton	127	M2
Walton-on-Trent	286	F1
Wardlow	84	F8
Warhill	16	E7
Warmbrook	183	H2
Wash	60	F1
Waterhouses	190	D1
Waterloo	145	L6
Waterside	44	B7
Wensley	155	K3
Wessington	174	B2
West Broughton	249	J3
West Edge	143	G7
Westfield	73	H3
West Hallam	229	J2
West Handley	91	M2
Westhouses	175	L2
Weston-on-Trent	270	C5
Weston Underwood	211	K8
Westthorpe	74	A6
Westwood	189	G7
Wetmore	274	C5
Whaley	114	F7
Whaley Bridge	58	F3
Whaley Thorns	115	K7
Whatstandwell	185	G1
Wheatcroft	173	K3
Wheston	83	H5
Whirlow	54	C8
Whirlow Brook	53	M7
Whitehough	59	M2
White Moor	199	M5
Whittington Moor	110	D2
Whitwell	96	D4
Wigley	108	C6
Wilday Green	89	L8
Willesley	291	H8
Williamthorpe	145	M2
Willington	266	E4
Willslock	247	K7
Wilson	279	J4
Wilsthorpe	260	D2
Windlehurst	42	B1
Windley	212	A3
Windmill	84	C2
Wingerworth	128	C6
Wingfield Park	186	A2
Winshill	274	D6
Winsick	129	H4
Winster	154	F5
Wirksworth	183	J2
Wirksworth Moor	184	A1
Woodall	74	F4
Woodend	42	F2
Woodend	162	A5
Woodhouse	57	M3
Woodhouses	278	C5
Woodlinkin	202	A4
Woodseats	24	D4
Woodside	113	H3
Woodside	215	G6
Woodthorpe	93	M8
Woodville	283	H7
Woolley	159	H4
Woolley Bridge	17	G6
Wootton	205	H3
Wormhill	102	A1
Wyaston	221	G1
Yeaveley	221	G5
Yeldersley Hollies	209	J6
Youlgreave	138	D1

USING THE STREET INDEX

Street names are listed alphabetically. Each street name is followed by its postal town or area locality, the Postcode District, the page number, and the reference to the square in which the name is found.

Example: Abbey Brook Ct *SHEFS* S8 .... 70 B1 🔟

Some entries are followed by a number in a blue box. This number indicates the location of the street within the referenced grid square. The full street name is listed at the side of the map page.

GENERAL ABBREVIATIONS

ACC	ACCESS	COM	COMMON	EXPY	EXPRESSWAY	HOSP .... HOSPITAL	MKT .... MARKET
ALY	ALLEY	COMM	COMMISSION	EXT	EXTENSION	HRB .... HARBOUR	MKTS .... MARKETS
AP	APPROACH	CON	CONVENT	F/O	FLYOVER	HTH .... HEATH	ML .... MALL
AR	ARCADE	COT	COTTAGE	FC	FOOTBALL CLUB	HTS .... HEIGHTS	ML .... MILL
ASS	ASSOCIATION	COTS	COTTAGES	FK	FORK	HVN .... HAVEN	MNR .... MANOR
AV	AVENUE	CP	CAPE	FLD	FIELD	HWY .... HIGHWAY	MS .... MEWS
BCH	BEACH	CPS	COPSE	FLDS	FIELDS	IMP .... IMPERIAL	MSN .... MISSION
BLDS	BUILDINGS	CR	CREEK	FLS	FALLS	IN .... INLET	MT .... MOUNT
BND	BEND	CREM	CREMATORIUM	FLS	FLATS	IND EST ... INDUSTRIAL ESTATE	MTN .... MOUNTAIN
BNK	BANK	CRS	CRESCENT	FM	FARM	INF .... INFIRMARY	MTS .... MOUNTAINS
BR	BRIDGE	CSWY	CAUSEWAY	FT	FORT	INFO .... INFORMATION	MUS .... MUSEUM
BRK	BROOK	CT	COURT	FWY	FREEWAY	INT .... INTERCHANGE	MWY .... MOTORWAY
BTM	BOTTOM	CTRL	CENTRAL	FY	FERRY	IS .... ISLAND	N .... NORTH
BUS	BUSINESS	CTS	COURTS	GA	GATE	JCT .... JUNCTION	NE .... NORTH EAST
BVD	BOULEVARD	CTYD	COURTYARD	GAL	GALLERY	JTY .... JETTY	NW .... NORTH WEST
BY	BYPASS	CUTT	CUTTINGS	GDN	GARDEN	KG .... KING	O/P .... OVERPASS
CATH	CATHEDRAL	CV	COVE	GDNS	GARDENS	KNL .... KNOLL	OFF .... OFFICE
CEM	CEMETERY	CYN	CANYON	GLD	GLADE	L .... LAKE	ORCH .... ORCHARD
CEN	CENTRE	DEPT	DEPARTMENT	GLN	GLEN	LA .... LANE	OV .... OVAL
CFT	CROFT	DL	DALE	GN	GREEN	LDG .... LODGE	PAL .... PALACE
CH	CHURCH	DM	DAM	GND	GROUND	LGT .... LIGHT	PAS .... PASSAGE
CHA	CHASE	DR	DRIVE	GRA	GRANGE	LK .... LOCK	PAV .... PAVILION
CHYD	CHURCHYARD	DRO	DROVE	GRG	GARAGE	LKS .... LAKES	PDE .... PARADE
CIR	CIRCLE	DRY	DRIVEWAY	GT	GREAT	LNDG .... LANDING	PH .... PUBLIC HOUSE
CIRC	CIRCUS	DWGS	DWELLINGS	GTWY	GATEWAY	LTL .... LITTLE	PK .... PARK
CL	CLOSE	E	EAST	GV	GROVE	LWR .... LOWER	PKWY .... PARKWAY
CLFS	CLIFFS	EMB	EMBANKMENT	HGR	HIGHER	MAG .... MAGISTRATE	PL .... PLACE
CMP	CAMP	EMBY	EMBASSY	HL	HILL	MAN .... MANSIONS	PLN .... PLAIN
CNR	CORNER	ESP	ESPLANADE	HLS	HILLS	MD .... MEAD	PLNS .... PLAINS
CO	COUNTY	EST	ESTATE	HO	HOUSE	MDW .... MEADOWS	PLZ .... PLAZA
COLL	COLLEGE	EX	EXCHANGE	HOL	HOLLOW	MEM .... MEMORIAL	POL .... POLICE STATION

298

PR PRINCE
PREC PRECINCT
PREP PREPARATORY
PRIM PRIMARY
PROM PROMENADE
PRS PRINCESS
PRT PORT
PT POINT
PTH PATH
PZ PIAZZA
QD QUADRANT
QU QUEEN
QY QUAY
R RIVER
RBT ROUNDABOUT
RD ROAD
RDG RIDGE
REP REPUBLIC
RES RESERVOIR
RFC RUGBY FOOTBALL CLUB
RI RISE
RP RAMP
RW ROW
S SOUTH
SCH SCHOOL
SE SOUTH EAST
SER SERVICE AREA
SH SHORE
SHOP SHOPPING
SKWY SKYWAY
SMT SUMMIT
SOC SOCIETY
SP SPUR
SPR SPRING
SQ SQUARE
ST STREET
STN STATION
STR STREAM
STRD STRAND
SW SOUTH WEST
TDG TRADING
TER TERRACE
THWY THROUGHWAY
TNL TUNNEL
TOLL TOLLWAY
TPK TURNPIKE
TR TRACK
TRL TRAIL
TWR TOWER
U/P UNDERPASS
UNI UNIVERSITY
UPR UPPER
V VALE
VA VALLEY
VIAD VIADUCT
VIL VILLA
VIS VISTA
VLG VILLAGE
VLS VILLAS
VW VIEW
W WEST
WD WOOD
WHF WHARF
WK WALK
WKS WALKS
WLS WELLS
WY WAY
YD YARD
YHA YOUTH HOSTEL

POSTCODE TOWNS AND AREA ABBREVIATIONS

ABRD Abbeydale Road
ALFN Alfreton
ASH Sutton in Ashfield/Kirkby in Ashfield
ASHB Ashbourne
ASHZ Ashby-de-la-Zouch
AU/AST/KP Aughton/Aston/Kiveton Park
BKWL Bakewell
BLID/ED Blidworth/Edwinstowe
BPR/DUF Belper/Duffield
BRAM/HZG Bramhall/Hazel Grove
BSTN/STPLFD Beeston/Stapleford
BSVR Bolsover
BUT Burton upon Trent
BUTN/AL/TUT Burton upon Trent north/Alrewas/Tutbury
BUX Buxton
BWSH/BRSTN Borrowash/Breaston
CDLE Cheadle (Staffs)
CDON/KEG Castle Donington/Kegworth
CFTN/RUD Clifton/Ruddington
CHF/WBR Chapel-en-le-Frith/Whaley Bridge
CHNE Chesterfield north & east
CHSW Chesterfield south & west
CLCR Clay Cross
COAL Coalville
CRTAM Central & Rural Tamworth
DERBY Derby
DERBYE Derby east
DERBYSE Derby southeast
DERBYW Derby west
DIN Dinnington
DRON Dronfield
ECC Ecclesall
ECK/KIL Eckington/Killamarsh
EDL/UDV Edale/Upper Derwent Valley
EWD/SEL/PNX Eastwood/Selston/Pinxton
FUL Fulwood
GLSP Glossop
GLV Gleadless Valley
HACK/IN Hackenthorpe/Intake
HAN/WDH Handsworth/Woodhouse
HATH/EY Hathersage/Eyam
HEANOR Heanor
HOLM/MEL Holmfirth/Meltham
HYDE Hyde
ILK Ilkeston
LEEK Leek
LGEAT Long Eaton
MCFLDN Macclesfield north
MCFLDS Macclesfield south
MCKLVR Mickleover
MELB/CHEL Melbourne/Chellaston
MOS Mosborough
MPL/ROM Marple/Romiley
MSFD Mansfield
MSFDW Mansfield Woodhouse
MSHM Measham
MTLK Matlock
NM/HAY New Mills/Hayfield
NORM/LIT Normanton/Littleover
POY/DIS Poynton/Disley
RCH Rural Chesterfield
RDERBYSW Rural Derby southwest
RIPLEY Ripley
SBK/MW Shirebrook/Market Warsop
SHEF Sheffield
SHEFP/MNR Sheffield Park/Manor
SHEFS Sheffield south
ST/HB/BR Stannington/Hillsborough/Bradfield
STKB/PEN Stocksbridge/Penistone
STLY Stalybridge
STPNHL/WNHL Stapenhill/Winshill
STV/CWN Staveley/Clowne
SWAD Swadlincote
TOT/DORE Totley/Dore
UPML Uppermill
UTXR Uttoxeter
WOL/BIL/BRX Wollaton/Bilborough/Broxtowe
WRKN Worksop north
WRKS Worksop south

Abb - Anc

Index - streets

A

Abbey Brook Ct SHEFS S8 70 B1 [1]
Abbey Brook Dr SHEFS S8 70 B1
Abbey Cl ASHZ LE65 291 J4
HOLM/MEL HD7 9 K3
SHEFS S8 70 B1
UTXR ST14 218 D7
Abbey Ct HOLM/MEL HD7 9 K3
MSFD NG18 165 J3
Abbey Crs ABRD S7 69 L1
Abbey Cft ABRD S7 69 L1
Abbeydale Dr MSFD NG18 165 G7
Abbeydale Park Crs
TOT/DORE S17 69 J4
Abbeydale Park Ri
TOT/DORE S17 69 H3
Abbeydale Rd SHEFS S8 55 J3
Abbeydale Rd South SHEFS S8 69 L1
TOT/DORE S17 69 K4
Abbey Dr ASHZ LE65 291 J4
Abbeyfields Cl
DERBYW DE22 226 D8 [1]
Abbey Gdns HYDE SK14 16 C7
Abbey Gra ABRD S7 69 L1
RCH S42 109 K3
Abbey Gv HYDE SK14 16 C7
Abbey Hl DERBYW DE22 226 E6
Abbeyhill Cl CHSW S40 109 J6
Abbey Hill Rd DERBYW DE22 226 A8
Abbey La DERBYW DE22 240 D1
ECC S11 54 D7
SHEFS S8 70 B1
Abbey Lane Dell SHEFS S8 69 L1
Abbey Lodge Cl SWAD DE11 282 D3 [1]
Abbey Pl ECK/KIL S21 93 M2
Abbey Rd EWD/SEL/PNX NG16 203 L8
MSFD NG18 165 H3
UTXR ST14 218 C7
Abbey St BUT DE14 274 A8 [1]
DERBYW DE22 4 D6
ILK DE7 217 J8
Abbey View Rd SHEFS S8 55 K7
Abbey Yd DERBYW DE22 240 D1 [1]
Abbot Cl DERBYE DE21 227 H8
Abbot Rd ILK DE7 229 M4
Abbots Cft MSFDW NG19 164 B1
Abbotsford Ms ILK DE7 217 G7 [1]
Abbotsford Rd ASHZ LE65 291 M5
Abbots Meadow MOS S20 73 K1 [1]
Abbot St EWD/SEL/PNX NG16 217 M6
Abbott Lea MSFDW NG19 164 A2
Abbott Rd ALFN DE55 175 L7
MSFDW NG19 164 A2
Abbotts Barn Cl DERBYW DE22 4 D5 [1]
Abbotts Cl SWAD DE11 282 D4 [1]
Abbotts Rd SWAD DE11 282 D4
Abbott St HEANOR DE75 216 B1
LGEAT NG10 261 G4
Abel La MTLK DE4 170 F1
Abells RIPLEY DE5 214 F1
Abercrombie St CHNE S41 3 G2
Aberdare Cl DERBYE DE21 227 M8 [1]
Abingdon St DERBYSE DE24 256 F2
Abington Av ASH NG17 163 J5
Ablard Gdns BSTN/STPLFD NG9 245 M8
Abney Cl CHSW S40 109 M4 [1]
MCKLVR DE3 239 J8 [1]
SHEFS S8 55 M4 [1]
Abney Crs MSHM DE12 295 M6
Abney Dr MSHM DE12 295 M6
SHEFS S8 55 M4
Abney Rd SHEFS S8 55 M4
Acacia Av MCKLVR DE3 255 H1
STV/CWN S43 111 K2
SWAD DE11 282 E3
Acacia Ct MSFDW NG19 165 H1
Acacia Crs ECK/KIL S21 73 L5
Acacia Dr CLCR S45 145 L7
MELB/CHEL DE73 278 D2
Acer Cl ECK/KIL S21 73 M5
EWD/SEL/PNX NG16 176 F7
Acer Cft DERBYE DE21 227 H7 [1]
Acorn Av EWD/SEL/PNX NG16 217 L2
Acorn Cl DERBYSE DE24 257 H7
Acorn Dr BPR/DUF DE56 199 K5
Acorn Rdg CHSW S40 127 M3 [1]
MTLK DE4 156 E3
SBK/MW NG20 133 G5
Acorn Wy BPR/DUF DE56 199 K5 [1]
DERBYE DE21 241 M1
MSFD NG18 165 L6
Acreage La SBK/MW NG20 133 H8
Acrefield Wy MELB/CHEL DE73 257 L8
Acre La BWSH/BRSTN DE72 271 G3
Acresford Rd MSHM DE12 289 L8
Acres Rd CLCR S45 145 M7
The Acres CLCR S45 145 M6
Acre St GLSP SK13 25 M3 [1]
Acres View Cl CHNE S41 110 C3
Acton Gv LGEAT NG10 261 H4 [1]
Acton Rd DERBYW DE22 239 J4
LGEAT NG10 261 H3
Adale Rd HEANOR DE75 215 L2
Adam Bede Crs MTLK DE4 183 H4 [1]
Adams Cl HEANOR DE75 216 A3
Adams Ct ILK DE7 217 H7
Adam's Rd ASHB DE6 238 D2
Adam St ILK DE7 230 D4 [1]
Adamsway MSFD NG18 165 K7
Adastral Av HACK/IN S12 56 D8
Adderley Rd GLSP SK13 25 J1
Addie Rd BUTN/AL/TUT DE13 273 L4
Addison Dr ALFN DE55 175 L6
Addison Rd ALFN DE55 160 C7
DERBYSE DE24 256 E2
Addison Sq MTLK DE4 171 K5 [1]
Addison St ALFN DE55 161 K3
Adelaide Cl
BSTN/STPLFD NG9 245 J1 [1]
MCKLVR DE3 239 H6
Adelaide Crs
STPNHL/WNHL DE15 275 G8 [1]
Adelaide Rd ECC S11 55 G4
Adelaide Wk
EWD/SEL/PNX NG16 188 C6
Adelphi Cl NORM/LIT DE23 255 K4 [1]
Adelphi Wy STV/CWN S43 112 B2
Adin Av BSVR S44 113 J4
Adler Ct DERBY DE1 240 E3 [1]
Adlington Av RCH S42 128 F8
Adlington La HATH/EY S32 86 F2
Admiral Cl HEANOR DE75 202 B8 [1]
Adrian Cl BSTN/STPLFD NG9 261 J1
Adrians Cl MSFD NG18 165 H5
Adrian St DERBYSE DE24 257 G4
Adwick Cl MCKLVR DE3 238 F8
Agard St DERBY DE1 4 C2
Agden Rd ABRD S7 55 H2
Agnes Meadow La ASHB DE6 195 G6
Agricultural Wy BKWL DE45 123 H5
Aimploy Ct NORM/LIT DE23 256 D1 [1]
Ainley Cl DERBYSE DE24 257 J3
Ainsty Rd ABRD S7 55 J3 [1]
Ainsworth Dr NORM/LIT DE23 256 B3
Aintree Av ECK/KIL S21 72 E7
Aintree Cl BUT DE14 280 D3 [1]
Airedale Cl LGEAT NG10 260 D4
Airedale Ct BSTN/STPLFD NG9 245 K6
Aisthorpe Rd SHEFS S8 55 J7
Aizlewood Rd SHEFS S8 55 J3 [2]
Akley Bank Cl TOT/DORE S17 69 J5
Alabaster La MTLK DE4 171 K4
Alandale Av SBK/MW NG20 133 J5
Alan Dr MPL/ROM SK6 32 B4
Albany Cl MSFDW NG19 164 F1
Albany Ct BSTN/STPLFD NG9 245 H1
Albany Dr MSFDW NG19 164 E1
Albany Pl MSFDW NG19 164 F1
Albany Rd ABRD S7 55 J3
DERBYW DE22 239 M6
Albany St ILK DE7 230 D4
Albemarle Rd DERBYE DE21 241 L4
Alberta Av EWD/SEL/PNX NG16 189 J3
Albert Av BSTN/STPLFD NG9 245 G3
EWD/SEL/PNX NG16 188 E6
STV/CWN S43 92 A7
Albert Crs DERBYE DE21 241 L6 [1]
Albert Rd BWSH/BRSTN DE72 259 L3
DERBYE DE21 241 K5
HACK/IN S12 57 L7
LGEAT NG10 244 E4
LGEAT NG10 261 G3
RIPLEY DE5 186 F8
SHEFS S8 55 K4
STV/CWN S43 92 A7
SWAD DE11 282 D8
Albert St ALFN DE55 176 D4
ALFN DE55 187 L2
ASH NG17 162 F4
BPR/DUF DE56 199 J6 [1]
BSTN/STPLFD NG9 245 G3
BUT DE14 273 M6
DERBY DE1 4 F4
ECK/KIL S21 73 G8
EWD/SEL/PNX NG16 203 J7
GLSP SK13 17 K5
ILK DE7 230 B2
MSFD NG18 164 E5
MSFDW NG19 149 M6
RIPLEY DE5 201 H1
Albine Rd SBK/MW NG20 133 H4
Albion Cl MSHM DE12 290 D6
Albion Rd ASH NG17 163 J8
CHSW S40 2 F3
LGEAT NG10 261 H2
NM/HAY SK22 43 M3
Albion St DERBY DE1 4 F4
ILK DE7 230 C1 [1]
MSFDW NG19 164 D1
RIPLEY DE5 201 H1
SWAD DE11 283 J8
Alcester Rd ABRD S7 55 J3 [3]
Alcock Av MSFD NG18 165 G3
Aldam Cl TOT/DORE S17 69 H6 [1]
Aldam Cft TOT/DORE S17 69 H6
Aldam Rd TOT/DORE S17 69 H6
Aldam Wy TOT/DORE S17 69 H6 [2]
Alder Brook CHF/WBR SK23 45 H8
Alderbrook Cl
BUTN/AL/TUT DE13 264 F6
Aldercar La
EWD/SEL/PNX NG16 202 E6
Alder Cl DERBYE DE21 227 H8
MSFDW NG19 165 H1
SBK/MW NG20 133 G5
Alder Ct MSFDW NG19 164 A5
Alderdale Dr MPL/ROM SK6 42 B3
Alderfen Cl DERBYSE DE24 257 G7
Alder Gv BUX SK17 99 K2
MSFDW NG19 149 L5
STPNHL/WNHL DE15 281 J3
Alder La ASHB DE6 210 D7
Alderley Ct DERBYE DE21 227 K8 [1]
Alderney Rd SHEFP/MNR S2 55 K3 [1]
Aldern Wy BKWL DE45 123 H3
Alder Ri CHF/WBR SK23 59 G2
Alder Rd BPR/DUF DE56 199 K7
Alders Av CHF/WBR SK23 60 B1
Alders Brook RDERBYSW DE65 265 G1
Aldersgate DERBYW DE22 239 J3 [1]
NM/HAY SK22 43 L2
Aldersgreen Av MPL/ROM SK6 42 C3
Alderslade Cl
BWSH/BRSTN DE72 270 E1
Alders La CHF/WBR SK23 45 H8
MTLK DE4 157 K7
Aldersley Cl RDERBYSW DE65 266 F1
Alderson Pl SHEFP/MNR S2 55 K2
Alderson Rd SHEFP/MNR S2 55 K2
Alderson Rd North
SHEFP/MNR S2 55 K2 [1]
Alders Rd POY/DIS SK12 42 D3
Alder Wy ASH NG17 163 G7
SBK/MW NG20 133 G5
Aldred Cl ECK/KIL S21 74 B2
Aldred's La HEANOR DE75 216 D1
Aldridge Cl
BSTN/STPLFD NG9 245 H8 [1]
Aldwark Rd BUX SK17 99 M5
Aldwych DERBYW DE22 239 K4 [1]
Alexander Av
EWD/SEL/PNX NG16 189 G3 [1]
Alexander Rd BUX SK17 81 J1
Alexander Ter
EWD/SEL/PNX NG16 188 F1
Alexandra Av ASH NG17 163 J6 [1]
MSFD NG18 164 E6
MSFDW NG19 149 L5 [1]
Alexandra Crs UTXR ST14 247 L2
Alexandra Gdns
NORM/LIT DE23 240 E8 [1]
Alexandra Rd BUX SK17 99 M5
DRON S18 70 E8 [1]
LGEAT NG10 261 G2 [1]
MSHM DE12 289 L6
SHEFP/MNR S2 55 L3
STPNHL/WNHL DE15 274 D7
SWAD DE11 282 E7
Alexandra Rd East CHNE S41 3 L7
Alexandra Rd West CHSW S40 2 E3
Alexandra St
BSTN/STPLFD NG9 245 G4
EWD/SEL/PNX NG16 203 J8 [1]
Alexandra Ter ASH NG17 162 F4
Alexandre Cl NORM/LIT DE23 256 A4 [1]
Alford Cl CHSW S40 109 M7 [1]
Alfred Rd BPR/DUF DE56 214 D2
Alfred St ALFN DE55 175 J7
ALFN DE55 188 A4 [1]
ASH NG17 163 J6
BUT DE14 273 M8
EWD/SEL/PNX NG16 176 F6
RIPLEY DE5 187 H8
Alfreton Rd ALFN DE55 161 H5
ALFN DE55 175 M2
ASH NG17 177 L3
DERBYE DE21 226 F7
EWD/SEL/PNX NG16 189 L8
MTLK DE4 157 G6
RIPLEY DE5 201 M1
Algar Cl SHEFP/MNR S2 56 B3
Algar Crs SHEFP/MNR S2 56 C3
Algar Dr SHEFP/MNR S2 56 B3
Algar Pl SHEFP/MNR S2 56 B3
Algar Rd SHEFP/MNR S2 56 B3
Alicehead Rd CLCR S45 126 C8
Alice St DERBY DE1 5 G2
Alice's Vw RCH S42 145 K2
Alice Wy DRON S18 91 H5
Alison Cl DERBYE DE21 241 J3
Alison Crs SHEFP/MNR S2 56 E1
Allan Av NORM/LIT DE23 255 H2
Allandale Rd HEANOR DE75 202 A8 [1]
Allcroft St MSFDW NG19 149 M6
Allenby Cl SHEFS S8 70 B3 [1]
Allenby Dr SHEFS S8 70 B3
Allendale ILK DE7 230 B3
Allendale Rd RCH S42 128 C7
Allendale Wy MSFDW NG19 165 H1 [1]
Allen Dr MSFD NG18 165 J5
Allen Hl MTLK DE4 156 E4
Allen La ASHB DE6 223 M1
BPR/DUF DE56 185 L4
MTLK DE4 157 M3
Allens Cft UTXR ST14 249 H8
Allen's Green Av
EWD/SEL/PNX NG16 189 J4
Allen's La UTXR ST14 249 H8
Allen St DERBYSE DE24 257 H5
Allestree Cl DERBYSE DE24 257 H2
Allestree Dr DRON S18 89 M1 [1]
Allestree La DERBYW DE22 226 A8
Allestree St DERBYSE DE24 257 H2
The Alley MTLK DE4 171 G6 [1]
Alley Wk ASHB DE6 223 J3
Allington Dr MSFDW NG19 164 A3
Allison Av SWAD DE11 282 E8
Allissa Av RIPLEY DE5 201 H3
Allpits Rd BSVR S44 111 J7
All Saints Ct MCKLVR DE3 255 G1 [1]
All Saints Cft BUT DE14 280 F2
All Saints Rd BUT DE14 280 E1
MTLK DE4 156 E4
Allsops Pl CHNE S41 110 C2
Allwood Cl MSFD NG18 165 H2
Alma Crs DRON S18 70 D7
Alma Hts MCKLVR DE3 255 H1
Alma Rd BUX SK17 83 M5
EWD/SEL/PNX NG16 189 J5
RCH S42 145 K2
SWAD DE11 282 C4
Alma St ALFN DE55 175 K7
BUT DE14 273 M8
BUX SK17 100 A2
DERBYW DE22 4 D5
MELB/CHEL DE73 278 D3
RCH S42 145 H4
RIPLEY DE5 187 G8
Alma St West CHSW S40 2 D5
Almond Av RIPLEY DE5 201 G2
SBK/MW NG20 133 H5 [1]
Almond Cl BSVR S44 111 K7
Almond Ct BUTN/AL/TUT DE13 274 B1
Almond Crs STV/CWN S43 93 M6
Almond Dr ECK/KIL S21 73 M5
Almond Gv ALFN DE55 187 K2 [1]
SWAD DE11 282 C5
Almond Ri MSFDW NG19 165 H1
Almond St NORM/LIT DE23 240 C8
Almshill Crs ECC S11 54 C7 [1]
Almshill Dr ECC S11 54 C7
Almshill Gld ECC S11 54 C7
Alms Hill Rd ECC S11 54 C7
Alms Rd ASHB DE6 248 F1
Alnwick Dr HACK/IN S12 56 F5 [1]
Alnwick Rd HACK/IN S12 56 E5
Alpine Ct WRKS S80 77 L8
Alpine Gv STV/CWN S43 111 K1
Alport Av BUX SK17 100 A3
HACK/IN S12 57 H6
Alport Cl ASHB DE6 196 C7
BPR/DUF DE56 199 L5
Alport Dr HACK/IN S12 57 H5
Alport Gv HACK/IN S12 57 H5
Alport La BKWL DE45 138 F5
BPR/DUF DE56 183 M5
Alport Pl HACK/IN S12 57 H6
MSFD NG18 165 L3
Alport Ri DRON S18 70 A8
Alport Rd HACK/IN S12 57 H5
Alsager Cl DERBYE DE21 241 K1
Alsfeld Wy NM/HAY SK22 43 K2
Alsop Pl BUX SK17 100 B3 [1]
Alsop Wy BUX SK17 100 B3
Alstonfield Dr DERBYW DE22 240 B1
Alston Rd CHF/WBR SK23 60 E5
Althorp Cl ALFN DE55 187 J3
Althorp Wy
BUTN/AL/TUT DE13 274 A2 [1]
Alton Cl CHSW S40 127 L2 [1]
DERBYW DE22 226 A7
DRON S18 90 A2 [1]
ECC S11 54 D8
Alton Hl RCH S42 143 L5
Alton La CLCR S45 143 M6
Alton Ri MTLK DE4 156 C3
Alton Rd BPR/DUF DE56 199 M6
UTXR ST14 218 A4
Alton Wy ASHZ LE65 291 M5
Alts Nook Wy
BWSH/BRSTN DE72 271 H1
Alum Chine Cl CHNE S41 128 F2 [1]
Alum Cl DERBYSE DE24 257 M3
Alvaston St DERBYSE DE24 257 L2
Alvenor St ILK DE7 230 C1
Alverton Cl MCKLVR DE3 254 F1 [1]
Alward's Cl DERBYSE DE24 257 K4
Ambaston La
BWSH/BRSTN DE72 258 E5
Amber Cl BPR/DUF DE56 185 L5
Amber Ct BPR/DUF DE56 199 K4
Amber Crs CHSW S40 127 M1
Amber Cft STV/CWN S43 111 M3 [1]
Amberdene MTLK DE4 157 G4 [1]
Amber Dr EWD/SEL/PNX NG16 202 E8
Amber Gv ALFN DE55 175 J8 [1]
Amber Hts RIPLEY DE5 186 F8
Amber Hl MTLK DE4 185 J3
Amber La CLCR S45 142 F8
Amberley Cl ILK DE7 230 C4
Amberley Dr BUX SK17 99 M5
DERBYSE DE24 256 C5
Amber Pl CLCR S45 144 D6
Amber Rd BPR/DUF DE56 185 L4
DERBYW DE22 240 A1
Amber St DERBYSE DE24 256 F3 [1]
Amber View Rd BPR/DUF DE56 185 L3
Amberwood SWAD DE11 282 D5
Ambleside Cl CHNE S41 109 M3
MOS S20 73 H4 [1]
Ambleside Dr
EWD/SEL/PNX NG16 203 G7 [1]
Ambrose Ter DERBY DE1 4 B3
Amen Aly DERBY DE1 4 E3
Amesbury Cl CHNE S41 110 B3 [1]
Amesbury La DERBYE DE21 227 H8
Ameycroft La MTLK DE4 156 D2
Amilda Av ILK DE7 230 C2
Amy St DERBYW DE22 4 A6
Anchor Av CHF/WBR SK23 60 F4
Anchor Fold CHF/WBR SK23 61 G4 [1]
Anchor Rd EWD/SEL/PNX NG16 202 F7

Anderby Gdns *SWAD* DE11 ...... 282 C8
Anderson Cl *STV/CWN* S43 ...... 92 B7 🗓
Anderson St *DERBYSE* DE24 ...... 257 J3
Andover Rd *MSFDW* NG19 ...... 164 A4
Andrew Av *ILK* DE7 ...... 230 D2
Andrew Cl *NORM/LIT* DE23 ...... 255 H2
Andrew La *MPL/ROM* SK6 ...... 42 B1
Andrews Dr
  EWD/SEL/PNX NG16 ...... 202 D6
  ILK DE7 ...... 228 D1
Andwell La *FUL* S10 ...... 53 H5
Anfield Cl *BSTN/STPLFD* NG9 ...... 245 K8
Angel Yd *CHSW* S40 ...... 3 G4
Angerford Av *SHEFS* S8 ...... 55 K6
Anglers' La *DERBYE* DE21 ...... 242 B8
Anglesey Rd *BUT* DE14 ...... 273 M8 🗓
  DRON S18 ...... 90 D2 🗓
Anglesey St
  BUTN/AL/TUT DE13 ...... 273 J6 🗓
  DERBYE DE21 ...... 241 G2
Angleton Av *SHEFP/MNR* S2 ...... 56 F2 🗓
Angleton Gdns
  SHEFP/MNR S2 ...... 56 F2 🗓
Angleton Gn *SHEFP/MNR* S2 ...... 56 F2 🗓
Angleton Ms *SHEFP/MNR* S2 ...... 56 F2 🗓
Anglia Wy *MSFD* NG18 ...... 165 L7
Ankerbold Rd *RCH* S42 ...... 145 H2
Anncroft Rd *BUX* SK17 ...... 99 C5
Anne Potter Cl
  BWSH/BRSTN DE72 ...... 242 F5 🗓
Annesley Cl *CHNE* S41 ...... 3 L9
  SHEFS S8 ...... 70 C3 🗓
Annesley La
  EWD/SEL/PNX NG16 ...... 189 L4
Annesley Wy *MSFDW* NG19 ...... 164 A4
Anns Rd *SHEFP/MNR* S2 ...... 55 K3
Anns Rd North *SHEFP/MNR* S2 ...... 55 L3
Ann St *WRKS* S80 ...... 115 H1
Annwell La *ASHZ* LE65 ...... 284 C8
Ansell Rd *ECC* S11 ...... 54 D4
Anslow Av *NM/HAY* SK22 ...... 163 J5
Anslow La *BUTN/AL/TUT* DE13 ...... 264 D8
Anslow La *BUTN/AL/TUT* DE13 ...... 262 D7
Anson Ct *BUT* DE14 ...... 274 B7
Anstee Rd *LGEAT* NG10 ...... 260 F6
Anstey Ct *DERBYE* DE21 ...... 241 K1 🗓
Anthony Crs *DERBYSE* DE24 ...... 257 J4
Anthony Dr *DERBYSE* DE24 ...... 257 J4
Antill St *BSTN/STPLFD* NG9 ...... 245 G4
Apiary Ga *CDON/KEG* DE74 ...... 271 L7
Appian Cl *BWSH/BRSTN* DE72 ...... 258 F1
Appian Wy *CLCR* S45 ...... 144 B3
  DERBYSE DE24 ...... 258 A4
Appin Rd *MSFDW* NG19 ...... 164 A5
Appleby Cl *ILK* DE7 ...... 230 C4
Appleby Gld *SWAD* DE11 ...... 282 A8
Appleby Wy *MSFDW* NG19 ...... 148 C4
Applecross Ct
  DERBYSE DE24 ...... 256 B7 🗓
Appledore Dr *DERBYE* DE21 ...... 241 L1 🗓
Applegarth Cl
  BSTN/STPLFD NG9 ...... 245 K1
  CHSW S40 ...... 109 K5 🗓
Applegarth Dr *HAN/WDH* S13 ...... 56 E4 🗓
Applegarth Dr *HACK/IN* S12 ...... 56 D4
Applegate Cl *DERBYE* DE21 ...... 227 L7 🗓
Applemead Cl *DERBYE* DE21 ...... 227 H8
Appleton Cl *DERBYE* DE21 ...... 241 K3
  SWAD DE11 ...... 282 C4 🗓
Appleton Dr *BPR/DUF* DE56 ...... 199 L4
  GLSP SK13 ...... 26 C2
Appletree Cl
  BWSH/BRSTN DE72 ...... 258 F1
Appletree Dr *DRON* S18 ...... 90 D1
Apple Tree Rd *NM/HAY* SK22 ...... 33 M8
Appletree Rd *BSVR* S44 ...... 113 L1
  RDERBYSW DE65 ...... 263 M1
Applewood Cl *BPR/DUF* DE56 ...... 199 L5
  UTXW ST14 ...... 247 K1 🗓
Aragon Wy *MPL/ROM* SK6 ...... 32 B4
Arbor Cl *DERBYW* DE22 ...... 4 D6
Arboretum St *NORM/LIT* DE23 ...... 5 G8 🗓
Arbor Gv *BUX* SK17 ...... 99 J4
Arbour Cl *CHNE* S41 ...... 129 C4
Arbour Hl *ILK* DE7 ...... 229 H7
Arbourthorne Rd
  SHEFP/MNR S2 ...... 56 B4
Arcadia St *SBK/MW* NG20 ...... 133 H5
Archaeological Wy
  MSFDW NG19 ...... 132 C8
  SBK/MW NG20 ...... 115 G8
  STV/CWN S43 ...... 95 M6
  WRKS S80 ...... 96 A5
Archdale Cl *SHEFP/MNR* S2 ...... 56 E2
Archdale Pl *SHEFP/MNR* S2 ...... 56 D2 🗓
Archdale Rd *SHEFP/MNR* S2 ...... 56 D1
Archer Av *ABRD* S7 ...... 55 G5
Archer Rd *BSTN/STPLFD* NG9 ...... 245 H5
  SHEFS S8 ...... 55 G7
Archer St *DERBYE* DE24 ...... 241 H8
  ILK DE7 ...... 217 H7
Archibald Rd *ABRD* S7 ...... 55 H4 🗓
Arden Cl *CHSW* S40 ...... 109 M6
  NORM/LIT DE23 ...... 240 B8 🗓
Arden Rd *NM/HAY* SK22 ...... 43 M3
Ardleigh Cl *MCKLVR* DE3 ...... 255 C2
Ardsley Dr *HEANOR* DE75 ...... 202 D8 🗓
  MOS S20 ...... 57 J8
Ardsley Gv *MOS* S20 ...... 57 J8 🗓
Ardsley Rd *CHSW* S40 ...... 109 L7
Argyle Rd *SHEFS* S8 ...... 55 K5
Argyle St *DERBYW* DE22 ...... 4 C8 🗓
  EWD/SEL/PNX NG16 ...... 202 E6
  MSFD NG18 ...... 165 H4
Argyll Cl *DERBYE* DE21 ...... 242 C5
Argyll Rd *RIPLEY* DE5 ...... 187 H8
Arklow Cl *CHNE* S41 ...... 3 K9
Arkwright Av *BPR/DUF* DE56 ...... 199 M4
Arkwright Cl *MTLK* DE4 ...... 140 F7 🗓
Arkwright Dr *MPL/ROM* SK6 ...... 32 D4
Arkwright Rd *MPL/ROM* SK6 ...... 32 C4
Arkwright St *DERBYSE* DE24 ...... 256 F3 🗓
  MTLK DE4 ...... 183 H2
Arleston La *DERBYSE* DE24 ...... 256 B7
  DERBYSE DE24 ...... 257 J4
Arleston St *NORM/LIT* DE23 ...... 256 C3
Arlington Dr *ALFN* DE55 ...... 187 J3

Arlington Rd *NORM/LIT* DE23 ...... 256 A1
Armitage Dr *LGEAT* NG10 ...... 261 K5 🗓
Armscote St *DERBYE* DE24 ...... 257 J3
Arms Park Dr *MOS* S20 ...... 73 J4 🗓
Armstrong Rd *MSFDW* NG19 ...... 164 A3
Armthorpe Rd *ECC* S11 ...... 54 C2
Arncliff Cl *WOL/BIL/BRX* NG8 ...... 231 M6 🗓
Arnfield La *GLSP* SK13 ...... 17 J3
Arnhem Ter *DERBYE* DE21 ...... 242 B7 🗓
Arnold Av *HACK/IN* S12 ...... 71 L1
  LGEAT NG10 ...... 260 D6
Arnold Cl *SWAD* DE11 ...... 289 H3
Arnold Crs *LGEAT* NG10 ...... 260 D6
Arnot Rd *BUT* DE14 ...... 280 D3
Arnside *CHNE* S41 ...... 110 A1
  MPL/ROM SK6 ...... 42 B2 🗓
  SWAD DE11 ...... 289 H1
Arnside Rd *SHEFS* S8 ...... 55 H5
Arran Cl *BSTN/STPLFD* NG9 ...... 231 H8 🗓
  DERBYSE DE24 ...... 256 B7
Arran Ct *ALFN* DE55 ...... 161 J5
Arridge Rd *DERBYE* DE21 ...... 241 J3
Arrunden La *HOLM/MEL* HD7 ...... 9 J1
Arthington St *SHEFS* S8 ...... 55 K4 🗓
Arthur Av *BSTN/STPLFD* NG9 ...... 245 J2
Arthur Hind Cl *DERBYW* DE22 ...... 240 C3
Arthur Mee Rd
  BSTN/STPLFD NG9 ...... 245 H5 🗓
Arthurs Ct
  BUTN/AL/TUT DE13 ...... 265 H8 🗓
Arthur Short Cl *WRKS* S80 ...... 96 A4
Arthur St *ALFN* DE55 ...... 175 J5
  BUT DE14 ...... 273 M5
  BWSH/BRSTN DE72 ...... 259 J3
  DERBY DE1 ...... 240 C3
  EWD/SEL/PNX NG16 ...... 177 G7 🗓
  MSFD NG18 ...... 164 F4
  SWAD DE11 ...... 289 H3
Artisan Vw *SHEFS* S8 ...... 55 K4
Arundel Cl *HYDE* SK14 ...... 16 C7
Arundel Av *HYDE* SK14 ...... 16 C7
Arundel Av *MCKLVR* DE3 ...... 239 J8
Arundel Cl *CHNE* S41 ...... 110 C2
  DRON S18 ...... 90 A1
  LGEAT NG10 ...... 244 E6 🗓
Arundel Dr *BSTN/STPLFD* NG9 ...... 231 L8
  DERBYE DE21 ...... 242 C5
  MSFDW NG19 ...... 164 C2
Arundel Gra *GLSP* SK13 ...... 25 K1
Arundel St *DERBYW* DE22 ...... 240 A7
  GLSP SK13 ...... 25 J2
Ascot Cl *STPNHL/WNHL* DE15 ...... 274 D7
Ascot Dr *DERBYSE* DE24 ...... 257 G3
  MSFD NG18 ...... 165 J3
Ascot Pl *ILK* DE7 ...... 229 M5
Ascot Rd *SHEFP/MNR* S2 ...... 55 K1 🗓
Ascott Dr *SWAD* DE11 ...... 282 D3
Ash Acre *BPR/DUF* DE56 ...... 200 A6
Ashbourne Av *CLCR* S45 ...... 144 D5 🗓
Ashbourne Cl
  BSTN/STPLFD NG9 ...... 245 K1
  CHSW S40 ...... 109 K5 🗓
Ashbourne Dr *MPL/ROM* SK6 ...... 42 B4
  SWAD DE11 ...... 289 J1 🗓
Ashbourne Gv *HAN/WDH* S13 ...... 57 J1 🗓
Ashbourne La *CHF/WBR* SK23 ...... 61 G4
Ashbourne Rd *ASHB* DE6 ...... 206 F3
  ASHB DE6 ...... 223 M5
  ASHB DE6 ...... 235 H3
  BPR/DUF DE56 ...... 197 M8
  BUX SK17 ...... 100 A6
  DERBYW DE22 ...... 239 G1
  EWD/SEL/PNX NG16 ...... 189 K8
  HAN/WDH S13 ...... 57 J1
  RDERBYSW DE65 ...... 251 K1
  UTXW ST14 ...... 218 C6
Ashbourne St *SBK/MW* NG20 ...... 133 J6
  STPNHL/WNHL DE15 ...... 281 K1
Ashbrook Av
  BWSH/BRSTN DE72 ...... 242 F8
Ashbrook Cl *DERBYW* DE22 ...... 225 M7
  UTXW ST14 ...... 247 M4 🗓
Ashburton Cl *HYDE* SK14 ...... 16 B8
Ashbury La *SHEFS* S8 ...... 55 M8
Ashbury La *SHEFS* S8 ...... 55 M8
Ashby La *SWAD* DE11 ...... 290 F1
Ashby Rd *ASHZ* LE65 ...... 284 A8
  MELB/CHEL DE73 ...... 277 J8
  MSFD NG18 ...... 290 E5
  STPNHL/WNHL DE15 ...... 274 F8
Ashby Rd East
  STPNHL/WNHL DE15 ...... 282 B1
Ashby St *DERBYSE* DE24 ...... 257 H4
Ash Cl *BWSH/BRSTN* DE72 ...... 270 E3
  DERBYW DE22 ...... 226 A6
  ECK/KIL S21 ...... 73 M5
  EWD/SEL/PNX NG16 ...... 177 G8
  HYDE SK14 ...... 16 D6
Ashcombe Gdns
  DERBYE DE21 ...... 241 L1 🗓
Ash Crs *ECK/KIL* S21 ...... 92 E1
  RIPLEY DE5 ...... 201 G2
Ashcroft Cl *DERBYSE* DE24 ...... 257 J3 🗓
Ashcroft Dr *CHNE* S41 ...... 91 L8
Ashdale Cl *STPNHL/WNHL* DE15 ...... 281 K2
Ashdale Rd *ILK* DE7 ...... 230 D4
Ashdown Dr *CHSW* S40 ...... 2 B1
Ash Dr *MSHM* DE12 ...... 295 M4
Ashe La *RDERBYSW* DE65 ...... 253 K5
Ashe Pl *NORM/LIT* DE23 ...... 256 C1
Asher La *RIPLEY* DE5 ...... 186 F5
Asher Rd *ABRD* S7 ...... 55 J2 🗓
Ashes Av *ASHB* DE6 ...... 196 B7
Ashes La *ASHB* DE6 ...... 193 K1
  ASHB DE6 ...... 262 A3
  GLSP SK13 ...... 17 L8
Ashfield Av *ALFN* DE55 ...... 188 A1
  DERBYE DE21 ...... 241 H2
  MSFD NG18 ...... 164 E2 🗓
Ashfield Cl *HACK/IN* S12 ...... 56 C6
Ashfield Dr *HACK/IN* S12 ...... 56 C6
  MSHM DE12 ...... 290 E4
Ashfield Gv *MPL/ROM* SK6 ...... 32 B3 🗓
Ashfield Rd *ASH* NG17 ...... 162 E7
  CHF/WBR SK23 ...... 61 G4 🗓
  CHNE S41 ...... 129 G2
  GLSP SK13 ...... 17 H7

Ashfield St *ASH* NG17 ...... 163 K5
Ashford Av *RCH* S42 ...... 145 K3
Ashford Cl *ILK* DE7 ...... 229 G2
Ashford La *BKWL* DE45 ...... 104 A7
Ashford Ms *GLSP* SK13 ...... 25 G1 🗓
Ashford Pl *ILK* DE7 ...... 217 H5 🗓
Ashford Ri *ASH* NG17 ...... 163 H6
  BPR/DUF DE56 ...... 199 L4
Ashford Rd *BUTN/AL/TUT* DE13 ...... 273 K4
  DRON S18 ...... 90 A2
  ECC S11 ...... 55 G2
Ashforth Av *HEANOR* DE75 ...... 216 D1
Ashfurlong Cl *TOT/DORE* S17 ...... 69 J3
Ashfurlong Dr *TOT/DORE* S17 ...... 69 J3
Ashfurlong Pk *TOT/DORE* S17 ...... 69 J3
Ashfurlong Rd *TOT/DORE* S17 ...... 69 J3
Ashgate *ASH* NG17 ...... 163 G7
Ashgate Av *CHSW* S40 ...... 2 C2
Ashgate Av *CHSW* S40 ...... 109 M7
Ashgate Rd *CHSW* S40 ...... 109 M7
Ashgate Valley Rd *CHSW* S40 ...... 2 B2
Ash Gv *ASH* NG17 ...... 163 G5
  BSTN/STPLFD NG9 ...... 245 G4
  CHF/WBR SK23 ...... 60 B1
  EWD/SEL/PNX NG16 ...... 203 G5
  LGEAT NG10 ...... 244 D3
  LGEAT NG10 ...... 260 F4
  MPL/ROM SK6 ...... 32 B5
  SBK/MW NG20 ...... 133 G5
  STV/CWN S43 ...... 93 L6
Ashgrove Ct *DERBYE* DE21 ...... 241 L1 🗓
Ash Grove La *RDERBYSW* DE65 ...... 265 M4
Ash House La *TOT/DORE* S17 ...... 69 L1
Ashland Rd *ABRD* S7 ...... 55 H5
  ASH NG17 ...... 162 F7
  ECK/KIL S21 ...... 73 H7
Ashland Rd (West) *ASH* NG17 ...... 162 E7
Ashlands Cl *ASH* NG17 ...... 162 E7
Ash La *ASHB* DE6 ...... 252 C7
  DRON S18 ...... 71 J7
  ECK/KIL S21 ...... 91 M2
Ashlea Dr *ASHB* DE6 ...... 206 F3
Ashleigh Av *GLSP* SK13 ...... 17 L8
  HACK/IN S12 ...... 56 C5
  SWAD DE11 ...... 282 C5 🗓
Ashleigh Ct *ECK/KIL* S21 ...... 92 F1
Ashleigh Dr *HACK/IN* S12 ...... 56 C5
Ashleigh Dr *HACK/IN* S12 ...... 56 C5
  MELB/CHEL DE73 ...... 257 J8
  UTXW ST14 ...... 247 J1
Ashleigh Pl *HACK/IN* S12 ...... 56 C5 🗓
Ashleigh Rd *STV/CWN* S43 ...... 94 D3
Ashley Cl *ECK/KIL* S21 ...... 74 A4 🗓
  MSHM DE12 ...... 289 L7 🗓
  MTLK DE4 ...... 157 K6
  STPNHL/WNHL DE15 ...... 274 D7 🗓
Ashley Gdns *MPL/ROM* SK6 ...... 42 A2
Ashley La *ECK/KIL* S21 ...... 74 A4
Ashley St *DERBYW* DE22 ...... 239 M5
Ashlyn Rd *DERBYE* DE21 ...... 5 J4
Ashmeadow
  BWSH/BRSTN DE72 ...... 258 E1
Ashmeadow Ct *ASHB* DE6 ...... 208 A2 🗓
Ashmore Av *ASH* NG17 ...... 162 F6
  ECK/KIL S21 ...... 72 E6
Ash Mount Rd
  EWD/SEL/PNX NG16 ...... 202 E7 🗓
Ashop Rd *BPR/DUF* DE56 ...... 200 A5
Ashopton Av *NORM/LIT* DE23 ...... 256 C5
Ashopton Dr *EDL/UDV* S33 ...... 50 E6
Ashopton Rd *EDL/UDV* S33 ...... 50 D5
Ashover Cl *DERBYE* DE21 ...... 241 J2 🗓
Ashover New Rd *ALFN* DE55 ...... 159 G2
Ashover Rd *CLCR* S45 ...... 143 H6
  CLCR S45 ...... 144 A6
  DERBYW DE22 ...... 226 A3
  STV/CWN S43 ...... 111 M4
  SWAD DE11 ...... 282 B5
Ashover Vw *ALFN* DE55 ...... 175 M1
Ashpool Cl *HAN/WDH* S13 ...... 57 K4
Ash St *BUT* DE14 ...... 280 E1
  BUX SK17 ...... 99 L4 🗓
  ILK DE7 ...... 217 H6
  MOS S20 ...... 72 F5
Ashton Cl *ALFN* DE55 ...... 187 J3
  CHSW S40 ...... 127 M2
  ECK/KIL S21 ...... 73 M4
  MCKLVR DE3 ...... 238 F7 🗓
Ashton Ct *ASH* NG17 ...... 163 K5
Ashton Gdns *RCH* S42 ...... 144 K4
Ashton St *GLSP* SK13 ...... 25 K3
Ashton Wy *BPR/DUF* DE56 ...... 200 A6
Ashtree Av *DERBYSE* DE24 ...... 256 F4
Ash Tree Cl *BPR/DUF* DE56 ...... 213 H5 🗓
  CHSW S40 ...... 109 M7
  ILK DE7 ...... 227 H6 🗓
  SWAD DE11 ...... 282 C4 🗓
Ash Tree Crs *MSFDW* NG19 ...... 149 M5
Ashurst Cl *RCH* S42 ...... 109 J5
Ash V *CHSW* S40 ...... 109 L7
Ashview Cl *LGEAT* NG10 ...... 260 D2 🗓
Ash View Cl *RDERBYSW* DE65 ...... 253 L6 🗓
Ashwater Cl *DERBYSE* DE24 ...... 256 C8 🗓
Ashwell Rd *HAN/WDH* S13 ...... 57 K4
Ashwood *GLSP* SK13 ...... 25 J2
Ashwood Cl *BUX* SK17 ...... 99 M3
Ashwood Crs *MPL/ROM* SK6 ...... 32 C3
Ashwood Rd *BUX* SK17 ...... 100 A1
  POY/DIS SK12 ...... 43 G4 🗓
  WRKS S80 ...... 77 L8
Ashworth Av *DERBYE* DE21 ...... 241 J5
  STPNHL/WNHL DE15 ...... 274 F8
Ashworth La *HYDE* SK14 ...... 16 C7
Askerfield Av *DERBYW* DE22 ...... 225 M6
Asker La *MTLK* DE4 ...... 157 G4
Askew Gv *RDERBYSW* DE65 ...... 267 G8
Asline Rd *SHEFP/MNR* S2 ...... 55 K2
Aspen Cl *BUX* SK17 ...... 99 L1
  ECK/KIL S21 ...... 73 M4
Aspen Ct *MSFDW* NG19 ...... 165 H2
Aspen Dr *DERBYE* DE21 ...... 241 M6
Aspen Ri *ALFN* DE55 ...... 175 G1
Aspen Rd *BUTN/AL/TUT* DE13 ...... 286 A2
  ECK/KIL S21 ...... 92 E1
Aspenshaw Rd *NM/HAY* SK22 ...... 34 B6
Aspen Wy *MPL/ROM* SK6 ...... 42 D3
Aspenwood Cl *MPL/ROM* SK6 ...... 32 B3 🗓
Aspley Cl *CHSW* S40 ...... 2 B1
Aspley Rd *MSFD* NG18 ...... 163 G7
Asquith Ms *MSFD* NG18 ...... 165 H4
Astcote Cl *HEANOR* DE75 ...... 216 D1 🗓

Astil St *STPNHL/WNHL* DE15 ...... 281 J1
Astlow Dr *BPR/DUF* DE56 ...... 199 L4 🗓
Aston Br *ASHB* DE6 ...... 250 B7
  MELB/CHEL DE73 ...... 269 K2
Aston Dr *SWAD* DE11 ...... 282 D3
Aston Gn *BSTN/STPLFD* NG9 ...... 245 H7
Aston Hall Dr
  BWSH/BRSTN DE72 ...... 270 D3
  MELB/CHEL DE73 ...... 250 D5
  MELB/CHEL DE73 ...... 270 F2
  EDL/UDV S33 ...... 50 A7
  MTLK DE4 ...... 156 A4
Aston Rd *NORM/LIT* DE23 ...... 255 M5
Astorville Gdns
  EWD/SEL/PNX NG16 ...... 203 J7
Athersley Gdns *MOS* S20 ...... 57 K8
Atherstone Rd *MSHM* DE12 ...... 295 M3
Atherton Av *HYDE* SK14 ...... 16 C7
Atherton Cl *SHEFP/MNR* S2 ...... 56 C4
Atherton Gv *HYDE* SK14 ...... 16 D7 🗓
Atherton Rd *ILK* DE7 ...... 216 F7
  SHEFP/MNR S2 ...... 56 C4
Athlestan Wy
  BUTN/AL/TUT DE13 ...... 273 M1
Athlone Cl *DERBYE* DE21 ...... 241 G2
Athol Cl *CHSW* S40 ...... 127 L2 🗓
  DERBYSE DE24 ...... 256 B6
Athol Rd *SHEFS* S8 ...... 55 H6
Atkin La *MSFD* NG18 ...... 164 E7
Atkin Pl *SHEFP/MNR* S2 ...... 55 K2 🗓
Atkinson Cl *ASHZ* LE65 ...... 291 J3
Atkins Wy *UTXW* ST14 ...... 218 C7
Atlantic Dr *SHEFS* S8 ...... 70 B4
Atlantic Rd *SHEFS* S8 ...... 70 A4
Atlantic Wy *SHEFS* S8 ...... 70 B4
Atlow Brow *ASHB* DE6 ...... 194 A7
Atlow Cl *CHSW* S40 ...... 109 L5
Atlow La *ASHB* DE6 ...... 195 K5
Atlow Rd *DERBYE* DE21 ...... 241 H5
Attenborough La
  BSTN/STPLFD NG9 ...... 245 M7
Attewell Cl *BWSH/BRSTN* DE72 ...... 259 L3
Attewell Rd
  EWD/SEL/PNX NG16 ...... 217 L5
  CDON/KEG DE74 ...... 271 K4
Attlebridge Cl *DERBYE* DE21 ...... 241 G2 🗓
Attlee Av *MSFDW* NG19 ...... 165 K1
Attlee St *STV/CWN* S43 ...... 111 L3
Atworth Gv *NORM/LIT* DE23 ...... 255 J3 🗓
Auburn Cl *ILK* DE7 ...... 228 E2
Auckland Cl *MCKLVR* DE3 ...... 239 J7
Auckland Dr *MOS* S20 ...... 73 G4
Auckland Ri *MOS* S20 ...... 73 H4
Auckland Wy *MOS* S20 ...... 73 H4
Auden Cl *RDERBYSW* DE65 ...... 251 K2 🗓
Audens Wy *SWAD* DE11 ...... 282 F4
Audley Cl *ILK* DE7 ...... 217 G7 🗓
Audrey Crs *MSFDW* NG19 ...... 149 L5
Audrey Dr *DERBYE* DE21 ...... 241 K2
Audrey Rd *HAN/WDH* S13 ...... 56 F3
Aughton Cl *HAN/WDH* S13 ...... 57 G3
Aughton Crs *HAN/WDH* S13 ...... 56 F2 🗓
Aughton Dr *HAN/WDH* S13 ...... 56 F2 🗓
Augusta St *NORM/LIT* DE23 ...... 240 F8 🗓
Aukley Rd *SHEFS* S8 ...... 55 J5
Ault Hucknall La *BSVR* S44 ...... 147 K5
Aults Cl *RDERBYSW* DE65 ...... 254 F8
Austen Av *LGEAT* NG10 ...... 260 F5
  NORM/LIT DE23 ...... 255 L2
Austin Cl *MSFD* NG18 ...... 165 H2
Austins Dr *LGEAT* NG10 ...... 244 E6
Austin Sq *NORM/LIT* DE23 ...... 256 C3
Austin St *SBK/MW* NG20 ...... 133 G6
Autumn Gv *DERBYE* DE21 ...... 241 J5
Avenue 1 *CHNE* S41 ...... 128 E2 🗓
Avenue 2 *CHNE* S41 ...... 128 E2 🗓
Avenue 3 *CHNE* S41 ...... 128 E2 🗓
Avenue 4 *CHNE* S41 ...... 128 E2 🗓
Avenue 5 *CHNE* S41 ...... 128 E2 🗓
Avenue 6 *CHNE* S41 ...... 128 E2 🗓
Avenue Cl *ASHZ* LE65 ...... 291 K5
  BPR/DUF DE56 ...... 213 H5
  CHNE S41 ...... 110 D2
The Avenue *ASHB* DE6 ...... 179 K6
  ASHB DE6 ...... 205 H5
  BKWL DE45 ...... 123 G5
  BWSH/BRSTN DE72 ...... 270 B5
  CHF/WBR SK23 ...... 60 B8
  DERBY DE1 ...... 4 F6 🗓
  DERBYE DE21 ...... 241 J5
  DRON S18 ...... 70 E8
  ECK/KIL S21 ...... 74 A8
  GLSP SK13 ...... 17 K6
  HATH/EY S32 ...... 86 D7
  MSFD NG18 ...... 164 E4
  MTLK DE4 ...... 140 E4
Averham Cl *DERBYE* DE21 ...... 241 L1 🗓
  MSFDW NG19 ...... 164 A4
Avertoun Wy *DERBYSE* DE24 ...... 257 J2
Aviation La *BUTN/AL/TUT* DE13 ...... 272 F6
Aviemore Cl *STV/CWN* S43 ...... 92 B6
Aviemore Wy *DERBYSE* DE24 ...... 256 B6 🗓
Avis Av *HEANOR* DE75 ...... 216 C3
Avocet Ct *DERBYSE* DE24 ...... 256 A6 🗓
Avocet Gv *WRKN* S81 ...... 77 M4
Avon Cl *DERBYSE* DE24 ...... 256 A8
  DRON S18 ...... 70 E7
  MPL/ROM SK6 ...... 32 B5
  SWAD DE11 ...... 282 E4
Avondale Cl *LGEAT* NG10 ...... 260 D4 🗓
Avondale Rd *BSVR* S44 ...... 131 K2
  CHSW S40 ...... 109 L6
  DERBYE DE21 ...... 242 A4
  ILK DE7 ...... 229 M5
  NORM/LIT DE23 ...... 4 E7
Avonlea Cl *ILK* DE7 ...... 230 E4 🗓
Avonmouth Dr *DERBYSE* DE24 ...... 257 H2
Avon Rd *DERBYSE* DE24 ...... 257 H2
Avon Wy *MSFD* NG18 ...... 165 K5
  RDERBYSW DE65 ...... 265 H1
  STPNHL/WNHL DE15 ...... 281 K1

Awburn Rd *HYDE* SK14 ...... 24 B1
Awdishaw La *ASHB* DE6 ...... 234 E5
Awsworth La
  EWD/SEL/PNX NG16 ...... 217 M7
Awsworth Rd *ILK* DE7 ...... 217 K7
Aycliffe Gdns *DERBYSE* DE24 ...... 257 J6
Aylesbury Av *DERBYE* DE21 ...... 241 J3
Aylward Cl *SHEFP/MNR* S2 ...... 56 C3
Aylward Rd *SHEFP/MNR* S2 ...... 56 C3
Ayncourt Rd *RCH* S42 ...... 145 L3
Ayr Cl *DERBYE* DE21 ...... 242 A6
Ayton Gdns *BSTN/STPLFD* NG9 ...... 245 M8
Azalea Av *ALFN* DE55 ...... 187 K2
Azalea Ct *ALFN* DE55 ...... 176 B7
Azalea Ct
  EWD/SEL/PNX NG16 ...... 217 M2 🗓

B

Babbacombe Cl *DERBYSE* DE24 ...... 257 M3
Babbington Cl
  BUTN/AL/TUT DE13 ...... 263 M5
Babbington St *ALFN* DE55 ...... 161 K4
Babbs La *ASHB* DE6 ...... 248 F1
Babington Cl *SHEFP/MNR* S2 ...... 56 C3
Babington Ct
  BSTN/STPLFD NG9 ...... 245 M5 🗓
  SHEFP/MNR S2 ...... 56 C3 🗓
Babington La *DERBY* DE1 ...... 4 E6
Bacchus Wy *ALFN* DE55 ...... 160 E5
Back Bridge St *NM/HAY* SK22 ...... 43 M1
Back Cft *CLCR* S45 ...... 145 H8
Backhill La *ASHB* DE6 ...... 168 B6
Back La *ALFN* DE55 ...... 161 J4
  ALFN DE55 ...... 174 B2
  ASH NG17 ...... 162 C7
  ASH NG17 ...... 163 J4
  ASHB DE6 ...... 166 A7
  ASHB DE6 ...... 205 J3
  ASHB DE6 ...... 222 A5
  ASHB DE6 ...... 236 E7
  BKWL DE45 ...... 138 D4
  BPR/DUF DE56 ...... 183 M6
  BSVR S44 ...... 129 L2
  BSVR S44 ...... 131 L4
  BUX SK17 ...... 167 G5
  CDLE ST10 ...... 191 H1
  CDON/KEG DE74 ...... 271 K4
  CLCR S45 ...... 145 M8
  DRON S18 ...... 91 J1
  ECK/KIL S21 ...... 72 F7
  GLSP SK13 ...... 25 H4
  HATH/EY S32 ...... 66 D5
  HYDE SK14 ...... 16 D7
  ILK DE7 ...... 217 H8
  MELB/CHEL DE73 ...... 257 K8
  MTLK DE4 ...... 141 K3
  MTLK DE4 ...... 154 B4
  RDERBYSW DE65 ...... 252 F8
  RIPLEY DE5 ...... 186 F4
  WRKS S80 ...... 76 E4
Back Moor *HYDE* SK14 ...... 16 D6
Backmoor Crs *SHEFS* S8 ...... 55 M8
Backmoor Rd *SHEFS* S8 ...... 55 M8
Back Rd *DRON* S18 ...... 91 J1
Back Sitwell St *DERBY* DE1 ...... 4 F5
Back South St *STV/CWN* S43 ...... 92 A7 🗓
Back St *EDL/UDV* S33 ...... 48 F8 🗓
  HAN/WDH S13 ...... 57 M4
Back Ter *ALFN* DE55 ...... 159 J6
Back Union Rd *NM/HAY* SK22 ...... 43 M3
Back Westlands Rd *UTXW* ST14 ...... 247 L4
Back Wyver La
  BPR/DUF DE56 ...... 199 J5 🗓
Bacon Cl
  EWD/SEL/PNX NG16 ...... 217 K2 🗓
Bacon La *RIPLEY* DE5 ...... 186 E3
Bacons La *CHSW* S40 ...... 128 D2
Baden Powell Av *CHSW* S40 ...... 2 F8
Baden Powell Rd *CHSW* S40 ...... 3 G6
Badger Cl *DERBYE* DE21 ...... 242 C4 🗓
  HAN/WDH S13 ...... 57 M3
Badger Dr *HAN/WDH* S13 ...... 57 M3
Badger La *ALFN* DE55 ...... 159 G2
  CLCR S45 ...... 158 F2
Badger Pl *HAN/WDH* S13 ...... 57 M3
Badger Ri *HAN/WDH* S13 ...... 57 M3
Badger Rd *HAN/WDH* S13 ...... 57 M3
Badger Wy *MSFDW* NG19 ...... 165 M3
Badway La *RDERBYSW* DE65 ...... 251 L2
Bage Hl *RCH* S42 ...... 127 H4
Baggaley Crs *MSFDW* NG19 ...... 164 E1
Bag La *ASHB* DE6 ...... 219 H3
  UTXW ST14 ...... 249 G8
Bagot St *ILK* DE7 ...... 228 F2
Bagshawe Av *CHF/WBR* SK23 ...... 60 C4
Bagshaw Hl *BKWL* DE45 ...... 123 G4
Bagshaw La *BUX* SK17 ...... 61 L4
Bagshaw's Rd *HACK/IN* S12 ...... 56 E4 🗓
Bagshaw St *DERBYSE* DE24 ...... 257 H2
  MSFDW NG19 ...... 148 E5
Bagshot St *ECC* S11 ...... 55 G2
Bagthorpe La *RCH* S42 ...... 108 D7
Bailey Av *MSHM* DE12 ...... 289 K7
Bailey Brook Crs
  EWD/SEL/PNX NG16 ...... 202 D7 🗓
Bailey Brook Dr
  EWD/SEL/PNX NG16 ...... 202 D7
Bailey Crs *MSFDW* NG19 ...... 164 B3
Bailey Dr *ECK/KIL* S21 ...... 74 B2
Bailey Gv *BUX* SK17 ...... 100 B3
Bailey Grove Rd
  EWD/SEL/PNX NG16 ...... 203 G8
Bailey St *BSTN/STPLFD* NG9 ...... 244 F4
  BUT DE14 ...... 281 G1
  NORM/LIT DE23 ...... 4 D8 🗓
Bainbridge Rd *BSVR* S44 ...... 131 J1
Bainbridge St *NORM/LIT* DE23 ...... 4 E8 🗓
Baines Wood Cl *CHNE* S41 ...... 109 M2
Bains Dr *BWSH/BRSTN* DE72 ...... 259 G1 🗓
Bakeacre La *RDERBYSW* DE65 ...... 255 H7
Bakehouse La
  BWSH/BRSTN DE72 ...... 242 E5
Baker Av *ASHZ* LE65 ...... 291 H4
  HEANOR DE75 ...... 216 C3
Baker Cl *ALFN* DE55 ...... 188 A3 🗓
Baker Dr *ECK/KIL* S21 ...... 73 M4

Baker Rd *EWD/SEL/PNX* NG16 .... 217 M2
  MSFDW NG19 .... 149 M4
Bakers Hl *BPR/DUF* DE56 .... 200 B1 🅸
Baker's La *ASHB* DE6 .... 248 F1
  MTLK DE4 .... 171 K5
  MTLK DE4 .... 172 D2
Baker St *DERBYSE* DE24 .... 257 J2
  ILK DE7 .... 230 C1
  STPNHL/WNHL DE15 .... 281 H3
  SWAD DE11 .... 282 F7 🅸
  WRKS S80 .... 96 B8
Bakestone Moor *WRKS* S80 .... 96 B5
Bakewell Cl *MCKLVR* DE3 .... 239 G7
Bakewell Dr *CDON/KEG* DE74 .... 271 K8
Bakewell Gn *SWAD* DE11 .... 282 E1
Bakewell Ms *GLSP* SK13 .... 25 G1 🅸
Bakewell Rd *BKWL* DE45 .... 106 B6
  BUX SK17 .... 99 M2
  LGEAT NG10 .... 261 H5
  MTLK DE4 .... 156 C3
  STV/CWN S43 .... 111 M5
Bakewell St *DERBYW* DE22 .... 4 C1
Balaclava Rd *NORM/LIT* DE23 ...... 256 D3
Balance St *UTXR* ST14 .... 247 M3
Baldwin St
  EWD/SEL/PNX NG16 .... 217 M1 🅸
Balfour Rd *BSTN/STPLFD* NG9 ..... 245 G4
  NORM/LIT DE23 .... 256 D2
Balfour St *BUTN/AL/TUT* DE13 ...... 273 M4
Balkham La *MSFDW* NG19 .... 132 D8
Ballacraine Dr *RIPLEY* DE5 .... 201 J1
Ballards Wy *BWSH/BRSTN* DE72 .. 259 G1
Ballater Cl *DERBYSE* DE24 .... 258 B6
  MSFDW NG19 .... 149 H8 🅸
Balleny Cl *DERBYE* DE21 .... 227 J8 🅸
Ball Hl *ALFN* DE55 .... 176 F4
Ballidon Cl *CHSW* S40 .... 109 M4 🅸
Ballfield Av *HAN/WDH* S13 .... 57 K1
Ballfield Cl *HAN/WDH* S13 .... 57 L1
Ballfield Crs *HAN/WDH* S13 .... 57 L1
Ballfield Dr *HAN/WDH* S13 .... 57 L1
Ballfield Pl *HAN/WDH* S13 .... 57 L1
Ballfield Rd *HAN/WDH* S13 .... 57 K1
Ballfield Wy *HAN/WDH* S13 .... 57 L1
Ball La *BWSH/BRSTN* DE72 .... 258 D5
Balmoak La *CHNE* S41 .... 110 F5
Balmoral Av *HEANOR* DE75 .... 215 M1
  LGEAT NG10 .... 244 E7
  NORM/LIT DE23 .... 239 L8
Balmoral Crs *DRON* S18 .... 70 A8
  WOL/BIL/BRX NG8 .... 231 M5
Balmoral Dr *BSTN/STPLFD* NG9 ... 231 L8
  MPL/ROM SK6 .... 42 B3
  MSFDW NG19 .... 149 H8
Balmoral Rd
  BWSH/BRSTN DE72 .... 258 F1 🅸
  HAN/WDH S13 .... 57 M4
  ILK DE7 .... 230 A5 🅸
  STPNHL/WNHL DE15 .... 274 D7 🅸
Balmoral Wy *STV/CWN* S43 .... 92 B6
Baltimore Cl *SWAD* DE11 .... 282 D3 🅸
Bamborough Cl
  BUTN/AL/TUT DE13 .... 274 A3 🅸
  DERBYE DE21 .... 242 A6 🅸
Bamford Av *NORM/LIT* DE23 .... 256 B2
  RCH S42 .... 145 J3
Bamford Dr *MSFDW* NG19 .... 165 L4
Bamford Fold *GLSP* SK13 .... 25 H1 🅸
Bamford Gn *GLSP* SK13 .... 25 H1 🅸
Bamford Ms *GLSP* SK13 .... 25 H1 🅸
Bamford St *ALFN* DE55 .... 161 K7
  RIPLEY DE5 .... 201 G3
  STV/CWN S43 .... 92 A6 🅸
Banbury Av *BSTN/STPLFD* NG9 .... 245 J7
Banchory Cl *MSFDW* NG19 .... 149 H8 🅸
Bancroft Dr *DERBYW* DE22 .... 225 M6
Bancroft La *MSFD* NG18 .... 164 D3
The Bancroft *RDERBYSW* DE65 ..... 253 G8
Bangor St *DERBYW* DE22 .... 241 H2
Bankbottom *GLSP* SK13 .... 17 K5
Bank Cl *ABRD* S7 .... 55 H4
  ALFN DE55 .... 161 J5
  BSVR S44 .... 113 K7
  SBK/MW NG20 .... 133 J6 🅸
  UTXR ST14 .... 247 M4
  WRKS S80 .... 115 G1
Bank Ct *DERBYW* DE22 .... 240 B2
Bankerwall La *ASHB* DE6 .... 205 M3
Bankfield Dr *BSTN/STPLFD* NG9 .. 245 M1
Bankfield Dr *ILK* DE7 .... 229 L4
Bank Gdns *MTLK* DE4 .... 156 E4
Bankholmes Cl
  DERBYE DE24 .... 256 B8 🅸
Bank House Ct *ASHB* DE6 .... 181 K8 🅸
Bank La *GLSP* SK13 .... 17 K3
Bank Mellor Rd *NM/HAY* SK22 .... 48 K1 🅸
  MTLK DE4 .... 156 F5
Banksburn Cl *HEANOR* DE75 .... 215 M1 🅸
Bankside *ASHB* DE6 .... 205 M1
  BKWL DE45 .... 138 C5
Bank Side *BUX* SK17 .... 151 G4
  DERBYE DE22 .... 226 B8
Bankside *HYDE* SK14 .... 24 A1
Bankside Cl *MPL/ROM* SK6 .... 32 C1 🅸
Banks Rd *BSTN/STPLFD* NG9 ...... 245 H8
Bank St *ALFN* DE55 .... 187 M2
  CHSW S40 .... 2 D4
  EWD/SEL/PNX NG16 .... 202 F6
  GLSP SK13 .... 17 J5 🅸
  GLSP SK13 .... 26 A2
  LGEAT NG10 .... 261 H3
  NM/HAY SK22 .... 35 G4
  STV/CWN S43 .... 111 G2
  SWAD DE11 .... 289 K2
Bankswood Cl *GLSP* SK13 .... 17 K6
The Bank *GLSP* SK13 .... 26 A2 🅸
  HATH/EY S32 .... 86 C6
  MTLK DE4 .... 170 F1
Bank Top La *HATH/EY* S32 .... 86 E2
Bank Vw *BUX* SK17 .... 83 L5
Bank View Rd *BPR/DUF* DE56 ...... 185 M8
  DERBYE DE22 .... 240 C2
Bank Wood Cl *CHSW* S40 .... 109 L3

Bankwood Cl *SHEFS* S8 .... 56 A5
Bankwood Rd *SHEFP/MNR* S2 .... 56 A5
Banmoor La *HATH/EY* S32 .... 66 B2
Bannels Av *NORM/LIT* DE23 .... 255 L3
Banner Ct *ECC* S11 .... 54 E4
Banner Cross Dr *ECC* S11 .... 54 E4 🅸
Bannerdale Cl *ECC* S11 .... 54 F4 🅸
Bannerdale Rd *ECC* S11 .... 54 F4
Bannerdale Vw *ECC* S11 .... 54 F4
Banton's La *MELB/CHEL* DE73 ..... 277 K6
Banwell Cl *MCKLVR* DE3 .... 238 F7
Barber Cl *ILK* DE7 .... 217 H7 🅸
Barber's La *ECK/KIL* S21 .... 74 A2
Barber St *EWD/SEL/PNX* NG16 .... 203 K8
  GLSP SK13 .... 17 L5
Barbon Cl *CHSW* S40 .... 110 B5
Barcheston Cl *DERBYE* DE21 .... 227 L8 🅸
Barclay Ct *ILK* DE7 .... 217 G7 🅸
Bar Cft *CHSW* S40 .... 110 A4 🅸
Barden Dr *DERBYW* DE22 .... 226 C8
Bardolph Cl *SWAD* DE11 .... 282 C7
Bardsey Ct *DERBYE* DE21 .... 227 L7 🅸
Bardsley Cl *HYDE* SK14 .... 16 B8 🅸
Bardsley Gate Av *STLY* SK15 .... 16 B4
Bare Jarnett Rd *BUX* SK17 .... 120 D1
Bare La *BWSH/BRSTN* DE72 .... 242 F5
Barf Cl *MCKLVR* DE3 .... 255 H1 🅸
Bargate Cl *EDL/UDV* S33 .... 48 F8
Bargate La *RDERBYSW* DE65 .... 266 E5
Bargate Rd *BPR/DUF* DE56 .... 199 L8
Barker Av *ASH* NG17 .... 163 G4
  EWD/SEL/PNX NG16 .... 188 E6
Barker Av East *LGEAT* NG10 .... 244 E4
Barker Av North *LGEAT* NG10 .... 244 D4
Barker Cl *ILK* DE7 .... 228 E1
Barker Fold *CHSW* S40 .... 2 B4
Barker Ga *ILK* DE7 .... 217 J8 🅸
Barker's Rd *ECC* S11 .... 55 G4
Barklam Cl *MSHM* DE12 .... 295 H1
Barlborough Cl *STV/CWN* S43 .... 95 G5
Barley Gv *HACK/IN* S12 .... 57 M7
Barley Cl *BUT* DE14 .... 274 B4
  DERBYE DE21 .... 226 F2
Barley Corn Cl *DERBYE* DE21 .... 227 M8
Barleycorn Cl
  STPNHL/WNHL DE15 .... 281 K1 🅸
Barley Cft *ALFN* DE55 .... 176 E6
  BPR/DUF DE56 .... 199 L8
Barleycroft *GLSP* SK13 .... 17 J6
Barley Cft *MELB/CHEL* DE73 .... 269 J1
Barley Dale Dr
  BSTN/STPLFD NG9 .... 231 G8
Barley La *CHSW* S40 .... 109 K5
Barley Ms *DRON* S18 .... 89 M1 🅸
Barling Dr *ILK* DE7 .... 216 F8
Barlow Crs *MPL/ROM* SK6 .... 32 C6
Barlow Dr *EWD/SEL/PNX* NG16 ... 217 L6
Barlow Dr (North)
  EWD/SEL/PNX NG16 .... 217 L6
Barlow Dr South
  EWD/SEL/PNX NG16 .... 217 L6
Barlow Lees La *DRON* S18 .... 90 C3
Barlow Rd *CHF/WBR* S23 .... 60 F4
  CHNE S41 .... 109 J1
  STV/CWN S43 .... 93 H8 🅸
Barlow St *DERBY* DE1 .... 5 H8
Barlow Vw *DRON* S18 .... 90 E3
Barlow Wood Dr *MPL/ROM* SK6 ... 32 E7
Barmouth Rd *ABRD* S7 .... 55 H5
Barms Wy *BUX* SK17 .... 100 A1
Barnard Av *DRON* S18 .... 71 G7
Barnard Rd *DERBYE* DE21 .... 241 G1
Barncliffe Cl *FUL* S10 .... 53 M2
Barncliffe Crs *FUL* S10 .... 53 L1
Barncliffe Gln *FUL* S10 .... 53 L2
Barncliffe Gln *FUL* S10 .... 53 L2
Barncliffe Rd *FUL* S10 .... 53 M2
Barn Cl *CDON/KEG* DE74 .... 271 K7
  CHSW S40 .... 109 M4
  DERBYW DE22 .... 225 M4
  GLSP SK13 .... 26 A3
  MSFD NG18 .... 165 J5
  RDERBYSW DE65 .... 255 G8
Barn Cft *BSTN/STPLFD* NG9 .... 245 L4
Barnes La *DRON* S18 .... 70 A8
Barnes La *BKWL* DE45 .... 138 F5
  DRON S18 .... 69 L6
  DRON S18 .... 70 A7
Barnes Rd *CHNE* S41 .... 129 H1
Barnet Av *ECC* S11 .... 54 B5
Barnet Rd *ECC* S11 .... 54 B5
Barnett La *RCH* S42 .... 146 B2
  STV/CWN S43 .... 93 H8
Barnfield Dr *HATH/EY* S32 .... 66 C3
Barnfields *HATH/EY* S32 .... 66 C3
Barnham Ct *CHSW* S40 .... 127 L2
Barnhill Gv *NORM/LIT* DE23 .... 255 K3 🅸
Barnsdale Av *MOS* S20 .... 57 K8
Barnsfold Rd *MPL/ROM* SK6 .... 32 C7
Barnsley Boundary Wk
  HOLM/MEL HD7 .... 9 M6
Barnsley La *BPR/DUF* DE56 .... 183 K8
Barnstaple Cl *DERBYE* DE21 .... 227 K8 🅸
Barnwell La *MTLK* DE4 .... 171 K5
Barnwood Cl *MCKLVR* DE3 .... 238 F8 🅸
Baron Cl *DERBYE* DE21 .... 228 A7 🅸
Baron St *SHEF* S1 .... 55 K1 🅸
Barrack Rd *DRON* S18 .... 91 K1
Barrack Yd *ALFN* DE55 .... 188 A3 🅸
Barratt Rd *ECK/KIL* S21 .... 73 G8
Barrett St *DERBYSE* DE24 .... 257 K3
Barrie Dr *DERBYSE* DE24 .... 256 C5
Barringer Rd *MSFD* NG18 .... 165 H2
Barrington Cl
  BUTN/AL/TUT DE13 .... 273 M1 🅸
Bar Rd *BKWL* DE45 .... 106 C4
  HATH/EY S32 .... 87 H8
Barrons Ct
  BWSH/BRSTN DE72 .... 258 D5 🅸
Barron's Wy
  BWSH/BRSTN DE72 .... 258 F1 🅸
The Barroon *CDON/KEG* DE74 ..... 271 L7
Barrow La *MELB/CHEL* DE73 .... 268 F4
Barrows Hill La
  EWD/SEL/PNX NG16 .... 189 G5
Barrow St *STV/CWN* S43 .... 93 J8

Barry Rd *STV/CWN* S43 .... 111 J6
Bartle Av *HACK/IN* S12 .... 56 C6
Bartle Dr *HACK/IN* S12 .... 56 C6
Bartle Rd *HACK/IN* S12 .... 56 C6
Bartle Wy *HACK/IN* S12 .... 56 C6
Barton Cl *MSFDW* NG19 .... 165 L2
Barton Crs *CHSW* S40 .... 109 K4
Barton Hl *MTLK* DE4 .... 154 F1
Barton Knowle
  BPR/DUF DE56 .... 200 A6 🅸
Barton La *BSTN/STPLFD* NG9 ...... 261 M1
Barton Ldg
  BUTN/AL/TUT DE13 .... 286 B1 🅸
Barton Rd *LGEAT* NG10 .... 261 K3 🅸
  SHEFS S8 .... 55 K4
Bartons *EWD/SEL/PNX* NG16 ...... 203 M8
Barton St *BUT* DE14 .... 280 F2
  STV/CWN S43 .... 95 J6
Barton Turn
  BUTN/AL/TUT DE13 .... 286 D1
Barway *ASHB* DE6 .... 233 H2
Basegreen Av *HACK/IN* S12 .... 56 E7
Basegreen Cl *HACK/IN* S12 .... 56 F7
Basegreen Crs *HACK/IN* S12 .... 56 E7
Basegreen Dr *HACK/IN* S12 .... 56 E7
Basegreen Pl *HACK/IN* S12 .... 56 E7 🅸
Basegreen Rd *HACK/IN* S12 .... 56 F8 🅸
Basegreen Wy *HACK/IN* S12 .... 56 F7 🅸
Basil Cl *CHNE* S41 .... 3 H2
Basildon Cl *DERBYSE* DE24 .... 257 J5
Baskin La *BSTN/STPLFD* NG9 ...... 245 M6
Baslow Cl *LGEAT* NG10 .... 260 D5
Baslow Dr *DERBYW* DE22 .... 226 C7
Baslow Gn *SWAD* DE11 .... 282 B5 🅸
Baslow Gv *BUX* SK17 .... 100 A4
Baslow Ms *GLSP* SK13 .... 25 H1 🅸
Baslow Rd *BKWL* DE45 .... 123 H1
  HATH/EY S32 .... 86 F8
  HATH/EY S32 .... 106 A1
  RCH S42 .... 126 F1
  TOT/DORE S17 .... 68 F6
Baslow Wy *MSFD* NG18 .... 165 L5
Bassettbarn La *RCH* S42 .... 143 K3
Bassett Cl *ILK* DE7 .... 216 F7 🅸
Bassett La *FUL* S10 .... 53 H4
The Bassett *BSK/MW* NG20 .... 133 H4 🅸
Bassford Av *HEANOR* DE75 .... 202 C8 🅸
Bassingham Cl *DERBYE* DE21 ...... 241 L1 🅸
Bassledene Rd *SHEFP/MNR* S2 ...... 56 D2
Bass's Crs *SWAD* DE11 .... 289 H3
Bass St *DERBYW* DE22 .... 240 A4
Batch La *ASHB* DE6 .... 248 F3
Bateman Cl *STV/CWN* S43 .... 92 A6
Bateman St *DERBY* DE1 .... 5 J9
Batemill Rd *NM/HAY* SK22 .... 34 A8
Batemoor Cl *SHEFS* S8 .... 70 D4
Batemoor Dr *SHEFS* S8 .... 70 D4
Batemoor Pl *SHEFS* S8 .... 70 D4 🅸
Batemoor Rd *SHEFS* S8 .... 70 D4
Bate Wood Av *STV/CWN* S43 ...... 111 L5
Batham Ga *BUX* SK17 .... 81 J6
Batham Gate Rd *BUX* SK17 .... 81 L5
Batham Rd *EDL/UDV* S33 .... 64 D2
Bath La *CLCR* S45 .... 143 H4
  MSFD NG18 .... 164 F3
  MSFDW NG19 .... 133 M8
  MSHM DE12 .... 290 A6
Bath Rd *BUX* SK17 .... 99 L4
  MCKLVR DE3 .... 239 H8
Bath St *ASH* NG17 .... 163 J6
  BKWL DE45 .... 123 G4
  DERBY DE1 .... 240 D3
  ILK DE7 .... 217 H8
  MSFD NG18 .... 164 E4
Bathurst Rd *BSVR* S44 .... 131 H2
Bathurst Ter *SBK/MW* NG20 .... 115 K8
Bathwood Dr *ASH* NG17 .... 148 B5 🅸
  MSFD NG18 .... 164 B5 🅸
Batley La *MSFDW* NG19 .... 148 B5
Batt St *SHEFP/MNR* S2 .... 55 K2 🅸
Baulk La *BSTN/STPLFD* NG9 .... 245 K4
  HATH/EY S32 .... 66 D2
Baum's La *MSFD* NG18 .... 164 E5
Baverstock Cl
  MELB/CHEL DE73 .... 257 J7
Baxter Hl *MSFDW* NG19 .... 148 C7
Baxter Sq *NORM/LIT* DE23 .... 256 C4
Baycliff Dr *CHSW* S40 .... 109 M7
Bay Ct *ECK/KIL* S21 .... 73 M5
Bayfield Cl *HOLM/MEL* HD7 .... 9 L2
Bayleaf Crs *DERBYE* DE21 .... 227 L7 🅸
Baysdale Cft *MOS* S20 .... 73 G3
Bayswater Cl *DERBYW* DE22 .... 239 J4 🅸
Beackden Cl *BPR/DUF* DE56 .... 200 B6 🅸
Beacon Dr *BUTN/AL/TUT* DE13 ... 264 E7
Beacon Rd *BUTN/AL/TUT* DE13 ... 264 E7
Beaconsfield Rd
  BUTN/AL/TUT DE13 .... 273 K3
Beaconsfield St *LGEAT* NG10 .... 261 H3 🅸
Beacon Vw *MPL/ROM* SK6 .... 32 C2
Beam Cl *BUTN/AL/TUT* DE13 .... 273 K1
Beamhill Rd
  BUTN/AL/TUT DE13 .... 273 H2
Beamwood Cl *DERBYE* DE21 .... 241 J1
Bear Bones Rd *HOLM/MEL* HD7 ..... 9 L5
Beardall St *MSFD* NG18 .... 164 D3 🅸
Beard Crs *NM/HAY* SK22 .... 44 A2
Beardmore Cl *DERBYE* DE21 .... 227 J8 🅸
Beards Rd *SWAD* DE11 .... 282 D4
Bearwood Hill Rd
  STPNHL/WNHL DE15 .... 274 C7
Beatrix Dr *GLSP* SK13 .... 17 H7
Beatty St *DERBYSE* DE24 .... 257 J2
Beauchief Abbey La *SHEFS* S8 ...... 69 M2
Beauchief Dr *SHEFS* S8 .... 69 M3
Beauchief Gdns *ALFN* DE55 .... 188 A2 🅸
Beauchief Ri *SHEFS* S8 .... 69 M1
Beaufit La *EWD/SEL/PNX* NG16 ... 177 K7
Beaufort Cl *HYDE* SK14 .... 16 B8 🅸
Beaufort Dr
  BSTN/STPLFD NG9 .... 245 M5 🅸
Beaufort Rd *DERBYE* DE24 .... 255 M8
  HYDE SK14 .... 16 B8
  STPNHL/WNHL DE15 .... 274 E8
Beaufort St *DERBYE* DE21 .... 241 G2
Beaulieu Wy *ALFN* DE55 .... 187 K2 🅸
Beauly Dr *MSFDW* NG19 .... 164 A5
Beaumaris Ct *DERBYE* DE21 .... 242 C5

Beaumaris Dr
  BSTN/STPLFD NG9 .... 245 L6
Beaumont Av *ASHZ* LE65 .... 291 J5
  MSFD NG18 .... 165 J5
Beaumont Cl
  BSTN/STPLFD NG9 .... 245 H1 🅸
  MELB/CHEL DE73 .... 268 D5 🅸
Beaumont Dr *BUX* SK17 .... 81 J7 🅸
Beaumont Ms *SHEFP/MNR* S2 .... 56 E1 🅸
Beaurepaire Crs
  BPR/DUF DE56 .... 199 L5 🅸
Beauvale Dr *DERBYW* DE22 .... 226 B7 🅸
Beauvale *EWD/SEL/PNX* NG16 .... 203 M8
Beauvale Dr *ILK* DE7 .... 217 H5
Beauvale Ri
  EWD/SEL/PNX NG16 .... 203 L7 🅸
Beaver Av *HAN/WDH* S13 .... 57 L2
Beaver Cl *HAN/WDH* S13 .... 57 L2
Beaver Dr *HAN/WDH* S13 .... 57 L2
Beaver Hill Rd *HAN/WDH* S13 .... 57 L2
Beazley Av *MSFD* NG18 .... 164 C3
Becher La *NORM/LIT* DE23 .... 256 D5
Beck Cl *BSVR* S44 .... 113 M8
Beck Crs *MSFDW* NG19 .... 164 B3
Beckdale *UTXR* ST14 .... 247 K2
Beckenham Wy *DERBYW* DE22 ... 239 L4
Becket Rd *SHEFS* S8 .... 70 B4
Becket St *DERBY* DE1 .... 4 D4
Beckett Av *MSFDW* NG19 .... 164 B1
Becket Well La *DERBY* DE1 .... 4 E4
Beckitt Cl *DERBYSE* DE24 .... 257 K2 🅸
Beck La *ASH* NG17 .... 163 L4
Becksitch La *BPR/DUF* DE56 .... 199 J8
Bedale Ct *BSTN/STPLFD* NG9 ...... 245 K6 🅸
Bedale Rd *SHEFS* S8 .... 55 J4
Bedehouse La *MTLK* DE4 .... 171 K5
Bedford Av *MSFD* NG18 .... 164 B1
Bedford Cl *DERBYW* DE22 .... 240 A7 🅸
Bedford Ct
  BSTN/STPLFD NG9 .... 245 H1 🅸
Bedford St *DERBYW* DE22 .... 240 A7
Bedgebury Cl *MOS* S20 .... 73 L1 🅸
Bedgrave Cl *ECK/KIL* S21 .... 74 C2
Beech Av *BPR/DUF* DE56 .... 214 E2 🅸
  ASH NG17 .... 162 D7
  ASHB DE6 .... 196 C7 🅸
  BUTN/AL/TUT DE13 .... 274 C2
  BWSH/BRSTN DE72 .... 242 F7
  BWSH/BRSTN DE72 .... 260 C2
  DERBYSE DE24 .... 257 L3
  DERBYW DE22 .... 225 K2
  EWD/SEL/PNX NG16 .... 177 M7
  GLSP SK13 .... 25 K2
  LGEAT NG10 .... 244 E3
  LGEAT NG10 .... 261 H1
  MELB/CHEL DE73 .... 278 E2
  MPL/ROM SK6 .... 32 A4
  MSFD NG18 .... 164 E5
  NM/HAY SK22 .... 44 A1
  RDERBYSW DE65 .... 266 D5
  RIPLEY DE5 .... 186 F8
  WRKS S80 .... 115 J1
Beech Ct *DERBYE* DE21 .... 242 A5
  EWD/SEL/PNX NG16 .... 189 G8
Beech Crs *BSVR* S44 .... 147 L2
  ECK/KIL S21 .... 73 K5
  ECK/KIL S21 .... 92 E1
Beechcroft *ILK* DE7 .... 227 G6
Beechdale Av *ASH* NG17 .... 163 J6
Beechdale Cl *CHSW* S40 .... 2 B1
Beechdale Rd *ALFN* DE55 .... 175 M7
Beech Dr *ASHB* DE6 .... 208 A2 🅸
  BSVR S44 .... 112 A7
  BUTN/AL/TUT DE13 .... 274 B2
  DERBYE DE22 .... 240 C2
  RDERBYSW DE65 .... 253 M6 🅸
  RDERBYSW DE65 .... 267 H1
Beeches Av *DERBYE* DE21 .... 242 A5
  SHEFP/MNR S2 .... 55 M2
Beeches Dr *SHEFP/MNR* S2 .... 55 M2
The Beeches *HEANOR* DE75 .... 215 M2
  MTLK DE4 .... 185 J1
Beechfield Rd *GLSP* SK13 .... 17 J7 🅸
Beech Hill Av *MSFDW* NG19 .... 164 C1
Beech Hill Crs *MSFDW* NG19 .... 164 D1
Beech Hill Dr *MSFDW* NG19 .... 164 C1
Beech La *BUTN/AL/TUT* DE13 ...... 274 B2
  BUX SK17 .... 81 H2
  ILK DE7 .... 229 G3
Beechley Dr *DERBYE* DE21 .... 241 L1
Beech Ri *CHF/WBR* S23 .... 58 F5
Beech Rd *BUTN/AL/TUT* DE13 ..... 286 A2
  CHF/WBR S23 .... 59 H3
  EWD/SEL/PNX NG16 .... 189 K7
  MPL/ROM SK6 .... 42 C3 🅸
Beech St *ASH* NG17 .... 163 G3
  BUT DE14 .... 280 E1
  STV/CWN S43 .... 111 K1
Beech Tree Av *MSFDW* NG19 .... 149 L5
Beech Tree Dr *STV/CWN* S43 .... 95 J3
Beech Wk *MTLK* DE4 .... 171 K4
  NORM/LIT DE23 .... 256 A1
Beech Wy *CLCR* S45 .... 145 H8
  DRON S18 .... 70 D7
Beechway *MPL/ROM* SK6 .... 42 C3
Beechwood *GLSP* SK13 .... 25 J3 🅸
Beechwood Cl *ASH* NG17 .... 163 K5
  BPR/DUF DE56 .... 199 H5
  MSFDW NG19 .... 165 K1 🅸
Beechwood Crs
  NORM/LIT DE23 .... 255 M1 🅸
Beechwood Dr *MPL/ROM* SK6 .... 32 A4
Beechwood Gv *ASH* NG17 .... 163 K5
Beechwood Rd *DRON* S18 .... 90 C1
Beehive Av *MSHM* DE12 .... 290 D6
Beehive Rd *CHSW* S40 .... 2 A4
The Bee Hives *SWAD* DE11 .... 282 D3
Beeley Cl *BPR/DUF* DE56 .... 199 G4
  DERBYW DE22 .... 226 A3
  MSFD NG18 .... 165 L4
  RCH S42 .... 145 K3 🅸

  STV/CWN S43 .... 111 M4 🅸
  WRKS S80 .... 114 F1
Beeley La *CLCR* S45 .... 125 M8
Beeley St *SHEFP/MNR* S2 .... 55 J1 🅸
Beeley Vw *STV/CWN* S43 .... 92 C5
Beelow Cl *BUX* SK17 .... 61 J8
Beelow La *CDLE* ST10 .... 204 A3
Beeston Cl *DRON* S18 .... 69 M8 🅸
Beeston Fields Dr
  BSTN/STPLFD NG9 .... 245 M2
Beeton St *SHEFS* S8 .... 55 J5
Beetwell St *CHSW* S40 .... 3 H5
Beggarway Ct *BKWL* DE45 .... 104 D6
Beighton Cl *MSFD* NG18 .... 165 L5
Beighton Rd *HACK/IN* S12 .... 57 L7
Beighton Rd East *MOS* S20 .... 57 M7
Beighton St *ASH* NG17 .... 163 J7
  RIPLEY DE5 .... 201 H1
Beldon Cl *SHEFP/MNR* S2 .... 56 A3
Beldon Pl *SHEFP/MNR* S2 .... 56 A3
Beldon Rd *SHEFP/MNR* S2 .... 56 A3
Belfield Rd *RDERBYSW* DE65 ...... 253 M7
  SWAD DE11 .... 282 E5
Belfield St *ILK* DE7 .... 217 J8
Belfit Dr *RCH* S42 .... 128 C8
Belf Moor Cl *WRKS* S80 .... 96 D5
Belfry *MCKLVR* DE3 .... 255 J1 🅸
The Belfry *BUTN/AL/TUT* DE13 .... 273 M1
Belgrade Av *CHF/WBR* S23 .... 60 B1
Belgrave Av *MPL/ROM* SK6 .... 32 C4 🅸
Belgrave Cl *BPR/DUF* DE56 .... 199 M5 🅸
Belgrave Rd *FUL* S10 .... 54 A1
Belgrave Rd *FUL* S10 .... 54 A1
Belgrave Sq *NORM/LIT* DE23 .... 4 E8
Belgrave St *NORM/LIT* DE23 .... 4 E8
Belklane Dr *ECK/KIL* S21 .... 74 B3
Bellamy Rd *MSFD* NG18 .... 165 K7
Bell Av *BWSH/BRSTN* DE72 .... 270 D3
Belle Vue Av *RIPLEY* DE5 .... 200 F4
Belle Vue Rd *ASHB* DE6 .... 207 L4
Bellhouse La
  BUTN/AL/TUT DE13 .... 272 B4
Bell House La *STV/CWN* S43 .... 93 J7
Bellingham Ct
  DERBYE DE22 .... 225 M8 🅸
Bell La *ASHB* DE6 .... 248 F2
  ILK DE7 .... 215 K6
  MTLK DE4 .... 170 F1
Bells End Rd *MSHM* DE12 .... 287 G1
Bellsfield Cl *WRKS* S80 .... 96 D5 🅸
Belmont Av *BWSH/BRSTN* DE72 .. 260 B2
Belmont Cl *BSTN/STPLFD* NG9 ... 245 L6
Belmont Dr *BWSH/BRSTN* DE72 .. 258 E1
  MPL/ROM SK6 .... 32 C1
  STV/CWN S43 .... 93 J8
Belmont St *SWAD* DE11 .... 282 F6
Belmot Rd *BUTN/AL/TUT* DE13 ... 263 L6
  BUTN/AL/TUT DE13 .... 272 C1
Belond La *CLCR* S45 .... 127 G8
Belper La *BPR/DUF* DE56 .... 199 H4
Belper Rd *ALFN* DE55 .... 159 M8
  ASHB DE6 .... 208 A1
  BPR/DUF DE56 .... 200 B8
  BPR/DUF DE56 .... 213 M1
  DERBY DE1 .... 240 C2
  ILK DE7 .... 228 D1
  SHEFS S8 .... 55 J4 🅸
Belper St *ILK* DE7 .... 230 C3
Belper Wy *MSFD* NG18 .... 165 G3 🅸
Belsize Cl *DERBYW* DE22 .... 239 J4 🅸
Belsize Rd *ECC* S11 .... 54 A2
Belton Cl *DRON* S18 .... 89 M1 🅸
  LGEAT NG10 .... 244 E6 🅸
Belvedere Av *CHSW* S40 .... 2 C9
Belvedere Cl *ALFN* DE55 .... 187 J3
  MCKLVR DE3 .... 239 G7
  RCH S42 .... 127 K2
Belvedere Rd
  BUTN/AL/TUT DE13 .... 273 K4
  SWAD DE11 .... 283 J8
Belvoir Cl *BUTN/AL/TUT* DE13 .... 273 L5
  BWSH/BRSTN DE72 .... 259 M3
  ILK DE7 .... 230 H5 🅸
  LGEAT NG10 .... 261 H5 🅸
Belvoir Crs *SWAD* DE11 .... 282 D4
Belvoir Dr *ASHZ* LE65 .... 291 L5 🅸
Belvoir Rd *BUTN/AL/TUT* DE13 ... 273 K5
Belvoir St *NORM/LIT* DE23 .... 240 C3
Belvoir Wy *ALFN* DE55 .... 187 M1
Bembridge Ct
  BSTN/STPLFD NG9 .... 245 K2 🅸
Bembridge Dr *DERBYSE* DE24 ..... 257 M5
Bemrose Ga *EDL/UDV* S33 .... 50 D4
Bemrose Rd *DERBYSE* DE24 .... 257 H3
Benbow Av
  MELB/CHEL DE73 .... 278 D2 🅸
Bench Rd *BUX* SK17 .... 100 A2
Bendall Gn *NORM/LIT* DE23 .... 255 M5
Bend Oak Dr
  STPNHL/WNHL DE15 .... 274 F6
Benenden Wy *ASHZ* LE65 .... 291 K3
Benington Dr
  WOL/BIL/BRX NG8 .... 231 M7
Beninmoor Wy *CHSW* S40 .... 2 D9
Benmore Ct *DERBYE* DE21 .... 227 L7 🅸
Benmore Dr *MOS* S20 .... 73 L1 🅸
Benner Av *ILK* DE7 .... 230 D5
Bennerley Av *ILK* DE7 .... 217 J6
Bennett Av *MSFD* NG18 .... 165 J4 🅸
Bennetts La *MTLK* DE4 .... 185 K2
  UTXR ST14 .... 246 F3
Bennett St *BUX* SK17 .... 99 M3
  DERBYSE DE24 .... 257 G5
  HYDE SK14 .... 17 G5 🅸
  LGEAT NG10 .... 244 E4
  SHEFP/MNR S2 .... 55 J2 🅸
Bennion Gv *UTXR* ST14 .... 218 B5
Bennison Gdns *CLCR* S45 .... 145 G7 🅸
Bensley Cl *MELB/CHEL* DE73 ...... 269 K1
Benson St *DERBYSE* DE24 .... 257 H3
Bentfield Rd *BPR/DUF* DE56 .... 199 M1
Bentham Rd *CHSW* S40 .... 110 B5
Benthead La *ABRD* S6 .... 196 C1
Bentinck Dr *STV/CWN* S43 .... 95 K6
Bentinck St *ASH* NG17 .... 163 J7
  MSFD NG18 .... 165 G4
Bentinck Cl *WRKS* S80 .... 114 F1 🅸
Bent La *ASHB* DE6 .... 179 M6
  BPR/DUF DE56 .... 183 M4

HOLM/MEL HD7 .... 9 K2
MTLK DE4 .... 140 F6
MTLK DE4 .... 156 E3
RDERBYSW DE65 .... 251 M3
STV/CWN S43 .... 93 K7
Bentley Br MTLK DE4 .... 157 H3
Bentley Cl ALFN DE55 .... 175 L2 ⊡
MTLK DE4 .... 157 G3
Bentley Dl SWAD DE11 .... 283 K7
Bentley Rd CDON/KEG DE74 .... 271 J6
RDERBYSW DE65 .... 265 H1 ⊡
UTXR ST14 .... 247 J1
Bentley St DERBYSE DE24 ...... 257 H4
Benton Dr MPL/ROM SK6 .... 32 F2
Bents Cl ECC S11 .... 54 B5
Bents Crs DRON S18 .... 70 F7
ECC S11 .... 54 C6
Bents Dr ECC S11 .... 54 C6
Bents Green Av ECC S11 .... 54 B4
Bents Green Pl ECC S11 .... 54 B5 ⊡
Bents Green Rd ECC S11 .... 54 C5
Bentside Rd POY/DIS SK12 ...... 43 G5
Bents La DRON S18 .... 70 F7
Bents Rd ECC S11 .... 54 C5
The Bent HATH/EY S32 .... 87 G7
Beowulf Covert
BUTN/AL/TUT DE13 .... 273 L1 ⊡
CHF/WBR SK23 .... 60 F4
Beresford Av ASHB DE6 .... 194 A8
CHF/WBR SK23 .... 60 F4
Beresford Cl CLCR S45 .... 145 G8
Beresford Dl SWAD DE11 .... 282 C8
ILK DE7 .... 217 H5
Beresford Dr DERBYE DE21 .... 242 B6 ⊡
ILK DE7 .... 217 H5
Beresford Pl BPR/DUF DE56 .... 185 L5
Beresford Rd CHF/WBR SK23 .... 60 F4
LGEAT NG10 .... 260 D5
MSFDW NG19 .... 149 L8
Beresford St MSFD NG18 .... 165 G4 ⊡
Berkeley Av LGEAT NG10 .... 260 F5
Berkeley Cl NORM/LIT DE23 .... 256 A3
Berkshire St DERBYE DE21 ...... 241 G2
Berle Av HEANOR DE75 .... 202 B7
Bermuda Av DERBYE DE24 ...... 226 F4 ⊡
Bernard Av MSFDW NG19 ...... 149 L5
Bernard Cl STV/CWN S43 .... 111 J1
Bernard Rd MSFDW NG19 .... 164 A2
Bernard St GLSP SK13 .... 25 M1
SWAD DE11 .... 283 G7
Berners Cl SHEFP/MNR S2 ...... 56 B5
Berners Dr SHEFP/MNR S2 ...... 56 B4
Berners Pl SHEFP/MNR S2 ...... 56 B4
Berners Rd SHEFP/MNR S2 ...... 56 A4
Berresford Rd ECC S11 .... 55 G2 ⊡
Berridge La ALFN DE55 .... 158 E6
Berrisford La ALFN DE55 .... 159 G3
Berristow La ALFN DE55 .... 176 F2
Berry Av ECK/KIL S21 .... 72 F7
MELB/CHEL DE73 .... 279 K7
Berry Gdns
STPNHL/WNHL DE15 .... 274 F6
Berry Hedge La
STPNHL/WNHL DE15 .... 274 F6
Berry Hill Cl MSFD NG18 .... 165 G6
Berry Hill Gdns MSFD NG18 .... 165 G6
Berry Hill La MSFD NG18 .... 165 G6
Berry Hill Ms MSFD NG18 ...... 165 G6
Berry Hill Rd MSFD NG18 ...... 164 F5
Berry Park Cl DERBYW DE22 .... 240 B1
Berry Park Lea MSFD NG18 .... 165 G7
Berry St RCH S42 .... 145 H4
Bertrand Av CHSW S40 .... 127 M3
DERBYE DE21 .... 240 F3
MSFDW NG19 .... 164 A2 ⊡
Berwick Av CHSW S40 .... 127 M2
DERBYSE DE24 .... 257 L5
Berwick Cl CHSW S40 .... 127 M3
Berwick Dr DERBYSE DE24 .... 256 A7
Berwick Rd BUX SK17 .... 99 L5
Berwin Cl LGEAT NG10 .... 260 D1 ⊡
Berwyn Cl CHSW S40 .... 109 M5
Bessalone Dr BPR/DUF DE56 .... 199 K5
Bessell La BSTN/STPLFD NG9 .... 244 F5
Bessie La EDL/UDV S33 .... 64 E4
Besthorpe Cl DERBYE DE21 .... 241 L1
Bestwick Av HEANOR DE75 .... 216 E1 ⊡
Bestwood Dr CLCR S45 .... 144 F7 ⊡
Bestwood Rd
EWD/SEL/PNX NG16 .... 177 H8
Bethulie Rd NORM/LIT DE23 .... 256 D2
Betjeman Gdns ECC S11 .... 54 F1 ⊡
Betlingspring La ASHB DE6 .... 207 G2
Betony Cl ECK/KIL S21 .... 73 L5
Bevan Dr STV/CWN S43 .... 111 L3
Bevan Rd CLCR S45 .... 145 G8
Bevan St ALFN DE55 .... 175 H1
Beverley Cl
WOL/BIL/BRX NG8 .... 231 L6 ⊡
Beverley Rd BUT DE14 .... 280 C3
Beverleys Rd SHEFS S8 .... 55 K6
Beverley St DERBYE DE24 ...... 241 G8 ⊡
Bewdley Cl MELB/CHEL DE73 .... 257 K7
Bexley Cl GLSP SK13 .... 17 M7 ⊡
Bicester Av DERBYSE DE24 .... 255 M8
Bickley Moss DERBYE DE21 .... 241 L1 ⊡
Bideford Cl RIPLEY DE5 .... 186 F8
Bideford Dr NORM/LIT DE23 .... 256 A4
Bidston Cl MTLK DE4 .... 156 F3
Big Barn La MSFD NG18 .... 165 J5
Biggart Cl BSTN/STPLFD NG9 .... 245 M8
Biggin La ASHB DE6 .... 196 E6
Bigginmill La BPR/DUF DE56 .... 196 F8
The Biggin CDON/KEG DE74 .... 271 L7 ⊡
Big La ASHB DE6 .... 181 K6
Bilborough Rd MSFDW NG18 .... 165 G3
WOL/BIL/BRX NG8 .... 231 L5 ⊡
Bilby La STV/CWN S43 .... 111 J1
Billam St ECK/KIL S21 .... 72 E7
Billingsley Av
EWD/SEL/PNX NG16 .... 176 F7
Binfield Rd SHEFS S8 .... 55 J5
Bingham Av ILK DE7 .... 163 K5
Bingham Park Crs ECC S11 .... 54 D2
Bingham Park Rd ECC S11 ...... 54 D3
Bingham Rd MSFD NG18 .... 165 K7
SHEFS S8 .... 55 J8 ⊡
Bingham St DERBYSE DE24 .... 257 H4
Bings Rd CHF/WBR SK23 .... 59 H3

Bingswood Rd CHF/WBR SK23 .... 59 H3
Binscombe La DERBYE DE21 .... 227 J7 ⊡
ILK DE7 .... 230 D3 ⊡
SWAD DE11 .... 282 D3
Birch Cl ALFN DE55 .... 174 B2
ALFN DE55 .... 175 K5
BUT DE14 .... 280 D2 ⊡
BUX SK17 .... 99 L1
DERBYE DE21 .... 242 D4
ECK/KIL S21 .... 73 M5
RCH S42 .... 129 J7
RIPLEY DE5 .... 201 C2
UTXR ST14 .... 218 A4
Birchen Cl CHSW S40 .... 110 A5
DRON S18 .... 90 A1
Birchen Holme ALFN DE55 .... 176 D7
Birches Av ALFN DE55 .... 174 C5
Birches Cl BUTN/AL/TUT DE13 .... 274 A2
Birches Fold DRON S18 .... 70 F6 ⊡
Birches La ALFN DE55 .... 174 B3
DRON S18 .... 70 F6
Birches Rd DERBYW DE22 ...... 226 A7
Birch Farm Av SHEFS S8 .... 70 D2
The Birches NM/HAY SK22 ...... 34 F8
Birchfield Cl MELB/CHEL DE73 .... 257 J8
Birchfield Dr WRKS S80 .... 77 L8
Birchfield Pk HEANOR DE75 .... 216 C3
Birchfield Rd
STPNHL/WNHL DE15 .... 281 H4
Birch Gn GLSP SK13 .... 26 B1
RDERBYSW DE65 .... 252 A8
SBK/MW NG20 .... 133 G5
Birch Gv MSFD NG18 .... 165 J6
Birch Holt Gv DRON S18 .... 91 H5
The Birchills WRKS S80 .... 114 F1 ⊡
Birchitt Cl TOT/DORE S17 ...... 69 M5
Birchitt Pl TOT/DORE S17 ...... 69 M5
Birchitt Rd TOT/DORE S17 ...... 69 M5
Birch Kiln Cft STV/CWN S43 .... 111 J2
Birchlands MSFD NG18 .... 165 J1
Birchlands Dr ECK/KIL S21 .... 74 A5
Birchover Edge MTLK DE4 .... 154 E3
Birchover La MTLK DE4 .... 154 E3
Birchover Pl ILK DE7 .... 217 H5 ⊡
Birchover Ri DERBYE DE21 .... 241 J1
Birchover Rd MTLK DE4 .... 139 M8
WOL/BIL/BRX NG8 .... 231 M5
Birchover Wy DERBYW DE22 .... 240 A1
Birchside Av GLSP SK13 .... 17 L8
Birchvale Rd HACK/IN S12 ...... 57 G7
Birchview Cft BPR/DUF DE56 .... 199 L8 ⊡
Birchway MPL/ROM SK6 .... 42 C3
Birchwood HEANOR DE75 ...... 201 M6
Birchwood Av
BWSH/BRSTN DE72 .... 260 C3
LGEAT NG10 .... 260 F4
NORM/LIT DE23 .... 256 A4
Birchwood Cl ALFN DE55 ...... 176 D6
CHSW S40 .... 128 C3
Birchwood Crs ALFN DE55 .... 188 A1
CHSW S40 .... 128 C3
Birchwood Cft MOS S20 .... 73 H2
Birchwood Dr ASH NG17 ...... 185 L6
BPR/DUF DE56 .... 185 L6
Birchwood Gdns MOS S20 .... 73 H2 ⊡
Birchwood Gv MOS S20 .... 73 H2
Birchwood La ALFN DE55 ...... 188 B2
Birchwood Ri MOS S20 .... 73 H2 ⊡
ECK/KIL S21 .... 72 B6
WOL/BIL/BRX NG8 .... 231 M6
Birchwood Vw ASHB DE6 ...... 193 M7 ⊡
MOS S20 .... 73 H2
Birchwood Wy ALFN DE55 .... 175 M8
MOS S20 .... 73 H2 ⊡
Bircumshaw's Rd
HEANOR DE75 .... 202 B8 ⊡
Birdcage Wk DERBYW DE22 .... 239 J4
Bird Cl MSFD NG18 .... 164 F7
Birdcroft La ILK DE7 .... 230 C5
Birdholme Crs CHSW S40 ...... 128 D2
Birding St MSFDW NG19 .... 149 L8
Birdsgrove La ASHB DE6 .... 193 G7
Bird St STV/CWN S43 .... 93 J8
Birdwood St NORM/LIT DE23 .... 256 C1 ⊡
Birkdale Av BUT DE14 .... 280 D4
Birkdale Cl ILK DE7 .... 230 A1
MCKLVR DE3 .... 239 K8 ⊡
Birkdale Dr CHSW S40 .... 127 M2
Birkin Av BSTN/STPLFD NG9 .... 245 K5 ⊡
RCH S42 .... 144 F1
Birkin La CLCR S45 .... 143 H3
RCH S42 .... 129 J8
Birkin La West RCH S42 .... 129 J8
Birkinstyle La ALFN DE55 ...... 160 C7
Birkinstyle La ALFN DE55 ...... 160 B7
Birklands Av HAN/WDH S13 .... 57 H1
Birklands Cl HAN/WDH S13 .... 57 H1
Birklands Dr HAN/WDH S13 .... 57 H1
Birkland St MSFD NG18 .... 165 L4
Birks Av HAN/WDH S13 .... 57 L4 ⊡
Birks Cl WRKS S80 .... 96 F4
Birks Rd MSFDW NG19 .... 164 A3
Birley Brook Dr CHSW S40 .... 109 L3
Birley La HACK/IN S12 .... 57 H8
HATH/EY S32 .... 51 J8
Birley Moor Av HACK/IN S12 .... 57 H7
Birley Moor Cl HACK/IN S12 .... 57 H7 ⊡
Birley Moor Crs HACK/IN S12 .... 57 H7
Birley Moor Pl HACK/IN S12 .... 57 H8
Birley Moor Pl HACK/IN S12 .... 57 H8
Birley Moor Rd HACK/IN S12 .... 57 H7
Birley Moor Wy HACK/IN S12 .... 57 H7
Birley Spa Cl HACK/IN S12 .... 57 L6
Birley Spa La HACK/IN S12 .... 57 L6
Birley St BSTN/STPLFD NG9 .... 245 G5
Birley Vale Av HACK/IN S12 .... 56 F6
Birley Vale Cl HACK/IN S12 .... 56 F6
Birstall Cl CHSW S40 .... 109 M3
Biscay Ct DERBYE DE21 .... 227 M8 ⊡
Bishopdale Cl LGEAT NG10 .... 260 D4
Bishopdale Ct MOS S20 .... 72 D2 ⊡
Bishopdale Dr HACK/IN S12 .... 72 D2 ⊡
Bishopdale Ri HACK/IN S12 .... 72 D2 ⊡

Bishop Gdns HAN/WDH S13 .... 57 K4
Bishop Hl HAN/WDH S13 .... 57 K4
Bishops Ct MELB/CHEL DE73 .... 278 E5 ⊡
SHEFS S8 .... 55 K5
Bishopscourt Rd SHEFS S8 .... 55 K5
Bishop's Dr DERBYE DE21 ...... 227 H8
Bishops La BUX SK17 .... 99 H3
Bishop St ALFN DE55 .... 175 J5
ASH NG17 .... 163 H7
EWD/SEL/PNX NG16 .... 203 J8 ⊡
MSFD NG18 .... 165 J5
Bispham Dr BSTN/STPLFD NG9 .... 245 J7
Bitham St BUTN/AL/TUT DE13 .... 273 M1
Bitham La BUTN/AL/TUT DE13 .... 273 M1
Blaby Cl NORM/LIT DE23 ...... 256 A4
Blacka Moor Crs TOT/DORE S17 .... 68 F4
Blacka Moor Rd TOT/DORE S17 .... 68 F4
Blacka Moor Vw TOT/DORE S17 .... 68 F4
Blackberry Wy BPR/DUF DE56 .... 200 C8
Blackbird Cl UTXR ST14 .... 247 M4
Blackbird Cl UTXR ST14 .... 247 M4
Blackbird Rw BPR/DUF DE56 .... 213 M1
Blackbrook Av FUL S10 .... 53 J1
Blackbrook Dr FUL S10 .... 53 J1
Blackbrook La CHF/WBR SK23 .... 53 L1
Blackbrook Rd FUL S10 .... 53 K1
Blackburn Hl ILK DE7 .... 217 H7 ⊡
Blackdown Av CHSW S40 ...... 109 L5 ⊡
Black Field Cliff Cl WRKS S80 .... 96 D5
Blackfordby La MSHM DE12 .... 290 E4
Black Harry La HATH/EY S32 .... 85 M8
Black Hills Dr ILK DE7 .... 230 C4
Blackmore St NORM/LIT DE23 .... 256 C5
Blackmount Ct
DERBYSE DE24 .... 256 A7 ⊡
Blackpit La ASHB DE6 .... 248 E2
Blackpool St BUT DE14 .... 280 F2
Blackrocks Av MTLK DE4 ...... 156 C3
Blackrod Cl BSTN/STPLFD NG9 .... 245 K8 ⊡
Blackshaw Rd GLSP SK13 ...... 18 B8
Blacksmith La STV/CWN S43 .... 111 K7
Blacksmith's La
RDERBYSW DE65 .... 265 K4
STPNHL/WNHL DE15 .... 275 M2
SWAD DE11 .... 283 J7
Blackstock Cl SHEFS S8 .... 56 A8
Blackstock Crs GLV S14 .... 56 A8
Blackstock Dr SHEFS S8 .... 56 A8
Blackstock Rd SHEFP/MNR S2 .... 56 A5
SHEFS S8 .... 56 A5
Blackstone Cl ALFN DE55 ...... 188 A3
Blackthorn Cl CHNE S41 .... 129 G3
Blackthorn Cl
BPR/DUF DE56 .... 200 C8 ⊡
Blackthorne Cl
BPR/DUF DE56 .... 200 C8 ⊡
Blackthorne Dr
EWD/SEL/PNX NG16 .... 203 H8
Blackthorn Rd
STPNHL/WNHL DE15 .... 281 H4
Blackthorn Wy ASH NG17 ...... 177 M1
Black Tor Rd MTLK DE4 .... 171 G3
Blackwall La BPR/DUF DE56 .... 196 D2
Blackwell La BKWL DE45 ...... 120 E7
MELB/CHEL DE73 .... 278 E3
Blackwell Rd ASH NG17 .... 162 B7
Bladon St STPNHL/WNHL DE15 .... 281 J4
Bladon Vw BUTN/AL/TUT DE13 .... 265 J8
Blagdon Cl MTLK DE4 .... 140 F7
Blagreaves Av NORM/LIT DE23 .... 255 M5
Blagreaves La NORM/LIT DE23 .... 255 M5
Blair Athol Rd ECC S11 .... 54 E4
Blair Gv LGEAT NG10 .... 244 D6
Blakebrook Dr
MELB/CHEL DE73 .... 257 K7 ⊡
Blake Ct LGEAT NG10 .... 260 E5 ⊡
Blake Crs MSFD NG18 .... 165 G3
Blakeley La DERBYSW DE65 .... 253 L8
Blakelow Dr
RDERBYSW DE65 .... 253 L7 ⊡
Blakelow La ASHB DE6 .... 205 L1
MTLK DE4 .... 155 K7
Blakemere La MTLK DE4 ...... 170 C1
Blakemore Av
MELB/CHEL DE73 .... 278 E2 ⊡
Blakeney Cl DERBYE DE21 .... 241 M1
Blakeney Dr MSFD NG18 ...... 164 F6
Blake Rd BSTN/STPLFD NG9 .... 245 H4
Blake St ILK DE7 .... 230 C1
MSFDW NG19 .... 149 L8
Blanch Cft MELB/CHEL DE73 .... 278 E3
Blandford Av LGEAT NG10 .... 260 E5
Blandford Cl DERBYSE DE24 .... 258 A4 ⊡
Blandford Dr CHNE S41 .... 110 B3
Blandford Rd
BSTN/STPLFD NG9 .... 245 M5
Blankney Cl DERBYSE DE24 .... 256 A8
Blaxton Cl MOS S20 .... 57 K8
Blazley Rd SHEFP/MNR S2 .... 56 C4
Bleach Ml MSHM DE12 .... 295 M7
Bleak Hills La MSFD NG18 .... 164 C6
Bleak Hill Wy MSFD NG18 .... 164 B6
Blencathra Dr MCKLVR DE3 .... 255 H2
Blenheim Av ALFN DE55 ...... 187 K2
MSFDW NG19 .... 165 G1 ⊡
STPNHL/WNHL DE15 .... 274 F7 ⊡
SWAD DE11 .... 282 D3 ⊡
Blenheim Ct BPR/DUF DE56 .... 200 A5 ⊡
Blenheim Dr BSTN/STPLFD NG9 .... 245 M7
DERBYW DE22 .... 225 M7
Blenheim Gdns ECC S11 .... 54 D5 ⊡
Blenheim Pde DERBYW DE22 .... 226 B6 ⊡
Blenheim Pl ASH NG17 .... 162 B7
Blenheim Rd ASHB DE6 .... 208 B3
Blenheim St LGEAT NG10 ...... 244 E6 ⊡
Blind La ASHB DE6 .... 182 C6
BSVR S44 .... 113 J7
BWSH/BRSTN DE72 .... 260 A2
MTLK DE4 .... 156 B3
MTLK DE4 .... 183 J2
Blissworth Wy ALFN DE55 .... 187 J3
Blithe Cl RDERBYSW DE65 .... 265 H1 ⊡
Blithfield Gdns
MELB/CHEL DE73 .... 257 K8 ⊡
Bloomer Wood Vw ASH NG17 .... 177 L1
Bloomfield Cl DERBY DE1 ...... 5 H8
RDERBYSW DE65 .... 265 G1

Bloomfield Rd ALFN DE55 ...... 187 K2 ⊡
Bloomfield St DERBY DE1 ...... 5 J7 ⊡
Bloomsgrove Rd ILK DE7 ...... 217 J2 ⊡
Blore Cl ASHB DE6 .... 208 A2
Blount's Dr UTXR ST14 .... 247 K4
Bluebank Vw CHNE S41 .... 92 A7
Bluebell Cl ALFN DE55 .... 176 B7
ASH NG17 .... 162 E4
DERBYSE DE24 .... 255 M6
EWD/SEL/PNX NG16 .... 189 J8 ⊡
Bluebell Hl ALFN DE55 .... 159 M6 ⊡
Bluebell Wood Wy
ASH NG17 .... 177 M1 ⊡
Bluebird Ct DERBYSE DE24 .... 256 A6 ⊡
Blue Lodge Cl STV/CWN S43 .... 111 L5
Bluestone La
STPNHL/WNHL DE15 .... 281 J3
Blundering La MTLK DE4 ...... 172 D8
Blunt Av STV/CWN S43 .... 93 M6
Blunt St ILK DE7 .... 215 K8 ⊡
Blyth Cl CHSW S40 .... 127 L2
Blyth Gv MSFDW NG19 .... 164 A1
Blythfield BUT DE14 .... 274 B7 ⊡
Blyth Pl DERBY DE21 .... 241 G1 ⊡
Boam La MTLK DE4 .... 156 C2
Boardman Rd SWAD DE11 .... 282 B7
Boarhill Gv ASH NG17 .... 177 M1
Boarslack La BUX SK17 .... 84 B8
Boarstones La BUX SK17 ...... 100 B3
Boat La EWD/SEL/PNX NG16 .... 202 D3
Boatmans Cl ILK DE7 .... 217 L6 ⊡
Bobbinmill Hl BPR/DUF DE56 .... 185 L3
Bobbin Mill La CHSW S40 ...... 2 A1 ⊡
Bochum Pkwy SHEFS S8 ...... 70 F2
Bocking La SHEFS S8 .... 70 A1
Bocking La SHEFS S8 .... 70 A1
Bocking Ri SHEFS S8 .... 70 B2 ⊡
Boden St NORM/LIT DE23 ...... 5 G9
Bodmin Cl DERBYSE DE24 .... 256 A7 ⊡
Bodmin Wy CHSW S40 .... 109 M5 ⊡
Body Rd BSTN/STPLFD NG9 .... 245 L7
Boggard La GLSP SK13 .... 25 G5
Bogguard Rd MPL/ROM SK6 .... 33 K6
Boguard Rd RDERBYSW DE65 .... 251 K3
Bog La MELB/CHEL DE73 ...... 278 B5
Bohem Rd LGEAT NG10 .... 244 F7
Boiley La ECK/KIL S21 .... 73 L6
Boland Rd TOT/DORE S17 ...... 70 A5
Bold La DERBY DE1 .... 4 E3
Bolehill La ECK/KIL S21 .... 72 D8
RCH S42 .... 143 H5
Bolehill Rd MTLK DE4 .... 171 K7
Bolsover Cl RIPLEY DE5 .... 201 H1
Bolsover St MSFD NG18 .... 165 G4
Bolton Av BSTN/STPLFD NG9 .... 245 M6
Bolton St ALFN DE55 .... 187 G3
Boman's La BPR/DUF DE56 .... 198 B1
Bonchurch Cl
DERBYSE DE24 .... 257 M5 ⊡
Bondfield Rd STV/CWN S43 .... 111 M3
Bondgate CDON/KEG DE74 .... 271 L7
Bondhay La WRKS S80 .... 75 M8
Bond St BUT DE14 .... 281 G1
STV/CWN S43 .... 111 M2
Bonington Ri MPL/ROM SK6 .... 32 E2
Bonington Rd MSFDW NG19 .... 164 A4
Bonner's Rd
EWD/SEL/PNX NG16 .... 217 L6
Bonnie Prince Charlie Wk
ASHB DE6 .... 208 F8
DERBYW DE22 .... 239 H4
Bonnington Dr ALFN DE55 .... 188 A2
Bonnyrigg Dr DERBYE DE21 .... 227 K8 ⊡
Bonsal Ct MSFD NG18 .... 165 L4 ⊡
Bonsall Av NORM/LIT DE23 .... 256 A2
Bonsall Dr ALFN DE55 .... 188 A2 ⊡
MCKLVR DE3 .... 239 H7
Bonsall La ALFN DE55 .... 175 J6
MTLK DE4 .... 155 H6
Bonsallmoor La MTLK DE4 .... 155 G6
Bonsall St LGEAT NG10 .... 261 H2
Bonser Cl ASH NG17 .... 162 B7
Bonser Gdns ASH NG17 .... 163 G8
Booker Rd SHEFS S8 .... 55 H8 ⊡
Booth Av MSFDW NG19 .... 148 D5
Boothbright Crs
MSFDW NG19 .... 149 G8 ⊡
Boothby Av ASHB DE6 .... 193 M8 ⊡
Booth Crs MSFDW NG19 ...... 149 G8
Boothgate BPR/DUF DE56 .... 188 A2
Boot Hl RDERBYSW DE65 ...... 266 F8
Boothorpe La SWAD DE11 .... 290 D2
Booth St DERBYSE DE24 ...... 257 J3
HYDE SK14 .... 16 F5 ⊡
MSFDW NG19 .... 149 L7
RIPLEY DE5 .... 187 H8
Boots Yd ASH NG17 .... 162 C7
Border Cl STV/CWN S43 .... 95 J7
Border Crs DERBYSE DE24 .... 257 L6
Border La BSVR S44 .... 114 B2
STV/CWN S43 .... 95 J7
Borlace Crs BSTN/STPLFD NG9 .... 245 H4
Borough Rd BUT DE14 .... 273 M7
Borough St CDON/KEG DE74 .... 271 L7
Borrowash By-pass
DERBYE DE21 .... 241 L7
Borrowash Rd DERBYE DE21 .... 242 C7
Borrowdale Av MOS S20 .... 73 H4 ⊡
Borrowdale Cl MOS S20 .... 73 H4 ⊡
MSFD NG18 .... 165 G7 ⊡
Borrowdale Dr LGEAT NG10 .... 260 D4
MOS S20 .... 73 H4
Borrowdale Rd DERBYE DE21 .... 242 B7
Borrowfields
BWSH/BRSTN DE72 .... 258 E1 ⊡
Boscastle Rd DERBYSE DE24 .... 257 L4
Bostock La BSTN/STPLFD NG9 .... 244 D8
LGEAT NG10 .... 244 D8
Boston Cl DERBYE DE21 ...... 241 M4
Boston St SHEFP/MNR S2 ...... 55 J1
Boswell Cl MSFD NG18 .... 164 F7
Boswell Sq NORM/LIT DE23 .... 256 C3
Bosworth Av
NORM/LIT DE23 .... 256 B4 ⊡

Bosworth Dr
BUTN/AL/TUT DE13 .... 273 L4
EWD/SEL/PNX NG16 .... 203 L7
Bosworth Rd CDON/KEG DE74 .... 271 J7
Bosworth Wy LGEAT NG10 .... 261 G5
Botanical Rd FUL S10 .... 54 F1
Botany Av ILK DE7 .... 217 J3
Bothe Cl LGEAT NG10 .... 260 F4
Bottom Cliff HATH/EY S32 ...... 86 C6
Bottomhill Rd BUX SK17 .... 84 B8
Bottom Rd RCH S42 .... 128 B8
Boughton Cl ASH NG17 .... 163 J5 ⊡
Boughton Dr ALFN DE55 ...... 187 J2
Boughton La STV/CWN S43 .... 95 G6
Boughton Rd WRKS S80 .... 77 K5
Bould St MSFDW NG19 .... 164 C2
The Boulevard HYDE SK14 .... 17 G5
Boulton Ct RCH S42 .... 109 K5
Boulton Dr DERBYSE DE24 .... 257 K4
Boulton La DERBYSE DE24 .... 257 K4
Boundary Cl SBK/MW NG20 .... 133 H4
STV/CWN S43 .... 93 K7 ⊡
Boundary Gdns ALFN DE55 .... 161 J5
Boundary La
EWD/SEL/PNX NG16 .... 202 F7 ⊡
Boundary Rd DERBYW DE22 .... 4 A5
RDERBYSW DE65 .... 266 A2
Boundary Wk SBK/MW NG20 .... 133 J1
Bourne Av ECK/KIL S21 .... 73 G6
Bournebrook Av MTLK DE4 .... 183 J5
Bourne Cl
BUTN/AL/TUT DE13 .... 263 L4 ⊡
STV/CWN S43 .... 111 K2 ⊡
Bourne Mill Cl STV/CWN S43 .... 94 E3
Bourne Sq BWSH/BRSTN DE72 .... 260 B2 ⊡
Bourne St DERBY DE22 .... 4 F6
Bowbridge Av NORM/LIT DE23 .... 255 M5
Bowden Av HYDE SK14 .... 24 B1
Bowden Crs NM/HAY SK22 .... 44 A2
Bowden La CHF/WBR SK23 .... 60 F3
MPL/ROM SK6 .... 32 F3
Bowden Rd GLSP SK13 .... 17 M7
Bowdon Av STV/CWN S43 ...... 94 D4
Bower Gdns STLY SK15 .... 16 A2 ⊡
Bower St DERBYSE DE24 ...... 257 J2
Bowes Well Rd ILK DE7 .... 217 H8
Bowfell Dr MPL/ROM SK6 ...... 42 B2
Bowland Dr CHSW S40 .... 127 L3
Bowland Rd GLSP SK13 .... 25 K2
Bowler Ct NORM/LIT DE23 .... 255 H3 ⊡
Bowler Dr BPR/DUF DE56 ...... 214 D3 ⊡
Bowler La MTLK DE4 .... 156 D1
Bowler Rd MTLK DE4 .... 140 F7 ⊡
Bowler St RIPLEY DE5 .... 201 G3
Bowling Aly BPR/DUF DE56 .... 200 B1
Bowlingalley La ASHB DE6 .... 219 G2
Bowling Alley La ASHB DE6 .... 233 K6
Bowling Cl ILK DE7 .... 244 B2
Bowling Gn MTLK DE4 .... 181 K1 ⊡
Bowling Green La MTLK DE4 .... 183 J1 ⊡
Bowling St MSFD NG18 .... 165 G4
Bowman Cl HACK/IN S12 ...... 56 C8
Bowman La BPR/DUF DE56 .... 185 L4
Bowmer La BPR/DUF DE56 .... 185 L4
Bowmer Rd DERBYSE DE24 .... 241 H8 ⊡
Bown Cl BPR/DUF DE56 .... 214 D2
Bowness Cl CHNE S41 .... 110 A3
DRON S18 .... 90 B1
Bowness Rd CHNE S41 .... 110 A3
Bowne St ASH NG17 .... 163 J7
Bowns Hl MTLK DE4 .... 185 K1
Bowns Yd ALFN DE55 .... 188 A2 ⊡
Bowood Rd ECC S11 .... 55 G2
Bowshaw Av SHEFS S8 .... 70 D5
Bowshaw Cl SHEFS S8 .... 70 D5
Bowshaw Vw SHEFS S8 .... 70 D5
Boxmoor Cl NORM/LIT DE23 .... 255 J3 ⊡
Boyd Gv MELB/CHEL DE73 .... 269 K2
Boyer St DERBYW DE22 .... 4 C8
Boylestone Rd NORM/LIT DE23 .... 255 M5
Boythorpe Av CHSW S40 ...... 2 C6
Boythorpe Crs CHSW S40 ...... 2 E7
Boythorpe Mt CHSW S40 ...... 2 E6
Boythorpe Ri CHSW S40 .... 2 C6
Boythorpe Rd CHSW S40 ...... 2 D6
Brabyns Brow MPL/ROM SK6 .... 32 D3
Bracken Av BSVR S44 .... 146 C1
Bracken Cl HYDE SK14 .... 17 G4
LGEAT NG10 .... 260 E1
MPL/ROM SK6 .... 32 F3
Brackendale Cl CLCR S45 ...... 145 H8 ⊡
STV/CWN S43 .... 111 G3
Brackendale La ASHB DE6 .... 180 F5
Brackendale Rd ALFN DE55 .... 187 J2
Brackenfield Av
EWD/SEL/PNX NG16 .... 217 L3 ⊡
Brackenfield Gv HACK/IN S12 .... 57 G6
Brackenfield La ALFN DE55 .... 174 A1
Bracken Hl MSFD NG18 .... 165 K5
Bracken La MTLK DE4 .... 172 E5
Bracken Rd LGEAT NG10 ...... 260 E1
Brackens Av DERBYE DE21 .... 257 J4
Brackensdale Av DERBYW DE22 .... 239 L5
Bracken's La DERBYSE DE24 .... 257 J4
STV/CWN S43 .... 94 E4
Bracken Wy GLSP SK13 .... 26 C3
Brackenwood Rd
STPNHL/WNHL DE15 .... 281 H4
Brackley Dr DERBYE DE21 .... 242 B5
Brackley Ga ILK DE7 .... 214 D8
Brackmills Cl MSFDW NG19 .... 165 H1 ⊡
Bracknell Dr DERBYSE DE24 .... 257 J5
Bradbourne Cl STV/CWN S43 .... 111 M2
Bradbury Cl
BWSH/BRSTN DE72 .... 258 F2 ⊡
Bradbury Dr RCH S42 .... 128 A6
Bradbury St SHEFS S8 .... 55 K4 ⊡
Bradder Wy MSFD NG18 ...... 164 D5
Braddon Av BSTN/STPLFD NG9 .... 245 H1
Bradforth Av MSFD NG18 ...... 165 K3
Bradgate Cl LGEAT NG10 ...... 244 E6 ⊡
Bradgate Ct NORM/LIT DE23 .... 256 B4 ⊡
Bradgate Dr RIPLEY DE5 ...... 200 E1
Brading Cl DERBYSE DE24 .... 258 A5
Bradley Cl MTLK DE4 .... 154 E1
Bradley Dr BPR/DUF DE56 .... 199 L6
Bradley La DRON S18 .... 89 L6

Bradley St *DERBYW* DE22 ..... **240** B2 🔲
  LGEAT NG10 ..... **244** F5
  STPNHL/WNHL DE15 ..... **281** H3
Bradley Vw *ASHB* DE6 ..... **194** A7
Bradley Wy *STV/CWN* S43 ..... **111** H3
Bradmoor Gv
  MELB/CHEL DE73 ..... **257** L8 🔲
Bradmore Rd
  BUTN/AL/TUT DE13 ..... **273** L5
Bradshaw Av *ALFN* DE55 ..... **188** A4
Bradshaw Crs *MPL/ROM* SK6 ..... **32** D3 🔲
Bradshaw Cft *BPR/DUF* DE56 ..... **199** H4
Bradshaw Dr *BPR/DUF* DE56 ..... **213** M4
Bradshaw La *HATH/EY* S32 ..... **85** H3
Bradshaw Meadow
  RDERBYSW DE65 ..... **263** M1 🔲
  STV/CWN S43 ..... **111** L4
Bradshaw Rd *MPL/ROM* SK6 ..... **32** C3
Bradshaw St *LGEAT* NG10 ..... **260** E5
Bradshaw Wy *DERBY* DE1 ..... **5** C6
Bradway Dr *TOT/DORE* S17 ..... **69** L5
Bradway Dr *TOT/DORE* S17 ..... **69** L5 🔲
Bradway Grange Rd
  TOT/DORE S17 ..... **69** M5 🔲
Bradway Rd *TOT/DORE* S17 ..... **69** M4
Bradwell Cl *DRON* S18 ..... **89** M1
  EWD/SEL/PNX NG16 ..... **217** M2 🔲
  MCKLVR DE3 ..... **255** H1
Bradwell Gv *CLCR* S45 ..... **160** A1
Bradwell Head Rd *ASHB* DE6 ..... **64** D2
Bradwell Pl *STV/CWN* S43 ..... **111** M3
Bradwell St *SHEFP/MNR* S2 ..... **55** L3
Bradwell Wy *BPR/DUF* DE56 ..... **199** L5
Braefield Cl *ILK* DE7 ..... **229** M5
Braelsford Wy
  BSTN/STPLFD NG9 ..... **261** M1
Braintree Cl *DERBYE* DE21 ..... **227** C8
Braithwell Cl *DERBYW* DE22 ..... **226** C8 🔲
Bramah Edge Ct *GLSP* SK13 ..... **17** J4
Bramall La *SHEFP/MNR* S2 ..... **55** L1
Brambleberry Ct
  DERBYE DE21 ..... **227** L7 🔲
Bramble Cl *BSVR* S44 ..... **146** C1 🔲
  LGEAT NG10 ..... **260** E1
  SBK/MW NG20 ..... **133** H4
Bramble Cft *ASH* NG17 ..... **177** M1
Bramble La *MSFD* NG18 ..... **165** K5
Bramble Ms *MCKLVR* DE3 ..... **255** G1 🔲
Bramble St *DERBY* DE1 ..... **4** D4
Bramble Wk *MSHM* DE12 ..... **289** K7
Bramble Wy *ALFN* DE55 ..... **176** C7
  BPR/DUF DE56 ..... **200** C8
Brambling Cl *MSFD* NG18 ..... **165** H5 🔲
  UTXR S80 ..... **247** M4 🔲
Brambling Ct *CHNE* S41 ..... **3** M5
The Bramblings *WRKN* S81 ..... **77** M3
Bramcote La
  BSTN/STPLFD NG9 ..... **245** M4
Bramell Cl *BUT* DE14 ..... **280** C3
Bramfield Av *DERBYW* DE22 ..... **4** A8
Bramhall Rd *WOL/BIL/BRX* NG8 ..... **231** M4
Bramham Rd *MPL/ROM* SK6 ..... **32** C6
Bramley Av *HAN/WDH* S13 ..... **57** J2
Bramley Cl *DERBYE* DE21 ..... **227** M7 🔲
  MOS S20 ..... **72** F4
Bramley Ct *ASH* NG17 ..... **163** J7
  RDERBYSW DE65 ..... **263** M1 🔲
Bramley Dl *SWAD* DE11 ..... **282** C8
Bramley Dr *HAN/WDH* S13 ..... **57** J1
Bramley Hall Rd *HAN/WDH* S13 ..... **57** J2
Bramley La *BKWL* DE45 ..... **105** L3
  HAN/WDH S13 ..... **57** J1
Bramleymoor La *ECK/KIL* S21 ..... **92** B1
Bramley Park Cl *HAN/WDH* S13 ..... **57** J2
Bramley Park Rd *HAN/WDH* S13 ..... **57** J1
Bramley Rd *BSVR* S44 ..... **147** H1
  ECK/KIL S21 ..... **92** B1
Bramley Wk *MSFD* NG18 ..... **164** A3
Bramlyn Cl *STV/CWN* S43 ..... **95** G5
Bramlyn Ct *STV/CWN* S43 ..... **95** G5
Brampton Av *HEANOR* DE75 ..... **202** D8 🔲
Brampton Ct *MCKLVR* DE3 ..... **238** F7
Brampton Ct *BPR/DUF* DE56 ..... **200** C8 🔲
  MOS S20 ..... **57** K8 🔲
Brampton Dr
  BSTN/STPLFD NG9 ..... **245** H5
Bramshall Rd *UTXR* ST14 ..... **247** H2
Bramshill Cl *MOS* S20 ..... **73** K1
Bramshill Ct *MOS* S20 ..... **73** K1 🔲
Bramshill Ri *CHSW* S40 ..... **2** B7
Bramway *MPL/ROM* SK6 ..... **42** C3
Bramwith Rd *ECC* S11 ..... **54** C2 🔲
Branch La *CLCR* S45 ..... **146** B5
Brancliffe La *WRKN* S81 ..... **77** J2
Brandelhow Ct
  DERBYE DE21 ..... **227** L7 🔲
Brandene Cl *STV/CWN* S43 ..... **111** K7
Brand La *ASH* NG17 ..... **162** F5
Brandreth Av *ASH* NG17 ..... **163** G6
Brandreth Dr
  EWD/SEL/PNX NG16 ..... **217** K3
Branksome Av *DERBYSE* DE24 ..... **257** M3
Bransdale Av *MSFDW* NG19 ..... **165** H1
Bransdale Cl *LGEAT* NG10 ..... **260** E4
Branston Rd *BUT* DE14 ..... **280** F2
Branton Cl *CHSW* S40 ..... **2** E8
Brassington Cl *BKWL* DE45 ..... **138** F5
  EWD/SEL/PNX NG16 ..... **217** L3 🔲
  ILK DE7 ..... **229** H2
Brassington Rd
  DERBYE DE21 ..... **241** J1 🔲
Brassington St *CLCR* S45 ..... **145** G6
Brassington La *RCH* S42 ..... **144** F4
Brayfield Av *NORM/LIT* DE23 ..... **256** A2
Brayfield Rd *NORM/LIT* DE23 ..... **255** M2
Breach Cl *BUTN/AL/TUT* DE13 ..... **273** L5
Breach La *ASHB* DE6 ..... **250** F4
  MELB/CHEL DE73 ..... **278** B1

  RDERBYSW DE65 ..... **252** A7
Breach Rd *HEANOR* DE75 ..... **216** D2
  RIPLEY DE5 ..... **201** J6
Breadsall Cl *SWAD* DE11 ..... **282** D3 🔲
Breamfield La *BPR/DUF* DE56 ..... **183** L5
Brearley Av *CHNE* S41 ..... **92** A7
Brearley St *CHNE* S41 ..... **91** M7
Breaston La
  BWSH/BRSTN DE72 ..... **244** A6
Brechin Ct *MSFDW* NG19 ..... **149** L4
Breckbank *MSFDW* NG19 ..... **165** H1
Breckland Rd *CHSW* S40 ..... **127** L2
Breck La *ECK/KIL* S21 ..... **92** F2
Brecon Cl *CHSW* S40 ..... **109** M5
  DERBYE DE21 ..... **242** B4
  LGEAT NG10 ..... **260** D2
Bredon Cl *LGEAT* NG10 ..... **260** D2
Breedon Av *NORM/LIT* DE23 ..... **256** A5
Breedon Hill Rd *NORM/LIT* DE23 ..... **4** C8
Breedon St *LGEAT* NG10 ..... **244** E8
Brenden Av *ALFN* DE55 ..... **187** M3
Brenden Cl *ALFN* DE55 ..... **187** M2 🔲
Brendon Dr *CHSW* S40 ..... **109** M6 🔲
Brendon Cl *GLSP* SK13 ..... **25** K2 🔲
Brendon Wy *ASHZ* LE65 ..... **291** L5
  LGEAT NG10 ..... **260** D1
Brent Cl *CHSW* S40 ..... **110** A5
Brentford Dr *DERBYW* DE22 ..... **239** L4
Brentwood Av *ECC* S11 ..... **55** G4 🔲
  EDL/UDV S33 ..... **50** E7 🔲
Brentwood Rd *ECC* S11 ..... **55** G4
  EDL/UDV S33 ..... **50** E7
Bren Wy *RDERBYSW* DE65 ..... **253** H8
Bretby Cl *MSFD* NG18 ..... **165** L4 🔲
Bretby La *STPNHL/WNHL* DE15 ..... **275** G8
Bretby Rd *CHSW* S40 ..... **109** K4 🔲
  SWAD DE11 ..... **282** C3
Bretby Sq *NORM/LIT* DE23 ..... **255** M5
Bretby Vw *SWAD* DE11 ..... **283** K6
Bretland Gdns *HYDE* SK14 ..... **24** B1 🔲
Bretlands Wy
  STPNHL/WNHL DE15 ..... **281** K4
  NORM/LIT DE23 ..... **239** M8
Bretton Av *BSVR* S44 ..... **113** M8
Bretton Cl *CHSW* S40 ..... **109** K5 🔲
Bretton Gv *HACK/IN* S12 ..... **57** G7
Bretton Rd *BPR/DUF* DE56 ..... **200** B5 🔲
Brewery St *CHNE* S41 ..... **3** H3
Breydon Ct *DERBYSE* DE24 ..... **257** G6
Briar Av *LGEAT* NG10 ..... **244** D7
Briar Briggs Rd *BSVR* S44 ..... **113** J7
Briar Cl *ALFN* DE55 ..... **175** M7
  ASH NG17 ..... **162** E4
  BWSH/BRSTN DE72 ..... **258** F1
  DERBYE DE21 ..... **241** L5
  SBK/MW NG20 ..... **133** H8
  SWAD DE11 ..... **282** C5
  WRKS S80 ..... **77** M8
Briardene Ct *RCH* S42 ..... **109** J5 🔲
Briarfield Av *HACK/IN* S12 ..... **56** D7
Briarfield Crs *HACK/IN* S12 ..... **56** D8
Briar Ga *LGEAT* NG10 ..... **244** D8
Briargrove Rd *NM/HAY* SK22 ..... **34** A4
Briar La *MSFD* NG18 ..... **165** K6
Briar Lea *WRKS* S80 ..... **77** M8
Briar Lea *DERBYSE* DE24 ..... **256** C6
Briar Rd *ABRD* S7 ..... **55** H4
  EWD/SEL/PNX NG16 ..... **217** L2
Briars Cl *ECK/KIL* S21 ..... **74** A5
Briarsgate *DERBYW* DE22 ..... **226** A8 🔲
Briars' La *MTLK* DE4 ..... **185** K4
Briars Wy *RIPLEY* DE5 ..... **201** G2
Briar Vw *STV/CWN* S43 ..... **111** H3
Briarwood Cl *MSFDW* NG19 ..... **165** L1 🔲
Briarwood Crs *MPL/ROM* SK6 ..... **32** C6
Briarwood Wy *NORM/LIT* DE23 ..... **255** M4
Brickbridge Rd *MPL/ROM* SK6 ..... **32** D5
Brickfields La *MTLK* DE4 ..... **171** K6 🔲
Brickfield St *GLSP* SK13 ..... **17** L5
Brickhouse La *TOT/DORE* S17 ..... **68** F7
Brickhouse Yd *CHSW* S40 ..... **2** C4
Brick-kiln La *ASHB* DE6 ..... **195** M5
  ASHB DE6 ..... **222** C1
  BUTN/AL/TUT DE13 ..... **264** D7
Brickkiln La *ILK* DE7 ..... **227** L2
Brick Kiln La *MSFDW* NG19 ..... **164** A3
Brick Rw *DERBYW* DE22 ..... **240** D1
Brick St *DERBY* DE1 ..... **4** B2
Brickyard La *ALFN* DE55 ..... **176** D4
  BPR/DUF DE56 ..... **214** C1
  RIPLEY DE5 ..... **201** J1
The Brickyard *ILK* DE7 ..... **228** E1
Bricky Ct *STV/CWN* S43 ..... **95** G5
Bridby St *HAN/WDH* S13 ..... **57** M4
Bridge Bank Cl *CHSW* S40 ..... **110** A4 🔲
Bridge Cl *SWAD* DE11 ..... **282** F8 🔲
  WRKS S80 ..... **96** D5
Bridge End Av
  EWD/SEL/PNX NG16 ..... **189** J2
Bridge Fld *BWSH/BRSTN* DE72 ..... **259** M7
Bridgeford Gv *BPR/DUF* DE56 ..... **199** H5
Bridge Hl *BPR/DUF* DE56 ..... **199** H5
Bridgend Cl *BSTN/STPLFD* NG9 ..... **245** J8
Bridgeness Rd *NORM/LIT* DE23 ..... **255** J4
Bridgeport Rd *DERBYE* DE21 ..... **241** M4
Bridge Rd *UTXR* ST14 ..... **248** A3
Bridgeside *BUTN/AL/TUT* DE13 ..... **274** B1
Bridge St *BKWL* DE45 ..... **123** G4
  BPR/DUF DE56 ..... **199** J6
  BUT DE14 ..... **274** B7
  BUTN/AL/TUT DE13 ..... **263** M7
  BUTN/AL/TUT DE13 ..... **274** B1
  CHF/WBR SK23 ..... **59** H3
  CHSW S40 ..... **3** H9
  CLCR S45 ..... **145** M8
  DERBY DE1 ..... **4** C2
  ECK/KIL S21 ..... **74** A3
  EDL/UDV S33 ..... **64** D3 🔲
  EWD/SEL/PNX NG16 ..... **202** F7
  ILK DE7 ..... **217** J6
  LGEAT NG10 ..... **244** F5
  LGEAT NG10 ..... **261** G1
  MSFD NG18 ..... **165** G4
  NM/HAY SK22 ..... **43** M1
  RCH S42 ..... **145** G1
  SWAD DE11 ..... **282** F8
  SWAD DE11 ..... **289** H2
  UTXR ST14 ..... **247** M3

Bridge Vw *BPR/DUF* DE56 ..... **213** K3
Bridgewater St *RCH* S42 ..... **144** F1
Bridgeway *CHF/WBR* SK23 ..... **60** E6
Bridgford Av *BUT* DE14 ..... **280** C3
Bridgford St *MSFD* NG18 ..... **165** J5
Bridgnorth Wy
  BSTN/STPLFD NG9 ..... **245** H7
Bridgwater Cl
  DERBYE DE24 ..... **257** M3 🔲
Bridle Cl *ASH* NG17 ..... **162** E4
  MELB/CHEL DE73 ..... **269** K1
Bridle La *ALFN* DE55 ..... **187** L3
  BPR/DUF DE56 ..... **186** D8
  RIPLEY DE5 ..... **187** H7
  STPNHL/WNHL DE15 ..... **281** K5
Bridle Rd *BSTN/STPLFD* NG9 ..... **245** L2
  BSVR S44 ..... **94** E8
  STV/CWN S43 ..... **93** L8
Bridle Stile *MOS* S20 ..... **72** F3
Bridle Stile *MOS* S20 ..... **72** F3 🔲
Bridle Stile Gdns *MOS* S20 ..... **72** F3 🔲
Brier Cl *MOS* S20 ..... **73** G1
Brierfield Rd *HACK/IN* S12 ..... **56** D7
Brierfield Wy *MCKLVR* DE3 ..... **255** H2
Brierley Cl *STV/CWN* S43 ..... **112** B1
Brierley Pk *CHF/WBR* SK23 ..... **59** L1
Brierley Rd *ALFN* DE55 ..... **160** B7
  DRON S18 ..... **91** H4
Brierly Rd *ASH* NG17 ..... **163** G6
Brigden Av *DERBYSE* DE24 ..... **257** H3
Bright Meadow *MOS* S20 ..... **73** K5
Brighton Rd *DERBYSE* DE24 ..... **257** J2
Brightstone Cl
  DERBYE DE24 ..... **258** A5 🔲
Bright St *ALFN* DE55 ..... **176** C5
  DERBYW DE22 ..... **240** A5 🔲
  ILK DE7 ..... **217** H7
  RCH S42 ..... **145** J3
Brimington Rd *CHNE* S41 ..... **3** K2
  CHNE S41 ..... **110** E5 🔲
Brimington Rd North
  CHNE S41 ..... **110** D2
Brimmesfield Dr
  SHEFP/MNR S2 ..... **56** B2 🔲
Brimmesfield Rd
  SHEFP/MNR S2 ..... **56** B3
Brimmsfield Ct *SHEFP/MNR* S2 ..... **56** C3
Brincliffe Cl *CHSW* S40 ..... **127** L1
Brincliffe Crs *ECC* S11 ..... **54** F3
Brincliffe Edge Cl *ECC* S11 ..... **54** E4
Brincliffe Edge Rd *ECC* S11 ..... **54** E4
Brincliffe Gdns *ECC* S11 ..... **54** F3
Brincliffe Hl *ECC* S11 ..... **54** E3
Brindley Av *MPL/ROM* SK6 ..... **32** C5
Brindley Cl *STV/CWN* S43 ..... **95** K6
Brindley Cl *ECK/KIL* S21 ..... **73** M4 🔲
Brindley Crs *SHEFS* S8 ..... **55** J3
Brindley Rd *CHNE* S41 ..... **110** D4 🔲
  WOL/BIL/BRX NG8 ..... **231** M5
Brindley Wy *STV/CWN* S43 ..... **93** J8
Brinkburn Cl *TOT/DORE* S17 ..... **69** J4 🔲
Brinkburn Dr *TOT/DORE* S17 ..... **69** J4
Brinkburn Vale Rd
  TOT/DORE S17 ..... **69** J4
Brinsley Hl *EWD/SEL/PNX* NG16 ..... **188** F8 🔲
Brisbane Cl *MSFDW* NG19 ..... **149** M4
Brisbane Dr *BSTN/STPLFD* NG9 ..... **245** H1
Brisbane Rd *MCKLVR* DE3 ..... **239** H6
Briset Cl *DERBYSE* DE24 ..... **256** B8 🔲
Bristol Av *ASHZ* LE65 ..... **291** K6
Bristol Dr *MCKLVR* DE3 ..... **239** H8
Bristol Rd *ECC* S11 ..... **54** F1
  ILK DE7 ..... **230** B1
Britannia Av *RIPLEY* DE5 ..... **201** K3 🔲
Britannia Dr
  BUTN/AL/TUT DE13 ..... **274** A2
Britannia Rd *CHSW* S40 ..... **128** C3
  LGEAT NG10 ..... **261** G1
Briton Lodge Cl *MSHM* DE12 ..... **290** C6
Brittain Dr *RIPLEY* DE5 ..... **201** K1
Brittany Av *ASHZ* LE65 ..... **291** K3
Brizlincote La
  STPNHL/WNHL DE15 ..... **282** A1
Brizlincote St
  STPNHL/WNHL DE15 ..... **281** J1
Broadacre *STLY* SK15 ..... **16** B4
Broad Bank *DERBYW* DE22 ..... **240** B2 🔲
Broadbent Gv *HYDE* SK14 ..... **16** B8 🔲
Broadbottom Rd *HYDE* SK14 ..... **16** C8
Broad Elms Cl *ECC* S11 ..... **54** C6 🔲
Broad Elms La *ECC* S11 ..... **54** B7
Broadfield Av *SHEFS* S8 ..... **55** J4
Broadfields Cl *DERBYE* DE22 ..... **240** C2 🔲
Broadgorse Cl *CHSW* S40 ..... **128** C3
Broadhey Vw *NM/HAY* SK22 ..... **43** L1
Broadholme La *BPR/DUF* DE56 ..... **199** K3
Broadlands *ALFN* DE55 ..... **176** D6
  BUTN/AL/TUT DE13 ..... **274** A2 🔲
  LGEAT NG10 ..... **244** E6
Broadlands Av *MOS* S20 ..... **57** K8
Broadlands Cl *MOS* S20 ..... **57** L8
Broadlands Cft *MOS* S20 ..... **57** L8 🔲
Broadlands Ri *HACK/IN* S12 ..... **57** L8 🔲
Broad La *BWSH/BRSTN* DE72 ..... **258** C6
  EWD/SEL/PNX NG16 ..... **203** H2
  WRKS S80 ..... **96** H4
Broadleaf Cl *DERBYE* DE21 ..... **227** H8 🔲
Broadley Rd *HAN/WDH* S13 ..... **57** E3
Broad Oak Dr
  BSTN/STPLFD NG9 ..... **245** G4
  EWD/SEL/PNX NG16 ..... **203** G2
Broadoaks Cl *CHNE* S41 ..... **3** K5
Broad Pavement *CHSW* S40 ..... **3** H4
Broad Pl *WRKS* S80 .... **96** H4
Broadstairs Rd
  BSTN/STPLFD NG9 ..... **245** J8 🔲
Broadstone La
  MELB/CHEL DE73 ..... **277** M5
Broad St *LGEAT* NG10 ..... **261** G3
Broad Wk *MSFD* DE4 ..... **140** F7
Broady Wy *BPR/DUF* DE56 ..... **196** E2
Broadway *ALFN* DE55 ..... **187** J3
  BPR/DUF DE56 ..... **213** G8
  DERBYW DE22 ..... **240** C2
  HEANOR DE75 ..... **216** B1
  ILK DE7 ..... **217** H7
  RIPLEY DE5 ..... **187** H8
Broadway Av *RIPLEY* DE5 ..... **201** H1
Broadway La *BUX* SK17 ..... **102** D5

Broadway Park Cl
  DERBYW DE22 ..... **240** B2 🔲
Broadway St *BUT* DE14 ..... **280** F2
Broadway Rd *MPL/ROM* SK6 ..... **42** C3
Brocco Bank *ECC* S11 ..... **54** F2
Brockenhurst Rd *MSFDW* NG19... **164** A4
Brockhall Ri *HEANOR* DE75 ..... **216** D1
Brockholes *GLSP* SK13 ..... **25** H1 🔲
Brockhurst La *CLCR* S45 ..... **142** F4
Brocklehurst Av *SHEFS* S8 ..... **70** F2
Brocklehurst Piece *CHSW* S40 ... **2** A4
Brockley *DERBYE* DE21 ..... **242** B5
Brockley Av *BSVR* S44 ..... **113** J4
Brockwell La *CHSW* S40 ..... **110** A5
  RCH S42 ..... **109** J3
Brockwell Pl *CHSW* S40 ..... **2** C1
The Brockwell *ALFN* DE55 ..... **176** E6
Brockwood Cl *HAN/WDH* S13 ... **57** M3 🔲
Bromehead Wy *CHNE* S41 ..... **110** A3
Bromley Cl *DERBYW* DE22 ..... **240** B3
Brompton Rd *DERBYW* DE22 ..... **239** L4
Bromwich Rd *SHEFS* S8 ..... **55** H8
Bronte Cl *BUT* DE14 ..... **274** A3 🔲
  LGEAT NG10 ..... **260** D3
Bronte Pl *NORM/LIT* DE23 ..... **255** L2
Bronte St *ALFN* DE55 ..... **159** M5 🔲
Brook Av *ALFN* DE55 ..... **175** L7
Brookbank Av *CHSW* S40 ..... **95** J6
Brook Bottom Rd *NM/HAY* SK22 ... **43** J1
Brook Cl *ALFN* DE55 ..... **175** L7
  ASHB DE6 ..... **248** F2
  DERBYW DE22 ..... **225** M6
  EWD/SEL/PNX NG16 ..... **217** L1
  LGEAT NG10 ..... **261** H5
  RCH S42 ..... **127** G3
  RDERBYSE DE65 ..... **252** A8
  RDERBYSW DE65 ..... **267** G1
Brookdale Av *MPL/ROM* SK6 ..... **32** D6
Brookdale Rd *ASH* NG17 ..... **163** K7
  SWAD DE11 ..... **283** K6
Brook Dr *STV/CWN* S43 ..... **111** J5
Brook End *RDERBYSW* DE65 ..... **266** F7
Brook St *ALFN* DE55 ..... **161** K4
  ILK DE7 ..... **230** E4
  LGEAT NG10 ..... **244** E5
Brookfield Av *ASH* NG17 ..... **163** G6
  CHSW S40 ..... **109** K8
  DERBYE DE21 ..... **241** L2
  NORM/LIT DE23 ..... **256** A4
Brookfield Cl *RIPLEY* DE5 ..... **201** L1
Brookfield Crs *SBK/MW* NG20 ... **133** H5
Brookfield La *BKWL* DE45 ..... **123** H2
  SHEFS S8 ..... **55** J3
Brookfields *BPR/DUF* DE56 ..... **214** B3 🔲
  HATH/EY S32 ..... **105** M1
Brookfields Dr *ILK* DE7 ..... **227** G6
Brookfield Wy *HEANOR* DE75 ..... **216** E1
  MTLK DE4 ..... **157** J6
Brook House Dr *HACK/IN* S12 ..... **57** L8
Brookhill Av
  EWD/SEL/PNX NG16 ..... **177** G6
Brookhill La
  EWD/SEL/PNX NG16 ..... **177** H5
Brookhill Leys Rd
  EWD/SEL/PNX NG16 ..... **203** G3 🔲
Brookhill Rd
  EWD/SEL/PNX NG16 ..... **177** G8
Brookhill St *BSTN/STPLFD* NG9 ... **245** G5
Brookhouse Dr *HACK/IN* S12 ..... **57** L7
Brookhouse Hl *ECC* S11 ..... **54** C3
Brook House Ms *SWAD* DE11 ..... **282** D3
Brookhouse St
  DERBYE DE24 ..... **257** G5 🔲
Brookland Av *MSFDW* NG18... ..... **164** C3
Brooklands *BUX* SK17 ..... **99** M2 🔲
Brooklands Av *CHF/WBR* SK23 ... **61** G4
  FUL S10 ..... **53** L3
  HEANOR DE75 ..... **202** C8
  MTLK DE4 ..... **183** J5
Brooklands Bank *BKWL* DE45 ..... **123** H4
Brooklands Crs *FUL* S10 ..... **53** M3
Brooklands Dr *FUL* S10 ..... **53** L3 🔲
  NORM/LIT DE23 ..... **255** M2
Brooklands Rd *CHF/WBR* SK23... ... **61** G4
Brook La *ALFN* DE55 ..... **175** L7 🔲
  ASHB DE6 ..... **252** D2
  HACK/IN S12 ..... **57** L7
  RDERBYSW DE65 ..... **251** M7
  RIPLEY DE5 ..... **201** G3
  STV/CWN S43 ..... **95** J6
Brook Lea *MTLK* DE4 ..... **156** F6
Brookleton *BKWL* DE45 ..... **138** F5 🔲
Brooklyn Dr *CHSW* S40 ..... **2** B2
Brooklyn Pl *SHEFS* S8 ..... **55** K5 🔲
Brooklyn Rd *SHEFS* S8 ..... **55** K5 🔲
Brook Meadow *GLSP* SK13 ..... **26** B1
Brook Ri *BWSH/BRSTN* DE72 ..... **258** E1
  SHEFS S8 ..... **55** J5
Brook Side *BKWL* DE45 ..... **123** G4
  BPR/DUF DE56 ..... **199** J7
  BUTN/AL/TUT DE13 ..... **264** C6
Brookside *ASHB* DE6 ..... **194** B8
  CHF/WBR SK23 ..... **59** K2
  EDL/UDV S33 ..... **64** D3
  EWD/SEL/PNX NG16 ..... **203** J6 🔲
  GLSP SK13 ..... **25** L2 🔲
  MTLK DE4 ..... **124** E7
  NM/HAY SK22 ..... **34** B3
  STPNHL/WNHL DE15 ..... **274** E5
Brookside Cl *MSFDW* NG19 ..... **149** M5
Brookside Bar *CHSW* S40 ..... **109** J8
Brookside Cl *DERBYW* DE22 ..... **240** B3
  GLSP SK13 ..... **17** J6 🔲
  HACK/IN S12 ..... **57** L7
  LGEAT NG10 ..... **260** E2
  RDERBYSW DE65 ..... **267** G6 🔲
Brookside Gv *BUX* SK17 ..... **99** G5
Brookside Rd *CHF/WBR* SK23 ..... **60** C5
  SHEFS S8 ..... **55** J4
  UTXR ST14 ..... **248** A3
Brookside Wy *ASH* NG17 ..... **177** H1
Brooks Rd *STV/CWN* S43 ..... **95** H6

Brook St *ASH* NG17 ..... **163** H8
  ASHZ LE65 ..... **291** L4
  BPR/DUF DE56 ..... **185** M8
  BPR/DUF DE56 ..... **200** B1
  BUT DE14 ..... **274** A7
  CLCR S45 ..... **144** D6
  DERBY DE1 ..... **4** C1
  ECK/KIL S21 ..... **93** M3
  GLSP SK13 ..... **25** H1 🔲
  HEANOR DE75 ..... **201** L5
  SWAD DE11 ..... **282** D7
  SWAD DE11 ..... **282** B4 🔲
  SWAD DE11 ..... **283** K3
Brookvale Av *RIPLEY* DE5 ..... **200** D8
  RIPLEY DE5 ..... **201** L2
Brook Vale Cl *DRON* S18 ..... **90** A7
Brookvale Cl *MSFD* NG18 ..... **165** K4
Brookvale Ri *RIPLEY* DE5 ..... **200** D8
Brook Vale Rd
  EWD/SEL/PNX NG16 ..... **202** F8
Brookvale Rd *RIPLEY* DE5 ..... **200** D8
Brookview Ct *DRON* S18 ..... **70** D7
Broom Av *ALFN* DE55 ..... **187** J3
  CLCR S45 ..... **145** M8
Broombank Pk *DRON* S18 ..... **91** G7
Broombank Rd *DRON* S18 ..... **91** G7
Broom Cl *BPR/DUF* DE56 ..... **199** H5
  CHNE S41 ..... **110** A3 🔲
  DERBYSE DE24 ..... **256** A8
  ECC S11 ..... **55** J1
  MELB/CHEL DE73 ..... **257** J8
Broomcroft Pk *ECC* S11 ..... **54** C7 🔲
Broom Dr *RCH* S42 ..... **129** H8
Broome Acre *ALFN* DE55 ..... **176** E6
Broomfield Av *CHNE* S41 ..... **91** J8
Broomfield Cl *LGEAT* NG10 ..... **244** D5 🔲
Broomfield La *ASHB* DE6 ..... **205** J8
Broom Gdns *STV/CWN* S43 ..... **111** J3
Broomhall Rd *FUL* S10 ..... **55** H1
Broomhill Av *ILK* DE7 ..... **230** D4 🔲
Broomhill Cl *ECK/KIL* S21 ..... **72** E7
  MCKLVR DE3 ..... **239** C7
Broomhill La *MSFDW* NG19 ..... **164** C2
Broomhill Rd *CHNE* S41 ..... **91** J8
Broomhills La *RDERBYSE* DE65 ... **276** A1
Broom La *ASHB* DE6 ..... **196** B5
Broom's La *ASHB* DE6 ..... **250** E8
Brosscroft *GLSP* SK13 ..... **17** K4
Brosscroft Village *GLSP* SK13 ..... **17** K4
Brougham Av *MSFDW* NG19 ..... **149** G8
Brough La *EDL/UDV* S33 ..... **64** F1
Brough Rd
  STPNHL/WNHL DE15 ..... **274** F7
Brough St *DERBYW* DE22 ..... **240** A5
Broughton Av *NORM/LIT* DE23 ... **256** A1
Broughton Cl *ILK* DE7 ..... **217** H8 🔲
Broun Swinfen *MSFD* NG18 ..... **164** F7 🔲
Brow Crs *MOS* S20 ..... **73** H3
Brown Av *MSFDW* NG19 ..... **149** L5
Brown Crs *ASH* NG17 ..... **163** K6
Brown Edge Rd *BUX* SK17 ..... **99** H1
Brownhill La *HOLM/MEL* HD7 ..... **8** E1
Brown Hills La *FUL* S10 ..... **53** H2
Brownhills La *RCH* S42 ..... **143** L6
Browning Dr *MSHM* DE12 ..... **295** L7
Browning Rd *SWAD* DE11 ..... **282** F5
Browning St *MSFD* NG18 ..... **164** D3 🔲
  NORM/LIT DE23 ..... **256** C4
Brown La *BUX* SK17 ..... **116** E7
  CLCR S45 ..... **158** E2
  DRON S18 ..... **70** F7
Brownlow Rd *MSFDW* NG19 ..... **164** C2
Brown's La *BPR/DUF* DE56 ..... **214** A3
Browns Rd *LGEAT* NG10 ..... **261** H2
Brown St *MSFDW* NG19 ..... **164** C2
Broxholme Rd *SHEFS* S8 ..... **55** J7 🔲
Broxtowe Dr *MSFD* NG18 ..... **164** F4
Bruce Rd *ECC* S11 ..... **55** G2 🔲
Brunel Av *EWD/SEL/PNX* NG16 ... **203** K7
Brun La *ASHB* DE6 ..... **238** E2
The Brunnen *ALFN* DE55 ..... **176** E6
Brunner Av *SBK/MW* NG20 ..... **133** J7
Brunswick Dr
  BSTN/STPLFD NG9 ..... **245** J5 🔲
Brunswick St *CHNE* S41 ..... **3** G1
  CLCR S45 ..... **160** F1 🔲
  NORM/LIT DE23 ..... **256** C1
Brunswood Cl *DERBYE* DE21 ..... **242** B5
Brunswood La *ASHB* DE6 ..... **209** L2
Brunswood Rd *MTLK* DE4 ..... **156** E8 🔲
Brunton Cl *MCKLVR* DE3 ..... **254** F1
Brunt La *ASHB* DE6 ..... **238** E6
Brushfield Gv *HACK/IN* S12 ..... **57** G6
Brushfield Rd *RCH* S42 ..... **109** J5
Brussells Ter *ILK* DE7 ..... **230** B1 🔲
Brydges Rd *MPL/ROM* SK6 ..... **32** B5
Bryn Lea *CHNE* S41 ..... **3** M5
Brynsmoor Rd
  EWD/SEL/PNX NG16 ..... **203** H3
Bryony *BUT* DE14 ..... **280** E2
Bryony Cl *DERBYE* DE21 ..... **227** K8
  ECK/KIL S21 ..... **73** L4
Bubnell Rd *BKWL* DE45 ..... **106** A3
Buchanan St *DERBY* DE1 ..... **4** E1 🔲
Buchan St *DERBYSE* DE24 ..... **257** G3
Buckden Cl *CHSW* S40 ..... **2** B1
Buckfast Cl *ALFN* DE55 ..... **187** H2
Buckford La *RDERBYSW* DE65 ..... **267** H2
Buckhazels La *ASHB* DE6 ..... **224** D4
Buckingham Av
  DERBYE DE21 ..... **241** G2 🔲
Buckingham Cl *ALFN* DE55 ..... **187** K3
  BUTN/AL/TUT DE13 ..... **274** A2 🔲
  DRON S18 ..... **70** A8 🔲
Buckingham Ct *LGEAT* NG10 ..... **244** D7 🔲
Buckingham Rd *LGEAT* NG10 ..... **244** D7
Buckland Cl *DERBYW* DE22 ..... **4** A2
Buckleather La *HATH/EY* S32 ..... **107** M1
Buckley Cl *MSHM* DE12 ..... **295** M5
  SWAD DE11 ..... **283** J8
Bucklow Cl *HYDE* SK14 ..... **24** C1
Buckminster Dr *DERBYE* DE21 ... **227** J8
Buckminster Rd *ILK* DE7 ..... **229** M6
Buck Wood Vw *SHEFP/MNR* S2 ... **56** A5
Budby Av *MSFD* NG18 ..... **165** J4
Bullace Ct *MSFDW* NG19 ..... **165** H1 🔲
Bullbridge Hl *BPR/DUF* DE56 ..... **185** L4
Buller St *ILK* DE7 ..... **230** D4
  NORM/LIT DE23 ..... **240** B8

Bullgap La *ASHB* DE6 .... **191** M7
 ASHB DE6 .... **192** A5
Bullhill La *BPR/DUF* DE56 .... **197** H6
Bullhurst La *ASHB* DE6 .... **211** J8
Bulling La *MTLK* DE4 .... **185** J1
Bullock Crs *MSFDW* NG19 .... **149** L5
Bullock La *ALFN* DE55 .... **188** B5
 ASHB DE6 .... **223** J3
Bullpit La *BPR/DUF* DE56 .... **226** D2
Bulltor Cl *ALFN* DE55 .... **174** L1
Bumpmill La *ASHB* DE6 .... **174** L1
Bun Aly *BKWL* DE45 .... **105** M8
Bunker S HI *ECK/KIL* S21 .... **74** B4
Bunkers Hill Rd *HYDE* SK14 ...... **24** B1
Bunting Cl *CHSW* S40 .... **127** L1
 ILK DE7 .... **229** M4
 MCKLVR DE3 .... **239** K7
 SHEFS S8 .... **70** E1
 UTXR ST14 .... **247** L4
Buntingfield La *CLCR* S45 .... **142** E3
Bunting Nook *SHEFS* S8 .... **55** L8
Bunyan Crs *ALFN* DE55 .... **160** C7
Bunyan Green Rd
 BPR/DUF DE56 .... **200** A6
 DRON S18 .... **70** A8 **🖪**
Burbage Cl *MSFD* NG18 .... **165** L4
Burbage Gv *HACK/IN* S12 .... **57** C5
Burbage Pl *DERBYSE* DE24 ...... **257** J3
Burbage St *STV/CWN* S43 .... **111** M3
Burcot Cl *ILK* DE7 .... **229** H2
Burcot Rd *SHEFS* S8 .... **55** J5
Burdekin Cl *CHF/WBR* SK23 .... **60** F4 **🖪**
Burdett Wy *RDERBYSW* DE65 ...... **267** G7
Burdock Cl *DERBYE* DE21 .... **227** H8 **🖪**
Burgess Cl *CHNE* S41 .... **129** C3
Burgh Hall Cl
 BSTN/STPLFD NG9 .... **245** M8
Burghley Cl *MELB/CHEL* DE73 .... **257** J8
Burghley Wy *NORM/LIT* DE23 ... **255** H4
Burke Dr *ALFN* DE55 .... **188** A2
Burkitt Dr *STV/CWN* S43 .... **93** L7
Burland Green La *ASHB* DE6 .... **211** M5
Burleigh Crs *ALFN* DE55 .... **187** J2
Burleigh Dr *DERBYE* DE22 .... **240** C2
Burleigh St *ILK* DE7 .... **230** C1 **🖪**
Burley Bank La *HOLM/MEL* HD7 ... **8** B4
Burley Cl *CHSW* S40 .... **128** D3
Burley Dr *DERBYW* DE22 .... **226** B3
Burley HI *DERBYW* DE22 .... **226** B4
Burley La *DERBYW* DE22 .... **226** A3
Burlington Av *SBK/MW* NG20 .... **133** H4
Burlington Cl
 BWSH/BRSTN DE72 .... **260** A2
Burlington Gln *TOT/DORE* S17 ... **69** H3 **🖪**
Burlington Gv *TOT/DORE* S17 ..... **69** H3
Burlington Rd *BUX* SK17 .... **99** K3
 TOT/DORE S17 .... **69** H3
Burlington St *CHSW* S40 .... **3** H1
Burlington Wy *MCKLVR* DE3 ...... **255** G1
Burlow Av *BUX* SK17 .... **99** M7
Burlow Rd *BUX* SK17 .... **100** A8
The Burma Rd *ASHB* DE6 .... **223** L4
Burnaby St *DERBYSE* DE24 ...... **257** J2
Burnaston Cl *DRON* S18 .... **89** M1 **🖪**
Burnaston Rd *MSFD* NG18 .... **165** L4
Burnbridge Rd *CHNE* S41 .... **91** M8
Burncroft *ILK* DE7 .... **229** H3 **🖪**
Burnell St *STV/CWN* S43 .... **111** J3
Burnett La *MTLK* DE4 .... **156** D2
Burney La *MELB/CHEL* DE73 ...... **278** F8
Burnham Cl *ASHZ* LE65 .... **229** G2 **🖪**
Burnham Ct *MSFD* NG18 .... **164** F6
Burnham Dr *MCKLVR* DE3 .... **238** F8
Burns Av *MSFDW* NG19 .... **149** M8
Burns Cl *CHSW* S40 .... **128** C3
 MSHM DE12 .... **295** L7
 NORM/LIT DE23 .... **255** L2 **🖪**
Burns Dr *DRON* S18 .... **90** F2
 RCH S42 .... **129** H7
Burnside *BUTN/AL/TUT* DE13 .... **264** E6
 GLSP SK13 .... **17** J6
 STLY SK15 .... **16** A3
Burnside Av *ALFN* DE55 .... **174** F1
 SHEFS S8 .... **55** M5
 STLY SK15 .... **16** A3
Burnside Cl *DERBYSE* DE24 ...... **256** A7 **🖪**
 DERBYE DE21 .... **242** C8
Burnside St *DERBYSE* DE24 ...... **257** K2
Burns St *HEANOR* DE75 .... **202** A8
 ILK DE7 .... **230** B2
 MSFD NG18 .... **164** D3
Burn St *ASH* NG17 .... **163** K7
Burnt House Rd *HEANOR* DE75 ... **216** A1
Burnwood Av *MSFD* NG18 .... **165** K3
Burre Cl *BKWL* DE45 .... **123** H4
Burrfields Rd *CHF/WBR* SK23 .... **60** E4
Burr La *ILK* DE7 .... **230** C1
Burrows La *ASHB* DE6 .... **223** J8
 MTLK DE4 .... **170** F5
The Burrows *SWAD* DE11 .... **282** C5 **🖪**
Burrs Wood Cft *CHSW* S40 ...... **109** L3 **🖪**
Bursdon Cl *CHNE* S41 .... **110** E1 **🖪**
Burton Cl *ASH* NG17 .... **163** G6
Burton Close Dr *BKWL* DE45 .... **123** H6 **🖪**
Burton Edge *BKWL* DE45 .... **123** G6
Burton Rd *ASH* NG17 .... **162** F7
 ASHZ LE65 .... **291** K4
 BUT DE14 .... **280** C1
 BUTN/AL/TUT DE13 .... **264** A5
 DERBY DE1 .... **4** E6
 MELB/CHEL DE73 .... **277** J6
 MSHM DE12 .... **287** M3
 MSHM DE12 .... **295** L5
 NORM/LIT DE23 .... **240** A8
 NORM/LIT DE23 .... **255** M1
 RDERBYSW DE65 .... **254** F7
 RDERBYSW DE65 .... **266** D1
 RDERBYSW DE65 .... **275** K1
 SWAD DE11 .... **282** E3 **🖪**
 SWAD DE11 .... **289** H2
Burton St *BUTN/AL/TUT* DE13 ... **263** M4
 HEANOR DE75 .... **202** B8 **🖪**
Burwell Cl *GLSP* SK13 .... **25** K2

Bushey Wood Rd *TOT/DORE* S17... **69** H4
Bushton La *BUTN/AL/TUT* DE13 ... **263** L7
Bushy Cl *LGEAT* NG10 .... **260** D4
Butcher's La *MTLK* DE4 .... **141** J6
Bute St *GLSP* SK13 .... **18** B7
Butler Ct *BUT* DE14 .... **273** L7 **🖪**
Butler Crs *MSFDW* NG19 .... **149** G8
Butler Wy *ECK/KIL* S21 .... **73** M3
Butterfield Crs *ALFN* DE55 ...... **187** J3
Butterfield La *ALFN* DE55 .... **174** C1
Butterhall Cl *WRKS* S80 .... **96** D5 **🖪**
Butterley Hl *RIPLEY* DE5 .... **187** H7
Butterley La *CLCR* S45 .... **158** C5
 RIPLEY DE5 .... **187** G6
Buttermead Cl
 BSTN/STPLFD NG9 .... **231** G8 **🖪**
Buttermere Cl *CHNE* S41 .... **110** A3
 LGEAT NG10 .... **244** D8 **🖪**
Buttermere Dr *DERBYW* DE22 ... **226** C7
 DRON S18 .... **90** B1 **🖪**
Buttermere Rd *SHEFS* S8 .... **55** H6
Buttermilk La *BSVR* S44 .... **112** F7
Butterpot La *ASHB* DE6 .... **237** G7
Butterton Cl *ILK* DE7 .... **230** D3 **🖪**
Butterton Dr *CHSW* S40 .... **109** K5 **🖪**
Buttonoak Dr
 MELB/CHEL DE73 .... **257** K7
 ILK DE7 .... **230** D6
Butts HI *WRKS* S80 .... **96** C4
Butt HI *WRKS* S80 .... **96** C4
Butt Hill Cl *WRKS* S80 .... **96** C4
Butts Cl *SWAD* DE11 .... **290** D1
Butts Dr *MTLK* DE4 .... **157** C6
Butts HI *TOT/DORE* S17 .... **69** G6
Butt's La *CDLE* ST10 .... **190** C2
Butts Pillar *MTLK* DE4 .... **183** H2
Butts Rd *BKWL* DE45 .... **123** G5
 CLCR S45 .... **143** H7
 MTLK DE4 .... **140** E7
The Butts *BPR/DUF* DE56 .... **199** K7
Butt St *LGEAT* NG10 .... **244** E5 **🖪**
Butts Vw *BKWL* DE45 .... **123** G5
Buxton Av *HEANOR* DE75 .... **216** C3 **🖪**
Buxton Cl *SWAD* DE11 .... **282** D3
Buxton Dr *DERBY* DE1 .... **213** M8
 MCKLVR DE3 .... **239** H7
Buxton La *MPL/ROM* SK6 .... **32** B5
Buxton Ms *GLSP* SK13 .... **25** H1
Buxton Old Rd *POY/DIS* SK12 ... **43** G4
Buxton Rd *ASHB* DE6 .... **193** C7
 BKWL DE45 .... **122** D3
 BUX SK17 .... **81** J3
 BUX SK17 .... **83** M7
 BUX SK17 .... **134** E3
 CHF/WBR SK23 .... **59** H1
 CHF/WBR SK23 .... **61** G4
 DERBYE DE21 .... **241** J1
 MSFDW NG19 .... **164** A1
 NM/HAY SK22 .... **43** L4
Buxton Rd West *HYDE* SK14 ...... **17** C5 **🖪**
Buxton Ter *HYDE* SK14 .... **17** C5 **🖪**
Buzzard Cl *MSHM* DE12 .... **295** L6
Byfield Cl *DERBYE* DE21 .... **227** L8
Byley Rd *WOL/BIL/BRX* NG8 ..... **231** L5
Byng Av *NORM/LIT* DE23 .... **256** C3
Byrd's La *UTXR* ST14 .... **247** J2
Byrkley St *BUT* DE14 .... **273** L6
Byron Av *ALFN* DE55 .... **175** L6
 ASH NG17 .... **163** L6
 LGEAT NG10 .... **244** E7
 MSFDW NG19 .... **149** M8
 STPNHL/WNHL DE15 .... **281** H3
Byron Cl *DRON* S18 .... **90** F3
 RCH S42 .... **129** H7
Byron Crs *BSTN/STPLFD* NG9 ... **245** H1 **🖪**
Byron Crs
 EWD/SEL/PNX NG16 .... **217** M6 **🖪**
 MSHM DE12 .... **295** M7
Byron Gv *EWD/SEL/PNX* NG16 ... **217** M6 **🖪**
Byron Rd *ABRD* S7 .... **55** G4
 CHSW S40 .... **128** D2
 SWAD DE11 .... **282** F4
Byron St *ALFN* DE55 .... **174** F1
 BUX SK17 .... **99** L4
 CHSW S40 .... **3** H7
 ILK DE7 .... **230** C1
 MSFD NG18 .... **164** D3
 NORM/LIT DE23 .... **4** D9
 SBK/MW NG20 .... **133** H6
Bythorn Cl *ASH* NG17 .... **163** L5
Bywell La *BPR/DUF* DE56 .... **214** C2

C

Cacklehill La *ASHB* DE6 .... **206** F8
Cadeby Ct *ALFN* DE55 .... **187** M4 **🖪**
Cadgwith Dr *DERBYW* DE22 ..... **226** D8
Cadley Hill Rd *SWAD* DE11 ...... **282** B7
Cadman Cl *MOS* S20 .... **73** C4
Cadman Rd *HACK/IN* S12 .... **56** F5
Cadman St *MOS* S20 .... **73** C4
Cadwell Cl *DERBYSE* DE24 ...... **258** A4
Caerhays Ct *DERBYSE* DE24 ..... **256** A7 **🖪**
Caernarvon Cl
 BUTN/AL/TUT DE13 .... **274** A2
 CHSW S40 .... **127** M1 **🖪**
 DERBYE DE21 .... **242** C5
Caernarvon Pl
 BSTN/STPLFD NG9 .... **245** L6 **🖪**
Caernarvon Rd *DRON* S18 .... **90** D2
Caesar St *DERBY* DE1 .... **240** E3
Cairn Dr *STV/CWN* S43 .... **92** A6
Cairngorm Cl *STV/CWN* S43 ..... **92** A6
Cairngorm Dr *DERBYSE* DE24... **256** A7
Cairns Cl *MCKLVR* DE3 .... **239** H7
Cairnsmore Cl *LGEAT* NG10 .... **260** D1 **🖪**
Caistor La *BUTN/AL/TUT* DE13 ... **273** L4
Caldbeck Dr *BSTN/STPLFD* NG9 .. **245** L6
Calder Cl *DERBYW* DE22 .... **226** C7
Calderdale Dr *LGEAT* NG10 ..... **260** D4
Calderdale *WOL/BIL/BRX* NG8 ... **231** L7
Caldermill Dr *DERBYE* DE21 ..... **227** K8

Caldey Rd *DRON* S18 .... **90** D2
Cale Rd *NM/HAY* SK22 .... **44** A2
Calesdale Cl *BUX* SK17 .... **99** L5 **🖪**
Calf Cft *WRKS* S80 .... **96** D5
Calgary Crs
 STPNHL/WNHL DE15 .... **275** G7
California Gdns
 DERBYW DE22 .... **239** M6 **🖪**
California La *STV/CWN* S43 ...... **94** D3
Calke Ri *RIPLEY* DE5 .... **201** J1
Calladine La *ASH* NG17 .... **177** L2
 BPR/DUF DE56 .... **197** M5
 ILK DE7 .... **215** G4
Calladine Rd *HEANOR* DE75 ..... **202** A8 **🖪**
Callan's La *ASHZ* LE65 .... **285** H4
Callington Cl *HYDE* SK14 .... **16** B8 **🖪**
Callington Dr *HYDE* SK14 .... **16** B8
Callingwood La
 BUTN/AL/TUT DE13 .... **272** B6
The Callis *ASHZ* LE65 .... **291** L3
Callow Dr *SHEFP/MNR* S2 .... **56** A5
Callow Hill Wy *NORM/LIT* DE23 .. **255** J3
Callow La *MTLK* DE4 .... **182** F5
Callow Mt *SHEFS* S8 .... **55** M5 **🖪**
Callow Rd *SHEFP/MNR* S2 ...... **55** M5 **🖪**
Callywhite La *DRON* S18 .... **90** F1
Calow Brook Dr *CHNE* S41 ..... **129** H2
Calow La *BSVR* S44 .... **129** H1
 CHNE S41 .... **129** H2
Calver Av *RCH* S42 .... **145** K3
Calver Cl *BPR/DUF* DE56 .... **199** L4
 DERBYE DE21 .... **227** H7
Calver Ms *GLSP* SK13 .... **17** G8
Calver Rd *BKWL* DE45 .... **106** A4
Calverton Cl *BSTN/STPLFD* NG9 .. **245** K8
 DERBYSE DE24 .... **257** H7
Calvert St *DERBYSE* DE24 ...... **257** K5
Calvin Cl *DERBYSE* DE24 .... **257** K5
Camberwell Av *DERBYW* DE22 ... **239** K4
Camborne Cl *DERBYE* DE21 .... **241** H1
Camborne Rd *HYDE* SK14 ...... **16** B7
Cambrian Cl *CHSW* S40 .... **110** A4
Cambrian Wy *ASHZ* LE65 ...... **291** L5
 SWAD DE11 .... **282** D7
Cambria Rd *MSFDW* NG19...... **148** A5
Cambridge Crs
 BSTN/STPLFD NG9 .... **231** G8 **🖪**
 BSVR S44 .... **147** H1
Cambridge Dr *SHEFS* S8 .... **55** L4
 STV/CWN S43 .... **111** J2 **🖪**
Cambridge St *ALFN* DE55 .... **176** B1 **🖪**
 BUT DE14 .... **280** E1
 DERBYE DE21 .... **242** B7
 MSFD NG18 .... **164** D5
 NORM/LIT DE23 .... **240** D8
Camdale Cl *BSTN/STPLFD* NG9 .. **245** L3
Camdale Ri *HACK/IN* S12 .... **72** C1
Camdale Vw *HACK/IN* S12 ...... **72** C1
Camden St *DERBYW* DE22 ...... **240** A6
Camellia Cl *MCKLVR* DE3 .... **239** G7
Camelot Cl
 BUTN/AL/TUT DE13 .... **265** H8 **🖪**
Cameron Cl
 STPNHL/WNHL DE15 .... **281** L1 **🖪**
Cameron Rd *NORM/LIT* DE23 ... **256** C2
The Camerons *MSFDW* NG19 ... **164** A5 **🖪**
Cameroy Wy *STV/CWN* S43 ...... **92** A5
Cam Height *ECC* S11 .... **53** G7
Camms Cl *ECK/KIL* S21 .... **73** G6 **🖪**
Campbell Dr *STV/CWN* S43 ..... **92** E6
Campbell St *BPR/DUF* DE56 .... **199** J7
 DERBYSE DE24 .... **257** G4
 EWD/SEL/PNX NG16 .... **202** F6 **🖪**
Camping La *SHEFS* S8 .... **55** H8
Campion Dr *ECK/KIL* S21 .... **73** M4 **🖪**
Campion Hl *CDON/KEG* DE74 ... **271** K6
Campion Rd *SWAD* DE11 .... **283** H6
Campion St *DERBYSE* DE24 ..... **256** A7 **🖪**
Campsie Cl *DERBYSE* DE24 ..... **256** A7 **🖪**
Camp St *DERBY* DE1 .... **240** D3
Canada St *BPR/DUF* DE56 ...... **199** K8
Canal Bank *BWSH/BRSTN* DE72.. **271** K1
Canal Br *ECK/KIL* S21 .... **74** A4
 RDERBYSW DE65 .... **266** D4
Canal St *BUT* DE14 .... **273** M8 **🖪**
 CHF/WBR SK23 .... **59** J3
 DERBY DE1 .... **5** H6
 ILK DE7 .... **230** D1
 LGEAT NG10 .... **244** E5
 LGEAT NG10 .... **260** F1
 MPL/ROM SK6 .... **32** M1
 MSHM DE12 .... **295** K3
Canal Whf *CHNE* S41 .... **3** J1
Canberra Cl
 BSTN/STPLFD NG9 .... **245** J1 **🖪**
 MCKLVR DE3 .... **239** H8
Cannell Ct *CLCR* S45 .... **144** E6
Canner Cl *SWAD* DE11 .... **283** K8
Cannock Wy *LGEAT* NG10 .... **261** K3
Cannon St *HYDE* SK14 .... **16** F5
 MSFDW NG19 .... **164** C1
Canon Cl *ILK* DE7 .... **217** H5
Canon's Wk *DERBYW* DE22 ..... **226** C8 **🖪**
Cantelupe Rd *ILK* DE7 .... **230** C2
Canterbury Av *FUL* S10 .... **53** M2
Canterbury Cl *MSFDW* NG19 .... **149** M5
Canterbury Crs *FUL* S10 .... **53** M2
Canterbury Dr *ASHZ* LE65 ...... **291** K3
 FUL S10 .... **53** M2
Canterbury Rd *MTLK* DE4 ...... **183** J2
 SHEFS S8 .... **55** L5
 STPNHL/WNHL DE15 .... **274** F7
Canterbury St *DERBYE* DE21 ... **241** H1
Canterbury Ter *MTLK* DE4 ...... **183** J2
Cantley Cl *DERBYSE* DE24 ...... **257** G1 **🖪**
Cantley Rd *ALFN* DE55 .... **187** M4
Canver Cl *WOL/BIL/BRX* NG8 ... **231** M4 **🖪**
Canwick Cl
 WOL/BIL/BRX NG8 .... **231** M5 **🖪**
Capel Ri *STV/CWN* S43 .... **111** G2 **🖪**
Capesthorne Rd *MPL/ROM* SK6... **42** B3
Cape St *MSFD* NG18 .... **164** C5
Captain's La
 BUTN/AL/TUT DE13 .... **286** A2
Capthorne Cl *RCH* S42 .... **109** J3
Cardales Cl *RDERBYSW* DE65 ... **255** G8 **🖪**
Cardean Cl *DERBY* DE1 .... **240** E3 **🖪**
Carder Gn *BUX* SK17 .... **134** E4 **🖪**

Cardigan St *DERBYE* DE21 ...... **241** G3
Cardinal Cl *DERBYE* DE21 ...... **227** J8
Cardlemere La *BUX* SK17 .... **152** C8
Cardrona Cl *DERBYE* DE21 ..... **227** J8
Cardwell Av *HAN/WDH* S13 ..... **57** J3
Cardwell Dr *HAN/WDH* S13 ..... **57** J3
Carfield Av *SHEFS* S8 .... **55** L5
Carfield La *SHEFS* S8 .... **55** M5
Carisbrook Av *MSFD* NG18 ...... **165** K3
Carisbrooke Gdns
 NORM/LIT DE23 .... **255** M4 **🖪**
Carley Dr *MOS* S20 .... **73** J1
Carlin Cl *BWSH/BRSTN* DE72 .... **260** B2
Carlin St *HAN/WDH* S13 .... **57** H5
Carlisle Av *NORM/LIT* DE23 .... **255** L2
Carlisle Cl *CHNE* S41 .... **91** H7
Carlisle Av *SHEFS* S8 .... **99** K2
Carlisle Rd *BUX* SK17 .... **99** K3
Carlton Av *DERBYSE* DE24 ..... **257** H6
 MTLK DE4 .... **140** D4
Carlton Cl *CLCR* S45 .... **145** G8
 HEANOR DE75 .... **202** D7 **🖪**
 MOS S20 .... **72** F4
Carlton Dr *DERBYSE* DE24 ..... **257** H6
Carlton Gdns *DERBYSE* DE24 ... **257** H6
Carlton Rd *CHSW* S40 .... **128** C4
 LGEAT NG10 .... **260** E5
 NORM/LIT DE23 .... **256** A1
Carlton St *BUTN/AL/TUT* DE13 ... **273** L4
 MSFD NG18 .... **164** F1
Carlyon Gdns *CHSW* S40 .... **128** C2 **🖪**
Carnarvon Gv *ASH* NG17 .... **162** E7
Carnarvon La *ASH* NG17 .... **162** C8
Carnarvon St *ASH* NG17 .... **162** E3
Carnegie St *NORM/LIT* DE23 ... **256** D2 **🖪**
Carnfield Hl *ALFN* DE55 .... **176** A5
Carnforth Cl *BSTN/STPLFD* NG9 .. **245** G5
 MCKLVR DE3 .... **255** H1 **🖪**
Carnoustie Av *CHSW* S40 ...... **127** M2
Carnoustie Cl *MCKLVR* DE3 .... **239** J8 **🖪**
Carol Crs *DERBYE* DE21 .... **241** J6
Caroline Cl *DERBYSE* DE24 .... **257** M3
Caroline Ct *ILK* DE7 .... **230** D4
The Carousels *BUT* DE14 ...... **273** M5
Carpenter Av *MSFDW* NG19 .... **149** C8
 STV/CWN S43 .... **93** L7
Carpenter Cl
 STPNHL/WNHL DE15 .... **281** M1
Carpenter Cft *HACK/IN* S12 .... **56** F4 **🖪**
Carpenter Gdns *HACK/IN* S12 .. **56** F4 **🖪**
Carper La *ASHB* DE6 .... **210** C7
Carr Bank Cl *ECC* S11 .... **54** C2
Carr Bank Dr *ECC* S11 .... **54** C2 **🖪**
Carr Bank La *ECC* S11 .... **54** B2
Carr Brow *MPL/ROM* SK6 .... **42** D3
Carr Cl *ALFN* DE55 .... **176** D3
Carrfield Av *BSTN/STPLFD* NG9 .. **261** J1
 LGEAT NG10 .... **261** J2
Carrfield Cl *ASH* NG17 .... **163** G7 **🖪**
Carrfield La *SHEFP/MNR* S2 .... **55** L4
Carrfield Rd *SHEFS* S8 .... **55** L4
Carr Flds *ILK* DE7 .... **214** F3
Carrfield St *SHEFP/MNR* S2 .... **55** L4
Carr Forge Cl *HACK/IN* S12 .... **57** L6
Carr Forge La *HACK/IN* S12 .... **57** L6
Carr Forge Mt *HACK/IN* S12 .... **57** L6
Carr Forge Pl *HACK/IN* S12 .... **57** L6
Carr Forge Rd *HACK/IN* S12 .... **57** L6
Carr Forge Ter *HACK/IN* S12 ... **57** L6
Carr Forge Vw *HACK/IN* S12 ... **57** L6
Carrhouse La *HYDE* SK14 ...... **16** F2
The Carriage Dr *GLSP* SK13 .... **17** H6
Carriers Rd *RDERBYSW* DE65 ... **265** M3
Carrington Rd *ECC* S11 .... **54** C2
Carrington St *DERBY* DE1 ...... **5** H6
Carr La *ALFN* DE55 .... **159** C7
 ALFN DE55 .... **176** A3
 BSVR S44 .... **131** K4
 DRON S18 .... **69** M8
 EDL/UDV S33 .... **50** C4
 EDL/UDV S33 .... **51** H8
 MTLK DE4 .... **173** H8
 MTLK DE4 .... **173** H8 **🖪**
Car Rd *TOT/DORE* S17 .... **88** C5
Carron Cl *DERBYSE* DE24 ...... **256** B6
Carrs Cl *CDON/KEG* DE74 ...... **271** K7 **🖪**
Carr Vale Rd *BSVR* S44 .... **131** J4
Carrwood Rd *DRON* S18 .... **90** F6
 ECK/KIL S21 .... **93** L2
Carsick Gv *FUL* S10 .... **54** A1
Carsick Hill Crs *FUL* S10 ...... **54** A1
Carsick Hill Dr *FUL* S10 .... **54** B1
Carsick Hill Rd *FUL* S10 .... **54** A1
Carsick Hill Wy *FUL* S10 .... **54** A1
Carsick View Rd *FUL* S10 ...... **54** A1
Carsic La *ASH* NG17 .... **163** H7
Carsic Rd *ASH* NG17 .... **163** G5
Carsington Cl *CHSW* S40 ...... **109** L5
Carsington Crs *DERBYW* DE22 .. **226** A8
Carsington Ms *DERBYW* DE22 .. **240** A1
Carson Mt *HACK/IN* S12 ...... **56** E7
Carson Rd *DERBYE* DE21 ...... **241** L4 **🖪**
Carter Cl *LGEAT* NG10 .... **260** E3
Carter Hall La *HACK/IN* S12 ... **56** E8
Carterhall Rd *HACK/IN* S12 .... **56** E8
Carter Knowle Av *ECC* S11 .... **54** C5
Carter Knowle Rd *ECC* S11 .... **54** C5
Carter La East *ALFN* DE55 ..... **176** E4
Carter La West *ALFN* DE55 .... **176** E5
 SBK/MW NG20 .... **133** G6
Carter Lodge Av *HACK/IN* S12 .. **57** K6
Carter Lodge Dr *HACK/IN* S12 .. **57** K6
Carter Lodge Pl *HACK/IN* S12 .. **57** L6
Carter Lodge Ri *HACK/IN* S12 .. **57** L6
Carter Pl *SHEFS* S8 .... **55** L4
Carter Rd *BSTN/STPLFD* NG9 ... **245** K7 **🖪**
 SHEFS S8 .... **55** K4
Carter St *DERBYSE* DE24 ...... **257** G4
 UTXR ST14 .... **247** M3
Cartledge La *DRON* S18 .... **89** K2
Cartmel Cl *DRON* S18 .... **90** B1 **🖪**
Cartmel Crs *CHNE* S41 .... **110** A2
Cartmell Rd *SHEFS* S8 .... **55** H7
Cartmel Rd *SHEFS* S8 .... **55** H7 **🖪**

Cartworth Moor Rd
 HOLM/MEL HD7 .... **9** H2
Cartwright La *ALFN* DE55 ...... **177** K3
Cartwright St *WRKN* S81 .... **77** H3
Car Vale Dr *SHEFP/MNR* S2 .... **56** F2
Car Vale Vw *SHEFP/MNR* S2 .... **56** F2
Carver Cl *AU/AST/KP* S26 ...... **75** H3
Carver Dr *MPL/ROM* SK6 .... **32** B5
Carver Rd *BUTN/AL/TUT* DE13 .. **273** M4
 MPL/ROM SK6 .... **32** B5
Carver Wy *AU/AST/KP* S26 ..... **75** H4
Cary Rd *ECK/KIL* S21 .... **72** E7
 SHEFP/MNR S2 .... **56** C2
Cascade Gv *NORM/LIT* DE23 ... **255** K3 **🖪**
Casey La *BUT* DE14 .... **273** L6
Casson Av *DERBYSE* DE24 ..... **257** K4
Casson Dr *AU/AST/KP* S26 ..... **75** H3
Casson St *EWD/SEL/PNX* NG16 .. **188** B6
Castings Rd *NORM/LIT* DE23 ... **256** E2 **🖪**
Castlebeck Av
 SHEFP/MNR S2 .... **56** F1 **🖪**
Castlebeck Cft
 SHEFP/MNR S2 .... **56** F2
Castlebeck Dr *SHEFP/MNR* S2 .. **56** F2
Castle Cl *BWSH/BRSTN* DE72 ... **243** G8 **🖪**
Castlecraig Ct
 DERBYSE DE24 .... **256** B8 **🖪**
Castle Cft *DERBYSE* DE24 ..... **258** A5
Castledale Cr *SHEFP/MNR* S2 .. **56** E2 **🖪**
Castledale Gv *SHEFP/MNR* S2 .. **56** E2 **🖪**
Castledale Pl *SHEFP/MNR* S2 .. **56** E2 **🖪**
Castle Dr *ALFN* DE55 .... **188** A2
 BKWL DE45 .... **123** H3
 RIPLEY DE5 .... **201** M2
Castle Edge Rd *NM/HAY* SK22 ... **33** M8
Castle Farm La *WRKS* S80 ..... **97** M3
Castlefields
 EWD/SEL/PNX NG16 .... **188** C7
Castlegate La *BKWL* DE45 ...... **103** M4
Castle Gn *BSVR* S44 .... **131** L2
Castle Hayes La
 BUTN/AL/TUT DE13 .... **263** K6
Castle HI *BPR/DUF* DE56 .... **213** H6
 CDON/KEG DE74 .... **271** L6
 ECK/KIL S21 .... **73** G6
 GLSP SK13 .... **18** B7
 RDERBYSW DE65 .... **267** G1
Castle Hill Cl *ECK/KIL* S21 ..... **73** G6
Castle La *BSVR* S44 .... **131** J1
 EWD/SEL/PNX NG16 .... **188** B8
 MELB/CHEL DE73 .... **278** E3
Castle Ms *MELB/CHEL* DE73 .... **278** E3
 MSFDW NG19 .... **149** L7
The Castle Ms *SWAD* DE11 ..... **282** D5 **🖪**
Castle Mount Crs *BKWL* DE45 .. **123** G4 **🖪**
Castle Mount Wy
 BKWL DE45 .... **123** H4 **🖪**
Castle Orch *BPR/DUF* DE56 .... **213** H6
Castle Park Rd
 BUTN/AL/TUT DE13 .... **273** L3
Castlerigg Wy *DRON* S18 ...... **90** B1 **🖪**
Castle Rd *SWAD* DE11 .... **289** J2
Castlerow Cl *TOT/DORE* S17 ... **69** K4
Castlerow Dr *TOT/DORE* S17 ... **69** L4
Castleshaw Dr *NORM/LIT* DE23 .. **255** H3
Castle St *BKWL* DE45 .... **123** G4
 BSVR S44 .... **113** K8
 BUTN/AL/TUT DE13 .... **263** L3
 DERBY DE1 .... **5** G5
 EDL/UDV S33 .... **48** E8
 EWD/SEL/PNX NG16 .... **217** K1
 GLSP SK13 .... **17** K6
 MELB/CHEL DE73 .... **278** E3
 MSFD NG18 .... **164** C3
 MSFDW NG19 .... **149** L7
Castleton Av *ALFN* DE55 ...... **187** L4
 ILK DE7 .... **217** H5 **🖪**
 NORM/LIT DE23 .... **256** C7
Castleton Cl *MSFDW* NG19 .... **149** M6
Castleton Crs *GLSP* SK13 ..... **25** H1
Castleton Dr *MPL/ROM* SK6 .... **42** C4
Castleton Gv *STV/CWN* S43 .... **111** G3
Castleton Rd *EDL/UDV* S33 .... **49** G7
 HATH/EY S32 .... **66** B2
Castle Vw *ECK/KIL* S21 .... **73** G7
 EWD/SEL/PNX NG16 .... **202** D6
Castleview *RDERBYSW* DE65 ... **263** M2 **🖪**
Castle View Dr *MTLK* DE4 ..... **171** M4
Castle Wy *ASHZ* LE65 .... **291** K6
The Castle Wy
 RDERBYSW DE65 .... **266** B5
Castlewood Crs *FUL* S10 ...... **53** L2 **🖪**
Castlewood Dr *FUL* S10 .... **53** L2
Castle Yd *CHSW* S40 .... **3** G5
Cat And Fiddle La *ILK* DE7 ... **229** G4
Catchford Vw *CHSW* S40 ...... **109** L3 **🖪**
Catcliff Cl *BKWL* DE45 .... **123** G6
Cathedral Rd *DERBY* DE1 ..... **4** D2
Cathedral Vw *NORM/LIT* DE23 .. **240** E8 **🖪**
Catherine Av *ILK* DE7 .... **230** C4 **🖪**
 MSFDW NG19 .... **149** M7
Catherine St *ASHB* DE6 .... **193** L8
Catherine St *ALFN* DE55 ...... **175** M6
 CHSW S40 .... **2** D4
 NORM/LIT DE23 .... **240** E8 **🖪**
Catholme La
 BUTN/AL/TUT DE13 .... **286** B4
Catkin Dr *EWD/SEL/PNX* NG16 .. **217** M3
Cat La *SHEFS* S8 .... **55** M5
Caton Cl *ASH* NG17 .... **163** G7
Cator La North
 BSTN/STPLFD NG9 .... **245** M4
Cator Rd *MSFDW* NG19 .... **148** F7
Catterick Dr *MCKLVR* DE3 ..... **254** F1
Catton La *MSHM* DE12 .... **287** L5
Caudwell Cl *RCH* S42 .... **145** G2 **🖪**
Caudwell Dr *MSFD* NG18 ...... **164** E7
Cauldon Dr *CHSW* S40 .... **109** K5 **🖪**
Cauldwell Rd *ASH* NG17 ...... **164** C8
 MSHM DE12 .... **288** D4
Caunton Cl *MSFD* NG18 ...... **164** C4
Caunt's Crs *ASH* NG17 .... **163** C7
Causeway *DERBYW* DE22 ...... **226** B8
Causeway Gdns
 TOT/DORE S17 .... **68** F2 **🖪**
Causeway Gld *TOT/DORE* S17 .. **68** F2 **🖪**
Causeway Head Rd
 TOT/DORE S17 .... **68** F2
Causeway La *MTLK* DE4 ...... **173** J5
The Causeway *CLCR* S45 ..... **143** G6 **🖪**
 HATH/EY S32 .... **86** B5

Causeway The *MTLK* DE4 .... 183 J2
The Causeway *TOT/DORE* S17 ... 69 G3
Cavan Dr *DERBYE* DE21 .... 241 L6
Cavell Dr *CLCR* S45 .... 145 H8
Cavendish Av *ASH* NG17 .... 163 H7
  BUX SK17 .... 99 J4
  DERBYW DE22 .... 226 C7
  TOT/DORE S17 .... 69 H3
Cavendish Cl *ASHB* DE6 .... 248 F1
  BPR/DUF DE56 .... 213 G8
  BWSH/BRSTN DE72 .... 259 K8
  CDON/KEG DE74 .... 271 K8
  RCH S42 .... 146 B1
  SWAD DE11 .... 282 D3
Cavendish Ct
  BWSH/BRSTN DE72 .... 271 K1
  DERBY DE1 .... 4 D3
Cavendish Crs
  BSTN/STPLFD NG9 .... 231 G8
  RIPLEY DE5 .... 200 F1
  STV/CWN S43 .... 95 K6
Cavendish Dr *ASHB* DE6 .... 208 A2
Cavendish Pl *STV/CWN* S43.... 92 E7
Cavendish Ri *DRON* S18 .... 90 C2
Cavendish Rd *BSVR* S44 .... 131 L2
  ECC S11 .... 54 F3
  ILK DE7 .... 230 C4
  LGEAT NG10 .... 244 F8
  MTLK DE4 .... 156 F4
Cavendish St *ASH* NG17 .... 163 K6
  CHSW S40 .... 3 H4
  DERBY DE1 .... 4 D3
  MSFD DE18 .... 164 C5
  MSFDW NG19 .... 149 K7
  SBK/MW NC20 .... 133 J2
  STV/CWN S43 .... 111 M2
Cavendish St North *CHNE* S41 ... 91 K8
Cavendish Wy *MCKLVR* DE3 ..... 239 H8
Caversfield Cl *NORM/LIT* DE23 ... 255 K2
Caversham Wy *ILK* DE7 .... 229 G2
Cavill Rd *SHEFS* S8 .... 55 K7
Cawdor Rd *SHEFP/MNR* S2...... 56 C4
Cawthorne Cl *SHEFS* S8 .... 55 H7
Cawthorne Gv *SHEFS* S8 .... 55 H7
Cawthorne Wy *MSFD* NG18 ..... 165 J3
Caxterway La *BUX* SK17 .... 101 H7
Caxton Cl *CHNE* S41 .... 92 A4
Caxton Ct *NORM/LIT* DE23 ..... 256 B3
Caxton St *NORM/LIT* DE23 ..... 256 B3
Cecil Av *DRON* S18 .... 70 D8
Cecil Cl *WRKS* S80 .... 77 K6
Cecil Rd *DRON* S18 .... 70 D8
  SWAD DE11 .... 282 C5
Cecil Sq *DERBY/MNR* S2 .... 55 J2
Cecil St *DERBYW* DE22 .... 240 A5
Cedar Av *ALFN* DE55 .... 175 K5
  CHSW S40 .... 110 A3
  LGEAT NG10 .... 260 F5
  MSFDW NG19 .... 149 L5
  RIPLEY DE5 .... 201 G1
Cedar Cl *ASH* NG17 .... 163 G3
  ASHB DE6 .... 208 A3
  BSVR S44 .... 147 L1
  ECK/KIL S21 .... 72 E8
  GLSP SK13 .... 17 L8
  LGEAT NG10 .... 244 E3
  SBK/MW NC20 .... 133 J6
  UTXR ST14 .... 247 J1
Cedar Cft *BPR/DUF* DE56 .... 214 E3
Cedar Dr *BWSH/BRSTN* DE72 ... 242 F6
  BPR/DUF DE56 .... 199 K8
  MSHM DE12 .... 288 C4
  MSHM DE12 .... 290 E4
  SWAD DE11 .... 282 D5
Cedar Pk *ILK* DE7 .... 230 B2
Cedar Park Dr *BSVR* S44 .... 113 M8
Cedar Rd *BUTN/AL/TUT* DE13 ... 286 A1
  CDON/KEG DE74 .... 271 L8
  MPL/ROM SK6 .... 32 B6
  SWAD DE11 .... 289 H3
Cedar St *ALFN* DE55 .... 159 M5
  DERBYW DE22 .... 240 B3
  MSFD DE18 .... 164 F5
  STV/CWN S43 .... 111 K3
Cedarwood Ct *DERBYE* DE21 ... 227 H8
Celandine Cl *DERBY* DE21 .... 227 J8
Celandine Ct *TOT/DORE* S17 ... 69 K5
Celandine Gdns *TOT/DORE* S17 ... 69 K5
Celandine Pl *SWAD* DE11 .... 283 H7
Celanese Rd *DERBYE* DE21 ..... 241 M7
Cemetery Av *ECC* S11 .... 55 G1
Cemetery Hill Nottingham Rd
  DERBYE DE21 .... 5 M2
Cemetery La *MTLK* DE4 .... 183 J2
  RIPLEY DE5 .... 201 G1
  STV/CWN S43 .... 112 B1
Cemetery Rd *ALFN* DE55 .... 187 L3
  BPR/DUF DE56 .... 199 K4
  BSTN/STPLFD NG9 .... 245 H3
  CHNE S41 .... 3 L5
  CLCR S45 .... 145 H8
  DRON S18 .... 90 E2
  ECC S11 .... 55 H2
  GLSP SK13 .... 17 M6
Cemetery Ter *STV/CWN* S43 ... 111 H3
Cenotaph Wy *ASHB* DE6 .... 212 A8
  BPR/DUF DE56 .... 213 L8
  ILK DE7 .... 229 M3
Central Av *ALFN* DE55 .... 176 C5
  BSTN/STPLFD NG9 .... 245 H2
  BWSH/BRSTN DE72 .... 258 E1
  CHSW S40 .... 2 D6
  ILK DE7 .... 228 C2
  LGEAT NG10 .... 244 E4
  MSFD DE18 .... 164 F5
  WRKS S80 .... 115 G2
Central Cl *DRON* S18 .... 91 H4
  SBK/MW NC20 .... 133 H7
Central Dr *ALFN* DE55 .... 176 B1
  BSVR S44 .... 111 J7
  BUX SK17 .... 100 A5
  CHNE S41 .... 3 L8
  RCH S42 .... 128 C7
  SBK/MW NC20 .... 133 H7
Central Rd *ALFN* DE55 .... 175 K6
Central St *ASH* NG17 .... 163 L6
  CHNE S41 .... 3 L8
  RCH S42 .... 146 B2
Central Wk *STV/CWN* S43 ...... 111 G3

Centre Ct *DERBY* DE1 .... 5 H8
Centre St *BSVR* S44 .... 147 G1
Century Av *MSFD* NG18 .... 164 C5
Chaddesden Cl *DRON* S18 .... 89 M1
Chaddesden La *DERBYE* DE21 ... 241 J5
Chaddesden Park Rd
  DERBYE DE21 .... 241 J4
Chadfield Rd *BPR/DUF* DE56 ... 213 H5
Chadwick Dr *DERBYE* DE24 ..... 257 H5
Chadwick Hl *MTLK* DE4 .... 154 D4
Chadwick Nick La *MTLK* DE4 ... 185 J3
Chadwick St *HAN/WDH* S13 .... 56 F3
Chadwick St *GLSP* SK13 .... 25 L2
  MPL/ROM SK6 .... 32 C5
Chaffinch Cl *DERBY* DE21 .... 242 C4
  MSFD NG18 .... 165 J3
Chaffinch Dr *UTXR* ST14 .... 247 M4
Chaffinch Ms *WRKN* S81 .... 77 M3
Chaff La *ASHB* DE6 .... 205 M1
Chain Bar La *MCKLVR* DE3 ...... 239 K8
  NORM/LIT DE23 .... 255 K1
Chalfont Sq *DERBYE* DE21 ...... 227 L8
Chalkley Rd *DERBYSE* DE24 .... 257 J5
Challands Cl *CHNE* S41 .... 3 M9
Challands Wy *CHNE* S41 .... 3 M9
Challis Av *DERBYE* DE21 .... 241 L3
Challoner Gn *MOS* S20 .... 73 H2
Challoner Wy *MOS* S20 .... 73 H2
Chalons Cl *ILK* DE7 .... 230 C1
Chalons Wy *ILK* DE7 .... 230 C2
Chambers Av *ILK* DE7 .... 230 E3
Chambers Ct *HYDE* SK14 .... 16 D7
Chambers St *DERBYSE* DE24 ... 257 H7
Champion Av *ILK* DE7 .... 216 F7
Champion Crs *MSFDW* NG19 ... 164 C2
Champion Hl *BPR/DUF* DE56 ... 216 F7
Chancery Cl *ASH* NG17 .... 163 K4
The Chancery
  BSTN/STPLFD NG9 .... 245 M3
Chancet Wood Cl *SHEFS* S8 .... 70 C2
Chancet Wood Dr *SHEFS* S8 ... 70 C2
Chancet Wood Ri *SHEFS* S8 .... 70 C2
Chandler Hill La *RCH* S42 .... 126 F1
Chandlers Ford *DERBYE* DE21 ... 227 J8
Chandos Crs *ECK/KIL* S21 .... 73 M4
Chandos Pole St
  DERBYE DE21 .... 240 A4
Chandres Ct *DERBYW* DE22 .... 226 B6
Chandwick Ct
  DERBYSE DE24 .... 256 A7
Chaneyfield Wy *CHSW* S40 ..... 109 L3
Chantrey Av *CHNE* S41 .... 110 C4
Chantrey Rd *SHEFS* S8 .... 55 J7
Chantry Cl *LGEAT* NG10 .... 260 D6
  MCKLVR DE3 .... 254 F1
  POY/DIS SK12 .... 43 H5
Chantry Fold *POY/DIS* SK12 ... 43 H4
Chantry La *BUX* SK17 .... 83 M6
Chantry Rd *POY/DIS* SK12 ...... 43 G4
The Chantry *MSFD* NG18 .... 165 J5
  GLSP SK13 .... 25 H4
Chapel Brow *GLSP* SK13 .... 17 K3
Chapel Cl *BKWL* DE45 .... 138 E5
  FUL S10 .... 54 C1
  RDERBYSW DE65 .... 266 E4
  STV/CWN S43 .... 95 H6
Chapel Cft *MTLK* DE4 .... 154 B4
  MTLK DE4 .... 171 G5
Chapel Ga *EDL/UDV* S33 .... 47 H6
Chapel Hl *CLCR* S45 .... 143 J6
  MTLK DE4 .... 124 E7
  MTLK DE4 .... 171 G5
Chapel La *ASHB* DE6 .... 179 L4
  ASHB DE6 .... 207 J4
  ASHB DE6 .... 234 D6
  ASHB DE6 .... 236 E2
  BKWL DE45 .... 125 G5
  BUTN/AL/TUT DE13 .... 262 C8
  BUTN/AL/TUT DE13 .... 264 E6
  BUTN/AL/TUT DE13 .... 272 D5
  DERBYE DE21 .... 241 K3
  DRON S18 .... 91 K1
  GLSP SK13 .... 17 J5
  MELB/CHEL DE73 .... 268 D4
  MELB/CHEL DE73 .... 269 K1
  MTLK DE4 .... 171 G6
  MTLK DE4 .... 183 J1
  MTLK DE4 .... 185 J2
  RDERBYSW DE65 .... 251 L2
Chapel La East *CHNE* S41 .... 129 G3
Chapel La West *CHSW* S40 ..... 109 M8
Chapel Mews Ct
  BSTN/STPLFD NG9 .... 245 L2
Chapel Rd *BSVR* S44 .... 131 J1
  CHF/WBR SK23 .... 59 J5
  EWD/SEL/PNX NG16 .... 189 H4
  NM/HAY SK22 .... 45 H1
  RCH S42 .... 129 H7
Chapel Rw
  BWSH/BRSTN DE72 .... 242 E8
Chapel St *ALFN* DE55 .... 160 D6
  ALFN DE55 .... 175 K6
  ALFN DE55 .... 187 M3
  ALFN DE55 .... 187 H3
  ASHZ LE65 .... 284 C7
  BKWL DE45 .... 120 E8
  BPR/DUF DE56 .... 185 L4
  BPR/DUF DE56 .... 199 J7
  BPR/DUF DE56 .... 213 M3
  BPR/DUF DE56 .... 213 J6
  BPR/DUF DE56 .... 214 D2
  BSTN/STPLFD NG9 .... 245 L2
  BUX SK17 .... 99 J3
  BUX SK17 .... 134 E4
  CHF/WBR SK23 .... 59 H2
  CHNE S41 .... 110 D2
  DERBY DE1 .... 4 D2
  DERBYE DE21 .... 242 B5
  EWD/SEL/PNX NG16 .... 189 K3
  GLSP SK13 .... 25 M1
  HAN/WDH S13 .... 57 L4
  HEANOR DE75 .... 216 D2
  ILK DE7 .... 230 C1
  LGEAT NG10 .... 261 H3
  MELB/CHEL DE73 .... 277 K5
  MELB/CHEL DE73 .... 278 E3
  MOS S20 .... 72 F4

MSFDW NG19 .... 148 D3
  MSHM DE12 .... 288 A7
  MSHM DE12 .... 295 J4
  MSHM DE12 .... 295 M5
  NM/HAY SK22 .... 34 F8
  NM/HAY SK22 .... 34 B3
  NM/HAY SK22 .... 43 L4
  RIPLEY DE5 .... 187 G8
  SBK/MW NC20 .... 115 K7
  STV/CWN S43 .... 111 J2
  SWAD DE11 .... 282 C4
  SWAD DE11 .... 283 H8
  SWAD DE11 .... 289 K1
  SWAD DE11 .... 289 H2
Chapel Ter *FUL* S10 .... 54 C1
Chapel Wk *HATH/EY* S32 .... 87 H8
Chapel Yd *ALFN* DE55 .... 174 B7
  DRON S18 .... 70 D8
Chaple Wy *GLSP* SK13 .... 17 J5
Chapman Av *DERBYSE* DE24 ... 257 L4
Chapman La *RCH* S42 .... 129 H7
Chapman Rd *HYDE* SK14 .... 24 B1
Chapmans Cft *MSHM* DE12 .... 288 A7
Chapmans Mdw *ASHZ* LE65 ... 291 M6
Chapter Cl *DERBYE* DE21 .... 227 G8
Chardin Av *MPL/ROM* SK6 ...... 32 F2
Charing Ct *DERBY* DE1 .... 240 E3
Charingworth Rd
  DERBYE DE21 .... 227 L8
Chariot Cl *DERBYSE* DE24 .... 258 A5
Charity Rd *ALFN* DE55 .... 187 L5
Charlbury Rd *NORM/LIT* DE23 ... 255 K2
Charles Ashmore Rd *SHEFS* S8 ... 70 C4
Charles Av *BSTN/STPLFD* NG9 ... 245 J2
  BSTN/STPLFD NG9 .... 245 M7
  DERBYE DE21 .... 242 A4
  EWD/SEL/PNX NG16 .... 217 L1
  LGEAT NG10 .... 244 E4
Charles Cl *ILK* DE7 .... 230 E4
Charles La *GLSP* SK13 .... 18 B8
Charles St *ALFN* DE55 .... 175 J5
  ALFN DE55 .... 187 M3
  ASH NG17 .... 163 K7
  BUX SK17 .... 99 M2
  CHSW S40 .... 2 C4
  GLSP SK13 .... 25 M1
  LGEAT NG10 .... 261 C4
  MSFDW NG19 .... 149 M6
  MSFD NG18 .... 164 D1
  SWAD DE11 .... 282 C4
Charleston Cl *SWAD* DE11 ...... 282 D3
Charleston Rd *DERBYE* DE21 ... 241 M4
Charlestown Dr *DERBYW* DE22 ... 226 A6
Charlestown Rd *GLSP* SK13 .... 25 M2
Charlesworth Crs
  CHF/WBR SK23 .... 44 A7
Charlesworth Rd *CHF/WBR* SK23 ... 44 A7
Charlesworth St *BSVR* S44 ..... 131 K2
Charley La *EDL/UDV* S33 .... 64 D3
Charlotte La *BPR/DUF* DE56 ... 199 J7
Charlotte Rd *SHEF* S1 .... 55 K1
  SHEFP/MNR S2 .... 55 L1
Charlotte St *ILK* DE7 .... 217 H7
  NORM/LIT DE23 .... 240 D8
Charlton Av *LGEAT* NG10 .... 261 J2
Charlton Cl *MSHM* DE12 .... 288 F4
Charnley Av *ECC* S11 .... 54 F5
Charnley Cl *ECC* S11 .... 54 E4
Charnley Dr *ECC* S11 .... 54 F5
Charnley Ri *ECC* S11 .... 54 F5
Charnock Av *HACK/IN* S12 ..... 56 E8
Charnock Crs *HACK/IN* S12 .... 56 D7
Charnock Dale Rd *HACK/IN* S12 ... 56 D8
Charnock Dr *HACK/IN* S12 ...... 56 D7
Charnock Gv *HACK/IN* S12 ...... 56 E8
Charnock Hall Rd *HACK/IN* S12 ... 56 E8
Charnock View Rd *HACK/IN* S12 ... 56 E8
Charnock Wood Rd *HACK/IN* S12... 56 E8
Charnwood Av *BPR/DUF* DE56 ... 199 J6
  BWSH/BRSTN DE72 .... 242 F8
  CDON/KEG DE74 .... 271 M7
  LGEAT NG10 .... 244 D6
  LGEAT NG10 .... 260 E6
  NORM/LIT DE23 .... 256 A5
Charnwood Cl *ALFN* DE55 ...... 187 J3
Charnwood Dr *RIPLEY* DE5 ..... 200 F1
Charnwood Gv *MSFD* NG18 .... 165 K3
  MSFDW NG19 .... 149 L5
Charnwood Rd
  BUTN/AL/TUT DE13 .... 273 L3
Charnwood St *ASH* NG17 .... 177 M1
  DERBY DE1 .... 4 E7
Charterhouse Cl
  DERBYE DE21 .... 227 J7
Charter Pk *ILK* DE7 .... 230 B3
Charterstone La
  DERBYW DE22 .... 226 B6
Chartwell Av *RCH* S42 .... 128 A5
Chartwell Dr *DERBYE* DE21 .... 5 K3
Chasecliff Cl *CHSW* S40 .... 110 A5
Chase Rd *BPR/DUF* DE56 .... 185 J6
The Chase *BPR/DUF* DE56 ...... 214 E2
  DERBYE DE21 .... 214 A8
  DERBYSE DE24 .... 256 C6
Chase Vw *MTLK* DE4 .... 185 J1
Chatfield Cl
  STPNHL/WNHL DE15 .... 281 M1
Chatfield Rd *SHEFS* S8 .... 55 H8
Chatham Av *ALFN* DE55 .... 175 M7
Chatham Ct *BPR/DUF* DE56 ... 200 A6
Chatham St *NORM/LIT* DE23... 256 D2
Chatsworth Av
  BSTN/STPLFD NG9 .... 245 M8
  CHSW S40 .... 109 L8
  EWD/SEL/PNX NG16 .... 189 K3
  LGEAT NG10 .... 260 D1
  MTLK DE4 .... 156 C3
  MTLK DE4 .... 185 J1
  SBK/MW NC20 .... 133 H4
Chatsworth Cl *ALFN* DE55 ...... 163 J5
  ASH NG17 .... 163 J5
  BSVR S44 .... 113 M8
  LGEAT NG10 .... 244 E6
  MSFD NG18 .... 165 K1
Chatsworth Ct *ILK* DE7 .... 229 H2
  STV/CWN S43 .... 112 A2
Chatsworth Crs
  BPR/DUF DE56 .... 185 L5
  DERBYE DE22 .... 226 C8

Chatsworth Dr
  BUTN/AL/TUT DE13 .... 263 M4
  DERBYE DE21 .... 214 A8
  MCKLVR DE3 .... 239 H7
  MSFD NG18 .... 165 J8
  RCH S42 .... 145 J4
Chatsworth Park Av
  HACK/IN S12 .... 56 D5
Chatsworth Park Dr
  HACK/IN S12 .... 56 D5
Chatsworth Park Gv
  HACK/IN S12 .... 56 D5
Chatsworth Park Rd
  HACK/IN S12 .... 56 D5
Chatsworth Pl *DRON* S18 .... 70 A8
Chatsworth Rd *BUX* SK17 ...... 100 A3
  CHSW S40 .... 2 C4
  MPL/ROM SK6 .... 42 C4
  MTLK DE4 .... 140 D1
  SWAD DE11 .... 282 D4
  TOT/DORE S17 .... 69 H4
  WRKS S80 .... 114 F1
Chatsworth St *ALFN* DE55 ...... 161 K4
  ASH NG17 .... 163 K7
  NORM/LIT DE23 .... 256 B7
Chatteris Dr *DERBYE* DE21 ..... 241 G1
Chatterton La *MPL/ROM* SK6 ... 33 M3
Chaucer Cl *BUT* DE14 .... 274 A4
Chaucer Crs *ASH* NG17 .... 163 L6
Chaucer Dr *DRON* S18 .... 90 F5
Chaucer Rd *CHNE* S41 .... 110 C2
Chaucer St *ILK* DE7 .... 230 C1
  NORM/LIT DE23 .... 256 B3
Chavery Rd *CLCR* S45 .... 145 H6
Cheadle Cl *NORM/LIT* DE23 .... 255 L1
Cheadle Rd *UTXR* ST14 .... 247 L1
Cheam Cl *DERBYW* DE22 .... 239 H4
Cheapside *BPR/DUF* DE56 ...... 199 J7
  DERBY DE1 .... 4 D3
Chedworth Dr
  DERBYE DE24 .... 258 A4
Cheedale Av *CHSW* S40 .... 110 A5
Cheedale *BUX* SK17 .... 100 A3
Cheedale Cl *CHSW* S40 .... 110 A4
  STPNHL/WNHL DE15 .... 274 D5
Cheetham Av *DRON* S18 .... 91 H5
Chellaston La
  BWSH/BRSTN DE72 .... 270 B2
  MELB/CHEL DE73 .... 269 M1
Chellaston Park Ct
  MELB/CHEL DE73 .... 269 J1
Chellaston Rd
  DERBYSE DE24 .... 257 H6
Chelmarsh Cl
  MELB/CHEL DE73 .... 257 K7
Chelmorton Pl *DERBYE* DE21 ... 241 J2
Chelmsford Cl *MCKLVR* DE3 ... 238 F7
Chelsea Cl *ECC* S11 .... 54 F3
Chelsea Ri *ECC* S11 .... 54 F3
Chelsea Rd *ECC* S11 .... 54 F4
Cheltenham Cl
  BSTN/STPLFD NG9 .... 245 J8
Cheltenham Ct *MSFD* NG18 ... 165 J5
Cheltenham Dr *ASHZ* LE65 ..... 291 K3
Chelwood Rd *MELB/CHEL* DE73... 257 J8
Chepstow Cl *CHSW* S40 .... 128 C2
Chepstow Wk *MSFD* NG18 ..... 165 J3
Chequer La *BPR/DUF* DE56 ..... 198 A1
Chequers La *DERBYE* DE21 ..... 5 L3
Chequers Rd *DERBYE* DE21 .... 5 K3
Cheribough Rd
  CDON/KEG DE74 .... 271 K8
Cheriton Cl *HYDE* SK14 .... 16 A3
  MSFDW NG19 .... 164 B1
Cheriton Dr *ILK* DE7 .... 216 F7
Cheriton Gdns
  NORM/LIT DE23 .... 255 H3
Cherry Bank Rd *SHEFS* S8 ...... 55 K7
Cherrybrook Dr *DERBYE* DE21 ... 227 L2
Cherry Cl *ALFN* DE55 .... 176 E3
  BWSH/BRSTN DE72 .... 260 B2
  SBK/MW NC20 .... 133 H4
Cherry Ct *BUT* DE14 .... 280 C2
Cherrycroft *MPL/ROM* SK6 ..... 32 B1
Cherry Gv *MSFD* NG18 .... 164 B4
Cherry Leys
  STPNHL/WNHL DE15 .... 274 F6
Cherry St *SHEFP/MNR* S2 ...... 55 K2
Cherry St South *SHEFP/MNR* S2 ... 55 K2
Cherry Tree Av *ALFN* DE55 ..... 187 K3
  BPR/DUF DE56 .... 199 K4
  RIPLEY DE5 .... 201 G2
  WRKN S81 .... 77 J3
Cherry Tree Cl *BSVR* S44 .... 131 M1
  BWSH/BRSTN DE72 .... 244 C6
  ECC S11 .... 55 G3
  EWD/SEL/PNX NG16 .... 203 H2
  ILK DE7 .... 230 A4
  MSFDW NG19 .... 149 L6
  RDERBYSW DE65 .... 253 G8
  SWAD DE11 .... 282 C4
Cherry Tree Ct *MSHM* DE12 ... 290 E4
Cherry Tree Dell *ECC* S11 .... 55 G3
  BSVR S44 .... 112 C6
  BUX SK17 .... 100 A1
  ECK/KIL S21 .... 73 M5
Cherry Tree Gv *RCH* S42 .... 145 J5
  STV/CWN S43 .... 93 M7
Cherry Tree Ms *DERBYE* DE21 ... 241 L6
Cherry Tree Rd *ABRD* S7 .... 55 G3
Cherrytree Rd
  STPNHL/WNHL DE15 .... 281 J4
Chertpit La *BKWL* DE45 .... 103 M4
Chertsey Cl *CHSW* S40 .... 128 C2
Chertsey Ct *ILK* DE7 .... 229 G2
Chertsey Rd *MCKLVR* DE3 ...... 238 F8
Cherwell Cl *STV/CWN* S43 ...... 111 H1
Chesapeake Rd *DERBYE* DE21 ... 241 L4
Chesham Cl *GLSP* SK13 .... 17 K5
Chesham Dr *BSTN/STPLFD* NG9 ... 231 L8
Cheshire Ring Canal Wk
  MPL/ROM SK6 .... 32 C2
Cheshire St *DERBYSE* DE24 .... 257 G5
Cheshire Wy
  EWD/SEL/PNX NG16 .... 188 F6
Chessel Cl *SHEFS* S8 .... 55 K6

Chester Av *DERBYW* DE22 ...... 226 E5
Chesterfield Av *LGEAT* NG10 ... 261 J3
  STV/CWN S43 .... 92 B7
  SWAD DE11 .... 282 B4
Chesterfield Dr *MSHM* DE12 ... 288 F4
Chesterfield Rd *ALFN* DE55 .... 159 M7
  ALFN DE55 .... 175 J4
  ASH NG17 .... 162 A5
  BPR/DUF DE56 .... 186 B7
  BPR/DUF DE56 .... 199 K5
  BSVR S44 .... 111 L8
  BSVR S44 .... 113 H5
  CHNE S41 .... 110 F4
  DRON S18 .... 90 F2
  ECK/KIL S21 .... 92 C1
  MSFDW NG19 .... 148 D5
  MTLK DE4 .... 124 D7
  MTLK DE4 .... 140 D1
  MTLK DE4 .... 141 G8
  MTLK DE4 .... 157 G4
  RCH S42 .... 129 M8
  SHEFS S8 .... 55 J4
  STV/CWN S43 .... 94 D5
  STV/CWN S43 .... 111 M2
  STV/CWN S43 .... 111 H3
Chesterfield Rd North
  MSFDW NG19 .... 149 G8
Chesterfield Rd South
  MSFDW NG19 .... 164 C2
  SHEFS S8 .... 70 D4
Chesterford Ct
  NORM/LIT DE23 .... 255 J4
Chester Gdns *SWAD* DE11 ...... 282 E8
Chester Gn *BSTN/STPLFD* NG9 ... 245 H8
Chester Green Rd *DERBY* DE1 ... 240 D5
Chesterman Cl
  EWD/SEL/PNX NG16 .... 217 L6
Chester St *CHSW* S40 .... 2 C3
  MSFDW NG19 .... 164 B2
Chesterton Av *DERBYE* DE23 ... 256 B3
Chesterton Rd *BUT* DE14 .... 274 A4
  DERBYE DE21 .... 242 B4
Chestnut Av *ALFN* DE55 .... 188 A5
  BPR/DUF DE56 .... 199 K8
  ECK/KIL S21 .... 72 E8
  ECK/KIL S21 .... 73 L5
  MCKLVR DE3 .... 239 H7
  NORM/LIT DE23 .... 4 E9
  RIPLEY DE5 .... 201 G2
  SWAD DE11 .... 282 E4
Chestnut Cl *BPR/DUF* DE56 .... 213 H8
  BUX SK17 .... 99 L1
  DRON S18 .... 90 E2
  ILK DE7 .... 214 F3
  MSHM DE12 .... 290 E5
  NM/HAY SK22 .... 44 B1
Chestnut Dr *ALFN* DE55 .... 176 E6
  ASHB DE6 .... 208 A3
  EWD/SEL/PNX NG16 .... 189 J3
  MSFD NG18 .... 165 H8
  RDERBYSW DE65 .... 267 M8
  SBK/MW NC20 .... 133 G6
  STV/CWN S43 .... 95 G6
  WRKS S80 .... 96 A8
Chestnut Gn *SWAD* DE11 .... 282 E8
Chestnut Gv *ALFN* DE55 .... 161 J5
  BWSH/BRSTN DE72 .... 242 F7
  LGEAT NG10 .... 244 D3
  MSFDW NG19 .... 149 L5
  RDERBYSW DE65 .... 253 L6
Chestnut Hl *MSFD* NG18 .... 165 H8
Chestnut La *CRTAM* B79 .... 293 H8
Chestnut Ms *MSFD* NG18 .... 165 H8
Chestnut Rd
  EWD/SEL/PNX NG16 .... 202 D7
  STPNHL/WNHL DE15 .... 281 J3
The Chestnuts *LGEAT* NG10 ... 260 D2
Chestnut Wy *ALFN* DE55 .... 187 J2
  RDERBYSW DE65 .... 266 F8
Chetwynd Rd
  BSTN/STPLFD NG9 .... 245 L7
  BSTN/STPLFD NG9 .... 245 K8
Chevely Ct *DERBYE* DE21 .... 241 G2
Cheverton Cl *DERBYSE* DE24 ... 258 A5
Chevin Av *BWSH/BRSTN* DE72 ... 242 F8
  MCKLVR DE3 .... 239 J8
Chevin Bank *BPR/DUF* DE56 ... 213 G4
Chevin Pl *DERBYW* DE22 .... 240 C3
Chevin Rd *BPR/DUF* DE56 ...... 199 G6
  BPR/DUF DE56 .... 213 H5
  DERBYW DE22 .... 240 C3
The Chevin
  BUTN/AL/TUT DE13 .... 273 M1
Chevin V *BPR/DUF* DE56 .... 213 H5
Cheviot Av *EWD/SEL/PNX* NG16... 188 C7
Cheviot Cl *SWAD* DE11 .... 282 D7
Cheviot Rd *LGEAT* NG10 .... 260 D1
Cheviot St *DERBYW* DE22 .... 239 M5
Cheviot Wy *CHSW* S40 .... 109 M5
Chewton Av
  EWD/SEL/PNX NG16 .... 217 K1
Chewton St
  EWD/SEL/PNX NG16 .... 217 K1
Cheyenne Gdns *DERBYE* DE21 ... 241 L5
Chichester Cl *ILK* DE7 .... 230 D2
  .... 163M4
Chigwell Wy *STV/CWN* S43 .... 92 E7
Chilson Dr *MCKLVR* DE3 .... 238 F7
Chiltern Cl *CHSW* S40 .... 109 M6
  RCH S42 .... 129 J7
Chiltern Dr *ILK* DE7 .... 229 H2
Chiltern Gdns *LGEAT* NG10 .... 260 D1
Chiltern Ri *ASHZ* LE65 .... 291 L5
Chiltern Rd *SWAD* DE11 .... 282 D8
Chilton Crs *MSFDW* NG19 ...... 149 M4
Chilwell La *BSTN/STPLFD* NG9 ... 245 L3
Chime Cl *DERBYE* DE21 .... 227 H8
China House Yd *MTLK* DE4 ..... 183 J2
The Chine *ALFN* DE55 .... 176 E7
Chingford Ct *DERBYE* DE22 .... 239 L4
Chinley Rd *DERBYE* DE21 .... 241 K1
Chippinghouse Rd *ABRD* S7 ... 55 J3
  SHEFS S8 .... 55 J3
Chirnside *MSFDW* NG19 .... 164 A5
Chiswick Cl *DERBYW* DE22 ..... 239 J4
Chiverton Cl *DRON* S18 .... 70 D8

Choppards Bank Rd
HOLM/MEL HD7 .... 9 K1
Chorley Av FUL S10 .... 53 M2
Chorley Dr FUL S10 .... 53 M2
Chorley Pl FUL S10 .... 53 M3
Chorley Rd FUL S10 .... 54 A2
Chrysalis Wy
EWD/SEL/PNX NG16 .... 202 F7
Chunal La GLSP SK13 .... 25 M4
Church Aly BKWL DE45 .... 123 G5
Church Av ASH NG17 .... 163 G8
BUX SK17 .... 81 L5
BUX SK17 .... 83 M6
CLCR S45 .... 145 H7
RDERBYSW DE65 .... 264 A2
SWAD DE11 .... 282 E7
Church Bank CDLE ST10 .... 190 C3
HATH/EY S32 .... 66 D2
Church Bk CHF/WBR SK23 .... 59 G3
Church Broughton Rd
RDERBYSW DE65 .... 251 M7
Church Brow CHF/WBR SK23 .... 60 E4
HYDE SK14 .... 16 D7
Church Cl ALFN DE55 .... 175 M2
BSTN/STPLFD NG9 .... 245 K6
BUX SK17 .... 62 D7
ECK/KIL S21 .... 93 L2
GLSP SK13 .... 18 B8
MELB/CHEL DE73 .... 269 K1
RCH S42 .... 128 D6
RDERBYSW DE65 .... 266 E5
STPNHL/WNHL DE15 .... 274 E6
STV/CWN S43 .... 95 J7
SWAD DE11 .... 290 E2
UTXR ST14 .... 249 J8
Church Ct SBK/MW NG20 .... 133 H7
Church Crs BSTN/STPLFD NG9 .... 245 K6
Church Cft MSHM DE12 .... 287 M7
RIPLEY DE5 .... 187 G8
Churchdale Av
BSTN/STPLFD NG9 .... 245 H1
Churchdale Rd HACK/IN S12 .... 57 C2
Churchdown Cl
DERBYE DE21 .... 227 L8
Church Dr ILK DE7 .... 217 G5
LGEAT NG10 .... 244 E3
SBK/MW NG20 .... 133 H7
Church Hi ALFN DE55 .... 176 D1
ASH NG17 .... 163 H8
MSFDW NG19 .... 149 M7
RDERBYSW DE65 .... 253 L5
Church Hill Av MSFDW NG19 .... 149 M8
Church Hill St
STPNHL/WNHL DE15 .... 274 E7
Churchill Av MTLK DE4 .... 171 G4
Churchill Cl ASHZ LE65 .... 291 J4
BWSH/BRSTN DE72 .... 260 A2
Churchill Crs MPL/ROM SK6 .... 32 A3
RDERBYSW DE65 .... 253 H8
Churchill Dr BSTN/STPLFD NG9 .... 245 H2
Churchland Av RCH S42 .... 146 A2
Church La ALFN DE55 .... 159 C8
ALFN DE55 .... 160 C5
ALFN DE55 .... 161 J3
ALFN DE55 .... 174 C6
ASH NG17 .... 163 H8
ASHB DE6 .... 193 G1
ASHB DE6 .... 205 K6
ASHB DE6 .... 206 F4
ASHB DE6 .... 208 D5
ASHB DE6 .... 211 H8
ASHB DE6 .... 222 A2
ASHB DE6 .... 224 B8
ASHB DE6 .... 248 D1
ASHB DE6 .... 252 E1
BKWL DE45 .... 104 D6
BKWL DE45 .... 106 B5
BKWL DE45 .... 123 G5
BKWL DE45 .... 136 F1
BPR/DUF DE56 .... 199 J6
BSTN/STPLFD NG9 .... 245 M3
BSVR S44 .... 111 J7
BSVR S44 .... 130 E7
BSVR S44 .... 131 G7
BUTN/AL/TUT DE13 .... 262 D6
BUTN/AL/TUT DE13 .... 286 A1
BUX SK17 .... 62 D7
BUX SK17 .... 84 A6
BUX SK17 .... 100 E3
BUX SK17 .... 119 L2
CDLE ST10 .... 190 C3
CDON/KEC DE74 .... 271 L2
CFTN/RUD NG11 .... 261 L7
CHF/WBR SK23 .... 60 E4
CHSW S40 .... 3 H4
DERBYE DE21 .... 226 F3
DERBYE DE21 .... 241 K4
DERBYW DE22 .... 226 D8
DERBYW DE22 .... 239 J2
ECK/KIL S21 .... 74 B4
EWD/SEL/PNX NG16 .... 189 J3
EWD/SEL/PNX NG16 .... 189 K7
EWD/SEL/PNX NG16 .... 203 K8
EWD/SEL/PNX NG16 .... 217 M8
HACK/IN S12 .... 57 M7
HAN/WDH S13 .... 57 L4
ILK DE7 .... 215 G4
ILK DE7 .... 227 H6
ILK DE7 .... 228 B4
ILK DE7 .... 244 B1
MELB/CHEL DE73 .... 268 C8
MELB/CHEL DE73 .... 277 K6
MPL/ROM SK6 .... 32 C4
MSFD NG18 .... 164 F4
MSFDW NG19 .... 148 D5
MSHM DE12 .... 288 B3
MSHM DE12 .... 294 B7
MTLK DE4 .... 124 D6
MTLK DE4 .... 140 B1
NM/HAY SK22 .... 43 M2
RCH S42 .... 129 L7
RCH S42 .... 145 J5
STPNHL/WNHL DE15 .... 275 G2
STV/CWN S43 .... 95 J7
TOT/DORE S17 .... 69 G4
UTXR ST14 .... 218 C7
Church La North CHNE S41 .... 91 K7
DERBYW DE22 .... 226 C7
Churchmead ASH NG17 .... 162 C7

Church Mdw BSVR S44 .... 111 J7
RCH S42 .... 145 J5
Church Ms ASH NG17 .... 163 H8
DERBYE DE21 .... 242 A6
ECK/KIL S21 .... 74 B3
MOS S20 .... 73 C3
RDERBYSW DE65 .... 264 A1
Church Paddock RCH S42 .... 145 J5
Church Ri ALFN DE55 .... 159 M6
Church Rd ASHB DE6 .... 206 F7
BSVR S44 .... 113 K4
BSVR S44 .... 113 L3
BUT DE14 .... 280 B3
BUTN/AL/TUT DE13 .... 264 C5
BUTN/AL/TUT DE13 .... 265 H8
DERBYW DE22 .... 225 M4
DERBYE DE21 .... 24 F4
HYDE SK14 .... 17 G6
MPL/ROM SK6 .... 33 H4
MTLK DE4 .... 140 E8
NM/HAY SK22 .... 43 M3
RDERBYSW DE65 .... 251 K2
RDERBYSW DE65 .... 265 L6
SWAD DE11 .... 282 D4
Church Side BSVR S44 .... 111 J7
Church Mdw CHNE S41 .... 129 C4
RDERBYSW DE65 .... 266 D5
Churchside La CHNE S41 .... 129 C4
Church Sq MELB/CHEL DE73 .... 278 E4
Church St ALFN DE55 .... 160 A8
ALFN DE55 .... 175 J6
ALFN DE55 .... 176 D4
ALFN DE55 .... 188 A4
ASH NG17 .... 163 H8
ASHB DE6 .... 166 B6
ASHB DE6 .... 193 L8
BKWL DE45 .... 120 F8
BKWL DE45 .... 122 C2
BKWL DE45 .... 138 F5
BPR/DUF DE56 .... 185 L4
BPR/DUF DE56 .... 186 A8
BPR/DUF DE56 .... 213 M4
BPR/DUF DE56 .... 214 C2
BSTN/STPLFD NG9 .... 245 G3
BSTN/STPLFD NG9 .... 245 L2
BSVR S44 .... 111 J7
BUTN/AL/TUT DE13 .... 263 M4
BUX SK17 .... 85 M6
BUX SK17 .... 134 E4
BUX SK17 .... 151 G5
BWSH/BRSTN DE72 .... 242 F6
CLCR S45 .... 143 J7
CLCR S45 .... 160 F1
CRTAM B79 .... 293 H8
DERBYE DE21 .... 214 C5
DERBYE DE21 .... 242 A6
DERBYSE DE24 .... 257 M3
DRON S18 .... 90 D1
DRON S18 .... 91 H3
ECK/KIL S21 .... 73 H6
EDL/UDV S33 .... 64 E4
EWD/SEL/PNX NG16 .... 217 H1
GLSP SK13 .... 17 K6
GLSP SK13 .... 17 J3
GLSP SK13 .... 18 A8
HATH/EY S32 .... 86 A5
HEANOR DE75 .... 216 C1
ILK DE7 .... 217 H6
LGEAT NG10 .... 244 E3
MELB/CHEL DE73 .... 278 E3
MPL/ROM SK6 .... 32 C4
MPL/ROM SK6 .... 32 D5
MSFD NG18 .... 164 D3
MSFDW NG19 .... 148 E5
MSFDW NG19 .... 149 L7
MSHM DE12 .... 287 M7
MSHM DE12 .... 294 C4
MSHM DE12 .... 295 H2
MTLK DE4 .... 156 F6
MTLK DE4 .... 157 K5
MTLK DE4 .... 171 G1
MTLK DE4 .... 172 D3
MTLK DE4 .... 181 J1
NM/HAY SK22 .... 35 G8
NORM/LIT DE23 .... 240 D8
NORM/LIT DE23 .... 255 M1
RIPLEY DE5 .... 187 G8
RIPLEY DE5 .... 201 K3
RIPLEY DE5 .... 214 F1
SBK/MW NG20 .... 115 K8
STV/CWN S43 .... 93 H8
STV/CWN S43 .... 94 E3
STV/CWN S43 .... 95 H7
STV/CWN S43 .... 111 H3
SWAD DE11 .... 282 F6
SWAD DE11 .... 282 D4
SWAD DE11 .... 283 L4
SWAD DE11 .... 289 K1
UTXR ST14 .... 247 M3
WRKS S80 .... 115 H1
Church St East
EWD/SEL/PNX NG16 .... 177 G7
Church St North CHNE S41 .... 91 K7
Church St South CHSW S40 .... 128 D3
GLSP SK13 .... 18 B8
Church St West CHSW S40 .... 109 M8
EWD/SEL/PNX NG16 .... 177 G7
Church Vw ASH NG17 .... 163 G4
ASHB DE6 .... 207 J4
BSVR S44 .... 147 L2
BUTN/AL/TUT DE13 .... 273 M3
BWSH/BRSTN DE72 .... 260 B3
CHSW S40 .... 109 M8
ECK/KIL S21 .... 74 B3
HAN/WDH S13 .... 57 M4
HEANOR DE75 .... 201 L6
HYDE SK14 .... 16 D7
ILK DE7 .... 230 B3
MSFDW NG19 .... 148 C3
STV/CWN S43 .... 94 D3
STV/CWN S43 .... 95 J7
Church View Dr BKWL DE45 .... 106 B5
Church Wk ALFN DE55 .... 188 B4
BPR/DUF DE56 .... 213 J8
EWD/SEL/PNX NG16 .... 203 J8
EWD/SEL/PNX NG16 .... 203 H4
Church Wy CHNE S41 .... 3 H4
Churnet Cl ASHB DE6 .... 206 F7

Churnet Ct BUT DE14 .... 274 B7
Churston Rd CHSW S40 .... 2 A3
Cinder Bank
EWD/SEL/PNX NG16 .... 188 C6
Cinderhill La SHEFS S8 .... 70 F2
Cinder La ECK/KIL S21 .... 74 C3
MTLK DE4 .... 183 H4
Cinder Rd ALFN DE55 .... 188 A3
Circle Cl SHEFP/MNR S2 .... 56 E2
The Circle DERBYE DE24 .... 256 B5
SHEFP/MNR S2 .... 56 E1
Circular Dr ECK/KIL S21 .... 93 L2
Circular Rd CHNE S41 .... 128 C2
STV/CWN S43 .... 111 M2
City Rd DERBY DE1 .... 240 D3
The City SWAD DE11 .... 283 J8
Civic Wy SWAD DE11 .... 282 E6
Clamp Dr SWAD DE11 .... 282 E7
Clapgun St CDON/KEC DE74 .... 271 L7
Clara Mount Rd HEANOR DE75 .... 216 D1
Clarehaven BSTN/STPLFD NG9 .... 245 H5
Claremont Av
BSTN/STPLFD NG9 .... 245 M2
Clarence La SHEFP/MNR S2 .... 55 M1
Clarence Rd CHSW S40 .... 2 F4
NORM/LIT DE23 .... 256 B1
LGEAT NG10 .... 260 F4
Clarence St ALFN DE55 .... 160 E6
BUT DE14 .... 280 C1
CHSW S40 .... 2 E4
MSFD NG18 .... 164 D4
MSFDW NG19 .... 148 F7
Clarendon Rd ECC S11 .... 54 B3
MSFDW NG19 .... 164 B2
STV/CWN S43 .... 111 M3
Clarke Av HEANOR DE75 .... 201 M7
Clarke Dell FUL S10 .... 55 G1
Clarke Dr FUL S10 .... 55 G1
LGEAT NG10 .... 260 D6
Clarkehouse Rd FUL S10 .... 54 F1
Clarke's Cl UTXR ST14 .... 247 L1
Clarkes La BWSH/BRSTN DE72 .... 270 E2
Clarke Sq SHEFP/MNR S2 .... 55 J2
Clarke St DERBY DE1 .... 5 H1
Clarkson Av CHSW S40 .... 2 F9
Clatterway MTLK DE4 .... 171 H2
Claverhouse Rd
STPNHL/WNHL DE15 .... 274 D8
Claxton St HEANOR DE75 .... 202 A8
Claxton Ter HEANOR DE75 .... 202 A8
Claye St LGEAT NG10 .... 261 H3
Claylands Av WRKN S81 .... 77 L3
Claylands Cl HYDE SK14 .... 17 G6
Claylands Gv WRKS S80 .... 96 B5
Claylands Pl WRKS S80 .... 96 B5
Claylands Rd WRKS S80 .... 96 B5
Clay La CLCR S45 .... 144 E6
HEANOR DE75 .... 202 C8
Claymar Dr SWAD DE11 .... 282 D3
Claymills Rd
BUTN/AL/TUT DE13 .... 265 J8
Claypit La RCH S42 .... 126 B2
Clay's La BUT DE14 .... 280 C3
Clay St ALFN DE55 .... 175 H1
BWSH/BRSTN DE72 .... 259 K3
STPNHL/WNHL DE15 .... 281 J1
Clay St East
STPNHL/WNHL DE15 .... 281 K1
Clayton Gv HEANOR DE75 .... 201 M6
Clayton St CHNE S41 .... 3 K6
Claywood Rd SHEFP/MNR S2 .... 55 M1
Cleave Rd BUT DE14 .... 280 D2
Clegg Hill Dr ASH NG17 .... 162 B6
Clematis Crs
STPNHL/WNHL DE15 .... 281 K2
Clement La EDL/UDV S33 .... 63 M4
Clement Rd ILK DE7 .... 214 F3
MPL/ROM SK6 .... 32 E3
Clerkson St MSFD NG18 .... 164 E4
Cleve Av BSTN/STPLFD NG9 .... 245 H7
MTLK DE4 .... 156 C3
Cleveland Av
BWSH/BRSTN DE72 .... 259 J3
DERBYE DE21 .... 241 L5
LGEAT NG10 .... 261 J2
Cleveland Cl SWAD DE11 .... 282 D7
Cleveland Rd ALFN DE55 .... 160 C7
Cleveland Wy CHSW S40 .... 109 L6
Cleveleys Rd
BSTN/STPLFD NG9 .... 245 H7
Clewley Rd BUT DE14 .... 280 C2
Cliffash La BPR/DUF DE56 .... 197 H4
Cliffe Farm Dr ECC S11 .... 54 D3
Cliffefield Rd SHEFS S8 .... 55 J5
Cliffe Hill Av BSTN/STPLFD NG9 .... 245 C3
Cliffe La BUX SK17 .... 83 M6
HATH/EY S32 .... 66 C2
Cliffe Rd GLSP SK13 .... 26 A3
Cliff Hl STV/CWN S43 .... 94 F7
Cliff La EWD/SEL/PNX NG16 .... 177 J7
HATH/EY S32 .... 106 A1
MTLK DE4 .... 154 A2
Cliff Ml BUX SK17 .... 99 M3
Clifford Cl CHSW S40 .... 109 L8
LGEAT NG10 .... 260 E6
Clifford Rd ECC S11 .... 54 A5
Clifford St LGEAT NG10 .... 261 H3
Cliff Rd BUX SK17 .... 100 A2
Cliff St ECC S11 .... 55 H5
MSFD NG18 .... 164 F3
Clifton Av ASHZ LE65 .... 291 K2
LGEAT NG10 .... 261 K3
STV/CWN S43 .... 94 D3
Clifton Cl MSHM DE12 .... 289 K7
SWAD DE11 .... 282 C8
Clifton Dr ASHZ LE65 .... 291 K3
BUX SK17 .... 99 M6
MCKLVR DE3 .... 239 H7
MPL/ROM SK6 .... 32 C3
Clifton Gv MSFD NG18 .... 165 J6
Clifton Pl MSFD NG18 .... 164 E3
Clifton Rd ASHB DE6 .... 207 J4
ASHB DE6 .... 207 J3
BUX SK17 .... 99 M3
DERBYW DE22 .... 226 A7
MSHM DE12 .... 294 A4
MTLK DE4 .... 171 K2
Clifton St CHSW S40 .... 2 C4
DERBY DE1 .... 5 J8
Clinthill La WRKS S80 .... 96 B3

Clinton Av EWD/SEL/PNX NG16 .... 203 G4
Clinton Pl FUL S10 .... 55 H1
Clinton St DERBYE DE21 .... 5 M2
Clipstone Av ASH NG17 .... 163 K6
MSFD NG18 .... 164 F2
Clipstone Gdns DERBYE DE21 .... 227 L8
Clipstone Rd West
MSFDW NG19 .... 165 J2
Clodhall La HATH/EY S32 .... 87 J8
RCH S42 .... 107 M5
Cloisters Ct DERBYE DE21 .... 227 J8
The Cloisters
STPNHL/WNHL DE15 .... 281 J1
Cloonmore Cft SHEFS S8 .... 70 E1
Cloonmore Dr SHEFS S8 .... 70 F1
Close Quarters
BSTN/STPLFD NG9 .... 245 M2
The Close BKWL DE45 .... 104 C6
BUTN/AL/TUT DE13 .... 263 L4
DERBYW DE22 .... 226 C8
MPL/ROM SK6 .... 32 D1
MSHM DE12 .... 288 F5
NORM/LIT DE23 .... 240 A8
SBK/MW NG20 .... 133 J5
SWAD DE11 .... 290 A2
Cloud Av BSTN/STPLFD NG9 .... 245 J3
Cloudside Rd LGEAT NG10 .... 244 D3
Cloudwood Cl NORM/LIT DE23 .... 255 L1
Clough Av MPL/ROM SK6 .... 32 F4
Clough Bank SHEFP/MNR S2 .... 55 L2
Clough End Rd HYDE SK14 .... 24 B1
Clough Foot La HOLM/MEL HD7 .... 9 K3
Clough La ECC S11 .... 53 K5
MTLK DE4 .... 154 F2
NM/HAY SK22 .... 34 F5
Clough Rd SHEF S1 .... 55 L1
Clough Side MPL/ROM SK6 .... 32 F5
Cloughside POY/DIS SK12 .... 43 H4
The Clough CHNE S41 .... 129 H1
EDL/UDV S33 .... 51 C5
Clover Cl DERBYE DE21 .... 242 C5
Clover Ct BWSH/BRSTN DE72 .... 259 H8
Clover Dl SWAD DE11 .... 282 E3
Cloverdale Dr DERBYSE DE24 .... 256 C8
Clover Nook Rd ALFN DE55 .... 176 A8
Clover Ri EWD/SEL/PNX NG16 .... 217 L1
Cloverslade RDERBYSW DE65 .... 266 F1
Cloves Hi ILK DE7 .... 214 F8
Clowne Rd BSVR S44 .... 113 K2
STV/CWN S43 .... 94 F4
Club Garden Rd ECC S11 .... 55 J2
Club Garden Wk ECC S11 .... 55 J1
Club La MELB/CHEL DE73 .... 268 D5
Club St ECC S11 .... 55 J2
Clumber Av
EWD/SEL/PNX NG16 .... 203 H1
Clumber Cl STV/CWN S43 .... 95 K6
Clumber Ct ILK DE7 .... 217 J5
MSFDW NG19 .... 149 H8
Clumber Crs ASH NG17 .... 162 F4
Clumber Dr MSFDW NG19 .... 149 H8
Clumber Pl STV/CWN S43 .... 111 M4
Clumber Rd FUL S10 .... 54 B1
Clumber St ASH NG17 .... 163 G8
MSFDW NG19 .... 149 H8
MSFDW NG19 .... 164 E3
Clune St STV/CWN S43 .... 95 K5
Cluster Rd BPR/DUF DE56 .... 199 J6
Clusters Ct BPR/DUF DE56 .... 199 J6
Clyde St SHEFS S8 .... 55 J4
Coach Dr DERBYSE DE24 .... 256 A7
EWD/SEL/PNX NG16 .... 203 J6
Coachhouse Ms SWAD DE11 .... 282 D3
Coach Rd HYDE SK14 .... 16 F5
RIPLEY DE5 .... 187 J7
Coach Wy RDERBYSW DE65 .... 266 F5
Coachways ILK DE7 .... 216 B7
Coalfields Cl ASH NG17 .... 177 M1
Coal La SWAD DE11 .... 284 A2
Coalpit La BKWL DE45 .... 138 F4
MSHM DE12 .... 288 A7
Coarses Vw CHF/WBR SK23 .... 60 F3
Coastbill La ECC S11 .... 53 K1
Coasthill MTLK DE4 .... 185 J1
Cobden Rd CHSW S40 .... 2 F7
Cobden St DERBYW DE22 .... 240 A5
LGEAT NG10 .... 261 G3
RIPLEY DE5 .... 186 F8
Cobham Cl DERBYSE DE24 .... 256 A7
Cobnar Av SHEFS S8 .... 55 K8
Cobnar Dr CHNE S41 .... 110 A2
SHEFS S8 .... 55 K8
Cobnar Gdns SHEFS S8 .... 55 J8
Cobnar Rd SHEFS S8 .... 55 K8
Cobthorn Dr DERBYW DE22 .... 225 M6
Cockayne Cl LGEAT NG10 .... 244 F7
Cockayne La ASHB DE6 .... 195 L1
Cockayne Pl SHEFS S8 .... 55 J6
Cockayne St North
DERBYSE DE24 .... 257 H4
Cockayne St South
DERBYSE DE24 .... 257 H4
Cockerhouse Rd
EWD/SEL/PNX NG16 .... 203 H6
Cockers La STLY SK15 .... 16 A2
Cock Hl ASHB DE6 .... 207 H4
BKWL DE45 .... 106 C5
Cockington Rd
WOL/BIL/BUX NC8 .... 231 M5
Cockleys LGEAT NG10 .... 260 F4
Cockshead La ASHB DE6 .... 219 M3
Cockshut La MELB/CHEL DE73 .... 278 C5
SBK/MW NG20 .... 115 K6
Cockshutt Av SHEFS S8 .... 70 A2
Cockshutt Dr SHEFS S8 .... 70 A2
Cockshutt La ALFN DE55 .... 188 C3
Cockshutt Rd SHEFS S8 .... 70 A2
Cockstubbles UTXR ST14 .... 247 L2
Cod Beck Cl DERBYSE DE24 .... 257 M4
Codnor-denby La RIPLEY DE5 .... 201 K5
Codnor Ga RIPLEY DE5 .... 201 L1
Codnor Rd RIPLEY DE5 .... 187 M8
Coffin La BPR/DUF DE56 .... 196 E1
Coisley Hi HAN/WDH S13 .... 57 J5
Coisley Rd HAN/WDH S13 .... 57 K4
Coit La ECC S11 .... 54 A7
Cokayne Av ASHB DE6 .... 193 M8
Coke St DERBYW DE22 .... 240 A5

Colbourne Gv HYDE SK14 .... 16 E7
Coldharbour La CLCR S45 .... 158 C5
Cold Side EDL/UDV S33 .... 22 D8
Coldwall Br ASHB DE6 .... 192 E2
Coldwell St MTLK DE4 .... 183 J1
Cole La BWSH/BRSTN DE72 .... 242 F6
Coleman St DERBYSE DE24 .... 257 H3
Coleraine Cl DERBYE DE21 .... 241 L6
Coleridge St NORM/LIT DE23 .... 256 C5
Colin Av RIPLEY DE5 .... 201 L2
Colin St ALFN DE55 .... 175 K6
Colledge St ALFN DE55 .... 187 M4
College Av STV/CWN S43 .... 112 A1
College Ms DERBY DE1 .... 4 A4
College Rd BUX SK17 .... 99 K4
ECK/KIL S21 .... 93 M1
UTXR ST14 .... 218 B4
College St LGEAT NG10 .... 244 F7
College Wy BUX SK17 .... 100 A8
Collegiate Crs FUL S10 .... 55 G1
Collier Av MSFDW NG19 .... 149 L5
Collier Cl HYDE SK14 .... 24 B1
Collier La BWSH/BRSTN DE72 .... 242 F6
Colliers Cl HAN/WDH S13 .... 57 L4
Collier St GLSP SK13 .... 25 M2
Colliers Trek STV/CWN S43 .... 94 F5
Colliers Wy CLCR S45 .... 144 E6
Colliery La MSHM DE12 .... 289 G5
Colliery Rd ALFN DE55 .... 176 C1
SWAD DE11 .... 289 K1
WRKS S80 .... 115 H2
Colliery Rw
EWD/SEL/PNX NG16 .... 177 G8
Collin Av LGEAT NG10 .... 244 E6
Collingbourne Av MOS S20 .... 73 K1
Collingbourne Dr MOS S20 .... 73 K1
Collingham Gdns
DERBYW DE22 .... 239 K5
Collingham Rd MSFDW NG19 .... 164 A1
Collingwood Crs MTLK DE4 .... 156 D4
Collingwood Rd LGEAT NG10 .... 261 G4
Collins Av ALFN DE55 .... 176 D3
Collinson Rd
BUTN/AL/TUT DE13 .... 286 A1
Collin St UTXR ST14 .... 247 L3
Collis Cl DERBYSE DE24 .... 257 H3
Collishaw Cl CHNE S41 .... 3 M9
Collumbell Av
BWSH/BRSTN DE72 .... 242 F5
Colne Mt UTXR ST14 .... 247 L3
Colombo St NORM/LIT DE23 .... 256 E1
Colonsay Cl BSTN/STPLFD NG9 .... 231 G7
Colston Rd MSFD NG18 .... 165 K8
Colton Cl CHNE S41 .... 110 B1
Coltsfoot Dr DERBYSE DE24 .... 256 C8
Coltsworth La STV/CWN S43 .... 95 G2
Colyear St DERBY DE1 .... 4 E4
Combs Cl NM/HAY SK22 .... 43 K2
Combs La CHF/WBR SK23 .... 80 B1
Combs Ms GLSP SK13 .... 25 G1
Combs Rd CHF/WBR SK23 .... 60 B7
Comfrey Cl NORM/LIT DE23 .... 255 J4
Commerce St DERBYSE DE24 .... 257 J2
MELB/CHEL DE73 .... 278 D3
Commercial Ga MSFD NG18 .... 164 E4
Commercial Rd BUX SK17 .... 83 M6
Commercial St MSFD NG18 .... 164 E4
Common La ALFN DE55 .... 159 M7
BSTN/STPLFD NG9 .... 245 K4
BUX SK17 .... 119 J1
CDLE ST10 .... 191 H4
ECC S11 .... 54 A5
ILK DE7 .... 228 D3
MSFDW NG19 .... 148 E3
MSFDW NG19 .... 149 K6
RCH S42 .... 109 H1
RDERBYSW DE65 .... 252 C2
SBK/MW NG20 .... 133 G5
Commonpiece La ASHB DE6 .... 236 E8
Common Piece La
RDERBYSW DE65 .... 267 H1
Common Rd ASH NG17 .... 162 C8
AU/AST/KP S26 .... 75 K5
SWAD DE11 .... 289 L1
WRKS S80 .... 76 C5
Commons Cl
EWD/SEL/PNX NG16 .... 217 K2
Common Side
EWD/SEL/PNX NG16 .... 189 J2
SWAD DE11 .... 282 E8
Commonside Rd DRON S18 .... 89 M8
The Common ALFN DE55 .... 176 D5
DERBYW DE22 .... 225 M2
MTLK DE4 .... 185 K2
Common Wd MTLK DE4 .... 156 E7
Compass Crs CHNE S41 .... 91 M7
Compton Av
BWSH/BRSTN DE72 .... 270 D2
Compton Cl DERBYSE DE24 .... 257 M4
Compton Gv WRKS S80 .... 115 G1
Compton Gv BUX SK17 .... 99 L4
Compton Rd BUX SK17 .... 99 L4
Compton St ASHB DE6 .... 193 M8
CHSW S40 .... 2 E2
RCH S42 .... 146 B3
SBK/MW NG20 .... 133 J2
Conalan Av TOT/DORE S17 .... 69 L5
Condliff Rd ILK DE7 .... 83 L5
Condor Rd ILK DE7 .... 230 C6
Conduit La BSVR S44 .... 131 K2
Conduit St GLSP SK13 .... 17 J3
Coniston Av DERBYE DE21 .... 242 B4
Coniston Crs DERBYE DE21 .... 227 G8
Coniston Dr CLCR S45 .... 144 E7
ILK DE7 .... 230 A5
Coniston Gdns ASHZ LE65 .... 291 M5
Coniston Rd CHNE S41 .... 110 B2
DRON S18 .... 90 B1

LGEAT NG10 — 244 D8
MPL/ROM SK6 — 42 A2
SHEFS S8 — 55 H5
Coniston Ter SHEFS S8 — 55 H5
Coniston Wy CHNE S41 — 110 B2
Conjoint La BUX SK17 — 84 B5
Conksbury Av BKWL DE45 — 138 F3
Conksbury La BKWL DE45 — 138 F3
Connaught Ct ALFN DE55 — 175 L7
Connaught Rd DERBYW DE22 — 239 M6
Connery Ms BSTN/STPLFD NG9 — 261 L1
Consort Gdns DERBYE DE21 — 227 M7
Constable Av DERBYW DE22 — 239 M4
Constable Cl DRON S18 — 90 B2
GLV S14 — 56 B8
Constable Dr MPL/ROM SK6 — 32 E2
NORM/LIT DE23 — 239 L8
SHEFS S8 — 56 A8
Constable La NORM/LIT DE23 — 239 M8
Constable Pl GLV S14 — 56 B8
Constable Rd SHEFS S8 — 56 A8
Constable Wy SHEFS S8 — 56 A8
Convent Cl STPNHL/WHNL DE15 — 281 J2
Conway Av BWSH/BRSTN DE72 — 243 G8
Conway Cl BUTN/AL/TUT DE13 — 274 A2
MSFDW NG19 — 164 A2
Conway Rd LGEAT NG10 — 261 J2
Conway St LGEAT NG10 — 261 J2
Conygree La ASHB DE6 — 207 G3
Coo In HAN/WDH S13 — 57 M4
Cook Cl BPR/DUF DE56 — 200 B5
Cook Dr ILK DE7 — 230 D4
Cooke Cl LGEAT NG10 — 260 E3
RCH S42 — 144 E4
Cookfield BPR/DUF DE56 — 200 B2
Cookham Cl MCKLVR DE3 — 238 F8
Cook La ASHB DE6 — 248 L1
Cooks Rd CDON/KEG DE74 — 271 K7
Coombes Av MPL/ROM SK6 — 32 C5
Coombes La GLSP SK13 — 24 F5
Coombes Vw HYDE SK14 — 24 C2
Coombs Rd BKWL DE45 — 123 K6
Co-operative St ASH NG17 — 162 F4
LGEAT NG10 — 261 H3
NORM/LIT DE23 — 4 D9
Cooper's Cl ASHB DE6 — 193 M8
BWSH/BRSTN DE72 — 259 G1
Coopers Cft RDERBYSW DE65 — 263 M1
Cooper St DERBYW DE22 — 239 M4
GLSP SK13 — 25 L2
Copeland Av BSTN/STPLFD NG9 — 245 H2
Copeland St DERBY DE1 — 5 G5
Copes Wy DERBYE DE21 — 241 K2
UTXR ST14 — 247 J1
Cophills Cl MSHM DE12 — 295 M8
Copley Cft ASHB DE6 — 194 A7
Coplow La RDERBYSW DE65 — 251 G4
Copperas Rd SWAD DE11 — 282 A5
Copper Beech Dr GLSP SK13 — 25 H1
Copper Beeches RIPLEY DE5 — 186 E8
Copperleaf Cl DERBYW DE22 — 4 C6
Copper Yd RIPLEY DE5 — 201 J8
Coppice Av ILK DE7 — 217 G5
Coppice Cl BPR/DUF DE56 — 214 D2
CHNE S41 — 129 G4
DERBYW DE22 — 240 C1
Coppice Dr EWD/SEL/PNX NG16 — 203 H7
HEANOR DE75 — 216 C3
POY/DIS SK12 — 42 D4
Coppice La POY/DIS SK12 — 42 D4
Coppice Side SWAD DE11 — 282 F7
The Coppice CHF/WBR SK23 — 59 J5
SBK/MW NG20 — 133 G2
Coppice Vw ALFN DE55 — 176 D6
Copse Cl MTLK DE4 — 183 J7
Copse Gv NORM/LIT DE23 — 255 K3
Copse Ri SWAD DE11 — 282 S3
Copseside Cl LGEAT NG10 — 260 D2
The Copse ASH NG17 — 162 F5
BSTN/STPLFD NG9 — 245 H1
ILK DE7 — 217 G5
MPL/ROM SK6 — 32 F2
Copsewood ALFN DE55 — 176 C6
Copthurst Rd HOLM/MEL HD7 — 9 G2
Coral Wy CLRC S45 — 145 G6
Corbar Rd BUX SK17 — 99 L2
Corbar Woods La BUX SK17 — 99 K3
Corbel Cl DERBYE DE21 — 227 H8
Corbridge Gv NORM/LIT DE23 — 255 K3
Corby Cl DERBYSE DE24 — 257 J5
Corden Av BUTN/AL/TUT DE13 — 274 C2
MCKLVR DE3 — 239 K8
Corden St NORM/LIT DE23 — 240 D8
Cordville Cl DERBYE DE21 — 241 L5
Cordwell Av CHNE S41 — 109 M2
Cordwell Cl CDON/KEG DE74 — 271 J7
STV/CWN S43 — 112 A2
Cordwell La DRON S18 — 89 H5
Cordy La EWD/SEL/PNX NG16 — 203 J3
Corfe Cl NORM/LIT DE23 — 256 A4
Corfield Av HEANOR DE75 — 216 C3
Coriander Gdns NORM/LIT DE23 — 256 A6
Corinium Cl DERBYSE DE24 — 258 A5
Corker Rd HACK/IN S12 — 56 D5
Corks La POY/DIS SK12 — 43 H5
Corley La ASHB DE6 — 194 F8
Corn Cl ALFN DE55 — 176 E4
Cornel Ct MSFDW NG19 — 165 H1
Corner Cft ASH NG17 — 162 D7
Corner Farm ASHB DE6 — 223 H2
Cornfield ALFN DE55 — 176 D6
Cornfield Av ALFN DE55 — 176 D6
Cornfield Cl CHSW S40 — 109 K5
Cornflower Dr DERBYE DE21 — 227 K8
Cornhill DERBYE DE22 — 226 C6
Cornhill Dr ALFN DE55 — 175 L6
Corn Market DERBY DE1 — 4 F3
Cornmill Bank BUTN/AL/TUT DE13 — 264 A4
Cornmill Cl BSVR S44 — 113 M8
DERBYSE DE24 — 258 A5
HATH/EY S32 — 105 M1

Cornmill La BUTN/AL/TUT DE13 — 263 M4
Corn Mill La BUTN/AL/TUT DE13 — 264 A4
Corn St GLSP SK13 — 26 A1
Cornwall Av BUX SK17 — 100 B3
MSFD NG18 — 165 J4
STV/CWN S43 — 111 J2
Cornwall Cl MPL/ROM SK6 — 42 B5
STV/CWN S43 — 111 J2
Cornwall Dr RCH S42 — 129 J7
STV/CWN S43 — 111 J2
Cornwallis Cl LGEAT NG10 — 261 G4
Cornwall Rd DERBYE DE21 — 5 M1
STPNHL/WHNL DE15 — 281 H4
WRKN S81 — 77 J3
Coronation Av BPR/DUF DE56 — 199 K5
DERBYSE DE24 — 257 M5
LGEAT NG10 — 244 D3
MSFDW NG19 — 148 C3
MSHM DE12 — 290 E4
Coronation Cl MELB/CHEL DE73 — 278 D2
Coronation Crs UTXR ST14 — 218 D6
Coronation Dr ALFN DE55 — 176 S3
Coronation Rd EWD/SEL/PNX NG16 — 217 L8
ILK DE7 — 217 K8
ILK DE7 — 228 E4
STV/CWN S43 — 111 H2
Coronation St ALFN DE55 — 174 B2
ILK DE7 — 230 C2
MSFD NG18 — 165 G4
MSHM DE12 — 289 K6
NORM/LIT DE23 — 256 E2
SWAD DE11 — 282 D5
WRKS S80 — 96 D4
Coronet Ct DERBYE DE21 — 228 A7
Corporation Rd ILK DE7 — 230 D5
Corporation St CHNE S41 — 3 J4
DERBY DE1 — 4 F3
MSFD NG18 — 164 D3
Cortworth Rd ECC S11 — 54 D6
Corve Wy RCH S42 — 109 J5
Corwen Pl HAN/WDH S13 — 57 K4
Cosgrove Av ASH NG17 — 163 K5
Cossall Rd BSTN/STPLFD NG9 — 230 F2
Costobadie Cl HYDE SK14 — 16 C7
Cote Bottom La RDERBYSW DE65 — 251 K3
Cotefield Cl MPL/ROM SK6 — 32 C5
Cote Green La MPL/ROM SK6 — 32 E1
Cote Green Rd MPL/ROM SK6 — 32 E1
Cote Hilloc MTLK DE4 — 140 D3
Cote La HOLM/MEL HD7 — 9 J1
NM/HAY SK22 — 35 G7
Cotes Park La ALFN DE55 — 175 M8
Cotgrave Av HACK/IN S12 — 57 K7
Cotleigh Av HACK/IN S12 — 57 K7
Cotleigh Crs HACK/IN S12 — 57 K7
Cotleigh Dr HACK/IN S12 — 57 K7
Cotleigh Gdns HACK/IN S12 — 57 K7
Cotleigh Pl HACK/IN S12 — 57 K7
Cotleigh Rd HACK/IN S12 — 57 K7
Cotleigh Wy HACK/IN S12 — 57 K7
Cotman Dr MPL/ROM SK6 — 32 C7
Cotmanhay Rd ILK DE7 — 217 J7
Coton La MSHM DE12 — 288 A6
Coton Pk MSHM DE12 — 288 F1
Coton Rd MSHM DE12 — 287 H4
Cotswold Av GLSP SK13 — 25 K2
Cotswold Cl LGEAT NG10 — 260 E2
NORM/LIT DE23 — 255 M7
SWAD DE11 — 282 D7
Cotswold Dr RCH S42 — 129 H7
Cotswold Gv MSFD NG18 — 165 L4
Cotswold Rd BUT DE14 — 280 C3
Cotswold Wy ASKE11 DE65 — 291 L5
Cottage Cl BPR/DUF DE56 — 200 B3
ILK DE7 — 217 G7
STV/CWN S43 — 112 D2
SWAD DE11 — 282 D4
Cottage Garden La HEANOR DE75 — 202 A8
Cottage La ECC S11 — 53 M5
GLSP SK13 — 17 H8
Cottam Crs MPL/ROM SK6 — 32 E3
Cottam Gv MSFDW NG19 — 164 A4
Cotterdale Cl MSFDW NG19 — 165 H1
Cotterhill La STV/CWN S43 — 111 H3
Cottesmore Rd STPNHL/WHNL DE15 — 281 K1
Cottisford Cl NORM/LIT DE23 — 255 K2
Cotton Brook Rd NORM/LIT DE23 — 256 E2
Cotton La DERBYSE DE24 — 256 E2
Cotton Mill Hl RCH S42 — 127 H3
Cotton St BSVR S44 — 131 K1
Coulton's Av ASH NG17 — 162 F7
Coulton's Cl ASH NG17 — 162 F7
Countess Rd SHEF S1 — 55 K1
Counting House Rd POY/DIS SK12 — 43 H5
Countisbury Dr DERBYE DE21 — 227 K8
Coupe La CLRC S45 — 144 D5
Coupe St RIPLEY DE5 — 201 J2
Coupland Pl ALFN DE55 — 187 M1
Court Farm La BUT DE14 — 280 B3
Court-field Rd ASH NG17 — 163 K4
Courtfield Rd ASH NG17 — 163 K4
Courtland Dr DERBYSE DE24 — 257 L4
Courtland Gdns DERBYSE DE24 — 257 L4
Courtland Rd RDERBYSW DE65 — 253 M7
Court La BKWL DE45 — 122 B2
Courtney Av BPR/DUF DE56 — 200 A5
Court Pl STV/CWN S43 — 111 M2
Court St SWAD DE11 — 283 H7
The Court DERBYSE DE24 — 257 L4
Court Vw STV/CWN S43 — 95 H7
Court Yd BSTN/STPLFD NG9 — 245 J7
Coventry La SWAD DE11 — 283 G4
Coventry La BSTN/STPLFD NG9 — 231 J8
WOL/BIL/BRX NG8 — 231 L5
Covert Pl SWAD DE11 — 289 M2
The Covert DERBYE DE21 — 242 B6
Cowbrook Av GLSP SK13 — 26 B1

Cowburn Dr NM/HAY SK22 — 43 M1
Cowdray Cl DERBYSE DE24 — 256 A8
Cowham Cl ALFN DE55 — 175 M7
Cow La BSTN/STPLFD NG9 — 245 M2
CDLE ST10 — 190 C2
ECC S11 — 54 D7
STV/CWN S43 — 111 H1
Cowley Bottom DRON S18 — 90 B2
Cowley Gdns MOS S20 — 73 H2
Cowley La DRON S18 — 89 L2
Cowley St DERBYW DE22 — 240 B5
Cowlishaw Cl BWSH/BRSTN DE72 — 271 H1
Cowlishaw Rd ECC S11 — 54 F2
Cowlow La CHF/WBR SK23 — 60 C8
Cown Edge Wy GLSP SK13 — 24 F8
HYDE SK14 — 24 B3
MPL/ROM SK6 — 32 F6
Cowpasture La ASH NG17 — 163 H8
Cowper Rd EWD/SEL/PNX NG16 — 217 K2
Cowper St DERBYSE DE24 — 256 D5
Cowpes Cl ASH NG17 — 163 G6
Cowpingle La STV/CWN S43 — 111 H1
Cowsell Dr CLRC S45 — 145 H8
Cowsley Rd DERBYE DE21 — 241 G3
Coxbench Rd DERBYE DE21 — 214 B6
Cox Green Ct NORM/LIT DE23 — 255 J3
Coxmoor Rd ASH NG17 — 163 L7
Coxon St DERBYE DE21 — 242 B5
Cox's La MSFDW NG19 — 149 K5
Crabtree Av BLK DE7 — 43 H5
Crabtree Cl CDON/KEG DE74 — 271 K8
DERBYW DE22 — 225 M6
MTLK DE4 — 183 H3
Crab Tree Hl DERBYE DE21 — 226 F2
Crabtree Hill Keddleston Rd DERBYW DE22 — 225 M7
Cracken Cl CHF/WBR SK23 — 60 A1
Craddock Av DERBYSE DE24 — 242 B7
Craddock Ms SHEFP/MNR S2 — 56 B3
Craddock Rd SHEFP/MNR S2 — 56 B3
Cragdale Gv MOS S20 — 73 G3
Cragg La ALFN DE55 — 161 K8
Craggon Dr STV/CWN S43 — 92 A6
Craggs Dr STV/CWN S43 — 95 H7
Craggs Rd BSVR S44 — 113 K7
Craglands Gv RCH S42 — 109 K5
Crags Rd WRKS S80 — 96 F3
WRKS S80 — 115 K1
Crags Vw WRKS S80 — 115 J1
Craig Dr CHF/WBR SK23 — 59 H4
Craiglee Cl DERBYSE DE24 — 256 A7
Craigs Gn MSFDW NG19 — 164 B5
Craig St LGEAT NG10 — 261 H3
Crampton Cl ASH NG17 — 162 E7
Crampton Rd MSFD NG18 — 165 H2
Cranberry Gv NORM/LIT DE23 — 255 J4
Cranborne Cl MSFDW NG19 — 163 M3
Cranborne Rd CHNE S41 — 110 B3
Cranbourne Cl BSTN/STPLFD NG9 — 231 G8
Cranbrook Cl MSFDW NG19 — 149 M4
Cranfleet Wy LGEAT NG10 — 260 E3
Cranford St MOS S20 — 57 K8
Cranford Dr HACK/IN S12 — 57 K7
Cranford Gdns MPL/ROM SK6 — 32 C7
Cranhill Cl NORM/LIT DE23 — 255 J4
Cranleigh Rd STV/CWN S43 — 93 L8
Cranmer Gv MSFDW NG19 — 149 G7
Cranmer Rd DERBYE DE21 — 5 J3
Cranmer St ILK DE7 — 230 C1
LGEAT NG10 — 261 G1
Cranston Rd BSTN/STPLFD NG9 — 245 M1
Craven La DRON S18 — 110 C5
Craven St BUTN/AL/TUT DE13 — 273 M4
Crawford Av BSTN/STPLFD NG9 — 245 C2
Crawford Rd SHEFS S8 — 55 J6
Crawley Rd DERBYSE DE24 — 257 J5
Crawshaw Av SHEFS S8 — 70 A2
Crawshaw Gv SHEFS S8 — 70 A2
Crayford Rd DERBYSE DE24 — 257 K5
Cray's Hl ALFN DE55 — 187 K5
Craythorne Cl SWAD DE11 — 282 D3
Craythorne Rd BUTN/AL/TUT DE13 — 264 F7
Creamery La ASHB DE6 — 180 A1
Cream St SHEFP/MNR S2 — 55 L1
Crecy Cl NORM/LIT DE23 — 239 M7
Crescent Dr ABRD S7 — 55 H3
Crescent Dr CHF/WBR SK23 — 44 A8
Crescent Kingsley ALFN DE55 — 160 C7
Crescent Rd ABRD S7 — 55 H3
EWD/SEL/PNX NG16 — 189 G4
RCH S42 — 127 G3
The Crescent ALFN DE55 — 175 L7
ASH NG17 — 163 G3
ASHB DE6 — 207 G3
ASHB DE6 — 222 A3
BSTN/STPLFD NG9 — 245 H1
BSTN/STPLFD NG9 — 245 M7
BUX SK17 — 99 L3
BWSH/BRSTN DE72 — 259 M3
CHF/WBR SK23 — 60 F3
CLRC S45 — 144 F8
DERBYE DE21 — 241 J5
DERBYSE DE24 — 257 H4
DRON S18 — 89 K2
EDL/UDV S33 — 49 K7
EDL/UDV S33 — 64 E2
EWD/SEL/PNX NG16 — 203 K8
ILK DE7 — 214 F5
ILK DE7 — 228 E1
MELB/CHEL DE73 — 279 H8
MSFD NG18 — 164 F7
NM/HAY SK22 — 43 L2
RCH S42 — 127 G3
RDERBYSW DE65 — 267 G8
SBK/MW NG20 — 133 J8
STLY SK15 — 16 A4
STV/CWN S43 — 94 F4
STV/CWN S43 — 111 G3
SWAD DE11 — 282 B4
TOT/DORE S17 — 69 H5
Cressbrook Av RCH S42 — 145 L3
Cressbrook Wy DERBYE DE22 — 227 L7
Cresswell Av NM/HAY SK22 — 43 M1
Cresswellpart La EDL/UDV S33 — 64 A3

Cresswell Rd BSTN/STPLFD NG9 — 245 L5
Cresswell St NM/HAY SK22 — 43 M2
Cressy Rd ALFN DE55 — 175 K6
Crest Cl BUTN/AL/TUT DE13 — 274 B1
The Crest DERBYW DE22 — 226 B8
MSHM DE12 — 288 F4
Crestwood Cl BUTN/AL/TUT DE13 — 274 A2
Creswell Rd STV/CWN S43 — 95 H6
STV/CWN S43 — 95 K6
Creswick Cl CHSW S40 — 127 L2
Crewe St SHEF S1 — 55 L1
Crewton Wy DERBYSE DE24 — 257 J5
Crich Av ALFN DE55 — 175 K6
NORM/LIT DE23 — 239 L8
Crich La BPR/DUF DE56 — 199 K1
Crich Pl RCH S42 — 145 J4
Crich Rd BPR/DUF DE56 — 185 K4
STV/CWN S43 — 111 M3
Crichton Av BUTN/AL/TUT DE13 — 274 A3
Crich Vw ALFN DE55 — 161 K6
BPR/DUF DE56 — 200 B2
BSVR S44 — 131 L2
Crich Wy SWAD DE11 — 282 B5
Cricket Cl STPNHL/WHNL DE15 — 275 H2
Cricketers Cl STPNHL/WHNL DE15 — 281 J2
Cricket Vw STV/CWN S43 — 95 H8
Cricklewood Rd DERBYW DE22 — 239 L4
Crimicar Av FUL S10 — 53 L2
Crimicar Cl FUL S10 — 53 M3
Crimicar Dr FUL S10 — 53 M3
Crimicar La FUL S10 — 53 M3
Cringle Ms DERBYE DE21 — 227 H8
Cripton La CLCR S45 — 143 H5
Crispin Cl HACK/IN S12 — 56 D1
Crispin Gdns HACK/IN S12 — 56 D6
Crispin Rd HACK/IN S12 — 56 D6
Critchley St ILK DE7 — 230 C1
Croft Abbey ECK/KIL S21 — 93 M2
Croft Av ASHB DE6 — 180 A1
MSFD NG18 — 164 F8
Croft Cl BUTN/AL/TUT DE13 — 264 E6
BWSH/BRSTN DE72 — 242 F6
DERBYE DE21 — 242 C4
ECC S11 — 54 C7
EWD/SEL/PNX NG16 — 176 F7
ILK DE7 — 229 J8
MSHM DE12 — 294 C5
Croft Crs EWD/SEL/PNX NG16 — 217 M5
Croft End DERBYE DE21 — 226 F2
Crofters Cl ECK/KIL S21 — 73 M6
Crofters Ct DERBYE DE21 — 227 H8
Croft Gv UTXR ST14 — 247 L1
Croft La DERBYE DE21 — 227 G7
ECC S11 — 54 C7
Croft Lea DRON S18 — 69 M8
Croft Mnr GLSP SK13 — 26 B1
Crofton Cl DRON S18 — 90 C1
Crofton Ri DRON S18 — 90 C1
Crofton Rd BKWL DE45 — 104 D6
HACK/IN S12 — 56 E5
Croftstead Av UTXR ST14 — 218 A4
Croft Vw STV/CWN S43 — 95 H7
STV/CWN S43 — 111 M5
Cromarty Cl DERBYSE DE24 — 256 B6
MSFDW NG19 — 164 A5
Cromarty Ri DRON S18 — 70 A8
Cromdale Av STV/CWN S43 — 92 A6
Cromer Cl MCKLVR DE3 — 254 F1
MSFD NG18 — 164 D6
Cromford Av MSFD NG18 — 164 D6
Cromford Cl EWD/SEL/PNX NG16 — 202 E6
LGEAT NG10 — 260 D5
RCH S42 — 145 L3
Cromford Dr MCKLVR DE3 — 239 G6
STV/CWN S43 — 111 L2
Cromford Hl MTLK DE4 — 171 K6
Cromford Ms MPL/ROM SK6 — 42 B3
Cromford Rd CLCR S45 — 144 D5
DERBYE DE21 — 241 K2
EWD/SEL/PNX NG16 — 202 D6
MTLK DE4 — 171 J8
MTLK DE4 — 173 J8
MTLK DE4 — 183 J1
RIPLEY DE5 — 187 G8
Cromford St SHEFP/MNR S2 — 55 L1
Cromley Rd MPL/ROM SK6 — 42 B3
Crompton Cl MPL/ROM SK6 — 32 C3
Crompton Rd ILK DE7 — 230 E7
MSFDW NG19 — 149 G7
STV/CWN S43 — 93 J8
Crompton St ASH NG17 — 162 E5
DERBY DE1 — 4 D5
MSFDW NG19 — 148 C3
Cromwell Av ALFN DE55 — 176 B1
CHF/WBR SK23 — 60 D5
ILK DE7 — 230 D5
RDERBYSW DE65 — 255 G8
Cromwell Cl BUTN/AL/TUT DE13 — 263 M5
Cromwell Dr ALFN DE55 — 187 G3
Cromwell Hl MTLK DE4 — 171 K4
Cromwell Rd BSVR S44 — 131 L2
CHSW S40 — 2 E1
NORM/LIT DE23 — 4 C9
Cromwell St EWD/SEL/PNX NG16 — 217 M2
LGEAT NG10 — 261 J1
RCH S42 — 144 E2
Crookes Av MSFDW NG19 — 148 D5
Crook's Av MSFDW NG19 — 149 M7
Crook Stile MTLK DE4 — 156 D3
Cropper La ASHB DE6 — 236 E7
Cropton Cl DERBYSE DE24 — 257 M4

Crosby Rd SHEFS S8 — 55 H8
Crosby St DERBYW DE22 — 240 A6
Cross Chantrey Rd SHEFS S8 — 55 K7
Cross Cliffe GLSP SK13 — 26 B2
Cross Cl NORM/LIT DE23 — 255 M2
Crossdale Gv DERBYE DE21 — 227 M7
Cross Dr HAN/WDH S13 — 57 L4
Crossfield Gv MPL/ROM SK6 — 32 E1
Crossgate La GLSP SK13 — 17 J3
Crosshill RIPLEY DE5 — 201 L4
Crosshill Dr ILK DE7 — 229 M5
Crossings Av CHF/WBR SK23 — 60 C4
Crossings Rd CHF/WBR SK23 — 60 C4
Crossland Dr HACK/IN S12 — 56 D7
Crossland Pl HACK/IN S12 — 56 D6
Crossland Rd HATH/EY S32 — 66 C3
Cross La ALFN DE55 — 174 C2
ALFN DE55 — 175 H2
ASH NG17 — 162 C8
BUTN/AL/TUT DE13 — 264 C1
BUX SK17 — 120 A3
DRON S18 — 70 F7
DRON S18 — 90 E1
HATH/EY S32 — 86 E8
MPL/ROM SK6 — 32 B5
MTLK DE4 — 170 B3
RIPLEY DE5 — 201 L3
SHEFS S8 — 70 F5
TOT/DORE S17 — 68 F2
Crossley Av ASH NG17 — 162 D7
Crossley St RIPLEY DE5 — 201 G1
Cross London St STV/CWN S43 — 92 A7
Crosslow La ASHB DE6 — 167 H6
Cross Myrtle Rd SHEFP/MNR S2 — 55 L3
Cross Park Rd SHEFS S8 — 55 K5
Cross Ri GLSP SK13 — 26 B2
Cross Rd UTXR ST14 — 247 L1
Cross Road Banner ECC S11 — 54 E5
Cross Rw ASH NG17 — 162 F4
Cross Side ASHB DE6 — 207 J3
Cross St BSVR S44 — 147 G1
BUT DE14 — 273 M8
BUX SK17 — 100 A1
CHF/WBR SK23 — 60 D4
CHSW S40 — 2 E2
CLCR S45 — 144 F7
DERBYW DE22 — 240 A4
ECK/KIL S21 — 74 C3
EDL/UDV S33 — 48 E8
EWD/SEL/PNX NG16 — 203 K8
GLSP SK13 — 17 K6
GLSP SK13 — 25 M2
HAN/WDH S13 — 57 L4
HYDE SK14 — 17 G6
LGEAT NG10 — 244 F4
LGEAT NG10 — 261 K2
MELB/CHEL DE73 — 279 J8
MSFDW NG19 — 149 L8
NM/HAY SK22 — 43 M2
RCH S42 — 129 H7
RCH S42 — 145 H4
STV/CWN S43 — 111 H2
SWAD DE11 — 289 H2
The Cross GLSP SK13 — 17 K5
Crossways La ASHB DE6 — 196 E8
The Crossways SHEFP/MNR S2 — 56 E1
Cross Wellington St STV/CWN S43 — 92 A7
Crow Croft Rd CLCR S45 — 145 M8
Crowcroft Wy LGEAT NG10 — 244 D8
Crowden Drive GLSP SK13 — 17 K5
Crowestones BUX SK17 — 99 H3
Crowfoot La RDERBYSW DE65 — 251 H1
Crow Hl MSFDW NG19 — 148 E5
Crow Hill St MSFDW NG19 — 164 E2
Crow Hill Dr MSFDW NG19 — 164 E2
Crowhill La BKWL DE45 — 122 D4
Crow Hill La MSFDW NG19 — 149 L8
Crow La ALFN DE55 — 159 K5
CHNE S41 — 3 K3
DRON S18 — 91 H3
Crowley Cl WOL/BIL/BRX NG8 — 231 M4
Crown Av MSFDW NG19 — 165 K2
Crown Cl CHNE S41 — 92 A7
LGEAT NG10 — 260 D3
Crown Farm Wy MSFDW NG19 — 165 M2
Crown Hill Wy ILK DE7 — 228 E2
Crownland Dr MELB/CHEL DE73 — 257 K8
Crown Ms DERBYW DE22 — 4 B7
Crown Rd CHNE S41 — 110 D5
Crown St BPR/DUF DE56 — 213 H6
DERBYW DE22 — 4 B7
MPL/ROM SK6 — 32 C7
MSFD NG18 — 165 J4
STV/CWN S43 — 95 H7
Crown Ter BPR/DUF DE56 — 199 J6
Crowshaw St DERBYSE DE24 — 256 E2
DERBYSE DE24 — 256 F2
Crowstones Rd MTLK DE4 — 140 E7
Crowther Pl SHEFP/MNR S2 — 55 J2
Crowtrees Dr ASH NG17 — 177 M1
Croxton Cl MPL/ROM SK6 — 32 B5
Croydon St ECC S11 — 55 J2
Cruck Cl DRON S18 — 70 B8
Cruise Rd ECC S11 — 54 C2
Crummock Cl BSTN/STPLFD NG9 — 245 M2
Crummock Rd SHEFS S8 — 55 H5
Cubley La ASHB DE6 — 233 J1
Cuckoo Holt WRKN S81 — 77 M3
Cuckoostone La MTLK DE4 — 157 J1
Cuckoo Wy AU/AST/KP S26 — 76 A1
CHNE S41 — 110 E5
ECK/KIL S21 — 73 L5
STV/CWN S43 — 93 J7
STV/CWN S43 — 110 F2
Cuillin Cl LGEAT NG10 — 260 D1
Culcheth Av MPL/ROM SK6 — 32 C4
Cullabine Rd SHEFP/MNR S2 — 56 D3
Cullamore La UTXR ST14 — 247 K6
Culland Rd BUT DE14 — 280 E3
Culland Vw MTLK DE4 — 185 K2
Cullen Av ASHB DE6 — 207 M1
Cullumbell La CLCR S45 — 135 H5
Culworth Cl BPR/DUF DE56 — 200 A6

Cumberhills Rd *DERBYW* DE22 ..... 225 L1
Cumberland Av *DERBYE* DE21 ..... 241 H4
Cumberland Cl *BUX* SK17 .... 100 A5
   EWD/SEL/PNX NG16 .... 188 F6 🲆
Cumberland Crs
   BWSH/BRSTN DE72 .... 258 E1
Cumberland Dr *MSFDW* NG19 ..... 164 A3
Cumberland Rd
   STPNHL/WHNL DE15 .... 281 C4
Cummings St *NORM/LIT* DE23 .... 4 E9
Cundy Rd *BSVR* S44 .... 113 K7
Cunliffe St *DRON* S18 .... 70 F6
Cunnery La *MTLK* DE4 .... 157 M7
The Cunnery *ASHB* DE6 .... 224 C8
Cunningham Pl *BKWL* DE45 .... 122 F4 🲆
Curbar Cl *RCH* S42 .... 145 K3
Curbar Curve *STV/CWN* S43 ...... 111 L4
Curbar Hl *HATH/EY* S32 .... 106 A1
Curborough Dr *DERBYSE* DE24 ... 257 H4
Curlew Av *ECK/KIL* S21 .... 72 E7
Curlew Cl *DERBYSE* DE24 .... 256 A6 🲆
   UTXR S14 .... 247 M4
Cursham St *ASH* NG17 .... 163 J8
Cursley Wy *BSTN/STPLFD* NG9 .. 245 M8
Curtis Gv *GLSP* SK13 .... 17 K5
Curtis Wy *BUT* DE14 .... 273 L6
Curzon Av *DRON* S18 .... 90 C2
Curzon Cl *DERBYW* DE22 .... 225 M6
   ECK/KIL S21 .... 74 A4
Curzon La *BPR/DUF* DE56 .... 213 C7
   DERBYSE DE24 .... 257 K2
Curzon Rd *BUX* SK17 .... 99 M3
   DERBYE DE21 .... 241 J3
Curzon St *BUT* DE14 .... 273 M7
   DERBY DE1 .... 4 D4
   DERBYW DE22 .... 4 C4
   LGEAT NG10 .... 244 E8
Curzon St West *BUT* DE14 ...... 273 L7 🲆
Cuscas La *ASHB* DE6 .... 210 B5
Cutler Cl *ECK/KIL* S21 .... 73 L3 🲆
Cutler La *ASHB* DE6 .... 224 D2
Cuttholme Rd *CHSW* S40 .... 109 K3
Cutthorpe Gft *RCH* S42 .... 109 K3
Cutthorpe Rd *RCH* S42 .... 109 J3
Cutthroat Br *EDL/UDV* S33 .... 40 F7
Cuttings Av *ASH* NG17 .... 177 L2
The Cutting *SWAD* DE11 .... 283 J6
Cuttlebrook Cl
   NORM/LIT DE23 .... 256 B4 🲆
Cutts Ter *SHEFS* S8 .... 55 J5 🲆
Cynthia Av *MPL/ROM* SK6 .... 32 C5
Cypress Av *SHEFS* S8 .... 70 F1
Cypress Cl *ECK/KIL* S21 .... 73 M5 🲆
Cypress Wy *MPL/ROM* SK6 .... 42 D3
Cyprus Rd *SHEFS* S8 .... 55 K5 🲆
Cyril Av *BSTN/STPLFD* NG9 ..... 245 C3

D

Dade Av *STV/CWN* S43 .... 111 L4
Dag La *MSHM* DE12 .... 293 C3
Dagnall Gdns *BKWL* DE45 .... 123 C5
Dagnam Cl *SHEFP/MNR* S2 .... 56 C4
Dagnam Crs *SHEFP/MNR* S2 .... 56 C3
Dagnam Dr *SHEFP/MNR* S2 ...... 56 C3
Dagnam Pl *SHEFP/MNR* S2 .... 56 C4 🲆
Dagnam Rd *SHEFP/MNR* S2 ...... 56 C3
Dahlia Av *ALFN* DE55 .... 159 M6
Dahlia Dr *DERBYE* DE21 .... 227 M7
Dairy House Rd
   NORM/LIT DE23 .... 256 D1
Daisy Farm Rd
   EWD/SEL/PNX NG16 .... 217 L2
Daisy Lee La *HOLM/MEL* HD7 ..... 9 M3
Daisymere Cl *BUX* SK17 .... 81 J8
Daisy Wy *MPL/ROM* SK6 .... 42 C3
Dakeyne Cl *MTLK* DE4 .... 156 B1
Dakin Av *BUX* SK17 .... 100 A1
Dalbury Rd *DRON* S18 .... 89 L1
Dalby Gdns *MOS* S20 .... 73 K1
Dale Av *ALFN* DE55 .... 161 K7
   ALFN DE55 .... 187 M4
   LGEAT NG10 .... 261 C1
Dale Bank Crs *CHNE* S41 .... 92 A7 🲆
Dalebank La *CLCR* S45 .... 158 E2
Dale Brook *RDERBYSW* DE65 ... 265 H1 🲆
Dalebrook Rd
   STPNHL/WHNL DE15 .... 274 D5
Dale Cl *ALFN* DE55 .... 160 E6
   ASH NG17 .... 163 K5 🲆
   BWSH/BRSTN DE72 .... 260 A2
   MTLK DE4 .... 185 K4
   SBK/MW NG20 .... 133 J1
   STV/CWN S43 .... 111 M2
Dale Ct *BPR/DUF* DE56 .... 214 C2 🲆
Dale Crs *HATH/EY* S32 .... 66 E2
   RCH S42 .... 144 F1
Dale End *MTLK* DE4 .... 183 J1 🲆
Dale End La *RDERBYSW* DE65... 252 F6
Dalefield Dr *SWAD* DE11 .... 282 E7 🲆
Dale La *ASHB* DE6 .... 191 H5
   BUX SK17 .... 100 B2
   CDLE ST10 .... 191 C4
   MSFDW NG19 .... 148 A3
Dale Park Av *BPR/DUF* DE56 ... 214 C2
Dale Rd *BUX* SK17 .... 81 K2
   BUX SK17 .... 99 M3
   DERBYE DE21 .... 242 D5
   DERBYSE DE24 .... 257 M3
   DRON S18 .... 90 E2
   ECK/KIL S21 .... 74 B4
   ILK DE7 .... 228 F6
   ILK DE7 .... 229 M8
   MPL/ROM SK6 .... 32 B3
   MTLK DE4 .... 156 E5
   MTLK DE4 .... 171 L1
   NM/HAY SK22 .... 43 M4
   NORM/LIT DE23 .... 240 C8
   RCH S42 .... 144 F1
Dale Rd North *MTLK* DE4 .... 140 D3
Dale Rd South *MTLK* DE4 .... 156 A1
Dales Av *ASH* NG17 .... 163 J5
Dalesfield *MTLK* DE4 .... 156 D4 🲆
Dale Side *BUX* SK17 .... 99 L3
Daleside *STPNHL/WHNL* DE15 .. 281 L1 🲆
Dalesthorpe Av *MSFDW* NG19 ... 164 A1 🲆
Dalestorth Cl *ASH* NG17 .... 163 K5

Dalestorth Gdns *ASH* NG17 ..... 163 K5
Dalestorth Rd *ASH* NG17 .... 163 K5
Dalestorth St *ASH* NG17 .... 163 K6
Dale St *BUT* DE14 .... 273 M8
   ILK DE7 .... 230 C3 🲆
   MSFDW NG19 .... 164 E1
Daleswood Crs *ALFN* DE55 ...... 176 D7
Dale Ter *BUX* SK17 .... 99 L4 🲆
   HATH/EY S32 .... 86 B6
The Dale *HATH/EY* S32 .... 66 F2
   MTLK DE4 .... 170 F1
   MTLK DE4 .... 183 H1
   STV/CWN S43 .... 55 J7
Dale Vw *ALFN* DE55 .... 159 M6
   BUX SK17 .... 84 B7
   BUX SK17 .... 118 E7
   ILK DE7 .... 230 B4
Dale View Gdns *BPR/DUF* DE56 .. 214 C2
Dale View Rd *CLCR* S45 .... 145 L6
Daleview Rd *SHEFS* S8 .... 55 G8
Dalewood Av *SHEFS* S8 .... 69 M1
Dalewood Cl *CHNE* S41 .... 129 H1
Dalewood Dr *SHEFS* S8 .... 69 L1
Dalewood Rd *SHEFS* S8 .... 69 M1
Dalkeith Av *DERBYSE* DE24 ..... 257 J5
Dallas St *MSFD* NG18 .... 164 D4
Dalley Cl *BSTN/STPLFD* NG9 ... 245 H2
Dalley La *BPR/DUF* DE56 .... 198 F4
Dallimore Rd *ILK* DE7 .... 230 A6
Dallow Cl *BUT* DE14 .... 273 M5
Dallow Crs *BUT* DE14 .... 273 M5
Dallow St *BUT* DE14 .... 273 M5
Dalmore Rd *ECC* S11 .... 54 F5
Dalness Ct *DERBYSE* DE24 ...... 256 A7 🲆
Dalston Rd *SWAD* DE11 .... 282 D5
Dalton Av *DERBYW* DE22 .... 239 M7
   STPNHL/WHNL DE15 .... 281 L1
Dalton Cl *BSTN/STPLFD* NG9 ... 245 H5 🲆
Dalton Ct *SHEFS* S8 .... 55 J3 🲆
Daltons Cl *EWD/SEL/PNX* NG16 .. 202 D6
Dalvey Wy *STV/CWN* S43 .... 92 A6
Dame Flogan St *MSFD* NG18 .... 164 E4 🲆
Dam La *ALFN* DE55 .... 175 J1
   ASHB DE6 .... 166 F7
Damon Cl *CLCR* S45 .... 160 F1
Damon Dr *STV/CWN* S43 .... 111 J2
Damsbrook Dr *STV/CWN* S43 .... 95 H7
Damsbrook La *BSVR* S44 .... 114 A2
Danbury Gv *RCH* S42 .... 129 H7
Danby Av *CHNE* S41 .... 91 L8
Dane Bank Dr *POY/DIS* SK12 ..... 43 G4
Danebridge Crs *DERBYE* DE21 .. 241 K1
Danebrook Dr *SHEFP/MNR* S2 ... 56 F1 🲆
Dane Gv *BUX* SK17 .... 99 M6
Dane Hill Cl *POY/DIS* SK12 .... 43 G5
Danesby Crs *RIPLEY* DE5 .... 214 C1
Danesby Ri *RIPLEY* DE5 .... 214 D1
Danesway *CHF/WBR* SK23 .... 60 E4
Danewood Av *SHEFP/MNR* S2 ... 56 F1
Danewood Cft *SHEFP/MNR* S2 .. 56 F1
Danewood Gdns *SHEFP/MNR* S2.. 56 F1
Daniel Crs *MSFD* NG18 .... 164 C3
Dannah Crs *RIPLEY* DE5 .... 201 H1
Dannah St *RIPLEY* DE5 .... 187 H8
Darby St *NORM/LIT* DE23 .... 4 D9
Darcy Rd *ECK/KIL* S21 .... 72 F7
Daresbury Dr *SHEFP/MNR* S2 ... 56 A4
Daresbury Pl *SHEFP/MNR* S2 ... 56 A4
Daresbury Rd *SHEFP/MNR* S2 ... 56 A4
Daresbury Vw *SHEFP/MNR* S2 ... 56 A4
Darfield Av *MOS* S20 .... 57 J8
Darfield Cl *MOS* S20 .... 57 J8 🲆
Darfield Dr *HEANOR* DE75 .... 202 D8
Darfield Rd *BSTN/STPLFD* NG9 . 245 H5
Darklands La *SWAD* DE11 .... 282 D6
Darklands Rd *SWAD* DE11 .... 282 E5
Dark La *ALFN* DE55 .... 158 E4
   ASHB DE6 .... 195 K7
   BKWL DE45 .... 139 G3
   BPR/DUF DE56 .... 183 G7
   BPR/DUF DE56 .... 213 K4
   BSVR S44 .... 111 J8
   CHNE S41 .... 111 H6
   CLCR S45 .... 145 M8
   MTLK DE4 .... 171 J6
   MTLK DE4 .... 173 J5
   RCH S42 .... 145 K3
Darley Abbey Dr
   DERBYW DE22 .... 226 D8 🲆
Darley Av *BSTN/STPLFD* NG9 ... 245 H7
   MTLK DE4 .... 140 F7
   MTLK DE4 .... 145 K3
Darley Cl *AU/AST/KP* S26 .... 75 H4 🲆
   STPNHL/WHNL DE15 .... 281 M1
   STV/CWN S43 .... 93 H8 🲆
   SWAD DE11 .... 289 K1 🲆
Darley Dl *SWAD* DE11 .... 282 C8
Darleydale Cl *MSFD* NG18 ...... 164 F7
Darley Dr *ILK* DE7 .... 229 H2 🲆
   LGEAT NG10 .... 260 D5
   RIPLEY DE5 .... 186 F7
Darley Gv *DERBY* DE1 .... 240 D3
   DERBYW DE22 .... 240 D1
Darley La *DERBY* DE1 .... 4 E1
Darley Lodge Dr *MTLK* DE4 .... 156 B2 🲆
Darley Park Av *DERBYW* DE22 .. 240 C1
Darley Park Rd *DERBYW* DE22 .. 240 C1
Darley Rd *CLCR* S45 .... 126 C8
Darley Sq *ILK* DE7 .... 217 H5
Darley St *DERBYW* DE22 .... 240 D1
Darley Wy *BUX* SK17 .... 100 B4
Darlton St *MSFDW* NG19 .... 164 A4
Darsway *CDON/KEG* DE74 .... 271 K6
Dartford Pl *DERBYSE* DE24 ...... 257 K5
Dartnall Cl *POY/DIS* SK12 .... 42 D4
Darwent Rd *CHNE* S41 .... 110 F4
Darwin Av *BUX* SK17 .... 99 M3
   CHNE S41 .... 110 B5
   DERBYSE DE24 .... 257 G6
   ILK DE7 .... 230 B3
Darwin Cl *MSFD* NG18 .... 164 F7
   STPNHL/WHNL DE15 .... 281 M1 🲆
Darwin Rd *CHSW* S40 .... 2 E1
   LGEAT NG10 .... 260 E5
   MCKLVR DE3 .... 239 H7
Darwood La *BSVR* S44 .... 131 K2
Dashwood St *NORM/LIT* DE23 ... 4 F8 🲆
Datchet Rd *DERBYSE* DE24 ...... 255 K2

Davenport Rd *DERBYSE* DE24 ... 256 F2
   RCH S42 .... 144 F2
Daventry Cl *MCKLVR* DE3 .... 238 F7
Davey Ct *BSVR* S44 .... 113 J7
Davey Rd *MSFD* NG18 .... 164 C3
Davian Wy *CHSW* S40 .... 128 B2
David La *FUL* S10 .... 53 K3
David's Cl *MELB/CHEL* DE73 .... 269 H1
Davids Dr *RCH* S42 .... 128 B6
Davies Av *ASH* NG17 .... 163 H7 🲆
Davies Dr *STV* S14 .... 247 J1
Davis Rd *BSTN/STPLFD* NG9 .... 245 L7
   SWAD DE11 .... 282 E6
Dawber La *ECK/KIL* S21 .... 74 C3
Dawgates La *ASH* NG17 .... 163 J1
Dawlands Cl *SHEFP/MNR* S2 ... 56 E1 🲆
Dawlands Dr *SHEFP/MNR* S2 ... 56 E1 🲆
Dawlish Cl *HYDE* SK14 .... 16 B7
Dawlish Ct *DERBYSE* DE24 ...... 257 M3
   EWD/SEL/PNX NG16 .... 203 G7
Dawn Vw *BSTN/STPLFD* NG9 .. 231 G8 🲆
Dawsmere Cl *DERBYE* DE21 .... 241 G1 🲆
Dawson Cl *EWD/SEL/PNX* NG16.. 217 K1
Daybell Rd *MSHM* DE12 .... 290 D6
Dayfield La *ASHB* DE6 .... 195 K5
Day Gv *HYDE* SK14 .... 16 D7
Daylesford Cl
   NORM/LIT DE23 .... 255 K2 🲆
Days La *BPR/DUF* DE56 .... 199 J7
Days Mill La *MTLK* DE4 .... 156 D4
Dayton Cl *DERBYE* DE21 .... 241 M5
Deacon Cl *ALFN* DE55 .... 187 H3
   DERBYE DE21 .... 227 H8 🲆
Dead La *EWD/SEL/PNX* NG16 .. 231 G1
Deadman's Dr *DERBYSE* DE24 .. 241 G8
Deakins Wk *FUL* S10 .... 54 C1
Deamon St *ALFN* DE55 .... 176 B1
Dean Cl *MSFD* NG18 .... 164 F6
   NORM/LIT DE23 .... 239 K8
Deanhead Ct *MOS* S20 .... 57 K8 🲆
Deanhead Dr *MOS* S20 .... 57 J8
Dean Rd *BPR/DUF* DE56 .... 185 J8
Deans Cft *BSTN/STPLFD* NG9 ... 245 L1
Deans Dr *BWSH/BRSTN* DE72 .. 242 E8
Deansgate *MSFDW* NG19 .... 148 D5
Dean St *DERBYW* DE22 .... 4 A7 🲆
   EWD/SEL/PNX NG16 .... 202 F7
Dearleap La *CLCR* S45 .... 144 A7
Debdale Ga *MSFDW* NG19 ...... 149 K8
Debdale La *MSFDW* NG19 ...... 149 K8
Deben Cl *CHSW* S40 .... 127 M2 🲆
Deborah Dr *DERBYE* DE21 ...... 241 K3
Deddington La
   BSTN/STPLFD NG9 .... 231 M8
Dee Cl *DERBYSE* DE24 .... 256 B6
Dee La *RDERBYSW* DE65 .... 254 C3
Deepdale *EWD/SEL/PNX* NG16 .. 188 C6
Deepdale *BSTN/STPLFD* NG9 .. 245 G4
Deepdale Cl
   STPNHL/WHNL DE15 .... 274 E5
   STV/CWN S43 .... 93 J7
Deepdale Gdns *ASH* NG17 ...... 163 J6
Deepdale La *ASHB* DE6 .... 206 D8
Deep Dale La *DERBYSE* DE24 .. 256 B8
Deepdale Rd *BPR/DUF* DE56 ... 199 L5
   BSVR S44 .... 113 J7
   DERBYE DE21 .... 242 C7
   LGEAT NG10 .... 260 D5 🲆
   MSFDW NG19 .... 165 H1 🲆
Deepdale St *ASH* NG17 .... 163 J6
Deep La *CLCR* S45 .... 146 F3
Deepsick La *BSVR* S44 .... 129 M1
Deepwell Av *MOS* S20 .... 73 J4
Deepwell Bank *MOS* S20 .... 73 J4
Deepwell Ct *MOS* S20 .... 73 J4
Deepwell Vw *MOS* S20 .... 73 J4
Deerlands Rd *CHSW* S40 .... 109 L7
   RCH S42 .... 128 C7
Deerpark Crs *RCH* S42 .... 128 C7
Deer Park Vw *DERBYE* DE21 ... 242 C4
De Ferrers Cft
   BUTN/AL/TUT DE13 .... 274 A2
Degge St *DERBY* DE1 .... 4 E5
Deincourt Cl *DERBYE* DE21 ..... 242 D4
Deincourt Crs *RCH* S42 .... 145 J3
Delamere Cl *ALFN* DE55 .... 187 J3 🲆
   BWSH/BRSTN DE72 .... 260 A2
   DERBYE DE21 .... 241 K1 🲆
   MSFD NG18 .... 164 F6
Delamere Dr *MSFD* NG18 .... 164 F6
Delf St *SHEFP/MNR* S2 .... 55 L3 🲆
Delhi Cl *STPNHL/WHNL* DE15 .. 274 F7 🲆
Dell Lea *MSFD* NG18 .... 165 J7
The Dell *CHF/WBR* SK23 .... 60 B3
Delph Bank *CHSW* S40 .... 2 C9
Delph Cl *HATH/EY* S32 .... 86 A4 🲆
The Delph *MELB/CHEL* DE73 ... 279 J7
Delven La *CDON/KEG* DE74 ..... 271 K7
Delves Av *HACK/IN* S12 .... 57 M7
Delves Bank Rd *ALFN* DE55 .... 187 K3
Delves Cl *CHSW* S40 .... 2 A8
   HACK/IN S12 .... 57 M6
Delves Dr *HACK/IN* S12 .... 57 M7
Delves Pl *HACK/IN* S12 .... 57 L7
Delves Rd *ECK/KIL* S21 .... 73 M4
   HACK/IN S12 .... 57 M7
   HEANOR DE75 .... 216 A2
Delves Ter *HACK/IN* S12 .... 57 M7
The Delves *ALFN* DE55 .... 187 J3
De Morgan Cl
   EWD/SEL/PNX NG16 .... 189 K8
Denacre Av *LGEAT* NG10 .... 261 J1
Denacre La *MTLK* DE4 .... 141 H7
Denarth Av *DERBYSE* DE24 ..... 257 H7
Denbigh Cl
   BUTN/AL/TUT DE13 .... 274 A3
Denbigh St *DERBY* DE21 .... 241 H3
Denby Common *RIPLEY* DE5 ... 201 J8
Denby Dr *MSFD* NG18 .... 165 C8
Denby La *RIPLEY* DE5 .... 214 E1
Denby St *STV/CWN* S43 .... 111 M4
Denby St *SHEFP/MNR* S2 .... 55 J1
Denefield Cl *MPL/ROM* SK6 ..... 32 E1 🲆
The Dene *WRKS* S80 .... 77 M8
Deneway *MPL/ROM* SK6 .... 42 C3
Denewood Av
   BSTN/STPLFD NG9 .... 231 M8
Denham Rd *FUL* S10 .... 55 H1
Denham St *CLCR* S45 .... 145 G7
Denison Gdns *DERBYE* DE21... 241 L4

Denman Crs *HATH/EY* S32 .... 86 D7 🲆
Denmark Rd *SHEFP/MNR* S2 .... 55 L4
Dennis Cl *NORM/LIT* DE23 ...... 255 H3
Denstone Cl *ASHZ* LE65 .... 291 K2 🲆
Denstone Dr *DERBYSE* DE24 ... 257 K6
Dentdale Dr *WOL/BIL/BRX* NC8 . 231 L6
Dent La *MOS* S20 .... 57 J8
Denton Av *LGEAT* NG10 .... 244 D4 🲆
Denton Cl *MSFDW* NG19 .... 165 J1
Denton Ri *BUTN/AL/TUT* DE13 .. 273 K3
Denton Rd *BUTN/AL/TUT* DE13 . 273 K4
   SHEFS S8 .... 55 J6 🲆
Denton Wy *ALFN* DE55 .... 187 J2
Denver Ct *BSTN/STPLFD* NG9 .. 245 H1
Denver Rd *MCKLVR* DE3 .... 239 G7
Depedale Av
   BWSH/BRSTN DE72 .... 242 F8
   ILK DE7 .... 230 A5
Depot St *NORM/LIT* DE23 .... 4 F9
Derby La *ASHB* DE6 .... 222 B2
   ASHB DE6 .... 234 C1
   BKWL DE45 .... 136 F3
   NORM/LIT DE23 .... 256 C2
Derby Pl *SHEFP/MNR* S2 .... 55 M4 🲆
Derby Rd *ALFN* DE55 .... 187 J1
   ASHB DE6 .... 208 A2
   ASHB DE6 .... 232 D8
   ASHB DE6 .... 249 J5
   ASHZ LE65 .... 284 D6
   ASHZ LE65 .... 291 L4
   BPR/DUF DE56 .... 185 J8
   BPR/DUF DE56 .... 197 H1
   BPR/DUF DE56 .... 213 J5
   BPR/DUF DE56 .... 214 B3 🲆
   BSTN/STPLFD NG9 .... 226 C1
   BSTN/STPLFD NG9 .... 244 F4
   BSTN/STPLFD NG9 .... 245 M1
   BUT DE14 .... 274 A5
   BUTN/AL/TUT DE13 .... 274 C3
   BWSH/BRSTN DE72 .... 242 D8
   BWSH/BRSTN DE72 .... 243 L6
   BWSH/BRSTN DE72 .... 258 D7
   BWSH/BRSTN DE72 .... 270 D2
   CHSW S40 .... 3 H9
   CHSW S40 .... 128 D4
   DERBYE DE21 .... 214 A5
   DERBYE DE21 .... 227 C1
   DERBYE DE21 .... 241 L6
   EWD/SEL/PNX NG16 .... 202 F7
   EWD/SEL/PNX NG16 .... 203 G7 🲆
   HEANOR DE75 .... 216 A1
   ILK DE7 .... 230 A3
   LGEAT NG10 .... 260 F2
   MELB/CHEL DE73 .... 257 J8
   MELB/CHEL DE73 .... 278 D2
   MSFD NG18 .... 164 F8
   MTLK DE4 .... 171 L4
   MTLK DE4 .... 185 H3
   NM/HAY SK22 .... 44 A1
   RCH S42 .... 128 E6
   RCH S42 .... 144 F1
   RDERBYSW DE65 .... 251 M8
   RDERBYSW DE65 .... 265 L7
   RIPLEY DE5 .... 187 H5
   RIPLEY DE5 .... 201 H4
   SWAD DE11 .... 282 F6
   SWAD DE11 .... 284 B3
   UTXR S14 .... 248 A2
Derbyshire Av
   BSTN/STPLFD NG9 .... 231 G6
   ILK DE7 .... 229 H2
Derbyshire Cl *ILK* DE7 .... 229 H2 🲆
Derbyshire Dr
   EWD/SEL/PNX NG16 .... 188 F6
   ILK DE7 .... 230 B4
Derbyshire La *SHEFS* S8 .... 55 K7
Derbyshire Level *SHEFS* S8 .... 55 K7
Derbyshire Rd *POY/DIS* SK12 .... 42 A5
Derby St *BUT* DE14 .... 273 M6
   GLSP SK13 .... 25 M2
   ILK DE7 .... 230 C2 🲆
   MPL/ROM SK6 .... 32 C5
   MSFD NG18 .... 164 F4
   SHEFP/MNR S2 .... 55 L4
Derby St East *BUT* DE14 .... 273 M6
Derby Ter *SHEFP/MNR* S2 .... 55 M4
Derriman Av *ECC* S11 .... 54 E6
Derriman Cl *ECC* S11 .... 54 E6
Derriman Dr *ECC* S11 .... 54 E6
Derriman Gln *ECC* S11 .... 54 D6
Derriman Gv *ECC* S11 .... 54 E6
Derrington Leys
   DERBYSE DE24 .... 258 A4
De Ruthyn Cl *MSHM* DE12 ...... 290 D6
Derventio Cl *DERBY* DE1 .... 240 D3 🲆
Derwent Av *BPR/DUF* DE56 .... 213 J2
   BWSH/BRSTN DE72 .... 242 F7
   DERBYW DE22 .... 226 D6
   HATH/EY S32 .... 86 F3
   ILK DE7 .... 217 G8
   ILK DE7 .... 229 H2
   MSFD NG18 .... 165 K5
   MTLK DE4 .... 140 F6
Derwent Cl *BUT* DE14 .... 274 B6
   DERBYW DE22 .... 226 D6 🲆
   DRON S18 .... 70 E1
   GLSP SK13 .... 26 C2
   HATH/EY S32 .... 86 F2
   MSFDW NG19 .... 165 K5 🲆
   SWAD DE11 .... 289 K1 🲆
Derwent Dr *BPR/DUF* DE56 ..... 199 L6 🲆
   RDERBYSW DE65 .... 266 D4
Derwent Crs *CHNE* S41 .... 110 A3
Derwent Dr *ALFN* DE55 .... 161 J4
   BKWL DE45 .... 106 A4
   CHF/WBR SK23 .... 60 A1
   DERBYSE DE24 .... 256 A8
   EWD/SEL/PNX NG16 .... 189 G3 🲆
Derwent Gdns *ASHB* DE6 .... 208 A2
   ASHZ LE65 .... 291 M6
Derwent Gv *ALFN* DE55 .... 175 J8
   ASHZ LE65 .... 291 M6
Derwent La *EDL/UDV* S33 .... 39 L3
   HATH/EY S32 .... 66 B2
Derwent Pl *CLCR* S45 .... 144 D5 🲆
Derwent Ri *DERBYE* DE21 .... 242 C6
Derwent Rd *BUX* SK17 .... 99 M4
   DERBYE DE21 .... 242 A7 🲆
   DRON S18 .... 70 E7
   MPL/ROM SK6 .... 42 B2

   RIPLEY DE5 .... 200 F1
   STPNHL/WHNL DE15 .... 281 K1
Derwent Sq *CHF/WBR* SK23 .... 60 A1
Derwent St *BPR/DUF* DE56 ..... 199 H7
   BWSH/BRSTN DE72 .... 259 G3
   DERBY DE1 .... 5 G3
Derwent V *BPR/DUF* DE56 ...... 199 J8 🲆
Derwent Vw *BPR/DUF* DE56 .... 199 J5
   STV/CWN S43 .... 93 M7 🲆
Desborough Rd
   EWD/SEL/PNX NG16 .... 189 G3
De Sutton Pl *AU/AST/KP* S26 ... 75 H5
Dethick La *MTLK* DE4 .... 172 E1
Devas Gdns *DERBYE* DE21 ...... 242 A5
Deveron Cl
   BUTN/AL/TUT DE13 .... 273 M1 🲆
Deveron Rd *MOS* S20 .... 73 J5
Devizes Cl *CHSW* S40 .... 128 C2
Devon Cl *DERBYE* DE21 .... 5 M1
   EWD/SEL/PNX NG16 .... 203 L8 🲆
   LGEAT NG10 .... 244 E5
   MSHM DE12 .... 290 E4
   RCH S42 .... 129 J7 🲆
   STPNHL/WHNL DE15 .... 281 H4
Devon Dr *MSFDW* NG19 .... 164 C3
   STV/CWN S43 .... 111 J2
Devon Park Vw *STV/CWN* S43 .. 111 J2
Devonshire Av
   BWSH/BRSTN DE72 .... 242 F8
   DERBYW DE22 .... 226 C7
   LGEAT NG10 .... 261 K2
   MTLK DE4 .... 156 C3
   RIPLEY DE5 .... 186 F8
Devonshire Av East *CHNE* S41 .. 128 F2
Devonshire Av North
   STV/CWN S43 .... 92 A7
Devonshire Cl *ASH* NG17 .... 162 D8
   CHNE S41 .... 110 C2
   DRON S18 .... 90 C2 🲆
   ILK DE7 .... 217 H5 🲆
   STV/CWN S43 .... 93 H8 🲆
   TOT/DORE S17 .... 69 J4 🲆
Devonshire Ct *STV/CWN* S43 .. 111 G3 🲆
Devonshire Dr *ALFN* DE55 ...... 187 L3
   BPR/DUF DE56 .... 213 G8
   BSTN/STPLFD NG9 .... 231 G8
   CHF/WBR SK23 .... 45 G8 🲆
   EWD/SEL/PNX NG16 .... 203 J8 🲆
   MCKLVR DE3 .... 239 H7
   SBK/MW NG20 .... 133 J1
   TOT/DORE S17 .... 69 H5
   WRKS S80 .... 114 F1
Devonshire Gln
   TOT/DORE S17 .... 69 J4 🲆
Devonshire Gv *TOT/DORE* S17 .. 69 H4 🲆
Devonshire Rd *BUX* SK17 .... 99 L2
   TOT/DORE S17 .... 69 J5
Devonshire Rd East
   CHNE S41 .... 128 F2 🲆
Devonshire Rd North
   STV/CWN S43 .... 92 A7
Devonshire Sq *MTLK* DE4 .... 124 D7 🲆
Devonshire St
   BPR/DUF DE56 .... 185 J8 🲆
   CHNE S41 .... 3 H3
   MSFDW NG19 .... 148 D3
   STV/CWN S43 .... 93 H8
Devon St *ILK* DE7 .... 230 D5
Dewar Dr *ABRD* S7 .... 54 F4
De Warren Pl *AU/AST/KP* S26 ... 75 J5
Dewchurch Dr *NORM/LIT* DE23 . 255 J3
Dewint Av *MPL/ROM* SK6 .... 32 E2
Dew Pond La *BUX* SK17 .... 100 B3
Dewsnap La *HYDE* SK14 .... 16 D4
Dewy La *MTLK* DE4 .... 173 J1
Dexter St *NORM/LIT* DE23 .... 5 J9
Dialstone *EDL/UDV* S33 .... 64 D3 🲆
Diamond Dr *DERBYE* DE21 ...... 227 J7
Diamond Ter *MPL/ROM* SK6 ..... 32 C7
Dibble Rd *BUT* DE14 .... 274 A4 🲆
Dickens Cl *BUT* DE14 .... 274 A4 🲆
Dickens Ct
   EWD/SEL/PNX NG16 .... 203 L7 🲆
Dickens Dr *RCH* S42 .... 146 A1
   SWAD DE11 .... 282 F5 🲆
Dickenson Rd *CHNE* S41 .... 3 K7
Dickens Sq *NORM/LIT* DE23 .... 256 C1
Dickinson's La *ASHB* DE6 .... 252 L1
Dickinson St *DERBYSE* DE24 ... 241 G8
Dicklant La *CLCR* S45 .... 158 L1
Didcot Cl *CHSW* S40 .... 128 C2
Digby St *ILK* DE7 .... 230 D1
Diglands Av *NM/HAY* SK22 .... 44 A1
Diglee Rd *CHF/WBR* SK23 .... 43 M7
Digmire La *ASHB* DE6 .... 192 F5
Dig St *ASHB* DE6 .... 193 L8
   BUX SK17 .... 151 C4
Dimple Crs *MTLK* DE4 .... 156 D4
Dimple La *MTLK* DE4 .... 185 K3
Dimple Rd *MTLK* DE4 .... 156 D4
Dingle Cl *GLSP* SK13 .... 25 K2
Dingle La *CHNE* S41 .... 129 H1
The Dingle *STPNHL/WHNL* DE15 281 H4
Dinmore Gra *SWAD* DE11 .... 283 K4
Dinnington Rd *SHEFS* S8 .... 55 J6 🲆
Dinting La *GLSP* SK13 .... 25 K1
Dinting Rd *GLSP* SK13 .... 17 L3
Discovery Wy *CHNE* S41 .... 110 C3
Diseworth Cl
   MELB/CHEL DE73 .... 257 K8 🲆
Dish La *ASHB* DE6 .... 252 E3
Dishwell La *AU/AST/KP* S26 ..... 75 H5
The Ditch *BUX* SK17 .... 119 H2 🲆
Division Rd *SBK/MW* NG20 ...... 133 H6
Division St *STV/CWN* S43 .... 111 M2
Dix Av *ILK* DE7 .... 215 J4
Dixie St *EWD/SEL/PNX* NG16 .. 188 E6
Dixon's Rd *CHNE* S41 .... 3 J5
Dobbin Hl *ECC* S11 .... 54 D4
Dobbin La *DRON* S18 .... 89 M4
Dobb Top Rd *HOLM/MEL* HD7 .... 8 E1
Dobcroft Av *ABRD* S7 .... 54 E8
Dobcroft Cl *ECC* S11 .... 54 D6
Dobcroft Rd *ECC* S11 .... 54 D6
Dobholes La *ILK* DE7 .... 215 H4
Dobson Pl *STV/CWN* S43 .... 111 L4
Dockholm Rd *LGEAT* NG10 ..... 244 F8
Dock Wk *CHSW* S40 .... 2 D5
Doctor La *AU/AST/KP* S26 .... 75 H5

Dodburn Ct DERBYSE DE24 256 A6
Dodslow Av
BUTN/AL/TUT DE13 264 E7 1
Doe Hill La ALFN DE55 160 F5
Doehole La MTLK DE4 158 C7
Doe La ECK/KIL S21 71 L6
SHEFS S8 71 M5
Doe Lea Br BSVR S44 131 H3
Doghole La MTLK DE4 170 F6
Dogkennel La ASHB DE6 209 H4
Dog La ASHB DE6 196 A6
CDLE ST10 191 K2
MELB/CHEL DE73 279 H4
MSHM DE12 294 C4
Dogmoor La CDLE ST10 191 J2
Dolby Rd BUX SK17 100 A8
Doles La ASHB DE6 207 J3
RDERBYSW DE65 254 F7
WRKS S80 96 E2
Dolly La CHF/WBR SK23 44 D8
Dolly Wood Cl CHF/WBR SK23 59 L1
Dolphin Cl DERBYE DE21 242 D4
Dominion Rd SWAD DE11 282 E5
Dominoe Gv HACK/IN S12 57 G5
Donald Hawley Wy
BPR/DUF DE56 213 J7
Doncaster Av LGEAT NG10 244 E4
Doncaster Gv LGEAT NG10 261 J1
Donetsk Wy HACK/IN S12 57 L8
Donington Cl
NORM/LIT DE23 256 B5 3
Donington Dr ASHZ LE65 291 K5
NORM/LIT DE23 256 B5
Donington La
BWSH/BRSTN DE72 271 M2
CDON/KEG DE74 271 M3
Donisthorpe La MSHM DE12 290 A7
Donithorne Cl
BUTN/AL/TUT DE13 273 M3
Donner Crs ILK DE7 217 H5
Donnington Rd SHEFP/MNR S2 56 A1
Don Vw STKB/PEN S36 15 G1
Dorchester Av DERBYE DE21 241 H3
Dorchester Cl MSFD NG18 165 G8
Dorchester Dr MSFD NG18 165 G8
Dore Cl TOT/DORE S17 69 K3
Doreen Dr ASH NG17 163 G8 1
Dore Hall Cft TOT/DORE S17 69 G3 1
Dore La HATH/EY S32 66 C3
Dore Rd TOT/DORE S17 69 H2
Doris Rd ILK DE7 230 D3
Dorking Rd DERBYW DE22 239 L4
Dormy Cl BSTN/STPLFD NG9 245 M3
Dorothy Av
EWD/SEL/PNX NG16 203 K7
LGEAT NG10 244 E5
MSFDW NG19 164 F1
Dorothy Dr MSFDW NG19 165 J1
Dorothy V CHSW S40 109 M6
Dorrien Av NORM/LIT DE23 256 C3
Dorset Av STV/CWN S43 111 J2
Dorset Cl BUX SK17 100 A6
STPNHL/WNHL DE15 281 H4 1
Dorset Dr MSHM DE12 290 F4
STV/CWN S43 111 J2
Dorset St DERBYE DE21 5 L1
Dorset Wy MSFD NG18 165 K6
Dorterry Crs ILK DE7 230 D5
Douglas Av
EWD/SEL/PNX NG16 217 M5
HEANOR DE75 201 M8
Douglas Rd ALFN DE55 188 A2
ASH NG17 163 G8
CHNE S41 110 E4
LGEAT NG10 260 E1
Douglas St NORM/LIT DE23 5 J9
Douse Croft La FUL S10 53 J4
Douthwaite Dr MPL/ROM SK6 32 B1
Dovecliff Crs
BUTN/AL/TUT DE13 265 J8 1
Dovecliff Rd
BUTN/AL/TUT DE13 265 H6
Dove Cl BPR/DUF DE56 214 D2 2
MCKLVR DE3 239 K7 2
SWAD DE11 283 J7
Dovecote MELB/CHEL DE73 279 L7
Dovecote Dr
BWSH/BRSTN DE72 242 D8
Dovecote Rd
EWD/SEL/PNX NG16 203 L8
Dovecotes CLCR S45 143 J7
The Dovecote DERBYE DE21 214 C4
MELB/CHEL DE73 279 J8
Dovedale Av ASHB DE6 208 A1
DERBYSE DE24 257 M3
LGEAT NG10 260 D4
STV/CWN S43 111 L5
Dovedale Cir ILK DE7 217 H5
Dovedale Cl MPL/ROM SK6 42 B3
MSFD NG18 165 G7
RIPLEY DE5 201 G4
STPNHL/WNHL DE15 274 D6
Dovedale Ct GLSP SK13 26 C1 1
LGEAT NG10 260 E4
Dovedale Crs BPR/DUF DE56 199 L5
BUX SK17 99 J4
Dovedale Ri DERBYW DE22 240 A1
Dovedale Rd ABRD S7 55 G5
DERBYE DE21 242 B7
Dove Dr EWD/SEL/PNX NG16 189 K3
Dovefields UTXR ST14 218 C7
Dove Flds UTXR ST14 248 A2
Dove Gv RDERBYSW DE65 265 K5 1
Dove House Gn ASHB DE6 193 L8
Dove La LGEAT NG10 260 F2
UTXR ST14 218 D6
Dove Lea BUTN/AL/TUT DE13 264 E6 1
Dovercourt Rd SHEFP/MNR S2 56 B1
Doveridge Cl CHNE S41 91 K8 2
Doveridge Gv BUX SK17 100 B4
Doveridge Rd
STPNHL/WNHL DE15 274 E8
Dove Ri RDERBYSW DE65 252 F8 1
Dove Rd RIPLEY DE5 200 F1
Dover Rd BUTN/AL/TUT DE13 273 L3
FUL S10 54 F1
Dover St NORM/LIT DE23 256 D1 2
WRKS S80 96 B8
Dove Side RDERBYSW DE65 264 A2
Dove St ASHB DE6 205 L8
Dove Vw BUTN/AL/TUT DE13 263 M4
Dove Wk UTXR ST14 248 A2
Dowcarr La AU/AST/KP S26 74 F5
Dowdeswell St CHNE S41 3 G1
Dower Cl DERBYW DE22 240 D1 2
Dowie Wy MTLK DE4 173 J8
Downham Cl MCKLVR DE3 255 H1 4
Downing Cl DERBYW DE22 239 J4 4
Downing Rd DERBYE DE21 5 M4
SHEFS S8 70 B2
The Downings AU/AST/KP S26 75 J5
Downing St ALFN DE55 176 D4
ASH NG17 163 J6
Downlands STV/CWN S43 111 G3
Downlee Cl CHF/WBR SK23 60 C5
Downmeadow
BPR/DUF DE56 200 B2 2
Downside Dr ASHZ LE65 291 K3
The Downs MSFDW NG19 165 J1
Drabbles Rd MTLK DE4 156 D4
Drage St DERBY DE1 240 E3
Draycott Cl HEANOR DE75 201 M6 1
Draycott Dr MCKLVR DE3 238 F7
Draycott Pl DRON S18 90 A2 2
Draycott Rd
BWSH/BRSTN DE72 258 F1
LGEAT NG10 260 C5
RCH S42 145 J3
Drayton Av DERBYW DE22 239 J4 5
MSFDW NG19 164 A1 2
Drayton St SWAD DE11 282 F6
Dresden Cl MCKLVR DE3 238 F8
Drewry Ct DERBYW DE22 4 C4
Drewry La DERBYW DE22 4 B5
Dreyfus Cl DERBYE DE21 242 C5 1
Drift Cl SWAD DE11 290 E2
Drift Side SWAD DE11 290 E3
The Drive BPR/DUF DE56 198 C7
MPL/ROM SK6 32 B4
Dronfield Pl ILK DE7 217 H5 5
Dronfield Rd ECK/KIL S21 72 D8
Drovers Wy BPR/DUF DE56 185 L5
Drummond Rd ILK DE7 230 A1
Drury Av DERBYE DE21 242 A6
Drury La BUX SK17 151 M8
DRON S18 70 F7
TOT/DORE S17 69 G3
Dryden Av CHSW S40 128 C2
Dryden Cl MPL/ROM SK6 32 C6
MSHM DE12 295 M6
Dryden St NORM/LIT DE23 256 C4
Dryhurst Dr POY/DIS SK12 43 G4 2
Dryhurst La POY/DIS SK12 43 G4
Drysdale Rd MCKLVR DE3 239 G7
Duchess Rd SHEFP/MNR S2 55 L1
Duchess St WRKS S80 96 D4
WRKS S80 115 J2
Duchy Cl BUTN/AL/TUT DE13 274 B2 1
Duckmanton Rd BSVR S44 112 D5
Duck Rw BKWL DE45 105 M7
Ducksett La ECK/KIL S21 73 G7
Duck St RDERBYSW DE65 265 K4
Dudwood La MTLK DE4 154 C2
Duesbury Cl DERBYSE DE24 257 H3
The Duesbury ALFN DE55 176 E6 1
Duffield Bank BPR/DUF DE56 213 K6
Duffield Cl LGEAT NG10 260 D5
Duffield Rd BPR/DUF DE56 226 E1
DERBYW DE22 226 D7
DERBYW DE22 240 C1
Duke Crs EWD/SEL/PNX NG16 217 M1
Dukeries Cl WRKN S81 77 M4
Dukeries Ct STV/CWN S43 95 J7 1
Dukeries La DERBYE DE21 227 L8
Dukeries Wy WRKN S81 77 M4
Dukes Cl ASH NG17 163 M8
RCH S42 146 B1
Duke's Dr BSVR S44 147 K4
BUX SK17 100 A5
CHNE S41 110 B4
HATH/EY S32 87 G8
The Duke's Dr BKWL DE45 122 B2
Duke's La LEEK ST13 190 A1
Dukes Pl ILK DE7 217 H6
Dukes St GLSP SK13 25 M2
Duke St ALFN DE55 176 E4
ASH NG17 162 D7 2
ASH NG17 163 H8 2
BUT DE14 273 M8
BUTN/AL/TUT DE13 263 M4
BUX SK17 99 H4
CHNE S41 110 D2 2
DERBY DE1 4 F1
ILK DE7 217 J7
MOS S20 73 G4
MTLK DE4 171 G5
STV/CWN S43 93 H8
STV/CWN S43 95 K6
WRKS S80 96 D4
WRKS S80 115 J1 2
Duluth Av DERBYE DE21 241 K3
Dulverton Av
DERBYSE DE24 255 M8 1
Dulwich Rd DERBYW DE22 239 H4
Dumb Hall La AU/AST/KP S26 76 D6
WRKS S80 76 D5
Dumbles Cl ILK DE7 229 M4
Dumbles La RIPLEY DE5 201 J8
Dumbles Rd BSVR S44 131 J1
The Dumbles ASH NG17 177 M1 2
Dumbleton Rd ECK/KIL S21 74 B5
Dumble Wood Gra
CHSW S40 109 M3 1
Dunbar Cl DERBYSE DE24 256 B8
Dunbar Dr MSFDW NG19 164 A5
Duncan Cl BPR/DUF DE56 199 L4
Duncan Rd NORM/LIT DE23 256 C2
Duncombe Dr ASHB DE6 207 M2
Dundee Dr MSFDW NG19 149 L4
Dundee Rd SWAD DE11 283 G5
Dundonald Rd CHSW S40 3 H8 1
Dunedin Cl MCKLVR DE3 239 H7
Dunedin Crs
STPNHL/WNHL DE15 274 F8
Dunedin Gln MOS S20 73 H4
Dunedin Gv MOS S20 73 H4
Dunelm Cl ASH NG17 162 F7
Dunford Rd HOLM/MEL HD7 9 L3
Dungley Hl BPR/DUF DE56 186 A8
Dungreave Av MTLK DE4 140 D5
Dunkeld Rd ECC S11 54 E5
Dunkery Ct DERBYE DE21 227 K8 4
Dunkirk DERBYW DE22 4 D5 2
Dunlin Ct WRKN S81 77 M4
Dunlow La HATH/EY S32 85 M5
Dunne La GLSP SK13 18 B8 1
Dunnett Rd MSFDW NG19 164 B5
Dunnicliffe La
MELB/CHEL DE73 278 D3
Dunnsmoor La SWAD DE11 283 G3
Dunoon Cl DERBYSE DE24 256 B7 2
Dunoon Rd MSFDW NG19 164 B5
Dunsa La BKWL DE45 124 A1
Dunsford Rd ALFN DE55 175 L5
Dunsil Rd EWD/SEL/PNX NG16 177 G8
Dunsmore Dr DERBYE DE21 227 H8
Dunsmore Wy SWAD DE11 283 G5
Dunstall Brook
STPNHL/WNHL DE15 281 K1
Dunstall Park Rd
DERBYSE DE24 257 G2
Dunster Rd
EWD/SEL/PNX NG16 203 L8
Dunston Ct CHNE S41 110 C1
Dunston La CHNE S41 110 A1
Dunston Pl CHNE S41 110 C1 1
Dunston Rd CHNE S41 109 L1
Dunvegan Av CLCR S45 145 H8
Dunvegan Cl DERBYSE DE24 256 A8 2
Dunwoody Cl MSFD NG18 165 J3
Duper La HATH/EY S32 65 G5
Durban Cl
STPNHL/WNHL DE15 274 F7 2
Durham Av DERBYE DE21 241 H4
RCH S42 129 J7
Durham Cl CHNE S41 92 A7
MSFDW NG19 149 M6
SWAD DE11 283 H5
Durham St ILK DE7 230 C1 2
Durley Cl DERBYSE DE24 257 M3 2
Durlstone Cl HACK/IN S12 56 D5 4
Durlstone Crs HACK/IN S12 56 D5
Durlstone Dr HACK/IN S12 56 C5
Durlstone Gv HACK/IN S12 56 D5
Durrant Rd CHNE S41 3 H3
Durvale Ct TOT/DORE S17 69 H4
Durward Cl DERBYSE DE24 256 F3 3
Dyche Cl SHEFS S8 70 E4 1
Dyche Dr SHEFS S8 70 E4
Dyche La SHEFS S8 70 D3
Dyche Pl SHEFS S8 70 E4 2
Dyche Rd SHEFS S8 70 E4
Dye House La NM/HAY SK22 43 M2
Dykes Cl BSVR S44 113 K8
Dyke Vale Av HACK/IN S12 57 K6
Dyke Vale Cl HACK/IN S12 57 K6
Dyke Vale Pl HACK/IN S12 57 K6
Dyke Vale Rd HACK/IN S12 57 J5
Dyke Vale Wy HACK/IN S12 57 J6
Dymond Gv RCH S42 129 J7
Dyson Pl ECC S11 55 G2 4
Dysons Cl MSHM DE12 295 L6
Dystelegh Rd POY/DIS SK12 43 G4

E

Each Well La ALFN DE55 175 J7
Eagle Cl MSHM DE12 295 L6
UTXR ST14 247 L4
Eagle Hts STPNHL/WNHL DE15 275 G7
Eagle Pde BUX SK17 99 L3
Eagle Rd ILK DE7 230 C6
Eagle St BPR/DUF DE56 186 B8
Eakring Cl MSFD NG18 165 J3
Eakring Rd MSFD NG18 165 J4
Ealing Cl DERBYW DE22 239 K4 2
Eardley Cl DERBYE DE21 241 L5
Earl Dr EWD/SEL/PNX NG16 217 M1
Earls Cl WOL/BIL/BRX NG8 231 M5
Earls Ct BUTN/AL/TUT DE13 274 A2 6
Earls Crs DERBYE DE21 227 L8
Earlsway CDLE ST10 190 E2
Earlswood Cl
BWSH/BRSTN DE72 260 A2 1
Earlswood Dr MCKLVR DE3 239 J6
Earnshaw St HYDE SK14 17 G6
Easedale Cl RCH S42 109 J5 2
East Av BSVR S44 113 L1
MCKLVR DE3 239 G7
East Bank MTLK DE4 154 E5
East Bank Cl SHEFP/MNR S2 56 A4 1
East Bank Pl SHEFP/MNR S2 56 A4
East Bank Rd SHEFP/MNR S2 55 M3
East Bank Vw SHEFP/MNR S2 56 A4 2
East Bank Wy SHEFP/MNR S2 56 A4 3
Eastbrae Rd NORM/LIT DE23 256 B3
Eastbrook Cl CHF/WBR SK23 60 F4
East Cl DERBYW DE22 226 B8
Eastcote Av BSTN/STPLFD NG9 231 L8
East Crs BPR/DUF DE56 213 M2 1
BSVR S44 112 D4
East Croft Av NORM/LIT DE23 256 A5
Eastcroft Cl MOS S20 73 J2
Eastcroft Dr MOS S20 73 H3
Eastcroft Gln MOS S20 73 J2 1
Eastcroft Vw MOS S20 73 J3 2
Eastcroft Wy MOS S20 73 J2 2
East Dr ASHB DE6 248 E1
MPL/ROM SK6 32 C7
East End MTLK DE4 154 B4
East End Dr SWAD DE11 282 F6
Eastern Av BSVR S44 131 L2
BUTN/AL/TUT DE13 274 C2
SHEFP/MNR S2 56 B3
Eastern Crs SHEFP/MNR S2 56 A4
Eastern Dr SHEFP/MNR S2 56 A3
Eastfield Dr ALFN DE55 176 D5
Eastfield Rd DRON S18 90 F2
RIPLEY DE5 201 K1
SWAD DE11 282 F4
Eastfield Side ASH NG17 163 K6
Eastfields Rd UTXR ST14 248 A2
East Glade Av HACK/IN S12 57 H7
East Glade Cl HACK/IN S12 57 H7
East Glade Crs HACK/IN S12 57 H6
East Glade Pl HACK/IN S12 57 H7
East Glade Rd HACK/IN S12 57 H6
East Glade Sq HACK/IN S12 57 H7 2
East Glade Wy HACK/IN S12 57 H6
Eastgrove Rd FUL S10 55 G1
East Lawn RDERBYSW DE65 255 G8
Eastleigh Ct CHNE S41 129 G2 1
Eastleigh Dr MCKLVR DE3 239 H8
MSFDW NG19 149 L4
Eastmoor Rd STV/CWN S43 111 J6
East Nelson St HEANOR DE75 202 B8 4
East Pde WRKS S80 96 D5
East Rd SHEFP/MNR S2 55 L3
East Service Rd DERBYE DE21 241 L8
Eastside Cl CHNE S41 110 E3
East Smedley St MTLK DE4 156 F4
East St ASH NG17 163 K7
BSVR S44 132 B4
BSVR S44 147 G1
CLCR S45 145 G6
DERBY DE1 4 F4 1
ECK/KIL S21 93 L2
HEANOR DE75 216 D2
ILK DE7 230 C2
LGEAT NG10 261 J2
STPNHL/WNHL DE15 274 E7
STV/CWN S43 95 K5
WRKS S80 115 G1
East V MPL/ROM SK6 32 D5
East Vw CHSW S40 3 H5
SBK/MW NG20 133 J4
East View Av ECK/KIL S21 72 F8
East View Rd BPR/DUF DE56 200 B1
Eastway CDON/KEG DE74 271 L7
Eastwood Av
NORM/LIT DE23 239 M8 1
Eastwood Cl CHNE S41 3 M9
Eastwood Dr BSVR S44 111 L8
NORM/LIT DE23 239 M8
Eastwood La CLCR S45 143 L8
Eastwood Park Dr CHNE S41 129 G2
Eastwood Rd ECC S11 55 G2 5
Eather Av MSFDW NG19 149 M6
Eaton Av DERBYW DE22 226 D5
ILK DE7 230 A4
Eaton Bank BPR/DUF DE56 213 K8
Eaton Cl ASHB DE6 196 B7
DERBYW DE22 226 D5
RDERBYSW DE65 264 A1
Eaton Ct BPR/DUF DE56 213 H8
DERBY DE1 4 B1
Eaton Dr BKWL DE45 106 C5
Eaton Fold HATH/EY S32 86 C7
Eaton Grange Dr LGEAT NG10 260 D2
Eaton Hl BKWL DE45 106 C5
Eaton La CLCR S45 142 E5
Eaton Pl BKWL DE45 106 C5
Eaton Rd CDON/KEG DE74 271 L7
UTXR ST14 218 C7
Eatons Rd BSTN/STPLFD NG9 245 G4
Eaton St UTXR ST14 247 M1
Eaves Av CHF/WBR SK23 60 E5
Eaves Knoll Rd NM/HAY SK22 43 K1
Ebenezer St
EWD/SEL/PNX NG16 202 E7 2
GLSP SK13 25 M3
ILK DE7 217 J7
Ecclesall Rd ECC S11 54 F2
Ecclesall Rd South ECC S11 54 D5 2
Ecclesbourne Av
BPR/DUF DE56 213 J7
Ecclesbourne Cl
BPR/DUF DE56 213 H7
Eccles Bourne Cl MTLK DE4 183 J3
Ecclesbourne Dr BUX SK17 99 K4
Ecclesbourne La
BPR/DUF DE56 197 J5
Ecclesbridge Rd MPL/ROM SK6 32 C6
Eccles Cl CHF/WBR SK23 59 G2
EDL/UDV S33 49 K6
Eccles Fold CHF/WBR SK23 60 D4
Eccles Rd CHF/WBR SK23 59 J5
Eccles Ter CHF/WBR SK23 60 A2
Eckington Cl ILK DE7 229 H2 5
Eckington Rd DRON S18 71 G7
MOS S20 73 J2
STV/CWN S43 93 J8
Eckington Wy MOS S20 73 J3
Edale Av DERBYSE DE24 257 L3
MCKLVR DE3 239 G8
NORM/LIT DE23 240 B8
Edale Cl DERBYW DE22 240 A1
LGEAT NG10 260 E4
MSFD NG18 165 K7
Edale Ct ASH NG17 163 H6
Edale Crs GLSP SK13 17 H8
Edale Dr ALFN DE55 176 E3
DERBYE DE21 242 C7
Edale Gv BUX SK17 100 B3 2
Edale Ms BUX SK17 100 B3 3
Edale Ri BSTN/STPLFD NG9 245 H6
Edale Rd ECC S11 54 D4
EDL/UDV S33 49 H1
MSFD NG18 165 L4
NM/HAY SK22 35 K8
STV/CWN S43 93 M6
Edale Sq ILK DE7 217 H5
Eddery Vw MSFD NG18 165 J3
Eden Av MPL/ROM SK6 42 B3
Edenhall Rd SHEFP/MNR S2 56 C3
Eden Rd DERBYE DE21 241 L6 5
Eden St BUX SK17 99 K4
Edensor Av BUX SK17 100 B3
Edensor Cl RCH S42 145 J4
Edensor Dr BPR/DUF DE56 199 M5
Edensor Sq DERBYW DE22 4 C6 1
Eden St DERBYSE DE24 257 L2
RCH S42 128 B7
Edenthorpe Dell HACK/IN S12 57 L8
Edenthorpe Gv MOS S20 57 M8
Edes Farm Dr UTXR ST14 218 C6
Edgar Av MSFD NG18 164 F2
Edgbaston Ct
NORM/LIT DE23 255 M2 1
Edgebrook Rd ECC S11 55 G4
Edgecote Dr SWAD DE11 282 D3
Edgedale Rd ABRD S7 55 H5
Edgefield Rd ABRD S7 55 H5
Edgefold Rd MTLK DE4 156 E5
Edge Hl MELB/CHEL DE73 257 J7
Edge Hill Ct LGEAT NG10 261 G6
Edgehill Gv MSFDW NG19 149 M8
Edge Hill Rd ABRD S7 55 G4
Edge La EDL/UDV S33 64 E4
HYDE SK14 16 B7
Edgelaw Ct DERBYSE DE24 256 A7 10
Edgemount Rd ABRD S7 55 H5 5
Edge Rd HATH/EY S32 86 A4
MTLK DE4 156 E4
Edge View Cl HATH/EY S32 86 F3 1
Edge View Dr BKWL DE45 104 D6
Edgware Rd DERBYW DE22 239 J4
Edinburgh Ct ALFN DE55 187 J3
Edinburgh Rd CHNE S41 110 C5
RCH S42 128 B6
Edinburgh Wy
BUTN/AL/TUT DE13 274 A2
Edingale Ct
BSTN/STPLFD NG9 231 L6 2
Edingley Av MSFDW NG19 164 A3
Edith Wood Cl DERBYSE DE24 257 L5
Edlaston La ASHB DE6 207 K7
Edlington Dr
WOL/BIL/BRX NG8 231 M7
Edmonton Pl
STPNHL/WNHL DE15 275 G7
Edmund Av TOT/DORE S17 69 M4
Edmund Cl TOT/DORE S17 70 A4
Edmund Dr TOT/DORE S17 69 M4
Edmund Rd DERBYE DE21 242 C7
SHEFP/MNR S2 55 L2
Edmund St CHNE S41 110 C2
Ednaston Av NORM/LIT DE23 256 A5
Edward Av ASH NG17 163 J6
DERBYE DE21 241 K5
EWD/SEL/PNX NG16 188 E6
Edward Rd
EWD/SEL/PNX NG16 203 K8
LGEAT NG10 261 G2
Edwards Cl MPL/ROM SK6 32 B5 1
Edwards Crs BPR/DUF DE56 214 D2
Edward St BPR/DUF DE56 199 K5
BSTN/STPLFD NG9 245 G3
BUT DE14 273 L6
DERBY DE1 4 D1
ECK/KIL S21 73 G7
EWD/SEL/PNX NG16 202 E7
GLSP SK13 25 M1
MPL/ROM SK6 32 D1
MSHM DE12 289 L6 1
STV/CWN S43 111 M2
SWAD DE11 283 K7
SWAD DE11 289 M1
Edwards Wy MPL/ROM SK6 32 B5
Edwin Av CHSW S40 2 B9
Edwin Rd SHEFP/MNR S2 55 M4
Edwinstowe Dr
EWD/SEL/PNX NG16 189 L3 1
Edwinstowe Rd DERBYE DE21 241 K1
Edwin St ASH NG17 163 H7
Efflinch La BUTN/AL/TUT DE13 286 B1
Egerton Cl MSFD NG18 165 J3
Egerton Dr BSTN/STPLFD NG9 231 G8
Egerton Rd DRON S18 70 E8 2
Eggesford Rd DERBYSE DE24 256 A8
Eggington Rd RDERBYSW DE65 253 L7
RDERBYSW DE65 265 L1
Egmanton Cl DERBYE DE21 241 L1 7
Egmanton Rd MSFD NG18 165 K8
Egreaves Av HEANOR DE75 201 M6
Egstow Pl CLCR S45 145 G6
Egstow St CLCR S45 145 G6
Ehlinger Av GLSP SK13 17 K5
Eider Cl SBK/MW NG20 133 G7
Eighth Av BUT DE14 280 C2
MSFDW NG19 165 K2
Eland Cl DERBYE DE21 242 D4
Eland Rd SBK/MW NG20 133 J5
Elder Cl ALFN DE55 187 K2
UTXR ST14 247 L4
Elder Ct ECK/KIL S21 73 M5
Elder St ASH NG17 163 G3
Elder Wy CHSW S40 3 H4
Eldon Cl CHF/WBR SK23 60 F4
Eldon La BUX SK17 62 E5
Eldon Rd BSTN/STPLFD NG9 261 M1
Eldon St CLCR S45 144 F6
STPNHL/WNHL DE15 274 E7
Eleanor Av ILK DE7 230 D5
Eleanor Crs BSTN/STPLFD NG9 245 J3
Electric St BUT DE14 274 B5
Eley Cl ILK DE7 216 F8 1
Elford St ASHZ LE65 291 L4 1
Elgar Dr LGEAT NG10 260 E5
Elgin Av NORM/LIT DE23 255 K1 1
Elgin Cl CHSW S40 127 M3
Eliot Cl LGEAT NG10 260 E5 2
MTLK DE4 183 H2 1
STV/CWN S43 111 J5
Eliot Dr ILK DE7 230 A5
Eliot Rd NORM/LIT DE23 255 L2
Elizabeth Av
BUTN/AL/TUT DE13 264 E7
BUX SK17 100 A3
POY/DIS SK12 43 G5
Elizabeth Cl DERBYE DE21 241 L5
ILK DE7 229 G2
Elizabeth Pk
EWD/SEL/PNX NG16 188 C6
Elizabeth Rd BSTN/STPLFD NG9 245 K7
Elkstone Cl DERBYE DE21 227 L8 5
Elkstone Rd CHSW S40 109 K5
Ella Bank Rd HEANOR DE75 216 C1
Ellastone Gdns DERBYSE DE24 257 L3
Ellastone Rd CDLE ST10 190 A6
Ellendale Rd DERBYE DE21 241 L3
Ellerslie Gv LGEAT NG10 244 D5
Ellesmere Av ALFN DE55 175 L6
DERBYSE DE24 257 G1
MPL/ROM SK6 32 C4 4
Ellesmere Dr
BSTN/STPLFD NG9 230 F5
Ellesmere Rd MSFDW NG19 165 J2
Ellin St SHEF S1 55 K1
Elliott Av EDL/UDV S33 64 D2
Elliott Dr STV/CWN S43 111 M4
Ellis Cl LGEAT NG10 260 E4
Ellison Av BWSH/BRSTN DE72 270 D3
Ellison Cl HYDE SK14 17 G5
Ellisons Rd ECK/KIL S21 74 B2
Ellison St GLSP SK13 26 A1
Elm Av BPR/DUF DE56 199 L8 2
LGEAT NG10 244 E3

LGEAT NG10 ...... 260 F1
MTLK DE4 ...... 156 C3
Elm Cl ASHB DE6 ...... 248 C1
BSVR S44 ...... 131 M1
BUT DE14 ...... 280 C2
CHNE S41 ...... 110 C3
ECK/KIL S21 ...... 73 M5
EWD/SEL/PNX NG16 ...... 177 G7
HYDE SK14 ...... 16 D6
Elm Crs MOS S20 ...... 72 F2
Elm Dr ECK/KIL S21 ...... 73 M5
RDERBYSW DE65 ...... 253 C8
Elmfield CHF/WBR SK23 ...... 60 D5
Elmfield Dr MPL/ROM SK6 ...... 32 B4
Elm Gv CLCR S45 ...... 145 C7
DERBYE DE21 ...... 241 L5
DERBYW DE22 ...... 226 A5
GLSP SK13 ...... 17 L8
MSHM DE12 ...... 290 E4
Elmhurst RDERBYSW DE65 ...... 265 K5
Elmhurst Av ASH NG17 ...... 176 C5
Elmhurst Cl ALFN DE55 ...... 176 C6
Elmhurst Dr ASH NG17 ...... 162 D7
Elmhurst Rd MSFDW NG19 ...... 165 J1
Elm Lodge Farm Cl CHNE S41 ...... 110 C3
Elm Rd CLCR S45 ...... 160 F1
ECK/KIL S21 ...... 72 F8
MPL/ROM SK6 ...... 42 C3
Elms Av ALFN DE55 ...... 175 K6
NORM/LIT DE23 ...... 239 L8
RIPLEY DE5 ...... 201 C2
Elms Cl ALFN DE55 ...... 175 K5
Elmsdale Rd SWAD DE11 ...... 283 K7
Elms Dr NORM/LIT DE23 ...... 255 L5
Elmsfield Av HEANOR DE75 ...... 202 D8
Elms Gv RDERBYSW DE65 ...... 253 M4
Elmslea Av MSHM DE12 ...... 288 A7
Elmsleigh Cl SWAD DE11 ...... 282 E4
Elmsleigh Dr SWAD DE11 ...... 282 E4
Elmsleigh Gn SWAD DE11 ...... 282 E4
Elms Rd MSHM DE12 ...... 287 M7
STPNHL/WNHL DE15 ...... 274 C8
Elms St DERBY DE1 ...... 240 C3
Elm St BWSH/BRSTN DE72 ...... 242 E8
RCH S42 ...... 129 L6
STV/CWN S43 ...... 111 K1
Elmsway MPL/ROM SK6 ...... 42 B4
Elmton Cl STV/CWN S43 ...... 95 J7
WRKS S80 ...... 115 C2
Elmton La BSVR S44 ...... 113 L8
Elmton Rd WRKS S80 ...... 115 H1
Elm Tree Av ALFN DE55 ...... 174 F1
BPR/DUF DE56 ...... 214 D3
MSFDW NG19 ...... 149 K6
SBK/MW NG20 ...... 133 C6
Elmtree Av DERBYSE DE24 ...... 256 E3
DERBYSE DE24 ...... 256 E3
EWD/SEL/PNX NG16 ...... 189 J3
Elmtree Av WRKN S81 ...... 77 J3
Elm Tree Crs DRON S18 ...... 70 D7
Elm Tree Dr RCH S42 ...... 128 C6
Elm Tree St MSFD NG18 ...... 164 F3
Elmwood Dr ALFN DE55 ...... 175 M7
DERBYE DE21 ...... 226 F8
MOS S20 ...... 73 C4
Elnor Av CHF/WBR SK23 ...... 59 H5
Elnor La CHF/WBR SK23 ...... 59 J5
Elnor St EWD/SEL/PNX NG16 ...... 202 F8
Elstead La SWAD DE11 ...... 290 E1
Elston Cl MSFDW NG19 ...... 164 A1
Elstree Dr HACK/IN S12 ...... 56 E6
Elstree Rd HACK/IN S12 ...... 56 E6
Elton Cl BSTN/STPLFD NG9 ...... 245 C2
MSFD NG18 ...... 165 L4
RCH S42 ...... 128 C6
Elton Gv BUX SK17 ...... 100 B4
Elton Rd DERBYSE DE24 ...... 256 E3
MSFD NG18 ...... 165 J4
MTLK DE4 ...... 154 E4
Elton St CHSW S40 ...... 3 C6
Elton Vw STV/CWN S43 ...... 112 A2
Elvaston Cl DRON S18 ...... 89 L1
Elvaston Ct MSFD NG18 ...... 165 L4
Elvaston Dr LGEAT NG10 ...... 260 C6
Elvaston La BWSH/BRSTN DE72... 258 D3
DERBYSE DE24 ...... 257 L3
Elvaston Rd RCH S42 ...... 145 J5
Elvaston St BWSH/BRSTN DE72 ...... 259 L3
Elveden Dr ILK DE7 ...... 216 F6
Elvin Wy RCH S42 ...... 144 F2
Elwood Rd TOT/DORE S17 ...... 69 M4
Elwyn Cl BUTN/AL/TUT DE13 ...... 274 A1
Ely Cl SWAD DE11 ...... 283 G4
Elyn Av RCH S42 ...... 145 L3
Embankment Cl
DERBYW DE22 ...... 239 J3
Ember La MTLK DE4 ...... 171 H1
Embridge Cswy BUX SK17 ...... 78 E5
Emerald Cl DERBYE DE21 ...... 227 J8
MSFDW NG19 ...... 164 C1
Emerson Sq NORM/LIT DE23 ...... 256 C4
Emery Cl MSHM DE12 ...... 289 G5
Emmas Williams Ct
RIPLEY DE5 ...... 201 G1
Emmetfield Cl CHSW S40 ...... 128 C2
Emmett Carr Cl ECK/KIL S21 ...... 93 M5
Emmett Carr Dr ECK/KIL S21 ...... 93 M2
Emmett Carr La ECK/KIL S21 ...... 93 M2
Empingham Cl
BSTN/STPLFD NG9 ...... 245 L8
Empire Rd ABRD S7 ...... 55 J3
SHEFS S8 ...... 55 J4
STPNHL/WNHL DE15 ...... 275 C2
Empire St MSFD NG18 ...... 165 G4
Empress Av MPL/ROM SK6 ...... 32 C5
Empress Rd NORM/LIT DE23 ...... 4 C8
Emsworth Cl ILK DE7 ...... 217 C2
Endcliffe Av ECC S11 ...... 54 E1
Endcliffe Crs ECC S11 ...... 54 E1
Endcliffe Edge FUL S10 ...... 54 L1
Endcliffe Glen Rd ECC S11 ...... 54 F1
Endcliffe Grove Av FUL S10 ...... 54 D1
Endcliffe Hall Av FUL S10 ...... 54 D1
Endcliffe Rise Rd ECC S11 ...... 54 F1
Endcliffe Terrace Rd ECC S11 ...... 54 F1
Endcliffe Vale Av ECC S11 ...... 54 F2
Endcliffe Vale Rd FUL S10 ...... 54 E1
Enderby Crs MSFD NG18 ...... 165 J4
Enderby Ri BUTN/AL/TUT DE13 ...... 273 K3
Endowood Rd ABRD S7 ...... 54 E8

CHSW S40 ...... 127 K2
Endsleigh Gdns
DERBY DE1 ...... 239 J4
The End STPNHL/WNHL DE15 ...... 275 H3
Enfield Cl RDERBYSW DE65 ...... 253 H8
Enfield Rd CHNE S41 ...... 110 D5
DERBYW DE22 ...... 239 L3
Engine La EWD/SEL/PNX NG16 ...... 203 L6
England Crs HEANOR DE75 ...... 202 D8
Englishe Rd MTLK DE4 ...... 156 E6
Ennerdale Av MOS S20 ...... 73 H4
Ennerdale Cl DRON S18 ...... 90 B1
Ennerdale Cl CHNE S41 ...... 109 M3
Ennerdale Dr MOS S20 ...... 73 H4
Ennerdale Rd LGEAT NG10 ...... 244 E8
Ennis Cl DERBYE DE21 ...... 241 M3
Enoch Stone Dr
DERBYE DE21 ...... 241 L6
Enslet La ASHB DE6 ...... 181 L8
Ensor Wy NM/HAY SK22 ...... 43 M3
Enterprise Dr RCH S42 ...... 146 A1
Epping Cl DERBYW DE22 ...... 239 H4
Epping Wy MSFDW NG19 ...... 165 L2
Epsom Cl BUT DE14 ...... 280 C3
Epsom Rd BSTN/STPLFD NG9 ...... 245 H7
Epsom St MSFD NG18 ...... 165 J4
Epworth Dr DERBYSE DE24 ...... 257 K6
Erdington Wy
BSTN/STPLFD NG9 ...... 245 H7
Erewash Dr ILK DE7 ...... 230 D4
Erewash Gv BSTN/STPLFD NG9 ...... 261 J1
Erewash Rd
EWD/SEL/PNX NG16 ...... 177 H8
Erewash Sq ILK DE7 ...... 230 D4
Erewash St ALFN DE55 ...... 188 D4
LGEAT NG10 ...... 261 H1
Erica Dr ALFN DE55 ...... 176 E3
Erin Rd BSVR S44 ...... 112 E3
STV/CWN S43 ...... 112 D2
Ernest Hall Wy SWAD DE11 ...... 282 F6
Ernocroft La MSHM DE12 ...... 24 B7
Ernocroft Rd MPL/ROM SK6 ...... 32 C1
Errington Av SHEFP/MNR S2 ...... 56 B3
Errington Cl SHEFP/MNR S2 ...... 56 B4
Errington Crs SHEFP/MNR S2 ...... 56 B4
Errington Rd CHSW S40 ...... 128 A2
SHEFP/MNR S2 ...... 56 B3
Errington Wy SHEFP/MNR S2 ...... 56 B3
Errwood Av BUX SK17 ...... 99 K4
Erskine Cl SHEFP/MNR S2 ...... 55 M3
Erskine Rd SHEFP/MNR S2 ...... 55 M3
Erskine Vw SHEFP/MNR S2 ...... 55 M4
Eskdale Cl DRON S18 ...... 90 B1
LGEAT NG10 ...... 260 E5
Eskdale Dr BSTN/STPLFD NG9 ...... 245 K6
Essendine Crs SHEFS S8 ...... 55 L7
Essex Rd SHEFP/MNR S2 ...... 56 A1
STPNHL/WNHL DE15 ...... 281 C4
Essex St DERBYE DE21 ...... 5 L1
EWD/SEL/PNX NG16 ...... 203 J8
Estwic Av EWD/SEL/PNX NG16... 203 J7
Etherow Brow HYDE SK14 ...... 24 E2
Etherow Wy GLSP SK13 ...... 17 H5
Eton Cl ASHZ LE65 ...... 291 K2
BUT DE14 ...... 274 B4
Eton Ct ILK DE7 ...... 229 G2
Eton Rd BUT DE14 ...... 274 A4
Eton St DERBYSE DE24 ...... 257 H1
Etruria Gdns DERBY DE1 ...... 240 D3
Etta's Wy RDERBYSW DE65 ...... 253 L6
Ettrick Cl CHSW S40 ...... 109 M5
Ettrick Dr DERBYSE DE24 ...... 256 B8
Etwall Cl CHSW S40 ...... 109 K4
Etwall La RDERBYSW DE65 ...... 254 C1
Etwall Rd MCKLVR DE3 ...... 254 F1
RDERBYSW DE65 ...... 265 L4
Etwall St DERBYW DE22 ...... 240 A5
Eureka Cl SWAD DE11 ...... 283 C5
Euston Dr DERBY DE1 ...... 240 E3
Evans Av ASH NG17 ...... 162 F7
DERBYW DE22 ...... 226 D5
Evans Cl EDL/UDV S33 ...... 64 D3
Evanston Gdns DERBYE DE21 ...... 241 L4
Evelyn Gv DERBYE DE21 ...... 241 K5
Everard Av TOT/DORE S17 ...... 69 K4
Everard Dr TOT/DORE S17 ...... 69 K5
Everard Gld TOT/DORE S17 ...... 69 K5
Everest Dr ALFN DE55 ...... 188 A3
Everett Cl STV/CWN S43 ...... 111 H3
Evergreen Cl DERBYE DE21 ...... 227 K7
Evershill Cl ALFN DE55 ...... 160 C5
Evershill La ALFN DE55 ...... 160 C4
Eversleigh Ri MTLK DE4 ...... 155 L2
Everton Rd ECC S11 ...... 54 F2
Everton St MSFDW NG19 ...... 164 B1
Evesham Av GLSP SK13 ...... 17 K5
Evesham Cl DERBYE DE21 ...... 241 H1
Evesham Ct
BSTN/STPLFD NG9 ...... 261 K1
Ewart La ALFN DE55 ...... 175 J7
Ewe Lamb Cl
BSTN/STPLFD NG9 ...... 245 J1
Ewe Lamb La
BSTN/STPLFD NG9 ...... 245 J1
Excelsior Av DERBYSE DE24 ...... 257 J4
Exchange Rw MSFD NG18 ...... 164 E3
Exchange St DERBY DE1 ...... 4 F4
Exeter Cl SWAD DE11 ...... 283 H4
Exeter Dr OWL S3 ...... 55 J1
Exeter Pl DERBY DE1 ...... 5 G3
Exford St MSFDW NG19 ...... 149 M4
Exlowmere La MTLK DE4 ...... 154 B5
Export Dr ASH NG17 ...... 177 J2
Extension St ILK DE7 ...... 230 C3
Eyam Cl BSTN/STPLFD NG9 ...... 231 M8
MSFD NG18 ...... 165 L4
RCH S42 ...... 145 K2
STPNHL/WNHL DE15 ...... 274 E8
Eyam Ms GLSP SK13 ...... 17 G8
Eyre Gdns CHNE S41 ...... 2 F1
Eyre's Gdn ILK DE7 ...... 217 J8
Eyre St CLCR S45 ...... 144 F7
SHEF S1 ...... 55 K1
WRKS S80 ...... 115 C3
The Eyrie DERBYSE DE24 ...... 256 B8
STPNHL/WNHL DE15 ...... 274 F7

F

Fabis Cl SWAD DE11 ...... 282 D7
Fabric Vw RCH S42 ...... 146 A2
Fackley Rd ASH NG17 ...... 162 E3
Fackley Wy ASH NG17 ...... 162 E4
Factory La ILK DE7 ...... 217 H8
POY/DIS SK12 ...... 43 H5
Factory St CHSW S40 ...... 2 B5
Fairacres Rd MPL/ROM SK6 ...... 42 B2
Fairbourne Dr MCKLVR DE3 ...... 239 C6
Fairburn Cl WOL/BIL/BRX NG8 ...... 231 M6
Fairburn Croft Crs STV/CWN S43... 94 E4
Faircroft Av LGEAT NG10 ...... 244 E5
Fairdale Dr
EWD/SEL/PNX NG16 ...... 203 L8
Fairdene NORM/LIT DE23 ...... 240 C8
Faires Cl BWSH/BRSTN DE72 ...... 259 G1
Faire St DERBYW DE22 ...... 4 B8
Fairfax Rd MPL/ROM SK6 ...... 32 A3
Fairfax Dr SHEFP/MNR S2 ...... 56 E2
Fairfax Rd NORM/LIT DE23 ...... 4 C9
SHEFP/MNR S2 ...... 56 E2
Fairfield Av ALFN DE55 ...... 160 D6
ALFN DE55 ...... 176 F1
BUTN/AL/TUT DE13 ...... 265 C6
BWSH/BRSTN DE72 ...... 242 F7
Fairfield Cl SBK/MW NG20 ...... 115 K8
STV/CWN S43 ...... 111 C2
Fairfield Crs LGEAT NG10 ...... 260 D6
SWAD DE11 ...... 282 B5
Fairfield Dr CHSW S40 ...... 109 J6
MSFD NG18 ...... 165 K3
RCH S42 ...... 145 J4
Fairfield Rd ASH NG17 ...... 163 L7
BSVR S44 ...... 131 K2
BUX SK17 ...... 99 M2
CHSW S40 ...... 2 E3
ILK DE7 ...... 214 F3
ILK DE7 ...... 230 D1
NORM/LIT DE23 ...... 240 B8
UTXR ST14 ...... 247 L2
Fairford Cl CHSW S40 ...... 128 C3
Fairford Gdns
NORM/LIT DE23 ...... 255 K4
Fairham Rd BUTN/AL/TUT DE13... 274 C1
Fairholme Dr MSFDW NG19 ...... 164 B1
Fairholmes MTLK DE4 ...... 157 C5
Fairisle Cl DERBYE DE21 ...... 227 M7
Fairlawns BPR/DUF DE56 ...... 213 G7
MSFD NG18 ...... 165 L3
Fair Lea Cl LGEAT NG10 ...... 261 C4
Fairleigh SHEFP/MNR S2 ...... 56 D2
Fairlie Av MSFDW NG19 ...... 164 A5
Fairmount Gdns HACK/IN S12... 57 K7
Fair Vw CHSW S40 ...... 2 C1
Fairview
EWD/SEL/PNX NG16 ...... 189 J8
Fairview Cl BPR/DUF DE56 ...... 214 E3
MPL/ROM SK6 ...... 32 C3
NORM/LIT DE23 ...... 255 K2
Fairview Dr MPL/ROM SK6 ...... 32 D4
Fairview Gra BPR/DUF DE56 ... 214 E3
Fairview Ri MTLK DE4 ...... 185 K2
Fairview Rd DRON S18 ...... 70 D7
Fairway BUT DE14 ...... 280 E4
Fairway Cl DERBYW DE22 ...... 226 A8
Fairway Crs DERBYW DE22 ...... 226 A8
Fairways Cl GLSP SK13 ...... 26 C1
The Fairways CLCR S45 ...... 145 H7
The Fairway FUL S10 ...... 53 K1
SWAD DE11 ...... 282 B5
Fairwood Dr DERBYSE DE24... 258 A4
Fairy Bank Crs NM/HAY SK22 ...... 35 G7
Fairy Bank Rd NM/HAY SK22 ...... 35 C7
Falaise Wy RDERBYSW DE65 ... 253 H8
Falcon Cl BUT DE14 ...... 274 B5
NM/HAY SK22 ...... 44 A2
Falcon Ri DRON S18 ...... 71 C7
Falcon Rd DRON S18 ...... 70 F7
Falcons Ri BPR/DUF DE56 ...... 199 M5
Falcon Wy DERBYSE DE24 ...... 256 B8
SWAD DE11 ...... 283 J7
Faldo Cl BUT DE14 ...... 280 E4
Falkland Ri DRON S18 ...... 90 D2
Falkland Rd ECC S11 ...... 54 D4
Fallowfield Rd CHNE S41 ...... 92 A7
Fallow Rd DERBYE DE21 ...... 242 C4
Fall Rd HEANOR DE75 ...... 202 B7
Falmouth Rd ABRD S7 ...... 55 H5
DERBYSE DE24 ...... 257 M5
Fanny Av ECK/KIL S21 ...... 74 B5
Fan Rd STV/CWN S43 ...... 112 C1
Fanshaw Av ECK/KIL S21 ...... 72 F8
Fanshaw Bank DRON S18 ...... 90 D1
Fanshaw Dr ECK/KIL S21 ...... 72 F8
Fanshaw Gate La DRON S18...... 89 G2
Fanshaw Rd DRON S18 ...... 70 E8
ECK/KIL S21 ...... 72 F8
Fanshaw Wy ECK/KIL S21 ...... 72 F8
Faraday Av
BUTN/AL/TUT DE13 ...... 274 A2
Faraday Rd MSFD NG18 ...... 165 H5
Far Cft BWSH/BRSTN DE72 ...... 260 A2
Far Croft Av ASH NG17 ...... 162 F7
Far Cross MTLK DE4 ...... 156 F3
Farfield La MSFDW NG19 ...... 147 M5
Far Gn MTLK DE4 ...... 156 E4
Far Hl EDL/UDV S33 ...... 64 D3
Farish Pl SHEFP/MNR S2 ...... 55 L4
Far La BWSH/BRSTN DE72 ...... 243 C5
DRON S18 ...... 89 H8
Far Laund BPR/DUF DE56 ...... 199 L4
Farley Hl MTLK DE4 ...... 156 D2
Farley La CDLE ST10 ...... 204 A7
MTLK DE4 ...... 141 M6
Farley Rd NORM/LIT DE23 ...... 240 B8
Farm Cl ALFN DE55 ...... 187 M2
BPR/DUF DE56 ...... 199 M6
BPR/DUF DE56 ...... 214 D2
BUTN/AL/TUT DE13 ...... 273 L3
CHSW S40 ...... 128 C4
DRON S18 ...... 70 E6
HACK/IN S12 ...... 56 D8
ILK DE7 ...... 230 D2
LGEAT NG10 ...... 261 H5
RIPLEY DE5 ...... 186 E4

Farm Close Gv STV/CWN S43 ...... 111 H3
Farm Crs MOS S20 ...... 72 F4
Farm Croft Rd MSFDW NG19 ...... 148 D8
Farm Dr DERBYSE DE24 ...... 257 K5
Farmfields Cl BSVR S44 ...... 113 H7
Farm La MTLK DE4 ...... 156 F4
Farmhouse Rd DERBYSE DE24... 256 E8
Farmlands La NORM/LIT DE23 ...... 255 L8
Farm Mill Cl HATH/EY S32 ...... 105 M1
Farmoor Gdns MOS S20 ...... 73 L1
Farm Rd BUTN/AL/TUT DE13 ...... 273 M3
SHEFP/MNR S2 ...... 55 L1
Farm Side SWAD DE11 ...... 282 C5
Farm St DERBYW DE22 ...... 4 C7
Farm Vw RCH S42 ...... 145 C2
Farm View Dr HACK/IN S12 ...... 57 L7
Farm View Gdns HACK/IN S12 ...... 57 L7
Farmway MSFDW NG19 ...... 149 M8
Farnah Green Rd
BPR/DUF DE56 ...... 199 C7
Farnborough Gdns
DERBYW DE22 ...... 226 E6
Farncombe La DERBYE DE21 ...... 227 J7
Farndale Cl ASH NG17 ...... 163 J5
LGEAT NG10 ...... 260 D5
Farndale Dr WOL/BIL/BRX NG8 ... 231 L6
Farndale Rd ASH NG17 ...... 163 J5
STV/CWN S43 ...... 93 H6
Farndon Dr
BSTN/STPLFD NG9 ...... 245 J7
Farndon Wy MSFDW NG19 ...... 164 B3
Far New Cl LGEAT NG10 ...... 244 E5
Farneworth Rd MCKLVR DE3 ...... 238 F7
Farnham Cl MCKLVR DE3 ...... 238 F8
Farningham Cl
DERBYE DE21 ...... 242 C5
Farnon Cl CHSW S40 ...... 3 J8
Farnsley La HATH/EY S32 ...... 85 L7
Farnsworth Gv ASH NG17 ...... 162 C8
Farnsworth St CHNE S41 ...... 128 F2
Farnway DERBYW DE22 ...... 240 B1
Farrar Rd SHEFS S8 ...... 55 J3
Farrendale Cl MSFDW NG19 ...... 165 C1
Farrier Gdns NORM/LIT DE23 ...... 255 K3
Farriers Cft ILK DE7 ...... 216 F7
Farringdon Cl DERBYW DE22 ...... 239 J4
Farthing Ct LGEAT NG10 ...... 260 E3
Farwater Cl DRON S18 ...... 90 D2
Farwater La DRON S18 ...... 90 C1
Far Woodseats La GLSP SK13 ...... 24 C4
BUTN/AL/TUT DE13 ...... 262 E4
Fauld La BUTN/AL/TUT DE13 ...... 263 K4
Fauvel Rd GLSP SK13 ...... 25 M1
Faversham Cl DERBYSE DE24 ...... 257 J5
Faversham Rd
BUTN/AL/TUT DE13 ...... 273 K4
Fawn Cl RCH S42 ...... 128 C4
Fawns Keep STLY SK15 ...... 16 B4
Fay Gdns GLSP SK13 ...... 17 H6
Faywood Dr MPL/ROM SK6 ...... 32 D4
Fearn Av RIPLEY DE5 ...... 201 H1
Fearn Cl BWSH/BRSTN DE72 ...... 260 D3
RDERBYSW DE65 ...... 251 K2
Featherbed La BSVR S44 ...... 113 K5
WRKS S80 ...... 77 H8
Featherstone Cl MSFD NG18 ...... 164 A4
Fellbrigg Rd SHEFP/MNR S2 ...... 56 A3
Fellow Lands Wy
MELB/CHEL DE73 ...... 257 K8
Fellside BPR/DUF DE56 ...... 199 K6
DERBYE DE21 ...... 242 C5
Fellview Cl HATH/EY S32 ...... 66 D3
Felly Mill La (North)
EWD/SEL/PNX NG16 ...... 189 L8
Felly Mill La (South)
EWD/SEL/PNX NG16 ...... 203 K1
Felstead Ct
BSTN/STPLFD NG9 ...... 245 M1
Felton Av MSFDW NG19 ...... 149 M4
Felton Cl BSTN/STPLFD NG9 ...... 245 L5
Fenchurch Wk DERBYW DE22 ...... 239 L4
Fen Cl ALFN DE55 ...... 161 K7
Fenland Wy CHSW S40 ...... 128 B2
Fennel St BKWL DE45 ...... 122 B2
Fenney La ECC S11 ...... 54 B8
Fenton Av SWAD DE11 ...... 290 E1
Fenton Gdns MSHM DE12 ...... 295 L7
Fenton Crs MSHM DE12 ...... 295 M7
Fenton Rd MCKLVR DE3 ...... 238 F8
Fenton St ECK/KIL S21 ...... 72 E8
Fentonville St ECC S11 ...... 55 H2
Fenwick St DERBYSE DE24 ...... 257 C3
Ferguson Av MSFDW NG19 ...... 149 L6
Ferguson Cl
BSTN/STPLFD NG9 ...... 245 M8
Fern Av RDERBYSW DE65 ...... 266 C4
STV/CWN S43 ...... 111 M2
Fernbank EDL/UDV S33 ...... 64 D3
Fern Bank Av ALFN DE55 ...... 176 B1
Fernbank Dr ECK/KIL S21 ...... 72 E7
Fern Cl BSTN/STPLFD NG9 ...... 245 L3
BSVR S44 ...... 146 C1
ECK/KIL S21 ...... 73 M5
MPL/ROM SK6 ...... 32 C4
RDERBYSW DE65 ...... 266 F4
SBK/MW NG20 ...... 133 H4
Fern Crs
EWD/SEL/PNX NG16 ...... 203 H7
Ferncroft Av MOS S20 ...... 72 F3
Ferndale Av BUX SK17 ...... 81 L6
Ferndale Cl DRON S18 ...... 71 C7
Ferndale Ri DRON S18 ...... 71 G7
Ferndale Rd BUX SK17 ...... 81 L5
DRON S18 ...... 71 G7
Ferndene Dr LGEAT NG10 ...... 260 D3
Ferneydale Av BUX SK17 ...... 99 M6
Fernhill MPL/ROM SK6 ...... 32 C4
Fernhill Cl GLSP SK13 ...... 18 A7
Fernilee Cl MELB/CHEL DE73 ...... 245 F7
Fernilee Cl ILK DE7 ...... 229 H2
NM/HAY SK22 ...... 43 M1
Fern Lea ALFN DE55 ...... 159 M7
Fernlea Cl GLSP SK13 ...... 17 H6
Fernleigh Ri MSFDW NG19 ...... 165 C1
Fern Rd BUX SK17 ...... 99 L5

Fern St ASH NG17 ...... 163 H6
Fernway BUX SK17 ...... 99 M6
Fern Wy ECK/KIL S21 ...... 72 E7
Fernwood MPL/ROM SK6 ...... 32 F3
Fernwood Cl ALFN DE55 ...... 160 A7
MSFDW NG19 ...... 165 K3
NORM/LIT DE23 ...... 255 M2
Fernwood Crs
WOL/BIL/BRX NG8 ...... 231 M6
Ferrers Av BUTN/AL/TUT DE13 ...... 263 L5
Ferrers Cl ASHZ LE65 ...... 291 J5
CDON/KEG DE74 ...... 271 K7
Ferrers Crs BPR/DUF DE56 ...... 213 C2
Ferrers Wy DERBYW DE22 ...... 226 B8
RIPLEY DE5 ...... 186 F7
Ferry Gn RDERBYSW DE65 ...... 266 C5
Ferry St STPNHL/WNHL DE15 ...... 281 H2
Ferry Vale Cl
STPNHL/WNHL DE15 ...... 281 H2
Festival Av BWSH/BRSTN DE72 ...... 259 M3
Festival Rd BUT DE14 ...... 280 B3
ILK DE7 ...... 229 H2
Fettes Cl ASHZ LE65 ...... 291 K2
Fiddler's La BUTN/AL/TUT DE13 ...... 264 F3
Fiddle St BUX SK17 ...... 99 M1
Fidlers Cl EDL/UDV S33 ...... 50 E6
Fidlers Well EDL/UDV S33 ...... 50 E6
Field Av ECK/KIL S21 ...... 93 L2
RDERBYSW DE65 ...... 263 M1
Field Cl BSTN/STPLFD NG9 ...... 245 L6
BUTN/AL/TUT DE13 ...... 273 K3
BWSH/BRSTN DE72 ...... 242 E7
BWSH/BRSTN DE72 ...... 242 E7
DRON S18 ...... 69 M8
MPL/ROM SK6 ...... 32 A5
RDERBYSW DE65 ...... 253 C8
Field Ct BPR/DUF DE56 ...... 214 D3
Field Crs DERBYSE DE24 ...... 257 K5
Field Dr DERBYSE DE24 ...... 257 K5
SBK/MW NG20 ...... 133 H8
Fielden Av MSFDW NG19 ...... 149 C8
Field End MTLK DE4 ...... 181 K1
Field End Cl STLY SK15 ...... 16 A2
Fieldfare Ct NORM/LIT DE23 ...... 255 K4
Fieldfare Dr WRKN S81 ...... 77 M3
Fieldgate Dr DERBYE DE21 ...... 227 J8
Fieldhead La HOLM/MEL HD7 ...... 8 C1
Fieldhead Rd SHEFP/MNR S2 ...... 55 K3
Fieldhead Wy CHSW S40 ...... 109 M4
Field Head Wy DERBYE DE21 ...... 227 L3
Field House La MPL/ROM SK6 ...... 32 D4
Fielding's Rd WRKS S80 ...... 115 J1
Field La ASHB DE6 ...... 205 M2
BPR/DUF DE56 ...... 196 E5
BPR/DUF DE56 ...... 199 J6
BSTN/STPLFD NG9 ...... 245 K6
BUTN/AL/TUT DE13 ...... 273 J4
DERBYE DE21 ...... 241 K3
DERBYSE DE24 ...... 257 L4
ECK/KIL S21 ...... 73 L5
MELB/CHEL DE73 ...... 279 L7
MSFDW NG19 ...... 147 M4
SWAD DE11 ...... 283 M8
Fieldon Cl ASHB DE6 ...... 224 C8
Field Ri BUTN/AL/TUT DE13 ...... 273 K3
NORM/LIT DE23 ...... 255 M3
Field Rd ILK DE7 ...... 230 C3
Field Rw BPR/DUF DE56 ...... 199 J6
Fields Crs HYDE SK14 ...... 17 C4
Fields Farm La HYDE SK14 ...... 24 A1
Fields Farm Rd HYDE SK14 ...... 16 A8
LGEAT NG10 ...... 260 F5
Fields Gv HYDE SK14 ...... 17 C5
Fields La SWAD DE11 ...... 289 J4
The Fields MTLK DE4 ...... 171 C6
Field St RIPLEY DE5 ...... 201 L3
Fieldsway Dr DERBYE DE21 ...... 227 C8
Field Ter RIPLEY DE5 ...... 201 C1
Field Vw ALFN DE55 ...... 176 C3
ASH NG17 ...... 177 M1
STV/CWN S43 ...... 95 J7
Fife St DERBYSE DE24 ...... 257 H2
Fifth Av MSFDW NG19 ...... 165 K2
Fincham Cl DERBYE DE21 ...... 241 C3
Finch Cl SWAD DE11 ...... 283 J7
Finch Crs MCKLVR DE3 ...... 254 F2
Finchley Av DERBYW DE22 ...... 239 L4
Findern Cl BPR/DUF DE56 ...... 199 L4
DERBYW DE22 ...... 240 A1
Findern Ct MSFD NG18 ...... 165 L4
Findern La RDERBYSW DE65 ...... 254 D5
RDERBYSW DE65 ...... 266 F3
Findern St DERBYW DE22 ...... 240 A5
Finley Wy ALFN DE55 ...... 176 E6
Finmere Cl NORM/LIT DE23 ...... 255 K2
Finney Cl MSHM DE12 ...... 295 H1
Finningley Dr DERBYW DE22 ...... 226 B8
Finningley Rd MSFD NG18 ...... 165 K8
Finny La ASHB DE6 ...... 221 L5
Finsbury Av DERBYW DE22 ...... 226 E7
Finsbury Rd BSTN/STPLFD NG9... 231 M7
Firbank Ct BSTN/STPLFD NG9... 245 L5
Firbeck Av MSFD NG18 ...... 165 J5
Firbeck Rd SHEFS S8 ...... 55 H7
WOL/BIL/BRX NG8 ...... 231 M6
Fir Cl SBK/MW NG20 ...... 133 H4
Firemen's Rw ASH NG17 ...... 163 H6
Firestone BPR/DUF DE56 ...... 213 C2
Firfield Av BWSH/BRSTN DE72 ...... 260 B2
Fir Pl ECK/KIL S21 ...... 73 M5
Fir Rd ECK/KIL S21 ...... 72 E8
SBK/MW NG20 ...... 32 B6
Firs Av ALFN DE55 ...... 175 K5
ASHB DE6 ...... 196 C7
RIPLEY DE5 ...... 201 G1
Firs Crs DERBYW DE22 ...... 226 B5
Firs Gdns ALFN DE55 ...... 175 K6
Firs Pde MTLK DE4 ...... 156 F5
Firs St LGEAT NG10 ...... 260 D6
First Av BWSH/BRSTN DE72 ...... 244 C5
MSFDW NG19 ...... 165 K1
The Firs ASHB DE6 ...... 207 M1
Fir St STV/CWN S43 ...... 111 L3
Firth Dr BSTN/STPLFD NG9 ...... 245 M8
Firthwood Av DRON S18 ...... 71 C7
Firthwood Cl DRON S18 ...... 71 C7
Firthwood Rd DRON S18 ...... 71 G7
Fir Tree Av ALFN DE55 ...... 159 M6
Firtree Gv DERBYE DE21 ...... 227 L8
Firvale AU/AST/KP S26 ...... 75 H5

Firvale Rd CHSW S40 ... 127 L2
Fisher Cl CHSW S40 ... 128 B3
RDERBYSW DE65 ... 267 G8 2
Fisher Ct ILK DE7 ... 217 J6
Fisher La BPR/DUF DE56 ... 213 H6
MSFD NG18 ... 164 F5
Fishers Br NM/HAY SK22 ... 35 G8 1
Fisher St DERBYSE DE24 ... 257 H4 1
Fishpond La
BUTN/AL/TUT DE13 ... 263 M4
RDERBYSW DE65 ... 265 K5
Fishponds Cl RCH S42 ... 128 C8
Fishponds Rd HAN/WDH S13 ... 56 F2
Fishponds Rd West
HAN/WDH S13 ... 56 F3
Fiskerton Wy DERBYE DE21 ... 241 L2
Fitzalan Rd HAN/WDH S13 ... 57 J1
Fitzalan St GLSP SK13 ... 25 M1
Fitzhubert Rd SHEFP/MNR S2 ... 56 D2
Fitzroy Rd SHEFP/MNR S2 ... 55 L4
Fitzwalter Rd SHEFP/MNR S2 ... 55 M1
Five Lands Rd
STPNHL/WNHL DE15 ... 281 J2
Five Pits Trail RCH S42 ... 129 K6
Five Trees Cl TOT/DORE S17 ... 69 K4
Five Trees Dr TOT/DORE S17 ... 69 K4
Flackets La ASHB DE6 ... 249 L2
Flagg La BUX SK17 ... 120 C3
Flagg Wood Av MPL/ROM SK6 ... 32 A3
Flagshaw La ASHB DE6 ... 224 C7
Flake La ILK DE7 ... 244 B1 1
Flamstead Av HEANOR DE75 ... 201 L6
Flamstead La RIPLEY DE5 ... 215 G1
Flamstead Rd ILK DE7 ... 230 C1
Flamstead St DERBYSE DE24 ... 257 G4
Flamsteed Crs CHNE S41 ... 110 D4
Flash La MTLK DE4 ... 125 L8
MTLK DE4 ... 141 L4
Flather La ASHB DE6 ... 206 A1
Flat La BUX SK17 ... 119 L2
The Flat BPR/DUF DE56 ... 214 C2
Flatts Cl BUTN/AL/TUT DE13 ... 273 L4 1
Flatts La CHF/WBR SK23 ... 58 C6
EWD/SEL/PNX NG16 ... 189 G7
The Flatts BPR/DUF DE56 ... 196 E1 1
BSTN/STPLFD NG9 ... 245 L5 2
Flaxholme Av
BPR/DUF DE56 ... 226 C1 1
Flaxpiece Rd CLCR S45 ... 144 F7
Fleet Crs BPR/DUF DE56 ... 199 J7 2
Fleet Pk BPR/DUF DE56 ... 199 K7
Fleet St BUT DE14 ... 274 A8
NORM/LIT DE23 ... 240 D8
The Fleet BPR/DUF DE56 ... 199 J8
Fleetway Cl
EWD/SEL/PNX NG16 ... 217 L1 1
Fletcher Av DRON S18 ... 90 D1
Fletcher Dr POY/DIS SK12 ... 42 C4
Fletcher St HEANOR DE75 ... 202 B8
LGEAT NG10 ... 261 G2
RIPLEY DE5 ... 187 H8
Fletchers Wy MSFDW NG19 ... 165 L2
The Fletches
BUTN/AL/TUT DE13 ... 273 L1 2
Fleury Cl GLV S14 ... 56 B6
Fleury Crs GLV S14 ... 56 B6
Fleury Pl GLV S14 ... 56 B6
Fleury Ri GLV S14 ... 56 B6
Fleury Rd GLV S14 ... 56 B6
Flight Hl HOLM/MEL HD7 ... 9 M5
Flint Av MSFDW NG19 ... 165 J1
Flint La MTLK DE4 ... 155 L2
Flintson Av CHNE S41 ... 92 A6
Flint St DERBYSE DE24 ... 257 G4
Flockton Av HAN/WDH S13 ... 57 L2
Flockton Crs HAN/WDH S13 ... 57 L2
Flockton Dr HAN/WDH S13 ... 57 M2
Flockton Rd HAN/WDH S13 ... 57 M2
Flood St BWSH/BRSTN DE72 ... 242 F6
Florence Av LGEAT NG10 ... 261 J1
Florence Cl RCH S42 ... 128 C4
Florence Dr ASHB DE6 ... 248 E2
Florence Gladwin Cl MTLK DE4 ... 154 F4
Florence Rd CLCR S45 ... 145 H6
RCH S42 ... 128 B6
SHEFS S8 ... 55 J8
Florence Wy HYDE SK14 ... 17 G5 3
Florin Gdns LGEAT NG10 ... 260 E3
Flowery Leys La ALFN DE55 ... 175 L7
Flowright Cl SHEFP/MNR S2 ... 56 A5
Fly Hl BKWL DE45 ... 123 G4
Folds Crs SHEFS S8 ... 69 M1
Folds Dr SHEFS S8 ... 69 M1 1
Folds La CHF/WBR SK23 ... 59 J8
SHEFS S8 ... 69 M1
Folds Yd MTLK DE4 ... 173 J8
The Fold HATH/EY S32 ... 86 C6
Foljambe Av CHSW S40 ... 128 A2
Foljambe Rd CHSW S40 ... 2 E4
STV/CWN S43 ... 111 H2
Folkestone Dr DERBYSE DE24 ... 257 K5
Folly Rd DERBYW DE22 ... 240 E1
Fonton Hall Dr ASH NG17 ... 177 L2
Fontwell Rd BUT DE14 ... 280 C3 2
Foolow Av CHSW S40 ... 2 E8
Forbes Cl LGEAT NG10 ... 261 H5
Ford Av HEANOR DE75 ... 201 M6
Fordbridge La ALFN DE55 ... 176 D3
Ford Cl RIPLEY DE5 ... 200 F2
Ford Gv HYDE SK14 ... 16 D6
Ford La DERBYE DE21 ... 226 F6
DERBYW DE22 ... 226 E5
HACK/IN S12 ... 72 B5
RDERBYSW DE65 ... 266 F5
Ford Rd ECC S11 ... 54 E4
ECK/KIL S21 ... 72 B6
Ford St BPR/DUF DE56 ... 199 J6
DERBY DE1 ... 4 D3
RCH S42 ... 145 G3
STPNHL/WNHL DE15 ... 281 H3
Fordwells Cl NORM/LIT DE23 ... 255 K2 4
Foremark Av NORM/LIT DE23 ... 256 B2
Forest Av BUX SK17 ... 99 M4
MSFD NG18 ... 164 F5
Forest Cl BPR/DUF DE56 ... 199 L5
EWD/SEL/PNX NG16 ... 189 L3
Forest Ct STV/CWN S43 ... 94 E4
Forest Dr CLCR S45 ... 145 M8
Forester Cl BSTN/STPLFD NG9 ... 245 M6
Forester St DERBY DE1 ... 4 D5
Foresters Wy RIPLEY DE5 ... 186 F8
Forest Hl MSFD NG18 ... 164 F8
Forest La BUX SK17 ... 64 A8
Forest Rd ASH NG17 ... 163 K5
BUTN/AL/TUT DE13 ... 273 G6
MSFD NG18 ... 164 F5
Forest St ASH NG17 ... 163 H8
Forge Cl RDERBYSW DE65 ... 267 G8 3
Forge La BUTN/AL/TUT DE13 ... 265 J8
ECK/KIL S21 ... 73 L3
SHEF S1 ... 55 K1 4
Forge Rd CHF/WBR SK23 ... 59 H3
The Forge BSTN/STPLFD NG9 ... 230 E5
Forman Cl SWAD DE11 ... 282 E6
Forman St DERBY DE1 ... 4 D4
DERBYW DE22 ... 4 C4
Forrester Av
BWSH/BRSTN DE72 ... 270 C5 1
Forrester's La DRON S18 ... 70 F6 2
Forshaw Cl ASHB DE6 ... 207 M2
Forth Av DRON S18 ... 70 A8
Forties La ASHZ LE65 ... 284 C6
Forty Foot La
MELB/CHEL DE73 ... 279 J3
Forty Horse Cl RIPLEY DE5 ... 187 K8
Forum Cl DERBYSE DE24 ... 258 A5 5
Fosbrook Dr CDON/KEG DE74 ... 271 J6
Fosbrooke Dr LGEAT NG10 ... 261 G5
Fossdale Rd ABRD S7 ... 55 G5
Fosse Cl BWSH/BRSTN DE72 ... 258 F1
Foster Rd SWAD DE11 ... 283 J8
Foster St MSFD NG18 ... 164 F4 1
Foston Av BUTN/AL/TUT DE13 ... 273 K4
Foston Cl MSFD NG18 ... 165 L4
RDERBYSW DE65 ... 263 M1
Foston Dr CHSW S40 ... 109 L5
Foundry La BPR/DUF DE56 ... 213 J3
Foundry St CHNE S41 ... 110 D2
Fountain Rd ASHB DE6 ... 262 A4 1
Fountains Cl DERBYW DE22 ... 226 D6 2
Fountain Sq BUX SK17 ... 83 M6 4
Fountain St BUX SK17 ... 99 L3
Four La HYDE SK14 ... 16 D6
Fourth Av MSFDW NG19 ... 165 K2
Four Wells Dr HACK/IN S12 ... 57 K7
Fowler Av DERBYE DE21 ... 242 A6
Fowler St BWSH/BRSTN DE72 ... 259 L3
CHNE S41 ... 91 J8
DERBYW DE22 ... 4 B2 1
Foxbrook Cl RCH S42 ... 109 J5 3
Foxbrook Ct CHSW S40 ... 127 L1
Foxbrook Dr CHSW S40 ... 127 L2
Fox Cl BUT DE14 ... 280 E2 1
DERBYSE DE24 ... 256 A8
LGEAT NG10 ... 261 G5
Foxcote Wy CHSW S40 ... 127 M1
Fox Covert Cl ASH NG17 ... 177 M1
Fox Covert Wy MSFD NG18 ... 165 L3
MSFDW NG19 ... 165 L3
Fox Cft ALFN DE55 ... 161 J5
Foxcroft Cha ECK/KIL S21 ... 73 M4
Foxcroft Dr ECK/KIL S21 ... 73 M4
Foxcroft Gv ECK/KIL S21 ... 73 M4
Foxdell Wy MELB/CHEL DE73 ... 257 L8
Foxes Wk DERBYW DE22 ... 226 B6 4
Foxfields Dr DERBYE DE21 ... 227 H8
Foxglove Av
STPNHL/WNHL DE15 ... 281 K2
UTXR ST14 ... 247 L4
Foxglove Cl BSVR S44 ... 111 K7
Foxglove Dr DERBYE DE21 ... 227 J7
Foxglove Rd
EWD/SEL/PNX NG16 ... 217 L2
Foxhall La FUL S10 ... 53 J4
Fox Hl BSVR S44 ... 132 C3
Foxhill Cl ASH NG17 ... 162 E7
Foxholes La ASHB DE6 ... 194 E3
MTLK DE4 ... 157 K3
Foxlands Av DERBYW DE22 ... 226 C8
Fox La DRON S18 ... 88 F4
HACK/IN S12 ... 56 F7
HATH/EY S32 ... 88 D8
TOT/DORE S17 ... 70 A4
Fox Lane Ct HACK/IN S12 ... 56 F6 1
Fox Lane Vw HACK/IN S12 ... 56 F6
Foxlea GLSP SK13 ... 25 J2
Foxley Ct DERBYE DE21 ... 227 K8 5
Fox Low Av BUX SK17 ... 99 M5
Foxpark Vw ALFN DE55 ... 161 H5
Fox Rd CDON/KEG DE74 ... 271 J6
WRKS S80 ... 96 D4
Foxstone Cl STV/CWN S43 ... 112 A2
Fox St ASH NG17 ... 163 J7
DERBY DE1 ... 5 G1
Foxton Cl ILK DE7 ... 216 F7 5
Foxwood Av HACK/IN S12 ... 56 E4
Foxwood Cl CHNE S41 ... 110 B1
CHNE S41 ... 129 G4
Foxwood Dr HACK/IN S12 ... 56 E5
Foxwood Gv HACK/IN S12 ... 56 E5
Foxwood Rd CHNE S41 ... 91 H8
HACK/IN S12 ... 56 E4
Foxwood Wy CHNE S41 ... 91 H8
Foyle Av DERBYE DE21 ... 241 K6
Framlingham Pl SHEFP/MNR S2 ... 56 A3
Frampton Gdns
NORM/LIT DE23 ... 255 J4 5
Frances Dr RCH S42 ... 128 B6
Frances St EWD/SEL/PNX NG16 ... 203 G1
Franchise St DERBYW DE22 ... 4 A6
Francis Cl STV/CWN S43 ... 111 G3
Francis St DERBYE DE21 ... 5 L2
MSFD NG18 ... 165 H3 2
Frank Av MSFD NG18 ... 164 C5
Franklin Av WRKS S80 ... 96 C5
Franklin Cl STPNHL/WNHL DE15 ... 281 L1
Franklin Crs WRKS S80 ... 96 C5
Franklin Rd
EWD/SEL/PNX NG16 ... 188 D6
Franklyn Dr DERBYSE DE24 ... 257 K4
STV/CWN S43 ... 93 J7
Franklyn Rd CHSW S40 ... 2 C2
Fraser Cl SHEFS S8 ... 55 H7 2
Fraser Crs SHEFS S8 ... 55 H7
Fraser Dr SHEFS S8 ... 55 J7
Fraser Rd SHEFS S8 ... 55 H7
Frazer Cl DERBYE DE21 ... 242 B4
Frecheville St STV/CWN S43 ... 112 A1
Frederic Av HEANOR DE75 ... 216 C3
Frederick Av DERBYSE DE24 ... 257 J4
ILK DE7 ... 230 D5
Frederick Rd
BSTN/STPLFD NG9 ... 245 G3
Frederick St ALFN DE55 ... 175 K5
ALFN DE55 ... 187 M5
ASH NG17 ... 177 L1
DERBYW DE22 ... 240 A4 2
LGEAT NG10 ... 261 J3
MSFD NG18 ... 164 F4
RCH S42 ... 129 H7 1
STPNHL/WNHL DE15 ... 281 H2
SWAD DE11 ... 283 H7
Freebirch Vw CHSW S40 ... 109 L3 4
Freehold St DERBYW DE22 ... 4 A6
Freeland Cl
BSTN/STPLFD NG9 ... 245 J7 2
Freeman Av NORM/LIT DE23 ... 256 B4
Freemantle Rd MCKLVR DE3 ... 239 H7 1
Freesia Cl MCKLVR DE3 ... 255 H1 3
Freetown GLSP SK13 ... 26 A3 1
French La DERBYE DE21 ... 214 C5
French St ILK DE7 ... 230 D4 3
NORM/LIT DE23 ... 240 B8
French Ter SBK/MW NG20 ... 115 K8
Fresco Dr NORM/LIT DE23 ... 255 J3
Fresh Ct GLSP SK13 ... 25 J3 2
Freshfield Cl MPL/ROM SK6 ... 32 E1 2
Fretson Rd SHEFP/MNR S2 ... 56 D2 2
Freydon Wy STV/CWN S43 ... 111 K7
Friar Ga DERBY DE1 ... 4 D3
Friar Gate Ct DERBY DE1 ... 4 C3
Friar Gv BUX SK17 ... 99 M4
Friars Cl DERBYW DE22 ... 226 C8 3
EWD/SEL/PNX NG16 ... 189 L3
Friars Ct ILK DE7 ... 229 M4
Friar St LGEAT NG10 ... 261 G3
Friary Av DERBYSE DE24 ... 257 H5
Friary Cft SWAD DE11 ... 282 D3
Friary St DERBY DE1 ... 4 C4
Frickley Rd ECC S11 ... 54 C2
Friesland Dr
BWSH/BRSTN DE72 ... 244 C5
Frinton Cl CHSW S40 ... 128 C3
Frisby Av LGEAT NG10 ... 261 H4
Fritchley Ct MSFD NG18 ... 165 L4 5
Fritchley La BPR/DUF DE56 ... 185 K4
Frith Cl HACK/IN S12 ... 56 E5
Frith Gv MSFDW NG19 ... 164 B3
Frithhall La RCH S42 ... 108 F8
Frith Rd HACK/IN S12 ... 56 E5
Frith Vw CHF/WBR SK23 ... 60 C5
Frithwood La SBK/MW NG20 ... 115 H4
Frizams La MELB/CHEL DE73 ... 267 J3
Froggatt Cl DERBYW DE22 ... 226 D5
STV/CWN S43 ... 111 M4
Froggett Cl ALFN DE55 ... 188 A3 1
Front St BPR/DUF DE56 ... 185 L4
Front Ter ALFN DE55 ... 159 J7
Frood Cl CHF/WBR SK23 ... 60 E3 1
Frost Av EWD/SEL/PNX NG16 ... 202 D6
Fryar Rd EWD/SEL/PNX NG16 ... 203 J6
Fulbrook Rd NORM/LIT DE23 ... 255 K3
Fulford Cl CHSW S40 ... 127 M2
Fulham Rd DERBYW DE22 ... 239 K5
Fullbrook Av
BUTN/AL/TUT DE13 ... 286 A2
Fuller Cl MSFD NG18 ... 164 E6
Fuller Dr CHNE S41 ... 110 F4 1
Full St DERBY DE1 ... 4 E2
Fullwood Av ILK DE7 ... 230 B1 2
Fullwood Cl
BSTN/STPLFD NG9 ... 245 M6 1
Fullwood Stile La EDL/UDV S33 ... 49 K3
Fullwood St ILK DE7 ... 230 B1
Fulmar Cl MCKLVR DE3 ... 239 H8
Fulmar Wy WRKN S81 ... 77 M3
Fulmer Rd ECC S11 ... 54 F3
Fulney Rd ECC S11 ... 54 C2
Fulwood Cha FUL S10 ... 54 B2 1
Fulwood Dr LGEAT NG10 ... 260 D3
Fulwood Head Rd FUL S10 ... 53 H4
Fulwood La FUL S10 ... 53 G4
Fulwood Ri ASH NG17 ... 177 K2
Fulwood Rd ECC S11 ... 54 A3
FUL S10 ... 54 D1
Fulwood Rd North ASH NG17 ... 177 J2
Fulwood Rd (South) ASH NG17 ... 177 J2
Furlong Cl BSTN/STPLFD NG9 ... 245 G2
Furlong La ASHB DE6 ... 195 K3
Furnace Cl RCH S42 ... 129 H8
Furnace La DRON S18 ... 90 C7
HEANOR DE75 ... 201 M6
MSHM DE12 ... 290 B7
STV/CWN S43 ... 111 J4
Furnace Rd ILK DE7 ... 230 E3
Furnall Av BKWL DE45 ... 104 D7 1
Furness Cl GLSP SK13 ... 26 C2 5
Furness Lodge Cl
CHF/WBR SK23 ... 44 A6
Furniss Av TOT/DORE S17 ... 69 G4
Furniss Ms TOT/DORE S17 ... 69 H4
Furrows Cl DERBYE DE21 ... 227 M7 5
Further La HYDE SK14 ... 16 B7
Fyfield Rd STPNHL/WNHL DE15 ... 281 H3
Fylde Cl BSTN/STPLFD NG9 ... 245 H8

G

Gable Ct MCKLVR DE3 ... 255 H2 1
Gables Cl RCH S42 ... 146 A2
The Gables ASHZ LE65 ... 291 M6
SWAD DE11 ... 282 B5 5
Gadley Cl BUX SK17 ... 99 J2
Gadley La BUX SK17 ... 99 J2
Gadsby Cl ILK DE7 ... 230 D6
Gadsby Ri BPR/DUF DE56 ... 185 M8
Gag La ASHB DE6 ... 179 G1
Gainsborough Av
MPL/ROM SK6 ... 32 E2 1
Gainsborough Cl
BSTN/STPLFD NG9 ... 245 H4
DERBYE DE21 ... 241 L1 3
LGEAT NG10 ... 261 H5 3
Gainsborough Rd ABRD S7 ... 55 G3
DRON S18 ... 90 B2
Gainsborough Wy
STPNHL/WNHL DE15 ... 274 E7
Gairloch Cl DERBYSE DE24 ... 256 A8
Galahad Dr
BUTN/AL/TUT DE13 ... 265 H8 3
Gallery La RCH S42 ... 126 F3
Galley Dr MOS S20 ... 73 G1
Gallowsclough Rd STLY SK15 ... 16 B4
Gallows Inn Cl ILK DE7 ... 230 D5 1
Gallowstree La ASHB DE6 ... 206 F1
Galway Av DERBYE DE21 ... 241 L6
Gamston Rd MSFD NG18 ... 165 L7
SHEFS S8 ... 55 J3
Gang La BSVR S44 ... 132 B5
Gannow Cl ECK/KIL S21 ... 74 C3
Gapsick La WRKS S80 ... 95 L4
Garden Av ECK/KIL S21 ... 93 L3
ILK DE7 ... 230 C5
MSFDW NG19 ... 148 C3
SBK/MW NG20 ... 133 H6
Garden Cl STV/CWN S43 ... 92 A7 5
Garden Crs ALFN DE55 ... 176 C6
CDON/KEG DE74 ... 271 L7
Garden La ASH NG17 ... 163 K7
Garden Rd EWD/SEL/PNX NG16 ... 203 K7
MSFD NG18 ... 164 E4
Garden Rw BSVR S44 ... 147 G1
The Gardens RIPLEY DE5 ... 201 G3
Garden St DERBY DE1 ... 4 D1
Gardinia Cl
BSTN/STPLFD NG9 ... 245 K8 4
Gardner Pl UTXR ST14 ... 247 K1 5
Gardom Cl DRON S18 ... 90 A1 1
Garfield Av BWSH/BRSTN DE72 ... 259 K3
Garfield Cl BSTN/STPLFD NG9 ... 245 H1
NORM/LIT DE23 ... 255 M4 2
Garland Cl MOS S20 ... 73 H3
Garland Cft MOS S20 ... 73 H3
Garland Mt MOS S20 ... 73 H2 6
Garland Wy MOS S20 ... 73 H3
Garner La MTLK DE4 ... 173 M8
Garnett Av HEANOR DE75 ... 202 C8
Garnett Cl HYDE SK14 ... 16 C7
Garnett Rd HYDE SK14 ... 16 C7
Garnham Cl ALFN DE55 ... 176 A8
Garnon St MSFD NG18 ... 164 B5
Garratt Av MSFD NG18 ... 164 F3
Garrick St DERBYSE DE24 ... 257 K3
Garry Cl DERBYSE DE24 ... 256 A8
Garside Av ASH NG17 ... 163 G8
Gartan Rd BUT DE14 ... 280 D2
Garth Crs DERBYSE DE24 ... 257 L4 2
Garthorpe Ct DERBYE DE21 ... 227 J8 5
Garth Rd MPL/ROM SK6 ... 32 D4
MSFD NG18 ... 164 D6
Garth Wy DRON S18 ... 90 C1 2
Gartland Cl BSTN/STPLFD NG9 ... 245 L5 3
Gartrice Gdns MOS S20 ... 73 K5
Gartrice Gv MOS S20 ... 73 J5
Gary Cl NORM/LIT DE23 ... 256 A5
Gascoigne Dr DERBYE DE21 ... 242 A6
Gashouse La MOS S20 ... 73 G5
Gaskell Av NORM/LIT DE23 ... 256 B3
Gasny Av CDON/KEG DE74 ... 271 L5
Gas St HYDE SK14 ... 17 G5
LGEAT NG10 ... 244 F4
UTXR ST14 ... 247 M2
Gatcombe Cl
BUTN/AL/TUT DE13 ... 274 A1
DERBYE DE21 ... 227 K8
Gatcombe Gv LGEAT NG10 ... 244 D7
Gate Brook Cl RIPLEY DE5 ... 201 L1 1
Gatefield Cl CHSW S40 ... 109 M3
Gatefield Rd ABRD S7 ... 55 H4 2
Gateford Pl BSTN/STPLFD NG9 ... 231 L8
Gateford Rd WRKN S81 ... 77 M3
Gateland La DRON S18 ... 90 B5
Gauledge La BUX SK17 ... 134 E4
Gaunt Cl ECK/KIL S21 ... 73 M4
GLV S14 ... 56 A7
Gaunt Dr GLV S14 ... 56 A7
Gaunt Pl GLV S14 ... 56 A6
Gaunt Rd GLV S14 ... 56 A6
Gaunt Wy GLV S14 ... 56 A7
Gawain Gv
BUTN/AL/TUT DE13 ... 265 H8 4
Gawsworth Cl GLSP SK13 ... 17 K5 5
Gayrigg Ct BSTN/STPLFD NG9 ... 245 L6 2
Gayton Av NORM/LIT DE23 ... 256 A4
Gayton Thorpe Cl
NORM/LIT DE23 ... 255 J3 3
Geary La STPNHL/WNHL DE15 ... 275 J8
Geer La HACK/IN S12 ... 71 M5
Gelderd Pl DRON S18 ... 90 D2
Gell Rd BSTN/STPLFD NG9 ... 245 K7
Gema Cl DERBYW DE22 ... 226 D6
Genista Cl STPNHL/WNHL DE15 ... 281 K2
Gentshill Av CLCR S45 ... 145 H8 2
George Av LGEAT NG10 ... 261 J2
George Crs ALFN DE55 ... 187 M4
George Elliott Cl UTXR ST14 ... 247 M4
George Holmes Wy SWAD DE11 ... 282 D7
George Percival Pl CLCR S45 ... 144 D6
George Rd MTLK DE4 ... 156 F4
George St ALFN DE55 ... 175 K6
ALFN DE55 ... 176 C5
ALFN DE55 ... 188 A4
ALFN DE55 ... 188 A2 5
ASH NG17 ... 162 E7
ASHB DE6 ... 207 L2
BPR/DUF DE56 ... 199 J6
BUT DE14 ... 274 A7 1
BUX SK17 ... 99 L2 1
CHF/WBR SK23 ... 59 H3
CHNE S41 ... 91 J8
DERBY DE1 ... 4 D3
EWD/SEL/PNX NG16 ... 176 F6
EWD/SEL/PNX NG16 ... 202 E7
GLSP SK13 ... 25 M2
MELB/CHEL DE73 ... 278 D3
MSFDW NG19 ... 164 C2
MSFDW NG19 ... 165 K1
RCH S42 ... 145 H3
SBK/MW NG20 ... 115 K8
STV/CWN S43 ... 111 H2
SWAD DE11 ... 282 D8
Gerard Cl CHSW S40 ... 127 M1
DERBYE DE21 ... 242 C4 2
SHEFP/MNR S2 ... 55 L4 2
Gerard Ct DERBY DE1 ... 4 D5
Gerard Gv RDERBYSW DE65 ... 253 M6 2
Gerard St DERBY DE1 ... 4 D6
SHEFS S8 ... 55 L4
Gertrude Rd
BWSH/BRSTN DE72 ... 259 K3
DERBYE DE21 ... 241 K2
Gervase Av SHEFS S8 ... 70 B4
Gervase Dr SHEFS S8 ... 70 B4
Gervase Pl SHEFS S8 ... 70 B4 1
Gervase Rd SHEFS S8 ... 70 B4
Ghost House La
BSTN/STPLFD NG9 ... 245 L5
Gibb La ASHB DE6 ... 250 B5
MPL/ROM SK6 ... 33 H5
Gibbons Av BSTN/STPLFD NG9 ... 245 G3
Gibbons Dr SHEFS S8 ... 56 B8
Gibbons Rd MSFD NG18 ... 164 C5
Gibbons Wy SHEFS S8 ... 56 B8 2
Gibb St LGEAT NG10 ... 261 H3
Gibfield La ASHB DE6 ... 196 A4
BPR/DUF DE56 ... 199 J8 2
Gifford Rd SHEFP/MNR S2 ... 55 K3 3
Gilbert Av CHSW S40 ... 128 A2
Gilbert Cl DERBYE DE21 ... 242 A6
Gilbert Crs BPR/DUF DE56 ... 213 H8
Gilbert St DERBYSE DE24 ... 257 L5
Gilcroft St ASH NG17 ... 163 H4
MSFD NG18 ... 164 F4 2
Gilderdale Wy DERBYE DE21 ... 227 L7
Gillamoor Ct DERBYSE DE24 ... 258 A4 3
Gilleyfield Av TOT/DORE S17 ... 69 H3
The Gillies MSFDW NG19 ... 164 B5
Gill La MTLK DE4 ... 140 F6
Gillott St HEANOR DE75 ... 216 D2
Gill's La RCH S42 ... 129 H8
Gill St ASH NG17 ... 162 F8
EWD/SEL/PNX NG16 ... 189 K4
Giltbrook Crs
EWD/SEL/PNX NG16 ... 217 M2
Giltway EWD/SEL/PNX NG16 ... 217 M3
Gimson Cl ILK DE7 ... 216 F7 4
Gin Close Wy
EWD/SEL/PNX NG16 ... 217 M5
Gin La CLCR S45 ... 158 C2
Gipsyhill La WRKS S80 ... 95 M1
Gipsy La CHNE S41 ... 110 E1
DRON S18 ... 91 K1
Girdon Cl BUX SK17 ... 99 J4
Girton Ct MSFD NG18 ... 165 L7
Gisborne Cl MCKLVR DE3 ... 239 H6
Gisborne Crs DERBYW DE22 ... 226 C6
Gisborne Gn DERBY DE1 ... 4 B1
Gisborne Rd ECC S11 ... 54 E4
Gisbourne Dr CHF/WBR SK23 ... 60 E5
Gisburn Gv MSFDW NG19 ... 165 L2 1
Glade Cl CHSW S40 ... 110 B5 1
Glade Cft HACK/IN S12 ... 56 D5
Glade Lea HACK/IN S12 ... 56 D6
The Glade BUX SK17 ... 99 K2
CHSW S40 ... 2 B3
Gladstone Av ALFN DE55 ... 176 B1
HEANOR DE75 ... 202 B8
Gladstone Cl MELB/CHEL DE73 ... 257 J7
Gladstone Dr
EWD/SEL/PNX NG16 ... 203 H3 1
Gladstone Ms FUL S10 ... 54 B1 1
Gladstone Rd ALFN DE55 ... 175 J7 1
CHSW S40 ... 2 E2
DERBYE DE21 ... 242 B5
FUL S10 ... 54 B1
Gladstone St ALFN DE55 ... 176 E4
EWD/SEL/PNX NG16 ... 202 F7 2
GLSP SK13 ... 17 K6 2
GLSP SK13 ... 25 M2
HEANOR DE75 ... 202 B8
LGEAT NG10 ... 261 G4
MSFD NG18 ... 165 G3
MSFDW NG19 ... 149 M8 1
NORM/LIT DE23 ... 256 B1
Gladstone St East ILK DE7 ... 230 C3 3
Gladstone St West ILK DE7 ... 230 C3 4
Gladstone Ter MSFDW NG19 ... 149 M8
Gladwin Gdns CHSW S40 ... 128 A2 1
Glamis Cl BUTN/AL/TUT DE13 ... 274 A2 8
DERBYE DE21 ... 227 L8
Glapwell La BSVR S44 ... 147 L1
Glasshouse Hl RIPLEY DE5 ... 201 L2
Glasshouse La CHNE S41 ... 92 A5
STV/CWN S43 ... 92 A5
Glastonbury Rd DERBYSE DE24 ... 257 M3
Gleadless Av HACK/IN S12 ... 56 C6
Gleadless Bank HACK/IN S12 ... 56 C6 1
Gleadless Common HACK/IN S12 ... 56 C5
Gleadless Ct SHEFP/MNR S2 ... 55 L4 3
Gleadless Crs HACK/IN S12 ... 56 C5
Gleadless Dr HACK/IN S12 ... 56 C6
Gleadless Mt HACK/IN S12 ... 56 D7 1
Gleadless Rd HACK/IN S12 ... 56 B5
SHEFP/MNR S2 ... 56 A4 4
SHEFS S8 ... 55 K4 3
Gleadmoss La DERBYE DE21 ... 241 K1 1
Glebe Av AU/AST/KP S26 ... 75 H3
BKWL DE45 ... 104 D7
EWD/SEL/PNX NG16 ... 177 G7
ILK DE7 ... 215 J4
RIPLEY DE5 ... 186 F8
Glebe Cl ALFN DE55 ... 176 D5
ASHB DE6 ... 237 H1
ASHB DE6 ... 248 F2 1
BUTN/AL/TUT DE13 ... 264 D6
MSHM DE12 ... 287 M7
RCH S42 ... 146 A2
WRKS S80 ... 77 M7
Glebe Crs ILK DE7 ... 228 E4
ILK DE7 ... 230 D3
Glebe Farm Cl AU/AST/KP S26 ... 75 H3
Glebe Field Cl MTLK DE4 ... 185 J1
Glebe Gdns RCH S42 ... 145 J5
Glebe Ri NORM/LIT DE23 ... 255 M1
Glebe Rd BUX SK17 ... 100 A2
Glebe St SWAD DE11 ... 282 E7
The Glebe EWD/SEL/PNX NG16 ... 217 L6
MSHM DE12 ... 287 M4
Glebe Vw MSFD NG18 ... 165 H2
STV/CWN S43 ... 94 E4
The Glebe Wy CHNE S41 ... 91 K8
Gledhill Cl DRON S18 ... 90 D1
Glenalmond Cl ASHZ LE65 ... 291 K3
Glenalmond Rd ECC S11 ... 54 E3
Glen Av BPR/DUF DE56 ... 213 M3
EWD/SEL/PNX NG16 ... 217 L1
Glenavon Cl STV/CWN S43 ... 92 A5
Glenbrook Hl GLSP SK13 ... 17 M8

Glen Cl *ALFN* DE55 ...... 161 K7
Glencoe Wy *CHSW* S40 .... 109 L6
Glencroft Cl *BUT* DE14 .... 280 E3
Glencroft Dr *DERBYE* DE24 .... 242 C5
Glendale Dr *DERBYE* DE21 .... 242 C5
Glendon Rd *DERBYSE* DE24 .... 256 A7
  ILK DE7 .... 229 M6
Glendon St *ILK* DE7 .... 228 D1
Gleneagles Cl *CHSW* S40 .... 127 M2
  MCKLVR DE3 .... 239 J8
Gleneagles Dr
  BUTN/AL/TUT DE13 .... 273 M1
Glenfield Crs *CHNE* S41 .... 110 C3
  MCKLVR DE3 .... 238 F8
Glenfield Ri
  BUTN/AL/TUT DE13 .... 273 L3
Glenfield Rd *LGEAT* NG10 .... 261 C5
Glengarry Wy *DERBYE* DE24 .... 256 A6
Glenholme Pl *HAN/WDH* S13 .... 57 J3
Glenholme Rd *HAN/WDH* S13 .... 57 J3
Glenholme Wy *HAN/WDH* S13 .... 57 H2
Glenmoor Rd *BUX* SK17 .... 99 M1
Glenmore Cft *HACK/IN* S12 .... 56 E4
Glenmore Dr *DERBYE* DE24 .... 256 A6
Glenmoy Cl *NORM/LIT* DE23 .... 256 A3
Glenn Wy *BWSH/BRSTN* DE72 .... 271 H1
Glenorchy Ct *ABRD* S7 .... 55 C5
Glenorchy Rd *ABRD* S7 .... 55 C5
Glen Ri *BUTN/AL/TUT* DE13 .... 273 K3
Glen Rd *ABRD* S7 .... 55 H4
  MTLK DE4 .... 185 C1
Glenside *BSTN/STPLFD* NG9 .... 231 M8
Glen St *ASH* NG17 .... 163 H6
The Glen *ECC* S11 .... 54 E7
Glenthorn Rd *WRKN* S81 .... 77 H3
Glenthorne Cl *CHSW* S40 .... 109 M8
Glentilt Rd *ABRD* S7 .... 55 C5
Glen Vw *BPR/DUF* DE56 .... 199 J8
Glen View Rd *SHEFS* S8 .... 70 B2
Glen Vine *RIPLEY* DE5 .... 201 K1
Glenwood Rd *MELB/CHEL* DE73 .. 269 G2
Glinton Av *ASH* NG17 .... 163 H5
Glossop Av *MSFD* NG18 .... 165 L4
Glossop Brook Rd *GLSP* SK13 .... 25 L1
Glossop Rd *GLSP* SK13 .... 24 B6
  GLSP SK13 .... 25 C2
  MPL/ROM SK6 .... 32 F1
  NM/HAY SK22 .... 34 F1
Glossop's Cft *CHNE* S41 .... 91 L8
Glossop St *DERBYSE* DE24 .... 256 C8
Gloster Rd *DERBYSE* DE24 .... 241 H8
Gloucester Av *CHNE* S41 .... 110 C4
  LGEAT NG10 .... 244 D6
  MPL/ROM SK6 .... 32 C4
Gloucester Rd *CHNE* S41 .... 110 C5
Gloucester Wy *GLSP* SK13 .... 26 C2
  STPNHL/WNHL DE15 .... 281 L1
Glover Rd *SHEFP/MNR* S2 .... 55 K3
  TOT/DORE S17 .... 69 J5
Gloves La *ALFN* DE55 .... 176 B1
Glumangate *CHSW* S40 .... 3 C3
Goathland Dr *HAN/WDH* S13 .... 57 M3
Goathland Rd *DERBYSE* DE24 .... 256 A8
Goddard La *GLSP* SK13 .... 17 K4
  NM/HAY SK22 .... 34 B3
Godfrey Dr *ILK* DE7 .... 229 M4
Godfrey St *HEANOR* DE75 .... 216 B1
Godkin Dr *EWD/SEL/PNX* NG16 .... 202 D6
Godward Rd *NM/HAY* SK22 .... 43 L2
Gold Cl *MTLK* DE4 .... 155 L2
Goldcrest Dr *DERBYE* DE21 .... 242 C4
Goldcrest Ri *WRKN* S81 .... 77 M3
Golden Va *ILK* DE7 .... 214 E4
Goldfinch Cl *MSFD* NG18 .... 165 H3
Goldhill *MTLK* DE4 .... 157 K6
Gold La *DERBYW* DE22 .... 239 H2
Goldsmith St *MSFD* NG18 .... 164 D3
Goldstone Ct *DERBYE* DE21 .... 242 B6
Golf Club Rd *ILK* DE7 .... 244 D1
Golf La *BPR/DUF* DE56 .... 213 H5
Gomersal La *DRON* S18 .... 90 D1
Goodacre St *MSFD* NG18 .... 164 F3
Goodale St *NORM/LIT* DE23 .... 256 D1
Goodhand Crs *MSFD* NG18 .... 164 B4
Goodman Cl
  EWD/SEL/PNX NG16 .... 217 M2
Goodman St *BUT* DE14 .... 274 A1
Goodrington Rd
  DERBYE DE21 .... 227 M7
Goodsmoor Rd *DERBYSE* DE24 .. 256 B5
Goods Rd *BPR/DUF* DE56 .... 199 H8
Goods Yd *BPR/DUF* DE56 .... 213 J1
Goodwin Cl *LGEAT* NG10 .... 244 D4
Goodwin Rd *SHEFS* S8 .... 55 K4
Goodwin's Cft *BPR/DUF* DE56 .... 212 F1
Goodwood Cl
  BUTN/AL/TUT DE13 .... 273 M1
Goodwood Dr
  BSTN/STPLFD NG9 .... 245 J8
  DERBYE DE24 .... 257 M4
Goodwood Rd *MPL/ROM* SK6 .... 32 C5
Goodwood Wy *MSFD* NG18 .... 165 J3
Gooker La *ALFN* DE55 .... 175 J7
Goole Av *ILK* DE7 .... 230 A5
Goose Green La *ALFN* DE55 .... 160 A8
Goosehill *EDL/UDV* S33 .... 48 E8
Goose La *EWD/SEL/PNX* NG16 .... 202 A2
Gordon Av *MSFD* NG18 .... 165 H4
  SHEFS S8 .... 55 K8
Gordonbrae *MSFD* NG18 .... 164 F7
Gordon Crs *DERBYSE* DE24 .... 176 E6
Gordondale Rd *MSFDW* NG19 .... 164 E1
Gordon Rd *ALFN* DE55 .... 187 J2
  BUX SK17 .... 83 M7
  BWSH/BRSTN DE72 .... 258 C4
  ECC S11 .... 55 G2
  NORM/LIT DE23 .... 4 D8
Gordon St *BUT* DE14 .... 273 M6
  ILK DE7 .... 230 C1
Gore La *EDL/UDV* S33 .... 64 D2
Gorman Cl *CHNE* S41 .... 110 B2
Gorse Av *MPL/ROM* SK6 .... 32 B4
  MSFD NG18 .... 165 L5
Gorsebank La *BKWL* DE45 .... 106 C3
Gorse Cl *EWD/SEL/PNX* NG16 .... 217 L1
  LGEAT NG10 .... 244 E8
  NORM/LIT DE23 .... 255 L4

Gorse Dr *ECK/KIL* S21 .... 74 A5
Gorse La *ASHB* DE6 .... 195 M6
  FUL S10 .... 53 J3
  MSHM DE12 .... 290 B4
Gorse Ridge Dr *BKWL* DE45 .. 106 B4
Gorses *BPR/DUF* DE56 .... 197 C4
Gorse Valley Rd *CHNE* S41 .... 129 H3
Gorse Valley Wy *CHNE* S41 .... 129 H3
Gorse Wy *GLSP* SK13 .... 26 B2
Gorsey Bank *BPR/DUF* DE56 .... 183 J3
Gorsey Brigg *DRON* S18 .... 90 A1
Gorsey Brow *HYDE* SK14 .... 24 D1
Gorsey Cl *BPR/DUF* DE56 .... 199 H4
Gorsey Intakes *HYDE* SK14 .... 24 D1
Gorsey La *BPR/DUF* DE56 .... 196 C1
  MSHM DE12 .... 294 D2
Gorsty Leys
  RDERBYSW DE65 .... 267 C1
Gosber Rd *ECK/KIL* S21 .... 73 G7
Gosber St *ECK/KIL* S21 .... 73 G7
Goseley Av *SWAD* DE11 .... 283 K6
Goseley Crs *SWAD* DE11 .... 283 K6
Gosforth Cl *DRON* S18 .... 90 C1
Gosforth Crs *DRON* S18 .... 90 C1
  DRON S18 .... 90 A2
Gosforth Dr *DRON* S18 .... 90 C1
Gosforth Gn *DRON* S18 .... 90 C1
Gosforth La *DRON* S18 .... 90 C1
Gosforth Rd *DERBYE* DE24 .... 257 H3
Goshawk Rd *ILK* DE7 .... 230 D7
Gough Side *BUT* DE14 .... 274 A8
Gowan Cl *BSTN/STPLFD* NG9 .. 245 M8
Gower Crs *CHSW* S40 .... 109 M5
Gower St *DERBY* DE1 .... 4 E5
Goyt Av *MSFD* NG18 .... 32 C6
Goytlands *BUX* SK17 .... 99 J4
Goyt Pl *CHF/WBR* SK23 .... 59 H3
Goyt Rd *CHF/WBR* SK23 .... 59 H4
  MPL/ROM SK6 .... 32 C6
  NM/HAY SK22 .... 43 M4
  POY/DIS SK12 .... 43 G5
Goyt Side *CHSW* S40 .... 2 B6
Goyt's Ln *BUX* SK17 .... 79 K7
Goyt Vw *NM/HAY* SK22 .... 43 L4
Goyt Wy *MPL/ROM* SK6 .... 32 C1
  NM/HAY SK22 .... 43 M4
Grace Crs *HEANOR* DE75 .... 216 C1
Grafham Cl *MELB/CHEL* DE73 .. 257 K8
Grafton Cl *ASH* NG17 .... 163 L5
Grafton Rd
  STPNHL/WNHL DE15 .... 281 L1
Grafton St *NORM/LIT* DE23 .... 240 B8
Graham Cl *BUT* DE14 .... 280 F3
Graham Dr *POY/DIS* SK12 .... 42 F3
Graham Rd *ECC* S11 .... 54 C2
  FUL S10 .... 54 B2
Graham St *ILK* DE7 .... 230 C3
Grammer St *RIPLEY* DE5 .... 201 K6
Grampian Crs *CHSW* S40 .... 109 L6
Grampian Wy *DERBYSE* DE24 .. 256 A7
  LGEAT NG10 .... 260 D2
Granary Cl *RCH* S42 .... 109 K2
Granby Av *CHF/WBR* SK23 .... 60 B1
  MSFDW NG19 .... 164 E2
Granby Cl *CLCR* S45 .... 145 M8
Granby Cft *BKWL* DE45 .... 123 G5
Granby Rd *BKWL* DE45 .... 123 G5
  BUX SK17 .... 100 A3
  EDL/UDV S33 .... 64 C3
Granby St *ILK* DE7 .... 217 H8
Grandfield St *HEANOR* DE75 .. 201 M6
Grandstand Rd *DERBYE* DE21 .. 5 K1
Grange Av *ASHB* DE6 .... 196 C7
  BWSH/BRSTN DE72 .... 260 C4
  CHF/WBR SK23 .... 60 E5
  DRON S18 .... 90 B1
  MSFD NG18 .... 164 C5
  NORM/LIT DE23 .... 256 B3
Grange Cliffe Cl *ECC* S11 .... 54 E6
Grange Cl *ALFN* DE55 .... 176 C8
  ASH NG17 .... 162 E2
  ASHZ LE65 .... 291 K5
  BUT DE14 .... 273 L6
  MELB/CHEL DE73 .... 277 K6
  MELB/CHEL DE73 .... 278 E2
Grange Ct *RDERBYSW* DE65 .. 265 L5
Grange Crs *ECC* S11 .... 55 H2
Grange Crescent Rd *ECC* S11 .. 55 H2
Grange Dl *MTLK* DE4 .... 169 M2
Grange Dr *CDON/KEG* DE74 .. 271 K7
  LGEAT NG10 .... 261 J2
Grange Farm Cl
  BSTN/STPLFD NG9 .... 261 K1
  CDON/KEG DE74 .... 271 M5
Grange La *DRON* S18 .... 108 D1
  MTLK DE4 .... 170 A2
Grangelea Gdns
  BSTN/STPLFD NG9 .... 245 L3
Grangemill Pl *STV/CWN* S43 .. 111 M2
Grange Park Av *CHF/WBR* SK23 .. 60 E5
  STV/CWN S43 .... 111 J6
Grange Park Rd *CHF/WBR* SK23 .. 60 E5
Grange Rd *BUX* SK17 .... 99 L3
  CLCR S45 .... 145 M8
  DERBYSE DE24 .... 257 L5
  ECC S11 .... 55 H2
  LGEAT NG10 .... 261 J2
  SWAD DE11 .... 282 B5
  UTXR S14 .... 247 K1
Grange St *ALFN* DE55 .... 175 K7
  BUT DE14 .... 273 L7
  NORM/LIT DE23 .... 5 H9
The Grange *ALFN* DE55 .... 176 D6
  ASHZ LE65 .... 291 M4
  BUT DE14 .... 273 L7
  CHSW S40 .... 109 J6
  HEANOR DE75 .... 215 M2
Grange Vw
  EWD/SEL/PNX NG16 .... 203 J7
Grange Wk *RCH* S42 .... 129 H8
Grangewood Av *ILK* DE7 .... 230 C3
Grangewood Dr
  BPR/DUF DE56 .... 213 K3
Grangewood Rd *CHSW* S40 .. 128 C3
  WOL/BIL/BRX NG8 .... 231 M7
Grant Av *RIPLEY* DE5 .... 241 L5
Grantham Av *DERBYE* DE21 .. 241 H1
Grantham Cl
  EWD/SEL/PNX NG16 .... 217 M3
Granton Ri *MSFDW* NG19 .... 164 A5

Granville Av *LGEAT* NG10 .... 261 G1
Granville Cl *BPR/DUF* DE56 .. 213 H7
  CHNE S41 .... 129 G2
  RDERBYSW DE65 .... 264 A1
Granville Rd *SHEFP/MNR* S2 .. 55 M1
Granville St *DERBY* DE1 .... 4 A4
  SWAD DE11 .... 283 H7
Grasmere Av *CLCR* S45 .... 144 E7
  DERBYE DE24 .... 242 B4
Grasmere Cl *CHNE* S41 .... 110 A3
  STPNHL/WNHL DE15 .... 281 L1
Grasmere Crs *DERBYSE* DE24 .. 256 B6
  MPL/ROM SK6 .... 42 B1
Grasmere Rd *DRON* S18 .... 90 B1
  LGEAT NG10 .... 244 B8
  LGEAT NG10 .... 260 E1
  SHEFS S8 .... 55 H5
Grasmere St *LGEAT* NG10 .... 244 E5
Grassdale Vw *HACK/IN* S12 .. 57 J7
Grassington Cl *HACK/IN* S12 .. 57 L7
Grassington Dr *HACK/IN* S12 .. 57 K7
Grassmoor Cl *GLSP* SK13 .... 17 G8
Grassthorpe Cl *DERBYE* DE21 .. 241 L1
Grassthorpe Rd *HACK/IN* S12 .. 56 D3
Grassy La *MCKLVR* DE3 .... 254 D3
Gratton La *BKWL* DE45 .... 153 M3
Gravelly Bank Ms *ASHB* DE6 .. 221 G5
Gravel Pit La *DERBYE* DE21 .. 242 B6
Gray Cl *HYDE* SK14 .... 16 C7
Gray Fallow *ALFN* DE55 .... 176 E6
Grayling St *NORM/LIT* DE23 .... 5 H9
Gray St *MOS* S20 .... 72 F3
  STV/CWN S43 .... 95 J6
Grayswood Cl *ALFN* DE55 .... 187 K3
Greasley Av
  EWD/SEL/PNX NG16 .... 203 M8
Great Central Rd *MSFD* NG18 .. 164 F4
Great Common Cl *STV/CWN* S43 .. 94 E3
Great Cft *DRON* S18 .... 70 A8
Great Hoggett Dr
  BSTN/STPLFD NG9 .... 245 K4
Great Lea *DRON* S18 .... 69 M8
Great Northern Rd *DERBY* DE1 .. 4 A4
  EWD/SEL/PNX NG16 .... 203 G8
Greatorex Av *DERBYE* DE24 .. 257 H3
Greave Rd *HOLM/MEL* HD7 .... 9 K2
Greaves La *ASHB* DE6 .... 262 A5
  BKWL DE45 .... 122 B1
  BUTN/AL/TUT DE13 .... 262 B7
Greaves St *ALFN* DE55 .... 175 H1
  RIPLEY DE5 .... 187 G8
Greenacre *ASH* NG17 .... 162 F4
Greenacre Av *HEANOR* DE75 .. 202 D7
Greenacres *NORM/LIT* DE23 .. 255 L2
Greenacres Cl *DRON* S18 .... 90 F3
  EWD/SEL/PNX NG16 .... 203 M8
Greenacres Dr *ALFN* DE55 .... 176 E4
The Greenacre *ASHB* DE6 .... 207 J3
Green Av *MELB/CHEL* DE73 .. 269 K1
Greenaway Dr *BSVR* S44 .... 131 J2
Greenaway La *MTLK* DE4 .... 156 B1
Greenbank *DERBYE* DE21 .. 242 A6
Greenbank Cl *ASH* NG17 .... 163 H6
  CHSW S40 .... 109 M6
Greenbank Rd *MPL/ROM* SK6 .. 32 E1
Greenbeech Cl SK13 NG6 .... 32 B3
Greenburn Cl *NORM/LIT* DE23 .. 255 M4
Green Cha *ECK/KIL* S21 .... 72 F7
Green Cl *ALFN* DE55 .... 161 K7
  DRON S18 .... 91 H4
  MTLK DE4 .... 156 E4
  RDERBYSW DE65 .... 266 D4
Green Crs *EWD/SEL/PNX* NG16.. 189 H4
Green Cross *DRON* S18 .... 70 E8
Greendale Av *RCH* S42 .... 127 H2
Greendale Cl *ASH* NG17 .... 162 F4
Green Ends La
  RDERBYSW DE65 .... 263 L1
Green Farm Cl *CHSW* S40 .... 109 M4
Green Farm Rd
  EWD/SEL/PNX NG16 .... 189 G4
Greenfield Cl *WRKS* S80 .... 96 F4
Greenfield Cl *MSFDW* NG19 .... 165 L1
  NM/HAY SK22 .... 43 K2
  SHEFS S8 .... 70 C3
Greenfield Dr *MSHM* DE12 .... 288 F4
  SHEFS S8 .... 70 C3
  UTXR S14 .... 247 K2
Greenfield Rd *SHEFS* S8 .... 70 C3
Greenfields *BPR/DUF* DE56 .. 185 L3
  ECK/KIL S21 .... 72 F7
  EWD/SEL/PNX NG16 .... 202 D6
  UTXR S14 .... 218 A4
Greenfields Av
  NORM/LIT DE23 .... 255 L3
Greenfield St *GLSP* SK13 .... 17 K4
Greenfinch Cl *DERBYE* DE21 .. 242 C4
Greenfinch Dl *WRKN* S81 .... 77 M3
Greengate Cl *CHSW* S40 .... 109 M8
Greengate La *HAN/WDH* S13 .. 57 M4
Green Gln *CHSW* S40 .... 109 M8
Greenhall Rd *ECK/KIL* S21 .... 72 F7
Greenhead Crs *BUX* SK17 .... 151 M8
Green Hl *MTLK* DE4 .... 183 H1
Greenhill Av *RIPLEY* DE5 .... 201 H2
  SHEFS S8 .... 70 B2
Greenhill La *ALFN* DE55 .... 187 M5
Greenhill Main Rd *SHEFS* S8 .. 70 D3
Greenhill Pkwy *SHEFS* S8 .... 70 B4
  TOT/DORE S17 .... 70 A4
Greenhill Rd *SHEFS* S8 .... 55 H8
Greenhills Av
  EWD/SEL/PNX NG16 .... 203 K7
Greenhills Rd
  EWD/SEL/PNX NG16 .... 203 K7
Greenhill Wk *POY/DIS* SK12 .. 43 G4
Greenhouse La *FUL* S10 .... 53 J5
Greenland Av *DERBYW* DE22 .. 239 L3
Greenland Cl *RCH* S42 .... 145 K3
Greenland Crs
  BSTN/STPLFD NG9 .... 245 M6
Greenland Rd *ASH* NG17 .... 163 H3
Green Lands *SWAD* DE11 .... 282 E3

Green La *ASHB* DE6 .... 166 F8
  ASHB DE6 .... 181 L8
  ASHB DE6 .... 207 H2
  ASHB DE6 .... 211 J8
  ASHB DE6 .... 219 J2
  BKWL DE45 .... 121 M7
  BPR/DUF DE56 .... 183 M1
  BPR/DUF DE56 .... 199 J6
  BUTN/AL/TUT DE13 .... 263 M5
  BUTN/AL/TUT DE13 .... 273 L3
  BUX SK17 .... 81 L8
  BUX SK17 .... 99 K4
  BUX SK17 .... 120 A2
  BWSH/BRSTN DE72 .... 242 F5
  CDLE S70 .... 191 K2
  CHF/WBR SK23 .... 60 B1
  CHNE S41 .... 111 C6
  CLCR S45 .... 145 M7
  DERBY DE1 .... 4 E5
  DERBYE DE24 .... 257 M2
  DRON S18 .... 70 E8
  ECK/KIL S21 .... 73 M6
  GLSP SK13 .... 17 G3
  GLSP SK13 .... 25 J2
  HYDE SK14 .... 16 F4
  ILK DE7 .... 230 D3
  MELB/CHEL DE73 .... 268 D6
  MELB/CHEL DE73 .... 278 F8
  MSFD NG18 .... 164 F7
  MSFDW NG19 .... 148 B2
  MSHM DE12 .... 289 J6
  MSHM DE12 .... 292 E4
  MTLK DE4 .... 140 E7
  MTLK DE4 .... 157 K5
  MTLK DE4 .... 170 B2
  POY/DIS SK12 .... 43 G5
  RCH S42 .... 109 H3
  RCH S42 .... 145 G2
  RDERBYSW DE65 .... 254 C6
  UTXR S14 .... 249 K7
  WRKS S80 .... 96 F6
Green Lea *DRON* S18 .... 69 M8
Green Mdw *MPL/ROM* SK6 .... 32 C3
Green Meadows Dr
  MPL/ROM SK6 .... 32 C3
Green Oak Av *TOT/DORE* S17 .. 69 H6
Green Oak Crs *TOT/DORE* S17 .. 69 H6
Green Oak Dr *TOT/DORE* S17 .. 69 G6
Green Oak Rd *TOT/DORE* S17 .. 69 H7
Green Pk *DERBYW* DE22 .... 239 K4
Green Park Av *CHF/WBR* SK23 .. 60 E4
The Green *ASHB* DE6 .... 193 M7
  ASH NG17 .... 177 J1
  ASHB DE6 .... 223 H3
  ASHB DE6 .... 237 M1
  BUTN/AL/TUT DE13 .... 274 B1
  BWSH/BRSTN DE72 .... 270 E3
  CDON/KEG DE74 .... 271 K7
  CHNE S41 .... 128 F4
  CLCR S45 .... 146 C7
  DERBYE DE22 .... 240 A1
  EDL/UDV S33 .... 64 E4
  GLSP SK13 .... 25 K3
  HATH/EY S32 .... 86 F5
  MELB/CHEL DE73 .... 279 H8
  MPL/ROM SK6 .... 32 D7
  MSFDW NG19 .... 149 K5
  MTLK DE4 .... 139 M5
  MTLK DE4 .... 154 E1
  MTLK DE4 .... 171 G5
  MTLK DE4 .... 185 G1
  RDERBYSW DE65 .... 266 E4
  STV/CWN S43 .... 95 H6
  STV/CWN S43 .... 111 H5
  TOT/DORE S17 .... 69 G6
Greenvale Cl
  STPNHL/WNHL DE15 .... 281 J2
Greenview *MTLK* DE4 .... 181 K1
Greenview Cl *MSFDW* NG19 .. 165 L1
Green Wy *RDERBYSW* DE65 .... 255 C8
  UTXR S14 .... 247 L2
Greenway *ASHB* DE6 .... 193 M7
  MPL/ROM SK6 .... 32 B1
  MTLK DE4 .... 181 K1
  RCH S42 .... 128 F8
  STPNHL/WNHL DE15 .... 274 D6
  WRKS S80 .... 96 C4
Greenway Cl
  BWSH/BRSTN DE72 .... 242 E7
Greenway Cft *MTLK* DE4 .... 183 J1
Greenways *CHSW* S40 .... 127 M2
The Greenway
  DERBYE DE24 .... 258 A5
  LGEAT NG10 .... 244 E4
  SHEFS S8 .... 70 C1
Greenwich Dr North
  DERBYW DE22 .... 239 L5
Greenwich Dr South
  DERBYW DE22 .... 239 K5
Greenwood Av *ASH* NG17 .... 162 C8
  DERBYE DE21 .... 241 J3
  ILK DE7 .... 230 D3
  MSFDW NG19 .... 149 L6
Greenwood Cl
  DERBYSE DE24 .... 257 G5
Greenwood Rd
  STPNHL/WNHL DE15 .... 281 H2
Greer La *MSFDW* NG19 .... 148 A1
Gregg Av *HEANOR* DE75 .... 202 B8
Greggs Av *CHF/WBR* SK23 .... 60 C5
Gregory Av *BWSH/BRSTN* DE72 .. 259 M2
Gregory Cl *BSTN/STPLFD* NG9 .. 245 J1

Gregory Ct
  BSTN/STPLFD NG9 .... 245 L6
Gregory La *STV/CWN* S43 .... 111 C1
Gregory Rd *SHEFS* S8 .... 55 K4
Gregory St *ILK* DE7 .... 230 D1
Gregorys *BPR/DUF* DE56 .... 199 M5
Gregson Cl *SWAD* DE11 .... 282 E5
Gregson Gdns
  BSTN/STPLFD NG9 .... 261 L1
Gregson Rd *BSTN/STPLFD* NG9 .. 245 L8
Grendon Cl *BPR/DUF* DE56 .. 199 L4
Grendon Wy *ASH* NG17 .... 163 L5
Grenfell Av *NORM/LIT* DE23 .. 256 B4
Grenville Cl *UTXR* S14 .... 247 J1
Grenville Dr *BSTN/STPLFD* NG9 .. 245 H2
  ILK DE7 .... 217 J7
Grenvoir Dr *RIPLEY* DE5 .... 201 K1
Gresham Rd *DERBYE* DE24 .. 256 F2
Gresley Rd *ILK* DE7 .... 230 C1
  SHEFS S8 .... 70 B5
Gresley Woodlands *SWAD* DE11.. 282 D8
Gresley Wood Rd *SWAD* DE11 .. 282 D8
Gretton Av *BUTN/AL/TUT* DE13 .. 274 B1
Gretton Rd *BUX* SK17 .... 100 A2
Greystoke Dr
  WOL/BIL/BRX NG8 .... 231 M4
Greystones Av *ECC* S11 .... 54 E3
Greystones Cl *AU/AST/KP* S26 .. 75 G4
Greystones Ct *AU/AST/KP* S26 .. 75 G4
Greystones Crs *ECC* S11 .... 54 D3
Greystones Dr *ECC* S11 .... 54 D3
Greystones Grange Crs
  ECC S11 .... 54 D3
Greystones Grange Rd *ECC* S11.. 54 D3
Greystones Hall Rd *ECC* S11 .. 54 D3
Greystones Ri *ECC* S11 .... 54 D3
Greystones Rd *ECC* S11 .... 54 C3
Grey St *DERBYW* DE22 .... 4 D6
  EWD/SEL/PNX NG16 .... 217 K1
Grid La *MPL/ROM* SK6 .... 33 H1
Griffin Cl *DERBYSE* DE24 .... 257 J3
  NM/HAY SK22 .... 43 M4
  STV/CWN S43 .... 112 B2
Griffon Rd *ILK* DE7 .... 230 C6
Griggs Gdns *MTLK* DE4 .... 183 J3
Grimshaw Av *DERBYSE* DE24 .. 257 L3
Grindlow Av *CHSW* S40 .... 2 E8
Grindlow Cl *SHEFS* S8 .... 55 M4
Grindlow Dr *SHEFP/MNR* S2 .. 55 M4
Grindlow Rd *DERBYE* DE21 .. 241 M5
Grindon Cl *CHSW* S40 .... 109 M5
Grindslow Av *ILK* DE7 .... 229 H2
Grinlow Cl *BUX* SK17 .... 99 M7
Grin Low Rd *BUX* SK17 .... 99 K6
Grisedale Ct
  BSTN/STPLFD NG9 .... 245 K6
Grisedale Rd *BKWL* DE45 .... 104 D6
Grisedale Rd West *BKWL* DE45 .. 104 C6
Gritstone Rd *MTLK* DE4 .... 157 G3
Grizedale Cl *MSFDW* NG19 .. 165 L2
Groome Av *HEANOR* DE75 .... 201 M6
Grosvenor Av *ASH* NG17 .... 163 H6
  BWSH/BRSTN DE72 .... 260 C2
  LGEAT NG10 .... 260 D6
Grosvenor Dr *NORM/LIT* DE23 .. 255 K4
Grosvenor Rd
  EWD/SEL/PNX NG16 .... 203 J8
  MPL/ROM SK6 .... 32 C3
  RIPLEY DE5 .... 201 C1
Grosvenor Sq *SHEFP/MNR* S2 .. 55 J2
Grosvenor St *DERBYSE* DE24 .. 256 F1
Groveburry Dr *NORM/LIT* DE23 .. 255 M5
Grove Cl *BWSH/BRSTN* DE72.. 258 C6
Grove Ct *RIPLEY* DE5 .... 201 C1
Grove Gdns *STV/CWN* S43 .... 111 J6
Grove House Ct
  TOT/DORE S17 .... 69 H5
Grove La *ASHB* DE6 .... 249 H1
  BUX SK17 .... 99 M4
  MTLK DE4 .... 156 B2
  RCH S42 .... 108 E6
Grove Pk *RDERBYSW* DE65 .... 253 C6
Grove Pl *BKWL* DE45 .... 138 C5
Grove Rd *ABRD* S7 .... 54 F7
  ASH NG17 .... 163 L7
  CHNE S41 .... 110 D3
  STV/CWN S43 .... 111 H5
  TOT/DORE S17 .... 69 H5
Groves Nook
  MELB/CHEL DE73 .... 269 H1
Grove St *CHNE* S41 .... 128 F2
  MSFD NG18 .... 164 E4
  MSFDW NG19 .... 149 L7
  NM/HAY SK22 .... 43 L3
  NORM/LIT DE23 .... 4 F8
  SWAD DE11 .... 282 E6
The Grove *BWSH/BRSTN* DE72 .. 260 C2
  GLSP SK13 .... 17 G6
  MCKLVR DE3 .... 239 J8
  STV/CWN S43 .... 112 D2
  TOT/DORE S17 .... 69 G5
Grove Wy *MSFDW* NG19 .... 149 L7
  STV/CWN S43 .... 111 J5
Grundy Av *EWD/SEL/PNX* NG16.. 189 G3
Grundy Nook *WRKS* S80 .... 96 D3
Grundy Rd *CLCR* S45 .... 144 F7
Grunmore Dr
  BUTN/AL/TUT DE13 .... 265 H8
Guernsey Rd *SHEFP/MNR* S2 .. 55 K3
Guest Rd *ECC* S11 .... 54 F2
Guildford Av *CHSW* S40 .... 2 A9
  MSFDW NG19 .... 149 M4
  SHEFP/MNR S2 .... 56 A3
  SWAD DE11 .... 283 H4
Guildford Cl *CLCR* S45 .... 145 H7
  SHEFP/MNR S2 .... 56 A2
Guildford Dr *SHEFP/MNR* S2 .. 56 A2
Guildford La *CLCR* S45 .... 145 H7
Guildford Ri *SHEFP/MNR* S2 .. 56 A2
Guildford Vw *SHEFP/MNR* S2 .. 56 B2
Guildford Wy *SHEFP/MNR* S2 .. 56 A3
Guildhall Dr
  EWD/SEL/PNX NG16 .... 177 H8
Guild St *BUT* DE14 .... 274 A7
Guinea Cl *LGEAT* NG10 .... 260 D3
Guinevere Av
  BUTN/AL/TUT DE13 .... 265 J2
Gunby Hl *MSHM* DE12 .... 294 C1
Gunhills La *BPR/DUF* DE56 .. 212 B4
Gun La *BPR/DUF* DE56 .... 185 L7

Gun Rd MPL/ROM SK6 .... 24 F8
 NM/HAY SK22 .... 33 M3
Gunthorpe Ct MSFD NG18 .... 165 L7
Gurney Av NORM/LIT DE23 .... 256 A4
Guy Cl BSTN/STPLFD NG9 .... 245 J4
Gypsum Wy ASHB DE6 .... 262 A4
Gypsy La BWSH/BRSTN DE72 .... 259 H2
 WRKS S80 .... 115 H1

H

Hackett Cl ASHZ LE65 .... 291 K4
Hack La ASH NG17 .... 163 H8
Hackney La DRON S18 .... 90 C8
Hackney Rd MTLK DE4 .... 156 C2
Hackthorn Rd SHEFS S8 .... 55 J7
Hackworth Cl
 EWD/SEL/PNX NG16 .... 203 L7
Haddon Cl ALFN DE55 .... 175 J7
 BPR/DUF DE56 .... 185 L4
 CHSW S40 .... 109 M8
 DERBYW DE22 .... 226 A7
 DRON S18 .... 90 E1
 ILK DE7 .... 229 H2
 MPL/ROM SK6 .... 42 B4
Haddon Ct ASHB DE6 .... 208 A2
Haddon Crs BSTN/STPLFD NG9 .... 245 J4
 DERBYE DE21 .... 242 C6
 DERBYW DE22 .... 226 A7
 MCKLVR DE3 .... 239 H7
Haddon Dr BKWL DE45 .... 123 H6
Haddon Ms GLSP SK13 .... 17 G8
Haddon Nurseries ILK DE7 .... 217 H1
Haddon Pl SBK/MW NG20 .... 133 H4
 STV/CWN S43 .... 112 A2
Haddon Rd BKWL DE45 .... 122 F4
 BUX SK17 .... 100 A2
 MSFDW NG19 .... 164 E2
 RCH S42 .... 145 K2
Haddon St ALFN DE55 .... 161 K4
 ASH NG17 .... 163 H6
 ILK DE7 .... 217 H7
 NORM/LIT DE23 .... 256 B1
Haddon Wy LGEAT NG10 .... 260 C6
Hade La BUX SK17 .... 120 B3
Hadfield Pl GLSP SK13 .... 25 M2
Hadfield Rd GLSP SK13 .... 17 J6
Hadfields Av HYDE SK14 .... 17 G5
Hadfield Sq GLSP SK13 .... 25 M2
Hadfield St GLSP SK13 .... 25 M2
Hadleigh Cl BSTN/STPLFD NG9 .... 245 H8
Hadley La ASHB DE6 .... 209 G2
Hadley St ILK DE7 .... 230 C2
Hadstock Cl LGEAT NG10 .... 244 E6
Hady Crs CHNE S41 .... 3 M4
Hady Hl CHNE S41 .... 3 M5
Hady La CHNE S41 .... 111 G8
Hag Bank La POY/DIS SK12 .... 43 G3
Hagg La ILK DE7 .... 229 C6
Hag La BPR/DUF DE56 .... 197 M8
Hague Av ECK/KIL S21 .... 93 L2
Haguebar Rd NM/HAY SK22 .... 43 J2
Hague Fold Rd NM/HAY SK22 .... 43 J2
Hague Rd HYDE SK14 .... 24 E1
Hague St GLSP SK13 .... 26 A3
Haigh Moor Cl HAN/WDH S13 .... 57 K2
Haigh Moor Rd HAN/WDH S13 .... 57 J2
Haig St DERBYSE DE24 .... 257 J2
Hailebury Av ASHZ LE65 .... 291 K3
Hailsham Cl MCKLVR DE3 .... 239 G7
Haines Cl DERBYSE DE24 .... 256 C6
Halam Cl MSFDW NG19 .... 164 A3
Halcyon Ap RCH S42 .... 128 F8
Halcyon Cl HACK/IN S12 .... 57 J7
Halcyon Wy BUT DE14 .... 273 L6
Haldane Cl WRKS S80 .... 96 B8
Haldane Crs BSVR S44 .... 113 J8
Hale St SHEFS S8 .... 55 J4
Halesworth Cl CHSW S40 .... 127 L2
Half Acre La DRON S18 .... 91 G2
Half Cft STV/CWN S43 .... 111 J3
Halfmoon La MTLK DE4 .... 182 E7
Halfway Dr MOS S20 .... 73 H3
Halfway Gdns MOS S20 .... 73 H3
Halifax Cl RDERBYSW DE65 .... 253 H8
Hallam Flds CDON/KEG DE74 .... 271 L8
Hallam Fields Rd ILK DE7 .... 230 D6
Hallam Grange Cl FUL S10 .... 53 M2
Hallam Grange Crs FUL S10 .... 53 M1
Hallam Grange Ri FUL S10 .... 53 M1
Hallam Grange Rd FUL S10 .... 53 M1
Hallam Rd UTXR ST14 .... 247 J1
Hallamshire Cl FUL S10 .... 53 L2
Hallamshire Dr FUL S10 .... 53 L2
Hallamshire Rd FUL S10 .... 53 L2
Hallams Rw BUT DE14 .... 273 M6
Hallam Wy ILK DE7 .... 229 G2
Hall Bank BUX SK17 .... 99 L3
 BUX SK17 .... 151 C5
Hallcliff La RCH S42 .... 126 B1
Hall Cl DRON S18 .... 69 M8
 HYDE SK14 .... 16 D5
 RCH S42 .... 109 H2
 SWAD DE11 .... 290 F2
Hall Ct ILK DE7 .... 229 H3
Hall Croft Av MSHM DE12 .... 289 L6
Halldale La ALFN DE55 .... 141 H7
Hall Dale Vw MTLK DE4 .... 141 L8
Hall Dr ASHB DE6 .... 248 D1
 HYDE SK14 .... 16 D5
 LGEAT NG10 .... 244 E4
Hall Dyke DERBYE DE21 .... 242 B5
Hall End La BKWL DE45 .... 122 C2
Hall Farm Cl CDON/KEG DE74 .... 271 K7
 CHNE S41 .... 129 G3
 SWAD DE11 .... 282 F6
Hall Farm Rd BPR/DUF DE56 .... 213 H8
 SWAD DE11 .... 282 F6
Hallfield Cl RCH S42 .... 128 D6
Hallfieldgate La ALFN DE55 .... 174 F1
Hallfield Rd ALFN DE55 .... 161 K7
Hallfields Ri ALFN DE55 .... 174 F1
Hallfields Rd SWAD DE11 .... 282 A6
Hallflash La BSVR S44 .... 129 K2
Hall Gdns BSTN/STPLFD NG9 .... 245 L3

UTXR ST14 .... 249 H8
Hallgate Cl DERBYE DE21 .... 227 M7
Hallgate La CLCR S45 .... 145 L8
Hall Gate Vw EDL/UDV S33 .... 64 D2
Hall Green Av
 BUTN/AL/TUT DE13 .... 265 H8
Hallington Dr HEANOR DE75 .... 216 A1
Hall La ALFN DE55 .... 161 K7
 ASHB DE6 .... 193 M8
 ASHB DE6 .... 205 J3
 ASHB DE6 .... 222 A1
 ASHB DE6 .... 223 K4
 ASHB DE6 .... 248 E1
 ASHZ LE65 .... 291 L8
 BPR/DUF DE56 .... 185 M7
 BUX SK17 .... 84 B7
 EWD/SEL/PNX NG16 .... 203 G3
 MSHM DE12 .... 295 H3
 RDERBYSW DE65 .... 266 E5
 STV/CWN S43 .... 92 F6
Hall Leys La MELB/CHEL DE73 .... 279 G1
Hall Meadow Cft MOS S20 .... 73 J5
Hall Meadow Dr MOS S20 .... 73 J5
Hall Meadow Gv MOS S20 .... 73 J5
Hall Meadow Rd GLSP SK13 .... 18 A8
Hallmoor Rd MTLK DE4 .... 140 F6
Hallowes Cl DRON S18 .... 90 L1
Hallowes Dr DRON S18 .... 90 L2
Hallowes La DRON S18 .... 90 L2
Hallowes Ri DRON S18 .... 90 F7
Hall Pk MELB/CHEL DE73 .... 268 D5
Hall Park Rd NORM/LIT DE23 .... 255 L1
Hall Ri ASHB DE6 .... 194 A7
 MTLK DE4 .... 141 G7
Hall Rd BUTN/AL/TUT DE13 .... 264 D6
 STV/CWN S43 .... 111 H3
 UTXR ST14 .... 247 K2
 UTXR ST14 .... 249 H7
Halls La EWD/SEL/PNX NG16 .... 217 K2
Halls Rd BSTN/STPLFD NG9 .... 245 G4
Hallsteads BUX SK17 .... 81 J1
Hallsteads Cl BUX SK17 .... 81 J1
Hall St ALFN DE55 .... 175 J6
 ASH NG17 .... 163 H4
 DERBYSE DE24 .... 257 K3
 MSFD NG18 .... 165 H4
 NM/HAY SK22 .... 43 L2
 SWAD DE11 .... 282 A8
The Hall MTLK DE4 .... 171 G5
Hall Vw CHNE S41 .... 110 B4
Hallyburton Cl
 SHEFP/MNR S2 .... 55 M4
Hallyburton Dr
 SHEFP/MNR S2 .... 55 M4
Hallyburton Rd SHEFP/MNR S2 .... 55 M4
Halstead Cl
 BSTN/STPLFD NG9 .... 245 M6
Halstock Dr DERBYSE DE24 .... 257 M2
Halton Cl CHNE S41 .... 110 B1
Halton Ct HACK/IN S12 .... 57 M7
Hambledon Cl CHSW S40 .... 109 M5
Hambledon Dr
 DERBYSE DE24 .... 256 A8
Hambleton Av RCH S42 .... 145 J4
Hambleton Cl ASHB DE6 .... 207 M2
 LGEAT NG10 .... 260 D1
Hamblin Crs DERBYSE DE24 .... 256 C6
Hamil Cl RCH S42 .... 145 J3
Hamilton Cl BSTN/STPLFD NG9 .... 245 J4
 MCKLVR DE3 .... 239 J7
Hamilton Dr SWAD DE11 .... 282 F5
Hamilton Flds
 STPNHL/WNHL DE15 .... 274 D8
Hamilton La ASH NG17 .... 163 H8
 DERBYE DE21 .... 242 C4
 LGEAT NG10 .... 261 G2
 NORM/LIT DE23 .... 4 C9
 STPNHL/WNHL DE15 .... 274 D8
Hamilton St MSFD NG18 .... 165 H4
Hamilton Ter
 RDERBYSW DE65 .... 266 E5
Hamilton Wy MSFD NG18 .... 164 B7
Hamlet La ALFN DE55 .... 176 D5
The Hamlet ALFN DE55 .... 176 D5
 HEANOR DE75 .... 202 B8
Hammersmith RIPLEY DE5 .... 187 G7
Hammonds Ct MTLK DE4 .... 183 J2
Hampden St
 EWD/SEL/PNX NG16 .... 217 L2
 NORM/LIT DE23 .... 256 D2
Hampshire Cl GLSP SK13 .... 26 C2
Hampshire Ct
 EWD/SEL/PNX NG16 .... 188 E6
Hampshire Dr LGEAT NG10 .... 244 E5
Hampshire Rd DERBYE DE21 .... 240 F2
Hampstead Dr DERBYW DE22 .... 239 K4
Hampton Cl BSTN/STPLFD NG9 .... 245 H7
 DERBYE DE21 .... 242 C5
 ILK DE7 .... 229 G3
Hampton Ct HEANOR DE75 .... 202 A8
Hampton St CHNE S41 .... 129 C3
Hanbury Av
 RDERBYSW DE65 .... 264 A1
Hanbury Cl CHSW S40 .... 109 K5
 DRON S18 .... 90 C1
Hanbury Crs MSFD NG18 .... 165 L4
Hanbury Hl BUTN/AL/TUT DE13 .... 262 D5
Hanbury Rd DERBYE DE21 .... 241 H4
Hanchurch Cl
 STPNHL/WNHL DE15 .... 274 D6
Handby St CHNE S41 .... 129 G2
Handel St DERBYSE DE24 .... 256 F2
Handford St DERBYW DE22 .... 240 A5
Handley Ar MSFD NG18 .... 164 E3
Handley Cl STV/CWN S43 .... 92 A6
 BKWL DE45 .... 123 L2
 CLCR S45 .... 159 H2
Handley Rd ECK/KIL S21 .... 92 A4
 STV/CWN S43 .... 95 J7
Handsacre Cl SWAD DE11 .... 282 C7
Hand's Rd HEANOR DE75 .... 216 C1
Handsworth Grange Cl
 HAN/WDH S13 .... 57 K2
Handsworth Grange Crs
 HAN/WDH S13 .... 57 K1
Handsworth Grange Rd
 HAN/WDH S13 .... 57 K1

Handyside St DERBY DE1 .... 4 E1
Hangar Hl WRKS S80 .... 96 D4
Hanger Bank
 BWSH/BRSTN DE72 .... 270 E2
Hanging Water Cl FUL S10 .... 54 C2
Hangingwater Rd ECC S11 .... 54 C3
Hangram La ECC S11 .... 53 L6
Hankin Av EWD/SEL/PNX NG16 .... 189 K8
Hanley Av BSTN/STPLFD NG9 .... 245 L2
Hanley Cl HACK/IN S12 .... 57 L7
 POY/DIS SK12 .... 43 G5
Hanover Sq DERBYW DE22 .... 239 K4
Hanslynn BWSH/BRSTN DE72 .... 258 C6
Hanstubbin Rd
 EWD/SEL/PNX NG16 .... 189 J4
Hanwell Wy DERBYW DE22 .... 239 J4
Harbin Rd MSHM DE12 .... 287 G2
Harbord Cl SHEFS S8 .... 55 H8
Harborough Av SHEFP/MNR S2 .... 56 D1
Harborough Wy SHEFP/MNR S2 .... 56 D1
Harbury St BUTN/AL/TUT DE13 .... 273 K4
Harcourt Pl CDON/KEG DE74 .... 271 L6
Harcourt Rd BUT DE14 .... 280 C2
Harcourt St DERBY DE1 .... 4 D6
 MSFD NG18 .... 165 G4
Hardacre Cl
 MELB/CHEL DE73 .... 278 D2
Hardcastle Dr HAN/WDH S13 .... 57 K3
Hardcastle Gdns HAN/WDH S13 .... 57 K3
Hardcastle Rd HAN/WDH S13 .... 57 K4
Hardhurst Rd DERBYSE DE24 .... 257 L5
 DRON S18 .... 91 H5
Hardie Av ALFN DE55 .... 176 D4
Hardie Pl STV/CWN S43 .... 112 A2
Hardie St ECK/KIL S21 .... 73 G8
Harding's Cl BPR/DUF DE56 .... 196 E1
Harding's La BUX SK17 .... 151 K5
Hard La AU/AST/KP S26 .... 75 H1
Hard Meadow La CLCR S45 .... 143 K8
Hardrake La BKWL DE45 .... 104 E5
Hardstoft Rd CLCR S45 .... 146 B8
Hardwick Av ASH NG17 .... 163 K4
 BSVR S44 .... 147 L2
 CHNE S41 .... 92 A7
 DERBYW DE22 .... 226 A7
 ILK DE7 .... 229 H2
 SBK/MW NG20 .... 133 H6
Hardwick Cl ALFN DE55 .... 176 A1
 ASH NG17 .... 163 K4
 DRON S18 .... 70 E8
 MPL/ROM SK6 .... 42 C4
 RCH S42 .... 146 B2
 RIPLEY DE5 .... 186 F7
 STV/CWN S43 .... 95 K6
Hardwick Crs ECC S11 .... 54 F2
Hardwick Dr BSVR S44 .... 112 A7
 EWD/SEL/PNX NG16 .... 189 L3
 MCKLVR DE3 .... 239 H8
Hardwicke Rd
 BSTN/STPLFD NG9 .... 245 M7
Hardwick La CLCR S45 .... 143 G4
Hardwick Mt BUX SK17 .... 99 L3
Hardwick Pl ILK DE7 .... 229 M5
Hardwick Sq East BUX SK17 .... 99 M3
Hardwick Sq West BUX SK17 .... 99 L3
Hardwick St ALFN DE55 .... 161 K3
 ASH NG17 .... 163 J8
 BUX SK17 .... 99 L2
 CHNE S41 .... 3 H1
 DERBYSE DE24 .... 256 F2
 MSFD NG18 .... 165 G3
 SBK/MW NG20 .... 133 K6
Hardwick Vw ASH NG17 .... 163 K4
Hardwick View Rd RCH S42 .... 146 C2
Hardy Barn HEANOR DE75 .... 216 E3
Hardybarn La BUX SK17 .... 81 L7
Hardy Cl BUTN/AL/TUT DE13 .... 286 B3
 LGEAT NG10 .... 261 L2
Hardy Crs RIPLEY DE5 .... 201 L2
Hardy Pl MSFD NG18 .... 164 C4
Hardy St ALFN DE55 .... 175 J5
Harebell Cl DERBYE DE21 .... 227 K7
Harefield Rd ECC S11 .... 55 G2
Harehedge La
 BUTN/AL/TUT DE13 .... 273 L2
Harehill Crs RCH S42 .... 128 A6
Harehill Rd CHSW S40 .... 128 C3
Hareholme St MSFDW NG19 .... 164 D2
Harepit Cl DERBYSE DE24 .... 257 K5
Harewood Cl BPR/DUF DE56 .... 200 A5
 LGEAT NG10 .... 244 E6
Harewood Crs CLCR S45 .... 144 D5
 RCH S42 .... 144 D4
Harewood Rd DERBYW DE22 .... 226 A7
 RCH S42 .... 126 B5
Harewood Wy ECC S11 .... 54 D8
Hargate Hill La GLSP SK13 .... 25 G3
Hargate Rd BUX SK17 .... 99 J4
 STPNHL/WNHL DE15 .... 281 M1
Hargrave Av
 BWSH/BRSTN DE72 .... 242 F5
Harland Rd FUL S10 .... 55 H1
Harlaxton Dr LGEAT NG10 .... 261 K1
Harlaxton St
 BUTN/AL/TUT DE13 .... 273 K4
Harlech Cl DERBYE DE21 .... 242 D5
 ILK DE7 .... 216 F7
Harlech Ri BSTN/STPLFD NG9 .... 245 L6
Harlech Wy BUTN/AL/TUT DE13 .... 274 A2
Harlequin Ct
 EWD/SEL/PNX NG16 .... 203 G7
Harlesden Av DERBYW DE22 .... 239 K3
Harlesthorpe Av STV/CWN S43 .... 95 J6
Harlesthorpe La STV/CWN S43 .... 95 H5
Harley Rd ECC S11 .... 54 C5
Harlow Cl ASH NG17 .... 163 J4
 DERBYSE DE24 .... 257 J6
 MSFDW NG19 .... 149 M4
Harlow Ct ILK DE7 .... 229 G3
Harold Av EWD/SEL/PNX NG16 .... 202 G6
Harper Av BUTN/AL/TUT DE13 .... 273 M5
Harperhill Cl CHSW S40 .... 128 C3
Harpole Cl ALFN DE55 .... 187 J2
Harpswell Cl DERBYW DE22 .... 240 B4
Harpur Av MELB/CHEL DE73 .... 277 K6
 NORM/LIT DE23 .... 255 L3
Harpur Hill Rd BUX SK17 .... 99 M5
Harrier Rd BPR/DUF DE56 .... 199 M5
Harrier Wy DERBYSE DE24 .... 256 B7
Harriet St NORM/LIT DE23 .... 4 F8

Harriet St BSTN/STPLFD NG9 .... 245 G2
Harrimans Dr
 BWSH/BRSTN DE72 .... 260 C2
Harringay Gdns
 DERBYW DE22 .... 239 M4
Harrington Av
 BWSH/BRSTN DE72 .... 242 F8
Harrington Rd
 NORM/LIT DE23 .... 255 M1
 SHEFF/MNR S2 .... 55 K2
Harrington St
 BWSH/BRSTN DE72 .... 259 L3
 DERBYSE DE24 .... 257 H4
 LGEAT NG10 .... 260 E5
 MSFD NG18 .... 164 C4
 NORM/LIT DE23 .... 256 C2
Harris Av RIPLEY DE5 .... 186 F8
Harris Cl RIPLEY DE5 .... 200 F1
Harrison Cl BUT DE14 .... 280 E2
Harrison Dr MTLK DE4 .... 183 J1
Harrison La ALFN DE55 .... 161 J4
 FUL S10 .... 53 J3
Harrison Rd BSTN/STPLFD NG9 .... 245 G2
 MSFD NG18 .... 164 B4
Harrison St DERBYW DE22 .... 4 A7
Harris Rd BSTN/STPLFD NG9 .... 245 M5
 BUX SK17 .... 99 M7
Harrogate Crs DERBYE DE21 .... 241 G1
Harrop Edge Rd HYDE SK14 .... 16 B6
Harrop La FUL S10 .... 53 J4
Harrop White Rd MSFDW NG19 .... 164 C2
Harrots La BUX SK17 .... 151 G4
Harrow Cl ASHZ LE65 .... 291 K2
Harrow Dr BUT DE14 .... 280 F3
 ILK DE7 .... 230 E6
Harrow Rd SWAD DE11 .... 282 E3
Harrow St DERBYSE DE24 .... 241 H8
 ECC S11 .... 55 J1
Hart Av LGEAT NG10 .... 244 D5
Hartfield Cl CHNE S41 .... 128 E3
Hartford Cl SHEFS S8 .... 55 K7
Hartford Rd SHEFS S8 .... 55 K7
Harthill Field Rd AU/AST/KP S26 .... 75 J5
Harthill La AU/AST/KP S26 .... 95 H1
Harthill Rd AU/AST/KP S26 .... 75 M3
 HAN/WDH S13 .... 56 E3
Hartill Dr MSFDW NG19 .... 164 C5
Hartington Av ABRD S7 .... 54 F7
Hartington Cl ILK DE7 .... 229 H2
Hartington Ct STV/CWN S43 .... 95 K6
Hartington Dr ASH NG17 .... 163 L6
 CHF/WBR SK23 .... 60 B1
 EWD/SEL/PNX NG16 .... 189 K3
 WRKS S80 .... 114 F1
Hartington Pl ILK DE7 .... 217 H5
Hartington Rd ABRD S7 .... 54 F7
 BUX SK17 .... 99 L4
 CHNE S41 .... 3 L6
 DRON S18 .... 70 E8
 MPL/ROM SK6 .... 42 B4
Hartington St NORM/LIT DE23 .... 4 F7
 SBK/MW NG20 .... 133 J2
Hartington Vw STV/CWN S43 .... 93 J7
Hartland Dr NORM/LIT DE23 .... 256 A4
Hartland Wy CHNE S41 .... 110 D1
Hartley St SHEFP/MNR S2 .... 55 K3
Hartopp Av SHEFP/MNR S2 .... 55 M4
Hartopp Cl SHEFP/MNR S2 .... 55 M4
Hartopp Dr SHEFP/MNR S2 .... 56 A4
Hartopp Rd SHEFP/MNR S2 .... 55 M4
Hartshay Hl RIPLEY DE5 .... 186 F7
Harthill Rd SWAD DE11 .... 283 K6
Hartsmoorne Rd NORM/LIT DE23 .... 255 M5
 RDERBYSW DE65 .... 276 B2
 SWAD DE11 .... 283 J7
Hartside Cl CHSW S40 .... 110 A5
Hartside Gdns LGEAT NG10 .... 260 D2
Hartwood Dr
 BSTN/STPLFD NG9 .... 245 G1
Harvest Gv MSHM DE12 .... 290 D5
Harvest Hl SWAD DE11 .... 282 E3
Harvest Wy CHSW S40 .... 109 K5
 DERBYE DE21 .... 227 M7
Harvey Clough Ms SHEFS S8 .... 55 K7
Harvey Clough Rd SHEFS S8 .... 55 K7
Harvey Ct BSVR S44 .... 113 J8
Harvey Cft
 BSTN/STPLFD NG9 .... 230 F6
Harvey Pl UTXR ST14 .... 247 L1
Harvey Rd BUT DE14 .... 280 D2
 CDON/KEG DE74 .... 271 L6
 CHNE S41 .... 111 H8
 DERBYSE DE24 .... 257 K3
 MSFD NG18 .... 165 H5
Harwell Rd SHEFS S8 .... 55 J3
Harwich Rd SHEFP/MNR S2 .... 56 C1
Harwood Av BUT DE14 .... 280 C2
 SHEFP/MNR S2 .... 55 J2
Harwood Dr MOS S20 .... 73 G1
Harwood Gdns MOS S20 .... 73 H1
Harwood Pl ASH NG17 .... 163 K6
Harwood St SHEFP/MNR S2 .... 55 K2
Harworth Cl MSFDW NG19 .... 164 A1
Hasgill Cl DERBYE DE21 .... 227 M7
Haslam St BSVR S44 .... 113 J8
Haslam Crs SHEFS S8 .... 70 B4
Haslam's La DERBYW DE22 .... 226 D8
Hasland Cl CHNE S41 .... 3 J6
Haslemere Ct NORM/LIT DE23 .... 5 H9
Haslemere Rd LGEAT NG10 .... 260 E2
Haslin Rd BUX SK17 .... 100 A3
Hassall Rd RDERBYSW DE65 .... 264 A1
Hassock La North
 HEANOR DE75 .... 216 E4
Hassock La South
 HEANOR DE75 .... 216 F4
Hassocky La RCH S42 .... 129 L5
Hassop Cl CHSW S40 .... 109 M4
 DRON S18 .... 70 F8
Hassop Rd BKWL DE45 .... 105 G8
 DERBYE DE21 .... 241 K2
 STV/CWN S43 .... 93 J8
Hastilar Cl SHEFP/MNR S2 .... 56 C2
Hastilar Rd SHEFP/MNR S2 .... 56 C2
Hastilar Rd South HAN/WDH S13 .... 56 C2
 SHEFP/MNR S2 .... 56 C2

Hastings Cl CHSW S40 .... 110 A4
 MELB/CHEL DE73 .... 279 H8
Hastings Mt ABRD S7 .... 54 F6
Hastings St ABRD S7 .... 54 F6
 BUX SK17 .... 99 M6
 SWAD DE11 .... 282 E7
Hastings Wy CDON/KEG DE74 .... 271 L8
 NORM/LIT DE23 .... 256 D1
Hastings Wy ILK DE7 .... 291 M5
Haston Dr ALFN DE55 .... 188 A2
Hatchmere Cl DERBYE DE21 .... 241 K1
Hatfield Av LGEAT NG10 .... 244 E6
 DERBYSE DE24 .... 257 J5
Hathaway Cl RCH S42 .... 144 E4
Hathern Cl LGEAT NG10 .... 261 C5
 NORM/LIT DE23 .... 256 B5
 SWAD DE11 .... 111 J6
Hathersage Av LGEAT NG10 .... 260 C5
 DERBYSE DE24 .... 256 B2
Hathersage Crs GLSP SK13 .... 17 H8
Hathersage Dr ALFN DE55 .... 188 C1
 GLSP SK13 .... 26 C1
Hathersage Rd HATH/EY S32 .... 66 A2
 TOT/DORE S17 .... 68 F1
Hathersage Wy ASH NG17 .... 163 H6
Hattersley Rd East HYDE SK14 .... 24 A1
Hatton Cl DRON S18 .... 90 A2
Hatton Cl MELB/CHEL DE73 .... 278 D3
 MSFD NG18 .... 165 L4
Hatton Crofts LGEAT NG10 .... 260 F4
Hatton Dr CHSW S40 .... 109 L5
Haugh La ECC S11 .... 54 C5
Haughton Rd SHEFS S8 .... 55 J8
Haulton Dr CDON/KEG DE74 .... 271 K6
Havelock Rd NORM/LIT DE23 .... 256 C2
Havelock St ILK DE7 .... 230 C3
 RIPLEY DE5 .... 187 G8
Haven Baulk Av
 NORM/LIT DE23 .... 255 H3
Haven Baulk La MCKLVR DE3 .... 255 G3
Haven Cl ASH NG17 .... 163 G7
Haven Ct DERBYSE DE24 .... 258 A4
Havercroft Rd SHEFS S8 .... 55 H6
Havercroft Ter ECK/KIL S21 .... 73 L3
Hawfield La
 STPNHL/WNHL DE15 .... 274 F7
Hawke St DERBYW DE22 .... 239 M5
Hawkesworth Av
 MSFDW NG19 .... 165 L1
Hawk Green Rd MPL/ROM SK6 .... 32 C7
Hawkhill Rd HATH/EY S32 .... 86 A4
Hawking La BSVR S44 .... 146 D3
Hawkins Dr BPR/DUF DE56 .... 185 L7
Hawkins La BUT DE14 .... 274 A6
Hawk Rd NM/HAY SK22 .... 44 A2
Hawksdale Cl
 MELB/CHEL DE73 .... 257 K8
Hawk's Dr STPNHL/WNHL DE15 .... 275 G7
Hawkshead Av DERBYE DE21 .... 241 G1
 DRON S18 .... 90 A1
Hawkshead Rd GLSP SK13 .... 18 B8
Hawksley Av CHSW S40 .... 2 E1
Hawksley Dr
 BUTN/AL/TUT DE13 .... 264 E6
 MTLK DE4 .... 140 E7
Hawksway ECK/KIL S21 .... 72 F7
Hawkswood Cl
 BSTN/STPLFD NG9 .... 245 L6
Hawleys Cl MTLK DE4 .... 157 H4
Hawley St DRON S18 .... 91 K1
Hawson Wy WRKN S81 .... 77 M3
Hawthorn Av
 BWSH/BRSTN DE72 .... 260 C2
 DERBYSE DE24 .... 257 K3
 MOS S20 .... 73 G1
 MPL/ROM SK6 .... 32 A4
 MSHM DE12 .... 294 C3
 RIPLEY DE5 .... 201 G2
 STV/CWN S43 .... 93 M6
Hawthorn Bank GLSP SK13 .... 17 J6
Hawthorn Cl ASHB DE6 .... 208 A2
 CHF/WBR SK23 .... 60 B1
 RDERBYSW DE65 .... 255 G8
 STV/CWN S43 .... 95 G6
Hawthorn Crs
 RDERBYSW DE65 .... 255 G8
 STPNHL/WNHL DE15 .... 281 J4
Hawthornden Av UTXR ST14 .... 247 J2
Hawthornden Cl UTXR ST14 .... 247 K2
Hawthornden Gdns UTXR ST14 .... 247 J2
Hawthorn Dr MTLK DE4 .... 171 K4
 ALFN DE55 .... 161 L2
 BSTN/STPLFD NG9 .... 245 G4
 BSVR S44 .... 147 L2
 BWSH/BRSTN DE72 .... 242 E7
 DRON S18 .... 70 D7
 LGEAT NG10 .... 260 F3
 SBK/MW NG20 .... 133 G6
 WRKS S80 .... 96 A7
Hawthorne Av ALFN DE55 .... 159 G2
 ASH NG17 .... 162 E4
 BPR/DUF DE56 .... 200 C8
 ECK/KIL S21 .... 74 A5
 MSHM DE12 .... 295 M5
 STV/CWN S43 .... 94 D4
Hawthorne Rd
 EWD/SEL/PNX NG16 .... 177 G7
Hawthornes Av ALFN DE55 .... 176 C5
Hawthorne St CHSW S40 .... 3 H8
Hawthorn Gv HYDE SK14 .... 17 G4
Hawthorn Hl STV/CWN S43 .... 93 J4
Hawthorn Ri
 EWD/SEL/PNX NG16 .... 217 L6
 SWAD DE11 .... 282 C3
Hawthorn Rd CDON/KEG DE74 .... 271 L6
 ECK/KIL S21 .... 72 F7
The Hawthorns
 CHF/WBR SK23 .... 60 E6
 DERBYE DE21 .... 227 G2
Hawthorn St DERBYSE DE24 .... 256 F2
Hawthorn Wy RCH S42 .... 109 J5
Hawton Cl MSFDW NG19 .... 164 C1
Hawtrey Gdns
 DERBYSE DE24 .... 257 K4
Haxby Cl HAN/WDH S13 .... 57 H4
Haxby Pl HAN/WDH S13 .... 57 H4
Haxby St HAN/WDH S13 .... 57 H5
Haybank La CDLE ST10 .... 204 B5

Haybrook Ct TOT/DORE S17 69 H5
Haycock Cl STLY SK15 16 B3 2
STLY SK15 16 A3 1
Hayden Fold GLSP SK13 25 G4
Haydn Rd DERBYE DE21 241 J2
Haydock Cl BUT DE14 280 D3 2
Haydock Park Rd
DERBYSE DE24 257 H2
Hayes Av BWSH/BRSTN DE72 259 L3
NORM/LIT DE23 256 A2
Hayes Cl EWD/SEL/PNX NG16 176 F7
ILK DE7 229 H2 5
Hayes Ct MOS S20 73 H4
Hayes Crs ALFN DE55 187 J4
Hayes Dr MOS S20 73 G4
Hayes La ALFN DE55 187 J3
The Hayes RDERBYSW DE65 266 F1
Hayes Wood Rd ILK DE7 228 E1
Hayfield Cl BPR/DUF DE56 199 L5 2
DRON S18 90 A1 2
RCH S42 128 C7
STV/CWN S43 93 J7
Hayfield Crs HACK/IN S12 57 G7 1
Hayfield Dr HACK/IN S12 56 F7
Hayfield Pl HACK/IN S12 57 G7
Hayfield Rd CHF/WBR SK23 45 J4
NM/HAY SK22 44 B1
Hayfield Vw ECK/KIL S21 72 E7
Hayford Wy STV/CWN S43 112 B1
Hay La ASHB DE6 205 H6
CLCR S45 158 E3
RDERBYSW DE65 251 H4
Hayley Cft BPR/DUF DE56 226 C1
Hayling Cl ILK DE7 216 F7 6
Haynes Av BSTN/STPLFD NG9 230 F5
Hays Cl ILK DE7 217 G8 1
Hays La ASHB DE6 196 B1
The Hays RDERBYSW DE65 251 M8
Hay Wain La SWAD DE11 282 E3
Haywards Cl GLSP SK13 17 M7
Haywood Cl DERBYSE DE24 257 K5 2
Hayworth Rd LGEAT NG10 244 E5
Hazel Av CLCR S45 145 L7
ECK/KIL S21 73 M5
NORM/LIT DE23 256 A4
Hazelbadge Crs HACK/IN S12 57 H7 3
Hazel Bank MSFD NG18 165 H2
Hazelby Rd WRKS S80 115 H2
Hazel Cl ASHB DE6 208 A2
DRON S18 90 F2 1
HEANOR DE75 216 A1
MPL/ROM SK6 32 B6
MSHM DE12 295 M5
RDERBYSW DE65 255 H8 1
UTXR ST14 247 L4
Hazel Ct DRON S18 90 E2
Hazel Crs SBK/MW NG20 133 G6
Hazeldene Cl BPR/DUF DE56 213 H5
Hazel Dr CHSW S40 2 B9
DERBYE DE21 242 D4
RCH S42 128 E7
Hazel Gv ALFN DE55 176 E5
BPR/DUF DE56 213 H7 1
HATH/EY S32 86 F8
MSFDW NG19 149 L5
MSHM DE12 290 E4
MTLK DE4 157 G5
STV/CWN S43 93 M6
Hazelhurst CHNE S41 129 G4 1
Hazelmere Rd WRKS S80 95 M8
Hazelrigg Cl CDON/KEG DE74 271 J6
Hazel Rd ECK/KIL S21 72 F8 2
Hazel St ASH NG17 163 G3
Hazeltree Cl RIPLEY DE5 200 F2
Hazelwood Cl DRON S18 89 M1 6
EWD/SEL/PNX NG16 203 L8
Hazelwood Hl BPR/DUF DE56 212 E2
Hazelwood Rd BPR/DUF DE56 212 F3
DERBYE DE21 241 J2 3
STPNHL/WNHL DE15 281 H4 2
Hazlebarrow Cl SHEFS S8 70 E3
Hazlebarrow Ct SHEFS S8 70 E3 1
Hazlebarrow Crs SHEFS S8 70 E3
Hazlebarrow Dr SHEFS S8 70 E3
Hazlebarrow Gv SHEFS S8 70 F3 1
Hazlebarrow Rd SHEFS S8 70 E4 3
Hazlehurst Av CHNE S41 110 D5
Hazlehurst La CHNE S41 110 D5
SHEFS S8 71 J3
Headingley Ct
NORM/LIT DE23 255 M2 3
Headland Cl STV/CWN S43 111 H3
Heage La RDERBYSW DE65 253 M3
Heage Rd RIPLEY DE5 200 E1
Healaugh Wy CHSW S40 3 J9
Healdswood St ASH NG17 163 G3
Heanor Gate Rd HEANOR DE75 216 A2
Heanor Rd HEANOR DE75 202 A7
ILK DE7 215 K3
ILK DE7 217 H7
RIPLEY DE5 201 K7
Heaps Farm Ct STLY SK15 16 A2
Hearthcote Rd SWAD DE11 282 C7
Hearthstone La MTLK DE4 157 G8
Heath Av ECK/KIL S21 74 A5
MSFD NG18 165 L3
NORM/LIT DE23 239 M8
Heathcote Cl DERBYSE DE24 257 M5 2
Heathcote Dr CHNE S41 129 H2
Heath Ct DERBYSE DE24 256 B7 3
Heather Av BSVR S44 130 C8
Heather Bank Cl GLSP SK13 25 K3
Heather Brow STLY SK15 16 B3
Heather Cl ALFN DE55 176 D7 1
ALFN DE55 187 K2
BSVR S44 111 K7
DERBYSE DE24 256 A8 2
EWD/SEL/PNX NG16 217 L1
MSFD NG18 164 D4
Heather Ct HEANOR DE75 216 E1 2
Heather Crs
BWSH/BRSTN DE72 260 C3 1
NORM/LIT DE23 255 M4
Heather Gdns CHNE S41 129 H3 1
Heather Gv HYDE SK14 17 G4
Heather Lea Av TOT/DORE S17 68 F3
Heather Lea Pl TOT/DORE S17 68 F3
Heatherley Dr MSFDW NG19 165 H1
Heathermead Cl DERBYE DE21 241 J1
Heather Vale Cl CHNE S41 129 H3 2
Heather Vale Rd CHNE S41 129 H3
Heather Wy MPL/ROM SK6 32 B5
MSFD NG18 165 K4
RCH S42 127 G3
Heathfield MTLK DE4 156 F3 1
Heathfield Av CHSW S40 2 B3
ILK DE7 230 D2
Heathfield Cl DRON S18 90 C2 2
RCH S42 128 E6 1
Heathfield Gdns ALFN DE55 161 K3
Heathfield Gv
BSTN/STPLFD NG9 245 M7
Heathfield Nook Rd BUX SK17 100 B8
Heathfield Rd HACK/IN S12 57 G6
UTXR ST14 247 L2
Heath Gdns BWSH/BRSTN DE72 260 D2
Heath Gv BUX SK17 99 M4
Heathland Cl MSFD NG18 165 K4
Heathlands Dr UTXR ST14 247 L1 2
Heath La ASHZ LE65 284 D5
RDERBYSW DE65 267 G1
SWAD DE11 284 B6
SWAD DE11 290 F1
Heath Park Rd BUX SK17 99 M3
Heath Rd GLSP SK13 17 M7
RCH S42 146 B1
RIPLEY DE5 201 H1
STPNHL/WNHL DE15 281 H3
UTXR ST14 247 L1
Heath St BUX SK17 99 L4
The Heath
EWD/SEL/PNX NG16 217 K2 3
Heath Wy RDERBYSW DE65 264 A1
Heathy La ST/HB/BR S6 41 K5
Heaton Cl DRON S18 90 A1
Heaton St CHSW S40 109 M8
Heavygate La BPR/DUF DE56 198 B2
Hebden Cl NORM/LIT DE23 255 J4
Hebden Dr GLSP SK13 26 C2 3
Hebrides Cl DERBYSE DE24 256 A7 11
Hedgebank Ct
DERBYE DE21 227 M7 3
Hedge Gv SWAD DE11 282 E3 3
Hedgerow Cl ASH NG17 177 M1
Hedgerow Gdns
DERBYE DE21 227 M7 3
Hedges Dr ILK DE7 230 C6
Hedingham Wy MCKLVR DE3 254 F2
Hedley Dr STV/CWN S43 111 G2
Heeley Bank Rd SHEFP/MNR S2 55 L3
Heeley Gn SHEFP/MNR S2 55 L4
Heigham Cl DERBYSE DE24 257 G7
Helmsdale Cl MSFDW NG19 164 B5 2
Helmsley Av MOS S20 73 G3
Helmton Dr SHEFS S8 55 K7
Helmton Rd SHEFS S8 55 J8
Helston Cl CHNE S41 3 K9
DERBYSE DE24 257 L4 3
MSHM DE12 289 G5
Helston Ri ABRD S7 54 F6
Helvellyn Wy LGEAT NG10 244 E8 2
Heming Av CLCR S45 145 M8 1
Hemington Hl CDON/KEG DE74 271 M6
Hemingway Cl
EWD/SEL/PNX NG16 217 M1
Hemlock Av BSTN/STPLFD NG9 245 H2
LGEAT NG10 261 G1
Hemlock Cl DERBYE DE21 227 K7
Hemlock La ILK DE7 230 A5 3
Hemper Gv SHEFS S8 70 A3 1
Hemper La SHEFS S8 70 A4
Hemp Yd BPR/DUF DE56 196 E1
Hemsley Dr
EWD/SEL/PNX NG16 203 G7 4
Hemsworth Rd SHEFS S8 55 M8
Hendon St HAN/WDH S13 57 J1
Hendon Wy DERBYW DE22 239 L4
Henhurst Hl
BUTN/AL/TUT DE13 272 E6
Henhurst Rdg
BUTN/AL/TUT DE13 272 F6
Henley Av SHEFS S8 70 E2
Henley Gdns
BSTN/STPLFD NG9 245 H1 5
Henley Wy ILK DE7 229 G2
Henmore Pl ASHB DE6 193 M8 2
Henning La ASH NG17 177 L1
Hennymoor Cl WRKS S80 96 D5
Hennymoor La WRKS S80 96 E8
Henry Av MSFDW NG19 149 L5
MTLK DE4 156 F4
Henry Crs ALFN DE55 175 M7
Henry St CHNE S41 110 E2
DERBY DE1 4 D1
ECK/KIL S21 73 G7
GLSP SK13 25 M1
RCH S42 129 H7
RIPLEY DE5 187 G8
Henshaw Av ILK DE7 230 A5 4
Henshaw Pl ILK DE7 217 H6
Herbert Rd ABRD S7 55 H4 3
Herbert St MSFD NG18 164 D4 1
STPNHL/WNHL DE15 274 E7
Herdings Ct HACK/IN S12 56 D7 2
Herdings Rd HACK/IN S12 56 D7
Herdings Vw HACK/IN S12 56 D7
Herdsmans Cl ASHB DE6 194 B4
Hereford Av MSFDW NG19 149 M5
Hereford Cl BUX SK17 99 M6 1
Hereford Crs SWAD DE11 283 G4
Hereford Dr STV/CWN S43 111 J2
Hereford Rd BUX SK17 99 M5
DERBYE DE21 241 G2
Hereford St SHEF S1 55 K1 3
Hereford Wy STLY SK15 16 A3 2
Herewood Cl SBK/MW NG20 133 J6
Heritage Dr STV/CWN S43 95 G5
Heritage Wy
STPNHL/WNHL DE15 281 K1
Hermitage Av ALFN DE55 187 M5
BWSH/BRSTN DE72 242 F8
MSFD NG18 164 B5
Hermitage Ct DERBYE DE21 241 L1
Hermitage La ASHB DE6 206 E4
MSFD NG18 164 B5
Hermitage Park Wy
SWAD DE11 282 D3 10
Hermitage St SHEFP/MNR S2 55 J1 3
Hermitage Wk ILK DE7 230 C4
Hermitage Wy MSFD NG18 164 B6
Herne St ASH NG17 163 K6
Hernstone La BUX SK17 62 E7
Heron Dr SWAD DE11 283 J7 1
UTXR ST14 247 M4
Heron Gld WRKN S81 77 M3 4
Heronswood Dr
DERBYE DE21 242 A4 1
Heron Wy MCKLVR DE3 239 K8
Herriot Dr CHSW S40 3 J8
Herrods Vw ASH NG17 162 F4 1
Herschell Rd SHEFS S8 55 J3 3
Hessey St HAN/WDH S13 57 J4
Hewers Holt STV/CWN S43 94 E4
Hewitt Pl AU/AST/KP S26 75 H5
Hexham Av ILK DE7 230 D6
Hexham Cl MSFD NG18 165 J5
Heyden Br GLSP SK13 13 G4
Heydon Cl BPR/DUF DE56 199 L4 3
Heyford Ct HEANOR DE75 216 D1 2
Hey La BPR/DUF DE56 183 L4
Heysbank Rd POY/DIS SK12 43 G5
Hey St LGEAT NG10 260 E6
Heyward St MSFD NG18 165 G3 2
Heywood St MSFD NG18 165 G3 3
STV/CWN S43 111 H2
Heyworth Rd CHF/WBR SK23 60 F4
Heyworth St DERBYW DE22 239 M4
Hibbert Crs ASH NG17 163 K7
Hibbert La MPL/ROM SK6 32 C5
Hibbert Rd MSFD NG18 165 G3
Hibbert St NM/HAY SK22 43 L4 2
Hickings La BSTN/STPLFD NG9 245 H2
Hickingwood La STV/CWN S43 95 K5
Hickinwood Crs STV/CWN S43 95 J5
Hickleton Cl RIPLEY DE5 200 F1
Hickling Cl DERBYSE DE24 257 G7 2
Hickmott Rd ECC S11 55 G2 3
Hickton Dr BSTN/STPLFD NG9 261 L1
Hickton Rd ALFN DE55 187 J4
Hide La BUX SK17 151 G4
Hides Gn BSVR S44 113 K8
Higger La HATH/EY S32 66 C2
Higgins Rd SWAD DE11 282 C4
Higg La BPR/DUF DE56 184 E4
Higgott Cl BUT DE14 280 D2
Higham La ALFN DE55 160 B6
Highashes La CLCR S45 143 H1
Highbank GLSP SK13 17 J3
High Bank RIPLEY DE5 201 J8
High Bank Av STLY SK15 16 A3
Highbank Rd GLSP SK13 26 C3
High Bank Rd
STPNHL/WNHL DE15 274 E7
Highbury Cl DERBYW DE22 239 J4 3
Highbury Rd CHNE S41 110 C5
Highcliffe Av SBK/MW NG20 133 G6
Highcliffe Dr ECC S11 54 C3
Highcliffe Pl ECC S11 54 C4
Highcliffe Rd ECC S11 54 C3
Highcroft Cl LGEAT NG10 261 H5
Highcroft Dr
BUTN/AL/TUT DE13 273 J6
WOL/BIL/BRX NG8 231 L5
High Cross BUX SK17 151 J5
High Edge Dr BPR/DUF DE56 200 B2
Higher Albert St CHNE S41 3 G1
Higher Barn Rd GLSP SK13 17 H6
Higher Hallsteads BUX SK17 61 J7
Higher La CHF/WBR SK23 58 A7
POY/DIS SK12 42 C3
Highfield BKWL DE45 122 B2
Highfield Av BUX SK17 81 H1
CHNE S41 110 B5
MSFDW NG19 164 E1
SBK/MW NG20 133 G7
Highfield Cl BKWL DE45 122 F5
BUTN/AL/TUT DE13 273 K3 1
HEANOR DE75 201 L5
MSFDW NG19 164 E1
Highfield Dr ALFN DE55 176 E5
BKWL DE45 122 F5 1
ILK DE7 229 L5
MTLK DE4 157 G4
STPNHL/WNHL DE15 274 C7
Highfield Gdns DERBYW DE22 240 C2
HYDE SK14 17 G5
Highfield La ASHB DE6 211 K5
BUX SK17 151 J7
CHNE S41 110 B4
DERBYE DE21 241 H5
Highfield Pl SHEFP/MNR S2 55 K2
Highfield Rd ALFN DE55 187 G4
ASH NG17 162 F7
ASHB DE6 196 C7
ASHB DE6 207 K2
BPR/DUF DE56 199 J8
BPR/DUF DE56 214 C2
BSTN/STPLFD NG9 245 K7 2
BSVR S44 131 K1
CHNE S41 110 C5
DERBYE DE21 226 F3
DERBYW DE22 240 C3
GLSP SK13 26 A2
MPL/ROM SK6 32 C4 5
NM/HAY SK22 35 G7
NORM/LIT DE23 255 M3 1
SWAD DE11 282 E7
Highfields RIPLEY DE5 201 L2 1
Highfields Cl ASHZ LE65 291 J4
Highfields Crs DRON S18 90 D2 3
Highfields Dr MSHM DE12 288 F4
Highfields Rd DRON S18 90 D2
Highfield St LGEAT NG10 260 F1
SWAD DE11 282 E7
Highfields Wy RCH S42 146 A2
Highfield Ter MSFD NG18 164 E4 3
NM/HAY SK22 44 A2
Highfield View Rd CHNE S41 110 C5
Highfield Wy MSFD NG18 164 D5
RIPLEY DE5 200 F2
Highgate ASHZ LE65 291 K2
Highgate Dr DRON S18 90 F3
ILK DE7 216 F7
Highgate La DRON S18 90 F3
Highgate Rd NM/HAY SK22 35 G8
High Grounds Rd WRKS S80 77 M6
High Grounds Wy WRKS S80 77 L6
High Gv BPR/DUF DE56 200 A6
Highgrove Cl
BUTN/AL/TUT DE13 274 A1 1
Highgrove Dr MELB/CHEL DE73 257 J8
High Hazels Cl CLCR S45 145 H6
High Hazels Rd STV/CWN S43 94 D5
High Hazles Dr ASH NG17 162 D8
High Hill Rd NM/HAY SK22 44 A1
High Holborn ILK DE7 217 H7 2
High Holborn Rd RIPLEY DE5 201 K1
Highland Cl BUX SK17 99 M5
MSFDW NG19 149 M7
Highland Rd MSFD NG18 165 H8
STV/CWN S43 92 A5
Highlands Dr
STPNHL/WNHL DE15 274 D6
High La GLSP SK13 25 H3
HACK/IN S12 72 B1
MTLK DE4 158 B7
MTLK DE4 172 F5
RCH S42 127 H5
High Lane Central ILK DE7 229 J1
High La East ILK DE7 229 L2
High La West ILK DE7 229 G2
High Lee Rd NM/HAY SK22 43 K2
High Leys Rd STV/CWN S43 95 H8
Highlightley La DRON S18 89 L5
Highlow Cl CHSW S40 109 M5
High Meadow GLSP SK13 25 L3
High Meadow Cl RIPLEY DE5 201 C2 2
High Oakham Dr MSFD NG18 164 E7
High Oakham Hl MSFD NG18 164 D6
High Oakham Rd MSFD NG18 164 E7
High Pavement ASH NG17 163 H8
BPR/DUF DE56 199 K7 1
High Peak Trail BUX SK17 119 K7
MTLK DE4 152 F7
MTLK DE4 168 D2
MTLK DE4 171 M5
High Rdg MTLK DE4 156 F3
High Rd ALFN DE55 174 C6
BSTN/STPLFD NG9 261 K1
Highstairs La ALFN DE55 159 L2
Highstone La BUX SK17 119 L4
High Storrs Cl ECC S11 54 C4
High Storrs Crs ECC S11 54 D3
High Storrs Dr ECC S11 54 C4
High Storrs Ri ECC S11 54 D3
High Storrs Rd ECC S11 54 C4
High St ALFN DE55 160 D6
ALFN DE55 161 J4
ALFN DE55 175 J6
ALFN DE55 187 H3
ALFN DE55 188 B5
ASH NG17 162 F4
ASH NG17 163 H8 4
ASHB DE6 248 E1
ASHZ LE65 291 M8
BKWL DE45 105 L7
BPR/DUF DE56 199 K6
BPR/DUF DE56 214 D2
BSTN/STPLFD NG9 245 H3 1
BSVR S44 131 K1
BUT DE14 274 A8
BUTN/AL/TUT DE13 263 M4
BUX SK17 83 M6
BUX SK17 99 L3
BUX SK17 134 E4
CDON/KEG DE74 271 K8
CHF/WBR SK23 60 D4
CHNE S41 91 K8 3
CHSW S40 3 G4
CLCR S45 144 F7
DRON S18 70 C8
DRON S18 91 K1
ECK/KIL S21 73 G7
EWD/SEL/PNX NG16 203 G1
HATH/EY S32 105 L1
HEANOR DE75 201 M6
ILK DE7 230 C2 4
LGEAT NG10 261 H2
MELB/CHEL DE73 269 K1 3
MELB/CHEL DE73 277 J6
MOS S20 72 F3
MSFD NG18 164 E4 4
MSFDW NG19 148 E7
MSHM DE12 288 E5
MSHM DE12 295 M5
MTLK DE4 156 A8
NM/HAY SK22 43 M2
RDERBYSW DE65 267 G8
RIPLEY DE5 201 L2
STV/CWN S43 92 A7
STV/CWN S43 111 J2
SWAD DE11 282 D4
SWAD DE11 283 J8
TOT/DORE S17 69 G3
UTXR ST14 218 C7
UTXR ST14 247 M2
UTXR ST14 249 H8
WRKS S80 96 C4
High St East GLSP SK13 26 A1
High St West GLSP SK13 25 L1
High Tor ASH NG17 163 H3
High Tor Rd MTLK DE4 156 E8
High Trees TOT/DORE S17 69 G3
Highview GLSP SK13 25 K3
High View Cl CHNE S41 111 G8
High View Rd ALFN DE55 176 F3
Highway La ASHB DE6 168 C8
Highwood Av BPR/DUF DE56 213 L1
High Wood Bank
BPR/DUF DE56 213 M1
Highwood Cl GLSP SK13 25 K2
High Wood Fold MPL/ROM SK6 32 F3
Highwood La WRKS S80 95 M4
Highwood Pl ECK/KIL S21 72 F7
Highwood Rd UTXR ST14 248 A5
High Wray Cl ECC S11 54 E6
Hilary Cl BPR/DUF DE56 200 B5
Hilcote La ALFN DE55 176 C1
Hilcote St ALFN DE55 176 D2
Hilderstone Cl DERBYSE DE24 258 A4
Hillary Pl ILK DE7 229 L5
Hillberry RIPLEY DE5 201 J1
Hillberry Ri RCH S42 128 C4
Hill Brow DERBY DE1 4 E5
Hillcliff La BPR/DUF DE56 197 J8
Hill Cl BPR/DUF DE56 197 L8
DERBYE DE21 242 B6
EWD/SEL/PNX NG16 217 M1
ILK DE7 228 D1
UTXR ST14 247 J1
Hillcote Cl FUL S10 54 A1
Hillcote Dr FUL S10 54 A1
Hillcote Ms FUL S10 54 A1
Hillcote Ri FUL S10 54 A1
Hillcourt Rd MPL/ROM SK6 42 B3
Hill Crs ASH NG17 163 K6
Hillcrest BUTN/AL/TUT DE13 263 L5
Hill Crest MTLK DE4 185 K1
SBK/MW NG20 133 G7
Hill Crest Av ALFN DE55 174 B2
Hillcrest Av ALFN DE55 176 C6
ASHB DE6 196 C7 2
STPNHL/WNHL DE15 274 D6
Hillcrest Dr BPR/DUF DE56 214 D2
RIPLEY DE5 201 L2
Hillcreste Dr
MELB/CHEL DE73 257 J7 1
Hillcrest Gv STV/CWN S43 93 J7
Hillcrest Rd CHNE S41 129 G3
Hill Crest Rd DERBYE DE21 241 G3
Hill Croft Dr BWSH/BRSTN DE72 242 F6
Hill Cross BKWL DE45 122 C2
Hill Cross Av NORM/LIT DE23 255 M3
Hill Cross Dr NORM/LIT DE23 255 L3
Hill Dr CHF/WBR SK23 59 G2
Hillend La HYDE SK14 24 C1
Hillfield La BUTN/AL/TUT DE13 274 C1
Hillfield Rd BSTN/STPLFD NG9 245 J2
Hill Flds ALFN DE55 176 D6
Hillfoot Rd TOT/DORE S17 68 F5
Hill Green Cl MSHM DE12 288 A7 2
Hill Gv STV/CWN S43 92 E6
Hillhead La BUX SK17 118 B1
Hillhouses La RCH S42 128 B7
Hill La HATH/EY S32 66 B2
Hillman Dr STV/CWN S43 111 M4
Hillmoor St MSFDW NG19 148 E6
The Hillocks ASH NG17 163 L7 2
The Hillock HATH/EY S32 87 H8
Hill Ri BSTN/STPLFD NG9 230 F6
Hill Rise Cl NORM/LIT DE23 256 A3
Hill Rd BSTN/STPLFD NG9 245 L8
CLCR S45 143 J6
HEANOR DE75 216 A1
Hillsdale Rd
STPNHL/WNHL DE15 274 E5
Hillside BUTN/AL/TUT DE13 263 L4
BUX SK17 100 A7
CLCR S45 143 K6
EWD/SEL/PNX NG16 202 D7
MOS S20 72 F3
MTLK DE4 171 G6
MTLK DE4 181 J1
RDERBYSW DE65 255 G8
WRKS S80 96 C5
Hillside Av ASHB DE6 193 M7
DERBYE DE21 241 K5
DRON S18 90 D2
Hillside Cl GLSP SK13 17 H7
POY/DIS SK12 43 G4
WRKS S80 96 C5
Hillside Ct MELB/CHEL DE73 279 J8 2
Hillside Crs DERBYE DE21 242 B6
Hillside Dr CHSW S40 2 A7
LGEAT NG10 260 E2
STV/CWN S43 93 M7
Hillside Gdns SWAD DE11 282 C8
Hillside Gv LGEAT NG10 244 D4
MPL/ROM SK6 32 E1
Hillside Ri BPR/DUF DE56 199 J8
Hillside Rd BSTN/STPLFD NG9 245 L7
DERBYE DE21 242 B6
MSHM DE12 288 F4
Hillside Vw NM/HAY SK22 43 K2
Hills Rd BWSH/BRSTN DE72 259 L2
The Hills EDL/UDV S33 64 D4
Hill St ASHZ LE65 291 K4
CLCR S45 144 F7
MSHM DE12 295 H1
RIPLEY DE5 187 G7
SHEFP/MNR S2 55 J1
STPNHL/WNHL DE15 281 H3
SWAD DE11 282 D4
Hillsway MELB/CHEL DE73 257 J7
NORM/LIT DE23 255 L1
SBK/MW NG20 133 G7
Hillsway Crs MSFD NG18 164 D6
The Hill BSVR S44 147 K1
DERBYW DE22 240 D1 3
Hilltop BPR/DUF DE56 185 L3 2
Hill Top BSVR S44 113 K8
DERBYE DE21 227 G8
Hilltop Cl BSVR S44 147 L2
Hill Top Crs MOS S20 73 G1
Hilltop La ASHB DE6 237 G5
BPR/DUF DE56 200 B8
Hill Top Ri CHF/WBR SK23 58 F2
Hill Top Rd ALFN DE55 187 M5
HOLM/MEL HD7 9 J1
Hilltop Rd CHNE S41 91 L8
CLCR S45 143 J5
DRON S18 90 D2
EWD/SEL/PNX NG16 176 F7
GLSP SK13 17 L7
RCH S42 128 A6
Hilltops Vw MTLK DE4 157 G5
Hill Top Vw HOLM/MEL HD7 9 L2
Hill Top View ASH NG17 177 M1
Hillwood Dr DRON S18 90 D3
Hill Turrets Cl ECC S11 54 C6
Hill Vw BPR/DUF DE56 213 G7 1
CHF/WBR SK23 58 F2
RDERBYSW DE65 267 H8
STLY SK15 16 A4
Hill View Cl ILK DE7 214 E3 3
Hill View Gv DERBYE DE21 242 B5 1
Hill View Rd BSTN/STPLFD NG9 245 K8
STV/CWN S43 111 H2
Hillwood Cl WRKS S80 77 L8
Hillwood Dr GLSP SK13 26 C2
Hilton Cl LGEAT NG10 260 C6
MCKLVR DE3 255 G1
SWAD DE11 282 D3
Hilton Park Dr ALFN DE55 187 M2
Hilton Rd POY/DIS SK12 42 E3
RDERBYSW DE65 253 L6
RDERBYSW DE65 265 K3
Hinckley Ct MTLK DE4 140 C1

Hind Av BWSH/BRSTN DE72 ...... 259 M3
Hindersitch La MTLK DE4 ...... 185 C1
Hindlow Ct MSFD NG18 ...... 165 L4 [7]
Hindscarth Crs MCKLVR DE3 ... 255 H1 [8]
Hipley Cl CHSW S40 ...... 109 L5
Hipper St CHSW S40 ...... 3 H5
Hipper St South CHSW S40 ...... 3 H5
Hipper St West CHSW S40 ...... 2 C5
Hixon's La ILK DE7 ...... 243 L1
Hoades St RCH S42 ...... 144 F2
Hoare Rd BSTN/STPLFD NG9 ...... 245 L8
Hoargate La ASHB DE6 ...... 236 B1
Hobart Cl MCKLVR DE3 ...... 239 J8
  STPNHL/WNHL DE15 ...... 274 F8
Hobart St ECC S11 ...... 55 J2
Hob Hl BPR/DUF DE56 ...... 212 E2
Hobhill Mdw GLSP SK13 ...... 26 A3
Hobhouse Rd MSFDW NG19 ...... 149 C8
Hobkirk Dr DERBYE DE24 ...... 256 B8
Hob La BPR/DUF DE56 ...... 197 G2
Hobsic Cl EWD/SEL/PNX NG16 ...... 203 J2
Hobsic La EWD/SEL/PNX NG16... 189 C2
Hobson Dr ILK DE7 ...... 230 B4
Hobson Moor Rd HYDE SK14 ...... 16 C4
Hockerley Cl CHF/WBR S23 ...... 59 C2 [1]
Hockerley La CHF/WBR S23 ...... 59 C2 [1]
Hockley La CLCR S45 ...... 143 K8
  RCH S42 ...... 128 D3
Hockley Wy ALFN DE55 ...... 175 L8
Hodge Beck Cl DERBYSE DE24 ... 257 M4
Hodge La CLCR S45 ...... 142 B3
  HYDE SK14 ...... 24 C2
Hodmire La BSVR S44 ...... 147 G3
Hodthorpe Cl DERBYE DE21 ...... 241 K1 [3]
Hogarth Cl
  BSTN/STPLFD NG9 ...... 245 H4 [1]
Hogarth Rd MPL/ROM SK6 ...... 32 E2
Hogbarn La HEANOR DE75 ...... 202 A5
Hoggarth Ri DRON S18 ...... 90 C1
Hoggetts Cl
  BSTN/STPLFD NG9 ...... 245 L4 [3]
Hogshaw Villas Rd BUX SK17 .. 99 M2 [3]
Holbeach Dr CHSW S40 ...... 2 D9
Holbeck Av BSVR S44 ...... 113 M8
Holbeck St WRKS S80 ...... 115 C1
Holbein Cl DRON S18 ...... 90 C2
Holborn Dr DERBYW DE22 ...... 239 K3
Holborn Vw RIPLEY DE5 ...... 201 K2
  RCH S42 ...... 145 K3
Holbrook Cl CHSW S40 ...... 127 M2 [3]
  MSFDW NG19 ...... 148 D5 [2]
Holbrook Ct MSFD NG18 ...... 165 L4 [3]
Holbrook Dr HAN/WDH S13 ...... 56 E4 [5]
Holbrook Gn MOS S20 ...... 73 K1 [8]
Holbrook Pl STV/CWN S43 ...... 111 M3 [8]
Holbrook Ri MOS S20 ...... 73 J1
Holbrook St BPR/DUF DE56 ...... 199 J8
  DERBYE DE24 ...... 257 L4
  HAN/WDH S13 ...... 56 E3
Holbrook Vw BPR/DUF DE56 ... 214 D2 [3]
Holburn Av DRON S18 ...... 70 D8
Holcombe St NORM/LIT DE23 ...... 256 E1
Holden Av BWSH/BRSTN DE72 ... 270 D2
Holden Gdns
  BSTN/STPLFD NG9 ...... 245 H4 [3]
Holden St MSFD NG18 ...... 164 D4
Holderness Cl DERBYSE DE24 ... 256 A8
The Holdings SWAD DE11 ...... 289 K1 [3]
Holdon Cft MSHM DE12 ...... 287 M4
Holestone Gate Rd CLCR S45 ... 142 F8
Holker Av BUX SK17 ...... 99 M2
Holker Rd BUX SK17 ...... 99 M2
Holkham Av BSTN/STPLFD NG9 .. 245 M5
Holkham Cl ILK DE7 ...... 216 F7 [7]
Holkham Ri ECC S11 ...... 54 C8
Holland Cl ALFN DE55 ...... 160 C5
Holland Crs
  EWD/SEL/PNX NG16 ...... 189 L3
Holland Meadow
  LGEAT NG10 ...... 261 G6 [3]
Holland Pl SHEFP/MNR S2 ...... 55 K2 [3]
Holland Rd CHNE S41 ...... 91 J8
  SHEFP/MNR S2 ...... 55 K2
Hollens Wy RCH S42 ...... 109 J5 [6]
Hollies Cl ASHB DE6 ...... 207 L4
  DRON S18 ...... 90 F2
  STPNHL/WNHL DE15 ...... 275 H2
Hollies Dr MPL/ROM SK6 ...... 32 D5
Hollies La ASHB DE6 ...... 219 L5
Hollies Rd DERBYE DE22 ...... 226 A7
The Hollies BWSH/BRSTN DE72 .. 244 D5
Hollin Cl CHNE S41 ...... 109 M2 [3]
Hollin Cross La GLSP SK13 ...... 25 M2
Hollindale Dr HACK/IN S12 ...... 56 F5
Hollin Dr CHF/WBR SK23 ...... 60 E5
Hollington Cl DERBYE DE21 ...... 241 H3 [6]
Hollington Wy MSFD NG18 ...... 165 L4
Hollingwood Crs STV/CWN S43 .. 111 K1
Hollingworth Av LGEAT NG10 ... 244 F7
Hollingworth Dr MPL/ROM SK6 .. 32 C7
Hollinhey Ter HYDE SK14 ...... 16 F5
Hollin Hl STV/CWN S43 ...... 95 K7
Hollinsclough Rake BUX SK17 .. 117 J7
Hollinsend Av HACK/IN S12 ...... 56 F5
Hollinsend Pl HACK/IN S12 ...... 56 F5 [2]
Hollinsend Rd HACK/IN S12 ...... 56 D6 [3]
Hollins Green MPL/ROM SK6 .. 32 E3
Hollins La MPL/ROM SK6 ...... 32 E3
  MTLK DE4 ...... 173 K6
Hollins Ms GLSP SK13 ...... 17 C8
Hollinsmoor Rd NM/HAY SK22 .. 33 M3
Hollins Mt MPL/ROM SK6 ...... 32 E2
Hollins Spring Av DRON S18 ...... 90 D2
Hollins Spring Rd DRON S18 ...... 90 D2
Hollins St BUX SK17 ...... 99 L4
The Hollins MTLK DE4 ...... 172 C4
Hollins Wood Cl MTLK DE4 ...... 172 D5
Hollinwood La MPL/ROM SK6 .. 32 E8
Hollis Cft HACK/IN S12 ...... 57 K4 [1]
Hollis La CHNE S41 ...... 3 J5
  CHSW S40 ...... 3 J5
Hollis St DERBYSE DE24 ...... 257 K2
Holloway Rd BPR/DUF DE56 ...... 213 C6
  DERBYSE DE24 ...... 257 J3

Hollow Brooks DERBYE DE21 .. 226 F3 [1]
Hollow Crs
  STPNHL/WNHL DE15 ...... 274 F6 [1]
Hollowford Rd EDL/UDV S33 ...... 48 E7
Hollow Ga EDL/UDV S33 ...... 64 D3
Hollow La ASHB DE6 ...... 206 F1
  ASHB DE6 ...... 262 A4
  MOS S20 ...... 73 C4
  STPNHL/WNHL DE15 ...... 274 F6 [2]
Hollowood Av NORM/LIT DE23 .. 255 M2
Hollow O'the Moor BUX SK17 .. 102 B6
Hollow Rd MELB/CHEL DE73 ... 279 H7 [1]
The Hollows LGEAT NG10 ...... 261 K2 [1]
The Hollow ASHB DE6 ...... 219 H4
  CDON/KEG DE74 ...... 271 L6
  EDL/UDV S33 ...... 50 E7
  MCKLVR DE3 ...... 255 C2
  MTLK DE4 ...... 172 E5
  NORM/LIT DE23 ...... 255 L1
  UTXR ST14 ...... 247 M4
Holly Av BWSH/BRSTN DE72 ... 260 C1
  RIPLEY DE5 ...... 201 C2
Holly Bank HYDE SK14 ...... 17 C5
Hollybank Av HACK/IN S12 ...... 56 F4
Holly Bank Cl ALFN DE55 ...... 174 E8
Hollybank La HACK/IN S12 ...... 57 C4
  SWAD DE11 ...... 282 D3 [1]
Hollybank Crs HACK/IN S12 ...... 56 F4
Hollybank Rd HACK/IN S12 ...... 56 F4
Hollybank Wy HACK/IN S12 ...... 57 C4
Hollybush Wy NORM/LIT DE23 .. 255 J4
Holly Bush HYDE SK14 ...... 17 C5
Holly Bush La BPR/DUF DE56 .. 184 F6
Holly Cl ASHB DE6 ...... 208 A2 [3]
  BWSH/BRSTN DE72 ...... 259 K3
  ECK/KIL S21 ...... 73 L5
  MOS S20 ...... 290 E4
Holly Ct BSTN/STPLFD NG9 ...... 245 M2
  MCKLVR DE3 ...... 255 C1 [3]
  MSFDW NG19 ...... 165 H1
  SWAD DE11 ...... 283 J8
Holly Dr MSFDW NG19 ...... 165 K1
Holly Gdns HACK/IN S12 ...... 56 F4
Holly Gn STPNHL/WNHL DE15 .. 281 J2
Holly Gv ALFN DE55 ...... 187 J2
  HACK/IN S12 ...... 56 F4
Holly Hill Rd
  EWD/SEL/PNX NG16 ...... 189 J4
Hollyhock Wy BUT DE14 ...... 280 B3
Hollyhouse Dr ALFN DE55 ...... 176 E4
Holly House La BPR/DUF DE56... 198 F6
Hollyhurst La ASHB DE6 ...... 233 L3
Holly La BPR/DUF DE56 ...... 184 F6
  MTLK DE4 ...... 157 K6
Hollymoor Dr MELB/CHEL DE73.. 257 H8
  MPL/ROM SK6 ...... 42 B3
  MSHM DE12 ...... 295 M5
  UTXR ST14 ...... 247 K2
Holly St STPNHL/WNHL DE15 .. 281 J2
Hollythorpe Crs SHEFS S8 ...... 55 K6
Hollythorpe Rd SHEFS S8 ...... 55 L6
Hollywell Av RIPLEY DE5 ...... 201 L3
Hollywell Rd MPL/ROM SK6... 33 H2
Holm Av DERBYE DE21 ...... 226 E3
Holmbank Cl CHSW S40 ...... 2 C2
Holme Bank East CHSW S40 ...... 2 C2
Holmebank Vw CHSW S40 ...... 109 M4
Holme Bank West CHSW S40 .. 2 C2
Holme Cl ILK DE7 ...... 217 C8
  MTLK DE4 ...... 172 D5
  RDERBYSW DE65 ...... 263 M1
Holme Cft ILK DE7 ...... 229 H3
Holme Farm Av
  STPNHL/WNHL DE15 ...... 281 J2
Holmefield Crs ILK DE7 ...... 230 D2
Holmefield Rd WRKS S80 ...... 96 D4
Holme Hall Crs CHSW S40 ...... 109 L5
Holme La BKWL DE45 ...... 123 C3
  DERBYE DE21 ...... 241 M8
Holme Park Av CHSW S40 ...... 109 L3
Holme Rd CHNE S41 ...... 110 D4
  MTLK DE4 ...... 171 K1
Holmes Cl
  EWD/SEL/PNX NG16 ...... 202 D7 [1]
Holmesdale Cl DRON S18 ...... 70 F7
Holmesdale Rd DRON S18 ...... 70 E7
Holmesfield Cl MTLK DE4 ...... 157 K5 [1]
Holmesfield Dr HEANOR DE75 ... 216 D2
  MCKLVR DE3 ...... 239 J8 [1]
Holmesfield Rd DRON S18 ...... 89 L1 [1]
Holmes St BWSH/BRSTN DE72 .. 260 A3
Holmes St HEANOR DE75 ...... 202 A8
  NORM/LIT DE23 ...... 4 E9
Holme Styes La HOLM/MEL HD7 .. 9 H1
Holme Valley Circular Wk
  HOLM/MEL HD7 ...... 8 E2
  HOLM/MEL HD7 ...... 9 M5
Holmewood Dr
  EWD/SEL/PNX NG16 ...... 217 L2 [1]
Holme Woods La HOLM/MEL HD7.. 8 C5
Holmfield BUX SK17 ...... 99 H4
  NORM/LIT DE23 ...... 256 B3
Holmfield Rd
  BSTN/STPLFD NG9 ...... 245 M7
Holmgate Rd CLCR S45 ...... 144 B7
Holmhirst Cl SHEFS S8 ...... 55 H8
Holmhirst Dr SHEFS S8 ...... 55 H7
Holmhirst Rd SHEFS S8 ...... 55 H7
Holmhirst Wy SHEFS S8 ...... 55 H8
Holm La ALFN DE55 ...... 174 D6
Holmley Bank DRON S18 ...... 70 D7
Holmley La DRON S18 ...... 70 D7
Holmoak Cl DERBYE DE21 ...... 227 L7 [1]
Holmshaw Dr HAN/WDH S13 .. 57 H1
Holmshaw Gv HAN/WDH S13 ... 57 H1
Holt Av DERBYSE DE24 ...... 257 M4
Holt Dr MTLK DE4 ...... 156 C4
Holtlands Dr DERBYSE DE24... 257 J5
Holt La MTLK DE4 ...... 156 E6 [4]
  MTLK DE4 ...... 172 E5
Holt Rd MTLK DE4 ...... 156 C1
Holt's La BUTN/AL/TUT DE13 ... 263 L5
Holyhead Dr DERBYW DE22 ...... 227 L8
Holyoake Av RCH S42 ...... 127 H1
Holyoake Dr LGEAT NG10 ...... 261 J3

Holyrood Cl DERBYE DE21 ...... 242 C5
Holywell BKWL DE45 ...... 123 H5
Holywell Av ASHZ LE65 ...... 291 K3
Holywell La BKWL DE45 ...... 138 C5
Holywell La ILK DE7 ...... 216 F7
Holywell St CHSW S41 ...... 3 H5
Homecroft Av ASH NG17 ...... 163 J4
Home Croft Dr ASHZ LE65 ...... 291 L8
Homecroft Dr
  BSTN/STPLFD NG9 ...... 245 L3
The Home Cft
  BSTN/STPLFD NG9 ...... 245 L3
Home Farm Av HYDE SK14 ...... 24 C1
Homefarm Cl
  BWSH/BRSTN DE72 ...... 242 F5
Home Farm Ct SWAD DE11 ...... 289 C1 [1]
Home Farm Dr DERBYW DE22 ... 226 D6
Homeport Ms CHNE S41 ...... 3 H1
Homer Dr MPL/ROM SK6 ...... 32 E2
Homestead
  EWD/SEL/PNX NG16 ...... 202 D6 [1]
Homestead Rd POY/DIS SK12... 42 F4
Honeycroft Cl
  BPR/DUF DE56 ...... 199 L8 [3]
Honeycroft Ct ALFN DE55 ...... 176 E6 [1]
Honeyfield Dr RIPLEY DE5 ...... 201 J2
Honeysuckle Cl SWAD DE11 ... 282 D4 [3]
Honeysuckle Vw
  STPNHL/WNHL DE15 ...... 281 K3 [1]
Honeywall La ASHB DE6 ...... 206 B2
Honingham Rd ILK DE7 ...... 216 F7
Honister Cl MSFD NG18 ...... 164 F6
Honiton Cl
  BSTN/STPLFD NG9 ...... 245 K8 [1]
Hoober Av ECC S11 ...... 54 D5
Hoober Rd ECC S11 ...... 54 D5
Hoodcroft La BSVR S44 ...... 94 D8
Hoole St CHNE S41 ...... 129 C2
Hooley St LGEAT NG10 ...... 260 E4
Hooleyhey La MCFLDN SK10 .. 78 A8
Hooley St EWD/SEL/PNX NG16... 189 C4
Hoon Rd RDERBYSW DE65 ...... 264 A2
Hoonwell La ASHB DE6 ...... 196 C5
Hope Av MCKLVR DE3 ...... 239 C8
Hopedale Rd HACK/IN S12 ...... 57 C6
Hopefield Av HACK/IN S12 ...... 57 C6
Hope Rd EDL/UDV S33 ...... 50 D8
Hope St CHSW S40 ...... 2 C4
  DERBY DE1 ...... 5 C5
  GLSP SK13 ...... 18 B8
  ILK DE7 ...... 230 C3 [2]
  MELB/CHEL DE73 ...... 278 C3
  MSFD NG18 ...... 165 G4 [3]
Hope Ter MTLK DE4 ...... 171 L1
Hopetoun St NORM/LIT DE23 ... 256 C2
Hopewell Rd MELB/CHEL DE73.. 256 F4
Hopewell Wk ILK DE7 ...... 217 J5
The Hop Inge AU/AST/KP S26 .. 75 H5
Hopley Rd BUTN/AL/TUT DE13 .. 272 C5
Hopmeadow La
  STPNHL/WNHL DE15 ...... 281 K1 [1]
Hopping Hl BPR/DUF DE56 ...... 213 J2
Hopping La BKWL DE45 ...... 138 E7
Hopton Cl DERBYE DE21 ...... 241 K1
Hoptonwood Cl MTLK DE4 ...... 171 G2 [3]
Hopwell Rd BWSH/BRSTN DE72 .. 259 K1
Horace Av BSTN/STPLFD NG9 ... 244 B3
Horderns La CHF/WBR SK23 ... 60 D5
Horderns Park Rd
  CHF/WBR SK23 ...... 60 D5
Hordron Rd STKB/PEN S36 ...... 15 H5
Hornbeam Cl DERBYE DE21 ...... 227 H8 [7]
The Hornbeams UTXR ST14 ... 247 K1 [3]
Hornbrook Cl
  BUTN/AL/TUT DE13 ...... 273 L2 [1]
Hornbrook Rd
  BUTN/AL/TUT DE13 ...... 273 L2
Horncastle Rd DERBYE DE21 ... 241 C1
Horner Rd SHEFS S8 ...... 55 J3
Horninglow Rd BUT DE14 ...... 273 M4
Horninglow Rd North
  BUTN/AL/TUT DE13 ...... 273 L3
Horninglow St BUT DE14 ...... 274 A6
Hornscroft Rd BSVR S44 ...... 131 K1
Hornsea Rd DERBYE DE21 ...... 241 G1
Hornthorpe Rd ECK/KIL S21 ... 72 E8
Hornton Rd
  BUTN/AL/TUT DE13 ...... 273 L3 [1]
Horridge St ILK DE7 ...... 217 J6 [1]
Horsecroft Cl ILK DE7 ...... 216 F8 [1]
Horse Fair Av CHF/WBR SK23 .. 60 C4
Horsehead La BSVR S44 ...... 113 L4
Horse La BKWL DE45 ...... 121 C7
Horseshoe Av BUX SK17 ...... 81 J1
The Horse Shoes
  CDON/KEG DE74 ...... 271 M6
Horses La MSHM DE12 ...... 295 M6
Horsewood Rd CHSW S40 ...... 127 L2
Horsley Cl CHSW S40 ...... 109 K5
Horsley Crs BPR/DUF DE56 ... 213 M3 [3]
  EWD/SEL/PNX NG16 ...... 202 D7
Horsleygate La DRON S18 ...... 89 G4
Horsleygate Rd TOT/DORE S17 .. 88 F4
Horsley La DERBYE DE21 ...... 214 B6
Horsley Rd DERBYE DE21 ...... 214 C4
Horton Av BUTN/AL/TUT DE13 .. 274 C3
Horton Cl ALFN DE55 ...... 187 J2
  MOS S20 ...... 73 H3 [1]
Horton Dr MOS S20 ...... 73 H3
Horton St NORM/LIT DE23 ...... 5 J9
Horwood Av NORM/LIT DE23 ... 240 A8
Hoselett Field Rd LGEAT NG10.. 261 H5
Hospital La MCKLVR DE3 ...... 254 C3
Houfton Crs BSVR S44 ...... 113 J7
Houfton Rd BSVR S44 ...... 113 J7
  MSFD NG18 ...... 165 H2
Houghton Av ILK DE7 ...... 216 F7 [1]
Houghton Ct DERBYE DE21 ...... 227 J8
Houldsworth Crs BSVR S44 ...... 113 J5
Houldsworth Dr CHNE S41 ...... 111 H8
Hoult St DERBYW DE22 ...... 240 A6
Houndkirk Rd ECC S11 ...... 68 D1
Hounslow Rd DERBYW DE22 ... 239 L4
Hoveton Cl DERBYSE DE24 ...... 257 G7
Howard Cl GLSP SK13 ...... 17 L8
  LGEAT NG10 ...... 261 H3 [1]
Howard Dr CHNE S41 ...... 91 K8
  RCH S42 ...... 145 J5 [1]
Howard Rd MSFDW NG19 ...... 164 C2

Howard St ASH NG17 ...... 163 J6
  GLSP SK13 ...... 25 M1
  NORM/LIT DE23 ...... 4 D9
Howarth Cl LGEAT NG10 ...... 260 D3
Howden Cl MCKLVR DE3 ...... 254 F1
  STV/CWN S43 ...... 93 J8
Howden Rd NM/HAY SK22 ...... 43 M1
Howell-jones Rd
  BSTN/STPLFD NG9 ...... 245 L7
Howells Pl STV/CWN S43 ...... 93 L7
Howe St DERBYW DE22 ...... 240 A5
Howitt Crs UTXR ST14 ...... 247 L1
Howitt St HEANOR DE75 ...... 202 C8
  NORM/LIT DE23 ...... 261 H3 [5]
How La EDL/UDV S33 ...... 48 F7
Howth Cl DERBYE DE21 ...... 241 K6
Hoylake Av CHSW S40 ...... 127 M3 [5]
Hoylake Cl MCKLVR DE3 ...... 238 F7
Hoylake Dr MCKLVR DE3 ...... 238 F7
Hoyland Ct BPR/DUF DE56 ...... 200 B5 [5]
Hubert Shaw Cl
  DERBYSE DE24 ...... 257 H6 [2]
Huckerby Rd ILK DE7 ...... 216 F8
Hucklow Av CHSW S40 ...... 2 E9
  RCH S42 ...... 145 K2
  STV/CWN S43 ...... 111 M3
Hucklow Ct DERBYE DE21 ...... 227 L7 [11]
  MSFD NG18 ...... 165 L4 [2]
Hucknall Av CHSW S40 ...... 109 M6
Huddale La CDLE ST15 ...... 190 F3
Hudson Cl AU/AST/KP S26 ...... 75 H3 [1]
Hudson Mt BSVR S44 ...... 131 L2
Hufton's Ct HEANOR DE75 ...... 216 D3
Hugh La EDL/UDV S33 ...... 64 D3
Hulland St DERBY DE1 ...... 5 J7
Hulland Vw DERBYW DE22 ...... 240 A1
Humber Cl DERBYSE DE24 ...... 257 M4 [3]
Humber Rd LGEAT NG10 ...... 260 F1
Humberston Rd
  WOL/BIL/BRX NG8 ...... 231 M7
Humbleton Dr DERBYW DE22 .. 239 K5
Humphrey Rd SHEFS S8 ...... 70 B2
Hundall La CHNE S41 ...... 91 K4
  DRON S18 ...... 91 J3
Hungerhill La CLCR S45 ...... 126 E3
Hunger La ASHB DE6 ...... 211 H7
Hungry La EDL/UDV S33 ...... 64 D4
  HATH/EY S32 ...... 66 E2
Hunloke Av CHSW S40 ...... 2 B8
Hunloke Crs CHSW S40 ...... 2 C7
Hunloke Rd RCH S42 ...... 146 B1
Hunloke Vw RCH S42 ...... 128 E6 [2]
Hunsdon Rd ECK/KIL S21 ...... 72 F7
Hunstone Av SHEFS S8 ...... 70 D3
Hunt Av HEANOR DE75 ...... 202 B8
Hunter Dr BPR/DUF DE56 ...... 214 C2
Hunter Hill Rd ECC S11 ...... 54 E3
Hunter House Rd ECC S11 ...... 54 E3
Hunter Rd BPR/DUF DE56 ...... 200 A5
Hunters Cft DERBYSE DE24 ... 256 B8
Hunters Green Cl CHF/WBR S23.. 60 B1
Hunters La GLSP SK13 ...... 25 J2
  HAN/WDH S13 ...... 56 F4
Hunter St BUT DE14 ...... 274 A5
Huntingdon Av BSVR S44 ...... 131 L1
Huntingdon Ct
  MELB/CHEL DE73 ...... 278 C2
Huntingdon Crs ECC S11 ...... 55 H2
Huntingdon Dr
  CDON/KEG DE74 ...... 271 K6
Huntingdon Gn DERBYE DE21 .. 5 K2
Huntingdon Rd ASHZ LE65 ...... 291 J5
  STPNHL/WNHL DE15 ...... 281 G4
Huntingdon Wk LGEAT NG10 .. 244 E5 [5]
Huntingdon Wy
  BSTN/STPLFD NG9 ...... 245 J8 [2]
  MSHM DE12 ...... 295 K6
Huntingtower Rd ECC S11 ...... 54 E4
Hunt La CLCR S45 ...... 158 E2
Huntley Av DERBYE DE21 ...... 242 D4
Huntley Cl STV/CWN S43 ...... 111 L2
Huntley Gv ECC S11 ...... 54 C4
Huntley Rd ECC S11 ...... 54 D4
Hunts La MSHM DE12 ...... 294 B2
Huntsman Rd STV/CWN S43 ... 93 H8
Huntspill Rd RDERBYSW DE65 .. 265 H1
Hurdlow Ms GLSP SK13 ...... 25 C1 [3]
Hurds Hollow MTLK DE4 ...... 156 D3
Hurker Ri MTLK DE4 ...... 156 F3
Hurl Dr HACK/IN S12 ...... 56 C5
Hurley Ct ILK DE7 ...... 229 H2
Hurlfield Av HACK/IN S12 ...... 56 D5
Hurlfield Ct HACK/IN S12 ...... 56 D5
Hurlfield Dr HACK/IN S12 ...... 56 C4
Hurlfield Rd HACK/IN S12 ...... 56 C5
Hurlingham Cl ABRD S7 ...... 54 F6
Hursley Cl MOS S20 ...... 73 K1 [1]
Hursley Dr MOS S20 ...... 73 K1
Hurstbrook Cl GLSP SK13 ...... 26 C1
Hurstclough La HATH/EY S32 .. 51 G8
Hurst Dr BUTN/AL/TUT DE13 ... 274 B1
  ILK DE7 ...... 228 F4
Hurst La ALFN DE55 ...... 176 C5
Hurst Lea Rd NM/HAY SK22 ... 43 M3 [1]
Hurst Ri MTLK DE4 ...... 157 C5
Hurst Rd GLSP SK13 ...... 26 C1
Huss's La LGEAT NG10 ...... 261 J3 [3]
Hutchings Crs STV/CWN S43 ... 95 C5 [1]
Hutchinson La SHEFS S8 ...... 55 C7 [1]
Hutchinson Rd SHEFS S8 ...... 55 C7 [3]
Hutcliffe Dr SHEFS S8 ...... 55 C8 [1]
Hutcliffe Wood Rd SHEFS S8 .. 55 C8
Huthwaite La ALFN DE55 ...... 161 L8 [1]
Huthwaite Rd ASH NG17 ...... 162 F7
Hut La CLCR S45 ...... 143 H4
  ECK/KIL S21 ...... 74 C5
Hutmoor Butts BKWL DE45 ... 120 D7
Hutton St DERBYSE DE24 ...... 257 H4
Hyde Bank Rd NM/HAY SK22 ... 43 M2 [1]
Hyde Park Rd DERBYW DE22 .. 239 K4
Hydro Cl BKWL DE45 ...... 106 C4 [1]
Hylton Cl BUT DE14 ...... 280 D3 [3]
Hyndley Rd BSVR S44 ...... 113 J7

Ian Av MTLK DE4 ...... 183 J3
Ians Wy CHSW S40 ...... 109 M6
Ibbotsons Cft HATH/EY S32 ... 66 D2 [3]
Ibsley Dr DERBYSE DE24 ...... 257 M4
Ibstock St BUTN/AL/TUT DE13 .. 273 L4 [1]
Ida's Rd ECK/KIL S21 ...... 73 C6
Ilam Cl STV/CWN S43 ...... 111 M4
Ilam Ct ASHB DE6 ...... 208 A2
Ilam Moor La ASHB DE6 ...... 178 B5
Ilam Sq ILK DE7 ...... 217 H5
Ilford Cl ILK DE7 ...... 217 H5
Ilford Rd DERBYW DE22 ...... 239 K5
Ilion St MSFDW NG19 ...... 149 J8
Ilkeston Rd BSTN/STPLFD NG9 .. 230 F6
  BSTN/STPLFD NG9 ...... 245 K1
  HEANOR DE75 ...... 216 C2
  ILK DE7 ...... 215 H8
  ILK DE7 ...... 230 C7
  ILK DE7 ...... 244 F2
Imperial Ct DERBYW DE22 ...... 226 A5
Imperial Rd MTLK DE4 ...... 156 E5
Inchwood Cl
  BSTN/STPLFD NG9 ...... 245 J8 [1]
Independent Hl ALFN DE55..... 175 J7
Industrial St NORM/LIT DE23 .. 4 E9 [1]
Infirmary Rd CHNE S41 ...... 3 J1
Ingham Dr MCKLVR DE3 ...... 255 C2
Ingham Rd LGEAT NG10 ...... 244 F8
Ingleborough Gdns
  LGEAT NG10 ...... 260 D2 [3]
Ingleby Av NORM/LIT DE23 ...... 256 C3
Ingleby Cl DRON S18 ...... 89 M1
  SWAD DE11 ...... 282 C7
  WOL/BIL/BRX NG8 ...... 231 L6 [3]
Ingleby La MELB/CHEL DE73 ... 277 K5 [1]
Ingle Rd LGEAT NG10 ...... 260 C5
Ingle Cl DERBYE DE21 ...... 242 B5
Ingleden Cl DERBYE DE21 ...... 241 H1 [1]
Ingle Dr ASHZ LE65 ...... 291 J3
Inglefield Rd ILK DE7 ...... 230 C4
Ingle's Channel
  BPR/DUF DE56 ...... 199 K6 [1]
Ingles Hl ASHZ LE65 ...... 291 J3
Ingleton Rd CHSW S41 ...... 128 E3
Inglewood Av MCKLVR DE3 ... 239 C6
  MOS S20 ...... 73 K1 [3]
Inglewood Ct MOS S20 ...... 73 K1 [3]
Inglewood Dell MOS S20 ...... 73 K1 [7]
Ingliston Cl DERBYSE DE24 ...... 258 A4 [1]
Inham Circ
  BSTN/STPLFD NG9 ...... 245 M4 [1]
Inham Cl BSTN/STPLFD NG9 ... 245 K5
Inham Rd BSTN/STPLFD NG9 .. 245 K5
Inkerman Rd
  EWD/SEL/PNX NG16 ...... 189 J5
Inkerman St
  EWD/SEL/PNX NG16 ...... 189 J5
Inkersall Dr MOS S20 ...... 73 H2
Inkersall Green Rd
  STV/CWN S43 ...... 111 L2
Inkersall Rd STV/CWN S43 ...... 112 B4
Inn La DERBYE DE22 ...... 225 L4
Inns La ALFN DE55 ...... 174 B6
Institute La ALFN DE55 ...... 175 K6 [1]
Institute St ASH NG17 ...... 162 F4
Instow Dr NORM/LIT DE23 ...... 256 A5
Intake La ASHB DE6 ...... 210 F4
Intake La BKWL DE45 ...... 123 H7
  MTLK DE4 ...... 171 L4
Inveraray Cl DERBYSE DE24 ... 256 A7
Invernia Cl NORM/LIT DE23 ... 256 B5 [1]
Iona Cl ALFN DE55 ...... 161 J5
  DERBYSE DE24 ...... 256 E6
Iona Dr BSTN/STPLFD NG9 ...... 231 G7
Ireland Cl STV/CWN S43 ...... 93 J3
Ireland St STV/CWN S43 ...... 93 J8
Iron Cliff Rd BSVR S44 ...... 113 J7
Iron Ga DERBY DE1 ...... 4 E3
Ironside Cl GLV S14 ...... 56 M1
Ironside Pl GLV S14 ...... 56 B7
Ironside Rd GLV S14 ...... 56 B7
Ironwalls La
  BUTN/AL/TUT DE13 ...... 263 M5
Irvine Cl DERBYSE DE24 ...... 256 A7
Irving Pl DERBYSE DE24 ...... 257 J3
Isaac's La BSTN/STPLFD NG9 ... 245 G3
Isherwood Dr MPL/ROM SK6 ... 32 A4
Islay Cl BSTN/STPLFD NG9 ...... 231 G8
Islay Rd DERBYSE DE24 ...... 256 A6
Isleworth Dr DERBYW DE22 ... 239 J4
Ismay Rd DERBYE DE21 ...... 241 J4
Ivan Brook Cl DRON S18 ...... 89 M1 [2]
Ivanhoe Cl RCH S42 ...... 145 C1
Ivanhoe Rd ASHZ LE65 ...... 291 J4
Ivanhoe Wy ASHZ LE65 ...... 285 C5
Ivonbrook Cl MTLK DE4 ...... 155 L2
Ivybridge Cl DERBYE DE21 ...... 227 M7 [3]
Ivy Cl BUTN/AL/TUT DE13 ...... 273 M3
  CHNE S41 ...... 91 K8
  MSHM DE12 ...... 295 H1
  RDERBYSW DE65 ...... 266 D5
  UTXR ST14 ...... 247 K2
Ivy Cottage La ECC S11 ...... 53 M4
Ivy Ct RDERBYSW DE65 ...... 265 C1 [1]
  SHEFS S8 ...... 55 H1
Ivycroft GLSP SK13 ...... 17 H6
Ivy Gv RIPLEY DE5 ...... 201 C1
Ivy La EWD/SEL/PNX NG16 ...... 203 H8
  MTLK DE4 ...... 154 B4
Ivy Lodge Cl
  STPNHL/WNHL DE15 ...... 281 H3
Ivy Side Cl ECK/KIL S21 ...... 74 A4
Ivyside Gdns ECK/KIL S21 ...... 74 A4
Ivy Spring Cl RCH S42 ...... 128 E6 [3]
Ivy Sq NORM/LIT DE23 ...... 5 J9

J

Jackass La BPR/DUF DE56 ...... 184 D5
Jacklin Cl BUT DE14 ...... 280 D4 [1]
Jacksdale Cl DERBYW DE22 ... 240 A1
Jackson Av BUTN/AL/TUT DE13 .. 274 C1
  ILK DE7 ...... 230 B1
  LGEAT NG10 ...... 244 D4
  MCKLVR DE3 ...... 239 K8
  RCH S42 ...... 144 F2
Jackson Rd BSVR S44 ...... 147 G1

CLCR S45 .... 145 H7
MTLK DE4 .... 156 E4
Jacksons Edge Rd POY/DIS SK12 .. 42 D3
Jackson's La BPR/DUF DE56 ... 200 A3
BPR/DUF DE56 .... 213 H5
RDERBYSW DE65 .... 253 M8
RIPLEY DE5 .... 186 D2
Jackson St DERBYW DE22 .. 4 B5 ⑥
GLSP SK13 .... 17 M5
GLSP SK13 .... 25 M3 ②
HYDE SK14 .... 16 D7 ②
Jackson Tor Rd MTLK DE4 .. 156 E4
Jackys La AU/AST/KP S26 .. 75 H4
Jacobean Ct
STPNHL/WNHL DE15 ... 274 F6 ③
Jagger's La HATH/EY S32 .. 66 B2
MTLK DE4 .... 141 M4
Jago Av STV/CWN S43 .. 95 K6
James Andrew Cl SHEFS S8 .. 70 C3
James Andrew Crs SHEFS S8 .. 70 B3
James Andrew Cft SHEFS S8 .. 70 C3 ②
James Brindley Wy
BUTN/AL/TUT DE13 .. 274 C2
James Cl DERBY DE1 .. 4 A3
James's La ASHB DE6 .. 252 E1
James St ALFN DE55 .. 187 M3
BUT DE14 .... 273 M8
CHNE S41 .... 110 C4
GLSP SK13 .... 25 M2 ②
SWAD DE11 .... 283 C5
UTXR ST14 .... 247 L2
Jane La BKWL DE45 .. 124 B2
Jap La BKWL DE45 .. 124 B2
Jardine Ct
BWSH/BRSTN DE72 .. 259 L3 ②
The Jardines BSTN/STPLFD NG9.. 245 M1
The Jarnett BUX SK17 .. 120 C2
Jarrow Rd ECC S11 .. 55 G2 ②
Jarvey's La DERBYSE DE24 .. 239 H2
Jarvis Rd DERBYSE DE24 .. 256 B8
Jasmin Cl MTLK DE4 .. 133 G4
Jasmine Cl ALFN DE55 .. 187 J3
DERBYE DE21 .. 241 L5
STPNHL/WNHL DE15 .. 281 K3
Jaspers La MTLK DE4 .. 181 K1 ①
Jaunty Av HACK/IN S12 .. 56 E7
Jaunty Cl HACK/IN S12 .. 56 E7
Jaunty Crs HACK/IN S12 .. 56 E6
Jaunty Dr HACK/IN S12 .. 56 E7
Jaunty La HACK/IN S12 .. 56 E6
Jaunty Mt HACK/IN S12 .. 56 E7
Jaunty Pl HACK/IN S12 .. 56 E7
Jaunty Rd HACK/IN S12 .. 56 E7
Jaunty Vw HACK/IN S12 .. 56 E7
Jaunty Wy HACK/IN S12 .. 56 E6
Jawbone La MELB/CHEL DE73 .. 278 C4
Jaw Bones Hl CHSW S40 .. 3 H9
Jebb Gdns CHSW S40 .. 109 M8 ②
Jebb's La BPR/DUF DE56 .. 197 J2
Jedburgh Cl DERBYSE DE24 .. 256 B8 ③
Jefferson Pl DERBYSE DE24 .. 257 J3
Jeffery St SHEFP/MNR S2 .. 55 L4 ②
Jeffrey La EDL/UDV S33 .. 64 C5
Jeffries La MTLK DE4 .. 185 J1
Jeffries La MTLK DE4 .. 185 J1 ①
Jellicoe Cl SBK/MW NG20 .. 115 K8
Jemison Cl NORM/LIT DE23 .. 255 H3 ⑤
Jenford St MSFD NG18 .. 164 B4
Jenkins Av NORM/LIT DE23 .. 164 A3
Jennings Wy BUT DE14 .. 273 K7
Jennison St MSFDW NG19 .. 164 D1
Jenny Beckett's La MSFD NG18.. 165 H3
Jenny's Ct BPR/DUF DE56 .. 199 M5 ②
Jephson Rd BUT DE14 .. 280 E3
Jermyn Av HACK/IN S12 .. 57 H6
Jermyn Cl HACK/IN S12 .. 57 J7
Jermyn Crs HACK/IN S12 .. 57 J7
Jermyn Dr HACK/IN S12 .. 57 J7
Jermyn Wy HACK/IN S12 .. 57 J7
Jersey Rd SHEFP/MNR S2 .. 55 K3 ②
Jervis Pl STV/CWN S43 .. 111 L4
Jesop Dr DERBYSE DE24 .. 256 B8 ②
Jesses La BPR/DUF DE56 .. 198 F3
Jessop Av EWD/SEL/PNX NG16 .. 188 C4
Jessop Dr MPL/ROM SK6 .. 32 C2
Jessop St RIPLEY DE5 .. 201 K3
Joan Av HEANOR DE75 .. 202 B8
Joan La EDL/UDV S33 .. 50 F7
Jodrell Av BPR/DUF DE56 .. 200 A6
Jodrell Meadow CHF/WBR SK23 .. 59 G2
Jodrell Rd CHF/WBR SK23 .. 59 G2
Jodrell St NM/HAY SK22 .. 43 L3
John Bank La BKWL DE45 .. 122 C3
John Berrysford Cl
DERBYE DE21 .. 241 J5
John Dalton St GLSP SK13 .. 17 H5 ③
John F Kennedy Gdns
DERBYE DE21 .. 241 M4 ①
John Kennedy Gdn
HYDE SK14 .. 16 D7 ③
John Kennedy Rd HYDE SK14.. 16 C7 ③
John Lombe Dr DERBY DE1 .. 240 D3
Johnnygate La DRON S18 .. 89 J7
John O'Gaunts Wy
BPR/DUF DE56 .. 200 A5
John Port Cl
RDERBYSW DE65 .. 253 M6 ②
Johnson Av DERBYSE DE24 .. 257 H3
MSFD NG18 .. 164 F7
Johnson Dr HEANOR DE75 .. 202 C8
MSFD NG18 .. 164 F7
Johnson La BKWL DE45 .. 121 J3
BPR/DUF DE56 .. 197 H3
Johnson Rd UTXR ST14 .. 247 L1
Johnson St CHF/WBR SK23 .. 59 H2 ③
Johnson Wy CHF/WBR SK23 .. 61 G5
Johnstone Cl CHSW S40 .. 2 F8
John St ALFN DE55 .. 175 K6
ALFN DE55 .. 187 M2
ASH NG17 .. 163 J6
CHSW S40 .. 2 C4
CLCR S45 .. 145 G6
DERBY DE1 .. 5 H6
ECK/KIL S21 .. 73 G7
GLSP SK13 .. 25 M2
HEANOR DE75 .. 202 A8
ILK DE7 .. 230 C1
MPL/ROM SK6 .. 32 D5
MTLK DE4 .. 156 E4
RCH S42 .. 145 H3
SHEFP/MNR S2 .. 55 K1

STV/CWN S43 .. 95 G7
STV/CWN S43 .. 111 H2
SWAD DE11 .. 282 F5
UTXR ST14 .. 247 L2 ②
WRKS S80 .. 115 H1
John Turner Rd MTLK DE4 .. 140 F7
Jolly La ASHB DE6 .. 195 K4
Jones St GLSP SK13 .. 17 K5
Jordan Av BUTN/AL/TUT DE13 .. 265 J8
Jordan St GLSP SK13 .. 26 B1
Jordanthorpe Gn SHEFS S8 .. 70 F4
Jordanthorpe Pkwy SHEFS S8 .. 70 D5
Jordanthorpe Vw SHEFS S8 .. 70 F3 ②
Joseph St BPR/DUF DE56 .. 199 J6
ECK/KIL S21 .. 73 G7
MPL/ROM SK6 .. 32 D4 ③
NORM/LIT DE23 .. 256 D1
Joshua Rd DERBYW DE22 .. 55 H3
Jowitt Rd ECC S11 .. 54 E4
Joyce Av BSTN/STPLFD NG9 .. 245 H4
Jubalton Cl DERBYSE DE24 .. 257 H4 ③
Jubilee Av RIPLEY DE5 .. 200 F1
Jubilee Cl MELB/CHEL DE73 .. 278 E3
Jubilee Ct BPR/DUF DE56 .. 199 K8
MTLK DE4 .. 183 H3 ②
Jubilee Crs ECK/KIL S21 .. 74 B3
STV/CWN S43 .. 95 K6
Jubilee Gdns NM/HAY SK22 .. 43 M3
WRKS S80 .. 96 C5
Jubilee Pl WRKS S80 .. 96 C5 ⑥
Jubilee Rd ASH NG17 .. 163 G7
Jubilee Sq ASHB DE6 .. 207 G3
Jubilee St NM/HAY SK22 .. 43 M3
Jubilee Wy South MSFDW NG19 .. 164 A7
Judson La BSTN/STPLFD NG9 .. 245 J4
Judy Hl MTLK DE4 .. 156 C1 ①
Julia Crs ALFN DE55 .. 160 C7
Julian Cl ILK DE7 .. 230 D4
Julie Av HEANOR DE75 .. 216 E1
Jumble Rd ECC S11 .. 53 J8
Junction Rd ASH NG17 .. 163 M8
ECC S11 .. 54 F2
LGEAT NG10 .. 261 K4 ②
Juniper Ct
EWD/SEL/PNX NG16 .. 217 M2 ②
Juniper Ri ECK/KIL S21 .. 73 M5
Jura Av RIPLEY DE5 .. 187 G8
Jury St DERBY DE1 .. 4 D3

K

Katherine Dr
BSTN/STPLFD NG9 .. 245 J7
Kay Dr SWAD DE11 .. 282 C5 ③
Kaye Rd MSFDW NG19 .. 164 A3
Kays Wood Rd MPL/ROM SK6 .. 32 A4
Kean Pl DERBYSE DE24 .. 257 J3
Kearsley Rd SHEFP/MNR S2 .. 55 K2
Keats Av ASH NG17 .. 162 E7
NORM/LIT DE23 .. 255 K1
Keats Cl LGEAT NG10 .. 260 D6
Keats Dr SWAD DE11 .. 282 F5
Keats Rd ALFN DE55 .. 160 C7
CHNE S41 .. 110 C2
Keats Wy RCH S42 .. 129 H6
Keble Cl DERBY DE1 .. 5 H8
STPNHL/WNHL DE15 .. 274 F8
Kedleston Cl
BSTN/STPLFD NG9 .. 245 M5 ①
BUTN/AL/TUT DE13 .. 273 M1 ②
DERBYW DE22 .. 240 A1
LGEAT NG10 .. 260 D6
RIPLEY DE5 .. 186 F5
Kedleston Ct ALFN DE55 .. 161 L4
Kedleston Dr ILK DE7 .. 217 G1
Kedlestone Cl ASH NG17 .. 162 C8
Kedleston Old Rd
DERBYW DE22 .. 240 A2 ①
Kedleston Rd BUX SK17 .. 99 M3 ①
DERBY DE1 .. 240 C3 ①
DERBYW DE22 .. 225 M8
DERBYW DE22 .. 225 G3
DERBYW DE22 .. 240 A1
Kedleston St DERBY DE1 .. 4 C1
Keeling Cl
EWD/SEL/PNX NG16 .. 217 L1 ③
Keeling La MTLK DE4 .. 154 E1
Keepers La DRON S18 .. 90 B7
Keeton's Hl SHEFP/MNR S2 .. 55 J1 ②
Kegworth Av
NORM/LIT DE23 .. 255 M4 ③
Keilder Ct CHSW S40 .. 2 B8
Kelburn Av CHSW S40 .. 127 M1
Keldholme La
DERBYSE DE24 .. 257 M3 ③
Kelgate MOS S20 .. 73 G4
Kelham Rd MSFD NG18 .. 164 B3
Kelham Wy
EWD/SEL/PNX NG16 .. 203 H7 ②
Kelmoor Rd DERBYSE DE24 .. 257 L3
Kelso Cl ASHZ LE65 .. 291 M4
Kelsons Av BUX SK17 .. 99 M5
Kelstedge Dr MSFD NG18 .. 165 L4
Kelstedge La CLCR S45 .. 143 G5
Kelvedon Dr NORM/LIT DE23 .. 255 K4 ③
Kelvin Cl BSTN/STPLFD NG9 .. 244 F5
Kemble Pl DERBYSE DE24 .. 257 J3 ③
Kemp Cl ECK/KIL S21 .. 73 M4 ③
Kemp Rd MPL/ROM SK6 .. 32 F2
Kempton Park Rd
DERBYSE DE24 .. 257 G2
Kempton Rd MSFD NG18 .. 165 J3
STPNHL/WNHL DE15 .. 274 D7
Kenbourne Gv ABRD S7 .. 55 H3 ②
Kenbourne Rd ABRD S7 .. 55 H3
Kendal Cl BUX SK17 .. 99 M6
Kendal Dr DRON S18 .. 90 B1
Kendal Rd CHNE S41 .. 110 B2
Kendon Av NORM/LIT DE23 .. 255 L3
Kendray Cl BPR/DUF DE56 .. 200 A5 ③
Kendricks Cl SWAD DE11 .. 283 K3
Kenilworth Av ASH NG17 .. 163 L6
NORM/LIT DE23 .. 255 H3
NORM/LIT DE23 .. 256 C2
Kenilworth Cl MPL/ROM SK6 .. 32 C2 ①

Kenilworth Dr ASHZ LE65 .. 291 M5 ②
ILK DE7 .. 229 M5
Kenilworth Pl ECC S11 .. 54 F2 ①
Kenilworth Rd RIPLEY DE5 .. 200 F1 ①
Kenmere Cl CLCR S45 .. 145 G6
Kenmore Cl MSFDW NG19 .. 164 B5 ③
Kennack Cl ALFN DE55 .. 176 F4
Kennedy Av LGEAT NG10 .. 260 F5
Kennedy Cl DERBYE DE21 .. 241 K3 ③
Kennedy Dr BSTN/STPLFD NG9 .. 245 H1
Kennedy Rd SHEFS S8 .. 55 H8
Kennett Gv BUX SK17 .. 99 H4 ①
Kenning Hall Ct
SHEFP/MNR S2 .. 56 A3 ①
Kenninghall Dr SHEFP/MNR S2 .. 56 A3
Kenninghall Mt
SHEFP/MNR S2 .. 56 A3 ②
Kenninghall Pl SHEFP/MNR S2 .. 56 A3 ③
Kenninghall Rd SHEFP/MNR S2 .. 56 A3 ④
Kenning St CLCR S45 .. 144 F7
Kensal Ri DERBYW DE22 .. 239 L4
Kensington Av HEANOR DE75 .. 215 M1
Kensington Cl
BSTN/STPLFD NG9 .. 261 K1 ③
Kensington Gdns ILK DE7 .. 230 C3
Kensington Rd LGEAT NG10 .. 244 E6
STPNHL/WNHL DE15 .. 274 D7 ③
Kensington St DERBYW DE22.. 4 C4
ILK DE7 .. 230 C4
Kent Av EWD/SEL/PNX NG16 .. 188 E6
Kent Cl CHNE S41 .. 110 C5
Kent House La HACK/IN S12 .. 72 B2
Kentish Ct DERBY DE1 .. 240 E3 ①
Kentmere Cl DRON S18 .. 90 B1 ②
Kent Rd EWD/SEL/PNX NG16 .. 217 J4
GLSP SK13 .. 26 A1 ①
SHEFS S8 .. 55 L4
STPNHL/WNHL DE15 .. 281 G4
Kent's Bank Rd BUX SK17 .. 99 M4
Kent St CHNE S41 .. 128 F2
DERBYE DE21 .. 241 G3
Kenwell Dr TOT/DORE S17 .. 69 L5
Kenwood Av ABRD S7 .. 55 H3 ⑥
Kenwood Bank ECC S11 .. 55 H2
Kenwood Park Rd ABRD S7 .. 55 H3
Kenwood Rd ABRD S7 .. 55 G3
ECC S11 .. 55 H2
Kenworthy Cl HYDE SK14 .. 16 B8
Kenyon Rd CHNE S41 .. 129 H1
Kepple Ga RIPLEY DE5 .. 201 J3
Kernel Cl NORM/LIT DE23 .. 255 K2
Kerry Dr ILK DE7 .. 215 J4
Kerry St DERBYE DE21 .. 241 G3
Kerry's Yd BPR/DUF DE56 .. 214 C2 ③
Kershaw St GLSP SK13 .. 25 M2 ③
Kershope Dr DERBYE DE21 .. 227 L7 ①③
Kerwin Cl TOT/DORE S17 .. 68 F2
Kerwin Dr TOT/DORE S17 .. 68 F2
Kerwin Rd TOT/DORE S17 .. 68 F2
Kestral Rd MSFD NG18 .. 164 B6
Kestrel Av ASHB DE6 .. 283 J7
Kestrel Cl ECK/KIL S21 .. 73 L3
ILK DE7 .. 230 C6
MPL/ROM SK6 .. 32 C4
UTXR ST14 .. 247 L4 ②
Kestrel Dr ECK/KIL S21 .. 72 F2
Kestrel Hts
EWD/SEL/PNX NG16 .. 188 C5
Kestrels Cft DERBYSE DE24 .. 256 A7
Kestrel Wy
STPNHL/WNHL DE15 .. 274 F6
Keswick Av NORM/LIT DE23 .. 256 B4
Keswick Cl ILK DE7 .. 230 C6
Keswick Ct LGEAT NG10 .. 244 E8 ③
Keswick Dr CHNE S41 .. 109 M3
Keswick Pl DRON S18 .. 90 A1
Keswick Rd MPL/ROM SK6 .. 42 B2
Ketton Av SHEFS S8 .. 55 K7
Kevin Cl DERBYE DE21 .. 241 L2
Kew Crs HACK/IN S12 .. 56 C8
Kew Gdns DERBYW DE22 .. 239 L5 ①
Keyhaven Cl DERBYE DE21 .. 241 G2
Keynsham Cl DERBYSE DE24 .. 257 H2
Keys Rd ALFN DE55 .. 175 L8
Keys St DERBY DE1 .. 5 G2
Keyworth Cl MSFDW NG19 .. 164 B3
Keyworth Dr MSFDW NG19 .. 165 L1
Keyworth Pl HAN/WDH S13 .. 57 K4
Khartoum Rd ECC S11 .. 55 G2
Kibworth Cl DERBYE DE21 .. 241 L2 ③
Kidd Rd GLSP SK13 .. 26 B4
Kidsley Cl CHSW S40 .. 109 K5
Kilburn Cl BSTN/STPLFD NG9 .. 231 L8
Kilburn Dr ILK DE7 .. 217 G2 ③
Kilburn La BPR/DUF DE56 .. 200 A7
Kilburn Rd BPR/DUF DE56 .. 199 M6 ①
DRON S18 .. 89 M1
Kilburn Wy SWAD DE11 .. 282 C5
Kildale Gdns MOS S20 .. 73 G3 ②
Kildare Rd DERBYE DE21 .. 241 L6
Kildonan Gv HACK/IN S12 .. 56 F7
Killamarsh La ECK/KIL S21 .. 74 D4
Killingworth Av
DERBYSE DE24 .. 256 C6 ④
Killis La BPR/DUF DE56 .. 214 A2
Kiln Bent Rd HOLM/MEL HD7 .. 8 D4
Kiln Cl ILK DE7 .. 229 H1
Kiln Cft RDERBYSW DE65 .. 253 M6
Kilnhouse Bank La
HOLM/MEL HD7 .. 8 E1
Kiln La ASHB DE6 .. 168 A4
GLSP SK13 .. 17 K5
Kilnsey Ct NORM/LIT DE23 .. 255 J4
Kiln Wy SWAD DE11 .. 283 J4
Kilverston Rd LGEAT NG10 .. 244 D3
Kilvington Av HAN/WDH S13 .. 56 E3 ①
Kilvington Crs HAN/WDH S13 .. 56 E3
Kilvington Rd HAN/WDH S13 .. 56 E3
Kilwardby St ASHZ LE65 .. 291 K4
Kimberley Dr
STPNHL/WNHL DE15 .. 274 F7
UTXR ST14 .. 247 J3
Kimberley Rd
BWSH/BRSTN DE72 .. 242 E8
Kinder Av GLSP SK13 .. 25 K2
Kinder Crs BPR/DUF DE56 .. 185 L5
Kinder Dr MPL/ROM SK6 .. 32 C4
Kinder Fold STLY SK15 .. 16 A4 ②

Kinder Gv BUX SK17 .. 99 K4
Kinder Rd NM/HAY SK22 .. 35 H8
STV/CWN S43 .. 111 L4
Kinder Wy BUX SK17 .. 100 B3
Kindlewood Dr
BSTN/STPLFD NG9 .. 261 L1 ③
King Alfred St DERBYW DE22 .. 4 C5
King Charles Ct GLSP SK13 .. 26 A3
King Ecgbert Rd TOT/DORE S17 .. 69 H5
King Edward Av GLSP SK13 .. 26 A1
MSFD NG18 .. 164 E6
King Edward Pl BUT DE14 .. 273 L7
King Edward St LGEAT NG10 .. 244 E4
MTLK DE4 .. 183 K1
SBK/MW NG20 .. 133 J6
Kingfield Rd ECC S11 .. 55 G3
Kingfisher Av SWAD DE11 .. 283 J7 ③
Kingfisher Cl MCKLVR DE3 .. 254 E3 ⑥
Kingfisher Wk WRKN S81 .. 77 M3
Kingfisher Wy UTXR ST14 .. 247 L4
King George Av ILK DE7 .. 230 B2
King George St ALFN DE55 .. 174 B2 ①
MTLK DE4 .. 183 H3
King George V Av MSFD NG18 .. 165 H5
Kingsbridge Wy
BSTN/STPLFD NG9 .. 245 M4
Kingsbury Cl
STPNHL/WNHL DE15 .. 274 D6 ③
Kingsbury Rd DERBYW DE22 .. 239 K4
Kingsclere Av DERBYE DE21 .. 227 L8
King's Cl BUX SK17 .. 100 A2
HEANOR DE75 .. 215 M1 ②
Kingsclere Cft DERBYSE DE24 .. 226 C6
Kings Coppice TOT/DORE S17 .. 69 G4
Kings Cft DERBYW DE22 .. 226 C6
Kingscroft Cl TOT/DORE S17 .. 69 H2
Kingsdale Cl LGEAT NG10 .. 260 D5 ③
Kingsdale Cft
BUTN/AL/TUT DE13 .. 274 A2 ②
Kings Dr EWD/SEL/PNX NG16 .. 203 H3
MCKLVR DE3 .. 239 L8
MPL/ROM SK6 .. 32 B3
Kingsfield Rd MTLK DE4 .. 183 H3
Kingsgate HATH/EY S32 .. 86 F8
Kings Hl MTLK DE4 .. 169 K8
Kingsland Cl DERBYE DE21 .. 227 J8 ⑥
Kingsley Av SWAD DE11 .. 283 J7 ③
Kingsley Crs LGEAT NG10 .. 260 F6
Kingsley Park Av ABRD S7 .. 54 E6
Kingsley Park Gv ECC S11 .. 54 E6
Kingsley Rd BUT DE14 .. 274 A3
DERBYW DE22 .. 226 A7
Kingsley St DERBYSE DE24 .. 256 C5
Kings Lodge Dr MSFD NG18 .. 164 B6
Kingsmead Av
MSFDW NG19 .. 165 H1 ②
King's Mead Cl DERBY DE1 .. 4 D1
Kingsmede Av CHSW S40 .. 2 B8
Kings Ms ECK/KIL S21 .. 73 H7
King's Mill La
BWSH/BRSTN DE72 .. 270 C6
MSFD NG18 .. 164 A6
Kings Mill Rd East ASH NG17 .. 163 L5
Kings Mill Wy MSFD NG18 .. 164 B6
Kingsmoor Flds GLSP SK13 .. 18 A7
Kingsmoor Rd GLSP SK13 .. 18 A8
Kingsmuir Rd MCKLVR DE3 .. 238 F7
King's Rd BUX SK17 .. 100 A2
LGEAT NG10 .. 244 E4
SWAD DE11 .. 282 E5
Kingsthorpe Cl
MSFDW NG19 .. 165 H1 ②
Kingston Av ILK DE7 .. 230 G2
Kingston Cl HYDE SK14 .. 16 B8
Kingston Ct ILK DE7 .. 229 C2
Kingston Rd MSFD NG18 .. 165 G3
STPNHL/WNHL DE15 .. 274 E8
Kingston St DERBY DE1 .. 240 C3
King St ALFN DE55 .. 161 K3
ALFN DE55 .. 175 J7
ALFN DE55 .. 176 C5
ASH NG17 .. 162 E7
ASH NG17 .. 163 H8
ASHB DE6 .. 193 M8 ③
MTLK DE4 .. 171 G5
STV/CWN S43 .. 95 H7
STV/CWN S43 .. 111 J1
WRKS S80 .. 96 F4
WRKS S80 .. 115 J1
King St North CHNE S41 .. 110 D3
King St South CHSW S40 .. 128 D3
Kingsway BUT DE14 .. 280 E2
DERBYW DE22 .. 239 M6
HEANOR DE75 .. 202 A8
ILK DE7 .. 230 D5
MSFDW NG19 .. 165 K1
Kingsway Crs
BPR/DUF DE56 .. 214 D2 ③
Kingsway Park Cl
DERBYW DE22 .. 239 M6
Kingswood Av
BPR/DUF DE56 .. 199 M4 ③
MOS S20 .. 57 K8
Kingswood Cl CHNE S41 .. 110 A2
MOS S20 .. 57 K8 ③
Kingswood Cft MOS S20 .. 57 K8 ③
Kingswood Gv MOS S20 .. 57 K8
King William St
EWD/SEL/PNX NG16 .. 188 C6 ①
Kinross Av DERBYE DE21 .. 240 F2
Kintyre Dr DERBYSE DE24 .. 256 A7
Kinver Cl ASHB DE6 .. 206 F2 ①

Kinver Rd STPNHL/WNHL DE15 .. 274 D6
Kipling Cl DRON S18 .. 90 F3
Kipling Dr MCKLVR DE3 .. 255 G1
Kipling Rd CHNE S41 .. 110 C2 ③
Kipling St MSFD NG18 .. 164 D3
Kirby Cl EWD/SEL/PNX NG16 .. 203 K7
Kirby La MTLK DE4 .. 155 L3
Kirby Rd EWD/SEL/PNX NG16 .. 203 K7
Kirkbride Ct
BSTN/STPLFD NG9 .. 245 L6 ②
Kirkby Av HACK/IN S12 .. 56 D6 ①
ILK DE7 .. 230 C4
Kirkby Dr HACK/IN S12 .. 56 D6
Kirkby La EWD/SEL/PNX NG16 .. 177 J7
Kirkby Rd ASH NG17 .. 163 H8
HACK/IN S12 .. 56 D6
Kirkby Vw HACK/IN S12 .. 56 D7
Kirk Cl RIPLEY DE5 .. 200 F2
Kirkcroft Av ECK/KIL S21 .. 74 A3
Kirkcroft Dr ECK/KIL S21 .. 74 A4
Kirkcroft La ECK/KIL S21 .. 74 A4
Kirk Dale Av DERBYE DE21 .. 242 C7
Kirkdale Cl CHSW S40 .. 3 J9
WOL/BIL/BRX S40 .. 231 L6 ②
Kirkdale Crs HAN/WDH S13 .. 57 L1
Kirkdale Dr HAN/WDH S13 .. 57 L1
Kirkdale Gdns LGEAT NG10 .. 260 E4
Kirkdale Rd LGEAT NG10 .. 260 E4
Kirkewhite Av LGEAT NG10 .. 261 G3
Kirkfell Dr MPL/ROM SK6 .. 42 B2 ③
Kirkfield Dr BWSH/BRSTN DE72 .. 260 C2
Kirkham Cl HEANOR DE75 .. 216 A1 ①
Kirkham Dr BSTN/STPLFD NG9 .. 245 L8
Kirkham La BPR/DUF DE56 .. 185 L3
Kirkistown Cl
DERBYSE DE24 .. 257 M4 ④
Kirkland Av MSFD NG18 .. 164 C4
Kirkland Cl CDON/KEG DE74 .. 271 J2
Kirkland Dr BSTN/STPLFD NG9 .. 245 L8
Kirkland Wy DERBYSE DE24 .. 256 A7
Kirk Leys Av North
DERBYE DE21 .. 242 B6
Kirk Leys Av South
DERBYE DE21 .. 242 B6
Kirkman Rd HEANOR DE75 .. 201 M6
Kirkpatrick Dr WRKN S81 .. 77 M3
Kirk's La BPR/DUF DE56 .. 199 L7
Kirkstall Rd ECC S11 .. 54 F2
Kirkstead Cl DERBYE DE21 .. 241 L1
EWD/SEL/PNX NG16 .. 177 G7
Kirkstead Rd
EWD/SEL/PNX NG16 .. 177 G7
Kirkstone Ct LGEAT NG10 .. 244 E8
Kirkstone Rd BUX SK17 .. 99 M7
CHNE S41 .. 109 M2
Kirk St DERBY DE1 .. 240 E4
Kirton Av LGEAT NG10 .. 261 G3
Kirton Cl MSFDW NG19 .. 164 A3
Kishfield La CHF/WBR SK23 .. 58 D5
Kitchener Av NORM/LIT DE23 .. 256 C3
Kitchener Dr MSFD NG18 .. 164 F4
Kitchener Ter SBK/MW NG20 .. 115 K8
Kitling Greaves La
BUTN/AL/TUT DE13 .. 273 K2
Kitson Av EWD/SEL/PNX NG16 .. 188 F6
Knab Cl ECC S11 .. 54 F5
Knab Cft ECC S11 .. 54 F5
Knabhall La MTLK DE4 .. 157 K2
Knab Ri ECC S11 .. 54 F5
Knab Rd ECC S11 .. 54 F5
MTLK DE4 .. 141 J7
Knapp Av EWD/SEL/PNX NG16 .. 217 J1
Knaresboro Rd ABRD S7 .. 54 F7
Knifesmithgate CHSW S40 .. 3 G4
Knighton St RCH S42 .. 145 H4
Knightsbridge DERBYW DE22 .. 239 K4
Knightsbridge Wy
BUTN/AL/TUT DE13 .. 274 A2
DERBYSE DE24 .. 256 B8
Knights Cl ASHZ LE65 .. 291 J3
DERBYSE DE24 .. 256 B8
Knights Ct
BUTN/AL/TUT DE13 .. 265 H8 ②
Knightsfield Rd
BUTN/AL/TUT DE13 .. 262 B8
Knight's La RDERBYSW DE65 .. 275 K2
Knightwake Rd NM/HAY SK22 .. 43 K2
Kniveton La ASHB DE6 .. 194 F5
Kniveton Pk ILK DE7 .. 230 A3
Knob Flds SWAD DE11 .. 289 H2
Knob La BPR/DUF DE56 .. 183 M5
Knoll Cl NORM/LIT DE23 .. 255 K2
Knoll St NM/HAY SK22 .. 43 L2
The Knoll CHSW S40 .. 109 J8
DRON S18 .. 71 G7
MSFD NG18 .. 164 B4
MTLK DE4 .. 157 K5
SBK/MW NG20 .. 133 G7
SWAD DE11 .. 282 E4
Knowl Av BPR/DUF DE56 .. 199 H4
Knowle Av CHF/WBR SK23 .. 60 C5
Knowle Cl ECK/KIL S21 .. 54 D5
Knowle Gn TOT/DORE S17 .. 68 F3
Knowle La ECC S11 .. 54 C5
Knowle Rd MPL/ROM SK6 .. 32 F4
Knowles Cl BUX SK17 .. 100 B2
Knowles Crs BUX SK17 .. 100 B2
Knowles Hl BUTN/AL/TUT DE13 .. 264 E7
Knowleston Pl MTLK DE4 .. 156 F6
Knowle Top MOS S20 .. 73 H3 ②
Koppe Cl MSHM DE12 .. 290 E4 ②
Kye La AU/AST/KP S26 .. 75 H4
Kyle Gv DERBY DE21 .. 227 L7 ③
Kynance Cl ALFN DE55 .. 176 F4
DERBYSE DE24 .. 257 M5 ③

L

Laburnum Av SBK/MW NG20 .. 133 H5
Laburnum Cl ALFN DE55 .. 176 E5 ①
BSVR S44 .. 131 L1
LGEAT NG10 .. 244 E8 ②
MTLK DE4 .. 140 F7 ②
WRKS S80 .. 115 J1
Laburnum Ct BSVR S44 .. 111 K7 ④
Laburnum Crs ALFN DE55 .. 187 K2
DERBYW DE22 .. 226 A5
Laburnum Gv DERBYW DE22 .. 239 K5
ECK/KIL S21 .. 73 M5

MSFDW NG19 149 K6 1
Laburnum Rd
STPNHL/WNHL DE15 281 J4
SWAD DE11 282 C4
Laburnum St STV/CWN S43 111 L1
Lacey Cl ILK DE7 216 F7
Lacey Fields Rd HEANOR DE75 216 D1
Ladbroke Gdns DERBYW DE22 239 J4
Ladies Spring Gv
TOT/DORE S17 69 K3 1
Ladle End La MSHM DE12 287 G1
Ladybank Rd MCKLVR DE3 238 F7
MCKLVR DE3 254 F1
MOS S20 73 G4 1
Ladybank Vw ECK/KIL S21 73 G6
Ladybower Cl SWAD DE11 282 D8 1
Ladybower Dr HATH/EY S32 66 D3
Ladybower La STV/CWN S43 112 A2
Ladybower Rd DERBYE DE21 242 C6
Ladybrook La MSFDW NG19 164 B3
Ladycroft BUX SK17 99 M1
Ladycroft Paddock
DERBYW DE22 226 B6 5
Lady Field Rd AU/AST/KP S26 75 M1
Ladyfields SWAD DE11 282 F4
Ladyflatts Rd MTLK DE4 183 H3
Lady Grove Rd MTLK DE4 141 J8
Lady Hole La ASHB DE6 208 D4
Lady Ida's Dr ECK/KIL S21 72 D6
MOS S20 72 F6
Lady La RIPLEY DE5 215 G1
Ladylea Cl WRKS S80 77 L8
Lady Lea Hl DERBYE DE21 214 D5
Lady Lea Rd ILK DE7 214 D4
Ladylea Rd LGEAT NG10 260 D6
Lady Mantle Cl
MELB/CHEL DE73 257 H8 1
Lady Meadow Cl UTXR ST14 218 B5
Ladypit Rd CHF/WBR SK23 44 C6
Ladysmith Av ABRD S7 55 G4
Ladysmith Rd
BWSH/BRSTN DE72 242 E8
Ladythorn Av MPL/ROM SK6 32 D5
Lady Wk WRKN S81 77 M3
Ladywell Cl BUTN/AL/TUT DE13 274 B1
Ladywood Av BPR/DUF DE56 199 L5
Ladywood Dr CHSW S40 109 M3 3
Ladywood Rd ILK DE7 229 J6
ILK DE7 230 A5
Lake Av HEANOR DE75 201 M6
MSFDW NG19 164 A3
Lake Dr ASHB DE6 248 D1
NORM/LIT DE23 256 C2
Lake Lands RCH S42 128 C8
Lakeside ASHB DE6 193 M8
BKWL DE45 122 E3
GLSP SK13 17 K4
RCH S42 128 C8
Lakeside Av LGEAT NG10 260 F6
Lakeside Crs LGEAT NG10 260 F5
Lakeside Dr NORM/LIT DE23 255 J3
Lakes Rd MPL/ROM SK6 32 D4
Lake View Av CHSW S40 127 M2 4
Lamb Close Dr
EWD/SEL/PNX NG16 203 K6
Lamb Crs RIPLEY DE5 201 J1
Lambcroft Rd
EWD/SEL/PNX NG16 177 G7
Lambcroft Vw HAN/WDH S13 57 M4
Lambert Rd UTXR ST14 247 J1
Lambgates GLSP SK13 17 K5 6
Lamb Hill Cl HAN/WDH S13 57 G3
Lambhouse La BPR/DUF DE56 198 B5
Lambley Av MSFD NG18 165 J4
Lambley Dr DERBYW DE22 225 M8
Lambourn Cl DERBYW DE22 226 D7 1
Lambourn Dr DERBYW DE22 226 D6
Lambourne Av ASHB DE6 208 A2
Lambpart La EDL/UDV S33 64 A5
Lambrook Cl MCKLVR DE3 238 F8
Lambton Cl ILK DE7 217 H7
Lammas Cl ASH NG17 163 H8 5
Lammas Rd ASH NG17 163 H8
Lamond Cl MSFDW NG19 164 A5
Lampad Cl MELB/CHEL DE73 278 D2 5
Lampeter Cl DERBYE DE21 227 L8 6
Lanark St DERBYE DE21 241 H3
Lancaster Av
BSTN/STPLFD NG9 245 H4
LGEAT NG10 244 D6
Lancaster Dr
BUTN/AL/TUT DE13 263 L5
RDERBYSW DE65 253 H8 3
Lancaster Rd CHNE S41 110 B2 1
Lancaster St BSVR S44 147 H1
Lancaster Wk DERBYE DE21 242 D4 1
Lancelot Cl CHSW S40 128 A2
Lancelot Dr BUTN/AL/TUT DE13 274 B1
Lancing Rd SHEFP/MNR S2 55 L2 1
Lander La BPR/DUF DE56 199 K6
Landmere Cl ILK DE7 216 F7 9
Landsdowne Av CHNE S41 110 B3
MSFD NG18 165 G8
Landsdown Gv LGEAT NG10 261 J1
Landseer Cl DRON S18 90 B2
SHEFS S8 56 A8 2
Landseer Dr MPL/ROM SK6 32 E3 1
SHEFS S8 56 A8
Landseer Pl GLV S14 56 B8 3
Lane Head BUX SK17 134 E3
Lanehead Rd CHF/WBR SK23 58 F5
Lane Head Rd TOT/DORE S17 68 F6
Laneside Av BSTN/STPLFD NG9 245 H8
Laneside Cl CHF/WBR SK23 60 D5
Laneside Rd NM/HAY SK22 34 B4
NM/HAY SK22 44 B3
The Lanes MTLK DE4 171 K7
The Lane ECK/KIL S21 94 A1
EWD/SEL/PNX NG16 217 M6
MTLK DE4 139 M5 1
Laneward Cl ILK DE7 216 F6
Langar Pl MSFDW NG19 165 L2
Langdale Cl MPL/ROM SK6 42 B2
RCH S42 109 J5 5
Langdale Dr DERBYE DE21 227 G8
DRON S18 70 F7
LGEAT NG10 260 D4
Langdale Rd SHEFS S8 55 H5
Langdale Sq STV/CWN S43 111 G2 4
Langdon Cl LGEAT NG10 260 D1 5
Langdon St ECC S11 55 J2
Langer Cl BUT DE14 280 D4 2
Langer Field Av CHSW S40 128 D3
Langer La CHSW S40 128 C4
RCH S42 128 B7
Langford Rd MCKLVR DE3 239 G7
MSFDW NG19 164 A4
Langford St ASH NG17 163 H7
Langham Pl MSFD NG18 164 C3 1
Langhurst Rd CHSW S40 2 A2
Langley Av ALFN DE55 187 M2
ILK DE7 217 G5
Langley Cl CHSW S40 109 K5 7
MSFDW NG19 164 B1
Langley Ct GLSP SK13 17 K5
Langley Dr GLSP SK13 26 C2 6
Langley Rd DERBYE DE21 242 B7
Langley St DERBYW DE22 240 A5
Lang Rd DERBYSE DE24 257 J4
Langsett Dr MELB/CHEL DE73 257 K8
Langstone Av BSVR S44 131 M1
Langton Hollow
EWD/SEL/PNX NG16 189 G4
Langton Rd ASH NG17 163 H8
Langtree Av CHNE S41 110 D1
Langwith Dr SBK/MW NG20 133 J1
Langwith Maltings
SBK/MW NG20 133 J2
Langwith Rd BSVR S44 131 K1
BSVR S44 132 B2
SBK/MW NG20 133 J5
Lansbury Av CLCR S45 160 F1
STV/CWN S43 93 L6
Lansbury Dr ALFN DE55 176 D4
Lansbury Rd ECK/KIL S21 73 G7
Lanscombe Park Rd
DERBYW DE22 240 B1 1
Lansdown Cl
BSTN/STPLFD NG9 245 L6
Lansdowne Av
DERBYSE DE24 257 J5 2
Lansdowne Rd BUT DE14 280 C3
BUX SK17 99 L1
STV/CWN S43 111 G3
SWAD DE11 282 D7
Lansing Gdns DERBYE DE21 241 L4 2
Lantern Vw NM/HAY SK22 43 L1
Lant La CLCR S45 157 L1
Lapwing Cl DERBYSE DE24 256 B8
Larch Av ECK/KIL S21 73 M5
MSFDW NG19 149 L5
RIPLEY DE5 201 G1 4
SBK/MW NG20 133 G6
Larch Cl DERBYW DE22 226 A7
MPL/ROM SK6 32 B5
Larch Crs EWD/SEL/PNX NG16 203 H8
Larchdale Cl ALFN DE55 176 D6
Larch Dr LGEAT NG10 244 E3 2
Larch Rd BPR/DUF DE56 214 E3
ECK/KIL S21 72 E8
SWAD DE11 282 C3
Larch Wy CHSW S40 110 A5
GLSP SK13 26 C2 7
Larchway MPL/ROM SK6 42 C3
Larges St DERBY DE1 4 B3
Lark Cl BSTN/STPLFD NG9 245 K5
NORM/LIT DE23 255 M4
Larkhall Pl MSFDW NG19 164 A5
Larkhill ALFN DE55 187 J2
Larkhill Cl ALFN DE55 187 J2
Larkhill Crs DERBYSE DE24 256 C6 2
Larkland's Av ILK DE7 230 D3
Lark Ri UTXR ST14 247 L4
Lark Spinney WRKN S81 77 M4 1
Larkspur Cl ALFN DE55 176 D6 1
Larkspur Ct DERBYE DE21 227 K7 2
Larpit Gn WRKS S80 96 D5
Lascelles Rd BUX SK17 99 L2
Lashley Gdns DERBYE DE21 227 J8
Latham Cl
STPNHL/WNHL DE15 274 F8 1
Latham Sq ECC S11 54 B5
Lathbury Cl DERBYE DE21 241 G1
Lathkil Dr ALFN DE55 176 C5
Lathkil Gv ALFN DE55 161 J4
BUX SK17 100 A3
Lathkill Av DERBYSE DE24 257 M3
ILK DE7 217 H5
STV/CWN S43 111 L4
Lathkill Cl HAN/WDH S13 56 F3
ILK DE7 229 H2
Lathkill Dl SWAD DE11 282 C8
Lathkilldale Crs LGEAT NG10 260 D5
Lathkill Dr ASHB DE6 208 B2
EWD/SEL/PNX NG16 189 J3
RIPLEY DE5 200 A3
Lathkill Gv CLCR S45 160 A1
Lathkill Rd DERBYE DE21 241 J2
HAN/WDH S13 56 F3
Latimer Cl NORM/LIT DE23 255 H3 4
Latimer Dr BSTN/STPLFD NG9 231 L7
Latimer St DERBYSE DE24 257 G4
Latrigg Cl MCKLVR DE3 255 H1 7
Lauder Cl DERBYSE DE24 256 B8
Launceston Rd DERBYSE DE24 257 L5
Laund Av BPR/DUF DE56 199 L4
Laund Cl BPR/DUF DE56 199 L5 3
Laund Hl BPR/DUF DE56 199 K5
Laund Nook BPR/DUF DE56 199 K5
Launds Av EWD/SEL/PNX NG16 189 G3
Laurel Av BSVR S44 112 A8
MSFD NG18 164 F5
MSFDW NG19 165 J1
RIPLEY DE5 201 G1
Laurel Cl ALFN DE55 187 K2
ECK/KIL S21 72 F8
SBK/MW NG20 133 G4
Laurel Crs ILK DE7 229 L1
LGEAT NG10 260 F3
STV/CWN S43 111 K1
Laurel Dr ECK/KIL S21 73 M6
Laurel Garth Cl CHNE S41 91 L7
Laurel Gv ALFN DE55 176 D6
STPNHL/WNHL DE15 281 H5
Laurence Cl CHNE S41 91 K8
Laurie Pl DERBYSE DE24 257 H3
Lavender Gdns
HEANOR DE75 216 E1 3
Lavender Rd ALFN DE55 187 K2
Lavender Rw DERBYW DE22 240 C1
Laverack St HAN/WDH S13 57 J1
Laverdene Av TOT/DORE S17 69 J5
Laverdene Cl TOT/DORE S17 69 H6 5
Laverdene Dr TOT/DORE S17 69 J6
Laverdene Rd TOT/DORE S17 69 H6
Laverdene Wy TOT/DORE S17 69 J6 1
Laverick Rd
EWD/SEL/PNX NG16 188 D6
Laverstoke Ct DERBYW DE22 4 B5
Lawn Av ASH NG17 163 K8
DERBYW DE22 226 A8
RDERBYSW DE65 253 M5
Lawn Cl HEANOR DE75 202 C8
Lawnfold GLSP SK13 17 H6 1
Lawn Heads Av
NORM/LIT DE23 239 M8
Lawn La ASH NG17 163 J8
Lawnlea Cl NORM/LIT DE23 256 B5
Lawn Rd ASH NG17 163 L7
Lawns Dr SWAD DE11 282 D3
Lawnside DERBYE DE21 242 C5
The Lawns
BUTN/AL/TUT DE13 264 E7 2
BWSH/BRSTN DE72 270 E2 1
ECC S11 54 E4
Lawnswood Cl
NORM/LIT DE23 255 M2 4
The Lawn DRON S18 70 E8
Lawn Vls BSVR S44 111 K7
Lawrence Av
BWSH/BRSTN DE72 260 A2
DERBYE DE21 241 L3
EWD/SEL/PNX NG16 203 J8
EWD/SEL/PNX NG16 217 M5
MSFDW NG19 149 L6
RCH S42 146 A1 1
RIPLEY DE5 200 F2
Lawrence Crs ASH NG17 163 L6
Lawrence Dr
EWD/SEL/PNX NG16 203 G2
Lawrence Pk
EWD/SEL/PNX NG16 189 L7
Lawrence St BSTN/STPLFD NG9 245 G4
LGEAT NG10 244 F3 1
LGEAT NG10 261 G2
NORM/LIT DE23 256 C2 1
Lawson Av LGEAT NG10 261 H3
Laxfield Cl CHSW S40 127 M2 5
Layton Av MSFD NG18 164 D3
Layton Dr CHNE S41 110 E1
Lea Bank ALFN DE55 176 D6
Leabrook Rd DRON S18 89 M1
Leabrooks Rd ALFN DE55 187 M2
Lea Cl DERBYW DE22 226 B7
Lea Ct WRKS S80 77 M8
Lea Crs ALFN DE55 187 M4
Leacroft Rd MTLK DE4 154 F4
NORM/LIT DE23 256 E1
Leadale Av ALFN DE55 187 K3
Leadbeater Dr HACK/IN S12 56 D5 5
Leadbeater Rd HACK/IN S12 56 C5
Leadmill Rd SHEFP/MNR S2 55 L1 5
Lea Dr DERBYE DE21 241 J4 1
MCKLVR DE3 239 H7
Leafe Cl BSTN/STPLFD NG9 245 M8
Leafenden Cl DERBYW DE22 226 D8 3
Leafgreen Cl NORM/LIT DE23 255 M4
Leafield Rd POY/DIS SK12 42 F4
Leafy La HEANOR DE75 216 C1
Leake St DERBYW DE22 240 A5 4
Lea La EWD/SEL/PNX NG16 189 J4
Lea Main Rd MTLK DE4 172 F2
Leamington Cl NORM/LIT DE23 256 A1
Leamington Dr ALFN DE55 176 E5
BSTN/STPLFD NG9 245 M6
Leamington Rd BUT DE14 280 B3
Leamington St RIPLEY DE5 187 H8
Leamoor Av ALFN DE55 187 L2
Lea Moor Rd MTLK DE4 173 H3
Leander Cl NORM/LIT DE23 256 A3 1
Leander Ri STPNHL/WNHL DE15 281 K2
Leaper St DERBY DE1 4 B1
Leapley La ASHB DE6 220 F8
Lea Rd DRON S18 90 D1
MTLK DE4 172 A3
NM/HAY SK22 34 F7
Leas Av MSFDW NG19 148 D5
Leas Gn BWSH/BRSTN DE72 270 D2
Leashaw MTLK DE4 172 F6
Leashaw Rd MTLK DE4 172 E6
Lea St NM/HAY SK22 43 K2
Leathersley La ASHB DE6 250 E7
Lea V ALFN DE55 176 C6
The Leaway SBK/MW NG20 133 G7
Lea Wood Cft MTLK DE4 172 D5
Leawood Gdns DERBYE DE21 227 L7
Leawood Rd SWAD DE11 283 G5
Leche Cft BPR/DUF DE56 200 A6
Lechlade Cl ILK DE7 229 G2
Ledbury Cha DERBYSE DE24 256 A8
Ledo Av RIPLEY DE5 187 G8
Ledstone Rd SHEFS S8 55 H6
Lee Crs ILK DE7 230 E2
Lee Dl BUX SK17 99 M7
Leedhams Cft MSHM DE12 287 G2 1
Leeds Pl DERBY DE1 5 J6
Leeds Rd WRKN S81 77 J3
Lee Farm Cl
MELB/CHEL DE73 269 J1 2
Leefield Rd CHF/WBR SK23 60 E5
Lee Head GLSP SK13 24 F5
Leek Rd BUX SK17 99 H5
BUX SK17 134 E4
Lee La HEANOR DE75 216 E1
Leeming La South
MSFDW NG19 149 M8
Leeming Pk MSFDW NG19 149 M7
Leeming St MSFD NG18 164 E3
Lee Mt GLSP SK13 25 M3
Leen Valley Dr SBK/MW NG20 133 H7
Lee Rd CHNE S41 111 H8
Lees Av MSFDW NG19 164 A3
Lees Hall Av SHEFS S8 55 K6
Lees Hall Pl SHEFS S8 55 L5
Lees Hall Rd SHEFS S8 55 L5
Lees House Ct SHEFS S8 55 K6 1
Lees La ALFN DE55 176 C4
Lees Rd MTLK DE4 139 M5
MTLK DE4 140 B7
The Lees DERBYSE DE24 258 A5
Leeswood Cl CHNE S41 110 A2 1
Lee Vale Dr GLSP SK13 25 G3
Leeway DERBYE DE21 242 A6
Legh Rd POY/DIS SK12 42 D4
Legion Dr ASH NG17 163 G3
Leicester Dr GLSP SK13 26 C3
Leicester Rd ASHZ LE65 291 M4
Leicester St BUT DE14 280 F2
DERBYW DE22 4 A7
LGEAT NG10 261 H4
Leigh Av MPL/ROM SK6 32 B4
Leigh La UTXR ST14 246 E2
Leigh Rd BSTN/STPLFD NG9 245 J7
Leighton Dr GLV S14 56 C7
MPL/ROM SK6 32 F2
Leighton Pl GLV S14 56 C7
Leighton Rd GLV S14 56 B5
UTXR ST14 247 M4
Leighton Vw SHEFP/MNR S2 56 B5
Leigh Wy RCH S42 145 J3
Leman St DERBYW DE22 4 B7
Lemont Rd TOT/DORE S17 69 H6
Leniscar Av HEANOR DE75 201 M6
Lens Rd DERBYW DE22 225 M8
Lenton Av DERBYE DE21 241 J4
Lenton St LGEAT NG10 244 F4
SHEFP/MNR S2 55 L1 4
Leominster Dr
DERBYE DE21 227 M8 3
Leonard Cl NORM/LIT DE23 4 F7
SHEFP/MNR S2 56 D3
Leonard St NORM/LIT DE23 5 G7
Leopold St DERBY DE1 4 F6
LGEAT NG10 261 G2
Lescar La ECC S11 54 F2
Leslie Cl NORM/LIT DE23 255 H2
Lesser La BUX SK17 100 B2
Letchworth Crs
BSTN/STPLFD NG9 245 M6
Level La BUX SK17 99 G5
Leven Cl DERBYSE DE24 256 C8
Levens Wy CHNE S41 110 B2
Leveret Cl MELB/CHEL DE73 257 L8 2
Leverton Dr ECC S11 55 J1
Leverton Gdns
SHEFP/MNR S2 55 J1 5
Leverton Rd MSFDW NG19 164 B3
Lewcote La ILK DE7 229 K1
Lewis Dr BUTN/AL/TUT DE13 273 L3
Lewis Rd HAN/WDH S13 56 F3
Lewis St NORM/LIT DE23 256 C1
Lewiston Rd DERBYE DE21 241 L5
Lexington Rd DERBYE DE21 241 L5
Ley Av ALFN DE55 175 L7
Leyburn Cl CHSW S40 110 A5
SWAD DE11 289 L1 1
Leyburn Rd SHEFS S8 55 J4
Ley Cft RDERBYSW DE65 263 M1 3
Leyfield Rd TOT/DORE S17 69 G3
Ley Gdns ALFN DE55 175 L7
Leygate Vw NM/HAY SK22 43 L2
Ley Hey Av MPL/ROM SK6 32 C3
Ley Hey Rd MPL/ROM SK6 32 C3
Leyland Cl BSTN/STPLFD NG9 245 J8 5
Leylands La HYDE SK14 24 B4
Leyland St DERBYW DE22 240 B3
Ley La MPL/ROM SK6 32 F2
Leys Ct BPR/DUF DE56 200 A6 5
Leys Field Gdns
MELB/CHEL DE73 257 K8
Leys La MTLK DE4 170 C1
The Leys DERBYE DE21 214 A8
SWAD DE11 282 B4
Leyton Av ASH NG17 163 K5
Leytonstone Dr DERBYW DE22 239 K5
Liber Cl MSFDW NG19 165 J2
Lichfield Av MSFD NG18 164 F8
SWAD DE11 283 H5
Lichfield Cl
BSTN/STPLFD NG9 245 H7 2
MSFD NG18 164 F8
Lichfield Dr DERBYSE DE24 257 K3
Lichfield La MSFD NG18 165 G8
Lichfield Rd BUT DE14 280 A5
BUTN/AL/TUT DE13 286 C2
CHSW S40 2 A9
CHSW S40 127 M2
Lichfield St BUT DE14 274 A8
BUT DE14 281 G1
Lichford Rd SHEFP/MNR S2 55 M4
Lickpenny La MTLK DE4 158 B6
Lidgate Cl MCKLVR DE3 254 F1
Lid La ASHB DE6 219 H3
CLCR S45 142 D4
Liffs Rd BUX SK17 151 L7
Light Alders La POY/DIS SK12 42 D3
Lightfoot Rd UTXR ST14 247 J1
Lightwood Av BUX SK17 99 M2 3
Lightwood Rd BUX SK17 80 E8
ECK/KIL S21 72 B8
Lilac Av DERBYW DE22 239 K5
Lilac Cl BSVR S44 130 C8
DERBYSE DE24 257 K4
UTXR ST14 247 L4 3
Lilac Gv ALFN DE55 176 D6
BSVR S44 131 M1
BSVR S44 147 L2
HEANOR DE75 216 B1
SBK/MW NG20 133 H5
STPNHL/WNHL DE15 281 J4
Lilac Ms ILK DE7 217 G7 6
Lilac St STV/CWN S43 111 K1
Lilac Wy ALFN DE55 175 G1
Lilley St DERBYSE DE24 257 L4
Lillymead Cl RCH S42 128 C4 1
Lilybank Cl MTLK DE4 156 F5 2
Limbersitch La
RDERBYSW DE65 252 C3
Limb La TOT/DORE S17 69 G2
Lime Av ASH NG17 162 D7
ASH NG17 163 J6
BPR/DUF DE56 213 H6
DERBY DE1 4 D7
DERBYE DE21 227 G8
EWD/SEL/PNX NG16 202 F8
MSHM DE12 295 M4
NM/HAY SK22 44 A1
RIPLEY DE5 201 G1
STV/CWN S43 112 B1
Lime Cl ASHB DE6 248 E2
BSVR S44 111 K7
EWD/SEL/PNX NG16 176 F7
Lime Crs BPR/DUF DE56 199 L8 4
Limecroft Vw RCH S42 128 D7
Limedale Av DERBYE DE21 227 L7
Lime Gv ALFN DE55 176 D5
ASHB DE6 207 M2
BSTN/STPLFD NG9 245 G5
BWSH/BRSTN DE72 259 J3
DERBYE DE21 241 L5
LGEAT NG10 244 E4
LGEAT NG10 261 G2
MSFDW NG19 165 M1
MTLK DE4 140 F7
RDERBYSW DE65 264 A1
STPNHL/WNHL DE15 281 H4
Lime Grove Av MTLK DE4 156 F5 3
Lime Grove Wk MTLK DE4 156 E5
Limekiln Fields Rd BSVR S44 113 K8
Lime Kiln La BPR/DUF DE56 211 L2
MPL/ROM SK6 32 D5
Limekiln Wy STV/CWN S43 94 E4
Lime La DERBYE DE21 227 K7
ILK DE7 228 A5
Limerick Rd DERBYE DE21 241 L6
Lime Rd ECK/KIL S21 92 E1
Limes Av ALFN DE55 175 K6
MCKLVR DE3 255 G1
SBK/MW NG20 115 K8
The Limes Cl MTLK DE4 156 F5
Limes Ct ASH NG17 163 M8
Limes Crs SBK/MW NG20 133 G5
Limes Pk RIPLEY DE5 200 F1
The Limes ILK DE7 216 B7
Limestone Cl SWAD DE11 283 J7
Limestone Wy ASHB DE6 192 E2
BKWL DE45 136 F2
BKWL DE45 138 D6
BUX SK17 102 A8
BUX SK17 120 C6
EDL/UDV S33 63 J2
MTLK DE4 155 J7
MTLK DE4 156 E5
UTXR ST14 218 D5
Lime St ASH NG17 163 K6
ILK DE7 230 C3
Lime Ter LGEAT NG10 261 G2
Lime Tree Av ASH NG17 163 G4
BSVR S44 147 L2
ECK/KIL S21 73 M5
MSFDW NG19 149 K6
SWAD DE11 282 E3
Limetree Cl STV/CWN S43 111 J5
Lime Tree Gv BSVR S44 112 A7
CLCR S45 145 H8
Lime Tree Pl MSFD NG18 164 F4 5
Limetree Ri ILK DE7 229 M4
Lime Tree Rd MTLK DE4 156 F5
Lime Wk NORM/LIT DE23 256 A1
Linacre Av CLCR S45 145 G8
Linacre Rd CHSW S40 109 K6
Linacres Dr MELB/CHEL DE73 257 K8
Linacre Wy GLSP SK13 26 C3
Linbery Cl ALFN DE55 174 E6
Linburn Rd SHEFS S8 55 J8
Linby Av MSFDW NG19 164 A4
Lincoln Av DERBYSE DE24 257 K2
LGEAT NG10 244 D6
Lincoln Cl ALFN DE55 161 K4
BSTN/STPLFD NG9 245 H1
Lincoln Gn MELB/CHEL DE73 257 J8 1
Lincoln Rd STPNHL/WNHL DE15 281 G3
Lincoln St ALFN DE55 161 K4
ALFN DE55 175 J7
CHSW S40 128 D2
Lincoln Wy GLSP SK13 26 C2 8
RCH S42 145 J4
SWAD DE11 283 H5
Lindale Rd CHNE S41 110 A2
Linden Av CHSW S40 127 L1
CLCR S45 145 G8
DRON S18 70 E7
SHEFS S8 55 H8
Linden Cl BPR/DUF DE56 214 E2
Linden Ct CLCR S45 145 G8
Linden Dr CHNE S41 129 H4
Linden Gv BSTN/STPLFD NG9 245 H4
LGEAT NG10 244 D3
MTLK DE4 156 F5
SBK/MW NG20 133 J5
Linden Park Gv CHSW S40 2 C3
Linden Rd BUTN/AL/TUT DE13 286 A1
MSFDW NG19 165 J2
STLY SK15 16 A3
WRKS S80 96 B8
Linden St MSFDW NG19 164 D1
SBK/MW NG20 133 J5
Linden Wy MPL/ROM SK6 42 D3
Lindford Cl DERBYE DE21 227 J7
Lindholme Gdns MOS S20 57 M8 1
Lindholme Wy ASH NG17 163 J5
Lindhurst La MSFD NG18 165 J6
Lindisfarne Cl
DERBYSE DE24 256 A7 12
Lindisfarne Rd DRON S18 90 E2 1
Lindley St EWD/SEL/PNX NG16 189 G4
EWD/SEL/PNX NG16 203 L6
MSFD NG18 164 D3
Lindon Dr DERBYSE DE24 257 M4
Lindrick Cl MCKLVR DE3 255 J1 2
Lindrick Gdns CHSW S40 127 M2 6
Lindsay Cl MSFD NG18 164 D4 2
Lindsey Cl DERBYE DE21 241 H4
Lindsey Dr MSFD NG18 165 K7
Lindway La ALFN DE55 173 L1
Linford Ct BSTN/STPLFD NG9 231 L6
Lingfield Cl MSFD NG18 165 J5
Lingfield Ri MCKLVR DE3 238 F7 5
Lingfield Rd BUT DE14 280 C3 5
Lingfoot Av SHEFS S8 70 E4
Lingfoot Cl SHEFS S8 70 E4 4
Lingfoot Crs SHEFS S8 70 E4
Lingfoot Dr SHEFS S8 70 F4 1
Lingfoot Pl SHEFS S8 70 E4
Lingforest Cl MSFD NG18 165 K5
Lingforest Rd MSFD NG18 165 K4
Ling La BSVR S44 131 M6
Linglongs Av CHF/WBR SK23 58 F5
Linglongs Rd CHF/WBR SK23 58 F5
Ling Rd CHSW S40 128 A2

Lings Crs RCH S42 145 K2
Lingwood Gv MSFD NG18 165 J3
Linkin Rd BSTN/STPLFD NG9 245 M4
Linkmel Rd
EWD/SEL/PNX NG16 203 G7 5
Links Cl DERBYSE DE24 256 C6
Links Rd CHF/WBR SK23 60 C5
DRON S18 90 E2
MPL/ROM SK6 32 C6
The Links MSFD NG18 165 K4
Linley La HACK/IN S12 57 H5 1
Linnet Cl DERBYE DE21 242 C4 4
Linnet Hl MCKLVR DE3 254 F3
Linnets Dr MSFD NG18 165 H3
Linscott Cl CHNE S41 110 A3
Linscott Rd SHEFS S8 55 H8
Linsdale Cl WOL/BIL/BRX NG8 231 L5
Linshaws Rd HOLM/MEL HD7 9 J5
Linton Cl MSFD NG18 165 L4
Linton Heath MSHM DE12 289 H5
Linton Rd CHSW S40 127 M2
MSHM DE12 288 B5
SWAD DE11 289 H3
Linwood Crs
EWD/SEL/PNX NG16 217 J1 2
Lipp Av ECK/KIL S21 73 M3
Liskeard Dr DERBYW DE22 226 A6
Lismore Ct DERBYSE DE24 256 A7 13
MSFDW NG19 164 A5
Lismore Gv BUX SK17 99 K3
Lismore Pk BUX SK17 99 K3
Lismore Rd BUX SK17 99 K3
SHEFS S8 55 L5
Lissett Av ILK DE7 230 B3 1
Lister Av HACK/IN S12 56 E6
Lister Cl HACK/IN S12 56 E7 2
Lister Crs HACK/IN S12 56 E7
Lister Dr HACK/IN S12 56 E7
Lister Pl HACK/IN S12 56 E7 3
Lister Wy HACK/IN S12 56 E6
Liston Dr DERBYW DE22 240 C2 2
Litchen Cl ILK DE7 217 J8
Litchfield Cl LGEAT NG10 261 K3 3
Litchurch La DERBYSE DE24 240 F8
Litchurch St DERBY DE1 5 H7 1
NORM/LIT DE23 5 G7
Little Barn Ct MSFD NG18 165 J4
Little Barn Gdns MSFD NG18 165 J5
Little Barn La MSFD NG18 165 J5
Little Bolehill MTLK DE4 171 K8
Little Breck ALFN DE55 176 D6
Little Bridge St DERBY DE1 4 C2
Little Brind Rd CHSW S40 109 L3
Littlebrook Cl GLSP SK13 17 K6
Little Burton East BUT DE14 274 A6
Little Burton West BUT DE14 274 A6
Little Cl SWAD DE11 282 E5
Little Common La ECC S11 54 C7
Littledale Cl DERBYE DE21 227 M7 11
Little Debdale La MSFDW NG19 149 J8
Little Edge HATH/EY S32 85 M4
Little Fen ALFN DE55 161 J5
Littlefield La ASHB DE6 205 J8
ASHB DE6 206 E6
Littlefield Rd RDERBYSW DE65 251 L3
Littlefields HYDE SK14 16 D6
Little Hallam Hl ILK DE7 230 B5
Little Hallam La ILK DE7 230 C4
Little La ASH NG17 162 B8
BKWL DE45 122 B1
BUX SK17 84 A7
HACK/IN S12 56 E4
MSFDW NG19 148 E5
SBK/MW NG20 133 G6
WRKS S80 76 E4
Little London MTLK DE4 172 D5
Little London Pl SHEFS S8 55 J4 3
Little London Rd SHEFS S8 55 H5
Little Longstone Cl
MCKLVR DE3 239 J8 5
Little Meadow Rd
MELB/CHEL DE73 257 K8
Littlemoor CHNE S41 110 B3 2
ECK/KIL S21 73 H7
Littlemoor Crs CHNE S41 110 A3
Littlemoor La ALFN DE55 161 K7
MTLK DE4 172 C1
Littlemoor Rd HYDE SK14 16 D8
Little Morton Rd RCH S42 145 J4
Little Norton Av SHEFS S8 70 D3
Little Norton Dr SHEFS S8 70 D2
Little Norton La SHEFS S8 70 D2
Little Norton Wy SHEFS S8 70 D3
Littleover Av MSFD NG18 165 L4
Littleover Crs NORM/LIT DE23 256 A2
Littleover La NORM/LIT DE23 256 A2
Littlewell La ILK DE7 244 C1
Little Woodbury Dr
NORM/LIT DE23 255 J4 6
Little Wood Dr GLV S14 56 C7
Little Wood La AU/AST/KP S26 76 B5
Littlewood La MSFDW NG19 149 K3
Little Wood Rd GLV S14 56 D7 3
Littleworth MSFD NG18 164 F5
Litton Av ASH NG17 163 K5
Litton Cl BPR/DUF DE56 199 L5 4
ILK DE7 217 H6
STV/CWN S43 111 M2
Litton Dr DERBYE DE21 242 C7
Litton Ms GLSP SK13 25 H1
Liverpool St DERBYE DE21 241 H2 1
Liversage Pl DERBY DE1 5 G6
Liversage Rd DERBY DE1 5 G6
Liversage St DERBY DE1 5 G5
Livingstone Rd NORM/LIT DE23 256 B1
Loadshead La RCH S42 126 A2
Loads Rd RCH S42 126 D3
Lochinvar Cl DERBYE DE21 242 C6
Lock Cl ILK DE7 229 M4
Lockington Cl
MELB/CHEL DE73 257 J8 2
Lock La LGEAT NG10 244 E5
LGEAT NG10 260 E6
Lockoford La CHNE S41 110 D4
Locko La CLCR S45 146 A7
Locko Rd DERBYE DE21 242 B3
Lockside MPL/ROM SK6 32 D4
Locksley Cl ASHZ LE65 291 K3
Lockton Av HEANOR DE75 216 B2
Lockton Cl ASHZ LE65 291 M3
Lockwood Rd DERBYW DE22 226 A6
Lode La ASHB DE6 166 B6
Lodes La BUX SK17 81 M2
Lodge Av ASHB DE6 207 K2
Lodge Bank GLSP SK13 17 K4
Lodge Cl ASHZ LE65 291 K5
BPR/DUF DE56 213 H7 2
RDERBYSW DE65 253 M6
STV/CWN S43 111 K6
Lodge Ct HYDE SK14 16 D6
Lodge Dr BPR/DUF DE56 199 H5
RCH S42 128 D6
Lodge Farm Cha ASHB DE6 207 L2
Lodge Farm Cl CHSW S40 127 M3
Lodge Hl BUTN/AL/TUT DE13 264 B7
Lodge La ASHB DE6 178 A6
ASHB DE6 224 D6
BPR/DUF DE56 198 A2
DERBY DE1 4 D2
DERBYE DE21 242 A7
DERBYW DE22 224 F4
EWD/SEL/PNX NG16 202 B4
Lodge Moor Rd FUL S10 53 H2
Lodge Pl STV/CWN S43 111 M4
Lodge Rd EWD/SEL/PNX NG16 217 K2
ILK DE7 216 B7
LGEAT NG10 260 F5
MSHM DE12 294 A1
Lodge St BWSH/BRSTN DE72 259 K3
The Lodge BUX SK17 83 M7
GLSP SK13 17 K4
Lodge Wy MCKLVR DE3 239 G8
Lohengrin Ct
BUTN/AL/TUT DE13 265 H8 6
Loire Cl ASHZ LE65 291 K3
Lombard St DERBYW DE22 239 J4 9
Lomond Av DERBYSE DE24 256 C8
London Rd BUX SK17 99 L4
BWSH/BRSTN DE72 271 J1
DERBY DE1 4 F5
DERBYSE DE24 257 J1
SHEFP/MNR S2 55 J1
London Rd South SHEFS S8 55 K3
London St CHNE S41 92 A7
Longacre Cl MOS S20 73 K1
Longacre Rd DRON S18 90 D3
Long Acre Vw MOS S20 73 K2
Longacre Wy MOS S20 73 K2
Longbow Cl
BUTN/AL/TUT DE13 273 M1 6
Long Bridge La DERBYSE DE24 257 G2
Longbridge La HEANOR DE75 202 A7
Long Cswy HATH/EY S32 51 M5
Longcliff Wk CHSW S40 109 M4 3
Longclough Dr GLSP SK13 25 K2
Longcourse La BSVR S44 112 D8
Long Cft BWSH/BRSTN DE72 270 D2
Longcroft Av DRON S18 69 L8
Longcroft Cl RCH S42 145 G2
Longcroft Crs DRON S18 69 M8
Long Croft Rd DRON S18 69 M8
Longcroft Vw WRKS S80 96 C4
Longdale MSFDW NG19 165 H1 8
Longdale Dr HYDE SK14 16 D7
Longden Cl BSTN/STPLFD NG9 231 J8
Longdendale Trail GLSP SK13 12 B8
STKB/PEN S36 14 D5
Longedge Gv RCH S42 128 E7
Longedge La RCH S42 128 C7
Longedge Ri RCH S42 128 D6
Longfellow Cl BUT DE14 274 A3 5
Longfield Crs ILK DE7 230 C5
Longfield La ILK DE7 230 C5
Longford Cl DERBYW DE22 226 A8
TOT/DORE S17 69 K5 3
Longford Crs TOT/DORE S17 69 K5
Longford Dr TOT/DORE S17 69 J6
Longford La ASHB DE6 236 C4
Longford Rd TOT/DORE S17 69 J6
Longford Spinney
TOT/DORE S17 69 J6
Longford St DERBYW DE22 240 A2
Long Gallery MTLK DE4 124 B4
Longgreave La BKWL DE45 104 E7
Longhedge La
BUTN/AL/TUT DE13 273 J1
MSFDW NG19 148 C6
Long Hl CHF/WBR SK23 79 J3
MTLK DE4 140 F6
Longhurst La MPL/ROM SK6 32 E3
Longhurst Vw WRKS S80 96 C5
Long Ing Rd HOLM/MEL HD7 9 K3
Longlands BSVR S44 113 L8
RDERBYSW DE65 267 H8
Longlands Dr NM/HAY SK22 43 L2 1
Longlands La RDERBYSW DE65 266 F1
Longlands Rd NM/HAY SK22 43 L2
SWAD DE11 283 G3
Long La ASHB DE6 236 B2
BUX SK17 102 B6
CHF/WBR SK23 59 L7
CLCR S45 143 J3
ECK/KIL S21 74 B4
ECK/KIL S21 91 M1
GLSP SK13 24 F3
ILK DE7 217 G4
MTLK DE4 172 D3
SBK/MW NG20 133 H7
Longleat Crs BSTN/STPLFD NG9 245 M6
Longley Edge La HOLM/MEL HD7 9 L1
Longley Edge Rd HOLM/MEL HD7 9 L1
Longley La DERBYE DE21 242 A4
HOLM/MEL HD7 9 K1
Long Line ECC S11 53 L8
ECC S11 68 F1
Longload La MTLK DE4 171 G5
Longmeade Dr CHF/WBR SK23 60 E6
Long Meadow La BUX SK17 103 H1
Long Meadow Rd ALFN DE55 175 J7
Longmead Rd
BUTN/AL/TUT DE13 273 M4
Longmoor Gdns LGEAT NG10 244 E8 4
Longmoor La
BWSH/BRSTN DE72 260 B1
LGEAT NG10 244 E7
Longmoor Rd GLSP SK13 25 K3
LGEAT NG10 244 D8
Longnor Ms GLSP SK13 17 G8
Long Rake BKWL DE45 137 G6
Longridge La BUX SK17 81 K4
Longrose La ASHB DE6 180 D8
Long Rw BPR/DUF DE56 199 J6
BWSH/BRSTN DE72 259 L8
Long Shambles CHSW S40 3 H4
Longshaw Cl RCH S42 145 J4
STV/CWN S43 112 A3
Longshaw La CDLE ST10 204 B4
Longshaw Rd MSFD NG18 165 L4
Longside Rd RCH S42 126 B4
Longson Rd CHF/WBR SK23 60 F4
Longster La SBK/MW NG20 133 M7
Longstock Cl DERBYE DE21 241 H1 2
Longstone Crs HACK/IN S12 57 G6
Longstone La BKWL DE45 122 C1
Longstone Ri BPR/DUF DE56 199 L4 4
Longstone Wy MSFDW NG19 164 A4
Long Stoop Wy MSFDW NG19 165 L3
Long St STPNHL/WNHL DE15 281 H3
Longthorpe Cl
NORM/LIT DE23 255 K3 6
Longwalls La BPR/DUF DE56 198 F4
Longwood Rd
EWD/SEL/PNX NG16 177 H7
Lonsdale Dr BSTN/STPLFD NG9 245 H8
Lonsdale Gv MTLK DE4 156 C3
Lonsdale Pl DERBYW DE22 240 A6
Lonsdale Rd BUT DE14 280 E2
CLCR S45 145 L8
Loom Cl BPR/DUF DE56 199 M5
Loosemore Dr HACK/IN S12 56 C5
Lord Haddon Rd ILK DE7 230 B1
Lord Roberts Rd CHSW S40 3 H8
Lords Cl BSVR S44 131 K1
Lordsmill St CHNE S41 3 J6
CHSW S40 3 J4
Lord St DERBYSE DE24 257 G4
GLSP SK13 25 M1
HYDE SK14 17 G6
MSFD NG18 164 E5
Lordswell Rd
BUTN/AL/TUT DE13 273 H6
Lorne Cl DRON S18 70 A8
Lorne St DERBYW DE22 4 C8
Lorraine Cl DERBYSE DE24 257 H7 1
Loscoe-denby La RIPLEY DE5 201 L6
Loscoe Gra HEANOR DE75 201 M7
Loscoe Rd DERBYE DE21 241 K1
HEANOR DE75 202 A7
Losk La BSVR S44 131 M7
Lothian Pl CDON/KEG DE74 271 K7 3
DERBYE DE21 241 G3
Lothlorien Cl NORM/LIT DE23 255 L3 2
Loudon St NORM/LIT DE23 4 F8
Loudoun Pl CDON/KEG DE74 271 K6 1
Loudoun Wy ASHZ LE65 291 J5
Loundes Rd DRON S18 91 H4
Loundes Wood Av CHNE S41 109 M2
Lound House Cl ASH NG17 163 J5 4
Loundsley Green Rd CHSW S40 109 L6
Lount La BUTN/AL/TUT DE13 273 H1
Lousie Greaves La
DERBYE DE21 242 B4
Louth Rd ECC S11 54 E3
Louvain Rd NORM/LIT DE23 239 M7
Lovatt Cl BUTN/AL/TUT DE13 265 J8 2
Love La ALFN DE55 160 F6
Lowburn Rd HAN/WDH S13 56 F3
Low Common ECK/KIL S21 94 A3
Lowedges Crs SHEFS S8 70 C4 1
Lowedges Dr SHEFS S8 70 C4 2
Lowedges Pl SHEFS S8 70 D4 2
Lowedges Rd SHEFS S8 70 C4
Lower Bagthorpe
EWD/SEL/PNX NG16 189 H7
Lower Bank GLSP SK13 26 A2
Lower Bank Cl GLSP SK13 17 J7
Lower Barn Rd GLSP SK13 17 H6
Lower Beauvale
EWD/SEL/PNX NG16 203 K7
Lower Bloomsgrove Rd
ILK DE7 217 J8 2
Lower Broadacre STLY SK15 16 B4
Lower Brook St LGEAT NG10 261 H3
Lower Chapel St ALFN DE55 160 E6
ILK DE7 230 C1
Lower Church St ASHZ LE65 291 L4 2
Lower Clara Mount Rd
HEANOR DE75 216 D1
Lower Dale Rd NORM/LIT DE23 240 C8
Lower Dr ALFN DE55 187 G3
Lower Dunstead Rd
EWD/SEL/PNX NG16 202 D7
Lower Eaves Vw
CHF/WBR SK23 60 F5 1
Lower Eley St DERBY DE1 4 D7
Lower Fold MPL/ROM SK6 32 E3
Lower Gladstone St
HEANOR DE75 202 B8 6
Lower Granby St ILK DE7 217 J8 3
Lower Gn RDERBYSW DE65 267 G1
Lower Greenshall La
POY/DIS SK12 43 H3
Lower Grove Rd CHSW S40 2 F4
Lower Hague NM/HAY SK22 43 H2
Lower Hall Cl BPR/DUF DE56 213 M4 1
Lower High St
BUTN/AL/TUT DE13 263 M3
Lower La CHF/WBR SK23 60 A1
Lowerlea POY/DIS SK12 42 F4
Lower Macclesfield Rd
CHF/WBR SK23 59 G4
Lower Mantle Cl CLCR S45 145 G6
Lower Maples HEANOR DE75 216 D2 1
Lower Middleton St ILK DE7 230 D1
Lower Nelson St HEANOR DE75 202 A8
Lower Oakham Wy MSFD NG18 164 B7
Lower Orchard St
BSTN/STPLFD NG9 245 G3 1
Lower Outwoods Rd
BUTN/AL/TUT DE13 273 J5
Lower Packington Rd
ASHZ LE65 291 L5
Lower Park St
BSTN/STPLFD NG9 244 F4 1
Lower Rd DERBYW DE22 239 H2
Lower Smithy La BUX SK17 102 D7
Lower Somercotes ALFN DE55 188 B3
Lower Stanton Rd ILK DE7 230 C4
Lower St ASHB DE6 248 E2
Lower Strines Rd MPL/ROM SK6 32 D5
Lower Terrace Rd BUX SK17 83 L5 1
Lower Whitworth Rd
ILK DE7 230 C4 2
Lowes Hl RIPLEY DE5 187 G7
Lowes La MELB/CHEL DE73 269 G1
Lowe St DERBYSE DE24 257 H3
Loweswater Gv ASHZ LE65 291 M6
Lowfield Av HACK/IN S12 72 B1
Lowfields STV/CWN S43 93 K8 1
Lowgates STV/CWN S43 93 J8
Lowlands Lea HEANOR DE75 202 C8
Lowlands Rd BPR/DUF DE56 199 L6
Low Lea Rd MPL/ROM SK6 32 E3
Low Leighton Rd NM/HAY SK22 44 A3
Low Meadow CHF/WBR SK23 59 G2
Low Pavement CHSW S40 3 G4
Low Rd ASH NG17 163 J3
STV/CWN S43 94 E8
Lowry Dr DRON S18 90 C1
MPL/ROM SK6 32 E2 2
Lowry Gv HYDE SK14 16 C7
Lowside HATH/EY S32 86 F8
Lowside Cl HATH/EY S32 86 E8 1
Low's La ILK DE7 230 D8
Low St ASH NG17 163 J8 1
Loxley Cl CHSW S40 109 L7
DERBYE DE21 227 L8
Loxley Dr MSFD NG18 165 K7
Loxley La UTXR ST14 246 F4
Loxton Ct MCKLVR DE3 238 F7
Loyne Cl DERBYSE DE24 256 C8
Lucas La RDERBYSW DE65 253 H8
Lucas Rd CHNE S41 110 B5
Luccombe Dr DERBYSE DE24 258 A5
Lucerne Rd DERBYE DE21 227 M7
Lucknow Dr ASH NG17 163 L8
MSFD NG18 164 B5 4
Ludgate St BUTN/AL/TUT DE13 263 M4
Ludgate Wk DERBYW DE22 239 H5
Ludham Cl CHNE S41 110 C3
Ludlam Av
EWD/SEL/PNX NG16 217 K3 1
Ludlow Cl DERBYE DE21 242 C5 3
Luke La ASHB DE6 223 H2
Lullington Rd CRTAM B79 292 B5
CRTAM B79 293 H7
MSHM DE12 289 K7
Lulworth Cl NORM/LIT DE23 256 A4 3
Lumber La BPR/DUF DE56 197 G8
Lumb La BPR/DUF DE56 197 M8
BPR/DUF DE56 198 F8
MTLK DE4 140 E4
Lumsdale MTLK DE4 157 G6
MTLK DE4 157 H3
Lumsdale Crs MTLK DE4 157 G5
Lumsdale Rd STV/CWN S43 111 M2
Lums Hill Ri MTLK DE4 157 G4
Luna Cft HACK/IN S12 56 C8
Lunch La BUX SK17 103 J2
Lundie Cl DERBYSE DE24 256 A8
Lundwood Cl MOS S20 57 M8 2
Lundwood Dr MOS S20 57 M8
Lundwood Gv MOS S20 57 M8
Lundy Rd DRON S18 90 D2
Lupin Cl DERBYE DE21 227 M7 12
Lupin Wy BSVR S44 111 K7
Lupton Crs SHEFS S8 70 C4
Lupton Dr SHEFS S8 70 C4
Lupton Rd SHEFS S8 70 C4
Luther Av ASH NG17 163 H8
Lychgate Cl DERBYE DE21 227 G8 1
Lydden Cl STV/CWN S43 111 H2 1
Lydford Av CHNE S41 110 E1 2
Lydford Rd ALFN DE55 175 L5
Lydgate HATH/EY S32 86 B5
Lydgate Dr RCH S42 128 B7
Lydia Gdns EWD/SEL/PNX NG16 217 H1
Lydstep Cl DERBYE DE21 227 M8
Lyme Gv MPL/ROM SK6 32 C5
Lyme Pk CHF/WBR SK23 45 H8
Lyme Rd POY/DIS SK12 42 D3
Lymewood Dr POY/DIS SK12 42 E4
Lymington Rd MSFDW NG19 164 A4
Lynam Cl CLCR S45 145 H7
Lynam Rd BPR/DUF DE56 185 M3
Lyncroft Av RIPLEY DE5 187 H8
Lyndale Dr RIPLEY DE5 201 K2
Lyndale Rd BSTN/STPLFD NG9 245 K2
Lynd Cl EWD/SEL/PNX NG16 189 L3
Lynden Av LGEAT NG10 261 G4
Lyndham Av
TPNHL/WNHL DE15 281 J1
Lyndhurst Cl ECC S11 54 F4
Lyndhurst Gv DERBYE DE21 241 K5
Lyndhurst Rd ECC S11 54 F4 2
Lyndhurst St NORM/LIT DE23 4 E9
Lyne Av GLSP SK13 25 K2
Lyne Ct BUT DE14 273 K7
Lynholmes Ri MTLK DE4 156 F5
Lynholmes Rd MTLK DE4 156 F5
Lynmouth Dr ILK DE7 217 G7
Lynmouth Rd ABRD S7 55 H5
Lynncroft EWD/SEL/PNX NG16 203 K8
Lynne Cl GLSP SK13 26 C2 9
Lynton Cl RIPLEY DE5 187 G7 1
Lynton Dr MPL/ROM SK6 42 B2
Lynton Rd BPR/DUF DE56 185 K7
BSTN/STPLFD NG9 245 M4
ECC S11 55 G2 10
Lynton St DERBYW DE22 4 B6
Lynwood Cl BUT DE14 280 C3 4
DRON S18 90 A1 3
Lynwood Rd BUT DE14 280 B3 2
DERBYSE DE24 256 C6
Lytham Cl DERBYE DE21 241 G1 4
Lyttelton St DERBYW DE22 239 L5

M

Mable St WRKS S80 77 L6
Macaulay St DERBYSE DE24 256 D5
Macclesfield Main Rd BUX SK17 99 G5
Macclesfield Old Rd BUX SK17 99 G5
Macclesfield Rd BUX SK17 99 J3
CHF/WBR SK23 58 F4
Macdonald Cl RCH S42 129 J7
Macdonald Sq ILK DE7 230 A5 5
Machin Gv WRKN S81 77 M3
Machins Ct DRON S18 70 D8 2
Machon Bank ABRD S7 55 H4
Machon Bank Rd ECC S11 55 G4
Mackenzie St DERBYW DE22 239 M4
ECC S11 55 H2 1
Mackinley Av
BSTN/STPLFD NG9 245 H1
Macklin St DERBY DE1 4 D4
Mackworth Cl SWAD DE11 282 E3 4
Mackworth Ct MSFD NG18 165 L5 1
Mackworth Rd DERBYW DE22 4 A1
Macready Pl DERBYSE DE24 257 J3 4
Maddock La MTLK DE4 181 K1
Madehurst Gdns
SHEFP/MNR S2 55 L3 2
Madehurst Ri SHEFP/MNR S2 55 L3 3
Madehurst Rd SHEFP/MNR S2 55 L3
Madehurst Vw
SHEFP/MNR S2 55 L3 4
Madeley Ct MCKLVR DE3 255 G1 4
Madeley St NORM/LIT DE23 240 D8
Madin Dr STV/CWN S43 111 L4
Madin St CHNE S41 3 G1
RCH S42 144 F2
Madison Av DERBYE DE21 241 H3
Madras Rd
STPNHL/WNHL DE15 274 F7 5
Mag La BPR/DUF DE56 197 G5
SBK/MW NG20 115 G5
Magnolia Wy ALFN DE55 187 J2
Magpie Cl WRKN S81 77 M3 5
Maguire Av GLSP SK13 17 K4
Maid Marian Av
EWD/SEL/PNX NG16 189 L3
Maidstone Dr DERBYSE DE24 257 J5
Maidwell Cl BPR/DUF DE56 199 L5
Main Av DERBYW DE22 226 C5
MSFDW NG19 165 K2
TOT/DORE S17 69 H6
Maine Dr DERBYE DE21 241 K4
Main Rd ALFN DE55 159 M4
ALFN DE55 160 A8
ALFN DE55 160 D5
ALFN DE55 187 M3
ALFN DE55 188 D4
ASHB DE6 207 G2
ASHB DE6 223 J3
ASHB DE6 250 B6
BSVR S44 130 D8
BUX SK17 102 C7
BUX SK17 120 B4
BWSH/BRSTN DE72 258 D4
CDLE ST10 190 B6
CRTAM B79 292 A5
DRON S18 89 K2
DRON S18 91 H3
ECK/KIL S21 72 B7
ECK/KIL S21 92 A3
EDL/UDV S33 50 E7
EDL/UDV S33 64 D3
EWD/SEL/PNX NG16 188 E6
EWD/SEL/PNX NG16 189 H7
HACK/IN S12 72 B3
HATH/EY S32 86 E7
HATH/EY S32 86 F3
ILK DE7 215 J7
MTLK DE4 155 M1
MTLK DE4 185 G1
RCH S42 109 H3
RIPLEY DE5 186 D7
RIPLEY DE5 186 E5
SBK/MW NG20 133 K1
Mainside Crs
EWD/SEL/PNX NG16 203 K1
Main St ALFN DE55 161 K6
ALFN DE55 176 D4
ASH NG17 162 C7
ASHB DE6 236 A2
ASHZ LE65 284 C7
BKWL DE45 104 D6
BPR/DUF DE56 196 E1
BSVR S44 131 K5
BSVR S44 131 J2
BSVR S44 132 B4
BUT DE14 280 B3
BUTN/AL/TUT DE13 272 E8
BUTN/AL/TUT DE13 272 F3
BUTN/AL/TUT DE13 274 B1
BUX SK17 119 K2
BWSH/BRSTN DE72 259 G4
BWSH/BRSTN DE72 260 A3
BWSH/BRSTN DE72 270 B6
CRTAM B79 293 H8
EWD/SEL/PNX NG16 203 M8
EWD/SEL/PNX NG16 203 G1
EWD/SEL/PNX NG16 217 J1
EWD/SEL/PNX NG16 217 M5
HACK/IN S12 57 L6
HATH/EY S32 105 M1
ILK DE7 214 E3
ILK DE7 216 B7
ILK DE7 244 C2
LGEAT NG10 261 H3
MELB/CHEL DE73 277 L5
MELB/CHEL DE73 278 F1
MELB/CHEL DE73 279 J8
MELB/CHEL DE73 279 H4
MSHM DE12 287 G1
MSHM DE12 287 M4
MSHM DE12 288 A7
MSHM DE12 288 B3
MSHM DE12 289 K7
MSHM DE12 289 G4
MSHM DE12 294 C3
MSHM DE12 295 K3
MTLK DE4 154 E1
MTLK DE4 154 F4
MTLK DE4 171 G7
RDERBYSW DE65 251 L2
RDERBYSW DE65 252 F8
RDERBYSW DE65 253 L6
RDERBYSW DE65 254 C5
RDERBYSW DE65 265 L5
RDERBYSW DE65 267 K8
RDERBYSW DE65 267 G1
RDERBYSW DE65 276 A1
SBK/MW NG20 115 K8
SBK/MW NG20 133 G7
STPNHL/WNHL DE15 275 G2
STPNHL/WNHL DE15 281 J2

SWAD DE11 .... 282 B4
SWAD DE11 .... 283 L4
SWAD DE11 .... 289 M1
SWAD DE11 .... 290 E2
WOL/BIL/BRX NG8 .... 231 L1
Mais Cl MTLK DE4 .... 157 K5
Makeney Rd BPR/DUF DE56 .. 213 M3
BPR/DUF DE56 .... 213 K4
BPR/DUF DE56 .... 213 J8
Malcolm Cl NORM/LIT DE23 .. 255 H2 ◆
Malcolm St NORM/LIT DE23 .... 240 E8
Maldon Cl BSTN/STPLFD NG9 .. 245 L6 ◆
Malham Cl CHSW S40 .... 110 A5
Malham Gdns MOS S20 .... 73 G3
Malham Gv MOS S20 .... 73 H3
Malham Rd NORM/LIT DE23 .... 255 J4 ◆
Malia Rd CHNE S41 .... 110 F4
Malin Cl DERBYSE DE24 .... 257 L5
Malinscommon La
BPR/DUF DE56 .... 183 M6
Malkin St CHNE S41 .... 3 J5
Mallard Cl MSHM DE12 .... 295 L6 ◆
SBK/MW NG20 .... 133 G7
UTXR ST14 .... 247 M4
Mallard Dr ECK/KIL S21 .... 73 L3 ◆
The Mallards WRKN S81 .... 77 M3 ◆
Mallard Wk MCKLVR DE3 ...... 254 F3
Mallatratt Pl MSFDW NG19 .... 149 L6 ◆
Mallens Cft UTXR ST14 .... 246 F3
The Mall STLY SK15 .... 16 B4
Malmesbury Av SWAD DE11 .... 283 C4
Malpas Rd MTLK DE4 .... 156 C4
Malpeton Wy ASH NG17 .... 163 K6
Malson Wy CHNE S41 .... 110 C4
Maltby Av ALFN DE55 .... 160 B5
Maltby Cl DERBYW DE22 .... 226 C8 ◆
Maltby Rd MSFD NG18 .... 165 H4
Malthouse Cl
EWD/SEL/PNX NG16 .... 217 J1 ◆
MTLK DE4 .... 171 J7
Malthouse La BPR/DUF DE56 .. 185 L8
CLCR S45 .... 143 J7
HATH/EY S32 .... 86 F5
RCH S42 .... 127 L7
RDERBYSW DE65 .... 252 A7
Malthouse Rd WRKS S80 .... 96 D4
The Maltings
BWSH/BRSTN DE72 .... 271 K1 ◆
STPNHL/WNHL DE15 .... 281 K1
Malton Pl DERBYE DE21 .... 241 G1
Malvern Av
STPNHL/WNHL DE15 .... 281 J1
Malvern Cl MCKLVR DE3 .... 239 G7 ◆
Malvern Crs ASHZ LE65 .... 291 K2
Malvern Gdns LGEAT NG10 .... 260 D2 ◆
MTLK DE4 .... 156 E4 ◆
Malvern Ri GLSP SK13 .... 17 K5
Malvern Rd CHSW S40 .... 2 D2
Malvern St
STPNHL/WNHL DE15 .... 281 J1
Malvern Wy DERBYE DE21 .... 241 G1
Manchester La SWAD DE11 .... 283 L5
Manchester Rd BUX SK17 ...... 83 K2
BUX SK17 .... 99 J1
CHF/WBR SK23 .... 59 M5
GLSP SK13 .... 17 J3
Manchester St DERBYW DE22 .. 240 A4
LGEAT NG10 .... 261 G4
Mandalay Gdns
MPL/ROM SK6 .... 32 A3 ◆
Mandeen Gv MSFD NG18 ...... 165 K6
Manifold Av ASHB DE6 .... 207 M1
STV/CWN S43 .... 112 A2
Manifold Dr DERBYSE DE24 .... 257 L2
EWD/SEL/PNX NG16 .... 189 J3
MPL/ROM SK6 .... 42 C4
Manifold Wy BUX SK17 .... 150 B7
CDLE ST10 .... 190 F1
Manitoba Wy
EWD/SEL/PNX NG16 .... 189 J3
Manknell Rd CHNE S41 .... 16 C7 ◆
Manley Gv HYDE SK14 .... 16 C7 ◆
Manners Av ILK DE7 .... 230 A1
Manners Cl CHF/WBR SK23 .... 45 G8
Manners Rd ILK DE7 .... 230 B1
Manners St ILK DE7 .... 230 D4 ◆
Manning Vw ILK DE7 .... 217 J8
Mannion Crs LGEAT NG10 ...... 260 C5
Manor Av BSTN/STPLFD NG9 .. 245 G2
DERBYW DE22 .... 239 M7
STV/CWN S43 .... 111 J3
Manor Cl ALFN DE55 .... 161 K7
ASH NG17 .... 162 F2
CLCR S45 .... 161 C1
MTLK DE4 .... 181 K1 ◆
STPNHL/WNHL DE15 .... 281 K4
UTXR ST14 .... 247 M2 ◆
WRKS S80 .... 77 M8
Manor Ct BWSH/BRSTN DE72 .. 260 A2
STV/CWN S43 .... 95 J7
Manor Court Rd BSVR S44 .... 113 J7 ◆
Manor Cl STY CHSW S40 .... 2 A4
DRON S18 .... 90 C1
STPNHL/WNHL DE15 .... 281 K4
RIPLEY DE5 .... 187 G6
Manor Dr BUT DE14 .... 274 B8
CHSW S40 .... 2 A4
STV/CWN S43 .... 111 J3
Manor Farm Rd
BWSH/BRSTN DE72 .... 270 E2
Manor Fields Dr ILK DE7 .... 230 A3
Manor Gv STV/CWN S43 .... 94 D3
WRKS S80 .... 77 M8
Manor Hill Rd MPL/ROM SK6 .. 32 C3
Manor House Rd LGEAT NG10 .. 261 J3
Manor La ALFN DE55 .... 186 C1
CRTAM B79 .... 292 M4
SHEFP/MNR S2 .... 56 B1
Manorleigh BWSH/BRSTN DE72 .. 260 B2
Manor Pk BWSH/BRSTN DE72 .. 258 D1
Manor Park Av SHEFP/MNR S2 .. 56 C1
Manor Park Cl SHEFP/MNR S2 .. 56 C1
Manor Park Ct
SHEFP/MNR S2 .... 56 C1 ◆
Manor Park Rd SHEFP/MNR S2 .. 56 C1 ◆
Manor Park Dr SHEFP/MNR S2 .. 56 C1
Manor Park Rd GLSP SK13 .... 26 B1

Manor Park Wy
DERBYW DE22 .... 239 L7 ◆
Manor Rd ALFN DE55 .... 56 C1 ◆
Manor Rd ALFN DE55 .... 174 B7
ASH NG17 .... 163 H5
ASHB DE6 .... 193 M7
AU/AST/KP S26 .... 75 K1
BPR/DUF DE56 .... 199 J7
BWSH/BRSTN DE72 .... 259 H5
CHSW S40 .... 2 A4
CHSW S40 .... 109 M8
ECK/KIL S21 .... 74 A5
ILK DE7 .... 230 B1
MELB/CHEL DE73 .... 269 J1
MPL/ROM SK6 .... 32 C3
MSFDW NG19 .... 149 K6
NORM/LIT DE23 .... 239 M8 ◆
STPNHL/WNHL DE15 .... 281 K4
STV/CWN S43 .... 94 D3
STV/CWN S43 .... 111 J3
UTXR ST14 .... 247 L2
Manor St ASH NG17 .... 163 H8
GLSP SK13 .... 26 A1 ◆
Manor Vw MOS S20 .... 73 H3 ◆
Manse Av WRKS S80 .... 115 G1
Manse Cl WRKS S80 .... 115 G2
Mansell Cl EWD/SEL/PNX NG16 .. 217 L1
Mansfeldt Crs CHNE S41 ...... 110 B4
Mansfeldt Rd CHNE S41 .... 110 B4
Mansfield Dr HACK/IN S12 .... 56 E4
Mansfield La ASH NG17 .... 163 K4
Mansfield Rd ALFN DE55 ...... 161 M3
ALFN DE55 .... 175 L6
ALFN DE55 .... 176 E5
ASH NG17 .... 163 H4
ASH NG17 .... 163 K4
BSVR S44 .... 114 A4
BSVR S44 .... 130 C7
BSVR S44 .... 130 E8
BSVR S44 .... 132 A4
BSVR S44 .... 147 M1
BSVR S44 .... 147 H1
BSVR S44 .... 147 M2
CHNE S41 .... 129 H3
DERBY DE1 .... 4 F1
DERBY DE1 .... 240 E3
DERBYE DE21 .... 227 J7
DERBYE DE21 .... 227 H7 ◆
DERBYE DE21 .... 240 F1
ECK/KIL S21 .... 74 C4
EWD/SEL/PNX NG16 .... 189 L3
EWD/SEL/PNX NG16 .... 203 J7
HACK/IN S12 .... 56 E4
HEANOR DE75 .... 202 C8
MSFDW NG19 .... 149 M8
MSFDW NG19 .... 163 M6
RCH S42 .... 129 K6
WRKS S80 .... 77 M8
WRKS S80 .... 97 J3
WRKS S80 .... 115 J1
Mansfields Cft
RDERBYSW DE65 .... 253 L6 ◆
Mansfield St ALFN DE55 .... 187 M2 ◆
DERBY DE1 .... 240 D3
Manston Wy WRKN S81 .... 77 M2
Manston Cl SWAD DE11 .... 282 C4 ◆
Manton St SHEFP/MNR S2 .... 55 L1 ◆
Manvers Av RIPLEY DE5 .... 201 H1 ◆
Manvers Rd STV/CWN S43 .... 111 K6
Manvers St MSFD NG18 .... 164 D2
MSFDW NG19 .... 149 K7
RIPLEY DE5 .... 201 H1
SBK/MW NG20 .... 133 K6
Manville Ct
BSTN/STPLFD NG9 .... 231 L7 ◆
Maple Av LGEAT NG10 .... 244 E3
MPL/ROM SK6 .... 32 C6
NORM/LIT DE23 .... 256 A4
POY/DIS SK12 .... 43 K4
RIPLEY DE5 .... 200 F2
Maplebeck Ct DERBY DE1 .... 4 F1
DERBY DE1 .... 240 D3 ◆
Maple Cl MSFDW NG19 .... 165 H1
Maple Gdns HEANOR DE75 .... 216 A1 ◆
Maple Gv BSVR S44 .... 147 K2
BWSH/BRSTN DE72 .... 260 C2
DERBYW DE22 .... 226 A5
STPNHL/WNHL DE15 .... 281 H5
Maple Rd SWAD DE11 .... 282 E4
SWAD DE11 .... 111 L2
Mapletoft Av MSFDW NG19 .... 149 K5
Mapleton Av DERBYE DE21 .... 241 J1
Mapleton Rd ASHB DE6 .... 193 K8
Mapleton Rd DERBYE DE21 .... 259 J2
Maple Vw MTLK DE4 .... 156 F7
Mapperley La ILK DE7 .... 216 B8
Mapperley Rd DRON S18 ...... 89 M1 ◆
Mappleton Dr MSFD NG18 .... 165 L1
Mapplewells Rd ASH NG17 .... 177 L1
Marchington Cl DERBYW DE22 .. 240 B1
Marchwood Cl CHSW S40 .... 2 D2
Mardale Cl CHNE S41 .... 110 B1
Marden Rd ABRD S7 .... 55 H4 ◆
Maree Cl DERBYSE DE24 ...... 256 B6
Marfleet Cl MCKLVR DE3 ...... 238 F7
Margaret Av DERBYE DE21 .... 241 H5
ILK DE7 .... 230 C2
LGEAT NG10 .... 244 E6
Margaret's Ct
BSTN/STPLFD NG9 .... 245 K2 ◆
Margaret St DERBY DE1 .... 240 D3 ◆
SHEF S1 .... 55 K1
Margery Cl ASHB DE6 .... 207 L2
Margreave Rd DERBYE DE21 .. 241 J3
Marigold Cl DERBYE DE21 .... 227 L7
Marina Dr DERBYE DE21 ...... 242 A5

DERBYSE DE24 .... 257 H5
Marina Rd HEANOR DE75 .... 215 L2
Marjorie Rd DERBYE DE21 .... 241 H2
Marjorie St WRKS S80 .... 77 K6
Marjory La ASHB DE6 .... 234 F8
Markeaton La DERBYW DE22 .. 239 L2
Markeaton St DERBYW DE22 .. 4 A1
Market Cl ALFN DE55 .... 176 D4
SBK/MW NG20 .... 133 J6
Market Head BPR/DUF DE56 .. 199 J7
Market House Pl MSFD NG18 .. 164 E3 ◆
Market Pl ALFN DE55 .... 176 D4
ALFN DE55 .... 187 M2
ALFN DE55 .... 188 B4
ASH NG17 .... 162 C7 ◆
BPR/DUF DE56 .... 199 K7 ◆
BSVR S44 .... 131 K1 ◆
BUT DE14 .... 274 B8
BUX SK17 .... 134 E4 ◆
CHF/WBR SK23 .... 60 E4
EDL/UDV S33 .... 48 F8
EWD/SEL/PNX NG16 .... 188 B6
HEANOR DE75 .... 216 B1
HYDE SK14 .... 16 D7 ◆
ILK DE7 .... 230 C2 ◆
MELB/CHEL DE73 .... 278 E3 ◆
MSFDW NG19 .... 149 M7
MTLK DE4 .... 183 J2 ◆
RIPLEY DE5 .... 201 L2
UTXR ST14 .... 247 M3
Market Sq HAN/WDH S13 .... 57 M4
Market St ALFN DE55 .... 176 D5
ASH NG17 .... 162 C7
ASH NG17 .... 163 H8
ASHZ LE65 .... 291 L4
BUX SK17 .... 99 L3
BWSH/BRSTN DE72 .... 259 K5
CHF/WBR SK23 .... 59 H3
CHF/WBR SK23 .... 60 E4
CLCR S45 .... 145 H6
ECK/KIL S21 .... 74 A5
GLSP SK13 .... 25 M1 ◆
HAN/WDH S13 .... 57 M4 ◆
HEANOR DE75 .... 202 B8
HYDE SK14 .... 16 D6
HYDE SK14 .... 17 C5
ILK DE7 .... 230 C2
NM/HAY SK22 .... 35 G7
NM/HAY SK22 .... 43 L3
POY/DIS SK12 .... 43 G4
SBK/MW NG20 .... 133 J6
STV/CWN S43 .... 93 H8
SWAD DE11 .... 282 E6
UTXR ST14 .... 247 M3
Markham Ct DERBYE DE21 .... 227 J8 ◆
Markham Crs STV/CWN S43 .. 93 J2
Markham La BSVR S44 .... 112 E6
Markham Pl MSFDW NG19 .... 164 A3
Markham Ri CLCR S45 .... 144 E6
Markham Rd BSVR S44 .... 112 E5
CHSW S40 .... 2 F5
Markham Ter SHEFS S8 .... 55 J4 ◆
Markland Av STV/CWN S43 .... 95 K6
Markland Crs STV/CWN S43 .. 95 K6
Markland La WRKS S80 .... 95 K7
Markland Vw WRKS S80 .... 96 A7
Mark La FUL S10 .... 53 K4
Mark's Cl NORM/LIT DE23 .... 256 A4
Mark St LGEAT NG10 .... 244 F5
Marlborough Cl
MPL/ROM SK6 .... 32 A3 ◆
Marlborough Crs
STPNHL/WNHL DE15 .... 281 J2
Marlborough Dr
BPR/DUF DE56 .... 199 M5
Marlborough Rd BUX SK17 .... 99 L2
BWSH/BRSTN DE72 .... 260 A3
DERBYSE DE24 .... 256 E5
LGEAT NG10 .... 261 J2
MSFDW NG19 .... 164 C1
Marlborough Wy ASHZ LE65 .. 291 K3
UTXR ST14 .... 247 J1
Marldon Cl
WOL/BIL/BRX NG8 .... 231 M5 ◆
Marley Rd SHEFP/MNR S2 .... 56 B1
Marlow Brow GLSP SK13 ...... 17 K6
Marlow Crs ILK DE7 .... 229 C2
Marlow St BUX SK17 .... 99 M2 ◆
GLSP SK13 .... 17 K6 ◆
Marlpit La ASHB DE6 .... 205 K7
ASHB DE6 .... 252 D2
BSVR S44 .... 113 M8
Marmion Rd ECC S11 .... 54 E3 ◆
Marple Hall Dr MPL/ROM SK6 .. 32 A3
Marple Rd GLSP SK13 .... 24 F5
Marples Cl SHEFS S8 .... 55 J3 ◆
Marples Dr SHEFS S8 .... 55 J3 ◆
Marriott Av BSTN/STPLFD NG9 .. 245 K5
MSFD NG18 .... 164 C4
Marriott Cl BSTN/STPLFD NG9 .. 245 K5
Marriott La SHEFS S8 .... 55 G7
Marriott Rd SHEFS S8 .... 55 G7
Marrison Dr ECK/KIL S21 ...... 73 M4
Marr Ter FUL S10 .... 54 C1
Marsden Cl BPR/DUF DE56 .... 213 H7 ◆
Marsden St CHSW S40 .... 3 C3
DERBYSE DE24 .... 257 H3 ◆
GLSP SK13 .... 17 K6 ◆
Marshall Dr BSTN/STPLFD NG9 .. 245 K2
Marshall Rd SHEFS S8 .... 55 J8
Marshall St ALFN DE55 .... 175 K6
HEANOR DE75 .... 202 B8
Marsham Dr MPL/ROM SK6 .... 32 D5 ◆
Marsh Av DRON S18 .... 70 E7
EDL/UDV S33 .... 49 J6 ◆
Marshaw Cl MCKLVR DE3 .... 255 H1 ◆
Marsh Cl MOS S20 .... 72 F4
Marshfield Gv STV/CWN S43 .. 93 K8 ◆
Marshgreen Cl
DERBYSE DE24 .... 258 A5 ◆
Marsh Green La CLCR S45 .... 143 H6
Marsh Hall La CHF/WBR SK23 .. 60 C5
Marsh Hollow ASHB DE6 ...... 222 B3
Marsh House Rd ECC S11 .... 54 C5
Marsh La ASHB DE6 .... 206 A2
BPR/DUF DE56 .... 199 L5
NM/HAY SK22 .... 44 A4
Marsh Lane Crs
BPR/DUF DE56 .... 199 L6 ◆

Marsh Vw ECK/KIL S21 .... 72 E8
Marsland Rd MPL/ROM SK6 .. 32 A3
Marston BUX SK17 .... 119 K3
Marston Brook
RDERBYSW DE65 .... 265 H1 ◆
Marston Cl BPR/DUF DE56 .... 199 M4
DRON S18 .... 90 A2
NORM/LIT DE23 .... 256 A5
Marstone Crs TOT/DORE S17 .. 69 H5
Marston La ASHB DE6 .... 232 F8
BUTN/AL/TUT DE13 .... 264 D6
RDERBYSW DE65 .... 264 B3
RDERBYSW DE65 .... 264 E2
Marston Old La
RDERBYSW DE65 .... 263 M2
Marston Ri
STPNHL/WNHL DE15 .... 281 J2
Martin Ct ECK/KIL S21 .... 72 F7
Martindale Ct
BPR/DUF DE56 .... 200 A5 ◆
Martin Dr DERBYE DE21 ...... 241 K2
Martin Ri ECK/KIL S21 .... 72 F7
Martin's La BUTN/AL/TUT DE13 .. 262 D6
RCH S42 .... 144 E2
Martlet Av POY/DIS SK12 .... 42 F4
Marton Rd BSTN/STPLFD NG9 .. 245 M7
Mary Ann St DRON S18 ...... 91 H6 ◆
Maryland Ct BSTN/STPLFD NG9 .. 245 H1
SWAD DE11 .... 282 D3 ◆
Maryland Rd DERBYE DE21 .... 241 L4
Marylebone Crs DERBYW DE22 .. 239 J5
Mary Rd EWD/SEL/PNX NG16 .. 217 L1
Mary St ECK/KIL S21 .... 73 G7
SBK/MW NG20 .... 115 K8
SHEF S1 .... 55 K1
WRKS S80 .... 77 K5
Masefield Av NORM/LIT DE23 .. 256 B5
RCH S42 .... 146 A2
SWAD DE11 .... 282 F4
Masefield Cl MSHM DE12 .... 295 L7
Masefield Crs BUT DE14 ...... 274 A3
Masefield Rd HAN/WDH S13 .. 56 F3
Mason Crs HAN/WDH S13 .... 57 G3
Mason Gv HAN/WDH S13 .... 57 G4
Mason Rd ILK DE7 .... 217 G8
Masons Gv GLSP SK13 .... 17 K4 ◆
Mason St ASH NG17 .... 163 L6
WRKS S80 .... 96 C4
Masson Cl CHSW S40 .... 110 A5 ◆
Masson La MTLK DE4 .... 171 K1
Mastin Av STV/CWN S43 ...... 94 F5
Mather's Wy RCH S42 .... 145 C1 ◆
Matlock Av MSFD NG18 .... 164 D5
Matlock Dr STV/CWN S43 .... 111 M5
Matlock Gn MTLK DE4 .... 156 F6
Matlock Rd ALFN DE55 .... 158 F8
BPR/DUF DE56 .... 185 J6
BPR/DUF DE56 .... 199 J5
CLCR S45 .... 143 H5
DERBYE DE21 .... 241 J1
Matlock St BKWL DE45 .... 123 C5
GLSP SK13 .... 17 J3
Matthew Cl DERBYE DE24 .... 257 J8
Matthews Ct ASHZ LE65 ...... 291 J4
Matthews Fold SHEFS S8 .... 70 F1 ◆
Matthews La SHEFS S8 .... 70 F1
Matthew St DERBYE DE24 .... 257 J8
MPL/ROM SK6 .... 32 D4 ◆
Matthew Wy
NORM/LIT DE23 .... 255 H3 ◆
Mauncer Crs HAN/WDH S13 .. 57 L3
Mauncer Dr HAN/WDH S13 .. 57 L3
Mauncer La HAN/WDH S13 .. 57 L4
Maundale Av ASH NG17 .... 163 L6
Maunleigh MSFDW NG19 ...... 165 H1
Maunside MSFD NG18 .... 164 C6
Maun Cl MSFD NG18 .... 164 C6
Maun Wy MSFD NG18 .... 164 C6
Mawfa Av SHEFS S8 .... 56 A8
Mawfa Crs SHEFS S8 .... 56 A8 ◆
Mawfa Dr SHEFS S8 .... 56 A8
Mawfa Rd SHEFS S8 .... 56 A8 ◆
Mawkin La EWD/SEL/PNX NG16 .. 177 J5
Mawson La BKWL DE45 .... 138 F6
Maxey Pl SHEFS S8 .... 55 K4 ◆
Max Rd DERBYE DE21 .... 241 H2
Maxwell Av DERBYW DE22 .... 240 A2
Maxwell St BWSH/BRSTN DE72 .. 260 C2
LGEAT NG10 .... 261 H3
May Av CHNE S41 .... 91 M7
Maybank Cl CHF/WBR SK23 .. 60 D1
Mayfair SWAD DE11 .... 282 B4
Mayfair Rd MSFD NG18 .... 165 G4
Mayfair Crs DERBYW DE22 .... 239 H4
Mayfield Av ASHB DE6 .... 206 F3
BPR/DUF DE56 .... 214 D2
HEANOR DE75 .... 216 B1
Mayfield Cl MSFD NG18 .... 165 L5 ◆
Mayfield Dr BSTN/STPLFD NG9 .. 231 J8
RCH S42 .... 145 J4
STPNHL/WNHL DE15 .... 281 J2
Mayfield Gv LGEAT NG10 ...... 261 H1
Mayfield Pl ASH NG17 .... 163 G8
Mayfield Rd ASHB DE6 .... 207 K1
CHSW S40 .... 109 M8
DERBYE DE21 .... 241 H3
FUL S10 .... 53 K3
MPL/ROM SK6 .... 32 E1
STPNHL/WNHL DE15 .... 270 D7
Mayflower Ct SBK/MW NG20 .. 133 H6 ◆
Mayflower Rd
EWD/SEL/PNX NG16 .... 217 L2
Mayhall Av MSFDW NG19 .... 149 K6
Maylands
BWSH/BRSTN DE72 .... 258 E1 ◆
Maylands Av
BWSH/BRSTN DE72 .... 260 B2
Maynard Rd CHSW S40 .... 2 F7
HATH/EY S32 .... 87 G1
Maynestone Rd CHF/WBR SK23 .. 45 H6
Maypole Hl SWAD DE11 ...... 282 D4 ◆
May St DERBYW DE22 .... 4 C7
May Tree Cl MOS S20 .... 73 H1
May Tree Cft MOS S20 .... 73 H1 ◆
May Tree La MOS S20 .... 73 H1
Mcadam Cl
STPNHL/WNHL DE15 .... 274 E8 ◆
Mcmahon Av STV/CWN S43 .. 111 L4

Mcneil Gv
BWSH/BRSTN DE72 .... 259 K3 ◆
Mead Cl DERBYSE DE24 ...... 256 C6
Mead Crs STPNHL/WNHL DE15 .. 281 K4
Meadow Av BUX SK17 .... 81 L5
MSFD NG18 .... 164 F5
RIPLEY DE5 .... 201 L2
Meadow Bank ALFN DE55 .... 176 D3 ◆
GLSP SK13 .... 25 J3
HYDE SK14 .... 17 G4
Meadowbank Ct
EWD/SEL/PNX NG16 .... 203 G7 ◆
Meadow Bank Rd ABRD S7 .. 55 G3 ◆
Meadowbank Wy
EWD/SEL/PNX NG16 .... 203 G7
Meadow Cl ALFN DE55 .... 161 L3
BSVR S44 .... 131 K2 ◆
BUX SK17 .... 81 H1
BWSH/BRSTN DE72 .... 259 K3
CHF/WBR SK23 .... 58 F2
CHNE S41 .... 92 A8
DERBYE DE21 .... 242 B6
DRON S18 .... 70 F6 ◆
EWD/SEL/PNX NG16 .... 203 K3 ◆
HATH/EY S32 .... 86 D7
ILK DE7 .... 215 G4
MPL/ROM SK6 .... 42 C2
RDERBYSW DE65 .... 255 G8 ◆
RDERBYSW DE65 .... 267 G8 ◆
Meadow Ct ALFN DE55 .... 176 C6 ◆
BPR/DUF DE56 .... 199 J6
BPR/DUF DE56 .... 214 D3 ◆
BWSH/BRSTN DE72 .... 259 C4
Meadow Crs CDON/KEG DE74 .. 271 L8
MOS S20 .... 72 E5 ◆
Meadowcroft HYDE SK14 .... 16 C6
Meadow Cft ASH NG17 .... 162 A2 ◆
Meadowcroft Gdns MOS S20 .. 73 H2
Meadowcroft Gld MOS S20 .. 73 H2 ◆
Meadowcroft Ri MOS S20 .... 73 H2 ◆
Meadow Dr ASH NG17 .... 162 F7 ◆
WRKS S80 .... 77 M8
Meadowfield CHF/WBR SK23 .. 58 F2
Meadowfield Cl GLSP SK13 .. 17 J3
Meadow Gdns MSHM DE12 .. 295 M7
Meadow Gate La MOS S20 .... 73 L1
Meadowgrass Cl
NORM/LIT DE23 .... 255 L4
Meadow Gv ALFN DE55 .... 161 K7
TOT/DORE S17 .... 69 H6
Meadow Grove Rd
TOT/DORE S17 .... 69 G6
Meadowhead SHEFS S8 .... 70 D3 ◆
Meadow Head Av SHEFS S8 .. 70 B3
Meadow Head Dr SHEFS S8 .. 70 C2
Meadow House Dr FUL S10 .. 54 A1
Meadowlands BSVR S44 ...... 113 M8
Meadow La ALFN DE55 .... 175 L6
ALFN DE55 .... 176 C3
ASHB DE6 .... 218 F3
BUTN/AL/TUT DE13 .... 274 D2
BUX SK17 .... 61 G7
BUX SK17 .... 102 D3
DERBY DE1 .... 5 H3
DERBYE DE21 .... 241 J5
DERBYSE DE24 .... 257 J1
LGEAT NG10 .... 261 K4
POY/DIS SK12 .... 43 G4
RDERBYSW DE65 .... 267 K6
SWAD DE11 .... 282 C5
Meadow Rd BUT DE14 .... 274 C6
CLCR S45 .... 144 D6
DERBY DE1 .... 5 G3
EWD/SEL/PNX NG16 .... 217M5
RIPLEY DE5 .... 201 G1
WRKS S80 .... 77 M8
Meadows Dr STV/CWN S43 .. 112 C2
Meadowside CHF/WBR SK23 .. 59 G2
NM/HAY SK22 .... 43 K4
Meadowside Cl ASHB DE6 .... 222 A3
RCH S42 .... 128 D6
Meadowside Dr BUT DE14 .... 274 B7 ◆
Meadows Rd NM/HAY SK22 .. 35 G8
The Meadows ALFN DE55 .... 187 H3
BUX SK17 .... 81 J1
HEANOR DE75 .... 216 B1 ◆
RCH S42 .... 109 J3
Meadow St
EWD/SEL/PNX NG16 .... 188 C5
ILK DE7 .... 230 C1
NM/HAY SK22 .... 43 M2 ◆
Meadow Ter ECC S11 .... 54 E2 ◆
Meadow V BPR/DUF DE56 .... 213 G7
Meadow Vw ALFN DE55 ...... 174 C5
ASHB DE6 .... 248 F2
BUTN/AL/TUT DE13 .... 264 F6
CHSW S40 .... 109 J3
MTLK DE4 .... 156 C3 ◆
RCH S42 .... 146 A2
STV/CWN S43 .... 95 J7
Meadow View Cl
DERBYE DE21 .... 227 L7 ◆◆
Meadow View Rd SHEFS S8 .. 70 C2
SWAD DE11 .... 282 C5
Meadow Wy MELB/CHEL DE73 .. 269 J1 ◆
SWAD DE11 .... 282 D4 ◆
The Meads SHEFS S8 .... 70 E2
Mead Wk STPNHL/WNHL DE15 .. 281 K4
Meadway MPL/ROM SK6 ...... 42 C2
STLY SK15 .... 16 B4
The Meadway TOT/DORE S17 .. 69 G3
Meakin St CHNE S41 .... 129 C2
Meal Hill Rd HOLM/MEL HD7 .. 8 C1
Meal St NM/HAY SK22 .... 43 M2
Mear Dr BWSH/BRSTN DE72 .. 258 E1
Mear Greaves La
STPNHL/WNHL DE15 .... 274 E6 ◆
Mease Cl MSHM DE12 .... 295M6
Mease La CRTAM B79 .... 292 E8
The Mease RDERBYSW DE65 .. 265 H1
Measham Rd ASHZ LE65 ...... 291 J8

MSHM DE12 .... 290 C7
MSHM DE12 .... 294 F4
MSHM DE12 .... 295 K2
Meath Av DERBYE DE21 .... 241 L6
Meden Av MSFDW NG19 .... 148 C3
Meden Bank ASH NG17 .... 162 E4
MSFDW NG19 .... 148 E5
Meden Cl MSFDW NG19 .... 148 E5
Meden Crs ASH NG17 .... 162 F6
Medina Cl DERBYSE DE24 .... 258 A5
Medlock Dr HAN/WDH S13 .... 57 K1
Medlock Rd HAN/WDH S13 .... 127 M2
HAN/WDH S13 .... 57 K1
Medway Cl BSTN/STPLFD NG9 .... 245 L5
Medway Dr DERBYW DE22 .... 226 D5
Meerbrook Cl DERBYE DE21 .... 241 K1
Meerbrook Pl ILK DE7 .... 229 M5
Meer Rd BSTN/STPLFD NG9 .... 245 K5
Meersbrook Av SHEFS S8 .... 55 J5
Meersbrook Park Rd SHEFS S8 .. 55 K4
Meersbrook Rd SHEFS S8 .... 55 J5
Meetinghouse Cft HAN/WDH S13 .... 57 M4
Meetinghouse La HAN/WDH S13 .. 57 M4
Megaloughton La DERBYE DE21 .... 241 M7
Megdale MTLK DE4 .... 156 D4
Melandra Castle Rd GLSP SK13 ... 25 G1
Melandra Crs GLSP SK13 .... 25 G2
Melandra Rd GLSP SK13 .... 17 G7
Melanie Cl GLSP SK13 .... 25 K2
Melbourn Cl BPR/DUF DE56 .... 213 H8
Melbourne Av DRON S18 .... 89 L1
STPNHL/WNHL DE15 .... 274 F8
Melbourne Cl BPR/DUF DE56 . 199 L8
DERBYW DE22 .... 240 A1
MCKLVR DE3 .... 239 J7
Melbourne Ct MSFD NG18 .... 165 L4
Melbourne La MELB/CHEL DE73 .... 277 M5
MELB/CHEL DE73 .... 279 L1
Melbourne Rd BSTN/STPLFD NG9 .... 231 H8
EWD/SEL/PNX NG16 .... 189 J3
MSFDW NG19 .... 149 M5
Melbreak Cl MCKLVR DE3 .... 255 H1
Melfort Cl DERBYSE DE24 .... 256 C8
Melling Cl CHSW S40 .... 128 C2
Melling Ct CHSW S40 .... 128 C2
Mellington Cl SHEFS S8 .... 55 M8
Mellor Dr UTXR ST14 .... 247 L1
Mellor La CHF/WBR SK23 .... 60 D4
Mellor Rd BUT DE14 .... 280 E3
NM/HAY SK22 .... 33 M7
Mellor's La BPR/DUF DE56 .... 213 M4
Mellors Rd MSFDW NG19 .... 164 A2
Mellor St DERBYSE DE24 .... 257 H4
Mellor Wy CHSW S40 .... 128 D3
Melrose Cl CHSW S40 .... 109 M7
DERBYSE DE24 .... 256 B8
Melrose Crs POY/DIS SK12 .... 42 A5
Meltham La CHNE S41 .... 110 E4
Melton Av MELB/CHEL DE73 .... 278 D2
NORM/LIT DE23 .... 255 M4
Melton Ct ALFN DE55 .... 187 M4
LGEAT NG10 .... 244 D5
Melton Gv HACK/IN S12 .... 57 K8
Melton Wy MSFD NG18 .... 164 B6
Melville Cl ASHB DE6 .... 196 C7
Melville Cr RDERBYSW DE65 .. 253 L7
Melville Crs STV/CWN S43 .... 111 J6
Melyncourt Rd HYDE SK14 .... 16 B7
Memorial Rd DERBYW DE22 .... 225 M8
Mendip Cl ASHZ LE65 .... 291 L5
LGEAT NG10 .... 260 D1
Mendip Ct DERBYE DE21 .... 227 H8
Mendip Crs CHSW S40 .... 109 L6
Menin Rd DERBYW DE22 .... 225 M8
Mentmore Cl ALFN DE55 .... 187 L3
Mercaston Cl CHSW S40 .... 109 K5
Mercaston La ASHB DE6 .... 210 E5
DERBYW DE22 .... 224 F3
Mercaston Rd DERBYE DE21 .... 241 J2
Mercer Crs ALFN DE55 .... 175 M7
Merchant Av DERBYE DE21 .... 242 A6
Merchant St DERBYW DE22 .... 4 A2
SBK/MW NG20 .... 133 K6
Mercia Cl RDERBYSW DE65 .... 264 A2
Mercia Dr RDERBYSW DE65 .... 266 E5
TOT/DORE S17 .... 69 H4
Mercian Ms DERBYE DE21 .... 242 A6
Mere Beck BWSH/BRSTN DE72 .. 259 C4
Meredith Cl BUT DE14 .... 274 A4
Meredith Ct BSTN/STPLFD NG9 .. 231 H8
Mereoak La SWAD DE11 .... 284 B3
Merepool Gdns CHF/WBR SK23 .. 59 K4
Mereside Gdns CHF/WBR SK23.. 59 K4
Meridian Cl ILK DE7 .... 217 H6
Merlin Dr UTXR ST14 .... 247 M4
Merlin Crs BUT DE14 .... 280 C2
Merlin Gn DERBYSE DE24 .... 256 A6
Merlin Wy ILK DE7 .... 230 D7
MCKLVR DE3 .... 254 E3
SWAD DE11 .... 283 J1
Merrial Cl BKWL DE45 .... 122 F6
Merrick Cl CHSW S40 .... 110 A5
Merridale Rd NORM/LIT DE23 .. 255 M3
Merrill Wy DERBYSE DE24 .... 256 F5
Merrybower Cl DERBYE DE24 .... 255 M7
Merrydale Rd STPNHL/WNHL DE15 .... 281 K2
Merryvale Dr MSFDW NG19 .... 164 A4
Mersey Bank Rd GLSP SK13 .... 17 J6
Merthyr Ct DERBYE DE21 .... 227 L8
Merton Ct BSTN/STPLFD NG9 .. 245 H1
Mervyn Rd STPNHL/WNHL DE15 .... 274 D7
Metcalfe Av ECK/KIL S21 .... 73 M4
Metcalfe Cl DERBYSE DE24 .... 257 L2
Metcalf Rd EWD/SEL/PNX NG16 .... 203 L7
Methley Cl SHEFP/MNR S2 .... 56 C4
Methuen Av MSFD NG18 .... 165 H4
Metro Av ALFN DE55 .... 161 K7
Mettesford MTLK DE4 .... 157 G5
Meverill Rd BUX SK17 .... 83 M5

Mevril Rd CHF/WBR SK23 .... 59 H5
Mews Pk MSFDW NG19 .... 149 M6
Meynell Cl STV/CWN S40 .... 109 M8
STPNHL/WNHL DE15 .... 281 L1
Meynell Ri DERBYW DE22 .... 225 M8
Meynell Ri ASHB DE6 .... 193 M7
Meynell Rd LGEAT NG10 .... 261 G5
Meynell St NORM/LIT DE23 .... 240 C8
SWAD DE11 .... 289 K1
Michael Cl RCH S42 .... 128 D5
Michael's La ASHB DE6 .... 205 M5
Michelle Cl DERBYSE DE24 .... 255 M7
Michigan Cl DERBYE DE21 .... 241 M5
Michlow Cl EDL/UDV S33 .... 64 D2
Michlow Dr EDL/UDV S33 .... 64 D2
Michlow La EDL/UDV S33 .... 64 C2
Micklebring St RIPLEY DE5 .... 200 F1
Micklecroft Gdns NORM/LIT DE23 .... 255 H3
Mickleden Edge STKB/PEN S36 ... 23 H1
Mickledon Cl LGEAT NG10 .... 260 E2
Mickleross Cl MCKLVR DE3 .... 239 G6
Mickleton Cl SWAD DE11 .... 289 L1
Mickley La ALFN DE55 .... 159 M5
TOT/DORE S17 .... 69 J6
Middlebeck Cl MELB/CHEL DE73.. 269 J1
Middlebrook Rd EWD/SEL/PNX NG16 .... 189 K6
Middlecliff Cl MOS S20 .... 73 H1
Middlecliff Ri MOS S20 .... 73 H1
Middlecliff Ri MOS S20 .... 73 H1
Middlecroft Rd STV/CWN S43... 111 M3
Middlefield Cl TOT/DORE S17 .. 68 F3
Middlefield Cft TOT/DORE S17 .. 68 F4
Middlegate Field Dr WRKS S80 ... 96 D5
Middle Hay Cl HACK/IN S12 .... 56 B5
Middle Hay Pl HACK/IN S12 .... 56 B5
Middle Hay Ri HACK/IN S12 .... 56 B5
Middle Hay Vw GLV S14 .... 56 B6
Middle Ox Cl MOS S20 .... 73 J4
Middle Ox Gdns MOS S20 .... 73 J4
Middle Rd RCH S42 .... 144 B1
Middle Shambles CHSW S40 .... 3 G4
Middle St BSVR S44 .... 131 M2
MTLK DE4 .... 139 M5
Middleton Av NORM/LIT DE23 .. 239 M8
RIPLEY DE5 .... 201 L5
Middleton Cl EWD/SEL/PNX NG16 .... 189 L3
Middleton Ct MSFD NG18 .... 165 L4
Middleton Dr NORM/LIT DE23 .... 239 M8
STV/CWN S43 .... 111 L5
Middleton La HATH/EY S32 .... 86 A7
Middleton Rd ILK DE7 .... 230 D5
MSFDW NG19 .... 149 M5
Middleton St EWD/SEL/PNX NG16 .... 217 M6
ILK DE7 .... 230 D1
Middlewood Rd MPL/ROM SK6 ... 42 A3
Midhill Rd SHEFP/MNR S2 .... 55 L3
Midhurst Cl BSTN/STPLFD NG9.. 245 M6
Midland Av BSTN/STPLFD NG9 .. 244 F5
Midland Pl DERBY DE1 .... 5 J6
Midland Rd ASH NG17 .... 163 L8
CHF/WBR SK23 .... 60 C4
DERBY DE1 .... 5 H7
EWD/SEL/PNX NG16 .... 203 J8
HEANOR DE75 .... 202 B8
SWAD DE11 .... 282 E5
Midland St LGEAT NG10 .... 261 H2
SHEF S1 .... 55 K1
Midland Ter BPR/DUF DE56 ... 185 J6
NM/HAY SK22 .... 43 M3
Midland Vw RCH S42 .... 145 J3
Midshires Wy BPR/DUF DE56 .. 184 D8
BPR/DUF DE56 .... 198 F4
ILK DE7 .... 228 E7
ILK DE7 .... 228 C4
Midway DERBYW DE22 .... 226 B8
Midway Rd DERBYW DE22 .... 282 F5
Midworth St MSFD NG18 .... 164 E4
Mikado Rd LGEAT NG10 .... 260 F5
Milbank Cl DERBYW DE22 .... 239 H4
Milburn Crt MOS S20 .... 73 K1
Milburn Gdns DERBYE DE21 .. 227 L7
Milburn Gv MOS S20 .... 73 K1
Milbury Cl DERBYE DE21 .... 227 J8
Mile Ash La DERBYW DE22 .... 240 C1
Milford BKWL DE45 .... 123 G4
Milford Av LGEAT NG10 .... 244 E7
Milford Crs MSFDW NG19 .... 164 A3
Milford Dr ILK DE7 .... 217 G7
Milford Rd BPR/DUF DE56 .... 213 H6
STV/CWN S43 .... 111 M5
Milford St DERBY DE1 .... 240 C3
Milken La CLCR S45 .... 143 L7
Milking La STV/CWN S43 .... 94 E7
Mill Acre Cl ILK DE7 .... 216 F8
Millash La WRKS S80 .... 96 E6
Mill Bank ASHZ LE65 .... 291 L8
Mill Bank Dr UTXR ST14 .... 218 D7
Millbeck Av WOL/BIL/BRX NG8 .... 231 M6
Mill Brow HYDE SK14 .... 24 D2
MPL/ROM SK6 .... 33 G2
Mill Brow Rd MPL/ROM SK6 .. 33 H2
Mill Cl ALFN DE55 .... 187 J3
ASH NG17 .... 162 D7
BPR/DUF DE56 .... 214 D2
BWSH/BRSTN DE72 .... 258 F1
RDERBYSW DE65 .... 255 G8
STPNHL/WNHL DE15 .... 275 H2
SWAD DE11 .... 282 E5
Mill Crs RDERBYSW DE65 .... 266 D5
RCH S42 .... 128 F7
WRKS S80 .... 96 D4
Mill Cft MCKLVR DE3 .... 239 G6
Millcross La DRON S18 .... 90 B7
Milldale Av BUX SK17 .... 99 J4
Milldale Cl CHSW S40 .... 109 M5
RIPLEY DE5 .... 201 G4
Milldale Ct ASHB DE6 .... 208 A2

BPR/DUF DE56 .... 199 L7
MSFD NG18 .... 165 K5
Milldale Rd DERBYE DE21 .... 242 C7
LGEAT NG10 .... 260 E4
TOT/DORE S17 .... 69 J5
Milldale Wk ASH NG17 .... 163 H6
Mildam La ASH NG17 .... 163 H6
Millennium Wy CHNE S41 .... 110 B1
Miller Av STV/CWN S43 .... 93 M6
Miller Cft HAN/WDH S13 .... 57 K4
Miller Rd SHEFS S8 .... 55 J3
MSFD NG18 .... 164 B6
Millersdale Av ILK DE7 .... 217 H5
MSFD NG18 .... 164 B6
Millersdale Cl BPR/DUF DE56 .. 199 L5
STPNHL/WNHL DE15 .... 274 E5
Millersdale Ct GLSP SK13 .... 26 C1
Millersdale Wy BUX SK17 .... 99 L4
Millers Gn MTLK DE4 .... 183 H4
Millers La ALFN DE55 .... 159 G8
BUT DE14 .... 273 M7
Millfield BWSH/BRSTN DE72 .. 259 L8
Millfield Cl ASHZ LE65 .... 291 K2
ILK DE7 .... 216 F7
Millfield Rd ILK DE7 .... 230 D3
Millfield St SWAD DE11 .... 283 K8
Millfield Vw WRKS S80 .... 77 M8
Mill Fleam RDERBYSW DE65 .. 265 H1
Mill Gdns WRKS S80 .... 77 M8
Mill Gn STV/CWN S43 .... 93 G8
Mill Hil BSVR S44 .... 130 E4
DERBYSE DE24 .... 257 M6
Mill Hill Gv HYDE SK14 .... 16 C8
Mill Hill La BWSH/BRSTN DE72 .. 260 B1
NORM/LIT DE23 .... 4 D8
STPNHL/WNHL DE15 .... 274 D6
Mill Hill Rd NORM/LIT DE23 .. 4 D8
Mill Holme ALFN DE55 .... 176 E6
Millhouse Ct BWSH/BRSTN DE72 .. 259 L3
Millhouses Ct ECC S11 .... 54 E6
Millhouses Gln ECC S11 .... 54 E6
Millhouses La ABRD S7 .... 54 F7
Mill La ASH NG17 .... 162 D8
ASHB DE6 .... 180 E4
ASHB DE6 .... 195 K3
ASHB DE6 .... 205 L8
ASHB DE6 .... 208 C1
ASHB DE6 .... 218 F2
ASHB DE6 .... 221 K5
ASHB DE6 .... 248 D2
ASHB DE6 .... 262 B1
BPR/DUF DE56 .... 199 L7
BSVR S44 .... 113 K7
BSVR S44 .... 113 J2
BSVR S44 .... 130 E8
BSVR S44 .... 146 F2
BUTN/AL/TUT DE13 .... 286 B2
BUX SK17 .... 150 F6
BUX SK17 .... 151 G5
CHSW S40 .... 2 B5
CLCR S45 .... 144 C5
CLCR S45 .... 144 E8
CLCR S45 .... 159 L1
CRTAM B79 .... 292 A6
DRON S18 .... 89 J5
DRON S18 .... 90 E1
ECK/KIL S21 .... 73 K8
EDL/UDV S33 .... 48 F7
EWD/SEL/PNX NG16 .... 176 F8
EWD/SEL/PNX NG16 .... 230 F1
HATH/EY S32 .... 66 C3
HATH/EY S32 .... 86 B5
LGEAT NG10 .... 244 E4
MCKLVR DE3 .... 239 G6
MTLK DE4 .... 172 D2
MTLK DE4 .... 172 D5
RCH S42 .... 128 F7
RDERBYSW DE65 .... 251 G3
RDERBYSW DE65 .... 252 F8
RDERBYSW DE65 .... 263 J1
RIPLEY DE5 .... 201 L2
TOT/DORE S17 .... 69 J5
UTXR ST14 .... 246 A7
WRKS S80 .... 96 D4
Mill Meadow Gdns MOS S20 .. 73 L1
Mill Meadow Wy RDERBYSW DE65 .... 253 L6
Mill Moor Cl MELB/CHEL DE73 .. 257 H8
Millmount Rd SHEFS S8 .... 55 J5
Millom Pl DERBYE DE21 .... 241 G5
Mill Rd BSTN/STPLFD NG9 .... 245 G2
ECK/KIL S21 .... 73 G2
EWD/SEL/PNX NG16 .... 203 L7
HEANOR DE75 .... 216 D2
MTLK DE4 .... 171 L4
Mills Cl BWSH/BRSTN DE72 .. 259 K3
Mills Cft MTLK DE4 .... 185 J1
Mills Cft ASHB DE6 .... 195 L8
Millstone Cl DRON S18 .... 70 A8
Millstone La ALFN DE55 .... 174 F8
Mill Stream Cl CHSW S40 .... 127 M1
Mill St ASH NG17 .... 163 H8
ASHZ LE65 .... 291 L8
BKWL DE45 .... 123 G4
BPR/DUF DE56 .... 199 J6
CHNE S41 .... 3 J4
DERBY DE1 .... 4 B2
DRON S18 .... 90 A7
GLSP SK13 .... 26 A1
HATH/EY S32 .... 86 D7
ILK DE7 .... 230 C1
MSFD NG18 .... 165 G4
MSHM DE12 .... 288 A7
STV/CWN S43 .... 95 H6
UTXR ST14 .... 218 D7
Millthorpe La DRON S18 .... 89 J4
Milltown GLSP SK13 .... 26 A1
Mill Wk BSVR S44 .... 113 K7
Millway MSFDW NG19 .... 165 G1
Millway La ASHB DE6 .... 166 B7
Mill Yd ALFN DE55 .... 187 M2
Milnbank Av BWSH/BRSTN DE72 .. 259 K3
RIPLEY DE5 .... 201 L5
Milner Rd LGEAT NG10 .... 261 G2
Milner St ASH NG17 .... 163 K4

Milnhay Rd EWD/SEL/PNX NG16 .... 202 F8
Milton Av ALFN DE55 .... 159 M6
ALFN DE55 .... 175 M6
ILK DE7 .... 217 H6
SWAD DE11 .... 282 F4
Milton Cl ASH NG17 .... 163 L6
MPL/ROM SK6 .... 32 C6
MSHM DE12 .... 295 M7
Milton Crs CHSW S40 .... 128 D2
Milton La CHF/WBR SK23 .... 59 L4
Milton Pl STV/CWN S43 .... 112 C1
Milton Rd ABRD S7 .... 55 H3
ILK DE7 .... 217 H6
MCKLVR DE3 .... 238 F7
RDERBYSW DE65 .... 267 G8
Milton St BUT DE14 .... 273 M8
DERBYW DE22 .... 240 A6
ILK DE7 .... 217 J6
LGEAT NG10 .... 261 C3
MSFD NG18 .... 164 D3
Milverton Dr UTXR ST14 .... 247 J1
Milward Rd HEANOR DE75 .... 201 M8
Mimosa Crs NORM/LIT DE23 .. 256 B5
Minster Gdns EWD/SEL/PNX NG16 .... 217 L1
Minster Rd DERBYE DE21 .... 227 H8
Minster Wy ALFN DE55 .... 187 H3
Mint Gv LGEAT NG10 .... 261 H4
Minton Cl BSTN/STPLFD NG9 .. 261 L1
Minton Pastures MSFDW NG19 .. 165 K1
Minton Rd CDON/KEG DE74 .. 271 J6
Mires La BKWL DE45 .... 104 C6
BUX SK17 .... 84 D7
The Mires MTLK DE4 .... 139 K8
Miriam Av RCH S42 .... 127 K2
Miry La RDERBYSW DE65 .... 251 M6
Misk Vw EWD/SEL/PNX NG16 .. 203 J3
Misterton Cl DERBYW DE22 .. 226 B8
Mitchell Av EWD/SEL/PNX NG16 .... 202 D6
Mitchell Rd SHEFS S8 .... 55 M3
Mitchell St LGEAT NG10 .... 261 H3
STV/CWN S43 .... 95 J6
Mitchell Ter ILK DE7 .... 230 D5
Mitchell Wy STV/CWN S43 .. 92 B7
Mitre Dr RDERBYSW DE65 .. 266 F5
Middletown Mdw STV/CWN S43 .. 94 D4
Moat Bank STPNHL/WNHL DE15 .... 275 G8
Moat St SWAD DE11 .... 282 B2
The Moat CDON/KEG DE74 .. 271 L6
Moffatt Rd SHEFP/MNR S2 .... 55 L3
Moira Cl DERBYE DE21 .... 241 K3
Moira Dr ASHZ LE65 .... 291 L4
MSHM DE12 .... 289 L7
SWAD DE11 .... 290 B2
Moira St MELB/CHEL DE73 .. 278 D3
Moisty La HATH/EY S32 .... 85 L7
UTXR ST14 .... 248 E7
Molineux Av STV/CWN S43 .. 112 A1
Molineux St NORM/LIT DE23 .. 240 B8
Molloy Pl SHEFS S8 .... 55 K5
Molloy St SHEFS S8 .... 55 K4
Monarch Cl BUTN/AL/TUT DE13 .... 274 B2
Monarch Dr DERBYE DE21 .... 228 A7
Monarch Wy HEANOR DE75 .. 202 A8
Mona Rd BUTN/AL/TUT DE13 .. 273 L5
Moncrieff Crs DERBYE DE21 .. 241 K2
Moncrieffe Rd ABRD S7 .... 55 H4
Mondello Dr DERBYSE DE24 .. 257 M4
Moneyhill Wy DERBYSE DE24 .. 291 L2
Monk Rd ALFN DE55 .... 175 L8
Monks Cl DERBYSE DE24 .... 255 M8
ILK DE7 .... 230 D2
Monksdale Cl BUX SK17 .... 83 L6
Monksdale La BUX SK17 .... 83 J8
Monks' Rd GLSP SK13 .... 25 H4
Monk St BUTN/AL/TUT DE13 .. 263 M4
DERBYW DE22 .... 4 C5
Monks Wy WRKN S81 .... 77 J3
Monkton Cl ILK DE7 .... 217 G7
Monkwood Rd CHNE S41 .... 110 A2
Monmouth Cl WOL/BIL/BRX NG8 .... 231 L6
Monmouth St DERBYE DE21 .... 5 L1
Monnies End STV/CWN S43 .. 94 F5
Monsal Av BUX SK17 .... 100 A3
Monsal Crs ALFN DE55 .... 161 J4
STV/CWN S43 .... 111 L4
Monsaldale Cl LGEAT NG10 .. 260 C3
STPNHL/WNHL DE15 .... 274 E6
Monsal Dr ALFN DE55 .... 176 C5
DERBYE DE21 .... 242 C7
Monsal Gv BUX SK17 .... 100 A3
Monsall Av BUX SK17 .... 100 A3
Monsal Trail BKWL DE45 .... 104 D3
BKWL DE45 .... 123 G2
BUX SK17 .... 101 M4
Monsdale La ASHB DE6 .... 168 B8
Monsom La RDERBYSW DE65 .. 267 G7
Montague St ECC S11 .... 55 H1
MSFD NG18 .... 165 G4
Monteith Pl CDON/KEG DE74 .. 271 L6
Montford Ms CDON/KEG DE74 .. 271 L6
Montgomery Av ABRD S7 .... 55 H3
Montgomery Cl BSTN/STPLFD NG9 .... 245 M8
RDERBYSW DE65 .... 253 H8
Montgomery Dr ABRD S7 .... 55 H3
Montgomery Wy ABRD S7 .... 55 H3
Montpelier DERBYW DE22 .... 226 A3
Montpelier Cl BUT DE14 .... 280 D3
Montpelier Pl BUX SK17 .... 100 A1
Montpelier Rd BPR/DUF DE56 .. 185 J7
Montrose Cl DERBYSE DE24 .. 256 F1
Montrose Ct BSTN/STPLFD NG9 .... 245 H1
Montrose Pl DRON S18 .... 70 A8
Montrose Rd ECC S11 .... 54 F5
Montrose Sq MSFDW NG19 .... 149 L4
Monument Hl EWD/SEL/PNX NG16 .... 188 C7
Monument La EWD/SEL/PNX NG16 .... 188 B8

Monyash Cl DERBYE DE21 .... 241 K2
ILK DE7 .... 217 H7
STV/CWN S43 .... 111 M3
Monyash Ms GLSP SK13 .... 25 G1
Monyash Rd BKWL DE45 .... 122 C8
Monyash Wy BPR/DUF DE56 .. 199 L5
Moonpenny Wy DRON S18 .... 90 D1
Moorbridge La BSTN/STPLFD NG9 .... 244 F1
Moorbrook La EDL/UDV S33 .. 64 C3
Moor Crs MOS S20 .... 72 F3
Moorcroft Cl FUL S10 .... 53 L2
Moorcroft Dr FUL S10 .... 53 L3
Moorcroft Pl FUL S10 .... 53 L3
Moorcroft Rd FUL S10 .... 53 L3
Moor Dr DERBYSE DE24 .... 257 K5
Moor Cl RCH S42 .... 146 A1
Mooredge Rd MTLK DE4 .... 157 G4
Mooredge Rd MTLK DE4 .... 173 K7
Moor End DERBYE DE21 .... 242 B5
Moor End MTLK DE4 .... 124 F6
Moor End MPL/ROM SK6 .... 33 K5
Moores Av LGEAT NG10 .... 244 F3
Moores Cl BUTN/AL/TUT DE13 .. 273 L4
Moore St NORM/LIT DE23 .... 4 E8
Moor Farm Av MOS S20 .... 72 F2
Moor Farm Garth MOS S20 .. 72 F2
Moor Farm Inn La BSTN/STPLFD NG9 .... 231 K8
Moor Farm Ri MOS S20 .... 72 F2
Moor Farm Rd (East) ASHB DE6 .. 208 B3
Moor Farm Rd (West) ASHB DE6 .... 208 B2
Moorfield MTLK DE4 .... 156 F3
Moorfield Av BSVR S44 .... 131 L1
STLY SK15 .... 16 A3
Moorfield Ct BSTN/STPLFD NG9 .... 245 H1
Moorfield Crs LGEAT NG10 .. 244 E5
Moorfield La SBK/MW NG20 .. 115 J6
Moorfield Rd BPR/DUF DE56 .. 213 M3
Moorfields Av EWD/SEL/PNX NG16 .... 203 J7
Moorfields Cl CDLE ST10 .... 190 B6
Moorfield Sq BSVR S44 .... 131 L1
Moorfield St HYDE SK14 .... 17 G4
Moorfield Ter HYDE SK14 .... 17 G5
Moorgate DERBYW DE22 .... 239 H4
Moorgate Crs DRON S18 .... 90 D2
Moorgreen EWD/SEL/PNX NG16 .... 203 M7
Moor Gv UTXR ST14 .... 247 K2
Moorhaigh La MSFDW NG19 .. 148 D7
Moorhall BKWL DE45 .... 122 F5
Moorhay Cl CHSW S40 .... 109 L3
Moorhead Av DERBYSE DE24 .. 257 J5
The Moorings POY/DIS SK12 .. 43 H4
Moorland Av BSTN/STPLFD NG9 .... 245 G4
Moorland Cl ASH NG17 .... 163 K4
Moorland Dr BSVR S44 .... 130 C8
Moorland Rd HATH/EY S32 .. 66 C3
MCKLVR DE3 .... 239 G7
Moorlands Cl LGEAT NG10 .. 244 E8
Moorlands Dr ASHB DE6 .... 206 F3
Moorlands La HATH/EY S32 .. 86 F5
STLY SK15 .... 16 A3
Moorland Vw DRON S18 .... 91 K1
HACK/IN S12 .... 56 D8
Moorland View Rd CHSW S40 .. 127 M1
Moor La ASHB DE6 .... 208 B4
ASHB DE6 .... 224 C8
BKWL DE45 .... 138 E5
BPR/DUF DE56 .... 182 D7
BPR/DUF DE56 .... 196 D1
BSTN/STPLFD NG9 .... 231 L8
BSVR S44 .... 129 M2
BSVR S44 .... 131 L1
BSVR S44 .... 132 C2
BUX SK17 .... 119 M1
BUX SK17 .... 120 B6
BWSH/BRSTN DE72 .... 242 F5
BWSH/BRSTN DE72 .... 270 E2
DERBYE DE21 .... 227 G1
DERBYSE DE24 .... 256 F4
DERBYSE DE24 .... 268 E1
MELB/CHEL DE73 .... 268 E3
MELB/CHEL DE73 .... 279 M7
MELB/CHEL DE73 .... 279 L8
MSFD NG18 .... 164 C4
MTLK DE4 .... 140 F6
MTLK DE4 .... 154 B5
MTLK DE4 .... 155 L8
MTLK DE4 .... 169 H1
Moorlawn Av RCH S42 .... 127 H3
Moorpark Av CHSW S40 .... 127 M2
Moorpool Crs BPR/DUF DE56 .. 213 M3
Moor Rd BKWL DE45 .... 104 C5
CLCR S45 .... 143 J6
EWD/SEL/PNX NG16 .... 203 H2
ILK DE7 .... 227 J4
Moorsholm Dr WOL/BIL/BRX NG8 .... 231 M6
Moorside FUL S10 .... 53 K2
Moorside Cl GLSP SK13 .... 25 L3
MOS S20 .... 72 F2
MTLK DE4 .... 171 K5
Moorside Crs DERBYSE DE24 .. 256 C6
Moorside La BPR/DUF DE56 .. 213 M2
Moor St BUT DE14 .... 273 M8
DERBYE DE21 .... 242 B5
MSFD NG18 .... 164 D4
The Moor EWD/SEL/PNX NG16 .. 203 G2
MTLK DE4 .... 170 F5
Moorthorpe Gdns MOS S20 .. 57 K8
Moorthorpe Gn HACK/IN S12 .. 57 J8
Moorthorpe Wy MOS S20 .... 57 K8
Moortop Rd DRON S18 .... 91 L1
Moor Va MOS S20 .... 57 J8
Moor Valley Cl HACK/IN S12 .. 72 E1
Moorview Cl RCH S42 .... 128 D7
STV/CWN S43 .... 111 G3
Moor View Dr SHEFS S8 .... 55 H8
Moor View Rd SHEFS S8 .... 55 H8

STV/CWN S43	93	K8
Moor View Ter ECC S11	54	B5 🔲
Moorway ILK DE7	227	H6
Moorway Cft		
NORM/LIT DE23	255	L3 🔲
Moorway La NORM/LIT DE23	255	K5 🔲
Moorwinstow Cft		
TOT/DORE S17	69	H3 🔲
Moorwood La TOT/DORE S17	68	E8
TOT/DORE S17	88	F1
Moorwoodmoor La ALFN DE55	174	A3
Moray PI DRON S18	70	A3
Moray Sq MSFDW NG19	164	A5
Mordaunt Rd SHEFP/MNR S2	56	C4
Morden Rd		
EWD/SEL/PNX NG16	217	M2
Morefern Dr DERBYE DE21	227	J8
Morland CI GLV S14	56	C7
Morland Dr GLV S14	56	C7
Morland PI GLV S14	56	C7
Morland Rd GLV S14	56	B7
NM/HAY SK22	34	D8
Morledge DERBY DE1	4	F4
Moreston St NORM/LIT DE23	5	J6
Morley Av CHSW S40	109	M6
Morley CI BPR/DUF DE56	200	B4
DRON S18	89	M1
MSFD NG18	165	L5
Morley Dr ILK DE7	217	L2
Morleyfields CI RIPLEY DE5	201	J1
Morley Gdns DERBYE DE21	241	L2
Morley La ILK DE7	227	J2
ILK DE7	228	E4
Morley Rd DERBYE DE21	241	K3
Morley's HI		
BUTN/AL/TUT DE13	273	L3 🔲
Morley St ASH NG17	162	F4
ASH NG17	163	J7
DERBYE DE22	239	M4
GLSP SK13	26	A2
Morlich Dr DERBYSE DE24	256	A6
Morningside CI		
DERBYE DE24	257	G6 🔲
Mornington Crs		
DERBYE DE22	239	L4 🔲
Mornington Ri MTLK DE4	156	F5
Mornington Rd RCH S42	146	A3
Morpeth Gdns DERBYE DE21	227	G8 🔲
Morrell Wood Dr		
BPR/DUF DE56	200	B5 🔲
Morris Av BSTN/STPLFD NG9	261	L1 🔲
CHNE S41	110	B5 🔲
Mortimer St DERBYSE DE24	256	E3
Morton CI CLCR S45	144	E6
Morton La ECK/KIL S21	91	M1
Morton Rd ALFN DE55	159	M4
ALFN DE55	160	F3
Morton St MSFDW NG19	164	B1
Morven Av ASH NG17	163	H8
BSVR S44	131	L1 🔲
MSFDW NG19	149	L8
Morven St WRKS S80	115	J2
Mosborough Hall Dr MOS S20	73	H5
Mosborough Moor MOS S20	72	E2
Mosborough Rd ASH NG17	177	K1
Moscar Cross Rd ST/HB/BR S6	41	L5
Mosedale CI DERBYSE DE24	257	J2 🔲
Moseley St RIPLEY DE5	187	G8
Moses La ILK DE7	228	B3
Moses Vw WRKN S81	77	H3
Mosgrove Av WRKN S81	77	M3
Mosley Dr UTXT S14	247	K1
Mosley St BUX SK17	99	L4
Mosley St BUT DE14	273	M8
Mossbank CI GLSP SK13	17	H6
Mossdale Av MOS S20	73	G3
Mossdale Rd MSFD NG18	165	H2
Moss Dr BSTN/STPLFD NG9	245	L3
ECK/KIL S21	74	C1
Moss Edge Rd HOLM/MEL HD7	8	F2
Moss La ASHB DE6	196	C7
HYDE SK14	24	C2
RIPLEY DE5	187	C7
Moss Rd ILK DE7	230	B3
TOT/DORE S17	68	E6
Moss St DERBYW DE22	4	A7
HYDE SK14	17	C5
Moss Vw MOS S20	72	E4
Moss View Rd CHF/WBR SK23	60	F4
Moss Wy MOS S20	73	G3
Mostyn Av NORM/LIT DE23	256	A1
Motehall Dr SHEFP/MNR S2	56	D1
Motehall PI SHEFP/MNR S2	56	E1
Motehall Rd SHEFP/MNR S2	56	E1
Motehall Wy SHEFP/MNR S2	56	D1 🔲
Mottistone CI DERBYE DE24	258	A5 🔲
Mottram Moor HYDE SK14	16	F6
Mottram Rd BSTN/STPLFD NG9	245	M4
HYDE SK14	24	D2
Mouldridge La MTLK DE4	153	K7
Moult Av DERBYE DE21	242	B6
Moulton CI ALFN DE55	187	J2
BPR/DUF DE56	200	A5 🔲
Mound Rd CHSW S40	3	C8
Mountbatten CI		
BUTN/AL/TUT DE13	274	A2 🔲
DERBYSE DE24	257	H6 🔲
Mountbatten Wy		
BSTN/STPLFD NG9	245	L8
Mount Carmel St NORM/LIT DE23	4	D8
Mountcastle St CHNE S41	110	C2
Mount Crs DERBYSE DE24	176	D7
Mount Dr MPL/ROM SK6	32	C5
Mountfield Av LGEAT NG10	244	D6
Mountfield Wy		
DERBYSE DE24	258	A6 🔲
Mountford Av MTLK DE4	183	H5
Mountford CI DERBYE DE21	227	L8 🔲
Mountford Cft TOT/DORE S17	69	H5 🔲
Mount Milner MSFD NG18	165	G4
Mount Pleasant ALFN DE55	188	A5
ASH NG17	163	J6
BKWL DE45	122	C3
CDON/KEG DE74	271	H7 🔲
ILK DE7	217	H6
MSFD NG18	164	D3 🔲

RIPLEY DE5	187	G8
Mount Pleasant Dr		
BPR/DUF DE56	199	H5
Mount Pleasant La		
MSHM DE12	294	D2
Mount Pleasant Rd		
HATH/EY S32	86	F3
RDERBYSW DE65	267	G8
SHEFP/MNR S2	55	J2 🔲
SWAD DE11	289	H3
Mount Rd STPNHL/WNHL DE15	275	K7
SWAD DE11	283	K6
SWAD DE11	289	G2
Mount St BSTN/STPLFD NG9	245	H3
BWSH/BRSTN DE72	260	C3
DERBY DE1	4	E7
ECC S11	55	J2
GLSP SK13	25	M2
HEANOR DE75	216	B1 🔲
MSFDW NG19	164	D2
STPNHL/WNHL DE15	274	D7
Mount View Av SHEFS S8	55	K7 🔲
Mount View Gdns SHEFS S8	55	K7 🔲
Mount View Rd SHEFS S8	55	K8
Mouselow CI GLSP SK13	17	J7
Mowbray Gdns		
DERBYSE DE24	256	F2 🔲
Mowbray St DERBYSE DE24	256	F2
Mowlands CI ASH NG17	163	L8
Moy Av DERBYSE DE24	256	C8
Moyne Gdns MELB/CHEL DE73	269	K2
Mudhurst La POY/DIS SK12	58	B1
Muirfield CI CHNE S41	110	E4
Muirfield Dr MCKLVR DE3	255	J1
Mulberries Ct DERBYW DE22	226	B6 🔲
Mulberry CI BPR/DUF DE56	199	L7 🔲
RCH S42	128	E6
Mulberry Ms RIPLEY DE5	200	F4 🔲
Mulberry Rd ECK/KIL S21	72	E8
Mulberry Wy ECK/KIL S21	73	L5 🔲
RDERBYSW DE65	253	H8
Mull Ct DERBYSE DE24	256	A7 🔲
Mullion PI DERBYSE DE24	257	L5
Mumford Dr ASHB DE6	208	A2
Mundella PI SHEFS S8	55	K7
Mundy CI DERBY DE1	4	B1
Mundy's Dr HEANOR DE75	216	C2
Mundy St DERBY DE1	4	B1
HEANOR DE75	216	B1
ILK DE7	217	J8 🔲
Munro CI ECK/KIL S21	74	A4
Murrayfield Dr MOS S20	73	H4 🔲
Murray Rd ECC S11	54	E4
ECK/KIL S21	74	B3 🔲
MCKLVR DE3	239	J6
Murray St DERBYSE DE24	257	J2 🔲
MSFD NG18	164	E5
Musard PI STV/CWN S43	112	A1
Muse La ASHB DE6	250	D1
Mushroom La SWAD DE11	290	A2
Muskham Av ILK DE7	217	J7
Muskoka Av ECC S11	54	B5
Musson Dr ECC S11	54	B4
Musson Dr ASHZ LE65	291	K6
Musters St SBK/MW NG20	133	K6
Muswell Rd DERBYW DE22	239	H5
Mycock La BUX SK17	120	C5
Myers CI DERBYE DE24	256	C6
Mylnhurst Rd ECC S11	54	D4
Mylor Rd ECC S11	54	D4
Myrtle Av BSTN/STPLFD NG9	245	H4
LGEAT NG10	260	F4
Myrtle CI SBK/MW NG20	133	H4
Myrtle Gv STV/CWN S43	111	K1
Myrtle Rd SHEFP/MNR S2	55	L2
SHEFP/MNR S2	55	L4
Myrtle Springs HACK/IN S12	56	E5
Mytham Br EDL/UDV S33	65	L1

N

Nailers Wy BPR/DUF DE56	199	M5
Nailor La MTLK DE4	156	A7
Nairn Av DERBYE DE21	241	G3
Nairn CI DERBYSE DE24	256	A7
Nairn Dr DRON S18	90	A1 🔲
Namur Ct DERBYW DE22	239	M7
Nan Gell's HI MTLK DE4	171	K7
Nankirk La BUTN/AL/TUT DE13	272	D4
Napier CI MCKLVR DE3	239	H6 🔲
Napier St BUT DE14	280	F1
DERBYW DE22	239	M5 🔲
ECC S11	55	H1
Narlow La ASHB DE6	179	J8
Narrow La MELB/CHEL DE73	277	J6
MSHM DE12	295	H2
UTXR S14	218	A4
Narrowleys La CLCR S45	143	J7
Naseby Dr LGEAT NG10	261	G5
Naseby Rd BPR/DUF DE56	200	A6
Nathan Ct MOS S20	73	J1
Nathaniel Rd LGEAT NG10	261	H3
Navan Rd SHEFP/MNR S2	56	D3
Navigation St MSHM DE12	295	M5
Neal Ct EWD/SEL/PNX NG16	202	D7 🔲
Neale Bank STV/CWN S43	111	G3
Neale St LGEAT NG10	261	H3
STV/CWN S43	95	J6
Near Meadow LGEAT NG10	261	H5
Nearwell CI CHF/WBR SK23	60	C1
Nearwood Dr DERBYE DE21	227	H7 🔲
Needham La RIPLEY DE5	201	L3
Needham Wy ECC S11	54	F5
Need Wood Av		
BSTN/STPLFD NG9	231	G8 🔲
Needwood CI BUT DE14	273	L6 🔲
Neighwood CI		
BSTN/STPLFD NG9	245	H8
Neill Rd ECC S11	54	F2
Neilson St DERBYSE DE24	257	J3
Nelper Crs ILK DE7	230	D5
Nelson St MCKLVR DE3	239	H7
CHNE S41	110	D4
DERBY DE1	5	J7 🔲
ILK DE7	217	J6
LGEAT NG10	261	G3
STPNHL/WNHL DE15	274	F7

SWAD DE11	282	E5
Nene CI BUTN/AL/TUT DE13	273	M1 🔲
Nene Wy RDERBYSW DE65	265	G2
Nesbit CI BSVR S44	131	L2
Nesfield CI CHNE S41	110	A2
DERBYSE DE24	257	M3
Nesfield St ILK DE7	230	B1
Ness Wk DERBYW DE22	226	B7
Nether Av ECK/KIL S21	73	M4
Nether Blindlow La BUX SK17	119	K5
Nether CI ALFN DE55	187	H3
BPR/DUF DE56	213	G5
EWD/SEL/PNX NG16	203	J6 🔲
RCH S42	128	D8
Netherclose St		
NORM/LIT DE23	256	D1 🔲
Nethercroft Dr ASHZ LE65	291	M8 🔲
Nethercroft La CLCR S45	145	H7 🔲
Nether Croft Rd STV/CWN S43	111	H3
Netherdene Rd DRON S18	90	D1
Nether Edge Rd ABRD S7	55	H5
Netherfield CI STV/CWN S43	93	K8
Netherfield Rd CHF/WBR SK23	61	G4
CHSW S40	127	K2
LGEAT NG10	244	E5
LGEAT NG10	260	E6
Netherfields Crs DRON S18	90	D2
Nether Gdns MTLK DE4	183	J2
Nethergreen Av ECK/KIL S21	74	A3
Nethergreen Ct ECK/KIL S21	74	A3 🔲
Nethergreen Gdns		
ECK/KIL S21	74	A3 🔲
Nethergreen Rd ECC S11	54	B2
Nether La ASHB DE6	196	D5
BPR/DUF DE56	196	E2
BPR/DUF DE56	212	D2
BPR/DUF DE56	214	A4
MTLK DE4	181	J3
Netherleigh Rd CHSW S40	109	L7
Nethermoor Av ECK/KIL S21	74	A3 🔲
Nethermoor Ct ECK/KIL S21	74	A3 🔲
Nethermoor Dr ECK/KIL S21	74	A3
Nethermoor La ECK/KIL S21	74	A3
Nethermoor Rd RCH S42	128	C8
RCH S42	144	F3
Netherseal Rd CRTAM B79	293	J8
MSHM DE12	294	C6
Netherside Dr		
MELB/CHEL DE73	257	K8
Nether Springs Rd BSVR S44	113	J7 🔲
Netherthorpe CI STV/CWN S43	93	K8
Netherthorpe La ECK/KIL S21	73	M4
Netherthorpe Rd STV/CWN S43	93	J8
Nether Thorpe Rd WRKS S80	76	D5
Nether Wy MTLK DE4	140	F7
Netherwood Ct		
DERBYW DE22	225	M7 🔲
Nettlefold Crs		
MELB/CHEL DE73	278	E1
Nettleham Rd SHEFS S8	55	J7
Nettleton La BUX SK17	100	A7
Neville CI BUTN/AL/TUT DE13	264	E7
Nevinson Av NORM/LIT DE23	256	A4
Nevinson Dr NORM/LIT DE23	256	A3
Nevis CI CHSW S40	2	A1
DERBYSE DE24	256	A8
Newall St BSTN/STPLFD NG9	245	M8
Newark CI MSFD NG18	165	J8
Newark Dr MSFD NG18	165	J8
Newark Rd DERBYE DE21	227	G8
Newark Wy MSFD NG18	165	J8
New Bank St GLSP SK13	17	K5
New Barlborough CI		
STV/CWN S43	95	G5 🔲
Newbarn St SBK/MW NG20	133	G8 🔲
New Bath Rd MTLK DE4	171	K2
New Beetwell St CHSW S40	3	G4
Newbery Av LGEAT NG10	261	J4
Newbold Av		
BWSH/BRSTN DE72	258	F1
CHNE S41	110	B4
Newbold Back La CHSW S40	110	A5
Newbold CI CHNE S41	2	D1
Newbold Dr CDON/KEG DE74	271	L5 🔲
CHSW S40	110	B4
Newbold Rd CHNE S41	2	D1
CHNE S41	109	L3
RCH S42	109	K2
Newborough Rd		
DERBYSE DE24	257	M4 🔲
Newbound La ASH NG17	147	K7
BSVR S44	147	J7
Newboundmill La		
MSFDW NG19	148	D6
New Breck Rd BPR/DUF DE56	199	K7
Newbridge CI ILK DE7	229	G2
Newbridge Ct CHNE S41	110	D1 🔲
Newbridge Crs DERBYSE DE24	257	H6
Newbridge Dr STV/CWN S43	111	G2
Newbridge La CHNE S41	110	E1
STV/CWN S43	110	F2
Newbridge St BPR/DUF DE56	185	J7
Newbury Dr		
BUTN/AL/TUT DE13	273	M1 🔲
Newbury St DERBYSE DE24	257	H2 🔲
Newby Rd CHNE S41	109	M2
Newcastle St ASH NG17	162	C7
MSFD NG18	164	D3 🔲
New Church St EDL/UDV S33	64	D3 🔲
New Cross Dr HAN/WDH S13	57	K4
New Cross St ASH NG17	163	K6
New Cross Wy HAN/WDH S13	57	K4
New Derby Rd		
EWD/SEL/PNX NG16	203	G8
Newdigate St ILK DE7	228	E7
ILK DE7	230	D4 🔲
NORM/LIT DE23	256	C2
New Eaton Rd		
BSTN/STPLFD NG9	245	G5
Newell Wy MTLK DE4	140	F7
New England Wy MSFDW NG19	148	E6
New Fall St ASH NG17	162	C7 🔲
Newfield Crs TOT/DORE S17	68	F3 🔲
Newfield Cft TOT/DORE S17	68	F2 🔲
Newfield Farm CI		
SHEFP/MNR S2	56	B5 🔲

Newfield Green Rd		
SHEFP/MNR S2	56	A4
Newfield La TOT/DORE S17	68	F3
Newfield Rd CHF/WBR SK23	59	H3
New Ga HOLM/MEL HD7	9	M1
Newgate Ct		
MELB/CHEL DE73	257	L8 🔲
Newgatefield La		
BUTN/AL/TUT DE13	273	C1
Newgate La MSFD NG18	165	G3
New Hall Rd CHSW S40	2	A5
CHSW S40	109	M8
Newhall Rd SWAD DE11	282	F5
Newham Av MSFDW NG19	149	L7
Newham CI HEANOR DE75	216	D1
Newhaven Av MSFDW NG19	149	L7
Newhaven CI CHSW S40	127	L1 🔲
Newhaven Rd DERBYE DE21	241	L4
New High St BUX SK17	100	A2 🔲
New Horwich Rd CHF/WBR SK23	59	H3
New Inn La DERBYE DE21	226	F3
New Lawn Rd ILK DE7	230	B2
New Linden St		
SBK/MW NG20	133	K6 🔲
Newlyn Dr ALFN DE55	161	M8
NORM/LIT DE23	256	C2 🔲
Newlyn PI SHEFS S8	55	J7
Newlyn Rd SHEFS S8	55	J7
Newman Dr BUT DE14	280	E2
Newmanleys Rd		
EWD/SEL/PNX NG16	217	H2
Newmanleys Rd (South)		
EWD/SEL/PNX NG16	217	H1
Newmarket Ct DERBYSE DE24	257	H1
Newmarket Dr DERBYSE DE24	257	H2
Newmarket La CLCR S45	144	B7
New Market St BUX SK17	99	L4
Newmarket St MSFD NG18	165	H4
Newmanleys Wy		
BSTN/STPLFD NG9	245	J8
New Mills Rd GLSP SK13	24	F6
NM/HAY SK22	34	E8
New Mount CI		
NORM/LIT DE23	256	A5 🔲
Newport Ct BUT DE14	274	A3
Newport Crs MSFDW NG19	148	A5
Newquay PI DERBYSE DE24	257	M5 🔲
New Queen St CHNE S41	2	F1
New Rd ASHB DE6	224	A1
BKWL DE45	138	D7
BPR/DUF DE56	185	L6
BPR/DUF DE56	197	J6
BPR/DUF DE56	199	J7
BPR/DUF DE56	200	A3
BSTN/STPLFD NG9	245	G1
CHF/WBR SK23	59	H4
DERBYW DE22	240	D1
DRON S18	89	K5
DRON S18	91	K1
EDL/UDV S33	50	E5
EDL/UDV S33	64	C6
EDL/UDV S33	64	E4
EWD/SEL/PNX NG16	188	C7
GLSP SK13	17	J3
HATH/EY S32	86	C5
MSHM DE12	287	M7
MTLK DE4	170	E5
MTLK DE4	171	J7
MTLK DE4	185	J2
RCH S42	127	G4
RCH S42	128	B7
RDERBYSW DE65	253	H8
RIPLEY DE5	188	A8
STV/CWN S43	94	E3
SWAD DE11	282	B4
SWAD DE11	283	H8
UTXR S14	247	K1
New Rd (Baslow Rd)		
BKWL DE45	122	C2 🔲
Newsham Rd SHEFS S8	55	J5
Newshaw La GLSP SK13	17	J7
New Station Rd BSVR S44	131	J1
Newstead Av DERBYE DE21	241	J4 🔲
HACK/IN S12	57	H8
Newstead Dr HACK/IN S12	57	H8
EWD/SEL/PNX NG16	189	L3
HACK/IN S12	57	H7 🔲
Newstead Gv HACK/IN S12	57	H7 🔲
Newstead PI HACK/IN S12	57	H8
Newstead Ri HACK/IN S12	57	H8
Newstead Rd HACK/IN S12	57	H8
LGEAT NG10	244	E7
Newstead Rd North ILK DE7	217	G7
Newstead Rd South ILK DE7	217	G7
Newstead St MSFDW NG19	164	A3
Newstead Wy HACK/IN S12	57	H7
New St ALFN DE55	159	M8
ALFN DE55	160	C5
ALFN DE55	161	K7
ALFN DE55	175	J6 🔲
ALFN DE55	176	D3
ALFN DE55	187	H3
ALFN DE55	187	M2
ASH NG17	162	C7
ASH NG17	163	H8
BKWL DE45	123	G4

BSVR S44	113	K7
BUT DE14	274	A8
BUX SK17	81	L5
BWSH/BRSTN DE72	242	F6
BWSH/BRSTN DE72	259	K3
CHSW S40	3	G6
CLCR S45	161	G1
DERBY DE1	5	H5
DERBYE DE21	226	F2 🔲
HYDE SK14	24	D2 🔲
LGEAT NG10	261	H2
MOS S20	73	K2
MSHM DE12	288	A4
MSHM DE12	295	K3
MSHM DE12	295	M4
MSHM DE12	295	H1
MTLK DE4	156	F5
NM/HAY SK22	43	M3
RCH S42	129	H7
RCH S42	145	J4
RIPLEY DE5	201	H1 🔲
SWAD DE11	282	E8
UTXR S14	247	L2
WRKS S80	96	B5
New Street Bus Link MOS S20	73	K2
New Ter LGEAT NG10	244	E4 🔲
MSFDW NG19	148	C5
Newthorpe Common		
EWD/SEL/PNX NG16	217	K2
Newton CI STPNHL/WNHL DE15	275	H2
WRKN S81	77	M3
Newtondale Av MSFDW NG19	165	H1
Newton Dr BSTN/STPLFD NG9	245	H4
Newton La		
STPNHL/WNHL DE15	275	H2
Newton Leys		
STPNHL/WNHL DE15	274	F6
Newton Ms		
STPNHL/WNHL DE15	274	C7
Newton Park CI SWAD DE11	282	D3
Newton Rd ALFN DE55	161	J5
STPNHL/WNHL DE15	274	D5
Newtons Croft Crs		
STV/CWN S43	94	E4
Newton's La		
EWD/SEL/PNX NG16	217	L7
Newton St MSFD NG18	164	F5
Newton's Wk DERBYW DE22	240	B2
Newtonwood La ALFN DE55	161	L5
New Tythe St LGEAT NG10	261	J7
New Zealand La BPR/DUF DE56	213	H4
New Zealand Sq		
DERBYW DE22	239	M5 🔲
Nicholas CI DERBYE DE21	242	B4
Nicholas St CHNE S41	129	G3 🔲
Nicholson PI SHEFS S8	55	L4 🔲
Nicholson Rd SHEFS S8	55	K4
Nicholson's Rw		
SBK/MW NG20	133	J7 🔲
Nicklaus Ct BUT DE14	280	D3 🔲
Nicola Gdns NORM/LIT DE23	256	A6
Nicolas CI BUX SK17	100	B2 🔲
Nidderdale		
WOL/BIL/BRX NG8	231	M6 🔲
Nidderdale CI		
WOL/BIL/BRX NG8	231	M7
Nields Wy MPL/ROM SK6	33	G6
Nightingale Av MSFDW NG19	148	D5
Nightingale CI CLCR S45	145	H8
MTLK DE4	172	C4
RIPLEY DE5	201	G1 🔲
Nightingale Crs		
EWD/SEL/PNX NG16	189	L4
Nightingale Dr MSFDW NG19	149	H8
SWAD DE11	283	J7 🔲
Nightingale Rd DERBYSE DE24	256	F3
Nilsson Rd BSTN/STPLFD NG9	245	L3
Ninelands Rd HATH/EY S32	66	D3
Ninth Av MSFDW NG19	165	K2
Nix's HI ALFN DE55	175	L8
Nobel CI WRKS S80	96	A1
Nodder Rd HAN/WDH S13	56	F3
Nodin Hill La BPR/DUF DE56	185	L7
Noehill PI SHEFP/MNR S2	56	E1 🔲
Noehill Rd SHEFP/MNR S2	56	E1
Noel St DERBYW DE22	240	A3 🔲
MSFD NG18	164	D3
No Man's Heath Rd		
MSHM DE12	294	B7
No Man's La ILK DE7	243	L2
Nook End Rd HEANOR DE75	216	A1
Nook La BSVR S44	111	L7
The Nook BPR/DUF DE56	213	M3 🔲
HATH/EY S32	86	D7 🔲
HEANOR DE75	201	M6 🔲
MELB/CHEL DE73	268	D4
SBK/MW NG20	133	G7
Nooning La BWSH/BRSTN DE72	259	H3
Norbett CI BSTN/STPLFD NG9	245	L7
Norbriggs Rd STV/CWN S43	93	M8
Norburn Dr ECK/KIL S21	74	C1
Norbury Av MPL/ROM SK6	32	B4
CHSW S40	109	L5
DERBYW DE22	240	A1
DRON S18	90	A1 🔲
Norbury Crs NORM/LIT DE23	255	M5 🔲
Norbury Dr MPL/ROM SK6	32	C4
MSFD NG18	165	H6
Norbury Hollow ASHB DE6	219	G1
Norbury Wy BPR/DUF DE56	199	M4 🔲
LGEAT NG10	244	D4
Norfolk Av BSTN/STPLFD NG9	261	K1
RCH S42	129	J8
Norfolk CI CHSW S40	127	L2
Norfolk Dr MSFDW NG19	164	E2
Norfolk Park Av SHEFP/MNR S2	56	A2
Norfolk Park Dr SHEFP/MNR S2	55	M1
Norfolk Park Rd SHEFP/MNR S2	55	M1
Norfolk Rd LGEAT NG10	261	J1
STPNHL/WNHL DE15	281	G3
Norfolk St GLSP SK13	26	A1
NORM/LIT DE23	5	G9
Norfolk Wk LGEAT NG10	244	E5
Norgreave Wy MOS S20	73	H3
Norman Av NORM/LIT DE23	256	B3
Normanby		
WOL/BIL/BRX NG8	231	M7
Norman CI BSTN/STPLFD NG9	245	M4
Norman Crs ILK DE7	217	H7

Normancroft Crs
SHEFF/MNR S2 .... 56 F1 🔢

Normancroft Dr
SHEFF/MNR S2 .... 56 E1 🔢

Normancroft Wy
SHEFF/MNR S2 .... 56 E1

Norman Dr
EWD/SEL/PNX NG16 .... 203 L8

Normandy Rd *RDERBYSW* DE65.. 253 H8

Normanhurst Pk *MTLK* DE4 ..... 156 B2

Norman Keep
BUTN/AL/TUT DE13 .... 263 M4 🔢

Norman Rd *ALFN* DE55 .... 188 B3
   BUTN/AL/TUT DE13 .... 263 M4
   RIPLEY DE5 .... 186 F8

Norman St *ILK* DE7 .... 217 H7

Normanton Av *ALFN* DE55 ...... 175 M7

Normanton Dr *MSFD* NG18 ..... 165 H4

Normanton Gv *HAN/WDH* S13 .... 57 J4

Normanton Hl *HACK/IN* S12 ...... 56 F4

Normanton La *NORM/LIT* DE23 .. 255 M1

Normanton Rd *DERBY* DE1.......... 4 E6
   NORM/LIT DE23 .... 4 E9

Normanton Spring Ct
HAN/WDH S13 .... 57 H4

Normanton Spring Rd
HAN/WDH S13 .... 57 H5

Norris Hl *MSHM* DE12 .... 290 A4

Northacre Rd *DERBYE* DE21 ...... 227 L8

Northam Dr *RIPLEY* DE5 .... 186 F8

North Av *ASHB* DE6 .... 193 L8
   DERBYW DE22 .... 226 D7
   LGEAT NG10 .... 244 D4
   MCKLVR DE3 .... 239 H7

North Brook Rd *GLSP* SK13 .... 17 H6

North Church St *BKWL* DE45 ...... 123 G4

Northcliffe Rd *ASHB* DE6.......... 193 L8

North Cl *ALFN* DE55 .... 176 C5
   DRON S18 .... 91 H4
   GLSP SK13 .... 17 J3
   MCKLVR DE3 .... 239 H7
   RDERBYSW DE65 .... 266 E5
   SWAD DE11 .... 290 E2

Northcote Av *SHEFS* S8 .... 55 L4

Northcote Rd *SHEFS* S8 .... 55 L4

Northcote St *LGEAT* NG10 .... 261 H3 🔢

North Crs *BSVR* S44 .... 112 D4
   ECK/KIL S21 .... 74 B2

Northdown Dr
BSTN/STPLFD NG9 .... 245 L1

Northedge La *RCH* S42 .... 143 L4

North End *MTLK* DE4 .... 183 J1

Northern Av *SHEFF/MNR* S2 ..... 56 B3

Northern Common *DRON* S18 .... 69 L7

Northern Dr *BSTN/STPLFD* NG9 .. 231 G2

Northern Rd *HEANOR* DE75 ..... 202 A8

Northern Vw *ASH* NG17.......... 163 H6

North Farm Cl *AU/AST/KP* S26 ... 75 J4

Northfield *BPR/DUF* DE56........ 200 C8
   DERBYSE DE24 .... 256 A7 🔢

Northfield Av *ILK* DE7 .... 217 H8
   LGEAT NG10 .... 260 D6
   MSFDW NG19 .... 149 J6
   UTXR ST14 .... 218 C6

Northfield Crs
BSTN/STPLFD NG9 .... 245 K6

Northfield La *BSVR* S44.......... 131 M4
   MSFDW NG19 .... 149 K5

Northfield Pk *MSFDW* NG19 ..... 149 L5

Northfield Rd
BSTN/STPLFD NG9 .... 245 K6
   BUTN/AL/TUT DE13 .... 273 L1

Northfields *ASHZ* LE65 .... 291 L2
   LGEAT NG10 .... 260 E6
   STV/CWN S43 .... 95 J7

Northfields Cl *ASH* NG17 .... 163 H7

Northgate St *ILK* DE7 .... 230 B1

North Gv *BSVR* S44 .... 112 D4

North Lands *AU/AST/KP* S26..... 75 J3

North La *ASHB* DE6 .... 210 A4
   BPR/DUF DE56 .... 199 G8
   BPR/DUF DE56 .... 213 H8
   RCH S42 .... 109 C5

North Leys *ASHB* DE6 .... 207 L1

Northmead Dr *DERBYW* DE22 ... 239 C7

Northmoor Cl *STV/CWN* S43 .... 111 J3 🔢

North Moor Vw *STV/CWN* S43 ... 111 J3

North Pde *DERBY* DE1 .... 240 D3 🔢
   MTLK DE4 .... 171 K1

North Pk *MSFD* NG18 .... 165 J7

North Rd *BSVR* S44 .... 111 J7
   BUX SK17 .... 100 A1
   GLSP SK13 .... 17 M7
   LGEAT NG10 .... 260 F4
   NM/HAY SK22 .... 35 G7
   STV/CWN S43 .... 95 H6

North Rw *DERBYW* DE22 .... 240 D1 🔢

North Side *RCH* S42 .... 144 F1

North St *ALFN* DE55 .... 161 J8
   ALFN DE55 .... 175 L7
   ALFN DE55 .... 176 C5
   ALFN DE55 .... 188 A4
   ASH NG17 .... 162 D7
   ASH NG17 .... 163 J7
   ASHZ LE65 .... 291 L4
   BSVR S44 .... 147 G1
   CLCR S45 .... 144 D5
   DERBY DE1 .... 240 C3
   EWD/SEL/PNX NG16 .... 177 G2
   EWD/SEL/PNX NG16 .... 202 E7
   EWD/SEL/PNX NG16 .... 203 M8
   ILK DE7 .... 230 C1 🔢
   MELB/CHEL DE73.................. 278 D3
   MTLK DE4 .... 171 K4
   NORM/LIT DE23 .... 239 M8
   RCH S42 .... 145 H4
   SBK/MW NG20 .... 115 K8
   STPNHL/WNHL DE15 .... 274 E7
   SWAD DE11 .... 282 E5 🔢

Northumberland Rd
STPNHL/WNHL DE15 .... 281 G3

Northumberland St
NORM/LIT DE23 .... 4 D9

North View *BSVR* S44 .... 131 H1

North Wingfield Rd *CHNE* S41 .. 129 H6

Northwood Av *ASH* NG17 ...... 163 G6
   DERBYE DE21 .... 241 H3
   MTLK DE4 .... 140 F6

Northwood La *ASHB* DE6 .... 205 M6
   MTLK DE4 .... 140 D4

Northwood Ri *ASHB* DE6......... 207 L2

Northwood St
BSTN/STPLFD NG9 .... 245 G2

Norton Av *BSVR* S44 .... 113 J4
   HACK/IN S12 .... 56 C8
   RCH S42 .... 127 K2
   SHEFS S8 .... 71 G1

Norton Church Glebe
SHEFS S8 .... 70 E1 🔢

Norton Church Rd *SHEFS* S8 .... 70 E1

Norton Green Cl *SHEFS* S8 .... 70 E3

Norton Hammer La *SHEFS* S8 .. 55 H6 🔢

Norton Lees Cl *SHEFS* S8 .... 55 K7 🔢

Norton Lees Crs *SHEFS* S8 .... 55 K6

Norton Lees La *SHEFS* S8 .... 55 J6

Norton Lees Rd *SHEFS* S8 .... 55 K6

Norton Lees Sq *SHEFS* S8 .... 55 K6

Norton Ms *SHEFS* S8 .... 70 F1

Norton Park Av *SHEFS* S8 ...... 70 E2 🔢

Norton Park Crs *SHEFS* S8 ...... 70 D2

Norton Park Dr *SHEFS* S8 .... 70 D2

Norton Park Rd *SHEFS* S8 .... 70 D3

Norton Park Vw *SHEFS* S8 ...... 70 D3

Norton Rd *BUTN/AL/TUT* DE13.. 273 K4
   SHEFS S8 .... 56 B8

Norwich St *DERBYE* DE21 ...... 241 G3

Norwood Av *CHNE* S41 .... 129 H3
   MPL/ROM SK6 .... 42 A3

Norwood Cl *ASH* NG17 .... 162 E7
   CHNE S41 .... 129 H4 🔢
   DERBYW DE22 .... 239 K5 🔢

Norwood Crs *AU/AST/KP* S26 .... 74 C3

Norwood Pl *ECK/KIL* S21 .... 74 C3

Nottingham Cl *RCH* S42 .... 128 E7 🔢

Nottingham Dr *RCH* S42 .... 128 E7

Nottingham La *ALFN* DE55 ..... 188 B5

Nottingham Rd *ALFN* DE55 ..... 175 L7
   ASHZ LE65 .... 285 M4
   ASHZ LE65 .... 291 M4
   BPR/DUF DE56 .... 199 K7 🔢
   BSTN/STPLFD NG9 .... 230 F6
   BSTN/STPLFD NG9 .... 231 K5
   BSTN/STPLFD NG9 .... 245 K5
   BSTN/STPLFD NG9 .... 261 L1
   BWSH/BRSTN DE72 .... 243 G8
   BWSH/BRSTN DE72 .... 258 E1
   DERBY DE1 .... 4 F2
   DERBYE DE21 .... 5 H2
   DERBYE DE21 .... 241 K5
   DERBYE DE21 .... 242 C7
   EWD/SEL/PNX NG16 .... 189 J4
   EWD/SEL/PNX NG16 .... 203 J8
   EWD/SEL/PNX NG16 .... 217 L1
   ILK DE7 .... 230 C3
   LGEAT NG10 .... 261 H2
   MSFD NG18 .... 164 E5
   MTLK DE4 .... 157 L6
   RIPLEY DE5 .... 201 H1

Nowill Ct *SHEFS* S8 .... 55 K4 🔢

Nowill Pl *SHEFS* S8 .... 55 K4 🔢

Nunbrook Gv *BUX* SK17 .... 99 M2 🔢

Nunn Brook Ri *ASH* NG17 ...... 177 H1

Nunn Brook Rd *ASH* NG17 ..... 162 B8

Nunn Cl *ASH* NG17 .... 177 H1

Nunsfield Dr *DERBYSE* DE24 ... 257 L3

Nunsfield Rd *BUX* SK17 .... 99 M2

Nun's St *DERBY* DE1................. 4 B2

The Nurseries
EWD/SEL/PNX NG16 .... 203 K8
   BSTN/STPLFD NG9 .... 245 M5
   BWSH/BRSTN DE72 .... 244 C5
   ILK DE7 .... 229 H3

Nursery Av *ASH* NG17 .... 162 F8

Nursery Cl *BWSH/BRSTN* DE72 . 242 E8
   GLSP SK13 .... 25 M2 🔢
   SWAD DE11 .... 282 E4

Nursery Cft *MTLK* DE4 .... 183 H4 🔢

Nursery Gdns *ALFN* DE55 ...... 176 F6

Nursery Hollow *ILK* DE7 .... 230 C4

Nursery La *BUX* SK17 .... 99 H3

Nursery St *MSFD* NG18 .... 164 F2

Nutbrook Crs *ILK* DE7 .... 230 A6

Nutbrook Trail *ILK* DE7 .... 216 F7
   ILK DE7 .... 230 B6

Nuthall Cir *ILK* DE7 .... 229 M6

Nuttall Cl *ALFN* DE55 .... 175 J7

Nuttall St *ALFN* DE55 .... 175 J7

Nuttall Ter *BSVR* S44 .... 147 G1

Nutwood Cl *DERBYW* DE22 .... 226 D7 🔢

O

Oadby Ri *BUTN/AL/TUT* DE13 .. 273 K4
   NORM/LIT DE23 .... 256 B4 🔢

Oak Acres *BSTN/STPLFD* NG9 .. 245 K5

Oak Apple Crs *ILK* DE7 .... 230 B4

Oak Av *EWD/SEL/PNX* NG16 .... 202 E5
   LGEAT NG10 .... 244 D3
   MSFD NG18 .... 164 F2
   POY/DIS SK12 .... 43 K4
   RIPLEY DE5 .... 201 G3
   SBK/MW NG20 .... 133 G6

Oak Bank Av *CHNE* S41 .... 91 L7

Oak Bank Cl *MSFDW* NG19 ...... 164 D3

Oakbank Ct *TOT/DORE* S17 ...... 69 H5 🔢

Oakbrook Rd *ECC* S11 .... 54 C2

Oak Cl *BPR/DUF* DE56 .... 213 H8
   BWSH/BRSTN DE72 .... 242 F5
   CHF/WBR SK23 .... 60 F5
   DERBYW DE22 .... 226 B6
   ECK/KIL S21 .... 73 M5
   EWD/SEL/PNX NG16 .... 176 F7
   HYDE SK14 .... 16 D6
   MSHM DE12 .... 295 M5
   STV/CWN S43 .... 111 G3
   SWAD DE11 .... 289 H3
   UTXR ST14 .... 247 J1

Oak Crs *ASHB* DE6 .... 207 M2
   NORM/LIT DE23 .... 255 L2
   RCH S42 .... 128 C7

Oakcroft *STLY* SK15 .... 16 B3

Oakdale Cl *CLCR* S45 .... 145 G8

Oakdale Dr *BSTN/STPLFD* NG9 . 245 M6

Oakdale Gdns *DERBYE* DE21 ... 227 L7 🔢

Oakdale Rd *ALFN* DE55 .... 176 D6

   ECC S11 .... 55 G4
   MSFDW NG19 .... 164 C3

Oakdell *DRON* S18 .... 71 G7

Oakdene Crs *MPL/ROM* SK6 ..... 32 C3

Oakdene Gdns *MPL/ROM* SK6 ... 32 C3

Oakdene Rd *MPL/ROM* SK6 ..... 32 C3

Oak Dr *ALFN* DE55 .... 175 L6
   ASHB DE6 .... 248 C1
   DERBYE DE24 .... 257 K4
   EWD/SEL/PNX NG16 .... 203 H8
   MCKLVR DE3 .... 239 H7
   MPL/ROM SK6 .... 32 A4 🔢
   RDERBYSW DE65 .... 253 G8

Oakerthorpe Rd *MTLK* DE4 ..... 171 K7

Oakes Park Vw *SHEFS* S8 ...... 71 G1 🔢

The Oakes *GLSP* SK13 .... 25 K3

Oakfield Av *CHSW* S40 .... 127 L1

Oakfield Cl *MSFD* NG18 .... 165 J8
   WOL/BIL/BRX NG8 .... 231 M7

Oakfield Ct *ILK* DE7 .... 215 K8 🔢

Oakfield Dr *LGEAT* NG10 .... 244 E7

Oakfield Rd *BSTN/STPLFD* NG9 . 245 G3
   GLSP SK13 .... 17 H7
   WOL/BIL/BRX NG8 .... 231 M7

Oakfields
BUTN/AL/TUT DE13 .... 262 D6 🔢

Oak Flatt *BSTN/STPLFD* NG9 .... 245 K5

Oak Grove Gn *TOT/DORE* S17 .. 69 H6

Oakham Cl *DERBYE* DE21 .... 241 G1 🔢
   MSFD NG18 .... 164 E6

Oakham Dr
EWD/SEL/PNX NG16 .... 189 L3

Oakham Gv *ASHZ* LE65 .... 291 K3

Oakham Wy *ILK* DE7 .... 217 G7

Oakhill Rd *ABRD* S7 .... 55 G4

Oakholme Ms *ECC* S11 .... 54 F1 🔢

Oakholme Rd *ECC* S11 .... 54 F1

Oakhurst Cl *BPR/DUF* DE56 ..... 199 G4

Oakland Av *ASH* NG17 .... 162 C8
   LGEAT NG10 .... 260 F5

Oakland Ct
BSTN/STPLFD NG9 .... 245 K1 🔢

Oakland Crs *ALFN* DE55 .... 188 A5

Oakland Rd *MSFDW* NG19 ...... 165 H2

Oaklands Av *HEANOR* DE75 .... 202 D8
   MPL/ROM SK6 .... 32 F2 🔢
   NORM/LIT DE23 .... 255 M5

Oaklands Rd *RDERBYSW* DE65 . 253 M6

The Oaklands *ALFN* DE55 .... 176 D6

Oakland St *ALFN* DE55 .... 175 L6

Oaklands Wy *MELB/CHEL* DE73 . 278 E2

Oakland Ter *LGEAT* NG10 .... 260 F5 🔢

Oak La *ASHB* DE6 .... 234 A6

Oaklea *BUX* SK17 .... 99 M5

Oakleaf Crs *ASH* NG17 .... 177 M1

Oaklea Rd *RCH* S42 .... 144 E4

Oakleigh Av *DERBYE* DE21 ...... 241 J4
   SWAD DE11 .... 282 C5

Oakley Av *CHSW* S40 .... 2 D2

Oakley's Rd *LGEAT* NG10 .... 261 H4

Oakover Dr *DERBYW* DE22 ..... 226 A7

Oakridge Cl *DERBYE* DE21 ...... 241 L3

Oakridge Cl *MSFDW* NG19 ..... 165 J1 🔢

Oak Rd *BUTN/AL/TUT* DE13 ..... 286 A1
   BWSH/BRSTN DE72 .... 258 C6
   HACK/IN S12 .... 56 D8
   MTLK DE4 .... 156 F5
   RCH S42 .... 129 J7
   UTXR ST14 .... 218 B4

Oaks Av *NM/HAY* SK22 .... 35 G8
   WRKS S80 .... 114 F2

Oaksedge La *BSVR* S44 .... 157 J4

Oaks Farm La *BSVR* S44 .... 111 K8

Oakside Wy *DERBYE* DE21 ...... 227 L7

Oaks La *CLCR* S45 .... 142 F5
   RCH S42 .... 108 C1

Oaks Rd *RDERBYSW* DE65 ...... 266 C4

Oakstedge La *CLCR* S45 .... 158 A4

The Oaks *DERBYE* DE21 .... 226 F2 🔢

Oak St *ASH* NG17 .... 163 G3
   BUT DE14 .... 280 E1
   GLSP SK13 .... 25 M1 🔢
   MOS S20 .... 72 F2
   NORM/LIT DE23 .... 240 D8
   SHEFS S8 .... 55 K3
   STV/CWN S43 .... 111 K1
   SWAD DE11 .... 282 D8

Oak Tree Av *BSVR* S44 .... 147 L3

Oaktree Av *DERBYSE* DE24 ..... 256 E5

Oaktree Cl *ALFN* DE55 .... 187 K2

Oak Tree Cl *BSVR* S44 .... 112 A7
   MSFD NG18 .... 165 L3

Oak Tree Ct *BWSH/BRSTN* DE72 . 258 F1

Oak Tree Gdns *MTLK* DE4 .... 157 K6

Oak Tree La *MSFD* NG18 .... 165 K4

Oaktree Rd *ALFN* DE55 .... 176 F1
   STV/CWN S43 .... 95 H8

Oak Tree Rd *ASH* NG17 .... 163 K6

Offridge Cl *STV/CWN* S43 .... 95 J8

Ogden St *HYDE* SK14 .... 24 E2

Ogston La *ALFN* DE55 .... 159 K6

Ogston New Rd *ALFN* DE55 ..... 159 H5

Okeover Av *ASHB* DE6 .... 208 A1

Oker Av *MTLK* DE4 .... 140 E7

Oker Dr *MTLK* DE4 .... 140 E7

Oker La *MTLK* DE4 .... 156 A4

Oker Rd *MTLK* DE4 .... 155 L3

Oldale Cl *HAN/WDH* S13 .... 57 M5

Oldale Ct *HAN/WDH* S13 .... 57 M4

Oldale Gv *HAN/WDH* S13 .... 57 M4

Old Bakery Cl *ASHB* DE6 .... 195 L1
   CHNE S41 .... 91 K8 🔢

Old Bank *ASHB* DE6 .... 207 G2

Old Barn Cl *DERBYE* DE21 ...... 226 F2 🔢

Oldbury Cl *DERBYE* DE21 .... 227 J8

Old Chapel La
EWD/SEL/PNX NG16 .... 189 K8

Old Chester Rd *DERBY* DE1 ..... 240 D2 🔢

Old Church Cl *DERBYW* DE22 ... 225 M5

Old Coach Rd *MTLK* DE4 .... 157 J6

Old Coalpit La *BUX* SK17 .... 119 H1

Old Colliery La *RCH* S42 .... 146 B2

Old Coppice Side *HEANOR* DE75.. 216 B3

Old Dam La *BUX* SK17 .... 82 E6

Old Derby Rd *ASHB* DE6 .... 207 M1 🔢
   EWD/SEL/PNX NG16 .... 203 G7 🔢

Old Derwent Av *MTLK* DE4 ..... 156 F8

Old Fall St *ASH* NG17 .... 162 C7 🔢

Oldfield Dr *SWAD* DE11 .... 282 F5

Oldfield La *ASHB* DE6 .... 181 L8
   ASHB DE6 .... 206 E7
   MTLK DE4 .... 155 K2
   RDERBYSW DE65 .... 265 J2

Old Fulwood Rd *ECC* S11 .... 54 A3

Old Ga *HOLM/MEL* HD7 .... 8 B3

Old Gate Av
BWSH/BRSTN DE72 .... 270 B5 🔢

Old Hackney La *MTLK* DE4 ...... 156 C2

Old Hall Av *BPR/DUF* DE56 ...... 213 C7
   CHF/WBR SK23 .... 59 H6
   DERBYSE DE24 .... 257 L3
   NORM/LIT DE23 .... 255 L1

Old Hall Cl *CLCR* S45 .... 145 M8
   GLSP SK13 .... 18 A8
   MTLK DE4 .... 140 F7 🔢

Old Hall Dr *RDERBYSW* DE65 ... 266 E5

Old Hall Gdns *HATH/EY* S32 ...... 86 D6
   SWAD DE11 .... 282 D8

Old Hall La *HYDE* SK14 .... 16 D5
   MPL/ROM SK6 .... 32 F5
   RDERBYSW DE65 .... 251 L2
   WRKS S80 .... 96 C4

Old Hall Rd *CHSW* S40 .... 2 A5
   NORM/LIT DE23 .... 255 M1

Old Hall Sq *GLSP* SK13 .... 17 K5 🔢

Old Hartshay Hl *RIPLEY* DE5 ... 186 F8

Oldhay Cl *TOT/DORE* S17 .... 69 G4

Old Hay La *TOT/DORE* S17 .... 68 F4

Old Hl *ASHB* DE6 .... 207 M1
   BSVR S44 .... 113 K8

Old Hillcliff La *BPR/DUF* DE56... 197 K7

Old House Rd *CHSW* S40 .... 110 A4 🔢

Oldicote La
STPNHL/WNHL DE15 .... 275 H7

Oldknow Rd *MPL/ROM* SK6 ..... 32 D4

Old La *BPR/DUF* DE56 .... 197 J7
   DERBYW DE22 .... 226 D8
   GLSP SK13 .... 25 K3
   MOS S20 .... 73 K3
   MTLK DE4 .... 171 J8

Old Lime Ct *MTLK* DE4 .... 156 F5 🔢

Old Longhill Rd *BUX* SK17 .... 79 L6

Old Manor Rd *MSFDW* NG19 ... 149 L7

Old Mansfield Rd *DERBYW* DE21 .. 240 F1

Old Market Pl *ALFN* DE55 ...... 176 D4 🔢

Old Mill Cl *BPR/DUF* DE56 ...... 213 H7
   BSTN/STPLFD NG9 .... 245 K8 🔢

Old Mill Dr *RCH* S42 .... 109 K3

Old Mill La *MSFDW* NG19 .... 149 M8

Old Park Av *SHEFS* S8 .... 70 A3

Old Park Rd *SHEFS* S8 .... 70 A3

Old Peveril Rd *BSVR* S44 .... 112 D5

Old Pit La *ILK* DE7 .... 215 K4

The Old Pond *HEANOR* DE75 ... 216 D2

Old Quarry Cl *STV/CWN* S43 .... 94 E4

The Old Railway Yd *SHEFS* S8 .. 55 G7

Old Retford Rd *HAN/WDH* S13 .. 57 M1

Oldridge Cl *CHSW* S40 .... 109 K4

Old Rd *ASH* NG17 .... 163 J4
   BPR/DUF DE56 .... 200 A2
   BUT DE14 .... 280 B3
   CHF/WBR SK23 .... 59 H4
   CHSW S40 .... 2 B5
   CHSW S40 .... 109 K7
   GLSP SK13 .... 17 K3
   HYDE SK14 .... 16 C5
   MTLK DE4 .... 155 M1

Old School Cl *BSVR* S44 .... 147 G1
   BUX SK17 .... 83 M5

Old School La *BSVR* S44 .... 111 J8 🔢
   MSFDW NG19 .... 148 D5

Old School Ms
BWSH/BRSTN DE72 .... 270 E2 🔢

Old Station Cl *MTLK* DE4 .... 140 C2 🔢

Old Storth La *ALFN* DE55 .... 176 E6

Old St *HYDE* SK14 .... 24 D2

Old Swanwick Colliery Rd
ALFN DE55 .... 187 J1

Old Ter *MSFDW* NG19 .... 148 C6

Old Vicarage Cl
NORM/LIT DE23 .... 255 M1 🔢

Old Vicarage La
DERBYW DE22 .... 225 M5 🔢

Oldwell Cl *TOT/DORE* S17 .... 69 G6

Old Whittington La *DRON* S18 ... 91 H4

Olive Av *LGEAT* NG10 .... 261 G1
   SBK/MW NG20 .... 133 G4

Olive Ct *ASH* NG17 .... 163 J6

Olive Crs *HACK/IN* S12 .... 56 D8

Olive Gv *MSFDW* NG19 .... 165 K2

Olive Grove Rd *SHEFF/MNR* S2 .. 56 C2

Oliver Cl *HEANOR* DE75 .... 202 E8

Oliver Rd *MOS* S20 .... 73 G3

Oliver Rd *ABRD* S7 .... 54 F6
   ILK DE7 .... 229 M5

Olive St *DERBYW* DE22............. 4 A6

Olivet Rd *SHEFS* S8 .... 55 J8

Olivier St *NORM/LIT* DE23 ...... 256 E1

Ollersett Av *NM/HAY* SK22 ...... 43 M2

Ollersett La *NM/HAY* SK22 .... 44 A2

Olton Rd *MCKLVR* DE3 .... 238 F6

Omberley Av *ASH* NG17 .... 163 L4

Onslow Rd *ECC* S11 .... 54 E3
   MCKLVR DE3 .... 239 C6

Ontario Dr *EWD/SEL/PNX* NG16 . 189 G1

Opal Cl *DERBYE* DE21 .... 227 K8

Openacre *EWD/SEL/PNX* NG16.. 188 C6

Openwoodgate *BPR/DUF* DE56.. 199 M6

Openwood Rd *BPR/DUF* DE56 ... 200 A4 🔢

Orange Cl *SBK/MW* NG20 .... 133 H4 🔢

Orange St *ALFN* DE55 .... 175 L6

Orchard Av *CDON/KEG* DE74 ... 271 K7
   CHF/WBR SK23 .... 59 G3

Orchard Cl *BPR/DUF* DE56 ...... 213 L2
   BSVR S44 .... 131 L1
   BWSH/BRSTN DE72 .... 242 F6
   BWSH/BRSTN DE72 .... 258 F2
   DERBYSE DE24 .... 257 M6 🔢
   ILK DE7 .... 227 G6 🔢
   ILK DE7 .... 229 G3
   MELB/CHEL DE73.................. 278 D3 🔢
   MSFD NG18 .... 164 F8
   MSHM DE12 .... 287 G1
   NORM/LIT DE23 .... 255 M3
   RDERBYSW DE65 .... 266 E4
   RIPLEY DE5 .... 201 K3
   SBK/MW NG20 .... 133 H5
   STV/CWN S43 .... 94 D3 🔢
   STV/CWN S43 .... 95 H7

Orchard Ct *DERBYE* DE21 .... 242 B5

Orchard Crs *ALFN* DE55 .... 187 G3 🔢
   BSTN/STPLFD NG9 .... 245 M5
   BSVR S44 .... 147 L2

Orchard Dr *GLSP* SK13 .... 25 H1
   WRKS S80 .... 96 B8

Orchard Hall *UTXR* ST14 .... 246 F3

Orchard La *ASHB* DE6 .... 221 G1

Orchard Lee *AU/AST/KP* S26 .... 75 H4

Orchard Pk *BUT* DE14 .... 274 A4

Orchard Pl *ECK/KIL* S21 .... 74 A4

Orchard Ri *HEANOR* DE75 ...... 202 C8 🔢

Orchard Rd *ALFN* DE55 .... 187 M4
   CHF/WBR SK23 .... 59 G3
   MTLK DE4 .... 156 B2
   MTLK DE4 .... 171 K1

Orchard Sq *DRON* S18 .... 70 A8

The Orchards *DERBYW* DE22 ... 226 A7 🔢

Orchard St *BSTN/STPLFD* NG9 .. 245 G3
   BUT DE14 .... 274 A4
   BUT DE14 .... 281 C1
   DERBY DE1 .... 4 D2 🔢
   EWD/SEL/PNX NG16 .... 202 E7 🔢
   EWD/SEL/PNX NG16 .... 217 K1 🔢
   ILK DE7 .... 230 C3
   LGEAT NG10 .... 261 H3 🔢
   MCKLVR DE3 .... 255 G1
   MSFDW NG19 .... 164 E1
   SWAD DE11 .... 282 C4

Orchards Wy *CHSW* S40 .... 2 A5
   CHSW S40 .... 127 M1

The Orchard *ASH* NG17 .... 163 L8
   BKWL DE45 .... 138 F5
   BPR/DUF DE56 .... 199 K6 🔢
   ILK DE7 .... 215 G4 🔢
   RIPLEY DE5 .... 201 L1

Orchard Vw *BSVR* S44 .... 131 H2
   MSFDW NG19 .... 149 L7

Orchard View Rd *CHSW* S40 .... 109 M6

Orchard Wy *ASH* NG17 .... 177 M2
   LGEAT NG10 .... 244 D7
   MELB/CHEL DE73.................. 257 J8
   MSHM DE12 .... 295 M5

Orchid Cl *BSVR* S44 .... 111 K7
   STPNHL/WNHL DE15 .... 281 K2

Ordish Av *DERBYE* DE21 .... 241 M5

Ordish Cl *BUT* DE14 .... 274 A8 🔢

Ordish St *BUT* DE14 .... 273 M8

Ordley La *ASHB* DE6 .... 206 C2

Oregon Wy *DERBYE* DE21 .... 241 M5

Orford Av *POY/DIS* SK12 .... 43 G4

Orford Cl *MPL/ROM* SK6 .... 42 B3

Orgreave Cl *HAN/WDH* S13 ..... 57 M1

Orgreave La *HAN/WDH* S13 ..... 57 K1

Orgreave Wy *HAN/WDH* S13.... 57 M2

Oriel Rd *FUL* S10 .... 53 M3

Orkney Cl *DERBYSE* DE24 .... 256 A7

Orly Av *CDON/KEG* DE74 .... 271 K8

Ormesby Cl *DRON* S18 .... 89 M1 🔢

Ormes Meadow *MOS* S20 .... 57 M8

Ormond Cl *CHSW* S40 .... 127 L3
   SHEFS S8 .... 70 E4

Ormond Dr *SHEFS* S8 .... 70 E4

Ormonde St
EWD/SEL/PNX NG16 .... 202 E6

Ormonde Ter
EWD/SEL/PNX NG16 .... 202 E6

Ormond Rd *SHEFS* S8 .... 70 E4

Ormond Wy *SHEFS* S8 .... 70 E3

Ormsby Rd *CHNE* S41 .... 110 C3

Ormskirk Ri *DERBYE* DE21 ...... 242 C6

Orpean Wy *BSTN/STPLFD* NG9 . 245 H8

Orpen Dr *SHEFS* S8 .... 56 B8

Orpen Wy *SHEFS* S8 .... 56 B8 🔢

Orton Av *BSTN/STPLFD* NG9 .... 245 M4

Orton Wy *BPR/DUF* DE56 .... 199 L4

Osberton Pl *ECC* S11 .... 54 F7

Osborne Cft *AU/AST/KP* S26 .... 75 J4
   LGEAT NG10 .... 244 E6 🔢

Osborne Pl *GLSP* SK13 .... 17 K5 🔢

Osborne Rd *ECC* S11 .... 54 F3

Osborne St *DERBY* DE1 .... 5 J8 🔢
   STPNHL/WNHL DE15 .... 274 D7

Osmaston Park Rd
DERBYSE DE24 .... 256 F3

Osmaston Rd *DERBY* DE1 .... 4 F5
   DERBYSE DE24 .... 256 F1
   DERBYSE DE24 .... 257 G4
   NORM/LIT DE23 .... 5 G7
   SHEFS S8 .... 55 J8 🔢

Osmaston St *LGEAT* NG10 ...... 244 F5

Osmund Rd *ECK/KIL* S21 .... 72 E7

Osprey Cl *DERBYSE* DE24 .... 256 B8
   STPNHL/WNHL DE15 .... 275 L4

Osterly Gn *DERBYW* DE22 .... 239 K5
Oswestry Cl *DERBYE* DE21 ...... 227 L7 **17**
Otterburn Dr *DERBYW* DE22.... 225 M8
Otter St *DERBY* DE1 .... 240 D3
Oulton Cl *DERBYSE* DE24 .... 257 C6
Oundle Cl *ASHZ* LE65 .... 291 J2
Oundle Dr *ILK* DE7 .... 230 D3
MSFDW NG19 .... 164 A1
Ousley La *ASHB* DE6 .... 205 M5
Outfield Rd
STPNHL/WNHL DE15 .... 281 J2
Outgang La *MSFDW* NG19........ 148 F4
Outlands Rd *EDL/UDV* S33 .... 64 C4
Out La *BSVR* S44 .... 146 B4
Outram Cl *MPL/ROM* SK6 .... 32 C6 **3**
Outram Rd *CHNE* S41 .... 110 C4
Outram St *ASH* NG17 .... 163 J7
RIPLEY DE5 .... 187 C8
Outram Wy *DERBYSE* DE24 ...... 256 B8
Outseats Dr *ASH* DE55 .... 175 L7
Outwoods La
BUTN/AL/TUT DE13 .... 272 F3
BUTN/AL/TUT DE13 .... 273 H4
Outwoods St *BUT* DE14............. 273 L5
Oval Ct *NORM/LIT* DE23 .... 255 M2
The Oval *ASH* NG17 .... 163 C6
Oven Hill Rd *NM/HAY* SK22 ...... 44 D2
Overcroft Ri *TOT/DORE* S17 ...... 68 F6
Overdale *MTLK* DE4 .... 157 C5
Overdale Av *ASH* NG17 .... 163 H3
BUX SK17 .... 100 A2
Overdale Gdns *TOT/DORE* S17 . 68 F4
Overdale Ri *TOT/DORE* S17 .... 68 F4 **3**
Overdale Rd *POY/DIS* SK12 ...... 43 J4
Overend Cl *GLV* S14 .... 56 A6
Overend Dr *GLV* S14 .... 56 A6
Overend Rd *GLV* S14 .... 56 A6
Overend Wy *GLV* S14 .... 56 A6
Over Hill Rd *NM/HAY* SK22 .... 44 D5
Over La *BKWL* DE45 .... 106 B4
BPR/DUF DE56 .... 198 D5
BPR/DUF DE56 .... 200 B5
Overlees *DRON* S18 .... 90 A7
Over Rd *BKWL* DE45 .... 106 B4
Oversetts Ct *SWAD* DE11 .... 282 C4
Oversetts Rd *SWAD* DE11 .... 282 B4
Overstone Cl *ASH* NG17 .... 163 J8
BPR/DUF DE56 .... 200 A6 **6**
Overton Cl *STV/CWN* S43 .... 93 J7
Owen Av *LGEAT* NG10 .... 261 K4
Owers Av *HEANOR* DE75 .... 216 C3
Owlcotes Vw *BSVR* S44 .... 131 K2
Owler Bar Rd *ECC* S11 .... 67 L5
TOT/DORE S17 .... 67 L6
Owler Car La *DRON* S18 .... 71 H6
SHEFS S8 .... 71 H5
Owlers La *DERBYW* DE22 .... 239 M8
Owlston Cl
EWD/SEL/PNX NG16 .... 203 J7 **11**
Owlswick Cl *NORM/LIT* DE23 ... 255 H3 **7**
Owlthorpe Av *MOS* S20 .... 72 E2
Owlthorpe Cl *MOS* S20 .... 72 E2 **11**
Owlthorpe Dr *MOS* S20 .... 72 E2
Owlthorpe Greenway *MOS* S20.. 73 H1
Owlthorpe Gv *MOS* S20 .... 72 E2
Owlthorpe La *MOS* S20 .... 72 E2
Owlthorpe Ri *MOS* S20 .... 72 E2
Ox Close Av *TOT/DORE* S17 ...... 69 K5
Oxclose Dr *DRON* S18 .... 89 M1 **10**
Oxclose La *ASHB* DE6 .... 166 F8
DRON S18 .... 89 M1
MSFDW NG19 .... 149 K7
Oxclose Park Rd *MOS* S20 .... 73 J3
Oxclose Park Rd North *MOS* S20.. 73 J4
Oxcroft La *BSVR* S44 .... 113 L7
WRKS S80 .... 114 D2
Oxenhope Cl
NORM/LIT DE23 .... 255 H3 **7**
Oxford Cl *STV/CWN* S43 .... 111 J2
Oxford Rd *STV/CWN* S43 .... 111 J2
Oxford St *ALFN* DE55 .... 176 B1
ASH NG17 .... 163 C8
BSVR S44 .... 147 J1
BUT DE14 .... 280 E1
DERBY DE1 .... 5 H7
DERBYE DE21 .... 242 B5
EWD/SEL/PNX NG16 .... 203 J8 **7**
ILK DE7 .... 230 C3 **8**
LGEAT NG10 .... 261 G2
MSFD NG18 .... 164 F1
RIPLEY DE5 .... 201 G1 **8**
SWAD DE11 .... 289 K1
Ox HI *MOS* S20 .... 73 K5
Oxley Rd *STPNHL/WNHL* DE15 .. 274 D7
Oxpasture La *SBK/MW* NG20 ... 114 E4
Oxton Cl *MSFDW* NG19 .... 164 B3
Oxwich Cl *DERBYE* DE21 ...... 227 L8 **8**
Ozier Holt *LGEAT* NG10 .... 260 F4

P

Packenham Bvd
RDERBYSW DE65 .... 251 K6
Packer's Rw *CHSW* S40 .... 3 H4
Pack Horse Rd
MELB/CHEL DE73.................... 278 E1
Packington Nook La *ASHZ* LE65.. 291 K6
Packman La *AU/AST/KP* S26 ..... 75 M6
AU/AST/KP S26 .... 75 L1
Paddock Cl *CDON/KEG* DE74..... 271 J7
CHF/WBR SK23 .... 58 C6
RCH S42 .... 128 C7
Paddock Crs *SHEFP/MNR* S2 .... 56 B5
Paddock Cft *DERBYE* DE21 ... 227 J8 **8**
Paddock Cl *CHF/WBR* SK23 ..... 58 C5
CHF/WBR SK23 .... 59 J5
Paddocks Cl *ALFN* DE55 .... 176 F5
The Paddocks *ASH* NG17 .... 162 C8
CLCR S45 .... 145 M8
LGEAT NG10 .... 244 D5
STV/CWN S43 .... 93 M7
SWAD DE11 .... 282 C5
Paddocks Vw *LGEAT* NG10 ...... 260 D2
The Paddock *ALFN* DE55 .... 176 C1
ASH NG17 .... 162 F5
BPR/DUF DE56 .... 213 M4
BSVR S44 .... 131 L1

Park Gv *DERBYW* DE22 .... 240 B2
Park Hall Av *CHSW* S40 .... 127 K2
Park Hall Cl *CHSW* S40 .... 127 L3
Park Hall Gdns *CHSW* S40 .... 127 L2
MSFDW NG19 .... 149 M5
Parkhall La *ECK/KIL* S21 .... 74 A8
Park Hall La *ILK* DE7 .... 216 A8
Park Hall Rd *MSFDW* NG19 ...... 149 M5
Parkhead Ct *ECC* S11 .... 54 C6
Parkhead Rd *ECC* S11 .... 54 C7
Park HI *ECK/KIL* S21 .... 73 H7
EWD/SEL/PNX NG16 .... 217 L5
Park Hill Cl *NM/HAY* SK22 .... 43 M1 **2**
Park Hill Dr *NORM/LIT* DE23 ..... 256 C3
Parkhouse Cl *CLCR* S45 .... 144 E6
Parkhouse Dr *ALFN* DE55 .... 176 B5
Parkhouse Rd *RCH* S42 .... 145 K5
Parkin St *ALFN* DE55 .... 175 L6
Parkland Av *NM/HAY* SK22 .... 43 M1
Parkland Cl *MSFD* NG18 .... 165 H8
Parkland Dr *RCH* S42 .... 128 D8
Parklands Dr
MELB/CHEL DE73 .... 269 K2 **2**
Park La *ALFN* DE55 .... 175 H1
ALFN DE55 .... 175 L3
ASHB DE6 .... 221 L6
ASHB DE6 .... 221 M1
BKWL DE45 .... 123 M8
BPR/DUF DE56........................ 200 C2
BUTN/AL/TUT DE13 .... 263 L4
BWSH/BRSTN DE72 .... 270 B6 **1**
CDON/KEG DE74 .... 271 C7
CHNE S41 .... 110 C3
DERBYW DE22 .... 226 C6
EWD/SEL/PNX NG16 .... 176 F7
EWD/SEL/PNX NG16 .... 189 L1
MSFD NG18 .... 164 E5
MTLK DE4 .... 139 M5
MTLK DE4 .... 141 G8
MTLK DE4 .... 173 M8
NM/HAY SK22 .... 35 G5
NORM/LIT DE23 .... 255 M1
SBK/MW NG20 .... 115 M4
Park Leys Ct *DERBYE* DE21 ...... 242 B6
Pastures Av *NORM/LIT* DE23 ... 255 J3
Pastures HI *NORM/LIT* DE23 .... 255 K2
The Pastures *BPR/DUF* DE56 .... 213 H6
RDERBYSW DE65 .... 266 F8
SWAD DE11 .... 282 C5 **8**
Patch Cl *BUTN/AL/TUT* DE13 .... 273 L4
The Patchills *MSFD* NG18 .... 165 H4
Patchwork Rw *SBK/MW* NG20... 133 J6
Paterson Av *DERBY* DE21 .... 241 K4
Patmore Sq *NORM/LIT* DE23 ... 256 C3 **7**
Paton Gv *STV/CWN* S43 .... 111 G2
Patrick Cl *ALFN* DE55 .... 289 G5
Patterdale Cl *DRON* S18 .... 90 B1 **6**
Patterson Pl *MSFD* NG18 .... 165 G3
Pattison St *BSVR* S44 .... 113 J4
Paul Av *MSFD* NG18 .... 165 K4
Paul's La *UTXR* ST14 .... 205 G8
Paulson's Dr *MSFD* NG18 .... 164 E3
Paulyn Wy *ASHZ* LE65 .... 291 J3
Pavilion Cl *STV/CWN* S43 .... 95 H8
Pavilion Gdns *MSFDW* NG19 .... 148 C2
Pavilion Rd *ILK* DE7 .... 217 H5
NORM/LIT DE23 .... 255 M2
Paxton Cl *MCKLVR* DE3 .... 254 F1
MTLK DE4 .... 156 C4
Paxton Rd *CHNE* S41 .... 110 F5
Payler Cl *SHEFP/MNR* S2 .... 56 D7
Payne Rd *BSTN/STPLFD* NG9 ... 245 K7
Payne St *DERBYW* DE22 .... 240 A4 **9**
Peacefield *MPL/ROM* SK6 .... 32 B5
Peach Av *ALFN* DE55 .... 176 E3
EWD/SEL/PNX NG16 .... 189 J4
Peache Wy *BSTN/STPLFD* NG9.. 245 L3
Peach St *DERBYW* DE22 .... 240 A5
HEANOR DE75 .... 216 A1
Peacock Cl *ECK/KIL* S21 .... 73 M4
GLSP SK13 .... 17 H6 **7**
Peacock Pl *ILK* DE7 .... 217 C6
Peacock St *MSFD* NG18 .... 164 D4
Peacock Wy *ALFN* DE55 .... 187 J2
Peacroft Ct *RDERBYSW* DE65 .. 253 C8
Peacroft La *RDERBYSW* DE65 .. 265 G1
Peak Av *ALFN* DE55 .... 187 L4
Peakdale Cl *LGEAT* NG10 .... 260 D4
RIPLEY DE5 .... 201 G4 **2**
Peakdale Crs *HACK/IN* S12 .... 57 H5
Peakdale Rd *GLSP* SK13 .... 17 H7
MPL/ROM SK6 .... 32 D6 **1**
Peak Dr *DERBYSE* DE24 .... 256 D5
Peaknaze Cl *GLSP* SK13 .... 25 K2
Peak Pl *STV/CWN* S43 .... 112 A3
Peak Rd *NM/HAY* SK22 .... 44 A2
The Peak *SBK/MW* NG20 .... 133 H7
Peaktor La *MTLK* DE4 .... 140 B2
Peak Vw *ALFN* DE55 .... 176 C5
STV/CWN S43 .... 95 C5
Peak View Dr *ASHB* DE6 .... 207 M1
Pearce La *RCH* S42 .... 127 M7
Pearl Bank *ASHB* DE6 .... 233 J2
Pearl Cl *DERBYE* DE21 .... 227 K8
Pearl St *ECC* S11 .... 55 H2
Pearson Av *BSTN/STPLFD* NG9.. 245 L5
Pearson Pl *SHEFS* S8 .... 55 J6
Pear St *ECC* S11 .... 55 H1
Peartree Av *RCH* S42 .... 128 B7
Pear Tree Av *RIPLEY* DE5 .... 200 F2
SWAD DE11 .... 282 C5
Peartree Cl *CDON/KEG* DE74 ... 271 K7 **6**
Pear Tree Cl *ECK/KIL* S21 .... 73 M5
GLSP SK13 .... 17 H6
MPL/ROM SK6 .... 32 E2
STV/CWN S43 .... 111 K2
Pear Tree Crs *NORM/LIT* DE23 .. 256 C3
Pear Tree Rd *MSHM* DE12 .... 288 F4
SBK/MW NG20 .... 133 C4
Peartree La *ALFN* DE55 .... 162 E1
Pear Tree Rd *CLCR* S45 .... 160 F1
NORM/LIT DE23 .... 256 D1
Pear Tree St *NORM/LIT* DE23 ... 256 D2

Pease Cl *ALFN* DE55 .... 175 L7
Pease Hl *ALFN* DE55 .... 175 L7
Peasehill Rd *RIPLEY* DE5 .... 201 H2
Peasunhurst La *CLCR* S45 .... 142 C1
Peatburn Av *HEANOR* DE75 ..... 215 M1
Peatfield Rd *BSTN/STPLFD* NG9.. 245 G1
ECK/KIL S21 .... 74 C3
Peat La *BPR/DUF* DE56 .... 184 A7
Peats Cl *BPR/DUF* DE56 .... 196 E1
Peckham Gdns
DERBYW DE22 .... 239 K5 **2**
Peck Mill Vw *AU/AST/KP* S26 .... 75 L3
Pecks HI *MSFD* NG18 .... 165 H3
Pedley Av *MOS* S20 .... 73 H1
Pedley Cl *MOS* S20 .... 73 H1 **3**
Pedley Dr *MOS* S20 .... 73 H2 **3**
Pedley Gv *MOS* S20 .... 73 H1
Pedley St *ILK* DE7 .... 230 C3
Peebles Cl *DERBYE* DE24 .... 256 B8 **8**
Peel Crs *MSFDW* NG19 .... 149 G8
Peel Rd *MSFDW* NG19 .... 164 B2
Peel St *ALFN* DE55 .... 176 E4
ASH NG17 .... 163 K7
BUT DE14 .... 280 F1 **1**
DERBYW DE22 .... 240 A4
EWD/SEL/PNX NG16 .... 202 E7
GLSP SK13 .... 17 M5
LGEAT NG10 .... 261 H2
Peers Cl *DERBYE* DE21 .... 227 L8
Pegasus Wy *RDERBYSW* DE65 .. 253 H8
Peggars Ct *STV/CWN* S43 .... 94 E4
Peggs La *MSHM* DE12 .... 295 M6
Peggy La *ALFN* DE55 .... 159 L5
Pegwell Cl *NORM/LIT* DE23 ...... 256 A3
Pelham Av *ILK* DE7 .... 230 B1 **8**
Pelham St *ASH* NG17 .... 163 G8
DERBYW DE22 .... 4 C6
ILK DE7 .... 230 B1 **8**
MSFD NG18 .... 164 F3
The Pemberton *ALFN* DE55 ...... 176 E6
Pembleton Dr *MSFDW* NG19 .. 164 A1 **8**
Pembrey Cl
BSTN/STPLFD NG9 .... 231 G8 **7**
Pembroke Cl *CHSW* S40 .... 127 M1 **2**
Pembroke Rd *DRON* S18 .... 90 D2
WRKN S81 .... 77 J5 **2**
Pembroke St *DERBYE* DE21 ...... 241 G2 **2**
DERBYE DE21 .... 241 G3 **1**
ECC S11 .... 55 H1 **2**
Penalton Cl *DERBYSE* DE24 ...... 257 H4
Pendean Cl *ALFN* DE55 .... 176 B1 **8**
Pendeen Rd *ECC* S11 .... 54 C2 **3**
Pendennis Cl *DERBYSE* DE24 ... 257 L4 **8**
Pendine Cl *ALFN* DE55 .... 176 F4
Pendlebury Dr *MCKLVR* DE3 .... 255 H1
Pendle Cft *MOS* S20 .... 73 L1 **8**
Pendleside Wy *NORM/LIT* DE23.. 255 H1
Pendleton La *BPR/DUF* DE56 ... 184 C3
Penfold Wy *ALFN* DE55 .... 160 E5
Penge Rd *DERBYW* DE22 .... 239 K3 **8**
Penhaligan's Cl
MELB/CHEL DE73 .... 269 J1 **8**
Penistone Gdns *CLCR* S45 .... 145 C8
Peniston Ri *MELB/CHEL* DE73 ... 278 D4
Penkridge Rd *SWAD* DE11 .... 289 L1
Penley St *ECC* S11 .... 55 J2 **7**
Penmore Cl *CHNE* S41 .... 3 L8
Penmore Gdns *CHNE* S41 .... 3 L9
Penmore La *CHNE* S41 .... 3 L9
Penmore St *CHNE* S41 .... 128 F2
Penncroft Dr *CLCR* S45 .... 145 H8
Penncroft La *CLCR* S45 .... 145 H7
Pennie Cl *LGEAT* NG10 .... 261 C6 **1**
Penniment La *MSFDW* NG19 .... 163 L1
Pennine Av *ALFN* DE55 .... 187 L3
Pennine Cl *ALFN* DE55 .... 161 J4 **1**
ASH NG17 .... 162 B6
LGEAT NG10 .... 260 D1
MSFDW NG19 .... 149 M6
Pennine Dr *ALFN* DE55 .... 176 C5
EWD/SEL/PNX NG16 .... 189 J3
Pennine Rd *GLSP* SK13 .... 25 K2
Pennine Vw *BPR/DUF* DE56 ..... 200 B2
BSVR S44 .... 131 K5 **1**
CHSW S40 .... 109 M5
EDL/UDV S33 .... 47 K2
GLSP SK13 .... 11 L8
GLSP SK13 .... 17 L8
NM/HAY SK22 .... 36 B3
RCH S42 .... 129 J7
STKB/PEN S36 .... 19 M6
SWAD DE11 .... 282 D8
Penn La *MELB/CHEL* DE73........ 278 D3
Penns Rd *SHEFP/MNR* S2 .... 55 M4
Penn St *ASH* NG17 .... 163 J7
BPR/DUF DE56 .... 199 K6
Pennycress Cl
NORM/LIT DE23 .... 255 K2 **7**
Pennycroft La *UTXR* ST14 .... 247 M1
Pennycroft Rd *UTXR* ST14 .... 247 K1
Penny Engine La *ECK/KIL* S21 ... 73 H6
Pennyfields Bvd *LGEAT* NG10 .. 260 C2
Penny Gn *WRKS* S80 .... 96 D5
Penny La *TOT/DORE* S17 .... 68 F5
Penny Long La *DERBYW* DE22 .. 240 B2
Pennyunk La *BKWL* DE45 .... 122 A1
Pennywell Dr *RCH* S42 .... 127 G3
Penrhyn Av *NORM/LIT* DE23 .... 256 A3
Penrhyn Crs *BSTN/STPLFD* NG9.. 245 L6
Penrhyn Rd *ECC* S11 .... 54 F3
Penrith Pl *DERBYE* DE21 ...... 227 G8 **8**
MSFDW NG19 .... 164 A2 **7**
Penrose Crs *BSVR* S44 .... 112 A3
Penrose Pl *NM/HAY* SK22 .... 57 K4
Pensgreave Rd
BUTN/AL/TUT DE13 .... 273 L4 **3**
Pentewen Cl *DERBYW* DE22 .... 226 B8
Penthorpe Cl *HACK/IN* S12 .... 56 E4 **1**
Pentland Cl *CHSW* S40 .... 109 M5 **8**
DERBYE DE21 .... 227 K8
Pentland Ct *MSFDW* NG19 .... 164 A5
Pentland Gdns *LGEAT* NG10 .... 260 D1
Pentland Rd *DRON* S18 .... 90 A1
Pentrich Rd *ALFN* DE55 .... 187 G3
RIPLEY DE5 .... 187 G8
Pentridge Dr *ILK* DE7 .... 216 F7
Penzance Pl *MSFD* NG18 .... 165 L3
Penzance Rd *DERBYSE* DE24 ... 257 L5 **8**

DERBYSE DE24 ...... 257 L5
DERBYSE DE24 ...... 257 L5
Pepper La ILK DE7 ...... 244 B1
Pepper St ASH NG17 ...... 163 L8
Percival Cl BUX SK17 ...... 152 A7
Percival Crs ASH NG17 ...... 163 H7
Percy St ASH NG17 ...... 163 G8
  DERBYW DE22 ...... 4 B7
  EWD/SEL/PNX NG16 ...... 203 K8
  ILK DE7 ...... 230 C3
Percy Wood Cl
  RDERBYSW DE65 ...... 252 F8
Peregrine Cl DERBYSE DE24 ...... 256 A6
  MSHM DE12 ...... 295 M6
  STPNHL/WHNL DE15 ...... 275 G7
Peregrine Wy SHEFS S8 ...... 55 H7
Perigree Rd SHEFS S8 ...... 55 H7
Periwood Av SHEFS S8 ...... 55 G7
Periwood Cl SHEFS S8 ...... 55 H7
Periwood Dr SHEFS S8 ...... 55 H7
Periwood Gv SHEFS S8 ...... 55 H7
Perlethorpe Av MSFDW NG19 ...... 164 C5
Pershore Dr BUT DE14 ...... 280 D2
Perth Cl MCKLVR DE3 ...... 239 H6
  MSFDW NG19 ...... 149 M5
  STPNHL/WHNL DE15 ...... 274 H1
Perth Dr BSTN/STPLFD NG9 ...... 245 H1
Perth St DERBYE DE21 ...... 241 G1
Peterborough Dr FUL S10 ...... 53 K2
Peterborough Rd FUL S10 ...... 53 K1
Peterborough St
  DERBYE DE21 ...... 241 J7
Peterdale Cl STV/CWN S43 ...... 111 H2
Peterdale Rd STV/CWN S43 ...... 111 H2
Peterlee Pl DERBYSE DE24 ...... 257 K4
Peter More Hl SWAD DE11 ...... 96 B7
Peters Av CLCR S45 ...... 144 E6
Peters Cl EWD/SEL/PNX NG16 ...... 203 M8
  MELB/CHEL DE73 ...... 279 L7
Peters Ct RDERBYSW DE65 ...... 264 A1
Petersfield Cl MSFDW NG19 ...... 164 A3
Petersgate Cl LGEAT NG10 ...... 244 D8
Petersgate Dr DERBYSE DE24 ...... 257 M4
Petersham Rd LGEAT NG10 ...... 244 D8
  LGEAT NG10 ...... 260 D1
Peter St ASHB DE6 ...... 207 H4
  GLSP SK13 ...... 17 K4
Petty Close La ASH DE6 ...... 223 M8
  ASHB DE6 ...... 237 M1
Pettyclose La CHNE S41 ...... 111 G5
Petworth Av
  BSTN/STPLFD NG9 ...... 245 J7
Petworth Dr ECC S11 ...... 54 C8
Pevensey Av CHNE S41 ...... 110 B4
Peveril Av BWSH/BRSTN DE72 ...... 242 F8
  NM/HAY SK22 ...... 43 M1
Peveril Cl ALFN DE55 ...... 187 L4
  EDL/UDV S33 ...... 48 F8
  MTLK DE4 ...... 140 F7
Peveril Ct GLSP SK13 ...... 26 C2
  RIPLEY DE5 ...... 200 F1
Peveril Crs ILK DE7 ...... 229 H2
  LGEAT NG10 ...... 260 C5
Peveril Dr ALFN DE55 ...... 187 M4
  ASH NG17 ...... 162 F8
  ILK DE7 ...... 217 G8
Peveril Gdns POY/DIS SK12 ...... 43 K4
Peveril Ms POY/DIS SK12 ...... 43 K4
Peveril Rd BSVR S44 ...... 161 J4
  BUX SK17 ...... 99 M3
  CHNE S41 ...... 110 C3
  ECC S11 ...... 54 E3
  ECK/KIL S21 ...... 73 H6
  EDL/UDV S33 ...... 48 F8
Peveril St DERBYSE DE24 ...... 257 G4
Pewit Cl RCH S42 ...... 146 A2
Pewit La ALFN DE55 ...... 160 F3
Pheasant Field Dr
  DERBYE DE21 ...... 242 D4
Pheasant Hl MSFDW NG19 ...... 164 D1
Philip Av EWD/SEL/PNX NG16 ...... 217 K1
Philip Howard Rd GLSP SK13 ...... 25 M2
Philips Cft BPR/DUF DE56 ...... 213 H6
Phoenix Ct HACK/IN S12 ...... 72 B1
Phoenix Rd HACK/IN S12 ...... 72 B1
Phoenix St ILK DE7 ...... 163 L6
  DERBY DE1 ...... 4 F2
Phyllis Gv LGEAT NG10 ...... 261 J3
Piccadilly La ASHB DE6 ...... 206 F1
Piccadilly Rd CHNE S41 ...... 3 K5
Pickard La BPR/DUF DE56 ...... 200 A1
Pickard St MSFD NG18 ...... 165 H3
Pickering Av
  EWD/SEL/PNX NG16 ...... 203 J8
Pickering Rd DERBYE DE21 ...... 240 F1
Pickford Pl CHF/WBR SK23 ...... 60 C4
Pickleys La ASHB DE6 ...... 248 F2
Picknalls UTXR ST14 ...... 247 L3
Pickton Cl CHSW S40 ...... 2 A6
Pictor Gv BUX SK17 ...... 100 A3
Pic Tor La MTLK DE4 ...... 156 F6
Pictor Rd BUX SK17 ...... 100 A3
Piddocks Rd
  STPNHL/WHNL DE15 ...... 281 L5
Pighills La DRON S18 ...... 70 E6
Pig La MTLK DE4 ...... 124 C5
Pike Cl CHSW S40 ...... 109 L5
Pike View Cl CHF/WBR SK23 ...... 45 H8
Pilgrim Ct WRKN S81 ...... 77 J3
Pilgrims Wy DERBYSE DE24 ...... 255 M8
Pilhough La MTLK DE4 ...... 139 M4
Pilhough Rd MTLK DE4 ...... 140 B4
Pilsley Cl BPR/DUF DE56 ...... 199 M4
Pilsley Rd ALFN DE55 ...... 160 E4
  CLCR S45 ...... 145 H1
Pimlico DERBYW DE22 ...... 239 L4
  ILK DE7 ...... 230 B7
Pimlico Cl BSTN/STPLFD NG9 ...... 231 L7
Pimm's Rd ASHB DE6 ...... 238 D2
Pinchom's Hill Rd
  BPR/DUF DE56 ...... 199 L7
The Pinch ASHB DE6 ...... 166 E7
Pindale Av STV/CWN S43 ...... 111 M3
Pindale Rd EDL/UDV S33 ...... 48 F8
  EDL/UDV S33 ...... 49 J3
Pine Av EWD/SEL/PNX NG16 ...... 202 D7

Pine Cl BUT DE14 ...... 280 D2
  DERBYE DE21 ...... 241 L6
  ECK/KIL S21 ...... 73 M5
  ILK DE7 ...... 215 J3
  MPL/ROM SK6 ...... 32 A7
  MSFDW NG19 ...... 149 M5
  RDERBYSW DE65 ...... 253 L6
  RIPLEY DE5 ...... 201 G1
  SBK/MW NG20 ...... 133 G4
  WRKS S80 ...... 115 J1
Pine Cft DERBYE DE21 ...... 207 M3
Pinecroft Ct DERBYE DE21 ...... 241 L1
Pine Gv SWAD DE11 ...... 282 C4
The Pines BWSH/BRSTN DE72 ...... 259 L3
  FUL S10 ...... 53 K2
Pine St STV/CWN S43 ...... 111 K2
Pine Vw CHSW S40 ...... 109 L7
  CLCR S45 ...... 145 H8
Pineview Cl MSFD NG18 ...... 165 J8
Pine Wk SWAD DE11 ...... 289 H3
  UTXR ST14 ...... 247 J2
Pinewood RIPLEY DE5 ...... 201 L3
Pinewood Cl ALFN DE55 ...... 175 M7
Pinewood Dr MSFD NG18 ...... 165 J8
Pinewood Rd BPR/DUF DE56 ...... 199 H4
  MTLK DE4 ...... 156 C3
  STPNHL/WHNL DE15 ...... 281 J4
Pinfold GLSP SK13 ...... 17 H6
Pinfold Cl BUTN/AL/TUT DE13 ...... 263 L5
  RCH S42 ...... 127 H2
  RDERBYSW DE65 ...... 267 G8
Pinfold Crs BUX SK17 ...... 83 M7
Pinfold Hl HATH/EY S32 ...... 87 H8
Pinfold La ASHB DE6 ...... 209 K2
  BSTN/STPLFD NG9 ...... 245 H3
  RDERBYSW DE65 ...... 267 G8
Pinfold Rd BUX SK17 ...... 83 M7
Pinfold St ECK/KIL S21 ...... 73 G7
  EWD/SEL/PNX NG16 ...... 217 M1
  UTXR ST14 ...... 247 M3
The Pinfold BKWL DE45 ...... 138 B7
  BPR/DUF DE56 ...... 199 M5
  BSVR S44 ...... 147 L1
  BWSH/BRSTN DE72 ...... 258 C6
Pinfold Vw BKWL DE45 ...... 122 F5
Pingle DERBYW DE22 ...... 226 B6
Pingle Av ABRD S7 ...... 54 F7
Pingle Crs BPR/DUF DE56 ...... 199 J5
Pingle Farm Rd SWAD DE11 ...... 282 C5
Pingle Gra STV/CWN S43 ...... 111 H3
Pingle La BPR/DUF DE56 ...... 186 C8
  BPR/DUF DE56 ...... 199 J5
Pingle Rd ABRD S7 ...... 54 F7
  ECK/KIL S21 ...... 74 B3
The Pingle DERBYE DE21 ...... 242 B6
  LGEAT NG10 ...... 261 G2
Pingot La HYDE SK14 ...... 16 F8
  HYDE SK14 ...... 24 E1
Pingot Rd NM/HAY SK22 ...... 44 B2
Pingott La GLSP SK13 ...... 17 K5
Pingreaves Dr
  MELB/CHEL DE73 ...... 257 K8
Pinner Rd ECC S11 ...... 54 F3
Pinxton Ct MSFD NG18 ...... 165 L5
Pinxton Gn
  EWD/SEL/PNX NG16 ...... 177 J7
Pinxton La ALFN DE55 ...... 176 E5
  ASH NG17 ...... 177 J4
  ASH NG17 ...... 177 L6
Pipe Hay La ASHB DE6 ...... 262 A5
Piper Av CLCR S45 ...... 145 H6
Piper La RCH S42 ...... 109 H7
Pipeyard La ECK/KIL S21 ...... 72 F7
Pipit Cl MSHM DE12 ...... 295 M6
Pippenwell Rd BUX SK17 ...... 119 K3
Pippin Hl RIPLEY DE5 ...... 215 H1
Pipworth Gv DERBYW DE22 ...... 295 M2
Pipworth La ECK/KIL S21 ...... 73 J6
Pitch Cl STV/CWN S43 ...... 95 H8
Pitchford La FUL S10 ...... 54 A1
Pit Close La
  MELB/CHEL DE73 ...... 269 K1
Pit Hill MY SBK/MW NG20 ...... 115 J8
Pithiviers Cl ASHZ LE65 ...... 291 K5
Pit La ALFN DE55 ...... 173 L4
  ALFN DE55 ...... 175 G3
  HAN/WDH S13 ...... 56 D4
  HEANOR DE75 ...... 216 E4
  RIPLEY DE5 ...... 201 K3
  RIPLEY DE5 ...... 201 H1
Pits La ASHB DE6 ...... 180 B1
Pittar St DERBYW DE22 ...... 4 C7
Pittlemere La BUX SK17 ...... 83 K1
Pitt St ECK/KIL S21 ...... 72 F8
Pittywood Rd MTLK DE4 ...... 183 H3
Placket La MTLK DE4 ...... 154 E4
Plackett Cl BSTN/STPLFD NG9 ...... 245 J2
  BWSH/BRSTN DE72 ...... 260 A2
Plains La BPR/DUF DE56 ...... 198 E6
Plainspot Rd
  EWD/SEL/PNX NG16 ...... 189 M8
The Plain ASHB DE6 ...... 223 J2
Plaistow Green Rd MTLK DE4 ...... 154 B1
Plane Tree Rd MPL/ROM SK6 ...... 32 A5
Plantain Gdns
  NORM/LIT DE23 ...... 255 M5
Plantation Cl WRKS S80 ...... 96 B5
Plantation Rd SHEFS S8 ...... 55 K4
  WOL/BIL/BRX NG8 ...... 231 L6
The Plantations LGEAT NG10 ...... 260 D2
Plantin Ri MOS S20 ...... 73 H3
The Plantin MOS S20 ...... 73 H3
Plant La LGEAT NG10 ...... 260 D6
Platts Av HEANOR DE75 ...... 215 M1
Platt St EWD/SEL/PNX NG16 ...... 176 F8
  GLSP SK13 ...... 17 L5
Pleasant Av BSVR S44 ...... 131 L3
Pleasant Cl HACK/IN S12 ...... 56 E4
Pleasant Rd HACK/IN S12 ...... 56 E4
Pleasley Rd ASH NG17 ...... 162 E2
  ASH NG17 ...... 163 K4
Plimsoll St DERBYW DE22 ...... 239 M4
Ploughfield Cl
  NORM/LIT DE23 ...... 255 L4
Plough Ga DERBYW DE22 ...... 226 C8
Plover Av SWAD DE11 ...... 283 J7
Plover Dene WRKN S81 ...... 77 M5
Plover Wy STV/CWN S43 ...... 111 J7

Plowman Ct
  BSTN/STPLFD NG9 ...... 245 G4
Plowright Dr SHEFP/MNR S2 ...... 56 A5
Plowright Mt SHEFP/MNR S2 ...... 56 A5
Plowright Wy SHEFP/MNR S2 ...... 56 A5
Plucksbridge Rd MPL/ROM SK6.. 32 D7
Plumbley Hall Ms MOS S20 ...... 72 F4
Plumbley Hall Rd MOS S20 ...... 72 F3
Plumbley La MOS S20 ...... 72 E4
Plummer Rd SWAD DE11 ...... 282 C4
Plumptre Cl
  EWD/SEL/PNX NG16 ...... 217 J1
Plumptre Rd
  EWD/SEL/PNX NG16 ...... 202 E5
Plumptre Wy
  EWD/SEL/PNX NG16 ...... 217 J1
Plum Tree La MSFDW NG19 ...... 165 L3
Plymouth Av
  EWD/SEL/PNX NG16 ...... 177 H8
Plymouth Rd ABRD S7 ...... 55 H5
Pocknedge La RCH S42 ...... 127 G1
Podnor La MPL/ROM SK6 ...... 33 K4
Pole Hl SHEFS S8 ...... 55 K8
Pole's Rd ASHB DE6 ...... 238 D2
Pollard Dr MSFD NG18 ...... 164 F3
Pollards Oaks
  BWSH/BRSTN DE72 ...... 258 E1
Polly Froggatt La
  HATH/EY S32 ...... 86 E8
Polyfields La BSVR S44 ...... 131 L2
Pomona St ECC S11 ...... 55 H1
Pond La RCH S42 ...... 128 B6
  RCH S42 ...... 145 G2
Pond St CHSW S40 ...... 3 G6
Pondwell Dr STV/CWN S43 ...... 111 J3
Ponsonby Ter DERBY DE1 ...... 4 B4
Pontefract St DERBYSE DE24 ...... 257 G3
Pontypool Cl DERBYSE DE24 ...... 227 L8
Pool Cl DERBYSE DE24 ...... 257 M6
  EWD/SEL/PNX NG16 ...... 177 G7
Pool Rd MELB/CHEL DE73 ...... 278 F4
Poolsbrook Av STV/CWN S43 ...... 112 D2
Poolsbrook Crs STV/CWN S43 .. 112 D2
Poolsbrook Rd BSVR S44 ...... 112 D4
Poolsbrook Vw STV/CWN S43 .. 112 D2
Pool's La ECK/KIL S21 ...... 91 M3
Pool St SWAD DE11 ...... 282 F8
Pope Carr Rd MTLK DE4 ...... 156 F5
Poplar Av CHSW S40 ...... 127 L1
  DERBYE DE21 ...... 242 B5
  LGEAT NG10 ...... 244 D3
  MSHM DE12 ...... 290 B8
  NM/HAY SK22 ...... 44 A1
  RIPLEY DE5 ...... 201 G2
  SWAD DE11 ...... 282 E4
Poplar Dr ILK DE7 ...... 227 M2
  LGEAT NG10 ...... 244 D3
Poplar Gv ASH NG17 ...... 177 M1
Poplar Nook DERBYW DE22 ...... 226 D6
Poplar Rd ALFN DE55 ...... 176 E4
  BWSH/BRSTN DE72 ...... 260 C1
  ECK/KIL S21 ...... 72 F8
Poplar Rw DERBYW DE22 ...... 240 D1
The Poplars WRKS S80 ...... 96 D5
Poplar St MSFDW NG19 ...... 149 M7
Poplar Wy ILK DE7 ...... 230 A5
  MPL/ROM SK6 ...... 42 D3
Porlock Cl SWAD DE10 ...... 260 D2
Porteous Cl MTLK DE4 ...... 141 G7
Porter Brook Vw ECC S11 ...... 55 G2
Porterhouse Rd RIPLEY DE5 ...... 201 J1
Porter La MTLK DE4 ...... 171 H7
Porter Rd NORM/LIT DE23 ...... 240 B8
Porter's La DERBYE DE21 ...... 227 J7
  RDERBYSW DE65 ...... 255 G8
Porter St STV/CWN S43 ...... 95 H8
Porthcawl Pl DERBYE DE21 ...... 227 M8
Portico Rd NORM/LIT DE23 ...... 255 K4
Portland Av BSVR S44 ...... 131 L5
  BUT DE14 ...... 280 D3
  WRKS S80 ...... 115 G1
Portland Cl MCKLVR DE3 ...... 239 G8
Portland Court Ms
  MSFDW NG19 ...... 149 M6
Portland Crs
  BSTN/STPLFD NG9 ...... 245 H4
  BSVR S44 ...... 131 L1
Portland Gv CHF/WBR SK23 ...... 45 H8
Portland Rd BSTN/STPLFD NG9 .. 261 K1
  EWD/SEL/PNX NG16 ...... 189 L8
  EWD/SEL/PNX NG16 ...... 217 L2
  ILK DE7 ...... 217 J7
  LGEAT NG10 ...... 260 D6
  NM/HAY SK22 ...... 44 A1
  SBK/MW NG20 ...... 133 G5
Portland Sq ASH NG17 ...... 163 G6
Portland St ASH NG17 ...... 163 H6
  MSFD NG18 ...... 164 E4
  MSFDW NG19 ...... 148 D3
  MSFDW NG19 ...... 149 M6
  NORM/LIT DE23 ...... 256 D2
  RDERBYSW DE65 ...... 253 L6
  STV/CWN S43 ...... 95 K6
  WRKS S80 ...... 96 C4
Portman Cha DERBYSE DE24 ...... 256 A8
Portreath Dr DERBYW DE22 ...... 226 B7
Port Wy DERBYE DE21 ...... 214 A9
Portway Cl DERBYE DE21 ...... 214 A9
Portway Dr BUTN/AL/TUT DE13.. 263 M5
Postern Rd BUTN/AL/TUT DE13 .. 272 E6
Postmans La RCH S42 ...... 129 L5
Post St GLSP SK13 ...... 17 L5
Posy La BWSH/BRSTN DE72 ...... 270 C1
Potato Pit La ILK DE7 ...... 243 K1
The Potlocks RDERBYSW DE65 .. 266 F4
Potter Rd GLSP SK13 ...... 17 H7
Potters Cl CHNE S41 ...... 91 L8
Potters La MTLK DE4 ...... 173 L5
Potters Nook WRKN S81 ...... 77 J3
Potter St ASH NG17 ...... 163 K6

  DERBYE DE21 ...... 242 A6
  MELB/CHEL DE73 ...... 278 E3
Pottery Cl BPR/DUF DE56 ...... 199 M5
Pottery La RIPLEY DE5 ...... 200 F7
Pottery La East CHNE S41 ...... 110 E2
Pottery La West CHNE S41 ...... 110 D3
Poulter St SBK/MW NG20 ...... 133 J1
Poulterwell La BSVR S44 ...... 131 L5
Pounder La MTLK DE4 ...... 156 A8
Powell Dr ECK/KIL S21 ...... 73 M4
Powell St NORM/LIT DE23 ...... 240 B8
Pown St BUX SK17 ...... 150 D4
Powtrell Pl ILK DE7 ...... 230 E4
Poynter Cl HEANOR DE75 ...... 215 M1
Poynton Wood Crs
  TOT/DORE S17 ...... 69 K4
Poynton Wood Gld
  TOT/DORE S17 ...... 69 K4
Poyser Av DERBYE DE21 ...... 241 K3
Poyser La ASHB DE6 ...... 238 D1
Pratt Cl MSFDW NG19 ...... 164 A1
Pratthall La BPR/DUF DE56 ...... 183 K4
Premier Av ASHB DE6 ...... 207 L2
Prescot Cl MCKLVR DE3 ...... 254 F1
Press La RCH S42 ...... 144 A4
Prestbury Cl DERBYE DE21 ...... 241 L1
Preston Av ALFN DE55 ...... 175 L6
Preston St SHEFP/MNR S2 ...... 55 K3
Prestop Dr ASHZ LE65 ...... 291 J4
Prestwold Av MSFDW NG19 ...... 165 L1
Prestwood La STV/CWN S43 ...... 113 J8
Prestwood Park Dr SWAD DE11.. 282 F5
Pretoria St BSVR S44 ...... 113 J4
Price St BUT DE14 ...... 273 K6
Pride Pkwy DERBYSE DE24 ...... 5 L6
Priestcliffe Rd BUX SK17 ...... 102 C6
Priestfield Gdns CHSW S40 ...... 109 L3
Priestland Av DERBYE DE21 ...... 242 A6
Priestley Av ALFN DE55 ...... 159 M5
Priestley St SHEFP/MNR S2 ...... 55 L1
Priestsic Rd ASH NG17 ...... 163 J7
Priest's Wy BUX SK17 ...... 101 G8
Primary Cl BPR/DUF DE56 ...... 199 K6
Prime Pkwy DERBY DE1 ...... 5 G1
  DERBY DE1 ...... 240 E3
Primrose Av
  EWD/SEL/PNX NG16 ...... 189 J8
  MPL/ROM SK6 ...... 32 A4
Primrose Dr ILK DE7 ...... 227 M2
Primrose Hl ALFN DE55 ...... 176 C1
  GLSP SK13 ...... 25 L2
  ILK DE7 ...... 217 H7
Primrose La ECK/KIL S21 ...... 74 B2
  GLSP SK13 ...... 25 K1
  UTXR ST14 ...... 247 L2
Primrose Meadow SWAD DE11 .. 282 E3
Primrose Ri
  EWD/SEL/PNX NG16 ...... 217 K2
Primrose St ILK DE7 ...... 217 H7
Primrose Ter GLSP SK13 ...... 25 L2
Primrose Wy ASH NG17 ...... 177 M1
Primula Wy NORM/LIT DE23 ...... 256 A6
Prince Charles Av
  DERBYW DE22 ...... 239 L3
Prince of Wales Rd
  SHEFP/MNR S2 ...... 56 E1
  NORM/LIT DE23 ...... 239 L8
Prince's Dr MPL/ROM SK6 ...... 32 A3
Prince's Rd BUX SK17 ...... 100 A3
  CHF/WBR SK23 ...... 45 H8
Princess Av ALFN DE55 ...... 176 D5
  MSFDW NG19 ...... 165 K2
  MSHM DE12 ...... 288 F5
Princess Cl SWAD DE11 ...... 283 J8
Princess Crs SHEFP/MNR S2 ...... 56 E2
Princess Dr BWSH/BRSTN DE72 .. 258 D1
  LGEAT NG10 ...... 244 E8
Princess Pl CLCR S45 ...... 144 F8
Princess St BUT DE14 ...... 273 M6
  CHNE S41 ...... 2 F1
  GLSP SK13 ...... 25 L2
  LGEAT NG10 ...... 261 G2
  STV/CWN S43 ...... 111 J1
  SWAD DE11 ...... 289 J2
Princes St EWD/SEL/PNX NG16 .. 203 J8
  MSFD NG18 ...... 164 D5
  NORM/LIT DE23 ...... 256 D2
Princess Wy
  BUTN/AL/TUT DE13 ...... 274 B2
Prince St ILK DE7 ...... 217 H6
  LGEAT NG10 ...... 261 G2
Printers Fold HYDE SK14 ...... 17 G5
Printers Pk HYDE SK14 ...... 17 H5
Prior Cl ASH NG17 ...... 163 L5
Priorfields DERBYE DE21 ...... 227 J7
Prior Park Rd ASHZ LE65 ...... 291 M5
Priors Barn Cl
  BWSH/BRSTN DE72 ...... 242 F8
Priorway Av
  BWSH/BRSTN DE72 ...... 242 F8
Priorway Gdns
  BWSH/BRSTN DE72 ...... 258 F1
Priory Av ECC S11 ...... 55 J3
Priory Cl ASHB DE6 ...... 221 G5
  BUTN/AL/TUT DE13 ...... 263 L5
  ILK DE7 ...... 229 M4
  MELB/CHEL DE73 ...... 269 K1
  SWAD DE11 ...... 282 D4
Priory Ct HACK/IN S12 ...... 57 L7
Priory Gdns ALFN DE55 ...... 187 K2
  DERBYE DE21 ...... 227 J7
Priory Lands
  BUTN/AL/TUT DE13 ...... 265 H8
Priory Pl ABRD S7 ...... 55 J3
Priory Rd ABRD S7 ...... 55 H3
  ALFN DE55 ...... 175 L6
  EWD/SEL/PNX NG16 ...... 176 C1
  MSFDW NG19 ...... 149 L7
Pritchard Cl HACK/IN S12 ...... 57 L7
Pritchard Dr BSTN/STPLFD NG9.. 245 H4
Pritchett Dr NORM/LIT DE23 ...... 255 H2
Private Dr STV/CWN S43 ...... 111 K2
Prospect Av ASH NG17 ...... 163 C5
Prospect Dr BPR/DUF DE56 ...... 199 J8

  MTLK DE4 ...... 156 D4
  SBK/MW NC20 ...... 133 H7
  TOT/DORE S17 ...... 69 J5
Prospect Pl ASH NG17 ...... 163 H8
  TOT/DORE S17 ...... 69 K4
Prospect Rd CHNE S41 ...... 91 J8
  CLCR S45 ...... 160 F1
  DRON S18 ...... 70 F7
  HEANOR DE75 ...... 216 D2
  RIPLEY DE5 ...... 214 D1
  SHEFP/MNR S2 ...... 55 K3
  SHEFS S8 ...... 55 K3
  TOT/DORE S17 ...... 69 K5
Prospect St ALFN DE55 ...... 175 L6
  MSFD NG18 ...... 165 G4
Providence Pl ALFN DE55 ...... 175 J7
  ILK DE7 ...... 230 B1
Providence Rd
  EWD/SEL/PNX NG16 ...... 188 D5
Providence St RIPLEY DE5 ...... 201 H2
Provident St NORM/LIT DE23 ...... 4 D9
Pryor Mede AU/AST/KP S26 ...... 75 H5
Psalter La ECC S11 ...... 54 E3
Pudding Bag La CLCR S45 ...... 143 J7
Pulborough Gdns
  NORM/LIT DE23 ...... 255 K4
Pullman Cl STV/CWN S43 ...... 93 J7
Pullman Rd DERBYE DE21 ...... 241 J6
Pump Cl MTLK DE4 ...... 156 F7
Pump Hollow La MSFD NG18 ...... 165 K3
Pump Hollow Rd MSFDW NG19.. 165 K2
Pump La ASHB DE6 ...... 248 E2
Purbeck Av CHSW S40 ...... 2 A1
Purbeck Cl LGEAT NG10 ...... 260 D2
  MSFDW NG19 ...... 149 M4
Purchase Av HEANOR DE75 ...... 201 M8
Purdy Meadow LGEAT NG10 ...... 260 C5
Purseglove Dr BUX SK17 ...... 84 A6
Pursglove Rd BUX SK17 ...... 83 M6
Putney Cl DERBYW DE22 ...... 239 H5
Pybus St DERBYW DE22 ...... 240 A4
Pye Av NORM/LIT DE23 ...... 164 A3
Pyegrove GLSP SK13 ...... 26 C1
Pyegrove Rd GLSP SK13 ...... 26 C1
Pye Hill Rd EWD/SEL/PNX NG16.. 188 D6
Pykestone Cl DERBYE DE21 ...... 227 J8
Pym Leys LGEAT NG10 ...... 260 C5
Pynot Rd CHNE S41 ...... 91 L8
Pytchley Cl BPR/DUF DE56 ...... 200 A6

Q

The Quadrant BUX SK17 ...... 99 L2
  TOT/DORE S17 ...... 69 H5
Quaker La MSFD NG18 ...... 164 E4
Quaker Wy MSFD NG18 ...... 164 E3
Quantock Cl DERBYSE DE24 ...... 256 A8
Quantock Rd LGEAT NG10 ...... 260 D1
Quantock Wy CHSW S40 ...... 109 L5
Quarndon Hts
  DERBYW DE22 ...... 225 M8
Quarndon Vw
  DERBYW DE22 ...... 225 M8
Quarn Dr DERBYW DE22 ...... 225 M7
Quarn St DERBY DE1 ...... 4 B1
Quarn Wy DERBY DE1 ...... 4 C1
Quarry Bank MTLK DE4 ...... 156 E3
Quarry Bank Rd CHNE S41 ...... 3 L6
Quarry Cl GLSP SK13 ...... 26 C1
Quarry Clough STLY SK15 ...... 16 A2
Quarrydale Av ASH NG17 ...... 163 H5
Quarrydale Dr ASH NG17 ...... 163 H5
Quarrydale Rd ASH NG17 ...... 163 J6
Quarry Gv WRKN S81 ...... 77 M3
Quarry Hl ECK/KIL S21 ...... 72 A8
  HACK/IN S12 ...... 72 D2
  ILK DE7 ...... 244 C2
Quarry Hill Rd ILK DE7 ...... 230 C5
Quarry La ALFN DE55 ...... 159 G4
  ALFN DE55 ...... 160 C6
  CHSW S40 ...... 109 M8
  ECC S11 ...... 54 F4
  MSFD NG18 ...... 164 D5
  MTLK DE4 ...... 157 H3
Quarry Rd ALFN DE55 ...... 187 M3
  BPR/DUF DE56 ...... 199 J8
  BSVR S44 ...... 113 K7
  DRON S18 ...... 91 K1
  ECK/KIL S21 ...... 73 M3
  ILK DE7 ...... 227 L1
  NM/HAY SK22 ...... 34 C7
  NM/HAY SK22 ...... 44 A3
  TOT/DORE S17 ...... 69 H5
Quarry Vale Gv HACK/IN S12 ...... 56 F6
Quarry Vale Rd HACK/IN S12 ...... 56 F6
Quarry Vd ASH NG17 ...... 163 H6
Queen Elizabeth Crs WRKS S80 .. 77 K6
Queen Elizabeth Wy ILK DE7 ...... 229 H5
Queen Mary Cl
  SHEFP/MNR S2 ...... 56 D3
Queen Mary Crs SHEFP/MNR S2 .. 56 D2
Queen Mary Gv
  SHEFP/MNR S2 ...... 56 C3
Queen Mary Ms
  SHEFP/MNR S2 ...... 56 D3
Queen Mary Rd CHSW S40 ...... 127 L1
  SHEFP/MNR S2 ...... 56 D3
Queen's Av BUX SK17 ...... 100 A3
  HEANOR DE75 ...... 202 A8
  ILK DE7 ...... 228 F4
  ILK DE7 ...... 230 D5
Queensbury Cha
  NORM/LIT DE23 ...... 255 K3
Queens Cl WRKS S80 ...... 96 E5
Queens Ct BUT DE14 ...... 280 E2
Queen's Dr BPR/DUF DE56 ...... 199 H5
  EWD/SEL/PNX NG16 ...... 203 H5
  GLSP SK13 ...... 26 C1
  ILK DE7 ...... 230 B3
  LGEAT NG10 ...... 244 E6
  NORM/LIT DE23 ...... 239 M8
  SWAD DE11 ...... 282 C5
Queensferry Gdns
  DERBYSE DE24 ...... 257 G6
Queensland Cl MCKLVR DE3 ...... 239 H6
Queensland Crs
  STPNHL/WHNL DE15 ...... 274 F8

Queens Ri
 BUTN/AL/TUT DE13 ...... 263 M4 🡒
Queen's Rd BUX SK17 ...... 100 A2
 SHEFF/MNR S2 ...... 55 L2
 WRKS S80 ...... 96 E4
Queens Rd North
 EWD/SEL/PNX NG16 ...... 203 J8
Queens Rd South
 EWD/SEL/PNX NG16 ...... 217 J1
Queen's Sq
 EWD/SEL/PNX NG16 ...... 203 J8 🡒
Queen's St MSHM DE12 ...... 295 M5
Queen St ALFN DE55 ...... 176 C5
 ALFN DE55 ...... 188 A2
 ASH NG17 ...... 163 J6
 BPR/DUF DE56 ...... 199 K7
 BUT DE14 ...... 280 F1
 BUX SK17 ...... 83 M6
 BUX SK17 ...... 134 E4 🡒
 CHSW S40 ...... 2 F7
 CLCR S45 ...... 144 F8
 CLCR S45 ...... 160 F1
 DERBY DE1 ...... 4 E2
 ECK/KIL S21 ...... 73 H7
 EWD/SEL/PNX NG16 ...... 176 F7
 EWD/SEL/PNX NG16 ...... 188 D6
 EWD/SEL/PNX NG16 ...... 202 F7
 GLSP SK13 ...... 17 K6
 GLSP SK13 ...... 25 L2
 ILK DE7 ...... 230 B2 🡒
 LGEAT NG10 ...... 261 G3
 MOS S20 ...... 72 F4
 MPL/ROM SK6 ...... 32 C4 🡒
 MSFD NG18 ...... 164 E3
 MTLK DE4 ...... 171 G6
 RIPLEY DE5 ...... 201 J3
 STV/CWN S43 ...... 111 J1
 STV/CWN S43 ...... 112 A2
 SWAD DE11 ...... 289 K1
 WRKS S80 ...... 115 H1
Queen St North CHNE S41 ...... 110 D2
Queensview Dr RIPLEY DE5 ...... 201 K3
Queen's Wk SBK/MW NG20 ...... 133 K1
Queensway ALFN DE55 ...... 160 C7
 CDON/KEG DE74 ...... 271 J6
 CLCR S45 ...... 160 F1
 DERBYW DE22 ...... 240 A3
 MELB/CHEL DE73 ...... 278 C2
 MSFDW NG19 ...... 165 K1
 RCH S42 ...... 146 B1 🡒
Queen Victoria Rd RCH S42 ...... 144 F7
 TOT/DORE S17 ...... 69 J5
Quenby La RIPLEY DE5 ...... 201 H1
Quentin Ri CHF/WBR SK23 ...... 60 F4
Quick Cl MELB/CHEL DE73 ...... 278 D3 🡒
Quick Hill Rd DERBYSE DE24... 255 M8 🡒
Quiet La ECC S11 ...... 53 L4
Quillings Wy
 BWSH/BRSTN DE72 ...... 259 G1 🡒
Quilow La ASHB DE6 ...... 208 A7
Quixhill Bank UTXR ST14 ...... 218 C2
Quixhill Cl ASHB DE6 ...... 207 L2
Quixhill La UTXR ST14 ...... 218 B3
Quoit Gn DRON S18 ...... 90 E1
Quorndon Crs LGEAT NG10 ...... 261 G5
Quorn Dr CHSW S40 ...... 109 K5 🡒
Quorn Ri NORM/LIT DE23 ...... 256 B4

R

Rabown Av NORM/LIT DE23 ...... 256 A2
Racecourse Mt CHNE S41 ...... 110 C2
Racecourse Rd CHNE S41 ...... 110 C1 🡒
 MSFD NG18 ...... 165 H5
Racecourse Rd East CHNE S41... 110 C2
Radbourne La ASHB DE6 ...... 238 F5
 DERBYW DE22 ...... 239 J3
Radbourne St DERBYW DE22 ...... 239 M4
Radburn Ct BSTN/STPLFD NG9... 245 H1
Radcliffe Av DERBYSE DE24 ...... 241 J3
Radcliffe Dr DERBYW DE22 ...... 240 A7
Raddle La CRTAM B79 ...... 292 A4
Radford Rd ILK DE7 ...... 215 J4
Radford St DERBYSE DE24 ...... 257 J3
 MSFD NG18 ...... 164 D4
Radmanthwaite Rd
 MSFDW NG19 ...... 149 G7
Rad Mdw LGEAT NG10 ...... 260 F4 🡒
Radnor Pl MSFDW NG19 ...... 148 F6
Radnor St DERBYE DE21 ...... 241 G3
Radstock Gdns
 DERBYE DE21 ...... 227 H8 🡒
Radstone Ct DERBYE DE21 ...... 227 L8 🡒
Raeburn Cl GLV S14 ...... 56 B8
Raeburn Dr BSTN/STPLFD NG9... 245 H8
 MPL/ROM SK6 ...... 32 E2 🡒
Raeburn Pl GLV S14 ...... 56 B7
Raeburn Rd GLV S14 ...... 56 B7
Raeburn Wy SHEFS S8 ...... 56 B8
Raglan Av DERBYW DE22 ...... 239 M5 🡒
Raglan Cl
 BUTN/AL/TUT DE13 ...... 274 A2 🡒
Raglan St ALFN DE55 ...... 175 K6
 EWD/SEL/PNX NG16 ...... 217 K1
Railway Av WRKS S80 ...... 115 C2
Railway Side SWAD DE11 ...... 289 L1
Railway St GLSP SK13 ...... 17 K5
 GLSP SK13 ...... 25 M1
Railway Ter DERBY DE1 ...... 5 J4
Rainbow Av HACK/IN S12 ...... 57 L6
Rainbow Crs HACK/IN S12 ...... 57 M6
Rainbow Dr HACK/IN S12 ...... 57 M6
Rainbow Gv HACK/IN S12 ...... 57 M6
Rainbow Pl HACK/IN S12 ...... 57 M6
Rainbow Rd HACK/IN S12 ...... 57 M6
Rainbow Wy HACK/IN S12 ...... 57 L6
Rainham Gdns DERBYSE DE24 ... 257 K5
Rainier Dr DERBYE DE21 ...... 241 K4 🡒
Rain's La MTLK DE4 ...... 170 F6
Rake La BKWL DE45 ...... 137 M8
 BKWL DE45 ...... 138 B7
Rakes La ASHB DE6 ...... 179 K4
Rakes Rd BKWL DE45 ...... 136 E1
The Rake BKWL DE45 ...... 136 E2
Raleigh Cl ILK DE7 ...... 217 J7 🡒
Raleigh Rd MSFDW NG19 ...... 164 A2

SHEFS S8 ...... 55 L4
Raleigh St DERBYW DE22 ...... 239 M5 🡒
Ralph Dr ALFN DE55 ...... 188 A3
Ralph Rd STV/CWN S43 ...... 93 K8
Ralston Ct MOS S20 ...... 73 G4 🡒
Ralston Cft MOS S20 ...... 73 H4 🡒
Ralston Gv MOS S20 ...... 73 G4 🡒
Rambler Cl SWAD DE11 ...... 282 D5 🡒
Ramblers Dr DERBYE DE21 ...... 227 M7
Ramper Av STV/CWN S43 ...... 95 H8
Rampton Rd ABRD S7 ...... 55 J3 🡒
Ramscliff Av MSHM DE12 ...... 295 J1
Ramsdean Dr DERBYE DE21 ...... 241 G2
Ramsden Cl GLSP SK13 ...... 17 M8
Ramsden Rd HOLM/MEL HD7 ...... 8 F7
Ramsey Av CHSW S40 ...... 2 B8
Ramsey Cl BSTN/STPLFD NG9... 231 H8
Ramshaw Cl CHSW S40 ...... 109 M3 🡒
Ramshaw Rd DRON S18 ...... 91 H4 🡒
Ramshorn Rd COLE S10 ...... 204 A2
Ranby Rd ECC S11 ...... 54 E3
Randall Dr SWAD DE11 ...... 282 E6 🡒
Randall Pl SHEFF/MNR S2 ...... 55 J2 🡒
Randall St ECK/KIL S21 ...... 72 E8 🡒
 SHEFF/MNR S2 ...... 55 K1
Randol Cl MSFD NG18 ...... 164 A6
Randolph Rd NORM/LIT DE23 ...... 256 C2
Ranelagh Dr ECC S11 ...... 54 E5
Ranelagh Gdns
 DERBYW DE22 ...... 239 L3 🡒
Raneld Mt CHSW S40 ...... 127 M2
Rangemoor La ASHB DE6 ...... 205 M4
Rangemore Dr MCKLVR DE3 ...... 239 H6
Rangemore St BUT DE14 ...... 273 L7
Range Rd ASHZ LE65 ...... 291 M4
Ranmoor Cliffe Rd FUL S10 ...... 54 B1
Ranmoor Cl CHNE S41 ...... 3 L9
Ranmoor Crs FUL S10 ...... 54 C1
Ranmoor Hl HATH/EY S32 ...... 66 B2
Ranmoor Park Rd FUL S10 ...... 54 C1 🡒
Ranmoor Rd FUL S10 ...... 54 C1 🡒
Ranmore Cl DERBYE DE21 ...... 242 C5 🡒
Rannoch Cl DERBYE DE21 ...... 226 B7
Rannoch Dr MSFDW NG19 ...... 164 A5
Ranson Rd BSTN/STPLFD NG9... 261 M1
Ranworth Ct DERBYSE DE24... 257 G7
Ratcher Wy MSFDW NG19 ...... 165 L2
Ratcliff Cl ASHZ LE65 ...... 291 K4 🡒
Ratcliffe Av BUT DE14 ...... 280 E2 🡒
Ratcliffe St ECC S11 ...... 55 G2
Ratcliffe St
 EWD/SEL/PNX NG16 ...... 203 J8
Raven Av ALFN DE55 ...... 161 J5
Raven Cl ECK/KIL S21 ...... 72 E7
Ravencarr Pl SHEFF/MNR S2 ...... 56 D1
Ravencarr Rd SHEFF/MNR S2 ...... 56 D1
Raven Cl ALFN DE55 ...... 187 M4 🡒
 MSHM DE12 ...... 295 L6
Ravenfield Cl MOS S20 ...... 57 K8
Ravenhill Cl
 BSTN/STPLFD NG9 ...... 245 L6 🡒
Raven Oak Cl BPR/DUF DE56 ...... 199 K8
Raven Rd ABRD S7 ...... 55 G4
Ravenscourt Rd DERBYW DE22 ... 239 L4
Ravenscroft Av HAN/WDH S13 ... 57 H2
Ravenscroft Cl HAN/WDH S13 ... 57 H2 🡒
Ravenscroft Ct
 HAN/WDH S13 ...... 57 H2 🡒
Ravenscroft Crs HAN/WDH S13 ... 57 H2
Ravenscroft Dr DERBYE DE21 ... 241 J4
 HAN/WDH S13 ...... 57 H2
Ravenscroft Ov
 HAN/WDH S13 ...... 57 H2 🡒
Ravenscroft Pl HAN/WDH S13 ... 57 H2 🡒
Ravenscroft Rd HAN/WDH S13 ... 57 H3
Ravenscroft Wy HAN/WDH S13 ... 57 H1
Ravensdale Av LGEAT NG10 ...... 244 E8
 MSFD NG18 ...... 165 G2 🡒
Ravensdale Cl STV/CWN S43... 111 M4
Ravensdale Dr
 WOL/BIL/BRX NG8 ...... 231 M7
Ravensdale Rd DERBYW DE22 ... 225 M7
 DRON S18 ...... 89 M1
 MSFD NG18 ...... 165 G2
Ravenstor Rd MTLK DE4 ...... 171 J8
Raven St DERBYW DE22 ...... 4 A7
Ravens Wy BUT DE14 ...... 273 L6 🡒
Ravenswood Rd RCH S42 ...... 109 K5 🡒
Rawdon Cl CDON/KEG DE74 ...... 271 K6 🡒
Rawdon Rd MSHM DE12 ...... 290 B5
Rawdon St NORM/LIT DE23 ...... 240 C8
Rawlinson Av NORM/LIT DE23 ... 256 D3
Rawson Gn BPR/DUF DE56 ...... 214 C1
Rawson St EWD/SEL/PNX NG16... 189 K4
Raylawn St MSFD NG18 ...... 165 K4
Rayleigh Av STV/CWN S43 ...... 111 G2
Raynald Rd SHEFF/MNR S2 ...... 56 D1
Rayneham Rd ILK DE7 ...... 216 F6
Raynesway DERBYE DE21 ...... 241 L6
 DERBYSE DE24 ...... 257 L3 🡒
 DERBYSE DE24 ...... 257 L3 🡒
Raynesway Park Dr
 DERBYE DE21 ...... 257 K1
Raynford Av BSTN/STPLFD NG9... 246 B1
Ray's Av HEANOR DE75 ...... 216 B1
Ray St HEANOR DE75 ...... 216 B1
Reader St DERBYE DE21 ...... 242 B5
Readman Rd
 BSTN/STPLFD NG9 ...... 245 K7
Recreation Cl ALFN DE55 ...... 176 B1
 STV/CWN S43 ...... 95 H6
Recreation Dr SBK/MW NG20 ...... 133 H4
Recreation Rd BUX SK17 ...... 83 M6
 LGEAT NG10 ...... 244 E4
 MSFDW NG19 ...... 148 C3
 MTLK DE4 ...... 183 H5
 SBK/MW NG20 ...... 133 H5
 STV/CWN S43 ...... 111 J3
Recreation St
 EWD/SEL/PNX NG16 ...... 189 L4
 LGEAT NG10 ...... 261 J2
 MSFD NG18 ...... 164 F3
Recreation Ter
 BSTN/STPLFD NG9 ...... 245 G4 🡒
Recreation Vw SBK/MW NG20... 133 H4
Rectory Cl BSVR S44 ...... 112 D7
 ECK/KIL S21 ...... 73 H6
 MELB/CHEL DE73 ...... 279 H8 🡒

Rectory Dr RCH S42 ...... 128 A6
Rectory Gdns AU/AST/KP S26 ...... 75 H4
 BWSH/BRSTN DE72 ...... 270 D3
 ECK/KIL S21 ...... 74 A4
Rectory La BPR/DUF DE56 ...... 196 E1
 ILK DE7 ...... 227 G6
 MSHM DE12 ...... 294 F6
Rectory Ms RDERBYSW DE65 ...... 265 L6
Rectory Rd BSVR S44 ...... 112 D6
 BWSH/BRSTN DE72 ...... 260 B2
 ECK/KIL S21 ...... 74 A4
 STV/CWN S43 ...... 93 H8
 STV/CWN S43 ...... 95 H6
Reculver Cl NORM/LIT DE23 ...... 256 A5
Redacre Cl BSVR S44 ...... 113 M8 🡒
Red Barn Cl ALFN DE55 ...... 161 L7
Redbarn La ALFN DE55 ...... 161 L7
Redbarn Wy ASH NG17 ...... 177 M1
Redbrook Av CHNE S41 ...... 3 J9
Redbrook Cft HACK/IN S12 ...... 57 K7 🡒
Redbrook Gv MOS S20 ...... 57 K7 🡒
Redbury Cl DERBY DE1 ...... 4 A5
Redcar Cl MSFD NG18 ...... 165 H5
Redcar Gdns DERBYE DE21 ...... 241 G1
Redcliffe Rd MSFD NG18 ...... 165 G4
Redcliffe St ASH NG17 ...... 163 K6
Reddish Av CHF/WBR SK23 ...... 58 F4
Reddish La CHF/WBR SK23 ...... 59 G4
Reddish Rd CHF/WBR SK23 ...... 59 G4
Redfern Av MOS S20 ...... 73 G1
 RIPLEY DE5 ...... 187 H8
Redfern Cl GLSP SK13 ...... 17 K4 🡒
Redfern Ct MOS S20 ...... 73 G1
Redfern Dr MOS S20 ...... 73 G1
Redfern Gv MOS S20 ...... 73 G1
Redfern Rd UTXR ST14 ...... 247 K1
Redfern St RCH S42 ...... 144 F5
Redgap La BUX SK17 ...... 100 D1
Redgate Cl GLSP SK13 ...... 17 M6
Redgate Ct MSFDW NG19 ...... 164 B2
Redgate St
 EWD/SEL/PNX NG16 ...... 177 G7
 MSFDW NG19 ...... 164 B2
Redgrove Wy CHSW S40 ...... 127 M2
Red Hl MTLK DE4 ...... 157 M6
Redhill La BUTN/AL/TUT DE13 ... 263 L5
Red Hill La MTLK DE4 ...... 158 A6
Redhill Lodge Rd
 SWAD DE11 ...... 282 D3 🡒
Redhouse Cl STV/CWN S43 ...... 92 A6 🡒
Redhouse La POY/DIS SK12 ...... 43 H4
Redland Cl BSTN/STPLFD NG9 ... 245 M6 🡒
 DERBYE DE24 ...... 256 C6 🡒
 ILK DE7 ...... 217 J8
Redland Dr BSTN/STPLFD NG9 ... 245 M7
Red La ALFN DE55 ...... 176 B7
 BPR/DUF DE56 ...... 213 L4
 CHNE S41 ...... 110 F1
 ECC S11 ...... 54 F1
 EWD/SEL/PNX NG16 ...... 203 H1
 POY/DIS SK12 ...... 42 E5
 RDERBYSW DE65 ...... 276 C4
Red Lion Hl MTLK DE4 ...... 181 K1 🡒
Redmires Dr MELB/CHEL DE73 ... 257 K8
Redmires La FUL S10 ...... 53 G1
Redmires Rd FUL S10 ...... 52 D2
Redmoor Cl RIPLEY DE5 ...... 201 L1
 STPNHL/WNHL DE15 ...... 274 E6
Rednall Cl CHSW S40 ...... 109 L5 🡒
Redmoor La NM/HAY SK22 ...... 43 L4
Redruth Cl WOL/BIL/BRX NG8 ... 231 M4
Redruth Dr MSFD NG18 ...... 165 K8
Redruth Pl DERBYSE DE24 ...... 257 M5 🡒
Redshaw St DERBYW DE22 ...... 240 B3
Redstart Cl DERBYE DE21 ...... 242 C4
Redthorn Rd HAN/WDH S13 ...... 57 J2
Redvers Buller Rd CHSW S40 ...... 3 G8
Redway Cft MELB/CHEL DE73 ... 278 D2 🡒
Redwing Cl WRKN S81 ...... 77 M4
Redwing Cft NORM/LIT DE23 ... 256 A3 🡒
Redwood Av ECK/KIL S21 ...... 73 M5
Redwood Cl STV/CWN S43 ...... 111 K2
Redwood Dr
 STPNHL/WNHL DE15 ...... 281 K2
Redwood Rd DERBYSE DE24 ...... 256 B7
Reedman Rd LGEAT NG10 ...... 260 E6
Reeves Rd NORM/LIT DE23 ...... 256 E1
Reform St ASH NG17 ...... 163 J8
Regan Rd MSHM DE12 ...... 295 K5
Regency Cl GLSP SK13 ...... 26 A1 🡒
 NORM/LIT DE23 ...... 256 E1
Regency Wy
 BUTN/AL/TUT DE13 ...... 274 A2 🡒
Regent Cl EWD/SEL/PNX NG16 ... 188 C6
Regent St ASH NG17 ...... 163 G8
 DERBY DE1 ...... 5 H7 🡒
 EWD/SEL/PNX NG16 ...... 202 E7 🡒
 GLSP SK13 ...... 26 A1 🡒
 ILK DE7 ...... 230 C3 🡒
 LGEAT NG10 ...... 244 F5
 LGEAT NG10 ...... 261 G2
 MSFD NG18 ...... 164 E3
 STV/CWN S43 ...... 95 G6
 SWAD DE11 ...... 289 K1
Reginald Rd North
 DERBYE DE21 ...... 241 J3
Reginald Rd South
 DERBYE DE21 ...... 241 J4
Reginald St NORM/LIT DE23 ...... 5 G9
Regis Cl DERBYE DE21 ...... 227 L8
Reigate Dr DERBYW DE22 ...... 239 J3
Reindeer St MSFD NG18 ...... 165 G4
Rembrandt Dr DRON S18 ...... 90 B1
Renals St NORM/LIT DE23 ...... 4 E8
Reney Av SHEFS S8 ...... 70 A4
Reney Dr SHEFS S8 ...... 70 A4
Reney Rd SHEFS S8 ...... 70 B3
Renfrew Ct MSFDW NG19 ...... 164 B5
Renfrew St DERBYE DE21 ...... 241 H3
Renishaw Rd STV/CWN S43 ...... 93 M5
Rennes Cl ASHZ LE65 ...... 291 K4
Renshaw Dr SWAD DE11 ...... 282 C5
Renshaw Rd ECC S11 ...... 54 D4
Repton Av HACK/IN S12 ...... 56 D3
 NORM/LIT DE23 ...... 256 B2
Repton Dr ILK DE7 ...... 230 E3 🡒
Repton Pl DRON S18 ...... 89 M1 🡒
Repton Rd LGEAT NG10 ...... 260 C6

 MSHM DE12 ...... 295 K5
 RDERBYSW DE65 ...... 266 D5
 SWAD DE11 ...... 283 J3
Reservoir Hl SWAD DE11 ...... 290 A3
Reservoir Rd
 BUTN/AL/TUT DE13 ...... 273 J6
 CHF/WBR SK23 ...... 59 G3
Rest Hvn SWAD DE11 ...... 282 E5 🡒
Retford Cl DERBYE DE21 ...... 227 G8 🡒
Retford Rd HAN/WDH S13 ...... 57 L1
Revill Cl ILK DE7 ...... 216 F8
Revill Crs BSTN/STPLFD NG9 ... 245 J2
Revill La HAN/WDH S13 ...... 57 M4
Rex Av ABRD S7 ...... 54 E6
Reynard Crs ECK/KIL S21 ...... 93 L2
Reynards La BUX SK17 ...... 151 G5
Reynolds Av RIPLEY DE5 ...... 201 J1
Reynolds Dr DRON S18 ...... 90 B2
Reynolds Dr MPL/ROM SK6 ...... 32 C2 🡒
Rhodes Av CHNE S41 ...... 110 C5 🡒
Rhodes St GLSP SK13 ...... 17 L5
Rhodes Wk MSFD NG18 ...... 164 B4
Rhodeswood Dr GLSP SK13 ...... 17 K4 🡒
Rhuddlan Pl CHF/WBR SK23 ...... 60 A1
Ribble Av MSFD NG18 ...... 165 H5
Ribblesdale ILK DE7 ...... 229 M5 🡒
Ribblesdale Cl
 DERBYW DE22 ...... 225 M8 🡒
Ribblesdale Dr HACK/IN S12 ...... 72 C1
Ribblesdale Rd LGEAT NG10 ...... 260 D5
Riber Av ALFN DE55 ...... 188 A2
Riber Bank GLSP SK13 ...... 25 H1 🡒
Riber Cl ILK DE7 ...... 229 H2
 LGEAT NG10 ...... 261 G5
 STV/CWN S43 ...... 111 M5
Riber Crs CLCR S45 ...... 144 E5
Riber Rd MTLK DE4 ...... 156 F8
 MTLK DE4 ...... 172 D2
Riber View Cl MTLK DE4 ...... 157 J5
Richard La BUX SK17 ...... 83 L7
Richards St SHEFF/MNR S2 ...... 55 L4 🡒
Richardson Dr ILK DE7 ...... 215 J4 🡒
Richardsons La ALFN DE55 ...... 188 A4
Richardson St DERBYW DE22 ... 240 A4 🡒
Richmond Av
 BWSH/BRSTN DE72 ...... 260 D2
 EWD/SEL/PNX NG16 ...... 203 L8
 HAN/WDH S13 ...... 57 H2
 ILK DE7 ...... 217 K6
 LGEAT NG10 ...... 244 D6
 NORM/LIT DE23 ...... 255 M2 🡒
Richmond Cl CHSW S40 ...... 128 B2 🡒
 GLSP SK13 ...... 17 K5 🡒
 ILK DE7 ...... 229 G2 🡒
 NORM/LIT DE23 ...... 255 K3 🡒
Richmond Dr BPR/DUF DE56 ... 213 G5 🡒
Richmond Farm Ms
 HAN/WDH S13 ...... 57 H2 🡒
Richmond Gv HAN/WDH S13 ... 57 H2 🡒
Richmond Hall Av
 HAN/WDH S13 ...... 57 G2
Richmond Hall Crs
 HAN/WDH S13 ...... 57 G3 🡒
Richmond Hall Dr
 HAN/WDH S13 ...... 57 G2 🡒
Richmond Hall Rd
 HAN/WDH S13 ...... 57 G2
Richmond Hall Wy
 HAN/WDH S13 ...... 57 G3 🡒
Richmond Hill Rd
 HAN/WDH S13 ...... 57 G3 🡒
Richmond Park Cl
 HAN/WDH S13 ...... 57 H1 🡒
Richmond Park Dr
 HAN/WDH S13 ...... 57 H1
Richmond Park Gv
 HAN/WDH S13 ...... 57 G1
Richmond Park Rd
 HAN/WDH S13 ...... 57 H1
Richmond Park Vw
 HAN/WDH S13 ...... 57 H2
Richmond Park Wy
 HAN/WDH S13 ...... 57 H1 🡒
Richmond Pl HAN/WDH S13 ...... 57 G2 🡒
Richmond Rd DERBYE DE21 ...... 241 J4 🡒
 HAN/WDH S13 ...... 57 H2
 HAN/WDH S13 ...... 57 H2
 NORM/LIT DE23 ...... 256 D1
Richmond St BUT DE14 ...... 273 M6
 MSFD NG18 ...... 165 J4
Richworth Rd HAN/WDH S13 ...... 57 J2
Ridding La UTXR ST14 ...... 205 H8
Riddings DERBYW DE22 ...... 226 B6
Riddings Cl SHEFF/MNR S2 ...... 56 E5
Riddings La ASHB DE6 ...... 223 L8
 ASHB DE6 ...... 262 B3
 HATH/EY S32 ...... 87 G6
Riddings St DERBYW DE22 ...... 4 C7
Ridd Wy RCH S42 ...... 128 D7
Ridge Av MPL/ROM SK6 ...... 32 D6
Ridge Cl ASH NG17 ...... 163 G7
 GLSP SK13 ...... 17 H6
Ridge Crs MPL/ROM SK6 ...... 32 C7
Ridgedale Rd BSVR S44 ...... 131 K1
Ridgedale Vw RIPLEY DE5 ...... 187 G8 🡒
Ridgehill Av HACK/IN S12 ...... 56 D5
Ridgehill Gv HACK/IN S12 ...... 56 E5
Ridge La BPR/DUF DE56 ...... 185 L6
Ridge La CHF/WBR SK23 ...... 80 A3
 MPL/ROM SK6 ...... 32 D6
The Ridge ALFN DE55 ...... 176 B1
 FUL S10 ...... 53 M1
Ridge Top La NM/HAY SK22 ...... 34 F8
Ridge Vw DRON S18 ...... 71 G7
 HEANOR DE75 ...... 216 C2 🡒
 MELB/CHEL DE73 ...... 269 K2
 STV/CWN S43 ...... 95 J7
Ridgeway Av BSVR S44 ...... 113 L8
 NORM/LIT DE23 ...... 255 M4
Ridgeway Cescent HACK/IN S12... 56 D4
Ridgeway Crs HACK/IN S12 ...... 56 D4
Ridgeway Dr HACK/IN S12 ...... 56 D4
 ILK DE7 ...... 229 L5
Ridgeway La BPR/DUF DE56 ...... 185 L6
Ridgeway Moor HACK/IN S12 ...... 72 B4
Ridgeway Rd HACK/IN S12 ...... 56 D4 🡒
 SHEFF/MNR S2 ...... 56 D4 🡒

 STPNHL/WNHL DE15 ...... 281 H4
The Ridgeways NM/HAY SK22 ...... 35 G8 🡒
The Ridgway POY/DIS SK12 ...... 42 F3
Ridgeway West STV/CWN S43 ...... 95 H8
Ridgewood Ct DERBYE DE21 .. 227 H8 🡒
Ridgewood Dr
 BSTN/STPLFD NG9 ...... 245 M6 🡒
 MTLK DE4 ...... 171 M4
Ridgway Rd ASHZ LE65 ...... 291 J5
Riding Bank MELB/CHEL DE73 ... 278 B3
Ridings Rd GLSP SK13 ...... 17 J5
The Ridings BWSH/BRSTN DE72... 242 F4
 MSFDW NG19 ...... 165 J1
Rigga La BPR/DUF DE56 ...... 226 D1
Riggotts Wy RCH S42 ...... 109 H3
Riggs La ASHB DE6 ...... 233 K3
Rigley Av ILK DE7 ...... 230 C1
Rigsby Ct MCKLVR DE3 ...... 238 F7
Riley Av ALFN DE55 ...... 174 A2
 ASH NG17 ...... 162 F7
Riley Back La HATH/EY S32 ...... 86 B5
Riley Cl ASH NG17 ...... 162 F7 🡒
Riley La RIPLEY DE5 ...... 186 E4
Rimsdale Cl DERBYSE DE24 ...... 256 B7
Ringer La STV/CWN S43 ...... 95 H7
Ringer Wy STV/CWN S43 ...... 95 H7
Ringinglow Rd ECC S11 ...... 53 L6
Ring-o-bells La POY/DIS SK12 ... 43 G4
Ringstone Wy CHF/WBR SK23 ...... 59 G2
Ringwood Av CHNE S41 ...... 110 B3
 MSFD NG18 ...... 164 F6
 STV/CWN S43 ...... 111 M2
Ringwood Rd STV/CWN S43 ...... 111 J3
Ringwood Vw STV/CWN S43 ...... 111 J3
Rink Dr SWAD DE11 ...... 282 E7
Ripley Rd BPR/DUF DE56 ...... 185 M5
 BPR/DUF DE56 ...... 200 C3
Ripon Crs DERBYE DE21 ...... 241 H2
Riseholme Av
 WOL/BIL/BRX NG8 ...... 231 M7
The Rises GLSP SK13 ...... 17 J5
The Rise CHF/WBR SK23 ...... 59 G2
 DERBYE DE24 ...... 226 B8
 SWAD DE11 ...... 282 C5
Risley La BWSH/BRSTN DE72 ... 244 A8
Rivenhall Cl NORM/LIT DE23 ... 255 J3 🡒
Riverbank MTLK DE4 ...... 140 C1 🡒
The Riverbank
 RDERBYSW DE65 ...... 266 E5
Riverbank Wy GLSP SK13 ...... 26 C3
Rivercroft Cl UTXR ST14 ...... 218 C2
Riverdale Av ECC S11 ...... 54 C2
Riverdale Cl
 STPNHL/WNHL DE15 ...... 274 E5
Riverdale Dr FUL S10 ...... 54 D1
Riverdale Rd ECC S11 ...... 54 D2
Rivergreen Cl
 BSTN/STPLFD NG9 ...... 231 M8 🡒
Rivergreen Crs
 BSTN/STPLFD NG9 ...... 231 M8
Riversdale BPR/DUF DE56 ...... 185 L6
Riversfield Dr UTXR ST14 ...... 218 C7
Riverside MSHM DE12 ...... 286 F1
Riverside Cl GLSP SK13 ...... 26 A1
 HATH/EY S32 ...... 106 A1 🡒
Riverside Crs RCH S42 ...... 127 G3
Riverside Dr BUT DE14 ...... 280 C3
 HATH/EY S32 ...... 106 A1 🡒
Riverside Rd DERBYSE DE24 ...... 5 L6
River St DERBY DE1 ...... 4 E1
River Vw BPR/DUF DE56 ...... 213 J3
Rivington Rd
 BSTN/STPLFD NG9 ...... 245 H8 🡒
Roach Rd ECC S11 ...... 54 F2
Roadmeadow Cl ASHB DE6 ...... 208 A2 🡒
Robert Av MSFD NG18 ...... 164 C5
Robert Rd SHEFS S8 ...... 70 C3
Roberts Av ASH NG17 ...... 162 C3
Roberts Dr ALFN DE55 ...... 175 L6 🡒
Robertson Rd BUX SK17 ...... 99 L4
Robertson's Av BSVR S44 ...... 112 D6
Roberts St ILK DE7 ...... 230 D4
Robert St DERBY DE1 ...... 5 G2
Robey Cl MSFDW NG19 ...... 165 L1
Robey Dr EWD/SEL/PNX NG16 ... 203 J7
Robian Wy SWAD DE11 ...... 282 D6
Robina Dr
 EWD/SEL/PNX NG16 ...... 217 L2 🡒
Robin Cl UTXR ST14 ...... 218 C7
Robincroft CHSW S40 ...... 128 C3 🡒
Robin Croft Rd DERBYW DE22 ... 226 B6
Robincroft Rd RCH S42 ...... 128 A6
Robin Down Cl MSFD NG18 ...... 165 G8
Robin Down La MSFD NG18 ...... 164 F8
Robinettes La
 EWD/SEL/PNX NG16 ...... 231 G1
Robin Hood Cl
 EWD/SEL/PNX NG16 ...... 217 J1 🡒
Robin Hood Pl SWAD DE11 ...... 282 F8
Robin Hood Rd MTLK DE4 ...... 172 F8
Robin Hood Wy
 BSTN/STPLFD NG9 ...... 231 K8
 WRKS S80 ...... 97 J8
 WRKS S80 ...... 115 L2
Robinia Cl DERBYE DE21 ...... 227 M7 🡒
Robinlands La EDL/UDV S33 ...... 48 G5
Robin Rd DERBYW DE22 ...... 240 C3
Robinscross
 BWSH/BRSTN DE72 ...... 258 E1 🡒
Robin's Cross La
 RDERBYSW DE65 ...... 276 B3
Robinson Rd SWAD DE11 ...... 282 C4
Robinson's Hl
 MELB/CHEL DE73 ...... 278 C4
Robridding Rd CLCR S45 ...... 142 D7
Robson Ct DERBYSE DE24 ...... 257 K3
Roby Lea CDON/KEG DE74 ...... 271 J4
Rochdale Ct MSFD NG18 ...... 165 K5 🡒
Rochester Ct DERBYSE DE24... 257 K5
 FUL S10 ...... 53 K1 🡒
 LGEAT NG10 ...... 260 D3 🡒
Rochester Dr FUL S10 ...... 53 K1
Rochester Rd FUL S10 ...... 53 K1
Rochley Ct DERBYE DE21 ...... 227 J7
Rock Bank BUX SK17 ...... 99 M7
 CHF/WBR SK23 ...... 59 H4
Rockbourne Cl DERBYSE DE24... 258 A4
Rockcliffe Cl SWAD DE11 ...... 289 L1
Rock Ct MSFD NG18 ...... 164 F3

Rock Crs *CLCR* S45 .... 144 D6
The Rockety *DERBYE* DE21 ... 214 B6
Rockfield Rd *BUX* SK17 ...... 100 A2
Rockford Ct
 BSTN/STPLFD NG9 .... 245 H1 ◳
Rock Hl *MSFD* NG18 .... 165 G4
Rockhouse Rd *DERBYSE* DE24 ... 257 K4
Rockingham Cl *ASHZ* LE65 ... 291 M5 ◲
 CHSW S40 .... 109 M7
 DERBYW DE22 .... 226 D6
 DRON S18 .... 89 M1 ◳
The Rocklands *SBK/MW* NG20 ... 133 H6
Rock La *RCH* S42 .... 130 B4
Rockley Av
 EWD/SEL/PNX NG16 .... 217 K1
Rockley Cl *CHSW* S40 .... 128 C3
Rockley Wy *SBK/MW* NG20 ... 133 H6
Rockside Vw *MTLK* DE4 ...... 156 F3
The Rocks *MTLK* DE4 .... 157 K5
Rock St *MSFD* NG18 .... 165 G4
 NM/HAY SK22 .... 43 M3 ◳
Rodge Cft *CHNE* S41 .... 91 K7
Rodger's La *ALFN* DE55 ...... 175 K5
Rodknoll La *RCH* S42 .... 125 M2
Rod Moor Rd *TOT/DORE* S17 ... 69 L6
Rodney Cl *RDERBYSW* DE65 ... 253 H8
Rodney Wy *ILK* DE7 .... 217 J6
Rodsley Cl *CHSW* S40 .... 109 L5 ◳
Rodsley Crs *NORM/LIT* DE23 ... 256 A5 ◲
Rodsley La *ASHB* DE6 .... 221 K5
Rodwood Av *STV/CWN* S43 ... 94 C3
Roebuck Dr *MSFD* NG18 ...... 164 E7
Roebuck Pl *CHF/WBR* SK23 ... 60 E4
Roecar Cl *CHNE* S41 .... 91 L8
Roe Cross Gn *HYDE* SK14 .... 16 C5
Roe Cross Rd *HYDE* SK14 .... 16 C5
Roedean Cl *ASHZ* LE65 ...... 291 K5
Roe Farm La *DERBYE* DE21 ... 241 H3
Roehampton Dr
 BSTN/STPLFD NG9 .... 231 G8
 DERBYW DE22 .... 239 K3
Roe's La *MTLK* DE4 .... 173 K8
Roe Wk *NORM/LIT* DE23 ...... 256 D1 ◳
Roger Cl *ASH* NG17 .... 163 J5
Rogers Av *WRKS* S80 .... 115 C1
Rolaine Cl *MSFDW* NG19 ..... 149 M6
Rolleston Dr
 EWD/SEL/PNX NG16 .... 217 K2
Rolleston La
 BUTN/AL/TUT DE13 .... 264 A5
Rolleston Rd
 BUTN/AL/TUT DE13 .... 273 L1
Rollet Cl *SHEFP/MNR* S2 .... 56 D2
Rollins La *MPL/ROM* SK6 .... 32 D1
Romandale Gdns
 SHEFP/MNR S2 .... 56 F1
Roman Rd *DERBY* DE1 .... 240 E3
Roman Wy *BWSH/BRSTN* DE72 ... 258 F1
Romeley Crs *STV/CWN* S43 ... 95 G7
Romney Dr *DRON* S18 .... 90 B1
Romney Gdns *SHEFP/MNR* S2 ... 55 L4 ◳
Romsey Pl *MSFDW* NG19 ...... 163 M4
Romsley Cl *MCKLVR* DE3 .... 239 G6 ◳
Rona Cl *DERBYSE* DE24 ...... 256 B6
 MSFDW NG19 .... 164 B5
Ronald Cl *NORM/LIT* DE23 ... 255 H3
Rood La *BPR/DUF* DE56 ...... 197 J4
 STV/CWN S43 .... 95 H7
Rookery La *STLY* SK15 ...... 16 B3
Rookery La *ASH* NG17 .... 162 F7
The Rookery *MSFD* NG18 ..... 164 D3 ◳
Rooley Av *DERBYE* DE21 ..... 241 J4
Rooley Dr *ASH* NG17 .... 162 F7
Rooley La *ASH* NG17 .... 162 E5
Roosevelt Av *DERBYE* DE21 ... 241 L4
 LGEAT NG10 .... 260 F5
Roosevelt Rd *ASH* NG17 ..... 163 L6
Rooth St *MSFD* NG18 .... 164 E4
Rope Cl *MTLK* DE4 .... 183 J3
Roper Av *HEANOR* DE75 ..... 216 C2
Roper Hl *FUL* S10 .... 53 G3
The Ropewalk *BUT* DE14 .... 280 F1
 ILK DE7 .... 228 C1
 ILK DE7 .... 230 D1
Ropsley La *ASHB* DE6 .... 235 L1
Rosamond Av *TOT/DORE* S17 ... 69 K4
Rosamond Cl *TOT/DORE* S17 ... 69 K4
Rosamond Dr *TOT/DORE* S17 ... 69 K5
Rosamond Gld *TOT/DORE* S17 ... 69 K4 ◳
Rosamond Pl *TOT/DORE* S17 ... 69 K4 ◳
Rosamond's Ride
 NORM/LIT DE23 .... 256 A2
Rose Av *BSVR* S44 .... 111 K7
 BUTN/AL/TUT DE13 .... 265 K8
 BWSH/BRSTN DE72 .... 258 F1
 ILK DE7 .... 217 H8
 STV/CWN S43 .... 95 K5
Rose Bank Cl *HYDE* SK14 .... 17 G5
Roseberry Ct *DERBYE* DE21 ... 241 L1 ◳
Rosebery Hl *MSFD* NG18 ..... 164 F4 ◳
Rose Cottage Dr *ASH* NG17 ... 162 C8
Rose Cottage Gdns
 BUT DE14 .... 281 G1 ◳
Rose Ct *LGEAT* NG10 .... 260 C2
Rose Crs *STV/CWN* S43 ...... 93 M6
Rosecroft Gdns *SWAD* DE11 ... 282 A5
Rosedale Av *CHSW* S40 ...... 3 J9
 DERBYSE DE24 .... 257 K4
Rosedale Cl *LGEAT* NG10 .... 260 L4
Rosedale Dr *WOL/BIL/BRX* NG8 ... 231 L6
Rosedale Gdns *ECC* S11 ..... 55 G2 ◳
Rosedale Rd *ECC* S11 .... 55 G2 ◳
Rosedale Vw *CHSW* S40 ...... 127 L3 ◳
Rose End Av *MTLK* DE4 ...... 171 K4
Roseheath Cl
 NORM/LIT DE23 .... 256 B5 ◳
Rose Hl *CHSW* S40 .... 2 F4
 MOS S20 .... 72 E2
 SWAD DE11 .... 283 H8
Rose Hill Av *MOS* S20 ...... 72 E2
Rose Hill Cl *MOS* S20 ...... 72 E2
Rosehill Ct *BSVR* S44 ...... 131 K1
Rose Hill Dr *MOS* S20 ...... 72 D2
Rose Hl East *CHSW* S40 ..... 3 G4
Rose Hl Nth *NORM/LIT* DE23 ... 4 F9
Rose Hl West *CHSW* S40 ..... 2 F4
Roseland La *SBK/MW* NG20 ... 132 E5

Rose La *MELB/CHEL* DE73 .... 277 K5
 MPL/ROM SK6 .... 32 B5
 MSFDW NG19 .... 149 M6
Roseleigh Crs *SWAD* DE11 ... 282 C4
Rosemary Av *MSFDW* NG19 ... 164 D2
Rosemary Dr *DERBYE* DE24 ... 257 K5
 UTXR ST14 .... 247 L4 ◳
Rosemary St *MSFDW* NG19 ... 164 D2
Rosemont Cl *ASH* NG17 ..... 163 H5
Rosemoor La *DERBYE* DE21 ... 241 L1
Rosemount Ct
 DERBYW DE22 .... 225 M7 ◲
Rosemount Rd
 STPNHL/WNHL DE15 .... 274 C7 ◳
Rosengrave St *DERBY* DE1 ... 4 D6
Rose Tree La
 STPNHL/WNHL DE15 .... 282 C3
Rosette Ct *DERBYE* DE21 .... 227 M7 ◳
Rose Va *SWAD* DE11 .... 282 D5
Rose Wy *ECK/KIL* S21 .... 74 A5
Rosewood Cl *ALFN* DE55 ..... 176 E3
Rose Wood Cl *CHNE* S41 .... 110 A2 ◳
Rosewood Cl *DERBYSE* DE24 ... 257 M3 ◳
Rosewood Crs *HEANOR* DE75 ... 202 E8
Rosewood Rd
 STPNHL/WNHL DE15 .... 281 H4
Rosier Crs *ALFN* DE55 ...... 187 K2
Rosling Wy *BSVR* S44 .... 112 A8
Rosliston Rd *MSHM* DE12 .... 287 K2
 STPNHL/WNHL DE15 .... 281 H4
Rosliston Rd South
 STPNHL/WNHL DE15 .... 281 H6
Roslyn Crs *HATH/EY* S32 .... 66 D3 ◳
Roslyn Rd *HATH/EY* S32 ..... 66 D3
Rossal Dr *ASHZ* LE65 .... 291 K3
Rossell Dr *BSTN/STPLFD* NG9 ... 245 H5
Rossendale *ILK* DE7 .... 217 H6 ◳
Rossendale Cl *CHSW* S40 .... 2 C9
Rosser Av *HACK/IN* S12 ..... 58 A8
Rossington Dr *NORM/LIT* DE23 ... 255 J4
Rossington Rd *ECC* S11 ..... 54 F2
Rosslyn Gdns *DERBYSE* DE24 ... 257 K4
Rostherne Av *MPL/ROM* SK6 ... 42 B2
Roston Cl *DRON* S18 .... 90 A1 ◳
 MSFD NG18 .... 165 L5
Rothay Cl *DRON* S18 .... 90 B2
Rothbury Av
 BSTN/STPLFD NG9 .... 231 C8 ◳
Rothbury Pl *DERBYE* DE21 ... 241 H1
Rother Av *STV/CWN* S43 ..... 111 G2
Rother Cl *CHSW* S40 .... 2 D9
Rother Cft *RCH* S42 .... 145 G2
Rotherham Cl *ECK/KIL* S21 ... 74 C2
Rotherham Rd *BSVR* S44 .... 132 B1
 ECK/KIL S21 .... 74 C2
 MOS S20 .... 73 J3
 MSFDW NG19 .... 148 D4
 STV/CWN S43 .... 95 H5
Rotherham Rd North
 MOS S20 .... 73 J3 ◳
Rother Rd *ECK/KIL* S21 ..... 73 J6
Rother St *CLCR* S45 .... 145 M8
Rothervale Rd *CHSW* S40 .... 3 H9
 CHSW S40 .... 128 D3
Rother Valley Wy *MOS* S20 ... 73 L2
Rother Wy *CHNE* S41 .... 110 E4
Rotherwood Dr *ASHZ* LE65 ... 291 K3
Rotherwood Rd *ECK/KIL* S21 ... 74 B3
Rothesay Cl *DERBYSE* DE24 ... 256 B6
Rothey Gv *RCH* S42 .... 109 J5
Rothwell La *BPR/DUF* DE56 ... 199 L6 ◳
Rothwell Rd *MCKLVR* DE3 .... 239 G7
Rouen Wy *ASHZ* LE65 .... 291 K4
Rough Heanor Rd *MCKLVR* DE3 ... 239 K7
Rough La *ASHB* DE6 .... 209 G4
Roughlow La *ASHB* DE6 ...... 219 G1
Roughpiece La *BPR/DUF* DE56 ... 184 A5
Roughton Cl *MCKLVR* DE3 .... 255 G2 ◲
Round Close Rd *HOLM/MEL* HD7 ... 9 L4
Round Hill Cl *GLSP* SK13 .... 17 J7 ◲
Round Wy *NM/HAY* SK22 ...... 44 A2 ◳
Rouse St *CLCR* S45 .... 161 G1
Routh Av *CDON/KEG* DE74 ... 271 L8 ◳
Rowan Av *BSTN/STPLFD* NG9 ... 245 H1
 RIPLEY DE5 .... 201 G2 ◲
Rowan Cl *DERBYE* DE21 ...... 241 L5
 DERBYSE DE24 .... 256 A7 ◳
 ILK DE7 .... 230 C5
 MSFDW NG19 .... 165 G1
 MSHM DE12 .... 290 E4 ◳
 MSHM DE12 .... 295 M5 ◲
 MTLK DE4 .... 140 E7 ◳
 WRKS S80 .... 96 A8
Rowan Cft *ASH* NG17 .... 162 C6
Rowan Dr *ALFN* DE55 .... 175 G1
 BPR/DUF DE56 .... 214 E2
 EWD/SEL/PNX NG16 .... 189 G4
 SBK/MW NG20 .... 133 G5
Rowan Park Cl *NORM/LIT* DE23 ... 256 A3
Rowan Rd *ECK/KIL* S21 ..... 92 F1
 STV/CWN S43 .... 93 M7 ◲
Rowan Tree Cl *ASHB* DE6 .... 207 M2
Rowan Tree Dell *TOT/DORE* S17 ... 69 H7
Rowan Tree Rd *ECK/KIL* S21 ... 73 M5
Rowan Wk *GLSP* SK13 .... 17 H6 ◲
Rowbury Dr
 STPNHL/WNHL DE15 .... 274 E8
Rowdale Crs *HACK/IN* S12 ... 57 G5 ◳
Rowditch Av *DERBYW* DE22 ... 240 A7
Rowditch Pl *DERBYW* DE22 ... 240 A6
Rowena Cl *DERBYSE* DE24 ... 257 J3
Rowena Dr *ASHZ* LE65 ...... 291 K3
Rowland Cl *ALFN* DE55 ..... 175 J6 ◲
Rowland Rd *SHEFP/MNR* S2 ... 55 K2
Rowland St *ALFN* DE55 ..... 175 K6
 DERBYSE DE24 .... 257 H4 ◳
Rowley Ct *SWAD* DE11 ...... 282 E6
Rowley Gdns
 NORM/LIT DE23 .... 255 M3 ◲
Rowley La *NORM/LIT* DE23 ... 255 M3 ◲
Rowley Wy *LGEAT* NG10 ..... 260 D5
Rowsley Crs *STV/CWN* S43 ... 111 M2
Rowsley Ms *GLSP* SK13 ...... 17 H8
Rowsley St *SHEFP/MNR* S2 ... 55 L1
Rowthorne Av *ALFN* DE55 ... 187 K2
Rowthorne La *BSVR* S44 .... 147 L3
Rowton Grange Rd
 CHF/WBR SK23 .... 60 E5
Rowton St *BUTN/AL/TUT* DE13 ... 273 M4

Roxburgh Av *DERBYE* DE21 ... 241 H3 ◲
Roxton Av *SHEFS* S8 .... 70 C2 ◲
Roxton Rd *SHEFS* S8 .... 70 B1
Royal Av *LGEAT* NG10 .... 261 G1
Royal Cl *BWSH/BRSTN* DE72 ... 258 E1
Royal Croft Dr *BKWL* DE45 ... 106 B4
Royale Cl *ECK/KIL* S21 ..... 73 H7
Royal Ga *BPR/DUF* DE56 ..... 200 A7
Royal Gv *DERBYE* DE21 ...... 228 A7 ◳
Royal Hill Rd *DERBYE* DE21 ... 242 A4
Royal Ms *BSTN/STPLFD* NG9 ... 245 M4
Royal Oak Dr
 EWD/SEL/PNX NG16 .... 189 L3
Royal Rd *POY/DIS* SK12 ..... 43 G5
Royal Wy *DERBYSE* DE24 .... 241 H7
Roydon Cl *MCKLVR* DE3 ..... 238 F6
Royds Crs *WRKS* S80 .... 77 K5
Royston Av *MOS* S20 .... 57 K8 ◲
Royston Cl *ASHB* DE6 ...... 207 M2
 MOS S20 .... 57 K8
Royston Cft *MOS* S20 ...... 57 K8 ◲
Royston Dr *BPR/DUF* DE56 ... 200 A5
Royston Gv *MOS* S20 .... 57 K8 ◲
Rubens Cl *DRON* S18 .... 90 C1
 MPL/ROM SK6 .... 32 F2
Ruddington Rd *MSFD* NG18 ... 165 K8
Rudyard Av *DERBYE* DE21 ... 242 B5
Rufford Av *BSTN/STPLFD* NG9 ... 245 K2
Rufford Cl *ASH* NG17 ...... 163 J5
 CHSW S40 .... 2 D7
Rufford Rd *LGEAT* NG10 .... 260 E6
Ruffstone La *BPR/DUF* DE56 ... 213 M3
Rugby Av *ALFN* DE55 .... 175 M7
Rugby Cl *ASHZ* LE65 .... 291 K2
 BUT DE14 .... 280 F2 ◲
Rugeley Av *LGEAT* NG10 .... 261 J5 ◲
Rundle Dr *ABRD* S7 .... 55 H3
Rundle Rd *ABRD* S7 .... 55 H3
Rupert Rd *ABRD* S7 .... 55 H5
 DERBYE DE21 .... 241 K3
Rupert St *CLCR* S45 .... 145 L6
 ILK DE7 .... 230 D1
Rushcliffe Av *DERBYE* DE21 ... 241 J1
Rushcliffe Gdns
 DERBYE DE21 .... 241 J4 ◲
Rushdale Av *NORM/LIT* DE23 ... 256 A4
 SHEFS S8 .... 55 K5
Rushdale Mt *SHEFS* S8 ..... 55 K5 ◳
Rushdale Rd *SHEFS* S8 ..... 55 K5 ◲
Rushdale Ter *SHEFS* S8 .... 55 K5 ◲
Rushen Mt *RCH* S42 .... 128 C4
The Rushes *GLSP* SK13 ..... 17 J6
Rushford Dr *WOL/BIL/BRX* NG8 ... 231 M6
Rushley Av *TOT/DORE* S17 ... 69 G2
Rushley Cl *TOT/DORE* S17 ... 69 G2
Rushley Dr *TOT/DORE* S17 ... 69 G2
Rushley Rd *TOT/DORE* S17 ... 69 G2
Rush Leys *LGEAT* NG10 ..... 261 G5 ◳
 LGEAT NG10 .... 261 G6 ◲
Rushley Vw *ASH* NG17 ...... 177 M1
Rushton Cl
 BUTN/AL/TUT DE13 .... 263 M4 ◳
 MPL/ROM SK6 .... 32 D5 ◳
Rushton Dr *MPL/ROM* SK6 ... 32 C6
Rushup Cl *DERBYW* DE22 .... 226 D5 ◳
Rushup La *CHF/WBR* SK23 ... 61 M1
Rushy La *LGEAT* NG10 ...... 244 C5
Ruskin Av *LGEAT* NG10 ..... 260 E5
Ruskin Pl *BUT* DE14 .... 274 A4 ◳
 MSFDW NG19 .... 149 G8
Ruskin Sq *SHEFS* S8 .... 55 K4
Ruskin Wy *NORM/LIT* DE23 ... 255 L2
Russell Av *MPL/ROM* SK6 ... 42 B3
Russell Ct *ECC* S11 .... 54 D8 ◲
Russell Gdns
 BSTN/STPLFD NG9 .... 245 M8 ◳
 RCH S42 .... 144 E4
Russell St *ASH* NG17 ...... 163 J7
 BUT DE14 .... 274 A8 ◳
 DERBYSE DE24 .... 256 F1
 LGEAT NG10 .... 261 G1
 SWAD DE11 .... 282 F7
Russet Cl *DERBYE* DE21 .... 241 L1
 RDERBYSW DE65 .... 263 M1 ◲
Russley Rd *BSTN/STPLFD* NG9 ... 245 K2
Rustlings Rd *ECC* S11 ..... 54 D2
Ruston Cl *CHSW* S40 .... 109 L4
 SWAD DE11 .... 282 E6 ◲
Rutherford Av *MSFD* NG18 ... 165 H5
Rutherford Rd *DERBYE* DE21 ... 227 J8 ◲
Ruthyn Av *STV/CWN* S43 ... 94 D3
Rutland Av *BSTN/STPLFD* NG9 ... 245 K8
 BSVR S44 .... 131 K1
 BWSH/BRSTN DE72 .... 242 F8
 MTLK DE4 .... 156 F4
 RIPLEY DE5 .... 200 F5
Rutland Cl *STPNHL/WNHL* DE15 ... 281 C4
Rutland Ct *MCKLVR* DE3 .... 239 G7 ◳
Rutland Gv *LGEAT* NG10 .... 244 F5
Rutland Pl *BPR/DUF* DE56 ... 185 L4
Rutland Rd *CHSW* S40 ...... 2 E4
 EWD/SEL/PNX NG16 .... 188 E6
Rutland St *CHNE* S41 ...... 91 K8 ◳
 ILK DE7 .... 230 C1
 MSFD NG18 .... 164 E5
 MTLK DE4 .... 156 F4
 NORM/LIT DE23 .... 256 D1
Rutland Ter *ILK* DE7 ...... 217 J8
Rutland Wy *CHF/WBR* SK23 ... 45 G8 ◲
Ryal Cl *BWSH/BRSTN* DE72 ... 242 F5
Ryan Cl *DERBYSE* DE24 ..... 256 B7 ◳
Rydal Av *LGEAT* NG10 ...... 244 E8
 MPL/ROM SK6 .... 42 B2
Rydal Cl *DERBYW* DE22 ..... 226 B6
 DRON S18 .... 90 A1
Rydal Crs *CHNE* S41 .... 110 B2
Rydale Gdns *ASHZ* LE65 .... 291 M6
Rydal Rd *SHEFS* S8 .... 55 K5
Rydal Wy *CLCR* S45 .... 144 E7 ◳
Ryder Cl *SWAD* DE11 .... 282 A8
Rye Butts *MELB/CHEL* DE73 ... 269 H1 ◳
Rye Cl *DERBYE* DE21 .... 227 H7 ◲
Rye Crs *CLCR* S45 .... 145 G7
Ryecroft *MTLK* DE4 .... 141 G8
Ryecroft Glen Rd *TOT/DORE* S17 ... 69 J3
Ryecroft St *BSTN/STPLFD* NG9 ... 245 H2
Ryecroft Vw *TOT/DORE* S17 ... 69 G2
Ryedale Av *MSFD* NG18 ..... 165 K5

Ryedale Gdns *NORM/LIT* DE23 ... 255 M6
Ryefield Gdns *ECC* S11 .... 54 D5
Rye Flatt La *CHSW* S40 .... 127 L1
Rye Flatts La *RDERBYSW* DE65 ... 264 A1
Ryegrass Cl *BPR/DUF* DE56 ... 200 A6 ◲
Ryegrass Rd *DERBYE* DE21 ... 227 M8
Rye Hill Av *CHSW* S40 ..... 109 K8
Ryemere Cl
 EWD/SEL/PNX NG16 .... 203 H8
Ryhill Dr *HACK/IN* S12 .... 57 K8
Rykneld Cl *CLCR* S45 ...... 144 F7 ◲
Rykneld Ct *NORM/LIT* DE23 ... 255 H3
Rykneld Ri *RCH* S42 .... 128 D7
Rykneld Wy *NORM/LIT* DE23 ... 255 H5
Rykneild Hl *RIPLEY* DE5 ... 200 E8
Rykneild Rd *BPR/DUF* DE56 ... 214 E3
Rylah Hl *BSVR* S44 .... 131 J5
Ryle Rd *ABRD* S7 .... 55 H4
Rylstone Cl *HACK/IN* S12 ... 57 L8 ◳
Rylstone Gv *HACK/IN* S12 ... 57 L8 ◲
Rymill Dr *DERBYE* DE21 .... 241 J1

S

Sacheveral La *MTLK* DE4 .... 154 C6
Sacheverall Av
 EWD/SEL/PNX NG16 .... 176 F7
Sacheverel St *DERBY* DE1 ... 4 E6
Sackerville Ter *ECK/KIL* S21 ... 73 L3
Sackville Cl *CHSW* S40 .... 127 L2 ◳
Sackville St *NORM/LIT* DE23 ... 256 C2
Saddler Av *MOS* S20 .... 73 G1
Saddler Cl *MOS* S20 .... 73 G1
Saddler Gn *MOS* S20 .... 73 G1 ◲
Saddler Gv *MOS* S20 .... 73 G1
Saddlers Cl *MSFDW* NG19 ... 165 J1
Sadler Ga *DERBY* DE1 ...... 4 E3
Sadler St *MSFDW* NG19 ..... 164 C2
Saffron Dr *DERBYE* DE21 ... 241 K1
Sage Dr *SWAD* DE11 .... 283 J6
St Agnes Av *DERBYW* DE22 ... 226 A6
St Aidan's Av *SHEFP/MNR* S2 ... 56 A2
St Aidan's Cl
 BUTN/AL/TUT DE13 .... 273 M2 ◳
 SHEFP/MNR S2 .... 56 B1 ◳
St Aidan's Dr *SHEFP/MNR* S2 ... 56 B1
St Aidan's Mt *SHEFP/MNR* S2 ... 56 B2 ◳
St Aidan's Pl *SHEFP/MNR* S2 ... 56 B2
St Aidan's Rd *SHEFP/MNR* S2 ... 56 A1
St Aidan's Wy *SHEFP/MNR* S2 ... 56 B2
St Albans Cl *FUL* S10 ..... 53 M1 ◳
 RCH S42 .... 146 B2
St Albans Ct
 BUTN/AL/TUT DE13 .... 273 M3 ◳
St Albans Dr *FUL* S10 ..... 53 L1
St Albans Pl *NM/HAY* SK22 ... 43 M3 ◳
St Albans Rd *DERBYW* DE22 ... 239 M7
 FUL S10 .... 53 M1
St Albans St *NM/HAY* SK22 ... 43 M2 ◲
St Alkmund's Cl
 BPR/DUF DE56 .... 213 H6 ◲
St Alkmunds Wy
 BPR/DUF DE56 .... 213 H6 ◲
 DERBY DE1 .... 4 F2
St Andrew's Cl *ABRD* S7 ... 55 G3 ◳
 CRTAM B79 .... 293 J8
St Andrews Crs *ASH* NG17 ... 163 J4
St Andrew's Dr *ALFN* DE55 ... 187 J5
 BUTN/AL/TUT DE13 .... 273 L2
St Andrew's Ri *DERBYE* DE21 ... 227 J8 ◲
 ILK DE7 .... 230 B2 ◲
St Andrews Ri *CHSW* S40 ... 127 M2 ◳
St Andrew's Rd *ABRD* S7 ... 55 G3
St Andrews Vw *DERBYE* DE21 ... 241 H2
St Andrew St *MSFD* NG18 ... 164 F5
St Annes Cl *WRKS* S80 ..... 77 M7
St Annes Dr *WRKS* S80 ..... 77 M8
St Anne's La *CDON/KEG* DE74 ... 271 L7 ◳
St Annes St *HYDE* SK14 .... 24 D2 ◳
St Annes Vw *WRKS* S80 ..... 77 M7
St Annes Wy *WRKS* S80 ..... 77 M8
St Ann's Cl *CHF/WBR* SK23 ... 60 C4 ◳
St Augustines Av *CHSW* S40 ... 3 C9
St Augustines Crs *CHSW* S40 ... 3 C9
St Augustines Dr *CHSW* S40 ... 3 C8
St Augustines Mt *CHSW* S40 ... 2 F9
St Augustines Ri *CHSW* S40 ... 3 C9
St Augustines Rd *CHSW* S40 ... 2 F9
St Augustine St
 NORM/LIT DE23 .... 256 C2
St Barnabas La
 SHEFP/MNR S2 .... 55 K2 ◲
St Barnabas Rd *SHEFP/MNR* S2 ... 55 K2
St Bride's Wk *DERBYW* DE22 ... 239 L4 ◳
St Catherine's Rd
 SWAD DE11 .... 282 C5 ◳
St Catherine St *MSFD* NG18 ... 164 F5 ◳
St Chad's Cl
 BUTN/AL/TUT DE13 .... 273 M2 ◳
 MSFD NG18 .... 164 F7
 UTXR ST14 .... 218 A4 ◳
St Chad's Rd
 BUTN/AL/TUT DE13 .... 273 M3 ◳
 NORM/LIT DE23 .... 4 B9
St Charles Cl *GLSP* SK13 ... 17 J5 ◳
St Clare's Cl *NORM/LIT* DE23 ... 240 A8
St Cuthbert's Rd *DERBYW* DE22 ... 239 M7
St David's Cl *DERBYW* DE22 ... 240 A7
St David's Dr
 BUTN/AL/TUT DE13 .... 273 M2
St David's Ri *CHSW* S40 ... 2 A9
St Davids Rd *CRTAM* B79 ... 293 J8
St Edmund's Av *MSFDW* NG19 ... 149 M7
St Edmund's Cl *DERBYW* DE22 ... 226 C8
St Edwards Ct *SWAD* DE11 ... 282 B5 ◳
St Edward's Rd
 CDON/KEG DE74 .... 271 L8 ◳
St Elizabeth Cl *SHEFP/MNR* S2 ... 55 L2 ◳
St Francis Cl
 BUTN/AL/TUT DE13 .... 274 A2 ◳
St Georges Dr
 BSTN/STPLFD NG9 .... 245 J8 ◳
St George's Pl
 BPR/DUF DE56 .... 199 J6 ◳
St George's Rd
 BUTN/AL/TUT DE13 .... 273 J5

 NM/HAY SK22 .... 43 M2
St Giles Cl *CHSW* S40 ..... 3 J9
St Giles Rd *NORM/LIT* DE23 ... 256 C1
St Giles Wk *MTLK* DE4 ..... 156 F6 ◳
St Helens Av
 EWD/SEL/PNX NG16 .... 176 F6
St Helen's Cl *CHNE* S41 ... 91 J8 ◳
 HATH/EY S32 .... 87 G2
 MTLK DE4 .... 140 E7
St Helen's Crs
 BSTN/STPLFD NG9 .... 230 F6
St Helen's Cft *HATH/EY* S32 ... 87 C2 ◳
St Helen's Dr
 EWD/SEL/PNX NG16 .... 189 G3
St Helen's La *BPR/DUF* DE56 ... 183 K2
St Helen's St *CHNE* S41 ... 3 G1
 DERBY DE1 .... 4 D2
St Hugh's Cl *DERBYW* DE22 ... 226 C8 ◳
St James Av *ILK* DE7 ...... 230 D3
St James Cl *BPR/DUF* DE56 ... 200 A6 ◳
 CHNE S41 .... 3 L8
 GLSP SK13 .... 25 M3 ◳
 RDERBYSW DE65 .... 266 F5 ◳
St James Ct *LGEAT* NG10 ... 244 E7 ◳
St James' Dr
 EWD/SEL/PNX NG16 .... 203 H2
St James' Rd
 BUTN/AL/TUT DE13 .... 286 A1
 NORM/LIT DE23 .... 256 C1
St James's St
 BSTN/STPLFD NG9 .... 244 F4 ◳
 DERBY DE1 .... 4 E4
St James' St *BUX* SK17 .... 99 L3 ◳
 NORM/LIT DE23 .... 256 D1
St James' Ter *BUX* SK17 ... 99 L5 ◳
St John's Av *DERBYE* DE21 ... 241 L5
St Johns Cl *CHSW* S40 ..... 127 L3
 DERBYW DE22 .... 226 B7 ◳
 EDL/UDV S33 .... 50 E7 ◳
 EWD/SEL/PNX NG16 .... 203 G1
 RIPLEY DE5 .... 187 J8
St John's Crs *STV/CWN* S43 ... 95 J7
St John's Dr *BPR/DUF* DE56 ... 214 D2 ◳
 SWAD DE11 .... 282 B5 ◳
St John's Mt *CHNE* S41 .... 110 C2
St Johns Pl *STV/CWN* S43 ... 112 A1
St John's Rd *BPR/DUF* DE56 ... 199 K6 ◳
 BUTN/AL/TUT DE13 .... 273 M2
 BUX SK17 .... 83 M6
 BUX SK17 .... 99 J5
 CHNE S41 .... 110 C2 ◳
 DRON S18 .... 91 H2
 ILK DE7 .... 215 J5
 ILK DE7 .... 230 D5
 MTLK DE4 .... 156 D7
 STV/CWN S43 .... 111 M1
St John's Sq *UTXR* ST14 ... 247 J1
St John's St *ASHB* DE6 .... 193 M8
 LGEAT NG10 .... 261 G3
 MTLK DE4 .... 183 J1
St John's Ter *DERBY* DE1 ... 4 B2
St John St *MSFD* NG18 ..... 164 D5
 NM/HAY SK22 .... 34 F8
St Joseph's St *MTLK* DE4 ... 156 F5 ◳
St Jude's Wy
 BUTN/AL/TUT DE13 .... 273 M2 ◳
St Katherines Cl *MTLK* DE4 ... 140 B1
St Laurence Ct *LGEAT* NG10 ... 261 H4 ◳
St Lawrence Av *BSVR* S44 ... 131 M2
St Lawrence Cl
 HEANOR DE75 .... 202 C8 ◳
St Lawrence Rd *RCH* S42 ... 145 J4
St Lawrence Vw *WRKS* S80 ... 96 C5
St Leonards Dr *CHNE* S41 ... 3 L8
St Leonards Pl *ALFN* DE55 ... 175 H1
St Leonards Wy *MSFDW* NG19 ... 155 L1
St Luke's Rd
 BUTN/AL/TUT DE13 .... 273 M2
 BUTN/AL/TUT DE13 .... 286 A1 ◳
St Margarets
 BUTN/AL/TUT DE13 .... 273 J5
St Margaret's Dr *CHSW* S40 ... 2 F3
St Margaret St *MSFD* NG18 ... 164 F6 ◳
St Marks St *MTLK* DE4 ..... 171 K4
St Mark's Rd
 BUTN/AL/TUT DE13 .... 273 M2 ◳
 CHSW S40 .... 2 C4
 DERBYE DE21 .... 241 G3
St Martin's Cl
 BUTN/AL/TUT DE13 .... 273 M2 ◳
St Martin's Rd *MPL/ROM* SK6 ... 32 D4
St Martin's Wk *WRKS* S80 ... 96 C5
St Mary's Cl
 BWSH/BRSTN DE72 .... 259 K3 ◳
St Mary's Cl *DERBYSE* DE24 ... 257 K4 ◳
Saint Mary's Cl
 STPNHL/WNHL DE15 .... 275 H2 ◳
St Mary's Ct *DERBY* DE1 ... 4 E1
St Mary's Crs *UTXR* ST14 ... 247 L1
St Mary's Dr
 BUTN/AL/TUT DE13 .... 265 J8
 BUTN/AL/TUT DE13 .... 273 M2
St Mary's Ga *CHNE* S41 .... 3 J4
 DERBY DE1 .... 4 E3
 MTLK DE4 .... 183 J2 ◲
 SHEFP/MNR S2 .... 55 J1
St Mary's Rd *ASH* NG17 ... 163 G7
 GLSP SK13 .... 25 M1
 NM/HAY SK22 .... 43 L2
 POY/DIS SK12 .... 43 G5
 SHEF S1 .... 55 K1
St Mary's Sq *SHEFP/MNR* S2 ... 55 J1 ◲
St Mary St *ILK* DE7 .... 230 D2
St Marys Wk
 EWD/SEL/PNX NG16 .... 188 E7
St Marys Wharf Rd *DERBY* DE1 ... 240 E3
St Matthew's St *BUT* DE14 ... 280 F2
St Matthew's Wk
 DERBYW DE22 .... 226 C8 ◲
St Mawes Cl *DERBYW* DE22 ... 226 A6
St Mellion *NORM/LIT* DE23 ... 255 J1 ◳
St Michael's Cl *ASHZ* LE65 ... 291 M5
St Michael's Dr
 BPR/DUF DE56 .... 213 M4 ◲
 DERBYSE DE24 .... 257 M3 ◳
 MTLK DE4 .... 173 J8 ◲
 RDERBYSW DE65 .... 266 F5
St Michael's Dr *ALFN* DE55 ... 176 D3
St Michael's La *DERBY* DE1 ... 4 E2
St Michaels Rd
 BUTN/AL/TUT DE13 .... 274 A2

St Michael's Sq
BSTN/STPLFD NG9 .... **245** L2 🖪
St Michael's St *ASH* NG17 .... **163** K7
St Michaels Vw
DERBYSE DE24 .... **257** M3 🖪
St Modwen's Cl
BUTN/AL/TUT DE13 .... **273** M3 🖪
St Nicholas Cl *DERBY* DE22 ..... **226** A8 🖪
St Norbert Dr *ILK* DE7 .... **230** A5
St Oswald Crs *ASHB* DE6 .... **207** M1
St Pancras Wy *DERBY* DE1 ..... **240** E3 🖪
St Patricks Rd
BUTN/AL/TUT DE13 .... **273** M2
St Pauls Av *CHNE* S41........... **129** G4
St Paul's Sq *BUT* DE14 .... **273** L7 🖪
St Paul's St West *BUT* DE14 ..... **273** L6
St Peter's Br *BUT* DE14 .... **281** G1
St Peter's Churchyard
DERBY **4** E4
St Peter's Cl *BPR/DUF* DE56 ... **199** K6 🖪
BSVR S44........................ **112** D6
St Peters Cre
STPNHL/WNHL DE15 .... **281** J1 🖪
St Peters Cft *BPR/DUF* DE56 ... **199** K6 🖪
St Peter's Rd *BUX* SK17 .... **100** A1
MELB/CHEL DE73............. **269** K1
WRKS S80 .... **76** B3 🖪
St Peter's St *DERBY* DE1 .... **4** F4
STPNHL/WNHL DE15 .... **281** J1
St Peter's Wy *MSFD* NG18....... **164** E4
St Philip's Dr *CHNE* S41 .... **128** E2 🖪
St Quentin Cl
NORM/LIT DE23 .... **239** M7 🖪
TOT/DORE S17 .... **69** L5
St Quentin Dr *TOT/DORE* S17 ... **69** L5
St Quentin Mt *TOT/DORE* S17 ... **69** L5
St Quentin Ri *TOT/DORE* S17 ... **69** L5
St Quentin Vw *TOT/DORE* S17 ... **69** L5
St Ronan's Av *BPR/DUF* DE56 ... **213** H7
St Ronan's Rd *ABRD* S7 .... **55** J3
St Stephens Cl
BWSH/BRSTN DE72 .... **258** E1
NORM/LIT DE23 .... **256** A4 🖪
St Stephens Ct
BUTN/AL/TUT DE13 .... **273** M3 🖪
SWAD DE11 .... **283** J7 🖪
St Swithin's Cl *DERBYW* DE22... **240** A7
St Thomas Cl *ILK* DE7............ **161** H5
St Thomas Rd *NORM/LIT* DE23 ... **256** D1
St Thomas' St *CHSW* S40 .... **109** M8
St Vincent Cl *LGEAT* NG10 .... **261** H4
St Werburgh's Vw
DERBY DE21 .... **242** A5 🖪
St Wilfrid's Rd *ILK* DE7 .... **229** H3
SHEFF/MNR S2 .... **55** K2
St Wystan's Rd *DERBYW* DE22 ... **239** M7
Salcey Cl *ALFN* DE55............. **187** J3
Salcey Dr *BSTN/STPLFD* NG9 ... **231** G8
Salcey Sq *CHSW* S40 .... **2** B7
Salcombe Cl
EWD/SEL/PNX NG16 .... **217** M1
Salcombe Rd *ALFN* DE55........ **175** L5
Sales Av *RCH* S42 .... **144** F3
Sales La *STPNHL/WNHL* DE15 ... **274** F7
Sale St *NORM/LIT* DE23 .... **240** E8
Salisbury Av *CHNE* S41 .... **110** B3
DRON S18 .... **90** D2
STPNHL/WNHL DE15 .... **274** F7
Salisbury Crs *CHNE* S41 .... **110** C3
Salisbury Dr *BPR/DUF* DE56 .... **200** A5 🖪
SWAD DE11 .... **283** H5
Salisbury La
MELB/CHEL DE73............. **278** E3 🖪
Salisbury Rd *DRON* S18 .... **90** E3
MSFDW NG19 .... **164** B2
Salisbury St *GLSP* SK13 .... **17** K5
LGEAT NG10 .... **261** H3 🖪
NORM/LIT DE23 .... **4** B3 🖪
Sallyfield La *ASHB* DE6........... **206** B1
Sallywood Cl *DERBYSE* DE24 ... **256** A8 🖪
Salmon St *ECC* S11 .... **55** J2 🖪
Saltbrook La *ASHB* DE6 .... **262** C2
Saltburn Cl *DERBYE* DE21 .... **240** F1
Salter Cl *CDON/KEG* DE74 .... **271** J6
Saltergate *CHSW* S40 .... **2** E3
Saltergate La *EDL/UDV* S33 ...... **50** E8
Salters La *MTLK* DE4 .... **156** D6
Salvin Crs *STV/CWN* S43 .... **95** H6
Samantha Ct *DERBYE* DE21 .... **241** L1 🖪
Sampson's La *MSFDW* NG19 ..... **148** E7
Sampsons Yd *ASH* NG17......... **162** C7 🖪
Samuel Cl *MSFDW* NG19 .... **164** C2
SHEFF/MNR S2 .... **56** A3 🖪
Samuel Ct *RIPLEY* DE5 .... **201** G2 🖪
Samuel Dr *SHEFF/MNR* S2 .... **56** A3 🖪
Samuel Pl *SHEFF/MNR* S2 .... **56** A3 🖪
Samuel Rd *SHEFF/MNR* S2 .... **56** A3 🖪
Samuel St *HYDE* SK14 .... **16** F6 🖪
Sancroft Av *DERBYE* DE21 ...... **242** B4
Sancroft Rd *DERBYE* DE21 ...... **242** C4
Sandalwood Cl
DERBYSE DE24 .... **257** M3 🖪
MSFD NG18 .... **165** L6
Sandalwood Rd
STPNHL/WNHL DE15 .... **281** L6
Sandbach Cl *DERBYE* DE21 ..... **241** L1 🖪
Sandbeck Pl *ECC* S11 .... **55** G3
Sandbed La *BPR/DUF* DE56 ..... **199** M8
Sandby Ct *BSTN/STPLFD* NG9 ... **245** M5
SHEFS S8 .... **56** B8 🖪
Sandby Cft *SHEFS* S8 .... **56** B8 🖪
Sandby Dr *MPL/ROM* SK6 .... **32** E2
SHEFS S8 .... **56** B8
Sandcliffe Pk *SWAD* DE11 .... **283** G3
Sandcliffe Rd *SWAD* DE11 .... **283** G3
Sandcroft Cl *SWAD* DE11 .... **283** G5
Sanders Av *MSFD* NG18 .... **165** H2
Sanderson Rd *DERBYE* DE21 ... **241** L4 🖪
Sandfield Cl *DERBYE* DE21 ...... **241** L2 🖪
MSFD NG18 .... **165** L6
Sandford Brook
RDERBYSW DE65 .... **265** H1 🖪
Sandgate Cl *DERBYSE* DE24 ... **257** L5 🖪
Sandhall La *BPR/DUF* DE56 ..... **184** B5
Sandham La *RIPLEY* DE5 .... **200** F1
Sandhill La *MPL/ROM* SK6 .... **33** L1

Sandhill Rd
EWD/SEL/PNX NG16 .... **189** L7
Sandhills Cl *MSHM* DE12 .... **295** M6 🖪
Sandhills Rd *BSVR* S44 .... **131** L5
Sandhurst Av *MSFD* NG18........ **164** E6
Sandhurst Dr
BSTN/STPLFD NG9 .... **245** L8
Sandiacre Rd
BSTN/STPLFD NG9 .... **244** F4
Sandiway Cl *MPL/ROM* SK6 ...... **32** C2
The Sandlands *SWAD* DE11 ..... **283** G4
Sand La *ASHB* DE6 .... **248** E1
Sandmartins *WRKN* S81 .... **77** M3
Sandown Av *MCKLVR* DE3 ...... **238** F7
Sandown Cl *BUT* DE14 .... **280** D3 🖪
ECK/KIL S21 .... **72** E7 🖪
Sandown Rd *ASH* NG17 .... **163** L7
BSTN/STPLFD NG9 .... **245** J7
DERBYSE DE24 .... **257** G2
MSFD NG18 .... **165** L6
Sandpiper Cl *UTXR* ST14 .... **247** L4 🖪
Sandringham Av
STPNHL/WNHL DE15 .... **281** K1
Sandringham Cl *STV/CWN* S43 ... **111** J6
Sandringham Ct
MSFDW NG19 .... **149** L4 🖪
Sandringham Crs
WOL/BIL/BRX NG8 .... **231** M5 🖪
Sandringham Dr
BSTN/STPLFD NG9 .... **245** M1
DERBYE DE21 .... **242** C6
MSFDW NG19 .... **149** L4
Sandringham Pl *ILK* DE7 .... **230** A5 🖪
Sandringham Rd *DERBYE* DE21 ... **241** H1
LGEAT NG10 .... **244** E6 🖪
Sands Cl *GLV* S14 .... **56** B6
HYDE SK14 .... **24** A1
Sandstone Av *CHSW* S40 .... **127** L2
Sandtop Cl *SWAD* DE11 .... **290** E2
Sandtop La *SWAD* DE11 .... **290** F2
Sandwell Cl *LGEAT* NG10 .... **260** D4
Sandwood Cl *ALFN* DE55 .... **161** K7 🖪
Sandy Acres Cl *MOS* S20 .... **73** J1
Sandy Acres Dr *MOS* S20 .... **73** H1
Sandy Bank Av *HYDE* SK14 ...... **24** A1
Sandybank Cl *GLSP* SK13 .... **17** H6
Sandy Bank Wk *HYDE* SK14 ..... **24** A1 🖪
Sandybrook Cl *ASHB* DE6 .... **193** M6 🖪
Sandycliffe Cl *MSFDW* NG19 ..... **165** J1
Sandy Cl *WRKS* S80 .... **96** B5
Sandyford La *BPR/DUF* DE56 ... **184** B6
Sandy Haven Cl *HYDE* SK14 ..... **24** A1
Sandyhill Cl *MELB/CHEL* DE73 ... **257** K8
Sandy La *DERBYE* DE21 .... **214** C6
GLSP SK13 .... **24** D6
MSFD NG18 .... **165** G3
MSHM DE12 .... **288** D2
MTLK DE4 .... **157** G2
MTLK DE4 .... **185** J2
WRKS S80 .... **96** C5
Sandypits La *RDERBYSW* DE65 ... **253** M6 🖪
Sanforth St *CHNE* S41 .... **110** D4
Santolina Dr *DERBYE* DE21 ..... **227** J8 🖪🖪
Sapperton Cl
NORM/LIT DE23 .... **256** A5 🖪
Sappertonfield La *ASHB* DE6 .... **234** F6
Sapperton La *RDERBYSW* DE65 ... **251** J1
Sarah Cl *ALFN* DE55 .... **187** M3
Sark Rd *SHEFF/MNR* S2 .... **55** K3 🖪
Saundby Av *MSFDW* NG19 ...... **164** A1
Saundersfoot Wy
DERBY DE21 .... **227** L8
Savage La *TOT/DORE* S17 .... **69** G3
Save Penny La *BPR/DUF* DE56 ... **213** K5
Saville Cl *BSTN/STPLFD* NG9 ... **245** H2 🖪
Saville Rd *ASH* NG17 .... **163** J4
Sawdon Rd *ECC* S11 .... **55** H1 🖪
Sawley Dr *MSFD* NG18 .... **165** L6
Sawley Rd *BWSH/BRSTN* DE72 ... **259** L3
Sawmand Cl *LGEAT* NG10 .... **260** F4 🖪
Saw Pit La *ALFN* DE55 .... **161** L4
Sawpit La *RDERBYSW* DE65 .... **251** M8
Saxby Dr *MSFD* NG18 .... **165** L6
Saxon Cl *MELB/CHEL* DE73 ..... **279** J8 🖪
STPNHL/WNHL DE15 .... **281** J3
Saxon Dr *HEANOR* DE75......... **202** C8
Saxondale Av *MCKLVR* DE3 ..... **238** F6 🖪
Saxon Gv *RDERBYSW* DE65 .... **266** D5
Saxonlea Av *SHEFF/MNR* S2 ..... **56** F1
Saxonlea Cl *SHEFF/MNR* S2 ..... **56** F1
Saxonlea Crs *SHEFF/MNR* S2 .... **56** F1
Saxonlea Dr *SHEFF/MNR* S2 ..... **56** E1 🖪
Saxon Rd *SHEFS* S8 .... **55** K4
Saxon St *STPNHL/WNHL* DE15 ... **281** J3
Saxon Wy *ASHZ* LE65 .... **291** K5
Saxton Av *HEANOR* DE75........ **202** C8
Scaddows La *MELB/CHEL* DE73 ... **277** G7
Scafell Cl *MPL/ROM* SK6 .... **42** B2
Scalby Cl *EWD/SEL/PNX* NG16 ... **203** G8
Scaliot Cl *NM/HAY* SK22 .... **43** L2 🖪
Scalpcliffe Cl
STPNHL/WNHL DE15 .... **274** C8
Scalpcliffe Rd
STPNHL/WNHL DE15 .... **274** C7
Scarborough Av *ILK* DE7 .... **230** A2
Scarborough Ri *DERBYE* DE21 ... **241** G1
Scarcliffe La *SBK/MW* NG20 ..... **132** E3
Scarcliffe St *MSFD* NG18 .... **165** G4
Scarcliffe Ter *SBK/MW* NG20 .... **115** K8
Scargill Av *EWD/SEL/PNX* NG16 ... **217** L1
Scargill Cl *EWD/SEL/PNX* NG16 ... **217** L1
Scargill Rd *ILK* DE7 .... **229** H2
Scargill Wk
EWD/SEL/PNX NG16 .... **203** J7 🖪
Scarsdale Av *DERBYW* DE22 .... **225** M7
NORM/LIT DE23 .... **239** M8
Scarsdale Cl *DRON* S18 .... **90** E2
Scarsdale Crs *STV/CWN* S43 .... **111** G3 🖪
Scarsdale Cross *DRON* S18 ...... **90** E1 🖪
Scarsdale Pl *BUX* SK17 .... **99** L3
Scarsdale Rd *BPR/DUF* DE56 ... **213** H7 🖪
CHNE S41 .... **110** D2 🖪
DRON S18 .... **90** E1
STV/CWN S43 .... **55** J7
Scarsdale St *BSVR* S44 .... **131** H2
Scarthin *MTLK* DE4............... **171** K4
Schofield Ct *MTLK* DE4 .... **140** C1

Schofield La *CRTAM* B79 .... **292** A5
Scholes Moor Rd *HOLM/MEL* HD7 .. **9** M1
School Av *MOS* S20 .... **73** H3
School Board La *CHSW* S40 .... **2** C4
School Cl *ALFN* DE55 .... **160** A8 🖪
ALFN DE55 .... **160** C7
ALFN DE55 .... **161** K7
ALFN DE55 .... **175** M1
ASHB DE6 .... **193** K1
MOS S20 .... **73** J1
MTLK DE4 .... **140** F7
SWAD DE11 .... **289** M1
School Cft *ALFN* DE55 .... **188** A4
School Green La *FUL* S10 .... **53** L3
Schoolhouse Hl *BPR/DUF* DE56 ... **200** A1
School La *ALFN* DE55 .... **158** F8
ALFN DE55 .... **176** E6
ASHB DE6 .... **207** L1
ASHB DE6 .... **250** B6
BKWL DE45 .... **105** J5
BKWL DE45 .... **106** B5
BPR/DUF DE56 .... **186** A8
BSTN/STPLFD NG9 .... **245** M6
BSVR S44 .... **112** A7
BUTN/AL/TUT DE13 .... **264** E6
BUX SK17 .... **102** C7
CDON/KEG DE74 .... **271** K6
DRON S18 .... **90** D1
ECK/KIL S21 .... **72** B7
HATH/EY S32 .... **66** D2
LGEAT NG10 .... **244** C3
MELB/CHEL DE73............. **124** E6
MTLK DE4 .... **139**M5
MTLK DE4 .... **140** C2
MTLK DE4 .... **185** K1
RCH S42 .... **108** B7
RIPLEY DE5 .... **200** F1
SHEFS S8 .... **70** F1
SHEFS S8 .... **70** C3 🖪
School Lane Cl *SHEFS* S8 .... **70** F1
School Rd *BUX* SK17 .... **81** L5
CHNE S41 .... **110** D3
EWD/SEL/PNX NG16 .... **189** K6
EWD/SEL/PNX NG16 .... **189** K3
MTLK DE4 .... **156** F5
UTXR ST14 .... **247** J1
School Sq *ILK* DE7 .... **229** H3 🖪
School St *ECK/KIL* S21 .... **73** G7
MOS S20 .... **73** G3
MSHM DE12 .... **290** C8
MSHM DE12 .... **295** L4
SWAD DE11 .... **282** E8
The Scotches *BPR/DUF* DE56 ... **199** J5
Scotia Cl *SHEFF/MNR* S2 .... **56** C2 🖪
Scotia Dr *SHEFF/MNR* S2 .... **56** C2 🖪
Scotland St *WRKS* S80 .... **96** C4
Scotswood Rd *MSFDW* NG19 .... **149** L4
Scott Cl *RCH* S42 .... **129** H6
Scott Crs *ALFN* DE55 .... **160** C7
Scott Dr *ALFN* DE55 .... **188** A2
BPR/DUF DE56 .... **200** B5
MPL/ROM SK6 .... **32** E2
Scotts Cl *ASHZ* LE65 .... **291** K3
The Scotts *SWAD* DE11 .... **289** G3
Scott St *NORM/LIT* DE23 .... **256** C1
SBK/MW NG20 .... **115** K8
Scowerdons Cl *HACK/IN* S12 .... **57** J5
Scowerdons Dr *HACK/IN* S12 .... **57** J5
Scratta La *WRKS* S80 .... **76** F8
Screetham La *CLCR* S45 .... **125**M8
Scropton Old Rd
RDERBYSW DE65 .... **263** M2
Scropton Rd *RDERBYSW* DE65 ... **263** L2
Seaburn Rd *BSTN/STPLFD* NG9 ... **245** H7
Seaford Wy *ILK* DE7 .... **217** J5
Seaforth Sq *MSFDW* NG19 ...... **164** A5
Seagram Wy *UTXR* ST14 .... **248** A3
Seagrave Av *HACK/IN* S12 .... **56** E6
Seagrave Cl *DERBYE* DE21 ...... **241** L2
Seagrave Crs *HACK/IN* S12 .... **56** D7
Seagrave Dr *HACK/IN* S12 .... **56** D6
Seagrave Rd *HACK/IN* S12........ **56** D6
Seale St *DERBY* DE1 .... **240** E3 🖪
Sealey Cl *RDERBYSW* DE65 ..... **266** F5
Seals Rd *MSHM* DE12 .... **295** H1
Seal Vw *MSHM* DE12 .... **288** F4
Sealwood La *MSHM* DE12 .... **289** H5
Seal Wood La *MSHM* DE12 ...... **289** G5
Seanor La *CLCR* S45 .... **145** K6
Searl St *DERBY* DE1 .... **4** C2
Searson Av *BSVR* S44 .... **131** K1
Searston Av *RCH* S42 .... **146** A2
Seascale Cl *DERBYE* DE21 ...... **241** G1
Seaton Cl *MCKLVR* DE3 .... **238** F7 🖪
Second Av *BUT* DE14 .... **280** B1
BWSH/BRSTN DE72 .... **244** B6
MELB/CHEL DE73............. **269** K2
MSFDW NG19 .... **165** K2
Sedbergh Crs *CHNE* S41 .... **110** G2 🖪
Sedgebrook Cl *DERBYE* DE21 ... **227** J8 🖪🖪
Sedgefield Rd *BUT* DE14 .... **280** C3
Sedgemoor Cl *CHSW* S40 .... **109** L6
Sedgwick Cl
EWD/SEL/PNX NG16 .... **177** G8
Sedgwick St
EWD/SEL/PNX NG16 .... **188** E5
EWD/SEL/PNX NG16 .... **202** E7
Sefton Av *BSTN/STPLFD* NG9 ... **245** H2
Sefton Cl *STPNHL/WNHL* DE15 ... **281** L1
Sefton Dr *DERBYE* DE21 .... **241** J4
ECC S11 .... **54** B3
Sefton Wy *GLSP* SK13 .... **25** M2 🖪
Selborne St *DERBYSE* DE24 ..... **241** G8 🖪
Selby Cl *BSTN/STPLFD* NG9 ..... **245** H7
CHSW S40 .... **127** M2
Selhurst Rd *CHNE* S41 .... **110** C5
Selina Cl *CDON/KEG* DE74 ...... **271** K6 🖪
Selina St *MELB/CHEL* DE73 ..... **278** D3
Selkirk St *DERBYE* DE21 .... **241** H3
Sellers St *SHEFS* S8 .... **55** J3 🖪
Selly Oak Gv *SHEFS* S8 .... **70** F4
Selly Oak Rd *SHEFS* S8 .... **70** F4 🖪
Selmer Ct *STV/CWN* S43 .... **111** G2 🖪
Selside Ct *BSTN/STPLFD* NG9 ... **245** K6
Selston Rd *EWD/SEL/PNX* NG16.. **188** E6
Selworthy Cl *DERBYE* DE21 ..... **227** K8 🖪
Selwyn St *BSVR* S44 .... **131** M2
DERBYW DE22 .... **239** M4 🖪
MSFD NG18 .... **165** H5

Senners La *BUX* SK17 .... **101** K8
Serina Av *NORM/LIT* DE23 ...... **256** A2 🖪
Serin Cl *UTXR* ST14 .... **247** M4 🖪
Serlby Dr *AU/AST/KP* S26 .... **75** C3
Serlby La *AU/AST/KP* S26 .... **75** H4
Serlby Rd *EWD/SEL/PNX* NG16 ... **203** K7
Setcup La *ECK/KIL* S21 .... **72** F8
The Settlement
BWSH/BRSTN DE72 .... **242** F5
Setts Wy *RCH* S42 .... **128** E6
Sett Valley Trail *NM/HAY* SK22 ... **34** C8
Sevenlands Dr *DERBYSE* DE24 ... **257** M6
Sevenoaks Av *DERBYW* DE22 ... **239** J5
Seven Oaks Crs
BSTN/STPLFD NG9 .... **245** L1
Seven Oaks Rd *ILK* DE7 .... **244** D1
Seven Stiles Dr *MPL/ROM* SK6 ... **32** B3
Seventh Av *MSFDW* NG19 .... **165** K2
Severals *BSTN/STPLFD* NG9 .... **245** J3
Severn Cl *BUTN/AL/TUT* DE13 ... **273**M1
Severn Crs *RCH* S42 .... **145** J5
Severn Dr *BUT* DE14 .... **274** B7 🖪
Severnale Cl *DERBYE* DE21 ..... **226** E5
Severn Cl *BUTN/AL/TUT* DE13 ... **273**M1
Severnside Dr *HAN/WDH* S13 .... **57** K3
Severnside Gdns *HAN/WDH* S13 .. **57** K3
Severnside Pl *HAN/WDH* S13 ..... **57** K3
Severn St *DERBYSE* DE24 .... **257** J2
Sewell Rd *MOS* S20 .... **73** J4
Sexton St *GLSP* SK13 .... **17** J3 🖪
Seymour Av
BUTN/AL/TUT DE13 .... **274** B3 🖪
Seymour Cl *DERBYW* DE22 ..... **239** M5 🖪
Seymour Gv *MPL/ROM* SK6 ...... **32** B4
Seymour La *STV/CWN* S43 .... **93** M8
Seymour Rd
EWD/SEL/PNX NG16 .... **217** J1
Shacklecross Cl
BWSH/BRSTN DE72 .... **258** F1 🖪
Shady Gv *RDERBYSW* DE65 ..... **252** F8 🖪
Shaef Cl *RDERBYSW* DE65 ...... **253** H8 🖪
Shaftesbury Av *CHSW* S40 .... **2** B3
LGEAT NG10 .... **244** D5
LGEAT NG10 .... **260** E6
NORM/LIT DE23 .... **164** A1
Shaftesbury Crs
NORM/LIT DE23 .... **256** E1
Shaftesbury St
NORM/LIT DE23 .... **256** F1 🖪
Shaftesbury St South
NORM/LIT DE23 .... **256** E2
Shafton Cl *CLCR* S45 .... **145** H6
Shakespeare Av *ALFN* DE55 .... **159** M6 🖪
MSFDW NG19 .... **149** L6
WRKS S80 .... **115** G1
Shakespeare Cl *SWAD* DE11 .... **282** F4 🖪
Shakespeare Crs *DRON* S18 ...... **90** F3
Shakespeare Dr *ALFN* DE55 .... **175** L6
Shakespeare Rd *BUT* DE14 ..... **274** A4
EWD/SEL/PNX NG16 .... **217** M5 🖪
Shakespeare St
DERBYSE DE24 .... **256** D5 🖪
LGEAT NG10 .... **260** F1
RCH S42 .... **129** H7
RCH S42 .... **146** A1
Shaldon Dr *NORM/LIT* DE23 .... **256** A1
Shalfleet Dr *DERBYSE* DE24 .... **257** M5
Shallcross Av *CHF/WBR* SK23 ... **59** H6
Shallcross Mill Rd
CHF/WBR SK23 .... **59** H5
Shallcross Rd *CHF/WBR* SK23 ... **59** H5
Shamrock Pl *STV/CWN* S43 .... **93** M6 🖪
Shamrock St *NORM/LIT* DE23 ... **256** F1
Shanklin Dr
BSTN/STPLFD NG9 .... **245** G3 🖪
Shannon Cl *NORM/LIT* DE23 .... **256** A4
Shap Cl *CHSW* S40 .... **109**M5
Shardlow Rd
BWSH/BRSTN DE72 .... **270** E3
DERBYSE DE24 .... **257** L4
Sharman Cl *DRON* S18 .... **91** K1
Sharnford Wy
BSTN/STPLFD NG9 .... **231** L6
Sharp Cl *ILK* DE7 .... **229**M4
LGEAT NG10 .... **260** F4
Sharpe Av *SHEFS* S8 .... **70** B2
Sharpswood Mnr *SWAD* DE11 ... **283** H6
Sharrard Cl
EWD/SEL/PNX NG16 .... **189** K8
HACK/IN S12 .... **56** E5
Sharrard Dr *HACK/IN* S12 .... **56** E5
Sharrard Gv *HACK/IN* S12 .... **56** E4
Sharrard Rd *HACK/IN* S12 .... **56** E5
Sharrow La *ECC* S11 .... **55** H2
Sharrow St *ECC* S11 .... **55** J2
Sharrow Vale Rd *ECC* S11 .... **54** F2
Sharrow Vw *ABRD* S7 .... **55** H2
Shatton La *EDL/UDV* S33 .... **50** D8
EDL/UDV S33 .... **49** K8
Shawcroft *ASHB* DE6 .... **193** M8 🖪
Shawcroft Av *ALFN* DE55 .... **187** M5
Shawfield Rd *GLSP* SK13 .... **17** J7
Shaw La *ASHB* DE6 .... **233** K1
BPR/DUF DE56 .... **213** L3
GLSP SK13 .... **17** J7
MTLK DE4 .... **172** F1
Shaws Hl *MTLK* DE4 .... **185** G1
Shaw's Rw *CHSW* S40 .... **2** A5
Shaw St *ALFN* DE55 .... **187** M4
CHNE S41 .... **110** D2
DERBYW DE22 .... **4** A2
GLSP SK13 .... **25** M2
HYDE SK14 .... **16** D6
MSFD NG18 .... **165** H3
Shaw St East *ILK* DE7 .... **230** D4 🖪
Shaw St West *ILK* DE7 .... **230** D4
Shaw's Yd *BPR/DUF* DE56 ...... **214** C2 🖪
Shaw Wood Vw *ALFN* DE55 .... **174** C7
Sheaf Bank *SHEFF/MNR* S2 ..... **55** K3 🖪
Sheaf Gdns *SHEFF/MNR* S2 ..... **55** L1 🖪
Sheardhall Av *POY/DIS* SK12 .... **43** H5
Sheards Cl *DRON* S18 .... **90** B1
Sheards Dr *DRON* S18 .... **90** B1 🖪
Sheards Wy *DRON* S18 .... **90** B1
Sheepbridge La *MSFD* NG18 .... **164** C5
Sheepcote Rd *ECK/KIL* S21 ...... **73** M4
Sheephill Rd *ECC* S11 .... **68** C1
Sheep La *ALFN* DE55 .... **174** F2
Sheeplea La *CLCR* S45 .... **143** G2
Sheepwash La *ASH* NG17 .... **163** L7 🖪

CLCR S45 .... **158** E2
Sheffield Pl *DERBY* DE1 .... **5** J6 🖪
Sheffield Rd *BKWL* DE45 .... **106** E3
CHF/WBR SK23 .... **61** G3
CHNE S41 .... **110** D3
CHNE S41 .... **110** D1 🖪
CHNE S41 .... **110** D2 🖪
DRON S18 .... **70** C7
DRON S18 .... **91** H6
ECK/KIL S21 .... **73** M3
ECK/KIL S21 .... **94** A3
ECK/KIL S21 .... **94** A2
GLSP SK13 .... **26** B1
HACK/IN S12 .... **57** J8
HAN/WDH S13 .... **57** K4 🖪
HATH/EY S32 .... **66** D3
HATH/EY S32 .... **107** G2
MOS S20 .... **73** G5
STV/CWN S43 .... **95** L7
Sheffield St *BUT* DE14 .... **280** F1
Shelden Ms *GLSP* SK13 .... **25** G1
Sheldon Cl *LGEAT* NG10 .... **244** E7 🖪
Sheldon Rd *ABRD* S7 .... **55** K1
CHSW S40 .... **109** L5 🖪
HEANOR DE75 .... **201** M5
Sheldon Cl *SHEFF/MNR* DE3 .... **238** F7
Shelford Hl *MSFDW* NG19 .... **164** B4
Shelford La *MTLK* DE4 .... **172** E3
Shellbrook Cl *ASHZ* LE65 .... **291** H4
Shelley Av *BUT* DE14 .... **274** A4
MSFDW NG19 .... **149** L6
Shelley Cl *BUT* DE14 .... **274** A4
MSHM DE12 .... **295**M7
Shelley Dr *DERBYSE* DE24 ...... **256** D5
DRON S18 .... **90** F3
Shelley Gv *ALFN* DE55 .... **160** C7
Shelley Rd *SWAD* DE11 .... **282** F5
Shelley St *RCH* S42 .... **146** A1
Shelmory Cl *DERBYSE* DE24 .... **257** G5
Shelton Cl *MSFDW* NG19 .... **164** B1 🖪
Shelton Dr *DERBYSE* DE24 ..... **257** J7
Shelton Rd *MSFD* NG18 .... **165** K8
Shenington Wy
DERBYE DE21 .... **227** L8 🖪
Shepherd's La *ASH* NG17 .... **162** B2
MELB/CHEL DE73............. **278** A4
Shepherds Oak *ASH* NG17 ...... **163** H4
Shepherd St
NORM/LIT DE23 .... **255** M1 🖪
Shepley La *MPL/ROM* SK6 .... **32** C6
Shepley St *CHSW* S40 .... **2** B5
GLSP SK13 .... **18** B8
Shepton Cl *ILK* DE7 .... **217** G7 🖪
Sheraton Wy *BUX* SK17 .... **99** L1
Sherbourne Av *CHNE* S41 .... **110** B2
Sherbourne Dr *ASHZ* LE65 ...... **291** K3 🖪
BPR/DUF DE56 .... **200** A5 🖪
BUT DE14 .... **280** D3 🖪
Sherbrooke Rd *POY/DIS* SK12 ... **43** G4
Sherbrook Gv *BUX* SK17 .... **99** M5 🖪
Sheridan Ct
BSTN/STPLFD NG9 .... **245** J1 🖪
Sheridan St *DERBYSE* DE24..... **256** C5
Sheriff Dr *MTLK* DE4............. **156** E4
Sheriff's Lea *BSTN/STPLFD* NG9 ... **245** M8
Sherman Dr *BSTN/STPLFD* NG9 ... **245** M8
Sherston Ct *DERBYE* DE21 ..... **227** L8 🖪🖪
Sherview Av *MSFD* NG18 .... **165** J3
Sherwin Rd *BSTN/STPLFD* NG9.. **245** J1
Sherwin St *DERBYW* DE22 ...... **240** B2
Sherwood Av
BWSH/BRSTN DE72 .... **242** F8
DERBYE DE21 .... **241** J3
NORM/LIT DE23 .... **256** B5 🖪
SBK/MW NG20 .... **133** H6
WRKS S80 .... **115** G1
Sherwood Cl *MPL/ROM* SK6 ..... **32** C6 🖪
MSFD NG18 .... **165** H3
Sherwood Copse *BUX* SK17 ..... **83** M6 🖪
Sherwood Dr *SBK/MW* NG20 .... **133** H7
Sherwood Fold *GLSP* SK13 .... **25** G3
Sherwood Gln *SHEFS* S8 .... **69** L1
Sherwood Hall Gdns
MSFDW NG19 .... **165** J2
Sherwood Hall Rd *MSFD* NG18 .. **165** H3
Sherwood Ri
EWD/SEL/PNX NG16 .... **217** J1
Sherwood Rd *BUX* SK17 .... **83** M6
BUX SK17 .... **99** M4
DRON S18 .... **90** A1
ECK/KIL S21 .... **74** B3
MTLK DE4 .... **156** F6 🖪
Sherwood St *ALFN* DE55 .... **159**M5
ALFN DE55 .... **161** L6
ALFN DE55 .... **187** M2
ASH NG17 .... **162** C7
BSVR S44 .... **131** H2
CHSW S40 .... **3** J8
DERBYW DE22 .... **4** B7
MSFD NG18 .... **164** B4
MSFDW NG19 .... **149** L7
Sherwood Wy
EWD/SEL/PNX NG16 .... **189** L3
Shetland Cl *DERBYE* DE21 ...... **240** F3 🖪
Shetland Rd *ALFN* DE55 .... **161** J5
DRON S18 .... **90** E2
Shields Crs *CDON/KEG* DE74 .... **271** J7
The Shieling *RDERBYSW* DE65 .. **251** M8
Shilling Wy *LGEAT* NG10 .... **260** D3
Shiloh Rd *NM/HAY* SK22 .... **33** M3
Shinwell Av *STV/CWN* S43 .... **111** L3
Shipley Cl *BUT* DE14 .... **280** D2
Shipley Common La *ILK* DE7 .... **216** F6
Shipley La *ILK* DE7 .... **216** C7
Shipman Ct *MOS* S20 .... **73** G3 🖪
Shipstone St *ILK* DE7 .... **230** E4
Shipton Dr *UTXR* ST14 .... **247** J2
Shirburn Av *MSFD* NG18 .... **164** F2
Shirebrook Dr *GLSP* SK13 .... **26** B2
Shirebrook Rd *SHEFS* S8 .... **55** K4
Shire La *BSVR* S44 .... **130** C6
Shireoaks *BPR/DUF* DE56 .... **199** G5
Shireoaks Rd *NORM/LIT* DE23 .. **255** M3 🖪
Shireoaks Common *WRKN* S81 .. **77** K3
Shireoaks Rd *DRON* S18 .... **70** F8
WRKN S81 .... **77** L5
WRKS S80 .... **77** L6
The Shires *MSFDW* NG19 .... **165** J1
Shire Wy *GLSP* SK13 .... **18** B7

Shirland Dr *MSFD* NG18............... 165 L6
Shirland St *CHNE* S41.......................... 3 H1
Shirley Av *MPL/ROM* SK6 .... 32 B4 ⑧
 CHSW S40 .... 109 L5
Shirley Cl *CDON/KEG* DE74 .... 271 K6
Shirley Crs *BWSH/BRSTN* DE72 ... 260 A2
Shirley Pk
 BWSH/BRSTN DE72 .... 270 E3 ⑧
Shirley Rd *ALFN* DE55 .... 187 J3
 DERBYE DE21 .... 241 H1
 RIPLEY DE5 .... 201 G1
Shirley St *LGEAT* NG10 .... 260 D6
Shobnall Ct *BUT* DE14 .... 273 L6
Shobnall Rd *BUT* DE14 .... 273 L7
 BUTN/AL/TUT DE13 .... 273 J6
Shobnall St *BUT* DE14 .... 273 L6
Shop La *BPR/DUF* DE56 .... 185 M8
Shop Stones
 BWSH/BRSTN DE72 .... 242 F5 ⑤
Shoreham St *SHEFF/MNR* S2 .... 55 K2
Short Av *DERBYW* DE22 .... 226 C5
Shortbrook Bank *MOS* S20 ...... 73 H2 ⑩
Shortbrook Cl *MOS* S20 .... 73 J3
Shortbrook Cft *MOS* S20 .... 73 J2 ⑧
Shortbrook Rd *MOS* S20 .... 73 H2
Shortbrook Wy *MOS* S20 .... 73 H2
Short Cl *RCH* S42 .... 127 G3
Shortheath *MSHM* DE12 .... 289 M8
Shortheath Rd *MSHM* DE12 .... 290 A7
Short Hl *MELB/CHEL* DE73 .... 279 J9
Short Lands *BPR/DUF* DE56 ..... 199 K6 ⑦
The Shortlands *MTLK* DE4........... 156 E6
Short La *BUTN/AL/TUT* DE13 ...... 286 A1
 CDON/KEG DE74 .... 271 H6
 UTXR ST14.. 246 A8
Shorts La *TOT/DORE* S17 .... 68 E4
Short St *ASH* NG17 .... 163 K7
 BPR/DUF DE56 .... 199 L6
 STPNHL/WNHL DE15 .... 281 H3
 UTXR ST14.. 247 L2
Shorwell Gdns *DERBYSE* DE24 ... 257 M5
Shotwoodhill La
 BUTN/AL/TUT DE13 .... 264 C1
Shrewsbury Cl
 DERBYE DE21 .... 227 M8 ⑧
Shrewsbury Rd
 BUTN/AL/TUT DE13 .... 265 J8
Shrewsbury St *GLSP* SK13 .... 25 M1
Shropshire Av *DERBYE* DE21 ...... 241 H3
 EWD/SEL/PNX NG16 .... 188 F6
Shropshire Dr *GLSP* SK13 .... 25 C2
The Shrubbery *SWAD* DE11 .... 283 K8 ⑨
Shubert Cl *HAN/WDH* S13 .... 57 L2
Shuckstone La *MTLK* DE4 .... 173 J3
Shunters Drift *STV/CWN* S43 .... 94 E4
Shuttlewood Rd *BSVR* S44 .... 113 J4
Shutts La *BKWL* DE45 .... 122 F6
 STLY SK15 .... 16 A2
Sibthorpe St *MSFD* NG18 .... 164 D5
Sicklebrook La *DRON* S18 .... 71 H6
Sickleholme Cl *STV/CWN* S43 .... 50 D4
Siddalls Dr *ASH* NG17 .... 162 E7
Siddalls St *STPNHL/WNHL* DE15 .. 274 E7
Siddals La *DERBYW* DE22 .... 226 C6 ⑧
Siddals Rd *DERBY* DE1 .... 5 H4
Siddons St *DERBYSE* DE24 ...... 257 K3 ⑨
Side End La *CHF/WBR* SK23 .... 58 C7
Sides La *ASHB* DE6 .... 206 D8
The Sidings *DERBYE* DE21 .... 241 K6
Sidings Wy *ALFN* DE55 .... 175 M1
Sidmouth Cl *DERBYSE* DE24 ...... 257 M3
Sidney St *DERBY* DE1 .... 5 H8
 LGEAT NG10 .... 261 G4
Siggate *EDL/UDV* S33 .... 64 A1
Silken Holme *ALFN* DE55 .... 176 E6 ⑧
Silk Hl *CHF/WBR* SK23 .... 59 J2
Silk Mill La
 BUTN/AL/TUT DE13 .... 263 M4 ⑧
 SWAD DE11 .... 289 L1
Silkstone Crs *HACK/IN* S12 .... 57 H6
Silkstone Dr *HACK/IN* S12 .... 57 G6
Silkstone Pl *HACK/IN* S12 .... 57 H6
Silkstone Rd *HACK/IN* S12 .... 57 H6
Silk St *ASH* NG17 .... 163 H8
 GLSP SK13 .... 26 B1
Silver Birch Av *FUL* S10 .... 53 M3 ⑧
Silver Birch Crs *ALFN* DE55 .... 175 M3
Silverburn Dr *DERBYE* DE21 ...... 227 K8
Silverdale Av *MSFDW* NG19 .... 149 L6
Silverdale Cl *CHNE* S41 .... 110 B1
 ECC S11 .... 54 D5
 MPL/ROM SK6 .... 42 B2
Silverdale Crs *ECC* S11 .... 54 D5
Silverdale Cft *ECC* S11 .... 54 D6
Silverdale Gdns *ECC* S11 .... 54 E6 ⑧
Silverdale Gld *ECC* S11 .... 54 D6 ⑧
Silverdale Rd *ECC* S11 .... 54 D6
Silverhill Cl *BUTN/AL/TUT* DE13 .. 273 M1
Silverhill La *ASH* NG17 .... 162 D2
Silverhill Rd *DERBYE* DE21 .... 242 B7
Silver Hill Rd *ECC* S11 .... 54 E5
 NORM/LIT DE23 .... 4 E9
Silverlands *BUX* SK17 .... 99 M3
Silverlands Cl *BUX* SK17 .... 99 M3
Silverlands Pk *BUX* SK17 .... 99 M3 ⑧
Silver La *BWSH/BRSTN* DE72 .... 258 C5
Silver Mill Rd *SHEFF/MNR* S2 .. 55 K2 ⑧
Silver St *MSHM* DE12 .... 295 K4
Silverton Cl *HYDE* SK14 .... 16 A8
Silverton Dr *DERBYSE* DE24 ..... 255 M8 ⑧
Silvey Gv *DERBY* DE21 .... 242 A6 ⑧
Simcoe Leys *MELB/CHEL* DE73 ... 257 J8
Simcrest Av *ECK/KIL* S21 .... 74 A5
Simmondley Gv *GLSP* SK13 .... 25 K2
Simmondley La *GLSP* SK13 .... 25 K3
Simmondley New Rd *GLSP* SK13 .. 25 K3
Simon Fields *ILK* DE7 .... 215 K8
Simons Cl *GLSP* SK13 .... 25 K2
Simpson Rd *MSFDW* NG19 .... 164 A3
Sims Av *DERBY* DE1 .... 4 A3
Sims Cft *CHNE* S41 .... 91 M7 ⑧
Sinai Cl *BUTN/AL/TUT* DE13 ...... 273 H6
Sinclair Cl *DERBYSE* DE24 .... 256 B6
 HEANOR DE75 .... 216 A2
Sinfin Av *DERBYSE* DE24 .... 257 G6

Sinfin Fields Crs
 DERBYSE DE24 .... 257 G5 ⑧
Sinfin La *DERBYSE* DE24 .... 256 C5
 MELB/CHEL DE73............................ 268 D4
 NORM/LIT DE23 .... 256 D3
Sinfin Moor La *DERBYSE* DE24 .. 256 D8
 MELB/CHEL DE73............................ 257 G8
Singleton Av *MSFD* NG18 .... 165 H2
Sir Frank Whittle Rd
 DERBYE DE21 .... 240 F3
Sir Henry's La *MELB/CHEL* DE73.. 278 D6
Sir Joseph's La *MTLK* DE4 .... 140 E6
Sir William Hill Rd *HATH/EY* S32 ... 85 K2
Siskin Cl *WRKN* S81 .... 77 M3
Siskin Dr *DERBYSE* DE24 .... 256 A6
 MSHM DE12 .... 295 L6
Sisley Av *BSTN/STPLFD* NG9 .... 245 H4
Sister's La
 BWSH/BRSTN DE72 .... 242 F5 ⑤
Sitch La *MTLK* DE4 .... 156 A3
 MTLK DE4 .... 182 D6
 NM/HAY SK22 .... 34 C7
Sitwell Av *CHSW* S40 .... 2 E8
Sitwell Cl *DERBYE* DE21 .... 242 A6
Sitwell Dr *BPR/DUF* DE56 .... 214 D3 ⑧
Sitwell Grange La *CLCR* S45 ...... 161 G1
Sitwell Pl *SHEFF/MNR* S2 .... 55 J2 ⑧
Sitwell Rd *ABRD* S7 .... 55 J2
Sitwell St *DERBY* DE1 .... 4 F5
 DERBYE DE21 .... 242 B6
 ECK/KIL S21 .... 72 F8
Sixth Av *MSFDW* NG19 .... 165 K2
Skeavington's La *ILK* DE7 .... 217 H5
Skegby La *MSFDW* NG19 .... 163 M4
Skegby Mt *MSFDW* NG19 .... 164 B5
Skegby Rd *ASH* NG17 .... 162 D7
 ASH NG17 .... 163 K6
Skeldale Dr *CHSW* S40 .... 128 E2
Skelton Dr *HAN/WDH* S13 .... 57 M5
Skelton Gv *HAN/WDH* S13 .... 57 L4
Skelton La *HAN/WDH* S13 .... 57 L4
Skelton Rd *SHEFS* S8 .... 55 K5
Skelwith Cl *CHNE* S41 .... 110 A2 ⑧
Skerry Hl *MSFD* NG18 .... 165 G3
Skiddaw Cl *CHSW* S40 .... 110 A4
Skiddaw Dr *MCKLVR* DE3............. 255 H1
Skinner St *WRKS* S80 .... 96 A8
Skipton Cl *ILK* DE7 .... 217 G7 ⑩
Skye Gdns *ALFN* DE55 .... 161 J3
Skylark Cl *MSHM* DE12 .... 295 L6
 UTXR ST14.. 247 M4
Skylark Wy *DERBYSE* DE24 .... 256 A6
Slackey La *MSHM* DE12 .... 289 M6
Slack La *ALFN* DE55 .... 174 A2
 ALFN DE55 .... 187 L5
 ASHB DE6 .... 206 E3
 ASHB DE6 .... 222 F1
 BPR/DUF DE56................................. 185 M7
 BSVR S44.. 130 C8
 CHSW S40 .... 109 L7
 CLCR S45 .... 142 F8
 DERBYW DE22 .... 226 C8
 DERBYW DE22 .... 240 A5
 HEANOR DE75 .... 216 B2
 RIPLEY DE5 .... 201 G1
 SWAD DE11 .... 283 L4
Slack Rd *ILK* DE7 .... 216 C7
Slack's La *CLCR* S45 .... 145 M8
 NM/HAY SK22 .... 34 F5
Slade Cl *ALFN* DE55 .... 176 E6
 ILK DE7 .... 230 C5
 RDERBYSW DE65 .... 253 M6
Slade Hollow La *ASHB* DE6 .... 205 M1
Slade Hollow Vw *ASHB* DE6 .... 222 D6
Slade Lands Dr
 MELB/CHEL DE73............................ 257 K8 ⑧
Slade La *ASHB* DE6 .... 224 B2
 MELB/CHEL DE73............................ 279 J4
Slag La *BSTN/STPLFD* NG9 .... 245 L5
Slag La *ECK/KIL* S21 .... 92 A4
Slaidburn Cl *MCKLVR* DE3 .... 255 H1 ⑧
Slaley La *MTLK* DE4 .... 170 F2
Slaney Cl *DERBYSE* DE24 .... 257 H3 ⑧
Slant Cl *GLSP* SK13 .... 26 A2
Slant La *MSFDW* NG19 .... 149 L6
 SBK/MW NG20 .... 133 G6
Slatelands Av *GLSP* SK13 .... 25 L2
Slatelands Rd *GLSP* SK13 .... 25 L2
Slatepit La *RCH* S42 .... 107 M3
Slater Av *DERBYW* DE22 .... 4 A3
Slater Crs *MTLK* DE4 .... 183 J3
Slater St *ASH* NG17 .... 163 J6
 CLCR S45 .... 144 F7
Slate St *SHEFF/MNR* S2 .... 55 L3 ⑧
Slayleigh Av *FUL* S10 .... 53 M2
Slayleigh Delph *FUL* S10 .... 53 M2
Slayleigh Dr *FUL* S10 .... 54 A2
Slayleigh La *FUL* S10 .... 53 M2
Slayley Hl *STV/CWN* S43 .... 94 F6
Slayley Vw *STV/CWN* S43 .... 94 F5 ⑧
Slayley View Rd *STV/CWN* S43 ... 94 E4
Slaypit La *WRKS* S80 .... 76 A4
Sledgegate La *MTLK* DE4 .... 172 E5
Sleepy La *MELB/CHEL* DE73 ...... 278 E1
Sleetmoor La *ALFN* DE55 .... 187 J1
Sleights La *EWD/SEL/PNX* NG16.. 176 F8
Slindon Cft *DERBYSE* DE24 .... 258 A4
Slipperlow La *BUX* SK17 .... 102 C8
Sloade La *HACK/IN* S12 .... 72 A3
Sloan Dr *BSTN/STPLFD* NG9 ..... 231 L8
Sloane Rd *DERBYW* DE22 .... 239 K4
Smalldale Head Rd
 EDL/UDV S33 .... 64 B3
Smalldale Rd *BUX* SK17 .... 81 M4
 HACK/IN S12 .... 57 H6
Smalley Cl *EWD/SEL/PNX* NG16... 189 K4
Smalley Dr *DERBYE* DE21 .... 227 L7
Smalley Mill Rd *ILK* DE7 .... 214 E6
Small Meer Cl
 MELB/CHEL DE73............................ 269 L7 ⑧
Smallthorn Pl *SWAD* DE11 ..... 283 J8 ⑧
Smeath Rd
 EWD/SEL/PNX NG16 .... 189 M3
Smeaton St *ECC* S11 .... 55 G5
Smeckley Wood Cl *DRON* S18.... 90 F7
Smedley Av *ALFN* DE55 .... 188 A1
Smedley Cl *ASHZ* LE65 .... 291 J5

Smedley Ct *RDERBYSW* DE65 ..... 265 L5
Smedley's Av *LGEAT* NG10 ..... 244 E5 ⑧
Smedley St *MTLK* DE4 .... 156 F4
Smedley St West *MTLK* DE4 ...... 156 D3
Smeeton St *HEANOR* DE75 .... 216 C1
Smelter Wood Cl
 HAN/WDH S13 .... 57 H3 ⑧
Smelter Wood Crs
 HAN/WDH S13 .... 57 J3
Smelter Wood Dr *HAN/WDH* S13 .. 57 H3
Smelter Wood La *HAN/WDH* S13 .. 57 J3
Smelter Wood Pl *HAN/WDH* S13 .. 57 J3
Smelter Wood Ri *HAN/WDH* S13 .. 57 J4
Smelter Wood Rd *HAN/WDH* S13 .. 57 J3
Smelter Wood Wy
 HAN/WDH S13 .... 57 H3
Smeltinghouse La *DRON* S18...... 90 B7
Smisby Rd *ASHZ* LE65 .... 291 K1
Smith Av *MELB/CHEL* DE73 .... 278 C2
 RIPLEY DE5 .... 201 L1
 STV/CWN S43 .... 111 L3
Smith Crs *CHNE* S41 .... 129 G1
Smith Dr *EWD/SEL/PNX* NG16 ... 202 D7
Smithfield Av
 BSTN/STPLFD NG9 .... 231 G6
 CHNE S41 .... 128 F3
Smithfield Rd *HACK/IN* S12 .... 56 D8
 UTXR ST14.. 247 L2
Smith-hall La *ASHB* DE6 .... 210 D1
Smith Rd *MTLK* DE4 .... 156 E4
Smithson Av *BSVR* S44 .... 131 L1
Smith St *MSFD* NG18 .... 165 H4
Smithurst Rd
 EWD/SEL/PNX NG16 .... 217 L2
Smithy Av *CLCR* S45 .... 144 F6
Smithy Cl *ASHB* DE6 .... 180 A1
 GLSP SK13 .... 26 A1
Smithy Cft *DRON* S18................ 69 M8 ⑧
Smithy Fold *GLSP* SK13 .... 26 A1 ⑧
Smithy Hl *EDL/UDV* S33 .... 64 D3
Smithy Knoll Rd *HATH/EY* S32 ... 86 F8
Smithy La *CRTAM* B79 .... 293 H8 ⑧
 MPL/ROM SK6 .... 33 J1
Smithy Mdw *HATH/EY* S32 .... 66 D2
Smithy Pl *RCH* S42 .... 129 J8
Smithy Wood Crs *SHEFS* S8 ... 55 J6 ⑧
Smithy Wood Rd *SHEFS* S8 .... 55 H6
Smuse La *MTLK* DE4 .... 157 H6
Snaithing La *FUL* S10 .... 54 B1
Snaithing Park Cl *FUL* S10 ...... 54 B1 ⑧
Snaithing Park Rd *FUL* S10 .... 54 B1
Snake La *BPR/DUF* DE56 .... 213 G7
Snake Pass *GLSP* SK13 .... 26 E2
Snake Rd *EDL/UDV* S33 .... 37 L2
 EDL/UDV S33 .... 39 J7
 GLSP SK13 .... 26 F2
 STKB/PEN S36 .... 28 B5
Snape Hl *DRON* S18 .... 70 D8
Snapehill Cl *DRON* S18 .... 70 D7 ⑧
Snapehill Crs *DRON* S18 .... 70 D7
Snape Hill Dr *DRON* S18 .... 70 E7 ⑧
Snape Hill La *DRON* S18 .... 70 D8
Snapes La *ASHB* DE6 .... 219 L2
Snelsmoor La *MELB/CHEL* DE73.. 257 L8
Snelston Cl *DRON* S18 .... 89 M1 ⑧
Snelston Crs *NORM/LIT* DE23 ... 239 M8
Snipe Cl *RCH* S42 .... 127 G3
Snipesmoor La *ASHB* DE6 .... 208 C3
Snitterton Rd *MTLK* DE4 .... 156 C5
Snittle Rd *HOLM/MEL* HD7 .... 9 L3
Snowberry Av *BPR/DUF* DE56 ... 199 H8
Snowdon La *ECK/KIL* S21 .... 71 L7
Snowdrop Va *MTLK* DE4 .... 183 H4 ⑧
Snowfield Vw *MTLK* DE4 .... 183 H4 ⑧
Soaper La *DRON* S18 .... 70 D8
Society Pl *NORM/LIT* DE23 .... 4 D9
Soft Water La *EDL/UDV* S33 .... 64 D3
Solney Cl *SWAD* DE11 .... 282 C7
Soloman Rd
 EWD/SEL/PNX NG16 .... 217 L8
Solomons Vw *BUX* SK17 .... 99 M3
Solway Cl *DERBYE* DE21 .... 227 K8 ⑦
Solway Ri *DRON* S18 .... 70 A8
Somerby Ct
 BSTN/STPLFD NG9 .... 231 L6 ⑧
Somerby Wy *DERBYE* DE21 .... 227 J8 ⑬
Somercotes Hl *ALFN* DE55 .... 188 A2
Somercotes Rd *HACK/IN* S12 .... 57 G5
Somersal Cl *DERBYSE* DE24 ..... 257 H7
Somersall La *CHSW* S40 .... 127 K1
Somersall Park Rd *CHSW* S40 .. 127 L1 ⑧
Somersall Rd *MSFDW* NG19 ..... 164 B3
Somersall Willows *CHSW* S40 .. 127 K1
Somersby Av *CHSW* S40 .... 127 L3
Somersby Ct *MSFD* NG18 .... 165 L5 ⑧
Somerset Cl *BUX* SK17 .... 99 M6 ⑧
Somerset Dr *STV/CWN* S43 .... 111 J2
 LGEAT NG10 .... 261 K2
Somerset Rd
 STPNHL/WNHL DE15 .... 281 G4
Somerset St *DERBY* DE21 .... 241 G3
Somme Rd *DERBYW* DE22 .... 225 L7
Sookholme La *HAN/WDH* S13 .... 57 M4
Sookholme Rd *SBK/MW* NG20 ... 133 J6 ⑧
Soresby St *CHSW* S40..................... 3 G4
Sorrel Cl *UTXR* ST14 .... 247 L4
Sorrel Dr *SWAD* DE11 .... 283 H6
Sough La *BUX* SK17 .... 120 A1
 HATH/EY S32 .... 86 E8
 MTLK DE4 .... 171 L8
Soughley La *FUL* S10 .... 53 H2
Sough Rd *ALFN* DE55 .... 176 E3
Southall St *SHEFS* S8 .... 55 K4 ⑪
Southard's La *AU/AST/KP* S26 ... 76 B5
South Av *ALFN* DE55 .... 187 J7
 DERBYE DE21 .... 242 B6
 DERBYW DE22 .... 226 B7
 MELB/CHEL DE73............................ 257 J7
 NORM/LIT DE23 .... 256 A1
 SBK/MW NG20 .... 133 J7
South Brae Cl *NORM/LIT* DE23 .. 256 A3
South Broadway St
 BUT DE14 .... 280 F2 ⑧
Southbrook Cl *GLSP* SK13 .... 17 H6
South Church St *BKWL* DE45 .... 122 F5
South Cl *DRON* S18........................ 91 H4
 GLSP SK13 .... 17 J3
 SWAD DE11 .... 290 E2

Southcote Dr *DRON* S18 .... 90 A1
South Crs *BSVR* S44 .... 112 D5
 BSVR S44.. 131 L1
 ECK/KIL S21 .... 74 B3
Southcroft *ALFN* DE55 .... 175 K6
 NORM/LIT DE23 .... 256 A5
Southcroft Gdns *SHEFS* S8 .... 55 J4 ⑧
Southdown Av *CHSW* S40 .... 109 M6
Southdown Cl
 DERBYSE DE24 .... 255 M8 ⑧
South Dr *DERBY* DE1 .... 240 C3
 DERBYE DE21 .... 241 K5
 MCKLVR DE3 .... 239 K8
 MELB/CHEL DE73............................ 257 J7
 SWAD DE11 .... 282 C4
South End *MTLK* DE4 .... 171 K3
Southend Rd *RCH* S42 .... 129 J8
Southend Rd *SHEFF/MNR* S2 .. 56 B1 ⑧
South Farm Av *AU/AST/KP* S26 .. 75 H4
Southfield Av *CHNE* S41 .... 129 G4
Southfield Cl *WRKS* S80 .... 96 C5
Southfield Dr *ALFN* DE55 .... 176 F5
 DRON S18.. 90 F2
Southfield La *WRKS* S80 .... 96 B5
Southfield Mt *DRON* S18 .... 90 F2 ⑧
Southfields *STV/CWN* S43 .... 95 J3
Southfields Av
 EWD/SEL/PNX NG16 .... 177 G7
Southgate *ECK/KIL* S21 .... 73 H7
Southgate Cl *MCKLVR* DE3 ...... 238 F7 ⑧
Southgate Ct *ECK/KIL* S21 .... 73 H7
Southgate Rd *STV/CWN* S43 ...... 95 J5
Southgate Wy *STV/CWN* S43 ..... 92 E6
Southgreen Cl *MSFD* NG18 ...... 165 H8
Southgreen Hl *MSFD* NG18 ...... 165 H8
Southgrove Rd *FUL* S10 .... 55 G1
South Head Dr *CHF/WBR* SK23 .. 60 F3
South Hl *ALFN* DE55 .... 159 J3
 BUTN/AL/TUT DE13 .... 265 G6
South Hill La *ALFN* DE55 .... 159 J4
South La *SHEF* S1 .... 55 K1
South Lodge Ct *CHSW* S40 .... 109 L7
South Marlow St *GLSP* SK13 ..... 17 K6
Southmead Wy
 DERBYW DE22 .... 239 L7 ⑧
Southmoor Cl *STV/CWN* S43 ..... 111 J6
South Oak St *BUT* DE14 .... 280 E2
South Pde *MTLK* DE4 .... 171 K1
Southpark Av *MSFD* NG18 .... 165 J8
South Pl *CHSW* S40 .... 3 H5
 RIPLEY DE5 .... 201 G1
South Ridge Dr *MSFD* NG18 ..... 165 G7
Southsea Rd *HAN/WDH* S13 ...... 57 K4
South St *ALFN* DE55 .... 161 J8
 ALFN DE55 .... 176 E4
 ALFN DE55 .... 187 H4
 ALFN DE55 .... 187 M5
 ASHB DE6 .... 207 M1
 ASHZ LE65 .... 291 L4
 BUX SK17 .... 99 L3
 BWSH/BRSTN DE72 .... 259 K3
 CHSW S40 .... 3 H5
 CLCR S45 .... 161 G1
 DERBY DE1 .... 4 B3
 EWD/SEL/PNX NG16 .... 203 H8
 EWD/SEL/PNX NG16 .... 217 M2
 ILK DE7 .... 230 B2
 LGEAT NG10 .... 261 H3
 MELB/CHEL DE73............................ 278 D5
 MOS S20 .... 73 G4
 SWAD DE11 .... 283 J8
South St North *STV/CWN* S43 .... 92 A6
South Uxbridge St *BUT* DE14 .... 280 E2
South Vw *BKWL* DE45 .... 105 M8
 EDL/UDV S33 .... 50 E6
 MOS S20 .... 73 K3
 WRKS S80 .... 96 C5
South View Crs *ABRD* S7 ...... 55 J3 ⑧
South View Rd *ECC* S11 .... 55 J2
Southview Rd *GLSP* SK13 .... 17 H3
Southwark Cl *DERBYW* DE22 ... 239 L5 ⑧
Southwell Ri
 EWD/SEL/PNX NG16 .... 217 L3 ⑧
Southwell Rd West *MSFD* NG18.. 165 K6
 MSFD NG18 .... 165 G4
Southwood Av *ASH* NG17 .... 163 G6
 DRON S18.. 90 D7
Southwood Dr *STV/CWN* S43 ..... 95 J7
Southwood St *DERBYSE* DE24 .. 257 H2
Sovereign Dr *BUT* DE14 .... 280 E2 ⑧
Sovereign Gv *LGEAT* NG10 .... 260 E3 ⑧
Sovereign Wy *DERBYE* DE21 .... 228 A7
 HEANOR DE75 .... 215 M1
Sowbrook La *ILK* DE7 .... 230 B7
Sowter Av *ASH* NG17 .... 163 H6
Sowter Rd *DERBY* DE1 .... 4 F2
Sowters Rw *CHSW* S40 .... 3 G4
Spa Brook Cl *HACK/IN* S12 .... 57 J6
Spa Brooke Dr *HACK/IN* S12 ..... 57 J5
Spa Cft *ALFN* DE55 .... 161 H5
Spa La *CHNE* S41 .... 3 J4
 DERBY DE1 .... 4 D7
 HAN/WDH S13 .... 57 M5
Spa Lane Cft *HAN/WDH* S13 ...... 57 M4
Spalden Av *ASHB* DE6 .... 193 M7
Spang La *ASH* NG17 .... 162 B6
Spanker La *BPR/DUF* DE56 .... 185 L8
Sparrow Cl *DERBYSE* DE24 ...... 256 A6
 ILK DE7 .... 230 D5
Spa View Av *HACK/IN* S12 .... 57 J7
Spa View Dr *HACK/IN* S12 .... 57 J7
Spa View Pl *HACK/IN* S12 .... 57 J7
Spa View Rd *HACK/IN* S12 .... 57 J7
Spa View Ter *HACK/IN* S12 ..... 57 J7 ⑧
Spa View Wy *HACK/IN* S12 .... 57 J7
Speedwell Cl *DERBYE* DE21 .. 227 M7 ⑩
 GLSP SK13 .... 17 J3
 SWAD DE11 .... 283 J6
Speetley Vw *STV/CWN* S43 .... 94 E3
Speighthill Crs *RCH* S42 .... 128 B6
Spenbeck Dr *DERBYW* DE22 ..... 226 D5
Spencer Av *BPR/DUF* DE56 .... 199 L6
 DERBYSE DE24 .... 257 G6
 LGEAT NG10 .... 244 E3
 STV/CWN S43 .... 93 L8
Spencer Cl *ASHB* DE6 .... 207 M2
 BUTN/AL/TUT DE13 .... 274 A1 ⑧
Spencer Crs *BSTN/STPLFD* NG9 .. 245 J7

Spencer Dr *ALFN* DE55 .... 188 A3
Spencer Gv *BUX* SK17 .... 99 L4
Spencer Rd *BPR/DUF* DE56 ...... 199 K6
 BUX SK17 .... 99 K4
 CHF/WBR SK23 .... 60 C4
 SHEFF/MNR S2 .... 55 K3
Spencer St *BSVR* S44 .... 131 J2
 CHSW S40 .... 3 G2
 DERBYSE DE24 .... 257 K2 ⑧
 ILK DE7 .... 215 J8
 MSFD NG18 .... 164 D4
Spend La *ASHB* DE6 .... 179 H7
 ASHB DE6 .... 193 K4
Sperry Cl *EWD/SEL/PNX* NG16 .. 189 J4
Spicer Cl *BSTN/STPLFD* NG9 .... 245 M8
Spindletree Dr *DERBYE* DE21 .. 227 H8
Spinkhill Av *HAN/WDH* S13 .... 56 F2
Spinkhill Dr *HAN/WDH* S13 .... 57 G2
Spinkhill La *ECK/KIL* S21 .... 73 M8
Spinkhill Rd *ECK/KIL* S21 .... 74 B6
 HAN/WDH S13 .... 57 G2
Spinnerbottom *NM/HAY* SK22 ... 34 C8
Spinners Wy *BPR/DUF* DE56 .... 199 M4
Spinney Cl *DERBYW* DE22 ...... 226 D8 ⑧
 GLSP SK13 .... 17 M8 ⑪
Spinney Crs *BSTN/STPLFD* NG9.. 245 J7
Spinney Dr *LGEAT* NG10 .... 244 F8 ⑧
Spinney Hl *MELB/CHEL* DE73 ... 278 D3
Spinney Ri *BSTN/STPLFD* NG9 ... 245 H7
Spinney Rd *BUT* DE14 .... 280 C2
 DERBYE DE21 .... 241 J3
 DERBYW DE22 .... 4 B8
 ILK DE7 .... 230 B4
 LGEAT NG10 .... 244 F8
The Spinney *BPR/DUF* DE56 ..... 199 K4
 BWSH/BRSTN DE72 .... 258 F1
 CDON/KEG DE74 .... 271 K6 ⑧
 ILK DE7 .... 230 B4
 SBK/MW NG20 .... 133 G7
Spire Hollin *GLSP* SK13 .... 17 M8
Spital Brook Cl *CHNE* S41 .... 3 M8
Spital Gdns *CHNE* S41 .... 3 L1
Spital La *CHNE* S41 .... 3 K5
Spitewinter La *HATH/EY* S32 .... 108 A2
Spittal *CDON/KEG* DE74 .... 271 K6
Spittal Gn *BSVR* S44 .... 131 K2
Spooner Dr *ECK/KIL* S21 .... 73 M4
Spooner La *HATH/EY* S32 .... 86 F4
Spoonley Wood Ct
 NORM/LIT DE23 .... 255 J3 ⑧
Sporton Cl *ALFN* DE55 .... 176 D3
Sporton La *ALFN* DE55 .... 176 D3
Spotswood Cl *GLV* S14 .... 56 B6 ⑧
Spotswood Dr
 SHEFF/MNR S2 .... 56 B5 ⑧
Spotswood Mt *GLV* S14 .... 56 B5 ⑧
Spotswood Pl *GLV* S14................. 56 A6
Spotswood Rd *SHEFS* S8............ 56 A6
Spout La *BPR/DUF* DE56 .... 183 M7
 MTLK DE4 .... 157 K6
Spridgeon Cl *LGEAT* NG10 ..... 244 E8 ⑧
Spring Bank *BKWL* DE45 .... 104 D6 ⑧
Springbank *GLSP* SK13 .... 17 J5 ⑧
Spring Bank Rd *CHSW* S40 .... 2 E3
 NM/HAY SK22 .... 43 M2
Spring Cl *BPR/DUF* DE56 .... 199 H4
 BWSH/BRSTN DE72 .... 259 M2
 ECK/KIL S21 .... 93 M3
 SWAD DE11 .... 289 J1
Spring Close Dell *GLV* S14 .... 56 C6
Spring Close Mt *GLV* S14 .... 56 C6
Spring Close Vw *GLV* S14........... 56 B6
 HACK/IN S12 .... 56 E5
 SHEFF/MNR S2 .... 55 K1
Spring Cottage Rd *MSHM* DE12 . 289 M5
Springdale Ct *MCKLVR* DE3 ... 255 H1 ⑩
Springdale Gdns
 BSTN/STPLFD NG9 .... 231 G8 ⑧
Springfarm Rd
 STPNHL/WNHL DE15 .... 281 K1
Springfield *GLSP* SK13 .... 24 F4
 NORM/LIT DE23 .... 239 L8
Springfield Av *ASHB* DE6 .... 208 A2
 CHSW S40 .... 2 B3
 ECC S11 .... 54 F5
 EWD/SEL/PNX NG16 .... 203 K8 ⑧
 HEANOR DE75 .... 201 L5
 LGEAT NG10 .... 244 D7
 LGEAT NG10 .... 261 J2
 SBK/MW NG20 .... 133 H5
Springfield Cl *ABRD* S7 .... 54 F6
 ECK/KIL S21 .... 72 F7
 GLSP SK13 .... 17 H6
 MSFD NG18 .... 165 K5 ⑧
 MTLK DE4 .... 185 K1
 STV/CWN S43 .... 95 H7
 SWAD DE11 .... 282 E5
Springfield Crs *ALFN* DE55 ...... 188 A3
 BSVR S44.. 113 J7
Springfield Dr
 BPR/DUF DE56 .... 213 G7 ⑧
Springfield Gdn *ILK* DE7 .... 217 J8
Springfield Ri *MTLK* DE4 .... 185 J1
Springfield Rd *ABRD* S7 .... 54 F6
 DERBYE DE21 .... 241 L5
 DRON S18.. 90 A7
 EDL/UDV S33 .... 64 D2
 MELB/CHEL DE73............................ 257 H8
 RCH S42 .... 146 A2
 RDERBYSW DE65 .... 253 L7
 RDERBYSW DE65 .... 267 G8
 SWAD DE11 .... 282 E5
 UTXR ST14.. 247 L2
Springfield Ter *RIPLEY* DE5 .... 201 H1 ⑧
Springfield Vw *RIPLEY* DE5 ...... 187 G8
Spring Gdns *BUX* SK17 .... 99 M2 ⑧
 DERBYE DE21 .... 241 J3
 GLSP SK13 .... 17 K5 ⑪
Spring Garden Ter *ILK* DE7 ..... 217 J8 ⑧
Springhill *SWAD* DE11 .... 283 K2
Springhill Wy *RIPLEY* DE5 .... 201 K2
Spring Hollow *BPR/DUF* DE56 ... 212 F3
Spring House Cl *RCH* S42 .... 109 J5
Spring La *HEANOR* DE75 .... 216 B1 ⑧
 SBK/MW NG20 .... 114 D8

SBK/MW NC20 .... **133** M4
SHEF/MNR S2 .... **56** B2
WRKN S81 .... **77** H5
WRKS S80 .... **77** J6
Springmeadow GLSP SK13 .... **25** G3
Spring Mt NM/HAY SK22 ...... **43** M2 🔟
Spring Ri GLSP SK13 .... **25** J3
Spring Rd ALFN DE55 .... **188** B4
ASH NG17 .... **163** H8
Spring St DERBYW DE22 ...... **4** C6
GLSP SK13 .... **25** L2
HYDE SK14 .... **16** F5
SWAD DE11 .... **289** K2
WRKS S80 .... **96** D4 🔟
Spring Terrace Rd
STPNHL/WHNL DE15 ...... **281** J1
The Spring LGEAT NG10 ...... **261** C5
Springvale Cl CLCR S45 ...... **145** G8
Springvale Rd CLCR S45 ...... **145** H8
Spring Vale NM/HAY SK22 ...... **35** G8
STV/CWN S43 .... **111** H2
Spring Water Av HACK/IN S12 ...... **57** J7
Spring Water Cl HACK/IN S12 ... **57** K7 🔟
Spring Water Dr GLSP SK13 ...... **17** H7
HACK/IN S12 .... **57** J6
Springwell Gdns HYDE SK14 ...... **24** B1
Springwell Rd ASH NG17 ...... **162** C8
Springwood GLSP SK13 ...... **25** J2
Springwood Dr DERBYE DE21 ...... **227** K8
Springwood Farm Rd
SWAD DE11 .... **282** E3
Springwood Rd SHEFS S8 ...... **55** K4 🔢
Springwood St ALFN DE55 ...... **129** L6
Springwood View Cl ASH NG17 ...... **162** F7
Sprinkswoods La ASHB DE6 ...... **207** H5
Spruce Av EWD/SEL/PNX N16 ...... **189** G4
Spruce Cl WRKS S80 .... **77** L8
Spruce Ri ECK/KIL S21 ...... **73** K5
Spurr St SHEF/MNR S2 ...... **55** L2
The Square BUX SK17 ...... **99** L3
DERBYW DE22 .... **240** D1
HATH/EY S32 .... **86** B5
MCKLVR DE3 .... **255** C1
MSHM DE12 .... **295** K3
STPNHL/WHNL DE15 ...... **275** L7
UTXR ST14 .... **249** H8
WRKS S80 .... **96** C4 🔟
Squires La EDL/UDV S33 ...... **48** F7
Squires Wk NORM/LIT DE23 ...... **255** K4
Squirrel La MELB/CHEL DE73 ...... **279** H7
Squirrel Wk MSHM DE12 ...... **289** L7
Stable Cl MTLK DE4 .... **172** E5
Stables Ct BSVR S44 .... **131** M1
Stables St DERBYW DE22 ...... **240** A5
Stacey Rd MSFDW NG19 ...... **149** G8
Staden La BUX SK17 .... **100** B6
Stadium Cl WRKN S81 .... **77** M4
Stadium Vw DERBYSE DE24 ...... **241** H7
Staffa Dr ALFN DE55 .... **161** J5
Stafford Cl DRON S18 ...... **69** M8 🔟
GLSP SK13 .... **26** C2 🔢
ILK DE7 .... **215** J4
Stafford Crs MTLK DE4 ...... **183** H5
UTXR ST14 .... **247** H5
Staffordshire Wy UTXR ST14 ...... **218** C4
UTXR ST14 .... **247** L8
UTXR ST14 .... **248** B1
Stafford St BUT DE14 .... **274** A5
DERBY DE1 .... **4** C4
LGEAT NG10 .... **261** J2
MSFDW NG19 .... **164** C2
NM/HAY SK22 .... **43** M1 🔟
Stagsden Crs
WOL/BIL/BRX NG8 ...... **231** M5
Staines Cl MCKLVR DE3 ...... **238** F8 🔟
Stainforth St MSFDW NG19 ...... **149** M8
Stainsbro' La MTLK DE4 ...... **182** E5
Stainsby Av HEANOR DE75 ...... **216** B1
ILK DE7 .... **215** H4
Stainsby Cl ASH NG17 ...... **146** C1
Stainsby Dr MSFDW NG18 ...... **165** K3
Stainsby Gv ASH NG17 ...... **162** C8
Stainton Rd ECC S11 ...... **54** E2
Stake Hill Rd ST/HB/BR S6 ...... **41** M3
Staker La MCKLVR DE3 ...... **255** C4
Staley Av ASHZ LE65 ...... **291** J6
Stalker Lees Rd ECC S11 ...... **55** C2
Stalybridge Rd HYDE SK14 ...... **16** D6
Stalyhill Dr STLY SK15 ...... **16** B3 🔟
Stamford Cl LGEAT NG10 ...... **261** G6
Stamford St DERBYSE DE24 ...... **257** C4 🔟
EWD/SEL/PNX N16 ...... **217** M1
EWD/SEL/PNX N16 ...... **217** M6
HEANOR DE75 ...... **202** B8 🔟
ILK DE7 .... **230** B1
Stamper Crs ASH NG17 ...... **163** J4
Stamps Cl
STPNHL/WHNL DE15 ...... **274** F7 🔟
Stanage Ct MSFDW NG18 ...... **165** L5 🔟
Stanage Gn MCKLVR DE3 ...... **255** J1 🔟
Stanage Ri HACK/IN S12 ...... **57** G5
Stanage Wy RCH S42 .... **109** J5 🔟
Stancliffe Av MTLK DE4 ...... **140** F7
Standing Butts Cl MSHM DE12 ...... **287** G2
Standlow La ASHB DE6 ...... **180** F8
Stand Rd CHNE S41 .... **110** C3
Stanedge Rd BKWL DE45 ...... **122** E5
Staneford Ct MOS S20 ...... **73** C1
Stanford Rd DRON S18 ...... **89** M1 🔢
Stanford Wy CHSW S40 ...... **127** L2
Stanhope St HACK/IN S12 ...... **56** F5
MCKLVR DE3 .... **239** H1
SWAD DE11 .... **282** E7
Stanhope St BSVR S44 ...... **147** H1
ILK DE7 .... **230** D4 🔢
ILK DE7 .... **244** B2
LGEAT NG10 .... **261** G2
NORM/LIT DE23 ...... **256** C1
STPNHL/WHNL DE15 ...... **274** E7
Stanier Wy DERBYE DE21 ...... **241** K7
Staniforth Av ECK/KIL S21 ...... **72** E7
Staniland Cl
BSTN/STPLFD NG9 ...... **245** M8 🔟
Stanleigh Rd MSHM DE12 ...... **289** L6
Stanley Av MPL/ROM SK6 ...... **32** A3
RIPLEY DE5 .... **187** H3
STV/CWN S43 .... **111** L3
Stanley Cl DERBYW DE22 ...... **240** C2

ILK DE7 .... **230** B3
MSHM DE12 .... **294** C3
SWAD DE11 .... **283** J7 🔟
Stanley Dr BSTN/STPLFD NG9... **245** K2
Stanley Hall La POY/DIS SK12 ...... **42** F3
Stanley La ASH NG17 ...... **147** G8
Stanley Rd DERBYE DE21 ...... **241** K5
DERBYE DE24 .... **257** H4
MSFD NG18 .... **164** E6
MSFDW NG19 .... **165** L1
SHEFS S8 .... **55** L5
Stanley St ALFN DE55 ...... **188** A3
BUT DE14 .... **273** M8
CHNE S41 .... **3** L6
DERBYW DE22 .... **240** A5
ECK/KIL S21 .... **74** A3
ILK DE7 .... **230** C3
LGEAT NG10 .... **261** H3 🔟
SWAD DE11 .... **282** F6
Stanhope La SWAD DE11 ...... **166** A8
Stanstead Rd MCKLVR DE3 ...... **238** F6
Stanton Av BPR/DUF DE56 ...... **199** L6
Stanton Cl MTLK DE4 ...... **140** E7 🔟
Stanton Crs ASH NG17 ...... **163** G6
HACK/IN S12 .... **57** G6 🔟
Stanton Ga ILK DE7 ...... **244** F1
Stantonhall La MTLK DE4 ...... **139** M2
Stanton HI MELB/CHEL DE73 ...... **277** M5
Stanton La ASHB DE6 ...... **206** C1
Stanton Moor Vw MTLK DE4 ...... **156** C3
Stanton Pl MSFD NG18 ...... **164** D3
MSFDW NG19 .... **148** C3 🔟
Stanton Rd ASHB DE6 ...... **208** A2
ILK DE7 .... **230** C4
LGEAT NG10 .... **244** C3
STPNHL/WHNL DE15 ...... **281** J3
Stanton St MSFDW NG19 ...... **148** C5
NORM/LIT DE23 ...... **256** C1
Stanwood Dr CHSW S40 ...... **127** L2 🔟
Stanyforth St GLSP SK13 ...... **17** K6
Stapenhill Rd
STPNHL/WHNL DE15 ...... **274** C8
Stapleford La
BSTN/STPLFD NG9 ...... **245** K8
Stapleford Rd
BSTN/STPLFD NG9 ...... **230** F6
BSTN/STPLFD NG9 ...... **231** G7
Stapleton Rd ILK DE7 ...... **217** H6
Star Bank CDLE ST10 ...... **204** A1
Starch La LGEAT NG10 ...... **244** E3
Starcross Ct MCKLVR DE3 ...... **238** F2
Starkholmes Rd MTLK DE4 ...... **156** F8
Starkie Av CDON/KEG DE74... **271** J7
Starling Gv WRKN S81 ...... **77** M4
Starr Av ASH NG17 ...... **163** G7
Startle Bank HEANOR DE75 ...... **202** C8
Starth La MTLK DE4 ...... **157** K7
Start La CHF/WBR SK23 ...... **58** F3
Statham Av RCH S42 ...... **144** F2
Statham St DERBYW DE22 ...... **240** B3
Station Ap BPR/DUF DE56 ...... **213** J6 🔢
BUX SK17 .... **99** L2
DERBY DE1 .... **5** H4
HATH/EY S32 .... **66** D3
Station Cl MELB/CHEL DE73 ...... **269** J1
Station Dr MSHM DE12 ...... **290** C6
Station HI MSFDW NG19 ...... **149** L7
Station La CHNE S41 ...... **91** K8
EWD/SEL/PNX N16 ...... **188** C7
MSHM DE12 .... **286** F1
RIPLEY DE5 .... **201** L4
Station New Rd RCH S42 ...... **145** G3
Station Rd ALFN DE55 ...... **160** E5
ASH NG17 .... **161** J4
ASHB DE6 .... **193** L8
BKWL DE45 .... **104** C6
BKWL DE45 .... **123** H3
BPR/DUF DE56 ...... **185** J6
BPR/DUF DE56 ...... **213** J6 🔢
BSVR S44 .... **113** H8
BSVR S44 .... **132** C4
BUTN/AL/TUT DE13 ...... **264** E6
BUTN/AL/TUT DE13 ...... **286** B1
BUX SK17 .... **81** H1
BUX SK17 .... **99** L2
BWSH/BRSTN DE72 ...... **258** E1
BWSH/BRSTN DE72 ...... **259** L3
CDLE ST10 .... **204** B8
CDON/KEG DE74 ...... **271** M5
CHF/WBR SK23 ...... **44** A6
CHF/WBR SK23 ...... **45** G8
CHF/WBR SK23 ...... **59** K1
CHF/WBR SK23 ...... **60** D4
CHNE S41 .... **3** J4
CHNE S41 .... **110** D2
CLCR S45 .... **161** G1
EDL/UDV S33 .... **49** L7
EDL/UDV S33 .... **50** E8
EWD/SEL/PNX N16 ...... **189** H1
EWD/SEL/PNX N16 ...... **202** E7
EWD/SEL/PNX N16 ...... **217** M5
GLSP SK13 .... **17** K5
HATH/EY S32 .... **66** D3
ILK DE7 .... **227** G6
ILK DE7 .... **228** F4
ILK DE7 .... **230** C1
LGEAT NG10 .... **244** E5
LGEAT NG10 .... **261** J2
MCKLVR DE3 .... **239** G7
MELB/CHEL DE73 ...... **269** J1
MELB/CHEL DE73... **278** E2
MOS S20 .... **73** J3
MOS S20 .... **73** G3 🔟
MPL/ROM SK6 ...... **32** C4
MPL/ROM SK6 ...... **42** C1
MSFD NG18 .... **164** E4
MTLK DE4 .... **140** F8
NM/HAY SK22 ...... **27** G5
NM/HAY SK22 ...... **43** L3
RCH S42 .... **145** H4
RDERBYSW DE65 ...... **264** A1
RIPLEY DE5 .... **200** E7
SBK/MW NG20 ...... **133** J6
SK/MW NG20 ...... **133** H4
STV/CWN S43 ...... **92** E7

STV/CWN S43 .... **95** H6
STV/CWN S43 .... **110** F2
STV/CWN S43 .... **111** K1
STV/CWN S43 .... **111** H2
SWAD DE11 .... **283** J8
UTXR ST14 .... **247** M3
WRKS S80 .... **96** D5
Station St ASH NG17 ...... **163** J8
ASHB DE6 .... **207** L1
BUT DE14 .... **274** A8
GLSP SK13 .... **26** A1 🔟
ILK DE7 .... **230** D1
LGEAT NG10 .... **261** J3
MSFD NG18 .... **164** E4
MSFDW NG19 .... **149** L7
SWAD DE11 .... **289** J7
Station Vw SBK/MW NG20 ...... **133** H7
Station Yd ASH NG17 ...... **163** J5
Staton La DRON S18 ...... **91** K1
Staunton Av NORM/LIT DE23 ...... **256** B4
Staunton Cl CDON/KEG DE74... **271** K6
Staunton La MELB/CHEL DE73... **284** C1
Staveley Cl DERBYSE DE24 ...... **257** H7
Staveley La ECK/KIL S21 ...... **92** C5
ECK/KIL S21 .... **93** H2
Staveley Rd BSVR S44 ...... **112** B6
SHEFS S8 .... **55** K5 🔟
STV/CWN S43 .... **92** B7
STV/CWN S43 .... **112** D2
Staverton Dr MCKLVR DE3 ...... **239** C6 🔟
Steade Rd ABRD S7 ...... **55** J3
Stead St ECK/KIL S21 ...... **73** G7
Steam Mill La RIPLEY DE5 ...... **201** K2
Steele Av STV/CWN S43 ...... **111** L4
Steel La BSVR S44 ...... **113** L8
Steel Rd ECC S11 ...... **54** F2
Steel's La BSVR S44 ...... **131** L4
Steeping Cl STV/CWN S43 ...... **111** H2
Steep La RCH S42 ...... **127** K6
Steeple Cl DERBYE DE21 ...... **227** H8
Steeple Gra MTLK DE4 ...... **171** J7
Steep Tpk MTLK DE4 ...... **156** F5
Steetley La WRKS S80 ...... **76** F8
WRKS S80 .... **77** K6
Stella St MSFD NG18 ...... **164** E5
Stemp St ECC S11 ...... **55** J2 🔢
Stenson Av NORM/LIT DE23 ...... **256** B4
Stenson Ct RIPLEY DE5 ...... **201** J1
Stenson Rd DERBYSE DE24... **255** M8
NORM/LIT DE23 ...... **256** B2 🔟
Stenton Rd SHEFS S8 ...... **70** C3
Stephenson Pl CHNE S41 ...... **3** H4 🔟
CLCR S45 .... **144** D6 🔟
Stephenson Rd STV/CWN S43 ... **112** B1
Stephensons Wy DERBYE DE21... **241** K7
Stephens Rd BUT DE14 ...... **280** E2
Stepping Cl DERBYW DE22... **240** A5
Stepping La DERBYW DE22... **240** A5
Sterland St CHSW S40 ...... **2** D4
Sterndale Cl BUX SK17 ...... **84** B7
Sterndale Rd ABRD S7 ...... **54** F7
LGEAT NG10 .... **260** E4
Sterry Cl STV/CWN S43 ...... **95** H4
Stevenage Cl DERBYSE DE24 ...... **257** J5
Steven Cl BSTN/STPLFD NG9... **245** K4
Stevens La BWSH/BRSTN DE72 .. **260** A2
Stevenson Av
BWSH/BRSTN DE72 ...... **259** L2
Stevenson Pl NORM/LIT DE23 ...... **255** L2
Stevenson Rd ASHB DE6 ...... **248** E2
Stevens Rd LGEAT NG10 ...... **244** D5
Steward Ga EDL/UDV S33 ...... **50** D4
Stewart Cl BUT DE14 ...... **280** D4
DERBYE DE21 .... **242** B4
Stewart Rd ALFN DE55 ...... **188** A5
Stewart St ALFN DE55 ...... **188** A5
Stile Cft MTLK DE4 ...... **171** G5 🔟
Stiles Av MPL/ROM SK6 ...... **32** B8
Stiles Cl GLSP SK13 ...... **17** H5 🔟
Stiles Rd DERBYSE DE24 ...... **257** L3
Stillman Cl CHNE S41 ...... **3** M9
Stinting La SBK/MW NG20 ...... **133** C8
Stirland St RIPLEY DE5 ...... **201** L1
Stirling Cl DERBYE DE21 ...... **240** F2 🔟
MSFDW NG19 ...... **164** B5
Stirling Gdns
BSTN/STPLFD NG9 ...... **245** L8 🔟
Stirling Ri BUTN/AL/TUT DE13... **274** A2
The Stitchings ASHB DE6 ...... **205** M1
Stockbrook Rd DERBYW DE22... **240** A7
Stockbrook St DERBYW DE22 ...... **4** B6
Stocker Av DERBYSE DE24 ...... **257** M3
Stockley La BSVR S44 ...... **131** J7
Stockley Vw BSVR S44 ...... **131** L2
Stockport Rd HYDE SK14 ...... **24** B1
Stock Rd SHEF/MNR S2 ...... **56** B1
Stocks Brow GLSP SK13 ...... **17** K3
Stocks Green Ct TOT/DORE S17 ... **68** F6
Stocks Green Dr
TOT/DORE S17 ...... **69** G6 🔟
Stocks La UTXR ST14 ...... **246** F3
The Stocks GLSP SK13 ...... **17** K3
Stockton Dr CHF/WBR SK23 ...... **60** B1
Stockwell Av AU/AST/KP S26 ...... **74** F1
Stockwell Ga MSFD NG18 ...... **164** D4
Stockwell La AU/AST/KP S26 ...... **74** E1
Stoddard Dr HEANOR DE75... **202** C8
Stoke Cl BPR/DUF DE56 ...... **200** A6
Stoke Ford HATH/EY S32 ...... **65** L7
Stollard St CLCR S45 ...... **145** G6
Stoneacre Av HACK/IN S12 ...... **57** L7
Stoneacre Cl HACK/IN S12 ...... **57** L7 🔟
Stoneacre Dr HACK/IN S12 ...... **57** L8
Stoneacre Ri HACK/IN S12 ...... **57** L7
Stonebench La BUX SK17 ...... **119** M7
Stonebroom La ALFN DE55... **160** E6
Stonechat Cl MCKLVR DE3 ...... **239** K7
Stonecliffe Pl SHEFP/MNR S2 ...... **56** D1
Stonecliffe Rd SHEFP/MNR S2 ...... **56** D1
Stone Cl DERBYE DE21 ...... **242** B4
DRON S18 .... **70** F7
Stone Crs MSFDW NG19 ...... **164** A3
Stonecroft Rd TOT/DORE S17... **69** H5
Stone Cross La ALFN DE55... **146** E4
Stonedale Cl MOS S20 ...... **73** G3 🔟
Stone Dell FUL S10 ...... **53** M1
Stonegravels La CHNE S41 ...... **110** D5 🔟

Stonegravels Wy MOS S20 ...... **73** J4
Stoneheads Ri CHF/WBR SK23... **59** G2
Stonehill CDON/KEG DE74 ...... **271** L8
Stone Hill Rd NORM/LIT DE23 ...... **4** C7
Stoneholes Dr CLCR S45 ...... **145** H8
Stoneleigh Wy ALFN DE55 ...... **187** H2
Stoneley Cl HACK/IN S12 ...... **71** K1
Stoneley Crs HACK/IN S12 ...... **71** L1
Stoneley Dell HACK/IN S12 ...... **71** L1
Stoneley Dr HACK/IN S12 ...... **71** L1
Stonelow Crs DRON S18 ...... **71** G8
Stonelow Rd DRON S18 ...... **70** E8
Stone Mdw LGEAT NG10 ...... **261** H5 🔟
Stonepit La ASHB DE6 ...... **181** K7
Stoneridge GLSP SK13 ...... **17** G5
Stone Rd DRON S18 ...... **70** F6
UTXR ST14 .... **247** L3
Stone Rw CHSW S40 ...... **2** B5
MPL/ROM SK6 ...... **32** D4
Stonerows La ALFN DE55 ...... **158** E4
Stonesby Cl DERBYE DE21 ...... **227** J8
Stones La MTLK DE4 ...... **185** J1
The Stones EDL/UDV S33 ...... **48** E8
Stone St MOS S20 ...... **73** G3
Stonewell La BUX SK17 ...... **151** G5
Stoney Cl BKWL DE45 ...... **123** C6
Stoneycroft La RCH S42 ...... **127** K6
Stoney Cross DERBYE DE21 ...... **242** B7
Stoneydale Cl SWAD DE11 ...... **282** C5 🔟
Stoney Flatts Crs
DERBYE DE21 ...... **241** K2 🔟
Stoneyford Rd ASH NG17 ...... **163** G4
Stoney Furlong Rd BKWL DE45... **106** B4
Stoney HI MTLK DE4 ...... **171** K8
Stoneyland Dr NM/HAY SK22 ...... **43** K2
Stoney La ASHB DE6 ...... **181** J8
ASHB DE6 .... **195** J1
BSTN/STPLFD NG9 ...... **230** E5
CDLE ST10 .... **190** A4
DERBYE DE21 ...... **242** C6
EWD/SEL/PNX N16 ...... **189** H3
EWD/SEL/PNX N16 ...... **202** F4
STV/CWN S43 .... **95** H8
STV/CWN S43 .... **111** J8
Stoney Wy MTLK DE4 ...... **156** F6
Stonyhurst Ct
DERBYSE DE24 ...... **257** H7 🔟
Stony La BPR/DUF DE56 ...... **213** M4
CDLE ST10 .... **191** C1
Stony Ridge Rd TOT/DORE S17 ... **67** L6
Stoodley Pike Gdns
DERBYW DE22 ...... **225** M8 🔟
Stoops Cl CHSW S40 ...... **110** A4 🔟
Stoppard Cl ILK DE7 ...... **217** C8
Storer La BPR/DUF DE56 ...... **183** K7
Stores Rd DERBYE DE21 ...... **240** E3
Store St SHEF/MNR S2 ...... **55** L1
Storforth La CHNE S41 ...... **128** F3
CHSW S40 .... **128** D3
Stormont Cl ALFN DE55 ...... **176** E6
Stornoway Cl
DERBYSE DE24 ...... **256** A7 🔟
Storrs Rd CHSW S40 ...... **109** L8
Storth Av FUL S10 ...... **54** B2
Storth Bank GLSP SK13 ...... **25** J3 🔟
Storthfield Wy ALFN DE55 ...... **176** E6
Storth La ALFN DE55 ...... **176** E6
FUL S10 .... **54** B1
Storth Meadow Rd GLSP SK13 ...... **25** J3
Storthholme Ms FUL S10 ...... **54** C3 🔟
Stotfield Rd WOL/BIL/BRX NC8 .. **231** L5
Stour Cl RDERBYSW DE65 ...... **265** H2 🔟
STV/CWN S43 .... **111** H2
Stourdale Cl LGEAT NG10 ...... **260** D4
Stourport Dr MELB/CHEL DE73... **257** K7
Stowe Av ABRD S7 ...... **54** F6
Stow Cl ASHZ LE65 ...... **291** K3
Stowmarket Dr DERBYE DE21... **241** G1
Stradbroke Av HAN/WDH S13... **57** G3
Stradbroke Crs HAN/WDH S13... **57** H3
Stradbroke Dr HAN/WDH S13... **57** H3
Stradbroke Pl HAN/WDH S13... **57** H3
Stradbroke Ri CHSW S40 ...... **127** M2
Stradbroke Rd HAN/WDH S13... **57** H3
Stradbroke Wy HAN/WDH S13... **57** H3
Strand DERBY DE1 ...... **4** E3
Stranfaer Cl ALFN DE55 ...... **187** J3
Stranraer Cl MSFDW NG19 ...... **149** M4
Stratford Cl DERBYE DE21 ...... **241** G1
Stratford Rd DERBYE DE21 ...... **227** G8
FUL S10 .... **54** A1
Stratford St ILK DE7 ...... **217** J6
Strathallan Cl MTLK DE4 ...... **140** F6
Strathaven Ct DERBYE DE21 ...... **242** B5
Strathmore Av DERBYSE DE24... **257** J4
Strathtay Rd ECC S11 ...... **54** E3
Stratton Rd BSVR S44 ...... **113** K4
Strawberry Bank ASH NG17 ...... **162** K6
Strawberry La MSHM DE12 ...... **288** A5
SWAD DE11 .... **290** E2
Strawberry Lee La
TOT/DORE S17 ...... **68** E5
Strawberry Wy MSFDW NG19... **165** L2
Straw La ALFN DE55 ...... **159** M2
Streatham Rd DERBYSE DE24... **239** K4
Street Farm Cl AU/AST/KP S26... **74** F1
Streetfield Crs MOS S20 ...... **73** C4 🔟
Streetfields MOS S20 ...... **73** H4
Street La RIPLEY DE5 ...... **200** D4
The Street BUX SK17 ...... **79** H6
Strelley Av RIPLEY DE5 ...... **200** E4
SHEFS S8 .... **70** A8
Strelley Rd SHEFS S8 ...... **70** A1
Stretfield Rd EDL/UDV S33 ...... **64** E1
Strettea La ALFN DE55 ...... **159** M8
Stretton Cl MCKLVR DE3 ...... **255** C1 🔟
Stretton Rd ALFN DE55 ...... **160** B5
CLCR S45 .... **144** F8
ECC S11 .... **54** F3
MSFDW NG19 ...... **149** L7
Striding Edge Cl LGEAT NG10... **244** E8 🔟
Strines Moor Rd HOLM/MEL HD7 .. **9** M3
Strines Rd MPL/ROM SK6 ...... **32** D5
Stringer Av HYDE SK14 ...... **16** C3
Stringer Cl HYDE SK14 ...... **16** C8

Stroma Cl DERBYSE DE24 ...... **256** C6 🔟
Struan Rd ECC S11 ...... **54** F5
Strutt St BPR/DUF DE56 ...... **199** J7
NORM/LIT DE23 ...... **4** F9
Stuart Av MSFDW NG19 ...... **165** J2
Stuart Cl CHNE S41 ...... **110** E4
Stuart St DERBY DE1 ...... **4** F2
MSFD NG18 .... **165** H3
Stuart Wy ASHZ LE65 ...... **291** L5
Stubben Edge La CLCR S45 ...... **158** F1
Stubbing Rd CHSW S40 ...... **128** C3
Stubbins La CHF/WBR SK23 ...... **45** G8
Stubbins Wd SBK/MW NG20... **133** H4
Stubbin Wood La
SBK/MW NG20 ...... **133** H4
Stubbs La ASHB DE6 ...... **191** M8
Stubley Cl DRON S18 ...... **70** B8
Stubley Cft DRON S18 ...... **70** A8
Stubley Dr DRON S18 ...... **70** B8
Stubley Hollow DRON S18 ...... **70** B8
Stubley La DRON S18 ...... **70** B8
Stubley Pl DRON S18 ...... **70** B8
Stubwood Hollow UTXR ST14... **218** A5
Stubwood La UTXR ST14 ...... **218** A6
Studbrook Cl CDON/KEG DE74... **271** J7
Studfarm Cl
MELB/CHEL DE73 ...... **279** H8 🔟
Stumperlowe Av FUL S10 ...... **54** B2 🔟
Stumperlowe Cl FUL S10 ...... **54** B2 🔟
Stumperlowe Crescent Rd
FUL S10 .... **54** A2
Stumperlowe Cft FUL S10 ...... **54** A1
Stumperlowe Hall Cha
FUL S10 .... **54** A1 🔟
Stumperlowe Hall Rd FUL S10... **54** A3
Stumperlowe La FUL S10 ...... **54** A2
Stumperlowe Park Rd FUL S10... **54** A2
Stumperlowe Vw FUL S10 ...... **54** A2
Sturge Cft SHEF/MNR S2 ...... **55** L4 🔟
Sturges La BWSH/BRSTN DE72... **258** C6
Sturston Rd ASHB DE6 ...... **207** M1
Sudbury Av ILK DE7 ...... **230** D3
LGEAT NG10 .... **244** D3
Sudbury Cl CHSW S40 ...... **109** L5
DERBY DE1 .... **4** B4
Sudbury Dr ASH NG17 ...... **162** C8
Sudbury Ms
EWD/SEL/PNX N16 ...... **217** H1 🔟
Sudbury Pk ASHB DE6 ...... **250** A3
Sudbury St DERBY DE1 ...... **4** A4
Sudhall Cl CHNE S41 ...... **110** A2
Suff La EWD/SEL/PNX N16 ...... **176** F7
Suffolk Av DERBYE DE21 ...... **241** H3
Suffolk Rd STPNHL/WHNL DE15.. **281** C3
Sugworth Rd ST/HB/BR S6 ...... **41** K3
ST/HB/BR S6 .... **42** A1
Sulleys Fld DERBYW DE22 ...... **226** A3 🔟
Summerbrook Ct
DERBYW DE22 ...... **4** C6 🔟
Summer Cross BUX SK17 ...... **83** L6
Summer Dr MTLK DE4 ...... **183** H5
Summerfield Crs STV/CWN S43... **111** H2
Summerfield Dr UTXR ST14 ...... **247** K2 🔟
Summerfield Rd CHSW S40 ...... **2** E7
DRON S18 .... **70** E7
Summerfield St FUL S10 ...... **55** H1
Summerfield Wy ILK DE7 ...... **216** F7
Summerfields Wy South
ILK DE7 .... **217** G8
Summer La MTLK DE4 ...... **183** G3
TOT/DORE S17 ...... **68** F6
Summerley Lower Rd DRON S18.. **71** H8
Summerley Rd DRON S18 ...... **71** H8
Summerskill Gn STV/CWN S43... **111** M3
Summer Wood Cl
NORM/LIT DE23 ...... **256** A3
Summerwood La DRON S18 ...... **70** C7
Summerwood Pl DRON S18 ...... **70** C7
Summit Dr SBK/MW NG20 ...... **133** H6
Sumner St GLSP SK13 ...... **25** M2
Sunart Cl DERBYSE DE24 ...... **256** C6
Sunderland St ECC S11 ...... **55** H1 🔟
Sundew Cl DERBYE DE21 ...... **242** C6
Sundial Cl HYDE SK14 ...... **16** A7
Sundown Av NORM/LIT DE23... **256** A4
Sundown Cl NM/HAY SK22 ...... **43** K2
Sundown Pl HAN/WDH S13 ...... **57** J2
Sundown Rd HAN/WDH S13 ...... **57** J2
Suningdale Cl
BUTN/AL/TUT DE13 ...... **273** M1 🔟
Sun La MTLK DE4 ...... **185** J2
Sunlaws St GLSP SK13 ...... **25** L2
Sunlea Crs BSTN/STPLFD NG9... **245** J5
Sunningdale Av DERBYE DE21... **242** A5
HEANOR DE75 ...... **216** C2
Sunningdale Cl CHSW S40 ...... **2** C9
Sunningdale Dr ILK DE7 ...... **229** L5
Sunningdale Mt ECC S11 ...... **54** E5
Sunningdale Ri CHSW S40 ...... **127** M2 🔟
Sunninghill Cl ILK DE7 ...... **229** G2 🔟
Sunny Bank ALFN DE55 ...... **161** J5 🔟
BKWL DE45 .... **104** D6 🔟
FUL S10 .... **55** H1
Sunnybank MTLK DE4 ...... **140** C7
Sunny Bank Gdns
BPR/DUF DE56 ...... **199** J8 🔟
Sunny Bank La BUX SK17 ...... **83** M7 🔟
Sunny Banks GLSP SK13 ...... **25** L2
Sunny Brook Cl STV/CWN S43... **95** H7
Sunny Gv DERBYE DE21 ...... **241** K5
Sunny HI BPR/DUF DE56 ...... **213** J3
Sunnyhill Av NORM/LIT DE23... **256** B4
Sunnyside STPNHL/WHNL DE15.. **282** B3
SWAD DE11 .... **282** B3
WRKS S80 .... **96** D3
Sunnyside Rd
BSTN/STPLFD NG9 ...... **245** M5 🔟
UTXR ST14 .... **247** L1
Sunny Springs CHNE S41 ...... **3** H1
Sunnyvale Av TOT/DORE S17... **69** G6
Sunnyvale Rd TOT/DORE S17... **69** G6
Sun St DERBYW DE22 ...... **4** C6
SWAD DE11 .... **283** J8
Sunwell Ter MPL/ROM SK6 ...... **32** C6 🔟
Surbiton Cl DERBYW DE22 ...... **239** K4 🔟
Surbiton Ct ILK DE7 ...... **229** G2
Surfleet Cl WOL/BIL/BRX NC8... **231** M7
Surgery La MTLK DE4 ...... **185** K1
Surrey Dr MSFDW NG19 ...... **164** C2
Surrey St DERBYW DE22 ...... **240** A4

GLSP SK13 ... 25 M1
Sussex Circ *DERBYE* DE21 ... 241 H2
Sussex Rd *STPNHL/WNHL* DE15 ... 281 G4
Sussex Wy *LGEAT* NG10 ... 244 E5
Sutherland Rd *DERBYE* DE23 ... 256 C2
Sutton Av *MELB/CHEL* DE73 ... 257 J7
Sutton Cl *ASH* NG17 ... 163 K5
  DERBYW DE22 ... 239 M4
Sutton Ct *EWD/SEL/PNX* NG16 ... 203 J8
Sutton Crs *STV/CWN* SK43 ... 111 M3
Sutton Dr *DERBYSE* DE24 ... 257 H6
Sutton Hall Rd *BSVR* SK44 ... 131 K2
Sutton La *BSVR* SK44 ... 130 A1
  RDERBYSW DE65 ... 252 F7
  RDERBYSW DE65 ... 252 B7
  RDERBYSW DE65 ... 252 E5
  RDERBYSW DE65 ... 253 L5
Sutton Rd *ASH* NG17 ... 162 D5
  MSFD NG18 ... 164 C5
  MSFDW NG19 ... 164 A5
  RDERBYSW DE65 ... 252 B3
Suttons La *MPL/ROM* SK6 ... 32 D5
Sutton Vw *BSVR* SK44 ... 131 L2
Sutton Wy *GLSP* SK13 ... 17 K5
Swaddale Av *CHNE* SK41 ... 110 F4
Swaddale Cl *CHNE* SK41 ... 110 E4
Swadlincote La *BUTN/AL/LIT* DE11 ... 289 G1
Swadlincote Rd *SWAD* DE11 ... 283 C2
Swaines Meadow *MTLK* DE4 ... 183 C2
Swalebank Cl *CHSW* SK40 ... 3 J9
Swaledale Rd *ABRD* S7 ... 55 G5
Swallow Cl *MCKLVR* DE3 ... 239 K7
  MSFD NG18 ... 165 L6
Swallowdale Rd
  DERBYSE DE24 ... 256 A6
Swallow House Crs
  NM/HAY SK22 ... 34 F7
Swallow House La *NM/HAY* SK22 ... 34 E7
Swallow Rd *SWAD* DE11 ... 283 J7
Swallow Wood Ct
  HAN/WDH S13 ... 57 K4
Swanbourne Cl *CHNE* S41 ... 3 L8
Swan Cl *WRKN* S81 ... 77 L3
Swan La *MSFDW* NG19 ... 149 L7
Swanmore Rd
  NORM/LIT DE23 ... 255 K2
Swannington St
  BUTN/AL/TUT DE13 ... 273 L4
Swann Yd *ASH* NG17 ... 162 C7
Swanson Av *ASH* NG17 ... 162 C7
Swanwick *DERBYE* DE21 ... 241 K1
Swanwick Av *SBK/MW* NG20 ... 133 J7
Swanwick Hl *ALFN* DE55 ... 187 H3
Swanwick Rd *ALFN* DE55 ... 187 L3
Swanwick St *CHNE* S41 ... 91 K8
Swarkestone Br
  MELB/CHEL DE73 ... 269 G5
Swarkestone Dr
  NORM/LIT DE23 ... 255 M5
Swarkestone Rd
  MELB/CHEL DE73 ... 268 D4
  MELB/CHEL DE73 ... 269 J3
Swathwick Cl *RCH* S42 ... 128 B6
Swathwick La *RCH* S42 ... 127 M4
Swayfield Cl *MCKLVR* DE3 ... 238 E7
Sweethill *MSHM* DE12 ... 290 D5
Sweetbriar Cl *DERBYSE* DE24 ... 257 K5
Swift Cl *MCKLVR* DE3 ... 239 K7
  SWAD DE11 ... 283 J7
Swift Ct *EWD/SEL/PNX* NG16 ... 203 J8
Swinburne St *DERBYE* DE1 ... 4 E7
Swinderby Dr *DERBYE* DE21 ... 241 L1
Swindon Cl
  EWD/SEL/PNX NG16 ... 217 L3
Swiney Wy *BSTN/STPLFD* NG9 ... 261 L1
Swinger La *CLCR* S45 ... 142 F5
Swinney Bank *BPR/DUF* DE56 ... 199 K5
Swinney La *BPR/DUF* DE56 ... 199 K5
Swinscoe Hl *ASHB* DE6 ... 192 C6
Swinscoe Wy *RCH* S42 ... 109 J5
Swinson Cl *UTXR* ST14 ... 218 D7
Sycamore Av *BSVR* SK44 ... 147 L2
  CHSW S40 ... 2 C7
  DERBYW DE22 ... 226 A7
  DRON S18 ... 70 D7
  RDERBYSW DE65 ... 255 G8
  RIPLEY DE5 ... 201 G2
  SWAD DE11 ... 282 D3
  WRKS S80 ... 96 B8
Sycamore Cl *ALFN* DE55 ... 159 M6
  BSVR S44 ... 113 M8
  BUX SK17 ... 99 L1
  EWD/SEL/PNX NG16 ... 177 C7
  NSHM DE12 ... 290 D6
  NM/HAY SK22 ... 44 B1
  RDERBYSW DE65 ... 253 M6
  UTXR ST14 ... 247 J3
Sycamore Ct *DERBYE* DE21 ... 242 B5
  RDERBYSW DE65 ... 266 E5
Sycamore Crs *LGEAT* NG10 ... 244 D3
Sycamore Dr *CHNE* S41 ... 111 C7
  ECK/KIL S21 ... 73 M5
  ILK DE7 ... 230 E3
  MSHM DE12 ... 290 D7
Sycamore La *STV/CWN* S43 ... 94 E4
  STV/CWN S43 ... 111 K1
Sycamore Rd *ASHB* DE6 ... 206 F3
  CDON/KEG DE74 ... 271 L5
  CHF/WBR SK23 ... 60 C6
  EWD/SEL/PNX NG16 ... 217 L6
  LGEAT NG10 ... 260 D5
  MSFDW NG19 ... 149 M5
  MTLK DE4 ... 156 C4
  NM/HAY SK22 ... 34 B8
  STPNHL/WNHL DE15 ... 281 H5
  STV/CWN S43 ... 111 J1
The Sycamores *ALFN* DE55 ... 176 D5
  EWD/SEL/PNX NG16 ... 217 H3
  GLSP SK13 ... 17 J7
Sycamore St *MOS* S20 ... 72 F2
Syda La *RCH* S42 ... 126 B2
Syday La *ECK/KIL* S21 ... 94 A1
Sydenham Rd *DERBYW* DE22 ... 239 K3
Sydney Cl *MCKLVR* DE3 ... 239 J7
  MSFDW NG19 ... 149 M4
Sydney Rd *BWSH/BRSTN* DE72 ... 259 K3
Sydney St *BUT* DE14 ... 274 A4
  CHSW S40 ... 2 C4

Sydnope Hl *MTLK* DE4 ... 141 K5
Syerscote La *CRTAM* B79 ... 292 E8
Syerston Rd *MSFD* NG18 ... 165 K8
Sylvan Cliff *BUX* SK17 ... 99 M3
Sylvan Cl *CHNE* S41 ... 3 L8
Sylvan Crs *ASH* NG17 ... 163 K5
Sylvan Dr *RCH* S42 ... 144 D4
Sylvan Pk *BUX* SK17 ... 99 M2
Sylvester Cl *HYDE* SK14 ... 16 B8
Sylvester St *MSFD* NG18 ... 164 C5
  SHEF S1 ... 55 K1
Sylvia Rd *DRON* S18 ... 91 G5
Sywell Cl *ALFN* DE55 ... 187 J2
  ASH NG17 ... 163 J5

T

Tabley Gdns *MPL/ROM* SK6 ... 32 D6
Tadcaster Gdns *SHEFS* S8 ... 55 J6
Tadcaster Rd *SHEFS* S8 ... 55 J6
Tadcaster Wy *SHEFS* S8 ... 55 J6
Taddington Rd *CHSW* S40 ... 109 L5
  DERBYE DE21 ... 241 H2
Taft Av *LGEAT* NG10 ... 244 E4
Tagg La *BKWL* DE45 ... 136 D1
Taggs Knoll *EDL/UDV* S33 ... 50 E6
Taghole La *HYDE* SK14 ... 16 B8
Tailby Dr *RDERBYSW* DE65 ... 266 D5
Talbot Crs *CHNE* S41 ... 129 G3
Talbot Dr *BSTN/STPLFD* NG9 ... 231 G8
Talbot Pl *MSHM* DE12 ... 295 H2
Talbot Pl *GLSP* SK13 ... 17 M8
Talbot St *CHNE* S41 ... 129 G3
  DERBYW DE22 ... 4 C4
  EWD/SEL/PNX NG16 ... 176 F8
  GLSP SK13 ... 25 M1
  MSFD NG18 ... 164 C6
  SWAD DE11 ... 289 K1
Talgarth Cl *DERBYE* DE21 ... 227 M8
Talmont Rd *ECC* S11 ... 54 E4
Tamar Av *DERBYW* DE22 ... 226 A6
Tamworth Rd *ASHZ* LE65 ... 291 K6
  LGEAT NG10 ... 260 F5
Tamworth St *BPR/DUF* DE56 ... 213 H7
Tandy Av *MSFD* NG18 ... 290 E5
Tanner's La *RDERBYSW* DE65 ... 266 F7
Tannery La *HAN/WDH* S13 ... 57 L4
Tannery St *HAN/WDH* S13 ... 57 L4
Tansley Av *ILK* DE7 ... 228 D1
Tansley Dr *CHSW* S40 ... 109 K5
Tansley House Gdns
  MTLK DE4 ... 157 K6
Tansley Ri *DERBYE* DE21 ... 241 J1
Tansley Rd *RCH* S42 ... 145 J5
Tansley Wy *STV/CWN* S43 ... 111 M4
Tants Meadow *BPR/DUF* DE56 ... 214 B4
Tantum Av *HEANOR* DE75 ... 201 M6
Tanwood Rd
  BSTN/STPLFD NG9 ... 261 L1
Tanyard Cl *CDON/KEG* DE74 ... 271 L6
Tap La *CHSW* S40 ... 2 D4
Taplow Cl *MCKLVR* DE3 ... 238 F8
Tapton La *CHNE* S41 ... 3 J5
Tapton Lock Hl *CHNE* S41 ... 110 E4
Tapton Park Rd *CHNE* S41 ... 110 D5
Tapton Ter *CHNE* S41 ... 110 F5
Tapton View Rd *CHNE* S41 ... 110 C5
Tapton Wy *STV/CWN* S43 ... 111 J6
Tarina Cl *MELB/CHEL* DE73 ... 269 K1
Tarnside Fold *GLSP* SK13 ... 25 K2
Tasman Cl *MCKLVR* DE3 ... 239 J7
Tatenhill Common
  BUTN/AL/TUT DE13 ... 272 A8
Tatenhill La *BUTN/AL/TUT* DE13 ... 280 A1
Tatham's La *ILK* DE7 ... 217 H8
Tattle Hl *ILK* DE7 ... 229 J8
Taunton Cl *DERBYSE* DE24 ... 257 M2
Taverners Crs *NORM/LIT* DE23 ... 256 A2
Tavern Rd *GLSP* SK13 ... 17 H7
Tavistock Av *RIPLEY* DE5 ... 186 F7
Tavistock Cl *DERBYSE* DE24 ... 256 A7
  HYDE SK14 ... 16 B8
Tavistock Rd *SHEFS* S8 ... 55 J4
Tavistock Sq *ALFN* DE55 ... 175 M5
Tawney Cft *MTLK* DE4 ... 157 K6
Tawny Wy *NORM/LIT* DE23 ... 255 K3
Tawton Av *HYDE* SK14 ... 16 B8
Taxal Moor Rd *CHF/WBR* SK23 ... 58 F6
Tay Cl *DERBYSE* DE24 ... 256 A8
  DRON S18 ... 70 A8
Taylor Av *MSHM* DE12 ... 290 D6
Taylor Crs *BSTN/STPLFD* NG9 ... 245 H7
  CHNE S41 ... 129 G1
Taylor La *HEANOR* DE75 ... 202 A7
Taylor's Cl *MSFD* NG18 ... 165 H2
Taylor's La *ASHB* DE6 ... 237 H4
  BPR/DUF DE56 ... 183 L7
Taylor St *DERBYSE* DE24 ... 241 G8
  HYDE SK14 ... 17 G5
  ILK DE7 ... 230 C1
Tayside Cl *DERBYSE* DE24 ... 256 A7
Tay Wk *DERBYW* DE22 ... 226 B7
T Benedict St *SHEF/MNR* S2 ... 56 A2
Teal Av *MSFD* NG18 ... 165 L6
Teal Cl *SBK/MW* NG20 ... 133 G7
Tean Cl *STPNHL/WNHL* DE15 ... 281 K1
Tedburn Dr *MSFD* NG18 ... 165 K8
Tedder Av *BUX* SK17 ... 100 A7
Tedgness Rd *HATH/EY* S32 ... 87 H1
Tedworth Av *DERBYSE* DE24 ... 256 A8
Teesbrook Dr
  WOL/BIL/BRX NG8 ... 231 L6
Teesdale Ct *BSTN/STPLFD* NG9 ... 245 K6
Teesdale La *HACK/IN* S12 ... 72 C1
  LGEAT NG10 ... 260 D4
Teignmouth Av *MSFD* NG18 ... 165 J4
Telford Cl *MCKLVR* DE3 ... 255 H1
Telford Crs *STV/CWN* S43 ... 111 J3
Telford Dr *EWD/SEL/PNX* NG16 ... 203 L7
Telma Rd *MPL/ROM* SK6 ... 32 D6
Telmah Cl
  BUTN/AL/TUT DE13 ... 274 A1
Temperance Hl *ALFN* DE55 ... 159 H3
Temperance St *HYDE* SK14 ... 16 B7
Templar Cl *DERBYSE* DE24 ... 255 M8
Temple Av *GLSP* SK13 ... 17 M5
Temple Cl
  BUTN/AL/TUT DE13 ... 274 B3

Templeoak Dr
  WOL/BIL/BRX NG8 ... 231 M7
Temple Rd *BUX* SK17 ... 99 K4
  MTLK DE4 ... 171 K1
Temple St *GLSP* SK13 ... 17 M5
  NORM/LIT DE23 ... 4 D8
Ten Dr *DERBYE* DE21 ... 227 M8
Ten Foot Cl *GLSP* SK13 ... 17 L8
Tennessee Rd *DERBYE* DE21 ... 241 K3
Tennyson Av *CHSW* S40 ... 2 F5
  MSFDW NG19 ... 149 M8
  SWAD DE11 ... 282 F4
Tennyson Cl *DERBYE* DE12 ... 295 L7
Tennyson Rd *BUT* DE14 ... 274 A3
  WRKS S80 ... 115 G1
Tennyson Sq
  EWD/SEL/PNX NG16 ... 217 M6
Tennyson St *ALFN* DE55 ... 159 M5
  DERBYE DE55 ... 257 G3
  ILK DE7 ... 217 H7
  MSFD NG18 ... 164 D3
  RCH S42 ... 146 A1
Tennyson Wy *RCH* S42 ... 129 H7
Tenter Cl *LGEAT* NG10 ... 261 G5
Tenter La *BPR/DUF* DE56 ... 200 A1
  MSFD NG18 ... 164 C5
Terminus Rd *SHEF* S7 ... 54 F7
Tern Av *SWAD* DE11 ... 283 J7
Terrace La *DERBYE* DE21 ... 257 J5
  CHNE S41 ... 110 C2
  STPNHL/WNHL DE15 ... 281 M1
Terrace Rd *BUX* SK17 ... 83 M5
  BUX SK17 ... 99 L3
  CHF/WBR SK23 ... 60 E4
  MSFD NG18 ... 164 F3
Terret Gv *BUX* SK17 ... 99 G5
Terry Rd *TOT/DORE* S17 ... 69 H5
Tetney Rd *FUL* S10 ... 54 C1
Teversal Av *MSFDW* NG19 ... 148 E6
Tevery Cl *BSTN/STPLFD* NG9 ... 245 H2
Teviot Pl *DERBYE* DE21 ... 227 K8
Tewkesbury Cl *DERBYE* DE21 ... 241 C2
Tewkesbury Rd *LGEAT* NG10 ... 261 H6
Thackeray Rd *ALFN* DE55 ... 160 C7
Thackeray St *DERBYE* DE24 ... 256 D5
Thames Cl *DERBYSE* DE24 ... 239 J5
Thanet Dr *DERBYSE* DE24 ... 257 K4
Thanet St *CLCR* S45 ... 144 F7
Thatchers La *MTLK* DE4 ... 157 L7
Theatre La *CHNE* S41 ... 3 J3
Thickley Cl *SBK/MW* NG20 ... 133 J5
Thimble Hl *ASHB* DE6 ... 211 K8
Third Av *RCH* S42 ... 280 C1
  MSFDW NG19 ... 165 K2
Thirlmere Av *DERBYW* DE22 ... 226 B7
Thirlmere Cl *LGEAT* NG10 ... 244 E8
Thirlmere Dr *DRON* S18 ... 70 D6
Thirlmere Gdns *ASHZ* LE65 ... 291 M5
Thirlmere Rd *CHNE* S41 ... 109 M3
  LGEAT NG10 ... 244 F8
  SHEFS S8 ... 55 H5
Thirlwell Rd *SHEFS* S8 ... 55 K4
Thirsk Pl *DERBYSE* DE24 ... 257 C3
Thistle Cl *EWD/SEL/PNX* NG16 ... 217 L2
  STLY SK15 ... 16 A6
Thistledown Cl
  DERBYW DE22 ... 226 D8
Thistle Green Cl *HEANOR* DE75 ... 216 E1
Thistle Rd *ILK* DE7 ... 230 D6
Thomas Cook Cl
  MELB/CHEL DE73 ... 278 D3
Thomas St *GLSP* SK13 ... 26 B1
Thompson Cl
  BSTN/STPLFD NG9 ... 245 M7
  CHNE S41 ... 110 C2
Thompson Rd *FUL* S10 ... 55 G1
Thompson St *CHNE* S41 ... 110 C2
  EWD/SEL/PNX NG16 ... 202 C7
Thomson Dr *RIPLEY* DE5 ... 200 A3
Thore Cl *DERBYE* DE21 ... 241 L1
Thoresby Av *SBK/MW* NG20 ... 133 H6
  STV/CWN S43 ... 95 K6
Thoresby Cl *RIPLEY* DE5 ... 201 H1
Thoresby Crs *ASH* NG17 ... 162 F4
  BWSH/BRSTN DE72 ... 259 K5
Thoresby Pl *STV/CWN* S43 ... 111 M4
Thoresby Rd *BSTN/STPLFD* NG9 ... 245 M1
  LGEAT NG10 ... 260 E3
  MSFDW NG19 ... 149 K6
Thoresby St *ASH* NG17 ... 163 K6
  MSFD NG18 ... 164 D3
Thorn Av *MSFDW* NG19 ... 164 C1
Thornborough Cl
  SHEF/MNR S2 ... 55 M3
Thornborough Pl
  SHEF/MNR S2 ... 55 M3
Thornborough Rd
  SHEF/MNR S2 ... 55 L3
Thornbridge Av *HACK/IN* S12 ... 57 G7
Thornbridge Cl *HACK/IN* S12 ... 57 G7
Thornbridge Crs *CHSW* S40 ... 128 C4
  HACK/IN S12 ... 57 H7
Thornbridge Dr *HACK/IN* S12 ... 57 G7
Thornbridge Gv *HACK/IN* S12 ... 57 G7
Thornbridge La *HACK/IN* S12 ... 57 H7
Thornbridge Pl *HACK/IN* S12 ... 57 G7
Thornbridge Ri *HACK/IN* S12 ... 57 G7
Thornbridge Wy *HACK/IN* S12 ... 57 H7
Thornbrook Rd *CHF/WBR* SK23 ... 60 E4
Thornbury Av *HYDE* SK14 ... 16 B8
Thornbury Dr *MSFDW* NG19 ... 164 A2
Thorncliffe Av *MTLK* DE4 ... 140 C4
Thorncliffe Rd *GLSP* SK13 ... 17 J7
Thorn Cl *BUX* SK17 ... 100 A2
  DERBYW DE22 ... 226 A6
Thorndene Cl *CHNE* S41 ... 110 C4
Thorndike Av *DERBYSE* DE24 ... 257 K3
Thorndon Cl *MCKLVR* DE3 ... 255 C2
Thorndon Wy *CHSW* S40 ... 127 M2
Thorn Dr *EWD/SEL/PNX* NG16 ... 217 L2
Thorne Cl *CHSW* S40 ... 109 J5
Thornell Cl *CHF/WBR* SK23 ... 60 F5
Thorne Rd *ABRD* S7 ... 55 H5
Thornescroft Gdns *BUT* DE14 ... 280 C1
Thorness *DERBYSE* DE24 ... 257 M5
Thornewill Dr
  BUTN/AL/TUT DE13 ... 274 C1
Thorneywood Rd *LGEAT* NG10 ... 261 J2
Thornfield Av *CHSW* S40 ... 127 L1
Thornhill Cl *BSTN/STPLFD* NG9 ... 231 L8

Thornhill La *EDL/UDV* S33 ... 50 C7
  EDL/UDV S33 ... 50 A6
Thornhill Rd *DERBYE* DE22 ... 239 M6
  NORM/LIT DE23 ... 255 M1
Thornholme Rd *MPL/ROM* SK6 ... 32 C6
Thornley St *BUT* DE14 ... 274 A5
Thornsett *NM/HAY* SK22 ... 34 A8
Thornsett Cl *BUX* SK17 ... 100 B2
Thornsett Gdns *TOT/DORE* S17 ... 69 J3
Thornsett Rd *ECC* S11 ... 55 H2
Thorn St *NORM/LIT* DE23 ... 240 C8
  SWAD DE11 ... 283 J8
Thornton Cl *MSFD* NG18 ... 165 L5
Thornton Pl *DRON* S18 ... 89 M1
Thorntop Cl *SWAD* DE11 ... 290 E2
Thorntree Cl
  BWSH/BRSTN DE72 ... 260 C1
Thorntree Gdns
  EWD/SEL/PNX NG16 ... 203 J6
Thorntree La *DERBY* DE1 ... 4 F4
Thorn Tree La
  STPNHL/WNHL DE15 ... 282 C2
Thornway *MPL/ROM* SK6 ... 42 C3
Thorp Cl *SHEFP/MNR* S2 ... 55 K2
Thorpe Av *DRON* S18 ... 70 F6
  WRKS S80 ... 96 C5
Thorpe Cl *BSTN/STPLFD* NG9 ... 244 F3
  CHNE S41 ... 110 C2
  STPNHL/WNHL DE15 ... 281 M1
Thorpe Cft *MTLK* DE4 ... 172 E5
Thorpe Downs Rd *SWAD* DE11 ... 289 L1
Thorpe Dr *MCKLVR* DE3 ... 239 H7
  MOS S20 ... 73 H1
Thorpe Gn *MOS* S20 ... 73 G1
Thorpe Hill Dr *HEANOR* DE75 ... 216 B3
Thorpe House Av *SHEFS* S8 ... 55 L6
Thorpe House Ri *SHEFS* S8 ... 55 K6
Thorpe House Rd *SHEFS* S8 ... 55 K6
Thorpelands Av *MSFDW* NG19 ... 165 H1
Thorpelands Dr
  DERBYW DE22 ... 240 B1
Thorpe La *WRKS* S80 ... 76 F4
Thorpe Leys *LGEAT* NG10 ... 261 G5
Thorpe Rd *AU/AST/KP* S26 ... 75 K3
  EWD/SEL/PNX NG16 ... 165 K8
  MSFD NG18 ... 165 K8
Thorpe's Rd *HEANOR* DE75 ... 216 A1
Thorpe Wy *BPR/DUF* DE56 ... 199 L5
Thorswood La *ASHB* DE6 ... 191 L8
Three Tunes Rd
  EWD/SEL/PNX NG16 ... 203 K8
Threshfield Wy *HACK/IN* S12 ... 57 L7
Thrift Rd *BUT* DE14 ... 280 E2
Throstle Gv *MPL/ROM* SK6 ... 32 B5
Throstle Nest Wy *ASHB* DE6 ... 223 J2
Thrumpton Av *LGEAT* NG10 ... 261 J3
Thrushton Cl
  RDERBYSW DE65 ... 254 F8
Thruxton Cl *DERBYSE* DE24 ... 257 M4
Thunderpit La *HATH/EY* S52 ... 85 K7
Thurcaton Wy *ALFN* DE55 ... 161 K7
Thurcroft Rd *DERBYW* DE22 ... 239 M4
Thurlow Cl *DERBYE* DE21 ... 241 L1
Thurman St *ILK* DE7 ... 230 D4
Thurstan Av *SHEFS* S8 ... 70 B2
Thurston Av *ALFN* DE55 ... 188 A2
Thurstone Furlong
  MELB/CHEL DE73 ... 269 H1
Thurvaston Rd *ASHB* DE6 ... 233 J1
Tiber Cl *DERBYSE* DE24 ... 258 A5
Tibshelf Rd *ALFN* DE55 ... 175 M1
  ASH NG17 ... 162 D3
  RCH S42 ... 146 A3
Tickham Av *DERBYSE* DE24 ... 255 M8
Ticknall La *RIPLEY* DE5 ... 214 E1
  SWAD DE11 ... 283 K3
Tideswell Cl *STV/CWN* S43 ... 111 L2
Tideswell Gn *SWAD* DE11 ... 282 B5
Tideswell La *HATH/EY* S32 ... 85 L5
Tideswell Rd *DERBYE* DE21 ... 241 J3
Tilbury Pl *DERBYSE* DE24 ... 257 K5
Tilford Rd *HAN/WDH* S13 ... 57 M4
Tiller Cl *NORM/LIT* DE23 ... 255 L4
Tillotson Cl *SHEFS* S8 ... 55 L4
Tillotson Ri *SHEFS* S8 ... 55 K4
Tilton Gv *ILK* DE7 ... 229 M5
Timber La *CLCR* S45 ... 146 A5
  UTXR ST14 ... 247 L4
Timbersbrook Cl *DERBYE* DE21 ... 241 K1
Timsbury Ct *DERBYE* DE21 ... 227 H8
Tinkerley La *BPR/DUF* DE56 ... 183 C8
Tinkley La *CLCR* S45 ... 143 M6
Tinsell Brook *RDERBYSW* DE65 ... 265 G1
Tinsley Rd *EWD/SEL/PNX* NG16 ... 217 C1
Tintagel Cl *BUTN/AL/TUT* DE13 ... 265 H8
  NORM/LIT DE23 ... 240 E8
Tipnall Rd *CDON/KEG* DE74 ... 271 K7
Tipper's La *RDERBYSW* DE65 ... 251 K2
Tiree Cl *ALFN* DE55 ... 161 J5
  BSTN/STPLFD NG9 ... 231 C8
  DERBYSE DE24 ... 256 C6
Tissington Cl *CHSW* S40 ... 109 L5
Tissington Dr *DERBYE* DE21 ... 227 L7
Tissington Trail *ASHB* DE6 ... 193 J2
  BUX SK17 ... 151 K2
  BUX SK17 ... 152 A6
Titchfield Av *ASH* NG17 ... 163 H8
Titchfield St *MSFDW* NG19 ... 146 E2
  WRKS S80 ... 96 C4
Tithe Barn Av *HAN/WDH* S13 ... 57 L3
Tithe Barn Cl *BUX* SK17 ... 83 M7
  HAN/WDH S13 ... 57 M3
Tithebarn La *ASHB* DE6 ... 236 F5
Tithe Barn La *HAN/WDH* S13 ... 57 M4
Tithe Barn Wy *HAN/WDH* S13 ... 57 L2
Tiverton Cl *MCKLVR* DE3 ... 239 G6
Tivoli Gdns *DERBYW* DE22 ... 240 B3
Toadmoor La *BPR/DUF* DE56 ... 185 J7
Tobermory Wy *DERBYSE* DE24 ... 256 A7
Todbrook Cl *CHF/WBR* SK23 ... 58 F4
Todwick Rd *SHEFS* S8 ... 55 H6
Toft Rd *BSTN/STPLFD* NG9 ... 245 K7
Toll Bar Av *HACK/IN* S12 ... 56 B5
Toll Bar Cl *HACK/IN* S12 ... 56 B5
Toll Bar Dr *HACK/IN* S12 ... 56 B5

Tollbridge Rd *STV/CWN* S43 ... 93 L8
Tollemache Cl *HYDE* SK14 ... 16 D5
Tollemache Rd *HYDE* SK14 ... 16 D5
Toll House Md *MOS* S20 ... 72 F3
Tom La *BSVR* S44 ... 112 C5
  FUL S10 ... 54 A1
Tomwood Ri *GLSP* SK13 ... 24 F4
Tonbridge Dr *DERBYSE* DE24 ... 257 K5
Tonge Gn *STLY* SK15 ... 16 B4
Tonge La *MELB/CHEL* DE73 ... 279 J7
Tongue La *BUX* SK17 ... 100 B2
Tontine Rd *CHSW* S40 ... 3 G5
Toothill La *MSFD* NG18 ... 164 E3
Toothill Rd *MSFD* NG18 ... 164 E3
  UTXR ST14 ... 248 B6
Top Farm Ct *BPR/DUF* DE56 ... 214 C2
Top Hagg La *BPR/DUF* DE56 ... 185 K4
Tophill La *MTLK* DE4 ... 170 A2
Tophole Rd *EDL/UDV* S33 ... 64 C5
Top La *BPR/DUF* DE56 ... 197 M1
  MSFDW NG19 ... 148 C8
  MSFDW NG19 ... 163 K1
  MTLK DE4 ... 185 L1
  RCH S42 ... 108 D7
Top Manor Cl
  BWSH/BRSTN DE72 ... 242 F5
Top Meadow *SWAD* DE11 ... 282 E3
Toppham Dr *SHEFS* S8 ... 70 C4
Toppham Ri *SHEFS* S8 ... 70 C4
Toppham Wy *SHEFS* S8 ... 70 C4
Top Pingle Cl *STV/CWN* S43 ... 111 K3
Top Rd *BSVR* S44 ... 111 K7
  RCH S42 ... 144 A1
Topshill La *BPR/DUF* DE56 ... 182 E8
Tor Av *ALFN* DE55 ... 159 F8
Tor Cl *MTLK* DE4 ... 156 F1
Torkington La *BRAM/HZG* SK7 ... 32 A7
Torrance Cl *BUT* DE14 ... 280 D4
Torrani Wy *RCH* S42 ... 145 J3
Torridon Cl *DERBYSE* DE24 ... 256 B6
Torrington Dr *HYDE* SK14 ... 16 A8
Tor Ri *MTLK* DE4 ... 156 E7
Torr St *BUX* SK17 ... 99 L3
Torrs Va *NM/HAY* SK22 ... 43 M3
Torr Top St *NM/HAY* SK22 ... 43 M3
Torrvale Rd *NM/HAY* SK22 ... 43 L3
Torry Cl *HAN/WDH* S13 ... 57 M4
Torside Wy *GLSP* SK13 ... 17 K5
The Tors *MTLK* DE4 ... 185 J1
Tor View Ri *MTLK* DE4 ... 171 K5
Torwood Dr *SHEFS* S8 ... 70 B3
Totland Rd
  BSTN/STPLFD NG9 ... 231 M8
Totley Brook Cl
  TOT/DORE S17 ... 69 G5
Totley Brook Cft
  TOT/DORE S17 ... 69 G5
Totley Brook Gln
  TOT/DORE S17 ... 69 G5
Totley Brook Gv *TOT/DORE* S17 ... 69 G5
Totley Brook Rd *TOT/DORE* S17 ... 69 G4
Totley Brook Wy
  TOT/DORE S17 ... 69 G5
Totley Grange Cl
  TOT/DORE S17 ... 69 G6
Totley Grange Rd *TOT/DORE* S17 ... 69 G6
Totley Hall La *TOT/DORE* S17 ... 69 G6
Totley La *TOT/DORE* S17 ... 69 L5
Totley Ms *GLSP* SK13 ... 25 G1
Totley Mt *STV/CWN* S43 ... 111 G2
Totnes Cl *BUTN/AL/TUT* DE13 ... 274 A3
Toton La *BSTN/STPLFD* NG9 ... 245 J5
Toulmin Dr *SWAD* DE11 ... 282 B6
Toulouse Pl *ASHZ* LE65 ... 291 K3
  SHEFP/MNR S2 ... 55 M2
Tower Cl *ALFN* DE55 ... 187 M2
Tower Crs *BSVR* S44 ... 131 L2
Tower Dr *SHEFP/MNR* S2 ... 55 M2
Tower Gdns *ASHZ* LE65 ... 291 K4
Tower Rd *STPNHL/WNHL* DE15 ... 274 E8
  SWAD DE11 ... 283 K4
Towers La *HATH/EY* S32 ... 66 B2
Tower St *DERBYSE* DE24 ... 257 G2
Towle Cl *BWSH/BRSTN* DE72 ... 258 E1
Towles Pastures
  CDON/KEG DE74 ... 271 K7
Towle St *LGEAT* NG10 ... 260 B6
Town End *ALFN* DE56 ... 196 E1
  BPR/DUF DE56 ... 196 E1
  BSVR S44 ... 113 K8
  BUX SK17 ... 100 A1
  DRON S18 ... 91 J1
Town End Rd
  BWSH/BRSTN DE72 ... 259 L3
Townfield La *EDL/UDV* S33 ... 65 G1
Town Fold *MPL/ROM* SK6 ... 32 E3
Town Ga *EDL/UDV* S33 ... 64 D3
Town Hall Yd *ASHB* DE6 ... 193 M8
Townhead La *EDL/UDV* S33 ... 50 C6
Townhead Rd *TOT/DORE* S17 ... 68 F4
Town La *ALFN* DE55 ... 161 K7
  EDL/UDV S33 ... 64 D2
  GLSP SK13 ... 25 G4
Townroe Dr *MSFDW* NG19 ... 164 A2
Townscliffe La *MPL/ROM* SK6 ... 32 E4
Townsend Gv
  MELB/CHEL DE73 ... 257 K3
Townside Cl *LGEAT* NG10 ... 260 E6
Town St *BPR/DUF* DE56 ... 213 M4
  BPR/DUF DE56 ... 213 H7
  BSTN/STPLFD NG9 ... 245 L2
  EWD/SEL/PNX NG16 ... 177 H7
  LGEAT NG10 ... 244 E4
  MPL/ROM SK6 ... 32 E3
The Town *DERBYE* DE21 ... 226 F3
Towson Av
  EWD/SEL/PNX NG16 ... 202 F8
Trafalgar Rd *LGEAT* NG10 ... 261 G4
Trafalgar Sq *LGEAT* NG10 ... 261 H3
Trafalgar Ter *LGEAT* NG10 ... 261 H3
Traffic St *DERBY* DE1 ... 5 G4
Trafford Wy *NORM/LIT* DE23 ... 255 M2
Tranker La *WRKN* S81 ... 77 L4
Tranmere Av *CLCR* S45 ... 145 G7
Trans Pennine Trail *ECK/KIL* S21 ... 93 L1
  HAN/WDH S13 ... 57 H1
  STV/CWN S43 ... 93 J7
Trap La *ECC* S11 ... 54 B4

Travers Rd *LGEAT* NG10 .... 244 D4
Travey Rd *SHEFP/MNR* S2 .... 56 D3 3
Tredcroft St *GLSP* SK13 .... 25 L2
Tredegar Dr *DERBYE* DE21 .... 227 L8
Treeneuk Cl *CHSW* S40 .... 109 L7 1
Trefoil Ct *NORM/LIT* DE23 .... 255 K3 10
Tregaron Cl *DERBYE* DE21............ 227 M8
Tregony Wy *DERBYSE* DE24 .... 256 A8
Tremayne Rd
WOL/BIL/BRX NG8........................ 231 M4
Trenchard Dr *BUX* SK17 .... 100 A7
Trent Av *BUX* SK17 .... 99 M6
RDERBYSW DE65 .... 266 F5
Trent Bridge Ct
NORM/LIT DE23 .... 255 M2 6
Trent Cl *DERBYSE* DE24 .... 256 A8
RDERBYSW DE65 .... 266 F5
Trent Dr *NORM/LIT* DE23 .... 256 A5
Trent Gv *ALFN* DE55 .... 175 K8
DRON S18 .... 70 E7
Trent La *BWSH/BRSTN* DE72 .... 270 B6
CDON/KEG DE74 .... 271 K5
LGEAT NG10 .... 261 J4
MELB/CHEL DE73.......................... 269 M8
STPNHL/WNHL DE15 .... 275 G2
Trenton Cl *BSTN/STPLFD* NG9....... 245 K1
Trenton Dr *LGEAT* NG10................. 261 K2
Trenton Green Dr
DERBYE DE21 .... 241 L4 4
Trent Ri *DERBYE* DE21 .... 242 C6
Trent Rd *ILK* DE7 .... 230 A6
Trent St *BUT* DE14 .... 280 F1
DERBYSE DE24.............................. 257 K3
LGEAT NG10 .... 261 H2
Trent Valley Wy
BSTN/STPLFD NG9........................... 261 M3
Trent Vslley Wy
CFTN/RUD NG11 .... 261 M5
Tresillian Cl *DERBYW* DE22 .... 226 B8
Tressall Cl *ILK* DE7.......................... 230 D2
Trevelyn Cl
STPNHL/WNHL DE15 .... 281 M1
Treveris Cl *DERBYE* DE21 .... 242 C6 2
Trevone Av *BSTN/STPLFD* NG9..... 245 H4
The Triangle *ILK* DE7 .... 230 D4
Trickett Cl *EDL/UDV* S33 .... 48 F7
Trinity Cl *ASHZ* LE65 .... 291 K5
CHNE S41 .... 2 F1
ILK DE7 .... 217 H7 8
Trinity Ct *ASHZ* LE65...................... 291 K4
Trinity Gv *SWAD* DE11 .... 282 E7
Trinity Pas *BUX* SK17 .... 99 M3
Trinity Rd *UTXR* ST14 .... 247 M3
Trinity St *DERBY* DE1 .... 5 H6
MPL/ROM SK6 .... 32 C5 3
Trinkey La *HATH/EY* S32 .... 86 D8
Tristram Gv *BUTN/AL/TUT* DE13.. 265 H8
Troon Cl *CHSW* S40......................... 127 M2
NORM/LIT DE23 .... 255 K2
Trot La *BUX* SK17 .... 84 C3
Troughbrook Rd *STV/CWN* S43 .. 111 L1
Troutbeck Crs
BSTN/STPLFD NG9......................... 245 M2
Troutbeck Gv
NORM/LIT DE23 .... 255 K3 11
Troutbeck Rd *SHEFS* S8................... 55 H6
Trowbridge Cl
DERBYE DE21 .... 227 H8 11
Trowell Av *ILK* DE7 .... 230 D5
WOL/BIL/BRX NG8........................ 231 L5
Trowell Gv *BSTN/STPLFD* NG9 ..... 231 G7
LGEAT NG10 .... 260 E1
Trowell Park Dr
BSTN/STPLFD NG9 .... 231 G8 10
Trowell Rd *BSTN/STPLFD* NG9 ..... 231 G8
WOL/BIL/BRX NG8........................ 231 M5
Trowels La *DERBYW* DE22.............. 239 M6
Trueman St *ILK* DE7 .... 217 J6 2
Truman St *ILK* DE7 .... 230 D1 1
Truro Cl *SWAD* DE11 .... 283 H5
Truro Crs *DERBYE* DE21................... 241 H2
Trusley Gdns *NORM/LIT* DE23......... 256 A5
Trustley Cl *BUT* DE14 .... 280 E3 4
Tuckers La *MSFDW* NG19................. 164 C2
Tudor Av *MSFDW* NG19 .... 165 J2
Tudor Cl *ASHZ* LE65......................... 291 L5
LGEAT NG10 .... 261 H1
Tudor Dr *MSFD* NG18 .... 164 F6
Tudor Falls *HEANOR* DE75.............. 202 B7
Tudor Field Cl
MELB/CHEL DE73 .... 269 K1 5
Tudor Hollow
BUTN/AL/TUT DE13 .... 274 A2 14
Tudor House Cl *SWAD* DE11 .... 282 D3
Tudor Pl *ILK* DE7 .... 229 M5
Tudor Ri *CRTAM* B79....................... 293 H8
Tudor Rd *DERBYE* DE21 .... 241 K4
Tudor St *STV/CWN* S43..................... 93 J8
Tudor Wy *SWAD* DE11 .... 282 D4
Tudsbury Ter *ASH* NG17.................. 163 K7
Tuffolds Cl *SHEFP/MNR* S2 .... 56 D3
Tufnell Gdns *DERBYW* DE22 ...... 239 L3 2
Tulip Rd *EWD/SEL/PNX* NG16 .... 217 L5
Tulla Cl *DERBYSE* DE24.................... 256 B8
Tullibardine Rd *ECC* S11 .... 54 E4
Tunstall Gn *CHSW* S40 .... 2 B7
Tunstall Wy *CHSW* S40....................... 2 B7
Tupton Wy *RCH* S42 .... 146 A1
Turf Lea Rd *MPL/ROM* SK6 .... 42 E1
Turlowfields La *ASHB* DE6.............. 195 L2
Turnberry Cl *BSTN/STPLFD* NG9.. 245 M4
CHSW S40 .... 127 M2 9
ILK DE7 .... 216 F8
Turnbury Cl *BUT* DE14 .... 280 D3
Turncliff Crs *MPL/ROM* SK6 .... 32 A3
Turncliffe Cl *BUX* SK17 .... 99 J4 2
Turner Av *EWD/SEL/PNX* NG16..... 202 D7
Turner Cl *BSTN/STPLFD* NG9......... 245 H4
DRON S18 .... 90 C1 5
Turner Dr *EWD/SEL/PNX* NG16..... 217 L3
STV/CWN S43 .... 111 L3
Turner Rd *LGEAT* NG10.................. 260 F6
MPL/ROM SK6 .... 32 C4
Turners La *ALFN* DE55 .... 187 K4
Turner St *DERBYSE* DE24................ 257 G4
Turnlee Cl *GLSP* SK13 .... 25 M3
Turnlee Dr *GLSP* SK13...................... 25 M3
Turnlee Rd *GLSP* SK13 .... 25 M3
Turnley Rd *ALFN* DE55 .... 176 F4
Turnoaks La *CHSW* S40 .... 128 D3
Turnpike Cl *MTLK* DE4 .... 156 F5 6
The Turnpike *MPL/ROM* SK6........... 32 A3
Turnstone Crs *MSFD* NG18 .... 165 L6 2
Turton Cl *EWD/SEL/PNX* NG16 ..... 202 D7
Tutbury Cl *ASHZ* LE65...................... 291 M5
Tutbury Rd *BUTN/AL/TUT* DE13 .. 264 D8
Tuxford Cl *DERBYE* DE21 .... 241 L1 15
Twayblade *BUT* DE14...................... 280 E2
Tweeds Muir Cl
DERBYE DE21 .... 227 J8 13
Twentylands
BUTN/AL/TUT DE13 .... 265 G6 1
Twentywell Dr *TOT/DORE* S17 .... 69 L4 1
Twentywell La *TOT/DORE* S17 .... 69 K3
Twentywell Ri *TOT/DORE* S17 .... 69 L3
Twentywell Rd *TOT/DORE* S17....... 69 L5
Twentywell Vw *TOT/DORE* S17 ..... 69 L5
Twickenham Cl *MOS* S20 .... 73 H4 9
Twickenham Ct *MOS* S20 .... 73 H4 10
Twickenham Crs *MOS* S20 .... 73 H5
Twickenham Dr
DERBYW DE22 .... 239 K4 5
Twickenham Gld *MOS* S20 .... 73 H4 11
Twickenham Gln *MOS* S20 .... 73 J5 2
Twickenham Gv *MOS* S20 .... 73 H4 12
Twin Oaks Cl *NORM/LIT* DE23 ...... 255 J3
Twin Oaks Dr *ASH* NG17 .... 162 F8
Twinyards Cl *ASH* NG17 .... 177 M1
Twisses Bank *ASHB* DE6 .... 234 D8
Twitchill Dr *HAN/WDH* S13 .... 57 L4
Twyford Cl *HEANOR* DE75 .... 215 M2
ILK DE7 .... 229 G2 5
RDERBYSW DE65 .... 266 F5
SWAD DE11 .... 282 C8
Twyford Rd *LGEAT* NG10 .... 260 C6
MELB/CHEL DE73.......................... 268 D4
RDERBYSW DE65 .... 266 F5
Twyford St *NORM/LIT* DE23 .... 4 F8
Tylden Rd *WRKS* S80 .... 77 L5 1
Tylden Wy *WRKS* S80 .... 77 K5 1
Tylney Rd *CHSW* S40 .... 127 L3
SHEFP/MNR S2 .... 56 A1
Tyndale Cha *DERBYSE* DE24 ... 255 M8 4
Tynedale Cl *LGEAT* NG10............... 260 D4
The Tythe *SWAD* DE11 .... 282 E3
Tyzack Rd *SHEFS* S8......................... 55 H8

U

Uffa Magna *MCKLVR* DE3 .... 254 F1 5
Uldale Gv *SWAD* DE11 .... 289 M1
Ulldale Ct *BSTN/STPLFD* NG9 .... 245 L6
Ulley Crs *HAN/WDH* S13.................. 56 E3
Ulley Rd *HAN/WDH* S13 .... 56 E3
Ullswater Av *MOS* S20...................... 73 H4
Ullswater Cl *DERBYE* DE21 .... 227 G8 5
DRON S18 .... 70 B8
MOS S20 .... 73 H4
Ullswater Crs *ASHZ* LE65 .... 291 M6
BSTN/STPLFD NG9........................ 245 M1
Ullswater Dr *DERBYE* DE21............ 242 B4
DRON S18 .... 90 B1
Ullswater Pl *DRON* S18 .... 70 B8
Ulverston Rd *CHNE* S41 .... 110 A3
SHEFS S8.. 55 H6
Undercliffe *BKWL* DE45 .... 123 G4
Underhill Av *NORM/LIT* DE23 .... 256 C3
Underhill Cl *NORM/LIT* DE23......... 256 B4
Underhill Rd *STV/CWN* S43 .... 94 E4
Undertown La *ASHB* DE6 .... 218 F4
Underwood Gdns *WRKS* S80 .... 77 M7
Underwood Rd *HYDE* SK14............... 16 A7
SHEFS S8.. 55 J6
Union Rd *ECC* S11 .... 55 G4
ILK DE7 .... 230 B3
MPL/ROM SK6 .... 32 C4 9
NM/HAY SK22 .... 43 L3
SWAD DE11 .... 282 E5
Union St *ALFN* DE55 .... 176 C6
ASH NG17 .... 163 J8
ASHB DE6 .... 193 L8
AU/AST/KP S26 .... 75 H3
BUT DE14 .... 274 A8
EWD/SEL/PNX NG16 .... 189 K3
GLSP SK13 .... 25 M2 5
LGEAT NG10 .... 261 H2
MELB/CHEL DE73.......................... 278 D3
MSFD NG18.................................... 164 D3
Unity Cl *SWAD* DE11 .... 289 K1
Unstone-dronfield By-pass
DRON S18 .... 70 C7
DRON S18 .... 90 C1
Unstone Hl *DRON* S18 .... 91 G2
Unstone Rd *DRON* S18...................... 91 J5
Unstone St *SHEFP/MNR* S2............. 55 K1
Unthank La *DRON* S18..................... 88 F6
Unwin Rd *ASH* NG17........................ 163 L7
Unwin St *ASH* NG17 .... 162 D7
Upland Ri *CHSW* S40 .... 2 A7
Uplands Av *NORM/LIT* DE23 .... 255 M4
Uplands Gdns *NORM/LIT* DE23....... 4 B9
Uplands Rd *GLSP* SK13 .... 26 A2
MSHM DE12 .... 295 M6
Upper Albert Rd *SHEFS* S8 .... 55 L5
Upper Bainbrigge St
NORM/LIT DE23 .... 4 D9
Upper Barn Cl *HEANOR* DE75 .. 202 C8 5
Upper Blindlow La *BUX* SK17 .... 119 K6
Upper Boundary Rd
DERBYW DE22 .... 4 A5
Upper Church Rd *ASHZ* LE65 .... 291 M4
Upper Croft Cl *STV/CWN* S43 .... 111 H3
Upper Dale Rd *NORM/LIT* DE23 .. 256 C1
Upper Dunstead Rd
EWD/SEL/PNX NG16 .... 202 E6
Upper End Rd *BUX* SK17 .... 81 M6
Upper Greenhill Gdns
MTLK DE4 .... 156 F4 1
Upper Hall Cl *BPR/DUF* DE56 .... 213 M4
Upper Hibbert La *MPL/ROM* SK6 .. 32 C6
Upper Hollow *NORM/LIT* DE23...... 255 M1
Upper House Rd *HOLM/MEL* HD7 .. 9 M2
Upper La *ASHB* DE6 .... 196 B6
Upper Mantle Cl *CLCR* S45 .... 144 F6
Upper Marehay Rd *RIPLEY* DE5 .. 200 F4
Upper Mexborough Rd
EWD/SEL/PNX NG16 .... 189 K3
Upper Moor Rd *DERBYSE* DE24 .. 257 H4
Upper Moor St *CHSW* S40 .... 109 L8 2
Upper Nelson St *HEANOR* DE75 .. 202 A8
Upper Newbold Cl *CHSW* S40 .. 109 L3 7
Upper Orchard St
BSTN/STPLFD NG9 .... 245 H3 2
Upper Packington Rd
ASHZ LE65 .... 291 M6
Upper School La *DRON* S18 .... 90 E2 3
DRON S18 .... 90 D2 4
Upperthorpe Rd *ECK/KIL* S21 .... 74 A5
Upper Town La *MTLK* DE4............ 154 E1
Uppertown La *MTLK* DE4 .... 170 F1
Upper Valley Rd *SHEFS* S8 .... 55 L5
Upper Wellington St
LGEAT NG10 .... 260 F1
Upperwood Rd *MTLK* DE4 .... 171 K1
Upper Yeld Rd *BKWL* DE45 .... 122 F6
Uppingham Dr *ASHZ* LE65............ 291 K3
Upton Cl *HEANOR* DE75 .... 216 D1 3
Upton Mt *MSFDW* NG19 .... 164 B1
Upwood Cl *CHSW* S40 .... 109 K5 13
Upwoods Rd *ASHB* DE6.................. 232 E8
Utah Cl *RDERBYSW* DE65 .... 253 H8 6
Uttoxeter New Rd
DERBYW DE22 .... 239 M7
Uttoxeter Old Rd *DERBY* DE1....... 240 A6
Uttoxeter Rd *ASHB* DE6 .... 250 F6
MCKLVR DE3 .... 239 H8 1
MCKLVR DE3 .... 255 H1 11
RDERBYSW DE65 .... 251 K7
Uxbridge St *BUT* DE14 .... 280 F1

V

Vale Cl *BSVR* S44 .... 131 K1
DRON S18 .... 90 E1 3
EWD/SEL/PNX NG16 .... 203 L8
MSFD NG18...................................... 165 H6
Vale Dr *SBK/MW* NG20 .... 133 J8
Vale House Dr *GLSP* SK13 .... 17 K4
Valentine Av
EWD/SEL/PNX NG16 .... 189 G3
Valerie Rd *BWSH/BRSTN* DE72 .... 270 C3
Vale Rd *MSFDW* NG19 .... 149 L6
SWAD DE11 .... 282 E4
SWAD DE11 .... 283 K7
The Vale *ILK* DE7 .... 217 H7
Vallance St *MSFDW* NG19 .... 149 L6
Valley Cl *CLCR* S45 .... 145 L6
Valley Dr *ECK/KIL* S21 .... 74 A3 5
EWD/SEL/PNX NG16 .... 217 L1
Valley Ri *DRON* S18......................... 90 A7
SWAD DE11 .... 282 D5
Valley Rd *BSTN/STPLFD* NG9......... 245 K5
BSVR S44....................................... 131 K2
CHNE S41 .... 3 L6
CLCR S45 .... 144 D6
DERBYE DE21 .... 241 L4
DRON S18 .... 90 A7
ECK/KIL S21 .... 74 A3
GLSP SK13 .... 25 J2 1
HACK/IN S12.................................... 57 M8
HYDE SK14 .... 24 B2
ILK DE7 .... 230 B5
MSHM DE12 .... 289 K7
NM/HAY SK22 .... 35 G8
NORM/LIT DE23 .... 256 A1
SBK/MW NG20 .... 133 H5
SHEFS S8.. 55 K4
STV/CWN S43 .... 93 M6
Valley Vw *BPR/DUF* DE56 .... 199 K8
ILK DE7 .... 230 B5
Valley View Cl *CHNE* S41 .... 129 H3
ECK/KIL S21 .... 72 F8 3
Valley View Dr *ILK* DE7 .... 228 D1
Valley View Rd *ALFN* DE55 .... 187 M6
Valmont Av *MSFD* NG18 .... 165 K4
Valmont Rd *BSTN/STPLFD* NG9 .. 245 K2
Vancouver Av *DERBYE* DE21 .... 242 A7
Vancouver Dr
STPNHL/WNHL DE15 .... 274 F7
Vanguard Rd *LGEAT* NG10 .... 261 G5 6
Vannes Gv *HYDE* SK14 .... 16 C7
Varley St *DERBYSE* DE24 .... 257 G3
Vaughan Pl *SBK/MW* NG20 .... 133 H4
Vaughan Rd *BSTN/STPLFD* NG9 .. 245 K6
CHF/WBR SK23................................. 59 H5
Vauxhall Av *DERBYW* DE22 .... 239 K3
Vellus Ct *ASH* NG17........................ 163 L8
Ventnor Pl *ABRD* S7 .... 55 J2 12
Venture Crs *ALFN* DE55 .... 175 K8
Venture Wy *CHNE* S41 .... 110 C1
Verbena Dr *NORM/LIT* DE23 .... 256 A6
Vere Av *ASH* NG17.......................... 163 H5
Vere Cl *RDERBYSW* DE65 .... 266 E5
Vermont Dr *DERBYE* DE21 .... 241 M4 2
Verney Cl *UTXR* ST14 .... 246 F3 2
Verney St *MSFDW* NG19 .... 148 C3
Verney Wy *MSFDW* NG19 .... 148 C3
Vernon Ct *SBK/MW* NG20 .... 133 K6
Vernon Dr *DERBYE* DE21 .... 242 C6 3
Vernongate *DERBY* DE1 .... 4 B3
Vernon Gn *BKWL* DE45.................. 122 E3
Vernon Ri *RCH* S42 .... 129 J8
Vernon Rd *CHSW* S40....................... 2 B4
TOT/DORE S17 .... 69 H4
Vernon St *DERBY* DE1 .... 4 B3
ILK DE7 .... 217 J6
SBK/MW NG20 .... 133 K6
Verona Ct *MSFD* NG18 .... 165 K7
Veronica Dr
EWD/SEL/PNX NG16 .... 217 M2 6
Veronne Dr *ASH* NG17 .... 163 K4
Vesper Ct *MSFDW* NG19 .... 165 J2
Vestry Rd *DERBYE* DE21 .... 227 H8
Vetchfield Cl *DERBYSE* DE24 .... 256 C8 2
Via Gellia Rd *MTLK* DE4 .... 170 F4
Vicarage Av *ILK* DE7 .... 217 G6
NORM/LIT DE23 .... 4 B9
Vicarage Cl *ALFN* DE55................. 187 H3
BPR/DUF DE56 .... 199 K6 8
BSVR S44.. 130 E8
DRON S18 .... 89 K2
ILK DE7 .... 215 J4
SBK/MW NG20 .... 133 H7 2
STPNHL/WNHL DE15 .... 274 E6
SWAD DE11 .... 290 F2 1
Vicarage Ct *ASH* NG17 .... 163 H3
MCKLVR DE3 .... 255 G1 6
Vicarage Dr *DERBYE* DE21 .... 241 K3
Vicarage Gdns *HEANOR* DE75....... 216 C1
SWAD DE11 .... 282 F6
Vicarage La *BKWL* DE45................ 122 B2
BPR/DUF DE56 .... 213 H6
DERBYE DE21 .... 226 E2
EWD/SEL/PNX NG16 .... 188 C6
MTLK DE4 .... 140 B1
NM/HAY SK22 .... 35 G8
TOT/DORE S17 .... 69 G3
Vicarage Ms *ALFN* DE55................ 188 B4
Vicarage Rd *BPR/DUF* DE56 .... 213 J2
MCKLVR DE3 .... 238 F8
MELB/CHEL DE73.......................... 257 J8
SWAD DE11 .... 283 H8
Vicarage St *ILK* DE7 .... 217 G6
Vicarage Wk *MSHM* DE12 .... 287 M4 1
Vicar La *ALFN* DE55....................... 161 K4
CHSW S40 .... 3 H4
HAN/WDH S13 .... 57 L3
Vicar Wy *MSFDW* NG19 .... 165 K2
Vicarwood Av
BPR/DUF DE56 .... 213 M3 4
DERBYW DE22 .... 240 C1
Victor Av *DERBYW* DE22 .... 240 C2
Victor Crs *LGEAT* NG10................. 244 F6
Victoria Av *BWSH/BRSTN* DE72 .. 242 E8
BWSH/BRSTN DE72 .... 259 K3 5
GLSP SK13 .... 17 K5 13
STV/CWN S43 .... 93 J7
Victoria Cl *MCKLVR* DE3 .... 239 H6
Victoria Crs *BUT* DE14 .... 273 M5
EWD/SEL/PNX NG16 .... 188 C6
Victoria Dr *ALFN* DE55 .... 161 H8
Victoria Gv *STV/CWN* S43 .... 111 J5
Victoria Hall Gdns *MTLK* DE4 .... 156 F4 2
Victoria Park Rd *BUX* SK17 .... 99 M2
STV/CWN S43 .... 111 J5
Victoria Rd *BUT* DE14 .... 273 M6
BWSH/BRSTN DE72 .... 259 K3
EDL/UDV S33 .... 50 E7
EWD/SEL/PNX NG16 .... 177 G7
EWD/SEL/PNX NG16 .... 189 J4
FUL S10 .... 55 H1
LGEAT NG10 .... 244 E5
RIPLEY DE5 .... 201 G1
Victoria St *ALFN* DE55 .... 175 L7
ALFN DE55 .... 176 D4
ALFN DE55 .... 187 M2
ASH NG17 .... 162 F4
ASH NG17 .... 163 H8 6
BSTN/STPLFD NG9 .... 245 G3 3
BSVR S44.. 131 L2
BUT DE14 .... 273 M6
CDON/KEG DE74 .... 271 L5
CHNE S41 .... 3 G2
DERBY DE1 .... 4 E4
DRON S18 .... 70 C8
EWD/SEL/PNX NG16 .... 188 C6
EWD/SEL/PNX NG16 .... 189 K3
EWD/SEL/PNX NG16 .... 202 F7
EWD/SEL/PNX NG16 .... 203 J7
GLSP SK13....................................... 25 M2
ILK DE7 .... 217 J7
LGEAT NG10 .... 260 E5
MELB/CHEL DE73.......................... 278 D3
MSFD NG18.................................... 164 D4
NM/HAY SK22 .... 43 L4 3
RIPLEY DE5 .... 187 J8
SBK/MW NG20 .... 133 J6
STV/CWN S43 .... 111 J1
WRKS S80 .... 115 J1
Victoria St North *CHNE* S41 .... 91 J8
Victoria St West *CHSW* S40.......... 109 M8
Victor Rd *TOT/DORE* S17 .... 69 J3
Victory Av *RIPLEY* DE5.................... 201 J1
Victory Cl *LGEAT* NG10 .... 261 G5
MSFDW NG19 .... 165 J1 2
Victory Dr *MSFDW* NG19 .... 165 J1
Victory Rd *DERBYSE* DE24 .... 256 E3
View Cl *MSFD* NG18 .... 165 G4
Viewdales Cl *ASHB* DE6 .... 196 C8
View Rd *SHEFS* S8 .... 55 K3
Vikinglea Cl *SHEFP/MNR* S2 ..... 56 E2 4
Vikinglea Dr *SHEFP/MNR* S2........... 56 E2
Vikinglea Gld *SHEFP/MNR* S2 ..... 56 E1 9
Vikinglea Rd *SHEFP/MNR* S2 .... 56 E1
Village St *NORM/LIT* DE23.............. 256 C2
The Village *ILK* DE7......................... 229 J8
ILK DE7 .... 229 H3
Villas Rd *BPR/DUF* DE56 .... 185 J7
BSVR S44.. 131 H1
Villa St *BWSH/BRSTN* DE72 .... 259 L3
Villiers Cl *SHEFP/MNR* S2 .... 56 B5
Villiers Dr *SHEFP/MNR* S2 .... 56 B4
Villiers Rd *MSFD* NG18 .... 165 H3
Vincent Av *DERBYE* DE21 .... 242 B7
ILK DE7 .... 230 C2
Vincent Cl *BPR/DUF* DE56 .... 214 D2 6
Vincent Crs *CHSW* S40 .... 109 L8
Vincent La *CHSW* S40.................... 109 L8
Vincent Rd *ECC* S11 .... 55 J2
Vincent St *NORM/LIT* DE23............ 256 C1
Vine Cl *NORM/LIT* DE23 .... 255 L3
Vine Crs *LGEAT* NG10 .... 244 E4
Vine Farm Cl *ILK* DE7 .... 230 A4
Viola Cl *DERBYE* DE21 .... 227 M7
Violet Av *EWD/SEL/PNX* NG16 ...... 217 L1
Violet Bank Rd *ABRD* S7 .... 55 H4 5
Violet Hl *MSFD* NG18 .... 165 K3
Violet St *NORM/LIT* DE23............... 256 C1
Violet Wy *STPNHL/WNHL* DE15...... 281 J2
Virginsalley La *ASHB* DE6 .... 219 M2
Vivian St *BSVR* S44 .... 113 J4
DERBYE DE21 .... 240 E2
Vulcan St *NORM/LIT* DE23 .... 256 E1 1
Vyse Dr *LGEAT* NG10...................... 260 F4

W

Wadbrough Rd *FUL* S10 .... 55 G1
Wade Av *ILK* DE7............................. 230 D3
NORM/LIT DE23 .... 239 M8
Wadebridge Gv
DERBYSE DE24 .... 257 M5 7
DERBYSE DE24 .... 257 M5 8
Wade Cl *MSFD* NG18....................... 164 F7
Wade Dr *MCKLVR* DE3 .... 239 H8
Wade St *NORM/LIT* DE23................ 255 M1
Wadsworth Av *HACK/IN* S12........... 56 F5
Wadsworth Cl *HACK/IN* S12 .... 57 G5 2
Wadsworth Dr *HACK/IN* S12............ 57 G4
Wadsworth Rd
BSTN/STPLFD NG9 .... 245 J2
HACK/IN S12 .... 56 F5 3
Wagstaff La
EWD/SEL/PNX NG16 .... 188 E6
Wagtail Cl *DERBYSE* DE24 .... 256 A6
Wain Av *RCH* S42 .... 145 K3
Wainfleet Cl *ILK* DE7 .... 216 F7
Waingroves Rd *RIPLEY* DE5 .... 201 L4
Wainhouse Brow
NM/HAY SK22 .... 35 G7 1
Wainwright Av *HAN/WDH* S13 ..... 57 G2
MSFDW NG19 .... 164 A1
Wainwright Crs *HAN/WDH* S13 .... 56 F2
Wakami Crs *MELB/CHEL* DE73 .... 257 K8
Wakefield Av
BUTN/AL/TUT DE13 .... 263 L4
Wakefield Cft *ILK* DE7 .... 216 F7
Wakelyn Cl *BWSH/BRSTN* DE72 .. 271 J1
Wake Rd *ABRD* S7............................. 55 H3
Walbrook Rd *NORM/LIT* DE23 ...... 256 C1
Walcote Cl *BPR/DUF* DE56 .... 199 M5
Waldene Dr *DERBYSE* DE24 .... 257 K4
Walden Rd *SHEFP/MNR* S2 .... 55 L3
Waldley La *ASHB* DE6..................... 233 H2
Waldorf Av *DERBYSE* DE24 .... 257 K3
Wales La *BUTN/AL/TUT* DE13 .... 286 A1
Walford Rd *BUTN/AL/TUT* DE13.. 265 G6
ECK/KIL S21 .... 73 M4
Walgrove Av *CHSW* S40.................... 2 B7
Walgrove Rd *CHSW* S40..................... 2 A7
Walk Cl *BWSH/BRSTN* DE72.......... 259 K3
Walkden St *MSFD* NG18................. 164 E3
Walker Av *RIPLEY* DE5 .... 187 H8
Walker Cl *ILK* DE7 .... 230 C6
Walker Gv *BSTN/STPLFD* NG9 .. 245 H4 4
Walker La *DERBY* DE1 .... 4 D2
Walkers Cl *MSFDW* NG19.............. 165 L1
Walkers La *ECK/KIL* S21 .... 74 A4
Walker St *BUT* DE14 .... 280 E1
EWD/SEL/PNX NG16 .... 203 K8
GLSP SK13....................................... 17 K5
Walk Mill Rd *NM/HAY* SK22 .... 35 G7 2
The Walk *BPR/DUF* DE56............... 214 E2
Wallace Gdns
BSTN/STPLFD NG9 .... 261 J1 1
Wallace St *DERBYW* DE22 .... 239 M5
Wallfields Cl *RDERBYSW* DE65 ..... 255 G7
Wallingbrook Ri *WRKS* S80 .... 77 L8
Wallis Cl *BWSH/BRSTN* DE72 .... 259 K3
Wallis Rd *MSFD* NG18..................... 164 F3
Wall Rd *BUT* DE14........................... 280 D2
Walls La *STV/CWN* S43 .... 95 H2
WRKS S80 .... 95 K2
Wall St *BUX* SK17 .... 100 A2 2
RIPLEY DE5..................................... 187 G8
Walnut Av *DERBYSE* DE24............... 257 L3
WRKN S81 .... 77 J3
Walnut Cl *BWSH/BRSTN* DE72...... 270 E2
ILK DE7 .... 230 D3
MELB/CHEL DE73 .... 268 D4 1
MELB/CHEL DE73........................... 269 K2
RDERBYSW DE65 .... 254 C5 1
RDERBYSW DE65 .... 267 J8
SWAD DE11 .... 282 D5 2
Walnut Dr *BSTN/STPLFD* NG9 ...... 245 L2
ECK/KIL S21 .... 73 M5 2
Walnut Rd *BPR/DUF* DE56 .... 199 L7
Walnut St *DERBYSE* DE24 .... 256 F3
Walpole St *DERBYE* DE21 .... 5 M1
Walseker La *AU/AST/KP* S26 .... 74 F3
Walsham Cl *BSTN/STPLFD* NG9...... 245 L8
Walsham Ct *DERBYE* DE21 .... 240 F2
Walters Av
EWD/SEL/PNX NG16 .... 203 H4 1
Walters Crs
EWD/SEL/PNX NG16 .... 189 G4
Walter St *BWSH/BRSTN* DE72........ 259 J3
DERBY DE1 .... 240 B3
Waltham Av *DERBYSE* DE24 .... 256 C6
Walthamstow Dr
DERBYW DE22 .... 239 L4
Waltheof Rd *SHEFP/MNR* S2 .... 56 D2
Waltin Rd *HOLM/MEL* HD7 .... 9 J1
Walton Av *DERBYSE* DE24............. 257 H6
Walton Back La *RCH* S42............... 127 J2
Walton Cl *CHSW* S40 .... 127 L2 5
DRON S18 .... 69 M8
MSFDW NG19 .... 165 L2
SWAD DE11 .... 282 D8
Walton Ct *ILK* DE7.......................... 229 G2
Walton Crs *ASHB* DE6.................... 208 A1
CHSW S40 .... 2 B7
Walton Dr *CHSW* S40 .... 2 C7
MPL/ROM SK6 .... 32 A3
NORM/LIT DE23 .... 256 B3
Walton Fields Rd *CHSW* S40 .... 2 A6
Walton Hl *CDON/KEG* DE74........... 271 J6
Walton Rd *CHSW* S40....................... 2 A8
DERBYE DE21 .... 241 J5
FUL S10 .... 55 G1
STPNHL/WNHL DE15 .... 281 G5
Walton St *ASH* NG17....................... 163 K7
LGEAT NG10 .... 261 G1
Walton Wk *CHSW* S40 .... 2 D6
Walton Wy *RCH* S42 .... 128 B6
Wansfell Cl *MCKLVR* DE3 .... 255 H1 12
Wapentake La *BPR/DUF* DE56 .... 182 F8
Warburton Cl *SHEFP/MNR* S2 ..... 55 M3 3
Warburton Gdns
SHEFP/MNR S2 .... 55 M3 4
Warburton Rd *SHEFP/MNR* S2...... 55 M3
Ward Dr *ALFN* DE55 .... 188 A3
Wardgate Wy *CHSW* S40............... 109 K5
Ward La *POY/DIS* SK12..................... 43 H6
STV/CWN S43 .... 74 E7
Wardle Brook Av *HYDE* SK14 .... 16 A7 2
Wardlow Av *DERBYE* DE21 .... 241 K2
Wardlow Cl *CHSW* S40 .... 2 F9
Wardlow Ms *GLSP* SK13.................... 25 G1
Wardlow Rd *HACK/IN* S12 .... 57 G5
ILK DE7 .... 217 G7
Ward Pl *MSFD* NG18 .... 164 B4
SHEFP/MNR S2 .... 55 J2 13
Ward's La *BWSH/BRSTN* DE72 ..... 260 A2

MELB/CHEL DE73 .... 269 J8
Ward St DERBY DE22 .... 4 B5
RCH S42 .... 145 G2
Wardswood Cl
BWSH/BRSTN DE72 .... 259 J4
Wardwick DERBY DE1 .... 4 E3
Warehouse La EDL/UDV S33 .... 49 C6
Warkton Cl
BSTN/STPLFD NG9 .... 245 M5 8
Warmbrook MTLK DE4 .... 183 J3
Warmbrook Rd CHF/WBR SK23 .... 60 F5
Warminster Cl SHEFS S8 .... 55 K6
Warminster Crs SHEFS S8 .... 55 K6
Warminster Dr SHEFS S8 .... 55 L7 2
Warminster Pl SHEFS S8 .... 55 L8
Warminster Rd SHEFS S8 .... 55 K6
Warmwells La RIPLEY DE5 .... 201 C3
Warner St CHNE S41 .... 3 K7
DERBYW DE22 .... 4 C8
MCKLVR DE3 .... 255 G1 7
Warney Rd MTLK DE4 .... 141 C8
Warren Av BSTN/STPLFD NG9 .... 245 G3
Warren Avenue Extension
BSTN/STPLFD NG9 .... 245 G3 3
Warren Cl ASH NG17 .... 162 D8
BUTN/AL/TUT DE13 .... 274 B1 2
CLCR S45 .... 145 M8
Warren Ct BSTN/STPLFD NG9 .... 245 G3 8
Warren Crs ECK/KIL S21 .... 72 B8
Warrender Cl
BSTN/STPLFD NG9 .... 245 M1
Warren Dr MSHM DE12 .... 288 E4
Warren La BUT DE14 .... 280 C3
CDON/KEG DE74 .... 260 D8
Warren Ri DRON S18 .... 70 F7
Warren St DERBYSE DE24 .... 257 J2 8
Warren Wy MSFDW NG19 .... 165 M3
Warsick La MELB/CHEL DE73 .... 277 J2
Warwick Av NORM/LIT DE23 .... 256 A1
Warwick Cl BUT DE14 .... 280 C2 8
GLSP SK13 .... 26 C2
SWAD DE11 .... 283 H4
Warwick Dr ILK DE7 .... 216 F7
MSFD DE11 .... 165 H3
Warwick Gdns BPR/DUF DE56 .... 200 A5
Warwick Rd ALFN DE55 .... 187 L1
LGEAT NG10 .... 261 J3 2
Warwick St BUTN/AL/TUT DE13 .... 273 M4
CHSW S40 .... 128 E3
DERBYSE DE24 .... 241 C8
Warwick Wy ASHZ LE65 .... 291 M5
Wasdale Av MOS S20 .... 73 H4 13
Wasdale Cl MOS S20 .... 73 H4
Washbrook La ASHB DE6 .... 179 J7
Washford Rd RDERBYSW DE65 .... 265 H2
Wash Gn MTLK DE4 .... 183 K2
Wash Hills Cl MTLK DE4 .... 181 K1 8
Washhouse Bottom BUX SK17 .... 64 A7
BUX SK17 .... 84 A3
Wash House La CHSW S40 .... 109 M8
Washington Av
DERBYE DE21 .... 241 L4 8
Washington Cl
MELB/CHEL DE73 .... 278 D3
Washington Dr
BSTN/STPLFD NG9 .... 245 J1
MSFDW NG18 .... 164 B5
Washington Rd ECC S11 .... 55 L2
Waste La ASHB DE6 .... 205 C6
ASHB DE6 .... 205 H7
Watburn Rd NM/HAY SK22 .... 44 A1
Watchorn La ALFN DE55 .... 175 J7
Watercress La CLCR S45 .... 145 C8
Waterfield Ms MOS S20 .... 73 H1 8
Waterfoot Cottages
HYDE SK14 .... 16 D6 8
Waterfoot La CHF/WBR SK23 .... 16 F4 8
Watergo La DERBYE DE21 .... 254 F3
Wateringbury Gv STV/CWN S43 .... 93 J8
Watering La BPR/DUF DE56 .... 214 A4
Water La ALFN DE55 .... 176 A4
BSVR S44 .... 131 J2
BUX SK17 .... 83 J4
EDL/UDV S33 .... 50 D8
HATH/EY S32 .... 86 B4
HYDE SK14 .... 17 C5
MSFDW NG19 .... 148 B1
MSFDW NG19 .... 148 E6
MTLK DE4 .... 170 F5
MTLK DE4 .... 171 K4
MTLK DE4 .... 183 J2
TOT/DORE S17 .... 69 J3
Waterloo Cl ALFN DE55 .... 176 F2
Waterloo Ct DERBY DE1 .... 240 E3 8
Waterloo La BSTN/STPLFD NG9 .... 231 H4
Waterloo Pl SWAD DE11 .... 282 E7
Waterloo Rd MTLK DE4 .... 171 K1
Waterloo St BSVR S44 .... 147 J1
BUT DE14 .... 273 M6
CLCR S45 .... 144 F6
Watermeade ECK/KIL S21 .... 72 E8
Water Meadow La CHSW S40 .... 109 L4
Watermeadow Rd
DERBYSE DE24 .... 257 K5
The Watermeadows
LGEAT NG10 .... 260 E2 8
The Water Mdw
MELB/CHEL DE73 .... 269 G4
Water Orton Cl
BSTN/STPLFD NG9 .... 245 H7
Waterpark Rd ASHB DE6 .... 248 E2 8
Waters Edge MPL/ROM SK6 .... 32 D2
Waterside EWD/SEL/PNX NG16 .... 188 C6
GLSP SK13 .... 17 K5
HYDE SK14 .... 16 A8
MPL/ROM SK6 .... 32 C5
STPNHL/WNHL DE15 .... 281 H3
Waterside Av MPL/ROM SK6 .... 32 C5 8
Waterside Cl DERBYW DE22 .... 226 D8 8
HYDE SK14 .... 16 A8 8
LGEAT NG10 .... 244 F7 8
Waterside Rd NM/HAY SK22 .... 43 H3
Water Slacks Cl HAN/WDH S13 .... 57 L4 8
Water Slacks La HAN/WDH S13 .... 57 L4
Water Slacks Rd HAN/WDH S13 .... 57 L4
Waterson Cl MSFD NG18 .... 165 J7
Waterson Oaks MSFD NG18 .... 165 J6

Water St BKWL DE45 .... 123 G5
BUX SK17 .... 99 L3
GLSP SK13 .... 18 B8
Waterswallows La BUX SK17 .... 81 J6
Waterswallows Rd BUX SK17 .... 81 J8
Waterthorpe Cl MOS S20 .... 73 J2 8
Waterthorpe Crs MOS S20 .... 73 J2
Waterthorpe Gdns MOS S20 .... 73 H2
Waterthorpe Gld MOS S20 .... 73 H2
Waterthorpe Gln MOS S20 .... 73 J2 8
Waterthorpe Ri MOS S20 .... 73 J2
The Waterway LGEAT NG10 .... 244 F6 8
Watery La ASHB DE6 .... 205 L7
ASHB DE6 .... 207 J1
ASHB DE6 .... 237 G4
HOLM/MEL HD7 .... 8 C2
RDERBYSW DE65 .... 251 H7
STPNHL/WNHL DE15 .... 275 M7
SWAD DE11 .... 282 A5
UTXR ST14 .... 246 D8
Watford Bridge Rd
NM/HAY SK22 .... 44 A1
Watford La NM/HAY SK22 .... 33 M8
Watford Rd BUX SK17 .... 99 J3
NM/HAY SK22 .... 33 M8
Wath Rd ABRD S7 .... 55 H4
Watkin Av GLSP SK13 .... 17 H6
Watkinson St HEANOR DE75 .... 202 A8
Watnall Crs MSFDW NG19 .... 164 B5
Watson Av HEANOR DE75 .... 202 C8
MSFD NG18 .... 164 F3
Watson La RCH S42 .... 127 M7
Watson Rd ILK DE7 .... 216 F8
Watson St BUT DE14 .... 281 G1
DERBY DE1 .... 4 B1
DERBYW DE22 .... 240 B3
Watten Cl DERBYSE DE24 .... 256 C8
Watts Gn BKWL DE45 .... 122 C2
Waveney Cl DERBYW DE22 .... 226 E5
Waverley La BUT DE14 .... 273 L7
Waverley Rd MSFD NG18 .... 164 E6
Waverley St ALFN DE55 .... 161 K3
DERBYSE DE24 .... 256 F3 4
LGEAT NG10 .... 261 H7
Wayfaring Rd DERBYE DE21 .... 241 K1
Wayford Av CHNE S41 .... 3 K9
Wayland Rd ECC S11 .... 55 G2
Wayside STV/CWN S43 .... 111 G2
Wayside Cl RCH S42 .... 145 K3
Wayside Ct STV/CWN S43 .... 111 G2 8
Wayzgoose Dr DERBY DE21 .... 5 K3
Weaddow La BKWL DE45 .... 138 C8
Weakland Cl HACK/IN S12 .... 57 J8
Weakland Crs HACK/IN S12 .... 57 J7
Weakland Dr HACK/IN S12 .... 57 J7
Weakland Wy HACK/IN S12 .... 57 J7 2
Weather Hill La HOLM/MEL HD7 .... 9 H2
Weatherley Dr MPL/ROM SK6 .... 32 A4
Weathern Rd MSHM DE12 .... 289 C5
Weaver Cl ASHB DE6 .... 207 M2
MTLK DE4 .... 185 J1 8
Weaver Rd UTXR ST14 .... 247 L1
Weavers Cl BPR/DUF DE56 .... 199 M4
BWSH/BRSTN DE72 .... 259 C1
The Weavers UTXR ST14 .... 218 A4
Weaving Av EDL/UDV S33 .... 48 F8
Webb Gv HYDE SK14 .... 24 B1
Webster Av
EWD/SEL/PNX NG16 .... 217 J1 8
Webster Cft CHNE S41 .... 91 L8 8
Webster St DERBY DE1 .... 4 D6
Wedding Dr WRKS S80 .... 97 M7
Wedgewood Cl
STPNHL/WNHL DE15 .... 281 L1 8
Wedneshough HYDE SK14 .... 16 F5
Weetwood Dr ECC S11 .... 54 E5 8
Weighbridge Rd MSFD NG18 .... 164 F4
Weightman Dr
EWD/SEL/PNX NG16 .... 217 L3 8
Weir Bank STPNHL/WNHL DE15 .... 281 H4
Weirfield Rd DERBYW DE22 .... 226 D8
Welbeck Av BUX SK17 .... 99 M4
ILK DE7 .... 230 A5
Welbeck Cl STV/CWN S43 .... 112 A4
Welbeck Dr RCH S42 .... 128 B6
Welbeck Gdns
BSTN/STPLFD NG9 .... 245 J7
Welbeck Gv DERBYW DE22 .... 226 A7
Welbeck Rd BSVR S44 .... 131 L1
LGEAT NG10 .... 244 E7
MSFDW NG19 .... 149 M7
Welbeck Sq ASH NG17 .... 162 F4
Welbeck St ASH NG17 .... 163 J8
MSFD NG18 .... 164 D3
WRKS S80 .... 96 D4
WRKS S80 .... 115 H1
Welbury Gdns MOS S20 .... 73 H4
Welby Pl SHEFS S8 .... 55 J6
Welch Av BSTN/STPLFD NG9 .... 245 H2
Weldbank Cl BSTN/STPLFD NG9 .... 245 L5
Welfare Av CHSW S40 .... 2 B4
Welfare St SBK/MW NG20 .... 133 H7
Welfitt Gv SBK/MW NG20 .... 115 H8
Welford La ASH NG17 .... 163 L5 8
Welford Ri BUTN/AL/TUT DE13 .... 273 K3
Welland Cl MCKLVR DE3 .... 239 G7
STPNHL/WNHL DE15 .... 274 D5
Welland Rd RDERBYSW DE65 .... 265 G1
Well Banks BPR/DUF DE56 .... 196 E5 8
Wellcarr Rd SHEFS S8 .... 55 K8
Well Cl ASHB DE6 .... 196 B7
Weldon St RIPLEY DE5 .... 201 K6
Wellesley Av NORM/LIT DE23 .... 256 A5
Wellfield MTLK DE4 .... 156 F4
Wellfield Cl HACK/IN S12 .... 72 B1
Wellfield Ct MTLK DE4 .... 156 F4 8
Well Ga GLSP SK13 .... 18 B8
Wellgate La BKWL DE45 .... 138 C1
Wellhead Rd SHEFS S8 .... 55 K4 19
Wellington Cl MTLK DE4 .... 157 G3 8
Wellington Ct BPR/DUF DE56 .... 199 J6 8
Wellington Pk MSFD NG18 .... 160 A8
Wellington Pl
EWD/SEL/PNX NG16 .... 203 J8 8
Wellington Rd BUT DE14 .... 280 D1
Wellington St
BSTN/STPLFD NG9 .... 244 F4

BUT DE14 .... 273 L7
DERBY DE1 .... 5 H7
DERBY DE1 .... 5 J6 8
EWD/SEL/PNX NG16 .... 203 J7 8
HEANOR DE75 .... 202 A8
LGEAT NG10 .... 244 F8
RIPLEY DE5 .... 201 H1
STV/CWN S43 .... 92 A6
Well La ALFN DE55 .... 159 M7
BPR/DUF DE56 .... 213 J3
RCH S42 .... 126 C3
RDERBYSW DE65 .... 275 M1
SWAD DE11 .... 290 E1
Wellow Cl MSFDW NG19 .... 164 A3
Well Pl SHEFS S8 .... 55 K4 16
Well Rd SHEFS S8 .... 55 K4 17
Well Rw HYDE SK14 .... 24 D2
Well Spring St STV/CWN S43 .... 111 H3 8
Wellspring Cl RCH S42 .... 128 C6
STV/CWN S43 .... 94 E4
Wellspring Dl
BSTN/STPLFD NG9 .... 245 H5
Wells Rd MCKLVR DE3 .... 239 H8
Well St BSVR S44 .... 131 M2
Well St DERBY DE1 .... 240 D5 8
MTLK DE4 .... 154 B3
MTLK DE4 .... 181 J3
NM/HAY SK22 .... 43 L2
RIPLEY DE5 .... 201 G1
STV/CWN S43 .... 94 D3
Wellwood Rd SWAD DE11 .... 282 D4
Welney Cl MCKLVR DE3 .... 255 G2 8
Welshpool Rd DERBYE DE21 .... 241 G1
Welwyn Av DERBYSE DE24 .... 257 H6
DERBYW DE22 .... 226 A7
Welwyn Cl CHSW S40 .... 2 A3
HACK/IN S12 .... 56 E6 8
Welwyn Rd HACK/IN S12 .... 56 E6
Wembley Gdns
BSTN/STPLFD NG9 .... 231 L8
DERBYW DE22 .... 239 K4
Wendover Cl MCKLVR DE3 .... 254 F1
Wenham La ASH NG17 .... 162 C6
Wenlock Cl CHSW S40 .... 109 M6
EWD/SEL/PNX NG16 .... 217 M2
MCKLVR DE3 .... 255 H1 13
Wenlock Crs CHSW S40 .... 109 M6
Wenlock Dr RCH S42 .... 129 J3
Wenlock St HAN/WDH S13 .... 57 J1 8
Wensleydale Cl
MSFDW NG19 .... 165 H1 9
Wensleydale Rd LGEAT NG10 .... 260 E4
Wensley Dr DERBYE DE21 .... 242 C7 1
Wensley Rd MTLK DE4 .... 154 F4
RCH S42 .... 145 J5
Wensley Wy STV/CWN S43 .... 111 M2
Wentbridge Dr MSFD NG18 .... 165 K6
Wentworth Av CHSW S40 .... 2 C9
CHSW S40 .... 128 B2
ECC S11 .... 54 D8 8
Wentworth Cl MCKLVR DE3 .... 255 J1 8
MPL/ROM SK6 .... 32 C2 8
Wentworth Cft
HEANOR DE75 .... 202 D7 8
Wentworth Dr
BUTN/AL/TUT DE13 .... 274 A1
Wentworth Rd
BUTN/AL/TUT DE13 .... 274 A1
DRON S18 .... 89 M1
Wentworth St ILK DE7 .... 217 K8
Werburgh Cl DERBYE DE21 .... 242 A6 8
Werburgh St DERBY DE22 .... 4 C5
Werneth Rd GLSP SK13 .... 25 K3
Wesleyan Chapel Wk
BSTN/STPLFD NG9 .... 245 G6
Wesley La
BWSH/BRSTN DE72 .... 242 F5 8
Wesley Pl BSTN/STPLFD NG9 .... 245 H7
Wesley Rd ALFN DE55 .... 160 C7
BPR/DUF DE56 .... 185 J7 8
DERBYSE DE24 .... 257 L5
Wesley St EWD/SEL/PNX NG16 .... 202 F7 8
GLSP SK13 .... 17 K5
GLSP SK13 .... 18 B8
ILK DE7 .... 217 H6
Wessex Gdns TOT/DORE S17 .... 69 G5
Wessington Dr STV/CWN S43 .... 111 M2
Wessington La ALFN DE55 .... 174 C3
Wessington Ms
DERBYW DE22 .... 240 B1 8
GLSP SK13 .... 17 H8 8
Westacre Dr SWAD DE11 .... 282 C8
West Av BSTN/STPLFD NG9 .... 245 H2
BWSH/BRSTN DE72 .... 259 J3
DERBY DE1 .... 4 C1
DERBY DE1 .... 240 C3 8
LGEAT NG10 .... 244 D4
MELB/CHEL DE73 .... 257 H7
RDERBYSW DE65 .... 252 F8
RIPLEY DE5 .... 200 F1
West Bank MTLK DE4 .... 154 E5
MTLK DE4 .... 171 K1
West Bank Av DERBYW DE22 .... 240 C2
MSFDW NG19 .... 164 E2
MTLK DE4 .... 185 J1 8
West Bank Cl DERBYW DE22 .... 240 B2 8
West Bank Lea MSFDW NG19 .... 164 E2
West Bank Link
MSFDW NG19 .... 164 E1 8
West Bank Rd DERBYW DE22 .... 226 B5
West Bank Wynd MSFDW NG19 .... 164 E2
West Bars CHSW S40 .... 2 E4
Westbourne Av ALFN DE55 .... 160 C6
Westbourne Gv CHSW S40 .... 109 L7
Westbourne Rd ASH NG17 .... 163 C7
EWD/SEL/PNX NG16 .... 189 K8
Westbourne Vw ASH NG17 .... 163 C7
Westbridge Rd STV/CWN S43 .... 94 D3
Westbrook Bank ECC S11 .... 55 G2
Westbrook Cl CHF/WBR SK23 .... 60 F4
CHSW S40 .... 109 J8
Westbrook Dr CHSW S40 .... 109 J8
Westbury Cl BSTN/STPLFD NG9 .... 245 M6
Westbury Ct DERBYW DE22 .... 240 A7 8
Westbury Dr MPL/ROM SK6 .... 32 B4
Westbury Gdns BPR/DUF DE56 .... 199 M5
Westbury St DERBYW DE22 .... 240 A7

West Cl DERBYW DE22 .... 226 B8
West Crs BSVR S44 .... 112 D5
MTLK DE4 .... 170 D4
West Croft Av NORM/LIT DE23 .... 256 A5
West Croft Cl BKWL DE45 .... 138 C5
West Croft Ct STV/CWN S43 .... 111 L5
Westcroft Crs MOS S20 .... 73 H2
West Croft Dr STV/CWN S43 .... 111 L5
Westcroft Gdns MOS S20 .... 73 H2
Westcroft Gln MOS S20 .... 73 H3 8
Westcroft Gv MOS S20 .... 73 H3
Westcross Av
BSTN/STPLFD NG9 .... 245 H2
Westdale Av ASH NG17 .... 163 K5
Westdale Cl LGEAT NG10 .... 260 D5 8
Westdale Rd
EWD/SEL/PNX NG16 .... 188 E6
MSFDW NG19 .... 164 E1
Westdene Av DERBYSE DE24 .... 257 G5
West Dr ASHB DE6 .... 248 D1
GLSP SK13 .... 17 H4
MCKLVR DE3 .... 239 C8
West Edge Cl CLCR S45 .... 143 C6
West End ALFN DE55 .... 175 K7
ASH NG17 .... 163 H8
EWD/SEL/PNX NG16 .... 176 F6
MTLK DE4 .... 154 A4
MTLK DE4 .... 181 J1
MTLK DE4 .... 183 H2
STV/CWN S43 .... 94 D3
West End Cl ALFN DE55 .... 175 K7
West End Crs ILK DE7 .... 230 A2
West End Dr
BWSH/BRSTN DE72 .... 271 H1
ILK DE7 .... 230 A2
West End St BSTN/STPLFD NG9 .... 244 F8
West End Vw ECK/KIL S21 .... 72 F8
Westerlands BSTN/STPLFD NG9 .... 245 J5
Western Av ALFN DE55 .... 187 G3
MSFD NG18 .... 164 C5
Western Cl ASHZ LE65 .... 291 L6
Western Dr HEANOR DE75 .... 216 C2
Western La CHF/WBR SK23 .... 59 K2
Western Rd MCKLVR DE3 .... 239 H8
NORM/LIT DE23 .... 4 D8
Westfield Av CHSW S40 .... 127 L1 8
HACK/IN S12 .... 57 M7
HEANOR DE75 .... 216 C2
West Field Bank STV/CWN S43 .... 94 D3
Westfield Centre MOS S20 .... 73 H2
Westfield Cl CHSW S40 .... 109 L8
ILK DE7 .... 229 M4 8
MSFDW NG19 .... 164 C2
Westfield Crs MOS S20 .... 73 G2
Westfield Dr ALFN DE55 .... 176 B1 8
ILK DE7 .... 217 G8
MSFDW NG19 .... 164 B2
Westfield Gdns CHSW S40 .... 109 L8 8
Westfield Gv HACK/IN S12 .... 57 L7 8
Westfield La ECK/KIL S21 .... 92 B2
MSFDW NG19 .... 164 B2
STV/CWN S43 .... 94 C3
Westfield Northway MOS S20 .... 73 H2
Westfield Rd
BUTN/AL/TUT DE13 .... 273 L3
DRON S18 .... 90 F2
ECK/KIL S21 .... 73 M5
SWAD DE11 .... 282 E5
Westfields CDLE ST10 .... 190 B6
Westfields Av ASHZ LE65 .... 291 J4
Westfield Southway MOS S20 .... 73 H2
Westfields Ter ASHZ LE65 .... 291 J3
West Ga HOLM/MEL HD7 .... 9 J2
LGEAT NG10 .... 261 H3 12
MSFD NG18 .... 164 B3
Westgreen Av DERBYSE DE24 .... 257 G5
West Gv DERBYSE DE24 .... 257 G5
Westhall Rd MCKLVR DE3 .... 239 G7
West Hl ASH NG17 .... 163 G4
MSFDW NG19 .... 164 D2
RIPLEY DE5 .... 201 L3
UTXR ST14 .... 247 M4
West Hill Av MSFD NG18 .... 164 E3
West Hill Dr MSFD NG18 .... 164 E3 8
Westhill La RCH S42 .... 129 H7
West Hill Pk MSFDW NG19 .... 149 L7 8
Westhorpe Dr LGEAT NG10 .... 260 F2
Westhouse La ASHB DE6 .... 205 H7
Westland Cl MOS S20 .... 73 H1
Westland Dr
EWD/SEL/PNX NG16 .... 176 F7
Westland Gdns MOS S20 .... 73 G1
Westland Gv MOS S20 .... 73 H2 11
Westland Rd MOS S20 .... 73 H1
Westlands Rd STV/CWN S43 .... 247 L4
West Lawn RDERBYSW DE65 .... 254 F8
West Lea ASHB DE6 .... 205 J7
West Lea CHSW S40 .... 109 L8 8
Westlea Vw STV/CWN S43 .... 95 G6
West Lees Rd EDL/UDV S33 .... 50 E6
Westleigh Av DERBYW DE22 .... 239 M4
Westleigh Cl CHSW S40 .... 2 D1
CHSW S40 .... 110 B5 8
Westley Crs DERBYE DE21 .... 214 A8
Westminster Av LGEAT NG10 .... 244 F5
Westminster Cl FUL S10 .... 53 L1 8
MPL/ROM SK6 .... 32 A3 8
Westminster Crs FUL S10 .... 53 L1
Westminster Dr
BUTN/AL/TUT DE13 .... 274 A2 18
Westminster St
DERBYSE DE24 .... 257 J2 8
Westminster Wy ASHZ LE65 .... 291 K2
Westmoor Rd STV/CWN S43 .... 111 J6
Westmorland Wy
EWD/SEL/PNX NG16 .... 188 C7
Weston Bank ASHB DE6 .... 233 J2
Weston Cl CHSW S40 .... 109 K4
Weston Crs LGEAT NG10 .... 260 C3
Weston Park Av BUT DE14 .... 274 A3
DERBYSE DE24 .... 257 G5
Weston Ri MELB/CHEL DE73 .... 269 K2 8
Weston Rd BWSH/BRSTN DE72 .... 270 C4
Weston Spot Cl RIPLEY DE5 .... 201 C3 8
Weston St HEANOR DE75 .... 216 D2 8
SWAD DE11 .... 282 E7
West Park Rd DERBYW DE22 .... 240 B2
Westray Cl BSTN/STPLFD NG9 .... 231 G7
West Rd BUX SK17 .... 99 L4
DERBYE DE21 .... 242 A5

West Rw DERBYW DE22 .... 240 D1 8
West Service Rd DERBYE DE21 .... 241 K8
West St ALFN DE55 .... 160 C6
ALFN DE55 .... 176 C5
ALFN DE55 .... 187 M4
BSVR S44 .... 147 G1
CHSW S40 .... 2 E2
CLCR S45 .... 144 D6
DRON S18 .... 70 C8 8
ECK/KIL S21 .... 72 F8
EWD/SEL/PNX NG16 .... 202 E7
GLSP SK13 .... 17 J3
HEANOR DE75 .... 202 A8
ILK DE7 .... 230 B3
SBK/MW NG20 .... 115 K7
STPNHL/WNHL DE15 .... 274 E7
STV/CWN S43 .... 95 K5
SWAD DE11 .... 282 E6
WRKS S80 .... 115 G1
West Ter ILK DE7 .... 230 C1 8
Westthorpe Fields Rd
ECK/KIL S21 .... 73 M6
Westthorpe Rd ECK/KIL S21 .... 74 A5
West Vw ALFN DE55 .... 161 J5
BSVR S44 .... 131 L2
STV/CWN S43 .... 94 D3
STV/CWN S43 .... 112 A1
UTXR ST14 .... 218 D7
West View Av NORM/LIT DE23 .... 255 L3
West View Cl TOT/DORE S17 .... 69 J4 8
West View La TOT/DORE S17 .... 69 J4 8
West View Rd CHSW S40 .... 110 B4
Westward Cl UTXR ST14 .... 247 L1
West Wy ALFN DE55 .... 187 M1
UTXR ST14 .... 247 J1
Westwell Pl MOS S20 .... 73 G4
Westwick Crs TOT/DORE S17 .... 70 A3
Westwick Gv SHEFS S8 .... 70 A3
Westwick La RCH S42 .... 109 G8
Westwick Rd SHEFS S8 .... 70 A3
WOL/BIL/BRX NG8 .... 231 M4
Westwick St ILK DE7 .... 230 D4
Westwood Av STV/CWN S43 .... 111 M2
Westwood Cl STV/CWN S43 .... 111 M5
Westwood Dr DERBYSE DE24 .... 257 G5
STV/CWN S43 .... 111 L5
WRKS S80 .... 77 L7
Westwood La STV/CWN S43 .... 111 J6
Westwood Pk SWAD DE11 .... 282 C5
Westwood Rd ECC S11 .... 54 C2
STV/CWN S43 .... 111 J6
Wetherby Ct BUT DE14 .... 280 C3 8
Wetherby Rd DERBYSE DE24 .... 257 G3
Wetherel Rd
STPNHL/WNHL DE15 .... 281 M1
Wetlands La CHNE S41 .... 111 H6
Wetmore La BUT DE14 .... 274 C4
Wetmore Rd BUT DE14 .... 274 B4
Weyacres BWSH/BRSTN DE72 .... 258 E1
Weybridge Cl ILK DE7 .... 229 G2 8
Whaley Bridge Cl
MSFD NG18 .... 165 M5 8
Whaley La CHF/WBR SK23 .... 58 F1
Whaley Rd SBK/MW NG20 .... 115 H8
Wharf Ct CHF/WBR SK23 .... 59 H3
Wharfdale Cl WOL/BIL/BRX NG8 .... 231 L7
Wharfedale Cl DERBYW DE22 .... 226 E6
CHNE S41 .... 3 H1
STV/CWN S43 .... 93 J7
Wharfedale Gdns MSFD NG18 .... 165 K5
Wharfedale Rd LGEAT NG10 .... 260 D4
Wharf La ALFN DE55 .... 161 M3
CHNE S41 .... 3 H1
STV/CWN S43 .... 93 J7
Wharf Rd ASH NG17 .... 162 F4
BUT DE14 .... 274 B5
CHF/WBR SK23 .... 59 H3
EWD/SEL/PNX NG16 .... 177 G8
MSFD NG18 .... 164 E4
The Wharf BWSH/BRSTN DE72 .... 271 K1
Wharmby Av MSFDW NG19 .... 149 G7
Wharncliffe Cl GLSP SK13 .... 17 J5
Wharncliffe Rd ILK DE7 .... 230 B2
Wheal La BUX SK17 .... 121 G3
Wheatbridge Rd CHSW S40 .... 2 C4
Wheatcroft GLSP SK13 .... 17 H6 8
Wheatcroft Cl CLCR S45 .... 145 G8
Wheatcroft La MTLK DE4 .... 173 J2
Wheatcroft Wy DERBYE DE21 .... 226 F8
Wheatfield STLY SK15 .... 16 B3
Wheatfields CHF/WBR SK23 .... 60 E3 8
Wheatfields Wy ASH NG17 .... 163 H5
RCH S42 .... 109 J5 8
Wheatgrass Rd
BSTN/STPLFD NG9 .... 245 L5
Wheathill Cl CHSW S40 .... 109 K5 14
CHSW S40 .... 109 J5 8
STV/CWN S43 .... 111 J6
Wheathill Gv NORM/LIT DE23 .... 255 K4 7
Wheathill La CHNE S41 .... 111 H6
Wheatland Cl
DERBYSE DE24 .... 255 M8 8
Wheatlands SWAD DE11 .... 282 E3 8
Wheatlands La BKWL DE45 .... 105 K5
Wheatlands Rd RCH S42 .... 128 B6
STPNHL/WNHL DE15 .... 281 H5
Wheatley Av ALFN DE55 .... 187 M1
Wheatley Cl MSFDW NG19 .... 165 J1
Wheatley Gdns MTLK DE4 .... 141 G8
Wheatley Gv HAN/WDH S13 .... 57 H1
Wheatley La
STPNHL/WNHL DE15 .... 274 E6
Wheatley Rd MTLK DE4 .... 141 F7
Wheatsheaf Cl
DERBYE DE21 .... 227 M8 8
Wheatsheaf La MTLK DE4 .... 185 J1
Wheatsheaf Rd
CHF/WBR SK23 .... 59 H4 8
Wheeldale Cl
WOL/BIL/BRX NG8 .... 231 L6 8
Wheeldon Av BPR/DUF DE56 .... 199 L5
DERBYW DE22 .... 240 B3
Wheeldon Crs STV/CWN S43 .... 111 G3
Wheeldon Wy ASHB DE6 .... 196 B7
Wheeler Av
EWD/SEL/PNX NG16 .... 217 L1
Wheelwright Cl
MPL/ROM SK6 .... 32 C2 8
Whenby Cl MCKLVR DE3 .... 238 F8 8
Whernside Cl DERBYSE DE24 .... 257 M4
Wheston Bank BUX SK17 .... 83 L6

332 Whe - Woo

Whetmorhurst Rd
MPL/ROM SK6 33 H6
Whilton Cl ASH NG17 163 K5 3
Whilton Ct BPR/DUF DE56 200 A6 10
Whilton Crs ILK DE7 229 G2
Whinacre Cl SHEFS S8 70 E4 5
Whinacre Pl SHEFS S8 70 E4
Whinbush Av DERBYSE DE24 257 H5
Whinfell Ct ECC S11 54 B8
Whirlow Court Rd ECC S11 54 C8
Whirlowdale Cl ECC S11 54 C8 2
Whirlowdale Crs ECC S11 54 E7
Whirlowdale Ri ECC S11 54 C8 3
Whirlowdale Rd ABRD S7 54 D8
ECC S11 54 C8
Whirlow Gv ECC S11 54 C8
Whirlow La ECC S11 54 C7 4
Whirlow Ms ECC S11 54 C7 5
Whirlow Park Rd ABRD S7 69 J1
Whiston St NORM/LIT DE23 240 D8
Whitaker Gdns NORM/LIT DE23 4 A9
Whitaker Rd NORM/LIT DE23 240 B8
Whitaker St NORM/LIT DE23 240 D8
Whitburn Rd
BSTN/STPLFD NG9 245 H7
Whitby Av DERBYE DE21 240 F1
Whitby Cl WOL/BIL/BRX NG8 231 L6 3
Whitby Rd EWD/SEL/PNX NG16 203 K7
Whitcombe Pl RIPLEY DE5 187 G8 3
Whitebank Cl CHNE S41 3 K8
White Carr La ALFN DE55 158 E5
Whitecoats Pk CHSW S40 2 E9
Whitecotes Cl CHSW S40 2 D9
Whitecotes La CHSW S40 128 B2
Whitecroft Rd MPL/ROM SK6 32 F8
Whitecross Av BUX SK17 83 M6 2
Whitecross Rd BUX SK17 84 A6
Whitecross St DERBY DE1 4 B1
White Edge Cl CHSW S40 110 A5
White Edge Dr BKWL DE45 106 B4
Whitefield La BUX SK17 120 B2
CDLE ST10 190 E1
CLCR S45 142 D5
White Gate Rd HOLM/MEL HD7 9 G1
White Gates RIPLEY DE5 201 L2
Whitegates Wy ASH NG17 162 B8
White Hart St MSFD NG18 164 E4
Whitehead Cl ILK DE7 217 G8
Whitehead Dr
EWD/SEL/PNX NG16 203 G2 1
Whitehead La ASH NG17 163 J4
Whitehead St STV/CWN S43 93 J8
White Horse La ALFN DE55 159 G3
Whitehough Head La
CHF/WBR SK23 60 A2
Whitehouse Cl DERBYSE DE24 257 G6
Whitehouse Ri BPR/DUF DE56 199 H4
Whitehouses CHNE S41 3 K7
Whitehurst St DERBYSE DE24 257 G3
White Knowle Rd BUX SK17 99 L5
White La BPR/DUF DE56 198 A7
HACK/IN S12 56 D7
Whitelea La MTLK DE4 157 K5
White Leas CHSW S40 109 L6
White Leas Av RCH S42 145 K3
Whiteleas Rd CHF/WBR SK23 59 G8
Whiteley La ECC S11 53 M3
Whiteley Rd RIPLEY DE5 201 J3
Whiteley Wood Cl ECC S11 54 B3
Whiteley Wood Rd ECC S11 54 B4
White Lodge La BKWL DE45 106 B4
Whitelow La MTLK DE4 170 A3
TOT/DORE S17 68 E3
Whitely Cl BSTN/STPLFD NG9 245 H3 3
Whitemoor Hall
BPR/DUF DE56 200 A5 5
Whitemoor La BPR/DUF DE56 200 A5
Whiteoak Cl MPL/ROM SK6 32 B3
White Rd NM/HAY SK22 43 M1
STV/CWN S43 93 K8
Whites Cl ALFN DE55 175 K8
Whitesmead Cl POY/DIS SK12 43 G5 1
Whitestone Cl MSFD NG18 165 K7
Whitestone La
BUTN/AL/TUT DE13 272 F1
White St DERBYW DE22 240 B3
Whitethorn Cl MPL/ROM SK6 32 B3 4
White Thorns Cl SHEFS S8 70 E4 6
White Thorns Dr SHEFS S8 70 E5
White Thorns Vw SHEFS S8 70 E4
White Tor Rd MTLK DE4 171 M1
Whiteway DERBYW DE22 226 B8 5
Whitewell Gdns
DERBYSE DE24 257 M5 8
Whitewells La BPR/DUF DE56 198 F2
Whitewells Rd BPR/DUF DE56 185 H8
White Woods Wy MTLK DE4 156 E7
Whitfield Av GLSP SK13 25 M3
Whitfield Cross GLSP SK13 26 A3
Whitfield La BKWL DE45 138 B8
Whitfield Pk GLSP SK13 25 M3
Whitfield Rd FUL S10 53 M3
Whiting Av
BSTN/STPLFD NG9 245 J8 7
Whiting St SHEFS S8 55 K4 18
Whitle Rd NM/HAY SK22 43 M1
Whitley Wy ASHB DE6 208 B2
Whitmore Av RCH S42 129 H7
Whitmore Rd DERBYE DE21 241 J4 5
Whitney Cl MSFDW NG19 165 L1 2
Whitstable Cl
NORM/LIT DE23 256 A3 3
Whittaker La DERBYE DE21 214 A8
Whittaker Rd
BSTN/STPLFD NG9 245 K7
Whittington Hl CHNE S41 110 D1
Whittington La DRON S18 91 J5
Whittington Rd STV/CWN S43 92 B6
Whittington St DERBYSE DE24 257 G5
Whittling Valley Rd CHNE S41 110 D1
Whittlebank Rd NM/HAY SK22 33 L8
Whittlebury Dr NORM/LIT DE23 255 J3
Whitton Cl
BSTN/STPLFD NG9 245 M8 2
Whitton Pl BSVR S44 112 D5
Whitwell Rd AU/AST/KP S26 76 D7
WRKS S80 76 D6
Whitworth Av MTLK DE4 140 F7
Whitworth Rd CHNE S41 110 C4 1
FUL S10 54 B1
ILK DE7 230 C4
MTLK DE4 140 E5
Whysall St HEANOR DE75 202 B8
Whyteleafe Gv
DERBYE DE21 241 L1 16
Wickersley Cl DERBYW DE22 226 B8 6
Wickfield Cl HACK/IN S12 57 J5
Wickfield Dr HACK/IN S12 57 H6
Wickfield Gv HACK/IN S12 57 H5
Wickfield Pl HACK/IN S12 57 H5
Wickfield Rd HACK/IN S12 57 J6
Wickins Pl STV/CWN S43 93 L7
Wicksteed Cl BPR/DUF DE56 200 A5
Widdop Cl HAN/WDH S13 57 G2
Widdop Cft HAN/WDH S13 57 G2
Widdybank Cl
DERBYW DE22 225 M8 6
Wideshaft SWAD DE11 282 F6
Widgeon Dr MSHM DE12 295 L6
Widmerpool St
EWD/SEL/PNX NG16 176 F8
Wigfull Rd ECC S11 54 F1
Wigley Rd STV/CWN S43 111 M4
Wigmore Cl MCKLVR DE3 238 F7 6
Wikeley Wy STV/CWN S43 111 G3
Wilberforce Rd
MSFDW NG19 149 G8 2
Wilcox Av MSFDW NG19 149 L5
Wilcox Dr EWD/SEL/PNX NG16 203 K1
Wildaygreen La DRON S18 89 K8
Wildbank Cha STLY SK15 16 B3
Wilde Crs EWD/SEL/PNX NG16 189 K4
Wilderbrook La BPR/DUF DE56 198 D2
Wilders Lea Ct BPR/DUF DE56 199 K8
Wildhay La ASHB DE6 205 K3
Wild Hl ASH NG17 162 A4
Wild La MTLK DE4 173 L6
Wildpark La ASHB DE6 223 M4
Wildsmith St DERBYSE DE24 257 K2
Wild St DERBYW DE22 240 A5
Wilford Rd MSFD NG18 165 K7
Wilfred Gdns ASHZ LE65 291 K5
Wilfred Pl ASHZ LE65 291 K5
Wilfred St NORM/LIT DE23 240 E8
Wilhallow La
EWD/SEL/PNX NG16 189 H7
Wilkes Av MSHM DE12 295 M6
Wilkin Hl DRON S18 109 H1
Wilkins Dr DERBYSE DE24 257 H3
Wilkinson Cl CHSW S40 128 D4 1
MSFDW NG19 148 D5
Wilkinson Dr STV/CWN S43 111 L3
Willbury Dr HACK/IN S12 56 D4
Willcock Rd BUT DE14 280 D3
Willersley Rd MTLK DE4 171 M3
Willesden Av DERBYW DE22 239 K3
Willesley Cl ASHZ LE65 291 J6
Willesley Gdns ASHZ LE65 291 J6
Willesley La ASHZ LE65 295 L1
MSHM DE12 290 E5
Willesley Wood Side
MSHM DE12 290 F8
Willetts Rd DERBYE DE21 241 K3
Willey La EWD/SEL/PNX NG16 203 K1
William Av EWD/SEL/PNX NG16 203 J8
William Cl MOS S20 73 G4 7
William Crs MOS S20 73 G3
William Nadin Wy SWAD DE11 282 C6
William Newton Cl
RDERBYSW DE65 265 L5
William Rd BSTN/STPLFD NG9 245 G3
Williams Cl ALFN DE55 188 A4
Williamson Av BUX SK17 99 M1
Williamson Crs
CHF/WBR SK23 59 G2 2
Williamson Rd CHF/WBR SK23 59 G2
ECC S11 55 G3
Williamson St MSFDW NG19 164 B3
Williams Rd BSTN/STPLFD NG9 245 L7
William St BPR/DUF DE56 199 J6
BUT DE14 273 M5
CHNE S41 110 D4 3
DERBY DE1 4 B1
ECK/KIL S21 73 G7
LGEAT NG10 244 F8
William St North CHNE S41 91 J8
Williamthorpe Cl RCH S42 145 K3
Williamthorpe Rd RCH S42 145 M2
William Wood La
SBK/MW NG20 133 M4
Willingham Cl MOS S20 73 K1
Willington Rd RDERBYSW DE65 253 M6
RDERBYSW DE65 266 E6
RDERBYSW DE65 266 F2
Willn St NORM/LIT DE23 256 C1
Willoughby Av LGEAT NG10 244 F8
Willoughby Cl
BWSH/BRSTN DE72 260 C2
Willoughby St ILK DE7 230 D1 2
Willow Av BSTN/STPLFD NG9 245 G4
LGEAT NG10 261 G1
MSFDW NG19 165 K1
RIPLEY DE5 201 G3
SBK/MW NG20 133 G5
Willowbath La MTLK DE4 183 J3
Willowbrook Cl ASHZ LE65 291 L2
RDERBYSW DE65 252 F8 4
Willowbrook Gra
MELB/CHEL DE73 269 K1
Willow Cl ALFN DE55 175 K5
ALFN DE55 176 E5
BWSH/BRSTN DE72 270 E3
CLCR S45 160 F1
DERBYW DE22 226 C8 8
EWD/SEL/PNX NG16 189 L3
MSHM DE12 290 E4 4
WRKS S80 115 J1 5
Willow Ct BSVR S44 111 K7
MPL/ROM SK6 32 C5 5
Willow Crs ASH NG17 163 G7
Willow Cft DERBYSE DE24 257 M6
Willowcroft Rd DERBYE DE21 242 A7
Willow Dr CHF/WBR SK23 60 E5
STV/CWN S43 93 M6
SWAD DE11 282 C3
Willowfields RDERBYSW DE65 253 G8
Willow Garth Rd CHNE S41 109 M2
Willow Gv BPR/DUF DE56 199 K8
MPL/ROM SK6 32 C5
RDERBYSW DE65 266 D4
Willowherb Cl
DERBYSE DE24 256 C8 3
Willow Meadow Rd ASHB DE6 207 M2
Willow Park Wy
BWSH/BRSTN DE72 270 D3
Willowpit La RDERBYSW DE65 253 G3
Willow Pl
STPNHL/WNHL DE15 281 H3 1
Willow Rd
BUTN/AL/TUT DE13 286 A1 2
CDON/KEG DE74 271 L5
ECK/KIL S21 73 M5
MPL/ROM SK6 42 C3
Willow Rw DERBY DE1 4 D2
Willows Av ALFN DE55 175 K5
Willowsend Cl
RDERBYSW DE65 267 G1 2
The Willows ASHB DE6 196 C7
MSFDW NG19 148 D4
Willow St ALFN DE55 174 F1
Willow Tree Dr STV/CWN S43 95 J8
Willow Wy MTLK DE4 140 E7
Willridding La ASHB DE6 205 M3
Will Shore's La MTLK DE4 155 M4
Willson Av NORM/LIT DE23 255 M2
Willson Dr ALFN DE55 187 L4
Willson Rd NORM/LIT DE23 255 M2
Wilmans Wk GLSP SK13 17 K4 6
Wilmington Av DERBYSE DE24 257 L5
Wilmore Rd DERBYSE DE24 256 D5
Wilmot Av BWSH/BRSTN DE72 270 B5
DERBYE DE21 241 J5
Wilmot Dr ILK DE7 215 J5
Wilmot Rd BPR/DUF DE56 199 K6
SWAD DE11 282 E7
Wilmot St DERBY DE1 4 F6
HEANOR DE75 216 B1
ILK DE7 230 B1 6
LGEAT NG10 260 D5
MTLK DE4 156 E4
Wilmslow Dr DERBYE DE21 241 L1 17
Wilne Cl LGEAT NG10 260 D6
Wilne La BWSH/BRSTN DE72 259 M6
BWSH/BRSTN DE72 271 L1
Wilne Rd BWSH/BRSTN DE72 259 K4
LGEAT NG10 260 C6
Wilshaw Cl CHF/WBR SK23 60 F5 5
Wilson Av ALFN DE55 176 B1
HEANOR DE75 201 L6
STV/CWN S43 95 K5
Wilson Cl CLCR S45 145 G8
MCKLVR DE3 254 F2
Wilson La BSVR S44 130 E8
Wilson Pl SHEFS S8 55 K4 19
Wilson Ri MELB/CHEL DE73 279 H4 1
Wilson Rd DERBYE DE21 241 J2
DRON S18 70 F6
ECC S11 54 F2
EWD/SEL/PNX NG16 217 J1
Wilson St ALFN DE55 175 K6
DERBY DE1 4 D5
DRON S18 90 E2 4
EWD/SEL/PNX NG16 177 G7
MSFDW NG19 149 G7
Wilsthorpe Rd
BWSH/BRSTN DE72 260 B2
DERBYE DE21 241 J3
LGEAT NG10 260 E2
LGEAT NG10 260 E4
Wilthorpe Gdns HACK/IN S12 57 K7 7
Wilton Cl DERBYSE DE24 255 M8 6
Wilton St ILK DE7 230 C1 10
Wiltshire Av
EWD/SEL/PNX NG16 188 E6
Wiltshire Dr GLSP SK13 26 C2
Wiltshire Rd DERBYE DE21 241 G3
Wimbledon Rd DERBYW DE22 239 K4
Wimborne Crs CHNE S41 110 C3
Wimbourne Cl
MELB/CHEL DE73 269 K1
Wimpole Gdns
DERBYW DE22 239 L4 5
Wimsey Wy ALFN DE55 175 K8
ALFN DE55 187 L1
Winborne Cl MSFDW NG19 164 A4
Wincanton Cl DERBYSE DE24 257 G1
Winchcombe Dr
STPNHL/WNHL DE15 281 L1 4
Winchcombe Wy DERBYE DE21 227 K8
Winchester Av FUL S10 53 L2
Winchester Cl MSFD NG18 165 K7
RCH S42 145 H4
Winchester Crs DERBYE DE21 241 G2
FUL S10 53 L2
ILK DE7 230 D2
Winchester Dr BUT DE14 280 F2 3
FUL S10 53 L2 2
MSHM DE12 289 G5
SWAD DE11 283 G4
Winchester Rd CHNE S41 110 B3
FUL S10 53 L2
Winchester Wy ASHZ LE65 291 K3
Windermere Av ASHZ LE65 291 M5
DRON S18 90 B1
ILK DE7 229 M5
Windermere Crs DERBYW DE22 226 B7
Windermere Dr
DERBYE DE21 242 B5 4
Windermere Rd CHNE S41 109 M3
CLCR S45 144 E7 3
LGEAT NG10 244 D8
MPL/ROM SK6 42 A1
SHEFS S8 55 H5 7
Winders Cnr STV/CWN S43 94 E5
Windlea Rd ALFN DE55 187 M4
Windle Edge STKB/PEN S36 14 D4
STKB/PEN S36 15 G1
Windlehurst Old Rd
MPL/ROM SK6 32 C8
Windlehurst Rd MPL/ROM SK6 42 A2
Windley Crs DERBYW DE22 240 C1
Windley Dr ILK DE7 217 G7 11
Windley La BPR/DUF DE56 197 H5
BPR/DUF DE56 211 K1
BPR/DUF DE56 212 B4
Windmere Rd CLCR S45 144 E7
Windmill Av BPR/DUF DE56 214 E2
Windmill Cl ASHZ LE65 291 M5
BSVR S44 113 K7 1
BWSH/BRSTN DE72 242 F5 3
CDON/KEG DE74 271 L8 2
DERBYSE DE24 258 A6
UTXR ST14 247 L1 3
Windmill Dr UTXR ST14 249 H7
Windmill Greenway MOS S20 73 H5
Windmill Hill La DERBYW DE22 239 M4
Windmill La ASHB DE6 193 M7
ASHB DE6 207 H7
BPR/DUF DE56 184 C4
BPR/DUF DE56 199 K6
DRON S18 91 K4
HATH/EY S32 85 M4
MSFD NG18 164 F2
Windmill Ri ALFN DE55 176 C5
ALFN DE55 188 A3
BPR/DUF DE56 199 K5
Windmill Rd RDERBYSW DE65 253 L7
Windmill St SWAD DE11 289 K1
Windmill Vw BPR/DUF DE56 200 B2 3
Windrush Cl DERBYW DE22 226 E5
Windsmoor Rd
EWD/SEL/PNX NG16 203 G2
Windsor Av ASH NG17 162 E7
MELB/CHEL DE73 278 D2
NORM/LIT DE23 255 L2
Windsor Cl ALFN DE55 187 K3
ASHB DE6 194 A7
BSTN/STPLFD NG9 230 E5 1
BWSH/BRSTN DE72 258 F1
CHSW S40 127 M1
HEANOR DE75 202 B7
SWAD DE11 282 D4
Windsor Ct ILK DE7 229 G2 7
LGEAT NG10 244 E6 11
MCKLVR DE3 239 G7 5
Windsor Crs BSTN/STPLFD NG9 245 H3
ILK DE7 230 A6
Windsor Dr DERBYE DE21 242 C4
DRON S18 89 M1
MPL/ROM SK6 32 B5 2
RCH S42 128 B6
STPNHL/WNHL DE15 281 J1
Windsor Gdns MSFD NG18 165 G5
Windsor Park Rd BUX SK17 100 A2
Windsor Rd ASHZ LE65 291 L5
BUX SK17 99 M2
EWD/SEL/PNX NG16 189 K2
MSFD NG18 165 G5
MSHM DE12 289 G5
SHEFS S8 55 J4
UTXR ST14 247 K2
Windsor St BSTN/STPLFD NG9 245 G3
Windsor Wk CHNE S41 3 M8
Windy Fields Rd RCH S42 127 G3
Windy House La SHEFP/MNR S2 56 C3
Windy La DERBYE DE21 226 F1
Windyridge BUX SK17 134 E4
Winfield Gv MPL/ROM SK6 32 E1 3
Wingerworth Av SHEFS S8 70 A3
Wingerworth Park Rd
DERBYE DE21 242 B5 5
Wingerworth St RCH S42 129 H7 2
Wingerworth Wy CHSW S40 128 C3
Wingfield Cl DRON S18 89 M2
Wingfield Crs HACK/IN S12 56 F5
Wingfield Dr DERBYE DE21 241 J1
ILK DE7 217 G7
Wingfield Gv GLSP SK13 26 C3 2
Wingfield Rd ALFN DE55 175 H7
MSFD NG18 165 K6
RCH S42 145 G2
Winhill Rd NM/HAY SK22 43 M1 7
Winifred St WRKS S80 77 K6
Winkburn Rd MSFDW NG19 164 C2
Winnat Pl STV/CWN S43 111 M3
Winnats EDL/UDV S33 48 B8
Winnats Cl CHSW S40 109 M5 7
GLSP SK13 26 C2
Winnats Rd EDL/UDV S33 48 D8
Winney Hl AU/AST/KP S26 75 H5
Winney La AU/AST/KP S26 75 H6
Winnington Rd MPL/ROM SK6 32 C2
Winn La ASHB DE6 195 J3
Winslow Av HYDE SK14 16 C8
Winslow Gn DERBYE DE21 241 L4
Winster Cl BPR/DUF DE56 199 L5 5
CLCR S45 144 D5
Winster Gn SWAD DE11 282 B5 8
Winster Gv BUX SK17 100 B3
Winster La MTLK DE4 154 C4
Winster Rd DERBYE DE21 241 H1
STV/CWN S43 111 M2
Winster Sq BUX SK17 100 B3 4
Winster Wy LGEAT NG10 260 C5
MSFD NG18 165 L5
Winston Cl BSTN/STPLFD NG9 245 H2
MPL/ROM SK6 32 A3
Winterbottom Gv HYDE SK14 16 C8 2
Winterbourne Dr
BSTN/STPLFD NG9 245 H1
Winter Closes
EWD/SEL/PNX NG16 203 J1
Wintercroft La ASHB DE6 193 G1
Wintergreen Dr
NORM/LIT DE23 255 J4
Winterton Gdns HACK/IN S12 57 M7
Winthorpe St MSFDW NG19 164 A4
Wire La ALFN DE55 161 L7
Wirksmoor Rd NM/HAY SK22 43 L3
Wirksworth Hall Gdns
MTLK DE4 183 J2 6
Wirksworth Rd BPR/DUF DE56 196 E1
BPR/DUF DE56 197 K5
BPR/DUF DE56 212 B1
BPR/DUF DE56 213 G7
ILK DE7 229 M6
MTLK DE4 172 E7
Wisbech Cl CHSW S40 2 D9
Wiseton Rd ECC S11 54 F1
Wisgreaves Rd DERBYSE DE24 257 J2
Wishing Stone Wy
MTLK DE4 157 H4 1
Witham Cl CHNE S41 110 F4 2
RDERBYSW DE65 253 H8
Witham Dr NORM/LIT DE23 256 A4 5
Withorn Ms MSFDW NG19 164 B3
Witney Cl DERBYSE DE24 256 F2 5
Witney St SHEFP/MNR S2 55 K2 6
Wittering Cl LGEAT NG10 261 H5
Witton Ct DERBYSE DE24 256 A6
Woburn Cl ALFN DE55 176 B1
ALFN DE55 187 J3
Woburn Cft LGEAT NG10 244 D6
Woburn Pl DERBYW DE22 239 L5 3
ECC S11 54 C8
MSFDW NG19 148 F6
Woburn Rd MSFDW NG19 148 F6
Wolds Ri MTLK DE4 156 F3
Wolds Rd MTLK DE4 157 G3 2
Wolfa St DERBYW DE22 4 C5
Wolfcote Cl CLCR S45 160 A1
Wolfe Cl CHSW S40 2 A7
Wolfscote Dl SWAD DE11 282 C8
Wollaton Av TOT/DORE S17 69 K5
Wollaton Dr TOT/DORE S17 69 K5 4
Wollaton Paddocks
WOL/BIL/BRX NG8 231 M6
Wollaton Rd DERBYE DE21 241 J2
TOT/DORE S17 69 K5
Wollaton V WOL/BIL/BRX NG8 231 L6
Wollen Cl WRKS S80 115 J1
Wolseley Ct ASH NG17 163 J7
Wolseley Rd SHEFS S8 55 J3
Wolverley Gra DERBYSE DE24 258 A4
Wolverley Rd HAN/WDH S13 57 K4
Woodale Cl NORM/LIT DE23 255 J4 3
Woodall La AU/AST/KP S26 74 F4
Woodall Rd ECK/KIL S21 74 C5
Wood Av LGEAT NG10 244 D4
WRKS S80 114 F2
Woodbank Crs SHEFS S8 55 J5
Woodborough Rd
MSFDW NG19 164 B1
Woodbourne Rd NM/HAY SK22 43 K5
Woodbridge Cl
MELB/CHEL DE73 269 J1
Woodbrook CHF/WBR SK23 59 H3
Woodbrook Ct CHF/WBR SK23 59 H3
Woodchester Dr
DERBYSE DE24 258 A4
Wood Cliffe ECC S11 53 L4
Wood Cl MSFDW NG19 165 J2
RCH S42 128 A6
Wood Close Camp
DERBYE DE21 226 F3 3
Wood Close Cobnar DRON S18 90 E7
Woodcock Gv GLSP SK13 26 B1 1
Woodcock Rd GLSP SK13 26 D1
Woodcock Wy ASHZ LE65 291 M3 1
Woodcote Wy NORM/LIT DE23 255 K3
Wood Ct BUT DE14 280 F1
Wood Cft NORM/LIT DE23 256 A2 2
Woodend Dr STLY SK15 16 A4
Woodend La STLY SK15 16 A3
Wood End Rd HEANOR DE75 202 B8 8
Woodfall La DERBYW DE22 212 C8
Wood Farm La SWAD DE11 283 H6 1
Woodfield Cl GLSP SK13 17 J5 4
Woodfield Dr RIPLEY DE5 201 K1
SWAD DE11 282 F5
Woodfield Rd
EWD/SEL/PNX NG16 177 G6
Woodford Rd DERBYW DE22 239 K3
Wood Gdns NM/HAY SK22 34 F7
Woodgate Dr
MELB/CHEL DE73 269 K1 6
Woodhall Cl MSFDW NG19 165 J2 1
Woodhall Dr NORM/LIT DE23 255 H2
Woodhall Gdns MSFD NG18 165 J2
Woodhead La CLCR S45 159 H1
Woodhead Rd GLSP SK13 17 L3
GLSP SK13 18 A7
HOLM/MEL HD7 8 B4
SHEFP/MNR S2 55 K2
Woodholm Pl ECC S11 54 E5 2
Woodholm Rd ECC S11 54 E5
Woodhouse Ct
MSFDW NG19 149 M8 2
Woodhouse La ASH NG17 163 K3
ASHB DE6 237 K5
BSVR S44 113 H6
HOLM/MEL HD7 9 G1
MTLK DE4 154 F4
RDERBYSW DE65 251 H3
STV/CWN S43 93 M5
Woodhouse Rd BPR/DUF DE56 214 D3
HACK/IN S12 56 E4
MSFD NG18 164 E2
MTLK DE4 140 C2
Woodhouse St SWAD DE11 283 G7
Woodhurst Cl DERBYE DE21 241 G1
Woodland Av ASH NG17 162 B6
BWSH/BRSTN DE72 242 F8
BWSH/BRSTN DE72 260 C2
ILK DE7 217 G6 1
Woodland Crs MSFD NG18 165 J6
Woodland Dr ASHB DE6 250 F6
HACK/IN S12 56 E8 1
MSFD NG18 165 J6
Woodland Gv MSFDW NG19 149 M6
RCH S42 144 E3
STV/CWN S43 94 D4
STV/CWN S43 95 K6 3
Woodland Pl TOT/DORE S17 69 J5
Woodland Rd DERBYW DE22 240 B2
MSFDW NG19 165 J1
SHEFS S8 55 L7
STPNHL/WNHL DE15 281 L4
Woodlands MTLK DE4 183 H2 2
STV/CWN S43 111 G3
Woodlands Av DERBYSE DE24 257 H6
Woodlands Brow ASHB DE6 194 A6 1
Woodlands Cl ASHB DE6 192 F1
DERBYE DE21 226 E2 1
GLSP SK13 17 J4
HYDE SK14 24 C1
MELB/CHEL DE73 278 D1
STLY SK15 16 A3
Woodlands Crs MSHM DE12 289 K6
Woodlands Gv HYDE SK14 24 C1
Woodlands La DERBYW DE22 226 A3
MELB/CHEL DE73 269 K2
Woodlands Rd CHF/WBR SK23 60 E6 2
DERBYW DE22 226 A4
MSHM DE12 289 L6
NM/HAY SK22 43 K2 1
POY/DIS SK12 42 D4
STLY SK15 16 A3
The Woodlands
MELB/CHEL DE73 278 E2

MSFDW NG19 ... 164 E1
SBK/MW NG20 ... 115 K6
Woodlands Wy ASH NG17 ... 177 M1
MELB/CHEL DE73 ... 278 D2
MSHM DE12 ... 290 E4
Woodland Vw HACK/IN S12 ... 56 E8
SBK/MW NG20 ... 115 K7
Woodland Views UTXR ST14 ... 249 H8
Woodland Wk RCH S42 ... 109 J3
Woodland Wy
EWD/SEL/PNX NG16 ... 203 H8
RCH S42 ... 144 C4
Wood La ASHB DE6 ... 194 D1
ASHB DE6 ... 223 K3
BPR/DUF DE56 ... 197 H2
BPR/DUF DE56 ... 213 J4
BSVR S44 ... 132 C4
ILK DE7 ... 215 G5
MPL/ROM SK6 ... 32 A5
MSFDW NG19 ... 149 J1
MTLK DE4 ... 170 B3
MTLK DE4 ... 172 D1
MTLK DE4 ... 173 L7
NM/HAY SK22 ... 34 F8
RIPLEY DE5 ... 186 D6
SWAD DE11 ... 282 C3
UTXR ST14 ... 246 A8
UTXR ST14 ... 248 B4
WRKS S80 ... 114 F2
WRKS S80 ... 115 G2
Woodlea Gv DERBYE DE21 ... 226 F2
Woodlea Rd GLSP SK13 ... 25 L3
Woodleigh Cl RCH S42 ... 109 J5 [7]
Woodleighton Gv
UTXR ST14 ... 247 M4 [7]
Woodmans Cft
RDERBYSW DE65 ... 263 M1
Woodminton Dr
MELB/CHEL DE73 ... 257 J7 [7]
Woodnook Cl CHSW S40 ... 109 J6
Wood Nook Cl
EWD/SEL/PNX NG16 ... 189 J4
Woodnook Gv ECK/KIL S21 ... 72 B8
Woodnook La RCH S42 ... 109 H4
Woodnook Wy CHSW S40 ... 109 J6
Woodpecker Hl ILK DE7 ... 229 K8
Woodrising Cl
DERBYE DE21 ... 227 L7 [13]
Wood Rd DERBYE DE21 ... 241 K2
DERBYE DE21 ... 242 D4
Woodrove Av HAN/WDH S13 ... 56 E3
Woodrove Cl HAN/WDH S13 ... 56 E3
Woodseats Cl SHEFS S8 ... 55 H6
Woodseats House Rd SHEFS S8 ... 55 J8
Woodseats La GLSP SK13 ... 24 F4
Woodseats Rd SHEFS S8 ... 55 H6
Woodsetts La WRKN S81 ... 77 K1
Woods Hl ASH NG17 ... 163 H6
Woodshop La
MELB/CHEL DE73 ... 269 G4
Woodside ASH NG17 ... 163 H3
ASHZ LE65 ... 291 J5
BUX SK17 ... 99 M3
EWD/SEL/PNX NG16 ... 203 H8
ILK DE7 ... 215 C7
Woodside Av DRON S18 ... 89 K2
ECK/KIL S21 ... 74 C3
MSFD NG18 ... 165 H4
RIPLEY DE5 ... 201 G2
Woodside Cl BKWL DE45 ... 123 G5

CHSW S40 ... 109 L6 [6]
Woodside Crs ILK DE7 ... 217 G5 [1]
ILK DE7 ... 260 E2
Woodside Dr BKWL DE45 ... 123 G5 [2]
DERBYW DE22 ... 226 D6
MPL/ROM SK6 ... 42 B3
Woodside Pl CLCR S45 ... 144 D6
Woodside Rd
BSTN/STPLFD NG9 ... 245 K6
LGEAT NG10 ... 244 D5
SBK/MW NG20 ... 133 H5
WRKN S81 ... 77 J3
Woodside Vw DRON S18 ... 89 K2
Woods La DERBYW DE22 ... 4 C7
STPNHL/WNHL DE15 ... 281 K1 [3]
STPNHL/WNHL DE15 ... 281 J2
Woods Meadow
DERBYE DE24 ... 258 A5 [2]
Woodsorrel Dr DERBYE DE21 ... 227 L7
Woodstock Cl DERBYW DE22 ... 226 A6
Woodstock Dr CHNE S41 ... 128 F2
Woodstock Ri CHNE S41 ... 3 M9
Woodstock Rd ABRD S7 ... 55 H4
BSTN/STPLFD NG9 ... 245 H7
Wood St ALFN DE55 ... 175 M6
ALFN DE55 ... 187 L2
ASHZ LE65 ... 291 M4
BUT DE14 ... 280 F1
DERBY DE1 ... 5 G2
EWD/SEL/PNX NG16 ... 203 J7
GLSP SK13 ... 25 M2
HYDE SK14 ... 17 G5
ILK DE7 ... 230 C1
MSFD NG18 ... 164 D3
MTLK DE4 ... 183 J2
NM/HAY SK22 ... 43 L3
RCH S42 ... 146 B1
RIPLEY DE5 ... 187 G8
RIPLEY DE5 ... 201 L2
RIPLEY DE5 ... 282 E8
Wood St North ALFN DE55 ... 175 M5
Woodthorne Av DERBYSE DE24... 257 H6
DERBYE DE21 ... 241 J4
Woodthorpe Av CLCR S45 ... 144 D6 [3]
DERBYE DE21 ... 241 J4
Woodthorpe Cl BSVR S44 ... 113 J4
HAN/WDH S13 ... 56 F3
STV/CWN S43 ... 93 M8
Woodthorpe Crs
HAN/WDH S13 ... 56 F2 [3]
Woodthorpe Rd BSVR S44 ... 113 H2
HAN/WDH S13 ... 56 F3
STV/CWN S43 ... 93 M8
Woodvale Cl CHSW S40 ... 127 K2
Woodvale Rd ECC S11 ... 54 E1
Woodview Cl RCH S42 ... 128 C7
Woodview Rd SWAD DE11 ... 282 A5
Woodview Ter ECC S11 ... 54 B2 [4]
Woodville Cl
BSTN/STPLFD NG9 ... 245 M4 [8]
Woodville Dr MPL/ROM SK6 ... 32 B6
Woodville Rd MSHM DE12 ... 289 L7
SWAD DE11 ... 283 K5
Woodward's Pl SWAD DE11 ... 282 F7
Woodyard La RDERBYSW DE65 ... 251 J6
RDERBYSW DE65 ... 251 M4
Woofindin Av ECC S11 ... 54 B3
Woofindin Rd ECC S11 ... 54 A3
Wooldale Cl MOS S20 ... 57 K8
Wooldale Cft MOS S20 ... 57 K8
Wooldale Dr MOS S20 ... 57 K8

Wooldale Gdns MOS S20 ... 57 K8
Wooley Cl RCH S42 ... 144 E3
Wooliscroft Wy ILK DE7 ... 216 F8 [8]
Woollaton La BUX SK17 ... 151 M8
Woolley Bridge Rd GLSP SK13 ... 17 H5
Woolley La HYDE SK14 ... 17 G6 [2]
Woolley La HYDE SK14 ... 16 F6
Woolley Mill La HYDE SK14 ... 17 G4
Woolley Rd MTLK DE4 ... 156 E5
Woolrych St NORM/LIT DE23 ... 240 C8
Woolsthorpe Crs ILK DE7 ... 230 A6
Woosnam Cl BUT DE14 ... 280 D4 [3]
Wootton La CDLE ST10 ... 204 A5
Worcester Av MSFDW NG19 ... 149 M4
Worcester Cl FUL S10 ... 53 L1 [2]
Worcester Crs DERBYE DE21 ... 241 G2
Worcester Dr FUL S10 ... 53 L1
Worcester Gv GLSP SK13 ... 26 C2 [3]
Worcester Rd FUL S10 ... 53 K1
STPNHL/WNHL DE15 ... 281 H4
Wordsworth Av ASH NG17 ... 162 E7
DERBYSE DE24 ... 256 B5
MSFDW NG19 ... 149 L6
SWAD DE11 ... 282 F4 [3]
Wordsworth Cl BUT DE14 ... 274 A4 [2]
Wordsworth Dr
DERBYSE DE24 ... 256 D5 [2]
Wordsworth Pl DRON S18 ... 90 F3
Wordsworth Rd CHNE S41 ... 110 C2
EWD/SEL/PNX NG16 ... 217 M5
Wordsworth Wy MSHM DE12 ... 295 J1
Works La BSVR S44 ... 111 L8
Worksop Rd STV/CWN S43 ... 93 L7
WRKS S80 ... 76 B3
WRKS S80 ... 96 D3
Works Rd STV/CWN S43 ... 92 E7
Worrall Av LGEAT NG10 ... 261 G1
Worthington Cl HYDE SK14 ... 16 B8 [3]
Worthington Wy BUT DE14 ... 274 A8
Wortley Av BSTN/STPLFD NG9 ... 231 G7
Wortley Cl ILK DE7 ... 230 D2
Wortley Ct EDL/UDV S33 ... 64 E5 [1]
Wostenholm Rd ABRD S7 ... 55 J3
Wragby Rd ECC S11 ... 54 D2
Wragley Wy DERBYSE DE24 ... 255 M8
DERBYSE DE24 ... 268 B1
Wreakes La DRON S18 ... 70 C8
Wrekin Cl ASHZ LE65 ... 291 M6
Wren Cl SWAD DE11 ... 283 J7
Wren Ct WRKN S81 ... 77 M3
Wren Nest Cl GLSP SK13 ... 25 L1
Wren Nest Ter GLSP SK13 ... 25 M1 [3]
Wren Park Cl BPR/DUF DE56 ... 199 G4
CHSW S40 ... 128 C3
HACK/IN S12 ... 72 B2
RDERBYSW DE65 ... 267 G1
Wrenpark Rd RCH S42 ... 128 A6
Wretham Cl MCKLVR DE3 ... 255 G2 [6]
Wright Av RIPLEY DE5 ... 201 J1
Wright's Hl SHEFP/MNR S2 ... 55 J1
Wrightson Cl ASH NG17 ... 163 L7
Wright St RIPLEY DE5 ... 201 L3
Wroughton Ct
EWD/SEL/PNX NG16 ... 203 K8 [3]
Wroxham Cl DERBYSE DE24 ... 257 G6
Wulfric Cl SHEFP/MNR S2 ... 56 C2
Wulfric Pl SHEFP/MNR S2 ... 56 C2
Wulfric Rd ECK/KIL S21 ... 72 F7

SHEFP/MNR S2 ... 56 C3
Wyaston Cl DERBYW DE22 ... 240 B1 [4]
Wyaston Rd ASHB DE6 ... 207 M2
Wyatt Av ECC S11 ... 54 F4
Wybersley Rd MPL/ROM SK6 ... 42 D1
Wychwood Dr
BSTN/STPLFD NG9 ... 231 G8
Wycliffe Rd ALFN DE55 ... 175 K7
Wye Bank BKWL DE45 ... 123 H6
Wye Bank Gv BKWL DE45 ... 123 H5
Wye Dl SWAD DE11 ... 282 C8
Wyedale Cl BKWL DE45 ... 123 H6
BUX SK17 ... 99 L4
Wyedale Crs BKWL DE45 ... 123 G6
Wyedale Dr BKWL DE45 ... 123 G6
Wyedale Vw BKWL DE45 ... 123 G6
Wye Gv BUX SK17 ... 99 K4
Wye Head Cl BUX SK17 ... 99 L3
Wyelands Cl BUX SK17 ... 99 K3
Wye St BUX SK17 ... 99 M2
DERBYSE DE24 ... 257 K2
Wyggeston St
BUTN/AL/TUT DE13 ... 273 L4
Wyndale Dr ILK DE7 ... 229 M4
Wyndham Crs
STPNHL/WNHL DE15 ... 274 F7 [7]
Wyndham St DERBYSE DE24 ... 257 K3
The Wynd ECK/KIL S21 ... 93 L3
Wynndale Dr MSFD NG18 ... 165 K5
Wynton Av DERBYSE DE24 ... 257 J2
Wyntor Av MTLK DE4 ... 154 F4
Wynward Cl ILK DE7 ... 216 F7 [11]
Wynwood Cl
BSTN/STPLFD NG9 ... 245 L8 [5]
Wynwood Rd
BSTN/STPLFD NG9 ... 245 L8 [6]
Wysall Cl MSFDW NG19 ... 164 B1
Wystan Ct RDERBYSW DE65 ... 267 G8
Wyston Brook
RDERBYSW DE65 ... 265 G1
Wythburn Rd CHNE S41 ... 109 M3
Wyver La BPR/DUF DE56 ... 199 J3
Wyvern Av LGEAT NG10 ... 261 G4 [1]
Wyvern Cl EWD/SEL/PNX NG16 ... 217 J1
MTLK DE4 ... 156 D4
Wyvern Gdns TOT/DORE S17 ... 69 H4
Wyvern Wy DERBYE DE21 ... 241 K7

Y

Yalding Dr WOL/BIL/BRX NG8 ... 231 M6
Yalding Gdns
WOL/BIL/BRX NG8 ... 231 M6
Yard Cl SWAD DE11 ... 282 E6 [3]
Yardley Cl ALFN DE55 ... 187 J2
Yardley Wy BPR/DUF DE56 ... 200 B6
Yarncliff Cl CHSW S40 ... 110 A5
Yarrow Cl DERBYSE DE24 ... 256 B8 [2]
Yarwell Cl DERBYE DE21 ... 241 C1
Yates Rd NM/HAY SK22 ... 43 M3
Yates St NORM/LIT DE23 ... 256 D1
Yeardsley Av CHF/WBR SK23 ... 44 A7
Yeardsley Gn CHF/WBR SK23 ... 59 C2
Yeardsley La CHF/WBR SK23 ... 44 A7
Yeld Cl BKWL DE45 ... 122 F6
Yeldersley Cl CHSW S40 ... 109 L5

Yeldersley La ASHB DE6 ... 209 G1
ASHB DE6 ... 222 E2
Yeld Rd ASHB DE6 ... 122 F5
The Yeld BKWL DE45 ... 122 F5
Yelt La ASHB DE6 ... 249 G2
Yeoman St MTLK DE4 ... 171 G1
Yeovil Cl DERBYSE DE24 ... 257 M3 [3]
Yerley Hl ASHB DE6 ... 192 D3
Yewdale Gv DERBYE DE21 ... 227 M3 [1]
Yews Cl MELB/CHEL DE73 ... 269 K1
Yew Tree Av
BWSH/BRSTN DE72 ... 243 G5
Yew Tree Cl CLCR S45 ... 143 J7 [1]
DERBYE DE24 ... 257 M3 [10]
MPL/ROM SK6 ... 32 B5
MTLK DE4 ... 140 E8
Yewtree Crs
STPNHL/WNHL DE15 ... 281 J3
Yew Tree Dr ASH NG17 ... 162 C8
ECK/KIL S21 ... 73 M5 [3]
RCH S42 ... 127 K2
RCH S42 ... 144 E4
SBK/MW NG20 ... 133 G6
Yew Tree Hl MTLK DE4 ... 172 E5
Yew Tree La ASHB DE6 ... 209 H1
BWSH/BRSTN DE72 ... 258 C6 [2]
Yew Tree Rd MSHM DE12 ... 287 M4
RDERBYSW DE65 ... 252 A8
Yewtree Rd SWAD DE11 ... 282 C3
Yokecliffe Av MTLK DE4 ... 183 H2
Yokecliffe Crs MTLK DE4 ... 183 H2
Yokecliffe Dr MTLK DE4 ... 183 H2
Yokecliffe Hl MTLK DE4 ... 183 H2
York Av EWD/SEL/PNX NG16 ... 188 E6
LGEAT NG10 ... 244 D5
York Cl MSHM DE12 ... 295 M5
SWAD DE11 ... 283 C4
York Crs BSVR S44 ... 147 H1
Yorke St MSFDW NG19 ... 149 L8
York Pl WRKN S81 ... 77 J3 [8]
York Rd DERBYE DE21 ... 241 J3
LGEAT NG10 ... 260 F1
SBK/MW NG20 ... 133 H7
SWAD DE11 ... 282 E8
Yorkshire Dr EDL/UDV S33 ... 50 C4
Yorkshire Wy GLSP SK13 ... 26 C2
York St ASH NG17 ... 163 H7
BUT DE14 ... 273 M6
CHNE S41 ... 128 F3
DERBY DE1 ... 4 B3
GLSP SK13 ... 26 B1
MSFD NG18 ... 164 D5
York Ter EWD/SEL/PNX NG16 ... 188 F1
GLSP SK13 ... 25 M2 [6]
Youlgreave Cl DERBYE DE21 ... 241 J1 [6]
Youlgreave Crs GLSP SK13 ... 25 G1
Youlgreave Dr HACK/IN S12 ... 57 G5
Young Crs ASH NG17 ... 163 L8
Young St NORM/LIT DE23 ... 256 C1
Ypres Rd DERBYW DE22 ... 225 M8

Z

Zetland Crs DERBYSE DE24 ... 255 M8

Index - featured places

Abbeydale Grange School
ABRD S7 ... 55 G6
Abbeydale Park Sports Club
TOT/DORE S17 ... 69 K3
Abbeydale Primary School
ABRD S7 ... 55 J4
Abbey Lane Primary School
SHEFS S8 ... 55 H8
Abbotsholme School
UTXR ST14 ... 218 E8
Abercrombie Primary School
CHNE S41 ... 3 G1
Acorn Business Park
MSFD NG18 ... 164 E4
Acorn Business Park
SHEFS S8 ... 55 H6
Acre Ridge Industrial Estate
ALFN DE55 ... 175 M5
Adam House Medical Centre
LGEAT NG10 ... 244 E5
The Agricultural
Business Centre
BKWL DE45 ... 123 H4
Albany Junior Mixed School
BSTN/STPLFD NG9 ... 245 J4
Albert Village County School
SWAD DE11 ... 289 M2
Albion Leisure Centre
ILK DE7 ... 230 C2
Aldercar Infant School
EWD/SEL/PNX NG16 ... 202 D6
Aldercar Secondary School
EWD/SEL/PNX NG16 ... 202 D6
Alderman White School
BSTN/STPLFD NG9 ... 245 M4
Alderwasley School
BPR/DUF DE56 ... 183 H6
Alfreton Clinic
ALFN DE55 ... 175 K7
Alfreton Golf Club
ALFN DE55 ... 175 G7
Alfreton Indoor Market Hall
ALFN DE55 ... 175 J6
Alfreton Leisure Centre
ALFN DE55 ... 175 J6
Alfreton Town Football Club
ALFN DE55 ... 175 L7
Allenpark Infant School
DERBYSE DE24 ... 257 H4
All Saints C of E First School
UTXR ST14 ... 218 B4

All Saints C of E Junior School
MTLK DE4 ... 156 D3
All Saints C of E Primary School
MPL/ROM SK6 ... 32 D5
All Saints RC School
MSFDW NG19 ... 164 C2
All Saints RC School
SHEFP/MNR S2 ... 55 M1
All Saints Road Surgery
BUT DE14 ... 280 F2
All Saints School
GLSP SK13 ... 18 A8
Alvaston & Boulton Sports Club
DERBYSE DE24 ... 257 K1
Alvaston Junior & Infant School
DERBYSE DE24 ... 257 M3
Alvaston Medical Practice
DERBYSE DE24 ... 257 L3
Amalgamated Sports Club
POY/DIS SK12 ... 42 E4
Amber Business Centre
ALFN DE55 ... 187 L5
Ambergate Primary School
BPR/DUF DE56 ... 185 J7
Amber Valley Rugby
Union Football Club
ALFN DE55 ... 188 C3
Anderstaff Industrial Estate
BUT DE14 ... 274 A5
Anglesey County
Primary School
BUT DE14 ... 280 E1
Anglia Way Industrial Estate
MSFD NG18 ... 165 L7
Anns Grove Primary School
SHEFS S8 ... 55 K3
Anthony Bek Primary School
MSFDW NG19 ... 148 C4
Anthony Gell School
MTLK DE4 ... 183 J2
Apperknowle County
Primary School
DRON S18 ... 91 J1
Appleby Glade Industrial Estate
SWAD DE11 ... 282 A8
Appletree Medical Practice
BPR/DUF DE56 ... 213 J7
Arboretum Primary School
NORM/LIT DE23 ... 240 D8
Arbourthorne Junior School
SHEFP/MNR S2 ... 56 A4

Arkwright Primary School
BSVR S44 ... 112 A7
Arthur Mee Secondary
Girls School
BSTN/STPLFD NG9 ... 245 G3
Art Theatre
NM/HAY SK22 ... 43 L3
Arundale Primary School
HYDE SK14 ... 16 C7
Ascot Park Estate
LGEAT NG10 ... 244 F4
Ashbourne Business Centre
ASHB DE6 ... 193 L8
Ashbourne Golf Club
ASHB DE6 ... 207 L4
Ashbourne Leisure Centre
ASHB DE6 ... 207 L1
Ashbourne P N E U School
ASHB DE6 ... 193 M7
Ashbrook Junior
& Infant School
BWSH/BRSTN DE72 ... 242 E8
Ashby De La Zouch
Grammar School
ASHZ LE65 ... 291 M4
Ashby & District Hospital
ASHZ LE65 ... 291 M4
Ashby Hill Top County
Primary School
ASHZ LE65 ... 291 J4
Ashby Museum
ASHZ LE65 ... 291 L4
Ashcroft Primary School
DERBYSE DE24 ... 256 B8
Ashfield Business Centre
ASH NG17 ... 163 H8
Ashfield College
ASH NG17 ... 163 G8
Ash Lodge Medical Centre
CHSW S40 ... 2 A5
Ashover Primary School
CLCR S45 ... 143 J7
Asian Mosque Centre
SHEFP/MNR S2 ... 55 K3
Assembly Rooms
DERBY DE1 ... 4 E3
Asterdale Leisure Centre
DERBYE DE21 ... 242 C7
Asterdale School
DERBYE DE21 ... 242 C7

Aston Hall Hospital
BWSH/BRSTN DE72 ... 270 D4
Aston on Trent Primary School
BWSH/BRSTN DE72 ... 270 D2
Athletics Club
MSFD NG18 ... 165 H7
Audley Centre
DERBY DE1 ... 4 F4
Avenue House Surgery
CHSW S40 ... 2 F3
The Avenue Medical Practice
SHEFS S8 ... 70 A3
Awsworth Junior
& Infant School
EWD/SEL/PNX NG16 ... 217 M6
Awsworth Trading Estate
ILK DE7 ... 217 J8
Babington Hospital
BPR/DUF DE56 ... 199 H7
Bagthorpe Primary School
EWD/SEL/PNX NG16 ... 189 K6
Bailey Brook Industrial Estate
HEANOR DE75 ... 202 E8
Bakewell C of E Infant School
BKWL DE45 ... 123 G4
Bakewell Golf Club
BKWL DE45 ... 123 H3
Bakewell Methodist
Junior School
BKWL DE45 ... 123 G6
Ballifield Primary School
HAN/WDH S13 ... 57 K2
Balloon Wood Industrial Estate
BSTN/STPLFD NG9 ... 231 L6
Bamford County School
EDL/UDV S33 ... 50 E6
Banks Road Infant School
BSTN/STPLFD NG9 ... 245 J8
Bankwood Primary School
SHEFS S8 ... 56 A5
Barlborough Hall School
STV/CWN S43 ... 94 E1
Barlborough Primary School
STV/CWN S43 ... 94 E3
Barlow C of E School
DRON S18 ... 90 B7
Barrow Hill Primary School
STV/CWN S43 ... 92 E7
The Basement Gallery
FUL S10 ... 53 M3

Baslow Road Surgery
TOT/DORE S17 ... 69 H5
Bass Museum
BUT DE14 ... 274 B6
Beauchief Golf Club House
SHEFS S8 ... 69 L1
Beaufort Junior
& Infant School
DERBYE DE21 ... 240 F2
Beaufort Street
Business Centre
DERBYE DE21 ... 5 L1
Becket Primary School
DERBYW DE22 ... 4 C6
Beech Hill School
MSFDW NG19 ... 164 C1
Belgrave Medical Centre
SHEFP/MNR S2 ... 55 K2
Belmont Primary School
SWAD DE11 ... 282 F6
Belper Long Row
Primary School
BPR/DUF DE56 ... 199 J5
Belper Meadows Sports Club
BPR/DUF DE56 ... 199 H6
Belper Natural Health Centre
BPR/DUF DE56 ... 199 H7
Belper Pottery Primary School
BPR/DUF DE56 ... 199 H6
Belper School
BPR/DUF DE56 ... 199 H6
Belper Sports Centre
BPR/DUF DE56 ... 200 B1
Belper Town Council
BPR/DUF DE56 ... 199 K6
Belvedere County
Junior School
BUT DE14 ... 273 L5
Bembrose Community School
RDERBYSW DE65 ... 252 F8
Bemrose Community School
DERBYW DE22 ... 240 A6
Bend Oak County
Junior School
STPNHL/WNHL DE15 ... 274 F7
Benjamin Outram
Business Centre
RIPLEY DE5 ... 201 L4
Bennerley Fields School
ILK DE7 ... 217 G2

Bennerley School
ILK DE7 .... 217 J6
Bents Green Special School
ECC S11 .... 54 B5
Berry Hill First School
MSFD NG18 .... 165 H6
Berry Hill Middle School
MSFD NG18 .... 165 H7
Biggin C of E School
BUX SK17 .... 152 A7
Bilborough Sixth Form College
WOL/BIL/BRX NG8 .... 231 M3
Birch Vale Industrial Estate
NM/HAY SK22 .... 34 D8
Birkdale Preparatory School
FUL S10 .... 55 H1
Birkdale School
ECC S11 .... 54 F1
Birkhill Primary School
ECK/KIL S21 .... 72 E8
Birley First School
HACK/IN S12 .... 57 G7
Birley Health Centre
HACK/IN S12 .... 57 G8
Birley Middle School
HACK/IN S12 .... 57 G7
Birley Primary School
HACK/IN S12 .... 57 G7
Birley Spa Primary School
HACK/IN S12 .... 57 J8
Bishop Lonsdale C of E School
DERBYW DE22 .... 4 A8
Bispham Drive Junior School
BSTN/STPLFD NG9 .... 245 H7
Bitham Special School
BUTN/AL/TUT DE13 .... 273 M1
Blackfordby C of E School
SWAD DE11 .... 290 E1
Blackwell County
Primary School
ALFN DE55 .... 176 C1
Blackwell Medical Centre
ALFN DE55 .... 176 B1
Bladon House School
STPNHL/WHNL DE15 .... 274 C4
Bluebell Gallery
DERBYW DE22 .... 226 D8
Bluestone Middle School
SHEFP/MNR S2 .... 56 A2
Bluestone Primary School
SHEFP/MNR S2 .... 56 A2
Boardman Industrial Estate
SWAD DE11 .... 282 B7
Boars Head Industrial Estate
DERBYE DE21 .... 5 H2
Bolsover Clinic
BSVR S44 .... 113 L8
Bolsover C of E Jm School
BSVR S44 .... 113 K8
Bolsover Infant School
BSVR S44 .... 113 L8
Bolsover Local Hospital
BSVR S44 .... 113 M8
Bondhay Golf & Country Club
WRKS S80 .... 96 A4
Bond's Picture Gallery
CHNE S41 .... 2 F2
Bonsall C of E (A)
Primary School
MTLK DE4 .... 171 G1
Borrow Wood Junior
& Infant School
DERBYE DE21 .... 242 C5
Boulton Clinic
DERBYSE DE24 .... 257 J4
Boulton Junior & Infant School
DERBYSE DE24 .... 257 K4
Brabyns School
MPL/ROM SK6 .... 32 D3
Brackenfield School
LGEAT NG10 .... 260 E1
Brackensdale Junior
& Infant School
DERBYW DE22 .... 239 L4
Bradley C of E Primary School
ASHB DE6 .... 209 J2
Bradshaw Retail Park
DERBY DE1 .... 4 F6
Bradwell C of E School
EDL/UDV S33 .... 64 E3
Bradwell County School
EDL/UDV S33 .... 64 D3
Brailsford C of E
Primary School
ASHB DE6 .... 223 H3
Bramble Business Centre
DERBY DE1 .... 4 E6
Bramcote C of E School
BSTN/STPLFD NG9 .... 245 L2
Bramcote Hills
Comprehensive School
BSTN/STPLFD NG9 .... 231 L8
Bramcote Hills Primary School
BSTN/STPLFD NG9 .... 245 L1
Bramcote Leisure Centre
BSTN/STPLFD NG9 .... 245 K1
Bramcote Park
Comprehensive School
BSTN/STPLFD NG9 .... 245 K1
Bramley Vale County
Primary School
BSVR S44 .... 147 H2
Brampton Junior
& Infant School
CHSW S40 .... 2 C4
Branston Golf & Country Club
BUT DE14 .... 280 E4
Brantwood Independent
School for Girls
ABRD S7 .... 55 G2
Brassington Primary School
MTLK DE4 .... 181 K1
Breadsall C of E
Primary School
ILK DE7 .... 227 H6
Breadsall Hilltop Junior
& Infant School
DERBYE DE21 .... 241 H1

Breedon Priory Golf Club
MELB/CHEL DE73 .... 279 H5
Bridge Street Industrial Estate
CLCR S45 .... 144 F6
Bridge Surgery
STPNHL/WNHL DE15 .... 281 H2
Brigg County Infant School
ALFN DE55 .... 176 E4
Brimington Clinic
STV/CWN S43 .... 111 H2
Brimington Manor
County Infant School
STV/CWN S43 .... 111 J5
Brinsley Primary School
EWD/SEL/PNX NG16 .... 203 H2
Broadbottom C of E
Primary School
HYDE SK14 .... 24 C2
Broad Elms School
ECC S11 .... 54 C6
Brockley Primary School
BSVR S44 .... 113 J3
Brockwell Junior School
CHSW S40 .... 2 A1
Brookfield Community School
CHSW S40 .... 109 K8
Brookfield County
Junior School
SBK/MW NG20 .... 133 H4
Brookfield Industrial Estate
GLSP SK13 .... 17 H7
Brookfield Industrial Estate
MTLK DE4 .... 157 J6
Brookfield Primary School
MCKLVR DE3 .... 255 G2
Brookhill Leys Infant School
EWD/SEL/PNX NG16 .... 217 K1
Brookhill Leys Junior School
EWD/SEL/PNX NG16 .... 203 K8
Brooklands County
Infant School
LGEAT NG10 .... 261 G4
Brooklands Junior School
LGEAT NG10 .... 261 G3
Brooklyn Surgery
HEANOR DE75 .... 202 C8
Brookside Business Park
UTXR ST14 .... 248 A2
Brookside Primary School
MPL/ROM SK6 .... 42 B4
Brookside School
ILK DE7 .... 227 H6
Broomfield College
DERBYE DE21 .... 227 L5
Broomhill First School
MSFDW NG19 .... 164 C2
Broxtowe Borough Council
EWD/SEL/PNX NG16 .... 203 K8
Brunts Business Centre
MSFD NG18 .... 164 F2
The Brunts School
MSFD NG18 .... 165 G2
Bull Farm First School
MSFDW NG19 .... 149 G8
Bull Farm Middle School
MSFDW NG19 .... 149 G8
Burbage CP School
BUX SK17 .... 99 J4
Burton Albion Football Club
BUT DE14 .... 274 A4
Burton Muslim Mosque
BUT DE14 .... 273 M6
Burton-on-trent Police Station
BUT DE14 .... 274 A6
Burton Road Surgery
SWAD DE11 .... 283 H7
Burton Rugby Club
BUT DE14 .... 274 A8
Burton Technical College
BUTN/AL/TUT DE13 .... 264 F6
Burton Tennis & Squash Club
STPNHL/WNHL DE15 .... 274 E8
Burton upon Trent Golf Club
STPNHL/WNHL DE15 .... 282 C1
Burton-upon-trent
Technical College
BUT DE14 .... 274 B8
Buxton Community School
BUX SK17 .... 99 K4
Buxton County Infant School
BUX SK17 .... 99 M3
Buxton Hospital
BUX SK17 .... 99 M5
Buxton Museum & Art Gallery
BUX SK17 .... 99 K3
Buxton Rugby Club
BUX SK17 .... 99 M3
Buxworth Primary School
CHF/WBR SK23 .... 59 K1
CAB
DERBY DE1 .... 4 F5
Caldwell Hall School
MSHM DE12 .... 288 C3
Calow C of E Junior School
BSVR S44 .... 111 J7
Camms Endowed
C of E Primary School
MOS S20 .... 73 G6
Canalside Industrial Estate
LGEAT NG10 .... 244 F3
Carfield Primary School
SHEFS S8 .... 55 K5
Carlyle Infant School
NORM/LIT DE23 .... 255 L2
Carrfield Medical Centre
SHEFP/MNR S2 .... 55 L4
Carsic Junior School
ASH NG17 .... 163 G7
Carsington & Hopton
C of E Primary School
MTLK DE4 .... 182 B3
Carsington Sailing Club Ltd
ASHB DE6 .... 181 M7
Carterknowle & Dore
Medical Practice
ABRD S7 .... 55 H5
Carter Knowle Junior School
ABRD S7 .... 55 G5

Carter Lane First School
MSFD NG18 .... 165 H4
Carver Theatre
MPL/ROM SK6 .... 32 C4
Castle
BUTN/AL/TUT DE13 .... 263 L3
Castle Donington
Community College
CDON/KEG DE74 .... 271 L7
Castle Gresley Infant School
SWAD DE11 .... 289 H4
Castle Park Infants School
BUTN/AL/TUT DE13 .... 273 L2
Castle Street Medical Centre
BSVR S44 .... 113 K8
Castleton C of E (C)
Primary School
EDL/UDV S33 .... 48 E8
Castle View Industrial Estate
RDERBYSW DE65 .... 263 M2
Cathedral Road Clinic
DERBY DE1 .... 4 D2
Cavendish Close Infant School
DERBYE DE21 .... 241 K2
Cavendish Close Junior School
DERBYE DE21 .... 241 K2
Cavendish Golf Club
BUX SK17 .... 99 J2
Cavendish Hospital
BUX SK17 .... 99 K2
Cavendish Junior School
CHNE S41 .... 110 C2
Chaddesden Medical Centre
DERBYE DE21 .... 241 H4
Chapel-en-le-Frith Golf Club
CHF/WBR SK23 .... 60 A5
Chapel-en-le-Frith High School
CHF/WBR SK23 .... 60 D5
Charlesworth School
GLSP SK13 .... 24 F4
Charlotte County Infant School
ILK DE7 .... 217 H8
Charlton House Medical Centre
LGEAT NG10 .... 261 J2
Charnock Hall Primary School
HACK/IN S12 .... 56 E8
Charnwood Surgery
DERBY DE1 .... 4 E6
Chatsworth House
BKWL DE45 .... 124 C1
Chatsworth Surgery
CHSW S40 .... 109 L8
Chaucer Infant School
ILK DE7 .... 230 C2
Chaucer Junior School
ILK DE7 .... 230 C1
Chellaston Infant School
MELB/CHEL DE73 .... 257 J8
Chellaston School
MELB/CHEL DE73 .... 269 J1
Cherry Tree Infant School
DERBYE DE21 .... 241 L5
Cherry Tree Junior School
DERBYE DE21 .... 241 L5
Chesterfield Borough Council
CHNE S41 .... 110 D4
Chesterfield Borough Council
CHSW S40 .... 2 E7
Chesterfield Bowl
CHSW S40 .... 128 E3
Chesterfield Caravan
& Leisure Centre
DRON S18 .... 91 G7
Chesterfield College of
Technology & Arts
CHNE S41 .... 3 H2
Chesterfield Football Club Ltd
CHSW S40 .... 2 E3
Chesterfield Museum
CHNE S41 .... 3 J4
Chesterfield Rugby Club
CHNE S41 .... 110 D5
Chesterfield Small
Business Centre
CHNE S41 .... 110 D3
Chevin Golf Club
BPR/DUF DE56 .... 213 H5
The Chilwell Alderman
Pounder Infant School
BSTN/STPLFD NG9 .... 245 L5
Chilwell Meadows Surgery
BSTN/STPLFD NG9 .... 261 L1
Chinley CP School
CHF/WBR SK23 .... 60 C1
Christchurch Infants School
BUT DE14 .... 273 M8
Christ Church School
CHNE S41 .... 110 D5
Christ the King RC School
ALFN DE55 .... 175 K5
Church Broughton C of E
Primary School
RDERBYSW DE65 .... 251 L2
Church Gresley County
Infant School
SWAD DE11 .... 282 E8
Church of England School
HATH/EY S32 .... 86 C7
Church Street Medical Centre
EWD/SEL/PNX NG16 .... 203 H8
Church Wilne Water
Sports Club
BWSH/BRSTN DE72 .... 260 A5
Cifford C of E Grammar School
ECC S11 .... 55 G2
Cinema
DERBY DE1 .... 4 E5
City Road Industrial Park
DERBY DE1 .... 240 D3
Civic Centre
MSFDW NG19 .... 164 D2
Civic Theatre
MSFD NG18 .... 164 F3
Clarke Industrial Estate
BUT DE14 .... 274 B6
Clay Cross Community Hospital
CLCR S45 .... 145 G6

Clay Cross Infant School
CLCR S45 .... 144 F7
Clay Cross Junior School
CLCR S45 .... 144 F7
Clay House Business Centre
BUT DE14 .... 274 B7
Cliff College
HATH/EY S32 .... 106 A1
Clifton C of E Primary School
ASHB DE6 .... 207 J4
Clocktower Business Centre
STV/CWN S43 .... 92 D7
Cloudside Junior School
LGEAT NG10 .... 244 E4
Clough House Medical Centre
SHEFP/MNR S2 .... 55 L1
Clowne Infant School
STV/CWN S43 .... 95 H7
Clowne Junior School
STV/CWN S43 .... 95 H7
Clowne Welfare Sports Club
STV/CWN S43 .... 95 G7
Cockshut Lane Business Centre
MELB/CHEL DE73 .... 278 D2
Codnor Infant & Junior School
RIPLEY DE5 .... 201 L2
C of E Junior School
ASHZ LE65 .... 291 K4
College Street Health Centre
LGEAT NG10 .... 260 F1
The College
DERBY DE1 .... 4 A5
Combs County School
CHF/WBR SK23 .... 80 B1
Concordia Industrial Estate
LGEAT NG10 .... 260 F5
Copthorne Infant School
ALFN DE55 .... 175 K5
Corfield C of E Infant School
HEANOR DE75 .... 216 A1
Cossall Industrial Estate
ILK DE7 .... 217 L8
Cotmanhay County
Infant School
ILK DE7 .... 217 H5
Cotmanhay County
Junior School
ILK DE7 .... 217 H5
Coton-in-the-elms
C of E Primary School
MSHM DE12 .... 288 A7
County Offices
MSFD NG18 .... 164 D3
County Offices
MTLK DE4 .... 156 F4
Creswell C of E Infant School
WRKS S80 .... 115 H1
Creswell Industrial Estate
WRKS S80 .... 115 H2
Creswell Leisure Centre
WRKS S80 .... 115 J1
Crich Carr C of E
Primary School
MTLK DE4 .... 184 F1
Crich C of E Controlled
Infant School
MTLK DE4 .... 185 J1
Crich County Junior School
MTLK DE4 .... 185 K1
Croft Infant School
ALFN DE55 .... 175 K6
Croft Primary School
ASH NG17 .... 163 J8
Cromford Road
Industrial Estate
EWD/SEL/PNX NG16 .... 202 E6
Cromford School
MTLK DE4 .... 171 L4
Crown Court
DERBY DE1 .... 4 E2
Crown Industrial Estate
BUT DE14 .... 273 L8
Crown Special School
BUTN/AL/TUT DE13 .... 274 A1
The Culvert Gallery
ECC S11 .... 55 G2
Curbar County School
HATH/EY S32 .... 106 A1
The Curtain Gallery
ECC S11 .... 55 G2
The Curzon C of E
Primary School
DERBYW DE22 .... 226 A4
Cutthorpe Primary School
RCH S42 .... 109 G3
Dale Medical Centre
NORM/LIT DE23 .... 4 D9
Dale Primary School
NORM/LIT DE23 .... 240 B8
The Dale Primary School
MPL/ROM SK6 .... 32 A3
The Dales Medical Centre
ILK DE7 .... 229 G3
Dallimore Primary School
ILK DE7 .... 230 A6
Dame Catherine
Harpurs School
MELB/CHEL DE73 .... 277 K5
Danesmoor County
Infants School
CLCR S45 .... 145 H7
Daneswood County
Junior School
ASH NG17 .... 163 G3
Darley Churchtown
C of E Primary School
MTLK DE4 .... 140 D7
Darley Dale Primary School
MTLK DE4 .... 141 G8
Davelanie Clinic
ASHB DE6 .... 193 M8
Debdale Surgery
MSFDW NG19 .... 149 G8
Deer Park Primary School
RCH S42 .... 128 B7
De Ferrers High School
BUTN/AL/TUT DE13 .... 273 M2

Deincourt School
RCH S42 .... 145 J2
The Delves School
ALFN DE55 .... 187 J4
Denby Free C of E Junior
& Infant School
RIPLEY DE5 .... 215 G1
The Derby Chest Clinic
DERBY DE1 .... 4 E5
Derby City Council
DERBY DE1 .... 4 D2
Derby City Council
DERBY DE1 .... 5 G2
Derby City Council
DERBYE DE21 .... 241 G3
Derby City Council
DERBYSE DE24 .... 256 F2
Derby City Council
DERBYSE DE24 .... 257 H1
Derby City Council
DERBYW DE22 .... 239 K4
Derby City Council
DERBYW DE22 .... 240 C3
Derby City General Hospital
DERBYW DE22 .... 239 L8
Derby College
DERBYE DE21 .... 5 L2
Derby College of Further
Education
DERBY DE1 .... 4 D6
Derby College Wilmorton
DERBYSE DE24 .... 241 J8
Derby County Football Club
DERBYSE DE24 .... 241 H7
Derby County Football Club
NORM/LIT DE23 .... 256 E1
Derby Crown Court
DERBY DE1 .... 5 G3
Derby Independent
Grammar School for Boys
NORM/LIT DE23 .... 255 J3
Derby Moor Community School
NORM/LIT DE23 .... 255 L3
Derby Playhouse Theatre
DERBY DE1 .... 5 G5
Derby Regional
Swimming Pool
DERBYSE DE24 .... 256 F4
Derby Road Business Park
BUT DE14 .... 274 B4
Derby Rowing Club
DERBY DE1 .... 240 D3
Derbyshire County Council
CHNE S41 .... 3 H2
Derbyshire County Council
CHSW S40 .... 2 E3
Derbyshire County Council
DERBYE DE21 .... 240 E3
Derbyshire County Council
DERBYE DE21 .... 241 L4
Derbyshire County Council
DERBYW DE22 .... 240 A7
Derbyshire County Council
ECK/KIL S21 .... 73 H7
Derbyshire County Council
GLSP SK13 .... 17 M8
Derbyshire County Council
LGEAT NG10 .... 261 G2
Derbyshire County Cricket Club
DERBYE DE21 .... 5 K1
Derbyshire Royal
Infirmary N H S Trust
DERBY DE1 .... 5 G6
Derbyshire Royal Infirmary
N H S Trust
DERBYSE DE24 .... 257 G2
Derby Small Business Centre
DERBY DE1 .... 5 H6
Derby Small Business Centre
NORM/LIT DE23 .... 256 E1
Derby & South Derbyshire
Magistrates Court
DERBY DE1 .... 4 F3
Derby Superbowl
NORM/LIT DE23 .... 256 D3
Derby Trading Estate
DERBYE DE21 .... 240 E3
Derek Topp Gallery
MTLK DE4 .... 140 D2
Derwent Bus Centre
DERBY DE1 .... 5 G1
Derwent Business Park
RIPLEY DE5 .... 201 G1
Derwent Community School
DERBYE DE21 .... 240 F3
Derwent Gallery
HATH/EY S32 .... 86 F2
Derwent Medical Centre
DERBY DE1 .... 4 E1
Derwentside Industrial Estate
BPR/DUF DE56 .... 213 J1
Devonshire Royal Hospital
BUX SK17 .... 99 L2
Dimple Head Medical Centre
MTLK DE4 .... 185 K1
Dinting C of E School
GLSP SK13 .... 25 K1
Disley CP School
POY/DIS SK12 .... 43 G4
Dobcroft Infant School
ECC S11 .... 54 E6
Dobcroft Junior School
ECC S11 .... 54 E7
Donisthorpe Primary School
MSHM DE12 .... 295 K1
Dore Junior & Infant School
TOT/DORE S17 .... 69 G4
Dovedale CP School
LGEAT NG10 .... 260 D4
Dovefields Industrial Estate
UTXR ST14 .... 248 A3
Dove First School
UTXR ST14 .... 218 D6
Dovercourt Surgery
SHEFP/MNR S2 .... 56 B1
Doveridge CP School
ASHB DE6 .... 248 C4

Dove River Practice
  ASHB DE6 .... 250 B5
The Dower House
  & Dove Clinic
  BUTN/AL/TUT DE13 .... 264 E6
Draycott Parish Council
  BWSH/BRSTN DE72 .... 259 L3
Draycott Primary School
  BWSH/BRSTN DE72 .... 259 K3
Dr John Bingham Junior
  & Infant School
  SHEFS S8 .... 70 D5
Dronfield County Junior School
  DRON S18 .... 90 D1
Dronfield Health Centre
  DRON S18 .... 90 D1
Dronfield Infant School
  DRON S18 .... 90 D1
The Dronfield School
  DRON S18 .... 70 B8
Dronfield Sports Centre
  DRON S18 .... 90 C1
Drs Rasheed & Masud Surgery
  ALFN DE55 .... 176 B1
Duckmanton Primary School
  BSVR S44 .... 112 C5
Duffield Art Gallery
  BPR/DUF DE56 .... 213 J7
Duffield Road Industrial Estate
  DERBYE DE21 .... 226 F4
Duke of Norfolk C of E School
  GLSP SK13 .... 26 A1
Dukeries Industrial Estate
  WRKN S81 .... 77 M4
Dunston Primary School
  CHNE S41 .... 110 A2
Dunston Trading Estate
  CHNE S41 .... 91 H8
Earl Sterndale School
  BUX SK17 .... 118 F7
East Derbyshire Magistrates
  ILK DE7 .... 230 B2
East Midlands Nuffield
  Hospital
  NORM/LIT DE23 .... 255 J4
East Staffordshire
  District Council
  BUT DE14 .... 273 L6
East Staffordshire
  District Council
  UTXR ST14 .... 247 M2
East View Industrial Estate
  SBK/MW NG20 .... 133 J4
Eastwood Comprehensive
  Lower School
  EWD/SEL/PNX NG16 .... 203 K7
Eastwood Comprehensive
  School
  EWD/SEL/PNX NG16 .... 203 H7
Eastwood Health Centre
  EWD/SEL/PNX NG16 .... 203 K8
Eastwood House Surgery
  STV/CWN S43 .... 95 H6
Eastwood Junior School
  EWD/SEL/PNX NG16 .... 203 J8
Eastwood & Kimberley
  Community College
  EWD/SEL/PNX NG16 .... 203 J7
Eastwood Town Cricket Club
  EWD/SEL/PNX NG16 .... 203 K7
Ecclesall Infant School
  ECC S11 .... 54 C4
Ecclesall Medical Centre
  ECC S11 .... 54 D5
The Ecclesbourne School
  BPR/DUF DE56 .... 213 H7
Ecclesbourne Surgery
  BPR/DUF DE56 .... 213 H7
Eckington Health Centre
  ECK/KIL S21 .... 73 H7
Eckington Junior School
  ECK/KIL S21 .... 73 G7
Eckington School
  ECK/KIL S21 .... 72 D7
Edale C of E (C) School
  EDL/UDV S33 .... 47 M2
Eden Surgery
  ILK DE7 .... 230 C4
Edge Hill Junior School
  STPNHL/WHNL DE15 .... 281 J3
Edward Revill Endowed
  School
  ALFN DE55 .... 159 M8
Egginton Primary School
  RDERBYSW DE65 .... 265 L5
Elite Business Park
  ALFN DE55 .... 175 L5
Elmsleigh County
  Infant School
  SWAD DE11 .... 282 E4
Elmwood Medical Centre
  BUX SK17 .... 99 J4
Elton C of E Primary School
  MTLK DE4 .... 154 B3
Elvaston Castle Working Estate
  Museum
  BWSH/BRSTN DE72 .... 258 D4
Elvaston Cricket Club
  BWSH/BRSTN DE72 .... 258 C3
Emmett Carr Surgery
  ECK/KIL S21 .... 93 L2
Endland Industrial Estate
  DERBYW DE22 .... 240 A6
English Martyrs RC School
  LGEAT NG10 .... 260 E1
Ensor Trading Estate
  NM/HAY SK22 .... 43 M4
Erewash Borough Council
  ILK DE7 .... 230 B3
Erewash Borough Council
  LGEAT NG10 .... 244 F5
Erewash Borough Council
  LGEAT NG10 .... 261 G2
Erewash Museum
  ILK DE7 .... 230 C2
Eskdale CP School
  BSTN/STPLFD NG9 .... 245 L5

Ethel Wainwright First School
  MSFDW NG19 .... 164 C2
Etherow Industrial Estate
  GLSP SK13 .... 17 H5
Eton Park Junior School
  BUT DE14 .... 274 A3
Etwall Leisure Centre
  RDERBYSW DE65 .... 253 L6
Etwall Primary School
  RDERBYSW DE65 .... 253 L6
Eureka Primary School
  SWAD DE11 .... 283 G5
Eyam C of E Primary School
  HATH/EY S32 .... 86 A5
The Eye Gallery
  DERBY DE1 .... 4 E3
Fairfield CP School
  BSTN/STPLFD NG9 .... 245 G4
Fairmeadows Gm Primary
  School
  SWAD DE11 .... 282 B5
Falkland House Surgery
  ECC S11 .... 54 D4
Family Medical Centre
  DERBYSE DE24 .... 257 K2
Farmilo First School
  MSFDW NG19 .... 148 F6
Fauld Industrial Estate
  BUTN/AL/TUT DE13 .... 263 H4
Femwork Industrial Estate
  BUT DE14 .... 274 B5
Field House County
  Infant School
  ILK DE7 .... 230 C4
Findern CP School
  RDERBYSW DE65 .... 267 H2
Firbeck School
  WOL/BIL/BRX NG8 .... 231 L6
Fire Brigade Sports Club
  BUT DE14 .... 273 M8
Firfield Primary School
  BWSH/BRSTN DE72 .... 260 B3
Firs Estate Primary School
  DERBYW DE22 .... 4 B8
The Fitzherbert C of E
  Primary School
  ASHB DE6 .... 193 K1
Flash Ce C Primary School
  BUX SK17 .... 116 E7
Flower Gallery
  DERBYW DE22 .... 4 A2
Forest Glade Primary School
  ASH NG17 .... 163 K6
Forest Town Primary School
  MSFDW NG19 .... 165 K1
Foxwood School
  BSTN/STPLFD NG9 .... 245 L1
Frederick Gent School
  ALFN DE55 .... 176 E5
Frederick Harrison
  Infant School
  BSTN/STPLFD NG9 .... 245 J2
Friargate Gallery
  DERBY DE1 .... 4 D3
Friar Gate Surgery
  DERBY DE1 .... 4 C3
Friargate Surgery
  DERBY DE1 .... 4 C2
Friesland School
  BWSH/BRSTN DE72 .... 244 C5
Fullivers Kingdom
  MTLK DE4 .... 171 K2
Furness Vale Industrial Estate
  CHF/WBR SK23 .... 44 A6
Furness Vale Primary School
  CHF/WBR SK23 .... 44 A7
Gainsbrough Galleries
  MPL/ROM SK6 .... 32 C4
The Gallery
  ASHB DE6 .... 193 L8
The Gallery
  DERBY DE1 .... 4 F4
The Gallery
  GLSP SK13 .... 25 M1
The Gallery
  ILK DE7 .... 230 B3
Gamesley County
  Primary School
  GLSP SK13 .... 17 H8
Gateway Christian School
  ILK DE7 .... 229 J8
Gayton Junior School
  NORM/LIT DE23 .... 256 A4
George Holmes Business Park
  SWAD DE11 .... 282 D7
George Spencer Secondary
  Mixed School
  BSTN/STPLFD NG9 .... 245 H5
Gilbert Heathcote
  Infant School
  CHNE S41 .... 110 C2
Gladys Buxton School
  DRON S18 .... 70 F8
Gleadless Clinic
  HACK/IN S12 .... 56 E7
Gleadless Primary School
  HACK/IN S12 .... 56 E5
Glebe County Junior School
  ALFN DE55 .... 176 D5
Glossop Cricket Club
  GLSP SK13 .... 25 M1
Glossopdale College
  GLSP SK13 .... 17 J6
Glossopdale Community
  College
  GLSP SK13 .... 17 M8
Glossop & District Golf Club
  GLSP SK13 .... 26 D2
Glossop Football Club
  GLSP SK13 .... 25 L1
Glossop Leisure Centre
  GLSP SK13 .... 26 A2
Glossop Rugby Club
  GLSP SK13 .... 25 H3
Goyt Medical Practice
  CHF/WBR SK23 .... 60 D4
Goyt Valley Industrial Estate
  CHF/WBR SK23 .... 44 A6

Goyt Valley Medical Practice
  CHF/WBR SK23 .... 59 H2
Granby CP Junior School
  ILK DE7 .... 217 H7
Grandby Gallery
  BKWL DE45 .... 123 G5
Grange County Infants School
  BUT DE14 .... 273 L6
Grange Primary School
  LGEAT NG10 .... 261 J2
Granville Community School
  SWAD DE11 .... 283 H6
Grassmoor Primary School
  RCH S42 .... 129 H8
Greasley Beauvale D H
  Lawrence Infant School
  EWD/SEL/PNX NG16 .... 203 L7
Greasley Beau Vale
  Junior School
  EWD/SEL/PNX NG16 .... 203 M8
Greasley Sports Centre
  EWD/SEL/PNX NG16 .... 203 L7
Greenbank Leisure Centre
  SWAD DE11 .... 282 E6
Greenhill Health Centre
  SHEFS S8 .... 70 B4
Greenhill Primary School
  SHEFS S8 .... 70 B3
The Green Infant School
  ALFN DE55 .... 176 D4
Green Lane Gallery
  DERBY DE1 .... 4 E6
Green Lane Surgery
  BPR/DUF DE56 .... 199 J6
Greenline Business Park
  BUT DE14 .... 273 L7
Greenway Natural
  Health Centre
  TOT/DORE S17 .... 69 G6
Greggs Mill First School
  MSFD NG18 .... 165 H4
Gresley Rovers Football Club
  SWAD DE11 .... 289 L1
Greystones First School
  ECC S11 .... 54 D3
Greystones Medical Centre
  ECC S11 .... 54 E3
Greystones Primary School
  ECC S11 .... 54 E3
Grindleford Primary School
  HATH/EY S32 .... 86 F2
Group Practice Centre
  MSFDW NG19 .... 164 D2
Group Surgery & Clinic
  DERBYW DE22 .... 226 A3
The Grove Hospital
  BWSH/BRSTN DE72 .... 271 J1
Hackenthorpe Medical Centre
  HACK/IN S12 .... 57 K7
Hade Edge Primary School
  HOLM/MEL HD7 .... 9 L2
Hadfield Clinic
  GLSP SK13 .... 17 K5
Hadfield Industrial Estate
  GLSP SK13 .... 17 J4
Hadfield Infant School
  GLSP SK13 .... 17 J6
Hady School
  CHNE S41 .... 111 G8
Haggonfields County
  Primary School
  WRKS S80 .... 77 K6
Hague Bar Primary School
  NM/HAY SK22 .... 43 J7
Halfway Infant School
  MOS S20 .... 73 H3
Halfway Junior School
  MOS S20 .... 73 H3
Hallam Fields Junior School
  ILK DE7 .... 230 C5
Hallam Primary School
  FUL S10 .... 53 M1
Hallamshire Business Park
  FUL S10 .... 55 H1
The Hallamshire Gallery
  ECC S11 .... 54 E3
Hallamshire Natural
  Health Centre
  ECC S11 .... 54 F2
Handsworth Branch Clinic
  HAN/WDH S13 .... 57 J1
Handsworth Road
  Medical Centre
  HAN/WDH S13 .... 57 J1
Hardwick Infant School
  NORM/LIT DE23 .... 256 C1
Harpur Hill Primary School
  BUX SK17 .... 99 M6
Harrington County
  Junior School
  LGEAT NG10 .... 260 E1
Harthill Junior & Infant School
  AU/AST/KP S26 .... 75 H1
Hartington C of E School
  BUX SK17 .... 151 H5
Hartington Industrial Estate
  STV/CWN S43 .... 93 H6
Hartshorne C of E
  Primary School
  SWAD DE11 .... 283 K4
Hasland Hall
  Community School
  CHNE S41 .... 129 G3
Hasland Primary Infant School
  CHNE S41 .... 128 F2
Hasland Primary Junior School
  CHNE S41 .... 128 F3
Hathersage Swimming Pool
  HATH/EY S32 .... 66 D3
Hattersley Health Clinic
  HYDE SK14 .... 16 B8
Hattersley High School
  HYDE SK14 .... 16 A8
Hatton School
  RDERBYSW DE65 .... 264 A1
Hayfield Parish Council
  NM/HAY SK22 .... 35 G7

Hayfield Primary School
  NM/HAY SK22 .... 34 F7
H C M Industrial Estate
  BUT DE14 .... 274 B6
Heage Primary School
  BPR/DUF DE56 .... 186 A8
Healdswood Infant School
  ASH NG17 .... 163 G4
Healdswood Surgery
  ASH NG17 .... 163 G4
Health Clinic
  HYDE SK14 .... 17 G5
Heanor Gate Industrial Estate
  HEANOR DE75 .... 216 A1
Heanor Gate School
  HEANOR DE75 .... 215 M1
Heanor Health Centre
  HEANOR DE75 .... 216 B1
Heanor & Langley Mill District
  Memorial Hospital
  HEANOR DE75 .... 216 C1
Heanor Leisure Centre
  HEANOR DE75 .... 216 C1
Heanor Town Sports Ground
  HEANOR DE75 .... 216 B1
Heatherley Primary School
  MSFDW NG19 .... 165 J1
Heath Fields Primary School
  RDERBYSW DE65 .... 263 M1
Heath House Clinic
  UTXR ST14 .... 247 L1
Heath Primary School
  BSVR S44 .... 146 C1
Heeley Business Centre
  SHEFP/MNR S2 .... 55 K2
Heeley Green Surgery
  SHEFP/MNR S2 .... 55 L4
Heeley Retail Park
  SHEFS S8 .... 55 J7
Heights of Abraham
  MTLK DE4 .... 156 D8
Hemsworth Primary School
  GLV S14 .... 56 A8
Henmore Trading Estate
  ASHB DE6 .... 207 K2
Henry Bradley County
  Infant School
  STV/CWN S43 .... 111 J2
The Henry Prince School
  ASHB DE6 .... 207 G3
Herbert Strutt Primary School
  BPR/DUF DE56 .... 199 H8
Herdings Primary School
  GLV S14 .... 56 B8
Highfield County Junior
  & Infant School
  LGEAT NG10 .... 244 F8
Highfield School
  BKWL DE45 .... 122 E6
Highfields Lower School
  MTLK DE4 .... 156 F7
Highfields School
  MTLK DE4 .... 157 H3
High Lane Medical Centre
  MPL/ROM SK6 .... 42 B3
High Lane Primary School
  MPL/ROM SK6 .... 42 B2
High Oakham Middle School
  MSFD NG18 .... 164 E7
High Peak Borough Council
  GLSP SK13 .... 25 L1
High Peak Golf Club
  BUX SK17 .... 100 B1
High Storrs School
  ECC S11 .... 54 C4
High Street Medical Centre
  STV/CWN S43 .... 93 H8
Hillocks Primary School
  ASH NG17 .... 163 L7
Hillside Medical Centre
  BSTN/STPLFD NG9 .... 245 J3
Hillstown Business Centre
  BSVR S44 .... 131 L3
Hill Street School
  STPNHL/WHNL DE15 .... 281 H2
Hilltop School
  ASHB DE6 .... 207 M2
Hilton Industrial Estate
  RDERBYSW DE65 .... 253 G7
Hilton Primary School
  RDERBYSW DE65 .... 253 G8
Hingorani Clinic
  STPNHL/WHNL DE15 .... 274 D7
Hodthorpe County
  Primary School
  WRKS S80 .... 96 F5
Holbrook C of E Infant School
  BPR/DUF DE56 .... 213 M3
Hollies Medical Centre
  ECC S11 .... 55 G3
Hollingwood Junior
  & Infant School
  STV/CWN S43 .... 111 K1
Hollingworth Primary School
  HYDE SK14 .... 16 F5
Hollinsclough School
  BUX SK17 .... 118 A8
Hollis Hospital
  TOT/DORE S17 .... 54 B8
Hollybrook Medical Centre
  NORM/LIT DE23 .... 255 J4
Hollyhill Primary School
  EWD/SEL/PNX NG16 .... 189 K3
Holly House School
  CHNE S41 .... 91 K7
Holly Primary School
  MSFDW NG19 .... 165 K1
Holme Hall Primary School
  CHSW S40 .... 109 L5
Holme School
  HOLM/MEL HD7 .... 8 B1
Holmgate Primary School
  CLCR S45 .... 144 D6
Holt House Infant School
  ABRD S7 .... 55 G6
Holymoorside Primary School
  RCH S42 .... 127 G3

Holy Rosary RC Primary
  School
  STPNHL/WHNL DE15 .... 274 C7
Holy Trinity C E Primary
  School
  BUT DE14 .... 274 B6
Hood Park Leisure Centre
  ASHZ LE65 .... 291 L3
Hope County Primary School
  EDL/UDV S33 .... 49 J6
Hope Valley College
  EDL/UDV S33 .... 49 J7
Horninglow Clinic
  BUTN/AL/TUT DE13 .... 273 L4
Horninglow County Infants
  Speech & Language Unit
  BUTN/AL/TUT DE13 .... 273 M3
Horninglow Infants School
  BUTN/AL/TUT DE13 .... 273 M4
Horning Low Surgery
  BUTN/AL/TUT DE13 .... 273 L4
The Horse Fair Gallery
  ALFN DE55 .... 175 J6
Horsley C of E Primary School
  DERBYE DE21 .... 214 C4
Horsley Lodge Golf Club
  ILK DE7 .... 214 E6
Horsley Woodhouse
  Primary School
  ILK DE7 .... 215 G4
Howard Street Group Practice
  GLSP SK13 .... 25 M1
Howitt House School
  BUTN/AL/TUT DE13 .... 262 B7
H S B C Sports Club
  TOT/DORE S17 .... 69 G1
Hulland C of E Primary School
  ASHB DE6 .... 196 C7
Hunloke Park Primary School
  RCH S42 .... 128 D6
Hunloke Secondary School
  CHSW S40 .... 128 D3
Hunters Bar Junior
  & Infant School
  ECC S11 .... 54 F2
Hurst Clough CP School
  HYDE SK14 .... 24 B1
Huthwaite All Saints
  C of E Infant School
  ASH NG17 .... 162 C6
Huthwaite Leisure Centre
  ASH NG17 .... 162 C6
Ilam C of E Primary School
  ASHB DE6 .... 178 B8
Ilkeston Bowl
  ILK DE7 .... 230 B3
Ilkeston Community Hospital
  ILK DE7 .... 217 G3
Ilkeston School
  ILK DE7 .... 230 A2
Ilkeston Swimming Pool
  ILK DE7 .... 230 B1
Industrial Estate
  HEANOR DE75 .... 216 A1
Industrial Estate
  RIPLEY DE5 .... 200 E1
Industrial Estate
  SWAD DE11 .... 289 K1
Industrial Museum
  DERBY DE1 .... 4 F2
Infant Welfare Clinic
  BUT DE14 .... 274 A8
Inkersall Primary School
  STV/CWN S43 .... 111 M3
Insley Industrial Estate
  BUT DE14 .... 273 K8
Intake Business Centre
  MSFD NG18 .... 164 C4
Intake Junior & Infant School
  HACK/IN S12 .... 56 E4
Ironbridge Industrial Estate
  HAN/WDH S13 .... 57 M2
Ironville & Codnor
  Park Primary School
  EWD/SEL/PNX NG16 .... 188 C6
Ivanhoe Industrial Estate
  ASHZ LE65 .... 291 K2
Ivanhoe School
  & Community College
  ASHZ LE65 .... 291 M3
Ivy Grove Surgery
  RIPLEY DE5 .... 201 G1
Ivy House School
  NORM/LIT DE23 .... 5 J9
Jamia Hanfia Taleem-ul-islam
  Ahle Sunnat Wal
  Jamaat Mosque
  NORM/LIT DE23 .... 4 D8
Jaunty Springs Health Centre
  HACK/IN S12 .... 56 E6
The Jessop Medical Practice
  RIPLEY DE5 .... 201 G1
John Carr Industrial Estate
  BUT DE14 .... 273 L8
John Davies Primary School
  ASH NG17 .... 162 C6
John Duncan School
  BUX SK17 .... 99 J1
John Flamsteed
  Community School
  RIPLEY DE5 .... 200 D8
John King Infant School
  EWD/SEL/PNX NG16 .... 177 G7
John of Rolleston
  Primary School
  BUTN/AL/TUT DE13 .... 264 E6
John Port School
  RDERBYSW DE65 .... 253 L6
Jordanthorpe Health Centre
  SHEFS S8 .... 70 E4
Junior & Infant School
  BPR/DUF DE56 .... 214 D2
Kedleston Hall (NT)
  DERBYW DE22 .... 225 H5
Kedleston Park Golf Club
  DERBYW DE22 .... 225 K4
Kensington Junior School
  ILK DE7 .... 230 D3

Killamarsh County Junior
& Infant School
ECK/KIL S21 .... **74** B3
Killamarsh Leisure Centre
ECK/KIL S21 .... **74** A3
Killamarsh Medical Centre
ECK/KIL S21 .... **73** M3
King Ecgbert Secondary
School
TOT/DORE S17 .... **69** G4
King Edward School
MSFD NG18 .... **164** F5
Kingsfield Industrial Estate
MTLK DE4 .... **183** H3
Kings Mead Clinic
DERBY DE1 .... **4** C1
Kingsmead Industrial Estate
DERBYW DE22 .... **240** A4
Kings Mead Infant School
DERBY DE1 .... **4** C1
Kings Mill Hospital
MSFDW NG19 .... **163** M6
Kings Mill Sailing Club
ASH NG17 .... **163** M8
Kingsway Hospital
DERBYW DE22 .... **239** M6
Kingsway Industrial Park
DERBYW DE22 .... **239** L5
Kingsway Retail Park
DERBYW DE22 .... **239** M5
Kirk Hallam Community School
ILK DE7 .... **230** A4
Kirk Hallam Ladywood
County School
ILK DE7 .... **230** A5
Kirk Ireton C of E School
BPR/DUF DE56 .... **196** E1
Kirk Langley C of E
Primary School
ASHB DE6 .... **224** C8
Kirkstead Junior School
EWD/SEL/PNX NG16 .... **177** G7
Kissing Gate Leisure Centre
SBK/MW NG20 .... **133** J6
Kniveton C of E Primary School
ASHB DE6 .... **180** F8
Knowles Fine Art Gallery
ASHB DE6 .... **209** L7
Knowles Industrial Estate
CHF/WBR SK23 .... **43** M7
Ladybrook Junior School
MSFDW NG19 .... **164** A2
Ladycross Infant School
LGEAT NG10 .... **244** E4
Ladylea Industrial Estate
ILK DE7 .... **214** E3
Lady Manners School
BKWL DE45 .... **122** F6
Lady Manners School
BKWL DE45 .... **123** G4
Lakeside Infant School
LGEAT NG10 .... **260** E5
Lammas School
ASH NG17 .... **163** H7
Lancaster Sports Centre
DERBY DE1 .... **4** D2
Landau Forte College
DERBY DE1 .... **4** F1
Langley Infant School
HEANOR DE75 .... **216** D1
Langley Mill Junior
Mixed School
EWD/SEL/PNX NG16 .... **202** E7
Langley Mill Junior School
EWD/SEL/PNX NG16 .... **202** D6
Langley Park Industrial Estate
EWD/SEL/PNX NG16 .... **202** E7
Lansdowne County
Infants School
BUT DE14 .... **274** A5
Lantern Theatre
ABRD S7 .... **55** H1
Larklands County Infant School
ILK DE7 .... **230** D2
The Lawrence Museum
EWD/SEL/PNX NG16 .... **203** J7
Leabrooks Medical Centre
ALFN DE55 .... **187** L3
Leander Rowing Club
BUT DE14 .... **274** C7
Lea Primary School
MTLK DE4 .... **172** D3
Lees Brook Community School
DERBYE DE21 .... **241** L2
Lenthall School
DRON S18 .... **70** B4
Leyfield Surgery
STV/CWN S43 .... **93** J8
Leys County Junior School
ALFN DE55 .... **175** M6
Lime Grove Medical Centre
MTLK DE4 .... **156** F5
Limes Medical Centre
ALFN DE55 .... **175** K6
Lime Tree Business Park
MTLK DE4 .... **156** F6
Linton Primary School
MSHM DE12 .... **289** G5
Little Eaton Primary School
DERBYE DE21 .... **226** F2
Littleover Community School
NORM/LIT DE23 .... **255** J2
Littleover Medical Centre
NORM/LIT DE23 .... **255** L1
Little Theatre Co
STPNHL/WNHL DE15 .... **281** J2
Littlewick Medical Centre
ILK DE7 .... **230** C3
Litton C of E Primary School
BUX SK17 .... **84** B7
Lodge Moor Medical Centre
FUL S10 .... **53** K1
Longdendale High School
HYDE SK14 .... **16** F5
Longdendale Recreation Centre
HYDE SK14 .... **16** C7
Long Eaton Community School
LGEAT NG10 .... **261** G3

The Long Eaton & District
Arts Council
LGEAT NG10 .... **261** H3
Longford Parochial C of E
Primary School
ASHB DE6 .... **236** A2
Longlane C of E Primary School
ASHB DE6 .... **237** G2
Longmoor Primary School
LGEAT NG10 .... **244** F7
Longstone C of E
Primary School
BKWL DE45 .... **104** C6
Longwood County
Infant School
EWD/SEL/PNX NG16 .... **188** F1
Lons County Infant School
RIPLEY DE5 .... **187** G8
Loscoe C of E Primary School
HEANOR DE75 .... **201** L6
Loughborough College
ASHZ LE65 .... **291** L4
Lowedges Primary School
SHEFS S8 .... **70** C4
Lower School
LGEAT NG10 .... **261** G4
Loxley Hall Special School
UTXR ST14 .... **246** F5
Ludworth Primary School
MPL/ROM SK6 .... **32** D2
Lum Farm Leisure Centre
RIPLEY DE5 .... **201** H5
Lyncroft Primary School
EWD/SEL/PNX NG16 .... **203** K7
Mackworth College Derby
DERBYW DE22 .... **239** J5
Main Line Industrial Estate
BUTN/AL/TUT DE13 .... **274** C4
Main Shopping Centre
DERBY DE1 .... **5** G4
Makki Mosque
SHEFS S8 .... **55** K4
Maltings Industrial Estate
BUT DE14 .... **274** B4
Manor Clinic
SHEFP/MNR S2 .... **56** C4
Manor House School
ASHZ LE65 .... **291** M4
Manor House Surgery
GLSP SK13 .... **26** A1
Manor Industrial Estate
BUT DE14 .... **274** A6
Manor Lodge Middle School
SHEFP/MNR S2 .... **56** B1
Manor Lodge Primary School
SHEFP/MNR S2 .... **56** B1
Manor School
MSFDW NG19 .... **149** M5
Manor School
MSHM DE12 .... **289** L7
Manor Top Medical Centre
HACK/IN S12 .... **56** D4
Mansfield Gas & Sports Club
MSFD NG18 .... **164** F4
Mansfield Lawn Tennis Club
MSFDW NG19 .... **164** D1
Mansfield Leisure Centre
MSFDW NG19 .... **164** D2
Mansfield Magistrate Courts
MSFDW NG19 .... **164** D2
Mansfield Town Football Club
MSFD NG18 .... **164** D5
Mapperley C of E
Primary School
ILK DE7 .... **216** C7
Mapplewells Junior
& Infant School
ASH NG17 .... **177** L1
Markeaton Primary School
DERBYW DE22 .... **240** B3
Market
DERBY DE1 .... **4** F4
Market Hall
BUT DE14 .... **274** B8
Marlpool Junior School
HEANOR DE75 .... **216** D1
Marple Clinic
MPL/ROM SK6 .... **32** C4
The Marple Cottage Surgery
MPL/ROM SK6 .... **32** C5
Marple Gallery
MPL/ROM SK6 .... **32** C4
Marsh Lane Primary School
ECK/KIL S21 .... **72** B7
Marsh Lane Trading Estate
NM/HAY SK22 .... **44** A3
Marston Montgomery C of E
Primary School
ASHB DE6 .... **233** H1
Mary Howitt Infant
Community School
HEANOR DE75 .... **202** A8
Mary Swanick Primary School
CHNE S41 .... **91** K7
Matlock All Saints C of E
Infant School
MTLK DE4 .... **156** E4
Matlock Bath Holy Trinity
C of E Primary School
MTLK DE4 .... **171** K2
Matlock County Infant School
MTLK DE4 .... **157** G4
Matlock Golf Club
MTLK DE4 .... **157** H2
Matlock Junior School
MTLK DE4 .... **157** G5
Matlock Town Football Club
MTLK DE4 .... **156** F5
Matthew Holland
Comprehensive School
EWD/SEL/PNX NG16 .... **189** J3
Maun Valley Industrial Estate
ASH NG17 .... **163** J.8
Meadow Brookes
Business Park
LGEAT NG10 .... **261** K4

Meadow Farm
Community Primary School
DERBYE DE21 .... **241** K6
Meadowhead School
SHEFS S8 .... **70** D3
Meadow Lane Industrial Estate
ALFN DE55 .... **175** L5
Meadows Community School
CHNE S41 .... **91** L7
The Meadows Primary School
BPR/DUF DE56 .... **213** G4
Measham Clinic
MSHM DE12 .... **295** M5
Meersbrook Bank
Primary School
SHEFS S8 .... **55** J5
Melbourne Junior
& Infant School
MELB/CHEL DE73 .... **278** E2
Mellor CP School
MPL/ROM SK6 .... **33** H4
Mellor Primary School
MPL/ROM SK6 .... **33** H4
Mellor Sports Club
MPL/ROM SK6 .... **33** G4
Memorial Hall School
SWAD DE11 .... **282** B4
Merlin Theatre
ABRD S7 .... **55** G3
The Merrill Community
School & Sixth Form College
DERBYSE DE24 .... **257** H4
Michael House School
HEANOR DE75 .... **216** D4
Mickleover Primary School
MCKLVR DE3 .... **239** G8
Mickleover Surgery
MCKLVR DE3 .... **239** H8
Mickley County Infant School
ALFN DE55 .... **159** M6
Middlecroft Leisure Centre
STV/CWN S43 .... **112** A3
Middleton County
Primary School
MTLK DE4 .... **171** G6
Middleton Top Visitor's Centre
MTLK DE4 .... **171** G7
Milford County School
BPR/DUF DE56 .... **213** K3
Millennium Business Centre
DERBYE DE21 .... **241** H6
Millview Surgery
MSFD NG18 .... **164** D3
Moira CP School
MSHM DE12 .... **290** E4
Molyneaux Business Park
MTLK DE4 .... **140** E7
Moneyash C of E (C)
Primary School
BKWL DE45 .... **136** F1
Montage Gallery
DERBY DE1 .... **4** E2
The Moore Clinic
BPR/DUF DE56 .... **199** J6
Moorgreen Industrial Park
EWD/SEL/PNX NG16 .... **203** L5
Moorhead Primary School
DERBYSE DE24 .... **257** J4
Moor Lane First School
MSFD NG18 .... **164** C5
Morley Primary School
ILK DE7 .... **228** A3
Mortimer Wilson
Secondary School
ALFN DE55 .... **175** K7
Mosaic Art & Craft Gallery
BUX SK17 .... **99** L3
Mosborough Medical Centre
MOS S20 .... **72** F3
Mosborough Primary School
MOS S20 .... **73** G3
Mosley County Primary School
BUTN/AL/TUT DE13 .... **272** E3
Mosque
BUT DE14 .... **280** F2
Mosque
NORM/LIT DE23 .... **4** F9
Mossbrook Special School
SHEFS S8 .... **70** F2
Mottram C of E Primary School
HYDE SK14 .... **16** D7
Mount St Marys College
ECK/KIL S21 .... **73** M8
Mugginton (C of E)
Primary School
ASHB DE6 .... **211** M4
Mundy C E Junior School
HEANOR DE75 .... **216** C1
Murray Park Community
School
MCKLVR DE3 .... **239** J2
Museum
ECC S11 .... **54** F2
Museum & Art Gallery
DERBY DE1 .... **4** E3
Museum & Art Gallery
MSFD NG18 .... **164** F4
National Tramway Museum
MTLK DE4 .... **173** H8
Nether Edge Hospital
ECC S11 .... **55** G4
Nether Green Infant School
FUL S10 .... **54** A2
Nether Green Junior School
FUL S10 .... **54** B2
Netherthorpe
Comprehensive School
STV/CWN S43 .... **93** K8
Nettleworth Infant School
MSFDW NG19 .... **149** M6
Newbold C of E School
CHNE S41 .... **110** B3
Newbold Community School
CHNE S41 .... **110** B3
Newchase Business Park
DERBYSE DE24 .... **256** F1
Newfield School
SHEFS S8 .... **55** M7

Newgate First School
MSFD NG18 .... **164** F3
Newhall County Infant School
SWAD DE11 .... **282** C3
Newhall County Junior School
SWAD DE11 .... **282** B4
Newhall Surgery
SWAD DE11 .... **282** C4
Newholme Hospital
BKWL DE45 .... **123** G3
New Mills CP School
NM/HAY SK22 .... **43** L2
New Mills Football Club
NM/HAY SK22 .... **44** A2
New Mills School & Sixth
Form Centre
NM/HAY SK22 .... **43** M3
New Mills Swimming Pool
NM/HAY SK22 .... **43** M2
New Mills Town Council
NM/HAY SK22 .... **43** L3
The New Surgery
BUX SK17 .... **83** M6
Newton Primary School
ALFN DE55 .... **161** K7
Newton Solney C of E
Infant School
STPNHL/WNHL DE15 .... **275** H2
Newtown CP School
NM/HAY SK22 .... **43** L4
New Whittington Infant School
STV/CWN S43 .... **92** A6
New Whittington Primary
Junior School
CHNE S41 .... **92** A7
Nightingale Business Park
DERBYSE DE24 .... **257** G2
Nightingale Infant School
DERBYSE DE24 .... **256** F3
Nightingale Junior School
DERBYSE DE24 .... **256** F2
Noel Baker Community School
DERBYSE DE24 .... **257** J6
Norbury C of E Primary School
ASHB DE6 .... **219** H2
Norfolk Middle School
SHEFP/MNR S2 .... **56** B2
Norfolk Park Health Centre
SHEFP/MNR S2 .... **55** M2
Normanton Junior School
NORM/LIT DE23 .... **256** B3
North Derbyshire College
WRKS S80 .... **115** H2
North Derbyshire
Health Authority
CHSW S40 .... **3** G2
North Derbyshire
Tertiary College
BSVR S44 .... **131** K1
North Derbyshire
Tertiary College
SBK/MW NG20 .... **133** H6
North Derbyshire
Tertiary College
STV/CWN S43 .... **95** H6
North East Derbyshire
District Council
CHSW S40 .... **2** F3
North East Derbyshire
District Council
DRON S18 .... **90** D1
North East Derbyshire
District Council
DRON S18 .... **90** E1
North East Derbyshire
District Council
RCH S42 .... **145** K3
Northfield Infant School
MSFDW NG19 .... **149** K5
Northfield Junior School
DRON S18 .... **70** F7
Northgate Surgery
UTXR ST14 .... **247** M2
Northside Business Park
BUT DE14 .... **274** B4
North Wingfield County
Junior School
RCH S42 .... **145** J3
North Wingfield County
Primary School
RCH S42 .... **145** J3
North Wingfield Infant School
RCH S42 .... **145** J3
Norton Free Primary School
SHEFS S8 .... **70** F1
Norton Oakes Cricket Club
SHEFS S8 .... **71** G1
Notre Dame School
FUL S10 .... **54** D1
Nottingham City Council
EWD/SEL/PNX NG16 .... **203** K8
Nursery
DERBY DE1 .... **4** E1
Nutbrook Cricket Club
ILK DE7 .... **229** L2
Oakes Park Special School
SHEFS S8 .... **55** M8
Oakthorpe Primary School
MSHM DE12 .... **295** L3
Oak Tree Lane First School
MSFD NG18 .... **165** L4
Oak Tree Lane Health Centre
MSFD NG18 .... **165** L6
Oak Tree Lane Leisure Centre
MSFD NG18 .... **165** L5
Oakwood Infant School
DERBYE DE24 .... **257** K4
Oakwood Junior School
DERBYE DE24 .... **257** K4
Oakwood Leisure Centre
DERBYE DE21 .... **227** K8
Oakwood Medical Centre
DERBYE DE21 .... **241** J1
Oakwood Surgery
DERBYE DE21 .... **241** K1
Oats Hill Surgery
ASH NG17 .... **163** J8

Ockbrook School
BWSH/BRSTN DE72 .... **242** F5
Odeon Cinema
BUT DE14 .... **274** A7
Ogden Sailing Club
ALFN DE55 .... **159** H4
The Old Bank Surgery
NM/HAY SK22 .... **35** G8
Old Church School
RCH S42 .... **129** J8
Oldfields Hall School
UTXR ST14 .... **247** K3
Old Forge Business Park
SHEFP/MNR S2 .... **55** K3
Old Hall Mill Business Park
DERBYE DE21 .... **226** F3
Old Vicarage School
DERBYW DE22 .... **226** C7
Ora Gallery
ECC S11 .... **55** G2
Orchard Business Park
ILK DE7 .... **230** A1
Orchard CP School
CDON/KEG DE74 .... **271** K6
Ormonde Fields Golf Club
RIPLEY DE5 .... **202** A2
Osmaston C of E
Primary School
ASHB DE6 .... **208** C6
Osmaston Road Surgery
DERBY DE1 .... **4** F6
Overseal CP School
MSHM DE12 .... **289** L6
Overseal Surgery
MSHM DE12 .... **289** L7
Owlthorpe Surgery
MOS S20 .... **57** K8
Packington C of E School
ASHZ LE65 .... **291** L8
Padfield County
Primary School
GLSP SK13 .... **17** L5
Paget County High School
BUT DE14 .... **280** D3
Parker Industrial Estate
DERBYE DE21 .... **240** E2
Park Farm Medical Centre
DERBYW DE22 .... **226** A8
Parkfields Surgery
DERBYSE DE24 .... **257** K2
Parkham Gallery
EWD/SEL/PNX NG16 .... **203** H7
Parkhouse Primary School
CLCR S45 .... **145** K6
Park Junior School
SBK/MW NG20 .... **133** G5
Parklands County
Infant School
LGEAT NG10 .... **260** E1
Park Lane Surgery
DERBYW DE22 .... **226** C6
The Park Medical Practice
BWSH/BRSTN DE72 .... **242** D8
The Park Medical Practice
DERBYE DE21 .... **241** K4
Parkside Community School
CHSW S40 .... **2** E7
Parkside County Junior School
ASHB DE6 .... **193** M8
Park Surgery
HEANOR DE75 .... **216** C1
Parkview Surgery
EWD/SEL/PNX NG16 .... **203** K8
Parkwood School
ALFN DE55 .... **175** J6
Parwich Primary School
ASHB DE6 .... **167** M8
Paulet County High School
STPNHL/WNHL DE15 .... **281** J3
Peacefield Primary School
MPL/ROM SK6 .... **32** B5
Peak Dale Primary School
BUX SK17 .... **81** L5
Peak District Mining Museum
MTLK DE4 .... **171** K1
Peak Forest C of E School
BUX SK17 .... **62** D7
Peakland Arts Gallery
MTLK DE4 .... **156** F5
Peak Practice
RIPLEY DE5 .... **201** K1
Peak School
CHF/WBR SK23 .... **45** J8
Pearsons Trading Estate
CHNE S41 .... **110** E1
Peartree Clinic
NORM/LIT DE23 .... **256** D1
Pear Tree Junior
& Infant School
NORM/LIT DE23 .... **256** D1
Pear Tree Medical Centre
NORM/LIT DE23 .... **256** D1
Penmore Business Centre
CHNE S41 .... **3** L9
Pennine Way Junior School
SWAD DE11 .... **282** D8
Perkins Industrial Estate
DERBYE DE21 .... **240** F2
Peter Baines Industrial Estate
DERBYW DE22 .... **4** D6
Peveril Castle
EDL/UDV S33 .... **63** L1
Peveril School of Art
ECC S11 .... **54** E2
Pickfords House Museum
DERBY DE1 .... **4** C3
Picknalls County First School
UTXR ST14 .... **247** K3
Picnic Area
MTLK DE4 .... **171** G2
Pilsley C of E Primary School
BKWL DE45 .... **105** L3
Pilsley Primary School
CLCR S45 .... **161** G1
Pinfold Junior & Infant School
HYDE SK14 .... **24** A1
Pinfold Trading Estate
BSTN/STPLFD NG9 .... **245** H2

The Pingle School
SWAD DE11.............................. 282 D5
Pipworth Junior School
SHEFP/MNR S2 .... 56 E1
Pleasley Surgery
MSFDW NG19...................... 148 D5
Police Museum
DERBY DE1.............................. 4 E2
Pomegranate Theatre
CHNE S41 .... 3 J4
Porter Croft School
ECC S11.............................. 55 H1
Portland Business Park
HAN/WDH S13 .... 57 H1
Portland Primary School
WOL/BIL/BRX NG8.................. 231 M4
Portway Infant School
DERBYW DE22 .... 226 B6
Portway Junior School
DERBYW DE22 .... 226 B6
Po Sorting Office
DERBY DE1.............................. 5 H7
Priestsic Primary School
ASH NG17.............................. 163 J7
Prime Business Centre
DERBYE DE21.......................... 241 L6
Prime Industrial Estate
NORM/LIT DE23 .... 240 F8
Prince Edward Middle School
SHEFP/MNR S2 .... 56 D3
Prince Edward Primary School
SHEFP/MNR S2 .... 56 D3
Priory RC Primary School
EWD/SEL/PNX NG16 .... 217 K1
Public Swimming Baths
ECK/KIL S21 .... 73 H7
Quarrydale School
ASH NG17.............................. 163 H5
Queen Elizabeth Lower School
ASHB DE6 .... 207 M2
Queen Elizabeth's
Grammar School
ASHB DE6 .... 193 M7
Queen St Baths
DERBY DE1.............................. 4 E2
Queens Hospital
BUTN/AL/TUT DE13.............. 273 K5
Queens Leisure Centre
DERBY DE1.............................. 4 E2
The Racecourse Gallery
UTXR ST14 .... 247 M3
Racecourse Industrial Park
DERBYE DE21.......................... 240 F2
Ragged School
CHSW S40 .... 3 G5
Rail Museum
ALFN DE55 .... 187 K6
Railway Staff Social
& Sports Club
STV/CWN S43 .... 111 J1
Ramcharia Sikh Temple
NORM/LIT DE23 .... 240 D8
Ravensdale Junior
& Infant School
MCKLVR DE3............................ 239 H7
Ravensdale School
MSFD NG18 .... 165 H2
Redgate Special School
MSFDW NG19.......................... 164 B3
Redhill Primary School
BWSH/BRSTN DE72 .... 243 G5
Red House Stables
Working Carriage Museum
MTLK DE4 .... 156 A1
Redwood Junior
& Infant School
DERBYSE DE24........................ 256 B7
Reflex Theatre
SHEFS S8 .... 55 K4
Reform Street
Industrial Estate
ASH NG17.............................. 163 J8
Reigate Junior & Infant School
DERBYW DE22 .... 239 J3
Renishaw Primary School
ECK/KIL S21 .... 93 L2
Repton Preparatory School
RDERBYSW DE65 .... 276 F1
Repton Primary School
RDERBYSW DE65 .... 267 H8
Repton School
RDERBYSW DE65 .... 266 F7
Repton SchoolI
RDERBYSW DE65 .... 266 F8
Repton Sports Club
RDERBYSW DE65 .... 266 F7
Revolution House
CHNE S41 .... 91 K7
Richardson Endowed
Primary School
ILK DE7 .... 215 J4
Richard Wakefield
C of E Primary School
BUTN/AL/TUT DE13.............. 263 M4
Richmond Medical Centre
HAN/WDH S13 .... 57 G3
Riddings Infant School
ALFN DE55 .... 187 M4
Riddings Junior School
ALFN DE55 .... 188 A4
The Ridge College
MPL/ROM SK6 .... 32 B5
Ridge Danyers College
MPL/ROM SK6 .... 32 C5
Ridgeway Infant School
NORM/LIT DE23 .... 256 A4
Ridgeway Primary School
HACK/IN S12............................ 72 B2
Ringstones Industrial Estate
CHF/WBR SK23 .... 44 A8
Ripley Hospital
RIPLEY DE5.............................. 200 F1
Ripley Junior and
Infant School
RIPLEY DE5.............................. 200 F2
Ripley Leisure Centre
RIPLEY DE5.............................. 201 G1

Ripley Mill Hill School
RIPLEY DE5.............................. 201 J2
Risley Lower Grammar
C of E Primary School
BWSH/BRSTN DE72 .... 244 B6
Riversdale Surgery
BPR/DUF DE56 .... 199 H6
Robert Sherborne
Infant School
BUTN/AL/TUT DE13................ 264 F6
Robert Sutton RC High School
STPNHL/WNHL DE15.............. 281 K3
Robinsons Industrial Estate
NORM/LIT DE23 .... 240 F8
Robirch Sports Centre
BUT DE14 .... 273 J7
Rock Mill Business Park
HATH/EY S32........................... 86 B6
Rose Avenue Surgery
BSVR S44 .... 111 K7
Rosehill Infant School
NORM/LIT DE23 .... 5 G8
Rose Hill Primary School
MPL/ROM SK6 .... 32 B4
Rosliston C of E
Primary School
MSHM DE12 .... 287 M4
Rother County Junior School
CHSW S40 .... 3 G9
Roundwood Surgery
MSFD NG18 .... 164 D3
Rowan School
TOT/DORE S17 .... 69 H4
Rowsley C of E
Controlled Primary School
MTLK DE4 .... 140 C2
Royal Crown Derby
NORM/LIT DE23 .... 5 G8
Rustlings Road Medical Centre
ECC S11.............................. 54 D2
Ryecroft Middle School
UTXR ST14 .... 218 B6
Rykneld CP School
BUT DE14 .... 280 B3
Rykneld Industrial Estate
BUTN/AL/TUT DE13................ 274 B4
Sailing Club
RDERBYSW DE65 .... 276 D6
S A I Medical Centre
NORM/LIT DE23 .... 240 D8
St Albans Primary School
DERBYE DE21.......................... 241 J4
St Andrews C of E CP School
CRTAM B79............................... 293 H8
St Andrews C of E
Methodist Aided School
DRON S18.............................. 90 A1
St Andrews C of E
Primary School
ASH NG17.............................. 163 J4
St Andrews C of E
Primary School
ILK DE7 .... 228 E5
St Andrews School
GLSP SK13.............................. 17 J6
St Andrews Special School
DERBYE DE21.......................... 241 H1
St Annes C of E Primary School
BKWL DE45.............................. 106 B5
St Annes RC School
BUX SK17 .... 99 L1
St Anne's Well
BUX SK17 .... 99 L2
St Anselms School
BKWL DE45.............................. 122 F4
St Augustines First School
ASHB DE6 .... 262 A5
St Bartholomews C of E
Primary School
BUX SK17 .... 134 E3
St Benedict School
& Sixth Form Centre
DERBYW DE22 .... 240 C1
St Catherines Preparatory
School
MPL/ROM SK6 .... 32 E3
St Chads C of E Infant School
NORM/LIT DE23 .... 4 D9
St Charles RC School
GLSP SK13.............................. 17 H5
St Clares School
MCKLVR DE3............................ 239 J8
St Edwards Junior School
CDON/KEG DE74 .... 271 L7
St Elizabeths School
BPR/DUF DE56 .... 199 J5
St Elphins School
MTLK DE4 .... 156 B1
St Georges C of E Primary
School
SWAD DE11.............................. 289 L1
St Georges C of E School
NM/HAY SK22.......................... 43 M2
St Georges RC School
NORM/LIT DE23 .... 255 M3
St Giles C of E (Aided)
Primary School
ECK/KIL S21 .... 73 M4
St Giles C of E (A)
Primary School
MTLK DE4 .... 156 F7
St Giles School
DERBYE DE21.......................... 240 F1
St Hardulphs School
MELB/CHEL DE73 .... 279 J8
St Helens Business Centre
DERBY DE1.............................. 4 D1
St James C of E Infant School
NORM/LIT DE23 .... 5 G7
St James RC Primary School
HYDE SK14.............................. 16 A8
St John Fisher RC Junior
& Infants School
HACK/IN S12............................ 57 K7
St John Fisher RC
Primary School
DERBYSE DE24........................ 257 M2

St John Houghton RC School
ILK DE7 .... 229 M4
St Johns Business Centre
CHNE S41 .... 110 C2
St Johns C of E Middle School
MSFD NG18 .... 164 E3
St Johns C of E Primary School
BPR/DUF DE56 .... 199 L5
St Johns C of E Primary School
RIPLEY DE5.............................. 187 J8
St Johns C of E School
BSTN/STPLFD NG9.................. 245 H3
St Johns College
BSTN/STPLFD NG9.................. 245 L3
St Johns RC CP School
CDLE ST10.............................. 204 B8
St Joseph Roman Catholic
Primary School
MTLK DE4 .... 157 G4
St Josephs Catholic School
SBK/MW NG20......................... 133 J5
St Josephs Convent School
CHSW S40 .... 2 F2
St Josephs RC CP School
UTXR ST14 .... 247 L2
St Josephs RC Primary School
STV/CWN S43 .... 112 A1
St Josephs School
NORM/LIT DE23 .... 4 D7
St Lawrence C of E Primary
School
LGEAT NG10 .... 261 G4
St Lukes Church
DERBYW DE22 .... 4 B6
St Lukes C of E Primary School
WRKN S81.............................. 77 J2
St Lukes School
GLSP SK13.............................. 17 L8
St Margarets RC School
GLSP SK13.............................. 25 G2
St Maries R C Primary School
FUL S10.............................. 54 D1
St Martins School
DERBYSE DE24........................ 257 J2
St Marys C of E First School
UTXR ST14 .... 247 L1
St Marys Primary School
ASH NG17.............................. 162 F7
St Marys RC High School
CHSW S40 .... 109 M3
St Marys RC Primary School
CHSW S40 .... 2 F2
St Marys RC Primary School
DERBY DE1.............................. 4 D1
St Marys RC Primary School
MPL/ROM SK6 .... 32 E3
St Marys RC Primary School
NM/HAY SK22.......................... 43 L2
St Marys RC School
GLSP SK13.............................. 26 A2
St Marys School
DRON S18.............................. 91 J2
St Michaels C of E School
HATH/EY S32........................... 66 D2
St Modwens RC Primary School
BUTN/AL/TUT DE13................ 273 L5
St Oswalds C of E Infant School
ASHB DE6 .... 193 L8
St Oswalds Hospital
ASHB DE6 .... 193 K8
St Peter & St Paul School
CHNE S41 .... 3 M5
St Peter & St Pauls RC
Junior & Infant School
SWAD DE11.............................. 282 E5
St Peters C of E First School
MSFD NG18 .... 165 K8
St Peters C of E First School
UTXR ST14 .... 249 J8
St Peters C of E Junior School
NORM/LIT DE23 .... 255 M1
St Peters C of E
Primary School
MSHM DE12 .... 294 C4
St Peters Retail Park
BUT DE14 .... 281 G1
St Peters & St Pauls School
CHNE S41 .... 3 L9
St Philip Howard RC School
GLSP SK13.............................. 25 L2
St Philip Neri with
St. Pedes Primary School
MSFDW NG19.......................... 164 D2
St Theresas School
SHEFP/MNR S2 .... 56 E3
St Thomas More RC School
BUX SK17 .... 99 L2
St Thomas of Canterbury
R C Primary School
SHEFS S8 .... 70 C2
St Thomas RC Primary School
ILK DE7 .... 230 B4
St Werburgh's Arcade
DERBY DE1.............................. 4 D3
St Werburghs C of E School
DERBYE DE21.......................... 242 A5
St Wilfrids RC Primary School
ABRD S7.............................. 54 F6
St Wystans School
RDERBYSW DE65 .... 266 F8
Sale & Davys C of E School
MELB/CHEL DE73 .... 268 D5
Saltergate Health Centre
CHSW S40 .... 3 G3
Salvation Army
DERBY DE1.............................. 4 F5
Sandiacre Friesland
Sports Centre
BWSH/BRSTN DE72 .... 244 C5
Sawley County Junior
& Infant School
LGEAT NG10 .... 260 D6
Sawmills Industrial Park
HEANOR DE75 .... 202 A7
Sawpit Industrial Estate
ALFN DE55 .... 161 M4
S B K Sports Club
BUT DE14 .... 273 L7

Scargill C of E Primary School
ILK DE7 .... 229 G3
The Schoolhouse Surgery
POY/DIS SK12........................... 42 F4
Sett Valley Medical Centre
NM/HAY SK22.......................... 43 M2
Shardlow Business Park
BWSH/BRSTN DE72 .... 271 G1
Shardlow County
Primary School
BWSH/BRSTN DE72 .... 271 H1
Sharley Park Leisure Centre
CLCR S45.............................. 145 G6
Sharpes Industrial Estate
SWAD DE11.............................. 282 E6
Sharrow Junior School
ECC S11.............................. 55 J2
Shawlands Surgery
STV/CWN S43 .... 95 J6
Sheaf Heaf Gardens
Industrial Estate
SHEFP/MNR S2 .... 55 L1
Sheepbridge Business Centre
CHNE S41 .... 91 H8
Sheffield Area Health
Authority Sports
& Social Club
ECC S11.............................. 54 A3
Sheffield City Council
HACK/IN S12............................ 57 H7
Sheffield City Council
HAN/WDH S13 .... 57 L4
Sheffield City Council
SHEFP/MNR S2 .... 55 L2
Sheffield City Council
SHEFP/MNR S2 .... 56 A5
Sheffield City Council
SHEFP/MNR S2 .... 56 D3
Sheffield City Council
SHEFS S8 .... 55 K5
Sheffield City Council
SHEFS S8 .... 70 B4
The Sheffield College
MOS S20.............................. 73 J2
The Sheffield College
SHEFP/MNR S2 .... 55 L1
The Sheffield College
SHEFS S8 .... 70 E3
Sheffield Natural Health Centre
SHEFS S8 .... 55 J3
Sheffield United AFC
SHEFP/MNR S2 .... 55 K1
Sherwin Sports Centre
NORM/LIT DE23 .... 256 E2
Sherwood Baths
MSFDW NG19.......................... 164 E1
Sherwood Hall Upper School
MSFDW NG19.......................... 165 J3
Shirebrook Business Park
SBK/MW NG20......................... 133 K8
Shirebrook Community School
SBK/MW NG20......................... 133 G5
Shire Hill Hospital
GLSP SK13.............................. 18 B7
Shireoaks Business Centre
WRKN S81.............................. 77 K4
Shireoaks Miners Welfare
& Sports Club
WRKN S81.............................. 77 J4
Shirland CP School
ALFN DE55 .... 160 A8
Shobnall County Primary
School
BUTN/AL/TUT DE13................ 273 J6
Shopping Centre
CHSW S40 .... 109 M5
Shortbrook Primary School
MOS S20.............................. 73 J2
Short Street Infants School
STPNHL/WNHL DE15.............. 281 H3
Showcase Cinemas
NORM/LIT DE23 .... 256 D3
Sickleholme Golf Club Ltd
EDL/UDV S33........................... 50 E8
Sidings Industrial Estate
BUT DE14 .... 274 B6
Silverdale School
ECC S11.............................. 54 B5
Silverhill Primary School
MCKLVR DE3............................ 238 F7
Simmondley Primary School
GLSP SK13.............................. 25 K2
Sinfin Community School
DERBYSE DE24........................ 256 B7
Sinfin Primary School
DERBYSE DE24........................ 256 C7
Sir Harold Jackson Primary
School
TOT/DORE S17 .... 69 L5
The Sloan Practice
SHEFS S8 .... 56 A8
The Smithy Surgery
HYDE SK14.............................. 17 G5
Sofa Gallery
DERBYSE DE24........................ 257 G1
Somercotes Infant School
ALFN DE55 .... 187 M2
Somercotes Medical Centre
ALFN DE55 .... 187 M1
Somerlea Park Junior School
ALFN DE55 .... 187 M2
South Darley C of E Primary
School
MTLK DE4 .... 155 L3
South Derbyshire
Health Authority
DERBY DE1.............................. 5 H7
South Derbyshire Mental
Health N H S Trust
DERBYW DE22 .... 239 L6
South East Derbyshire College
HEANOR DE75 .... 216 B1
South East Derbyshire College
ILK DE7 .... 230 C3
Southern Derbyshire
Health Authority
DERBY DE1.............................. 4 F5

Southern Derbyshire Health
Authority
DERBY DE1.............................. 4 F3
Southern Derbyshire
Mental Health N H S Trust
MCKLVR DE3............................ 239 L6
Southern Derbyshire
N H S Trust
ILK DE7 .... 230 B3
Southgate Infant School
DERBYSE DE24........................ 257 J2
South Wingfield Primary
School
ALFN DE55 .... 174 C7
Speedwell County Infants
School
STV/CWN S43 .... 112 B1
Sports Centre
ASHB DE6 .... 181 M6
Sports Centre
MPL/ROM SK6 .... 32 D3
Springfield County Junior
School
SWAD DE11.............................. 282 E5
Springfield Primary School
DERBYE DE21.......................... 242 A5
Springwell Community School
STV/CWN S43 .... 112 A3
Staden Business Park
BUX SK17 .... 100 A5
Staffordshire County Council
BUT DE14 .... 274 A7
Stalyhill Junior School
STLY SK15.............................. 16 A3
Stalyhill Primary School
STLY SK15.............................. 16 B3
Stancliffe Hall School
MTLK DE4 .... 140 E5
Stanley Common C of E
Primary School
ILK DE7 .... 228 D1
Stanton County Primary
School
STPNHL/WNHL DE15.............. 281 L5
Stanton-in-peak C of E
Primary School
MTLK DE4 .... 139 M5
Stanton Vale School
ILK DE7 .... 230 C4
Stapenhill Football Club
STPNHL/WNHL DE15.............. 281 M5
Stapleford Health Centre
BSTN/STPLFD NG9.................. 245 G4
Stapleford Town Council
BSTN/STPLFD NG9.................. 245 G3
Station Lane Industrial Estate
CHNE S41 .... 91 L8
Station Rd Industrial Estate
STV/CWN S43 .... 95 H6
Station Road Industrial Estate
RDERBYSW DE65 .... 263 M2
Staveley Council Office
STV/CWN S43 .... 93 H8
Staveley Health Clinic
STV/CWN S43 .... 112 B1
Staveley Junior School
STV/CWN S43 .... 112 A1
Staveley Norbriggs County
Infants School
STV/CWN S43 .... 93 M7
Staveley Urban District Council
STV/CWN S43 .... 112 B1
Steel Fabs Industrial Estate
BUT DE14 .... 273 M5
Stenson Fields Community
Primary School
DERBYSE DE24........................ 256 A8
Stephensons College
ASHZ LE65.............................. 291 L4
Stevenson Junior School
BSTN/STPLFD NG9.................. 245 J2
Stockport Metropolitan
Borough Council
MPL/ROM SK6 .... 32 D4
Stockport Road
Medical Practice
MPL/ROM SK6 .... 32 C4
Stokes Industrial Estate
MSFD NG18 .... 164 B6
Stonebroom Primary School
ALFN DE55 .... 160 D6
Stonedge Golf Club
CLCR S45.............................. 127 G6
Stonelow Junior School
DRON S18.............................. 70 E8
Stradbroke Primary School
HAN/WDH S13 .... 57 G9
Street Lane Primary School
RIPLEY DE5.............................. 200 E5
Stretton Handley C of E
Controlled Primary School
ALFN DE55 .... 159 G3
Stretton Hostel School
ALFN DE55 .... 159 L2
Stretton Surgery
BUTN/AL/TUT DE13................ 274 B1
Stud Farm Gallery Chatsworth
BKWL DE45.............................. 105 M8
Sudbury Primary School
ASHB DE6 .... 250 A6
Sunnyhill Infant School
NORM/LIT DE23 .... 256 B3
Sunnyside Primary
& Infant School
BSTN/STPLFD NG9.................. 245 L4
Superbowl
BUT DE14 .... 274 B7
Superbowl 2000
MSFD NG18 .... 164 E3
Sutton Centre
Comprehensive School
ASH NG17.............................. 163 J4
Sutton Recreation Centre
ASH NG17.............................. 163 H4
Sutton Road First School
MSFD NG18 .... 164 C4
Swadlincote Surgery
SWAD DE11.............................. 282 E6

Swanwick Hall School
ALFN DE55 .... 187 J3
Swanwick Primary School
ALFN DE55 .... 187 G4
Swarkestone Boat Club
MELB/CHEL DE73 .... 269 G6
Tansley County
Primary School
MTLK DE4 .... 157 K6
Tapton Golf Course
CHNE S41 .... 110 C3
Taxal Lodge School
CHF/WBR SK23 .... 59 G5
Temple House Clinic
NORM/LIT DE23 .... 4 E7
Temple Normanton
Primary School
RCH S42 .... 129 M6
The Temple
NORM/LIT DE23 .... 4 E9
Tertiary College
ECK/KIL S21 .... 73 G7
Thomas Alleynes High School
UTXR ST14 .... 247 M2
Thomas Russell Junior School
BUTN/AL/TUT DE13 .... 286 B1
Thornbridge School
HACK/IN S12 .... 57 G8
Thornsett CP School
NM/HAY SK22 .... 34 B7
Tibshelf Comprehensive School
ALFN DE55 .... 161 K3
Tibshelf Infant School
ALFN DE55 .... 161 K3
Tibshelf Town End
Junior School
ALFN DE55 .... 161 H5
Tintwistle C of E
Primary School
GLSP SK13 .... 17 K3
Tintwistle Parish Council
GLSP SK13 .... 17 J3
Tomlinson Industrial Estate
DERBYE DE21 .... 226 E8
Tongue Lane Industrial Estate
BUX SK17 .... 100 B2
Totley All Saints C of E
Primary School
TOT/DORE S17 .... 68 F6
Totley Primary School
TOT/DORE S17 .... 69 G6
Toton Chetwynd Road
Primary School
BSTN/STPLFD NG9 .... 245 K8
Tower Business Park
CLCR S45 .... 144 C6
The Towerview Primary School
STPNHL/WNHL DE15 .... 274 E7
Trent College
LGEAT NG10 .... 260 F1
Trent Industrial Estate
BUT DE14 .... 274 B6
Trent Lane Industrial Estate
CDON/KEG DE74 .... 271 L4
Trent Meadows
Medical Centre
BUT DE14 .... 280 F1
Trentside Cricket Club
BUT DE14 .... 280 E3
Trowell C of E School
BSTN/STPLFD NG9 .... 231 G6

Tupton Hall School
RCH S42 .... 144 F3
Tupton Primary School
RCH S42 .... 144 F1
Turnditch C of E
Primary School
BPR/DUF DE56 .... 197 L8
Turnoaks Business Park
CHSW S40 .... 128 E4
Tutbury Cricket Club
BUTN/AL/TUT DE13 .... 263 M3
Tutbury Health Centre
BUTN/AL/TUT DE13 .... 263 M4
Tynsel Parkes First School
UTXR ST14 .... 247 J1
U C I Cinemas
DERBYE DE21 .... 240 F1
Underwood C of E
Primary School
EWD/SEL/PNX NG16 .... 203 J1
University Centre of Mansfield
MSFD NG18 .... 164 C5
University of Derby
BUX SK17 .... 100 A8
University of Derby
DERBY DE1 .... 4 C2
University of Derby
DERBYW DE22 .... 4 A1
University of Derby
DERBYW DE22 .... 240 A4
University of Derby
NORM/LIT DE23 .... 4 A9
University of Nottingham
MSFD NG18 .... 164 C2
University of Sheffield
BUX SK17 .... 99 K8
University of Sheffield
ECC S11 .... 54 E1
Unstone Junior School
DRON S18 .... 91 H3
Uttoxeter Golf Club
UTXR ST14 .... 248 B4
Uttoxeter Leisure Centre
UTXR ST14 .... 247 L3
Valley Surgery
BSTN/STPLFD NG9 .... 245 M5
Vanguard Trading Estate
CHSW S40 .... 128 D3
Vernon Street Medical Centre
DERBY DE1 .... 4 B3
Victoria Gallery
ASHB DE6 .... 193 L8
Victoria Primary School
BUT DE14 .... 273 M6
Vidya Medical Centre
DERBY DE1 .... 4 F7
Viking Business Centre
NORM/LIT DE23 .... 256 C2
Village Hall School
BKWL DE45 .... 138 B7
Violet Lane County
Infants School
STPNHL/WNHL DE15 .... 281 J2
Volu-med Clinic
MSFD NG18 .... 164 E3
Waingroves Primary School
RIPLEY DE5 .... 201 K2
Walk Talk Galleries
ECC S11 .... 54 E2
Walter Evans C of E School
DERBYW DE22 .... 226 C8

Walton Hospital
CHSW S40 .... 128 B3
Walton on Trent C of E
Primary School
MSHM DE12 .... 287 G2
Warmbrook Junior School
CHF/WBR SK23 .... 60 F4
Warwick Street
Industrial Estate
CHSW S40 .... 128 E3
Waterside County
Junior School
STPNHL/WNHL DE15 .... 281 G3
Waterside Retail Park
ILK DE7 .... 230 D1
Waverley Street Clinic
DERBYSE DE24 .... 256 F3
Welfare Clinic
ECK/KIL S21 .... 73 G7
Wellside Medical Centre
DERBY DE1 .... 4 E6
Wessington Primary School
ALFN DE55 .... 174 A2
West Bridgford High School
MSFD NG18 .... 164 E3
Westbrook School
LGEAT NG10 .... 260 F3
Westfield Health Centre
MOS S20 .... 73 H2
Westfield Infant School
CHSW S40 .... 109 L8
West Hallam Cricket Club
ILK DE7 .... 229 G3
West Hallam Medical Centre
ILK DE7 .... 229 H3
Westhouses Primary School
ALFN DE55 .... 175 M1
West Nottinghamshire College
MSFD NG18 .... 164 F8
West Nottinghamshire College
MSFD NG18 .... 164 E3
Weston on Trent
Parochial Primary School
BWSH/BRSTN DE72 .... 270 B6
West Park Community School
DERBYE DE21 .... 242 A5
West Park Leisure Centre
LGEAT NG10 .... 260 E3
Westside Gallery
FUL S10 .... 55 G1
Wetmore Road Surgery
BUT DE14 .... 274 B7
Whaley Bridge Primary School
CHF/WBR SK23 .... 59 G3
Whaley Thorns
Secondary School
SBK/MW NG20 .... 115 K7
Wharf Road Industrial Estate
BUT DE14 .... 274 B5
Whitecotes Primary School
CHSW S40 .... 2 E9
White House Surgery
SHEFP/MNR S2 .... 56 E2
Whiteley Wood Clinic
ECC S11 .... 54 B3
Whitfield C of E Primary School
GLSP SK13 .... 25 L2
Whittington Medical Centre
CHNE S41 .... 91 K7

Whittington Moor Surgery
CHNE S41 .... 110 D2
Whittington Moor Surgery
CHNE S41 .... 110 E3
Whitwell Square Health Centre
WRKS S80 .... 96 D4
Whitworth Hospital
MTLK DE4 .... 156 C2
Wigley Primary School
RCH S42 .... 108 B6
Willersley Castle
MTLK DE4 .... 171 L3
Willesley CP School
ASHZ LE65 .... 291 K6
Willesley Park Golf Club
ASHZ LE65 .... 291 J6
William Allitt School
SWAD DE11 .... 282 B3
William Gilbert End
C of E Primary School
BPR/DUF DE56 .... 213 H6
William Hutson Junior School
BUTN/AL/TUT DE13 .... 273 L2
William Levick Infant School
DRON S18 .... 69 M8
William Levick Primary School
DRON S18 .... 69 M8
William Lilley Infant School
BSTN/STPLFD NG9 .... 245 G4
William Rhodes Primary School
CHSW S40 .... 2 D6
William Sharp School
WOL/BIL/BRX NG8 .... 231 M3
William Shrewsbury
County Primary School
BUTN/AL/TUT DE13 .... 265 J8
Willington County
Primary School
RDERBYSW DE65 .... 266 E5
Willington Surgery
RDERBYSW DE65 .... 266 D5
Willowbrook Medical Practice
ASH NG17 .... 163 G8
Willow Sports Centre
DERBY DE1 .... 4 D2
The Will Practice
BSTN/STPLFD NG9 .... 245 M7
Wilmorton Primary School
DERBYSE DE24 .... 257 G1
Wilson Street Surgery
DERBY DE1 .... 4 E5
Wilson Street Surgery
DERBYE DE21 .... 241 J1
Wilsthorpe
Comprehensive School
LGEAT NG10 .... 260 E1
Windermere Surgery
CHNE S41 .... 110 A3
Windmill Ridge Middle School
MSFD NG18 .... 165 H3
Windsor Industrial Estate
BUT DE14 .... 274 B6
Windsor Park C of E
Middle School
UTXR ST14 .... 247 L2
Wingerworth Surgery
RCH S42 .... 128 B7
Wingfield Manor House
ALFN DE55 .... 174 B8

Winshill Clinic
STPNHL/WNHL DE15 .... 274 E7
Winshill Infants School
STPNHL/WNHL DE15 .... 274 E6
Winster C of E Primary School
MTLK DE4 .... 155 G4
Wirksworth C of E
Infant School
MTLK DE4 .... 183 J1
Wirksworth Health Centre
MTLK DE4 .... 183 J2
Wirksworth Industrial Centre
MTLK DE4 .... 171 J7
Wirksworth Infant School
MTLK DE4 .... 183 J1
Wirksworth Junior School
MTLK DE4 .... 183 K1
Witness Gallery
BUX SK17 .... 99 L2
Woodbridge Junior School
ALFN DE55 .... 175 K7
Woodhouse Business Centre
SWAD DE11 .... 283 G7
Woodhouse Clinic
HAN/WDH S13 .... 57 L4
Woodhouse Medical Centre
HAN/WDH S13 .... 57 L4
Woodlands Community School
DERBYW DE22 .... 226 A6
Woodseats Medical Centre
SHEFS S8 .... 55 J8
Woodseats Primary School
SHEFS S8 .... 55 J7
Woods Hospital
GLSP SK13 .... 17 M7
Woodthorpe Community
Primary School
CHSW S40 .... 56 F3
Woodville C of E Junior School
SWAD DE11 .... 283 J8
Woodville County
Infant School
SWAD DE11 .... 283 H8
Works
EDL/UDV S33 .... 64 C1
Worksl
CHSW S40 .... 3 J6
Wren Park Primary School
MCKLVR DE3 .... 239 K8
Wynndale Drive Jmi School
MSFD NG18 .... 165 J5
Wyvern Business Park
DERBYE DE21 .... 241 K7
Yeoman Business Estate
BUT DE14 .... 274 B5
Yeoman Park School
MSFDW NG19 .... 149 M6
Yew Tree Gallery
ASHB DE6 .... 205 L7
York House Medical Centre
SHEFP/MNR S2 .... 56 C2
Youlegrave All Saints
C of E Primary School
BKWL DE45 .... 138 F5
Zen Gallery
LGEAT NG10 .... 261 G2
Zion School
GLSP SK13 .... 25 K1

Page 17

G6
1 Claylands Cl
2 Woolley Cl

H6
1 Lawnfold
2 Peacock Cl
3 Pinfold
4 Rowan Wk
5 Wheatcroft

J6
1 Brookside Cl

K4
1 Greenfield St
2 Masons Cv
3 Redfern Cl
4 Rhodeswood Dr
5 Wilmans Wk

K5
1 Blenheim Cl
2 Chesham Cl
3 The Cross
4 Evesham Av
5 Gawsworth Cl
6 Hebden Dr
7 Langley Dr
8 Larch Wy
9 Lincoln Wy
10 Lynne Cl
11 Richmond Cl
12 Spring Gdns
13 Torside Wy
14 Victoria Wy

Page 25

J2
1 Valley Rd

Page 26

C2
1 Ashbourne Ct
2 Derwent Cl
3 Furness Cl
4 Gloucester Wy
5 Hebden Dr
6 Langley Dr
7 Larch Wy
8 Lincoln Wy
9 Lynne Cl
10 Peveril Ct
11 Stafford Cl
12 Worcester Gv

Page 32

A4
1 Oak Dr

B4
1 Shirley Av

C4
1 Belgrave Av
2 Church St
3 Culchetch Av
4 Ellesmere Av
5 Gloucester Av
6 Highfield Rd
7 Queen St
8 Springfield Av
9 Union Rd

C5
1 Chadwick St
2 Cotefield Cl
3 Trinity St
4 Waterside Av
5 Willow Ct

D4
1 Canal St
2 Faywood Dr
3 Joseph St
4 Matthew St

D5
1 Church St
2 Marsham Dr
3 Rushton Cl

F2
1 Oaklands Av

Page 54

A1
1 Carsick Hill Wy
2 Stumperlowe Hall Cha

B1
1 Gladstone Ms
2 Snaithing Park Cl

B2
1 Fulwood Cha
2 Stumperlowe Av
3 Stumperlowe Ct
4 Woodview Ter

B5
1 Bents Green Rd
2 Moor View Ter

C1
1 Chapel Cl
2 Ranmoor Ri
3 Stortholme Ms

C2
1 Bramwith Rd
2 Carr Bank Dr
3 Hanging Water Cl
4 Pendeen Rd

C6
1 Broad Elms Cl

C7
1 Almshill Cres
2 Broomcroft Pk
3 Croft Cl
4 Whirlow La
5 Whirlow Ms

C8
1 Holkham Ri
2 Whirlowdale Cl
3 Whirlowdale Ri

D3
1 Cliffe Farm Dr
2 Greystones Grange Crs
3 Greystones Ri

D5
1 Blenheim Gdns
2 Ecclesall Rd South

D6
1 Silverdale Gld

D8
1 Harewood Wy
2 Russell Ct
3 Wentworth Av

E1
1 Endcliffe Edge
2 The Glen

E3
1 Marmion Rd

E4
1 Banner Cross Rd

E5
1 Weetwood Dr
2 Woodholm Pl

E6
1 Millhouses Glen
2 Silverdale Gdns

E7
1 Betjeman Gdns
2 Oakholme Ms

F2
1 Kenilworth Pl
2 Meadow Ter

F3
1 Osborne St

F4
1 Bannerdale Cl
2 Lyndhurst Rd

F5
1 Knab Cl

F7
1 Terminus Rd

Page 55

G1
1 Cemetery Av

G2
1 Ashford Rd
2 Berresford Rd
3 Bruce Rd
4 Dyson Pl
5 Eastwood Rd
6 Gordon Rd
7 Harefield Rd
8 Hickmott Rd
9 Jarrow Rd
10 Lynton Rd
11 Rosedale Gdns
12 Rosedale Rd

G3
1 Cherry Tree Cl
2 Cherry Tree Dell
3 Cherry Tree Dr
4 Cherry Tree Rd
5 Meadow Bank Av
6 St Andrew's Cl

G4
1 Brentwood Av

G7
1 Hutchinson La
2 Hutchinson Rd

G8
1 Hutcliffe Dr

H1
1 Parliament St
2 Pembroke St
3 Sawdon Rd
4 Sunderland St

H2
1 Mackenzie St

H3
1 Kenbourne Gv
2 Kenwood Av
3 Montgomery Dr

H4
1 Archibald Rd
2 Gatefield Rd
3 Herbert Rd
4 Marden Rd
5 Violet Bank Rd

H5
1 Coniston Ter
2 Crummock Rd
3 Edgemount Rd
4 Grasmere Rd
5 Thirlmere Rd
6 Thorne Rd
7 Windermere Rd

H6
1 Norton Hammer La

H6
1 Firbeck Rd
2 Fraser Cl
3 Periwood Cl
4 Periwood Dr
5 Periwood Gv

H8
1 Booker Rd
2 Moor View Dr

J1
1 Beeley St
2 Exeter Dr
3 Hermitage St
4 Keeton's Hl
5 Leverton Gdns
6 St Mary's Sq

J2
1 Asher Rd
2 Bennett St
3 Crowther Pl
4 Croydon St
5 Grosvenor Sq
6 Mount Pleasant Rd
7 Penley St
8 Salmon St
9 Sitwell Pl
10 Smeaton St
11 Stemp St
12 Ventnor Pl
13 Ward Pl

J3
1 Ainsty Rd
2 Aizlewood Rd
3 Alcester Rd
4 Brookfield Sq
5 Cutts Ter
6 Dalton Ct
7 Farrar Rd
8 Herschell Rd
9 Marples Dr
10 Marples Dr
11 Miller Rd
12 Kampton Rd
13 Sellers St
14 South View Crs

J4
1 Belper Rd
2 Empire Rd
3 Little London Pl
4 Markham Ter
5 Southcroft Gdns

J7
1 Denton Rd
2 Dinnington Rd
3 Smithy Wood Crs
4 Tadcaster Wy

J8
1 Broxholme Rd

J9
1 Bingham Rd
2 Cobnar Gdns
3 Osmaston Rd

K1
1 Ascot St
2 Baron St
3 Countess Rd
4 Forge La
5 Hereford St
6 Midland St

K2
1 Alderson Rd North
2 Atkin Pl
3 Batt St
4 Belgrave Rd
5 Harrington Rd
6 Holland Pl
7 St Barnabas La
8 Silver Mill Rd
9 Witney St

K3
1 Alderney Rd
2 Fieldhead Rd
3 Gifford Rd
4 Glover Rd
5 Guernsey Rd
6 Jersey Rd
7 Preston St
8 Sark Rd
9 Sheaf Bank

K4
1 Arthington St
2 Bradbury St
3 Gleadless Rd
4 Goodwin Rd
5 Gregory Rd
6 Maxey Pl
7 Molloy St
8 Nowill Cl
9 Nowill Pl
10 Plantation Rd
11 Southall St
12 Springwood Rd
13 Tillotson Cl
14 Tillotson Ri
15 Wellhead Rd
16 Well Pl
17 Well Rd
18 Whiting St
19 Wilson Pl

K5
1 Brooklyn Pl
2 Brooklyn Rd
3 Cross Park Rd
4 Cyprus Rd
5 Molloy St
6 Normancroft Dr
7 Prince Of Wales Rd
8 Saxonlea Dr
9 Vikinglea Gld

K6
1 Castledale Cft
2 Castledale Pl
3 Princess Ct
4 Vikinglea Cl

K7
1 Hartford Cl
2 Mount View Gdns
3 Norton Lees Cl

L1
1 Cream St
2 Cromford St
3 Leadmill Rd
4 Lenton St
5 Manton St
6 Sheaf Gdns

L3
1 Lancing Rd
2 St Elizabeth Ct

L4
1 Delf St
2 Madehurst Gdns
3 Madehurst Rd
4 Madehurst Vw
5 Slate St

L4
1 Farish Pl
2 Gerard Cl
3 Gleadless Ct
4 Jeffery St
5 Nicholson Pl
6 Richards Ct
7 Romney Gdns
8 Sturge Cft

L1
1 Warminster Dr

M1
1 Claywood Rd

M2
1 Tower Cl

M4
1 Abney Cl
2 Derby Pl
3 Hallyburton Cl
4 Hallyburton Dr
5 Hartopp Cl

M5
1 Callow Mt

Page 56

A2
1 T Benedict Ct

A3
1 Kenning Hall Cl
2 Kenninghall Mt
3 Samuel Cl
4 Samuel Dr

A4
1 East Bank Pl
2 East Bank Vw
3 East Bank Wy
4 Gleadless Rd
5 Hartopp Dr

A7
1 Hayfield Crs
2 Thornbridge Gv

A8
1 Constable Wy
2 Landseer Cl
3 Mawfa Crs
4 Mawfa Rd
5 Richmond Gv

B1
1 St Aidan's Cl
2 Southend Rd

B2
1 Brimmesfield Dr
2 Guildford Vw
3 St Aidan's Mt
4 St Aidan's Rd

B3
1 Cradock Ms

B5
1 Newfield Farm Cl
2 Spotswood Dr
3 Spotswood Mt
4 Toll Bar Av

B6
1 Spotswood Cl

C1
1 Manor Park Ct

C2
1 Scotia Cl
2 Scotia Dr

C3
1 Babington Cl
2 Queen Mary Gv

C4
1 Dagnam Pl

C5
1 Ashleigh Cl
2 Grassmoor Cl

D1
1 Motehall Wy

D2
1 Archdale Cl
2 Fretson Rd
3 Kingswood Cl
4 Royston Cft
5 Royston Gv

D3
1 Queen Mary Cl
2 Queen Mary Ms
3 Travey Rd

D4
1 Ridgeway Cl

D5
1 Chatsworth Park Av
2 Chatsworth Park Dr
3 Chatsworth Park Gv
4 Durnstone Cl
5 Leadbeater Rd

D6
1 Crispin Cl
2 Crispin Rd
3 Hollinsend Rd
4 Kirkby Av

D7
1 Gleadless Mt
2 Herdings Ct
3 Little Wood Dr

E1
1 Beaumont Wy
2 The Crossways
3 Dawlands Cl
4 Dawlands Dr
5 Noehill Pl
6 Normancroft Ct
7 Prince Of Wales Rd
8 Saxonlea Cl
9 Vikinglea Gld

E2
1 Castledale Cft
2 Danebrook Cl
3 Danebrook Dr
4 Normancroft Dr

E3
1 Kilvington Av

E4
1 Applegarth Cl
2 Bagshaw's Rd
3 Holbrook Dr
4 Penthorpe Cl
5 Pleasant Cl

E6
1 Welwyn Cl

E7
1 Basegreen Pl
2 Lister Cl
3 Lister Pl

E8
1 Woodland Cl

F1
1 Castlebeck Cft
2 Danebrook Cft
3 Danebrook Dr
4 Normancroft Dr

F2
1 Angleton Cl
2 Angleton Gdns
3 Angleton Ms
4 Aughton Dr
5 Woodthorpe Cres

F5
1 Carpenter Gdns

F6
1 Alnwick Dr
2 Hollinsend Pl
3 Wadsworth Rd

F7
1 Basegreen Wy

F8
1 Basegreen Rd

G2
1 Richmond Hall Dr

G3
1 Richmond Farm Ms
2 Richmond Hall Av
3 Richmond Hall Wy
4 Richmond Hill Rd
5 Richmond Pl

G5
1 Rowdale Crs
2 Wadsworth Dr

G6
1 Stanton Crs

G7
1 Hayfield Crs
2 Thornbridge Gv
3 Thornbridge Pl

H1
1 Farmstead Cl
2 Plowright Wy

H2
1 Richmond Park Cl

H3
1 Ravenscroft Cl
2 Ravenscroft Ct
3 Ravenscroft Ov
4 Ravenscroft Wy
5 Richmond Gv

H3
1 Smelter Wood Cl

H5
1 Linley La

H7
1 Birley Moor Cl
2 East Glade Sq
3 Hazelbadge Crs
4 Newstead Cl
5 Newstead Gv
6 Thornbridge La

J1
1 Ashbourne Gv
2 Parsley Hay Cl
3 Parsley Hay Dr
4 Wenlock St

J3
1 Glenholme Pl

J7
1 Spa View Ter
2 Weakland Wy

J8
1 Ardsley Gv
2 Darfield Cl

K1
1 Medlock Dr

K3
1 Hardcastle Dr

K4
1 Hollis Cft
2 Sheffield Rd

K7
1 Cotleigh Cl
2 Cotleigh Pl
3 Fairmount Gdns
4 Redbrook Cft
5 Redbrook Gv
6 Spring Water Cl
7 Withorpe Gdns

K8
1 Brampton Ct
2 Cranford Ct
3 Deanhead Ct
4 Kingswood Cl

L4
1 Birks Av
2 Cross Dr
3 Water Slacks La

L4
1 Farm View Cl
2 Grassington Cl
3 Greenside Ms
4 Stoneacre Cl
5 Threshfield Wy
6 Westfield Gv

Page 109

J6
1 Briardene Cl
2 Easedale Cl
3 Foxbrook Cl
4 Hollens Wy
5 Langdale Cl
6 Stanage Wy
7 Wheathall Wy
8 Woodleigh Cl

K5
1 Ashbourne Cl
2 Bretton Cl
3 Butterton Dr
4 Cauldon Dr
5 Cornfield Cl
6 Harvest Wy
7 Ladywood Dr
8 Mercaston Cl
9 Parwich Cl
10 Quorn Dr
11 Ravenswood Rd
12 Rednall Cl
13 Upwood Cl
14 Wheathill Cl

L5
1 Blackdown Av
2 Pike Cl
3 Honeyveld Cl
4 Sheldon Rd
5 Taddington Rd

M3
1 Dumble Wood Gra
2 Ennerdale Crs
3 Ladywood Dr
4 Ramshaw Cl
5 Thirlmere Rd

M4
1 Abney Cl
2 Ballidon Cl
3 Longcliff Wk

M5
1 Bodmin Wy
2 Cheviot Wy
3 Ettrick Cl
4 Grindon Cl
5 Pentland Cl
6 Sidlaw Cl
7 Windley Cl

Page 110

A2
1 Leeswood Cl
2 Rose Wood Cl
3 Skelwith Cl

A3
1 Broom Cl

A4
1 Bar Cft
2 Bridge Bank Cl
3 Cheedale Cl
4 Old House Rd
5 Stoops Cl

A7
1 Barker Fold

G3
1 Brocklehurst Piece
2 Pickton Cl
3 Shaw's Rw
4 Walgrove Rd

H1
1 Halton Cl

H3
1 Lancaster Rd

J2
1 Camms Cl

J3
1 Birchwood Cl
2 Birchwood Gdns
3 Birchwood Ri
4 Birchwood Wy
5 Challoner Gn
6 Garland Mt
7 Meadowcroft Gld
8 Meadowcroft Ri
9 Pedley Dr
10 Shortbrook Bank
11 Westland Cl

H4
1 Ambleside Cl
2 Borrowdale Av
3 Borrowdale Cl
4 Ennerdale Av
5 Ennerdale Dr
6 Murrayfield Dr
7 Oakworth Cl
8 Ralston Cft
9 Twickenham Cl
10 Twickenham Ct
11 Twickenham Gld
12 Twickenham Gv
13 Wasdale Av

K1
1 Abbots Meadow
2 Bramshill Ct
3 Collingbourne Av
4 Hursley Cl
5 Inglewood Av
6 Inglewood Cl
7 Inglewood Dell
8 Milburn Ct

L5
1 Mulberry Wy

Page 89

M1
1 Allestree Cl
2 Barley Ms
3 Belton Ct
4 Burnaston Cl
5 Chaddesden Cl
6 Hazelwood Cl
7 Ivan Brook Cl
8 Mapperley Rd
9 Newstead Cl
10 Ormesby Cl
11 Oxclose Dr
12 Repton Pl
13 Rockingham Cl
14 Snelston Cl
15 Stanford Rd
16 Thornton Pl

Page 90

B1
1 Buttermere Dr
2 Cartmel Cl
3 Castlerigg Wy
4 Kentmere Cl
5 Patterdale Cl
6 Sheards Dr

C2
1 Devonshire Cl
2 Heathfield Cl

E1
1 Hallowes Cl
2 Scarsdale Cross
3 Vale Cl

F2
1 Hazel Ct
2 Southfield Mt

Page 99

M2
1 Brooklands
2 Hogshaw Villas Rd
3 Lightwood Av
4 Marlow St
5 Nunbrook Gv
6 Spring Gdns

Page 109

L8
1 Broadlands Cft
2 Broadlands Ri
3 Rylstone Ct

M3
1 Brockwood Cl

M4
1 Market St

M7
1 Delves Ter

M8
1 Lindholme Gdns
2 Lundwood Cl

Page 69

G3
1 Dore Hall Cft

H6
1 Aldam Cl
2 Aldam Wy
3 Green Oak Crs
4 Green Oak Dr
5 Laverdene Cl

J5
1 Glover Rd

Page 70

A3
1 Hemper Gv

A8
1 Buckingham Cl
2 Burbage Cl
3 Chiltsworth Pl
4 Millstone Cl

E2
1 Norton Park Av

E4
1 Dyche Cl
2 Dyche Pl
3 Hazlebarrow Rd
4 Lingfoot Cl
5 Whinacre Cl
6 White Thorns Cl

E7
1 Derwent Cl
2 Snape Hill Dr

E8
1 Alexandra Rd
2 Egerton St

F1
1 Matthews Fold

F3
1 Hazlebarrow Gv
2 Jordanthorpe Vw

F4
1 Lingfoot Pl
2 Selly Oak Rd

F6
1 Birches Fold
2 Forrester's La
3 Meadow Cl

Page 73

G3
1 Church Ms
2 Kildale Gdns
3 Shipman Ct
4 Station Rd
5 Stonedale Cl

H3
1 Amesbury Cl
2 Littlemoor

B5
1 Glade Cl
2 Morris Av
3 Westleigh Ct

B7
1 Brickhouse Yd
2 Catherine St
3 Chatsworth Rd
4 Tap La

C1
1 Dunston Cl
2 Racecourse Rd

C4
1 Whitworth Rd

C5
1 Rhodes Av

C6
1 Compton St
2 Marchwood Cl
3 Newbold Rd
4 New Queen St
5 Princess St

C7
1 Foster St
2 Gilcroft St
3 Lime Tree Pl
4 Rosebery Hl

D1
1 Hartland Wy
2 Newbridge Ct
3 Sheffield Rd

D2
1 Chapel St
2 Duke St
3 Scarsdale Rd
4 Sheffield Rd
5 Thompson Cl

D5
1 Crown Rd
2 Stonegravels La

D6
1 Dowdeswell St
2 Homecroft Ms
3 St Helen's Cl
4 St Helen's St
5 Victoria St

D7
1 Broad Pavement
2 Marsden St
3 Rose Hl
4 Soresby St
5 Stephenson Pl

D8
1 Castle Yd
2 East Vw
3 South Pl
4 Tontine Rd

E1
1 Burdon Cl
2 Lydford Av

E4
1 Swaddale Cl

E5
1 Brimington Rd

E7
1 Corporation St
2 Devonshire St
3 Station Rd
4 Theatre La

F4
1 Fuller Rd
2 Witham Cl

F8
1 Brambling Ct
2 Quarry Bank Rd

Page 111

G3
1 Devonshire Ct
2 Moorview Cl
3 Scarsdale Crs

Page 127

M2
1 Deben Cl
2 Gleneagles Cl
3 Holbrook Cl
4 Lake View Av
5 Laxfield Cl
6 Lindrick Gdns
7 St Andrews Ri
8 Sunningdale Ri
9 Turnberry Cl

M4
1 Abney Cl
2 Ballidon Cl
3 Longcliff Wk

Page 128

C1
1 Foolow Av

C3
1 Harperhill Cl
2 Robincroft

D2
1 Dickenson Rd
2 Farnon Cl
3 Park Dr
4 Sylvan Cl
5 Warner St
6 Wayford Av
7 Whitehouses

G7
1 Avenue 1
2 Avenue 2
3 Avenue 3
4 Avenue 4
5 Avenue 5
6 Avenue 6
7 St Philip's Dr

F1
1 Central Cl
2 Central St
3 St James Cl

F2
1 Alum Chine Cl
2 Challands Cl
3 Colbshaw Cl
4 Devonshire Rd East
5 Farnsworth Cl
6 Ranmoor Cl
7 Woodstock Rd

G3
1 Weston Spot Cl

Page 156

F4
1 Upper Greenhill Gdns
2 Victoria Hall Gdns
3 Wellfield Ct

F5
1 Firs Pde
2 Lilybank Cl
3 Lime Grove Av
4 Old Lime Ct
5 St Joseph's St
6 Turnpike Cl

D7
1 Bailey Brook Crs
2 Carlton Cl
3 Chestnut Rd
4 Holmes Cl
5 Neal Ct
6 Wentworth Cft

Page 163

G7
1 Boughton Cl
2 Chatsworth Cl
3 Farndale Cl
4 Lound House Cl
5 Welbeck Cl

Page 164

B5
1 Bathwood Dr
2 Helmsdale Cl
3 Kenmore Cl
4 Thorpe Cl

C4
1 Peveril Pl

C5
1 Rhodes St

D3
1 Exchange Rw
2 Handley Ar
3 Market House Pl
4 West Hill Dr

J8
1 Alexandra St
2 Bishop St
3 Church Wk
4 Devonshire St
5 Essex St
6 Grosvenor Rd
7 Oxford St
8 Queen's Sq
9 Wellington St

M3
1 Horsley Crs
2 Moorpool Crs
3 The Nook
4 Vicarwood Av

Page 165

G4
1 Beresford St
2 Harcourt St
3 Hope St
4 Rock St

H1
1 Allendale Wy
2 Aspen Ct
3 Brackmills Cl
4 Bullace Ct
5 Cornel Ct
6 Deepdale Rd
7 Kingsthorpe Cl
8 Longdale
9 Wensleydale Cl

H4
1 Hamilton St

L4
1 Bonsal Ct
2 Bretby Ct
3 Elvaston Ct
4 Findern Ct
5 Fritchley Ct
6 Hatton Ct
7 Hindlow Ct
8 Holbrook Ct
9 Hucklow Ct
10 Millfield Cl
11 Wynnard Cl

L6
1 Swallow Cl
2 Turnstone Crs

M5
1 Whaley Bridge Cl

Page 183

J2
1 Causeway The
2 China House Yd
3 Hammonds Cft
4 Market Pl
5 St Mary's Ga
6 Wirksworth Hall Gdns

Page 199

J7
1 Cheapside
2 Fleet Crs

J8
1 Derwent V
2 Gibfield Ld
3 Quarry Rd
4 Sunny Bank Gdns

K6
1 Ingle's Channel
2 The Orchard
3 Primary Cl
4 St John's Rd
5 St Peter's Cl
6 St Peters Cft
7 Short Lands
8 Vicarage Cl

L5
1 Beaurepaire Crs
2 Hayfield Cl
3 Laund Cl
4 Lytton Cl
5 Winster Cl

L8
1 Birchview Cl
2 Elm Av
3 Honeyveld Cl
4 Lime Crs
5 Millbank Av
6 Redhill Cl

M4
1 Kingswood Cl
2 Norbury Wy
3 Pilsley Cl

Page 200

A5
1 Blenheim Ct
2 Courtney Wy
3 Harewood Cl
4 Kendray Cl
5 Martindale Cl
6 Moulton Cl
7 Salisbury Dr
8 Sherbourne Dr
9 Whitemoor Hall

H6
1 Rossendale

H8
1 Barber Cl
2 Barber Ct
3 Barber Pl
4 Blackburn Pl
5 Blackburn Rd
6 Haddon Nurseries
7 Haddon Nurseries
8 High Holborn
9 High Holborn Rd
10 Primrose Cl
11 Primrose Hl
12 Primrose Ri
13 Ryegrass Cl
14 Tennyson St
15 Tennyson St
16 Trinity St

J6
1 Horridge St
2 Horridge St
3 Trueman St
4 Trueman Pl

J7
1 Raleigh Cl

J8
1 Bloomsgrove Cres
2 Bloomsgrove Rd
3 Lower Bloomsgrove Rd
4 Lower Bloomsgrove Rd
5 Lower Granby St
6 Lower Granby St
7 Mundy St
8 Mundy St
9 Spring Garden Ter
10 Spring Garden Ter

K1
1 Orchard St

K2
1 Bacon Cl
2 Cowper Rd
3 The Heath

L2
1 Ludlam Av

Page 201

G1
1 Crossley St
2 Emmas Williams Ct
3 Field Ter
4 Larch Av
5 Nightingale Cl
6 Oxford St

G3
1 Weston Spot Cl

Page 202

A5
1 Admiral Cl
2 Bircumshaw's Rd
3 Burton St
4 East Nelson St
5 The Hamlet
6 Lower Gladstone St
7 Stamford St
8 Wood End Rd

D7
1 Bailey Brook Crs
2 Carlton Cl
3 Chestnut Rd
4 Holmes Cl
5 Neal Ct
6 Wentworth Cft

J8
1 Alexandra St
2 Bishop St
3 Church Wk
4 Devonshire St
5 Essex St
6 Grosvenor Rd
7 Oxford St
8 Queen's Sq
9 Wellington St

K1
1 Orchard St

K2
1 Bacon Cl
2 Cowper Rd
3 The Heath

L2
1 Ludlam Av

Page 203

G7
1 Ambleside Dr
2 Derby Rd
3 Harlequin Ct
4 Hemsley Dr
5 Linkmel Rd
6 Meadowbank Ct
7 Old Derby Rd

H2
1 Brackenfield Dr
2 Brassington Ct
3 Southwell Rd
4 Weightman Dr

L6
1 Chesterman Cl

Page 213

M1
1 Baldwin St

M2
1 Azalea Ct
2 Bradwell Cl
3 Cromwell St
4 Goodman St
5 Juniper Ct
6 Veronica Dr

M3
1 Grantham Cl

M4
1 Shakespeare Rd

M6
1 Byron Crs
2 Middleton St
3 Tennyson Sq

Page 214

D2
1 Coppice Cl
2 Dove Cl
3 Farm Cl
4 Holbrook Vw
5 Kingsway Crs
6 Mill Cl
7 St John's Dr
8 Vincent Cl

Page 216

F7
1 Bassett Cl
2 Champion Av
3 Foxton Cl
4 Gimson Cl
5 Harlech Cl
6 Hayling Cl
7 Holkham Cl
8 Houghton Av
9 Landmere Cl
10 Millfield Cl
11 Wynnard Cl

Page 217

G6
1 Woodside Cl

G6
1 Woodland Av

G7
1 Abbotsford Rd
2 Abbotsford Ms
3 Audley Cl
4 Audley Cl
5 Barclay Cl
6 Barclay Ct
7 Emsworth Cl
8 Ensworth Cl
9 Kilburn Dr
10 Kilburn Dr
11 Lilac Ms
12 Lilac Ms
13 Millbank Cl
14 Millbank Cl
15 Monkton Cl
16 Monkton Cl
17 Shepton Cl
18 Shepton Cl
19 Skipton Cl
20 Skipton Cl
21 Windley Dr
22 Windley Dr

G8
1 Hays Cl

H1
1 Sudbury Ms
2 The Sycamores

Page 227

H6
1 Ash Tree Cl

Page 226

B6
1 Blenheim Pde
2 Chandres Ct
3 Charterstone La
4 Foxes Wk
5 Ladycroft Paddock
6 Mulberries Ct

C1
1 Flaxholme Av

C8
1 Braithwell Cl
2 Canon's Wk
3 Hallfield Cl
4 Maltby Cl
5 Plough Ga
6 St Hugh's Cl
7 St Matthew's Wk
8 Willow Cl

D8
1 Abbeyfields Cl
2 Darley Abbey Dr
3 Leafenden Cl
4 Spinney Cl
5 Thistledown Cl
6 Waterside Cl

F2
1 New St
2 The Oaks
3 Old Barn Cl

F4
1 Bermuda Av

Page 227

H6
1 Ash Tree Cl

C2
1 Coronation St
2 Derby St
3 Hallcroft Rd
4 High St
5 Market Pl

C5
1 Dale St
2 Extension St
3 Gladstone St East
4 Gladstone St West
5 Grangewood Av
6 Havelock St
7 Hope St
8 Oxford St
9 Percy St
10 Regent St

C7
1 Catherine Ct
2 Lower Whitworth Rd

Page 229

H2
1 Burcot Cl
2 Chatsworth Dr
3 Darley Dr
4 Derbyshire Cl
5 Eckington Ct
6 Grindlow Av
7 Haddon Cl
8 Hartington Cl
9 Haves Cl

Page 230

A5
1 Balmoral Rd
2 Coniston Dr
3 Hemlock La
4 Henshaw Av
5 Macdonald Sq
6 Sandringham Pl

B2
1 Queen St
2 St Andrew's Dr

C1
1 Albion St
2 Burleigh St
3 Chalons Cl
4 Cranmer St
5 Gladstone St
6 Greasley Rd
7 North St
8 Taylor St
9 West Ter
10 Wilton St

C2
1 Coronation St
2 Derby St
3 Hallcroft Rd
4 High St
5 Market Pl

C5
1 Dale St
2 Extension St
3 Gladstone St East
4 Gladstone St West
5 Grangewood Av
6 Havelock St
7 Hope St
8 Oxford St
9 Percy St
10 Regent St

C7
1 Catherine Ct
2 Lower Whitworth Rd

Page 231

C8
1 Buttermead Cl
2 Cambridge Crs
3 Cavendish Crs
4 Cranbourne Cl
5 Dawn Vw
6 Newbery Av
7 Pembrey Cl
8 Rothbury Av
9 Spring Dale Gdns
10 Trowell Park Dr

H8
1 Blackthorn Cl
2 Broadleaf Cl
3 Burdock Cl
4 Cedarwood Cl
5 Crofters Ct
6 Deacon Cl
7 Hornbeam Cl
8 Radstock Gdns
9 Ridgewood Cl
10 Trowbridge Cl

J8
1 Balleny Cl
2 Beardmore Cl
3 Celandine Cl
4 Cloisters Ct
5 Garthorpe Cl
6 Kingsland Cl
7 Markham Cl
8 Paddock Cft
9 Rutherford Ri
10 Santolina Dr
11 Sedgebrook Cl
12 Trowbridge Cl

Page 239

G6
1 Mickleross Cl
2 Romsley Ct
3 Staverton Dr
4 Tiverton Cl

G7
1 Broomhill Cl
2 Hailsham Cl
3 Malvern Cl
4 Rutland Dr
5 Windsor Cl

H4
1 Epping Cl
2 Milbank Cl
3 Moorgate

H6
1 Napier Cl
2 Queensland Cl

H8
1 Freemantle Av

J3
1 Aldersgate Embankment Cl

J4
1 Bayswater Cl
2 Belsize Cl
3 Burlington Rd
4 Downing Cl
5 Drayton Av
6 Endsleigh Gdns
7 Farringdon Cl
8 Highbury Cl
9 Lombard St

J7
1 Hamilton Cl

J8
1 Abney Cl
2 Carnoustie Cl
3 Cleveleys Cl
4 Holmesfield Dr
5 Little Longstone Cl

K3
1 Penge Rd

K4
1 Aldwych
2 Ealing Cl
3 Green Pk
4 Surbiton Cl
5 Twickenham Dr

K5
1 Norwood Cl
2 Peckham Gdns

K7
1 Bunting Cl
2 Dove Cl
3 Swallow Cl
4 Swift Cl

K8
1 Birkdale Cl

L3
1 Ranelagh Gdns
2 Tufnell Gdns

L4
1 Chingford Ct
2 Mornington Crs
3 Pimlico
4 St Bride's Wk
5 Wimpole Gdns

L5
1 Cove Cl
2 Southwark Cl
3 Woburn Pl

L7
1 Manor Park Wy
2 Southmead Wy

M4
1 Cooper St
2 Harringay Gdns
3 Plimsoll St
4 Selwyn St

M5
1 Napier St
2 New Zealand Sq
3 Raglan Av
4 Raleigh St
5 Seymour Cl

C1
1 California Gdns

M7
1 St Quentin Cl

M8
1 Eastwood Av
2 Manor Rd
3 Middleton Dr

Page 240

A2
1 Kedleston Old Rd

A4
1 Chandos Pole St
2 Frederick St
3 Noel St
4 Payne St
5 Richardson St

A5
1 Bright St
2 Coke St
3 Findern St
4 Leake St

A7
1 Bedford St
2 Westbury St

B1
1 Lanscombe Park Rd
2 Thorpelands Dr
3 Wessington Ms
4 Wyaston Cl

B2
1 Bradley St
2 Broad Bank
3 Broadway Park Cl
4 Parkfields Dr
5 West Bank Cl

B4
1 Brick St
2 Bridge St
3 Buckland St
4 Fowler St
5 Gisborne Gn
6 Watson St
7 Whitecross St

B5
1 Larges St
2 Sudbury Cl

B6
1 Jackson St
2 Junction St
3 Laverstoke Cl
4 Redbury Cl

B7
1 Harrison St
2 Sherwood St
3 Spinney Rd

C1
1 Arden Cl
2 Uplands Gdns
3 Whitaker Gdns

C2
1 Broadfields Cl
2 Liston Dr

C3
1 Kedleston Rd
2 West Av

C4
1 Brook St
2 Edward St
3 Henry St
4 King's Mead Cl
5 Little Bridge St
6 Lodge La
7 Orchard St
8 Parker Ct
9 St Helen's St
10 St John's Ter
11 Walker La
12 Willow Rw

C5
1 Becket St
2 Bramble St
3 Cavendish Ct
4 Cavendish St
5 Curzon St
6 Drewry Ct
7 Forman St
8 Friar Gate Ct
9 George St
10 Kensington St
11 Monk St
12 Newland St

C6
1 Abbotts Barn Cl
2 Alma St
3 Copperleaf Cl
4 Dunkirk
5 Edensor Sq
6 Gerard Ct
7 Rosengrave St
8 Summerbrook St
9 Webster St

C7
1 Argyle St
2 Bailey St
3 Lime Av
4 Lorne St
5 Lower Eley St
6 Mill Hill Rd
7 Mount Carmel St
8 Temple St

C8
1 Fairdene
2 Northumberland St

D1
1 Abbey Yd
2 Dower Cl
3 The Hill
4 North Rw
5 Poplar Rw
6 West Rw

D2
1 Old Chester Rd

D3
1 Derventio Cl
2 Etruria Gdns
3 Maplebeck Ct
4 Margaret St
5 North Pde
6 Well St

D4
1 Buchanan St
2 Darley La
3 King St
4 Nottingham Rd
5 Phoenix St
6 Queen St
7 St Helen's St
8 St Mary's Ct
9 St Michael's La

D5
1 Albert St
2 Amen Alley
3 Becket Well La
4 Cheapside
5 Corn Market
6 East St
7 Exchange St
8 Green La
9 Sadler Ga
10 St James's St
11 St Peter's Churchyard
12 Strand
13 Thorntree La
14 Wardwick

D6
1 The Avenue
2 Babington La
3 Burton Rd
4 Crompton St
5 Degge St
6 Gower St
7 Green La
8 Harcourt St
9 Hill Brow
10 Leopold St
11 Osmaston Rd
12 Sacheverel St
13 Sitwell St

D7
1 Avondale Rd
2 Bainbridge St
3 Charnwood St
4 Dashwood St
5 Melbourne St
6 Mill Hill La
7 Renals St
8 Salisbury St

D8
1 Chestnut Av
2 Industrial St
3 Lyndhurst St
4 Provident St

E3
1 Adler Ct
2 Cardean Cl
3 Charing Cross
4 Euston Dr
5 Kentish Ct
6 St Pancras Wy
7 Seale St
8 Waterloo Ct

E4
1 Derwent St
2 Exeter St
3 Robert St
4 Wood St

E5
1 Morledge

E6
1 Bradshaw Wy
2 Carrington St
3 Castle St
4 Copeland St
5 Hope St
6 Liversage Av
7 Liversage Rd
8 New St
9 Traffic St
10 Trinity St

E7
1 Arboretum St
2 Centre Ct
3 Litchurch St
4 Morleston St
5 Regent St

E8
1 Alexandra Gdns
2 Augusta St
3 Catherine St
4 Haslemere Ct
5 Tintagel Cl

F2
1 Stirling Cl

F3
1 Shetland Cl

F4
1 Huntingdon Gn
2 Wayzgoose Dr

F6
1 Leeds Pl
2 Midland St
3 Sheffield Pl
4 Wellington St

F7
1 Barlow St
2 Bloomfield St
3 Carrington St

F8
1 Ivy Sq

Page 241

G1
1 Blyth Pl
2 Dawsmere Cl
3 Fincham Cl
4 Lytham Cl
5 Oakham Cl

G2
1 Attleridge Cl
2 Buckingham Av
3 Chevely Ct
4 Pembroke St

G8
1 Beverley St
2 Selborne St

H1
1 Evesham Cl
2 Longstock Cl

H2
1 Liverpool St
2 Peterborough St

H3
1 Hollington Cl
2 Roxburgh Av

H8
1 Bowmer Rd

J1
1 Brassington Rd
2 Tansley Ri
3 Tideswell Rd
4 Youlgreave Cl

J2
1 Ashover Cl
2 Chelmorton Pl
3 Hazelwood Rd

J4
1 Lea Dr
2 Newstead Av
3 Richmond Rd
4 Rushcliffe Av
5 Whitmore Rd

K1
1 Anstey Ct
2 Columbine Cl
3 Delamere Cl
4 Gleadmoss La
5 Hodthorpe Cl
6 Sandbach Cl
7 Swanwick
8 Thurlow Ct

K3
1 Stoney Flatts Crs

K5
1 Kennedy Cl
2 Moira Cl

K4
1 Church La
2 Rainier Cl

L1
1 Appledore Dr
2 Ashcombe Gdns
3 Ashgrove Cl
4 Avenham Cl
5 Bassingham Cl
6 Bickley Moss
7 Gainsborough Cl
8 Grasthorpe Cl
9 Prestbury Cl
10 Roseberry Cl
11 Samantha Ct
12 Swinderby Dr
14 Thore Cl
15 Tuxford Cl
16 Whyteleafe Cl
17 Wilmslow Dr

L2
1 Kibworth Cl
2 Sandfield Cl

L3
1 Atchison Gdns

L4
1 Carson Rd
2 Lansing Gdns
3 Sanderson Rd
4 Trenton Green Dr
5 Washington Av

L5
1 Cordville Cl
2 Grant Av

L6
1 Albert Crs
2 Cherry Tree Ms
3 Eden Rd
4 Enoch Stone Dr

M4
1 John F Kennedy Gdns
2 Vermont Dr

Page 242

A5
1 St Werburgh's Vw

A7
1 Derwent Rd

B5
1 Hill View Gv
2 Moor End
3 Sycamore Ct
4 Windermere Dr
5 Wingerworth Park Rd

C4
1 Badger Cl
2 Gerard Cl
3 Greenfinch Cl
4 Linnet Cl

F5
1 Anne Potter Cl
2 Hargrave Av
3 Sister's La
4 Wesley La
5 Windmill Cl

Page 244

E5
1 Butt St
2 Faircroft Av
3 Far New Cl
4 Grasmere St
5 Huntingdon Wk
6 Smedley's Av

E6
1 Arundel Cl
2 Belton Cl
3 Blenheim Ct
4 Bradgate Cl
5 Chatsworth Cl
6 Hadstock Cl
7 Harewood Cl
8 Osborne Cl
9 Princess Dr
10 Sandringham Rd
11 Windsor Cl

E8
1 Corse Cl
2 Helvellyn Wy
3 Keswick Ct
4 Longmoor Gdns
5 Spridgeon Cl
6 Striding Edge Cl

Page 245

G3
1 Lower Orchard St
2 Shanklin Dr
3 Victoria St
4 Warren Avenue Extension
5 Warren Ct
6 Wesleyan Chapel Wk

G4
1 Halls Rd
2 Plowman Ct
3 Recreation Ter

H1
1 Beaumont Cl
2 Bedford St
3 Byron Ct
4 Churchdale Av
5 Henley Gdns
6 Montrose Ct
7 Moorfield Ct
8 Rockford Ct

H2
1 Saville St

H3
1 High St
2 Upper Orchard St
3 Whitely Ct

H4
1 Hogarth Cl
2 Holden Gdns
3 Portland Cres
4 Walker Gv

H5
1 Arthur Mee Rd
2 Dalton Cl

H7
1 Cleveleys Rd
2 Dale St
3 Sandfield Rd

H8
1 Aldridge Cl
2 Rivington Rd
3 Sandfield Rd

J1
1 Adelaide Cl
2 Canberra Ct
3 Sheridan Ct

J5
1 Brunswick Dr

J7
1 Farndon Cl
2 Freeland Cl

J8
1 Broadstairs Rd
2 Cheltenham Cl
3 Huntingdon Wy
4 Inchwood Cl
5 Leyland Cl
6 St Georges Dr
7 Whiting Av

K1
1 Oakland St

K2
1 Bembridge Ct
2 Margaret's Ct

K6
1 Bedale Ct
2 Grisedale Ct

K7
1 Carter Rd
2 Highfield Rd

K8
1 Birkin Av
2 Blackrod Cl
3 Chetwynd Rd
4 Gardinia Cl
5 Honiton Cl
6 Old Mill Cl

L2
1 Chapel Mews Ct
2 St Michael's Sq

L4
1 Hoggetts Cl

L5
1 Firbank Cl
2 The Flatts
3 Garton Cl

L6
1 Caernarvon Pl
2 Gayrigg Ct
3 Gregory Ct
4 Hawkswood Cl
5 Kirkbride Cl
6 Maldon Cl
7 Ravenhill Cl

L8
1 Empingham Cl
2 Stirling Gdns
3 Wynwood Cl
4 Wynwood Rd

M1
1 Felstead Ct

M2
1 Close Quarters
2 Crummock Cl

M4
1 Inham Circ
2 Woodville Cl

M5
1 Babington Ct
2 Beaufort Dr
3 Kedleston Ct
4 Sunnyside Rd
5 Warkton Cl

M6
1 Fullwood Cl
2 Halstead Cl
3 Redland Cl
4 Ridgewood Dr

M7
1 Hardwicke Rd

M8
1 Chatsworth Av
2 Ferguson Cl
3 Gowan Cl
4 Montgomery Cl
5 Russell Gdns
6 Staniland Cl
7 Whitton Cl

Page 255

G7
1 All Saints Cl
2 Bramble Ms
3 Holly Ct
4 Madeley Cl
5 Stretton Cl
6 Vicarage Rd
7 Warner St

1 Roughton Cl
2 Thorndon Cl
3 Welney Cl
4 Wretham Cl

G8
1 Cardales Cl
2 Green Wy
3 Hawthorn Crs
4 Meadow Cl

H1
1 Barf Cl
2 Bowland Cl
3 Carnforth Cl
4 Downham Cl
5 Freesia Cl
6 Hindscarth Crs
7 Latrigg Cl
8 Melbreak Cl
9 Slaidburn Cl
10 Springdale Cl
11 Uttoxeter Rd
12 Wansfell Cl
13 Wenlock Cl

H2
1 Cable Cl
2 Malcolm Gv

H3
1 Bowlees Ct
2 Cheriton Gdns
3 Jemison Cl
4 Latimer Cl
5 Matthew Wy
6 Micklecroft Gdns
7 Oxenhope Cl

H8
1 Hazel Cl

J1
1 Belfry Cl
2 Lindrick Cl
3 St Mellion Cl
4 Stanage Ct
5 Wentworth Cl

J3
1 Atworth Cl
2 Boxmoor Cl
3 Gayton Thorpe Cl
4 Rivenhall Cl
5 Spoonley Wood Cl

J4
1 Chesterford Ct
2 Comfrey Cl
3 Cranberry Gv
4 Cranhill Cl
5 Frampton Gdns
6 Little Woodbury Dr
7 Malham Rd
8 Woodale Cl

K1
1 Elgin Av

K2
1 Caversfield Cl
2 Charlbury Cl
3 Daylesford Cl
4 Fordwells Cl
5 Swanmore Rd

K3
1 Barnhill Cl
2 Cascade Gv
3 Copse Gv
4 Corbridge Gv
5 Farrier Gdns
6 Longthorpe Cl
7 Pennycress Cl
8 Queensbury Cha
9 Richmond Cl
10 Trefoil Cl
11 Troutbeck Cl

K4
1 Adelphi Cl
2 Fairford Gdns
3 Fieldfare Cl
4 Kelvedon Dr
5 Palladium Dr
6 Pulborough Gdns
7 Wheathill Gv

L2
1 Burns Cl
2 Greenacres

L3
1 Greenfields Av
2 Lothlorien Cl
3 Moorway Cft

L4
1 Ploughfield Cl
2 Tiller Cl

M1
1 Beechwood Crs
2 Harrington Rd
3 Old Vicarage Cl
4 Shepherd St

M2
1 Edgbaston Ct
2 Fernwood Cl
3 Headingley Cl
4 Lawnswood Cl
5 Richmond Av
6 Trent Bridge Ct

M3
1 Highfield Rd
2 Rowley Gdns
3 Shireoaks Cl

M4
1 Carisbrooke Gdns
2 Carfield Cl
3 Kegworth Av

M5
1 Norbury Cl
2 Plantain Gdns

M7
1 Merrybower Cl
2 Michelle Cl

M8
1 Dulverton Cl
2 Silverton Dr
3 Southdown Cl
4 Tyndale Cha
5 Wheatland Cl
6 Wilton Cl

Page 256

A2
1 Serina Av
2 Wood Cft

A3
1 Leander Cl
2 Redwing Cft
3 Whitstable Cl

A4
1 Alexandre Cl
2 Corfe Cl
3 Lulworth Cl
4 St Stephen's La
5 Witham Dr

A5
1 New Mount Cl
2 Rodsley Crs
3 Sapperton Cl

A6
1 Avocet Cl
2 Bluebird Ct
3 Coriander Gdns
4 Curlew Cl
5 Glenmore Dr
6 Merlin Gn
7 Peregrine Cl

A7
1 Blackmount Cl
2 Bodmin Cl
3 Braemar Cl
4 Burnside Cl
5 Caerhays Ct
6 Campsie Ct
7 Chandwick Ct
8 Craiglee Ct
9 Dalness Ct
10 Edgelaw Ct
11 Hebrides Cl
12 Lindisfarne Cl
13 Lismore Ct
14 Mull Ct
15 Northfield
16 Padstow Cl
17 Rowan Cl
18 Stornoway Cl

A8
1 Cowdray Cl
2 Dunvegan Cl
3 Hambledon Dr
4 Heather Cl
5 Oakwood Cl
6 Sallywood Cl

B2
1 Stenson Rd

B3
1 Caxton Cl

B4
1 Bosworth Av
2 Bradgate Ct
3 Cuttlebrook Cl
4 Oadby Ri

B5
1 Butterwick Cl
2 The Circle
3 Donington Cl
4 Invernia Cl
5 Roseheath Cl
6 Sherwood Av

B6
1 Aviemore Wy

B7
1 Applecross Ct
2 Dunoon Cl
3 Heath Ct
4 Ryan Cl

B8
1 Bankholmes Cl
2 Briset Cl
3 Castlecraig Ct
4 The Eyrie
5 Hunters Cft
6 Jedburgh Cl
7 Jesop Dr
8 Peebles Ct
9 Yarrow Cl

C1
1 Birdwood St

C2
1 Lawrence St
2 Newlyn Cl

C6
1 Killingworth Av
2 Larkhill Crs
3 Redland Cl
4 Stroma Cl

C8
1 Ashwater Cl
2 Vetchfield Cl
3 Willowherb Cl

D1
1 Aimploy Cl
2 Dover St
3 Netherclose St
4 Roe Wk

D2
1 Carnegie St
2 Hampden St

D5
1 Shakespeare St
2 Wordsworth Dr

E1
1 Vulcan St

E2
1 Castings Rd
2 Coronation St
3 Crowshaw St

E3
1 Elmtree Av

F1
1 Shaftesbury St

F2
1 Crowshaw St
2 Mowbray Gdns
3 Witney Cl

F3
1 Amber St
2 Arkwright St
3 Durward Cl
4 Waverley St

Page 257

G3
1 Tennyson St

G4
1 Stamford St

G5
1 Brookhouse St
2 Greenwood Cl
3 Sinfin Fields Crs

G6
1 Morningside Cl

G7
1 Cantley Cl
2 Hickling Cl

H2
1 Newbury St

H3
1 Marsden St
2 Slaney Cl

H4
1 Fisher St
2 Harrington St
3 Jubalton Cl
4 Poole St
5 Rowland St

H6
1 Chellaston Rd
2 Hubert Shaw Cl
3 Mountbatten Cl

H7
1 Lorraine Cl
2 Stonyhurst Ct

H8
1 Lady Mantle Cl
2 Mill Moor Cl

J2
1 Mosedale Cl
2 Murray St
3 Warren St
4 Westminster St

J5
1 Ashcroft Cl
2 Jefferson Pl
3 Kemble Pl
4 Macready Pl

J6
1 Corby Cl
2 Lansdowne Av
3 Moorhead Av

J6
1 Harlow Cl

J7
1 Hillcreste Cl
2 Woodminton Dr

J8
1 Lincoln Gn
2 Lockington Cl
3 Newbold Cl

K2
1 Beckitt Cl
2 Spencer St

K3
1 Hawthorn Av
2 Siddons St

K4
1 Hawtrey Gdns
2 Rosedale Av
3 St Mary's Cl

K5
1 Harepit Cl
2 Haywood Cl
3 Sweetbriar Cl

K7
1 Blakebrook Dr
2 Chelmarsh Cl

K8
1 Blithfield Gdns
2 Crownland Dr
3 Diseworth Cl
4 Hawksdale Cl
5 Pingreaves Dr
6 Slade Lands Dr
7 Townsend Gv

L3
1 Poplar Cl
2 Raynesway

L4
1 The Court
2 Garth Crs
3 Helston Cl
4 Pendennis Cl

L5
1 Penzance Rd
2 Sandgate Cl

L6
1 Bradmoor Cl
2 Leveret Cl
3 Newgate Cl

M2
1 Taunton Cl

M3
1 Bridgwater Cl
2 Durley Cl
3 Keldholme La
4 Rosewood Cl
5 St Michaels Cl
6 St Michaels Vw
7 Sandalwood Cl
8 Sledmere Cl
9 Yeovil Cl
10 Yew Tree Cl

M4
1 Cod Beck Cl
2 Compton Cl
3 Humber Cl
4 Kirkistown Cl
5 Newborough Rd
6 Thruxton Cl

M5
1 Bonchurch Cl
2 Heathcote Cl
3 Kynance Cl
4 Newquay Pl
5 Redruth Cl
6 Thorness
7 Wadebridge Gv
8 Whitewell Gdns

M6
1 Orchard Cl

Page 258

A5
1 Brightstone Cl
2 Chariot Cl
3 Cheverton Cl
4 Cornmill Cl
5 Forum Cl
6 The Greenway
7 Marshgreen Cl
8 Mottistone Cl
9 Woods Meadow

Page 260

D1
1 Berwin Cl
2 Cairnsmore Cl
3 Cuillin Cl
4 Hambleton Cl
5 Langdon Cl
6 Mendip Cl

D2
1 Ashview Cl
2 Hartside Gdns
3 Ingleborough Gdns
4 Malvern Gdns
5 The Plantations
6 Porlock Cl
7 Purbeck Cl

F4
1 Clarence Rd
2 Cockleys
3 Hatten Crofts
4 Rad Mdw
5 Sawmand Cl

Page 261

G6
1 Pennie Cl
2 Rush Leys

H3
1 Beaconsfield St
2 Claye St
3 Clifford St
4 Howitt St
5 Northcote St
6 Orchard St
7 Salisbury St
8 Sandford Av
9 Stanley St
10 Trafalgar Sq
11 Trafalgar Ter
12 West Ga

L1
1 Connery Ms
2 Cregson Gdns
3 Kindlewood Dr
4 Minton Cl
5 Morris Av
6 Tanwood Rd

Page 273

L4
1 Flatts Cl
2 Moores Cl
3 Pensgreave Rd

M1
1 Barrington Cl
2 The Chevin
3 Deveron Cl
4 Gleneagles Dr
5 Kedleston Cl
6 Longbow Cl
7 Newbury Dr
8 Suningdale Cl

M3
1 St Albans Cl
2 St Chad's Rd
3 St Modwen's Cl
4 St Stephens Cl

Page 274

A1
1 Highgrove Cl
2 Spencer Cl
3 Telmah Cl

A2
1 Althorp Wy
2 Broadlands
3 Buckingham Cl
4 Conway Cl
5 Crestwood Cl
6 Earls Ct
7 Faraday Av
8 Glamis Cl
9 Kingsdale Cft
10 Mountbatten Cl
11 Raglan Cl
12 Regency Wy
13 St Francis Cl
14 Tudor Hollow
15 Westminster Dr

A3
1 Bamborough Cl
2 Bronte Cl
3 Crichton Av
4 Denbigh Cl
5 Longfellow Cl
6 Totnes Cl

A4
1 Dickens Cl
2 Meredith Cl
3 Ruskin Pl
4 Wordsworth Cl

A7
1 George St

A8
1 Abbey St
2 Gough Side
3 Orchard Pk
4 Ordish Cl
5 Russell St

B1
1 The Green
2 Warren Cl

B2
1 Duchy Cl
2 Monarch Cl

B3
1 Seymour Av
2 Temple Cl

B5
1 Falcon Cl

B7
1 Blythfield
2 Meadowside Dr
3 Severn Cl

C1
1 Thornewill Dr

C7
1 Rosemount Cl

D5
1 Cheedale Cl

D6
1 Hanchurch Cl
2 Kingsbury Cl

D7
1 Ashley Cl
2 Balmoral Rd
3 Kensington Rd

D8
1 Hamilton Rd

E5
1 Millersdale Cl

E6
1 Mear Greaves La
2 Monsaldale Cl

E8
1 Mcadam Cl

F6
1 Hollow Crs
2 Hollow La
3 Jacobean Ct

F7
1 Blenheim Cl
2 Delhi Cl
3 Durban Cl
4 The Eyrie
5 Madras Rd
6 Stamps Cl
7 Wyndham Cl

F8
1 Latham Cl
2 Queensland Crs

Page 280

E4
1 Faldo Cl

Page 281

L1
1 Cameron Cl
2 Daleside
3 Wedgewood Cl
4 Winchcombe Dr

M1
1 Darwin Cl

Page 282

B5
1 Baslow Gn
2 Brailsford Av
3 Dales Cl
4 The Fairway
5 The Cables
6 St Edwards Ct
7 St John's Dr
8 Winster Gn

C4
1 Appleton Cl
2 Ash Tree Cl
3 Cherry Tree Cl
4 Manton Cl

C5
1 Ashleigh Av
2 The Burrows
3 Kay Dr
4 The Paddocks
5 The Pastures
6 St Catherine's Rd
7 Stoneydale Cl

D3
1 Abbey Lodge Cl
2 Baltimore Cl
3 Blenheim Cl
4 Breadsall Cl
5 The Castle Ms
6 Cavendish Cl
7 Charleston Cl
8 Coachhouse Ms
9 Craythorne Cl
10 Hermitage Park Wy
11 Hollybank Cl
12 Maryland Ct
13 Redhill Lodge Rd

F5
1 Dickens Cl
2 Midway Rd

F7
1 Baker St

F8
1 Bridge Cl